SEXUALITY AND THE LAW

AMERICAN LAW AND SOCIETY
Series Editor: John W. Johnson
Volume 3

Garland Reference Library of Social Science
Volume 1272

American Law and Society

1. Mass Media and the Constitution
An Encyclopedia of Supreme Court Cases
Richard F. Hixson

2. Historic U.S. Court Cases, 1690–1990
An Encyclopedia
John W. Johnson

3. Sexuality and the Law
An Encyclopedia of Major Legal Cases
Arthur S. Leonard

Sexuality and the Law
An Encyclopedia of
Major Legal Cases

by
Arthur S. Leonard

GARLAND PUBLISHING
New York & London
1993

Library of Congress Cataloging-in-Publication Data

Leonard, Arthur S.
    Sexuality and the law : an encyclopedia of major legal cases /
by Arthur S. Leonard.
        p. cm. — (Garland reference library of social science ; vol. 1272.
American law and society ; vol. 3)
        Includes index.
        ISBN 0-8240-3421-X (acid-free paper)
        1. Sex and law—United States—Cases. 2. Gays—Legal status,
laws, etc.—United States—Cases. I. Title. II. Series: Garland reference
library of social science ; vol. 1272. III. Series: Garland reference library
of social science. American law and society ; vol. 3.

KF9325.A7L46   1993
346.7301'3—dc20
[347.30613]   92-45133

Printed on acid-free, 250-year-life paper
Manufactured in the United States of America

Design by Marc Shifflet

CONTENTS

FOREWORD

The formal law, its practitioners, and the culture it has engendered pervade the United States. The brilliant nineteenth-century French traveler and writer Alexis de Tocqueville maintained in *Democracy in America* that in this country virtually every political question sooner or later leads to a legal decision. Garland Publishing's American Law and Society series of one-volume encyclopedias, of which *Sexuality and the Law: An Encyclopedia of Major Legal Cases* is a part, goes Tocqueville one better. Those of us involved in this series believe that the prism of the law gathers, refracts, reflects, and (not infrequently) blurs American life. At its best, law provides a framework that enables us to make sense out of our physical and intellectual surroundings. At its worst, it confuses, frustrates, and impedes progress. Law has affected and continues to affect virtually everything we do or think about: giving birth, rearing and educating children, marriage, work, travel, business transactions, what we read and see, and, of course, how we get along with one another.

Although studying law in its social context might be a valuable approach to use in grappling with any country's history, it is particularly appropriate for the United States. That is, after all, the country with more statutes and published case law than any in the world. D.H. Lawrence, the great British writer and critic, once referred to America as a nation of "Thou Shalt Nots." The United States now has about 25 times as many lawyers per capita as Japan. Yet Americans are not totally comfortable with the law and those who perform what the legal philosopher Karl Llewellyn once called the "law jobs." For example, the first lawyer who arrived in the Pilgrim colony of Plymouth in the 1620s was quickly driven out of town for being too disputatious. This may have spawned the First American lawyer joke. Perhaps the residents of Plymouth were saying that law is too important to be left to the lawyers.

Sexuality and the Law: An Encyclopedia of Major Legal Cases is the third volume to appear in Garland's American Law and Society series. Consistent with the philosophy of the series, the more than 100 essay/entries in *Sexuality and the Law* deal with important legal issues without descending into jargon or lawyer's Latin. The essay/entries cover an enormous range of topics on this complex and controversial subject. The volume's author-editor, Arthur S. Leonard, has created a unique reference work; he not only sketches the facts of the cases and sets forth the legal issues in straightforward, unflinching prose, but he also offers his own reasoned opinions as to whether the judicial decisions treated advance or retard the right to privacy or the rights of individual litigants.

Arthur Leonard holds a J.D. degree from the Harvard University School of Law (1977) and a B.S. degree from Cornell University (1974). He is Professor of Law at the New York Law School and a member of the Association of the Bar of the City of New York. Among Professor Leonard's many publications are the textbook *AIDS Law in a Nutshell* (1991) and articles in law reviews and journals of opinion on such subjects as collective bargaining, discrimination in employment and business, the rights of gays and lesbians, and the ethical challenges of HIV infection.

John W. Johnson
University of Northern Iowa
Editor, American Law and Society Series

INTRODUCTORY NOTES

This book describes more than one hundred significant court decisions concerning sexuality. The case discussions necessarily include references to technical legal terms and assume basic understanding of legal procedures and the structure of the state and federal court systems. The discussions also assume some background knowledge of the history of sexuality. This brief note addresses both matters to provide better understanding of the text.

The U.S. court systems, whether on the state or the federal level, have a hierarchical structure. At the bottom of the hierarchy are trial courts. The trial courts in the federal system are referred to as district courts. State nomenclature varies, with the following names being used in different states: superior court, supreme court, circuit court, district court, commonwealth court, civil court, criminal court, court of civil claims, court of common pleas, etc. Regardless of the name, a trial court has the essential functions of determining the facts and applying the law to the facts. In cases where a jury is empaneled, the jury's role is to determine the facts and apply the law to the facts as instructed by the judge. The judge determines the appropriate law to apply by reference to the federal or state constitution, federal or state statutes (laws enacted by a legislative body), federal or state regulations (rules adopted by an executive body pursuant to legislative authorization), or the common law (the accumulated body of legal precedents concerning matters as to which there are no statutes or regulations).

In some cases discussed in this book, there was no trial. Rather, after being served with a complaint, the defendant moved the court to dismiss the case, usually on the ground that the complaint did not state a valid legal claim. When a court receives such a motion, it is supposed to determine whether the facts asserted in the plaintiff's complaint, if presumed to be accurate, would provide the basis for a valid legal claim along the lines described by the plaintiff. If the court decides that the plaintiff's allegations, even if true, would not provide the basis

for a valid legal claim, the court will dismiss the case without a trial. In some other cases, the trial court receives a motion for summary judgment before trial from one or both of the parties. The motion for summary judgment contends that there is no factual dispute between the parties and asks the court to determine the winner purely as a question of law. If the court finds that a relevant factual dispute still exists, it will deny the motion. Otherwise, it will proceed to decide the case without holding a trial.

In the federal system and most of the states, the losing party at the trial court level has a right to appeal to an intermediate appellate court. (In a few less populous states, there are no intermediate appellate courts and losers at trial may appeal directly to the state's highest court.) In the federal system, such courts are called circuit courts of appeals. Names of intermediate appellate courts vary on the state level, including court of appeals, appellate division, court of errors, etc. The role of the intermediate appellate court is to determine whether the trial court made an error of law significant enough to justify reversing its decision. In rare cases, an intermediate appellate court may order a reversal when it finds that the trial court's decision is based on factual determinations that have no support in the trial record. Trial court decisions come to an intermediate appellate court with a presumption of correctness. The burden is on the appellant (the party who files the appeal) to persuade the court that the trial court's decision should be reversed. Appeals are normally considered by a group of judges, called a panel, chosen at random from all the judges sitting on the appellate court. In the federal system, most appeals are heard by panels of three judges. In unusually important cases, or when the full appeals court decides to reconsider a case decided by a panel, an expanded panel will sit. This is referred to as a hearing *en banc*.

The loser in an intermediate appellate decision may try to obtain further review from the highest court in the jurisdiction. In the federal system and most state systems, this is the supreme court. In some states, the highest court is called the court of appeals. Appellate courts at the top of the hierarchy usually have control over the cases they will hear, so the appellant must petition for review. The procedures for doing this vary among jurisdictions. In the federal system, the petitioner files a petition for a writ of *certiorari* with the U.S. Supreme Court. If four Justices decide that the case merits review, the Court will grant the writ, ordering the court of appeals or state court from which the case has come to send the record of the case to the Supreme Court in Washington. Many states also use a *certiorari* system similar to the federal system. There are variations, however. In New York, where the highest court is the court of appeals, the losing party in the appellate division may request permission from the appeals panel that decided the case; alternatively, the losing party may directly petition the court of appeals for permission to have the case reviewed. In some states, such as California, a decision by the state's supreme court to grant review in a case automatically vacates the lower appeals court's decision.

It is not unusual in appellate litigation for parties other than the plaintiff and defendant to file briefs with the court. These parties are referred to as *amicus curiae*, which literally means "friends of the court." They are usually public interest organizations or professional or business associations whose members have a significant interest in the legal questions to be decided by the court. Rules for filing such briefs vary among jurisdictions. Normally, an *amicus* brief may only be filed with the permission of the court, and sometimes permission of the parties is also required.

When appellate courts issue their opinions, it is customary for one judge to take principal responsibility for drafting an opinion for consideration by his or her colleagues. If a majority of the judges agree with that opinion, it will be announced as the opinion of the court. Judges who would reach the same result by different reasoning may issue a concurring opinion. Judges who disagree with the result may issue a dissenting opinion. Sometimes, the panel of judges may decide to issue an opinion without identifying any single judge as the author. These are called *per curiam* opinions.

Most of the cases discussed in this book presented new legal questions for the courts to consider, most often in the realm of constitutional law. Constitutional law is the fundamental law of a society, concerned with the structure and power of government.

The U.S. Constitution establishes a framework for government and specifies the powers and responsibilities for each branch of the government. The first ten amendments, commonly called the Bill of Rights, contain express limitations on the power of government. As originally adopted in 1791, the Bill of Rights was understood as limiting the power of the federal government. After the Civil War, the nation adopted the Fourteenth Amendment, which significantly altered the relationship of the federal and state governments by adding restrictions on the power of state governments in their dealings with the people: the states were forbidden from depriving individuals of life, liberty, or property without due process of law, and were required to accord all persons equal protection of the laws.

During the second and third quarters of the 20th century, the Supreme Court further construed the Fourteenth Amendment as extending some of the principles of the Bill of Rights and applying them to the states. This was done by a process of selective incorporation of Bill of Rights principles as aspects of due process of law. For example, the Supreme Court ruled that under the Fourteenth Amendment a state could not abridge freedom of speech, incorporating the First Amendment's statement that "Congress shall make no law abridging the freedom of speech or of the press" as a requirement of due process of law.

In addition, during the last part of the 19th century the Supreme Court began to give independent substantive meaning to the due process clauses of the Fourteenth and Fifth Amendments. "Due process" originally referred to proper procedures, or "procedural due process." The Court began to take the view that legislation restricting the rights of property owners without sufficient justification violated their right not to be deprived of property without due process of law. This concept of "substantive due process" was eventually expanded to subject all legislation that might be seen as restricting liberty or property rights to judicial review. Any restriction on liberty or property rights was subject to the Court's review as to its reasonableness. During the 1930s, after a string of decisions declaring unconstitutional on due process grounds the major social welfare legislation of President Franklin D. Roosevelt's New Deal program, the Court changed course and decided that properly enacted statutes should be deemed constitutional so long as there was some rational basis for their enactment.

The Court eventually developed a complex due process jurisprudence, under which laws that were seen to interfere with fundamental individual rights (such as those described in the Bill of Rights) were subjected to more searching scrutiny than the minimal test of rationality. It was through this expansive substantive due process that the Court incorporated aspects of the Bill of Rights as limitations on state power. More significantly for the cases described in this book, it was through this process that the Court constructed a constitutional right of privacy that was used to strike down governmental regulation of reproductive and sexual conduct.

Another important element of the Fourteenth Amendment is the Equal Protection Clause, which requires that the states provide to all persons equal protection of the laws. The Supreme Court has declared that the concept of equal protection is actually an aspect of fundamental due process, and thus binding on the federal government as well as on the states because the Fifth Amendment obligates the federal government to afford due process of law to all residents of the United States.

As with due process, the Supreme Court has developed a complex jurisprudence of equal protection, recognizing that almost all governmental policies draw distinctions and treat people differently, and that not all instances of unequal treatment are constitutionally suspect. The keystone is whether persons protesting unequal treatment are similarly situated with respect to the policy in question, and whether the difference in treatment may be attributed

to factors that bear little relevance to legitimate governmental goals. Some members of the Court have spoken in terms of different levels of judicial scrutiny of governmental policies, based on the type of classification used or the type of interest abridged by the government's policy. During the middle years of the 20th century, most of the Justices came to the view that differential treatment based on race was inherently suspect and merited strict judicial scrutiny of the justifications offered for the challenged policy; only a compelling government interest could justify taking race into account, and then only when the governmental policy was "narrowly tailored" to meet that interest. The Supreme Court subsequently acknowledged other suspect classifications, and identified other characteristics as to which "heightened scrutiny" was justified, including sex. The appropriate treatment of sexuality or sexual orientation within this analytical framework is the subject of continuing debate.

The U.S. legal system is unusual, compared with the systems of many other advanced industrial countries, in its federalist nature. In addition to the national constitution, each state has its own constitution, specifying the powers and duties of state and local governments and, in many cases, imposing restrictions on those powers. The state courts are responsible for interpreting state constitutions and statutes. Decisions of the state courts are subject to review by the United States Supreme Court only when they concern matters of federal law, or when one of the parties claims that a state court decision has violated the federal constitution or a federal statute or policy. This explains why many significant cases discussed in this book were never taken to the U.S. Supreme Court for review. In many instances, the decisions concerned state law issues that raised no "federal question" within the jurisdiction of the U.S. Supreme Court.

* * * * *

This book refers frequently to a few significant events in the history of sexuality, which are here described to assist readers of the case discussions.

During the 1940s, Alfred Kinsey formed an institute for the scientific study of human sexuality. Kinsey, a zoologist by training, was interested in observing the broad variety of human sexuality, and sought out as many interview subjects as he could possibly find to document this variety. He enlisted other scientists in his efforts, and his most important books on sexual behavior in the male and female were co-authored by Pomeroy and Martin, but the works have always been associated in the public mind with Kinsey himself.

The first Kinsey book, on the male, was published in 1948. It created a sensation by suggesting that the frequency of nonprocreative sexual activity was much higher than had commonly been thought, and most significantly higher in the cases of homosexuality and bisexuality. Most writers on human sexual conduct had previously asserted that homosexuality and bisexuality were rare phenomena, involving only a small number of mentally disturbed people. Kinsey's research suggested that more than a third of American males had participated in homosexual behavior after puberty, and that as many as ten percent might be primarily homosexual in their orientation for much of their adult life. A subsequent book on women, published in 1953, suggested that female sexuality also exhibited considerable diversity in practice, although Kinsey's research showed a smaller percentage of the female population engaged in homosexual or bisexual activity. These two books, commonly referred to together as the Kinsey Reports, caused many professionals in the fields of medicine, mental health, religion, and law to take a new look at how their fields dealt with sexual issues.

Kinsey's work inspired others during the 1950s to explore the phenomenon of homosexuality. Perhaps the most prominent was Dr. Evelyn Hooker, whose work led to a National Institute of Mental Health Task Force report that concluded that homosexuality and bisexuality were not necessarily symptoms of mental illness. Together with other studies, the Kinsey Reports and the Hooker studies led members of the American Psychiatric Association and the American Psychological Association to vote in the early 1970s to remove homosexuality from their published lists of mental illnesses, and persuaded the American Bar Association to support the repeal of laws against same-sex sexual activity.

In both England and the United States, prominent law revision groups evaluated the role that criminal law played in controlling "deviant" sexual behavior during the 1950s. A special law revision committee appointed by the English Parliament, chaired by Lord Wolfenden, issued a report in 1957 recommending that consensual sexual activity between adults, whether homosexual or heterosexual, be freed from penal sanction as long as it was conducted in private. At about the same time, the American Law Institute, drafting a Model Penal Code for consideration by state legislatures, was also moved by the Kinsey Reports and subsequent studies to recommend that penal sanctions against consensual sodomy and other "victimless" sex crimes be removed. These law reform proposals were adopted by Parliament and many state legislatures in the United States during the 1960s. In some states, however, legislatures adopted the Model Penal Code but retained or reenacted criminal sanctions for nonmarital sexual activity, including fornication, prostitution, adultery, and sodomy (most frequently defined as anal or oral sex). In many cases, however, the penalties for sodomy were sharply reduced, since the crime was reclassified from felony to misdemeanor status in many states.

The 1960s was a decade of considerable social ferment in the United States, marked by powerful advocacy of civil rights for racial minorities and a new militancy by women seeking equal rights in the workplace and government. Although there was a small homosexual rights movement in the United States that had been begun by pioneering activists in Los Angeles, San Francisco, and New York during the 1950s, a militant, visible movement patterned on the efforts of racial minorities and women did not burst forth until the end of the 1960s. A key event, frequently mentioned in this book, was the Stonewall Riots of 1969.

The Stonewall Inn was a "gay bar" on Christopher Street in Greenwich Village, a bohemian neighborhood of New York City. At the time, New York State liquor regulations prohibited establishments with liquor licenses from knowingly serving homosexuals. Gay bar owners (many reputed to be fronts for organized crime groups) had to "pay off" local police officers to secure their cooperation in not reporting that homosexuals were congregating in their establishments. Police raids of gay bars would occur if the bar owner was slow in making a payment, or if politicians campaigning for reelection desired to show the public that they were "cracking down" on vice. By 1969, the liberation spirit had begun to grow among homosexuals, and a routine police raid at the Stonewall Inn on June 27, 1969, encountered unprecedented resistance from the patrons, a diverse collection of gays, transvestites, and other street people, leading to two nights of rioting in the neighborhood of the bar and the formation of the Gay Liberation Front, the first militant gay rights organization in the United States.

Although there was a growing movement among homosexuals for law reform prior to the Stonewall Riots, the Riots were the catalyst for a more widely based movement, leading to political organizing on a new scale on college campuses and in urban communities. Most writers on the history of the gay rights movement describe the Stonewall Riots as the key birthdate of the modern movement. Soon after, gay rights activists in New York started the National Gay Task Force, which actively lobbied governmental leaders for changes in the law, and the Lambda Legal Defense and Education Fund, which undertook test-case litigation to challenge inequitable treatment of individuals or groups on the basis of sexual orientation. The gay liberation movement of the 1970s also inspired the phenomenon of "coming out," by which homosexuals revealed and made an issue of their sexual orientation, which led to some of the significant gay rights litigation described in this book.

The gay rights movement of the 1970s, together with the more general "sexual revolution" of the 1960s and 1970s, had a direct impact on the development of law relative to sexuality in several respects. First, it helped to advance the trend of sodomy law reform by which almost half the states had decriminalized consensual sodomy, both homosexual and hetero-

sexual, by the end of the 1980s, and some other jurisdictions had reduced the classification of consensual sodomy from a felony to a misdemeanor. Second, it led to the enactment of laws forbidding discrimination on the basis of sexual orientation in several cities, and secured issuance of executive orders by several governors banning sexual orientation discrimination by executive agencies of their states. Third, it confronted courts for the first time with fierce opposition to discrimination against lesbian and gay parents, who began to contest attempts to deprive them of parental rights, producing some landmark decisions in the field of domestic relations law. And, on a more general level, it led to lesbians, gay men, bisexuals and other sexual minorities becoming generally more assertive about their rights to equal treatment under the law. Although this book discusses some significant cases predating the 1970s, the overwhelming majority of significant appellate decisions on issues of sexuality and law postdate the Stonewall Riots; prior to this time, there was not much direct litigation asserting the rights of sexual minorities.

In 1979 and 1980, doctors in San Francisco, Los Angeles, and New York began to observe strange disorders among otherwise healthy gay men. By 1981, the U.S. Centers for Disease Control, a division of the Public Health Service responsible for documenting outbreaks of epidemics, had determined that an apparently new sexually transmitted disease was spreading in the gay male community. At first called "gay-related immune deficiency," the new disease was eventually attributed to a blood-borne virus as cases sprang up among blood transfusion recipients, users of blood-clotting medication manufactured from donated blood, and intravenous drug users who shared needles. The disease was renamed acquired immune deficiency syndrome, or AIDS, and became a major factor in the history of sexual minorities beginning in the early 1980s.

Concerns about AIDS have come to play a role in a variety of issues discussed in this book, including parental rights of gay men, criminal regulation of nonmarital sexual conduct, and discrimination on the basis of sexual orientation in employment, housing, public services, and the military. Because AIDS raises significant issues apart from sexuality, this book does not deal directly with the growing body of cases defining the rights and responsibilities of persons infected with human immunodeficiency virus, the virus many scientists believe to be the cause of AIDS. However, as courts continue to address such issues as the constitutionality of sodomy laws and other sex crime laws, exclusionary employment policies, and parental rights, it seems inevitable that concerns about AIDS will play a major role.

* * * * *

The closing date for inclusion of new cases for discussion in this book was January 1, 1992.

* * * * *

The author gratefully acknowledges the encouragement and assistance of Gary Kuris, John Johnson, and Kevin Bradley at Garland Publishing, of copyeditor Paula Grant, and of the entire Garland staff. New York Law School students John William Cook and Otis Damslet provided helpful research assistance in compiling materials and reviewing first drafts. Special thanks go to former Dean James F. Simon and the trustees of New York Law School for faculty research grants in support of this project, and to Professor Wayne Dynes for suggesting to Garland that a book on sexuality and the law be part of its series of legal encyclopedias. This book is dedicated with love to my life partner, Timothy W. Nenno.

SEXUALITY AND THE LAW

CHAPTER 1
REPRODUCTION

The U.S. Supreme Court suggested that the federal Constitution might restrain the government from interfering with the reproductive capacity of an individual in *Skinner v. Oklahoma*, a 1942 case in which the State of Oklahoma sought to sterilize a man because he was a habitual petty thief. Out of the due process and equal protection theories articulated by some of the judges in *Skinner* grew a body of law developed by federal and state courts and legislators significantly deregulating private consensual sexual activities and decisions about reproduction. In this chapter are discussions of several leading cases on reproductive issues.

The cases on reproductive autonomy recognize that the decision whether to beget or bear a child is one of the most deeply personal and individualistic decisions that a person can make. By identifying such a decision as presenting issues of constitutional dimension, the Supreme Court injected the judicial system into one of the most emotionally perplexing issues facing 20th-century America: the role of the state with respect to the practices of contraception and abortion. The theoretical underpinnings of the reproductive rights cases have also served to change the law in other spheres, including interracial marriage, homosexual conduct, so-called unnatural (i.e., nonvaginal) sexual expression, and many issues related to the family and employment, which will be explored in subsequent chapters.

The cases selected for discussion provide a broad outline of the judicial debate on reproductive activity up to the advent of the new Supreme Court majority constructed through the appointments of Presidents Ronald W. Reagan and George H. W. Bush. Developments in the law governing reproductive freedom after January 1, 1992 (such as the "frozen embryos" controversy addressed by the Tennessee Supreme Court in *Davis v. Davis* (1992)), and the further adventures of the Supreme Court in confronting abortion, such as *Planned Parenthood v. Casey* (1992) are deferred to future editions of this work. However, it appears that the dissenting views expressed by Justices Byron R. White and William H. Rehnquist in *Roe v. Wade*, the landmark abortion decision of the 1970s, may be the majority views of the Supreme Court in the 1990s.

Reproduction: Readings

Bradley, T.S., "Prohibiting Payments to Surrogate Mothers: Love's Labor Lost and the Constitutional Right of Privacy," 20 *John Marshall Law Review* 715 (Summer 1987)

Collins, R.K.L., "Is There Life (Or Choice) After Roe ?," 3 *Constitutional Commentary* 91 (Winter 1986)

Dellinger, W., and G.B. Sperling, "Abortion and the Supreme Court: The Retreat From *Roe v. Wade*," 138 *U. Pennsylvania Law Review* 83 (November 1989)

Johnsen, D., "From Driving to Drugs: Governmental Regulation of Pregnant Women's Lives After *Webster*," 138 *University of Pennsylvania Law Review* 179 (November 1989)

Rubenfeld, J., "The Right of Privacy," 102 *Harvard Law Review* 737 (February 1989)

Schnably, S.J., "Beyond *Griswold*: Foucauldian and Republican Approaches to Privacy," 23 *Connecticut Law Review* 861 (Summer 1991)

Scott, E.S., "Sterilization of Mentally Retarded Persons: Reproductive Rights and Family Privacy," 1986 *Duke Law Journal* 806 (November 1986)

Sunstein, C.R., "Neutrality in Constitutional Law (With Special Reference to Pornography, Abortion, and Surrogacy)," 92 *Columbia L. Rev.* 1 (Jan. 1992)

1. CONSTITUTIONALITY OF EUGENIC STERILIZATION

Buck v. Bell, 274 U.S. 200 (1927), affirming 143 Va. 310, 130 S.E. 516 (1925).

Buck v. Bell probably represents the high point of the eugenic sterilization movement in the United States. Spurred by popular enthusiasm for Charles Darwin's theory of evolution, some propagandists argued that advances in modern medicine and living standards had unfortunately made it possible for genetically inferior persons to survive and reproduce, thus threatening the overall fitness of the human race and preventing the process of natural selection from allowing the race to adapt to changing conditions. Proponents of eugenic sterilization argued that it was imperative for the future health of the human race that people with inferior genes be identified and prevented from reproducing. They managed to persuade several state legislatures to authorize or require the sterilization of persons with mental impairments believed to be genetically based. Virginia enacted a sterilization act in 1924, which was promptly challenged in the case of *Buck v. Bell.*

The Virginia Sterilization Act (Act of 1924, chapter 394), after reciting that the welfare of the individual and society would be promoted by sterilizing mental defectives, authorized the superintendents of the various state institutions where "mental defectives" were housed to identify inmates suitable for sterilization and to apply to special boards of directors for an order to have women sterilized by salpingectomy (i.e., cutting and tying the fallopian tubes) and men sterilized by vasectomy (i.e., cutting and tying the vas deferens), thus terminating reproductive capacity without de-sexing the individual. The Act provided that the mental defective, any parents, and a legal guardian be entitled to appeal the board's order to the state's circuit courts and ultimately to the Virginia Supreme Court of Appeals.

Those seeking to test the validity of the law selected Carrie Buck, a 17-year-old unmarried mother who was confined to the State Colony for Epileptics and Feeble-Minded in 1924, having been adjudged feeble-minded on

January 23 of that year. Buck's infant daughter was also believed to be mentally defective, and her mother had previously been confined to the same institution. On September 10, Superintendent A. S. Priddy petitioned the special board of directors of the State Colony for an order to have Carrie Buck sterilized.

The board issued the order as requested, and Buck's guardian filed an appeal in the Amherst County circuit court, where she was represented by Lynchburg attorney I. P. Whitehead and the State Colony was represented by Aubrey E. Strode of the Lynchburg firm of Strode and Edmunds. Whitehead argued that the statute violated the due process and equal protection requirements of the Fourteenth Amendment and imposed a cruel and unusual punishment in violation of the Eighth Amendment, as well as parallel protections afforded under the Virginia Constitution. Strode countered that the Act was well within the police powers of the state that had not been surrendered to the federal government, in providing for the health and welfare of the state and its citizens. Because of her mental condition, Strode argued, it was likely that Buck would bear further mental defectives unless prevented from doing so. There were two ways this could be prevented: either she could be confined under segregation from sexual contact with men in the State Colony until she naturally became infertile with the passage of time (about thirty years) or she could be sterilized and allowed to live outside the Colony under appropriate supervision, free to engage in sexual activity without fear of producing defective offspring.

The circuit court entered judgment for the defendant, Dr. J. H. Bell, who had replaced Priddy as superintendent of the State Colony. Buck appealed, renewing her constitutional arguments before the Virginia Supreme Court of Appeals. In a unanimous opinion by Justice Jesse F. West issued November 12, 1925, the court rejected all grounds advanced on behalf of Buck, affirming the circuit court's sterilization order.

As to the due process allegations, the court held that all requisites of procedural due process were satisfied by affording a right of appeal to the circuit court where Buck was represented by counsel before an assertedly impartial tribunal. The court made no mention of any substantive due process considerations, such as whether there was a rational basis to sustain the statute, but it appeared from the tenor of the opinion (especially the discussion of equal protection) that the court would have so found.

The court was equally dismissive of Buck's argument that the Act imposed a cruel and unusual punishment. According to West, the constitutional prohibition on cruel and unusual punishment referred to criminal proceedings and had reference "to such bodily punishments as involve torture and are inhumane and barbarous." The Act was a civil statute, was not intended to punish, and indeed was intended for the benefit of both the mentally defective individual and society, since it would allow a feeble-minded person to live outside a mental institution by removing the fear of unwanted pregnancy. West stated that "the operation, practically speaking, is harmless and 100 per cent safe, and in most cases relieves the patient from further confinement in the colony."

As to the equal protection claim, the court found that Buck had not been treated differently from anybody similarly situated. Since the state was authorized under the police power to confine mentally defective people, it followed that the state could take steps to make it possible for such people to live outside institutions by subjecting them to sterilization. So long as the basis on which the state selected individuals for sterilization was "reasonable," those selected could not be heard to complain that they were being subjected to unequal treatment. Besides, the determination that an individual is feeble-minded required careful observation for two months after confinement in the institution and the use of an approved test of mentality to confirm the diagnosis. Until somebody was definitely judged to be feeble-minded, they were not subject to the Act, thus removing the possibility that people who were not similarly situated would be subjected to the same treatment.

Counsel for Buck promptly petitioned the U.S. Supreme Court for a writ of error, and the case was argued before the Court on April 22, 1927. Whitehead made a passionate argument, including the contention that upholding the Virginia law would impose in place of the constitution a version of "Plato's Republic" where the "experts" of medicine would rule instead of the people's representatives. Strode replied that the statute was merely intended to free the feeble-minded from confinement by removing the main impediment to their release; since the right of the state to confine the feeble-minded was unquestioned, it was absurd to argue that an enactment intended to enhance their opportunity for freedom was unconstitutional.

The Court's quickest writer, Justice Oliver Wendell Holmes, Jr., was assigned the opinion, approved by the Court and announced on May 2. Justice Pierce Butler dissented, but wrote no opinion.

Justice Holmes upheld the lower court opinions in a brief memorandum, which has become a classic statement of the limits of due process prior to the revolution in constitutional law that began to transform the field of individual liberties during the 1940s and 1950s. After reciting the facts of the case and stating conclusorily that the requirements of procedural due process had been served, Holmes devoted two paragraphs to disposing of Buck's substantive claims. Being bound by the factual finding that Carrie Buck "is the probable potential parent of socially inadequate offspring, likewise afflicted, that she may be sexually sterilized without detriment to her general health and that her welfare and that of society will be promoted by her sterilization," Holmes rejected the argument that as a matter of law, grounds did not exist for ordering the sterilization; given the factual findings of the circuit court, the result is justified.

"We have seen more than once that the public welfare may call upon the best citizens for their lives," said Holmes, a veteran of the Union Army in the Civil War who had been seriously wounded in combat and who was a devotee of Darwin's theories. "It would be strange if it could not call upon those who already sap the strength of the State for these lesser sacrifices, often not felt to be such by those concerned, in order to prevent our being swamped with incompetence." Holmes had accepted the rationale of the eugenics movement without hesitation. "It is better for all the world," he asserted, "if instead of waiting to execute degenerate offspring for crime, or to let them starve for their imbecility, society can prevent those who are manifestly unfit from continuing their kind." Invoking the Court's precedent in *Jacobson v. Massachusetts* (1905), which upheld a compulsory vaccination statute, Holmes stated with finality, "Three generations of imbeciles are enough."

Holmes dealt even more tersely with the equal protection claim, in effect stating that resort to equal protection is the last desperate refuge of those unable to make a successful due process argument. "[T]he answer is that the law does all that is needed when it does all that it can, indicates a policy, applies it to all within the lines, and seeks to bring within the lines all similarly situated so far and so fast as its means allow." That mentally defective persons who were not committed to state institutions were not subject to the Sterilization Act posed no equal protection barrier to the Act's enforcement, since "as far as the operations enable those who otherwise must be kept confined to be returned to the world, and thus open the asylum to others, the equality aimed at will be more nearly reached."

While *Buck v. Bell* marked a triumph for the pro-eugenics forces by affirming that the states had authority to compel the sterilization of mental defectives after affording procedural due process, doubts as to the ability of the medical profession to determine whether particular mental defects were due to inherited genetic causes helped to undermine the viability of the movement. Later scholars were able to show, for example, that Carrie Buck herself was not significantly retarded and that her infant daughter turned out to be of normal intelligence. By the 1940s, some members of the Court were ready to hold in *Skinner v. Oklahoma* (1942) that reproductive rights were so fundamental that more than "fair procedures" were necessary for government-ordered sterilization against the will of the individual. But *Buck v. Bell* continues to be cited, along with *Jacobson v. Massachusetts*, in support of the proposition that individual liberties must cede when the government determines that the general welfare requires the imposition of public health measures.

Case References

Jacobson v. Massachusetts, 197 U.S. 11 (1905)
Skinner v. Oklahoma, 316 U.S. 535 (1942)

2. CAN THE STATE STERILIZE CRIMINALS?

Skinner v. Oklahoma, 316 U.S. 535 (1942), reversing *Skinner v. State*, 115 P.2d 123 (Okla. 1941).

The eugenics movement of the early decades of the 20th century reached its height in the years between the World Wars. At first, the focus was on involuntary sterilization of those who seemed clearly mentally ill, presumably due to some inheritable genetic defect, with a particular focus on those confined in mental institutions. After the constitutionality of these practices was approved by the U.S. Supreme Court in *Buck v. Bell*, the movement gained new force and extended to the more controversial area of "inheritable criminality." Scientific "experts" were by no means unanimous on the question, but some contended that "habitual" criminality

could be traced to physical and mental characteristics with an inheritable genetic basis, and they persuaded the legislatures of several states that involuntary sterilization of such persons would enhance the public welfare.

One such state was Oklahoma, which passed its Habitual Criminal Sterilization Act in 1935. The Act provided that any person convicted of certain crimes amounting to felonies of "moral turpitude" and sentenced to prison could be subjected to an involuntary sterilization procedure, provided that the person had twice previously been convicted of felonies of moral turpitude and that a jury determined the procedure would not be injurious to the person's health. The Act required the attorney general to initiate such a procedure in every case that qualified for it by petitioning the district court. The Act was very particular about which felonies would or would not count for purposes of determining whether a repeat offender could be sterilized. For example, larceny was covered by the statute, but embezzlement was excluded, as were violations of the tax laws or political offenses.

The first case brought by Attorney General Mac Q. Williamson to enforce the law became a test case that ended up in the U.S. Supreme Court. The target was a young man named Jack T. Skinner, a "habitual criminal" if ever there was one. Skinner was convicted in 1926 while just a youth of stealing chickens and sentenced to a term in the Oklahoma State Reformatory. In 1929, he was convicted of armed robbery and again sentenced to the Reformatory. In 1934, he was again convicted of armed robbery and having attained the requisite age was sentenced to a term in the state penitentiary. The following year, the legislature passed the sterilization law, and in 1936 Williamson commenced proceedings in the Pittsburg County District Court before Judge R.W. Higgins to have Skinner vasectomized. Since there was no question that Skinner had been thrice convicted of felonies involving moral turpitude that were covered by the law, the only real question for the jury was "whether he might be rendered sexually sterile without detriment to his general health." The jury found that Skinner's general health would not be impaired by the operation, and Judge Higgins entered an order for Skinner's sterilization. Skinner's attorneys, Claud Briggs and John Morrison, of Oklahoma City, appealed this order to the Oklahoma Supreme Court.

Skinner's stated grounds for appeal were numerous. He argued that the sterilization law was in effect a punishment for his crimes and, as such, a "cruel and unusual punishment" in violation of the Oklahoma Constitution. (At that time, the U.S. Supreme Court had not yet applied the Eighth Amendment to the states by incorporation in the Due Process Clause of the Fourteenth Amendment, so Skinner raised no Eighth Amendment claim.) Since his offenses

had been committed before the Act was passed, he also contended that it was an unconstitutional ex post facto law or a bill of attainder, in violation of both the state and federal constitutions, and objected as well to having been compelled to testify at his hearing on grounds of self-incrimination. Skinner also argued that the Act violated the Due Process clauses of the state and federal constitutions, both procedurally and substantively, and denied him equal protection of the laws by singling out certain felonies and excluding others as a prerequisite for sterilization.

The Oklahoma Supreme Court divided sharply, 5–4, in its decision of February 18, 1941. Upholding the constitutionality of the Act and its application to Skinner, the five-member majority opinion written by Justice Thurman S. Hurst characterized the whole process as "civil" rather than "criminal" and held that Skinner had failed to overcome the strong presumption of constitutionality that attached to all legislation that was within the police power of the state. The dissenting opinion by Justice Monroe Osborn, joined by three others, contended that the Act was fatally defective under the Due Process Clause by its failure to require inquiry and findings on the question whether the individual sought to be sterilized possessed inheritable criminal traits.

Justice Hurst dealt first with whether the proceedings were civil or criminal in nature, which was deemed crucial to the issue of cruel and unusual punishment because various courts had held that sterilization was a cruel and unusual punishment. Indeed, if the Act were deemed criminal in nature, then sterilization of Skinner would be unconstitutional under the prohibition of *ex post facto* laws, because it would in effect be imposing on him a new punishment that had not been authorized at the time his crimes were committed. Imbued with the goals of the eugenics movement, the court was confident that the law had nothing to do with punishment and everything to do with the improved welfare of society. Not only did this law use the procedure in civil cases as opposed to criminal cases, it was applicable to all those who had been thrice convicted and sentenced, regardless whether they were presently confined. It was passed as "a eugenic measure to improve the safety and general welfare of the race by preventing from being born persons who will probably become criminals." As such, its goal was not punishment but rather the improvement of society.

To Skinner's objection that the failure of the law to require any hearing on whether he was likely "to beget criminal children" cut against any eugenic purpose, the court responded that this merely showed that the legislature had concluded that all habitual criminals were likely to beget criminal children. To the further objection that the law's application to all regardless of age or length of sentence belied a eugenic purpose, the court responded that the legislature might have been concerned that a prisoner could escape before the operation was carried out. The court also dismissed Skinner's objections to his required testimony and the unavailability of peremptory challenges against jurors. Since, in its opinion, this was a civil proceeding, these elementary violations of criminal procedure were not relevant.

As to the constitutional challenges under the Due Process and Equal Protection clauses, the court held that all procedural requirements of the Constitution were obeyed. Skinner was given a full hearing on the question whether the operation would injure his health, and it was reasonable for the legislature to have prescribed sterilization under these circumstances for the welfare of the people of Oklahoma. Sterilization laws had been passed in at least twenty-seven states, the court asserted, and in ten of those the laws applied to habitual criminals. "Thus it is seen that the sterilization of criminals as well as mental defectives as a eugenic measure may be effected under the police power of the state," commented Hurst, "provided the particular act fulfills the requirements of due process of law in its procedural aspects and the provisions thereof reasonably appear to bear a real and substantial relation to the public health, safety, morals or some other phase of the general welfare."

These requirements were met by the Oklahoma law, said the court, because it was reasonable for the legislature to have concluded, on the basis of current evidence from eugenic studies, that criminal tendencies were inheritable. "The discretion of the Legislature is very great in the exercise of the police power," said Hurst, and only an act infringing on "the inherent rights of life, liberty and property" would require the court to engage in supervisory scrutiny of the legislature's actions. Even then, "all the presumptions of validity" would apply to the law. "We must, therefore, assume that the Legislature had before it statistics, scientific works, and information from which it found as a fact that habitual criminals are more likely than not to beget children of like criminal tendencies who will probably become a burden upon society." It was not the job of the courts to usurp the fact-finding functions of "the coordinate branch of the government" which had "the duty to formulate the public policy of the state." "Every presumption must be indulged in favor of the existence of facts which the Legislature assumed and acted upon," said Hurst, "and we are not at liberty to strike down the act unless we can say beyond a reasonable doubt that the Legislature was clearly in error, and was wholly unwarranted and acted arbitrarily, in assuming or determining such facts."

Given such a tough barrier to judicial review, Skinner's effort to have the law declared unconstitutional was doomed to failure. That heredity plays an important role in "our mental, moral and physical make-up" is something that "we all know," said Hurst. What was less certain was whether criminality was hereditary; some experts believed it was, and presumably members of the legislature had acted on their beliefs. While the law's constitutionality might be even more certain if it required an individualized determination whether a particular habitual offender was capable of transmitting his criminal nature to his offspring, that could impose difficult issues of proof that the legislature might have wished to avoid. In any event, the opinions of the experts who would have testified on such issues could just as well be relied on by the legislature in drawing its conclusion that sterilization was justified in the case of all habitual criminals. That other states provided for such an inquiry in their statutes did not render the Oklahoma law defective. The legislature may have omitted such a provision "because it thought such a finding could not be based upon satisfactory proof," and it should be given the "latitude" to have made such a judgment. In any event, there was nothing in the record to justify the court finding that "the Legislature was clearly and beyond a reasonable doubt in error in assuming facts justifying the act as a proper exercise of the police power." The court's judgment on this was in no way superior to the legislature's, and it would violate the separation of powers for the court to substitute its judgment on the matter.

Finally, Hurst quickly disposed of the equal protection argument. This would "be dependent upon the reasonableness of the classification." Since the law applied to "all habitual criminals as therein defined," there was no classification problem, asserted Hurst, and no arbitrary or unlawful discrimination.

Justice Osborn's spirited dissent insisted that the extreme deference to legislative judgment shown by the court was not appropriate "when the inherent constitutional rights of citizens are involved." The police power "is subordinate to the organic law," he asserted, and could be exercised only to the extent it did not entrench on rights protected by such law. The legislature's omission to provide a hearing on the issue whether the individual was capable of passing on his objectionable traits to offspring was fatal. "The right to beget children is one of the highest natural and inherent rights, protected by" both the state and federal due process clauses, and it would violate that right to deprive somebody of his reproductive capability without at minimum making an individualized determination that such deprivation was necessary for the public welfare.

Curiously, neither the majority nor the dissenters gave any express consideration to the grounds upon which the case was eventually decided by the U.S. Supreme Court, which granted *certiorari* to review the ruling on January 12, 1942, on a petition filed for Skinner by Oklahoma attorneys W. J. Hulsey and Heba I. Aston. It took less than a month after the May 6, oral argument for a unanimous Court to announce on June 1 that it had found the law unconstitutional, although two of the Justices wrote separately to state alternative approaches to the case. For Justice William O. Douglas, writing for the Court, the most pressing flaw of the Oklahoma law was its list of excluded crimes. The state had mandated sterilization for those

who had thrice been convicted of some felonies and not others, and Douglas could not see how the degree of moral turpitude was any different for some crimes on one list and not on another. Although he did not come right out and say it, he certainly implied in his opinion that the legislation bore the marks of bigoted assumptions about human worthiness based on economic class that were unacceptable under the Equal Protection Clause.

Douglas seized on a comparison of embezzlement, a crime on the excluded list, and grand larceny, a crime included. Both essentially involved theft and were equally felonies under Oklahoma law. Indeed, it was likely that the theft of something over $20 in value and the embezzlement of something over $20 in value would be equally punished, all things considered. But the larcenist might be sterilized and the embezzler would not be. "A clerk who appropriates over $20 from his employer's till and a stranger who steals the same amount are thus both guilty of felonies," he pointed out. "If the latter repeats his act and is convicted three times, he may be sterilized. But the clerk is not subject to the pains and penalties of the Act no matter how large his embezzlements nor how frequent his convictions. A person who enters a chicken coop and steals chickens commits a felony; and he may be sterilized if he is thrice convicted. If, however, he is a bailee of the property and fraudulently appropriates it, he is an embezzler. Hence, no matter how habitual his proclivities for embezzlement are and no matter how often his conviction, he may not be sterilized." For Douglas, that "the nature of the two crimes is intrinsically the same" and both were dealt with as felonies meant that those convicted were similarly situated, as that term acquires relevance in an equal protection analysis, and the state could not single them out for different treatment in imposing a procedure "that involves one of the basic civil rights of man." Douglas stated:

Marriage and procreation are fundamental to the very existence and survival of the race. The power to sterilize, if exercised, may have subtle, far-reaching and devastating effects. In evil or reckless hands it can cause races or types which are inimical to the dominant group to wither and disappear. There is no redemption for the individual whom the law touches. Any experiment which the State conducts is to his irreparable injury. He is forever deprived of a basic liberty.

Thus, a fundamental constitutional right was involved, and "strict scrutiny of the classification which a State makes in a sterilization law is essential" to avoid "invidious discriminations . . . against groups or types of individuals" in violation of the Fourteenth Amendment. Since the offenses of embezzlement and larceny were intrinsically of "the same quality," it would offend equal protection to subject the larcenist to sterilization while letting the embezzler reproduce unhindered. Indeed, the only distinction Oklahoma recognized between the two crimes was the timing of when the "fraudulent intent to convert the property to the taker's own use" arises; should so basic a right as human reproduction turn on such a distinction, derived from common-law formalism? The law was unconstitutional, and Judge Higgins's sterilization order must be reversed.

For Chief Justice Harlan Fiske Stone, Douglas's approach to the issue was inadequate to the problems the law presented. Indeed, Stone rather disagreed with Douglas's analysis. He seriously doubted whether there was any equal protection problem with the law. It might be that the legislature could rationally pick and choose among various felonies and decide which ones would justify subsequent sterilization of repeat offenders. For Stone, "the real question we have to consider is . . . whether the wholesale condemnation of a class to such an invasion of personal liberty, without opportunity to any individual to show that his is not the type of case which would justify resort to it, satisfies the demands of due process." For Stone, this was purely a fundamental rights case, not an equal protection case.

Implicitly agreeing with the dissenting opinion of Justice Osborn, Stone found the law fatally flawed in failing to accord a hearing on the question whether the individual sought to be sterilized had inheritable criminal tendencies. The legislature could not just presume inheritability from the classification of the crimes committed. "Science has found and the law has recognized that there are certain types of mental deficiency associated with delinquency

which are inheritable," said Stone, but there was no evidence that "the criminal tendencies of any class of habitual offenders are universally or even generally inheritable." As such, "the most elementary notions of due process" required an individualized determination before the subject of the proceedings "is condemned to an irreparable injury in his person."

Justice Robert H. Jackson was clearly torn between the alternative theories of Douglas and Stone. He essentially agreed with both, and he wrote separately to make clear that while endorsing both opinions, he was opposed to each to the degree it might be read as rejecting the holding of the other. He also wanted to indicate that the statute suffered flaws other than those identified by Douglas and Stone. While the Court had upheld mandatory sterilization in *Buck v. Bell*, a case of "imbecility" where "the condition had persisted through three generations and afforded grounds for the belief that it was transmissible and would continue to manifest itself in generations to come," that was not the case with habitual criminal offenders statutes. "There are limits to the extent to which a legislatively represented majority may conduct biological experiments at the expense of the dignity and personality and natural powers of a minority—even those who have been guilty of what the majority define as crimes." But the Court need not describe those limits in this case, because the Oklahoma law fell so short of minimal due process and equal protection requirements as described by Justices Douglas and Stone.

Skinner v. Oklahoma was an opinion of enormous significance. By limiting the holding of *Buck v. Bell* and describing the right of procreation as having fundamental constitutional importance, the Court was providing a crucial foundation element for the right of sexual privacy that it would develop a quarter century later in the contraception and abortion decisions of the Warren and Burger courts. The opinion was also an early expression of the individual rights jurisprudence under the Fourteenth Amendment that would lie at the heart of the revolution in individual rights developed by the Warren Court. Justice Douglas's talk of "strict scrutiny" under the Equal Protection Clause where similarly situated persons were dealt with unequally concerning a "basic" issue of "human rights" would become a familiar feature of the civil rights rhetoric of the Court on a wide range of issues, and the Skinner opinion would become one of the most frequently invoked precedents in support of this mode of analysis.

Case Reference

Buck v. Bell, 274 U.S. 200 (1927)

3. THE RIGHT TO SEXUAL PRIVACY: A "DRY RUN"

Poe v. Ullman, 367 U.S. 497 (1961), dismissing appeal from *Buxton v. Ullman*, 147 Conn. 48, 156 A.2d 508 (1959).

When the U.S. Supreme Court issued its historic decision in *Griswold v. Connecticut* in 1965, finding that a constitutional right to privacy required striking down a Connecticut law against the use of contraceptives to prevent conception, it was confronting a question it had struggled to avoid just four years previously in *Poe v. Ullman*, a challenge to the very same statute. Four members of the Court, Justices Hugo L. Black, William O. Douglas, John M. Harlan, and Potter Stewart, wanted to reach the constitutional question in *Poe*, but, while four members can bring a case before the Court, it takes five to rule on the merits, and a fifth vote was not available. Nonetheless, *Poe* provoked a lengthy set of opinions, one from Justice Felix Frankfurter explaining for a plurality of the Court why it had decided not to rule on the merits, and two (by Justices Douglas and Harlan) that were the precursors of two main strands of the privacy theory that would finally surface triumphantly in *Griswold*.

Since 1879, Connecticut had forbidden as a criminal offense the use of contraceptives by any person for the purpose of preventing conception. By a general aiding and abetting statute read in combination with the contraception law, Connecticut authorities had prosecuted a family planning clinic in *State v. Nelson* (1940), winning a judgment from the state's highest court that the contraception law was constitutional and contained no exception, and in 1942 that court held in *Tileston v. Ullman* that the law did not even allow an exception for married couples when a physician determined that the health of the wife would be endangered if she became pregnant. The *Nelson* prosecution was brought at a time when there were eight such family planning clinics operating in Connecticut in defiance of the law. State authorities, who had never previously enforced the law, brought the case to "make an example," which was quite effective.

After the court decision, the other clinics closed down and, although contraceptives remained available through pharmacies (there was no law banning their distribution or sale), public or organized family planning activities in Connecticut were effectively deterred. The law had never been enforced directly against a husband and wife who used contraceptives privately. Enforcement would have been quite difficult, since testimonial privileges protected spouses from having to testify against each other, and only eyewitness testimony or personal confession would provide competent, admissible evidence of a violation.

Family planning advocates were ready to try again by the late 1950s. Dr. C. Lee Buxton, a prominent physician, and a group of his patients, got together with attorney Catherine G. Roraback of Canaan, Connecticut, to put together a trio of declaratory judgment complaints, which they filed in the superior court in New Haven, seeking an injunction against enforcement of the law. The plaintiffs alleged that the law violated Buxton's right to practice his profession by prescribing contraceptives in appropriate cases, and the rights of his patients (given pseudonyms for privacy purposes) to protect their health and control their reproductive activities. State's Attorney Abraham S. Ullman, the named defendant in the three companion cases, represented by Assistant Attorney General Raymond J. Cannon, moved to dismiss the complaints for failure to state a legal claim. Cannon argued that the constitutionality of the statute had already been determined by the state's highest court in 1940, and that mere passage of time or change of personnel on the court was not a sufficient basis for the superior court to consider a new challenge on the merits, being bound by the prior decision. Judge Frank Healey was persuaded by this, and dismissed the cases, which were promptly appealed to Connecticut's Supreme Court of Errors.

The Supreme Court of Errors unanimously affirmed the dismissal in an opinion by Chief Justice Raymond E. Baldwin issued on December 8, 1959. After reviewing the history of the litigation and past attacks on the Connecticut statute, Baldwin concluded that the difference, if any, between these declaratory judgment actions and the *Nelson* and *Tileston* cases "lies only in the fact that here each plaintiff is asserting his own constitutional right, while in the *Nelson* and *Tileston* cases the doctors were attempting to assert the right of their patients to receive treatment." Baldwin concluded that the court might take one of two courses in this case: reinterpret the statute to provide an exception for married couples, thus avoiding any constitutional question, or stick with its prior construction and confront the constitutional question. He saw no ground for abandoning the prior construction. Indeed, since those 1940s decisions, the legislature had reenacted the statute verbatim as part of two general law revisions and had uniformly rejected attempts to amend the contraceptive law on several occasions. This must mean that the court's prior interpretations were consistent with the intent of the legislature to enact a complete ban on contraceptive use for purposes of preventing conception. (The legislature had not, however, banned the use of contraceptives to prevent transmission of disease, and presumably a doctor would not be in violation of Connecticut

law for prescribing them for that purpose. As noted above, there was no law banning distribution or sale, and condoms and other contraceptive devices were available for sale in Connecticut pharmacies.)

Thus, Baldwin had to confront the constitutional questions, which were "presented more dramatically than they have ever been before," given the allegations that pregnancy would be potentially quite dangerous for one of the woman plaintiffs, and the other, based on past experience, was incapable of bearing genetically normal children. In both cases, denial of contraceptives would theoretically sentence the two women and their husbands to a marriage without normal sexual intercourse, since Connecticut laws also forbade abortion. But Baldwin did not believe that such a harsh result dictated a finding of unconstitutionality. "We cannot say that the legislature, in weighing the considerations for and against an exception legalizing contraceptive measures in cases such as the ones before us, could not reasonably conclude that, despite the occasional hardship which might result, the greater good would be served by leaving the statutes as they are." He continued:

> The plaintiffs' argument raises an issue of public policy. Each of the separate magistracies of our government owes to the others a duty not to trespass upon the lawful domain of the others. The judiciary has a duty to test legislative action by constitutional principles, but it cannot, in that process, usurp the power of the legislature.

Concluding that the challenged law was "a constitutional exercise of legislative power" to determine public policy, Baldwin affirmed dismissal of the complaint.

The plaintiffs appealed to the U.S. Supreme Court, which noted probable jurisdiction and set the case for argument on March 1 and 2, 1961. At this stage of the litigation, the plaintiffs were represented by Fowler V. Harper, an experienced appellate attorney, and the Court had also extended the privilege of oral argument to Harriet Pilpel, general counsel of Planned Parenthood of America, which, as potential operator of family planning clinics in Connecticut, was actually the most interested representative body in the whole litigation. The Court also received *amicus* briefs from a group of doctors and the American Civil Liberties Union, urging the unconstitutionality of the law. Cannon appeared for the state. On June 19, 1961, the Court announced by 5–4 vote that it would dismiss the appeal for lack of justiciability. According to five members of the Court, the lack of any prosecutions apart from *Nelson*, which they characterized as a "test case," suggested that there was no real controversy about the law's enforcement requiring a constitutional decision from the Court.

Justice Frankfurter wrote an opinion for a plurality of the Court, setting forth at length his favorite theories on federal jurisdiction and why it was not appropriately extended to this case. Although the defendant, State's Attorney Ullman, had indicated that he intended to enforce the law if violations were brought to his attention, Frankfurter contended that this was not sufficient to present the kind of "live controversy" required under Article III of the U.S. Constitution to invoke the Court's jurisdiction. At oral argument, it had come out that contraceptives were widely available in Connecticut through pharmacies and that the *Nelson* prosecution was the only one in the history of the statute. The plaintiffs were not really deprived of access to contraceptives. Frankfurter wrote:

> The undeviating policy of nullification by Connecticut of its anti-contraceptive laws throughout all the long years that they have been on the statute books bespeaks more than prosecutorial paralysis. What was said in another context is relevant here. "Deeply embedded traditional ways of carrying out state policy . . ."—or not carrying it out—"are often tougher and truer law than the dead words of the written text."

It was not only the Article III restriction of the Court's jurisdiction to actual "cases and controversies" that led the Court to decline jurisdiction here, said Frankfurter, but also the strong feeling that only real controversies produce the kind of sharply focused arguments conducive to constitutional decisionmaking: "the adjudicatory process is most securely founded when it is exercised under the impact of a lively conflict between antagonistic demands, actively pressed, which make resolution of the controverted issue a practical necessity."

Since it was the Court's long-stated preference to avoid making constitutional rulings, especially those invalidating statutes enacted by properly constituted and elected legislatures, unless such rulings were absolutely necessary to resolve a significant controversy, it seemed appropriate to refrain from such a ruling here, where the state's enforcement policies seemed to Frankfurter to represent at least a "tacit" policy of nonenforcement. Furthermore, the mere fact that the declaratory judgment proceeding was authorized by federal and state procedural codes did not represent any retreat from this policy. In some cases, prosecution practices gave a clear basis for finding that there was a live legal controversy, even though the particular plaintiff who brought suit for a declaratory judgment had not been actually prosecuted. But this was not such a case, because there was no evidence of a real threat of prosecution against Dr. Buxton or any of his anonymous patients.

Justice William J. Brennan, Jr., concurred in the judgment, but told the plaintiffs in his brief opinion just how they could get this controversy to the Court:

> The true controversy in this case is over the opening of birth-control clinics on a large scale; it is that which the State has prevented in the past, not the use of contraceptives by isolated and individual married couples. It will be time enough to decide the constitutional questions urged upon us when, if ever, that real controversy flares up again. Until it does, or until the State makes a definite and concrete threat to enforce these laws against individual married couples—a threat which it has never made in the past except under the provocation of litigation—this Court may not be compelled to exercise its most delicate power of constitutional adjudication.

Four members of the Court dissented. Justice Black issued a one-sentence dissent declaring that he believed that the constitutional issues should be reached and decided by the Court, without indicating how he would decide them. (Ultimately, in *Griswold*, he decided them in favor of upholding the statute.) Justice Stewart issued a brief statement agreeing with Douglas and Harlan in their reasons for asserting that the Court should decide the case, but indicating that since the appeal was being dismissed he need go no further in dissent, but "in refraining from a discussion of the constitutional issues, I in no way imply that the ultimate result I would reach on the merits of these controversies would differ from the conclusions of my dissenting Brothers."

Justices Douglas and Harlan dissented at length. In this case, they made rather an "odd couple." Douglas, the proponent of judicial activism in the cause of individual rights, and Harlan, the apostle of judicial restraint, both believed that the so-called nonenforcement of the law was actually nothing of the kind. By its selective prosecution of *Nelson*, Connecticut had effectively barred the establishment of family planning clinics throughout the state; because the law had this ongoing effect, and Connecticut officials reiterated that they would actively enforce it, Douglas and Harlan agreed that there was a live controversy worthy of constitutional adjudication, although there were shades of difference in their approach to this question. Where they differed more sharply, however, was over the constitutional theory by which they could reach the conclusion that the law, at least as applied to married couples and doctors counseling them, was unconstitutional.

For Douglas, the case first presented a significant First Amendment issue in the form of the aiding and abetting statute, when read in combination with the contraception law as it had been in *Nelson* and might be in the future against Dr. Buxton. "The right of the doctor to advise his patients according to his best lights seems so obviously within First Amendment rights as to need no extended discussion," he asserted. Such medical advice was clearly speech, and the First Amendment was not limited to the protection of political speech. "Of course," said Douglas, "a physician can talk freely and fully with his patient without threat of retaliation by the State. The contrary thought—the one endorsed *sub silentio* by the courts below— has the cast of regimentation about it, a cast at war with the philosophy and presuppositions of this free society." In a country with a First Amendment, no doctor could be required to go "underground" to prescribe contraceptives if his professional training led him to believe that their use was medically indicated. Douglas continued, "A society that tells its doctors under pain of criminal penalty what they may not tell their patients is not a free society. Only free exchange of views and information is consistent with 'a civilization of the dialogue,' to borrow a phrase from Dr. Robert M. Hutchins."

But, even more directly, Douglas found that the contraception law itself violated the right of a married couple to "liberty" as protected by the Due Process Clause of the Fourteenth Amendment. Here, Douglas reiterated his frequent argument that the Fourteenth Amendment's Due Process Clause incorporated the first eight amendments of the Bill of Rights and applied them to the states, and, through the use of the term "liberty," went beyond the rights specifically enumerated in those amendments to others that could rationally be inferred as emanating from them. He pointed to cases in which the Court had held that the Due Process Clause protected the right to travel between states, and the rights to marry and establish a home and bring up children. Indeed, in a recent dissent, Douglas had argued that the Due Process Clause included a right to privacy that would be infringed upon by a public transit authority subjecting its customers to radio broadcasts as part of a captive audience in a bus. "'Liberty' is a conception that sometimes gains content from the emanations of other specific guarantees or from experience with the requirements of a free society," insisted Douglas.

Facing the argument that what he was seeking was a revival of the dreaded "substantive due process" under which the Court had struck down protective labor legislation earlier in the century, Douglas insisted that there was nothing wrong with substantive due process when appropriately used:

> The error of the old Court, as I see it, was not in entertaining inquiries concerning the constitutionality of social legislation but in applying the standards that it did. Social legislation dealing with business and economic matters touches no particularized prohibition of the Constitution, unless it be the provision of the Fifth Amendment that private property should not be taken for public use without just compensation. If it is free of the latter guarantee, it has a wide scope for application. Some go so far as to suggest that whatever the majority in

the legislature says goes, that there is no other standard of constitutionality. That reduces the legislative power to sheer voting strength and the judicial function to a matter of statistics. . . . While the legislative judgment on economic and business matters is "well-nigh conclusive," it is not beyond judicial inquiry.

On the other hand, when it comes to rights of the individual against government regulation of private life, substantive due process had an appropriate role to play. Douglas stated:

The regime of a free society needs room for vast experimentation. Crises, emergencies, experience at the individual and community levels produce new insights; problems emerge in new dimensions; needs, once never imagined, appear. To stop experimentation and the testing of new decrees and controls is to deprive society of a needed versatility. Yet to say that a legislature may do anything not within a specific guarantee of the Constitution may be as crippling to a free society as to allow it to override specific guarantees so long as what it does fails to shock the sensibilities of a majority of the Court.

Douglas found the Connecticut legislation to be an excellent example of the distinctions he was urging. Connecticut might have made a commercial regulation regarding the distribution and sale of contraceptives, but that would present a different case, given the appropriate deference the Court normally paid these days to legislative judgments in matters of commercial regulation. On the other hand, the challenged law dealt solely with the use of contraceptives. Douglas wrote:

The regulation as applied in this case touches the relationship between man and wife. It reaches into the intimacies of the marriage relationship. If we imagine a regime of full enforcement of the law in the manner of an Anthony Comstock, we would reach the point where search warrants issued and officers appeared in bedrooms to find out what went on. It is said that this is not that case. And so it is not. But when the State makes "use" a crime and applies the criminal sanction to man and wife, the State has entered the innermost sanctum of the home. If it can make this law, it can enforce it. And proof of its violation necessarily involves an inquiry into the relations between man and wife. That is an invasion of the privacy that is implicit in a free society.

While Douglas could not identify any one phrase or provision of the Constitution as a source for this right of privacy, he insisted that "it emanates from the totality of the constitutional scheme under which we live." "Can there by any doubt," he asked, "that a Bill of Rights that in time of peace bars soldiers from being quartered in a home 'without the consent of the Owner' should also bar the police from investigating the intimacies of the marriage relation? The idea of allowing the State that leeway is congenial only to a totalitarian regime." Thus, Douglas dissented not only from the dismissal on jurisdictional grounds, but also from "our refusal to strike down this law."

Justice Harlan's dissent on the constitutionality of the statute was rather more finely tuned than Douglas's. Unlike his colleague, Harlan was less disposed to engage in sweeping pronouncements. Douglas's formulation might be taken to invalidate a wide range of state laws regulating private sexual conduct, and Harlan was not ready to take such a step, preferring to base his holding more solidly on the historic privacy accorded marital relations.

After a lengthy explanation of his reasons for concluding that there was a live controversy sufficient to invoke the Court's jurisdiction, he turned to the constitutionality issue and asserted that "a statute making it a criminal offense for *married couples* to use contraceptives is an intolerable and unjustifiable invasion of privacy in the conduct of the most intimate concerns of an individual's personal life." Harlan rejected the appellants' argument that the statute was unconstitutional as an arbitrary and unreasonable exercise of state police power, however, preferring to ground it in a right of marital privacy based on substantive due process.

Harlan asserted that it is "but a truism" to say that the Due Process Clauses, in both the Fifth and Fourteenth Amendments, were not "self-explanatory," and that history shed little light on their full intended meaning. He asserted that the Court had long rejected the view that the effect of the Fourteenth Amendment, implicated in this case, was solely procedural, or that it merely forbade to the states what had been forbidden to the federal government prior to its enactment. Thus, he rejected Douglas's attempt to give content to the Due Process

Clause primarily by reference to the Bill of Rights and "emanations" from the rights specified therein. "Again and again," he insisted, "this Court has resisted the notion that the Fourteenth Amendment is no more than a shorthand reference to what is explicitly set out elsewhere in the Bill of Rights." Indeed, this would be somewhat ridiculous; since the Fifth Amendment contains an identical due process provision, it was clear that "due process is a discrete concept which subsists as an independent guaranty of liberty and procedural fairness, more general and inclusive than the specific prohibitions" in the other amendments of the Bill of Rights.

For Harlan, due process could not be "reduced to any formula; its content cannot be determined by reference to any code." He looked for guidance mainly to history, to try to find the "balance" struck over the course of constitutional and social development between the necessary authority of the state and the independence and liberty of the people. He stated, "That tradition is a living thing. A decision of this Court which radically departs from it could not long survive, while a decision which builds on what has survived is likely to be sound. No formula could serve as a substitute, in this area, for judgment and restraint."

In this case, the plaintiffs had asserted that the Connecticut law deprived them of "a substantial measure of liberty in carrying on the most intimate of all personal relationships, and that it does so arbitrarily and without any rational, justifying purpose." The state, on the other hand, contended that it was acting to "protect the moral welfare of its citizenry, both directly, in that it considers the practice of contraception immoral in itself, and instrumentally, in that the availability of contraceptive materials tends to minimize 'the disastrous consequence of dissolute action,' that is fornication and adultery." Since Harlan saw the issue as one of "fundamental liberty," he concluded that "the mere assertion that the action of the State finds justification in the controversial realm of morals cannot justify alone any and every restriction it imposes." It was true that the state had an interest in promoting the morals of the public, and that protection of physical well-being was not the sole function of the state. Harlan stated:

Indeed to attempt a line between public behavior and that which is purely consensual or solitary would be to withdraw from community concern a range of subjects with which every society in civilized times has found it necessary to deal. The laws regarding marriage which provide both when the sexual powers may be used and the legal and societal context in which children are born and brought up, as well as laws forbidding adultery, fornication and homosexual practices which express the negative of the proposition, confining sexuality to lawful marriage, form a pattern so deeply pressed into the substance of our social life that any Constitutional doctrine in this area must build upon that basis.

Thus, in the realm of sexual morality, Harlan was ready, based on tradition, to draw a rather sharp line between traditional marriage, within which sexual conduct should be largely sheltered from state intervention, and nonmarital sex, whether heterosexual or homosexual, where he felt tradition provided no basis for constitutional protection.

There was quite a lot of moral disputation about contraception, and maybe it was difficult for the Court to say that its view on the matter was sounder than that of Connecticut legislators. In many cases, that would be reason enough for judicial abstention, but not where fundamental individual rights were concerned, asserted Harlan. The issue, brought sharply into focus by the complaint in this case, was that "the statute allows the State to enquire into, prove and punish married people for the private use of their marital intimacy." In such a case, where the most "fundamental aspect of 'liberty,' the privacy of the home in its most basic sense" is at stake, the statute must be subjected to "strict scrutiny," the approach endorsed by the Court in *Skinner v. Oklahoma*, a 1942 case regarding sterilization as a criminal punishment in which the Court had identified reproductive choice as an aspect of liberty protected by the Fourteenth Amendment. While it was true that the statute did not compel a literal invasion of the home by law enforcement authorities, it did something just as constitutionally offensive. To say that due process was concerned only with literal searches could be plausible only if due process "in this respect is limited to what is explicitly provided in the Constitution, divorced from the rational purposes, historical roots, and subsequent developments of the relevant provisions." Quoting Justice Louis D. Brandeis's famous statement in *Olmstead v. United States* (1928) on the "right to be let alone" as being among the "most comprehensive of rights and the right most valued by civilized men," Harlan asserted that "the sweep of the Court's decisions . . . amply shows that the Constitution protects the privacy of the home against all unreasonable intrusion of whatever character." To say that the protection extended only to intrusions by the police would be "an extreme instance of sacrificing substance to form."

Harlan characterized as "insubstantial" any distinction that depended on the lack of a physical intrusion by the state in this case, as opposed to the sorts of physical intrusions described in the Fourth Amendment's ban on unreasonable searches and seizures. He said,

> [I]f the physical curtilage of the home is protected, it is surely as a result of solicitude to protect the privacies of the life within. Certainly the safeguarding of the home does not follow merely from the sanctity of property rights. The home derives its pre-eminence as the seat of family life. And the integrity of that life is something so fundamental that it has been found to draw to its protection the principles of more than one explicitly granted Constitutional right.

On the other hand, perhaps unlike Douglas, Harlan was not ready to recognize an utterly unassailable personal right of privacy in the home:

> The right of privacy most manifestly is not an absolute. Thus, I would not suggest that adultery, homosexuality, fornication and incest are immune from criminal enquiry, however privately practiced. So much has been explicitly recognized in acknowledging the State's rightful concern for its people's moral welfare. But not to discriminate between what is involved in this case and either the traditional offenses against good morals or crimes which, though they may be committed anywhere, happen to have been committed or concealed in the home, would entirely misconceive the argument that is being made.

> Adultery, homosexuality and the like are sexual intimacies which the State forbids altogether, but the intimacy of husband and wife is necessarily an essential and accepted feature of the institution of marriage, an institution which the State not only must allow, but which always and in every age it has fostered and protected. It is one thing when the State exerts its power either to forbid extra-marital sexuality altogether, or to say who may marry, but it is quite another when, having acknowledged a marriage and the intimacies inherent in it, it undertakes to regulate by means of the criminal law the details of that intimacy.

While Connecticut had made arguments based on morality for sustaining its concern with contraception, Harlan felt that nothing in the Connecticut Supreme Court of Errors opinions sustaining this law "remotely suggests a justification for the obnoxiously intrusive means it has chosen to effectuate that policy." Indeed, the very history of nonenforcement suggested to Harlan Connecticut's own reservations about the statute. Even more important, Connecticut was apparently the only state in the Union that took the step of forbidding contraceptive use, although many others had enacted laws involving distribution or sale, further supporting the notion that this particular law did not have history or tradition on its side.

Justice Harlan's dissent in *Poe v. Ullman* has been particularly influential, both in providing an alternative theoretical underpinning for the subsequent *Griswold* decision (and its ultimate progeny, *Roe v. Wade* (1973) and other decisions supporting a woman's right to an abortion), and in limiting the sexual privacy right (as the Court subsequently did in *Bowers v. Hardwick* (1986), a sodomy case) to sexual intimacies having some claim on historical toleration or protection. Although the Court's decision in *Poe v. Ullman* did not decide anything in terms of substantive constitutional law, the dissents and Justice Brennan's concurrence laid the groundwork for *Griswold*, the case that was the opening shot in the Court's participation in the Sexual Revolution of the 1960s.

Case References

Bowers v. Hardwick, 478 U.S. 186 (1986)

Griswold v. Connecticut, 381 U.S. 479 (1965)

Olmstead v. United States, 277 U.S. 438 (1928)

Roe v. Wade, 410 U.S. 113 (1973)

Skinner v. Oklahoma, 316 U.S. 535 (1942)

State v. Nelson, 126 Conn. 412, 11 A.2d 856 (1940)

Tileston v. Ullman, 129 Conn. 84, 26 A.2d 582 (1942)

4. THE MODERN RIGHT OF SEXUAL PRIVACY IS BORN

Griswold v. Connecticut, 381 U.S. 479 (1965), reversing *State v. Griswold*, 151 Conn. 544, 200 A.2d 479 (1964).

During the 19th century, American doctors became an organized force crusading against a variety of common practices that were likely to cause serious injury in the hands of nonprofessionals. Most of the laws concerning abortion and contraception passed by state legislatures were inspired, at least in part, by arguments that the practices were unsafe under existing conditions of hygiene and medical science. In 1879, the state of Connecticut passed such a law, providing: "Any person who uses any drug, medicinal article or instrument for the purpose of preventing conception shall be fined not less than fifty dollars or imprisoned not less than sixty days nor more than one year or be both fined and imprisoned."

Early in the 20th century, proponents of family planning seeking to promote the use of artificial contraception ran into significant legal barriers because of such laws, and prominent figures, such as Emma Goldman and Margaret Sanger, risked imprisonment and ostracism for advocating the use of diaphragms and condoms. These attitudes began to break down with a new public health movement aimed at eradicating venereal disease. By the time of World War II, the military was distributing condoms to soldiers and public health advocates were calling for the repeal of outmoded legal restrictions. But many states, including Connecticut, continued to enforce their old statutes.

Several challenges, all unsuccessful, were mounted against the Connecticut law during the 1950s. Some of these failed on procedural grounds. Noting that the U.S. Supreme Court had been embracing a broader view of individual rights under the Due Process Clause with the leadership of Chief Justice Earl Warren and the appointment of William J. Brennan, Jr., Connecticut reformers decided to make another attempt at having the law invalidated. On November 1, 1961, the Planned Parenthood League of Connecticut opened an office in New

Haven for the specific purpose of providing information, instruction and medical advice in family planning for married couples. The clinic provided contraceptives to its clients and charged fees on a sliding scale based on client income. After ten days, the state closed down the clinic and indicted its operators, Estelle Griswold, the executive director, and C. Lee Buxton, the medical director, for aiding and abetting in violation of the law. Each defendant was fined $100.

Griswold and Buxton appealed their convictions, asserting that the law violated their due process rights, and urged the state's Supreme Court of Errors "to consider whether or not in the light of the facts of this case, the current developments in medicine, social and religious thought in this area, and the present conditions of American and Connecticut life, modification of the prior opinions of this Court might not 'serve justice better.'" The court refused this invitation, resting its decision on the police power of the state in matters of public safety and welfare. Associate Justice John M. Comley found that the statute was neither arbitrary nor unreasonable, so the conviction of Griswold and Buxton was "not an invasion of their constitutional rights." The opinion of the court was unanimous.

The defendants appealed to the U.S. Supreme Court, which had itself rejected various challenges to contraception laws in recent Terms on procedural grounds. They were supported in their appeal by several amicus parties, including the Planned Parenthood Federation of America, the American Civil Liberties Union, and the Catholic Council on Civil Liberties. Catherine G. Roraback, of New Haven, who had argued the case before the Connecticut Supreme Court on behalf of Griswold and Buxton, yielded her place to Yale Law School Professor Thomas I. Emerson. Julius Maretz, who had been prosecuting attorney in the state courts, yielded his place for oral argument, which carried over for two days (March 29 and 30, 1965), to his assistant prosecutor, Joseph B. Clark. The Court announced its opinion on June 7, 1965, reversing the Connecticut Supreme Court and vacating the criminal convictions of Griswold and Buxton.

Justice William O. Douglas announced the opinion of the Court, representing the views of five members. He premised the decision on a right of privacy in matters of sexuality and reproduction, which could be invaded by the state only for compelling reasons. Because privacy and reproductive freedom are not expressly mentioned in the U.S. Constitution, Douglas devoted much of his opinion to expounding a theory deriving such rights from a variety of provisions in the Bill of Rights, made applicable to the states by virtue of the Due Process Clause of the Fourteenth Amendment.

According to Douglas, several of the Articles of the Bill of Rights concern some aspect of personal privacy: the First Amendment's guarantee of freedom of association, the Third Amendment's prohibition against quartering troops in private homes during peacetime without the owner's consent, the Fourth Amendment's ban on unreasonable searches and seizures, the Fifth Amendment's protection against compelled self-incrimination. Furthermore, the Ninth Amendment indicates that the enumerated rights are not exclusive.

Douglas noted that the Court had throughout its history given the express rights meaning by interpretation; in his words, "specific guarantees in the Bill of Rights have penumbras, formed by emanations from those guarantees that help give them life and substance." In less colorful language, he was saying that the particular rights enumerated in the Bill of Rights would not have much value if given a narrow, literalistic interpretation. If they were to be meaningful, they should be interpreted as having natural extensions in their real-world application so as to assure the important freedoms they embodied. For Douglas, the various aspects of personal privacy expressly covered in the Bill of Rights implied a more general zone of privacy, and the privacy of intimacy within the marital relationship surely fell within that zone.

Having found that the Connecticut law intruded on a constitutionally protected zone of privacy, Douglas had to evaluate whether the state had a compelling interest for the intrusion. He held that the state had no such interest, but without analyzing in detail the state's arguments. He stated that a law forbidding the use of contraceptives "seeks to achieve its goals by means having a maximum destructive impact upon" the marital relationship and that such a law could not stand. "Would we allow the police to search the sacred precincts of marital bedrooms for telltale signs of the use of contraceptives?" he melodramatically inquired, and closed his opinion with purple prose about the nobility of marriage.

Justice Arthur J. Goldberg, joined by Chief Justice Warren and Justice Brennan, wrote a separate opinion, agreeing in all respects with Douglas's analysis applying a right of privacy to the states by incorporation of the Bill of Rights, but emphasizing the Ninth Amendment as the source of such a right. Douglas had merely given passing mention to the Ninth Amendment, concentrating his analysis on identifying other provisions of the Bill of Rights which could be considered source material for such a privacy right. For Goldberg, such a search was really unnecessary. He preferred to focus on the Ninth Amendment's statement that the enumerated rights were not exclusive. Other rights not mentioned in the document but considered so basic or fundamental as not to be questioned were retained by the people, and the Ninth Amendment could be the vehicle for the Court to restrain the states from invading those rights. Goldberg invoked the "fundamental rights" rhetoric of the Court in past Fourteenth Amendment adjudication and argued that exclusion of a right of marital privacy from the scope of the unenumerated rights protected by the Ninth Amendment would render that amendment a nullity, and indeed violate the language of the amendment if premised on the view that only enumerated rights were protected.

To identify which rights should be considered protected by the Ninth Amendment, Goldberg again reverted to the rhetoric of past "fundamental rights" decisions under the Fourteenth Amendment, invoking "tradition," "collective conscience of our people," "fundamental principles of liberty and justice which lie at the base of all our civil and political institutions," and similar phrases from past cases. He concluded that a right of marital privacy easily came within these formulations, thus invoking a compelling interest test for the state to meet in defense of the statute. He pointedly noted that the state's only argument in support of the statute was that it would prevent promiscuity and adultery, presumably by making such activities dangerously discoverable through unintended pregnancy. Goldberg asserted that the state could accomplish these ends without interfering in marital relations, as it had done by outlawing promiscuity and adultery, which it undoubtedly could constitutionally do. Consequently, he agreed with Douglas that the statute was unconstitutional and the convictions should be set aside.

Two other members of the Court concurred in the judgment but refused to join with their five brethren in Douglas's opinion. Justices John Marshall Harlan and Byron R. White objected to a process of purporting to find an unwritten right of marital privacy in the Bill of Rights and then to apply it to the states through the incorporation theory of the Fourteenth Amendment.

Harlan had previously voiced his disagreement with the incorporation theory, but had written in dissent in *Poe v. Ullman* (1961), a prior case concerning the Connecticut law, that the concept of "liberty" under the Due Process Clause of the Fourteenth Amendment could itself be used to invalidate the law. For him, a right of marital privacy was "implicit in the concept of ordered liberty," as described in prior Fourteenth Amendment case law, and the inquiry into the Bill of Rights was superfluous and even dangerous, since it implied that a statute would violate due process only if it could be found in contravention of some right rooted in the Bill of Rights. He did not expand further on the due process analysis, referring back to his *Poe v. Ullman* dissent, which had been liberally quoted in Justice Goldberg's concurring opinion.

Justice White, however, in a separate concurrence, did engage in further due process analysis. He agreed with Justice Harlan that

the case should be decided solely by reference to the Fourteenth Amendment. He went further, however, to contend that the legacy of the 1930s, when the Court formally eschewed substantive due process under the Fourteenth Amendment, required great deference to legislative bodies in both the economic and social spheres of their activities. Only an arbitrary and capricious statutory ban would fall under such an analysis.

For Justice White, the state's sole justification for the statute rendered it arbitrary and capricious. He concluded, "I wholly fail to see how the ban on the use of contraceptives by married couples in any way reinforces the State's ban on illicit sexual relationships." Connecticut had legislated against only the use of contraceptives, without concerning itself with their manufacture, sale, or possession. Furthermore, given the peculiar motivation-oriented wording of the statute, there had never been any clear ruling whether, without violating the law, contraceptives could be used for health purposes rather than for contraception. Under those circumstances, forbidding married couples from using them seemed ridiculous in light of the state's asserted purpose. Justice White was satisfied to strike down the law on this basis.

Justice Hugo L. Black and Justice Potter Stewart dissented, each in an opinion joined by the other.

For Justice Black, the majority had misused the incorporation doctrine and revived substantive due process in violation of the proper role of the Court. One must remember Justice Black's consistent and historic disposition in Fourteenth Amendment and Bill of Rights cases. He was President Franklin D. Roosevelt's first appointee to the Court after the battle over substantive due process and the invalidation of New Deal legislation by the conservative "Nine Old Men." For him, reviving substantive due process, even in the context of personal liberty rather than economic regulation, was anathema and he had consistently disagreed with such uses of the Fourteenth Amendment, contending that, viewed in isolation, that Amendment should be construed as largely procedural.

He was also an ardent advocate of the incorporation doctrine, but his approach to the

Bill of Rights was that of a literalist. If a right was not particularly mentioned, he was not one to find the right by implicating or to equivocate in enforcing those rights that were mentioned. Thus, he absolutely opposed restrictions on the freedom of the press mentioned in the First Amendment and found dangerous the formulations embraced by the Court to forbid certain publications for reasons of obscenity or security, but found no protection against wiretapping under the Fourth Amendment, since it was a procedure not mentioned nor within the contemplation of the drafters. Where the Bill of Rights meant to protect some aspect of privacy, that aspect of privacy was spelled out in the document, he insisted, and no penumbra theory could stretch the document to cover cases not enumerated.

Black found the Ninth Amendment arguments of Justice Goldberg to be as dangerous as the due process arguments of Justices Harlan and White. By engaging in some sort of "fundamental rights" or "natural law" argument, they were doing just the sort of thing that the conservative judges of the 1920s and 1930s did when they elevated "freedom of contract" to a fundamental unwritten constitutional right and used it to invalidate progressive economic legislation. Black argued that such a process was dangerous and unwarranted, leaving judges free to impose their personal views on the country without constitutional warrant. The Ninth Amendment, he insisted, was passed to narrow the powers of the federal government by negativing any implication that rights not expressly protected from federal intrusion were thus subject to such intrusion. Any argument that the Ninth Amendment expanded the powers of the federal government by authorizing the Court to strike down a particular state law was contrary to this history.

For Black, the argument that the Court had a responsibility to keep the Constitution up to date was unpersuasive. The Constitution provided an amendment process by which it was the responsibility of Congress and the people, through their state governments, to keep the Constitution up to date. He was in favor of judicial restraint in this case and would have held the Connecticut law constitutional.

Justice Stewart agreed with this dissent, but with somewhat less passion. "I think this is an uncommonly silly law," he said, and "obviously unenforceable, except in the oblique context of the present case." But he argued that it was not the role of the Supreme Court to strike down laws it considered silly unless they violated the Constitution, and he agreed with Justice Black that this one did not. He briefly echoed Black's argument that the right of privacy could not be precisely located anywhere in the Bill of Rights and that the law embodied no procedural violation under the Fourteenth Amendment. He was particularly dismissive of the Ninth Amendment argument, asserting that "the idea that a federal court could ever use the Ninth Amendment to annul a law passed by the elected representatives of the people of the state of Connecticut would have caused James Madison [its legislative author] no little wonder."

The Court's decision in *Griswold* marked the beginning of a long and controversial process by which the Court was to carve out over the next twenty years an expansive body of sexual privacy law, which reached its limit only in 1986 with *Bowers v. Hardwick*, and then began a narrowing process in 1989 with *Webster v. Reproductive Health Services*. The *Griswold* decision would eventually be extended to protect the right of unmarried persons to use contraceptives and to guarantee the right of women to decide whether to terminate a pregnancy. In other spheres, lower courts seized on *Griswold* to invalidate laws on cohabitation, adultery, sodomy, and private possession of obscene materials. As the "right to die" movement gained force during the 1980s, courts began to cite *Griswold* as authority for terminating life support and extraordinary measures to keep alive terminally ill people against their will, and the case was cited frequently during the AIDS (acquired immune deficiency syndrome) epidemic to support confidentiality of serologic test results for AIDS patients.

At the same time, however, *Griswold* inspired serious criticism in the legal academy and from some conservative quarters on the bench. While few quarreled with the result, the Court's theory of the case aroused considerable criticism, which intensifed greatly after abortion laws were struck down in reliance on

Griswold in *Roe v. Wade* (1973) less than ten years later. Robert H. Bork, a Yale Law School professor and later a judge of the U.S. Court of Appeals for the District of Columbia Circuit, was a leading critic of the "right of privacy" theory. In a 1985 case concerning a challenge to the discharge of a gay man by the Navy, he wrote a lengthy opinion criticizing the Court's privacy cases as "incoherent." His nomination to the Supreme Court in 1987 by President Ronald W. Reagan elevated the arguments about constitutional privacy to the level of national debate beyond the legal academy, as televised confirmation hearings exposed the nation to a dialogue over constitutional protection for privacy.

Bork's nomination was rejected, at least in part due to fears expressed by members of the Senate over his views on the *Griswold* decision. It seemed clear in the fall of 1987 that there was a national consensus in support of a right of privacy that extended at least to contraception. Even as the Court seemed poised in the 1990s to overrule *Roe v. Wade*, and to allow the states to decide whether to ban abortion under some or all circumstances, it seemed that the Court was reluctant to do so if such a step might endanger the contraception rights protected in *Griswold*.

Case References

Bowers v. Hardwick, 478 U.S. 186 (1986)
Poe v. Ullman, 367 U.S. 497 (1961)
Roe v. Wade, 410 U.S. 113 (1973)
Webster v. Reproductive Health Services, 492 U.S. 490 (1989)

5. REPRODUCTIVE FREEDOM FOR THE INDIVIDUAL

Eisenstadt v. Baird, 405 U.S. 438 (1972), affirming 429 F.2d 1398 (1st Cir. 1970), reversing 310 F. Supp. 951 (D. Mass. 1970), effectively overruling in part *Commonwealth v. Baird*, 355 Mass. 746, 247 N.E.2d 574 (1969), certiorari denied, 396 U.S. 1029 (1970).

After the U.S. Supreme Court decided *Griswold v. Connecticut* (1965), holding that the states could not prohibit married persons from using contraceptive articles or devices to prevent conception, the Massachusetts legislature decided to modify its antiquarian 19th-century law "Crimes Against Chastity, Morality, Decency and Good Order," to conform to what the legislature thought was the scope of the Supreme Court's ruling. The old Massachusetts law forbade the distribution of contraceptive devices for the purpose of preventing conception. After the 1966 amendments, the law (chapter 272, section 21, of the Massachusetts General Laws) forbade selling, lending, giving away, or exhibiting articles for the purpose of preventing conception (or offering to do any of these things), but made an exception for registered physicians, who were authorized to prescribe contraceptives for the use of married persons, and for licensed pharmacists, who were authorized to supply such articles upon the prescription of a registered physician. Violation of the law was a felony, with imprisonment up to five years authorized.

Birth control advocate Bill Baird was determined to challenge the law. Responding to an invitation, he presented a lecture on contraception at Boston University on April 6, 1967. As part of the lecture, he exhibited and discussed various articles used as contraceptives. At the end of the lecture, he invited members of the audience to come to the front of the auditorium and take any of the exhibited materials. Pointing out that what he was doing violated the new Massachusetts law, Baird handed a package of Emko vaginal foam to a young woman. A police officer arrested Baird and took him to police headquarters. He was subsequently indicted by a Suffolk County grand jury for exhibiting contraceptive articles and giving one away to the young woman. The facts being uncontested, Baird was convicted by Superior Court Judge MacCauley, sitting without a jury.

Since Baird had challenged the constitutionality of the law, the Superior Court delayed sentencing pending consideration of these challenges by the Massachusetts Supreme Judicial Court, which heard arguments on December 2, 1968. Joseph J. Balliro represented Baird, and Assistant District Attorney Joseph R. Nolan appeared for the state.

The unanimous Supreme Judicial Court ruled on May 1, 1969, that Baird's conviction for exhibiting contraceptive devices violated the First Amendment and would have to be set aside. In an opinion by Chief Justice Raymond S. Wilkins, the court ruled that the exhibition as illustration of a lecture was clearly expressive activity and as such was covered by *Griswold*, where the Supreme Court had clearly indicated that the state could not bar the transmission of information about contraception. (Indeed, the Massachusetts law did not forbid the use of contraceptives, merely their exhibition and distribution, so it would not be unlawful for Baird to advocate their use.) Wilkins noted that the New Jersey Supreme Court had recently unanimously struck down the conviction of Bill Baird, the defendant in this case, for displaying contraceptive devices, relying expressly on *Griswold*.

However, the court divided 4–3 on the constitutionality of the distribution ban as enacted by the legislature. Dissenting Justices Arthur E. Whittemore, R. Ammi Cutter, and Jacob J. Spiegel argued that the restriction of distribution to physicians and pharmacists was unnecessary to accomplish any legitimate purpose and that the prohibition of distribution to unmarried persons was discriminatory. Justice Spiegel's separate dissent anticipated many of the points that U.S. Supreme Court Justice William O. Douglas would make in his concurring opinion when this case finally reached the Supreme Court.

A majority, however, believed that the legislature was within its authorized power to protect public health and welfare when it restricted the dispensing of contraceptives to physicians and pharmacists, since some contraceptives were known to present health hazards. It noted that the Connecticut statute invalidated in *Griswold* had banned physicians from counseling their married patients regarding contraception and had, in fact, banned the use of contraceptives to

prevent conception. The Massachusetts law, as amended in 1966, banned neither activity. It was aimed solely at distribution, and it specifically excepted physicians and pharmacists acting on a physician's prescription (but no other persons) from the general ban on distribution. Baird was neither a physician nor a pharmacist. The majority asserted that it was "obvious" that the privacy right did not extend to the sexual activities of unmarried persons, so fault could not be found with the Massachusetts law's prohibition of distribution of contraceptives to unmarried persons. Thus, Baird's conviction was affirmed.

Baird petitioned the U.S. Supreme Court to review the case, but was rebuffed. Only Justice Douglas, author of the *Griswold* opinion, recorded his view that *certiorari* should have been granted. The Superior Court subsequently sentenced Baird to three months' imprisonment.

Baird immediately filed a petition for *habeas corpus* in the U.S. District Court for the District of Massachusetts, alleging that his imprisonment for violation of the Massachusetts law violated his federal constitutional rights under the First and Fourteenth amendments. Baird argued that the distribution of contraceptives incident to his lecture was protected expressive conduct under the First Amendment, that the prohibition on exhibiting contraceptives could not be severed from the rest of the statute, and that in any event the statute was unconstitutionally overbroad, vague, and violative of the privacy rights recently identified by the Supreme Court in *Griswold*. Joseph J. Balliro, of Boston, again represented Baird in the *habeas* action, with Assistant Attorney General Lawrence P. Cohen appearing in defense of the statute.

District Judge Anthony Julian issued his opinion on March 20, 1970, denying Baird's petition. Holding that it was common knowledge that some contraceptives may have harmful effects, Julian found that the legislature had a legitimate purpose in restricting their distribution so that those seeking to obtain them would have to seek medical advice. He agreed with the Supreme Judicial Court's narrow construction of the precedential effect of *Griswold*, noting as well that Massachusetts law forbade sexual intercourse between unmarried people (i.e., fornication) and that, in any event, Baird lacked standing to assert the interests of physicians who were prevented by the law from prescribing contraceptives for their unmarried patients. He rejected Baird's argument that giving away the Emko foam kit was constitutionally protected speech, relying on the celebrated Supreme Court precedent of *United States v. O'Brien* (1968), upholding a conviction for the burning of a draft card by an antiwar protester during a demonstration. Julian concluded that section 21 was constitutional as construed by the Supreme Judicial Court to remove the prohibition on exhibiting contraceptives, that this prohibition was severable from the remainder of the law, and that the conviction of Baird for being an unlicensed distributor was valid.

Baird appealed to the U.S. Court of Appeals for the First Circuit, retaining the services of Chester C. Paris as appellate counsel. The court ordered his release on bail pending its decision. Chief Judge Bailey Aldrich and Circuit Judges Edward H. McEntee and Frank M. Coffin heard oral argument on June 4, 1970. The court issued its decision unanimously reversing the district court in an opinion by Chief Judge Aldrich on July 6. While dismissing as unworthy of lengthy discussion Baird's claims that the law violated his First Amendment rights or could not survive the elimination of the ban on exhibition, the court held that the law failed the elemental test of due process: it did not bear "a real and substantial relation to the public health, safety, morals, or some other phase of the general welfare" and, in fact, was arbitrary and discriminatory in its prohibitions.

Aldrich asserted that it was difficult to believe that a law originally enacted solely to protect morality, as indicated by its original title, had suddenly been converted into a public health measure by the 1966 amendments. It was clear, he asserted, that the legislature's purpose in 1966 was to trim back the law from its prior total prohibition on the distribution of contraceptives to the extent necessary to comply with the *Griswold* decision, which clearly protected the right of physicians to counsel their married patients regarding contraception. In drawing the line between married and unmarried people, the state had betrayed any health justification for the law, since, in the words of

dissenting Justices Whittemore and Cutter of the Supreme Judicial Court, "If there is need to have a physician prescribe (and a pharmacist dispense) contraceptives, that need is as great for unmarried persons as for married persons." Even more tellingly, since the law authorized physicians to prescribe for married persons, it was clear that an absolute ban on distribution to unmarried persons was not required for health purposes. Both married and unmarried persons would use contraceptives in the same way, and their physical effects would not vary based on marital status.

Furthermore, Aldrich stated that the court could take notice that not all contraceptive devices presented health hazards in their use. Indeed, he noted, it had been 200 years since Casanova recorded the ubiquitous use of condoms, which nobody ever seriously contended presented a health hazard, and yet condoms were covered by the statutory ban. Since the legislature made no attempt to distinguish between those contraceptives that posed health hazards and those that did not, it was clear that the legislature had some purpose other than health in maintaining the restrictions on distribution.

Aldrich then focused on the state's alternative contention that the statute was supported by a legitimate purpose to protect morals. The state argued that by making acquisition of contraceptives difficult for them, the law would discourage unmarried persons from engaging in the forbidden act of fornication. Aldrich found this contention bizarre. Fornication was a misdemeanor, punishable by $30 or thirty days. It strained credulity that the state would pass a felony statute to discourage commission of a misdemeanor. If prevention of fornication was a purpose of the statute as originally passed, why had it been also extended to married persons? Clearly, the legislature considered the use of contraceptives immoral conduct, regardless of the identity of the users. The 1966 amendments exempted married persons from the distribution ban solely because the legislature felt constrained by *Griswold* to do so.

Aldrich asserted that the legislation was irrational as it stood: "To say that contraceptives are immoral as such, and are to be forbidden to unmarried persons who will nevertheless persist in having intercourse, means that such persons must risk for themselves an unwanted pregnancy, for the child, illegitimacy, and for society, a possible obligation of support." Aldrich asserted that such a result conflicted with "fundamental human rights," and "in the absence of demonstrated harm, we hold it is beyond the competency of the state." Only by removing the distinction between married and unmarried persons could the statute be justified as a health measure, but then, because many common contraceptives posed no health hazard, the statute would remain overbroad, and it would be inappropriate to leave in place an overbroad statute where fundamental rights were concerned. Consequently, the whole statute must be considered unconstitutional, and Baird must be released from serving the balance of his sentence. As to the state's argument that Baird lacked standing to present these constitutional arguments, Aldrich dismissed as unworthy the contention that one who had been imprisoned under a statute lacked standing to challenge its constitutionality.

The state appealed the decision to the U.S. Supreme Court, which noted probable jurisdiction on March 1, 1971. When the Court sat to hear arguments in the case on November 17 and 18, the cast of characters had changed considerably. Special Assistant Attorney General Joseph R. Nolan appeared to defend the statute, and Joseph D. Tydings represented Baird. Amicus briefs were filed in support of Baird's position by the Planned Parenthood Federation of America, the Planned Parenthood League of Massachusetts, the American Civil Liberties Union, and Human Rights for Women, Inc. The case was heard by a seven-member Court, since the vacancies created by the resignations and deaths of Justices Hugo L. Black and John Marshall Harlan had not yet been filled. (The subsequently appointed Justices Lewis F. Powell and William H. Rehnquist did not participate in deciding the case.)

The Court announced its decision affirming the court of appeals on March 22, 1972. Justice William J. Brennan, Jr., announced the opinion for the Court, joined by Justices Douglas, Potter Stewart, and Thurgood Marshall. Justice Douglas also filed a concurring opinion. Justice White filed an opinion concurring in

the result, which was joined by Justice Harry A. Blackmun. Chief Justice Warren E. Burger dissented.

Justice Brennan stated the Court's agreement with the court of appeals that "the goals of deterring premarital sex and regulating the distribution of potentially harmful articles cannot reasonably be regarded as legislative aims" of the Massachusetts law. However, Justice Brennan found an alternative method of striking down the law, relying on the Equal Protection Clause rather than on the substantive due process approach of the court of appeals. It is Justice Brennan's equal protection analysis that has made this opinion a frequently cited precedent on the sexual privacy rights of unmarried persons.

Before addressing the equal protection issue, Brennan disposed of the argument that Baird lacked standing to raise a constitutional challenge based on privacy by noting that, in fact, Baird and those situated similarly to him as possible distributors of contraceptives were those against whom the direct prohibition of the statute ran. As in *Griswold*, where the Court held that the director of Connecticut's Planned Parenthood chapter had standing to raise the privacy rights of married couples who desired to use the organization's counseling services, "the relationship between Baird and those whose rights he seeks to assert is not simply that between a distributor and potential distributees, but that between an advocate of the rights of persons to obtain contraceptives and those desirous of doing so." Indeed, since the Massachusetts statute forbade distribution but did not forbid use, Baird's standing argument was even stronger than Griswold's "because unmarried persons denied access to contraceptives in Massachusetts, unlike the users of contraceptives in Connecticut, are not themselves subject to prosecution and, to that extent, are denied a forum in which to assert their own rights."

Turning to the equal protection issue, Brennan asserted that the question for decision was "whether there is some ground of difference that rationally explains the different treatment accorded married and unmarried persons" under the law, thus implicitly accepting without further discussion that marital status was not a "suspect classification" requiring heightened scrutiny.

The first ground of difference asserted by the state was its interest in preventing premarital sex. Brennan agreed with the court of appeals that this was not very plausible. "It would be plainly unreasonable to assume that Massachusetts has prescribed pregnancy and the birth of an unwanted child as punishment for fornication, which is a misdemeanor" under state law. Brennan said that "it is abundantly clear that the effect of the ban on distribution of contraceptives to unmarried persons has at best a marginal relation to the proffered objective." For one thing, the statute did not forbid distribution of contraceptives for health purposes, only for purposes of preventing conception. For another, married persons could obtain contraceptives and then engage in extramarital sex with unmarried persons. Furthermore, Brennan, in agreement with the court of appeals, found it incredible to suppose that Massachusetts would authorize a five-year prison term as punishment for distributing contraceptives when the maximum sentence for fornication was a mere thirty days.

The state's attempt to justify the law as a health regulation was also unavailing. Brennan agreed with the court of appeals' conclusion that the law swept too broadly to be credible on that basis, being both invidiously discriminatory toward the unmarried and overbroad with regard to the married, who would have to obtain a prescription for so innocuous a contraceptive as a condom. Brennan also noted that section 21 was unnecessary as a health measure, since there was pervasive federal regulation of drugs through the Federal Food, Drug, and Cosmetic Act.

Finally, Brennan agreed with the court of appeals that the real legislative purpose seemed to be a prohibition on contraception *per se* as immoral, to the extent allowed after *Griswold*. After quoting the court of appeals' determinative paragraph finding that this purpose failed the substantive due process test, Brennan asserted that it was unnecessary to decide the substantive due process question because, "whatever the rights of the individual to access to contraceptives may be, the rights must be the same for the unmarried and the married alike."

While conceding that in *Griswold* the right of privacy "inhered in the marital relationship," Brennan denied that it could be given so narrow a construction as had been done by the Massachusetts Supreme Judicial Court. "Yet the marital couple is not an independent entity with a mind and heart of its own, but an association of two individuals each with a separate intellectual and emotional makeup. If the right of privacy means anything, it is the right of the *individual*, married or single, to be free from unwarranted governmental intrusion into matters so fundamentally affecting a person as the decision whether to bear or beget a child." Brennan cited *Stanley v. Georgia* (1969) and *Skinner v. Oklahoma* (1942) to support this contention, both cases in which, at least arguably, some members of the Court purported to base limitations on state intrusion in a constitutional privacy right that inhered in the individual.

Even if *Griswold* was interpreted as going only to state prohibitions on counseling and use, and as not affecting the issue of distribution, outlawing distribution to the unmarried but not the married would work an invidious underinclusion, since the "evil" of contraception would be the same in both cases and the state would have no basis for distinguishing. "By providing dissimilar treatment for married and unmarried persons who are similarly situated," Brennan concluded, the Massachusetts law violated the Equal Protection Clause.

Justice Douglas concurred separately to emphasize his view that the case could have been decided on a narrower First Amendment analysis, by which Baird's act of handing the Emko foam kit to a woman in the audience was merely a part of the educational strategy of his lecture. Douglas insisted that the record was ambiguous as to whether Baird intended the woman to take the material away from the lecture hall or merely to examine it. In dissent, Chief Justice Burger expressed bafflement at this conclusion, since Baird had been indicted and convicted of "distribution," not just "exhibition."

Justice White, with Justice Blackmun's concurrence, argued that the equal protection issue was not properly presented as a basis for decision. There was no indication in the record whether the young woman handed the contraceptive material by Baird was married or single. Baird's standing, as far as White was concerned, was limited to the question of whether the state had a rational basis for restricting distribution of contraceptives to registered physicians and licensed pharmacists. Here, he agreed with the court of appeals that such a restriction was irrational, since there were perfectly harmless contraceptives in wide use as to which no such health-related restriction was necessary. "I assume," he said, "that a State's interest in the health of its citizens empowers it to restrict to medical channels the distribution of products whose use should be accompanied by medical advice.... Had Baird distributed a supply of the so-called 'pill,' I would sustain his conviction under this statute." Thus, the statute was not unconstitutional on its face, but only as applied in this case to Baird, who had "distributed" a contraceptive as to which health regulation was unnecessary. Since the Court had identified a constitutional right for married couples to use contraceptives, and since some contraceptives did not require any particular medical advice to be used safely, it would unduly burden a constitutional right for a state to require a married person to go to a physician to obtain such a contraceptive.

Since it was possible to grant Baird's petition for *habeas corpus* on the narrow ground that there was no rational basis for restricting him from distributing vaginal foam, White asserted that there was "no reason for reaching the novel constitutional question whether a State may restrict or forbid the distribution of contraceptives to the unmarried."

Chief Justice Burger dissented, arguing that the Massachusetts Supreme Judicial Court's decision "sustaining appellee's conviction for dispensing medicinal material without a license seems eminently correct." To Burger, the only issue properly before the Court—the only issue as to which Baird had standing—was whether Massachusetts could properly limit to physicians the right to authorize distribution of contraceptives.

Burger argued that the state court's determination that the law was a health measure was an "authoritative" declaration not to be questioned by the federal courts as a binding interpretation of a state statute. As such, it was well

within the police power of the state. "So far as I am aware," he stated, "this Court has never before challenged the police power of a State to protect the public from the risks of possibly spurious and deleterious substances sold within its borders." It was not for the Court to decide by judicial notice that some contraceptives were harmful and some were not. "Even assuming no present dispute among medical authorities," he argued, "we cannot ignore that it has become commonplace for a drug or food additive to be universally regarded as harmless on one day and to be condemned as perilous on the next. It is inappropriate for this Court to overrule a legislative classification by relying on the present consensus among leading authorities. The commands of the Constitution cannot fluctuate with the shifting tides of scientific opinion."

Finally, Burger argued that even if it was definitely established that a particular contraceptive article was not dangerous, "the choice of a means of birth control, although a highly personal matter, is also a health matter in a very real sense, and I see nothing arbitrary in a requirement of medical supervision." He concluded by warning that the Court's opinion might open the door to wholesale invalidations of legislation intended to protect the public from quack medications and practitioners. Analogizing Baird to the old-time "medicine man . . . who attracted a crowd of the curious with a soapbox lecture and then plied them with 'free samples' of some unproved remedy," Burger commented, "Massachusetts presumably outlawed such activities long ago, but today's holding seems to invite their return."

Eisenstad v. Baird was a significant expansion on the privacy interest identified in *Griswold*. It was not surprising that the Massachusetts Supreme Judicial Court was able to give *Griswold* a narrow construction, for Justice Douglas's opinion in that case focused heavily on the marital relationship as the location for a right of sexual privacy. By imaginatively reaching out to such different contexts as *Stanley v. Georgia* and *Skinner v. Oklahoma*, Justice Brennan constructed a personal privacy right that seemed likely to topple many other state regulatory barriers, including those against abortion, fornication, and homosexual conduct.

As such, Eisenstadt, even more than *Griswold*, was the sword wielded by those who sought to attack state regulation of private consensual sexual conduct until *Bowers v. Hardwick* (1986) signaled the Court's retreat from a broad concept of individual privacy.

Case References

Bowers v. Hardwick, 478 U.S. 186 (1986)
Griswold v. Connecticut, 381 U.S. 479 (1965)
Skinner v. Oklahoma, 316 U.S. 535 (1942)
Stanley v. Georgia, 394 U.S. 557 (1969)
State v. Baird, 50 N.J. 376, 235 A.2d 673 (1967)
United States v. O'Brien, 391 U.S. 367, rehearing denied, 393 U.S. 900 (1968)

6. ABORTION AND THE RIGHT TO PRIVACY

Roe v. Wade, 410 U.S. 113 (1973), affirming 314 F. Supp. 1217 (N.D. Tex. 1970). *Doe v. Bolton*, 410 U.S. 179 (1973), modifying 319 F. Supp. 1048 (N.D. Ga. 1970).

The U.S. Supreme Court's decisions in *Griswold v. Connecticut* (1965) and *Eisenstadt v. Baird* (1972) held that a constitutional right of privacy barred the states from prohibiting adults, whether married or single, from obtaining or using contraceptives to prevent conception. These decisions came at a time when debate was mounting on the issue of abortion in the United States. In most states, abortion laws dating from the mid- to late-19th century were still in effect, making it a serious crime to abort a fetus except, in some states, where a doctor (or group of doctors) certified that the life of the mother was at stake.

Many of these statutes had been passed in response to strenuous lobbying efforts by the American Medical Association at a time when abortion was a dangerous medical procedure, and apparently represented a judgment that the operation had to be forbidden in defense of the health and welfare of American women. With the introduction of antiseptic operating procedures in the late 19th century and the refinement of surgical techniques in the 20th century, abortions had become much safer, and if performed early in pregnancy were actually as safe as, or safer than, childbirth.

By the 1960s, medical professionals and legal policy experts were engaged in heatedly debating over whether the traditional statutory regime should be allowed to continue. The American Law Institute (ALI) recommended, as part of its Model Penal Code, a liberalization of the law that would significantly expand the usual exception for circumstances where the life of the mother was seriously threatened. Under the ALI approach, a category of "justifiable abortion" was recognized:

A licensed physician is justified in terminating a pregnancy if he believes there is substantial risk that continuance of the pregnancy would gravely impair the physical or mental health of the mother or that the child would be born with grave physical or mental defect, or that the pregnancy resulted from rape, incest, or other felonious intercourse. All illicit intercourse with a girl below the age of 16 shall be deemed felonious for purposes of this subsection. Justifiable abortions shall be performed only in a licensed hospital except in case of emergency when hospital facilities are unavailable. [Additional exceptions from the requirement of hospitalization may be incorporated here to take account of situations in sparsely settled areas where hospitals are not generally accessible.]

While the ALI approach constituted a marked liberalization from the laws of many states, it still imposed substantial restrictions on the availability of abortion. The first two exceptions hinged on medical determinations, and the reasons available to a woman for terminating an abortion took no account of her other possible needs, in terms of economics, family situation, or career, except as they might seriously affect physical or mental health. Furthermore, the ALI draft required concurrence of two physicians in writing, and, with the exception of sparsely settled areas, seemed to rule out the idea of family planning clinics standing alone from hospitals being allowed to perform abortions. Some states—including Georgia, whose statute was challenged in *Doe v. Bolton*—basically adopted the ALI's recommended approach with some modifications. Others went their own way; many made no changes at all.

Court challenges to abortion statutes became increasingly common during the late 1960s and early 1970s, and soon it became necessary for the U.S. Supreme Court to confront the question whether existing legislative prohibitions were consistent with developing constitutional protection of individual rights. In 1971, the Court ruled in *United States v. Vuitch* that an abortion statute in the District of Columbia was not unconstitutionally vague in restricting abortions to those "necessary for the preservation of the mother's life or health and under the direction of a competent licensed practitioner of medicine." The Court found that the term "health" presented no problem of vagueness, where it was construed broadly to include mental as well as physical health. But the Court did not address the substantive question whether the government could restrict availability of abortions to situations where physicians believed that the operation was necessary to protect the mother's health. Two decisions by three-judge federal district courts in 1970 provided the vehicle for the Court to address these substantive questions.

The cases were brought by pregnant women, proceeding anonymously, denied abortions during the first three months of their pregnancies under criminal abortion laws in Georgia and Texas. The first to proceed to a district court decision was *Roe v. Wade*, the Texas case, in which Texas attorneys Linda N. Coffee and Sarah Weddington represented the pregnant woman as well as a married couple who alleged that their constitutional rights were "chilled" by the existence of the statute, and in which Fred Bruner and Ray L. Merrill, Jr., of Dallas, represented a doctor who had been frequently arrested for performing abortions and sought to intervene as a plaintiff in the case. Dallas Assistant District Attorney John B. Tolle and Texas Assistant Attorney General Jay Floyd represented the state. The plaintiffs requested a declaration that the Texas statute, which allowed abortions only to save the life of the mother, violated the constitutional right of privacy, and sought an injunction barring further enforcement of the law.

The three-judge panel, constituted as required by then-applicable federal rules in cases where the constitutionality of state laws was being challenged, issued a *per curiam* decision on June 17, 1970, holding the statute unconstitutional but refusing to issue an injunction. Rejecting the state's arguments that the plaintiffs lacked standing to bring the case or that the suit did not present a "case of actual controversy" as required to confer jurisdiction on the court, the panel agreed with the plaintiffs' argument that the Texas law deprived single women and married couples of "their right, secured by the Ninth Amendment, to choose whether to have children."

The panel relied on Justice Arthur J. Goldberg's concurring opinion in *Griswold*, which emphasized the Ninth Amendment's concept of fundamental rights reserved to the people as a source of the privacy right governing access to contraceptives. The panel noted that the California Supreme Court had ruled in *People v. Belous* (1969) that "the fundamental right of the woman to choose whether to bear children follows from the Supreme Court's and this court's repeated acknowledgment of a 'right to privacy' or 'liberty' in matters related to marriage, family, and sex," and quoted retired U.S. Supreme Court Justice Tom C. Clark's recent article on abortion in the *Loyola University Law Review* to the effect that the state would need to show "a compelling subordinating interest that outweighs the individual rights of human beings" if it wanted to interfere with "a person's marriage, home, children and day-to-day living habits."

> [Abortion] falls within that sensitive area of privacy—the marital relation [said Clark]. One of the basic values of this privacy is birth control, as evidenced by the *Griswold* decision. Griswold's act was to prevent formation of the fetus. This, the Court found, was constitutionally protected. If an individual may prevent conception, why can he not nullify that conception when prevention has failed?

The panel acknowledged that the state had presented compelling reasons to be involved in the abortion process, such as the requirement that abortions be performed by competent medical personnel in appropriate surroundings to protect the health of the mother. "Concern over abortion of the 'quickened' fetus may well rank as another such interest," said the panel, but Texas's law was too broadly prohibitory, failing the requirement that laws invading constitutional privacy be narrowly drafted to accomplish their compelling purpose. The panel found that not only was the Texas law overbroad in prohibiting all abortions save those necessary to preserve the life of the mother, but that the exception was itself unconstitutionally vague, since it left open questions of how likely death would have to be if the mother were to carry the fetus to term:

> How *likely* must death be? Must death be certain if the abortion is not performed? Is it enough that the woman could not undergo birth without an ascertainably higher possibility of death than would normally be the case? What if the woman threatened suicide if the abortion was not performed? How *imminent* must death be if the abortion is not performed? Is it sufficient if having the child will shorten the life of the woman by a number of years? These questions simply cannot be answered.

The panel found that by imposing criminal penalties on the basis of such a vague provision the state violated the Due Process Clause of the Fourteenth Amendment. However, the panel was unwilling to issue an injunction barring enforcement of the statute, citing "the strong reluctance of federal courts to interfere with the process of state criminal procedure" except in cases where "statutes are justifiably attacked on their face as abridging free expression" or where "statutes are justifiably attacked as applied for the purpose of discouraging protected activities." The panel found neither exception met in this case, and concluded that abstention was proper.

Meanwhile, the Georgia case, *Doe v. Bolton*, was also proceeding toward decision by a three-judge district court panel. The lead plaintiff was an anonymous pregnant woman who had been denied an abortion by the physician committee established by an Atlanta hospital pursuant to the state's abortion law; other plaintiffs included physicians and other health care workers who might be prosecuted under the statute for performing abortions, and ministers and social workers who might be prosecuted under the statute for advising women to have abortions. As in the Texas case, they sought both a declaration of the law's unconstitutionality and an injunction against its enforcement. Participating in the argument were Atlanta attorneys Margie Pitts Hames, Tobiane Schwartz, Elizabeth Rindskopf, and Bettye Kehrer for the plaintiffs; Georgia Attorney General Arthur K. Bolton, Atlanta Assistant District Attorney Tony H. Hight, and Atlanta Attorney Ralph H. Witt for the government defendants; and Ferdinand Buckley, an Atlanta attorney who had been appointed to represent the interests of "the unborn child of Mary Doe."

The panel issued a decision on July 31, 1970, holding the statute at least partially unconstitutional but denying injunctive relief. After resolving issues of standing and justiciability in favor of the plaintiffs, the panel cited the panoply of U.S. Supreme Court decisions on privacy. While indicating its agreement that they were relevant to the constitutionality of the abortion statute, however, the panel stated its agreement in guarded terms:

> While the court agrees that the breadth of the right to privacy encompasses the decision to terminate an unwanted pregnancy, we are unwilling to declare that such a right reposes unbounded in any one individual. Rather, we are of the view that although the state may not unduly limit the reasons for which a woman seeks an abortion, it may legitimately require that the decision to terminate her pregnancy be one reached only upon consideration of more factors than the desires of the woman and her ability to find a willing physician.

Although the privacy right identified in *Griswold* was clearly involved here, the case was distinguishable in an important way, said the panel, because "unlike the decision to use contraceptive devices, the decision to abort a pregnancy affects other interests than those of the woman alone, or even husband and wife alone." The fetus presented the prospect of "the potential of independent human existence," so "once the embryo has formed, the decision to abort its development cannot be considered a purely private one affecting only husband and wife, man and woman. A potential human life together with the traditional interests in the health, welfare and morals of its citizenry under the police power grant to the state a legitimate area of control short of an invasion of the personal right of initial decision."

The panel noted with approval that Georgia, by adopting the ALI recommendations, had made the issue of abortion primarily a "medical one." This seemed like a reasonable approach in addressing the health concerns the state was raising, so the panel endorsed most of the procedural requirements imposed by the statute, including the requirement of written concurrence on the desirability of an abortion by two doctors. The panel held that the state "certainly has a clear right to circumscribe a decision made by a woman alone or by a woman and a single physician and to guard against the establishment of transient 'abortion mills' by the occasional opportunistic or unethical practitioner and the concomitant dangers to his patrons and the public." Nonetheless, the state did not have the right to limit the grounds for abortion to the three exceptions based on the ALI draft, since that list was too narrow to encompass all the legitimate reasons for which a woman might seek to terminate her pregnancy. Thus, the panel struck down as unconstitutional the list of three exceptions, leaving intact the portion of the statute providing that an abortion could be performed where it was found, by the applicable multiple-physician and review committee process, to be "necessary." Having thus somewhat limited the prohibitory scope of the statute, the panel refused to issue an injunction against its enforcement, relying on a 1968 U.S. Supreme Court decision that held that once a state statute was held unconstitutional, the "vindication" of the parties' rights could be left to the operation of the state law enforcement and judicial systems.

In both cases, the challengers filed petitions with the U.S. Supreme Court seeking review for the purpose of gaining injunctive relief. In addition, of course, the Georgia challengers asserted that the district court had not gone far enough in striking down the statutory restrictions, especially the requirement for written doctor certification or committee approval prior to an abortion being performed. The state defendants reiterated their objections to standing and justiciability. On May 3, 1971, the Supreme Court indicated that it would hear the appeals in both cases, reserving the question of jurisdiction to its hearing on the merits. At the same time, the Court denied a petition from the state of Georgia for direct substantive review of the district court's decision, noting the Court's rule that state appeals from declaratory judgment actions where no injunctive relief had been awarded were properly brought first to the circuit courts of appeals, not to the Supreme Court.

The Court heard oral argument in the combined cases on December 13, 1971. Sarah Weddington presented the argument for the challengers of the statute in the Texas case, and Texas Assistant Attorney General Jay Floyd defended the law. Margie Pitts Hames argued on behalf of the challengers in the Georgia case, while Dorothy T. Beasley represented the government defendants. The Court decided to schedule a second round of oral argument, held on October 11, 1972, at which Robert C. Flowers replaced Jay Floyd as oral advocate for the state of Texas.

The Court issued its opinions in both cases on January 22, 1973, affirming the Texas district court decision and modifying the Georgia decision to strike down more of the statute. However, the Court denied injunctive relief, noting that its ruling on the merits would be binding on law enforcement authorities and lower courts, so there was no need for such relief.

Justice Harry A. Blackmun's opinion for the Court in *Roe v. Wade*, the Texas case, became instantly controversial for its extended discussion of medical history and opinion, appearing to the casual reader to be based on determinations as to which the Supreme Court could claim little particular competence. On more careful analysis, however, it would be seen that the discussion of medical history underlay traditional sorts of inquiries necessary to determine whether the claimed constitutional right could be logically derived from existing precedents.

Blackmun began his opinion by confirming the district court's finding that the pregnant woman had standing to sue and presented a justiciable controversy. The state argued that by the time of the hearing, it appeared that the plaintiff was no longer pregnant, and, in any event, would have been at such a late stage of pregnancy that she might not be personally eligible for an abortion even under the most expansive constitutional ruling without presenting evidence that carrying to term would endanger her life. Blackmun dismissed this technical argument, asserting that litigation about the rights of pregnant women, given the delays inherent in the legal system, were the quintessential examples of cases presenting issues capable of repetition but evading review because of the very transience of personal standing argued by the defendants. However, he did agree with the defendants that the district court should not have allowed the doctor to participate as a plaintiff, since his possible future prosecution under the Texas abortion law was entirely speculative, and he agreed with the district court that the married couple lacked standing, since their possible future need for abortion services was also speculative.

Turning to the merits, Blackmun quickly sketched out the existing scope of constitutional privacy in a one-paragraph summation of the Court's recent decisions, and then asserted that before addressing the claim that the constitutional privacy right extended to abortion, "we feel it desirable briefly to survey, in several aspects, the history of abortion, for such insight as that history may afford us, and then to examine the state purposes and interests behind the criminal abortion laws." The historic survey revealed some surprises. The Ancient World was apparently not consistent in its view of abortion, with some ancient Western cultures condemning it and others allowing it. The Hippocratic Oath, said to represent the views of ancient Greek medicine, was actually the viewpoint only of a minority sect, the Pythagoreans, who considered the embryo "animate" and thus a living thing from the moment of conception. By contrast, it appeared that most Greek thinkers, at least those who left written records, "commended abortion, at least prior to viability."

Blackmun's survey of English common-law authorities also revealed considerable tolerance for abortion. Abortion prior to "quickening" (i.e., the point in pregnancy at which the fetus can be detected as engaging in motion independent of the mother) was not a traditional common-law crime, since legal authorities considered the prequickening fetus merely a part of the mother's body, not an independent "soul." There was even a dispute as to whether postquickening abortion was treated as a felony under the common law, Blackmun noting that one common interpretation of old texts made it a misdemeanor. The common law received by the American colonies upon independence thus provided no criminal penalties for prequickening abortions, and only minor penalties for postquickening abortions.

England passed its first abortion statute in 1803, preserving the distinction between pre- and postquickening abortions by making a postquickening abortion a capital crime, but prescribing "lesser penalties" for prequickening abortions. In 1837, with the removal of the death penalty for this offense, the distinction in punishments was removed. A 1929 English statute focused on the destruction of "the life of a child capable of being born alive" as the primary element of the crime, and made it a felony, with the exception of abortions done "in good faith for the purpose only of preserving the life of the mother." In the Abortion Act of 1967, England had liberalized its abortion laws somewhat along the lines of the Model Penal Code in the United States, authorizing abortions where it could be shown that there would be an adverse effect on the physical or mental health of the mother or that the child would be born with gross deformities.

The U.S. statutory developments during the 19th and early 20th centuries had largely paralleled the English experience, with some lag time built in for ideas to cross the Atlantic. Connecticut was the first state to pass an abortion statute, in 1821, outlawing abortion performed on a woman "quick with child," but not imposing the death penalty. It was not until 1860 that Connecticut criminalized prequickening abortion. New York's 1828 law, characterized as a "model" for many other 19th-century abortion laws, made prequickening abortion a misdemeanor and postquickening abortion a felony as second-degree manslaughter, but allowed an exception for abortions necessary to preserve the mother's life. It was not until after the Civil War that there was a rapid increase in the number of states passing abortion laws. Most midcentury laws were rather lenient toward prequickening abortion, but toward the end of the century the distinction between pre- and postquickening abortions began to disappear and the laws became relatively stringent, making abortion a felony offense whenever performed, although many states provided an exception for situations where carrying the child to term would threaten the mother's life. During the 1960s, about a third of the states liberalized their laws along the lines recommended in the Model Penal Code.

Blackmun next turned to the views of medical and legal professional organizations. He asserted that the American Medical Association (AMA) was actually a strong moving force in the adoption of tough abortion laws during the 19th century, the doctors taking the view that abortions were dangerous operations that should be avoided in virtually all cases. This view seems to have been based, at least in part, on a literal following of the Hippocratic Oath, which banned abortion, and on the widespread view among 19th-century doctors that all abortions involved the "unwarrantable destruction of human life," according to a resolution adopted by the AMA at its 1859 annual convention. By the late 1960s, however, the doctors had taken note of the liberalizing trends and shifted the main focus of their concern to the conditions under which abortions might be performed, while insisting that abortions should be performed only when medically indicated for the health of the mother. In 1970, the AMA adopted the view that the decision whether to have an abortion should be arrived at jointly by doctor and patient; doctors should not merely acquiesce "in the patient's demand" without extensive discussion. In the same year, the American Public Health Association (APHA) had taken a more affirmative view, urging that abortion services be made available and that various procedural barriers to abortion be abandoned, although the APHA insisted that it was best that abortions be performed in a hospital where possible. The American Bar Association's position was best summed up by its approval in 1972 of a resolution recommending passage by the states of the Uniform Abortion Act drafted by the Commissioners on Uniform State Laws,

which paralleled in its approach that of the American Law Institute in the Model Penal Code. This Act was, in turn, based heavily on the law adopted by New York in response to the recommendations of a special commission appointed by Governor Nelson Rockefeller to review the subject.

Blackmun then turned to the justifications normally advanced for laws banning or sharply limiting access to abortion. The first was the state's concern in regulating sexual activity itself, a concern that may have played a role in the 19th century but was of decreasing significance in constitutional argumentation, especially in light of the Court's holdings in *Griswold* and *Eisenstadt* on the freedom of adults to make decisions about their private, consensual (heterosexual) activity. The second was protection of the health of the mother, which Blackmun noted was an issue that had undergone considerable change since the first criminal abortion laws were passed in America, because medical advances made abortion even safer than childbirth when it was performed early in pregnancy. However, Blackmun noted, it was clear that abortion remained a serious procedure presenting some danger as pregnancy advanced, and that a state would have a concomitantly accelerating interest in regulating the circumstances under which abortions were performed. The third state interest, protecting potential life, was also seen by Blackmun as increasing in weight as pregnancy progressed. Blackmun rejected the view, advanced particularly by some *amici* in the case, that life began at conception, thus making abortion murder and imposing on the state the duty to ban it under all circumstances, but indicated that it was not, in his view, necessary to accept or to reject this proposition in order to reach an appropriate decision in the case. He likewise rejected the argument that the protection of potential life was not a valid state interest because the 19th-century abortion statutes were, on their face, aimed at protecting maternal health rather than potential life. He noted, however, that the early abortion laws, with their distinction between pre- and postquickening abortion, seemed implicitly to embrace the view that human life begins no earlier than quickening, thus suggesting that the laws were, at least initially, concerned primarily with maternal health when they imposed penalties for prequickening abortion, not the "life" of the fetus.

Finally, Blackmun began his legal analysis. After again listing and characterizing the Court's prior significant privacy cases, Blackmun asserted that the right of privacy, "whether it be founded in the Fourteenth Amendment's concept of personal liberty and restrictions upon state action, as we feel it is, or, as the District Court determined, in the Ninth Amendment's reservation of rights to the people, is broad enough to encompass a woman's decision whether or not to terminate her pregnancy." However, the Court was unwilling to recognize that right, or any right, as absolute, finding "unpersuasive" the argument that the state has no "valid interest at all in regulating the abortion decision, or no interest strong enough to support any limitation upon the woman's sole determination." Blackman stated:

> The privacy right involved, therefore, cannot be said to be absolute. In fact, it is not clear to us that the claim asserted by some amici that one has an unlimited right to do with one's body as one pleases bears a close relationship to the right of privacy previously articulated in the Court's decisions. The Court has refused to recognize an unlimited right of this kind in the past.

As with the other privacy cases, the question was whether the state had a compelling interest that would justify abridging the privacy right to the extent necessary to accomplish that interest.

Thus, the question was whether the state had met its burden to justify the intrusion on a woman's privacy rights in the Texas abortion law. The state had argued that the fetus was a "person" protected by the Fourteenth Amendment. "If this suggestion of personhood is established," Blackmun observed, "the appellant's case, of course, collapses, for the fetus' right to life would then be guaranteed specifically by the Amendment." However, no prior decision by the Court had recognized such a status for the fetus, and a review of constitutional provisions and common-law doctrines indicated to Blackmun that it was not tenable, since it was clear that almost all legal rights that had ever been recognized in fetuses depended to some

extent on subsequent live birth, and most of the constitutional references to "persons" quite clearly intended reference to persons who had already been born. Thus, the Court could reject this defense argument.

The state had next contended that the privacy cases did not appropriately extend to abortion because abortion was a process that went beyond the confines of the privacy of the home and the intimate relation of two adults. The doctor and other attending health care workers were implicated in a procedure that most often took place outside the home, and the fetus, if not yet a born person, was potential life, particularly toward the later stages of pregnancy. Indeed, Texas urged that life begins at conception and thus the fetus was in effect a "third party" with an interest in the outcome. Blackmun was not willing to accept this argument, however, stating: "When those trained in the respective disciplines of medicine, philosophy, and theology are unable to arrive at any consensus, the judiciary, at this point in the development of man's knowledge, is not in a position to speculate as to the answer" of when life begins. For Blackmun, the safe path was to focus on "viability," that point when the fetus was well enough developed to have a fighting chance of surviving independently of the mother, "albeit with artificial aid." This point occurred normally at twenty-eight weeks of pregnancy, although it might occur as early as twenty-four weeks. Blackmun contended that at the point of viability, Texas's argument began to have significant weight, for it could plausibly be said that the fetus' interests as a "person" emerged. Looking to the common law, he noted that viability had become a significant point of demarcation in tort and criminal law.

Where did this leave Blackmun? Since he had advocated, in effect, a balancing of rights, it suggested to him that the constitutional doctrines governing state legislative power over abortion naturally subdivided into three temporal stages, or "trimesters," of pregnancy. During the first trimester, he contended, the state's interest in maternal health or protection of potential life was at its lowest, since abortion was no riskier than (and perhaps safer than) carrying a fetus to term in the early stages, and the fetus was merely a small growth in the mother's uterus at this point, far from viability during those first nine or ten weeks. During this stage, then, the state's interests were not sufficient to overcome the mother's right of choice.

As pregnancy continued, however, the state's interests became more and more compelling. During the second trimester, abortion became a more complicated and risky procedure, particularly if performed outside the context of a hospital under regulated standards. Thus, Blackmun would concede to the state's interest in maternal health the right to regulate abortion during the second trimester, at least to the extent "that the regulation reasonably relates to the preservation and protection of maternal health." This could include specification of the qualifications of those allowed to perform abortions and of the quality of facilities in which they could be performed. Finally, in the final trimester, when the fetus was near or at the point of viability, the state's interest in protecting potential life grew so compelling that the state could outlaw abortion, although Blackmun insisted on the widespread exception contained in most abortion laws for circumstances where the mother's life or health was in danger.

"Measured against these standards," said Blackmun, the Texas abortion law "sweeps too broadly," since it made no distinction between early and late-term abortions and limited legal abortions to only those necessary to save the life of the mother. Having found the law unconstitutional on its face, Blackmun found it unnecessary to deal with the alternative ruling by the district court that found the statutory exception unconstitutionally vague. After recapitulating his "trimester" system in summary form, Blackmun concluded:

> This holding, we feel, is consistent with the relative weights of the respective interests involved, with the lessons and examples of medical and legal history, with the lenity of the common law, and with the demands of the profound problems of the present day. The decision leaves the State free to place increasing restrictions on abortion as the period of pregnancy lengthens, so long as those restrictions are tailored to the recognized state interests. The decision vindicates the right of the physician to administer medical treatment according to his professional judgment up to the points where important state interests provide compelling justifications for intervention. Up to those points, the abortion decision in all its aspects is inherently, and primarily, a medical decision, and basic responsibility for it must rest with the physician. If an individual practitioner abuses the privilege of exercising proper medical judgment, the usual remedies, judicial and intra-professional, are available.

Finally, Blackmun asserted it was unnecessary to decide whether the district court should have issued an injunction, "for we assume the Texas prosecutorial authorities will give full credence to this decision that the present criminal abortion statutes of that State are unconstitutional."

Blackmun then turned to the Georgia statute in *Doe v. Bolton*, which now had to be measured against the test erected in *Roe v. Wade*. *Bolton* was critically important because the Georgia statute was based on the Model Penal Code abortion provisions, which had been adopted in some form or another by about a third of the states. The Georgia statute had authorized legal abortions only when continued pregnancy would endanger the life or health of the mother, the fetus would be born with significant defects, or the pregnancy resulted from forcible or statutory rape. In addition, Georgia (1) imposed a residency requirement (presumably out of fear that women from less liberal neighboring states would flood Georgia hospitals seeking abortions); (2) required written statements of medical judgment by the patient's doctor with written concurrence from two other doctors; (3) restricted performance of abortions to hospitals accredited both by the state and by a nongovernmental body, the Joint Commission on Accreditation of Hospitals; (4) required advance approval by a hospital staff committee and special certifications in rape cases; and (5) imposed special record-keeping and confidentiality requirements. The Georgia law also provided that law enforcement officers or relatives of "the unborn child" could initiate legal proceedings to halt an abortion by challenging whether the statute would allow it in a particular case.

After disposing of procedural and jurisdictional issues favorably to the plaintiffs,

Blackmun turned to the particular Georgia provisions challenged on appeal in light of the fundamental right/compelling interest analysis adopted by the Court in *Roe v. Wade*. Framing their arguments in terms of the district court's decision, the appellants had focused on the ways in which the various substantive and procedural provisions of the Georgia law imposed hardships on women seeking abortions, particularly unwed women. In particular, they focused on the ambiguity the district court had left in the statute when it removed the explicit exceptions listed by the legislature and left in place the requirement that a physician find abortion "necessary" in a particular case before the operation could be performed. As Blackmun summarized the effect of the district court's decision:

> The net result of the District Court's decision is that the abortion determination, so far as the physician is concerned, is made in the exercise of his professional, that is, his "best clinical," judgment in the light of *all* the attendant circumstances. He is not now restricted to the three situations originally specified. Instead, he may range farther afield wherever his medical judgment, properly and professionally exercised, so dictates and directs him.

Blackmun found this to be an acceptable result, noting that the Court's prior decision in *Vuitch* had upheld the District of Columbia law that authorized an abortion when the woman's physician found it necessary for her health to have one. "We agree with the district court," he said, "that the medical judgment may be exercised in the light of all factors—physical, emotional, psychological, familial, and the woman's age— relevant to the well-being of the patient."

Blackmun next turned to the procedural burdens imposed by the Georgia statute and found them, in the main, too onerous to withstand constitutional review, particularly as applied to first trimester abortions. For example, the requirement that abortions be performed only in specially accredited hospitals swept too broadly, considering that the statute made no distinction between early and later term abortions. Georgia had a legitimate interest under *Roe v. Wade* in specifying the facilities in which second trimester abortions could be performed, however. Thus, the Court held that the accredi-

tation provision had to fall, while expressing "no opinion on the medical judgment involved in any particular case, that is, whether the patient's situation is such that an abortion should be performed in a hospital, rather than in some other facility."

Blackmun similarly disposed of the requirement for advance approval by a hospital committee, the requirement that two doctors concur with the woman's doctor before an abortion could be performed, and the residence requirement. While he acknowledged that the state could make credible arguments supporting the utility of each of these requirements in some circumstances, once again the statute swept too broadly by applying them to all abortions, including first trimester abortions. It became increasingly clear in Blackmun's opinion that states seeking to regulate abortion to the extent permitted under *Roe v. Wade* would have to reenact their abortion laws after careful redrafting and could not rely on "limiting constructions" of existing laws. Blackmun concluded by noting that having set aside many of the impediments to abortion under Georgia law that had made abortions expensive, it was not necessary to rule on the appellants' contention that these requirements made abortion so expensive that poor people would suffer a deprivation of equal protection by their application. As in *Roe v. Wade*, Blackmun concluded that it was unnecessary for the Court to authorize injunctive relief, since it could be assumed that the state's prosecutors would abide by the Court's decision.

Justice Potter Stewart, who had been a reluctant convert in *Eisenstadt* to the view that constitutional privacy founded on the Fourteenth Amendment should be embraced as part of the Court's constitutional doctrine, wrote a separate concurrence, agreeing with Blackmun that the privacy right previously identified extended to this case. "It is difficult to imagine a more complete abridgment of a constitutional freedom than that worked by the inflexible criminal statute now in force in Texas," he commented. While noting that the state had legitimate interests at stake, he asserted that it would be soon enough for the Court to address those interests if called on to evaluate legislation, not now before it, tailored to meet the Court's decision in this case.

Chief Justice Warren E. Burger also concurred separately, indicating his concerns that the opinion for the Court took notice of much medical and scientific data, perhaps too much for his comfort, in reaching its conclusion. He stressed that the Court's decision did not, in his view, authorize "abortion on demand," and that there remained a legitimate sphere for state regulation of abortion procedures. The Texas and Georgia laws had to fall because they were either too rigid (Texas) or too demanding and time consuming in their procedural requirements (Georgia), although Burger, for himself, might have been inclined to support the requirement that more than one doctor be involved in the abortion decision.

Justice William O. Douglas also concurred separately, sketching out at some length his views on the various component parts of the constitutional right of privacy, which he had described in his opinion for the Court in *Griswold.* He located the rights involved in these cases as part of "the freedom of choice in the basic decisions of one's life respecting marriage, divorce, procreation, contraception, and the education and upbringing of children," as well as "the freedom to care for one's health and person, freedom from bodily restraint or compulsion, freedom to walk, stroll, or loaf." He focused most of his direct fire on the Georgia statute:

> The Georgia statute is at war with the clear message of these cases—that a woman is free to make the basic decision whether to bear an unwanted child. Elaborate argument is hardly necessary to demonstrate that childbirth may deprive a woman of her preferred lifestyle and force upon her a radically different and undesired future. For example, rejected applicants under the Georgia statute are required to endure the discomforts of pregnancy; to incur the pain, higher mortality rate, and aftereffects of childbirth; to abandon educational plans; to sustain loss of income; to forgo the satisfactions of careers; to tax further mental and physical health in providing child care; and, in some cases, to bear the lifelong stigma of unwed motherhood, a badge which may haunt, if not deter, later legitimate family relationships.

The problem, however, was that the state did have legitimate interests at stake, because "voluntary abortion at any time and place regardless of medical standards would impinge on a rightful concern of society," said Douglas. "The woman's health is part of that concern; as is the life of the fetus after quickening. These concerns justify the State in treating the procedure as a medical one." However, the statutes before the Court needed to be redrafted if they were to achieve these goals consistently with the woman's constitutional privacy rights, since as they stood they were drastically overbroad. Douglas was particularly concerned, however, with the way the Georgia statute intruded into the physician-patient relationship by requiring resort to committees and mandatory consultations before an abortion decision was made:

> The right of privacy has no more conspicuous place than in the physician-patient relationship, unless it be in the priest-penitent relationship. It is one thing for a patient to agree that her physician may consult with another physician about her case. It is quite a different matter for the state compulsorily to impose on that physician-patient relationship another layer or, as in this case, still a third layer of physicians. The right of privacy—the right to care for one's health and person and to seek out a physician of one's own choice protected by the Fourteenth Amendment—becomes only a matter of theory, not reality, when a multiple-physician approval system is mandated by the state.

Douglas insisted that the state must rest its interest in the hands of the individual physicians it licensed. If they abused that trust in making abortion decisions, it could regulate them through the licensing procedure. But it could not, consistent with the right of physician-patient privacy, require patients to open their medical affairs and decisions up to groups and committees of doctors beyond their chosen doctor. "Georgia has constitutional warrant in treating abortion as a medical problem," concluded Douglas, but "to protect the woman's right of privacy, however, the control must be through the physician of her choice and the standards set for his performance."

Two members of the Court dissented from this disposition of the two cases, Justices Byron R. White and the recently appointed William

H. Rehnquist. For White, the main issue was "those recurring pregnancies that pose no danger whatsoever to the life or health of the mother but are, nevertheless, unwanted for any one or more of a variety of reasons—convenience, family planning, economics, dislike of children, the embarrassment of illegitimacy, etc." To him, there was no constitutional warrant for saying that a state could not forbid a woman from aborting such a pregnancy under the rubric of "privacy," and he was harshly critical of the balance struck by the Court:

> During the period prior to the time the fetus becomes viable, the Constitution of the United States values the convenience, whim, or caprice of the pregnant woman more than the life or potential life of the fetus; the Constitution, therefore, guarantees the right to an abortion as against any state law or policy seeking to protect the fetus from an abortion not prompted by more compelling reasons of the mother. With all due respect, I dissent.

One senses from reading this short but biting dissent that White did not consider much respect due. He contended that this was a sensitive area of public policy where the people, through their legislatures, should be the ultimate decisionmakers.

Justice Rehnquist, who joined in White's dissent, also dissented separately at length, setting forth a much more limited view of the role of the Fourteenth Amendment than that embraced by Justice Blackmun on behalf of the Court. He disagreed that the plaintiffs had standing to bring these cases, that they were justiciable in any event, or that anything remotely characterized as "privacy" was involved in a procedure like abortion. Rehnquist asserted that the "liberty" interest in the Fourteenth Amendment that seemed to be the basis for the Court's decision did not impose on legislatures any tougher test than that their statutes have "a rational relation to a valid state objective," whether the regulation was economic or social in nature. While he would agree to strike down an abortion law that even forbade abortions when the mother's life was in danger (at least, as applied to such a case), he did not see that any lesser level of restrictiveness was so irrational as to be beyond the competence of the states to enact.

As he would later do in many other contexts, Rehnquist stated his preference for a more historically based view of the scope of the Fourteenth Amendment, a post-Civil War enactment intended primarily to guarantee full citizenship rights to newly freed slaves. At the time the Amendment was passed, there was no indication its framers expected it to have any reference to the issue of abortion, or that it would invalidate the abortion laws then in effect in many states. Furthermore, that a majority of the states had now forbidden abortions for more than a century significantly undermined the argument that a right to abortion was "so rooted in the traditions and conscience of our people as to be ranked as fundamental." That the right to have an abortion was the subject of so much fierce debate in state legislatures and other forums signified that it did not have that level of general acceptance.

Rehnquist also objected to the Court's handling of the Texas case, in that it was clear from the opinion that Texas could validly apply its law to third trimester abortions, but the Court struck down the law in its entirety. Given his concerns about standing and justiciability, Rehnquist contended that the law should have been left intact and merely held unconstitutional, if at all, as applied to the plaintiff Jane Roe. He also issued a brief paragraph dissent in *Doe v. Bolton*, protesting application of a "strict scrutiny" approach to the procedural components of Georgia's abortion law.

The decisions in *Roe v. Wade* and *Doe v. Bolton* had the instant effect of invalidating abortion laws in almost all the states, since few allowed first trimester abortions with the freedom suggested by the Court. However, the decisions did not by any means end the abortion debate. If anything, while freedom of choice proponents celebrated their victory, the antiabortion forces were organizing to battle in the court of public opinion and the state legislatures immediately to begin enacting less restrictive laws that would regulate abortion as far as possible under these decisions and test their boundaries. In two decades of legislation and litigation following *Roe v. Wade*, the forces opposed to abortion achieved widespread legislative success in imposing barriers to abortion, including eliminating much public funding and imposing onerous consent requirements, many struck down by the courts but some surviving constitutional challenge as the federal courts grew increasingly conservative during the 1980s.

By the 1990s, so many supporters of the decision in *Roe v. Wade* had retired from the Court to be replaced by appointees of staunchly anti-*Roe* presidents that it was widely believed that the privacy doctrine of *Roe v. Wade* would be entirely vitiated, if not overruled outright, by the end of the century, if not sooner. The Court took a major step in this direction in 1992, when a bare majority reaffirmed in *Planned Parenthood v. Casey* that the states could not forbid previability abortions outright, but rejected *Roe*'s trimester analysis in favor of a new test for abortion regulations: whether a particular regulation placed an "undue burden" on a woman's ability to obtain an abortion. Several of the regulations the Court upheld in *Casey* in applying this test had been specifically rejected in earlier post-*Roe* decisions. In the end, it seemed likely that Justice White and now-Chief Justice Rehnquist would prevail in their contention that the highly controversial issue of abortion could not be settled by judicial fiat, but must be resolved through the political process.

Case References

Eisenstadt v. Baird, 405 U.S. 438 (1972)
Griswold v. Connecticut, 381 U.S. 479 (1965)
People v. Belous, 458 P.2d 194, 80 Cal. Rptr. 354 (1969), certiorari denied, 397 U.S. 915 (1970)
Planned Parenthood v. Casey, 112 S. Ct. 4795 (1992)
United States v. Vuitch, 402 U.S. 62 (1971)

7. KIDS CAN GET CONDOMS, TOO!

Carey v. Population Services International, 431 U.S. 678 (1977), affirming 398 F. Supp. 321 (S.D.N.Y. 1975) (three-judge court).

Having decided in *Griswold v. Connecticut* (1965) that married adults are entitled to use contraceptives and in *Eisenstadt v. Baird* (1972) that contraceptives must be made available to unmarried persons on the same basis as married persons, both as an aspect of a right of privacy inhering in the guarantee of liberty in the Fourteenth Amendment of the Constitution, the U.S. Supreme Court proceeded to consider the right of minors to have access to nonprescription contraceptives (primarily condoms) in *Carey v. Population Services International*. This test case, brought by various persons and institutions interested in family planning issues, also concerned other restrictions on distribution and advertising contained in a New York law that drew its roots from almost a century of strict regulation of the availability of contraceptives in New York State.

New York State first sought to regulate the availability of contraceptive devices in the 19th century. The constitutionality of its efforts, which resulted in limiting distribution to physicians who could prescribe contraceptives only in connection with the treatment of disease, was first challenged by family planning advocate Margaret Sanger during World War I.

New York police suppressed an attempt to establish a family planning clinic where contraceptives would be distributed in violation of section 1142 of the New York Penal Law, which (as summarized by the state's highest court, the New York State Court of Appeals) made it "a misdemeanor for a person to sell, or give away, or to advertise or offer for sale, any instrument or article, drug or medicine, for the prevention of conception," or "to give information orally, stating when, where or how such an instrument, article or medicine can be purchased or obtained." Sanger was arrested and sentenced to "thirty days in the workhouse" for violation of this law. Her conviction was ultimately upheld by the Court of Appeals in January 1918, after Sanger's attorneys conceded that the law was within the police power so far as distribution to unmarried persons was concerned. They still contended that the law violated the rights of physicians and married persons. The court found the exception in section 1145, allowing physicians to prescribe contraceptives for the treatment of disease, sufficient to avoid any constitutional questions, and the U.S. Supreme Court affirmed *per curiam* by reference to its jurisdictional precedents. There things stood through subsequent amendments and enactments of the law until the new privacy doctrine announced in *Griswold* stimulated a new challenge.

The New York law, section 6811(8) of the Education Law, as amended after *Griswold*, made it a misdemeanor for

> any person to sell or distribute any instrument or article, or any recipe, drug or medicine for the prevention of conception to a minor under the age of sixteen years; the sale or distribution of such to a person other than a minor under the age of sixteen years is authorized only by a licensed pharmacist but the advertisement or display of said articles, within or without the premises of such pharmacy is hereby prohibited.

In essence, the law gave pharmacists a monopoly on the sale of contraceptives, prohibited their sale to persons under age 16, and absolutely forbade all display or advertising of contraceptive articles.

A test case to challenge this law was put together after Population Planning Association (PPA), a mail-order dealer in contraceptives, received a threat of prosecution from the New York State Board of Pharmacy after having placed advertisements for sale of condoms through the mail in a college newspaper in New York State as well as in several national magazines sold through mail subscription and over the counter in New York State. The American Civil Liberties Union (ACLU) and Planned Parenthood of New York City, Inc. (the organization founded by Sanger decades earlier) assisted in assembling a diverse roster of plaintiffs, including, in addition to PPA, Population Services International (which became the lead named plaintiff), an organization dedicated to contraceptive research and education; Reverend James B. Hagen, a Brooklyn pastor and coordinator of Sunset Action Group Against V.D., an organization that sold and distributed

contraceptives without the participation of a pharmacist; three physicians, active in treating adolescents under age 16, who wished to distribute contraceptives to their patients; and a John Doe parent plaintiff, who wanted to distribute contraceptives and information about them to his minor children.

This diverse roster of plaintiffs was considered necessary because of doubts as to which potential plaintiff might have standing to challenge the law. The concept of standing in federal court required that a plaintiff suffer an injury from the statute and have a constitutional right at issue. Since the theory of the case was primarily that the statute violated the constitutional rights of potential customers to receive information about contraception and to effectuate their decisions to use contraceptives to prevent conception, those putting together the test case knew they would have to rely on recent cases in which the Supreme Court had created exceptions to normal standing requirements in order to allow those whose constitutional rights were not directly in issue to represent those whose were. For example, in *Eisenstadt v. Baird*, the Court had allowed contraception advocate Bill Baird to challenge a Massachusetts law regulating the distribution of contraceptives as representative of the constitutional rights of those who desired to receive and use contraceptives. In addition to dealing with standing issues, the choice of plaintiffs was intended to dramatize the different ways in which the law failed to achieve (and actually was counterproductive regarding) the goals the state was expected to articulate in its defense.

The plaintiff group was represented by Michael N. Pollet of the New York City firm of Karpatkin, Pollet & Le Moult, with *amicus* support from ACLU attorneys Rena K. Uviller and Judith Mears, and Planned Parenthood attorneys Harriet F. Pilpel, Nancy F. Wechsler, and Eve W. Paul. They filed suit in the Southern District of New York, seeking designation of a three-judge district court as then required by federal statute for a challenge to the constitutionality of a state law. A three-judge court was designated, consisting of Senior Circuit Judge Henry J. Friendly of the Second Circuit and Southern District Judges Lawrence W.

Pierce and William C. Conner. New York attorney Arlene R. Silverman was designated by Attorney General Louis J. Lefkowitz (one of the named defendants, as enforcer of the law) to represent New York State. The other named defendants were Governor Malcolm Wilson and the executive director of the Board of Pharmacy, as well as the Board itself.

The three-judge court unanimously found the law to be unconstitutional in its entirety. District Judge Pierce wrote the court's opinion, which was announced on July 2, 1975.

The three-judge court had first to face arguments by the defendants concerning standing and capacity to be sued, all of which it decided in favor of the plaintiffs, resting the standing determination on the particular interests of PPA and Reverend Hagen. Since PPA had received a threat of prosecution for its advertising campaign, and Reverend Hagen alleged that he was in actual violation of the statute due to his activities in the V.D. prevention program, the court concluded that these two plaintiffs had the requisite standing to place the constitutionality of the statute in issue, making it unnecessary to pass on the standing of the other named plaintiffs. Relying primarily on *Eisenstadt*, the court found that PPA and Hagen were analogous to Baird in that case, and that it might be difficult to obtain constitutional review of the statute unless someone who was forbidden by the law to distribute contraceptives was given standing to assert the constitutional rights of potential recipients and users of the devices.

Proceeding to the merits, Pierce quickly summarized the Supreme Court's privacy precedents to that point, noting that "the reach of the constitutional right of privacy had yet to be determined," although the U.S. Court of Appeals for the Second Circuit had recently commented that the Supreme Court's decisions had made clear that protection extends to "the most intimate phases of personal life having to do with sexual intercourse and its possible consequences." While there might be some question as to whether the Court's opinions had actually recognized a specific constitutional right to access to contraceptives, at least those decisions had "forecast" the recognition of such a right, wrote Pierce. Since each of the restrictions contained in New York's law burdened the exercise of such a right, the Due Process Clause required "that the Court carefully scrutinize each provision of the statute to determine whether, as drafted, it is in fact sufficiently related to a legitimate State interest to justify its infringement of the right at stake." If the statute failed this basic rationality test, it would not be necessary for the court to take the next step and decide whether a fundamental right (which would trigger a "compelling interest" test) was at stake.

Pierce first considered the prohibition on sale or distribution to minors. Recognizing at the outset that, while the right of privacy extended to minors as well as to adults, the state had a greater interest in regulating the sexual activities of minors to protect their health and welfare, Pierce concluded nonetheless that the particular interests the state was articulating in this case were insufficient to provide a rational basis for the law. The state argued that it was interested in preventing teen promiscuity, and that preventing minors from getting contraceptives was part of its effort in this direction. Even the state conceded that all relevant evidence showed that making contraceptives available to teenagers had no discernible effect on the rate of sexual intercourse in which they engaged. Given this finding, it was not rational for the state to think that placing barriers to access to contraceptives would have any effect in achieving its goal of reducing such sexual activity. Furthermore, since venereal disease and pregnancy were more likely to occur if teenagers were denied access to contraceptives than if contraceptives were made available, the law actually might cause harm rather than provide protection for minors. Consequently, Pierce rejected the state's argument that the law should survive because the plaintiffs had not presented any solid proof disproving its theory of deterrence:

This Court concludes that where, as here, there is substantial evidence that harm may result from enforcement of particular legislation and that positive benefits may result from reversing that policy, and where the legislation in question burdens the exercise of a constitutionally protected right, it is not sufficient for the State to support its claim that the statute furthers some other legislative aim merely by asserting that the plaintiffs have not disproved that claim.

Furthermore, the state had created quite a few loopholes, which belied its argument that the barriers were necessary to protect teenagers from their immature decisions to have sex. Implementing various federal welfare and family programs, the state legislature had actually mandated that contraceptives be offered to teenagers under age 16 under a variety of circumstances, and it had also apparently authorized physicians to give contraceptives to their patients without any age restriction, a state law provision on which the defendants had relied in arguing that the plaintiff physicians had no standing in the case. These exceptions set up the statute for the kind of equal protection challenge that had succeeded in *Eisenstadt*, by saying that some minors could have contraceptives and others could not, depending on whether they were eligible by virtue of poverty for certain public assistance programs. Since the ban on distribution or sale to minors did not seem to advance any of the state's articulated interests, it failed to meet the rationality test and violated the Fourteenth Amendment.

Pierce next turned to the requirement that only licensed pharmacists distribute or sell nonprescription contraceptives. The state articulated two justifications for this policy: first, the restriction made it easier to police compliance with the other restrictions in the statute, by concentrating distribution of contraceptives in one type of regulated business; second, that pharmacists could provide appropriate professional advice about the quality and suitability of various kinds of contraceptives for their customers. Pierce found that neither of these justifications for the restriction carried much water. Apart from the fact that the Court found the other two restrictions in the statute to be unconstitutional, which would in effect remove the first justification, Pierce noted that courts had frequently found constitutional rights to override the "clear prospect of increased administrative inconvenience and burden." Even if the other portions of the law were deemed valid, convenience in enforcing them "does not serve as a sufficient basis for the significant restriction this provision imposes on the right of

access to non-prescription contraceptive products."

The state's other articulated justification was dismissed as irrational. There was a wide variety of nonprescription products and patent medicines sold outside pharmacies, as to which pharmacists's advice might be equally useful, but New York had imposed the sales restriction only on contraceptives. There was no evidence that their training made pharmacists any more capable to give professional advice regarding nonprescription contraceptives than other retailers. Even if some customers needed such advice, many might have no such need. When someone needed advice, pharmacists were available to give it, but requiring that all purchasers obtain their contraceptives from pharmacists, regardless whether they needed or desired such advice, did not seem to the court to justify so restricting the availability of contraceptives. If the state could show, as it had not, that there was some danger that nonpharmacists would distribute defective products due to improper handling of the product, that might provide a basis for some state regulation. Similarly, if the state could show that vandalism or improper storage provided a health justification for banning sales through vending machines, it might undertake such regulation. But, as with the ban on distribution or sale to minors, it did not appear that the state's interests were "sufficient to support the limitation contained in this provision of the subject statute."

Finally, the court considered the ban on display and advertising. Here the analysis was more complex, because the Supreme Court had just begun at that time to expand the First Amendment protection attaching to commercial speech, which display and advertising were deemed to be. In *Bigelow v. Virginia* (1975), the Court had recently struck down a state law banning advertising of the availability of abortion services, on the ground that the ban unduly burdened the exercise of the right of an individual to decide whether to terminate her pregnancy. However, the Court had premised its ruling on the idea that advertising about the availability of abortion services was not purely commercial speech, but had an important informational component independently deserving of constitutional protection. While Pierce concluded that after *Bigelow*, "it is still the law that purely commercial speech—whatever may be the scope of that term—does not enjoy constitutional protection," he concluded that the New York display and advertising ban was unduly broad because it extended to all advertising, whether purely commercial speech, a mingling of commercial and educational speech, or even promotional materials that were entirely educational with virtually no commercial content. Because the statute banned "public interest" and "mixed as well as purely commercial, advertising and display," it "runs afoul of the Constitution."

Pierce asserted that the analogy to the factual circumstances in *Bigelow* was so close that the Supreme Court's opinion provided a sound basis for striking down the statute on overbreadth grounds, without having to reach the question whether the state could more narrowly regulate the type and placement of contraceptive displays and advertising. "Regulations affecting protected freedoms must be narrowly drawn," said Pierce. "The New York statute operates to prohibit dissemination of information relating to the intimate phases of sexual life protected by the right of privacy and to such matters of public interest and importance as birth control, contraception, and population growth. Clearly, the statute is overbroad."

However, recognizing that New York would have a valid interest in adopting a more narrowly tailored regulation to protect the public from offensive or inappropriate advertising and display, the court decided to stay the effect of its decision as to the display and advertising ban for four months to give the legislature an opportunity to act accordingly. While declaring the entire statute unconstitutional, the court limited the immediate effect of its injunctive relief to the portions of the law forbidding distribution to minors and restricting distribution to licensed pharmacists.

The state appealed to the U.S. Supreme Court, which noted probable jurisdiction on June 7, 1976, and set the case for argument on January 10, 1977. Newly elected Governor Hugh Carey was substituted for retiring Governor Malcolm Wilson as the petitioner in the case. Attorneys Silverman and Pollet argued

before the Court, with *amicus* briefs urging affirmance filed again by the ACLU and Planned Parenthood. The Court announced its decision on June 9, 1977, upholding the district court's decision, although the Justices differed in some respects on the grounds of decision. Chief Justice Warren E. Burger and Justice William H. Rehnquist dissented, but only Rehnquist filed a dissenting opinion.

Justice William J. Brennan, Jr., wrote the opinion for the Court, which was joined in full by Justices Potter Stewart, Thurgood Marshall, Harry A. Blackmun, and in part by John Paul Stevens, Byron R. White, and Lewis F. Powell, Jr. Justices White, Stevens, and Powell wrote separately to articulate their different rationales for portions of the holding. All of the Justices in the majority concurred with Justice Brennan's handling of the standing issue. Brennan preferred to premise standing solely on PPA, which had been directly threatened with enforcement of the law against it due to its advertising activities. Brennan found a clear basis for standing by analogy to the Court's recent decision (postdating the district court's ruling) in *Craig v. Boren* (1976), where the Court had upheld the standing of a vendor of alcoholic beverages to challenge a state law that set a higher age for men than for women to be entitled to purchase alcoholic beverages. Because the statute limited the vendor's potential market, it inflicted on the vendor an "injury in fact," requiring it either to heed the statute or to subject itself to criminal penalties. As such, PPA was entitled to assert the constitutional rights of third parties who would be affected should its challenge to the law fail.

Moving to the merits, Brennan first wrote a brief summary of the Court's privacy jurisprudence, in which he emphasized that the right of privacy was broader than the particular instances of personal decisionmaking that the Court had protected thus far. Harking back to his statement in *Eisenstadt v. Baird* about the right of privacy being "the right of the *individual*, married or single, to be free of unwarranted governmental intrusion into matters so fundamentally affecting a person as the decision whether to bear or beget a child," Brennan stated that "decisions whether to accomplish or prevent conception are among the most private and sensitive." However, the individual's choices about conception would not automatically invalidate every state regulation. "The business of manufacturing and selling contraceptives may be regulated in ways that do not infringe protected individual choices," said Brennan. Even a burdensome regulation might be justified by a compelling state interest. "'Compelling' is of course the key word; where a decision as fundamental as that whether to bear or beget a child is involved, regulations imposing a burden on it may be justified only by compelling state interests, and must be narrowly drawn to express only those interests," he stated. Thus, Brennan was willing to go further than the district court and to hold that New York's regulations must meet the compelling interest test to survive constitutional scrutiny.

Brennan began his consideration of the individual restrictions in the statute with the restriction of distribution to licensed pharmacists and found the district court's analysis of the state interests to be justified. First addressing the state's argument that prior decisions of the Court had not created a constitutional right of access to contraceptives, Brennan responded that this mode of argument misunderstood the nature of the Court's rulings, which were concerned at bottom with the right of the individual to make important personal decisions. The question was not whether there was a right to contraceptives, but rather whether the state was justified in placing a particular burden on the individual's ability to make and effectuate personal decisions concerning reproduction. "Restrictions on the distribution of contraceptives clearly burden the freedom to make such decisions," insisted Brennan. While a total ban on sales would clearly violate the Constitution, so would any regulation that significantly limits access. "[T]he restriction of distribution channels to a small fraction of the total number of possible retail outlets renders contraceptive devices considerably less accessible to the public, reduces the opportunity for privacy of selection and purchase, and lessens the possibility of price competition." As Justice Powell pointed out in his concurring opinion, the prohibition of mail-order sales placed a particular burden on the exercise of the right of choice. At this point, Brennan responded as well to

Powell's contention, in his concurring opinion, that Brennan's opinion went too far in appearing to hold that the compelling interest test must be applied whenever a state regulation "implicates sexual freedom." In a frequently cited footnote that lower federal courts came to treat as a substantial gloss on the precedential scope of *Doe v. Commonwealth's Attorney for City of Richmond* (1976), Brennan disclaimed any such holding, referring to a subsequent footnote in a portion of his opinion that had the support of only four Justices, that stated that "the Court has not definitely answered the difficult question whether and to what extent the Constitution prohibits state statutes regulating [private consensual sexual] behavior among adults."

Brennan found that no compelling state interest was served by the regulation. Since the law applied to nonhazardous contraceptives, it bore no relation to any state interest in protecting health. The district court had adequately disposed of the arguments that the restriction was necessary to overall enforcement of the statute and that it facilitated provision of adequate advice to potential consumers. A new argument articulated by the state on appeal was that it expresses "a proper concern that young people not sell contraceptives." Brennan found this ludicrous, since it was entirely possible that a minor employed by a pharmacy could sell contraceptives without violating the statute.

Brennan next turned to the ban on distribution or sale to minors. Here, speaking only for himself and three other members of the Court, he agreed with the district court that the state had not adequately justified its intrusion on the privacy rights of minors regarding decisions about conception by articulating as its interest the discouragement of promiscuous sexual intercourse. Brennan argued that "the right to privacy in connection with decisions affecting procreation extends to minors as well as to adults." While the Court had long recognized that the state had a greater interest in regulating the conduct of minors than of adults, still state restrictions on minors' decisions in this area "are valid only if they serve 'any significant state interest . . . that is not present in the case of an adult,'" quoting from the Court's recent decision in *Planned Parenthood of Central Missouri v. Danforth* (1976), in which the Court had struck down certain restrictions on access to abortion for minors. Since *Danforth* had held that the state could not impose a blanket prohibition on access to abortion for minors, "the constitutionality of a blanket prohibition of the distribution of contraceptives to minors is *a fortiori* foreclosed," concluded Brennan. While the state was entitled to take a more active role in regulating the sexual conduct of minors than of adults, as for example by setting an age of consent for sexual activity, there was no evidence that banning distribution of contraceptives to minors had any impact on their sexual activities other than to expose them to the risk of venereal disease and pregnancy unnecessarily. Indeed, the statute on its face even banned the distribution of contraceptives to married minors, who were presumably licensed by the state to engage in sexual intercourse. Here, the state was imposing a burden on reproductive choice without making any showing that the burden had a rational relationship to the end it proclaimed to seek of reducing sexual promiscuity.

Brennan also rejected the argument that New York's statute was saved by the existence of so many loopholes, particularly the one allowing physicians to distribute contraceptives to their patients regardless of the age of the patient. Brennan held that the state had asserted "no medical necessity for imposing a medical limitation on the distribution of nonprescription contraceptives to minors." Since the contraceptives in question were not hazardous to health, there was no particular medical judgment that physicians would be making in deciding whether to give contraceptives to a particular minor. The state was in effect delegating to physicians the authority to disapprove of minors' sexual behavior, and this authority might be exercised arbitrarily, which was impermissible where a constitutional right was concerned.

Finally, on the issue of the display and advertising bans, Brennan noted that since the district court's decision was announced, the Court had decided *Virginia Pharmacy Board v. Virginia Citizens Consumer Council* (1976), which had substantially expanded recognition of constitutional protection for commercial speech. Information about the availability and price of an item was clearly information that itself was deserving of constitutional protection, particularly where the information pertained to an item relevant to a constitutionally protected choice. There were "substantial individual and societal interests" in "the free flow of commercial information." When stacked up against these interests, the state's articulated interests in preventing offensive advertising and avoiding appearing to "legitimate" promiscuous sexual activity by allowing contraceptive displays and advertisements could carry little weight, at least when contained in such a broad-sweeping prohibition as that contained in the New York law. At least none of the PPA advertisements introduced in evidence suggested any such problem. Stating "the availability of products and services that are not only entirely legal, but constitutionally protected" was itself constitutionally protected speech.

Justice White joined the portions of the opinion dealing with standing, the limitation of distribution to pharmacists, and the ban on advertising, while noting that he did "not regard the opinion, however, as declaring unconstitutional any state law forbidding extramarital sexual relations." He concurred separately in the result concerning distribution to minors, agreeing with Justice Stevens that he would describe as "frivolous" the arguments by the plaintiffs that "a minor has a constitutional right to put contraceptives to their intended use, notwithstanding the combined objection of both parents and the State." Nonetheless, he agreed that this portion of the law was unconstitutional because "the State has not demonstrated that the prohibition against distribution of contraceptives to minors measurably contributes to the deterrent purposes which the State advances as justification for the regulation."

Justice Powell concurred in the result, but did not join Brennan's opinion, because he believed that the opinion went too far in applying either the compelling state interest test or any form of heightened scrutiny to the New York statute's provisions on distribution and sale, "particularly to the young." Commenting that the Court "apparently would subject all state regulation affecting adult sexual relations to the strictest standard of judicial review," Powell felt that "the extraordinary protection the Court would give to all personal decisions in matters of sex is neither required by the Constitution nor supported by our prior decisions." For him, the compelling interest test should be restricted to state regulations that worked a direct and substantial interference with constitutionally protected rights. In this case, the regulation of distribution worked at best an indirect burden, particularly the limitation of distribution to pharmacists. In particular, said Powell, it was inappropriate to subject state regulations to heightened judicial review when they involved the sexual activity of youngsters, arguing that prior decisions had made clear that regulations held unconstitutional as to adults might frequently be upheld as applied to children. For him, it was sufficient to ask "whether the restriction rationally serves valid state interests."

Having said all this, apparently primarily to limit the precedential impact of the Court's ruling on subsequent cases, he agreed with the Court that the statute was unconstitutional. As to the ban on anyone other than a physician distributing contraceptives to minors, he found that it infringed upon the privacy interests of "married females between the ages of 14 and 16 . . . in that it prohibits the distribution of contraceptives to such females except by a physician." Since the state authorized marriage for women beginning at age 14, there was no legitimate state interest in preventing them from engaging in sexual activity or in burdening their decision to use contraceptives while doing so. Furthermore, the law violated the constitutionally protected parent-child relationship, which the Court had recognized in a variety of cases striking down state interference in that relationship, by forbidding parents from distributing contraceptives to their minor children. No state interest had been articulated justifying this interference.

However, although the law was facially unconstitutional for these two reasons, Powell argued that the state might be justified in imposing more narrowly tailored regulations. "Participation in sexual intercourse at an early age may have both physical and psychological consequences," he asserted, that could justify requiring minors to seek parental guidance before obtaining contraceptives. A parental consent requirement might be constitutional.

Powell also agreed that it was unconstitutional for New York to forbid anyone other than a pharmacist or a physician to distribute nonprescription contraceptives. He found particularly offensive the ban on mail-order sales: "In this respect, the statute works a significant invasion of the constitutionally protected privacy in decisions concerning sexual relations. By requiring individuals to buy contraceptives over the counter, the statute heavily burdens constitutionally protected freedom." In a footnote, Powell indicated that it was "not a satisfactory answer that an individual may preserve anonymity as one of a number of customers in a retail outlet." Implicitly invoking scores of books, films, and television shows in which the trauma of buying contraceptives from a pharmacist is portrayed, Powell concluded: "However impersonal the marketplace may be, it does not approach the privacy of the home."

Powell also agreed that the advertising ban was unconstitutional, but again argued that the Court's opinion swept too broadly. The state did have a legitimate interest in time, place, and manner restrictions when it came to the impact of contraceptive advertising on the young, and Powell wanted to make clear that the state was entitled to adopt appropriately tailored regulations to meet this interest.

Justice Stevens, who had joined Brennan's opinion in regard to issues of standing and the restriction of distribution outlets, wrote separately to articulate a different rationale for striking the ban on distribution to minors and to emphasize, as had Justice Powell, the degree to which the state retained authority to regulate the time, place, and manner of contraceptive advertising. Stevens felt that there remained a significant state interest in regulating the sexual activity of minors, and that the Constitution provided a greater measure of protection to a minor's decision to have an abortion than the decision to engage in sexual activity, primarily because of the consequences of those decisions. Stevens agreed with Powell that the statute violated the constitutional rights of married women under age 16 and of parents, but he also agreed with the Court that it violated as well the rights of the other plaintiffs. "It is almost unprecedented," he said, "for a State to require that an ill-advised act by a minor give rise to greater risk of irreparable harm than a similar act by an adult." By depriving minors access to contraceptives, the state was following just such a course. "Common sense" indicated that minors would engage in sexual activity regardless of the availability of contraceptives. By denying minors a choice that "if available, would reduce their exposure to disease or unwanted pregnancy" while itself acknowledging that the law did not have any direct effect on the rate of teen sexual activity, the state was engaging in "propaganda" legislation. Although the state is frequently a teacher, "it seems to me that an attempt to persuade by inflicting harm on the listener is an unacceptable means of conveying a message that is otherwise legitimate," said Stevens. "It is as though a State decided to dramatize its disapproval of motorcycles by forbidding the use of safety helmets. One need not posit a constitutional right to ride a motorcycle to characterize such a restriction as irrational and perverse."

Justice Rehnquist's dissent was primarily rhetorical in nature and seems to have been written mainly to dispute Justice Brennan's assertion that the Court had not yet ruled definitively on the issue of constitutional protection for consensual sexual activity by adults. In a footnote, he asserted: "While we have not ruled on every conceivable regulation affecting such conduct the facial constitutional validity of criminal statutes prohibiting certain consensual acts has been 'definitively' established," citing *Doe v. Commonwealth's Attorney* and *Hicks v. Miranda* (1975), the latter case holding that summary dispositions are binding on the merits despite the lack of a written opinion by the Court. Apart from that comment, Rehnquist's opinion was devoted mainly to expressing incredulity that the soldiers who fought the Revolution and the Civil War to establish the principles of due process of law "had enshrined in the Constitution the right of commercial vendors of contraceptives to peddle them to unmarried minors through such means as window displays and vending machines located in the men's room of truck stops, notwithstanding the considered judgment of the New York Legislature to the contrary." "The Court holds that New York may not use its police power to leg-

islate in the interests of its concept of the public morality as it pertains to minors," he said, urging that this "denial of a power so fundamental to self-government" should prove to be "but a temporary departure from a wise and heretofore settled course of adjudication to the contrary."

Justice Rehnquist's hope was not to be fulfilled until 1986, when the Court in *Bowers v. Hardwick* began its retreat from the expansive view of privacy articulated by Justice Brennan in *Carey*. In the interim, however, Brennan's opinion became perhaps the most frequently cited statement of the broad concept of privacy founded in the Fourteenth Amendment, and it was invoked in support of a wide range of privacy interests far beyond the sexual sphere. Since the opinion has not itself been directly repudiated by a majority of the Court, it remains a source of significant authority, although changes in the composition of the Court and its view of privacy make it unlikely that the reach of *Carey* will extend much further in the future than the precise issues decided in the case. Indeed, a new Puritanism reflected in decisions involving sexual conduct and speech might even lead to some retrenchment. *Carey* may stand as the high-water mark, then, of the Supreme Court's assertion of individual liberty rights against the state's attempt to restrict those rights in the name of a majoritarian vision of public morality.

Case References

Bigelow v. Virginia, 421 U.S. 809 (1975)

Bowers v. Hardwick, 478 U.S. 186 (1986)

Craig v. Boren, 429 U.S. 190 (1976), rehearing denied, 429 U.S. 1124 (1977)

Doe v. Commonwealth's Attorney for City of Richmond, 425 U.S. 901 (1976)

Eisenstadt v. Baird, 405 U.S. 438 (1972)

Griswold v. Connecticut, 381 U.S. 479 (1965)

Hicks v. Miranda, 422 U.S. 332 (1975)

People v. Sanger, 222 N.Y. 192 (1918), appeal dismissed, 251 U.S. 537 (1919)

Planned Parenthood of Central Missouri v. Danforth, 428 U.S. 52 (1976)

Virginia Pharmacy Board v. Virginia Citizens Consumer Council, 425 U.S. 748 (1976)

8. IS SURROGATE PARENTING "BABY SELLING"?

Surrogate Parenting Associates, Inc. v. Kentucky, 704 S.W.2d 209 (Ky. Sup. Ct. 1986).

A public debate sprang up during the 1980s over the legality of surrogate parenting agreements, under which men retained the services of women (to whom they were not married) to bear children for them. One aspect of the debate, addressed by the New Jersey Supreme Court in 1988 in the celebrated "Baby M" case, was whether such an agreement was legally enforceable as a contract if the "surrogate mother" refused to surrender custody of the baby to the contracting father. At an earlier point, the Kentucky Supreme Court, in one of the first appellate decisions to consider the phenomenon of surrogate parenting, responded to an attempt by Kentucky Attorney General David Armstrong to put out of business Surrogate Parenting Associates, Inc. (SPA), a Kentucky corporation that specialized in arranging surrogate agreements for a fee.

SPA operated a medical clinic to provide assistance to infertile couples desiring children who would be genetically related to one of the parents. This would be accomplished by identifying a fertile woman who was willing to be artificially inseminated with the husband's sperm, bear the child, and surrender custody to the father for a fee. In addition to the payment to the woman for her services, the father would bear the expenses of the pregnancy and childbirth and would pay a fee to SPA for its services in locating the surrogate mother and arranging for the insemination procedure. As part of the agreement, the surrogate mother would promise to yield custody of the child upon birth, and her husband, if any, would agree to waive all claims of custody to the child. (In Kentucky, as in many states, the law presumed that the husband of a woman was the father of any child born during the marriage, but the presumption could be overcome through evidence that the child was not genetically related to the husband.) Although no mention would be made in the surrogacy agreement of the contracting father's wife, or of her intention to adopt the child, it was understood between all parties that

adoption of the child by the wife was one of the goals of the arrangement. SPA's procedures required that both contracting father and surrogate mother be represented by counsel, and that the mother have the right to change her mind about giving up custody of the child.

The attorney general filed suit in March 1981 in the Franklin Circuit Court, seeking to have SPA's corporate charter revoked on the ground that its activities violated three Kentucky statutes: a law forbidding the sale, purchase, or procurement for sale or purchase of "any child for the purpose of adoption or any other purpose, including termination of parental rights"; a law prohibiting filing of a petition for voluntary termination of parental rights "prior to five (5) days after the birth of a child"; and a law providing that a "consent for adoption" would not be valid "if such consent for adoption is given prior to the fifth day after the birth of the child." Assistant Attorney General Joseph R. Johnson represented the state at trial, and David E. Roseberry and Joseph J. Leary represented SPA. There was no trial of the facts, since SPA and the attorney general agreed on a "Stipulation of Facts" that summarized the details of SPA's operations. The Franklin Circuit Court found that there was no statutory violation, and it dismissed the case.

For one thing, the contracting father was the biological father of the child, so there could be no question that the father was paying the surrogate to adopt a child. "Because of the existence of a legal relationship between the father and the child, any dealing between the father and the surrogate mother in regard to the child cannot properly be characterized as an adoption," said the court. Indeed, the surrogacy agreement did not on its face deal with adoption at all, so the circuit court found that the statutory provisions did not apply and reasoned that in the absence of legislative prohibition, the parties were free to contract.

On appeal, Attorney General Armstrong was able to persuade the court of appeals to reverse the circuit court's ruling. Criticizing the circuit court's decision as resting on "an improper conceptual framework," the appeals court asserted that the subsequent adoption by the contracting father's wife was an integral part of the arrangement, contemplated by all the parties, so the adoption statutes were directly implicated in the procedure. The court opined that the "termination of parental rights by the surrogate mother is simply a necessary predicate to a subsequent adoption by the infertile wife," so indeed the father was paying the surrogate mother to terminate her parental rights in order to make adoption by his wife possible. To the court of appeals, "the infertile wife of the biological father is the *sine qua non* of this procedure." "Artful draftsmanship designed to nominally include only the biological father, the surrogate, and the surrogate's husband so as to avoid the purview of [the adoption statutes] must fail," the court insisted.

SPA appealed to the Kentucky Supreme Court, which ruled by vote of 5–2 on February 6, 1986, that the court of appeals was mistaken in its conceptualization of the case. The court's opinion, by Justice Charles M. Leibson, focused on the question, "Has the legislature spoken?" Leibson said "no," agreeing with the circuit court that the legislative prohibitions, strictly construed, did not apply to the surrogate parenting agreements, at least as arranged by SPA under the stipulated procedures, and that in the absence of legislative prohibition there was no warrant for the court to engage in "judicial legislation" on the subject.

Leibson identified the legislative purpose for the law banning baby selling as an attempt "to keep baby brokers from overwhelming an expectant mother or the parents of a child with financial inducements to part with the child." Surrogate parenting presented an entirely different situation, since the child would be conceived solely for the purpose of providing a child for the infertile couple. "The essential considerations for the surrogate mother when she agrees to the surrogate parenting procedure are *not* avoiding the consequences of an unwanted pregnancy or fear of the financial burden of child rearing," said Leibson. Rather, "the essential consideration is to assist a person or couple who desperately want a child but are unable to conceive one in the customary manner to achieve a biologically related offspring." Leibson found little difference conceptually between surrogate parenting and the "reverse situation," where a husband was infertile and the wife was inseminated with sperm from a donor so that the couple could raise a child who was biologically related to one of them. Because there was no argument that such arrangements violated the existing laws, Leibson rejected the notion that the surrogacy arrangement could be held to violate those laws, since the U.S. Supreme Court had recognized in *Carey v. Population Services International* (1977) that "the decision whether or not to beget or bear a child is at the very heart. . . of constitutionally protected choices."

Leibson also found support in the legislature's 1984 decision to pass a law authorizing the procedure of *in vitro* fertilization (by which an egg extracted from a woman is fertilized in a test tube and then reinserted in the woman) in order to overcome problems a fertile couple might be having in conceiving through intercourse. The attorney general argued that because the legislature had not included an endorsement of surrogate parenting when it was legislating on the subject of artificially assisted conception, it was implicitly adopting a policy against surrogacy. Leibson rejected this suggestion, preferring the approach that what is not forbidden is allowed rather than the approach that what is not authorized is forbidden.

Turning to the adoption issue directly, Leibson noted that the surrogacy agreement, to which the contracting father's wife was not a party, concerned "custody" rather than "adoption," since the contracting father, as donor of the sperm, had no need to adopt the child who was biologically his. Although Kentucky laws seemed to preclude enforceable contracts on the custody of a child made earlier than five days after birth, SPA took the position that its surrogacy agreements were voidable by the mother, and that in fact the mother's final consent to surrender custody of the child was not obtained until after the five-day statutory period had passed, complying with the legislature's mandate. Leibson was satisfied that this arrangement met the statutory requirement.

The policy of the voluntary termination statute and the consent to adoption statute is to preserve to the mother her right of choice regardless of decisions made before the birth of the child. This policy is not violated by the existence of the contractual arrangements previously made. The policy of these statutes is carried out because the law gives the mother the opportunity to reconsider her decision to fulfill the role as surrogate mother and refuse to perform the voluntary termination procedure. Should she elect to do so, the situation would be no different than had she never entered into the procedure. . . . The parental rights and obligations between the biological father and mother, and the obligations they owe to the child, would then be the rights and obligations imposed by pertinent statutes rather than the obligations imposed by the contract now vitiated.

Since Kentucky law had traditionally taken the view that custody agreements were voidable, rather than void as a matter of law, this arrangement fell comfortably within the boundaries of accepted legal practice in the state. Leibson was opposed to construing the existing statutes in a narrow way that would block the forward advance of science, asserting that it was for the legislature, not the courts, to intervene if these new practices were deemed contrary to the public welfare. "It is only when a proposed solution violates individual constitutional rights that the courts have a place in the controversy," he insisted, and apparently neither Leibson nor the other judges in the majority found any threat to the constitutional rights of surrogate mothers in SPA's procedures. Leibson stated:

The courts should not shrink from the benefits to be derived from science in solving these problems simply because they may lead to legal complications. The legal complications are not insolvable. Indeed, we have no reason to believe that the surrogate parenting procedure in which SPA participates will not, in most instances, proceed routinely to the conclusion desired by all of the parties at the outset—a woman who can bear children assisting a childless couple to fulfill their desire for a biologically-related child.

Two members of the court, however, sharply disagreed with the majority's view and would have affirmed the decision by the court of appeals. In separate dissenting opinions, Justices Roy N. Vance and Donald C.

Wintersheimer argued that the legislature had, indeed, spoken, and that the court of appeals had correctly penetrated the "subterfuge" in SPA's procedures when it identified payment for adoption as a centerpiece of the surrogate parenting arrangement.

Justice Vance said, "When the activities of [SPA] are placed in their best light by the majority, the fact remains that its primary purpose is to locate women who will readily, for a price, allow themselves to be used as human incubators and who are willing to sell, for a price, all of their parental rights in a child thus born." To Vance, this was precisely what the baby-selling statute was all about.

Vance noted that the statute, which the majority had failed to quote in full in its opinion, prohibited not just "sale or purchase" of "any child for the purpose of adoption," but went on to forbid such sale or purchase for "any other purpose, including termination of parental rights." "I view the subsequent delivery of the child together with an agreed judgment terminating the parental rights of the natural mother in exchange for a monetary consideration to be no less than the sale of a child." Since SPA was an intermediary in this process, its activities were contrary to the public policy of Kentucky and revocation of its charter was an appropriate action, concluded Vance.

Justice Wintersheimer developed his views at much greater length, finding at the outset that "the legislative intent to prohibit the buying and selling of children is abundantly clear" and agreeing with Justice Vance's analysis of applicability of the baby-selling statute. "In my view," he proclaimed, "the people of the Commonwealth of Kentucky have not abdicated their sovereignty to a self-appointed group of scientists-kings. The tolerance of the many can easily lead to the tyranny of a few. The attractiveness of assistance to childless couples should not be a cosmetic facade for unnecessary tampering with human procreation. Animals are reproduced; human beings are procreated."

Wintersheimer found that the surrogate parenting arrangement was at heart a "commercial transaction," in which the contracting father "is obviously not adopting his own child but actually purchasing the right to have the child adopted by his own infertile wife. Regardless of the good intentions that may give rise to such a practice," he said, "the commercialization of this type of personal problem" was exactly what the baby-selling law was "intended to prevent." He also disputed Leibson's version of the legislative history of the 1984 statute on *in vitro* fertilization, noting that a proposed amendment was presented to the state Senate specifically to approve surrogate parenting arrangements and was defeated. The legislature had a chance to approve this procedure and chose not to do so, said Wintersheimer, who would draw from that a disapproval of surrogate parenting arrangements rather than legislative silence on the issue.

After reiterating at length the court of appeals' analysis of surrogate contracts as subterfuges for adoption contracts, and asserting that such arrangements were directly contrary to the legislature's intent in adopting the baby-selling law, Wintersheimer stated his recognition of the seriousness of the problem faced by infertile couples, but insisted that the majority was heading down a dangerous path in allowing SPA to continue to function in the state:

The fact that a woman's infertility can be cured is a matter that evokes serious questions of medical and public policy. The prospect of host-mothers with wombs for hire is immediately possible. There are already sperm banks and egg banks could be next. It is entirely possible, as we have seen in this case, that reproduction can be arranged by contract and financial payment. In my view the consequences which could arise from the opening of the human uterus to commercial medical technology does not contribute to the emancipation of women. In my opinion, the safeguarding of marriage and the family is essential to the continuation of human society as we know it. The possibility of exploitation of women as surrogate mothers is totally undesirable.

Wintersheimer rejected Leibson's assertions for the majority that the court should not stand in the way of the advance of science. Where Leibson saw progress, Wintersheimer saw an emerging system for the exploitation of poor women. "Our consideration of public policy in this regard should include the possible exploitation of financially-needy women," he said. "Although there may be some altruistic women who will volunteer as surrogate mothers, the greater prospect is that monetary payment will have to be made to surrogates," and that poor women would engage in this work solely for the monetary reward. "The price at which a woman will sell her reproductive capacity may depend on her financial status." In addition, Wintersheimer feared that allowing such arrangements to flourish would present a threat to the "stability of the family unit" which he saw as "a direct threat to society's stability." Wintersheimer believed that the existing statutory framework in Kentucky represented a legislative judgment that surrogate mothering "tends to violate public policy" by marking a departure from "the traditional family concept." He stated:

The decision to become pregnant parallels the fundamental right of reproductive privacy. The adopting couple's claimed right of reproductive privacy does not appear to be sufficiently similar. The emphasis in reproductive privacy is on the right of the individual to control his or her reproductive faculties. To give a second party the right to control another person's reproductive capacity would appear to be contradictory. Although a surrogate mother's decision to become pregnant is a fundamental right, another party would not have the right to contract for the control of her pregnancy.

Wintersheimer cited in support of this proposition an appellate decision in Michigan, *Doe v. Attorney General* (1981), which had taken an approach to surrogate parenting contrary to that of the Kentucky Supreme Court majority. Concluding that the majority had gone astray in its construction of the adoption statute, Wintersheimer would have preferred to affirm the decision of the court of appeals.

The Kentucky Supreme Court decided that surrogate parenting agreements are not unlawful, but it did not have to confront the question whether an agreement that purported to bind the surrogate mother prior to the birth of the child was specifically enforceable. This question soon arose in New Jersey in the "Baby M" litigation, which attracted nationwide attention. The New Jersey Supreme Court ruled in 1988 that surrogacy contracts involving payment of a fee by the father to the surrogate mother were unenforceable as against public policy, and that the appropriate role for the court when such a contractual arrangement broke down due to the mother's unwillingness to give up the child would be to decide the disputed custody issue solely with regard to the best interest of the child, according the noncustodial parent such visitation rights as would appear appropriate within the normal discretion of a court sitting in a contested custody dispute. In other words, for the New Jersey Supreme Court, while a surrogacy contract might not be illegal, it did not have the force of a binding contractual obligation. The father was entitled neither to specific enforcement of the agreement nor to damages for the mother's breach of contract.

However, in reviewing the factors normally considered in making custody determinations, the New Jersey Supreme Court in the "Baby M" case found that the father, who was in a better position to provide for the child financially and, probably, emotionally, should have sole custody. The dramatic factual setting of that case undoubtedly contributed to the decision, since the surrogate mother had "abducted" the child after changing her mind about relinquishing custody. As might commonly be the case in such situations, the father had significantly more financial resources than the mother, as well as a richer educational background, leading the court to believe that it would be in the best interest of the child to be raised in the father's household.

When the result in the SPA case is viewed in conjunction with the "Baby M" case, it is clear that the last judicial word cannot have been said on the issue of surrogate parenting, and it also seems likely that the debate will be long and difficult, for there are strong arguments made on both sides of the issue. One factor never expressly addressed by the majority in the SPA case, and only incompletely explored in the dissents, was the practical consequence of upholding a "voidable" contract under circumstances where the contracting parties were quite likely to be from very different social and economic strata of society. As Justice Wintersheimer observed, it seemed likely that the overwhelming majority of women willing to participate in surrogate arrangements would be financially needy, and, given the high fees involved, that most of the men would be relatively well-off financially. Since both the man and the woman would be biologically related to the child, the voidability of the contract might not make a great difference in subsequent litigation over custody, as the "Baby M" case demonstrated. The father, normally married and well-off, will usually score much higher than the mother on the factors courts consider in awarding custody "in the best interest of the child," especially when they weigh the factor that the child was conceived at the urgent instance of the father, desperately seeking offspring, and that the mother's motivation in participating at the inception of the agreement was most likely almost entirely mercenary.

While voidability of the contract means that the surrogate mother may have a fighting chance to obtain custody or at least visitation rights, it seems likely, as in the "Baby M" case (where the New Jersey court found the contract to be void rather than voidable), that most fathers will win disputed custody contests. Whether the surrogate parenting contracts are declared unenforceable as against public policy (as in the "Baby M" case) or voidable at the instance of the mother, the results may appear just as unsatisfactory: the surrogate mother will lose custody of the child and will never be paid the fee she was promised at the inception of the agreement. Some might see this result as predictable, given the overwhelmingly male composition of courts and legislatures.

In the absence of federal legislation or of any agreement by the courts that constitutional rights might somehow invalidate surrogate agreements, it seems likely that legal treatment of the surrogate issue will continue to develop on a state-by-state basis, producing a patchwork of laws that may result in people traveling to different states in order to enter into surrogate arrangements, just as people have traveled in the past to obtain legal abortions or legal divorces. Whether such a result is in the public interest remains a matter for prolonged societal debate.

Case References

In re Baby M, 109 N.J.2d 396, 537 A.2d 1227 (1988)

Carey v. Population Services International, 431 U.S. 678 (1977)

Doe v. Attorney General, 106 Mich. App. 169, 307 N.W.2d 438 (1981), leave to appeal denied, 414 Mich. 875 (1982), certiorari denied, 459 U.S. 1183 (1983)

9. RIGHTS OF THE DONOR AND RECIPIENT OF SEMEN

Jhordan C. v. Mary K., 179 Cal. App. 3d 386, 224 Cal. Rptr. 530 (1st Dist. 1986).

"Lesbians Choosing Motherhood" was the name given to a conference jointly convened in New York City in 1983 by Lambda Legal Defense and Education Fund and the Lesbian Rights Project. The conference name identified a growing phenomenon in the lesbian community, as the number of women desiring to conceive and raise children steadily grew. (Over three hundred women attended the conference, which explored alternative insemination techniques and issues, including donor selection and the legal issues arising from new reproductive technologies.) One of the most significant issues confronting these women was whether to obtain semen from a known donor directly or from an unknown donor through a "semen bank" or a physician specializing in donor insemination procedures. For many lesbians, the desire to select a donor personally outweighed the possible legal entanglements. These women, however, attended the conference and were thus relatively well informed about the risks they were taking. Mary K. and Victoria T., however, the California women whose case generated one of the first appellate decisions to deal with the asserted parental status, if any, of a known semen donor, were not well informed about the legal issues and suffered the consequences.

Mary and Victoria, described by the court as "close friends," decided late in 1978 to raise a child together by obtaining semen from an appropriate donor and inseminating Mary. Mary talked with many friends and acquaintances about the search for a suitable donor. From their suggestions, she identified three or four potential donors, interviewed them, and finally, in consultation with Victoria, settled on Jhordan C. At no point did Mary and Victoria involve a physician or a lawyer in their planning and selection process.

The discussions with Jhordan were informal, and no written agreement was made between the two women and Jhordan. When disputes arose later, they disagreed about what agreements they had reached. According to Mary, she had told Jhordan from the beginning that she did not want a donor who desired an ongoing involvement in raising the child, but that she was willing to let the donor see the child to satisfy his curiosity about how the child was turning out. Jhordan recollected a different understanding: that he and Mary would have an ongoing friendly relationship, which would give him ongoing contact with the child, and that he might care for the child as often as two or three times a week. Neither Mary, Victoria, nor Jhordan consulted a lawyer about their respective legal rights at any point in the process, and they were not aware that California had adopted a provision from the Uniform Parentage Act (UPA) governing the status of semen donors.

The UPA expressed a preference for having donor insemination handled with the assistance of a physician, purportedly for health reasons. As adopted by the California legislature, the statute provided that "the donor of semen provided to a licensed physician for use in artificial insemination of a woman other than the donor's wife is treated in law as if he were not the natural father of a child thereby conceived." This provision, adopted in 1975, had not been judicially construed in California when Mary and Victoria selected Jhordan as their donor, which made no difference to them, since they were totally unaware of it. The statute might have provided them a complete defense in the subsequent litigation had they been aware of it and used a physician as an intermediary in obtaining the semen.

Jhordan provided semen to Mary several times over a six-month period beginning in January 1979. Each time, he came to her house, spoke briefly with her, retired to another room to masturbate into a jar, turned over his product to her, and left. Mary, who was a nurse, would then perform the insemination either by herself or with Victoria's participation.

After Mary finally became pregnant, she maintained occasional contact with Jhordan, including, well into her pregnancy, attending a Christmas party at Jhordan's home. Jhordan visited Mary at the health center where she worked, and he took pictures of her during the pregnancy. At one point, Jhordan informed Mary in a telephone conversation that he had assembled a crib, playpen, and highchair for the child. Mary told him to keep those items at his home. At another point, Jhordan told Mary he intended to start a trust fund for the child and wanted to be appointed legal guardian in case Mary died. Mary did not agree to the guardianship arrangement, but did not disapprove of the trust fund idea. Victoria and Mary remained closely involved throughout the pregnancy. Victoria accompanied Mary to medical appointments and birthing classes, and they consulted together on issues of pregnancy, delivery, and child rearing.

When Mary gave birth to her son, Devin, on March 30, 1980, Victoria was present and assisted in the delivery. Mary's roommate telephoned Jhordan to let him know about the birth. Jhordan visited Mary and Devin the next day and took photos of the baby. When Jhordan called to arrange another visit five days later, Mary resisted at first, but finally agreed to let him visit, although she told him she was angry about this degree of involvement. Jhordan claimed a right to visit Devin, and Mary agreed to allow one visit a month. Jhordan conscientiously kept up the monthly visits until August, when Mary said they had to stop. Jhordan threatened to go to a lawyer if Mary barred him from seeing Devin. Mary tried to condition future visits on Jhordan's signing a contract indicating he would not seek paternity rights, which Jhordan refused to do. Jhordan obtained legal counsel, Annette Lombardi, of Santa Rosa, who filed his paternity petition in December 1980. Mary contacted the Lesbian Rights Project in San Francisco and obtained legal representation from the project's attorney, Roberta Achtenberg. The court appointed the office of Sonoma County Public Defender Marteen J. Miller to represent Devin's interest in the proceeding, with Stephany L. Joy appearing on his behalf. It became clear rather quickly that the Public Defender sided with Jhordan.

While the petition was pending in the Sonoma County Superior Court, the county brought an action against Jhordan for reimbursement to the county for certain public assistance benefits paid out for Devin's support, and an order to that effect was entered by stipulated judgment in June 1982, requiring Jhordan to pay, through the district attorney's office, $900 in arrearages and future support payments of $50 a month. During that proceeding, an amended birth certificate was filed by order of the court designating Jhordan as the father of Devin, and in November 1982 the court granted Jhordan weekly visitation rights with Devin.

Meanwhile, Devin had developed a close, parent-child-type relationship with Victoria and a sibling relationship with Victoria's 14-year-old daughter. Devin and Victoria were together several times a week, and Devin usually spent at least two days a week at Victoria's home. Victoria and Mary consulted daily about Devin, either in person or by telephone, and made joint decisions about his daily care and development. Vacations were taken jointly. Because of the antipathy between Mary and Jhordan, all of Jhordan's visitation arrangements were negotiated by Victoria.

In August 1983, Victoria moved to join as a party in the on-going paternity litigation, claiming that she should be recognized as a *de facto* parent of Devin. The concept of *de facto* parent had just been recognized by a California court of appeal in another case, *Guardianship of Phillip B.* (1983), in which the court held that if a genuine parent-child relationship existed between an unrelated adult and child, the adult might obtain some of the legal rights of parenthood with respect to that child. Victoria asserted that she should be designated by the court as sharing joint custody of Devin with Mary, based on their relationship. Jhordan subsequently amended his petition to seek a declaration of joint custody between himself and Mary.

After trial, Superior Court Judge Rex G. Sater entered judgment declaring Jhordan to be Devin's legal father, but awarding sole legal and physical custody to Mary, denying Jhordan any direct parenting role but granting substantial visitation rights on the recommendation of a court-appointed psychologist. However, the court rejected Victoria's claim of *de facto* parenthood, but also granted her visitation rights, on the psychologist's recommendation. Judge Sater held that the UPA provision did not apply to this situation, because Mary had not obtained Jhordan's semen through a licensed physician.

Mary and Victoria appealed the court's judgment, seeking to terminate Jhordan's visitation rights and to have Victoria designated as a *de facto* parent with joint custody of Devin. They claimed that the UPA provision should be broadly construed to quash the parental rights of a semen donor such as Jhordan, and that failing to adopt such an interpretation would violate Mary and Victoria's constitutional rights to equal protection, privacy, and reproductive choice. San Francisco attorney Catherine M. Steane filed an *amicus* brief in support of Mary and Victoria on behalf of the Lambda Legal Defense and Education Fund. The public defender filed a brief that was identical in all relevant respects to the brief filed by Lombardi on behalf of Jhordan, which earned a rebuke from the court: "We strongly disapprove of such conduct by counsel for a minor child in custody proceedings, as it substantially compromises counsel's independence."

The First District Court of Appeal issued its unanimous decision on March 28, 1986, affirming Judge Sater's rulings in an opinion by Justice Donald B. King. While disclaiming "any judicial preference toward traditional notions of family structure or toward providing a father where a single woman has chosen to bear a child," King asserted that the key policy decision in this case had been made by the legislature when it adopted the UPA provision requiring the participation of a licensed physician if the woman wanted to assure that the donor would have no parental rights.

Interpretation of the UPA provisions presented a new issue for the court. Achtenberg had argued on behalf of Mary and Victoria that the legislature did not intend to deprive mothers of the protection of the nonpaternity provision when they obtained semen directly from a donor without physician participation, contending that the legislature had erroneously assumed that all insemination procedures required medical assistance. She also argued that the apparent requirement of physician participation should be interpreted as being merely directive rather than mandatory. King rejected these arguments, which conflicted with the clear language of the statute and its legislative history. King noted that during the drafting of the UPA, the drafters had at first not included the physician's involvement, which was later added as a result of conscious discussion and debate about the health justifications for involving a physician. The UPA drafters indicated that a physician could obtain a complete medical history of the donor, which might reveal health problems or hereditary conditions that would suggest not using his semen. Involvement of a physician could also assist in documenting the terms of agreement between the donor and recipient over the role, if any, the donor would be expected to play in the child's life, conspicuously missing from this case.

King conceded that, as a practical matter, there was no need for a physician to perform donor insemination, and that required physician involvement might raise constitutional questions of privacy, equal protection, and autonomy, but he did not find that these factors militated against a construction of the statute consistent with its language. Furthermore, he noted that physician involvement as required by the statute need not be overly intrusive; insemination could still occur at home and be performed by the woman herself and her friend, since the statute required only that the semen be "provided" by the donor to the physician for use in insemination. Presumably, arrangements could be made for the donor to turn over the semen to the doctor who would then immediately turn it over to the woman. King stated:

> Regardless of the various countervailing considerations for and against physician involvement, our Legislature has embraced the apparently conscious decision by the drafters of the UPA to limit application of the donor nonpaternity provision to instances in which semen is provided to a licensed physician. The existence of sound justification for physician involvement further supports a determination the Legislature intended to require it.

King then turned to the constitutional arguments. Mary and Victoria had argued that California law discriminated in favor of mar-

SEXUALITY AND THE LAW

ried women, because their husbands were presumed to be the fathers of children conceived through donor insemination, while unmarried women were required to obtain the services of a physician in order to protect themselves from paternity claims by donors. While conceding that they had correctly characterized the effect of California law, King denied that this presented a cognizable equal protection claim because, in his view, married and unmarried women were not "similarly situated" with regard to this issue, and the insemination statute, standing alone, did not treat married and unmarried women unequally. "In the case of a married woman, the marital relationship invokes a long-recognized social policy of preserving the integrity of the marriage," said King. "No such concerns arise where there is no marriage at all. Equal protection is not violated by providing that certain benefits or legal rights arise only out of the marital relationship."

Mary and Victoria had also argued that they comprised a family unit with Devin, whose constitutionally protected autonomy would be violated by forcing Jhordan into that "unit" against their will. King said that this argument "begs the question of which persons comprise the family in this case for purposes of judicial intervention," because it was necessary first to characterize the family unit before deciding whether family autonomy was being infringed upon by the superior court's order. In this case, King found that Mary had allowed Jhordan to develop a relationship with Devin by allowing visitation for several months after Devin's birth. There was disagreement in the testimony about what, if any, understandings Mary and Jhordan had prior to Devin's birth, but the postbirth evidence showed a continuing involvement by Jhordan, with Mary approving the idea of Jhordan setting up a trust fund for the child. The parties' conduct thus led to a conclusion that Jhordan was in some way a part of the family unit. King stated:

> We would not purport to hold that an oral or written nonpaternity agreement between the parties would have been legally binding; that difficult question is not before us (and indeed is more appropriately addressed by the Legislature). We simply emphasize that for

purposes of the family autonomy argument raised by Mary, Jhordan was not excluded as a member of Devin's family, either by anonymity, by agreement, or by the parties' conduct.

King concluded that the court's order did not intrude on any right of Mary and Victoria to family autonomy, because, at least for purposes of resolving the custody dispute, Jhordan was not clearly excluded by the parties' conduct as a member of Devin's family.

Finally, King rejected the argument that the superior court's order violated the constitutional right of reproductive choice of Mary. King said that "the statute imposes no restriction on the right to bear a child," but merely recognized a situation in which a semen donor would not be entitled to assert parental rights. Mary was free to conceive through donor insemination, as the court had previously indicated, without ever seeing a physician. King noted that California law imposed no ban on such insemination procedures, unlike the laws of several other states that mandated physician participation. King also asserted that it was not necessary to make any kind of declaration regarding Victoria's status as a *de facto* parent, since the award to her of visitation rights by the trial court was sufficient to protect her interest in continuing contact with Devin. At the same time, King noted that his decision was not dictated by the result of the child support proceeding, since the legislature, in the interest of providing for the support of children without complicating other legal proceedings, had taken steps to insulate support proceedings and their results from any other litigation concerning parental rights over the child.

King concluded that the best forum for making public policy on the difficult questions raised by donor insemination was the legislature, not the courts, and that disagreements with the policy decisions of the legislature should not be brought to the courts. He stated:

> Our Legislature has already spoken and has afforded to unmarried women a statutory right to bear children by artificial insemination (as well as a right of men to donate semen) without fear of a paternity claim, through provision of the semen to a licensed physician. We simply hold that because Mary omitted to invoke Civil Code section 7005, subdivision (b), by

obtaining Jhordan's semen through a licensed physician, and because the parties by all other conduct preserved Jhordan's status as a member of Devin's family, the trial court properly declared Jhordan to be Devin's legal father.

The decision in *Jhordan C. v. Mary K.* shows the importance of careful planning prior to insemination for those who wish to preclude parental rights for the donor. The UPA nonpaternity provision was intended to supplant the common law and escape conflicts arising from differing state statutes. As such, its requirement of physician participation, at least in the collection of sperm for insemination purposes, is the kind of policy judgment that is unlikely to be suspended through legislative amendment, particularly on the evidence of a case like *Jhordan C.*, which illustrates the deeply emotional human issues of parenthood that would most likely stir sympathy in the male legislative majority for a man in the position of Jhordan. On the other hand, at least one appellate court subsequent to the *Jhordan* court—the Colorado Supreme Court in *In re R.C.* (1989)—found that the intention of the parties at the time of the semen donation regarding the parental role of the donor would take priority over whether a physician was involved in the insemination process.

The court in *Jhordan* disclaimed any ruling regarding the effect, if any, of a written agreement of nonpaternity executed by donor and recipient prior to insemination. The Colorado Supreme Court, on the other hand, appeared willing to give an unwritten agreement regarding paternity, if adequately proved, controlling effect, even though Colorado had adopted the same UPA provision and the mother had the insemination performed by a licensed physician. While some might argue that private "contracting" of parenting obligations and privileges should be rejected as contrary to the best interest of the child, which is normally the touchstone in all custody and visitation proceedings,

such considerations did not appear to bother the Colorado court.

On the other hand, neither the California Court of Appeal nor the Colorado Supreme Court expressly considered the constitutional issues that might be raised by denying a "biological" father (i.e., semen donor) the right of parents with regard to a child whom they are eager and willing to acknowledge as their biological descendant. In *McIntyre v. Crouch* (1989), the Oregon Court of Appeals held that an Oregon statute not based on the UPA, which effectively cut off all parental rights of sperm donors, regardless of the participation or lack of participation of a doctor in the insemination process, might violate the constitutional rights of the donor, at least if the donor and the mother had agreed prior to insemination that the donor would have some parental rights. The court's constitutional concerns were based on the U.S. Supreme Court's decisions in *Lehr v. Robertson* (1983) and *Stanley v. Illinois* (1972), cases holding that biological fathers do have constitutional due process rights with respect to their children.

Legal rights and responsibilities stemming from donor insemination constitute one of the newest areas of family law, where courts are increasingly called on to decide cases without firm precedent. At this stage, it would be futile to attempt to identify any particular legal rule as "firmly established," especially when the U.S. Supreme Court has yet to rule on the constitutional ramifications of decisions now emerging from state appellate courts.

Case References

Lehr v. Robertson, 463 U.S. 248 (1983)

McIntyre v. Crouch, 98 Or. App. 462, 780 P.2d 239 (1989)

Phillip B., Guardianship of, 139 Cal. App. 3d 407, 188 Cal. Rptr. 781 (1983)

R.C., In re (Upon Petition of J.R.), 775 P.2d 27 (Colo. 1989)

Stanley v. Illinois, 405 U.S. 645 (1972)

CHAPTER 2
CRIMINAL LAW AND SEXUAL CONDUCT

From earliest recorded history, religion and government have sought to regulate the expression of sexuality. Sometimes the regulation has gone so far as to prohibit particular sexual acts even between consenting, married adults. Biblical proscriptions, adopted as secular laws during the reign of Henry VIII in the Reformation, made anal-genital sexual intercourse a serious felony in 16th-century England, regardless of the gender of the participants or their marital status. At American independence, such sexual proscriptions (as well as proscriptions of adultery, prostitution, and other forms of nonmarital intercourse) in the English common law were "received" into the common law of the states. Vestiges of this early common law, including its ambiguous wording, have survived in statutes still on the books in some states, outlawing "crimes against nature," "wanton and dissolute persons," and the like.

During the 1950s, the American Law Institute (ALI), paralleling similar efforts in England, undertook a thorough study of American criminal law and recommended the adoption of a Model Penal Code that substantially revised the terminology and scope of sex crimes laws. In addition to providing clinically precise nomenclature to describe particular acts to be forbidden, the ALI recommended decriminalization of most consensual sexual activity between adults conducted in private. However, the Model Penal Code continued to provide penalties for public solicitation and sexual conduct involving minors. Illinois, in 1960, was the first state to enact a version of the Model Penal Code with the recommended sex crimes provisions virtually intact. Many other states have since adopted the Code, although some have refused to follow the ALI's recommendations regarding nonmarital or nonvaginal consensual sex and have specifically amended the Code to retain penalties for such activities. In a handful of jurisdictions, the legislatures decided to end regulation of the details of consensual marital sex, while retaining penalties for same-sex ac-

tivities and, in some cases, extra-marital heterosexual activities.

Regulation of sexual conduct is governed primarily by the states, as an aspect of their general police powers to preserve order and to protect the morality of society. While there are some federal criminal laws dealing with sexual conduct on federal property, the focus of modern litigation has been on the interpretation and validity of state laws. Most of the constitutionally based litigation has attempted to use the privacy themes sounded by the U.S. Supreme Court in its major reproductive rights decisions of the 1960s and early 1970s (see chapter 1) as a basis for finding a right of "sexual privacy" extending to nonmarital activities. The Supreme Court's 1986 decision in *Bowers v. Hardwick*, holding that the federal right of privacy does not extend to consensual homosexual sex, has diverted most litigation efforts to the state courts. By the time of the *Hardwick* decision, about half of the states had decriminalized nonvaginal intercourse, but the process of legislative reform seemed stalled, particularly in light of epidemics of sexually transmitted diseases such as AIDS, herpes, and hepatitis. By early 1992, when case selection for this encyclopedia ended, appeals were pending in the Supreme Courts of Kentucky and Texas from lower court decisions declaring laws against homosexual sodomy unconstitutional under state constitutional privacy theories.

Leading cases involving constitutional challenges to sex crimes laws are discussed in this chapter. Related cases discussed in other chapters include *Arcara v. Cloud Books, Inc.* (No. 45), *David M. v. Margaret M.* (No. 64), and *Dronenburg v. Zech* (No. 92).

Criminal Law and Sexual Conduct: Readings

Carrington, P.D., "A Senate of Five: An Essay on Sexuality and Law," 23 *Georgia Law Review.* 859 (Summer 1989)

Daly, K., "The Social Control of Sexuality: A Case Study of the Criminalization of Prostitution in the Progressive Era," 9 *Research in Law, Deviance & Social Control* 171 (1988)

Editorial Staff, "Survey on the Constitutional Right to Privacy in the Context of Homosexual Activity," 40 *University Miami Law Review* 521 (January 1986)

Goldstein, A.B., "History, Homosexuality, and Political Values: Searching for the Hidden Determinants of *Bowers v. Hardwick*," 97 *Yale Law Journal* 1073 (May 1988)

Koppelman, A., "The Miscegenation Analogy: Sodomy Law as Sex Discrimination," 98 *Yale Law Journal* 145 (November 1988)

Mohr, R.D., "Mr. Justice Douglas at Sodom: Gays and Privacy," 18 *Columbia Human Rights Law Review* 43 (Fall-Winter 1986)

Morris, J.A., "Challenging Sodomy Statutes: State Constitutional Protections for Sexual Privacy," 66 *Indiana Law Journal* 609 (Spring 1991)

Page, J.D., "Cruel and Unusual Punishment and Sodomy Statutes: The Breakdown of the *Solem v. Helm* Test*," 56 *University Chicago Law Review* 367 (Winter 1989)

Reinig, T.W., "Sin, Stigma & Society: A Critique of Morality and Values in Democratic Law and Policy," 38 *Buffalo Law Review* 859 (Fall 1990)

Richards, D.A.J., "Constitutional Legitimacy and Constitutional Privacy," 61 *New York University Law Review* 800 (November 1986)

———, "Liberalism, Public Morality, and Constitutional Law: Prolegomenon to a Theory of the Constitutional Right of Privacy," 51 *Law & Contemporary Problems* 123 (Winter 1988)

———, *Sex, Drugs, Death and the Law: An Essay on Human Rights and Overcriminalization* (1982)

Scharrer, J.R., "Covert Electronic Surveillance of Public Rest Rooms: Privacy in the Common Area? " 6 *Cooley Law Review* 495 (September 1989)

Spiegel, C., "Privacy, Sodomy, AIDS and the Schools: Case Studies in Equal Protection," 1986 *Annual Survey of American Law* 221 (April 1987)

Stoddard, T.B., "*Bowers v. Hardwick:* Precedent by Personal Predilection," 54 *University Chicago Law Review* 648 (Spring 1987)

10. REFORMING THE TEXAS SODOMY LAW

Buchanan v. Batchelor, 308 F. Supp. 729 (N.D. Tex. 1970), vacated and remanded sub nom., *Wade v. Buchanan* and *Buchanan v. Wade*, 401 U.S. 989 (1971); see also *Buchanan v. State*, 471 S.W.2d 401 (Tex. Crim. App. 1971), certiorari denied, 405 U.S. 930 (1972).

Article 524 of the Texas Penal Code provided as follows, under the heading "Sodomy":

> Whoever has carnal copulation with a beast, or in an opening of the body, except sexual parts, with another human being, or whoever shall use his mouth on the sexual parts of another human being for the purpose of having carnal copulation or who shall voluntarily permit the use of his own sexual parts in a lewd or lascivious manner by any minor, shall be guilty of sodomy, and upon conviction thereof shall be confined in the penitentiary not less than two (2) nor more than fifteen (15) years.

Some form of sodomy statute had existed in Texas for more than one hundred years when Alvin Leon Buchanan, a Dallas gay man, was arrested for having sex with another man in a public restroom in Dallas. After his second arrest on a similar charge, Buchanan decided to challenge the constitutionality of the statute and the validity of the police practices of surveillance and decoys that had led to his arrests. He retained counsel and filed a lawsuit on May 26, 1969, in the federal district court in Dallas, seeking a declaration that the law was unconstitutional, an injunction against prosecution of the two sodomy cases pending against him and the harassment tactics against homosexuals by the Dallas police, and other equitable relief. Since Buchanan was challenging the constitutionality of a state law in the federal court, he requested the designation of a three-judge court, as required at that time by 28 U.S.C. section 2281. Circuit Judge Irving Goldberg of the U.S. Court of Appeals for the Fifth Circuit and District Judges Sarah T. Hughes and W.M. Taylor, Jr., were designated. Buchanan named as defendants the Dallas police chief, Charles Batchelor, and the local prosecuting attorney, Henry Wade.

At a pretrial conference with counsel, the judges determined that the various allegations of police harassment were not appropriate for consideration by the three-judge court, which was limited to considering the constitutionality of the challenged state law, so those charges were severed and reserved for later consideration by a single judge. The request for injunction against the state court prosecutions was dismissed, since recent U.S. Supreme Court rulings had made clear that federal courts did not have authority to intervene in such proceedings. The state raised jurisdictional issues about suitability of the constitutional challenge under the federal jurisdiction statute, and the judges reserved judgment pending briefing and argument.

Meanwhile, civil libertarians seized on the pending litigation as a vehicle for sexual liberation in light of the Supreme Court's recent decision in *Griswold v. Connecticut* (1965), but realized that Buchanan, whose arrests were for having sex in a public restroom, did not present the ideal plaintiff. With the permission of Buchanan and his attorney, a married couple, Michael and Jannet Gibson, and another gay man, Travis Lee Strickland, intervened as plaintiffs. The Gibsons and Strickland alleged that they feared possible prosecution for committing in private acts prohibited by the statute. They believed that private commission of sodomy by consenting adults was constitutionally protected activity under *Griswold*. Relying on the references to the First Amendment in Justice William O. Douglas's opinion for the Supreme Court in that case, they sought to invoke the First Amendment overbreadth doctrine, under which the entire statute would have to be stricken if it seriously impinged on protected expression under the First Amendment in any of its applications. The intervenors' complaint requested that the court not only declare article 524 unconstitutional, but also enjoin its enforcement. (Lack of such a request for injunctive relief had been spotted as a jurisdictional flaw of Buchanan's original complaint.)

Attorneys Henry J. McCluskey, Jr., of Dallas, and George Schatzki, of Austin, represented the plaintiffs. Assistant District Attorneys John B. Tolle and Thomas B. Thorpe, of Dallas, represented their boss, Henry Wade, and Assistant Attorney General Bennie Bock, II, appeared on behalf of Texas Attorney General Crawford C. Martin, to defend the constitutionality of the Texas law.

The three-judge court issued its decision on January 21, 1970, in an opinion by District Judge Hughes. She wrote that the statute was unconstitutionally overbroad as applied to the Gibsons and other married couples whose interests they were representing. The court declared the law unconstitutional for overbreadth and enjoined Henry Wade from enforcing it in the future.

The first question that occupied the court was whether any or all of the plaintiffs had standing to challenge the law. Here, the intervention of the Gibsons was crucial to the case, since the state was arguing that Buchanan, who was prosecuted for public acts, had no standing to raise the rights of married persons or homosexuals who performed their sexual activities in private, and it was unlikely that existing precedents would support a constitutional right to commit homosexual acts in public restrooms. The Gibsons and Strickland clearly had the right to raise those privacy concerns, however. Nevertheless, the state argued that the court should abstain from deciding the case, pointing out that there had been no recorded prosecutions of married couples for violation of the law, and there seemed to have been none of homosexuals who kept their activities private. The state argued that there was no reason for the court to pronounce judgment on a law that was not being unconstitutionally enforced.

The court rejected this argument. Judge Hughes asserted: "To require such persons to await a state court's disposition of the prosecution of an offense of sodomy committed by either of these classes of persons would result in an unfair delay in determination of their rights and a substantial impairment of freedom of action." To the court, which was viewing this as primarily a First Amendment case, the problem of "chilling" protected expression was foremost. Furthermore, it was clear that the statute by its terms applied to every act of sodomy, regardless of who was performing it or where it was taking place. There was no basis for a state court to adopt a limiting construction, so principles of federalism did not dictate abstention pending construction by a state court in an appropriate case. Furthermore, if the allegations were true that the law was not being enforced against married couples, an opportunity for such interpretation might not arise.

Getting to the merits of the challenge, Hughes observed that the challenged statute "operates directly on an intimate relation of husband and wife" of the type protected from state criminal regulation in *Griswold*. Hughes noted that the U.S. Court of Appeals for the Seventh Circuit had suggested in a 1968 *habeas corpus* decision, *Cotner v. Henry*, that *Griswold* might make it unconstitutional to punish married persons for sodomy, and that the American Law Institute's proposed Model Penal Code "adopts the view that consensual private sexual conduct between adults should not ordinarily be subject to criminal sanction." On the other hand, a federal district court in Connecticut had ruled in *Travers v. Paton* (1966) that *Griswold*'s precedential scope was limited to the sexual relations of married couples, and the Ninth Circuit ruled in *Smayda v. United States* (1965) that "homosexuals committing acts of sodomy in a public rest-room" were not protected by the privacy right identified in *Griswold*.

Agreeing with the state's argument that it was "not the function of the court to determine the policy of the state as it relates to morals," nonetheless Hughes commented that the state's authority would have to give way when it used means "which sweep unnecessarily broadly and thereby invade the area of protected freedoms." Texas could have a sodomy law, but only so long as it was narrowly tailored to avoid penalizing constitutionally protected relations. "Sodomy is not an act which has the approval of the majority of the people," wrote Hughes. "In fact such conduct is probably offensive to the vast majority, but such opinion is not sufficient reason for the state to encroach upon the liberty of married persons in their private conduct. Absent some demonstrable necessity, matters of (good and bad) taste are to be protected from regulation." (Hughes's assertion that "sodomy" is probably offensive to a majority of the people has been disproven, at least in the context of heterosexual sodomy, by sex researchers who have documented that a majority of heterosexuals engage in such practices with each other.)

The strongest argument the state could mount against this constitutional challenge was that the Gibsons had no real fear of prosecu-

tion so long as they conducted their activities in private. The court, while noting the lack of prosecutions, did not feel that this alone answered the question of standing on the part of the Gibsons. "The law is on the books," said Hughes, "and so long as it remains there it is the duty of the State to carry out the laws. All public officials take an oath to perform the duties of the office . . . and certainly the major duty of the law enforcing officers is to enforce the criminal statutes." She invoked the precedent of *Dombrowski v. Pfister*, a 1965 decision by the Supreme Court which stated that "statutes are justifiably attacked on their face . . . as applied for the purpose of discouraging protected activities." In *Dombrowski*, the Court also stated that as long as the statute was available to the state "the threat of prosecutions of protected expression is a real and substantial one." While noting that the conduct protected in *Griswold* had not been characterized by the Court as expression, Hughes asserted that "it was identified as a vital interest protected by the First Amendment," thus allowing the Gibsons standing to invoke the overbreadth doctrine and claim that the possibility of future prosecution, however hypothetical, still existed sufficiently to give them standing to challenge the law.

The ultimate threat to justiciability, however, was *Poe v. Ullman*, a 1961 precursor of *Griswold* where declaratory judgment plaintiffs were challenging the same statute that was later invalidated in *Griswold*. The Supreme Court had dismissed the challenge in *Poe*, holding that a history of nonenforcement of the Connecticut law against contraception meant there was no justiciable controversy. Since the Connecticut law had been passed in 1879, the only reported litigation was a 1940 test case. The Court had ruled that the "mere existence" of the statute was "insufficient grounds" to give a federal court jurisdiction to consider its constitutionality "if real threat of enforcement is wanting." The three-judge court in *Buchanan v. Batchelor* was eager to rule on the merits, however, and distinguished *Poe* by noting that the Dallas police were vigorously enforcing the sodomy law, with at least 35 arrests every year since 1963, hitting a high point of 129 arrests in 1966. While none of these involved prosecution of married persons, "the statute is definitely being enforced and since the Gibsons have admitted being in violation there is a real threat of prosecution from a District Attorney who takes pride in the manner in which he has enforced the law." Furthermore, *Poe* preceded *Dombrowski* by several years, and the later case may have carved out an exception for First Amendment cases.

The court found that the law made no distinction between homosexuals or heterosexuals and married or unmarried persons, that it operated directly on the Gibsons, who "have reason to fear prosecution," and that the claims of Buchanan and Strickland lay outside the protected realm of marital sex. Consequently, the court ruled that the state was unconstitutionally overbroad by reaching the Gibsons' sexual activities and must be stricken on that basis.

Cross-appeals followed. District Attorney Wade filed an appeal contending that the court was without jurisdiction to decide the merits of the case. Buchanan and Strickland filed an appeal arguing that their conduct was also constitutionally protected. The North American Conference of Homophile Organizations, a recently formed loose federation of the scattering of gay rights groups that had sprung up during the 1960s, filed an *amicus* brief in support of Buchanan and Strickland. But the Supreme Court was not willing to get to the merits of the case, letting the appeals petitions sit along with many other cases while it considered the complicated question of federal jurisdiction to consider the constitutionality of state laws.

Finally, on February 23, 1971, the Court issued its landmark decisions in *Younger v. Harris* and accompanying cases on these issues. The Court held that persons who had not been indicted, arrested, or credibly threatened with prosecution under a state law could not use the federal courts to challenge the constitutionality of such laws, and that those who were undergoing prosecution could raise their federal constitutional claims within the state criminal court system, leaving access to federal judicial review until they had exhausted state court appeals. In particular, Justice Hugo L. Black's opinion for the Court adopted a narrow view of *Dombrowski*, commenting that "the existence of a 'chilling

effect,' even in the area of First Amendment rights, has never been considered a sufficient basis, in and of itself, for prohibiting state action." Only a statute that directly abridges free speech might provide the basis for a "fear of prosecution" standing theory. Black emphasized the concerns of federalism and comity between the federal and state court systems, especially in the enforcement of criminal statutes that were in the peculiar province of the states to enact under their police powers.

On March 29, the Court vacated and remanded a large number of pending appeals, including *Wade v. Buchanan* and *Buchanan v. Wade*, "for reconsideration in light of *Younger v. Harris*" and the other cases on similar points released the prior month. Justice William O. Douglas indicated that he would have dismissed the Wade appeal for untimeliness, but would have noted "probable jurisdiction" in Buchanan and Strickland's appeal, allowing the Court to consider the claims of the homosexual plaintiffs on the merits.

Meanwhile, things were happening back in Texas. Buchanan had been convicted on his public sex charges, and his conviction was subsequently upheld by the Texas Court of Criminal Appeals, with the U.S. Supreme Court refusing to review the decision. In other litigation, the Court of Criminal Appeals refused to follow the three-judge district court decision in *Pruett v. State* (1971), holding that article 524 was a valid, constitutional enactment, and the Supreme Court had dismissed an appeal of that ruling as failing to present a substantial federal question.

But legislative wheels were also grinding in Texas. The legislature was in the midst of its first general overhaul of the state's Penal Code since the 19th century, and the influence of the Model Penal Code was being felt. Article 524 was repealed and replaced with a new provision downgrading sodomy, now described as "deviate sexual intercourse," to a misdemeanor offense and limiting its application to persons of the same sex. Thus, heterosexual couples regardless of their marital status were no longer prohibited from engaging in oral or anal sexual activity in private, and the substantive basis for the three-judge court's finding of overbreadth had been removed. The state moved for dismissal of the remanded case as moot, and it was dismissed.

Buchanan v. Batchelor thus did not set any precedents, but the case is important for a variety of reasons. For one thing, it marked the first time that a federal appeals court had declared a sodomy law to be unconstitutional, on any basis, and sought to extend the holding in *Griswold* from the narrow issue of contraception to the broader question of sexual intercourse. Furthermore, the case provided a vehicle for encouraging the reform of a draconian sodomy law under which gay men had been sentenced to significant prison terms.

While some in the emerging gay activist community were opposed to such halfway measures as "reform" of sodomy laws from felony to misdemeanor status, the difference between a two-to-fifteen-year sentence and a sentence calculated in months with a small fine was significant. Older gay rights advocates, who had begun their legal struggles in the 1950s within the American Law Institute and by fighting for such elemental rights as the right of gay people to assemble in a public place such as a bar or a restaurant, saw "sodomy law reform" as a promising strategy for gradual liberation from repressive sex laws, especially since legislative action to repeal sodomy laws had been slow and scattered. Such legislative reform efforts began to bear fruit during the 1970s, and, side by side with isolated litigation successes, led to decriminalization of sodomy for homosexuals in about half the states by the end of the decade. The Texas legislature remained resolutely against further reform, however, and a test case was launched against the new Texas sodomy law in the 1980s. That case, *Baker v. Wade* (No. 26), is discussed later in this encyclopedia.

Case References

Cotner v. Henry, 394 F.2d 873 (7th Cir.), certiorari denied, 393 U.S. 847 (1968)

Dombrowski v. Pfister, 380 U.S. 479 (1965)

Griswold v. Connecticut, 381 U.S. 479 (1965)

Poe v. Ullman, 367 U.S. 497 (1961)

Pruett v. State, 463 S.W.2d 191 (Tex. Crim. App. 1971), appeal dismissed, 402 U.S. 902, rehearing denied, 403 U.S. 912 (1971)

Smayda v. United States, 352 F.2d 251 (9th Cir. 1965), certiorari denied, 382 U.S. 981 (1966)

Travers v. Paton, 261 F. Supp. 110 (D. Conn. 1966)

Younger v. Harris, 401 U.S. 37 (1971)

11. TOILET SEX AND SURREPTITIOUS SURVEILLANCE

People v. Triggs, 8 Cal. 3d 884, 106 Cal. Rptr. 408, 506 P.2d 232 (1973), reversing 102 Cal. Rptr. 725 (App., 2d Dist. 1972).

Even though it may be contrary to penal laws, consensual sexual activity is rarely prosecuted because it normally takes place where no third party can observe it and bear witness against the actors. The consensual activity most likely to be subject to prosecution is that which takes place in locations ordinarily deemed "public," but at times when the actors believe that they are not being observed. While some of these prosecutions result from complaints by members of the public who unwittingly stumble on sexual activity in public parks or in public restrooms, the overwhelming majority of such prosecutions result from the undercover activities or surreptitious surveillance of police officers specifically employed to discover these activities. The motivations for such police activity in the absence of complaints from the public have caused much speculation. At certain times and places, there has been a suspicious coincidence between waves of such arrests and imminent reelection campaigns for district attorneys and sheriffs.

Such police practices raise significant questions in a society that seeks to guarantee a certain level of protection for the privacy of its members. In a series of decisions culminating in *People v. Triggs*, the California Supreme Court sought to end police practices most likely to intrude on the privacy of "innocent" individuals (i.e., those not engaging in sexual activity while using public facilities).

Leroy Triggs went to Arroyo Seco Park in Los Angeles on the afternoon of December 19, 1970, looking for an opportunity to have sex. He went to the men's room in the park, which had open toilet stalls that lacked doors, and found there a man willing to have sex with him sitting in one of the stalls. Triggs and the other man, one David Crockett, got down to their business (oral sex). Nobody else was in the restroom, but, unknown to them, about ten minutes after Triggs had entered the restroom, plainclothes Los Angeles police officer Richard Aldahl had entered the "plumbing access area" of the building, separating the men's and women's facilities, where he was able to peer down into the room through an overhead vent and observe what was happening inside. Aldahl had been observing the restroom building, and decided to engage in the surreptitious surveillance from the overhead vent when he saw Triggs enter the facility and not exit after ten minutes had passed. Aldahl had no reason other than the amount of time that had passed to trigger his decision to discover what was happening within the restroom. After observing the sexual activity, Aldahl entered the men's room and arrested Triggs and Crockett.

Both men were convicted in the California Superior Court by Judge E. Talbot Callister of violating section 288a of the Penal Code. Triggs sought by motion to have the evidence of Officer Aldahl's observations suppressed, on the ground that it constituted an unconstitutional search in violation of his right of privacy under the federal and state constitutions. Aldahl had testified that he had entered the plumbing access area after noticing that Triggs had not come out of the restroom after ten minutes "to make an observation in case there was a crime committed." On the basis of several court of appeal decisions holding that there was no reasonable expectation of privacy in a restroom stall that lacked a door, Callister refused to suppress Aldahl's testimony, upon which Triggs pleaded guilty, was sentenced to probation on condition of a brief jail term and fine, and appealed his conviction to the Court of Appeal for the Second District.

The court of appeal received briefs and argument on the constitutionality of the search from Triggs's attorney, Herbert M. Porter, of Laguna Beach, and a team of attorneys from the state attorney general's office. It rendered a unanimous decision upholding Triggs's conviction on June 26, 1972. Acting Presiding Justice Harold W. Schweitzer indicated in his opinion that the two California Supreme Court decisions upon which Triggs primarily relied, *Bielicki v. Superior Court* (1962) and *Britt v. Superior Court* (1962), both involved police officers using overhead viewing access to discover sexual activity occurring in fully enclosed toilet stalls. In those situations, the police were able to view the activity because they had a vantage point not available to the general public; an incidental user of the restroom facility would not have been able to see the defendants engaged in sexual activity. By contrast, in this case there was no door on the toilet stall, so a member of the public (or a plainclothes police officer) who entered the restroom would have been able to observe the activity. Court of appeal decisions subsequent to *Britt* had concluded that "if an officer observed illegal conduct from a vantage point not open to the public, there is no unreasonable search if the illegal activity could have been observed had the officer been in an area open to the public."

The only case that seemed to have reached a contrary conclusion, *People v. Metcalf* (1971), was decided after the legislature passed a law banning the installation of "two way mirrors" in public restrooms. In that case, the court of appeal had found in that law a more general statement of public policy against the practice of surreptitious surveillance of public toilet facilities and held that police observations of sexual activities from a concealed vantage point could not be admitted in evidence. The attorney general had not appealed that decision, however, and Schweitzer was not persuaded by it:

In reaching this conclusion, the court made no analysis of the cases heretofore cited [i..e, upholding police surveillance activities involving doorless toilet stalls]; it set forth no reasons and cited no authorities for its conclusion. It is to be noted that two-way mirrors were not used by police in any recently reported case; each involved observations through vents, louvers, peepholes, etc. If the Legislature had intended to overrule these cases . . ., it could have been more explicit by reference to the types of surveillance used therein, instead of referring to only one type of surveillance that was not involved in the recently reported decisions.

Thus, the Second District Court of Appeal disagreed with the conclusion reached by the court in *Metcalf* and would not follow it.

Triggs applied for a hearing before the California Supreme Court, which was granted on August 30, 1972. On appeal, he received *amicus* support from the American Civil Liberties Union's Southern California affiliate. On February 2, 1973, the court announced its unanimous decision reversing the court of appeal and approving the approach taken by the *Metcalf* court.

Chief Justice Donald R. Wright's opinion for the court began with an analysis of the *Bielicki* and *Britt* precedents. In *Bielicki*, where the toilet stall was fully enclosed, it was "undisputed that the activities of petitioners witnessed by [the arresting officer] were not 'in plain sight' or 'readily visible and accessible.'" The court held that the search was "unreasonable" for federal and state constitutional purposes because "the officer had begun his observations on the night in question with 'no reasonable cause to arrest these petitioners . . . he spied on innocent and guilty alike.' Such a practice amounts to a general exploratory search conducted solely to find evidence of guilt, a practice condemned both by federal law and by the law of this state." However, the toilet stall in *Bielicki* was fully enclosed so that nobody physically present in the restroom could have seen what was happening in it.

To avoid the possibility that lower courts would give too restrictive a reading to *Bielicki*, the court granted review in another case, *Britt*, in which the toilet stall was constructed in such a way that a particularly curious person present in the restroom might discover that sexual activity was taking place by leaning down to see into the stall through the eight open inches between the bottom of the stall door and the floor. The arresting officer had not first observed the activity in that way, however, being

stationed in an overhead compartment with a concealed view into the top of the stall. The court rejected the government's attempt to distinguish *Britt* from *Bielicki* based on the differences in construction of the stalls: "The crucial fact in *Bielicki* was neither the manner of observation *alone* nor the place of commission *alone*, but rather the manner in which the police observed a place—and persons in that place—which is ordinarily understood to afford personal privacy to individual occupants."

But this apparently had not been clear enough to lower California courts. In the intervening years, several courts of appeal had taken the view that the reasonable expectation of privacy did not exist if the toilet stall lacked a door, even though there was nobody else in the restroom to observe the sexual activity between the defendants at the time it occurred. Several of these cases were appealed to the California Supreme Court, but for whatever unspecified reason the court had consistently denied hearings, which led the lower courts to conclude that the court agreed with their analysis. Indeed, in Triggs's case, the court of appeal had specifically relied on a statement by the Court of Appeal in *People v. Crafts* (1970) regarding the California Supreme Court's alleged "acquiescence" in this interpretation of *Bielicki* and *Britt*. Chief Justice Wright would now disabuse the lower courts of that notion:

> Preliminarily we declare that our refusal to grant a hearing in a particular case is to be given *no* weight insofar as it might be deemed that we have acquiesced in the law as enunciated in a published opinion of a Court of Appeal when such opinion is in conflict with the law as stated by this court. Our statements of law remain binding on the trial and appellate courts of this state and must be applied wherever the facts of a case are not fairly distinguishable from the facts of the case in which we have declared the applicable principle of law. Our refusal to grant a hearing in any given case must not be deemed a sub silentio overruling of our prior decisions.

Wright rejected the state's argument that "clandestine observation of doorless stalls in public restrooms" was not a Fourth Amendment "search," because the activity was being carried on in "plain view" of anyone who walked into the restroom. "This would permit the police to make it a routine practice to observe from hidden vantage points the restroom conduct of the public whenever such activities do not occur within fully enclosed toilet stalls and would permit spying on the 'innocent and guilty alike,'" he declared. "Most persons using public restrooms have no reason to suspect that a hidden agent of the state will observe them. The expectation of privacy a person has when he enters a restroom is reasonable and is not diminished or destroyed because the toilet stall being used lacks a door." Wright found support for this assertion in the U.S. Supreme Court's seminal Fourth Amendment ruling, *Katz v. United States* (1967), in which the Court held that a person using a public telephone booth had a reasonable expectation of privacy that would require the police to obtain a warrant based on probable cause before they could plant a listening device on the wall of the telephone booth that would pick up the defendant's end of the conversation. The inquiry focused on the reasonable expectation of the individual, not necessarily on whether it was possible that the individual could be observed by others.

Here, the police conduct was objectionable in itself, because it could result in violating the reasonable privacy expectations of any member of the public who went into the restroom "because occupants of toilet stalls can reasonably expect their activities within them to be private," regardless whether the stall in question had a door. While the occupant of a doorless stall knew that somebody who came into the restroom could see what he was doing, he had no reason to believe that he was being observed by a government agent (or anybody, for that matter) if the restroom was empty. Thus, observation from a concealed point, through a vent or other opening, "remained a search and hence subject to the Fourth Amendment's ban against exploratory searches, even if the interior of the stall might have been open to view from areas accessible to the public." Continuing, Wright also stated:

> In seeking to honor reasonable expectations of privacy through our application of search and seizure law, we must consider the expectations of the innocent as well as the guilty. When innocent people are subjected to illegal searches—including when, as here, they do not even know their private parts and bodily functions are being exposed to the gaze of the law—their rights are violated even though such searches turn up no evidence of guilt. Save through the deterrent effect of the exclusionary rule there is little courts can do to protect the constitutional right of persons innocent of any crime to be free of unreasonable searches.

The legislature's action in specifically banning the installation of two-way mirrors in toilets, motel rooms, hotel rooms, and the like merely reinforced this constitutional holding, said Wright. The *Metcalf* court had been correct in pointing to this statute as implementing the broader public policy, and in not restricting that policy to two-way mirrors. "The public policy declared [in the two-way mirror law] is incompatible with the carte blanche which the People claim for clandestine surveillance of all areas of restrooms not fully enclosed by three walls and a door."

Having determined that Triggs was subjected to a search, the court had to determine whether the search was legal. Did the police have "probable cause" to believe that by conducting this search they would uncover unlawful activity? Probable cause would exist only if "at the moment officers made an arrest or conduct a search 'the facts and circumstances within their knowledge and of which they had reasonably trustworthy information were sufficient to warrant a prudent man in believing that the [defendant] had committed or was committing an offense.'" In this case, Triggs had given the police "no cause to suspect him of criminal conduct aside from his prolonged stay in the restroom," behavior that "was susceptible to an innocent explanation." Such a search could not be validated *ex post facto* by reference to the fact that Triggs was actually engaging in sexual activity in the restroom, since the test was whether the police officer, at the time he decided to undertake the search, possessed information that would lead a "prudent man" to believe Triggs was committing a crime. A ten-minute stay in the restroom was not enough for that, concluded Wright.

Consequently, Officer Aldahl's testimony resulted from an illegal search and had to be excluded from Triggs's trial. Since Aldahl's testimony was the only evidence, the conviction had to be reversed.

The *Triggs* decision was an important landmark in ending the practice of surreptitious police surveillance of California restrooms. This case did not end the prosecution of men for restroom sex, since plain clothes police officers could always linger in restrooms themselves, seeking to observe (or stimulate) sexual activity by the users of the facilities. But at least the offensive practice of police spying on the activities of restroom users had been cut short. However, the *Triggs* decision was not always followed by the courts of other states, which have continued in some cases to allow such intrusive surveillance, sometimes using advanced electronic technology such as concealed miniature television cameras, in an attempt to identify and prosecute those who engage in sexual activities in public toilets.

Case References

Bielicki v. Superior Court, 57 Cal. 2d 602, 21 Cal. Rptr. 552, 371 P.2d 288 (1962)

Britt v. Superior Court, 58 Cal.2d 469, 24 Cal. Rptr. 849, 374 P.2d 817 (1962)

Katz v. United States, 389 U.S. 347 (1967)

People v. Crafts, 13 Cal. App. 3d 457, 91 Cal. Rptr. 563 (1970)

People v. Metcalf, 22 Cal. App. 3d 20, 98 Cal. Rptr. 925 (1971)

12. IS "CRIME AGAINST NATURE" TOO VAGUE?

Wainwright v. Stone, 414 U.S. 21 (1973), reversing 478 F.2d 390 (5th Cir. 1973).

When the American Law Institute studied sex crimes laws as part of its consideration of a proposed Model Penal Code during the 1950s, it found a degree of euphemism that seemed inappropriate under modern conceptions of due process of law. As early as 1926, the U.S. Supreme Court had taken on the problem of statutory vagueness, holding in *Connally v. General Construction Co.*, "[that the words of a criminal statute] must be sufficiently explicit to inform those who are subject to it what conduct on their part will render them liable to its penalties, is a well-recognized requirement, consonant alike with ordinary notions of fair play and the settled rules of law." Furthermore, it was not sufficient that one trained in the law would know what conduct a criminal law was intended to forbid; a statute had to be informative to the lay person, said the Court, holding that "a statute which either forbids or requires the doing of an act in terms so vague that men of common intelligence must necessarily guess at its meaning and differ as to its application violates the first essential of due process of law."

Applying this principle to laws against anal or oral intercourse yielded but one reasonable conclusion: only one knowledgeable about legislative history, archaic linguistic formulas, and court decisions would necessarily conclude from the term "abominable and detestable crime against nature, either with mankind or with beast," the standard formulation of many state laws, what the prohibited acts were. This was especially true because of judicial expansions of traditional common-law meanings. Under the English common law taken over by the early American states at the time of independence, this language would refer solely to anal intercourse, and the genders of the participants would not be an aspect of the crime. When various American states codified the common law of sodomy during the 19th century, they adopted the euphemistic "crime against nature" terminology, but frequently offered no explanation of what it meant, presuming that "everybody knows." But there were serious uncertainties. Some state courts held that this phrase prohibited only anal intercourse, while others applied it to oral intercourse. In some jurisdictions, it was generally believed that the described offense applied only to same-sex copulation, while most clung to the common-law application that disregarded gender. A person of "ordinary intelligence" without legal training or direct access to court decisions might have little conception, based solely on reading the statute, of what was prohibited.

The Model Penal Code drafters, while recommending that private consensual sexual activity be free of criminal sanctions, still needed to adopt a verbal formulation to describe the conduct that would be prohibited if imposed without consent or performed in public or with minors. They adopted the more descriptive term "deviate sexual intercourse," which they defined as sexual conduct consisting of "contact between the penis and the anus, the mouth and the penis, or the mouth and the vulva." As various states considered and adopted the Model Penal Code, the sex crimes provisions were the subject of much debate and were among those provisions most frequently modified or rejected on a state-by-state basis. Some states decriminalized only anal or oral intercourse involving married persons or opposite-sex couples, others completely decriminalized, and others, while adopting some provisions of the Model Penal Code, retained their crime-against-nature or other common-law derived formulations. Proponents of sodomy law reform began to attack the nonreformed language in the courts, alleging that under the standards adopted by the U.S. Supreme Court, crime-against-nature laws were unconstitutionally vague in violation of the Due Process Clause of the Fourteenth Amendment.

One of the early successful challenges came in Florida, whose sodomy law in 1971 stated: "Whoever commits the abominable and detestable crime against nature, either with mankind or with beast, shall be punished by imprisonment in the state prison not exceeding twenty years." This law had survived in the Florida statute books as originally drafted since 1868, more than one hundred years, when Alva Gene Franklin and Stephen F. Joyce became caught up in its net. A police officer saw Franklin and Joyce leaving a public restroom on the Municipal Pier in St. Petersburg, Florida, at about 2:45 a.m., drive in their separate cars to a deserted area and get together in one of the cars. When the officer approached the car and shined his flashlight inside, he observed the two men committing "a crime against nature," according to the charges filed against them. How "nature" was actually offended was not recorded. Both

men were convicted by Pinnellas County Circuit Judge B.J. Driver, who rejected their vagueness challenge to the sodomy law on the authority of a long line of Florida cases culminating in *Delaney v. State* (1966), which had been denied review by the U.S. Supreme Court. Both men appealed to the Florida District Court of Appeal, which certified their challenge directly to the Florida Supreme Court, as required by state procedural rules.

Walter R. Talley, the public defender representing the two men, argued the case before the Florida Supreme Court against Florida Attorney General Robert L. Shevin. Although it had only been five years since *Delaney*, something important had happened in the interim: the U.S. Supreme Court had begun to recognize that the private, consensual sex lives of adults might have some constitutional protection, ruling in *Loving v. Virginia* (1967) and *Griswold v. Connecticut* (1965) that the Due Process Clause could under certain circumstances be used substantively to invalidate state regulations interfering with marital and sexual choices. Thus, the question arose anew whether the state could invade what might be constitutionally protected privacy and liberty interests with statutes that were so unspecific about what conduct was prohibited.

In a *per curiam* opinion of December 17, 1971, from which only one member of the court dissented, the court concluded that if the Florida legislature wanted to punish anal or oral intercourse as a felony, it would have to say so more directly. Over the course of a hundred years, the language of the sodomy law, archaic to begin with, had become virtually meaningless to the modern-day everyman. "People's understandings of subjects, expressions and experiences are different than they were even a decade ago," said the court. "The fact of these changes in the land must be taken into account and appraised. Their effect and the reasonable reaction and understanding of people today relate to statutory language." Furthermore, the new privacy cases made it specially important for the legislature to be precise about what it was prohibiting. "The language in this statute could entrap unsuspecting citizens and subject them to 20-year sentences for which the statute provides. Such a sentence is equal to that for manslaughter and would no doubt be a shocking revelation to persons who do not have an understanding of the meaning of the statute," said the court.

While it was true that anyone "versed in the law" could figure out what the statute prohibited by reading the court's past opinions, "it seems to us that if today's world is to have brought home to it what it is that the statute prohibits, it must be set forth in language which is relevant to today's society and is understandable to the average citizen of common intelligence which is the constitutional test of such language." While hastening to assure the legislature that it was not passing judgment on the validity of laws prohibiting "historically forbidden sexual acts, homosexuality, or bestiality," the court argued that "the common man" was entitled to statutes that spelled out clearly what was prohibited. While the court would prefer to leave this whole issue to the legislature, the legislature had not paid attention to the need for clarification, because "there is no doubt on its face that this statute as worded cannot withstand the constitutional onslaught and must fall."

Nonetheless, invalidating the statute did not end the matter for Franklin and Joyce, because there was another law on the books in Florida under which they could be accused, penalizing "unnatural and lascivious acts" as a misdemeanor subject to fine or relatively brief imprisonment. The court remanded the case to the trial judge with directions to find the two men guilty and impose sentences under this statute as a "lesser included offense" of the invalidated felony sodomy law. The court seemed totally unconcerned with the idea that the "unnatural and lascivious acts" law presented the same vagueness questions! Furthermore, since prior decisions of the court had upheld the sodomy law as recently as five years before, the court concluded that its decision in this case should have only prospective effect.

Chief Justice B.K. Roberts supplemented the *per curiam* opinion with a brief concurring statement, quoting from a variety of sources on the need for specificity in criminal statutes to meet due process requirements. His statement was joined by most of the other justices in the majority.

All well and good, but what about the Floridians who had recently been convicted under the sodomy law and were now serving time in the state prison? If the law was void for vagueness, did not their continued confinement under it violate the due process clause? Two Florida prisoners, Raymond R. Stone and Eugene P. Huffman, whose attempts to challenge their convictions in the Florida courts had come to nothing, sought relief through petitions in the federal district court for *habeas corpus*. Stone had attempted to raise the *Franklin* case as the appeal of his conviction went up through the Florida court system, but the state courts resolutely applied the Florida Supreme Court's statement in *Franklin* that its ruling was to have only prospective effect. Each prisoner wrote his own petition for the writ of *habeas corpus*, articulating with varying degrees of clarity the argument that the sodomy law found vague in *Franklin* was undoubtedly vague at the times of their arrests and convictions. District Judge William A. McRae, Jr., agreed with them, ordering that the writ be issued. When Florida Attorney General Robert L. Shevin petitioned the U.S. Court of Appeals for the Fifth Circuit for review, Stone and Huffman obtained the services of the Legal Aid and Defender Clinic at the University of Florida College of Law in Gainesville, under the direction of Lynn E. Wagner.

The Fifth Circuit panel assembled to hear the case unanimously agreed with McRae and upheld his grant of the writ on April 19, 1973, in an opinion by Circuit Judge Irving L. Goldberg. Goldberg rejected the state's main argument, that the Florida Supreme Court had a right to make its invalidation of the sodomy law solely prospective, without interference from the federal courts. After reviewing the extraordinary range of legal challenges that had been mounted against sodomy laws in recent years, Goldberg pointed out that the proper role of the district judge in this case had been to make an independent determination on the validity of the Florida sodomy law, separate and apart from anything the Florida Supreme Court had said in *Franklin*. This McRae had done, although he also noted the *Franklin* opinion as confirming his view that the law was unconstitutionally vague. "In making this determination," said Goldberg, "Judge McRae's independent federal finding that the statute fails to advise those who may be convicted under it of precisely what behavior is proscribed was neither new or unsupported," because the Florida Supreme Court had independently come to the same conclusion. The court of appeals panel agreed with this conclusion as well. "Convictions obtained under this statute, rendered void by its vagueness, are repugnant to the Constitution and cannot stand," insisted Goldberg. The independent power of the federal judiciary to protect the federal constitutional rights of individual citizens against state encroachment by virtue of *habeas corpus* jurisdiction meant that the "prospective" language of *Franklin* was essentially irrelevant to the district court's role. As such, McRae had not been "applying" the *Franklin* decision, but applying an independent federal judgment on the constitutionality of the Stone and Huffman convictions. There was no question that, as a matter of federalism, federal courts were "bound" by state court constructions of state laws, but that was not this case; McRae was not construing a state law, but rather evaluating its constitutionality against a federal standard. "With all due deference to the sovereignty of the states," said Goldberg, "the power is not given unto any state to suspend, limit, or condition with prospectivity a *constitutional* right such as that before us . . . . Florida cannot veto, nullify, or suspend a right that the Constitution grants to all persons, and the revered Writ is ever at the ready to answer the distress calls of its wards." Circuit Judge Paul H. Roney specially concurred in a very brief opinion, stating his view that the case could be disposed of summarily because *Franklin* held the statute void "on its face," which left little room for doubt that prior convictions under it were unconstitutional.

The state, as then authorized by federal jurisdictional statutes, appealed as of right to the U.S. Supreme Court, which promptly reversed in a brief unanimous *per curiam* opinion on November 5, 1973. Apparently, the lower courts had misunderstood the Court's "void for vagueness" jurisprudence, to judge by the Court's brief explanation for the reversal. The Florida Supreme Court had upheld the state's sodomy laws in a series of decisions beginning

in 1921, when it had first described with requisite specificity the acts prohibited by the law. "The judgment of federal courts as to the vagueness or not of a state statute must be made in the light of prior state constructions of the statute," said the Court. "For the purpose of determining whether a state statute is too vague and indefinite to constitute valid legislation 'we must take the statute as though it read precisely as the highest court of the State has interpreted it,'" the Court insisted, citing its 1940 decision in *Minnesota ex rel. Pearson v. Probate Court*. When a state court had defined a state penal law to apply to particular conduct, adequately described, the vagueness problem did not arise, and the court of appeals was not free to ignore the line of cases culminating in *Delaney* in determining whether Florida had given fair notice of the conduct condemned by the statute.

While it was true that the Florida Supreme Court had changed its tune in *Franklin*, "this holding did not remove the fact that when appellees committed the acts with which they were charged, they were on clear notice that their conduct was criminal under the statute as then construed." Consequently, the Florida courts had correctly refused to upset Stone's conviction, relying on the expressly prospective ruling in *Franklin*. "The State Supreme Court did not overrule *Delaney* with respect to pre-*Franklin* convictions," said the Court, and it was not "constitutionally compelled to do so or to make retroactive its new construction of the Florida statute," since the question of retroactive application was one for state courts to make with regard to their own statutes.

The Supreme Court had cast a peculiar gloss on its due process jurisprudence. On the one hand, a law had to be specific enough for a person of "ordinary intelligence" to understand what was prohibited. On the other hand, it was not the constitutional duty of the legislature to communicate this. The common citizen could be held charged with knowing not only what his or her elected representatives in the legislature had decided to prohibit, but also, where the legislators hid their prohibitions in general euphemisms, to know how the state's courts had interpreted the vague language. Such a ruling significantly undermined the rationale of the void-for-vagueness doctrine. And, so far as the theory that crime-against-nature statutes were unconstitutionally vague went, the Court's brief *per curiam* essentially put an end to such arguments in most states. These laws had been around for a century or more in most jurisdictions where they persisted in the statute books, and over the course of those years had accumulated substantial track records of interpretation and explication in the state courts. While it might be plausible in some few states to argue that none of the prior judicial constructions had adequately described the conduct to be covered by the law, in most states such arguments would have little substance or credibility. Attacks on

sodomy laws would have to be substantive, focused on arguments that the legislatures did not have authority to penalize the described behavior, in order to avoid the precedential weight of *Wainwright v. Stone.*

Case References

Connally v. General Construction Co., 269 U.S. 385 (1926)

Delaney v. State, 190 So. 2d 578 (Fla. 1966), appeal dismissed, 387 U.S. 426 (1967)

Franklin v. State, 257 So. 2d 21 (Fla. 1971)

Griswold v. Connecticut, 381 U.S. 479 (1965)

Loving v. Virginia, 388 U.S. 1 (1967)

Minnesota ex rel. Pearson v. Probate Court, 309 U.S. 270 (1940)

13. WHAT IS "UNNATURAL" SEXUAL CONDUCT?

Commonwealth v. Balthazar, 318 N.E.2d 478 (Mass. 1974), writ of habeas corpus granted and conviction vacated sub nom. *Balthazar v. Superior Court*, 428 F. Supp. 425 (D. Mass. 1977), affirmed, 573 F.2d 698 (1st Cir. 1978).

The Victorian sensibilities underlying pre-Model Penal Code sex crime laws in the United States generated a host of problems as the due process revolution of the 20th century gathered force. Feeling that describing specific sexual acts to be prohibited "would be an offence against common decency," legislators had resorted to subjective terms such as "unnatural," whose meaning might shift over time with developing community attitudes. In some cases, issues of vagueness might be cured by long, specific usage. For example, it had been clear since colonial times that the old English common-law crime-against-nature referred to anal intercourse, although that term became more and more ambiguous as prosecutors tried to use crime-against-nature statutes to prosecute oral-genital sex of various types having nothing to do with penile penetration. However, even decades of interpretation might not suffice to give adequate definition to subjective statutory terms where the courts themselves continued the practice of speaking in euphemisms. Of course, states that adopted some version of the Model Penal Code could solve this problem by following the Code's practice of describing with

particularity the body parts that were forbidden to come into contact and the precise circumstances under which such contact was punishable.

Massachusetts, not a Model Penal Code jurisdiction, had a variety of antiquated sex crimes laws at the time Richard L. Balthazar stood trial in 1972 on the charge of committing an "unnatural and lascivious act with another person" under Massachusetts General Laws chapter 272, section 35. In addition to the broad proscription of "unnatural and lascivious acts" in section 35, section 34 proscribed "crimes against nature," which had been construed according to its English common-law roots as "sodomy" or "anal intercourse," and section 53 proscribed "lewd, wanton and lascivious" behavior. One would presume that each statute was aimed at different conduct, but each contained at least one descriptive word or concept in common with one of the others and provided for different levels of punishment. Furthermore, the statutes on their face made no distinction regarding whether the acts were consensual and where they were occurring. In light both of the broad due process developments and the specific case law of constitutional privacy growing from *Griswold v. Connecticut* (1965), this jumble of imprecise sex crimes laws seemed quite vulnerable to challenge as vague and confusing.

On July 9, 1972, Eileen Lomprez was walking penniless on a Boston street, having given her last remaining money to her younger sister for bus fare to Exeter, Massachusetts. She hoped to stop in at a friend's house and borrow money for the public transit fare to get to her home. According to her account of what happened, a car pulled over and a door opened. Lomprez, thinking she recognized the car of an acquaintance, got in. When she realized the driver was a stranger, she tried to get out, but he pulled a knife and told her to remain. The man drove her into a secluded area in the suburbs, told her to get out and undress, and threatened her with his knife when she hesitated. Then he forced her to perform fellatio on him and put her "tongue on his backside." He mentioned girls getting raped and killed and she started crying. They both got dressed and the man gave her a cigarette. They chatted about astrology and got back in the car, with a "friendly conversation" continuing until they got back to Boston, where the man dropped Lomprez off at a subway station with enough money for her fare home. They agreed to meet again the following Saturday at the bus terminal. When Lomprez got home, she confided in a friend and, the following day, went to the police, who arrested Richard L. Balthazar near the bus terminal the following Saturday at 1:30 p.m. Lomprez identified Balthazar in a police lineup. He was charged with assault and commission of "unnatural and lascivious acts with another person."

At the trial in Norfolk Superior Court, which lasted from June 7 to June 11, 1973, Balthazar's lawyer, Bruce R. Bono, of the Massachusetts Defenders Committee, presented the defense of mistaken identity. He centered his case, which did not include testimony by Balthazar, on that theory. He produced as his only witness Dr. A. Walter Ciani, an orthopedic surgeon who had examined Balthazar on April 9, 1973, and determined that a condition of weakness in Balthazar's right shoulder due to prior surgery would have made it impossible for Balthazar to have performed some of the physical acts described in the victim's testimony. Lomprez had testified that the car driven by her assailant was a manual shift car. Ciani testified that it would have been quite difficult for a person with Balthazar's shoulder problem to drive a manual shift car. Both parties stipulated that had Balthazar's father been called as a witness, he would have testified that Balthazar had suffered from the shoulder condition since 1955, had not owned an automobile for the past three years, had a driver's license limited to automatic transmission cars, and had not, to his father's knowledge, driven since his license had been suspended prior to the date of the alleged incident.

Because it would have been inconsistent with his defense theory and would have required Balthazar to waive his Fifth Amendment privilege and to testify, Bono decided not to pursue an alternative defense of consent, and did not ask the judge to charge on that basis. He did, however, move the court without success to declare the "unnatural and lascivious acts" statute unconstitutionally vague.

The prosecutor argued in closing: "We may have non-corroboration but we do not have denial as to the basic facts of this case, two basic facts, one, the knifepoint and threat and, two, an unnatural act. Those two facts have not been denied in this trial." Bono objected that these remarks violated Balthazar's Fifth Amendment rights, since he had an absolute right not to testify and, since there were no witnesses to the alleged acts, nobody else could be called to testify that they had not occurred. The judge instructed the prosecutor to "move off that particular point" and instructed the members of the jury that it was not up to the defendant to deny the prosecution's case, but up to the prosecution to prove its case beyond a reasonable doubt. At the end of the trial, the judge charged the members of the jury that if they believed the victim's testimony, they would be warranted in finding that the defendant committed an unnatural and lascivious act with her. Without having to go any further in defining the nature of acts covered by the statute, Judge Lynch asserted that the acts alleged fell "within the meaning of the statute." The jury found Balthazar innocent on the assault charge, evidently believing the testimony that his shoulder made it unlikely he could have wielded the knife as described in Lomprez's testimony, but convicted him on the "unnatural and lascivious acts" charge. No issue was made in the trial as to whether Lomprez might have consented to the sexual acts that allegedly took place.

Balthazar appealed his conviction to the Massachusetts Supreme Judicial Court, alleging again that the statute was unduly vague, that the trial judge gave an inadequate charge to the jury to clear up vagueness problems, and that the judge's remarks about the prosecutor's "denial" statement during his closing argument had not adequately cured the compromise of his Fifth Amendment rights. For the first time at oral argument, Balthazar's attorney also raised an alternative theory, arguing that Lomprez had consented to any acts that might have taken place. Malvine Nathanson, of the Defenders Committee, was lead counsel on the appeal, with Assistant District Attorney John P. O'Connor, Jr., appearing for the Commonwealth of Massachusetts. The Supreme Judicial Court heard arguments on September 16, 1974, and announced its unanimous decision affirming Balthazar's conviction on November 1, 1974, in an opinion by Justice Herbert P. Wilkins.

While the court affirmed Balthazar's conviction, however, it seemed to agree that section 35 was on its face a vague, subjective statute. To Balthazar's argument that the law failed "to state with particularity what conduct is made criminal," Wilkins responded, "We agree that today these words, standing alone, present some question as to their meaning, even if they had a generally understood signification in 1887 when they were first expressed in the statute from which section 35 is derived." After noting that similar statutes had been struck down on due process grounds in other states, Wilkins asserted that invalidation was not the only remedy for the problem, since judicial construction and past history of usage could give the law enough precision of meaning for "constitutional adequacy."

Wilkins pointed to the court's prior consideration of the statute in *Jaquith v. Commonwealth* (1954), in which the court had stated that "an unnatural and lascivious act" are "words of common usage and indicate with reasonable clarity the kind and character of conduct which

the Legislature intended to prohibit and punish. . . . [T]hese words have a well defined, well understood, and generally accepted meaning," signifying "irregular indulgence in sexual behavior, illicit sexual relations, and infamous conduct which is lustful, obscene, and in deviation of accepted customs and manners." The court said that "the common sense of the community, as well as the sense of decency, propriety, and morality which all respectable persons usually entertain, is sufficient to apply the statute to a situation and determine what particular kind of conduct offends." To be more specific in the statute itself, said the court, "would be an offence against common decency."

Thus, said Justice Wilkins, almost twenty years ago the court had adopted a limiting construction of the statute, applying it only to "sexual conduct which virtually all members of the community have regarded as offensive." Of course, the opinions of members of the community could change over time, resulting in a changing meaning to the statute. What was considered offensive in 1887 or 1954 might not be considered offensive in 1972. In addition, said Wilkins, the U.S. Supreme Court's articulation of "the constitutional right of an individual to be free from governmental regulation of certain sex-related activities" in cases such as *Griswold* and its progeny on contraception, sexually oriented books and films, and abortion required a narrow enough construction to avoid unduly burdening the right of privacy. Consequently, Wilkens stated,

> [W]e conclude that section 35 must be construed to be inapplicable to private, consensual conduct of adults. We do so on the ground that the concept of general community disapproval of specific sexual conduct, which is inherent in section 35, requires such an interpretation. We do not decide whether a statute which explicitly prohibits specific sexual conduct, even if consensual and private, would be constitutionally infirm.

Thus, the court was construing section 35 to apply only to sexual conduct that would be considered offensive by virtually the entire community if it was either nonconsensual, performed in public, or both. Assuming that Balthazar had been convicted of nonconsensual conduct, Wilkins stated that section 35 "clearly may apply" to the conduct "in which the defendant forced the victim to engage." A Massachusetts appeals court had ruled in 1972 in *Commonwealth v. Deschamps* that fellatio and cunnilingus were among the acts covered by section 35, so there was no vagueness problem in applying the statute to Balthazar, whose trial took place after that decision was rendered.

Turning to the issue of consent, Wilkins stated that it had not been raised in a timely manner. Since Balthazar had never made anything out of the consent issue at trial, it was inappropriate to raise it on appeal. Wilkins also rejected Balthazar's arguments concerning the charge to the jury and the prosecutor's remarks. By charging the jury that it could find a violation if it found that Balthazar had Lomprez suck his penis and lick his rear end, the trial judge had correctly included within the meaning of the statute nonconsensual fellatio and oral-anal sex acts, said Wilkins. The trial judge had also said all that was necessary concerning the prosecutor's remarks when he indicated to the jury that it was up to the state to prove guilt, not to the defense to disprove it.

Balthazar's attorney filed a petition for rehearing in light of the court's decision, arguing that by narrowing the statute to nonconsensual acts, the court had recognized a previously unavailable defense and that Balthazar should be allowed to try to establish that defense at trial. Since consent had not previously been recognized as a defense, argued trial attorney Bono in an affidavit filed with the court, he had not felt it would be worth waiving his client's Fifth Amendment right not to testify in order to establish the consent defense by his testimony. The court denied this petition without further comment.

Seeking further legal assistance, Balthazar contacted the Prisoner's Rights Project in Boston, which, together with attorneys from the Massachusetts Defenders Committee, represented him in his petition to the federal district court in Boston for a writ of *habeas corpus.* Balthazar's attorneys argued to District Judge Joseph L. Tauro that he was entitled at least to have his conviction vacated and remanded for a new trial on the issue of consent if the court disagreed with his argument that the vagueness of the statute was not itself grounds for setting aside the conviction. Appearing for the commonwealth, Assistant Attorney General Barbara A. H. Smith argued that Balthazar had failed to satisfy the jurisdictional prerequisite for a writ of *habeas corpus* of exhausting all state remedies, that the statute gave fair warning of the offenses covered, and that there was no error of constitutional dimensions at the trial. Judge Tauro agreed that as to the demand for a new trial Balthazar had not exhausted his state remedies, and he stayed the proceedings so that Balthazar could apply to the Massachusetts Superior Court for a new trial on the consent issue. When the Superior Court denied this motion, Balthazar renewed his application for the writ before Judge Tauro. This time, Assistant Attorney General Smith argued that Balthazar should be required to appeal the trial court's denial of his motion. Judge Tauro disagreed, holding that since the Supreme Judicial Court had denied Balthazar's petition for rehearing on this issue, it was unnecessary for Balthazar to toil any longer in the state courts before receiving a federal court consideration of his constitutional claims.

Proceeding to the merits in his final order of March 9, 1977, Tauro ruled that the statute was, indeed, unconstitutionally vague at the time Balthazar allegedly committed the sex acts at issue and even when he was tried the following year. Indeed, the Supreme Judicial Court had itself recognized the problems with the statute when it decided to adopt a narrowing construction. The prior interpretation in *Jaquith*, suggesting a relative meaning based on evolving community standards, struck Tauro as too imprecise standing alone to meet constitutional muster. While the more specific holding in *Deschamps* by a state intermediate appellate court provided some help by identifying specific acts that were prohibited—fellatio and cunnilingus—it was not quite enough. The statute failed the due process test, at least prior to the Supreme Judicial Court's decision in *Balthazar*, by using the vague term "unnatural" in such a way as to defy any precise definition at the time of Balthazar's conduct. *Jaquith* had not made things any clearer. Indeed, its "attempt at definition seems to compound rather than resolve the ambiguity." Tauro stated:

73

While a state may have a legitimate interest in protecting community sensibilities, criminal liability should only attach to clearly delineated transgression. Currents of community standards are constantly shifting. These changes are sometimes subtle. Standards are apt to vary from generation to generation without the specific awareness of either generation. This is true in the area of private sexual conduct, among others.

Tauro found that the Supreme Judicial Court's opinion in *Balthazar* itself reflected this phenomenon of shifting standards. The Supreme Judicial Court's acknowledgment that the *Jaquith* standard might "change with time" "underscores the point that the public should not be required at its peril to anticipate a judicial pronouncement that public standards of morality have changed." It was up to the legislature, not the courts, to determine precisely what the rules were to be regarding criminal conduct. The statute should be precise enough to establish the policy determination. Despite the lower appeals court ruling in *Deschamps*, which did not satisfy due process concerns because it was issued twelve months after Balthazar's alleged conduct took place, the state's highest court had not issued a ruling any more precise than the ambiguous, floating *Jaquith* standard at the time of Balthazar's trial. Surely, he could not be held to have to anticipate that conduct not specifically mentioned in the statute would be covered, or that the issue of consent would be relevant when it had never been identified as such by the state's highest court.

"The Massachusetts cases prior to July, 1972, the date of petitioner's conduct, did not perform that remedial function" of giving precise contours to the statute, asserted Tauro. "They did not serve to provide 'fair warning.' On the contrary, those cases are distinguished by their delicate and ambiguous discussions of the conduct involved in section 35 cases. No reported case in the Commonwealth had expressly applied the 'unnatural and lascivious' act prohibition to fellatio or oral-anal contact." Case law from other jurisdictions was no more helpful. Thus, as of July, 1972, section 35 was too vague to provide a basis for Balthazar's conviction, which would have to be set aside. Indeed, the indictment would be ordered vacated and dismissed, since the problem was not one

merely of whether a new trial was needed on the issue of consent. However, said Tauro, the combination of the Supreme Judicial Court's decision on the merits in *Balthazar* (which mentioned the lower appellate ruling in *Deschamps* with approval) and a subsequent Supreme Judicial Court decision in *Commonwealth v. LaBella* (1974) holding that cunnilingus was covered by section 35, had now given that section enough precise content so that it could be constitutionally applied to conduct that postdated those decisions. The dismissal of the case against Balthazar was based on the state of things at the time of his acts.

The commonwealth appealed to the U.S. Court of Appeals for the First Circuit, which announced on April 4, 1978, that it would affirm Judge Tauro's decision. In a decision by Senior District Judge Albert C. Wollenberg, of the Northern District of California, who was sitting on the panel by designation, the court ruled that Tauro had correctly decided to vacate and dismiss the criminal charges against Balthazar based on the state of construction of the statute at the time of the alleged acts. Regardless of the consent issue, as to which the commonwealth urged that it be allowed to retry Balthazar, "the question as to what forced acts were within the statutory sweep would remain," said Wollenberg. "If the set of all unnatural and lascivious acts is unconstitutionally vague, so will be the subset of forced acts no matter how clear the dividing line between forced and consensual acts."

Taking note of the U.S. Supreme Court's decision in *Rose v. Locke*, a 1975 case upholding the constitutionality against a vagueness challenge of a Tennessee crimes-against-nature law based on the long history of judicial construction, the court commented that no comparable record of construction had existed with respect to the Massachusetts law. Indeed, there was a Massachusetts crimes-against-nature statute, section 34, so it was clear that the long common-law history attaching to that phrase could not be borrowed to give meaning to section 35's somewhat different phrasing. The use of the term "unnatural" in section 35 had created a "fundamental ambiguity" as to the degree to which section 35 covered different behavior from section 34. The prior Massachusetts case law, especially *Jaquith* , did not "cure the ambiguity." "The District Court was rightly concerned," said Wollenberg, "that the use of constantly shifting community standards, as the test of what conduct falls within the terms of a criminal statute, places the public 'at its peril to anticipate a judicial pronouncement that public standards of morality have changed.'"

"Criminal statutes involving morals legislation often give rise to difficulties in the description of prescribed conduct," said Wollenberg, because of "the common practice of including subjective terminology, such as 'offensive,' 'indecent,' and 'unnatural' rather than explicit descriptions of the prohibited acts." This hesitancy to use sexually explicit words in statutes, whatever its cause, had been rejected by "forward-looking jurisdictions." The Supreme Judicial Court had itself recognized this problem in its *Balthazar* opinion. Since the law did not have an adequately precise, commonly understood meaning at the time of Balthazar's acts, it could not appropriately be applied to him, although "subsequent decisions" had since rendered the statute "sufficiently precise to survive a constitutional vagueness attack as applied today to the same conduct."

Circuit Judge Levin H. Campbell dissented from this disposition. It was clear from the nature of the charges against Balthazar that he was not being charged with consensual acts, and it should be equally clear to "any sane person" that the specific acts he was charged with committing—fellatio and oral-anal contact—came within the language of the *Jaquith* decision. For Campbell, the appropriate disposition would be to send the case back for a new trial so Balthazar would have a chance to show that Lomprez had consented to the sexual activity. That was the only legitimate basis for questioning the validity of his prior trial, given the Supreme Judicial Court's subsequent narrowing of the statute to ban only nonconsensual acts.

Commonwealth v. Balthazar was an important landmark in interpreting and applying pre–Model Penal Code sex crimes laws. Taken together with other decisions limiting the reach of Massachusetts's vintage sex crimes laws, it was part of a trend decriminalizing consensual sex between adults in private through judicial fiat that took the wind out of the sails of any attempt to achieve decriminalization by legislative action. By its receptivity to limiting constructions that had no particular basis in the language of the statutes, the Massachusetts court effectively seized the law-reform initiative away from the legislature. This approach was quite different from that of the state court in Alaska, which ruled in *Harris v. State* (1969) that the lack of a plausible limiting construction invalidated entirely a crime-against-nature statute.

Case References

Commonwealth v. Deschamps, 294 N.E.2d 426 (Mass. App. 1972)
Commonwealth v. LaBella, 306 N.E.2d 813 (Mass. 1974)
Griswold v. Connecticut, 381 U.S. 479 (1965)
Harris v. State, 457 P.2d 638 (Alaska 1969)
Jaquith v. Commonwealth, 120 N.E.2d 189 (Mass. 1954)
Rose v. Locke, 423 U.S. 48 (1975)

14. A FAILED ATTEMPT TO CHALLENGE A SODOMY LAW

Doe v. Commonwealth's Attorney for City of Richmond, 403 F. Supp. 1199 (E.D. Va. 1975), summarily affirmed without opinion, 425 U.S. 901, rehearing denied, 425 U.S. 985 (1976).

For ten years, the summarily affirmed three-judge district court decision in *Doe v. Commonwealth's Attorney for City of Richmond* was the Supreme Court's official precedent on whether state sodomy laws violated the federal Constitution. The enigma of *Doe v. Commonwealth's Attorney* dominated all discussion of this issue until the Supreme Court's 1986 decision in *Bowers v. Hardwick*.

Doe did not involve an actual prosecution. Several gay activists in Virginia, hoping that the doctrine of sexual privacy newly recognized by the U.S. Supreme Court in *Griswold v. Connecticut* (1965) could be extended to consensual homosexual activity in private, filed a class action suit in the U.S. District Court for the Eastern District of Virginia, contending that Virginia's "crimes against nature" statute violated their constitutional rights. The suit named the chief state prosecutor in the city of Richmond as defendant, and claimed that the threat of prosecution by local officials would violate due process, freedom of expression, and privacy, and would impose a cruel and unusual punishment. Attorneys John D. Grad and Philip J. Hirschkop, of Alexandria, Virginia, represented the plaintiffs. Assistant Attorney General Robert E. Shepherd, Jr., responded on behalf of the Commonwealth of Virginia.

The sodomy law, section 18.1–212 of the Code of Virginia, was first enacted in 1792 and continued in some form throughout the state's history. In its most recent form, it provided:

> If any person shall carnally know in any manner any brute animal, or carnally know any male or female person by the anus or by or with the mouth, or voluntarily submit to such carnal knowledge, he or she shall be guilty of a felony and shall be confined in the penitentiary not less than one year nor more than three years.

Thus, in common with most of the sodomy laws then and still in effect, the law outlawed all anal or oral intercourse, regardless of the sex of the participants, including such intercourse by married couples in private. The plaintiffs hoped that the overbreadth of the statute, intruding into areas clearly covered by the privacy right the Court articulated in *Griswold*, would lead to victory. That an overbreadth challenge was an important part of their strategy was clear from the complaint, which placed heavy emphasis on the First Amendment. The Court has traditionally applied the overbreadth doctrine most freely in First Amendment litigation. The plaintiffs cited the First Amendment as a source of the rights of freedom of expression and privacy, both of which they claimed to be violated by enforcement of the statute. Interestingly, given the grounds stated in the Court's opinion in *Griswold* for striking down the Connecticut law against artificial contraception, the plaintiffs invoked only the First and Ninth amendments in support of their privacy claim, making

a separate due process claim under the Fourteenth Amendment.

Because the suit challenged the constitutionality of a state law, the case was tried to a special three judge court including a member of the U.S. Court of Appeals for the Fourth Circuit, Senior Circuit Judge Albert V. Bryan. The two district court judges were Oren R. Lewis and Robert R. Merhige, Jr. (This procedure, then required by the federal judicial code for such constitutional cases, has since been abandoned.) In their decision announced on October 24, 1975, all three judges agreed that the case failed to meet the standards for class action certification under Rule 23(b)(1)(A) of the Federal Rules of Civil Procedure. Since any decision by the three-judge district court would be directly appealable to the U.S. Supreme Court under relevant federal rules, a resulting decision would be binding on all Virginia prosecutors (and, depending on the outcome of the case, precedentially binding on all law enforcement authorities in the nation), so there was no need to join as parties-plaintiff all gay people in Virginia as the plaintiffs requested.

After this procedural unanimity, however, the panel split over the merits of the case. Judges Bryan and Lewis held that there was no constitutional violation, while Judge Merhige argued strenuously in dissent that the law was clearly unconstitutional as an unjustified restriction on liberty in violation of the Due Process Clause of the Fourteenth Amendment.

Judge Bryan's opinion for the court was based almost entirely on Justice John Marshall Harlan's dissenting opinion in *Poe v. Ullman* (1961), a pre-*Griswold* challenge to Connecticut's contraception law that had failed on procedural grounds. Justice Harlan argued that the case was properly before the Supreme Court and further, in *dicta*, that the Connecticut law violated the protected intimacy of the marital relationship by depriving marital couples of the right to obtain and to use contraceptives in their sexual relations. Rather than argue for a broad right of sexual privacy, Harlan argued narrowly for a right of privacy within the marital relationship, and stressed that the question of state regulation of nonmarital sexuality was not an issue in the case. Indeed, in his dissent Justice Harlan specified that "adultery, homosexuality, and the like are sexual intimacies which the State forbids," and that requiring a husband and wife to answer in criminal court for their private sexual conduct "is surely a very different thing indeed from punishing those who establish intimacies which the law has always forbidden and which can have no claim to social protection." In addition, Justice Harlan observed that state laws regulating sexual activity had long drawn a distinction between sex within and outside the marital relationship, consistently banning fornication, homosexuality, and adultery while specifically licensing sexual intercourse within the marital relationship. Cautioning against misinterpreting his concept of sexual privacy, Harlan reiterated that he "would not suggest that adultery, homosexuality or fornication are immune from criminal enquiry, however privately practiced."

Although Justice Harlan was speaking in dissent, Judge Bryan asserted that his words "were authentically approved in *Griswold*" when they were cited and quoted at length in a concurring opinion by Justice Arthur J. Goldberg. Since the Court did not address the merits in *Poe v. Ullman*, it could not be argued that the Court had there disagreed with Harlan's *dicta*. And, of course, Justice Harlan's stature as a constitutional expositor was invoked as well. In addition, Bryan stressed that the opinion for the Court in *Griswold* by Justice William O. Douglas had specifically described the right protected in that opinion as founded on the marital relation.

Having found that a fundamental sexual privacy right founded on the *Griswold* opinion could extend only to "marriage, home or family life," and asserting without explanation that homosexuality was "obviously" not covered by such a right, Bryan proceeded to analyze the issue under the rational basis test required by the Due Process Clause to sustain all state legislation. Under the rational basis test as provided by Supreme Court precedents up to that time, little more was required to sustain a statute than to show that it was a type of legislation that had frequently been enacted and that some plausible justification could be articulated in its support. For Bryan and Lewis, it was enough to cite the state's interest in "the promotion of morality and decency" and the long, unbroken

history of the prohibition of sodomy by statute in Virginia since 1792. Rejecting any distinction based on the location of the sexual act, Bryan stated that "the State action is simply directed to the suppression of crime, whether committed in public or in private," and that the Supreme Court had, in *California v. LaRue* (1972), held that the location of criminal acts was of no consequence in deciding whether the state could suppress them.

Under the rational basis test, the state was not required to show that homosexuality causes moral delinquency; it was enough to "establish that the conduct is likely to end in a contribution to moral delinquency." Here, Bryan invoked the spectre of *Lovisi v. Slayton*, a case then on appeal to the Fourth Circuit, in which a married couple had advertised their desire to "meet people," had invited a man to join them in sexual activity (including fellatio), and had allowed the wife's teen-age daughters to observe the sexual activity. The Lovisis had set up a camera to record their exploits, and the photographs fell into their daughters' hands and were carried by them to school, thus alerting the authorities and resulting in criminal prosecution. Bryan cited this case as an example of the prohibited conduct leading to moral delinquency. Unmentioned, of course, is that the fellatio in question was heterosexual and had nothing to do with the sort of private conduct between same-sex partners specified in the Doe plaintiffs' complaint.

Finally, Bryan noted that in *Wainwright v. Stone* (1973), the Supreme Court had recently sustained another state's crime-against-nature statute against challenge on grounds of vagueness.

Judge Merhige's dissent sharply disputed the majority's contention that the constitutional right of privacy extended only to marriage, home, or family life. Unlike the majority, which limited its review of Supreme Court precedent to *Griswold* and its predecessor cases, Merhige observed that the Court had subsequently expanded the right of sexual privacy in *Eisenstadt v. Baird* (1972) and *Roe v. Wade* (1973) to apply to issues clearly outside the context of marital sexuality. In *Eisenstadt*, the Court struck down a Massachusetts contraception law that barred the sale of contraceptive devices to unmarried people, and in *Roe*, a case involving an unmarried pregnant woman, the Court held that the state could not criminalize first and second trimester abortions. Both cases were explicitly premised on the right of privacy articulated in *Griswold*, thus, in Merhige's view, implicitly disapproving the more restricted view of privacy Justice Harlan had articulated in his *Poe v. Ullman* dissent. Therefore, for the *Doe* majority to say that the right of privacy was limited to the factual premises of *Griswold* "places a distinction in marital-nonmarital matters which is inconsistent with current Supreme Court opinions," in Merhige's view. He asserted: "In significantly diminishing the importance of the marital-nonmarital distinction, the Court to a great extent vitiated any implication that the State can, as suggested by Mr. Justice Harlan in *Poe v. Ullman*, forbid extra-marital sexuality, and such implications are no longer fully accurate."

Merhige argued that both *Roe v. Wade* and *Eisenstadt*

> cogently demonstrate that intimate personal decisions or private matters of substantial importance to the well-being of the individuals involved are protected by the Due Process Clause. The right to select consenting adult sexual partners must be considered within this category. The exercise of that right, whether heterosexual or homosexual, should not be proscribed by state regulation absent compelling justification.

As to such justification, Merhige noted that the only specific justification advanced by the state was that the prohibition of homosexuality would encourage "new heterosexual marriages and would prevent the dissolution of existing ones." This, Merhige found "unworthy of judicial response. In any event, what we know as men is not forgotten as judges—it is difficult to envision any substantial number of heterosexual marriages being in danger of dissolution because of the private sexual activities of homosexuals."

On the basis of the record before the court, Merhige concluded that the only real state justification was "the promotion of morality and decency." Here, Merhige argued that the Supreme Court's decision in *Stanley v. Georgia* (1969), invalidating a prosecution for private possession of obscene materials, invalidated the promotion of private morality as an adequate justification for interfering with private sexual conduct. In *Stanley*, the Court had emphasized that conduct which could be subject to regulation when performed in public might be protected when performed in private, where the state's only justification for regulation had to do with the promotion of morality rather than with the prevention of harm. Merhige concluded that this precedent removed any constitutionally legitimate justification for Virginia's sodomy law, and that it should be declared violative of the right of privacy under the Due Process Clause.

The plaintiffs appealed the three-judge court opinion directly to the U.S. Supreme Court, as then authorized under federal procedural rules. On March 29, 1976, the Court announced that it was affirming the decision below based on the appeal papers and records. The plaintiffs never had an opportunity to file briefs or to present oral argument to the Court. Three members of the Court disagreed with this method of disposition. Justices William J. Brennan, Jr., Thurgood Marshall, and John Paul Stevens would have provided for briefing and oral argument before deciding the case. On May 19, 1976, the Court denied a petition by the plaintiffs to reconsider its ruling.

Because the Supreme Court summarily affirmed the three-judge court's decision without an opinion, the result was enigmatic. It was unclear whether a majority of the Court agreed with the three-judge court's analysis of the merits or whether the Court was merely treating this case consistently with others around that time in which it was stiffening the standing requirements for declaratory judgment actions against the constitutionality of state and federal statutes. Because none of the plaintiffs alleged that they had personally been threatened with or actually experienced prosecution for consensual sodomy in private, it was arguable that they did not have standing to challenge the law under the more restrictive approach the Court was crafting in the mid-1970s.

For ten years, the enigma of *Doe v. Commonwealth's Attorney* haunted state and federal courts facing challenges to the constitutionality of sodomy laws. The Justices who had disagreed with the Court's manner of dealing with the case fed the enigma by asserting that the Court had not yet decided whether the right of privacy encompassed private, consensual homosexual activity, while others asserted that nonetheless a summary affirmance is a decision on the merits, not a mere denial of review. It was not until the circuit courts split over the precedential significance of *Doe* in the mid-1980s that the Court finally decided to take a sodomy law challenge on the merits. Even then, in deciding *Bowers v. Hardwick*, Justice Byron R. White wrote that it was unnecessary for the Court to deal with the precedential effect of *Doe* because a majority had decided to deal with the constitutional issue on the merits in *Bowers*.

Case References

Bowers v. Hardwick, 478 U.S. 186 (1986)

California v. LaRue, 409 U.S. 109 (1972), rehearing denied, 410 U.S. 948 (1973)

Eisenstadt v. Baird, 405 U.S. 438 (1972)

Griswold v. Connecticut, 381 U.S. 479 (1965)

Lovisi v. Slayton, 363 F. Supp. 620 (E.D. Va. 1973), affirmed, 539 F.2d 349 (4th Cir.), certiorari denied, 429 U.S. 977 (1976)

Poe v. Ullman, 367 U.S. 497 (1961)

Roe v. Wade, 410 U.S. 113, rehearing denied, 410 U.S. 959 (1973)

Stanley v. Georgia, 394 U.S. 557 (1969)

Wainwright v. Stone, 414 U.S. 21 (1973)

15. IS ORAL-GENITAL SEX A "CRIME AGAINST NATURE"?

Rose v. Locke, 423 U.S. 48 (1975), summarily reversing 514 F.2d 570 (6th Cir. 1975). Conviction affirmed below, sub nom. *Locke v. State*, 501 S.W.2d 826 (Tenn. Crim. App.), certiorari denied (Tenn. 1973).

During the 19th century, many of the American states adopted crime-against-nature statutes, codifying the common-law offense derived from the sodomy law passed during the reign of King Henry VIII in 1533. When the old English statute was passed, the only behavior it was intended to condemn was anal intercourse. The American statutes did not specify the actual conduct prohibited, for reasons explained in 1897 by the Illinois Supreme Court:

> It was never the practice to describe the particular manner or the details of the commission of the act, but the offense was treated in the indictment as the abominable crime not fit to be named among Christians. . . . The existence of such an offense is a disgrace to human nature. The legislature has not seen fit to define it further than by the general term, and the records of the courts need not be defiled with the details of different acts which may go to constitute it. A statement of the offense in the language of the statute, or so plainly that its nature may be fully understood by the jury, is all that is required.

This reticence left unclear, however, whether the American statutes were intended solely to deal with anal intercourse, or whether, as urged

by some law enforcement authorities, it should be held more broadly to cover all "unnatural" intercourse (i.e., intercourse other than penile-vaginal intercourse, the argument being made that only penile-vaginal intercourse involved a use of the genitalia consistent with their natural function of reproduction). State courts were divided over the application of their crime-against-nature laws, but prior to the adoption of the Model Penal Code by many jurisdictions beginning in the 1960s, few state legislatures revised their laws to be more specific.

Such vague statutory language lent itself to repeated challenge by criminal defendants. Those who were charged with sex offenses other than anal intercourse frequently argued that their prosecution went beyond the bounds of statutory intent, and that, given the differences in opinion among the various state courts on the scope of crime-against-nature laws, such laws failed to give due warning consistent with the more expansive requirements of the Due Process Clause developed by the U.S. Supreme Court during the term of Chief Justice Earl Warren. In *Wainwright v. Stone* (1973), the

Supreme Court adopted the view that such due process challenges would fail when a state's highest court had previously and repeatedly construed its crime-against-nature law to apply to the particular conduct with which the defendant was charged. The Court held that prior interpretations should be treated as if they had become part of the statutory language, even though that would provide little warning to one reading the statute who was unaware of the court decisions. This objection was probably considered beside the point, since it was assumed that few lay persons read criminal statutes.

In *Rose v. Locke*, the Court encountered the next wrinkle in this problem: what about a situation where the defendant was charged with a sex offense that had never been the subject of a prior judicial construction of the statute? Would it offend due process to convict somebody under a crime-against-nature law when there was no prior construction of the statute that expressly included the charged offense?

One hot summer night in 1972, stirred by lust and longing for his neighbor Minnie R. Rogers, Harold Locke knocked on her door and asked to use her telephone. On gaining admission, he flashed a butcher knife and forced Mrs. Rogers onto her bed, where he proceeded to lick her vagina. Evidently this satisfied Locke's sexual urges of the moment, for he did not go any further. The shaken Mrs. Rogers contacted the police, and Locke was subsequently prosecuted and convicted of crime-against-nature in Knox County, Tennessee, Criminal Court before Judge Richard R. Ford on October 3, 1972. He was sentenced to five to seven years imprisonment under the felony crimes-against-nature statute, which had never previously been held by the Tennessee appellate courts to forbid cunnilingus (oral-vaginal contact).

Locke filed an appeal with the legal assistance of John D. Webb, James W. Bell, and Robert M. Stivers, Jr., Knoxville attorneys, arguing that the law under which he was convicted was unconstitutionally vague. The state fielded a large legal team to defend this application of its statute, including attorneys from the state attorney general's office as well as the local prosecutors from Knoxville, Ronald A. Webster and Lance D. Evans. On October 2,

1973, the Tennessee Court of Criminal Appeals rejected Locke's challenge to the statute in a 2–1 decision.

In his opinion for the court, Judge William Russell noted that the Tennessee Supreme Court had previously held in *Fisher v. State* that fellatio was covered by the law, and had, in *Sherrill v. State* (1959), expressly adopted the approach of the Maine Supreme Court in its 1938 decision, *State v. Cyr*, a landmark in the construction of vague crime-against-nature laws, holding that such a law brings "all unnatural copulation with mankind or a beast, including sodomy, within its scope." Indeed, in a subsequent 1950 decision, *State v. Townsend*, the Maine courts had applied their crime-against-nature law to cunnilingus. This seemed dispositive to Russell; "It would be a paradox of legal construction to say that fellatio, 'which in common language means sexual perversion committed with the male sexual organ and the mouth,' *Sherrill v. State, supra*, is proscribed as a crime against nature, but cunnilingus is not," insisted Russell.

While conceding that some state courts had strictly limited their crime-against-nature laws to the common-law offense of sodomy—anal intercourse—the majority had read their laws more broadly. In 1972, the Tennessee Court of Criminal Appeals had said in *Stephens v. State* that the Tennessee courts "probably accept the broader meaning since they have held that the proscribed acts may be per os as well as per anus." Without further explanation, Russell held that the law as written was not "unconstitutionally vague and indefinite." He did note that the court's decision should not be construed as expressing any view regarding the constitutionality of the law as applied to "the private acts of married couples" or "the application of the statute to consenting adults."

Judge Charles Galbreath dissented, arguing that the Tennessee laws on sex offenses needed to be modernized so as to describe accurately the conduct being prohibited. Surveying existing state laws, he found that fewer than half of the states had crime-against-nature laws. Two such laws had been declared unconstitutional recently on due process grounds, and of the ten states that had ruled on coverage of cunnilingus under such laws, the majority had held that cunnilingus "is not a form of sodomy." Of more significance to Galbreath, however, was the lack of specificity in the statute. Characterizing himself as a "strict constructionist," he asserted: "To hold that cunnilingus (an act approved by almost 90% of adults between 18 and 34 according to an exhaustive study) is a crime would seem to me to be judicial legislation of the plainest kind."

Galbreath noted that the Tennessee Supreme Court had once specifically held that when a statute is based on the common law, the courts had to look to the common law to determine the elements of the offense. This decided the case for him because under the common law the offense of crime-against-nature required penetration of the anus by the penis, and cunnilingus did not involve the penis. Indeed, the court of criminal appeals, in upholding the crime-against-nature law against a vagueness attack in *Stephens v. State*, had specifically relied on the fact that "the crime is well defined and described at common law," and had asserted: "There is no danger that some kind of sexual perversion apart from unnatural carnal copulation, unnatural sexual intercourse, could be embraced in the definition and description as plaintiff in error contends." Well, here was the danger. Now, the court of criminal appeals had gone beyond the common-law definition. This was "a direct refutation of what this Court said in *Stephens*," said Galbreath, "and points up the danger inherent in judicial legislation." He continued:

Where do we stop if we decree that any form of sexual activity is the equivalent of copulation or sexual intercourse so as to be unlawful if not confined to penis-vaginal connection? Even if we had the authority to legislate on the subject, where would we draw the line? Would we go so far as has the legislature of Indiana which has proscribed masturbation or self-pollution and thus condemned a practice that is so universally accepted now as normal under certain circumstances that the mature person who has never engaged in this type of activity would in all likelihood be considered biologically quite abnormal? I, for one, would certainly insist that such legislation proscribe, as do the Penal Codes of New York, Minnesota and Washington, what I personally consider the most loathsome, degrading and vile sexual activity imaginable, i.e., necrophilia or sexual intercourse with a dead body. The fact that neither of these acts [i.e., masturbation and necrophilia], the first of which must be conceded to be rather mild and innocuous, the second of which so horrible as to be repugnant to all but the most depraved, have as yet been legislated against in Tennessee might be a source of regret to some, but still the fact exists.

This did not mean that Galbreath felt Locke should not be prosecuted for something. After all, it was appropriate to punish somebody for forcing himself sexually upon another by threats and coercion, but existing statutes dealing with assault and battery were sufficient for that purpose. Galbreath also conceded that there was a role for the state to play in forbidding various forms of sex with minors. But the sex crimes laws should be clarified to specify exactly what was prohibited. "Surely we have progressed some from the dim past when Lord Coke spoke of sodomy as being 'a detestable and abominable sin among Christians not to be named,'" he said, "although affirmation here would seem to be a regression since not even Lord Coke and his fellow English jurists through the centuries have felt it legally permissible to include cunnilingus, or even fellatio, within the definition of sodomy." After quoting the Illinois Supreme Court's 1897 explanation of why the crime-against-nature law was not more specific, Galbreath argued that these reasons would not stand up to contemporary scrutiny:

This reason seems to suggest two fallacies to me. Firstly, that sodomy is the most abhorrent of all crimes, so much so that it may not even be defined in writing. Any person who believes that sodomy is more abhorrent than murder, which is sharply defined by statute, in my opinion has a misplaced sense of priority. Secondly, the attitude of the Maine Court, now adopted by the majority, seems to be "everyone knows what a crime against nature is, so why spell it out?" In the first place there have been so many disagreements as to what constitutes the offense that such reasoning falls under its own weight. (The legal paradox mentioned by the majority has not prevented some few states, at least two, from holding that while fellatio is proscribed as a crime against nature, cunnilingus is not [citations omitted].) Secondly, if there is no need to define this offense, why should it be necessary to define every other offense in our statutes exacting penal sanction? Are arson, rape, robbery, burglary, forgery, etc. so little understood that they must be carefully defined while the never before in this State judicially encountered activity involved here is so familiar to all that one accused of committing a "crime against nature" must of necessity know what he is supposed to have done so as to be able to prepare a defense?

Galbreath concluded that the action should be remanded for retrial on a charge of aggravated assault and battery. Hoping that this dissent would persuade the state supreme court, Locke petitioned for *certiorari*, but his petition was denied on November 5, 1973, and Locke reported to the authorities to serve his prison term. But hope sprung eternal, and he filed a petition for a writ of *habeas corpus* in the U.S. District Court for the Eastern District of Tennessee, once again arguing (*pro se*) that his conviction violated due process for two reasons: first, the statute was unconstitutionally vague and overbroad, and second, he had been convicted on the uncorroborated testimony of the victim. District Judge Robert L. Taylor, Jr., denied relief in an unpublished order relying on the Supreme Court's recent decision in *Wainwright v. Stone*, and Locke appealed to the U.S. Court of Appeals for the Sixth Circuit, where he obtained assistance of appointed counsel, Ray Lee Jenkins. The state appeared to defend its statute by Assistant Attorneys General Bart C. Durham, III, R. A. Ashley, Jr., and E. R. Trotter.

Locke found a friendlier reception in the Sixth Circuit, where the three-judge panel of Circuit Judges George C. Edwards, Jr., John W. Peck, and Pierce Lively unanimously held that his conviction was unconstitutional in a *per curiam* opinion issued April 4, 1975. Why a *per curiam* opinion rather than an opinion attributed by name to one of the judges? Courts issue *per curiam* opinions most often when the case requires little more than a brief application of existing precedent with no significant analysis. But sometimes they resort to this device, even though some analysis is required, where none of the judges wants to be personally associated with the opinion. Could the same Victorian sensibilities about discussing sex in public have led these three judges to avoid associating themselves personally with a pub-lished, public discussion of fellatio and cunnilingus?

Having to consider the precedential effect of the Supreme Court's decision in *Wainwright*, the court said that in its view *Wainwright* did not decide this case. There, the Supreme Court had held that a crime-against-nature law should be read as if all prior state court interpretations had become part of the statute, so that application of the law to a man charged with the offense of fellatio did not offend due process where the Florida courts had repeatedly applied the law to fellatio in the past. That was not this case, because the Tennessee courts had apparently never previously applied their crime-against-nature law to cunnilingus.

The *per curiam* opinion rejected Tennessee's argument that prior interpretations of the statute gave fair warning that cunnilingus would be covered by the law. Although the Tennessee courts in *Sherrill* had adopted the so-called liberal construction of the Maine courts deriving from *State v. Cyr, Cyr* was a fellatio case. "Moreover, *Sherrill* failed to cite *State v. Townsend*, which applied the Maine statute to cunnilingus," the court remarked. But even had the *Sherrill* court cited *Townsend*, "such citation most likely would still have failed in putting 'men of common intelligence' on notice of the court's cunnilingus-reaching interpretation." It just stretched due process too far to state that a vague law could be made constitutional by references to decisions in other states construing their vague laws.

In *Stephens*, which the opinion described as "the Tennessee courts' most candid attempt at outlining the scope" of the crime-against-nature law, the court had clearly said that the law should be construed by reference to the common-law offense of "sodomy," and that the courts of the state would "probably" follow the "broader" interpretation of sodomy, thus applying the statute to include fellatio. As far as the Sixth Circuit panel was concerned, even following the "broader view" of what comprised "sodomy" did not give "fair warning . . . of the proscription of cunnilingus." Consequently, the district court was reversed and the case was remanded to the Criminal Court of Knox County for further appropriate proceedings, which the court suggested might be "a prosecution for aggravated assault and battery." If the state did not initiate such proceedings within sixty days of the remand, the writ of *habeas corpus* should be issued and Locke should be discharged from prison.

The state was not about to take this lying down, and it immediately petitioned the U.S. Supreme Court for a writ of *certiorari*. Locke, who did not have an attorney to represent him in the Supreme Court, had filed a motion seeking to defend on his own. Apparently considering this case a mere extension of *Wainwright*, a majority of the Court decided that reversal was required and that neither full briefing on the merits nor oral argument was necessary to the determination. On November 17, 1975, the Court issued an order summarily reversing the Sixth Circuit's decision. Three members of the Court strongly disagreed with this disposition however, with Justices William J. Brennan, Jr., and Potter Stewart writing dissents, both of which Justice Thurgood Marshall joined. Having dissenting argument on the published record accusing the Court of virtual malpractice in its disposition of the case naturally provoked a lengthy *per curiam* opinion of justification from the Court, resulting in the somewhat unusual circumstance of a summary disposition accompanied by lengthy explanation.

The Court's *per curiam* opinion is no model of logic. Asserting that "[a]ll the Due Process Clause requires is that the law give sufficient warning that men may conduct themselves so as to avoid that which is forbidden," the Court insisted that such warning had been given by the state of Tennessee. "[The] phrase 'crime against nature' is no more vague than many other terms used to describe criminal offenses at common law and now codified in state and federal penal codes," the Court insisted. "The phrase has been in use among English-speaking people for many centuries . . . , and a substantial number of jurisdictions in this country continue to utilize it. Anyone who cared to do so could certainly determine what particular acts have been considered crimes against nature, and there can be no contention that the respondent's acts were ones never before considered as such." This argument, of course, assumed that if any state court anywhere had held that cunnilingus was a crime against nature, that interpretation

became part of Tennessee's statute. Given the independent and autonomous development of state law, such an argument was patently ridiculous.

The Court also rejected the suggestion that a "broad" definition of crime-against-nature was inherently "impermissibly vague," but that, of course, was not really Locke's argument. Engaging in a bit of revisionism, the Court revisited its opinion in *Wainwright v. Stone* and gave it a new reading not suggested by its original language:

> The Court of Appeals, relying on language in *Stone*, apparently believed these cases turned upon the fact that the state courts had previously construed their statutes to cover the same acts with which the defendants therein were charged. But although *Stone* demonstrated that the existence of previous applications of a particular statute to one set of facts forecloses lack-of-fair-warning challenges to subsequent prosecutions of factually identical conduct, it did not hold that such applications were a prerequisite to a statute's withstanding constitutional attack. If that were the case it would be extremely difficult ever to mount an effective prosecution based upon the broader of two reasonable constructions of newly enacted or previously unapplied statutes, even though a neighboring jurisdiction had been applying the broader construction of its identically worded provision for years.

Exactly, would reply the court of appeals and dissenting Justice Galbreath of Tennessee! It should not be up to judges to have to guess whether particular conduct was within the intent of the legislature when a statute uses language so vague and the decisions by judges in neighboring jurisdictions have no controlling weight in that determination. Each state has its own authority under the police power to describe the crimes it seeks to punish.

In this case, the Court believed it was sufficient that the Tennessee courts had previously embraced the "Maine approach," and that using this approach, the Maine courts had found cunnilingus to be forbidden by its crime-against-nature law. "[We] think the Tennessee Supreme Court had given sufficiently clear notice that [the crime-against-nature law] would receive the broader of two plausible interpretations, and would be applied to acts such as those committed here when such a case arose." The Court found this case distinguishable from another case relied on by the Sixth Circuit, *Bouie v. City of Columbus* (1964), in which the Supreme Court had found a due process violation when a court had expanded a relatively specific statute to punish conduct not previously believed to be within its scope. Here, said the Court, other states had construed language, admittedly vague standing alone, to include the conduct charged against Locke, so the analogy to *Bouie* was false. Furthermore, since the Tennessee Supreme Court had indicated in the past that it would give the law a "broad" reading, and "there was nothing to indicate, clearly or otherwise, that respondent's acts were outside the scope" of the law, there was "no possibility of retroactive lawmaking here."

This opinion drew a sharp-tongued dissent from Justice Brennan, joined by Justice Marshall. He argued that the Court had stood "on its head" the traditional test of vagueness, to supplant it with "a test of whether there is anything in the statute 'to indicate, clearly or otherwise, that respondent's acts were outside the scope of' the statute." These "extraordinary distortions of the principle that the Due Process Clause prohibits the States from holding an individual criminally responsible for conduct when the statute did not give fair warning that the conduct was criminal, are perpetrated without plenary review affording the parties an opportunity to brief and argue the issues orally," noted Brennan, exclaiming: "It is difficult to recall a more patent instance of judicial irresponsibility." Brennan continued:

> I simply cannot comprehend how the fact that one state court has judicially construed its otherwise vague criminal statute to include particular conduct can, without explicit adoption of that state court's construction by the courts of the charging State, render an uninterpreted statute of the latter State also sufficiently concrete to withstand a charge of unconstitutional vagueness.

Brennan found this holding to fly in the face of the Court's prior due process precedents.

Brennan also found the Court's discussion of the particular merits of Locke's argument regarding prior Tennessee cases to be incompetent. While the Tennessee courts had cited *Cyr*, the Maine decision upholding its sodomy

law as applied to fellatio, they had never previously cited *Townsend*, the Maine cunnilingus case. Brennan stated:

> Despite this significant failure of the Tennessee court to cite *Townsend*, and solely on the strength of the Tennessee court's general "equating" of the Maine statute with the Tennessee statute, this Court holds today that respondent had sufficient notice that the Tennessee statute would receive a "broad" interpretation that would embrace cunnilingus.

Characterizing this as a "1974 attempt to bootstrap 1950 Maine law for the first time into the Tennessee statute," Brennan asserted that it "must obviously fail if the principle of fair warning is to have any meaning."

Brennan also disputed the Court's "assumption that the 'broad interpretation' of the phrase 'crime against nature' is not unconstitutionally vague," since neither the *per curiam* opinion in *Wainwright v. Stone* nor the Court's dismissal of another vagueness case, *Crawford v. Missouri* (1972), was on point. In both cases, either prior judicial construction or legislative action had made it plausible to assert that at the time of the charged offense, there was "fair warning" that it was covered by the otherwise vague statutory language. That was just not the case here. Brennan argued that the requirement of "sufficient warning" in criminal statutes was "one of the great bulwarks of our scheme of constitutional liberty." "The Court's erosion today of that great principle without even plenary review reaches a dangerous level of judicial irresponsibility," he reiterated. Although he would have denied the petition for *certiorari*, since it had been granted by a majority of the Court, he would have affirmed the Sixth Circuit, or at least set the case for full briefing and argument before reaching a decision.

Justice Stewart's dissent lacked the passion of Brennan's, briefly noting that this case was "not of a piece with *Wainwright v. Stone*" because "the Tennessee courts had never ruled that the act that Locke was found to have committed was covered by the vague and cryptic language of the Tennessee statute." Neither the Maine Supreme Court decision in *Cyr* nor the Tennessee decision in *Stephens* would have given fair warning that cunnilingus was covered by the Tennessee law. Observing that Locke could be prosecuted under other laws, Stewart said he thought the Sixth Circuit was correct in holding that the Tennessee law was "unconstitutionally vague as here applied."

When it was issued, the Court's opinion in *Wainwright v. Stone* appeared to be rather narrow, in upholding crime-against-nature laws against vagueness attacks in instances where the defendant was charged with an offense that had previously (and repeatedly) been held by the state courts to be covered by the statute. The Court's opinion in *Locke*, however, widened the *Wainwright* holding to such a degree that future attacks on crime-against-nature laws from a vagueness perspective were virtually precluded. So long as a state's courts had previously indicated that their crime-against-nature law was subject to a broad interpretation, the Supreme Court seemed to be saying, a person charged with a sexual offense could not be heard to complain if the courts of another state had held the conduct charged to be within the scope of such a statute. Since there is enough case law under crime-against-nature laws for such "precedent" to be found for almost any kind of act that might be prosecuted under such laws, this

would virtually preclude vagueness challenges, unless the Court's opinion is strictly read to deal with instances where the courts of the charging state had at some time referred approvingly to the general approach taken by the courts of the state whose decision was now being cited as precedent. This convoluted approach to statutory interpretation is quite strange, and unlike the approach taken in any other area of law, suggests that the Court was implicitly adopting a special doctrine to deal with sex crimes laws. This reflects yet again the way laws dealing with sex seem to exist apart from many of the basic precepts of the U.S. legal system.

Case References

Bouie v. City of Columbus, 378 U.S. 347 (1964)

Crawford v. Missouri, 409 U.S. 811 (1972)

Fisher v. State, 197 Tenn. 594, 277 S.W.2d 340 (1955)

Sherrill v. State, 204 Tenn. 427, 321 S.W.2d 811 (1959)

State v. Cyr, 135 Me. 513, 198 A. 743 (1938)

State v. Townsend, 145 Me. 384, 71 A.2d 517 (1950)

Stephens v. State, 489 S.W.2d 542 (Tenn. Crim. App. 1972), certiorari denied (Tenn. 1973)

Wainwright v. Stone, 414 U.S. 21 (1973)

16. IS A "SODOMOUS" MÉNAGE À TROIS "PRIVATE"?

Lovisi v. Slayton, 539 F.2d 349 (4th Cir.) (en banc), certiorari denied sub nom. *Lovisi v. Zahradnick*, 429 U.S. 977 (1976), affirming 363 F. Supp. 620 (E.D. Va. 1973).

Aldo and Margaret Lovisi loved sexual adventure. They lived together in Virginia Beach with Margaret's two teen-age daughters from a previous marriage. The Lovisis sought out additional sexual partners and photographed their exploits. Eschewing the puritanical limitations of sex crimes laws, they included oral sex in their active repertory. They apparently had lots of fun until one of the girls found a sexually explicit photograph and brought it to school, stimulating litigation in the federal courts over whether a photographically documented *ménage à trois* that included oral sex could conceivably be covered by the constitutional right to pri-

vacy. Despite a sharply split *en banc* Fourth Circuit decision, the U.S. Supreme Court wanted nothing to do with this case!

In search of new partners, the Lovisis placed an advertisement in *Swinger's Life*, which Earl Romeo Dunn, a Jamaican native, answered. Dunn and the Lovisis really hit it off after first meeting in March 1969. The sex was so good that they got together three times altogether, the last an extended occasion that included a trip by the three to New York and back to Virginia Beach, where they topped things off with an enthusiastic session during which Margaret performed fellatio on both Aldo and Earl, and

Polaroid snapshots were taken to save the moments! This happy *ménage* might have continued had not Carolyn and Eugenia Acree, Margaret's daughters, brought a Polaroid snapshot to school showing one of the girls seated naked next to an equally unclad man. Alarmed school authorities confiscated the photograph and convened a meeting in the principal's office with the two girls, welfare officials, police officers, and Margaret Lovisi. The girls told the police officer that there were many pictures like that at home. The police obtained a search warrant and found in the Lovisi home literally hundreds of Polaroid snapshots, many of them depicting sexual activity, as well as numerous books and films with similarly explicit sexual content. Among the treasure horde were the Polaroids documenting the last tryst with Dunn, which the girls claimed credit for taking themselves, an assertion furiously denied by the Lovisis.

The Virginia Beach prosecutor now had a juicy little sex scandal to exploit. Dunn was deported back to Jamaica and Aldo and Margaret were prosecuted for sodomy and for corrupting the morals of Margaret's children. There was much contention in the trial as to the actual facts, including allegations by the police that sexy photographs were found all over the apartment while Aldo insisted he kept the really sexy ones locked up in a gun case. There was evidence that the gun case lock had been tampered with, however. The Lovisis also strenuously denied that the girls had ever been present during their sexual activities with Dunn. At any rate, the Lovisis were convicted on all counts and sentenced to two years imprisonment for committing sodomy with each other, while Margaret drew an additional three years for committing sodomy with Dunn. They appealed their convictions through the Virginia courts, contending that the sodomy law was unconstitutional on its face and as applied to them, but their claims were rejected at all levels and the U.S. Supreme Court refused to review their convictions.

After exhausting their direct appeals and reporting to the prison authorities, the Lovisis filed a petition for a writ of *habeas corpus* with the federal district court in Richmond, naming as defendant the state penitentiary superinten-dent, A. E. Slayton, Jr., alleging that their imprisonment deprived them of liberty without due process of law because the statute under which they were imprisoned was unconstitutional in forbidding sodomy between husband and wife. Two American Civil Liberty Union attorneys, Richard E. Crouch of Washington, and David Thelen, of Richmond, argued on their behalf. Virginia Assistant Attorney General Robert E. Shepherd, Jr., appeared in defense of the statute and the convictions.

District Judge Robert R. Merhige, Jr., determined that the state court trial left some unresolved factual issues and held a factual hearing on July 27, 1973, at which the Lovisis and other witnesses testified. On August 31, 1973, Merhige issued an opinion holding that the convictions of the Lovisis were constitutional and denying their application for the writ of *habeas corpus*.

Merhige expressed significant reservations about the constitutionality of the Virginia sodomy law in his opinion. (Indeed, in a subsequent case, *Doe v. Commonwealth's Attorney for City of Richmond* (1975), Merhige would vehemently argue in dissent that the sodomy law was unconstitutional as applied to consenting homosexuals conducting their activities in seclusion.) After disposing of procedural issues in the case, such as the purportedly binding effect of the Supreme Court having previously refused to consider a direct appeal of the Lovisis' convictions, Merhige initiated his discussion of the constitutional issues by noting that the Supreme Court had as of that time developed a firmly established theory of marital privacy that would ordinarily protect a married couple's choice of sexual activities when carried out in the privacy of their relationship, secluded from observation by others. While the Court had recognized the sanctity of the family in a variety of contexts drawn from different sections of the Bill of Rights and the Fourteenth Amendment, Merhige found the strongest basis for sexual privacy in marriage in the Court's contraception, marriage, and abortion decisions. He especially noted *Griswold v. Connecticut* (1965), *Loving v. Virginia* (1967), and *Roe v. Wade* (1973), with particular emphasis on Justice John Marshall Harlan's dissenting opinion in *Poe v. Ullman* (1961) and concurring opinion in *Griswold.* Harlan had focused on the Due Process Clause of the Fourteenth Amendment as a source of protection for "fundamental human values 'implicit in the concept of ordered liberty,'" which Merhige characterized as "the preferred view." "While other provisions of the Bill of Rights certainly give guidance to what values are to be so enumerated," he said, "the Court would be less than candid if it did not recognize that the process of defining those values represents at least in part a return to the ancient, if somewhat discredited, concept of natural law." Merhige emphasized Justice Harlan's assertion in dissent in *Poe,* that in the "whole 'private realm of family life' it is difficult to imagine what is more private or intimate than a husband and wife's marital relations. . . ." Clearly, a law that limited the married couple's choice of how they engaged in sex with each other would have to meet a stiff constitutional test.

Two elements of this case, however, added factors not clearly covered by the Supreme Court's sexual privacy opinions: the Lovisis had committed sodomy in the presence of a third person, Dunn, and had documented their acts photographically, allowing the photographs to come into the possession of Margaret's daughters, whence they ultimately found their way into the public domain, as it were. Could it credibly be argued that the aura of constitutional privacy still surrounded Margaret and Aldo's fellatious activities under the circumstances?

Merhige thought not. The defendants had "voluntarily relinquished the privacy that would normally have surrounded their acts," he said. While it was clear that the Virginia sodomy law "regulates no less than the actual form of sexual expression between husband and wife" and as such "doubtless threatens an invasion of the right to privacy," Merhige found that "the relations in this case were not private" and concluded that "the Lovisis have no right which they can assert. Their conduct was not constitutionally protected." He reached this result because he found that the element of "seclusion" was an essential part of the Court's rationale in protecting actual sexual conduct. While acknowledging that there were occasions when the sexual privacy focused on choice rather than

on location, such as the abortion issue, Merhige believed that when it came to constitutional protection for sexual activity, the activity must be conducted in a secluded manner as a "necessary prerequisite to that act's being protected from state regulation by the Constitution."

Surprisingly, however, Merhige reached the conclusion that the Lovisis had waived their right to privacy on this occasion not on the basis of Dunn's participation, but rather on the basis of the photographs. "It may be that Dunn, as a willing participant, was within the ambit of privacy protected by the Constitution." Dunn was a consenting adult, too, and in *Eisenstadt v. Baird* (1972) the Supreme Court had made clear that the private sexual activities of unmarried persons also had some element of protection. The only prosecution before him for review involved Margaret performing fellatio on Aldo, and as to that, the presence of another consenting adult did not bother Merhige unduly. Indeed, although he disbelieved their testimony about being present, Merhige suggested that even had the teen-age daughters been in the room, that would not necessarily have breached the requisite seclusion requirement. What concerned Merhige was that "the Lovisis took photographs of their sexual acts and then allowed these photographs to fall into their children's hands."

To secure constitutional protection for their otherwise private sexual activities, said Merhige, the Lovisis had to take appropriate steps to make sure that those activities did not become a matter of public knowledge. By photographing the activities and then failing to take care that the photographs remained private, the Lovisis had voluntarily sacrificed their claim to privacy protection:

> By electing to photograph their sexual relations, thus creating the possibility that the intimacy of their acts would be destroyed by future viewing by others, the Lovisis took upon themselves an especially heavy burden to protect their privacy. They did not meet that burden, the Court concludes, because of their failure to deny other persons access to the photographs.

That the teen-age daughters could gain access to the photographs and take one to school suggested that the Lovisis had not taken appropriate care to keep the photographs secluded. Indeed, one of the police officers who executed the search warrant testified at Merhige's hearing that "thousands of photographs were to be found all over the house," from which Merhige drew the conclusion that "the photos were freely available throughout the house to whomever lived there."

The Lovisis had argued, nonetheless, that since the sodomy law was clearly unconstitutional as applied to other heterosexual couples, married or otherwise, who carried on their activities in private, it could not be used to prosecute them. Merhige concluded that they did not have standing to make such an argument, since the photographs provided a significant distinguishing factor in their case. While it was true that in a limited range of cases, the Supreme Court had allowed litigants to raise constitutional challenges to statutes which could constitutionally be applied to their own conduct but which were facially unconstitutional as applied to others, Merhige believed that this was not an appropriate case for such an extension of standing. "The principal question surrounding this type of standing," he said, "is whether the party seeking to challenge an action or statute alleges that it is his rights which have been violated or rather those of some other party." Since the Virginia sodomy law would be unconstitutional only as applied to truly private activity, asserted Merhige, it was clear that the Lovisis were trying to assert other's rights, the rights of those who strived to maintain the privacy of their sexual activities. And sodomy laws such as Virginia's broadly phrased to apply to all acts of sodomy, whether public or private, were mainly used to punish those whose acts came to light due to inadequate seclusion, such as the Lovisis, so the law might in this sense be characterized as constitutional in the vast majority of its intended applications. Consequently, Merhige refused to treat this as an abstract attack on the statute due to the Lovisis' lack of standing to raise such an attack.

The case caused quite a commotion when the Lovisis appealed to the U.S. Court of Appeals for the Fourth Circuit, where argument was held on November 11, 1975. Court-appointed counsel Harvey Bines and Richard Crouch received *amicus* assistance from the American Civil Liberties Union. To judge by the resulting published opinions, it seems likely that the initial three-judge panel was inclined to reverse Merhige's opinion and grant the writ of *habeas corpus*, but a majority of the full circuit would not agree to that result and ordered resubmission of the matter for *en banc* consideration. On May 12, 1976, Chief Judge Clement F. Haynsworth, Jr., announced the *en banc* majority's affirmance of Merhige's decision. Three members of the Circuit were in strong dissent, with opinions from Circuit Judges Harrison L. Winter and J. Braxton Craven, Jr., each of whom joined the other's dissent and both of whom were joined by Circuit Judge H. Emory Butzner, Jr.

Haynsworth's opinion avoided the subtleties of Merhige's analysis and focused on the presence of Dunn as the deciding factor in exposing the Lovisis's conduct to state prosecution. Without much explanation, Haynsworth stated the court's agreement with Merhige's conclusion that the constitutional right of privacy as developed by the Supreme Court would protect "the marital intimacies shared by the Lovisis when alone and in their own bedroom. . . . What they do in the privacy of the marital boudoir is beyond the power of the state to scrutinize," he said, but the question the court faced was "whether they preserve any right of privacy when they admit others to observe their intimacies." Married couples could not be punished for talking about their private sex acts or for writing about them, even if they recounted them in explicit detail. "State law protects them from unwelcome intruders, and the federal constitution protects them from the state in the guise of an unwelcome intruder." But the federal constitutional protection extended only to circumstances where a right of privacy "may reasonably be expected," Haynsworth insisted, and that expectation was not reasonable once "a married couple admits strangers as onlookers." Regardless of the number in the "audience," "if the couple performs sexual acts for the excitation or gratification of welcome onlookers, they cannot selectively claim that the state is an intruder." Evidently, for Haynsworth, an invitation to one was an invitation to the world. Even "close friends" would break the bonds of marital seclusion if present during sex between the happy couple. Regardless how many or who was admitted, "the married couple has welcomed a stranger to the marital bedchamber, and what they do is no longer in the privacy of their marriage."

Haynsworth added a brief addendum to his opinion, commenting that after it was prepared but before it could be filed, the Supreme Court had announced its decision to affirm summarily the three-judge district court opinion upholding the Virginia sodomy statute in *Doe v. Commonwealth's Attorney*. While that constitutional challenge had only considered the law's application to homosexual conduct, one would infer that the Court probably intended its sexual privacy cases to protect conduct only within the marital relationship, suggested Haynsworth. "At least it reinforces our conclusion that the oral sexual activity of the Lovisis in the presence of Dunn and a camera was not within the area of the constitution's protection."

The two dissenting opinions were quite spirited. Judge Winter asserted, on behalf of his dissenting colleagues, that "we reject . . . the majority's implied premise that this marital right of privacy is restricted to those situations in which it is enjoyed in secret. In this regard, the majority's opinion is unsupported either by reason or by authority." For Winter, the question was relatively simple: could the state of Virginia tell a married couple, Aldo and Margaret Lovisi, what they could do in bed with each other in their bedroom? The presence of Dunn or a camera was irrelevant to this basic question. The only question properly before the court was whether married people could have oral sex with each other. After reviewing the Supreme Court precedents on sexual privacy within marriage, Winter stated:

> From these cases we would conclude that certainly within the marital relationship, and perhaps in some instances even without, the nature and kind of consensual sexual intimacy is beyond the power of the state to regulate or even to inquire. If the state may not restrict marital sexual relations to those whose object or risk is that of procreation, *Griswold, supra*, we think that the state is powerless to brand as sodomitic other consensual sexual practices within the marital relationship.

Winter rejected the contention that such a right of privacy was contingent on secrecy, because the right had a broader derivation than

the Fourth Amendment, under which the "reasonable expectation of privacy" analysis had been developed. If one carefully examined the factual contexts of many of the privacy cases, one noted that they involved third parties in many cases. In *Roe v. Wade*, for example, the privacy right to choose abortion and carry the choice through necessarily involved the woman, her doctor, and any attending health care workers. In *Griswold* and *Eisenstadt*, family planning advocates could participate with the individual woman or the marital couple in discussing and advocating birth control and demonstrating the use of contraceptive devices. From these cases, the dissenters "conclude that secrecy is not a necessary element of the right and that therefore the right exists, whether or not exercised in secret." Winter expressed puzzlement at how the majority reached a contrary conclusion, noting that it was "unsupported by any authority; nor do we think it supported by reason." Continuing, Winter stated:

> The majority assumes that the Lovisis have a constitutional right to practice marital sodomy in secret, and further suggests that this right would not be lost or "waived" if they talked or wrote about their sexual activities. Presumably, this protection would extend to non-obscene but explicit photographs and movies even if sold on a commercial basis; yet, if a husband and wife were to seek certain types of medical help in an attempt to save a marriage endangered by sexual maladjustment, or if due to economic necessity, or for any other reason, they share a bedroom with other family members, under the majority's holding the state may prosecute them for certain types of consensual marital acts. Surely these absurd results suggest that the presence of Dunn is irrelevant to the question before us. What would not be punishable sodomy in Dunn's absence is not rendered punishable sodomy by his presence, although his presence may, of course, give rise to other prosecution for other crimes.

Winter noted that the dissenters would be of another view if the Lovisis were prosecuted expressly for performing a sex act in public, where the public nature of the act was "the gravamen of the offense." What they objected to was the notion that the Lovisis could be prosecuted for "sodomy," where the "gravamen of the offense" was the particular body parts coming into contact, a matter as to which they believed the state had no legitimate concern, at least when a husband and wife were concerned.

Winter also commented unfavorably on Haynsworth's brief addendum referencing the Supreme Court's affirmance in *Doe v. Commonwealth's Attorney*. A summary affirmance provided no basis for the kind of speculation in which Haynsworth had engaged. Until the Supreme Court actually spoke to the merits of the issue, nobody could know exactly what its views might be of the application of a sodomy statute to a heterosexual couple. The case was precedential only with regard to homosexual sodomy.

Circuit Judge Craven was even more insistent in his dissenting opinion, asserting that "it is dangerous to withdraw from any citizen the protection of the Constitution because he or she is amoral, immoral, or just plain nasty." For Craven, it was clear that this case was not about group sex or "sexual activity, deviant or otherwise, in public." What the Lovisis were attacking was the ability of Virginia to make "their conduct *with each other while married* criminal— whether or not in public and without regard to the presence or participation of a third person." The majority opinion went off the track by focusing on irrelevancies, constituting "a narrative of the sort to be found in 'adult' bookstores." Had the case been properly tried in the Virginia courts, most of this "sordid story" would not even appear in the record, "because Dunn's participation is irrelevant and highly prejudicial to the question of the Lovisis' guilt of a violation of Virginia's crime against nature by their conduct *with each other*. Just as a jury cannot forget such evidence erroneously received, neither, apparently, can we." Under the Virginia law, the only question was which body parts came into contact, and the ability of Virginia to decree which body parts may come into contact between a married couple was the only legitimate issue in the case, insisted Craven.

Part of the problem may have been the nomenclature used by the courts in describing the right at issue here. The term "privacy," which does not appear in the Constitution, is a convenient but misleading shorthand for what was intended. Craven quoted from a speech recently given by the leading constitutional scholar, Professor Paul Freund, of Harvard, at a meeting of the American Law Institute:

> The theme of personhood is . . . emerging. It has been groping, I think, for a rubric. Sometimes it is called privacy, inaptly it would seem to me; autonomy perhaps, though that seems too dangerously broad. But the idea is that of personhood in the sense of those attributes of an individual which are irreducible in his selfhood. We all know the agonizing judgments that have had to be made and that will have to be made in such diverse areas as abortion and the death penalty, which it seems to me are aspects of this issue of personhood.

To Craven, "privacy" meant "the right to be let alone," drawn from Justice Louis D. Brandeis's famous dissent in *Olmstead v. United States* (1928), or Freund's concept of "personhood." Either way, Craven found it unclear

> why the Lovisis forfeit their right to be let alone in their conjugal relationship because they allowed a third person to be present. The only valid reason I can think of is a moral value judgment that deviant sex is so odious that not even the Constitution may be successfully interposed to protect a husband and wife so despicably disposed. However right the court may be as to morals, I do not believe it to be a proper principle of constitutional law. If there is any more fundamental right of personhood than the conjugal relationship of husband and wife, it does not occur to me. I do not believe it to be within the power of the state to make consensual physical contact between husband and wife criminal; and when convictions are predicated upon that fact alone, the writ must issue.

What the court had really done in this case, suggested Craven, was to amend the indictment "so as to charge the Lovisis with lewd and lascivious behavior in the presence of another and indecent exposure." Craven would agree that they were guilty of both these offenses (which, incidentally, are mere misdemeanors in most jurisdictions), but that was not what they were prosecuted for: felony sodomy, for which they drew multiyear prison sentences. The court should not now validate "convictions of offenses not charged," Craven angrily concluded.

On November 29, 1976, the Supreme Court denied a petition from the Lovisis to review the decision by the Fourth Circuit.

The opinion in *Lovisi v. Slayton* is frequently cited as authority for the proposition that any constitutional protection for the privacy of sexual activity will extend only to situations involving two people. While that is clearly the precedential scope of the *en banc* court's holding, it is hard to see how it is justified by the logic of the constitutional doctrine in the area of sexual privacy up to that time. As the dissenters convincingly demonstrated, the Lovisis were not prosecuted for public lewdness, but for having oral sex with each other. The prosecution of Margaret Lovisi for having oral sex with Dunn was not before the court on appeal, and neither was her prosecution for corrupting the morals of her children by letting them, albeit perhaps inadvertently, see photographs of her sexual activities with their stepfather and other men. Thus, it was quite inconsistent for the *en banc* court to say on the one hand that the Constitution probably would bar a sodomy prosecution against a heterosexual married couple who performed their conduct in private, but would allow such a prosecution of *them* if a third party, another consenting adult, was present and watching (and perhaps taking their picture at the time).

However, taking into account the erosion of sexual privacy doctrine represented by *Bowers v. Hardwick* (1986) and the Court's continuing refusal to review on the merits cases involving consensual heterosexual sodomy, it is uncertain how a case involving state prosecution of the participants in a *ménage à trois* situation would be decided. Is there anything inherently magical in the notion of two parties versus three parties engaging in sexual activity behind closed bedroom doors that would make the former protected while the latter is not? Does the presence of a third person truly make the event public? Can it plausibly be asserted, as Haynsworth did, that by inviting in a third willing sex partner the marital couple is inviting in the state? Only future litigation will tell.

Case References

Bowers v. Hardwick, 478 U.S. 186 (1986)

Doe v. Commonwealth's Attorney for City of Richmond, 403 F. Supp. 1199 (E.D. Va. 1975), summarily affirmed, 425 U.S. 901 (1976)

Eisenstadt v. Baird, 405 U.S. 438 (1972)

Griswold v. Connecticut, 381 U.S. 479 (1965)

Loving v. Virginia, 388 U.S. 1 (1967)

Olmstead v. United States, 277 U.S. 438 (1928)

Poe v. Ullman, 367 U.S. 497 (1961)

Roe v. Wade, 410 U.S. 113 (1973)

17. FORNICATION: "A GRUBBY LITTLE EXERCISE IN SELF-GRATIFICATION?"

State v. Saunders, 75 N.J. 200, 381 A.2d 333 (1977), reversing 142 N.J. Super. 287, 361 A.2d 111 (App. Div. 1976) and 130 N.J. Super. 234, 326 A.2d 84 (Essex County Ct. 1974).

When Charles Saunders and Bernard Busby had sex in a parked car in Newark with some women they had picked up on the street late at night, they certainly did not expect that they would stimulate a far-reaching decision by the New Jersey Supreme Court on the sexual freedom of the individual. Their "grubby little exercise in self-gratification," as it was described by one of the justices of the court, signaled the downfall of the state's power to regulate consensual adult sexuality. It also encouraged the legislature to

adopt the Model Penal Code's provisions decriminalizing most such conduct rather than to follow the approach of some neighboring states that had retained certain criminal prohibitions from existing law while adopting the modernized phrasing typical of the Code. A $50 fine for "fornication" led to a revolution in New Jersey criminal law that would be influential in many other jurisdictions.

Although the Cromwell government of 17th-century England had outlawed fornication (i.e., sex between persons not married to each other), upon the restoration of the monarchy the law was removed from the books. As Blackstone commented,

> But at the restoration, when men, from an abhorrence of the hypocrisy of the late times, fell into a contrary extreme of licentiousness, it was not thought proper to renew a law of such unfashionable rigour. And these offences have been ever since left to the feeble coercion of the spiritual court, according to the rules of the canon law.

The colonists in America were apparently less tolerant of "licentiousness," however, for the New Jersey Assembly outlawed fornication in 1704 in a burst of concern for "Suppressing Immorality," which, said the statute's preamble, had abounded too much "to the shame of Christianity and the great Grief of all good and sober men." The fornication prohibition was part of a general vice law that also prohibited adultery, drunkenness, cursing, swearing, and "breaking the Lord's day." Subsequent reenactments of the prohibition dropped the religious references but continued to describe the crime as one against public morality.

Saunders, Busby, and another man had spent the evening of July 22 and early hours of July 23, 1973, in New York City visiting friends. What happened next was contradicted in testimony, but the jury apparently believed Saunders and Busby rather than their accusers. They claimed that they stopped the car for two women walking along the street who "attracted their attention by calling out to their passing vehicle." The women asked if they had any reefers. Although the men did not have any marijuana with them, they decided to lie and see what happened. Thus encouraged, the women offered to have sex with the men in exchange for "reefers." Both Saunders and Busby testified that they had no weapons and used no force with the women. They drove to a deserted spot and all three men in the car had sex with the two women, after which they said they had no reefers. "Enraged, the women indignantly demanded $10 for each act of sexual intercourse. The men refused to pay and the argument became more heated. It ended abruptly when the men pushed the women out of the car and drove off."

The women went to the police, claiming that they had been forced to have sex at gunpoint. Saunders and Busby were arrested and indicted for rape, assault with intent to rape, and armed robbery. Saunders was represented at trial by Irvington attorney Robert A. Baime. Assistant Essex County Prosecutor David L. Rhoads presented the case for the state before County Court Judge Stanley Bedford. At the close of the defendants' evidence, Judge Bedford informed the lawyers that he was considering charging the jury on the crime of fornication as a lesser included offense of rape. Baime objected, pointing out that the fornication statute was in "disrepute" and rarely enforced. Rhoads took no position, apart from commenting that the charge might be "required" by the testimony of the defendants, who had freely admitted having intercourse with the women. After both sides had completed their summations, Judge Bedford said, "Here is a situation in which there appears to be, and it is up to the jury to decide, an open admission in court of fornication, and I don't think the Court can ignore it since it is in the statute." He charged the jury that the crime of fornication was "an act of illicit sexual intercourse by a man, married or single, with an unmarried woman," which the state had the burden to prove. Baime again objected, arguing that fornication was not a lesser included offense and that there was no evidence that the women were single. Judge Bedford responded that his "recollection" was that they were. Busby's attorney also objected to the fornication charge. The charge evidently puzzled the jury, which requested clarification after twenty minutes of deliberation. Bedford restated his charge, including that a finding of guilt on fornication would preclude a finding of guilt on rape. The jury returned a finding of not guilty on the indicted offenses, but guilty on fornication. Busby had been held in prison pending the trial and was sentenced to time served. Saunders was fined $50, the maximum allowed under the statute. Baime renewed his objection on behalf of Saunders to the fornication conviction, arguing that the statute was unconstitutional. Bedford set the objection down for hearing, at which Alan Silber argued on behalf of Saunders.

Silber summoned an impressive array of expert witnesses to testify about the fornication statute. Morton Hunt, a writer who had recently published his book, *Sexual Behavior in the 1970s*, with Playboy Press, testified about the survey that was the basis for his writing. Hunt had found widespread practice of and toleration for nonmarital sex among Americans, particularly those under age 35. A leading New Jersey matrimonial lawyer, Gary Skoloff, testified that a substantial portion of the divorce cases he handled involved couples who had engaged in extramarital sex. While this fact usually came out during the court proceedings, no judge in his experience had ever referred the matter for prosecution under the fornication laws. In Skoloff's experience, the police were loath to get involved in such cases. Dr. Richard Green, a professor of psychiatry (who testified as an expert witness in a variety of important cases mentioned in this book), testified about how the existence of laws regulating consensual sexual activity generated tensions that "result in personality problems traceable to those proscriptions," as Bedford summarized his testimony, and "[g]uilt feelings and anxiety are created, with residual psychological and sexual problems that are sometimes manifested many years later." Bedford also received documentary evidence tending to show that both in New Jersey and on a national scale prosecutions for fornication were rare, with different prosecutors taking widely different attitudes on whether to pursue such cases. In sum, the expert testimony and evidence showed a class of infrequently enforced criminal statutes that were viewed with disdain or widely ignored, but that were capable of generating significant psychological harm when invoked or considered by those engaging in such activity.

Accepting the evidence for what it showed, however, Judge Bedford was not convinced that it had much to do with his task of ruling on the constitutionality of the New Jersey fornication law. He said that "the constitutionality of a statute is not to be determined by a Gallup or Harris poll, taken periodically, reflecting a majority or minority view of the legislation." What was important to him was not whether the law was wise or harmful, but rather whether it was within the authority of the legislature to pass.

He rejected the argument of discriminatory enforcement. It was not enough to show that the law was rarely enforced, he said. The defendants had to show that there was a deliberate pattern of discriminatory enforcement based on some invidious or arbitrary classification. No such pattern could be found in this case or generally.

The New Jersey Supreme Court had recently dealt with two cases involving the fornication law, and in neither had the court questioned its constitutionality. In *State v. Lutz* (1971), the court had rejected the argument that the fornication statute was unconstitutional due to selective enforcement. In *State v. Clark* (1971), the court had declined to pass on the constitutionality of the law due to lack of an adequate record at trial on the issue, instead setting aside on self-incrimination grounds the prosecution of unmarried welfare recipients who had been prosecuted after testifying in civil proceedings about their sexual relations. After mentioning these cases, Bedford proceeded to consider the impact of recent federal sexual privacy cases on the substantive constitutionality of the fornication law and found that they did not provide a basis for striking it down. While the U.S. Supreme Court's then recent abortion decision, *Roe v. Wade* (1973), made clear that there was a federal constitutional right of privacy, Justice Harry A. Blackmun's opinion stated that the right of privacy was not absolute. Blackmun said that it did not give one "an unlimited right to do with one's body as one pleases," but could be restricted on the showing of a compelling state interest. Furthermore, in *Griswold v. Connecticut* (1965), Justice Arthur J. Goldberg's famed Ninth Amendment concurrence made clear that the constitutionality of adultery and fornication laws was "beyond doubt."

In light of these comments, said Judge Bedford, it was clear that the state's interests in prohibiting fornication were compelling and outweighed the individual right to privacy. For one thing, the spread of venereal diseases was a serious problem that a ban on extra-marital sex would address. For another, the state had a compelling interest in preventing illegitimacy, he asserted. Although the statute may have initially been enacted in the 18th century as a result of religious impulses, there were sufficient secular justifications to avoid any First Amendment Establishment Clause problems, Bedford concluded. Bedford noted that the legislature was now considering the Model Penal Code, which would decriminalize fornication if adopted as recommended by the American Law Institute, and asserted that the legislature, rather than a court, was the proper body to make such a decision. Bedford published his decision denying the motion to vacate the verdict on September 27, 1974. Silber filed an appeal, which was denied by the appellate division on June 21, 1976, just a week after hearing argument, in a brief *per curiam* opinion adopting Judge Bedford's reasoning and citing as additional precedent the Supreme Court's recent summary affirmance in *Doe v. Commonwealth's Attorney for City of Richmond*, in which a three-judge district court had upheld the constitutionality of Virginia's sodomy statute.

Saunders appealed to the New Jersey Supreme Court, which heard oral argument on April 26, 1977. Assistant Essex County Prosecutor Roy B. Greenman appeared to defend the conviction, while Silber argued for Saunders. The court voted 5–2 to reverse the conviction and to declare the fornication statute unconstitutional. In his opinion for the court, Justice Morris Pashman found the statute unconstitutional on both federal and state constitutional grounds. Concurring, Justice Sidney M. Schreiber preferred to rely solely on state constitutional grounds, finding that the federal constitutional right of privacy did not protect the conduct involved. Dissenting Justice Robert L. Clifford, joined by Justice Worrall F. Mountain, argued that the court had reached the constitutional issues prematurely and should have addressed itself to the question whether fornication was properly charged as a lesser included offence of rape, as to which he had serious doubts, reserving the constitutional question for possible consideration depending on how the statutory issue was resolved.

Pashman reviewed the U.S. Supreme Court privacy precedents, concluding that "the right of privacy is not confined to the private situations involved in each of these decisions," but rather "that the constitutional basis for the protection of such decisions is their relationship to

individual autonomy." He found this approach consistent with the New Jersey court's jurisprudence under its own constitution. In *In re Quinlan* (1976), the case in which the court recognized a personal right to refuse artificial life support, the court had held that the "underlying concern" of the right of privacy "was with the protection of personal decisions, and that it might be included within 'the class of what have been called rights of "personality." '" Pashman asserted, "Any discussion of the right of privacy must focus on the ultimate interest which protection the Constitution seeks to ensure—the freedom of personal development. . . . [T]he crux of the matter is that governmental regulation of private personal behavior under the police power is sharply limited." After quoting Justice Louis D. Brandeis's famous ode to privacy from his dissent in *Olmstead v. United States* (1928), Pashman said:

> We conclude that the conduct statutorily defined as fornication involves, by its very nature, a fundamental personal choice. Thus, the statute infringes upon the right of privacy. Although persons may differ as to the propriety and morality of such conduct and while we certainly do not condone its particular manifestations in this case, such a decision is necessarily encompassed in the concept of personal autonomy which our Constitution seeks to safeguard.

While the U.S. Supreme Court had never addressed the question whether fornication lay within the boundaries of federal constitutional privacy, Pashman found that such protection was reasonably derived from the contraception cases. "It would be rather anomalous," he declared, "if such a decision [i.e., whether to use contraception] could be constitutionally protected while the more fundamental decision as to whether to engage in the conduct which is a necessary prerequisite to child-bearing could be constitutionally prohibited." Furthermore, the New Jersey court's own opinions in *Lutz* and *Clark* had been superseded by the Supreme Court's subsequent decision in *Eisenstadt v. Baird* (1972), which made clear that the federal privacy right extended to unmarried persons, and *Roe v. Wade*, which extended it beyond the intimacy of the bedroom into the more public sphere of abortion. Finally, Pashman disputed the appellate division's unexplained citation of *Doe v. Commonwealth's Attorney* as a basis for upholding the conviction. "We are not inclined to read this controversial decision too broadly," he said. "Though the lower court's decision is technically binding as a precedent, it does not necessarily represent the reasoning of the Court." Pashman pointed to the disagreement within the Court as to the meaning of *Doe*, signaled by comments by Justice Brennan and Justice Rehnquist in *Carey v. Population Services International* (1977).

Clear as it was to Pashman that the federal right of privacy extended to this conduct, it was equally clear that the New Jersey constitutional privacy right applied. Although thus far the state constitutional privacy right had not been developed beyond the extent of the federal right, "the lack of constraints imposed by considerations of federalism permits this Court to demand stronger and more persuasive showings of a public interest in allowing the State to prohibit sexual practices than would be required by the United States Supreme Court."

What were the state's interests in outlawing fornication? The state advanced four interests: preventing the spread of venereal diseases, preventing illegitimacy, protecting public morality, and protecting the marital relationship. While acknowledging the strong interest of the state in preventing venereal disease, Pashman asserted that the fornication law was not "properly designed with that end in mind," since it was unlikely that a $50 fine or a six-month jail term under a statute almost never enforced against consenting adults in private would serve as any significant deterrent to sexual activity. Just as the U.S. Supreme Court had dismissed the notion that "the threat of an unwanted pregnancy would deter persons from engaging in extramarital sexual activities" if they were denied access to contraceptive devices, Pashman concluded that "the same is true for the possibility of being prosecuted under the fornication statute." Indeed, the statute was counterproductive, since the best way of achieving the state's purpose would be to encourage people to seek testing and treatment for venereal diseases, and people were unlikely to seek these out if they would thus render themselves liable for prosecution under the fornication law. Us-

ing a similar rationale, the court dismissed the prevention of illegitimacy as a sufficient justification of the law.

Pashman was even more dismissive of the other two justifications the state had articulated. The decision whether to marry is a private choice, he said, and it is entirely inappropriate for the state to enact a criminal law in order to coerce people to marry in order to gain access to sexual satisfaction. While the regulation of public morality was within the sphere of legislative authority, the fornication law was concerned with private morality. To the extent that the fornication law "serves as an official sanction of certain conceptions of desirable lifestyles, social mores or individualized beliefs," wrote Pashman, "it is not an appropriate exercise of the police power." Even though fornication might offend the moral beliefs of many people, that was not an adequate basis to criminalize it. Pashman stated:

> Private personal acts between two consenting adults are not to be lightly meddled with by the State. The right of personal autonomy is fundamental to a free society. Persons who view fornication as opprobrious conduct may seek strenuously to dissuade people from engaging in it. However, they may not inhibit such conduct through the coercive power of the criminal law.

Quoting Sir Francis Bacon's comment that "the sum of behavior is to retain a man's own dignity without intruding on the liberty of others," Pashman asserted: "The fornication statute mocks the dignity of both offenders and enforcers." Police had better things to do than "to search out adults who live a so-called 'wayward' life," said Pashman, who insisted that human dignity was offended by dragging such conduct into open court. "More importantly," he concluded, "the liberty which is the birthright of every individual suffers dearly when the State can so grossly intrude on personal autonomy."

Justice Schreiber emphasized what he saw as the narrowness and particularity of the federal privacy right, concurring solely on state constitutional grounds. Not only had Justice Goldberg said that the federal constitutionality of fornication statutes was "beyond doubt," but nothing in subsequent U.S. Supreme Court decisions persuaded Schreiber that the Court had moved beyond that point. The summary affirmance in *Doe v. Commonwealth's Attorney* was significant evidence of this, in his view. "I can discern no rational basis for excepting from the realm of 'individual autonomy' the private consensual conduct which, according to *City of Richmond*, may be constitutionally prohibited by the states." Without an opinion in that case from the Court, he had to conclude that "the Court continues to view the federal right of privacy as encompassing the narrower range of activity associated with choices related to childrearing and childbearing."

On the other hand, said Schreiber, the New Jersey privacy right had a broader basis in article 1, paragraph 1 of the state's constitution, which provided that "[a]ll persons are by nature free and independent, and have certain natural and unalienable rights, among which are those of enjoying and defending life and liberty . . . and of pursuing and obtaining safety and happiness." This language provided a clear textual basis for protecting individual autonomy in sexual matters, said Schreiber. He stated:

> The rights of two adults to make personal decisions are inherent in their freedom of thought. Implementation of those decisions in pursuit of their concept of happiness manifests an exercise of human liberty. Whatever else may be said of happiness, it is best obtained in a climate of free decision where each individual has the choice of consenting or not to acts or events which may affect him. Different persons have differing spiritual and moral views and so long as their personal conduct does not affect others, individuals have freedom to think, decide and act as they see fit. This freedom is an aspect of their right of privacy. Private consensual sexual conduct represents an exercise of that right.

Schreiber proceeded to review the early history of the New Jersey fornication law and concluded that the law had always been advanced by the legislature as a matter of religion or public morality. No object, "other than enforcing a particular moral code, motivated its adoption of the fornication statute." Although the state was now arguing public health, "there is no evidence that this statute was intended as anything but an attempt to regulate private morality." Indeed, even in the 18th century,

the fornication statute had been viewed as extending only to situations in which fornication had public consequences, such as the birth of an illegitimate child. Purely private consensual fornication was not commonly prosecuted. Schreiber concluded that these old cases provided the proper rule: the legislature could regulate only conduct with public consequences.

Justice Clifford's dissent appealed to the prudential policy of avoiding constitutional questions when they were not necessary to resolve a case. He expressed particular distaste for using this case as a vehicle to discuss the right of privacy in sexual matters:

> Bluntly put, this case is a wretched vehicle for addressing the questions which counsel for the respective parties would have us answer. It seems somehow incongruous to use the soaring phrases of Mr. Justice Brandeis in *Olmstead* . . . as support for the proposition that the State of New Jersey is powerless to prohibit, as a violation of [the fornication statute], indiscriminate group fornicating by—or indeed, among—complete strangers in the confined quarters of a parked automobile on a deserted lot in Newark.

While agreeing with the other justices that "absent a compelling state interest the State may not regulate a person's private decisions which have merely incidental effects on others," he would not reach the constitutional issues in this case involving "the grubby little exercise in self-gratification involved here" because he thought it was more appropriate to focus first on the propriety of applying the fornication law in a case where the indictment specified rape.

The New Jersey Supreme Court's decision in *State v. Saunders* sounded the death-knell for consensual sex crimes laws in New Jersey. The sweeping language of Justices Pashman and Schreiber clearly indicated that virtually all consensual sexual activity was likely to be protected to some extent by federal and state constitutional privacy rights. Even the dissent by Justice Clifford indicated general agreement with this proposition. Short of amending the state constitution to remove the right of privacy, the legislature apparently had no authority to legislate in this area. The impact on consideration of the Model Penal Code was decisive. The legislature repealed its consensual sex crimes laws, substituting the Model Penal Code's concern with nonconsensual situations and public sexual activity. A subsequent attempt by some conservative legislators to reenact the sodomy law was unsuccessful.

The *Saunders* decision was important not only for its ringing language but for its embrace of the concept that state constitutional privacy protection might be given a more sweeping reading than the federal rights identified by the U.S. Supreme Court. This was not only because of variations in language between the federal and state documents, but more significantly, as the New Jersey justices recognized, because of the differing roles of the federal and state governments under the U.S. federal system. Justice Schreiber made this point most explicitly when he wrote:

> Unlike the United States Constitution, the New Jersey Constitution is not a grant of enumerated powers, but rather a limitation of the sovereign powers of the State vested in the Legislature. That legislative authority is circumscribed by constitutional provisions, including those expressed in Article I, paragraph 1. Although the Legislature, in exercising its powers, may incidentally affect the natural and unalienable rights of individuals to liberty and the pursuit of happiness which have been recognized in Article I, the validity of any

statute directly limiting those rights should be carefully scrutinized in light of its legislative purposes.

In this difference between federal and state constitutions lay a significant justification for state courts to take a more aggressive role than they had been accustomed to taking in defense of individual rights. The U.S. Supreme Court had seized the initiative in this area under the leadership of Chief Justice Earl Warren in the 1950s and 1960s. Now, as the federal judiciary had become more restrained in protecting individual rights, it was the turn of the state courts to seize the initiative. *State v. Saunders* was an important step in that direction.

Case References

Carey v. Population Services International, 431 U.S. 678 (1977)

Doe v. Commonwealth's Attorney for City of Richmond, 425 U.S. 901 (1976), affirming 403 F. Supp. 1199 (E.D. Va. 1975)

Eisenstadt v. Baird, 405 U.S. 438 (1972)

Griswold v. Connecticut, 381 U.S. 479 (1965)

Olmstead v. United States, 277 U.S. 438 (1928)

Quinlan, In re, 70 N.J. 10, 355 A.2d 647 (1976)

Roe v. Wade, 410 U.S. 113 (1973)

State v. Clark, 58 N.J. 72, 275 A.2d 137 (1971)

State v. Lutz, 57 N.J. 314, 272 A.2d 753 (1971)

18. HOW TO PRESERVE A VAGUE SOLICITATION STATUTE

Pryor v. Municipal Court for Los Angeles County, 25 Cal. 3d 238, 158 Cal. Rptr. 330, 599 P.2d 636 (1979).

Repealing criminal sanctions against private, consensual adult sexual activity is only the first step in lifting the repressive regime of governmental interference in the sex lives of private citizens. In its law reform recommendations formulated during the 1950s, the American Law Institute drew a sharp distinction between public and private conduct and recommended continuing existing prohibitions on both public sexual activity, broadly defined, and public solicitation to engage in sexual activity, whether the solicited activity was to occur in public or in private. This recommendation rested on the

argument that the state retained a strong interest in regulating public conduct that might offend passers-by, to protect individuals from unwelcomed solicitations on public streets and in places of public accommodation, and to maintain a dignified, nonsexual atmosphere in such places.

Accordingly, as various states adopted the Model Penal Code or otherwise legislated to reform their sex crimes laws, they retained provisions banning public solicitation, usually using the sort of broad, subjective language that has long characterized such laws. In California, the legislature passed Penal Code section 647(a) in 1961, declaring that a person is guilty of a disorderly conduct misdemeanor "[w]ho solicits any one to engage in or who engages in lewd or dissolute conduct in any public place or in any place open to the public or exposed to public view." The Penal Code contained no specific description of the acts that would be considered "lewd" or "dissolute." At the time this law was passed, California penalized consensual sodomy between adults, regardless where the act was performed, but in 1975 the legislature passed the Brown Act, which made private consensual sexual activity between adults lawful.

Passage of the Brown Act now protected Californians from being prosecuted for what they did consensually in their bedrooms, but the law continued to penalize asking somebody to come home to do it. This law vested great discretion in law enforcement authorities to interpret the words "lewd" and "dissolute," and studies published in 1966, 1972, and 1974 indicated that the police disproportionately targeted homosexual men for enforcement of the solicitation law by sending plainclothes police decoys to known homosexual meeting places, hoping to entice gay men to solicit them to engage in sexual activity. Such decoy activity provided the main means of enforcing the law, because gay men rarely, if ever, approached anyone in a public place to solicit sexual activity who was not there specifically to engage in such solicitation activity, known in the gay community as "cruising," and so it was rare for anyone to be so offended by a solicitation as to complain to the police. In the case of Don Barry Pryor, however, the police targeted a man who was willing to fight back against the injustice of being entrapped for making a polite solicitation to engage in private sexual activity.

Pryor was arrested on May 1, 1976. He was hanging out in a popular "cruising" area. A handsome man parked his car near where Pryor was standing, but remained seated in the car, which is normally interpreted as a sign of interest in being "cruised." Pryor walked over and struck up a conversation with the man in the car, who, unknown to Pryor, was a plainclothes police officer. According to the officer, Pryor asked him to drive to a nearby parking lot and

have oral sex in the car; the officer suggested going to his home instead. The officer arrested Pryor after Pryor assented to the proposition and got in the car. According to Pryor, he never mentioned the parking lot and discussed having sex only at the driver's home. The officer searched Pryor incident to the arrest and found a small amount of marijuana. Pryor was charged with violating section 647(a) by soliciting "a lewd and dissolute act," and a provision of the Health and Safety Code involving possession of marijuana.

At his trial, Pryor argued that the solicitation law was unconstitutional and moved that the evidence of marijuana possession be suppressed because it was obtained by a search incident to an invalid arrest. When the trial judge denied his motion, Pryor pled guilty to the marijuana charge and appealed his conviction on that charge, but it was affirmed by the appellate department of the California Superior Court. Then trial began on the solicitation charge. After the testimony of the police officer and Pryor, the judge charged the jury that oral sex between males was "lewd or dissolute" under the statute as a matter of law, and that the solicitation law made it immaterial whether the sexual activity Pryor solicited was intended to take place in public or in private. Even though these instructions, taken with the points of overlap in the witness's testimony, virtually guaranteed conviction, the jury deadlocked, undoubtedly due to its unhappiness at being asked to enforce a vague and unjust law, and the judge had to declare a mistrial.

Pryor's attorney, Thomas F. Coleman (who was a co-author of one of the studies on selective enforcement of the solicitation law), then filed a petition with the California Supreme Court, seeking writs of prohibition and mandate concerning both the marijuana conviction and pending retrial of the solicitation charges. The court issued an alternative writ of prohibition, dealing solely with the solicitation charge, and set the matter for argument to consider the constitutionality of the solicitation law as enforced against Pryor. The National Committee for Sexual Civil Liberties filed an *amicus* brief prepared by a distinguished collection of national authorities on sex crimes law, led by Donald C. Knutson, founder of Gay Rights

Advocates, a public interest law firm. Los Angeles City Attorney Burt Pines, assisted by Deputy City Attorneys Laurie Harris and Mark L. Brown, appeared in defense of the law, with *amicus* assistance from San Diego City Attorney John W. Witt and three of his deputies.

In its decision announced September 7, 1979, the California Supreme Court adopted a new, narrow construction of the statute to save it from fatal constitutional flaws of vagueness and overbreadth, but refused to order the dismissal of charges against Pryor, since the conflicting testimony about his sexual proposition to the police made it possible that a jury could conclude his conduct was still covered under the narrow construction. In a unanimous opinion by Justice Mathew O. Tobriner, the court held that the words "lewd" and "dissolute" were unconstitutionally vague as used in the statute, but that the court could give them a definite meaning that would cure the vagueness problem for the future. In light of this problem, Justice Tobriner and six of his colleagues agreed that their ruling should have retroactive effect. Justice William P. Clark, Jr., dissented from the ruling on retroactivity.

The constitutionality of section 647(a) had been much litigated in the lower California courts in the almost twenty years since its enactment, but the supreme court had only once previously been called on directly to confront the issue, in *In re Giannini* (1968), a case involving a prosecution for nude dancing. In that case, having concluded that nude dancing that was not "obscene" was protected as communicative or expressive activity under the First Amendment, the court had adopted a narrowing construction of the law by which engaging in nonobscene dancing was protected from prosecution. However, said Tobriner, the court did not consider *Giannini* binding in Pryor's case, because the earlier decision was very much tied to its specific acts because of the important First Amendment interests implicated in Ms. Giannini's activities. Pryor was not charged as making a lewd, dissolute, or obscene communication, but rather with soliciting the commission of a lewd or dissolute act, so the "obscenity" standard of *Giannini* was not really relevant to his case. Thus, the court was facing as a matter of first impression whether the solicitation law

was unconstitutionally vague and would look to its language, legislative history, and prior constructions to make this determination.

First addressing the language of the statute, Tobriner asserted that it was vague because the words "lewd" and "dissolute," being "words of common speech" rather than "technical terms," did not "imply a definite and specific referent, but apply broadly to conduct which the speaker considers beyond the bounds of propriety." This was an inherently subjective standard, likely to shift from jury to jury depending on the opinions and life experience of particular jurors. If construction of the statute depended on its language alone, it would have to be declared unconstitutional.

Turning next to legislative history, Tobriner noted that the law actually derived from an earlier vagrancy statute of the type whose constitutionality had been cast into doubt by the U.S. Supreme Court's decision in *Papachristou v. City of Jacksonville* (1972), which made it clear that broadly phrased loitering and vagrancy laws, which left undue room for police discretion in deciding whom to arrest, offended elementary due process concerns. The California Supreme Court had anticipated the U.S. Supreme Court's decisions when in 1960 it ruled in *In re Newbern* that a provision of the California vagrancy law, a subsection of section 647, was void for vagueness. This, together with an influential study on vagrancy laws by Professor Arthur Sherry, had persuaded the California legislature to amend section 647 by abandoning the "status offense" nature of the old vagrancy law and replacing it with a specific requirement of behavior ("lewd or dissolute conduct" or soliciting same). The specific prohibition of solicitation was added for the first time with this 1960 amendment, although solicitation had been implicitly comprehended within the prior law. The legislative history made clear, however, that there was no intention to change or to give a narrower meaning to the words "lewd" and "dissolute" that had been carried forward from the prior statute. Since the old vagrancy laws had been drafted to give the police wide discretion in deciding whom to arrest, and had used the terms "lewd" and "dissolute" precisely because they were so broad and subjective, the legislature history gave no more help than the actual language of the statute in meeting the vagueness problem.

Finally, Tobriner turned to prior construction of the statute. Once again, he found little help in detecting the kind of specificity that would save the statute. Indeed, he said, examining these cases "is like opening a thesaurus." Rather than attempt to define "lewd" or "dissolute" by describing particular acts that would be covered by the law, the lower courts merely used "pejorative adjectives." For example, in *People v. Williams* (1976), one of the appeals courts had said that the words "lewd" and "dissolute" were synonymous, and meant "lustful, lascivious, unchaste, wanton, or loose in morals and conduct." This language was typical, although other courts of appeal had also referred to lack of "restraint," or conduct that was "lawless, loose in morals and conduct, recklessly abandoned to sexual pleasures, profligate, wanton, lewd, debauched." All these were colorful terms that undoubtedly raised images in peoples' minds, but none of them described particular acts so clearly that a person reading the statute would know precisely what was forbidden. "This impressive list of adjectives and phrases confers no clarity upon the terms 'lewd' and 'dissolute' in section 647," said Tobriner. Instructing a jury by using a string of adjectives "piles additional uncertainty upon the already vague words of the statute." In trying to let juries know what "lewd" and "dissolute" meant, courts were just compounding the problem by using more vague, subjective terms. The one court of appeal that tried to solve the problem by importing the "obscenity" test from *In re Giannini* had not solved the problem, since the standards for determining whether a particular communication was "obscene" had little logical relevance to the problem of sexual solicitation, and the other courts of appeal had accordingly not followed its lead.

Since the California decisions had failed to produce a clear or consistent definition of "lewd or dissolute conduct," or to adopt narrowing constructions of the statute that would increase its specificity, Pryor was correct in arguing that the law as it stood had constitutional problems. This creates special problems when the law "concerns speech, for uncertainty concerning its scope may then chill the exercise of pro-

tected First Amendment rights," said Tobriner. This was because the law did not ban only solicitations that were stated in obscene speech, but rather "any public solicitation, however discreet or diffident, of lewd or dissolute conduct," and lower court opinions had even applied the ban to solicitations "seeking private, lawful, and consensual conduct," as Pryor was claiming in his own case.

Herein lay a special vagueness problem, suggested Tobriner. "But what private, consensual, lawful sexual acts are nonetheless lewd or dissolute, such that public solicitation of them is criminal?" he asked.

> The answer of the prior cases—such acts as are lustful, lascivious, unchaste, wanton, or loose in morals and conduct—is no answer at all. Some jurors would find that acts of extramarital intercourse fall within that definition; some would draw the line between intercourse and other sexual acts; others would distinguish between homosexual and heterosexual acts. Thus one could not determine what actions are rendered criminal by reading the statute or even the decisions which interpret it. He must gauge the temper of the community, and predict at his peril the moral and sexual attitudes of those who will be called to serve on the jury.

Tobriner rejected the contention that all solicitations to engage in sexual activity are necessarily obscene or might constitute "fighting words," an exception to the First Amendment that the U.S. Supreme Court had recognized as justifying lack of protection for certain nonobscene speech. When the law banning solicitation was so vague, said Tobriner, it "creates the danger that police, prosecutors, judges and juries will lack sufficient standards to reach their decisions, thus opening the door to arbitrary or discriminatory enforcement of the law," which assumed particular importance in the present case. The National Committee for Sexual Civil Liberties' *amicus* brief had attached copies of the studies showing "both that the police selected techniques and locations of enforcement deliberately designed to detect a disproportionate number of male homosexual offenders, and that they arrested male homosexuals for conduct which, if committed by two women or by a heterosexual pair, did not result in arrest."

Indeed, aware of these problems, the Los Angeles city attorney had conceded in its brief that since 1977 it had adopted guidelines for prosecution which should, in future, effectively limit prosecution to offensive solicitations or those to minors. While impressed that such guidelines might reduce the problems of discretionary enforcement, Tobriner commented that the very need for such guidelines pointed up the constitutional vagueness problems with the statute. And, left unsaid, that the prosecutorial guidelines could not solve the problems of police harassment and entrapment, since police might continue to arrest gay men disproportionately as a method of street control that would chill the associational rights of the individuals subject to arrest, even though the city attorney was declining to prosecute their cases.

As a final blow to the constitutionality of the law, Tobriner noted that the court and other federal and state courts in California had declared unconstitutional an array of other statutes dealing with sexual matters that contained similarly vague language. Taken together, all these considerations of language, legislative history, and past construction suggested that the statute, as written and previously interpreted, was unconstitutionally vague. But that did not end the case because "the judiciary bears an obligation to construe enactments to give specific content to terms that might otherwise be unconstitutionally vague." If it was possible for the court to give section 647(a) a specific meaning that would solve the vagueness problem, there would be no need to strike the law from the books. And Tobriner found it possible to fashion a construction that observed all the constitutional niceties, even though it involved overruling a substantial body of prior California case law.

The word "solicitation" was not itself unconstitutionally vague, but there were difficulties stemming from past decisions holding that it applied to solicitation to engage in private conduct, especially since the Brown Act of 1975 had decriminalized most such private conduct. Those prior cases were inconsistent with the law reform, which now required a more limited construction of the statute. Consequently, said Tobriner, henceforth section 647(a) would be limited to "the solicitation of criminal sexual conduct," and more specifically "prohibits only solicitations which propose the commission of conduct itself banned by [that section], that is, lewd or dissolute conduct which *occurs* in a public place, a place open to the public, or a place exposed to public view." This construction saved the court from having to decide which private sexual conduct, if any, was to be deemed lewd or dissolute for purposes of the solicitation law and avoided the First Amendment difficulties which, according to Tobriner, "attend a statute which prohibits solicitation of lawful acts."

Giving more concrete meaning to "lewd or dissolute" was a bit more challenging, however. The court held that those terms should be construed as synonymous and limited to "sexually motivated conduct." Even though a past decision had held that a narcotics addict was a "dissolute" person, to extend the term to nonsexual activity was inconsistent with the requirement under Penal Code section 290 that anyone convicted under section 647(a) register as a sex offender. There was nothing about being a narcotics addict that would justify such a registration requirement, and the registration requirement evinced a legislative intent that section 647(a) be interpreted as applying to sexual activities. Finally, arriving at a carefully limited meaning for "lewd and dissolute," Tobriner held that these words referred to conduct that occurred "in public view" and involved "touching of the genitals, buttocks, or female breast, for purposes of sexual arousal, gratification, or affront." With such a definition, the police had little discretion to use the law selectively to target particular groups of people. Furthermore, said the Court, it was not enough that the conduct occur in a public place. It was appropriate to limit the reach of the law to conduct that occurred in the presence of somebody who might be offended by the conduct. Since enlightened jurisprudence usually held that a plainclothes police officer could not serve as such an "offended person," this should put an end to the entrapment problem insofar as inoffensive solicitation to engage in private sexual conduct was concerned.

Under the construction we have established in this opinion, [said Tobriner], section 647, subdivision (a), prohibits only the solicitation or commission of a sexual touching, done with specific intent when persons may be offended by the act. It does not impose vague and far-reaching standards under which the criminality of an act depends upon the moral views of the judge or jury, does not prohibit solicitation of lawful acts, and does not invite discriminatory enforcement. We are confident that the statute, as so construed, is not unconstitutionally vague.

Since the statute had now been saved through construction, the case would have to be remanded for a retrial of Pryor. The charges could not just be dismissed because of the conflict of testimony between the police officer and Pryor about the nature of Pryor's solicitation. Furthermore, if the jury believed the police officer's version, further evidence would be required about whether the parking lot setup allegedly proposed by Pryor would offend the statute. Under the court's construction, this would require evidence about the time of day, lighting, presence of others who might be offended, and the like. The court decided that there was no need to consider the other constitutional issues Pryor had raised, since they all addressed the old, broader construction of the law which the court had abandoned in this case.

Finally, the court held that its decision should apply to all pending prosecutions, not just Pryor's case. Since the new construction was adopted "to establish a specific, constitutionally definite test of what conduct does or does not violate that section," questions of guilt or innocence would turn on it and it would not be proper to allow prosecutions to go forward without reference to it. As to those who had been finally convicted under the old interpretation, they would be entitled to relief "by writ of habeas corpus only if there is no material dispute as to the facts relating" to their convictions and it appeared that the new construction did not prohibit their conduct.

Justice Clark briefly dissented from the ruling on retroactivity, which he characterized as "a windfall to defendants validly convicted under the statute." What about somebody convicted of soliciting private commission of sodomy prior to the Brown Act, who was validly convicted of soliciting criminal sexual activity at that time? Since the U.S. Supreme Court, in *Doe v. Commonwealth's Attorney for City of Richmond*, had ruled in 1976 that sodomy laws were

constitutional, there was no warrant for giving such convicted persons an opportunity to get their convictions vacated now, which Clark asserted was a consequence of the majority's decision.

The decision in *Pryor* helped to establish a major advance on the Model Penal Code's sexual law reform recommendations. While the Code's drafters saw a legitimate public order purpose in allowing states to continue to punish public solicitation to commit private sexual acts, the California court had embraced a broader vision of sexual freedom, recognizing that freedom of speech and of association were inappropriately burdened when persons were punished for soliciting lawful activity, even if members of the community might be offended to know that the solicitation was going on. The *Pryor* case became quite influential as it was cited against the constitutionality of solicitation and loitering statutes in other jurisdictions that had repealed their sodomy laws. But the case did not completely end selective enforcement against homosexuals as Tobriner suggested it would. Instead, it stimulated a shifting in police tactics, including *pro forma* allegations that solicitations to plainclothes policemen always involved a suggestion of public sex, and in many cases the police alleged that the defendants had made sexual gestures or exposed their genitals. To some extent, enforcement activity was shifted from the streets to public restrooms, where indecent exposure and solicitation for public sex allegations could more easily be pressed, and a more conservative California Supreme Court would subsequently prove amenable in *People v. Superior Court (Caswell)* (1988) to allowing prosecutions that might have appeared inappropriate to the liberal court of the late 1970s.

Case References

Doe v. Commonwealth's Attorney for City of Richmond, 425 U.S. 901 (1976), summarily affirming 403 F. Supp. 1199 (E.D. Va. 1975)

Giannini, In re, 69 Cal. 3d 563, 72 Cal. Rptr. 655, 446 P.2d 535 (1968)

Newbern, In re, 53 Cal. 2d 786, 3 Cal. Rptr. 364, 350 P.2d 116 (1960)

Papachristou v. City of Jacksonville, 405 U.S. 156 (1972)

People v. Superior Court (Caswell), 46 Cal. 3d 381, 250 Cal. Rptr. 515, 758 P.2d 1046 (1988)

People v. Williams, 59 Cal. App. 2d 225, 130 Cal. Rptr. 460 (1976)

19. DOING "IT" ON STAGE: THEATRICAL ORAL SEX

Commonwealth v. Bonadio, 415 A.2d 47 (Pa. 1980).

The Pennsylvania Supreme Court surprised just about everybody with its decision in *Commonwealth v. Bonadio* because the factual setting of this suit challenging the constitutionality of Pennsylvania's voluntary deviate sexual intercourse statute was an unlikely vehicle for such a constitutional challenge.

The case arose in March 1979, when plainclothes police officers raided the Penthouse Theater in downtown Pittsburgh, where "exotic dancers" Mildred Kannitz (known professionally as "Dawn Delight") and Shanne Wimbel engaged in oral sex with members of the paying audience. The officers arrested the dancers and two theater employees, Michael Bonadio and Patrick Gagliano. The women were charged with the misdemeanor offense of voluntary deviate sexual intercourse; the men with criminal conspiracy. "Deviate sexual intercourse" was defined in Pennsylvania law as "sexual intercourse per os or per anus between human beings who are not husband and wife, and any form of sexual intercourse with an animal."

Their attorneys, Carl Max Janavitz and Rochelle D. Friedman, of Pittsburgh, filed a motion in the court of common pleas to quash the indictments, arguing that the statute was an unconstitutional invasion of privacy on its face. To their surprise, the common pleas court dismissed the indictment in an unpublished memorandum, relying on the developing federal case law on sexual privacy, and apparently ignoring the precedent of *Paris Adult Theatre I v. Slaton* (1973), in which the U.S. Supreme Court had ruled that an "adult theater" could not be considered a "private place" for purposes of the constitutional privacy doctrine.

District Attorney Robert E. Colville promptly appealed the case to the state supreme court, which held oral arguments on March 7, 1980. The case attracted *amicus* briefs urging affirmance of the dismissals from the National Committee for Sexual Civil Liberties, the

American Civil Liberties Union of Pennsylvania, and the Eromin Center, Inc. The court was sharply split over the case, dividing 4–3, with the majority sustaining the dismissal on a theory that the statute was beyond the police powers of the state, while the dissenters argued that the court's opinion improperly ignored the factual setting of the arrests in its rush to invalidate the statute. The opinion for the court by Justice John P. Flaherty, Jr., issued on May 30, 1980, is one of the most sweeping endorsements of sexual freedom and limitation of the police power ever issued by a U.S. appellate court, and it reads at times more like a jurisprudence essay than a judicial opinion.

With virtually no discussion of the details of the arrests, Flaherty plunged into his constitutional analysis by quoting an old U.S. Supreme Court decision, *Lawton v. Steele* (1894), on the limits of state police power:

> To justify the State in thus interposing its authority in behalf of the public, it must appear, first, that the *interests of the public generally*, as distinguished from those of a particular class, require such interference; and, second, that the means are reasonably necessary for the accomplishment of the purpose, and *not unduly oppressive upon individuals*.

(The emphases were provided by Justice Flaherty.)

Thus, for Flaherty, "the threshold question in determining whether the statute in question is a valid exercise of the police power is to decide whether it benefits the public generally." Flaherty conceded that the state would have a valid interest in "protecting the public from inadvertent offensive displays of sexual behavior," preventing rape or other involuntary sexual contacts, "protecting minors from being sexually used by adults," and eliminating cruelty to animals, so laws against indecent exposure, open lewdness, rape, *involuntary* deviate sexual intercourse, indecent assault, statutory rape, corruption of minors, and cruelty to animals were clearly within the police power. But, he concluded, "the statute in question serves none of the foregoing purposes and it is nugatory to suggest that it promotes a state interest in the institution of marriage." Flaherty concluded that the law had "only one possible purpose: to regulate the private conduct of consenting adults." This purpose "exceeds the valid bounds of the police power while infringing the right to equal protection of the laws" under both the federal and state constitutions.

The state had argued that the law was a valid regulation of morals. Flaherty asserted that "the police power should properly be exercised to protect each individual's right to be free from interference in defining and pursuing his own morality but not to enforce a majority morality on persons whose conduct *does not harm others.*" Flaherty cited two sources of "authority" for this proposition: a comment from the Model Penal Code drafted by the American Law Institute, explaining why the ALI was recommending repealing penalties for all private, noncommercial consensual intercourse between adults, and a lengthy passage from John Stuart Mill's famous 1859 essay, "On Liberty."

Said Flaherty:

> Many issues that are considered to be matters of morals are subject to debate, and no sufficient state interest justifies legislation of norms simply because a particular belief is followed by a number of people, or even a majority. Indeed, what is considered to be "moral" changes with the times and is dependent upon societal background. Spiritual leadership, not the government, has the responsibility for striving to improve the morality of individuals. Enactment of the Voluntary Deviate Sexual Intercourse Statute, despite the fact that it provides punishment for what many believe to be abhorrent crimes against nature and perceived sins against God, is not properly in the realm of the temporal police power.

Flaherty quoted extensively from Mill's essay on the "harm principle," including the following passages which he highlighted: "The only part of the conduct of any one, for which he is amenable to society, is that which concerns others. In the part which merely concerns himself, his independence is, of right, absolute. Over himself, over his own body and mind, the individual is sovereign. . . . The only freedom which deserves the name, is that of

pursuing our own good in our own way, so long as we do not attempt to deprive others of theirs." "This philosophy," Flaherty asserted, "as applied to the issue of the regulation of sexual morality presently before the Court, or employed to delimit the police power generally, properly circumscribes state power over the individual."

In addition to exceeding the police power, the state had engaged in invidious and unconstitutional discrimination against single persons in this statute, the court concluded, by making unlawful when performed by unmarried persons sexual acts that were lawfully performed within a marriage. In a prior case, *Moyer v. Phillips* (1975), the Pennsylvania Supreme Court had commented that the equal protection clauses of both the federal and state constitutions denied the state "the right to legislate that different treatment be accorded to persons placed by statute into different classes on the basis of criteria wholly unrelated to the objective of the particular statute." The court had held that statutory classifications had to be "reasonable, not arbitrary, and must rest upon some ground of difference having a fair and substantial relation to the object of the legislation so that all persons similarly circumstanced shall be treated alike."

The state had argued that it exempted married couples from the penalties of the Voluntary Deviate Sexual Intercourse statute in pursuit of the strong state interest in protecting the "privacy interest inherent in the marital relationship." What the state had actually done, of course, was to recast its sex crimes laws in 1972 in response to the U.S. Supreme Court's *Griswold v. Connecticut* decision of 1965, which strongly suggested that any state regulation of voluntary marital sexuality violated the federal constitutional right of privacy. The Commonwealth of Massachusetts had followed a similar course, amending its laws restricting contraceptive distribution to exempt marital couples, but the Supreme Court had struck down that distinction in *Eisenstadt v. Baird* (1972), ruling that a restriction exempting married persons worked an equal protection violation against unmarried persons. Flaherty found the ruling of *Eisenstadt* controlling here:

[To] suggest that deviate acts are heinous if performed by unmarried persons but acceptable when done by married persons lacks even a rational basis, for requiring less moral behavior of married persons than is expected of unmarried persons is without basis in logic. If the statute regulated sexual acts so affecting others that proscription by law would be justified, then they should be proscribed for all people, not just the unmarried.

Flaherty was supported by short statements from Chief Justice Michael J. Eagen and Justices Rolf Larsen and Bruce W. Kauffman. Larsen, joined by Kauffman, additionally asserted, "I would like to point out that *all* public sexual intercourse should be illegal, not just those public sex acts entered into by single persons."

The court's action incensed the three dissenting justices. In a brief statement joined by Justice Henry X. O'Brien, Justice Samuel J. Roberts asserted that the record clearly showed that the defendants "engaged in the proscribed conduct on a stage before a public audience and in plain view of the arresting officers. Thus there is no basis, constitutional or otherwise, for the majority's hasty invalidation of our Legislature's Crimes Code."

Justice Robert N. C. Nix, Jr., dissented at greater length, characterizing the court's ruling as "novel and shocking," contending that the court's theory "ignores the facts of the case" because this "is not a case of private, intimate conduct between consenting adults." After providing a full statement of the facts (perhaps not so curiously omitted from Flaherty's opinion for the court), Nix criticized the court for avoiding the privacy issue "by reasoning that there was not a valid exercise of the state's police power in the prohibition of this type of conduct. The absurdity of such a position," he asserted, "does not require demonstration." Characterizing what had happened as "a public display of the most depraved type of sexual behavior for pay," Nix ridiculed the court's suggestion that "this is beyond the state's power to regulate public health, safety, welfare, and morals" as "incredible." "I assume that regulation

of prostitution and hard core pornography are also now prohibited by today's ruling," he huffed.

Finally, Nix characterized as a "red herring" the Court's conclusion that the statute offended equal protection. The marital exemption to the law involved private behavior, not this sort of public activity engaged in by the women for monetary compensation. "It is therefore clear that the marital status of the participants in this conduct would not have affected their culpability," he asserted. He continued:

To suggest that the marital exception was intended to insulate a marital couple who performed deviate sexual acts for public display for pay would distort the obvious legislative objective in providing for this exception. The marital exception was designed to protect the intimacy and privacy of the marital unit. It did not give married couples the license to publicly engage in lewd and lascivious public acts.

Actually, the *Bonadio* case was a peculiar vehicle for the court's holding, leading to speculation that at least four members of the court were really unconcerned with the factual context in which a sodomy appeal came to them, given their apparent eagerness to have an opportunity to strike down the statute. They might even have done so on privacy grounds, had not the factual context made that impossible due to the unmentioned *Paris Adult Theatre* precedent. By invoking the state constitution in parallel with the federal Constitution at every step, the majority of the court protected their decision from Supreme Court review, making it one of the leading precedents in the field of sexual liberty, frequently cited by courts in other states confronting constitutional challenges to voluntary sex crime laws.

Case References

Eisenstadt v. Baird, 405 U.S. 438 (1972)

Griswold v. Connecticut, 381 U.S. 479 (1965)

Lawton v. Steele, 152 U.S. 133 (1894)

Moyer v. Phillips, 462 Pa. 395, 341 A.2d 441 (1975)

Paris Adult Theatre I v. Slaton, 413 U.S. 49 (1973)

20. DEREGULATING SEXUAL SOLICITATION

Commonwealth v. Sefranka, 382 Mass. 108, 414 N.E.2d 602 (1980).

Old Puritan New England left a legacy of strict sexual regulation aimed at removing from the streets and separating from society those who did not meet the prim and proper requirements of the moral majority. In Massachusetts, laws deriving from 17th-century colonial enactments remain on the books. To read them is akin to an adventure in time travel:

> Common night walkers, both male and female, common railers and brawlers, persons who with offensive and disorderly act or language accost or annoy persons of the opposite sex, lewd, wanton and lascivious persons in speech or behavior, idle and disorderly persons, prostitutes, disturbers of the peace, keepers of noisy and disorderly houses and persons guilty of indecent exposure may be punished by imprisonment in a jail or house of correction for not more than six months, or by a fine of not more than two hundred dollars, or by both such fine and imprisonment. [Mass. Gen. L. ch. 272, 53.]

Before this law was "modernized" in the 1940s, it even referred to "rogues" and "vagabonds." These laws present a particular challenge to courts aware of contemporary requirements of due process of law and protection for freedom of speech, much expanded during the past forty years as the federal Bill of Rights was construed in relation to state police powers through the Fourteenth Amendment. In *Commonwealth v. Sefranka*, the Massachusetts Supreme Judicial Court confronted the quoted statute in a prosecution for the kind of conduct that for centuries has brought men into the hands of the police: street "cruising" for sexual companionship.

Edward J. Sefranka was out cruising for sex one fine night in April of 1978. He drove to a public rest area along Route 24 outside of Boston, where gay and bisexual men were known to play a game with their car headlights to establish contact for sexual purposes. Unknown to Sefranka, three plainclothes police officers were present in unmarked cars, having claimed to have received unspecified "complaints" about sexual activities at the rest stop. When the police arrived at the rest stop, they saw several parked cars with men in them. The men would flash their parking lights at each other, then one would get out of his car and walk over to another whose lights had been flashing, get inside the other car, and then the two men would "disappear" from sight for awhile in the car. The police officers watched as Sefranka approached two cars, but he did not get in either one, and he did not appear to be engaging in sexual activity.

The Supreme Judicial Court summarized what happened next as follows:

> The police officers decided that one of them should pull into the line of cars that were flashing lights and "try [his] luck." A while later, the defendant [Sefranka] pulled behind the unmarked cruiser and flashed his parking lights. After several minutes, the police officer flashed his lights back at the defendant. The defendant then approached the cruiser, conversed with the officer, and invited the officer to return with him to his home and engage in oral copulation. The officer responded that he did not want to leave the rest area and indicated that he preferred the sexual activity to take place at the rest area. Replying that it was not safe at the rest area, the defendant said, "Well, I guess I'll see you later," got into his parked car, and drove away. He was arrested a few minutes later and charged with being a disorderly person and a lewd, wanton, and lascivious person.

The police officers swore out a complaint against Sefranka on April 27, 1978, in the district court in Brockton. At some point in the proceedings, the "disorderly person" charge was dropped. Upon his conviction for being a "lewd, wanton and lascivious person in speech or behavior," Sefranka appealed to the Massachusetts Superior Court, where Judge Dwyer affirmed his conviction, despite his contention that the statute under which he was prosecuted was unconstitutionally vague and violated his right of free speech. Sefranka sought review in the appeals court, but the Massachusetts Supreme Judicial Court, which had evidently been looking for an opportunity to deal with the problems posed by section 53's vague provisions, reached out on its own initiative and asserted jurisdiction over the appeal, bypassing the intermediate appellate court. After hearing argument on September 8, 1980, from Stephen R. Wainwright for Sefranka and Assistant District Attorney Robert M. Payton for the commonwealth of Massachusetts, and considering an *amicus* brief submitted by George H. Butcher, III, and Andrea L. Davis on behalf of the Massachusetts Civil Liberties Union and other *amici*, the Supreme Judicial Court ruled on December 15, 1980, that Sefranka's conviction must be reversed.

The unanimous decision of the court, embodied in an opinion by Chief Justice Edward F. Hennessey, upheld the constitutionality of the statute by adopting a limiting construction that did not include the conduct charged against Sefranka. Following the lead of the California Supreme Court's then-recent decision in *Pryor v. Municipal Court for Los Angeles County* (1979), the Supreme Judicial Court held, in effect, that the law could be applied only to public conduct that involved sexual touching.

Turning first to the question whether the statute was unconstitutionally vague on its face, Hennessey asserted that the language "lewd, wanton and lascivious persons in speech or behavior," standing alone, "fails to inform a person of ordinary intelligence what conduct is proscribed, as there is no commonly accepted understanding of the quoted terms." Words such as "lewd" and "wanton" did not refer to specific conduct, but rather to any conduct "which the speaker considers beyond the bounds of propriety." As the California Supreme Court had indicated in *Pryor*, this left the meaning of the statute totally to the "temper of the community," and a defendant would have to "predict at his peril the moral and sexual attitudes of . . . the jury." Looking to the history of the statute in search of its intended application, Hennessey noted that its antecedent laws dated from 1699, and had been codified in 1787 under the general title of "An Act for suppressing and punishing of rogues, vagabonds, common beggars, and other idle, disorderly and lewd persons." In 1862, the Supreme Judicial Court had held in *Commonwealth v. Parker* that the gravamen of the various offenses was "being a person of the character and behavior described," rather than "doing a certain overt act." Clearly, the law was originally intended to create a sta-

tus offense of being a certain type of person. Legislative revisions in modern times had struck some of the more quaint terms from the statute and added "prostitution" as a separate offense. This addition was important, for previously the words used to charge Sefranka had most often been used to charge persons who were soliciting to engage in acts of prostitution.

Hennessey noted that most of section 53 had come under attack for vagueness at one time or another, but that the court had "saved many of the challenged provisions by examining statutory and case law concerning each provision to determine with specificity the elements of the charged crime." This did not work, however, in the case of the provisions on "lewd, wanton and lascivious persons" because the prior case law was conclusory and nonspecific regarding the elements of the offense. The only prior case that presented some assistance, *Commonwealth v. Templeman*, was decided in 1978. In that case, the court had limited the application of this provision to public conduct, in line with its 1974 decision in *Commonwealth v. Balthazar*, which, on grounds of constitutional free speech and privacy rights, had limited the "unnatural and lascivious acts" portion of the statute to conduct that took place in public. In 1977, a man charged (as was Sefranka) with soliciting a police officer to engage in oral sex had his conviction vacated by the Supreme Judicial Court in *Commonwealth v. Scagliotti* because the judge failed to charge the jury on the question whether "the defendant had offered to commit the act in a public place." Clearly, these cases indicated that the current interpretation of the law required public conduct, but there was no prior specification by the court of exactly what public conduct was to be prohibited. However, in *Templeman* the court had gone so far as to indicate that section 53 could not be applied to punish mere speech or other expressive conduct covered by the First Amendment, and that it could be used to punish only conduct, not status. Because the court had not yet spelled out exactly what conduct was to be punishable, however, the statute remained unduly vague.

This did not mean, however, that the court had to declare the statute unconstitutional, since an appropriate construction could render it specific enough to pass constitutional muster. "We have encountered great difficulty in attempting to define specifically the conduct proscribed by the 'lewd, wanton and lascivious persons' provision," said Hennessey. Because status offenses were not punishable under modern constitutional law, and changes in the statute, such as the addition of a distinct crime of "prostitution" had removed most of the conduct previously prosecuted under this part of the statute, "we are hard put to find sufficient legislative indication of what distinct function the provision serves today." This was so because the Massachusetts legislature and courts had been busy in recent years specifying precise forms of conduct prohibited in other statutes. There were separate laws covering "indecent exposure," "lewd and lascivious cohabitation by a man and woman not married to each other," "open and gross lewdness and lascivious behavior," fornication, crimes against nature, and unnatural and lascivious acts. The other, more specific statutes, had already been held to cover specific offenses of indecent exposure and sexual conduct with children, as well as public acts of fellatio and anal sex. What could be left to punish under the more general rubric of "lewd, wanton and lascivious" behavior? Hennessey answered:

> After examining all of the above statutes, and proceeding under the reasonable assumption that the Legislature intended a comprehensive and integrated approach, we can perceive for the challenged provision a function in the penal law which appears to be consistent with legislative intent. None of the above statutes, with the possible exception of "open and gross lewdness," . . . deals with a public sexual touching that does not rise to the level of a completed sexual act. Nor do these statutes encompass public solicitations of such conduct.

Hennessey concluded that section 53's proscription of "lewd, wanton and lascivious" conduct could be used to fill this "gap." He found support for such a construction in the California Supreme Court's *Pryor* decision, where the court had construed a similar statute to be limited to instances where one person had touched the "genitals, buttocks, or female breast" in a public place, "for purposes of sexual arousal, gratification, annoyance or offense," where the "toucher" knew or had reason to know of the

presence of persons (other than the touchee) who might be offended. Solicitation of such conduct as well as the conduct itself could be punished, so long as the solicitation was for the conduct to take place in public.

"In order to satisfy constitutional standards of specificity," said Hennessey, "we think a similarly definite construction is appropriate here. . . . As so construed, the provision does not impose generalized, indefinite behavioral standards under which the criminality of conduct depends on the personal predilections of the judge or the jury; nor does it invite discriminatory enforcement by police and prosecutors." Hennessey also asserted that this construction avoided First Amendment problems, by limiting the proscription to speech soliciting commission of an unlawful public act.

Turning finally to Sefranka's conviction, Hennessey noted that "the defendant's speech and conduct falls [*sic*] outside the statutory prohibition" as it had now been closely defined by the court. "No public sexual conduct took place, nor did the defendant solicit any such conduct." Consequently, his conviction had to be reversed and "a finding of not guilty entered."

The Massachusetts Supreme Judicial Court's decision in *Sefranka*, and others like it, such as *Pryor v. Municipal Court* and *State v. Kueny*, a similar Iowa decision from 1974, are a mixed blessing. While purporting to "cure" the vagueness problem inherent in antiquated laws of puritanical origin through limiting constructions, these decisions leave the vague laws on the books, where they can continue to be misconstrued and misapplied by police officers so long as things do not advance to the stage of actual prosecution. Indeed, all a police officer need do to save a prosecution is to swear falsely, as law enforcement officers have been known to do, that the defendant solicited the officer to engage in sexual activity on the spot. The police officers in Sefranka's case were apparently honest in reporting his conversation as the basis of the charge, but they undoubtedly believed that what he said constituted a violation of the statute as it had previously been construed and applied. Had they known that the truth would not sustain a conviction, they might have been more creative in their reporting of his speech. Thus, the process of "limiting construction" to save facially unconstitutional laws may well contribute to the continued harassment of sexual minorities.

Case References

Commonwealth v. Balthazar, 366 Mass. 298, 318 N.E.2d 478 (1974)

Commonwealth v. Parker, 4 Allen 313 (Mass. 1862)

Commonwealth v. Scagliotti, 373 Mass. 626, 371 N.E.2d 726 (1977)

Commonwealth v. Templeman, 376 Mass. 533, 381 N.E.2d 1300 (1978)

Pryor v. Municipal Court, 25 Cal. 3d 238, 158 Cal. Rptr. 330, 599 P.2d 636 (1979)

State v. Kueny, 215 N.W.2d 215 (Iowa 1974)

21. PRIVACY, EQUALITY, AND SEXUAL FREEDOM

People v. Onofre, 51 N.Y.2d 476, 434 N.Y.S.2d 947, 415 N.E.2d 936 (1980), certiorari denied sub nom. New York v. Onofre, 451 U.S. 987 (1981). Decisions below: People v. Onofre, 72 A.D.2d 268, 424 N.Y.S.2d 566 (4th Dept. 1980), People v. Peoples and Goss, People v. Sweat (Erie County Ct., unpublished, 1980).

After an attempt to invalidate the Virginia sodomy law in a declaratory judgment proceeding failed in Doe v. Commonwealth's Attorney for City of Richmond (1975), it seemed clear that the most appropriate vehicle to challenge sodomy laws in the courts would be through the appeal of actual convictions, which would assure the appellants' standing. One of the first such successful attempts came in People v. Onofre, a case in which a purely consensual relationship between consenting adult males became the subject of a criminal prosecution in Syracuse, New York.

Ronald Onofre had initiated a consensual sexual relationship with a 17-year-old male (unnamed in court papers) that deteriorated after some time. The young man, angry with Onofre, went to the police seeking revenge, alleging that he had been coerced into the relationship. Onofre, seeking to avoid prosecution for felony sodomy, showed Syracuse District Attorney Richard A. Hennessy, Jr., photographs of himself and his partner engaged in sexual activity in a successful attempt to convince Hennessy that their conduct was consensual. Nevertheless, Hennessy decided to charge Onofre under New York's misdemeanor consensual sodomy statute, which had been adopted in 1965 to accompany New York's enactment of the Model Penal Code. Although the Model Penal Code did

not include criminal penalties for consensual sodomy, it did, as adopted in New York, provide penalties for nonconsensual "deviate sexual intercourse," defined as "sexual conduct between persons not married to each other consisting of contact between the penis and the anus, the mouth and the penis, or the mouth and the vulva." Using this definition, New York made it a misdemeanor for anyone to engage in "deviate sexual intercourse" with anyone else under the rubric of "consensual sodomy."

Representing Onofre, Syracuse attorney Bonnie Strunk filed a motion to dismiss the charges, arguing that the consensual sodomy law violated the right to privacy and equal protection (the latter because it prohibited for unmarried persons conduct allowed to married persons). Onondaga County Court Judge Ormand N. Gale denied the motion, after having researched the question, and found no prior New York or federal precedents suggesting that the law might be unconstitutional. After Gale rendered his unpublished decision on the motion to dismiss, Onofre, who had admitted to Hennessy that he and his young friend had engaged in consensual sodomy, repeated his admission in court and was convicted by Gale. Onofre appealed to the New York Supreme Court's Appellate Division, Fourth Department.

While Onofre's case was working its way to the appellate level, Buffalo attorney William H. Gardner was defending one of several sodomy prosecutions in the Buffalo city courts. Gardner's case involved two gay men, Conde J. Peoples, III, and Philip S. Goss, who had been apprehended having oral sex in a parked car in the early morning hours; another pending case involved Mary Sweat, similarly apprehended having oral sex with a man in a parked car. Gardner's clients had been convicted in the city courts, and their convictions were upheld in the Erie County Court. Seeing the *Onofre* case as a vehicle for getting his clients' convictions reversed, Gardner filed an *amicus* brief on behalf of the National Committee for Sexual Civil Liberties, of which he was a member, in the Fourth Department's consideration of Onofre's challenge to the sodomy law. (The National Committee for Sexual Civil Liberties, later to become the American Association for Personal Privacy, was a voluntary organization of attorneys and others concerned with reforming sex crimes laws that had participated as litigant or *amicus* in a variety of cases around the nation as well as in lobbying efforts to obtain reform through repeal or amendment of existing laws.)

Onofre's appeal was heard by a five-judge panel of the Fourth Department. For some reason not explained in the published opinion, Presiding Justice Michael F. Dillon decided not to participate in issuing the opinion released on January 24, 1980, by his unanimous colleagues. The opinion by Justice John H. Doerr found the consensual sodomy law violative of due process and equal protection under both the federal and state constitutions. Strunk and Gardner had urged consideration of state as well as federal grounds, hoping that in the event the statute was held unconstitutional and the case ever got to the U.S. Supreme Court, there might be independent state grounds to insulate it from reversal. This course seemed prudent in light of the Supreme Court's summary affirmance in *Doe v. Commonwealth's Attorney.*

Doerr began his analysis by rejecting the prosecutor's contention that *Doe v. Commonwealth's Attorney* bound the court to reject Onofre's challenge. That case was a declaratory judgment action, said Doerr, while here the court was faced with "a defendant attacking the constitutionality of a penal statute under which he stands convicted of a crime." Besides, Onofre had also based his challenge on the state constitution, as to which *Doe* was not binding precedent.

Doerr then described the accumulating privacy precedents under the federal Constitution, noting that *Griswold v. Connecticut* (1965) and its progeny had converted "an interest given limited protection by certain constitutional provisions" into "an independent constitutional right." Tracing the growth of privacy doctrine through *Eisenstadt v. Baird* (1972), *Stanley v. Georgia* (1969), and *Roe v. Wade* (1973), Doerr concluded:

> Thus it is seen that the concept of personal freedom includes a broad and unclassified group of values and activities related generally to individual repose, sanctuary and autonomy and the individual's right to develop his personal existence in the manner he or she sees fit. Personal sexual conduct is a fundamental right, protected by the right to privacy because of the transcendental importance of sex to the human condition, the intimacy of the conduct, and its relationship to a person's right to control his or her own body. . . . The right is broad enough to include sexual acts between non-married persons . . . and intimate consensual homosexual conduct.

Significantly, in citing authority to support these propositions, Doerr appeared to rely as much on academic publications as on prior court decisions, citing law review articles as well as Professor Laurence Tribe's treatise on constitutional law, quoting extensively from Professor David Richards's article advocating extension of constitutional privacy doctrine to consensual sodomy in volume 45 of the *Fordham University Law Review.*

Having concluded that the right to privacy covered such activity, Doerr said, "To the extent that certain conduct has the potential for working harm, the State may restrict it," and turned to the issue of the state's interest in forbidding consensual sodomy to unmarried persons. "If the interest of the State is the general promotion of morality," he asserted, "we are then required to accept on faith the State's moral judgment." This Doerr was unwilling to do:

> Equally important in the community of man would seem to be some degree of toleration of ideas and moral choices with which one

disagrees. The State may have a paternalistic interest in protecting an individual from self-inflicted harm or self-degrading experiences. This again presupposes the validity of the State's judgment, and outright proscription of certain activity can easily become discriminatory governmental tyranny. Curtailing activity which offends the public is a legitimate State interest but the standard to be applied in such a case is the effect that behavior might have on a reasonable person, not the most sensitive member of the community. Conduct which is carried on in an atmosphere of privacy between two parties by mutual agreement has little likelihood of offending a public not embarked on eavesdropping. A State interest based upon the prevention of physical violence and disorder fails for the same reason. Sexual conduct with an unwilling partner or one incapable of consent is punishable by other statutes.

Doerr was similarly dismissive of Hennessy's argument that the state's interest in "preserving marriage and the nuclear family" required upholding the statute. While these interests would justify constitutionality of the adultery laws, said Doerr, it was not clear how the consensual sodomy law advanced these interests. He found "no empirical evidence" to support the view that "homosexual conduct" needed to be forbidden to bolster traditional family values. He found no evidence that the new sexual permissiveness had made heterosexual marriage "as an institution" less attractive; it appeared that most divorced people eventually remarried. "Further," he asserted, "there is no indication that the state of remaining unmarried has undermined the heterosexual family," noting that religious celibacy, a long-standing practice, had "not made the heterosexual family less stable." Again quoting from Richards's law review article, Doerr indicated that there was no "constitutional or moral duty to marry, or more generally to procreate," and any assertion of such a duty would clearly violate the constitutional right to privacy in matters of marital and reproductive choice already recognized by the Supreme Court.

Since none of the reasons suggested by the state as justification for the statute rose to the level necessary to justify intrusion on the right of privacy, the statute offended the due process requirements of both the federal and state constitutions. Doerr continued:

Moreover, if homosexual conduct is thus protected, heterosexual conduct between unmarried consenting adults in private is protected for the same reasons and in addition for the reason that the differentiation made between married and unmarried persons has no rational basis and is violative not only of due process but also the equal protection clause of the Constitution.

Consequently, Onofre's conviction must be reversed and the indictment dismissed.

District Attorney Hennessy sought and received permission to appeal to the court of appeals, where his case was consolidated with the pending appeals from the Erie County Court in Gardner's Buffalo sodomy conviction cases. The case at this point became something of a *cause célèbre*, attracting *amicus* briefs to the multiparty arguments held in Albany from the Association of the Bar of the City of New York, the National Committee for Sexual Civil Liberties, the New York Civil Liberties Union, and the Lambda Legal Defense and Education Fund. The court heard oral argument from District Attorneys Hennessy, of Syracuse, and Edward Cosgrove, of Buffalo, and defense attorneys Strunk, Gardner, and Buffalo attorney Dianne Bennett.

On December 18, 1980, the court of appeals issued its decision, affirming the Fourth Department, reversing the Erie County Court, and holding the consensual sodomy law unconstitutional as violative of due process and equal protection under the federal Constitution, but failing to mention the state constitution in its opinion. The opinion for the court by Judge Hugh R. Jones represented the views of four members. An additional member of the court, Judge Matthew J. Jasen, concurred in the result solely on equal protection grounds. Judge Domenick L. Gabrielli wrote a lengthy dissenting opinion, joined by Chief Judge Lawrence H. Cooke.

Jones dealt first with the issue of privacy, referring to the right of privacy as "a right of independence in making certain kinds of important decisions, with a concomitant right to conduct oneself in accordance with those decisions, undeterred by governmental restraint," which the court had referred to in an earlier case as "freedom of conduct." He grounded the right in Justice Louis D. Brandeis's famous dissenting opinion in *Olmstead v. United States* (1928), where it was described as "the most comprehensive of rights and the right most valued by civilized men," and traced its application to sexual decisions and behavior from *Griswold* in 1965 through *Roe v. Wade*. He particularly emphasized Justice William J. Brennan's comment in *Carey v. Population Services International* (1977) that the Supreme Court had not yet marked the "outer limits" of the federal constitutional privacy right.

The people were not contesting the existence of the right, said Jones, but only its scope as applied to this case. The district attorneys argued that the right of privacy in the sexual context applied only to marital intimacy and procreative choice. Jones asserted that this description failed to take account of *Stanley v. Georgia*, in which the Supreme Court had applied a right of privacy to the private possession and use of pornography, or of *Eisenstadt v. Baird*, in which the Court had indicated that the right of privacy attached to the individual person, including unmarried people, when it came to sexual decisionmaking. After quoting at more length from Justice Brandeis's *Olmstead* dissent, Jones said:

> In light of these decisions, protecting under the cloak of the right of privacy individual decisions as to indulgence in acts of sexual intimacy by unmarried persons and as to satisfaction of sexual desires by resort to material condemned as obscene by community standards when done in a cloistered setting, no rational basis appears for excluding from the same protection decisions—such as those made by defendants before us—to seek sexual gratification from what at least once was commonly regarded as "deviant" conduct, so long as the decisions are voluntarily made by adults in a noncommercial, private setting.

In a footnote, Jones disclaimed for the court any interest in getting into debates about the theological, moral, or psychological arguments concerning consensual sodomy. "These are aspects of the issue on which informed, competent authorities and individuals may and do differ," he said, but, contrary to the dissent, "it is not the function of the Penal Law in our governmental policy to provide either a medium for the articulation or the apparatus for the intended enforcement of moral or theological

values." He based this assertion on the Supreme Court's contraception decisions, arguing that they reflected a view that moral objections by some citizens to the use of contraceptives were not sufficient basis for a law penalizing their use. "We are not unmindful of the sensibilities of many persons who are deeply persuaded that consensual sodomy is evil and should be prohibited," he said, but insisted that was not the issue before the court, which was whether the federal Constitution "permits recourse to the sanctions of the criminal law for the achievement of that objective." He concluded on this point that individuals were entirely free to attempt to persuade others through noncoercive means not to engage in sodomy, but that the state could not resort to criminal laws for that purpose.

Jones rejected the contention that the state could justify invading this privacy right in order to "prevent physical harm which might otherwise befall the participants" in consensual sodomy, or to "uphold public morality" or to "protect the institution of marriage." While he found each of these objectives to be "commendable," he asserted that "there is nothing on which to base a conclusion that they are achieved" by the consensual sodomy law. The district attorneys had proceeded solely from argument, not from presentation of facts documenting the connection between the statute and the achievement of these goals. In fact, said Jones, as to the "physical harm" issue, the legislative history of the statute made it clear that the sole reason for enacting a consensual sodomy law at the time New York was adopting the Model Penal Code was the legislature's apprehension that repeal of the existing sodomy law without putting a new one in its place could be "construed as legislative approval of deviate conduct." Thus, the only justification advanced by the state plausibly founded in legislative intent was that of advancing public morality, but Jones asserted that *Eisenstadt v. Baird* had disposed of this sort of argument by sharply distinguishing between private and public morality as legitimate bases for governmental regulation. Said Jones:

> There is a distinction between public and private morality and the private morality of an individual is not synonymous with nor

necessarily will have effect on what is known as public morality.... So here, the People have failed to demonstrate how government interference with the practice of personal choice in matters of intimate sexual behavior out of view of the public and with no commercial component will serve to advance the cause of public morality or do anything other than restrict individual conduct and impose a concept of private morality chosen by the State.

Jones rejected on similar grounds the argument that the consensual sodomy law was necessary to promote or protect the institution of marriage; there were no empirical data showing a connection between the two.

In effect, the court of appeals was adopting the Millian "harm principle" (i.e., that one's liberty of action should be circumscribed only when the action harms others) as its basis for decision here. Jones asserted that the state had failed to show any harm to the individual or to society in allowing individual adults to engage in consensual sodomy in private with other adults, provided there was no commercial component to their decision. He concluded:

> Personal feelings of distaste for the conduct sought to be proscribed ... and even disapproval by a majority of the populace, if that disapproval were to be assumed, may not substitute for the required demonstration of a valid basis for intrusion by the State in an area of important personal decision protected under the right of privacy drawn from the United States Constitution—areas, the number and definition of which have steadily grown but, as the Supreme Court has observed, the outer limits of which it has not yet marked.

He also quickly disposed of Gabrielli's dissenting argument that the case was inconsistent with the court's recent decision in *People v. Shephard* (1980), in which it had upheld against constitutional challenge a law banning private possession of marijuana, on the ground that there was evidence that marijuana might be harmful to its users. Jones could not find any intrinsic harm in the sexual activity in question.

Turning next to the equal protection issue, Jones found the law discriminatory on its face in allowing married couples to do what it prohibited for unmarried persons. He found that there was no "ground of difference that rationally explains the different treatment accorded married and unmarried persons," noting that

the only justification advanced by the state for this disparate treatment was "a societal interest in protecting and nurturing the institution of marriage and what are termed 'rights accorded married persons.'" Jones was unpersuaded by this justification, noting again that there was no evidence that the sodomy law advanced those objectives in any way.

Seeking to cloak the court's decision in the garb of familiarity, Jones then invoked a variety of decisions from other states casting doubt on the constitutionality of laws regulating private consensual sexual activity between adults and discussed at length why the court believed that it was not bound by the Supreme Court's decision in *Doe v. Commonwealth's Attorney*. He concluded that the dismissal of Onofre's indictment should be affirmed and that the convictions of the Buffalo appellants should be reversed. (In a footnote, Jones had rejected the state's argument that the Buffalo defendants and Onofre had waived any privacy rights because the Buffalo defendants' acts took place in parked cars and Onofre had shown photographs of his sexual activity to the prosecutors; in any event, said Jones, the court's disposition on equal protection grounds made it unnecessary to get into detailed arguments about what constituted "public" or "private" activity.)

Judge Jasen concurred in the result separately, stating that he could not accept the majority's use of the right of privacy to achieve its result, but that he could "discern no rational basis upon which the Legislature could have decided to freely allow the conduct in issue among married people and to make identical conduct criminal among those for whom that estate is undesirable or unattainable." Thus, he saw an equal protection problem of equal significance for homosexuals and heterosexuals. "I hasten to add," he said, "that, in my opinion, the Legislature does have the power to make moral judgments," but in this case the moral judgment had not been made with "the requisite evenhandedness." In other words, if sodomy was wrong, it should either be prohibited for everybody or not at all.

Judge Gabrielli's lengthy dissent provided a foretaste of the Supreme Court's opinion six years later in *Bowers v. Hardwick*, for he made many of the same arguments, although, it must be said, with more eloquence and point than Justice Byron R. White in his 1986 opinion. Gabrielli was critical of the court's willingness to recognize what he believed to be a new, unprecedented right of sexual privacy without taking any steps to demarcate its scope. Gabrielli believed that use of the Supreme Court's existing privacy cases was not enough to justify this case as a mere extension of a previously identified right, for "the connection between this case and those decisions exists only on the most superficial level." For Gabrielli, none of the Supreme Court's cases stood for the proposition that "there is a generalized right of privacy or personal autonomy implicit in the Federal Bill of Rights" or in the Due Process Clause. To take such an approach was totally inconsistent with the court's recent *Shephard* decision on marijuana. He accused the majority of having conflated two steps in the constitutional analysis, by incorporating into its consideration of whether a fundamental right was at issue its discussion of the state's purported justifications for penalizing sodomy. Gabrielli feared that the majority's analysis would lead to finding a "fundamental right" for all private, consensual activity, thus imposing on the state too high a burden to justify a wide variety of criminal laws that had long, respected histories.

In reviewing the Supreme Court's decisions, Gabrielli found that those aspects of sexual choice protected by the Court had long histories of societal respect, only recently interrupted by state enactments. In the cases of contraception and abortion, the Court was dealing with the kinds of personal decisions that had essentially been left up to individuals until the mid- to late 19th century. By contrast, sodomy prohibitions extended far back in time, as part of the English common law taken over by the United States and subsequently codified in the various states. This difference in historical treatment was a critical distinction for Gabrielli, since it provided a method for rejecting the charge that courts had unfettered discretion under the Due Process Clause to strike down laws with which they disagreed. Rather, he asserted, the court's power was limited to striking down laws that interfered with long-venerated private rights.

Specifically disputing the court's reliance on *Stanley v. Georgia* as the critical case marking an extension of the right of privacy beyond marital and reproductive choice, Gabrielli characterized that case as grounded in First Amendment rather than Fourteenth or Fourth Amendment rights, as would Justice White in *Hardwick*. Invoking the spectre of the sort of "substantive due process" that had been discredited during the 1930s, under which protective labor legislation had been routinely invalidated by the Supreme Court to protect "freedom of contract," Gabrielli argued that while the privacy cases such as *Griswold* and *Roe v. Wade* clearly marked at least a limited revival of substantive due process, the Supreme Court had been careful to apply such an analysis "to matters that were traditionally insulated from governmental intrusion. To my view," he said, "it is precisely this limitation that differentiates the relatively recent 'fundamental right' concept from the long discarded and truly pernicious doctrine enunciated in *Lochner v. New York* [1905]." Contrary to decisions "relating to family life, matrimony and procreation, decisions involving pure sexual gratification have been subject to State intervention throughout the history of western civilization," asserted Gabrielli, invoking Blackstone's characterization of sodomy as an offense worse than rape and noting the ancient provenance of American sodomy laws in a statute of the reign of Henry VIII in 1553. Given this long history, Gabrielli considered the majority's decision in this case "an act of judicial legislation."

Buoyed by the strength of Gabrielli's dissenting opinion, the district attorneys petitioned the court for reargument and reconsideration, but the court refused to revisit the case. Then they filed a petition for *certiorari* with the Supreme Court, arguing that the decision, explicitly premised solely on the federal Constitution, was contrary to existing precedent. This petition raised great consternation in the gay legal community in New York, which had been celebrating its famous victory. Strunk and Gardner had both urged the court, in briefs and oral argument, to affirm the Fourth Department's conclusion that the consensual sodomy law violated the New York State Constitution, but the court had inexplicably neglected to mention the state document in its opinion. There was a great sigh of relief from around the state when the Supreme Court denied *certiorari* on May 18, 1981, making the decision *res judicata* and final in all respects.

The importance of the New York State Constitution became even clearer when the Supreme Court finally issued its first substantive decision on sodomy laws in 1986, upholding Georgia's statute in *Bowers v. Hardwick*. Because the *Onofre* decision was premised solely on federal constitutional law, and the New York State legislature had stoutly resisted any effort to repeal the sodomy law despite the decision, there were fears that *Hardwick* would, in effect, revive the sodomy law in New York. Attorney General Robert Abrams promptly moved to quell those fears, announcing that after study of the two decisions he concluded that the sodomy law had not been revived because of the equal protection component of the New York decision. (In *Hardwick*, the Supreme Court had ruled based only on privacy arguments.) The consensual sodomy law remains on the New York statute books, but is unenforceable as to private, consensual, and noncommercial activity in light of the *Onofre* decision.

The court of appeals' decision in *Onofre* was a historic landmark in sodomy litigation for several reasons. Perhaps most significantly, the court was willing to equate heterosexual and homosexual sodomy and deal with the issue on the level of sexual privacy, an approach eschewed by the Supreme Court in *Hardwick*, where the majority focused solely on "homosexual sodomy" despite the broad prohibition of all sodomy by Georgia's law. More importantly, the court articulated a broad theoretical basis for its decision, tying together the federal privacy cases in a way that vindicated extension of the privacy concept to conduct that had traditionally been subject to penal sanction in a way that contraception and abortion had not. By striking down the sodomy law of one of the largest states in the nation, the court gave new hope to those struggling for eventual decriminalization of consensual sodomy throughout the United States. Even though that hope appeared dashed at the federal level by the Supreme Court's *Hardwick* decision, it remained alive as litigators turned back to state courts and state constitutions to attack sodomy laws one jurisdiction at a time.

Case References

Bowers v. Hardwick, 478 U.S. 186 (1986)

Carey v. Population Services International, 431 U.S. 678 (1977)

Doe v. Commonwealth's Attorney for City of Richmond, 403 F. Supp. 1199 (1975), affirmed, 425 U.S. 901 (1976)

Eisenstadt v. Baird, 405 U.S. 438 (1972)

Griswold v. Connecticut, 381 U.S. 479 (1965)

Lochner v. New York, 198 U.S. 45 (1905)

Olmstead v. United States, 277 U.S. 438 (1928)

People v. Shephard, 50 N.Y.2d 640 (1980)

Roe v. Wade, 410 U.S. 113 (1973)

Stanley v. Georgia, 394 U.S. 557 (1969)

22. "STATUTORY RAPE" AND EQUAL PROTECTION

Michael M. v. Superior Court of Sonoma County, 450 U.S. 464 (1981), affirming 25 Cal. 3d 608, 159 Cal. Rptr. 340, 601 P.2d 572 (1979).

Teen-age sex is one of the most controversial issues in American society. The states have traditionally taken a strong role in regulating such conduct under the criminal law, although the strict statutory prohibitions are rarely enforced against teens who have consensual sex in private, and soaring teen pregnancy rates seem to indicate that the laws have little deterrent effect. However, with rare exception, judicial authorities agree that the states may maintain criminal penalties for teen-age sex on the books, even—as in California—when the pertinent statutes discriminate on the basis of gender.

From early days of statehood, California purported to impose criminal penalties on any man, of whatever age, who had sexual intercourse with a woman who was herself below a specified age, regardless of consent and regardless whether effective contraception was used. The California laws drew their basis from the common-law offense of statutory rape, dating from the reign of the English King Edward I at the end of the 13th century, at which time the age of consent for women was 12 years. The purpose of such laws was to protect underage females because of the belief that they were "too young to understand the nature and quality" of their acts and thus incapable of giving true consent. California enacted its first "statutory rape" law of this type in 1850, and it was reenacted in 1872 as part of a general Penal Code adoption. These early laws, echoing an English statute of 1576 that reduced the age of consent for women to 10, adopted that low age, but in 1889 the Penal Code was amended to raise the age of consent to 14. Later amendments in 1897 and 1913 raised the age of consent first to 16 and then to 18, where it remained at the time of the *Michael M.* litigation.

Late on the night of June 3, 1978, 16-year-old Sharon and her teen-age sister were waiting at a bus stop with a bag containing whiskey and soda when three teen-age boys, including 17-year-old Michael M., were riding by on their bicycles. The boys circled back, joined the girls (whom they did not know), and the group walked over to the railroad tracks, drinking. After a period of drinking and "making out," Sharon's sister and one of the other boys left. Michael, Sharon, and Bruce hung around together, with Bruce leaving after getting kissed by Sharon. Michael and Sharon ended up on a secluded park bench, with Michael attempting to "go all the way." At first Sharon protested, but after Michael hit her several times she gave in and they had intercourse.

Michael was brought before the municipal court upon a complaint by Sharon. That court determined that he was not a "fit and proper subject" to be dealt with under the juvenile court law, so he was charged by information with a felony violation of the Penal Code ban on sexual intercourse with a woman to whom the defendant is not married and bound over for trial in the Superior Court of Sonoma County. Michael's attorney, Gregory F. Jilka, of Rohnert Park, California, moved to set aside the information, contending that the statute violated Michael's right to equal protection of the laws, in that it provided for punishment only of the male partner in the sexual act. The superior court and the court of appeal rejected this contention in unpublished orders, and Michael applied to the California Supreme Court for a writ of prohibition seeking dismissal of the information against him.

The state supreme court heard argument from Jilka and Deputy Attorney General Sandy R. Kriegler, and subsequently ruled 4–3 that the law violated no constitutional right of Michael, who should be tried on the charge. The November 5, 1979, opinion by Justice Frank K. Richardson, while conceding that the statute discriminated on its face against men, found that the discrimination was justified by a compelling state interest in preventing teen pregnancy.

Since the statute clearly discriminated on the basis of sex by imposing a penalty only on men, it could be sustained only if found justified under the constitutional standards pertaining to sex discrimination. In *Sail'er Inn, Inc. v. Kirby* (1971), the California Supreme Court had held that sex was a "suspect classification," so that sexual classifications in statutes could be maintained only if supported by a compelling state interest and if there were no less discriminatory method to achieve that interest. In that case, the court struck down a law barring women from employment as bartenders, finding that there was no compelling state interest to support the discrimination. In this case, Richardson found that the "obviously discriminatory classification scheme is readily justified by an important state interest," the prevention of teen pregnancy. He stated:

> Unlike the sex-based classification which we invalidated in *Sail'er Inn*, and which reflected overbroad social generalizations regarding the appropriate roles of males and females, the law herein challenged is supported not by mere social convention but by the immutable physiological fact that it is the female exclusively who can become pregnant. This changeless physical law, coupled with the tragic human costs of illegitimate teenage pregnancies,

generates a compelling and demonstrable state interest in minimizing both the number of such pregnancies and their disastrous consequences. Accordingly, the Legislature is amply justified in retaining its historic statutory rape law because of the potentially devastating social and economic results which may follow its violation.

Richardson recited statistics showing the alarming rate of teen pregnancies and their consequences, including the high proportion of abortions in California performed on unmarried teen-age women, and the higher rate of medical complications during teen pregnancies than during pregnancies of more physically mature women. He also noted that among the nonmedical consequences of teen pregnancy were a high school drop-out rate much higher than for nonpregnant teens, and that there were additional psychological and social problems attendant on this phenomenon. Clearly, the legislature was attacking an important social problem when it sought to prevent teen pregnancy, and legislative bodies had a fairly wide degree of discretion in deciding how to address such problems. Said Richardson, "It may encourage sex education in schools and provide for the dissemination of relevant educational information and medical attention. . . . It may also, in our view, properly attack the problem more directly by expressly prohibiting acts of sexual intercourse performed by a male with a female, not the wife of the perpetrator, who is under the age of 18 years." Richardson insisted that once the legislature had identified pregnancy by teen-age girls as the problem it sought to prevent,

> it inevitably follows that sex is the only possible and therefore *necessary* classification which can be adopted in identifying offender and victim. The Legislature is well within its power in imposing criminal sanctions against males, alone, because they are the *only* persons who may physiologically cause the result which the law properly seeks to avoid.

(This last assertion was, of course, patently inaccurate, since an unmarried teen-age woman could impregnate herself by securing sperm from a donor. More significantly, of course, "it takes two to tango!")

Michael M. argued that the law was overbroad if this was its purpose because it even

covered situations where pregnancy was impossible or unlikely, due to the lack of fertility of one or more participant or the use of contraceptive techniques. Richardson rejected this argument, noting the significant burden of proof to which the state would be put, quoting from a Maine decision, *State v. Rundlett* (1978), where that state's supreme court said:

> We doubt that legislators, intent on use of the criminal law to prevent juvenile pregnancies, would throw such a roadblock in the way of effective prosecution as would be created by subjecting an under-age prosecutrix to cross-examination of such additionally embarrassing and uncertain details. Furthermore, we believe legislators' rejection of the defenses suggested . . . reflects their reluctance to rely, for accomplishment of their anti-pregnancy objective, upon the doubtful efficacy of contraceptives and the truth of the inevitable claim of nonemission by a male charged with statutory rape.

Richardson also rejected the opposite argument, that the statute was underinclusive because the woman was not also subject to prosecution. He asserted that the legislature could recognize "degrees of culpability," and, implicitly finding men more responsible than women, even where conduct was consensual, impose punishment only on the man. Richardson justified this approach by contending that the woman was subjected to more risk and adverse consequences from underage intercourse than the man, and thus more in need of protection by the state. "To hold otherwise," he insisted, "defies not only common sense and reality, but the fundamental laws of biology." This statute was part of an overall statutory scheme that had many other provisions dealing with sex involving minors, including provisions under which older women could be prosecuted if they engaged in sex with underage males. The statutory rape provision, commented Richardson, "merely provides additional protection for minor females in recognition of the demonstrably greater injury, physical and emotional, which they may suffer." Richardson rejected the precedential value of *Meloon v. Helgemoe*, a 1977 decision by the U.S. Court of Appeals for the First Circuit striking down a state law that provided no penalty for sex with an underage male but penalized men for having sex with underage women, contending that the California statutory scheme was not comparable.

Furthermore, said Richardson, there was an intensely practical reason for exempting the young woman from punishment. In a prosecution, the state would likely be relying on her to be the principal witness, indeed the "prosecutrix," and such a role was unlikely to be played by many women if they were subject to prosecution themselves. Punishing women might deter them from reporting unlawful sex acts, thus undermining achievement of the state's compelling purpose. Richardson rejected the contention that the statute created "adverse inferences concerning the capacity of minor females to make intelligent and volitional decisions," noting that both men and women could be prosecuted under the "forcible rape" law for nonconsensual cases and that the statutory rape provision was just one of many laws forbidding to minors various activities (such as purchasing tobacco products or participating in bingo games for money) that were allowed for adults. While it was possible that the legislature could adopt a gender-neutral statutory rape law, it "is not constitutionally compelled to do so," concluded Richardson, and a decision to do so should be left to the legislature. The defendant had introduced evidence that the overwhelming majority of states with statutory rape laws had reformed them over time to be gender neutral through legislative amendment; to Richardson, this was a good argument to bring to the legislature, not to the court.

Justice Stanley Mosk dissented, in an opinion joined by two other members of the court. "I cannot subscribe to the implied premise of the majority that the female of the human species is weak, inferior, and in need of paternalistic protection from the state," he proclaimed.

> That concept is an anachronism in a society in which females have achieved remarkable progress toward equality. The tutelary syndrome of Victorian days has yielded to a new era in which women are contributing their talents in every field of endeavor—as prime ministers, governors, legislators, judges, corporate executives, lawyers, scientists, medical doctors, police officers and professional athletes.

In this context, such a blatantly discriminatory statutory classification must fall under the hold-

ing in *Sail'er Inn* as violating the California Constitution's equal protection clause. The facts in this case, urged Mosk, showed the "fundamental unfairness of a law that always punishes the young man and never the young woman for a joint act of which she was often equally the cause."

Mosk was particularly dismissive of the "compelling interest" of preventing pregnancy advocated by the state as justification for the statute. Tracing the history of the law back to medieval times, he showed that preventing pregnancy was never its motivation, especially since in early times it applied only to sex with very young girls who were biologically incapable of becoming pregnant. The age of consent had been raised to cover young women capable of conceiving only in relatively recent times (the late 19th century), and nowhere in the legislative record was there any mention of preventing pregnancy as a reason for raising the age.

While conceding that preventing teen pregnancy was an important interest of the government, Mosk contended it could not be used to justify a statute without some evidence that it was "among its actual purposes." Clearly, based on both history and biology, it was not. "The true intent of the Legislature in adopting the California statutory rape law, rather, is revealed in the draftsmen's notes to the Penal Code of 1872" where, echoing the old common-law view, the drafter stated: "This provision embodies the well settled rule of the existing law; that a girl under ten years of age is *incapable of giving any consent* to an act of intercourse which can reduce it below the grade of rape." Said Mosk, "There was no mention whatever of pregnancy prevention," either in 1872 or later when the age was raised. The most plausible explanation for raising the age of consent, said Mosk, was not a concern about pregnancy but rather "because popular views changed both with regard to the suitable age of women for marriage and the age until which they were deemed appropriately subject to protective legislation." This was reflected in parallel changes in the law regarding the age of consent for marriage without parental consent. Applying the law in early cases from the 19th century, the California Supreme Court had stated that its "obvious purpose" was "the protection of society by protecting from violation the *virtue* of young and unsophisticated girls."

Mosk's crowning blow to the teen pregnancy justification, however, was the California Supreme Court's much more recent decision in *People v. Hernandez* (1964), where the court upheld the law against constitutional attack by affirming the presumption that a woman under age 18 could not give effective consent to sexual intercourse because "she is presumed too innocent and naive to understand the implications and nature of the act."

> The law's concern with her capacity or lack thereof to so understand is explained in part by a popular conception of the social, moral and personal values which are preserved by the abstinence from sexual indulgence on the part of a young woman [said the *Hernandez* court]. An unwise disposition of her sexual favor is deemed to do harm both to herself and the social mores by which the community's conduct patterns are established. Hence the law of statutory rape intervenes in an effort to avoid such a disposition.

Mosk noted that the law itself did not appear to have any concern with pregnancy, since it made no distinction between procreative and nonprocreative intercourse, including intercourse with young women who were not yet physically capable of becoming pregnant. While the objective of "reducing illicit pregnancies among teenage girls may well be a laudable governmental objective," said Mosk, it was "wishful thinking to believe that the California statutory rape law was actually enacted or reenacted for that purpose."

But even if preventing pregnancy were the purpose of the law, Mosk contended that discriminating on the basis of sex was not a rational way to proceed. Either the male or the female could be the instigator of the act, and, assuming it was consensual, both parties were equally responsible for the act occurring. While it was true that only females could become pregnant, "no compelling justification has been offered for holding the male but not the female criminally responsible for the same act," which left the law "impermissibly underinclusive." Mosk ridiculed the court's rationale that the woman should be exempted from the statutory prohibition because she would suffer greater consequences from teen sex that led to preg-

nancy than would the man; to Mosk, that she would run greater risks did not make her any less morally culpable than the man. "In our system of justice, offenders are not deemed less culpable merely because they may suffer additional punishment from sources outside the legal system," he exclaimed. He also labeled a *"non sequitur"* the contention that this law was merely one among many protecting minors from various forms of sexual abuse, pointing out that the other laws cited by the majority made no distinction based on the gender of the victim or perpetrator. "The fact that those statutes are gender-neutral does not somehow give the Legislature the right to enact an 'additional' law on the topic that invidiously discriminates on sexual grounds," he asserted.

Mosk also rejected the notion that penalizing women would deter enforcement of the statute and accomplishment of the goal. He found this an "exaggeration," since the testimony of the woman was not "the sole evidence of the offense in every case," prosecutors would have discretion in determining who was at fault and deserved to be charged, and women whose testimony was necessary to convict an aggressive male could be given immunity from prosecution in exchange for their testimony. Since 31 other states had gender-neutral statutory rape laws, Mosk was unpersuaded that California's discriminatory law was really "necessary" to achieve the purpose contended for by the state.

Mosk also disagreed with Richardson's denial that the law presumed women inferior to make sexual decisions. "As it presently reads," he said, "the California statutory rape law thus reflects a belief that the minor female is in need of special protection not only against the male but also against herself, against her 'voluntary' but presumptively imprudent decisions in matters of sex," since it treated her differently from a man solely because she was a woman. Mosk opined: "Such notions are obviously vestiges of a bygone era, remnants of the exploded myth of intrinsic male superiority. They are the product of conventional sex-stereotypical thinking, and revive an outmoded patriarchal view of 'the woman's role.'" He found these notions as a motivating force for legislation to violate the equal protection requirement of the Fourteenth Amendment and the California Constitution as well.

Michael M. petitioned the U.S. Supreme Court for review, and the petition was granted on June 9, 1980, with oral argument scheduled for November 4. The Supreme Court was as divided by the case as the California court had been, dividing 5–4 in its March 23 decision, upholding the California court while generating separate opinions from five of the justices and no one opinion for a majority of the Court.

Writing for himself and three others, then-Associate Justice William H. Rehnquist began by observing that the California Supreme Court had applied a higher standard of review in this case than the Supreme Court had adopted for dealing with cases involving sex discrimination. Sex was not a "suspect classification;" under such decisions as *Craig v. Boren* (1976), statutes that used sex classifications were not subjected to strict scrutiny. Rather, they would be upheld if the Court found that the sex classification bore a "substantial relationship" to "important governmental objectives," a standard Rehnquist found to be met in this case because the gender distinction was not, in his view, "invidious," but rather "realistically reflects the fact that the sexes are not similarly situated in certain circumstances."

Rehnquist asserted that "the fact that the California Legislature criminalized the act of illicit sexual intercourse with a minor female is a sure indication of its intent or purpose to discourage that conduct." Although the reason why the legislature wanted to discourage the conduct was not ideally clear, and legislators might have voted out of a wide variety of motives, the state's argument in this case that preventing teen pregnancies was a motivation for the law, accepted by the state's highest court, was entitled to considerable deference from the Supreme Court. Even if preserving "female chastity" was one of the motives for the statute at one time, noted Rehnquist, that did not mean that the Court could not accept other motivations that were a permissible basis for the legislation.

After reviewing briefly the statistics on the occurrence and consequences of teen pregnancy, Rehnquist addressed the issue of whether men and women were "similarly situated" with regard to this issue:

We need not be medical doctors to discern that young men and young women are not similarly situated with respect to the problems and the risks of sexual intercourse. Only women may become pregnant, and they suffer disproportionately the profound physical, emotional and psychological consequences of sexual activity. The statute at issue here protects women from sexual intercourse at an age when those consequences are particularly severe. The question thus boils down to whether a State may attack the problem of sexual intercourse and teenage pregnancy directly by prohibiting a male from having sexual intercourse with a minor female. We hold that such a statute is sufficiently related to the State's objectives to pass constitutional muster.

Rehnquist found it unexceptionable that the legislature would single out the male actor for punishment, since it was, after all, intending to protect the female, not punish her, and it was the male who normally suffered few, if any, consequences from engaging in illicit intercourse, while the female was stuck with the pregnancy, possible abortion, and all the other consequences spelled out in the California Supreme Court's opinion. Rehnquist thus rejected the argument that the statute was underinclusive, and as well the argument that California must be put to the burden of showing that a gender-neutral statute could not serve its purposes equally well, accepting the speculation that a gender-neutral statute would undermine enforcement by deterring women from reporting and testifying about offenses. Rehnquist also characterized as "ludicrous" the alternative contention that the statute was overbroad, since it covered women incapable of becoming pregnant, pointing out that California would have a legitimate interest in protecting young girls from possible physical injury due to premature intercourse. Finally, he rejected a new argument, that Michael M. should be exempt from punishment because he was also a minor, and the statute improperly presumed that the male minor would automatically be the aggressor in any sexual act with a female minor. To Rehnquist, there was no suggestion of such a presumption in the statute; it merely provided that the age of men was irrelevant, because the evil to be prevented was underage women having intercourse.

Finally, Rehnquist asserted that the need for equal protection scrutiny was normally focused on laws that discriminated invidiously against women, because "we find nothing to suggest that men, because of past discrimination or peculiar disadvantages, are in need of the special solicitude of the courts."

Justice Potter Stewart joined Rehnquist's opinion, but also concurred separately, emphasizing that the statute was part of a more general statutory scheme that also imposed liability on women for some sexual activities, so the discrimination was not so "complete" as the appellant alleged. More to the point, however, he hammered on the conclusion that men and women were not similarly situated with regard to the risks of illicit teen intercourse, thus justifying the state's decision to focus criminal liability on the male. He also contended that "experienced observation confirms the commonsense notion that adolescent males disregard the possibility of pregnancy far more than do adolescent females," and thus were in greater need of deterrence to accomplish the state's goal. That other states had decided to enact gender-neutral statutes did not go to the issue of constitutionality, he asserted, contending that "the Equal Protection Clause does not mean that the physiological differences between men and women must be disregarded."

Justice Harry A. Blackmun concurred in the result in a separate opinion, beginning by chiding the plurality a bit for placing so much weight in this case on the burdens of teen pregnancy but, in other cases, voting in favor of various federal and state restrictions that made it difficult for pregnant teen-agers to obtain abortions. In the abortion cases, as in this case, what the state was really after was "the control and direction of young people's sexual activities," asserted Blackmun. But he could not vote to strike down this law, he said, because he thought it was "a sufficiently reasoned and constitutional effort to control the problem at its inception." He found a significant difference between this law and a state law that reflected "a State's adamant and rigid refusal to face, or even to recognize, the 'significant consequences'—to the woman—of a forced or unwanted conception."

Blackmun had joined many of the opinions cited by Rehnquist in holding that sex discriminatory statutes were subject to a lower standard of review than race discriminatory statutes under the Equal Protection Clause, and he was not willing to depart from that position in this case. Quoting lengthy extracts from Sharon's testimony at the preliminary hearing in the municipal court, Blackmun asserted that "it is only fair, with respect to this particular petitioner, to point out that his partner, Sharon, appears not to have been an unwilling participant in at least the initial stages of the intimacies" and that there were a variety of factors that "should make this case an unattractive one to prosecute at all, and especially to prosecute as a felony." However, Blackmun "reluctantly" concluded that here the facts "may fit the crime," and he was content to let the prosecution go forward.

Justice William J. Brennan, Jr., dissented in an opinion joined by Justices Byron R. White and Thurgood Marshall. He said that it was "disturbing to find the Court so splintered on a case that presents such a straightforward issue." Even using the "mid-level" scrutiny of *Craig v. Boren*, it was clear to him that this law was unconstitutional. The plurality and the concurrers had focused too much on whether the state had a compelling interest, said Brennan, and not enough on the second part of the test: whether the sex-based classification was *substantially* related to the achievement of the state's goal. Summarizing the Court's precedents in sex discrimination cases, Brennan pointed out that the burden on the government was to show both "the importance of its asserted objective and the substantial relationship between the classification and that objective." Furthermore, "the State cannot meet that burden without showing that a gender-neutral statute would be a less effective means of achieving that goal."

To save the statute in this case, asserted Brennan, California would have to show that "because its statutory rape law punishes only males, and not females, it more effectively deters minor females from having sexual intercourse." The evidence for such an argument was not in the record or anywhere else. The plurality just assumed that a gender-neutral law would be less effective because it might create enforcement difficulties, but this assumption was seriously flawed. First, thirty-seven other states had gender-neutral laws, yet California had not obtained or presented any evidence that these laws were less effective than its own law in preventing teen pregnancies. This stood to reason, since the law involved consensual sex, and in most cases it was unlikely a woman who participated in such activity would complain to the authorities, regardless whether the statute was gender-neutral. Furthermore, California had been busy over the years amending its other sex crime laws to make them gender-neutral, but no reason had been given why gender-neutrality was not extended to statutory rape as it was to all other sex crimes. Finally, Brennan argued that a gender-neutral statute would logically be more effective, since it could directly deter both men and women from engaging in premarital teen sex, thus potentially deterring "twice as many potential violators." But, Brennan noted, for him there was even a serious constitutional question whether the state had any business meddling in the consensual sexual activities of people such as Michael M. and Sharon: "Minors, too, enjoy a right of privacy in connection with decisions affecting procreation," he observed, citing *Carey v. Population Services International* (1977). "Thus," Brennan concluded, "despite the suggestion of the plurality to the contrary, it is not settled that a State may rely on a pregnancy-prevention justification to make consensual sexual intercourse among minors a criminal act."

Brennan apparently found persuasive Justice Mosk's summary of the history of the California law, since he closely paraphrased it in the next portion of his dissent, making the point again that the law was not adopted or readopted over the years for the express purpose of preventing teen pregnancy but rather to protect the "chastity" of young women. That the statute was enacted to "further these out-moded sexual stereotypes" was perhaps the best explanation why California could not come up with a "substantial relationship between the classification and its newly asserted goal," Brennan contended.

Justice John Paul Stevens dissented separately, arguing in effect that all this talk of deterrence was rather beside the point, since "lo-cal custom and belief—rather than statutory laws of venerable but doubtful ancestry—will determine the volume of sexual activity among unmarried teenagers." The very evidence on the increasing volume of teen intercourse and pregnancy showed the "futility of the notion that statutory prohibition will significantly affect the volume of that activity or provide a meaningful solution to the problem created by it." He wrote separately from Justice Brennan, however, because he could not agree with Brennan's observation that the right of privacy might prevent a state from "prohibiting all unmarried teenagers from engaging in sexual intercourse. The societal interests in reducing the incidence of venereal disease and teenage pregnancy are sufficient, in my judgment, to justify a prohibition of conduct that increases the risk of those harms," said Stevens. The problem was that this law did not approach that task with the requisite "evenhandedness."

The problem with the plurality's decision, said Stevens, was that it seemed *sub silentio* to indulge the "rather fanciful notion" that the California legislature's action assumed that the greater risks faced by young women than by young men from illicit intercourse made it unnecessary to impose penalties to deter women from engaging in it. This stood things on its head, said Stevens. "In my judgment, the fact that a class of persons is especially vulnerable to a risk that a statute is designed to avoid is a reason for making the statute applicable to that class. The argument that a special need for protection provides a rational explanation for an exemption is one I simply do not comprehend." He found California's approach here to be "utterly irrational":

> In my opinion, the only acceptable justification for a general rule requiring disparate treatment of the two participants in a joint act must be a legislative judgment that one is more guilty than the other. The risk-creating conduct that this statute is designed to prevent requires the participation of two persons—one male and one female. In many situations it is probably true that one is the aggressor and the other is either an unwilling, or at least a less willing, participant in the joint act. If a statute authorized punishment of only one participant and required the prosecutor to prove that that participant had been the aggressor, I assume that the discrimination would be valid.

Stevens noted in passing his puzzlement with the California court's statement that males "are the *only* persons who may physiologically cause the result which the law properly seeks to avoid." As noted above, it takes two to tango!

Because the California law required no proof that the male is the aggressor as a prerequisite to punishment, it must be that the legislature presumed the male would always be the aggressor, which assumed that the male was the decisionmaker in every such case. Stevens found no support for that presumption however, either in the record of the case, in any scholarly study, or in any other reputable source. Its only support was in "traditional attitudes toward male-female relationships." But it was just such reliance on "traditional attitudes" that was constitutionally unacceptable as a basis for discriminatory treatment.

In its brief, the state of California had argued that prosecutors could be relied on to invoke the statute only in cases where it appeared that the male was the aggressor, most likely cases where forcible rape should be charged but evidence for a conviction was lacking. Stevens found this an unacceptable justification for the statute:

> That assumption implies that a State has a legitimate interest in convicting a defendant on evidence that is constitutionally insufficient. Of course, the State may create a lesser-included offense that would authorize punishment of the more guilty party, but surely the interest in obtaining convictions on inadequate proof cannot justify a statute that punishes one who is equally or less guilty than his partner.

By the same token, he rejected the argument that a gender-neutral statute would undermine enforcement by deterring women from informing on men, asking "what is the justification for defining the exempt class entirely by reference to sex rather than by reference to a more neutral criterion such as relative innocence? . . . If a discarded male partner informs on a promiscuous female, a timely threat of prosecution might well prevent the precise harm the statute is intended to minimize." For Stevens, the need for "evenhanded enforcement of the law" outweighed all the speculative arguments advanced by the state to justify the statute.

In *Michael M.*, a majority of the Supreme Court endorsed a dubious solution to the problems of teen sex and pregnancy, indulging sexist attitudes about the relative capabilities of men and women in their teen years to make decisions about their sexual activities. The decision accorded poorly with existing precedents involving both sex discrimination and sexual privacy. It also suggested the anomalous result that the state could imprison an unmarried teen father, even if he and his girlfriend produced a child to whose support he agreed to contribute. The Supreme Court's decision was characteristic, however, of the more conservative turn the Court was taking in sexual matters at the beginning of the 1980s as part of a trend to give the states more leeway in matters of criminal law and regulation.

Case References

Carey v. Population Services International, 431 U.S. 678 (1977)

Craig v. Boren, 429 U.S. 190 (1976)

Meloon v. Helgemoe, 564 F.2d 602 (1st Cir. 1977)

People v. Hernandez, 61 Cal. 2d 529, 39 Cal. Rptr. 361, 393 P.2d 673 (1964)

Sail'er Inn, Inc. v. Kirby, 5 Cal. 3d 1, 95 Cal. Rptr. 329, 485 P.2d 529 (1971)

State v. Rundlett, 391 A.2d 815 (Me. 1978)

23. THERE'S NO HARM IN ASKING?: SOLICITING LAWFUL SEX

People v. Uplinger, 58 N.Y.2d 936 (1983), certiorari dismissed as improvidently granted, 467 U.S. 246 (1984). Decisions below: *People v. Uplinger,* 111 Misc. 2d 403, 444 N.Y.S.2d 373 (Buffalo City Ct. 1981); *People v. Sanders,* 110 Misc. 2d 398, 442 N.Y.S.2d 46 (Buffalo City Ct. 1981); *People v. Butler,* 110 Misc. 2d 843, 443 N.Y.S.2d 40 (Buffalo City Ct. 1981); *People v. Uplinger,* 113 Misc. 2d 876, 449 N.Y.S.2d 916 (Erie County Ct. 1982).

In 1980, the New York Court of Appeals held unconstitutional the state's law penalizing the commission of "deviate sexual intercourse" as defined in New York's adaptation of the Model Penal Code, which included oral or anal intercourse engaged in between persons not married to each other. In *People v. Onofre,* the court held that prohibiting private consensual sexual activity between adults offended the federal constitutional right of privacy first recognized by the U.S. Supreme Court as applying to married couples and expanded in later cases to encompass unmarried individuals as well. The court also held that the state had shown no justification for penalizing unmarried persons for engaging in conduct that was lawful for married couples, and thus had offended the requirement of equal protection of the laws as well. In 1981, the Supreme Court refused to review the court of appeals' decision.

Robert Uplinger, a gay man who lived in Buffalo, New York, was out "cruising" for sex on the hot night of August 7, 1981. He wandered over to North Street between Delaware Avenue and Irving Street, in a neighborhood where many gay men wandered the streets in the early morning hours, hoping to make a sexual connection. At about 3 A.M., Uplinger was attracted to a handsome young man sitting on the steps of the Hotel Lenox. Uplinger walked over and said, "Hi, how are you?" The young man replied, and they had a brief conversation. Uplinger asked him if he wanted to "get high," and he said no. "What do you like to do?" asked Uplinger. "I don't know," said the object of his affections, "What do you like to do?" This banter continued for several minutes, until a police car drove up and the police officers told Uplinger, the young man, and others milling about the area to "move on." Uplinger followed the young man and asked

him if he wanted to go back to Uplinger's place. When the young man asked why, Uplinger said, "Well, do you just want to come over?" "No. I'm scared with the police. I'm going to leave," the young man replied. "If you drive me over to my place," offered Uplinger, "I'll blow you."

Those were the magic words! The young man was Buffalo police department undercover vice officer Steven Nicosia. He arrested Uplinger for violating section 240.35–3 of the New York Penal Code, which prohibited "loitering in a public place for the purpose of engaging in or soliciting another person to engage in deviate sexual intercourse or other sexual behavior of a deviate nature." Uplinger's arrest was part of a sustained campaign by the local police department, stimulated by Erie County District Attorney Richard J. Arcara, who had been one of the losing parties in the *Onofre* case. The police had received several complaints about the heavy sexual cruising activities of gay men in the residential neighborhood, and the undercover campaign was directed toward scaring the gay men away.

Uplinger retained Buffalo attorney William H. Gardner to represent him, and moved to dismiss on grounds that the law under which he was charged was unconstitutional as a result of the *Onofre* ruling. If it is legal to have oral intercourse with a consenting adult in my apartment, argued Uplinger, then it must be legal for me to ask him inoffensively on the street to come home for that purpose. City Judge Timothy J. Drury decided to reserve decision on this motion pending a full hearing of the charges against Uplinger. Assistant District Attorney Thomas Lokken appeared for the district attorney at the nonjury trial in Buffalo City Court on September 24. On November 9, Judge Drury issued his opinion, denying Uplinger's motion and convicting him of violating the penal law.

Drury's decision was quite a surprise, since just a month earlier, he had dismissed a charge under the same section of the penal law against Susan Butler, a "known prostitute" who had been arrested after she was discovered in a parked car performing oral sex with a customer after being spotted by police officers "waving at cars at the intersection of Genesee and Davis Streets," an area "frequented by prostitutes." Unable to prove the commercial element of the crimes of prostitution and soliciting prostitution, the authorities had charged Butler with soliciting to engage in deviate sexual intercourse. Drury had dismissed the charges, holding that the statute was unconstitutional as applied to Butler's situation. Drury noted that in actuality Butler had been arrested for exactly the same conduct (having oral sex in a parked car) that was involved in a "heterosexual" case that was consolidated with Ronald Onofre's homosexual sodomy prosecution in the court of appeals' decision. "And," he said, "there is nothing to indicate that the loitering aspect of the statute adds anything to the instant case or serves to distinguish it in any way from the *Onofre* decision." If the public was concerned with prostitution activities, it should pursue them under the prostitution statutes, since it would violate equal protection to use the loitering statute for this purpose, as well as leave the police too much discretion to decide which conduct violated the statute.

Uplinger's case presented different issues from Butler's, asserted Drury. While it is true that much of the apprehension concerning the activities of gay men in this residential neighborhood may be traced to the gay prostitutes among them, many of the men, like Uplinger, were not prostitutes, but merely out to find sexual contacts. The rationale of the *Butler* case was not controlling, said Drury. The behavior of the men would have to be analyzed apart from the activities of occasional male prostitutes, who, in any event, appeared to steer clear of noncommercial street traffic.

"The main reason" that residents of the neighborhood were protesting, concluded Drury, "is that the occasional soliciting of a teenager or others by homosexuals and the appearance of homosexuals outside homes reinforces the age-old fear that people have of ho-mosexuals and renews the offense they take at their activities." This was only partly because the conduct took place in public. While some of this opposition might be without foundation, since it appeared that the gay men were on the whole quite discrete and, like Uplinger, unlikely to proposition anybody for sex until having engaged in extended discussion, some of it was grounded in "the real possibility that a man or his son may be solicited, harassed or confronted at the very door to his house." Rejecting the argument that enforcement of the law targeted against gays was discriminatory, Drury stated that the burden was on Uplinger to prove that the law should be found unconstitutional. Given the "wide and well recognized latitude" of the state to enact "every sort of law, even stupid ones," this was a significant burden, which Drury found Uplinger had not met. Drury stated:

> The court finds that a sufficient connection exists between the public's loss of the use and enjoyment of its streets, businesses and homes and the activity at issue to warrant this ban. . . . The defendant cannot create an ideal test tube situation and ask that his conduct be viewed apart from its surrounding social implications, nor can he blame the public for its reaction to his activities when the reaction is in large measure understandable.

In other words, although Uplinger's conduct had been quiet and inoffensive, he could be constitutionally convicted of a "public order" offense because the public as a whole was presumed to be offended by groups of gay men cruising the streets at 3 A.M., when almost everybody else was asleep.

Uplinger appealed to the county court. There, his case was consolidated with District Attorney Arcara's appeal of Drury's dismissal of the *Butler* case and an appeal by another alleged prostitute, Fredericka Sanders, from a ruling by City Court Judge Parlato denying her motion to dismiss charges under the same loitering statute under which she was ultimately convicted. County Court Judge Joseph P. McCarthy heard the consolidated appeal, with attorney Gardner representing Uplinger and Sanders and Rose H. Sconiers, assisted by Joseph A. Shifflett and Michael C. Walsh, representing Butler. Assistant District Attorney

Ernest G. Anstey appeared for the prosecution. McCarthy issued his ruling May 3, 1982, holding that the law was constitutional as applied to all three defendants, affirming the rulings in Uplinger's and Sanders's cases and reversing the ruling in Butler's.

McCarthy dismissed the argument that because the underlying activity, oral intercourse, had been held constitutionally protected in *Onofre*, it necessarily followed that loitering in a public place to solicit such activity could be held constitutionally protected as well. The defendants had argued that while the state had a legitimate concern for public order that might extend to noisy, aggressive, or otherwise blatantly offensive soliciting, a "discreet, non-obtrusive invitation" should be found constitutionally protected as a matter of freedom of speech. McCarthy was not convinced. "Indiscriminate public solicitation for deviate sex constitutes a contemptuous disregard for community standards, facially defies moral and aesthetic sensibilities, and annoys individuals who do not wish to become involved in such activities," he thundered. "Surely the reasonable and legitimate expectations of citizens in public places may be protected from this undesired annoying behavior," he asserted, citing the Model Penal Code discussion of this point, where the drafters recommended decriminalizing consensual sexual activity but retaining prohibitions on public solicitation as a matter of public order and morality.

McCarthy also rejected the argument that the statute unduly intruded into the private sphere or authorized punishment of mere loitering without any overt conduct beyond that. The law extended only to conduct in public places, he held, and furthermore required an overt solicitation before the police would make an arrest, since otherwise they would not have the evidence to show the purpose of the loitering. He also rejected the argument that the statute unconstitutionally distinguished between deviate and nondeviate sexual intercourse. Surely, the defendants had argued, if the public was concerned with public order, there was no rational basis to distinguish between loitering to solicit oral sex as opposed to vaginal sex. Not so, said McCarthy: "The Legislature may have rationally concluded that solicitation by loitering for deviate sexual activity is more offensive to the standards of public morality and, thus, more egregious than is the solicitation to participate in non-deviate sexual conduct," basing his conclusion on "practical experience and common observation." McCarthy also rejected claims of selective enforcement and vagueness.

The defendants jointly petitioned the court of appeals for permission to appeal, bypassing the normal intermediate appellate stage of the Supreme Court's Appellate Division. Permission was granted. The New York Civil Liberties Union, the Center for Constitutional Rights, and the Lambda Legal Defense and Education Fund filed *amicus* briefs, urging that the loitering law be found unconstitutional. On February 23, 1983, by a vote of six to one, the court of appeals reversed the county court's decision. In a brief *per curiam* opinion, the court found that the loitering law "must be viewed as a companion statute to the consensual sodomy statute," which it had held unconstitutional in *Onofre*. The objective of the statute, said the court, "is to punish conduct anticipatory to the act of consensual sodomy." Because that conduct could not be deemed criminal after *Onofre*, "we perceive no basis upon which the State may continue to punish loitering for that purpose." Thus, the statute "suffers the same deficiencies as did the consensual sodomy statute." The loitering law could not properly be classified as a "harassment statute," said the court, because it "is devoid of a requirement that the conduct proscribed be in any way offensive or annoying to others." Thus, the loitering statute must be stricken as unconstitutional.

This brief opinion brought forth a lengthy dissent from Judge Matthew J. Jasen, who totally disagreed with the court's characterization of the statute and the basis on which it should be evaluated. For him, it was clear that the statute was not a "companion" to the sodomy law. This statute derived from a portion of the pre-Model Penal Code law concerned with public order, not with sexual offenses. While it referred to the sexual offenses provisions for its definition of "deviate sexual intercourse" as part of the modernization of New York criminal law when the state's version of the Model Penal Code was adopted, it was clear that the legislature had followed the Model Penal Code's recommendation to ban loitering for this purpose even as it rejected the Model Penal Code's recommendation to decriminalize consensual sodomy.

So long as the solicitation took place while the defendants were loitering in a public place, he asserted, they could not invoke the overbreadth doctrine, which he asserted that the court had implicitly used to invalidate the statute. (The majority denied this was what it was doing, stating that overbreadth had played no role in its analysis and that the legislature could enact a properly drawn law to prohibit aggressive or offensive sexual solicitation in public.) For Jasen, the law was clearly a harassment statute and, as such, addressed completely different concerns from those addressed in *Onofre*. "This statute embodies the Legislature's determination that public solicitation to engage in sexual conduct is necessarily offensive to others," said Jasen. If not the person solicited, then others observing the solicitation might be offended. (At 3 A.M.?)

Jasen argued that inasmuch as the statute applied to a range of conduct, some of it offensive and some perhaps inoffensive, the court should have refrained from striking the whole statute and instead ruled on it as applied to the particular facts. He also rejected the contention that the law was vague.

District Attorney Arcara promptly filed a petition with the U.S. Supreme Court seeking review of the court of appeals' ruling. Styling the case "*New York v. Uplinger*," he sought to avoid the denial of *certiorari* he had sustained in *Onofre* by specifically disclaiming any desire to have the Court address the underlying issue of the federal constitutionality of the consensual sodomy law. He asked the Court to address the question whether the states could maintain public order by forbidding loitering for the purpose of soliciting people to engage in deviate sexual intercourse in private. The Supreme Court granted a writ of *certiorari* in the case on October 3, 1983. After the writ was granted, New York State Attorney General Robert Abrams filed an *amicus* brief, arguing that while the statute as a whole should not have been declared unconstitutional on its face, it should have been held unconstitutional as applied to the defendants in the underlying prosecutions

as violative of freedom of speech and privacy. Other *amicus curiae* briefs urging that the court of appeals' decision be sustained were filed by the American Association for Personal Privacy (a sodomy law reform group), the American Civil Liberties Union, the American Psychological Association and other professional medical groups, the Committee on Sex and Law of the Association of the Bar of the City of New York, Lambda Legal Defense and Education Fund, and the Center for Constitutional Rights. Finally, the National Association of Business Councils filed a brief by Laurence R. Sperber and Jay M. Kohorn that took a strikingly different tack from the others, arguing that the writ of *certiorari* should be dismissed as improvidently granted, since a determination on the constitutionality of the underlying consensual sodomy law (declared unconstitutional in *Onofre*) was essential to this case, and such a deter-mination was not appropriate on this record.

At oral argument on January 18, 1984, the Court immediately focused on the contradictions between Arcara's position and that of Attorney General Abrams, asking Arcara whether he really represented New York State on this appeal. After some fumbling around, Arcara acknowledged that his position was quite different from that of the attorney general.

On May 30, the Court announced that the writ had been dismissed as improvidently granted, by a vote of five to four. As was made quite clear by Justice John Paul Stevens's concurring opinion, only four members of the Court—Chief Justice Warren E. Burger and Justices Byron R. White, William H. Rehnquist and Sandra Day O'Connor—had voted to grant the writ. They were persuaded that the Court should address the merits of the constitutional grounds on which the court of appeals had invalidated the statute, as Justice White asserted in a two-sentence dissent joined by the others. The majority, however, bemused at the split between Arcara and Abrams and puzzled as to the actual basis for the court of appeals' holding, essentially decided that they were uncertain what they were being asked to decide, and decided the most prudent course was not to decide.

"[T]he opinion of the Court of Appeals is fairly subject to varying interpretations, leaving us uncertain as to the precise federal constitutional issue the court decided," said the *per curiam* opinion of Justices William J. Brennan, Jr., Thurgood Marshall, Harry A. Blackmun, Lewis F. Powell, Jr., and Stevens. Furthermore, whatever basis there was for the decision, "it was clearly premised on the court's earlier decision in *People v. Onofre* and for that reason a meaningful evaluation of the decision below would entail consideration of the questions decided in that case." Since Arcara was not asking for such a consideration, "we are persuaded that this case provides an inappropriate vehicle for resolving the important constitutional issues raised by the parties."

Evidently addressing an issue hotly debated by the Justices in deciding how to dispose of this case, Justice Stevens commented at length in his concurring opinion on the "Rule of Four" by which the Court decided petitions for *certiorari*. If four members of the Court believe a case should be reviewed, the writ of *certiorari* is granted, but if five members of the Court decide, after briefing and argument, that a case should not be reviewed, the writ is dismissed as improvidently granted. The dissenters had evidently argued that this was wasteful of the Court's resources; once the writ was granted, the case should be decided on the merits. The *per curiam* opinion had noted that it was not until the *amicus* briefs came in that the Court learned that Attorney General Abrams was taking a different course from Arcara, or indeed that Arcara did not want to raise the issue of *Onofre*. Stevens dismissed this approach to the argument, asserting as to the Rule of Four that "its force is largely spent once the case has been

heard," at which point "a more fully informed majority of the court must decide whether some countervailing principle outweighs the interest in judicial economy in deciding the case."

While the Supreme Court did not rule on the merits in *Uplinger*, its decision left intact a ruling by New York's highest court that the government could not prosecute people for asking others to come home and have "deviate" sex. Since similar decisions had been reached by the highest courts in several other states, it contributed toward the trend of refuting the Model Penal Code suggestion that such loitering or solicitation laws could be independently justified as public order measures on the assumption that, regardless of the nature of the conduct involved, the public would be offended by it. Furthermore, by its reference to the "important constitutional issues" that were raised by the case, a majority of the Court might have been signaling that the underlying constitutional issues of sodomy laws themselves should not be considered to have been finally disposed of by the Court's 1976 summary affirmance in *Doe v. Commonwealth's Attorney for City of Richmond*, in which a three-judge district court had upheld the constitutionality of Virginia's law against consensual sodomy between adults in private.

Case References

Doe v. Commonwealth's Attorney for City of Richmond, 403 F. Supp. 1199 (E.D. Va. 1975), affirmed, 425 U.S. 901 (1976)

People v. Onofre, 51 N.Y.2d 476, 434 N.Y.S.2d 947, 415 N.E.2d 936 (1980), certiorari denied, 451 U.S. 987 (1981)

24. DOES THE CONSTITUTION PROTECT ADULTERERS?

Commonwealth v. Stowell, 389 Mass. 171, 449 N.E.2d 357 (1983).

As the U.S. Supreme Court identified and developed an apparent right of sexual privacy beginning in the 1960s and continuing through the 1970s in decisions concerning contraception and abortion, the population as a whole was experiencing a shift in sexual ethics, bringing into question many of the values that had previously seemed firmly entrenched and unshakable. Although Supreme Court Justices, such as John Marshall Harlan and Arthur J. Goldberg, had confidently asserted in opinions issued in the contraception cases that the right of privacy they were recognizing would not bar a state from condemning adultery, the adultery laws were rarely enforced, even though public authorities were aware that they were widely flouted. Surprisingly, there are few reported appellate decisions considering whether the right of privacy would protect an adulterer from criminal prosecution. The courts of many states, including Massachusetts, appeared willing to strike down fornication and sodomy laws when enforced against consenting adults who conducted their activities in private. Would the same willingness extend to adultery laws?

The Massachusetts Supreme Judicial Court faced this question in 1983 in the case of Judith Stowell, who had been convicted of adultery and fined $50 in the Central Worcester Division District Court. Police officers had spotted Stowell getting into a van on the afternoon of October 13, 1980, and they followed as the van drove off the highway onto a dirt road and stopped in a secluded, wooded area near a factory. The police lost sight of the van as it pulled into the woods. Nobody else was in the area, except a boy on a bicycle who stopped and asked the police officers what they were looking for. When the police officers asked the boy if he had seen a van and its occupants, the boy confirmed seeing the van but not the occupants. After the officers located the van, they looked into the rear window and observed Stowell and a man having sexual intercourse. The officers interrupted the act and asked if they were married to each other. When they indicated they were each married to somebody else, the officers arrested them. Both Stowell and her sexual partner were convicted of adultery and fined $50 apiece.

Stowell appealed her conviction, alleging that the adultery law violated the constitutional right of privacy, both on its face and as applied to her. District Judge Greenberg certified the question of the law's constitutionality to the appeals court. Before the case could be heard, Stowell's attorney, Margaret H. Van Deusen, of Boston, applied to the Massachusetts Supreme Judicial Court for direct appellate review, inasmuch as the matter was solely one of law. That court heard oral argument on May 13 from Van Deusen and Assistant District Attorney Jane Shepard. The unanimous court is-

sued its decision on May 13, 1983, upholding the constitutionality of the law and Stowell's conviction, in an opinion by Justice Neil L. Lynch.

Lynch first addressed the question whether the statute was unconstitutional on its face. The law provided:

> A married person who has sexual intercourse with a person not his spouse or an unmarried person who has sexual intercourse with a married person shall be guilty of adultery and shall be punished by imprisonment in the state prison for not more than three years or in jail for not more than two years or by a fine of not more than five hundred dollars.

Thus, adultery was treated in Massachusetts as a felony, potentially punishable by a relatively long confinement.

Lynch briefly reviewed the U.S. Supreme Court's privacy cases under the Due Process Clause of the Fourteenth Amendment up to that date, noting that they appeared to divide into two streams of privacy: the "individual interest in avoiding disclosure of personal matters," and "the interest in independence in making certain kinds of important decisions." Judith Stowell's appeal implicated the second stream, which could be summarized as a right, relatively free of state intervention, for the individual to make decisions relating to marriage, procreation, and family relations, as identified in cases such as *Griswold v. Connecticut* (1965) and *Eisenstadt v. Baird* (1972) (contraception), *Loving v. Virginia* (1967) (marriage), and *Roe v. Wade* (1975) (abortion). Lynch noted that the Supreme Court had never marked the "outer limits" of the right to make important personal decisions, and quoted Justice William J. Brennan's comment in *Carey v. Population Services International* (1977) that the Court had "not definitely answered the difficult question whether and to what extent the Constitution prohibits state statutes regulating [private consensual sexual behavior] among adults." However, the Court had indicated that "only personal rights that can be deemed 'fundamental' or 'implicit in the concept of ordered liberty'" were included in the constitutional "guarantee of personal privacy."

Without any further discussion or statement of reasons, Lynch asserted:

Whatever the precise definition of the right of privacy and the scope of its protection of private sexual conduct, there is no fundamental personal privacy right implicit in the concept of ordered liberty barring the prosecution of consenting adults committing adultery in private. [Citation of four federal trial court decisions omitted.] Therefore, the statute is not unconstitutional on its face.

Lynch evidently believed that there was no need to engage in explicit discussion of the changing sexual mores in American society that might lead one to argue that, whatever moral view might exist about the appropriateness of engaging in adultery as a matter of personal choice, the state's interest in applying the criminal law to adulterers was not compelling. The result was apparently self-evident to him. However, in his subsequent discussion of why the statute was constitutional *as applied* in Stowell's case, he did reveal the policy underpinnings of the court's decision.

Turning to that question, Lynch asserted that "the right of the State to regulate the institution of marriage under its police power is unquestioned where it does not infringe on fundamental rights," citing *Zablocki v. Redhail*, a 1978 U.S. Supreme Court decision, as well as *Loving v. Virginia* and *Griswold v. Connecticut*, both cases in which the Supreme Court, while striking down particular marital regulations, had explicitly recognized that the state does have authority in broad terms to define and regulate the marital relationship. From this, Lynch concluded that the state had a valid interest in preventing conduct that would "threaten" the institution of marriage, here citing prior Massachusetts decisions identifying the state's "strong public interest in ensuring that its rules governing marriage are not subverted" and that marital "integrity" is not "jeopardized." In 1916, in *Southern Surety Co. v. Oklahoma*, the U.S. Supreme Court had stated: "Adultery is an offense against the marriage relation and belongs to the class of subjects which each State controls in its own way." Despite the intervening decades of developing individual rights under the Due Process Clause, Lynch apparently found no weakening of this precedent.

Massachusetts, in common with many other states, made adultery a ground for divorce. "We

take judicial notice," said Lynch, "that the act of adultery frequently has a destructive impact on the marital relationship and is a factor in many divorces. We are not unaware that the public policy against adultery is most often expressed in these divorce proceedings and that the crime of adultery is rarely made the subject of criminal prosecution." But, as a lower Massachusetts court had recently commented, "To recognize that fact is not to say that [this statute has] become invalid or judicially unenforceable." After asserting that the failure to prosecute more aggressively under the law was "not presented by the legal questions" that had been certified to the court for review in Stowell's appeal, Lynch held that the adultery law "remains as a permissible expression of public policy." If the law's relative nonenforcement truly reflected "a general public disfavor with the statute," the legislature could address that disfavor by modifying or repealing the law. "In the absence of a constitutional violation, we have no power to invalidate the statute," Lynch concluded.

The court's decision in *Commonwealth v. Stowell* appears consistent with the developing body of sexual privacy law, in the sense that courts have normally justified striking down sex crimes laws when doing so seemed consistent with the "harm principle" espoused by the 19th-century philosopher John Stuart Mill, whose writing was specifically invoked in several significant sodomy law cases. Mill's "harm principle" could justify maintaining criminal penalties for adultery because sexual relations outside the marital relationship may inflict harm against a third (or in Stowell's case, even a fourth) person, the absent spouse, provided, of course, that the absent spouse is either unaware of or actually aware of and in opposition to this sexual activity. Marital infidelity can introduce sexually transmitted disease into the marital relationship, or result in a pregnancy imposing legal duties on the husband of a female adulterer, who will be presumed to be the father of any child born during the marriage (in some states, irrebutably presumed so).

Would the same considerations apply in situations where the nonmarital sexual activity takes place with the consent of the marital partner, or with his or her active participation?

Would the phenomenon of "swinging," an interesting 1970s spin-off of the sexual revolution, also be subject to criminal prosecution?

Case References

Carey v. Population Services International, 431 U.S. 678 (1977)

Eisenstadt v. Baird, 405 U.S. 438 (1972)
Griswold v. Connecticut, 381 U.S. 479 (1965)
Loving v. Virginia, 388 U.S. 1 (1967)
Roe v. Wade, 410 U.S. 113 (1973)
Southern Surety Co. v. Oklahoma, 241 U.S. 582 (1916)
Zablocki v. Redhail, 434 U.S. 374 (1978)

25. REPORTING TO BIG BROTHER?: REGISTRATION FOR SEX OFFENDERS

In re Reed, 33 Cal. 3d 914, 191 Cal. Rptr. 658, 663 P.2d 216 (1983) (en banc).

Laws against public sexual solicitation provide the main grounds for confrontation over sexuality between ordinary citizens and law enforcement personnel. Whether considering gay or bisexual men, transvestites, or prostitutes of either sex, most of those who find themselves caught up in the criminal justice system find their way there through the enforcement of such laws. Indeed, actual enforcement of laws banning private, consensual sexual activity was traditionally so infrequent, and contact with the police was always so involved with enforcement of public solicitation and lewdness laws, that the repeal or abrogation of sodomy laws actually had little effect on the continuing confrontational atmosphere between gays and law enforcement officials in many jurisdictions. In Illinois, for example, the first state to repeal its consensual sodomy law as part of adoption of the Model Penal Code, that repeal made little practical difference in the lives of gay men whose sexual lifestyles had previously brought them into contact with the police because the Model Penal Code continued to criminalize sexual solicitation in a public place and the rate of enforcement of that law did not decrease.

In a handful of states, law enforcement authorities asserted control and surveillance over the lives of "deviants" through a mechanism of entrapment followed by lifelong stigma and surveillance under sex offender registration laws tied in to the solicitation statutes. Using handsome plainclothes decoys, the police would lure gay men into making friendly conversation, and in some cases actual sexual advances, in public restrooms. Even a friendly glance or slight lingering in the restroom might be enough to trigger an arrest where nobody was present (apart from the defendant and the police officer) to counter the inevitable charge by the police officer of sexual advances or open masturbation in his presence. Subsequent charges of solicitation and public lewdness would confront the defendant with a cruel dilemma: seek vindication through a trial at the risk of publicity and incurring a maximum penalty or plead guilty (sometimes to a reduced misdemeanor charge) and preserve anonymity while securing a minimal penalty, perhaps even mere probation. In the handful of states with sex offender registration laws, even pleading guilty to a minor charge might create a lifetime obligation of continuing contact with the police, a permanent record, and the psychological weight of a skeleton in the closet that could never be removed.

California's sex offender registration provision, section 290 of the Penal Code, was particularly draconian. By the mid-1970s, law reform efforts had reduced the number of states with such laws to only a handful, and by 1978, after a reform effort in Arizona, only California required misdemeanor offenders under solicitation and lewdness statutes to register. In the other states with such laws, they were applied only to felony offenses. California's law required that the individual convicted of enumerated sex offenses register with the chief of police of the city in which he temporarily or permanently resided, furnishing a written statement accompanied by fingerprints and a photograph, which the local police would forward to the Department of Justice. Any change of address had to be reported within ten days, with failure to report being a separate misdemeanor offense. While the individual could apply for an order to relieve himself of the perpetual reporting obligation, the initial registration was permanent and irrevocable. Thus, over time, California police departments and the Department of Justice could compile and maintain an extensive list of gay and bisexual men who had been convicted (in most cases on a plea bargain) of sexual solicitation or public lewdness.

The other offenses for which registration was mandatory included loitering in or about public toilets for purposes of sexual solicitation; procuring female minors to commit prostitution; contributing to the delinquency of a minor; engaging in lewd or lascivious conduct with a child under age 14; committing oral copulation, indecent exposure, incest, sodomy, assault with intent to commit rape, or sodomy or forcible rape. The only other crimes for which California maintained a convict registration system involved narcotics. Sex-related crimes for which there was no registration requirement included child pornography, statutory rape, bigamy, bestiality, lewdness in the presence of a child, "Peeping Tom" offenses, pimping and pandering, and soliciting or engaging in prostitution where the parties were above the age of consent. The Penal Code required that the information compiled through the registration system be kept confidential within the police system, but this was little comfort to those forced to register, who knew that wherever they lived, the local police department would be aware of their status and would consider them prime suspects for sex crimes investigations or harassment.

Lawyers whose practices routinely included defending men caught in the police decoy game at public restrooms were eager to challenge the constitutionality of the registration requirement, since it was seen as an oppressive device stigmatizing gay men and generating the kind of information about them that could prove quite dangerous were the climate surrounding sexual matters to turn sharply more repressive, as well as a tool for continuing harassment. (For example, under the laws against loitering for

the purpose of sexual solicitation, registered sex offender status might be cited as justification for arresting somebody lingering "too long" at a public toilet even though that person had not engaged in any overt solicitation conduct.) The problem was finding a convicted sex offender who was willing to endure the publicity of an appeal to the state supreme court. Most of those caught up in this trap were quite fearful of publicity, and its potential adverse effects on their employment, housing, and associations.

The willing challenger finally materialized in the form of Allen Eugene Reed. Reed was a retired veteran of twenty-one years of service in the U.S. Air Force, a divorced father of three children who had for ten years been living with another man. He had been steadily employed since leaving military service and had no prior arrest record when he was entrapped in a restroom by a vice officer and charged with masturbating briefly in the officer's presence after brief conversation with the officer calculated to make Reed believe the officer was looking for sexual activity. Reed was convicted under section 647(a) of the Penal Code of soliciting "lewd or dissolute" conduct, a disorderly conduct misdemeanor. (The California Supreme Court had previously adopted a narrowing definition of "lewd or dissolute" conduct to save the constitutionality of the statute from vagueness and overbreadth challenge in *Pryor v. Municipal Court* (1979). The construction limited application of the statute to public solicitation or to performance of conduct "which involves the touching of the genitals, buttocks, or female breast, for purposes of sexual arousal, gratification, annoyance, or offense, by a person who knows or should know of the presence of persons who may be offended by the conduct.") The municipal court sentenced Reed to three years formal probation and ordered him to register with the Los Angeles Police Department as a sex offender.

After exhausting appeals opportunities in the lower courts, Reed filed a petition for a writ of *habeas corpus* with the California Supreme Court, challenging the constitutionality of the registration requirement. His attorney on the petition was Jay M. Kohorn, a Los Angeles lawyer whose practice involved many sexual solicitation defense cases. Although the case, and

Reed's standing to bring it, arose out of an actual arrest and conviction, it was conceptualized as a test case and *amicus* support was sought both from the lesbian and gay rights and civil rights communities and from the Los Angeles City Attorney's Office. The California Attorney General's Office appeared in the supreme court to defend the statute.

The court ruled on May 26, 1983, that automatic imposition of the registration requirement on those convicted under section 647(a), the "lewd and dissolute conduct" solicitation statute, violated the constitutional ban on "cruel or unusual punishment." Because it disposed of the case on this ground, the court refrained from commenting on the other grounds of unconstitutionality that Reed had asserted, including violation of equal protection, the rights to privacy and intrastate travel, and a broad due process claim, although the court's analysis of the cruel and unusual punishment issue actually embraced some aspects of the equal protection analysis. The court's opinion, by Justice Stanley Mosk, drew separate dissenting opinions from Justices Otto M. Kaus and Frank K. Richardson.

Reed's challenge to the statute presented two distinct issues for the court: first, was the registration requirement actually a "punishment" within the meaning of the constitutional prohibition, and second, if so, was it a "cruel or unusual" punishment of the type prohibited? (If the court had decided the first question in the negative, it would have had to proceed to consider the alternative theories under which the statute was challenged, and Mosk intimated that it might have been vulnerable to attack on those other grounds.) Whether registration was a punishment was the main point of contention between the majority of the court and Justice Richardson, whose dissent focused heavily on his view that while it might be inconvenient to the offender, the requirement worked no deprivation of liberty sufficient to be considered punitive rather than merely regulatory. For Mosk, however, the requirements of the registration statute were onerous enough to come within the sphere of punishment, as that term had been developed by the U.S. Supreme Court in *Kennedy v. Mendoza-Martinez*, a 1963 case in

which the Court described the following factors as relevant to that determination:

> Whether the sanction involves an affirmative disability or restraint, whether it has historically been regarded as a punishment, whether it comes into play only on a finding of *scienter*, whether its operation will promote the traditional aims of punishment—retribution and deterrence, whether the behavior to which it applies is already a crime, whether an alternative purpose to which it may rationally be connected is assignable for it, and whether it appears excessive in relation to the alternative purposes assigned are all relevant to the inquiry and may often point in differing directions.

Mosk asserted that the registration requirement was an "affirmative disability or restraint," noting that the court had treated it as such in at least one past case where it vacated a conviction under section 647(a). In that case, *In re Birch* (1973), Justice Matthew Tobriner's opinion stated that "although the stigma of a short jail sentence should eventually fade, the *ignominious badge* carried by the convicted sex offender can remain for a lifetime." Furthermore, Justice Kaus, dissenting in *Reed*, had written in a law review article: "Apart from the bother and loss of privacy which mere registration entails, the 'ready availability' to the police, if it serves its purpose, presumably means a series of command performances at lineups." "Needless to emphasize," wrote Mosk, "law enforcement 'command performances' involve compulsion and restraint." Furthermore, although the offender might obtain judicial relief from the perpetual obligation to file change of address notices, he could never get the initial registration expunged, so at least one police department would have a permanent record, including his photograph and fingerprints, on file.

While conceding that sex offender registration may not have "historically" been regarded as punishment, Mosk indicated that some of the other factors on the Supreme Court's list were present, and not all factors were required for a particular imposition to qualify as a punishment. The severity of a nonphysical punishment, particularly in relation to the underlying act that triggers it, was an important factor. For example, in describing postimprisonment penalties as an aspect of punishment in a 1910 case, *Weems v. United States*, the U.S. Supreme Court had commented that after leaving prison chains behind, the convicted felon

> goes from them to a perpetual limitation of his liberty. He is forever kept under the shadow of his crime, forever kept within voice and view of the criminal magistrate, not being able to change his domicile without giving notice to the "authority immediately in charge of his surveillance," and without permission in writing. He may not seek, even in other scenes and among other people, to retrieve his fall from rectitude. Even that hope is taken from him and he is subject to tormenting regulations that, if not so tangible as iron bars and stone walls, oppress as much by their continuity, and deprive of essential liberty.

While Mosk's invocation of this passage may have been a bit overdrawn, since the requirements imposed on convicted federal felons were somewhat more oppressive than those imposed by the California registration law, nonetheless the passage supported the assertion that the California requirements did impair the liberty of the individual.

Mosk asserted that several other factors specified by the Supreme Court in *Mendoza-Martinez* were "readily satisfied" in Reed's case. As narrowly construed by the court in *Pryor*, the solicitation statute had the requisite *scienter* requirement, the conduct to which registration applied was deemed criminal, and at least part of the legislature's intent in imposing the requirement was to deter recidivism and facilitate apprehending repeat offenders. As to whether the registration requirement might have a purpose other than punishment, Mosk suggested that its utility in helping the police solve subsequent sex crimes had not really been adequately demonstrated. In fact, the Los Angeles city attorney's *amicus* brief suggested that the registration requirement had actually proved counterproductive in sex crimes investigations because it loaded up the record system with "useless information" about petty misdemeanor offenders who were not really suspects in the kinds of serious sex crimes that would be under investigation. To Mosk, the imposition of the registration requirement was clearly excessive in relation to this alternative, "non-punitive" purpose, and he concluded that enough of the Supreme Court's enumerated factors had been

met to denominate it a "punishment," not a mere regulatory requirement.

The next question, then, was whether the requirement was a "cruel and unusual" punishment. Mosk said that the courts had recognized that this determination called for a "flexible and progressive standard for assessing the severity of punishment." It was not enough to ask whether the punishment was unusual or unduly severe in the context of the times when it was first imposed by the legislature. Rather, the assessment must be based on contemporary circumstances, and consider issues of proportionality and comparability. The California Supreme Court had described its approach to this issue in the 1972 case of *In re Lynch*, where it identified three "techniques" for accomplishing the proportionality determination:

> (1) an examination of "the nature of the offense and/or the offender, with particular regard to the degree of danger both present to society"; (2) a comparison of the challenged penalty with those imposed in the same jurisdiction for more serious crimes; and (3) a comparison of the challenged penalty with those imposed for the same offense in different jurisdictions.

Turning to the first "technique" of comparison, Mosk asserted that section 647(a) offenses were "relatively minor" by "contemporary standards." As little as "a gesture, a flirtation, an invitation for sexual favors, if accompanied by any touching and done in a public place, may suffice" for conviction. Most of those caught up in section 647(a) prosecutions were homosexual men whose underlying private sexual behavior had been decriminalized by the legislature in 1975. Even under the narrower interpretation of the law embraced in *Pryor*—where the "perpetrator" would have to know or have reason to know that the other person who was the subject of his attentions might be "offended"—this did not render the offense "violent or dangerous." Furthermore, since the overwhelming majority of these situations involved the "perpetrator" and a vice cop, with nobody else present, it was really a "victimless" crime, since the vice cop could hardly claim to be really "offended" when he had voluntarily placed himself there for the express purpose of being propositioned. The facts of Reed's own arrest confirmed this characterization, and his biography also confirmed that a punishment of lifetime registration obligations was wholly disproportionate. "Petitioner is not the prototype of one who poses a grave threat to society; nor does his relatively simple sexual indiscretion place him in the ranks of those who commit more heinous registrable sex offenses." Furthermore, Reed was not challenging all uses of the offender registration statute, merely its application to solicitation cases like his under section 647(a).

This point led naturally to the rather odd list of sex offenses either covered or not covered by the registration requirement. Statutory rape and prostitution, for example, did not require registration, while a relatively innocuous sexual solicitation, such as Reed's, did. "It is difficult to justify requiring a section 647(a) misdemeanant who masturbates in the presence of a police officer to register as a sex offender, while not imposing this additional penalty on those convicted under section 273g of lewd conduct in the presence of a child," commented Mosk. If recidivism was a concern motivating the registration requirement, why not require registration of those convicted of soliciting or engaging in prostitution, since their reliance on prostitution for their livelihood suggested they were likely to be recidivists. Mosk also noted that "more serious crimes not related to sex, such as robbery, burglary, or arson" did not require registration, even though they were more likely to involve violence and actual victimization. "A felon convicted of such crimes may serve his time and be done with it; while a misdemeanant convicted of a nonviolent section 647(a) offense in a semiprivate restroom, involving no victim as such, must carry the onus of sex offender registration for a lifetime. This discrepancy demonstrates the relative severity of the punishment imposed for section 647(a) violations."

Finally, law reform efforts around the country had resulted in the repeal or reform of most sex offender registration laws. With the recent Arizona reform, California remained the only state to require registration of those convicted of misdemeanor solicitation offenses. The few other states that retained registration requirements imposed them only on felons, in some cases only repeat felons. California's requirement was now quite unusual and much more severe than the punishment in other jurisdictions for the same offenses.

In *Lynch*, the California court had adopted the idea that the "punishment must fit both the crime and the criminal," said Mosk. By imposing a lifelong stigma on minor offenders, while punishing "equally or more serious offenses" with less severity, and standing virtually alone in imposing such punishments in these cases, California had adopted a penalty "out of all proportion to the crime of which petitioner was convicted," concluded Mosk. Section 290, the registration statute, was thus unconstitutional under article I, section 17, of the state constitution's ban on cruel and unusual punishments, insofar as it required registration of those convicted under section 647(a), and the municipal court should be instructed to remove the registration requirement from the conditions of probation imposed on Reed.

Justice Kaus's brief dissent disputed the court's apparent conclusion that it could invalidate any punishment which it felt did not "fit the crime," arguing that "the constitutional standards are more severe." He agreed that "reasonable men can differ over the wisdom or efficacy" of the registration requirement in sexual solicitation cases under section 647(a), but he could not agree that it met the constitutional standards established either by the United States or California Supreme Courts in prior cases, and urged that this was a matter best left to legislative judgment.

Justice Richardson dissented at much greater length, since he disagreed with both prongs of the court's opinion. First, as far as he was concerned, Mosk had significantly overstated the burden imposed by the registration requirement in denominating it a "punishment." He did not see the "compulsion and restraint" that Mosk saw in a mere requirement, after initial registration, to report changes of address to local police departments, a requirement from which the offender could be excused upon application if he behaved himself. He charged that the court had abandoned the proper approach of presuming the legitimacy of a statute in the absence of strong contrary evidence, instead indulging in unproven "presumptions" about things like whether the requirement had proven effective in assisting police in their sex crimes investigations.

In light of *Pryor*, he also thought that the court's characterization of section 647(a) violations as "relatively minor" offenses revealed "a disturbing and dangerous naivete." Where Mosk had stated that alleged "perpetrators" might be arrested for a nod or a glance, Richardson noted that as interpreted in *Pryor* the section now required proof of "an *offensive* touching of the genitals, buttocks or female breast for purposes of sexual arousal, gratification, annoyance or offense." Surely, such an offensive touching was not a relatively minor offense, asserted Richardson, and might actually be a prelude to more serious offenses. The legislature was entitled to draw the conclusion that requiring the performer of the preliminary offense to register could serve a purpose in both deterrence and future law enforcement, since people who engaged in the touching might commit the more serious offense at a later time. What Richardson overlooked, however, and Mosk seemed to grasp, was that the narrowing interpretation of *Pryor*, while a significant symbolic achievement, meant little in the cases of men whose only defense witnesses would be themselves and who feared the publicity of a trial at which the state would have to "prove" the elements of the offense. It was their shaky, nervous word against a police officer who was a practiced, cool witness. Those who obtained legal counsel and were willing to bargain hard with prosecutors might benefit from that narrowing interpretation, but many of those caught up in restroom solicitation cases would fear the contest, plead guilty without any real proof of "offensive" touching, and be subjected to lifetime registration requirements for doing nothing more than smiling a bit too long at a handsome young man in a public restroom where nobody else was present.

For Richardson, the cruel and unusual punishment provisions were meant to dispose of a punishment that "shocks the conscience and offends fundamental notions of human dignity." "Considering the relatively minor burdens imposed by section 290, the potential and continuing danger to the public, especially the young, posed by persons who have been convicted under section 647, subdivision (a), and the presumed utility of the registration device, the unconstitutionality of section 290 does not 'clearly, positively, and unmistakably' appear," he concluded, arguing that such a clear appearance of unconstitutionality was required before a statute could be invalidated.

The California Supreme Court's decision in *Reed* was both symbolic and practically important. In its symbolism, it lifted one of the few remaining penal laws in the nation that imposed a lifetime, recurring sex offender stigmatization process on those caught up in the most trivial sorts of offenses. In its practical significance, it removed part (although by no means all) of the incentive for the police to play these restroom entrapment games. More significantly, as Justice Mosk had noted, the continuing registration requirement cast a very real pall over the lives of these men, who had to expose the embarrassment of their past peccadillos to the police department wherever they might live and retain the constant fear of being picked up "on suspicion" for a variety of things having nothing to do with them. The California court's decision was an important advance toward first-class citizenship for sexual minorities.

Case References

Birch, In re, 10 Cal. 3d 314, 110 Cal. Rptr. 212, 515 P.2d 12 (1973)

Kennedy v. Mendoza-Martinez, 372 U.S. 144 (1963)

Lynch, In re, 8 Cal. 3d 410, 105 Cal. Rptr. 217, 503 P.2d 921 (1972)

Pryor v. Municipal Court, 25 Cal. 3d 238, 158 Cal. Rptr. 330, 599 P.2d 636 (1979)

Weems v. United States, 217 U.S. 349 (1910)

26. A SECOND CHALLENGE TO THE TEXAS SODOMY LAWS

Baker v. Wade, 553 F. Supp. 1121 (N.D. Tex. 1982), appeal dismissed, 743 F.2d 236 (5th Cir. 1984), motion to substitute class representative and reopen evidence denied, 106 F.R.D. 526 (N.D. Tex.), reversed en banc, 769 F.2d 289 (5th Cir. 1985), petition for rehearing denied, 774 F.2d 1285 (5th Cir. 1985), certiorari denied, 478 U.S. 1022, petition for rehearing denied, 478 U.S. 1035 (1986).

Baker v. Wade was the second attempt to reform Texas statutes criminalizing consensual sodomy. The first attempt had ultimately been at least partially successful, as the federal district court's opinion in *Buchanan v. Batchelor* (1970) contributed to the Texas legislature's decision, as part of a general penal code reform in 1974, to downgrade sodomy from a felony to a misdemeanor punishable by a $200 fine and to restrict application of the statute, section 21.06, to oral and anal intercourse between persons of the same sex.

This was actually the third sodomy statute in Texas's history. The first, dating from 1860, was a broad "crime against nature" statute which had been interpreted by Texas courts to track the old English common law, prohibiting only anal intercourse, regardless of the genders of the participants. This law was followed by article 524 of the Texas Penal Code, adopted in 1943. It prohibited "carnal copulation," defined to include all anal or oral intercourse between any persons, once again regardless of gender. This was the law held unconstitutional by the federal district court in *Buchanan*. After the U.S. Supreme Court vacated the *Buchanan* decision for reconsideration in light of various procedural issues, the Texas courts indicated that they would not follow that decision, but the legislature took matters into its own hands. Thus, for eighty-three years Texas had prohibited anal intercourse but allowed oral intercourse, regardless of the sex of the participants; then, for thirty-one years, Texas prohibited all persons from engaging in both anal and oral intercourse; finally, since 1974, Texas had allowed heterosexuals, regardless of marital status, to engage in sodomy, but had prohibited homosexuals from engaging in the same activity.

Gay rights advocates in Texas were determined to remove the criminal penalties for consensual sodomy entirely. When several attempts to secure repeal in the legislature were unsuccessful, a gay rights organization in Dallas decided to mount a new challenge to the law in federal court. They found their ideal plaintiff in Donald F. Baker, a young former Dallas schoolteacher, a military veteran with an excellent employment record, who was a sophisticated, articulate spokesman for their cause. They also found their ideal judge in Jerry Buchmeyer, a liberal maverick on the federal district bench in Dallas.

In the resulting case, Baker sued Henry Wade, the much-sued Dallas law enforcement official who had been a named defendant in *Buchanan v. Batchelor* (and was even more famous as the named defendant in the Supreme Court's 1973 landmark abortion decision, *Roe v. Wade*. *Baker v. Wade* became a major *cause célèbre* in Texas and the nation, although it would ultimately be eclipsed in public attention by *Bowers v. Hardwick*, the Georgia sodomy law challenge that reached the Supreme Court first. Judge Buchmeyer issued his opinion finding the statute unconstitutional on August 17, 1982.

Baker's attorney, James C. Barber, of Dallas, presented a case that was a textbook example of carefully planned test case litigation, replete with nationally credentialed expert witnesses, a virtual library of supporting affidavits and documentary exhibits, and, most importantly, a highly presentable plaintiff who was willing to tell his life story in excruciating, emotional detail on the witness stand while his parents sat in the courtroom. By contrast, the state, represented by Assistant District Attorney Charles Baldree and Dallas City Attorneys Joseph G. Werner and Kent S. Hofmeister, presented an "expert" who showed little sophisticated knowledge of the subject, and made little effort to secure the evidence of legislative intent necessary to meet the legal challenge.

Baker recounted his life story in moving detail. The grandson of an Assembly of God minister, Baker had been raised in a strongly religious household and was tormented well into adulthood by the growing knowledge that his sexual feelings were condemned by religious authorities and the criminal law. While fighting his feelings and shying away from any sexual activity, Baker continued church activities as a college student until he had his first sexual experience at age 20—an experience that so shook him that he retreated entirely from the world for two weeks. He was so traumatized by his experience, and the full realization of his homosexuality, that he left college and enlisted in the Navy at the height of the Vietnam War because "he needed to run away from what he was." He refrained form all sexual activity through a four-year hitch in the Navy, continuing to attend church regularly and to agonize about his "deviant" sexuality. He was convinced that if he continued a homosexual lifestyle "he wouldn't have a job, his family would reject him, and he would burn in hell." After his honorable discharge from the Navy in 1972, Baker left Texas to live with friends in Massachusetts.

For two years he continued to struggle with his identity, even contemplating suicide. It was not until 1974 when, as a student at the State University of New York at Cortland, Baker summoned the courage to attend a meeting of a student gay organization at Cornell University, thirty miles away in Ithaca, New York. "It was the first time Donald Baker had ever seen other human beings that he knew were homosexual, too, but who were not ashamed of that fact," found the Court. Baker began to come out of the closet. He devoted much of his time to studying the history, sociology, and psychology of homosexual issues, convinced himself that he could be a good Christian and a homosexual, and developed the self-confidence to return to Dallas and the teaching career that he wanted. He returned to Dallas in 1975, "came out" to his family, and taught in the public schools as a language arts and social studies teacher in grades 4–6 for four years until deciding to attend graduate school to obtain a master's degree. He received exuberantly positive ratings on his teaching, and the school district recommended him for the teaching fellowship that allowed him to undertake graduate studies.

While enrolled at Southern Methodist University, Baker became involved in gay rights activities in Dallas, becoming Vice President of the Dallas Gay Political Caucus and volunteering to be plaintiff in the sodomy law challenge, which was filed in November 1979. In 1980, the Caucus changed its name to Dallas Gay Alliance, and Baker became the president. He told the court that he would continue to engage in homosexual conduct in violation of section 21.06 of the Texas Penal Code, but would do so only in private with other consenting men. He testified that although the law was evidently not enforced against homosexuals who confined their activities to private places with consenting adults, it did have serious effects on him and other homosexuals by attaching the stigma of criminality to their lives and subjecting them to potential discrimination by employers, apartment owners, domestic relations courts, and others. Indeed, attorney Barber provided documentation in the form of an affidavit from the Dallas school board that it would not consider hiring a teacher known to violate the sodomy law.

Barber presented testimony from two nationally known authorities on the subject of homosexuality, psychiatrist Judd Marmor, a past president of the American Psychiatric Association and the author and editor of numerous scientific works on the subject, and William Simon, a sociologist who had published extensively on the subject. Both experts had a long record of research and study on the issues raised by homosexuality in their respective disciplines, and they provided a detailed background for the court's consideration. They pointed out that section 21.06 made at least 500,000 Texas men and 200,000 Texas women potential criminals; that medical scientists had adopted a majority view that homosexuality was not an illness, but rather a normal variation of human sexuality that became fixed quite early in life; and that variant sexuality was probably due to a variety of biological, genetic, and environmental factors having nothing to do with conscious choice on the part of the homosexual. They recited the impressive list of professional associations that had called for an end to criminal laws against consensual homosexual conduct between adults, including the American Medical Association and the American Bar Association. Simon testified that the experience of foreign countries and American states that had decriminalized homosexual conduct had shown no discernible adverse effects on public welfare or order, and no measurable increase in the occurrence of homosexuality itself. Marmor testified that laws against homosexual conduct, even if not enforced, resulted in stigma, emotional distress, and other adverse effects. Homosexuals suffered severe emotional problems, not from their sexuality as such, but from the fear and anxiety they experienced because of society's discriminatory attitudes toward them, which were compounded by the label of criminality.

Marmor and Simon both contended that there was no legitimate governmental interest to justify criminal sodomy laws. They argued that there was no rational basis for heterosexuals to fear homosexuals, who were not, contrary to popular belief, disproportionately responsible for sexual abuse of children or more likely to engage in criminal acts (apart from violation of sodomy laws, of course).

The state presented as its sole expert James Grigson, a psychiatrist who specialized in testifying in criminal proceedings, a specialty that he called "legal psychiatry." Apart from examinations undertaken in connection with such testimony and evaluation of arrestees for the prosecutors, Grigson had minimal experience in dealing with homosexuals. He had not undertaken any research on the subject of homosexuality and produced no "respected medical or psychiatric literature" in support of his opinions. Grigson asserted that the weight of psychiatric opinion was incorrect, in that homosexuality was a "sickness." He also asserted that, by criminalizing homosexual conduct, the statute benefitted the public welfare of Texas in two ways: the state induced homosexuals to seek treatment curing them of this condition, and further reinforced "the culture of society's norm pattern or expected pattern of behavior" which was salutary in the "growth and development"

of children. Grigson produced no evidence that either of these benefits had actually occurred.

Judge Buchmeyer had little trouble concluding that the plaintiff's experts were far more credible than the defense's experts. Indeed, his opinion of Grigson was rather scornful, noting that neither of the interests asserted by Grigson were particularly credible and that his assertions were contrary to the positions taken by the leading professional associations in the areas of medicine and criminal justice. Buchmeyer was particularly scornful of the notion "that children might become homosexuals or develop homosexual tendencies unless homosexual conduct is illegal and punished by a $200 fine." (Indeed, the Texas legislature's actions in reducing the penalties for homosexual conduct in 1974 weighed heavily with Judge Buchmeyer when it came to evaluating the purported justification for the statute. It seemed clear, in light of the state's inability or unwillingness to produce legislative history describing the reasons for the statute, that the prohibition of homosexual sodomy was retained for political reasons entirely unrelated to any purported state interest other than securing the enactment of a modern penal code.)

The testimony of District Attorney Henry Wade and City Attorney Lee Holt, as recounted in Buchmeyer's opinion, sounds even more like low comedy. Neither of these law enforcement authorities had a clue as to why the legislature retained the criminal penalties for homosexual conduct, and they were rather forthright in saying so. When asked what the social welfare interest was in having a law "that intrudes into the bedroom of consenting sexual adults," Wade responded, "I don't know of any. There may be some." Wade expressed surprise when told that Texas law allowed heterosexuals to engage in anal and oral sex but denied that right to homosexuals. When he was asked how a law prohibiting "deviate sexual intercourse" advanced the state's interest in procreation when it allowed such intercourse by heterosexuals but denied it to homosexuals, he replied, "I don't think procreation is involved in either one of them, is it?" Both Wade and Holt indicated that there must have been some public interest involved, or the legislature would not have passed the law, but they could not imagine what that interest was.

This created a puzzle for Buchmeyer, who noted that whatever interests might have been cited in "decency" or "morality" would seem to have equally applied to the 1943 law that the legislature had replaced in 1974, and there was no indication why an interest in decency or morality was served by letting heterosexuals commit sodomy but denying that activity to homosexuals. He also pointed out that section 21.06 itself was not concerned with all homosexual conduct, just oral and anal sex. "It did not prohibit homosexuals from kissing or sexually stimulating their partner with hands and fingers" and did not even prohibit the use of vibrators or dildos as originally passed, although the imaginative Texas legislators corrected this oversight by a 1981 amendment. Buchmeyer concluded that the retention of these penalties was based on purely political considerations having nothing to do with public welfare.

Turning to the legal theories under which the law was being attacked, Buchmeyer concluded that section 21.06 was unconstitutional under both theories: privacy and equal protection.

As to privacy, Buchmeyer quickly summarized the U.S. Supreme Court precedents stemming from *Griswold v. Connecticut* (1965) and concluded that the "outer limits" of the right of privacy had not been established by the Court, relying on *dicta* subscribed to by six Justices in a footnote in *Carey v. Population Services International* (1977). As to the application of the right of privacy to sodomy statutes, the Supreme Court had not "answered these questions in any opinion," asserted Buchmeyer, pointing out that there was no substantive discussion by the Court in its orders vacating the district court opinion in *Buchanan* or affirming the district court opinion in *Doe v. Commonwealth's Attorney for City of Richmond* (1975). Buchmeyer concluded that the question was open for him to consider, agreeing with those who contended that *Doe v. Commonwealth's Attorney*, whatever its substantive precedential scope, did not foreclose such consideration, in light of the comments in *Carey* and the subsequent decision by the New York Court of Appeals in *People v. Onofre* (1980), striking down that state's sod-

omy law, which the Supreme Court had refused to review. Buchmeyer particularly emphasized the similarity to the *Onofre* case, in that New York's law had allowed married couples to commit sodomy, thus presenting an equal protection issue also present in Texas but missing under the Virginia statute approved in *Doe v. Commonwealth's Attorney*.

Having satisfied himself that he was free of contrary precedent, Buchmeyer articulated a theoretical basis in the right of privacy to strike down the Texas law. Under the right of privacy flowing from the Supreme Court's decisions, he said, "Every individual has the right to be free from undue interference by the state in important and intimate personal matters. Decisions concerning a person's sexual needs or desires are 'in a field that by definition concerns the most intimate of human activities and relationships,'" quoting the *Carey* decision. This was obviously true for heterosexuals, "and, it is equally true as to a homosexual choosing to engage in sodomy in private with a consenting adult of the same sex," Buchmeyer asserted, noting Baker's detailed testimony and commenting that "it is evident that Baker's resulting decisions concerning his sexual needs and desires are of the most personal, intimate and important concern (just as they are for heterosexuals)." When one added the Supreme Court's decision in *Stanley v. Georgia* (1969), concerning the privacy of the home, to the sexual privacy precedents, it was clear that homosexual conduct in private came within the sphere of privacy suggested by the Supreme Court in its opinions. Furthermore, Buchmeyer could see no state interest other than raw politics to support enactment of section 21.06, and this was insufficient to justify criminalization of conduct that was so fundamental to a person's identity. Emphasizing that his opinion dealt only with section 21.06, and not with other statutes that might be used against homosexuals who engaged in sexual activity in public, by force or with minors, he found unavailing the state's contention that the law was justified by concerns with "morality and decency," public health, welfare and safety, or procreation. Summarizing the testimonies of Grigson, Wade, and Holt, Buchmeyer concluded that "under the record in this case, the defendants have nothing to rely upon but the assertion of general platitudes (morality, decency, etc.)," and that this was "totally inadequate" to justify the statute under the compelling interest standard he would apply. Indeed, even if one were to find no fundamental right implicated in the case, "this statute's condemnation of homosexual conduct is not even rationally related to a legitimate state interest," asserted Buchmeyer.

As an equal and alternative ground, Buchmeyer found that the statute also violated the equal protection rights of the homosexual citizens of Texas. While declining to find that sexual orientation was a suspect or even a quasi-suspect classification for equal protection purposes ("the Supreme Court has not even concluded yet that *sex* is a suspect class," noted Buchmeyer), Buchmeyer found that it was not necessary to apply any more than rationality review to find the statute unconstitutional on this basis. Under any version of equal protection, a statute that lacked any rational basis in a legitimate state interest had to fall. The defendants had argued in their brief that "it is undisputed that homosexual sodomy, far from being a proud and cherished tradition, is a practice which has been abhorred in western civilization and has long inspired an almost universal phobic response," thus justifying continued criminalization despite the challenged unequal treatment of homosexuals and heterosexuals under the law. In other words, the historical persecution of gays justified continued persecution. Buchmeyer criticized this as bad history and bad constitutional law. For one thing, condemnation of homosexual sodomy was not universal, as cross-cultural studies showed, and many countries and states had decriminalized this conduct. Furthermore, issues of constitutional law were not appropriately resolved by reference to "emotion" and "predilection," asserted Buchmeyer, quoting Justice Oliver Wendell Holmes, Jr.'s, famous admonition from his dissent in *Lochner v. New York* (1905) that the Constitution is made for people of fundamentally differing views and "the accident" of one finding certain opinions "novel and even shocking ought not to conclude one's judgment upon the question" of constitutionality.

Disposing briefly of Baker's contention that the sodomy law violated the First Amendment's Establishment Clause (there was no evidence that the legislature was motivated by religion in its enactment) and objections to standing and jurisdiction mounted by the state, Buchmeyer concluded that the law could not stand. "Homosexuality is an emotional and controversial issue in our society," he said. "It causes fear and disgust among many people. This may well result in condemnation of this decision—but, if so, the critics should at least have a clear understanding that this decision has little effect upon the general public." Buchmeyer emphasized that he was striking down a misdemeanor statute that imposed a mere $200 fine, no real deterrent to the private conduct involved, and that the decision left intact a wide range of laws penalizing public sexual behavior, sex offenses involving children, and forcible sex. He also emphasized that the state remained capable of punishing private activities that might be considered truly harmful, such as use of dangerous drugs. Buchmeyer supplemented his opinion with a lengthy appendix detailing the history of Texas sodomy laws.

Buchmeyer's opinion created jubilation in the gay community and consternation among Texas conservatives. The case had been certified as a class action, binding all Texas law enforcement officials. Although at the time of the class action ruling county prosecutors had been notified and offered the opportunity to participate in the defense of the case, none had taken up the offer. Now, however, as word spread that Attorney General Mark White was seriously considering not appealing the ruling, a conservative Dallas attorney, William Charles Bundren, went into action, persuading the newly elected district attorney of Potter County, Danny E. Hill, to allow Bundren to file a motion in Hill's name seeking permission to intervene, reopen the case, and appeal it to the U.S. Court of Appeals for the Fifth Circuit if necessary. Bundren was also representing a group of conservative doctors in Dallas, who contended that the recently discovered disease of acquired immune deficiency syndrome (AIDS), which at that time mainly affected the gay male community, provided a compelling interest for keeping the sodomy law in force.

On October 28, 1982, just weeks after Buchmeyer entered his final order in the case,

Bundren filed a notice of appeal in the Fifth Circuit on behalf of Hill. On November 1, Attorney General White filed a notice of appeal on behalf of the state, and gay rights groups stepped up their lobbying efforts to persuade White to drop his appeal. On February 23, 1983, the Dallas Doctors Against AIDS, represented by Bundren, filed a motion seeking leave to file an *amicus curiae* brief in the state's Fifth Circuit appeal. On March 9, 1983, White signaled that the state would drop its appeal, sending a letter to the Fifth Circuit to that effect. The next day, Bundren filed a new motion with the Fifth Circuit, seeking permission to substitute Hill for White as counsel of record for the state of Texas. Bundren alleged that Hill had standing in this situation as a local prosecutor sworn to enforce the law and that by withdrawing from the case White had failed adequately to represent the defendant class. Bundren filed a similar motion with the district court in April, accompanied by a motion to set aside the final judgment and to reopen the evidence. In this new motion, Bundren charged that the proceedings had been deficient in ignoring the issue of AIDS, "the lethal and epidemic disease" that was spread by "homosexual sodomy." (As it later appeared, all of this appeal activity on behalf of Hill was being funded by a handful of conservative Dallas physicians.) Hill never even executed the necessary affidavit in support of the motion to substitute him as counsel for the state, and the Dallas doctors' group, seeking to distance themselves from Bundren, substituted attorney Donovan Campbell, Jr., son of one of the doctors, as their counsel. A single Fifth Circuit judge granted Bundren's motion to appear on behalf of Hill pending a hearing on his motions by a panel of the court.

On September 21, a three-judge panel of the Fifth Circuit dismissed Hill's appeal. In an opinion by Circuit Judge Alvin B. Rubin, the panel held that Hill was not a proper representative of the state of Texas on this appeal. The attorney general was the proper person to decide whether an appeal of the district court's opinion was in the best interest of the state, asserted Rubin. Without expressing any opinion on the merits of Buchmeyer's decision, Rubin asserted that Hill had failed to meet the requirements of Rule 24(a)(2) of the Federal Rules of Civil Procedure, governing the circumstances when a party can intervene in litigation at the appellate level. Rubin concluded that Hill (actually Bundren) had failed to show that his interest in his official capacity as a Texas law enforcement official had been inadequately represented by Attorney General White. Noting that the attorney general had appeared and vigorously defended the sodomy law in the trial court, Rubin asserted that the subsequent decision not to appeal the ruling did not necessarily mean that the interests of Hill or the state were inadequately represented. Furthermore, Texas law "plainly designates the Attorney General as the official responsible for protecting the State's interest in litigation." It would be improper for the court of appeals to allow a local prosecutor to decide which cases the state should be appealing. Noting that Hill (or his predecessor) had been "content to rely on the efforts of others until the cause was lost and those who had hitherto fought the battle considered further litigation undesirable," Rubin concluded that Hill's motions should be dismissed.

Bundren promptly filed a petition for rehearing *en banc* and renewed his efforts to get Judge Buchmeyer to reopen the trial decision for receipt of new evidence about the AIDS epidemic. On January 28, 1985, the appeals court announced that a majority of the sixteen judges of the Circuit voted to rehear the case *en banc*. On July 1, 1985, Judge Buchmeyer denied Bundren's various pending motions. Buchmeyer ridiculed contentions that the materials about AIDS appended to his motions were "newly discovered evidence" sufficient to justify reopening the case. Noting that many of the appended articles were published while the trial was pending and could, with reasonable diligence, have been submitted by the state, Buchmeyer concluded that the established standards for granting such motions had not been met. Furthermore, reviewing materials submitted in opposition to the motion by Barber, including affidavits from public health authorities, Buchmeyer commented that the evidence seemed to indicate that maintaining the sodomy law in effect would have little or no utility in containing the AIDS epidemic, and might even be counterproductive, since criminalization of homosexual sodomy was likely to make research and prevention efforts more difficult while providing little independent deterrent to dangerous conduct. Indeed, the risk of death from infection by the Human Immunodeficiency Virus was likely to be more of a deterrent to anal intercourse than a threatened $200 fine for commission of a misdemeanor.

The Fifth Circuit's decision to rehear the case *en banc* sent alarm bells ringing throughout the gay legal community and brought *amicus* briefs to the court from the Texas Human Rights Foundation (a recently formed statewide gay rights group), Lambda Legal Defense and Education Fund, National Gay Rights Advocates, and the Medical Advisory Council of AIDS Project/Los Angeles (to counter the allegations in the *amicus* brief filed by Dallas Doctors Against AIDS). Attorney General White also filed a brief urging dismissal of the appeal on the grounds of the original panel decision.

On August 26, 1985, the court announced that ten judges had voted to grant Hill's motion to intervene and substitute himself as class representative and, on the merits, had voted to reverse the judgment of the district court. The brief opinion by Circuit Judge Thomas M. Reavley held that both Hill and Baker had standing, the former to represent the State of Texas on appeal, the latter to challenge the statute even though he had never been personally threatened with prosecution. Reavley made short work of the merits, ruling that *Doe v. Commonwealth's Attorney* was binding authoritative precedent on the privacy argument and refusing "to speculate, on the basis of the writings cited to us by the appellee, about what the Court might do today on this issue." Reavley was equally dismissive of the equal protection argument. Without any discussion or analysis, he said that "we refuse to hold that homosexuals constitute a suspect or quasi-suspect classification." The standard of review was thus the rationality test. "In view of the strong objection to homosexual conduct, which has prevailed in Western culture for the past seven centuries, we cannot say that section 21.06 is 'totally unrelated to the pursuit of' implementing morality, a permissible state goal," asserted Reavley. Thus, it did "not deprive Baker of equal protection of the laws." Reavley also noted that the issue of equal protection had been raised in the

jurisdictional statement presented to the Supreme Court in *Doe v. Commonwealth's Attorney*, implying that for whatever it was worth the Court may have considered the equal protection issue in deciding to affirm in that case. The court dissolved Judge Buchmeyer's injunction against enforcement of the law.

Judge Rubin dissented, in an opinion joined by five of his colleagues. Without taking any position on the merits of the case, which he contended had been improperly addressed by the court, Rubin reiterated his arguments from the panel opinion at great length, contending that the court, "[d]etermined to uphold the constitutionality of a Texas statute whatever obstacles bar the way, . . . tramples every procedural rule it considers." In addition to joining Judge Rubin's opinion, Circuit Judge Irving Goldberg, also a member of the three-judge panel, dissented separately to assert that inasmuch as the majority had reached the merits of the dispute, he would articulate his view that the Texas law was unconstitutional. Asserting that *Doe v. Commonwealth's Attorney* did not control the case, he said: "If ever there was a constitutional right to privacy, Texas has violated it by blatantly intruding into the private sex lives of fully consenting adults. Because this legislative trespass lacks a compelling state interest, I would hold this statute invalid on its face." The *en banc* court announced October 23 that it would refuse to reconsider its decision.

Reavley's opinion was met with outrage from gay rights attorneys. As contrasted to the lengthy, detailed opinion by District Judge Buchmeyer, the *en banc* opinion disposed of complicated constitutional issues in a bare two paragraphs, with no reasoned explanation. Indeed, the court of appeals had stated, in effect, that a history of objection to a particular practice was sufficient, under the rational basis test, to continue outlawing that practice. This was particularly galling in light of Judge Buchmeyer's detailed historical appendix, which showed that for most of the time since Texas first enacted a sodomy law in 1860, oral sex had been lawful and that not until 1974 had the Texas legislature singled out "homosexual sodomy" for particular criminalization. It also ignored Buchmeyer's careful documentation that many countries that are part of "western civilization" had decriminalized sodomy long ago. The skimpy appellate decision certainly seemed vulnerable to attack.

Now a major strategic issue loomed. Several grounds presented themselves for appealing the case to the U.S. Supreme Court. An appeal could focus on the issue of Hill's standing and the blatant violation of the concept of federalism when a federal appeals court substituted its judgment for that of the elected attorney general of Texas as to whether the state should appeal the district court's ruling. Alternatively, the appeal could emphasize the privacy and equal protection issues, which clearly distinguished this case from *Doe*, where the Virginia statute had resembled the 1943 Texas sodomy law in prohibiting conduct by all persons, heterosexual or homosexual, married or single. Complicating matters was the U.S. Supreme Court's decision to grant the writ of *certiorari* in *Bowers v. Hardwick*, which was scheduled for argument in March 1986. What would be the effect of *Hardwick* on *Baker*, or vice versa, if a *certiorari* petition was filed? Under the Supreme Court's rules, the filing of a petition would have to take place before the *Hardwick* case was argued. What if the Court decided to consolidate the cases for argument? Would that help or hurt the case for sodomy law reform?

These issues were considered at length at a meeting of attorneys for Hardwick and Baker together with representatives of the leading lesbian and gay rights legal organizations at the national headquarters of the American Civil Liberties Union shortly after the Fifth Circuit refused to reconsider its decision. After a tense discussion, Donald Baker decided to accept an offer from Harvard Law School Professor Laurence Tribe, who was representing Hardwick, to take over as lead counsel on his case and file a *certiorari* petition at the last possible moment under the Court's rules. Tribe hoped that the last-minute petition would not be consolidated, thus preserving for possible later argument the equal protection issues in the Texas case that were less obviously present in Georgia, where the sodomy law was not limited to homosexual conduct. Subsequent negotiations with the Texas attorney general's office led to multiple petitions being filed. Texas

filed a petition seeking reversal of the Fifth Circuit's decision that Hill could represent the state on appeal. Bundren eventually filed petitions on behalf of Hill against the state of Texas and against Baker, defending the Fifth Circuit's rulings on the merits and the procedural issues.

On June 30, 1986, the Supreme Court announced its decision in *Bowers v. Hardwick*, holding that the constitutional right of privacy did not extend to consensual homosexual sodomy in private. A week later, the Court announced that it was denying the petitions for writs of *certiorari* in *Baker v. Wade*, *Texas v. Hill*, *Hill v. Texas*, and *Hill v. Baker*, with Justice Thurgood Marshall noting that he would have granted *certiorari* in all four cases. Tribe, seizing on the Court's indication in *Hardwick* that it was not addressing equal protection issues in that case, filed a further petition for rehearing of the decision on the writ, arguing that *Hardwick* left open significant equal protection issues that deserved addressing by the Court, but the Court denied this petition on September 3, 1986.

Thus ended the extended, complex history of *Baker v. Wade*, in which the most sweeping, detailed constitutional condemnation of sodomy laws was overturned through the persistence of one man, William Charles Bundren, with the financial support of a small group of Dallas physicians. The determination of Texas gay rights organizations to challenge the sodomy law was not ended by this heartbreaking *dénouement*. The Texas courts had themselves indicated that the state constitution independently protected the right of privacy of Texans, so the Texas Human Rights Foundation went back to the drawing boards and filed a new challenge in state court, which led a Texas trial judge in Austin to declare late in 1990 that section 21.06 violated the state constitution. Virtually simultaneously, Lambda Legal Defense and Education Fund filed suit in Dallas on behalf of a woman whose offer of employment as a Dallas police officer had been withdrawn when it was learned she was a lesbian. Lambda alleged that the underlying reason for withdrawal of the offer (that as a lesbian, their client was presumptively a violator of section 21.06) was unconstitutional, because section 21.06 violated the Texas and federal constitutions. The challenges to Texas's misdemeanor sodomy law continued.

Case References

Bowers v. Hardwick, 478 U.S. 186 (1986)

Buchanan v. Batchelor, 308 F. Supp. 729 (N.D. Tex. 1970), vacated and remanded sub nom. Buchanan v. Wade, 401 U.S. 989 (1971)

Carey v. Population Services International, 431 U.S. 678 (1977)

Doe v. Commonwealth's Attorney for City of Richmond, 403 F. Supp. 1199 (E.D. Va. 1975), affirmed, 425 U.S. 901, rehearing denied, 425 U.S. 985 (1976)

Griswold v. Connecticut, 381 U.S. 479 (1965)

Lochner v. New York, 198 U.S. 45 (1905)

People v. Onofre, 51 N.Y.2d 476 (1980), certiorari denied, 451 U.S. 987 (1981)

Roe v. Wade, 410 U.S. 113, rehearing denied, 410 U.S. 959 (1973)

Stanley v. Georgia, 394 U.S. 557 (1969)

27. SEX AND THE SINGLE PERSON: A FEDERAL CONSTITUTIONAL FORUM?

Doe v. Duling, 782 F.2d 1202 (4th Cir. 1986), vacating 603 F. Supp. 960 (E.D. Va. 1985).

"Virginia is for lovers" scream the billboards and T-shirts, part of an effective promotional campaign to increase tourism. Not so, proclaimed some civil liberties activists in Richmond, pointing to 19th-century laws, still on the books, banning unmarried adults from having sex or living together in a sexual relationship. Although the most recent convictions under these statutes leave their traces in published appellate decisions also dating from the 19th century, their continued existence seemed an affront to a young generation raised in the libertarian ethos of the sexual revolution.

And these laws remained troublesome for other reasons. A young woman who was living with her boyfriend without benefit of marriage encountered difficulty being admitted to law practice, having to litigate the question to the state's highest court, which ruled in 1979 that "cohabitation," as prohibited by the statute, had "no rational connection to . . . fitness to practice law." While reassuring, the decision in Cord v. Gibb pointed up the hypocrisy of a legal code that was widely flouted and only really enforced against those who had sex in public places like parks or cars. All unmarried lovers were stigmatized, and the laws were likely to be cited in domestic relations disputes (including those over child custody) as well. Something had to be done about it.

Two young adults residing in separate houses in Richmond, proceeding anonymously as James Doe and Jane Doe, agreed to be plaintiffs in a test case brought by civil liberties attorneys Michael Morchower and John B. Boatwright, III, in the U.S. District Court for the Eastern District of Virginia. They were lucky to have their case assigned to one of the federal judiciary's leading advocates of sexual privacy, District Judge Robert R. Merhige, Jr., who had been the dissenting member of the three-judge panel that upheld the Virginia sodomy law in Doe v. Commonwealth's Attorney for City of Richmond (1975). They named as defendants Frank S. Duling, Richmond's Chief of Police, and Aubrey M. Davis, Jr., the commonwealth's attorney for the City of Richmond, who were represented in the suit by Assistant Commonwealth's Attorneys Michael L. Sarahan and James C. Wicker, Jr., and Assistant Attorney General Linwood T. Wells.

Alleging that the fornication and cohabitation statutes violated their rights to privacy, freedom of association, and freedom of expression as protected by the First, Fifth, Ninth, and Fourteenth amendments, the Does sought a judicial declaration that the laws were unconstitutional and an injunction against their enforcement. The defendants moved for dismissal, arguing that neither of the plaintiffs had standing to bring the lawsuit because they had not been prosecuted for violation of the laws and were not faced with the likelihood of prosecution. Prior to ruling on the motion, Judge Merhige had the parties conduct discovery on the issue of standing, and received depositions, documents, and a written factual stipulation on which to base his ruling.

In their depositions, the Does stated that they were single adults who had engaged in consensual sexual activity with other adults of the opposite sex in private places. They both indicated their desire and intent to continue such activities and to cohabit in the future "under conditions normally associated with living as husband and wife," but that they had put such activities on hold for the pendency of this suit because of their fear of potential prosecution. They acknowledged that the conduct covered by the laws was widespread, with little if any police enforcement against those who conducted their sexual activities in private, but they indicated that they would suffer embarrassment to their reputations were they to be prosecuted.

The plaintiffs deposed two Richmond police officers about enforcement of the laws. Lieutenant John Carlson, commander of the vice squad, testified that there had been several arrests under the fornication statutes during the previous five years, although all involved some element of prostitution. Police Officer William C. Bailey, a member of the vice squad, had participated in more than thirty fornication arrests. He testified that "almost" all of them involved prostitution, and those that did not involve prostitution involved sexual activity exposed to public view. None of the recent fornication arrests involved noncommercial sexual activity in a private home. Furthermore, there was no record of any arrest for cohabitation violations in the past ten years. Lt. Carlson testified to his belief that cohabitation had to involve open sexual conduct in order to violate the law. The officers testified that enforcement activities were focused mainly on public conduct, but that the police would respond to complaints about private conduct. Enforcement of these laws against parties acting in private was low on the police department's list of priorities, however.

Merhige heard oral arguments on the motion to dismiss and the merits of the constitu-

tional claims and issued his opinion February 27, 1985. He ruled that the Does did have proper standing, the court had jurisdiction of the matter, and the challenged laws were unconstitutional violations of the right of individual privacy protected by the federal Constitution.

Merhige broke down the jurisdictional issues to those of standing and ripeness. Standing refers to the personal interest the plaintiff has in the controversy, while ripeness concerns whether that interest is strong enough to create a real controversy for the court to decide as opposed to a merely hypothetical one. In the context of a declaratory judgment action placing in issue the constitutionality of a law, the plaintiff must face a "real threat of prosecution" because he or she is engaged in conduct covered by a statute that is presently being enforced in a way that makes it reasonably likely that it could be enforced against the plaintiff.

Merhige found that the Virginia statutes plainly applied to the type of conduct in which the Does swore they had engaged and would engage in the future. However, the Does testified that they had not and were not engaged in sexual activity with each other. The defendants argued that this meant future violations were hypothetical. Merhige disagreed, since both Does testified that they had present opportunities to engage in activity covered by the statute from which they were refraining while the lawsuit proceeded. Thus, at least theoretically, the plaintiffs had standing. Ripeness presented another question, since enforcement of the laws was spotty and virtually negligible when the conduct took place in a private home. The defendants argued that the patterns of enforcement indicated that the odds of prosecution against the Does were extremely low, thus failing to meet the ripeness requirements developed by the federal courts. Merhige disagreed, pointing to the U.S. Supreme Court decision in *Doe v. Bolton* (1973), a case in which plaintiffs were challenging a newly enacted antiabortion law that had never been enforced. The Virginia laws had been recently enforced, the police had not disavowed any intention of enforcing them, and they would respond to complaints if they were received. Consequently, he decided the issue was ripe for decision and held that the court had jurisdiction of the case.

Proceeding to the merits, Merhige first discussed the fornication statute. The defendants argued that two cases decided in the mid-1970s, *Doe v. Commonwealth's Attorney* and *Lovisi v. Slayton*, were dispositive of the issues. In *Doe v. Commonwealth's Attorney*, a three-judge district court, specially convened under the rules then prevailing to consider a test case challenge to the Virginia sodomy law, had concluded that the right to privacy previously articulated by the Supreme Court in *Griswold v. Connecticut* (1965) did not extend to consensual private sexual activity between adults of the same sex. The Supreme Court summarily affirmed that decision without issuing an opinion. In *Lovisi*, the U.S. Court of Appeals for the Fourth Circuit, which had binding precedential authority over the district court in Virginia, had ruled that the right of privacy did not apply to sexual activity between married adults when they allowed a third person to be present, observing and photographing their activity. From these cases, the defendants argued, it was clear that sexual activity between unmarried persons, or in the presence of somebody not married to the participants, was not protected by the right of privacy, thus demarking the limitations of *Griswold* to sexual activity between married persons.

Merhige rejected this characterization of the prior case law. As to *Doe v. Commonwealth's Attorney*, since the Supreme Court's affirmance had been without an opinion, the precedential value of the case should be limited to the precise issue decided (i.e., "that Virginia's sodomy statute as applied to adult males who consensually engage in homosexual sodomitic activity in privacy [for such were the anonymous plaintiffs in that case] is a constitutional exercise of state power"). That, of course, had nothing to do with the present case, in which the plaintiffs were challenging restrictions on heterosexual "sexual intercourse" which would include vaginal intercourse not covered by the sodomy law. *Doe v. Commonwealth's Attorney* had not addressed the particular issues this case would raise. As to *Lovisi*, the Fourth Circuit had "found it unnecessary to recognize a right of sexual privacy outside the marriage." Said Merhige,

"The majority in *Lovisi* implied, without deciding, that there was no such right. While the Court's instant task would be greatly lightened if it were so, *Lovisi* simply is not dispositive of this issue."

For Merhige, the line of cases beginning with *Griswold v. Connecticut* and extending through *Eisenstadt v. Baird* (1972) and *Carey v. Population Services International* (1977) indicated that the right of privacy would extend to cover the activities condemned by the fornication and cohabitation statutes. Although all three of these cases were about contraception and might be narrowly viewed as addressing only the right to prevent conception, to Merhige, the holding was not so limited. "Necessarily implicit in the right to make decisions regarding childbearing is the right to engage in sexual intercourse," he said. "To hold otherwise would result in the constitutional right to decide whether to bear or beget a child contingent on one's marital status," but *Carey* made clear that the Court had not approved such a limitation. In *Eisenstadt*, Justice William J. Brennan, Jr., had written, "If the right of privacy means anything, it is the right of the *individual*, married or single, to be free from unwarranted governmental intrusion into matters so fundamentally affecting a person as the decision whether to bear or beget a child." Since sexual intercourse was a prerequisite to "bearing a child," asserted Merhige, "[t]he decision to engage in sexual intercourse . . . is a matter fundamental to the decision whether to bear or beget a child." The decision to engage in intercourse, then, must also be covered by the same constitutional privacy right.

Of course, even "fundamental" rights are not absolute. The state is entitled to abridge them for compelling reasons if the abridgement is narrowly tailored to meet the state's articulated interest. Here, the state argued that the interest to be protected was in "encouraging, promoting and regulating traditional marital and family relationships as well as traditional moral values," and that the fornication law was also designed to protect the public from sexually transmitted diseases and to minimize illegitimate births. "As laudable as these state goals are," said Merhige, "they do not justify an absolute prohibition of the exercise of a constitutionally protected activity." The decision whether to marry, and whom to marry, "is a personal choice protected by the right of privacy," said Merhige, citing *Loving v. Virginia* (1967). He also rejected the notion that a state purpose to regulate "public morals" could be extended into "the privacy of one's home." "There is no showing," he asserted, "that fornication in private has any detrimental effect on society." Citing *Stanley v. Georgia* (1969) he said that even "socially condemned activity" would be shielded from state prohibition if it took place in private and had no such detrimental effect on society. At bottom, he said, while the state's goals here were desirable, they did not seem compelling, given the constitutional privacy protection for marital choice and the home.

The public health rationale also was unavailing, since the statute was overbroad in relation to that goal. "All single people who engage in sexual intercourse do not pose a threat of spreading sexual diseases," he said. As to the goal of preventing illegitimacy, he observed that the state could provide a procedure for legitimating children born out of wedlock. While it was legitimate for the state to encourage traditional family relationships, the encouragement could not come at the sacrifice of constitutionally protected privacy rights.

The cohabitation statute raised somewhat different issues. For one thing, the law's plain language ranged farther than punishing mere cohabitation, condemning "any persons, not married to each other, [who] lewdly and lasciviously associate and cohabit together [or], whether married or not, be guilty of open and gross lewdness and lasciviousness." The Does were not challenging the entire statute, merely that portion that specifically criminalized cohabitation. The defendants argued that the law in that regard was susceptible to a limiting interpretation, somewhat along the lines suggested by Lt. Carlson's deposition (i.e., that only open sexual conduct between cohabitants would subject them to prosecution). The problem with this interpretation was that the Virginia courts had not given the law such a limited meaning. Merhige found that the cases the defendants cited did not support the proposition that the Virginia courts had limited the application of the statute so as to protect individuals who lived

together in a sexual relationship that was quiet and discreet. Finding that the state's articulated interests in penalizing such behavior were "identical" to those underlying the fornication statute, Merhige found the statute equally invalid. Given the Supreme Court's implicit holdings that "all individuals have a constitutional right to decide whether to procreate," said Merhige, "[i]mplicit in this decision is the right to engage in private heterosexual intercourse. . . . It is irrational to limit such conduct, if partners are not married to each other, only to those persons who are *not* living together. Such a limitation hardly furthers the marital relationship and may even frustrate a family relationship—unmarried parents of a child would be deterred from living together." This last assertion was a bit unfair of Merhige; the Virginia legislators had not intended to set up such an irrational scheme, after all, for they had banned all sexual contact between unmarried adults, not just those living together. Merhige's decision to strike down the fornication law helped make the cohabitation law appear even more ridiculously outmoded.

Merhige ruled that both statutes were unconstitutional and enjoined the defendants from enforcing them. The defendants promptly appealed this ruling to the U.S. Court of Appeals for the Fourth Circuit in Richmond, which scheduled oral argument for October 10, 1985. The state substituted Mark R. Davis, an assistant attorney general, for Linwood T. Wells, in presenting its appeal. The appellate panel quickly concluded that Judge Merhige had erred in his determination regarding jurisdiction and issued an opinion on February 7, 1986, holding to that effect and vacating Merhige's declaratory judgment and injunction. The court's opinion, by Circuit Judge James Harvie Wilkinson, III, shows the difficulty of attempting to clear the statute books of antiquated enactments through litigation.

The problem, said Wilkinson, was that there did not appear even a remote possibility that the plaintiffs would be prosecuted for the kind of behavior to which they testified in their depositions. "To adjudge this fanciful dispute would undermine the proper role of federal courts in our system of government and usurp the position of state courts and legislatures as primary arbiters of state law," he said. Reviewing the arrest records that had been introduced before Merhige as evidence of recent enforcement, he pointed out that "none of these arrests involved fornication in a private residence." To the contrary, "All involved public conduct." It was clear that the statutes in question were not presently being enforced against those who conducted their sex life privately. To the extent that Merhige's ruling was premised on the privacy of the home, it was clear the privacy of the home was not being violated by enforcement of these laws and that "the Does face only the most theoretical threat of prosecution."

While the laws might have a "chilling effect" on their behavior, as they alleged in their depositions, every criminal law had some chilling effect, but "a subjective chill" was not the sort of "specific present objective harm or a threat of specific future harm" that had been identified by the Supreme Court in *Laird v. Tatum* (1972) as the necessary prerequisite for standing to challenge a statute, apart perhaps from "rare cases involving core First Amendment rights," and even there the Supreme Court had required a "credible threat of prosecution" before recognizing standing.

The case also presented a problem because of concerns for federalism. The Does were challenging a state law that had not been enforced against people in their position. They emphasized the symbolism and stigma of the law, but to Wilkinson, such an emphasis cut against standing, because the question whether to maintain such unenforced laws on the books was inherently one of policy best decided by the legislative branch, in his view. Noting that several states had recently repealed fornication laws, he saw this as a matter well suited to debate in the political arena:

> To many, the Virginia statutes here compromise the sacred component of privacy in sexual expression. They represent the potential intrusion of the state into the sanctity of the home or apartment, the potential for police action on nothing more than pretext and suspicion, and the imposition of antiquated attitudes about sex that bear little relevance to the diversity of individual lifestyles in a contemporary world. To others, these statutes express the value society places upon the life of the family and the institution of marriage, upon the realization of love through the

encouragement of sexual fidelity, and upon the prevention of sexually transmitted diseases brought on by promiscuity. They discern in old laws renewed relevance as traditional values come under siege.

"Each view has its adherents," said Wilkinson, "and the pendulum of social conscience will doubtless swing between the two indefinitely." But the institution under our form of government for locating the pendulum and adjusting the laws accordingly is the legislature of the state, not a federal court. The states were given primary responsibility under the federal system for "the protection of public health, welfare, safety and morals." It was not for a federal court to substitute its moral sense for that of the legislature. If the Virginia legislature refused to address the issue, those seeking repeal of the statutes could make it an issue in the future election of representatives.

In addition, there was the lack of recent appellate constructions of the law with regard to the kind of conduct described by the Does. Lacking that, the district court was making its decision in a vacuum. "Awaiting a threat of enforcement, by contrast, allows concrete application of state laws to specific instances of human behavior," argued Wilkinson, and "also provides an opportunity for limiting constructions of state law by state courts by which constitutional issues may be avoided." In fact, the state could avoid the necessity for such judicial constructions by adopting a limited construction in enforcement which would avoid "needless and premature friction" between the state and the federal courts. Wilkinson noted that the law had been enforced in ways not questioned in this lawsuit, against prostitution and public sexual activity. Although the law, by its terms, might be applied to activity that was recognized as constitutionally protected, "[b]y awaiting a concrete case or controversy, we decline to indulge the presumption that state authorities will pursue a constitutionally suspect course," said Wilkinson.

Declining "to make a symbolic pronouncement endorsing one of many possible visions of social governance and sexual morality," the court ruled that the Does were without standing to challenge the Virginia statutes, vacated Judge Merhige's decision, and ordered dismissal of the case.

While Merhige's substantive ruling on the merits of the constitutional challenge to the fornication and cohabitation laws was thus without precedential effect, his opinion had been published and provides a thoughtful and cogent analysis of the constitutional issues, as to which the court of appeals had pointedly refrained from ruling. The significance of the case, however, rests primarily on its illustration of the limitations of the federal judicial forum as a mechanism for the reconsideration of many of the sex crimes laws that remain on the books. Their enforcement is voluntarily restricted by law enforcement authorities in most instances due to lack of interest in prying into the private lives of peaceful citizens, but their symbolic importance is revived from time to time in other forums where the moral character of individuals might be drawn into question.

Case References

Carey v. Population Services International, 431 U.S. 678 (1977)

Cord v. Gibb, 219 Va. 1019, 254 S.E.2d 71 (1979)

Doe v. Bolton, 410 U.S. 179, rehearing denied, 410 U.S. 959 (1973)

Doe v. Commonwealth's Attorney for City of Richmond, 403 F. Supp. 1199 (E.D.Va. 1975), affirmed, 425 U.S. 901, rehearing denied, 425 U.S. 925 (1976)

Eisenstadt v. Baird, 405 U.S. 438 (1972)

Griswold v. Connecticut, 381 U.S. 479 (1965)

Laird v. Tatum, 408 U.S. 1, rehearing denied, 409 U.S. 824 (1972)

Loving v. Virginia, 388 U.S. 1 (1967)

Lovisi v. Slayton, 539 F.2d 349 (4th Cir.), certiorari denied, 429 U.S. 977 (1976)

Stanley v. Georgia, 394 U.S. 557 (1969)

28. CROSS-DRESSING AND THE CONSTITUTION

D.C. and M.S. v. City of St. Louis, 795 F.2d 652 (8th Cir. 1986).

The diversity of human sexuality expresses itself in a wide variety of behaviors, including cross-gender dressing as an expression of gender role nonconformity, labeled "transvestism." A strong desire to dress in a manner normal for the opposite sex has no necessary correlation with sexual orientation and is not necessarily an indication of transsexualism, contrary to the beliefs of many. According to sex researchers, a surprising number of men and women experience significant discomfort in having to dress in the manner socially prescribed for their sex, which is dispelled when they can abandon sexual dressing conventions. In addition, cross-dressing has a long and venerable history as a theater form, beginning in classical times and continuing through the "pants roles" performed by women and the "skirt roles" performed by men in 17th- and 18th-century opera (and recalled even in the 20th century by Richard Strauss in *Der Rosenkavalier*). "Drag shows" continue as an entertainment form, primarily appealing to gay men as customers but, in fact, drawing a diverse audience in many parts of the United States.

Official unhappiness with such practices is reflected in many parts of the country by penal laws prohibiting public cross-dressing. The sources of such laws are quite ancient, deriving from Old Testament prohibitions against cross-dressing, and most of these laws are rarely enforced relics. Do they cross the line of permissible regulation of such an intimate matter as personal appearance, a matter as to which the U.S. Supreme Court has held there is some degree of constitutional protection? In *Kelley v. Johnson* (1976), a Suffolk County, New York, police officer challenged official grooming standards as an invasion of his right to "liberty" under the Due Process Clause of the Fourteenth Amendment. The Court sustained the regulation as reasonably necessary for law enforcement purposes in the context of the "para-military" world of the police, indicating that it was possible that in a purely civilian context the Due Process Clause would render suspect a government-imposed grooming standard. In dissent, Justice Thurgood Marshall asserted that it was "clear" that the Fourteenth Amendment "does indeed protect against comprehensive regulation of what citizens may or may not wear."

The issue of governmental regulation of dress was raised more directly in St. Louis, Missouri, early in the 1980s, with the arrest of two men for violating a municipal ordinance regulating personal appearance. The ordinance provided:

Any person who shall, in this city, appear in any public place in a state of nudity or in a dress not belonging to his or her sex or in an indecent or lewd dress, or shall make an indecent exposure of his or her person, or be guilty of an indecent or lewd act or behavior shall be guilty of a misdemeanor.

The first case involved Daniel Clippard, a transvestite who was arrested for appearing dressed as a woman in public on October 25, 1982, and again on November 5, 1982. The official charge was appearing "in any public place . . . in a dress not belonging to his or her sex." Clippard pleaded guilty the first time and was released with "time served" (i.e., the time from his arrest to his conviction). On the second charge, Clippard pleaded not guilty and the municipal court dismissed the charge, finding the ordinance to be vague with regard to the cross-dressing prohibition.

In the second case, police arrested Michael Shreves, a "drag show" performer, on January 14, 1984. Undercover police attended the club show in which Shreves portrayed "Michelle Mouth," dressed in a variety of clothes during his act to impersonate women, and made erotic gestures. He was charged under the portion of the ordinance dealing with "an indecent or lewd act or behavior." Shreves moved to dismiss the charge against him, arguing that the ordinance was unconstitutionally vague. Responding to this motion, the city attorney dropped the prosecution.

A leading lesbian feminist attorney in St. Louis, Arlene Zarembka, filed an action in federal district court on behalf of both Clippard and Shreves, seeking a declaration that the ordinance was unconstitutional so far as it was used to harass, arrest, and prosecute individuals for cross-dressing in public or performing in drag shows. Zarembka also requested an award of damages to the two plaintiffs for violation of

their civil rights under color of law. The complaint named as defendants the city, the police officers who had arrested Clippard and Shreves, and Board of Police Commissioners, and various past and present members of the Board. The city attorney's office assigned Judith Ronzio to defend the ordinance before District Judge William L. Hungate.

Hungate disposed of various pretrial motions by dismissing the Board of Police Commissioners as a party defendant, granting the plaintiffs' motion for partial summary judgment with regard to the constitutionality of the cross-dressing provision, and denying the portion of the motion aimed at the "indecent and lewd conduct" provision under which Shreves had been charged. In an unpublished memorandum of March 21, 1985, Hungate explained why he found the cross-dressing provision to be unconstitutionally vague. Invoking the recent U.S. Supreme Court decision in *Kolender v. Lawson* (1983), where the Court held that a law would be found unconstitutionally vague when "it encourages arbitrary enforcement by failing to describe with sufficient particularity what a suspect must do in order to satisfy the statute," Hungate asserted that a blanket prohibition of appearing in public "in a dress not belonging to his or her sex" swept too broadly and gave police too much interpretive discretion in deciding what conduct violated the law:

For example, the wearing of clothing not belonging to a person's sex may conceivably include a stylish young woman in a man's fedora, the wearing of kilts in the St. Patrick's Day Parade, a teenage girl in her older brother's shirt, an actor wearing a dress is a stage role, or a woman lawyer in a pants suit. By facially permitting such unreasonable results, it is clear that the ordinance creates "a standardless sweep [that] allows policemen, prosecutors, and juries to pursue their personal predilections." . . . What is "dress not belonging to his or her sex?" Necklaces and earrings are not infrequently worn by both sexes.

The quotation was from a 1974 Supreme Court decision, *Smith v. Goguen*. Hungate concluded that "due to the lack of minimum standards on the face of this ordinance or in its construction, this clause of the ordinance fails to meet constitutional standards for definiteness and clarity" and must be declared unenforceable as written.

There may be a societal interest in enabling a person to identify a member of the opposite sex without being misled (i.e., a man looking for a mother for his children). However, there are methods far short of a cross-dressing ordinance that could accomplish the purpose of sexual identification. One could ask for a driver's license or a draft registration card.

Surprisingly, Hungate said nothing about the argument that this regulation of personal appearance might present substantive constitutional problems as a violation of "liberty" under the Due Process Clause, resting his decision solely on the asserted "vagueness" of the ordinance.

Hungate refused to grant the motion for summary judgment with respect to the "indecent or lewd conduct" provision, asserting that, "while more specificity might be desirable," the provision "is not so impermissibly vague on its face that it violates the due process clause of the fourteenth amendment." As to the other aspects of the ordinance, Hungate concluded that there was no constitutional bar to banning public nudity or obscene conduct.

The case then proceeded to trial before a jury. The jury found that the city had violated Clippard's constitutional rights, but pursuant to instructions from Hungate awarded no damages. The jury found against Shreves on all his claims, and Hungate denied a motion by Zarembka for judgment notwithstanding the jury's verdict. The plaintiffs' appeal to the U.S. Court of Appeals for the Eighth Circuit followed and was submitted on papers on February 12, 1986. (The city apparently decided not to appeal Hungate's ruling on the constitutionality of the cross-dressing provision.) A unanimous Eighth Circuit panel ruled on July 9, 1986, in an opinion by Circuit Judge Roger L. Wollman, that the "indecent or lewd act" provision was also unconstitutional.

Wollman first reviewed the reasons for requiring specificity in penal statutes, including both the notion that individuals have a right to know what conduct is prohibited and that the discretion of law enforcement authorities and courts should be constrained, since the decision whether to bar particular conduct properly belonged to the legislature. He then concluded that the terms "indecent" and "lewd"

did not have a contemporary meaning precise enough to achieve those goals. The plaintiffs had cited a 1974 decision by the Iowa Supreme Court, *State v. Kueny*, in which the court said that everyday usage of these words "has eroded the effective employment of such terms in any statutory enactment, absent an attendant specific definition thereof, as descriptions of proscribed ultimate criminal conduct." Wollman found that observation to be "persuasive."

Since the St. Louis ordinance contained no more precise definition of the terms, it could be saved only if the Missouri courts had provided a more precise definition through statutory interpretation, but Wollman found the reported Missouri cases dealing with statutes containing terms such as "lewdness" or "indecent" to be unhelpful in constructing a more precise meaning for the terms. For example, in *Mainstreet Enterprises, Inc. v. Supervisor of Liquor Control* (1984), the Missouri Court of Appeals dealt with a provision governing conduct of persons in retail liquor establishments that included the term "lewdness." That court had asserted that the term "has been held sufficient to inform actors what conduct will subject them to liability. Acts of lewdness constituted criminal offenses at common law and the word and its definition are of common use." Later Missouri cases had referred back to *Mainstreet Enterprises* as providing the "definition" of "lewdness." In another case arising under the predecessor of the St. Louis ordinance which used similar language, *City of St. Louis v. Mikes* (1963), the Missouri Court of Appeals upheld the law's constitutionality on the ground that "judges may know what falls within the classification of the decent, the chaste and the pure in either social life or in publications, and what must be deemed obscene and lewd and immoral and scandalous and lascivious." "With all due respect to the foregoing state court decisions," said Wollman, "we are not persuaded that they constitute a narrowing judicial interpretation of the challenged language . . . that would make constitutionally specific those terms that are otherwise unconstitutionally vague." Consequently, Shreves's motion to have the law declared unconstitutional should have been granted.

On the issue of damages, however, the panel had concluded that no more than nominal damages were due either plaintiff, so the case was remanded to Hungate for entry of an award of nominal damages. The opinion contained no discussion of the merits of Hungate's ruling that the cross-dressing provision was unconstitutional.

The Eighth Circuit's decision, in effect holding that a typical drag show could not be the subject of a prosecution for "indecent" or "lewd" conduct in public, left open the possibility that a more precisely drafted statute could pass constitutional muster. Similarly, Hungate's decision on the cross-dressing provisions, premised solely on the asserted "vagueness" of a statute that generally prohibits a person of one sex from dressing in the normal garb of the opposite sex, left open the possibility that a more precisely drafted statute could be enacted. Both Hungate and the court of appeals avoided the more difficult constitutional questions: whether a more precisely drafted statute outlawing wearing specified items of clothing in public might constitute a deprivation of "liberty" under the Due Process Clause, and what justifications the state might present for such a regulation.

Hungate's amusing comment that the state's interest in protecting people from being misled about the sex of those they encounter could be met by asking to see a driver's license or draft registration card is unlikely to stand up to serious consideration. Does the state have a legitimate interest along those lines, or, more broadly, in enforcing gender appearance conventions as an aspect of maintaining public order? The more permissive jurisprudence of the 1960s and 1970s might have found no sufficient state interest to abridge personal liberty in this manner, but it is harder to know how the more conservative courts of the 1990s might react.

Case References

City of St. Louis v. Mikes, 372 S.W.2d 508 (Mo. App. 1963)

Kelley v. Johnson, 425 U.S. 238 (1976)

Kolender v. Lawson, 461 U.S. 352 (1983)

Mainstreet Enterprises, Inc. v. Supervisor of Liquor Control, 665 S.W.2d 641 (Mo. App. 1984)

Smith v. Goguen, 415 U.S. 566 (1974)

State v. Kueny, 215 N.W.2d 215 (Iowa 1974)

29. A SODOMY LAW WITHSTANDS FEDERAL CONSTITUTIONAL PRIVACY CHALLENGE

Bowers v. Hardwick, 478 U.S. 186 (1986), reversing 760 F.2d 1202 (11th Cir. 1985).

The U.S. Supreme Court's 1976 action summarily affirming a three-judge court decision upholding Virginia's sodomy law from a wide-ranging constitutional challenge stood as an ambiguous barrier to constitutional progress for lesbian and gay rights for ten years. The Court's failure to explain why it was affirming the lower court in Doe v. Commonwealth's Attorney for City of Richmond left legal scholars and litigators speculating. For one thing, it seemed clear to many that the plaintiffs in Doe might be held to lack standing to initiate the lawsuit, since they had never suffered individual prosecution for engaging in sodomy in private with other adults and there seemed little likelihood they would suffer such prosecution in the future. While summary affirmances are rulings on the merits,

the practice was to accord such rulings the narrowest plausible precedential scope due to the lack of explanation, and some argued that the narrowest plausible precedential ruling in Doe, avoiding constitutional issues, would be an affirmance on procedural grounds. However, the lower court had not discussed the standing issue, it was not raised in opposition to the petition for certiorari, and some argued that had the Supreme Court wished to dispose of the case on standing grounds, it would have dismissed the appeal rather than summarily affirming the lower court's decision.

The more significant basis for attempting to limit the precedential value of Doe was found by tea-leaf readers in a cryptic comment in a footnote in the Court's 1977 decision in Carey *v. Population Services International*, a challenge to a law banning sales of nonprescription contraceptives by persons other than licensed pharmacists. A plurality of the Court joined the portion of the opinion containing footnote 5, which stated that "'the Court has not definitively answered the difficult question whether and to what extent the Constitution prohibits state statutes regulating [private consensual sexual] behavior among adults,' n. 17, *infra*, and we do not purport to answer that question now" (with the bracketed material coming from footnote 17). Furthermore, in *People v. Uplinger* (1983), dismissing as improvidently granted a writ of *certiorari* to review a New York Court of Appeals decision concerning a state law criminalizing loitering for the purpose of soliciting "deviate sexual intercourse" (the Model Penal Code description of sodomy), the Court noted *per curiam* that the case presented an "inappropriate vehicle" for resolving the "important constitutional issues" raised by the parties, which many contended necessarily included the constitutional validity of laws criminalizing sodomy. Four members of the Court (all of whom would eventually vote against Michael Hardwick's challenge to the Georgia sodomy law) had dissented from this disposition; presumably, they were the four who had voted to grant *certiorari* in the case to begin with. (Four votes are all that is needed to grant such a petition under the Supreme Court's operating procedures.) From the *Carey* footnote and the *Uplinger per curiam* comment, some argued that the Court was signaling that the constitutionality of sodomy laws remained an open question. Certainly the continued vitality and expansion of the privacy right identified in *Griswold v. Connecticut* (1965) and *Roe v. Wade* (1973), which had been reiterated many times during the decade after *Doe v. Commonwealth's Attorney* as the Court continued to strike down various impediments to women's abortion rights, gave hope to many that the Court might be receptive to a full frontal challenge to state sodomy laws. The Court's failure to grant *certiorari* in *People v. Onofre* (1981), a New York state court sodomy decision in which a law was invalidated on federal constitutional grounds, seemed counter to this theory, but some argued that the Supreme Court was waiting for a split in

lower court authority to develop. When such a split occurred, preferably at the level of the federal courts of appeals, the Court would be ready to tackle the issue. When the split developed in the mid-1980s, the Court was ready, granting *certiorari* in *Bowers v. Hardwick*.

The case stemmed from the summer of 1982, when Michael Hardwick was working at a gay bar in Atlanta, Georgia. As he later related the events to a national television audience on the *Phil Donahue Show*, Hardwick was staying late one night to help install a new sound system in the bar. He left the bar in the early morning hours holding an open can of beer. A police officer spotted him and gave him a summons for violating a municipal ordinance. Hardwick forgot to show up at his court date, and the police officer obtained a warrant for his arrest. When Hardwick remembered the summons, he went to court, paid his fine, and was told the summons would be quashed. But several weeks later, on August 3, the police officer knocked on Hardwick's door to arrest him using the invalid warrant. A friend from out of town was sleeping on the couch in Hardwick's living room when the officer knocked. The friend answered the door, and allowed the officer into the apartment, directing him toward the rear where the guest thought Hardwick might be in the bedroom. The friend was unaware that Hardwick had brought home a guest for sex. The officer approached Hardwick's bedroom. The door was ajar and the officer could see inside that Hardwick and another man were engaged in oral sex. The officer stood watching until Hardwick, suddenly aware of being watched, looked up and asked him what he was doing there. The officer replied that he had "caught you in the act of sodomy" and that Hardwick and his friend were under arrest. Hardwick was taken to the police station, booked, and held overnight in jail for arraignment in the municipal court, which bound him over to superior court for trial pending action of the grand jury on charges. Hardwick was released pending these events, but the district attorney's office eventually informed him that it would not present the case to the grand jury "unless further evidence developed" and once the statute of limitations ran out, he would be off the hook if he stayed out of trouble.

An arrest by a police officer in a private home for engaging in consensual fellatio with another adult was an extraordinary event, and Hardwick's case was a lively topic of discussion in Atlanta. In addition to the arrest, Hardwick had been beaten up by a group of strangers shortly after being issued the ticket, and he felt this event was connected to the other. Hardwick was persuaded by friends to meet with a local American Civil Liberties Union (ACLU) co-operating attorney, Kathleen L. Wilde, who offered to represent him in a lawsuit challenging the constitutionality of the sodomy law. To bring in all relevant arguments against the Georgia law, which penalized all anal or oral sex regardless of the gender or marital status of the participants, with a possible jail term up to twenty years, a married couple friendly with Hardwick agreed to be co-plaintiffs in the case under the pseudonym "John and Mary Doe."

The complaint, filed in federal district court against Georgia Attorney General Michael A. Bowers, Fulton County District Attorney Lewis R. Slaton, and Atlanta Public Safety Commissioner George Napper, alleged on behalf of Hardwick that as a practicing homosexual who regularly engaged in conduct prohibited by the statute, had been arrested for doing so, and intended to continue doing so, he had suffered a violation of his constitutional rights of privacy, equal protection, and freedom of association. Hardwick also alleged that the potential penalties under the law inflicted cruel and unusual punishment. John and Mary Doe alleged that their desire to engage in sexual activity prohibited by the statute, which they described as constitutionally protected, had been "chilled and deterred" by the existence of the statute and Hardwick's recent arrest under it. The plaintiffs sought a declaration that the statute was unconstitutional and an injunction against its enforcement.

The case was assigned to District Judge Robert H. Hall, who granted a motion by the defendants to dismiss the Does' claims for lack of standing and Hardwick's for failure to state a claim on which relief could be granted. The dismissal as to Hardwick cited *Doe v. Commonwealth's Attorney* as a binding precedent on the issues raised in Hardwick's complaint. Judge Hall did not produce a published opin-

ion. With the assistance of Nan Hunter, a staff attorney at the ACLU's New York headquarters who would subsequently become the first director of the ACLU's new Lesbian and Gay Rights Project, Wilde prepared an appeal to the U.S. Court of Appeals for the Eleventh Circuit and deemed herself extremely lucky when she learned the makeup of the three-judge panel for the case: Senior Circuit Judge Elbert P. Tuttle, a long-time civil libertarian and a hero of the civil rights movement who had served on the court since 1954; Frank M. Johnson, Jr., probably the most "liberal" member of the circuit, who had been elevated from the district court bench in 1979 by President Jimmy Carter (and would probably have been appointed to the Supreme Court had a vacancy occurred during the Carter Administration); and the only woman on the circuit, Phyllis A. Kravitch, who had also been appointed by Carter. Assistant Attorney General George M. Weaver and Assistant District Attorney H. Allen Moye represented the heads of their offices, while attorneys Marva Jones Brooks and George R. Ference represented the Atlanta law enforcement authorities.

The panel unanimously agreed on the merits of the challenge, but not on the ability of the court to reach the merits. In an opinion by Johnson issued on May 21, 1985, the court unanimously upheld Judge Hall's decision that the Does lacked standing to challenge the law but that Hardwick had such standing by virtue of the specific use of the law against homosexuals and his own experience under the law. Also crucial to the standing issue was Hardwick's statement that he would continue to engage in sexual activity covered by the law regardless of its legality, which meant he would continue to be subject to prosecution in the future. The Does, by contrast, alleged that their desire to engage in such conduct had been "chilled," so the likelihood of prosecution for them did not exist.

The more difficult question, on which the panel split, was whether, as Hall had held, *Doe v. Commonwealth's Attorney* precluded their reaching the merits of Hardwick's challenge. Johnson and Tuttle concluded that *Doe* did not have that effect, accepting the argument that it could be narrowly construed as a ruling on standing from which Hardwick's situation was distinguishable, and, even if it were more of a ruling on the constitutional merits, its precedential value had been vitiated by the Court's subsequent comments in *Carey* and *Uplinger*. Judge Kravitch dissented on this construction of *Doe* and its effect, agreeing with Hall that *Doe* had to be construed as a ruling on the merits, since there was no indication that the Court had considered it anything other than a ruling on the merits, and asserting that neither the *Carey* footnote nor the *Uplinger per curiam* satisfied the requirement for a clear disavowal or overruling that would remove *Doe's* precedential effect. "Whatever our personal views about the constitutionality of a law that permits the state to regulate the most private of human behavior within the confines of the home, unless and until the Supreme Court clearly indicates otherwise, we are bound by that Court's opinion in *Doe v. Commonwealth's Attorney*," she concluded, while noting in a footnote, "If I thought that this court were empowered to reach those issues, however, I would agree with the majority."

The majority, having concluded that it could reach the merits free of *Doe v. Commonwealth's Attorney's* precedent, proceeded to hold that the Georgia law infringed on a fundamental right of privacy protected by the Ninth and Fourteenth amendments, and could be upheld only upon trial and fact-finding by the district court as to whether the state of Georgia could "demonstrate a compelling interest in restricting this right and . . . that the sodomy statute is a properly restrained method of safeguarding its interests."

Summarizing the case law that had developed over the course of the 20th century leading to *Griswold* and then through cases on abortion, family living arrangements, and marriage and contraception, the court asserted that "the Constitution prevents the States from unduly interfering in certain individual decisions critical to personal autonomy because those decisions are essentially private and beyond the legitimate reach of a civilized society." Johnson noted that such decisions did not necessarily involve cloistered conduct, as such, but included such things as the right of a parent to direct a child's education or the right of a woman and her physician to agree on aborting a pregnancy.

"Hardwick desires to engage privately in sexual activity with another consenting adult," continued Johnson. "Although this behavior is not procreative, it does involve important associational interests." In *Griswold* and *Eisenstadt v. Baird* (1972), the Supreme Court had recognized as constitutionally protected a couple's decision to have nonprocreative sex through the use of contraceptives. Citing *Eisenstadt* and *Carey*, Johnson emphasized that the reasons for protecting these decisions went beyond the sanctity of the marital relationship to include "the opportunity for mutual support and self expression," which was not necessarily restricted to marital partners. "The benefits of marriage can inure to individuals outside the traditional marital relationship," he asserted. "For some, the sexual activity in question here serves the same purpose as the intimacy of marriage."

Furthermore, since Hardwick had asserted that he intended to carry out his sexual activities in private, there was an extra element of constitutional protection derived from the Supreme Court's 1969 decision in *Stanley v. Georgia*, where the Court had held that the state could not criminalize private possession of obscene materials. "Stanley's First Amendment interests, while not sufficient to allow the viewing of obscene material in public, prevented the State from deciding what he could view in private," said Johnson.

> This case presents a person asserting an interest at least as substantial as the one in *Stanley v. Georgia*. In both cases, the fact that the activity is carried out in seclusion bolsters its significance. This is not a case involving sexual activity with children or with persons who are coerced either through physical force or commercial inducement. The absence of any such public ramifications in this case plays a prominent part in our consideration of Hardwick's legal claim.

Without providing any detailed explanation for a textual basis in the U.S. Constitution of the right of privacy thus described, Johnson asserted that it was protected by the Ninth and Fourteenth amendments, citing Justice Arthur J. Goldberg's concurring opinion in *Griswold* and the Court's opinion in *Roe v. Wade*, and ordered the case remanded for trial to give the state an opportunity to meet its burden of justifying the statute under the "compelling interest" test used under the Fourteenth Amendment for evaluating laws restricting fundamental rights. The state petitioned for a rehearing and reconsideration by all dozen judges of the Eleventh Circuit, but the petition was denied on June 13, 1985. Later that summer, the state filed a petition for *certiorari* with the U.S. Supreme Court.

The Eleventh Circuit panel's decision was widely hailed by gay legal observers as the first time that a federal court of appeals had identified gay sex as being part of a fundamental right protected by the Constitution. The decision was particularly gratifying in light of the harsh defeat the previous year in the District of Columbia Circuit Court of Appeals, which had ruled in *Dronenburg v. Zech* that the Army's discharge of an enlisted man for engaging in private, consensual sex with another enlisted man on a military base did not violate their right of privacy. In the course of that opinion by Circuit Judge Robert H. Bork, the court had asserted that much of the Supreme Court's privacy case law since the 1960s was of dubious soundness, and in any event could not be extended to cover consensual sodomy. The doctrinal split between the two circuit courts, however, provided the impetus for the Supreme Court to agree to review the *Hardwick* decision. (No petition for review had been filed in the *Dronenburg* case, since gay litigants were eager to avoid consideration of this issue on the merits by an increasingly conservative Supreme Court.)

While preparations proceeded for consideration of Hardwick's challenge by the Supreme Court, gay rights advocates suffered another setback as the Fifth Circuit reaffirmed *en banc* a panel decision rejecting a due process and equal protection challenge to the Texas sodomy law in *Baker v. Wade*, a test case that had been successful in getting the law declared unconstitutional at the district court level. Representatives of the gay legal groups that had banded together to coordinate *amicus* brief strategy in the *Hardwick* case met for a tense strategy discussion at the ACLU headquarters in New York with Professor Laurence Tribe of Harvard Law School, whose offer to represent Hardwick on a *pro bono* basis in the Supreme Court argument had been accepted by Hardwick and the ACLU.

(Tribe had become involved in gay rights advocacy the previous Term when, at the invitation of National Gay Task Force Executive Director Virginia Apuzzo, he had represented the Task Force in its Supreme Court defense of a Tenth Circuit decision holding unconstitutional portions of an Oklahoma law that in essence barred the employment of public school teachers who were openly gay or advocates for gay rights.)

The tension focused on the potential interactions of the Georgia and Texas cases. Should the gay rights attorneys from Texas who had litigated the case appeal this negative ruling to the Supreme Court? After furious discussion, a consensus emerged that a petition should be filed at the latest possible moment under the Court's rules, so as to avoid the possibility that the Court might consolidate the two cases. Because the Texas sodomy law outlawed only same-sex conduct, it presented equal protection issues that were not expected to play a significant role in the Georgia case. If the cases were consolidated, the Court might decide to dispose of both Fourteenth Amendment theories in the same case, and if the Court rejected the challenge in both cases, that would preclude a wide range of litigation in the lower federal courts relying on either theory. However, the distinctions between the two cases might provide a possibility for a "second bite of the apple" if the Georgia case was unsuccessful and the Court was willing to hear the Texas case the following term. After caucusing separately, the Texas attorneys and their client, Don Baker, president of the Dallas Gay Alliance, returned to announce that they would accept Professor Tribe's offer to handle their case at the Supreme Court level and that they agreed to the strategy of filing an *amicus* brief at the latest possible time.

The Supreme Court heard argument in the case on March 31, 1986, with Michael E. Hobbs, a Georgia senior assistant district attorney, arguing for the state and Tribe arguing for Hardwick as a cooperating attorney for the ACLU. The Court had received *amicus* briefs urging reversal of the Eleventh Circuit's decision from the Catholic League for Religious and Civil Rights, the Rutherford Institute (a religious issues organization), and George

Washington University Law Professor David Robinson, Jr., who argued that the emerging AIDS epidemic presented a compelling state interest in criminalizing oral and anal sex, an argument he repeated in an article published later in 1986 based on his *amicus* brief. Two state attorneys general, Robert Abrams of New York and John Van de Kamp of California, filed a joint *amicus* brief urging affirmance. Other *amicus* briefs in support of Hardwick's position were filed by the American Jewish Congress, a group of medical and public health organizations led by the American Psychological Association, the Association of the Bar of the City of New York, the National Organization for Women, the Presbyterian Church (U.S.A.), and a coalition of lesbian and gay legal groups.

According to newspaper reports published after the Court's opinion was announced, the Court voted 5–4 at its Friday conference after the argument to affirm the court of appeals' decision, with Justice Harry A. Blackmun designated to draft an opinion for the Court. Over that weekend, however, Justice Lewis F. Powell, Jr., whose support had been shakily premised on his view that a twenty-year felony statute was absurdly disproportionate to this type of conduct under the Court's Eighth Amendment jurisprudence on "cruel and unusual punishment," had a change of heart. Powell, who had commented to his clerks that he had never met any gay people, decided that judicial restraint should be the order of the day on this kind of controversial issue. Since Hardwick was not actually prosecuted, the case was "trivial" in his estimation, and the Eighth Amendment issue was not really appropriately before the Court. On returning to his chambers Monday morning, he circulated a memo indicating he had changed his mind and would vote to reverse the court of appeals. Blackmun's opinion would now become a dissent, and Justice Byron R. White was designated by Chief Justice Warren E. Burger to write an opinion for the new majority.

White's opinion was announced on June 30, 1986, ironically just days before a massive national celebration of the centennial of the Statue of Liberty was scheduled to be held in New York Harbor. In a departure from recent custom, Justice Blackmun insisted on reading his impassioned dissent aloud at the Court's opinion session that morning. The lines were sharply drawn between the majority and the dissents (there was also a dissent by Justice John Paul Stevens) in a dispute that went much deeper than the question whether Georgia's sodomy law violated the Fourteenth Amendment. Indeed, the debate of the Justices foreshadowed the national debate that would occur a year later in response to President Ronald Reagan's nomination of Robert Bork, author of the *Dronenburg* opinion, to the Supreme Court. Was it appropriate for the Court to recognize and develop "fundamental rights" without a clear textual basis in the Constitution? Justice White, an uneasy participant in the *Griswold* majority, had become increasingly suspicious of the trend of privacy jurisprudence, dissenting in the abortion cases and arguing strongly in dissent just weeks before the *Hardwick* decision was announced that the sexual privacy cases were inherently illegitimate (in a case striking Pennsylvania abortion regulations by a 5–4 vote, *Thornburgh v. American College of Obstetricians and Gynecologists*).

Using language taken from his *Thornburgh* dissent, but this time speaking for the Court with the concurrence of Justice Powell, White asserted a sharp break from the developing privacy jurisprudence of the twenty years since *Griswold*. "The Court is most vulnerable and comes nearest to illegitimacy when it deals with judge-made constitutional law having little or no cognizable roots in the language or design of the Constitution," he insisted.

> That this is so was painfully demonstrated by the face-off between the Executive and the Court in the 1930's, which resulted in the repudiation of much of the substantive gloss that the Court had placed on the Due Process Clauses of the Fifth and Fourteenth Amendments. There should be, therefore, great resistance to expand the substantive reach of those Clauses, particularly if it requires redefining the category of rights deemed to be fundamental. Otherwise, the Judiciary necessarily takes to itself further authority to govern the country without express constitutional authority. The claimed right pressed on us today falls far short of overcoming this resistance.

As prelude to this assertion, White began his opinion by framing the issues for decision narrowly as "whether the Federal Constitution confers a fundamental right upon homosexuals to engage in sodomy and hence invalidates the laws of the many States that still make such conduct illegal and have done so for a very long time," but then more broadly as involving "some judgment about the limits of the Court's role in carrying out its constitutional mandate." Then he asserted, contrary to the court of appeals, that the Court's prior decisions had not necessarily answered the question, because those cases were not about a general "right of privacy," but rather were about child rearing and education, family relationships, procreation, marriage, contraception, and abortion. If the most recent cases were to be construed as having a conceptual link, that link was "a fundamental individual right to decide whether or not to beget or bear a child."

By limiting the precedential scope of prior "privacy" rulings narrowly to their subject matter, White could assert that the right "claimed" in this case "of homosexuals to engage in acts of sodomy" failed to bear "any resemblance" to the rights identified in the earlier cases. "No connection between family, marriage, or procreation on the one hand and homosexual activity on the other has been demonstrated," he said, "either by the Court of Appeals or by respondent." (Of course, since the case had been decided on a motion to dismiss without any trial record having been created, it was difficult to know how Hardwick or the lower court could have done more than assert such a connection. Judge Johnson's opinion had stated, as quoted above, "For some, the sexual activity in question here serves the same purpose as the intimacy of marriage." The "demonstration" of this would have to await compilation of a factual record at trial, which the Supreme Court was not willing to permit.)

Having satisfied himself and his concurring colleagues that the existing case law did not cover this case, White indicated that the majority of the Court was not inclined to recognize a new fundamental right. To avoid overreaching its role in construing the Due Process Clauses of the Fifth and Fourteenth amendments, said White, the Court had adopted a series of tests to determine whether an asserted right could be characterized as fundamental. In

Palko v. Connecticut (1937), the Court treated as fundamental "liberties that are 'implicit in the concept of ordered liberty,' such that 'neither liberty nor justice would exist if [they] were sacrificed.'" In *Moore v. City of East Cleveland* (1977), the Court asked whether a claimed liberty was "deeply rooted in this Nation's history and tradition." White stated that it was "obvious" that the right claimed by Hardwick was not covered by either formulation, but he really explained only his views on the second (i.e., historical justification for a claimed right). Broad sodomy prohibitions such as that contained in the Georgia statute were part of the common law received from England and were codified in all the states until 1960, when Illinois became the first state to repeal its sodomy law while adopting the Model Penal Code. Half the states continued "to provide criminal penalties for sodomy performed in private and between consenting adults." "Against this background," said White, "to claim that a right to engage in such conduct is 'deeply rooted in this Nation's history and tradition' or 'implicit in the concept of ordered liberty' is, at best, facetious."

This abbreviated analysis conveniently overlooked the arguments going to the first formulation cited by White, the idea of "ordered liberty" that, by its terms, appears to adopt a Millian approach to identifying what was in the public sphere and what was in the private sphere. "Ordered liberty" connotes a delicate balance between individual freedom and the needs of the community that would comprehend the right of persons in a free society to choose their sexual companions without state interference unless the state could show a need for intervention to prevent harms to *public* order or harm to unconsenting persons. History alone would not be sufficient to answer the question posed by the *Palko* formulation, but White's analysis appeared to rest on history alone.

White also disclaimed for the majority any interest in taking a more expansive view of how fundamental rights should be identified, producing the statements quoted above about how the Court veers nearest to illegitimacy when it undertakes such an effort. He also cast aside the argued relevance of *Stanley v. Georgia*, which

Johnson had invoked in the court of appeals' opinion, as being irrelevant to cases involving sexual conduct. *Stanley* was a First Amendment case, said White, and besides, there were many crimes that could be committed in a home for which the Constitution should afford no protection. Furthermore, if Hardwick was claiming constitutional protection for any sexual conduct of consenting adults at home, "it would be difficult, except by fiat, to limit the claimed right to homosexual conduct while leaving exposed to prosecution adultery, incest, and other sexual crimes even though they are committed in the home. We are unwilling to start down that road."

Since a fundamental right was not at issue, then, the statute must be sustained if there was some rational basis for it. Hardwick's argument that "the presumed belief of a majority of the electorate in Georgia that homosexual sodomy is immoral and unacceptable" did not provide a rational basis for the law did not impress White. Asserting that the law "is constantly based on notions of morality," the Court would be "very busy indeed" if it had to go about striking down all laws which were solely based on "essentially moral choices." "Majority sentiments" about "the morality of homosexuality" were enough to sustain this law and those of the other states that still had such laws. Finally, in a footnote, White asserted that "[r]espondent does not defend the judgment below based on the Ninth Amendment, the Equal Protection Clause, or the Eighth Amendment," even though Tribe had mentioned the first two in his brief and had responded to questioning from the bench about the source of Hardwick's claimed right with a reference to the Ninth Amendment. Since the Court had decided this appeal on substantive grounds, White said it was unnecessary to address the question that had so consumed the Eleventh Circuit panel and other lower courts: the precedential scope of *Doe v. Commonwealth's Attorney*, which had been rendered academic by the Court's ruling in Hardwick's case.

Chief Justice Burger concurred briefly with a moralistic lecture revealing apparent ignorance of the sources he cited about "decisions of individuals relating to homosexual conduct." Quoting Blackstone's description of "the infamous crime against nature" as an offense of "deeper malignity" than rape, Burger conveniently overlooked that the crime described by Blackstone was solely anal intercourse, only half the conduct covered by Georgia's statute and, incidently, not the conduct by Hardwick that had initiated the case. Burger proclaimed that invalidating the statute would "cast aside millennia of moral teaching."

Justice Powell's brief concurrence was more temperate but puzzling. Agreeing, without discussion, that "there is no fundamental right—i.e., no substantive right under the Due Process Clause—such as that claimed by respondent Hardwick," he indicated that had Hardwick actually been sentenced to any significant prison term, the Eighth Amendment might be offended, given the disproportion between the penalties authorized for sodomy and the much shorter terms authorized for more serious offenses. Powell also thought it significant that the last "reported decision" of a sodomy prosecution in Georgia dated from 1939, as if only published appellate decisions were significant in determining whether the law was being enforced by the police (as in Hardwick's own case) without matters ever proceeding to judicial review and published opinions. (The ACLU had determined that there were several inmates in the Georgia state prisons serving prison terms for "sodomy.") Overlooking Hardwick's broad-ranging complaint and focusing narrowly on the court of appeals' basis for decision and the consequent narrow privacy focus of Tribe's brief and oral argument, Powell commented that Hardwick had not raised the Eighth Amendment issue, so that argument was not before the Court.

Justice Blackmun's dissent, joined by Justices William J. Brennan, Jr., Thurgood Marshall, and John Paul Stevens, began by criticizing the way White had described the question presented in the case. This case was not about "a fundamental right to engage in homosexual sodomy," said Blackmun. Viewed that way, *Stanley* was about "a fundamental right to watch obscene movies" and *Katz v. United States*, a leading case about the protected zone of privacy under the Fourth Amendment, was merely about "a fundamental right to place interstate bets from a telephone booth." Rather, all these cases must be seen at a higher level of generality if constitutional law was to make any conceptual sense. The case was about "the most comprehensive of rights and the right most valued by civilized men . . . the right to be let alone" by the government, said Blackmun, quoting Justice Louis D. Brandeis's famous dissenting opinion in *Olmstead v. United States* (1928). The Georgia sodomy law "denies individuals the right to decide for themselves whether to engage in particular forms of private, consensual sexual activity." That such laws had a long historical basis was not a valid argument for upholding them, for each law must be evaluated based on the times in which the challenge was brought.

For Blackmun, the prior privacy case law of the Court was based on a set of general values that should be used to evaluate Hardwick's claims. Blackmun seemed particularly upset with the Court's "almost obsessive focus on homosexual activity." Contrary to the Court, Georgia had said nothing about homosexuality in its statute, which outlawed with impartiality all anal or oral sex, regardless whether homosexuals were involved. In fact, when Georgia had last amended this law in 1968, it had expanded its scope to ensure that all anal or oral sex was reached by the law. This was done by abandoning the archaic, ambiguous wording of the old common law concerning "crimes against nature" and instead adopting a clinical definition indicating which body parts had to come into contact for the law to be violated. Thus, the law was, in many of its aspects, actually quite new despite having "ancient roots." Furthermore, said Blackmun, the Court had improperly narrowed the question to be considered. Michael Hardwick's standing had nothing to do with the gender of the person with whom he was having sex when he was arrested. He could just as much have been arrested for having oral or anal sex with a woman. His standing was not thus limited to challenging the Georgia law as it applied to homosexuals.

Blackmun also protested the Court's decision to base its ruling entirely on the Due Process Clause. Given the procedural posture of the case, he said, it was inappropriate for the Court to dismiss the case in advance of trial leaving unexplored other possible constitutional grounds for attacking the statute. Because

Blackmun believed that the Georgia statute did violate the right of privacy, he did not undertake any detailed discussion of other possible claims, but he did include in a footnote the basis of an argument premised on equal protection and cruel and unusual punishment.

Blackmun then took on White's assertion that the existing privacy precedents did not extend to this case. He argued, contrary to White, that the privacy decisions could not be understood each as standing in isolation, but only made sense if understood as founded on a two-pronged underlying concept of privacy: "a privacy interest with reference to certain *decisions* that are properly for the individual to make," and "a privacy interest with reference to certain *places* without regard for the particular activities in which the individuals who occupy them are engaged."

Refuting White's assertion that the right claimed by Hardwick bore no "resemblance" to the rights protected in the prior sexual privacy cases, Blackmun asserted, "Only the most willful blindness could obscure the fact that sexual intimacy is 'a sensitive, key relationship of human existence, central to family life, community welfare, and the development of human personality,'" citing *Paris Adult Theatre I v. Slaton* (1973) and *Carey v. Population Services.* Since individuals "define themselves in a significant way through their intimate sexual relationships with others," there could be "many 'right' ways" of conducting sexual relationships in the diverse American society, and "much of the richness of a relationship will come from the freedom an individual has to *choose* the form and nature of these intensely personal bonds." As such, the right to choice in intimate sexual relationships must be considered an intrinsic part of the right to privacy identified in cases such as *Griswold* and *Roe v. Wade.*

As to the locational privacy aspect of the case, Blackmun contested White's claim that *Stanley v. Georgia* lacked relevance because it was a First Amendment case. For Blackmun, the Fourth Amendment had played a major role in *Stanley*, a case where the prosecution arose from a search that went beyond the scope of the search warrant issued to the police. The *Stanley* opinion had quoted Brandeis's dissent in *Olmstead*, a Fourth Amendment case, giving it a "central place" in the opinion, according to Blackmun. In fact, in *Paris Adult Theatre*, the Court had emphasized the Fourth Amendment aspect of *Stanley* in holding that *Stanley*, with its emphasis on the home, could not be extended to an adult movie theater.

Blackmun chastised the Court as well for its skimpy consideration of the state's proferred justifications for the statute. Indeed, White's opinion did not even mention the first justification the state articulated in its brief and at oral argument, the contention that prohibiting sodomy was necessary for the public health and welfare, as a means of blocking the spread of communicable diseases and preventing other criminal activity associated with sexual promiscuity. Blackmun argued that even if the case were to be decided under the standard of minimal rationality review, the relation of the statute to these purposes was a matter of hot dispute that could not be decided without compilation of a factual record at trial, noting that several prestigious *amici* had disputed the alleged public health connection. The state's alternative justification, the right of the state to legislate on moral questions founded in historical precedent, Blackmun found equally unconvincing. "I cannot agree that either the length of time a majority has held its convictions or the passions with which it defends them can withdraw legislation from this Court's scrutiny," said Blackmun, invoking the precedents of *Roe v. Wade*; *Loving v. Virginia* (1967), in which the Court invalidated miscegenation laws of long standing; and *Brown v. Board of Education of Topeka* (1954), which found unconstitutional the racially segregated public school systems that had existed in many states for almost a century. "It is precisely because the issue raised by this case touches the heart of what makes individuals what they are," said Blackmun, "that we should be especially sensitive to the rights of those whose choices upset the majority."

As to White and Burger's overly general "history" of sodomy laws, Blackmun responded that the history showed that these laws were rooted in religious proscriptions of a type that should not be considered as justification in a nation with a First Amendment. "A State can no more punish private behavior because of religious intolerance than it can punish such behavior because of racial animus," insisted Blackmun. He also found support in the Court's past decisions for the proposition that the unpopularity of a particular group would not be considered a rational basis for laws specifically directed against that group. Finally, he asserted, the Court must recognize some distinction between conduct that took place in private and in public. It was entirely appropriate to let the state ban the performance in public of acts which the Constitution might require it to tolerate when performed in private. For Blackmun, the Court had fatally failed to consider the "harm principle," and in this case that principle supported Hardwick's position because "the mere knowledge that other individuals do not adhere to one's value system cannot be a legally cognizable interest" and that was all that was involved here, since there was no showing that allowing sodomy as described in the Georgia statute was harmful as such to the participants or anybody else. Blackmun concluded with his hope that the Court would come to its senses and overrule this case in the future, opining that "depriving individuals of the right to choose for themselves how to conduct their intimate relationships poses a far greater threat to the values most deeply rooted in our Nation's history than tolerance of nonconformity could ever do." He asserted that the Court "today betrays those values."

Justice Stevens's separate dissenting opinion, concurred in by Justices Brennan and Marshall, was less impassioned but equally telling. His major emphasis was on the irrelevance of most of the history cited by the Court to the propositions for which it was cited, since most of the historical record showed no distinction between homosexuals and heterosexuals in its treatment of the topic. That being so, and taking the likelihood that sodomous conduct by heterosexual couples would be insulated from state sanction under the *Griswold* and *Eisenstadt* decisions (i.e., the right of heterosexuals to engage in nonprocreative sexual activity, as to which Stevens believed that sex with contraceptives was not constitutionally distinguishable from other forms of nonprocreative sex), Stevens believed that the case presented a fundamental equal protection issue that the Court had improperly overlooked. Since the Court's own precedents, such as *Loving v. Virginia*, showed that the general population's view that a practice was "immoral" could not alone sustain a law, even one of long vintage, it was inappropriate to ground this case in the historical record alone. Stevens was persuaded that the privacy line of cases was adequate for that purpose. Furthermore, since the Georgia law could not be enforced against consenting heterosexuals in private, the Equal Protection Clause burdened Georgia to explain why homosexuals should be forbidden to do what heterosexuals were entitled to do. "Either the persons to whom Georgia seeks to apply its statute do not have the same interest in 'liberty' that others have, or there must be a reason why the State may be permitted to apply a generally applicable law to certain persons that it does not apply to others," he asserted.

Since "every free citizen has the same interest in 'liberty' that the members of the majority share," it was "plainly unacceptable" to assert that Georgia had a right under the Equal Protection Clause to treat homosexuals differently in a nation founded on the principle that "all men are created equal." And a "habitual dislike for, or ignorance about, the disfavored group" had already been rejected by the Court in the past as the basis for singling out that group for unequal treatment by the government. The Court purported to discern "the presumed belief of a majority of the electorate in Georgia that homosexual sodomy is immoral and unacceptable." Stevens astutely noted that the text of the statute provided no basis for such an assumption, since it also outlawed heterosexual sodomy. It was not even credible to assert that the state believed that homosexuals who violated the statute in private should be prosecuted, since the police had caught Hardwick in the act yet decided not to prosecute him, and the state's attorney had actually told the Court that the statute was rarely enforced.

For Stevens, Georgia had failed to meet the most elemental burden in the case, having completely failed "to provide the Court with any support for the conclusion that homosexual sodomy, *simpliciter*, is considered unacceptable conduct in that State, and that the burden of justifying a selective application of the gener-

ally applicable law has been met." Concluding that at this stage of the litigation Hardwick had articulated "a constitutional claim sufficient to withstand a motion to dismiss," Stevens dissented from the dismissal of Hardwick's case.

The Court's decision in *Bowers v. Hardwick* dropped like a bomb on a nation that had assumed, without really thinking about it, that people were relatively free to do what they wanted sexually, as long as they did it in private and everybody consented. Prosecutions for such private conduct (as opposed to prosecutions for solicitation or sexual activity in parks, public restrooms, and the like) were so rare as to be virtually unheard of. Many people outside the gay community (and even some in the gay community) had assumed that such laws were a dead letter. The idea that people might be sent to prison for years for making love in private struck many as archaic and absurd. Public opinion polls showed that a majority of the public, while continuing to believe that homosexual conduct was "wrong," disagreed with the Court about whether the Constitution allowed a state to impose a prison term for it.

For the gay community, the *Hardwick* decision seemed a direct attack at a time when the community was struggling to win public support for the fight against AIDS. It signaled the probable end of the usefulness of the constitutional privacy theory that litigators had been advancing for years in their attempts to attack a variety of ways in which government discriminated against gay people. It caused the organized effort to challenge sodomy laws that had been conceived by the gay public interest firms to take a sharp strategic turn, abandoning the federal courts and initiating a new round of challenges in state courts founded on state constitutional provisions. It shocked significant numbers of hidden gay people into joining gay organizations and donating money for the first time in their lives, and helped to build an enormous march on Washington for lesbian and gay rights, which turned out over half a million people in the capital in October 1987. The events surrounding that march during the second weekend of October included a meeting of lesbian and gay lawyers and law students that launched the National Lesbian and Gay Law Association, and an activist demonstration at the Supreme Court that led to several hundred arrests. The Court, which was still perceived by many as a defender of civil liberties against the perceived deprivations of the politically reactionary national administration, was now perceived as "the enemy" by progressive forces.

Hardwick not only signaled a major setback in the fight against sodomy laws. By its crabbed approach to the procedures for identifying fundamental rights, and its particularistic application of the existing sexual privacy precedents, the decision threatened to unravel many of the gains of the reproductive rights movement. Legal observers were not so surprised when lower courts and the Supreme Court began to cite and quote from *Hardwick* as they chipped away at the substance of *Roe v. Wade*. The awakening to the danger posed to the right of privacy may have contributed to the defeat of President Reagan's nomination of Robert Bork to the Court the following year, and led to a litmus test imposed on subsequent Court nominees, but it seemed clear that the Senate's litmus test was not finely tuned enough to uncover nominees whose agreement with White's methodology might lead them to eschew a generalized right of privacy in future cases. (After all, White had concurred in *Griswold*, which, due to Bork's published attacks on it, had become the keystone of the Senate's confirmation test.) To those who saw *Hardwick* as the endpoint to the developing right of privacy, it was not surprising that the Court eschewed the doctrine of privacy totally in *Cruzan v. Director, Missouri Department of Health* (1990), upholding the right of a comatose individual to refuse life-sustaining medical treatment on an alternative "liberty" formulation without the normal resort to privacy precedents that had been cited to the Court in a host of *amicus* briefs.

Hardwick was influential not only in the continuing struggle over privacy rights. It began to be cited also as precedent for the proposition that homosexuals were not entitled to invoke heightened judicial scrutiny of government policies that discriminated on the basis of sexual orientation. Some courts reasoned that there could be no more basic discrimination against a group than outlawing the sexual conduct by which that group defined itself. If the Supreme Court was willing to state that such

penalization was constitutional, it would be "anomalous" to say that the group involved was a "suspect class" for Equal Protection Clause purposes. Furthermore, if "majoritarian morality" was sufficient justification to sustain the sodomy law in *Hardwick*, said some courts, it was sufficient justification to sustain other forms of discrimination against gays.

While strong arguments were mounted against this reasoning, it carried the day in several important federal court of appeals decisions issued in the years following the *Hardwick* decision. The *Hardwick* decision was also cited in a host of other contexts where gay litigants sought vindication of their legal rights, including child custody and visitation disputes, employment discrimination cases, and the continuing challenges to official exclusion of gays from the military.

Case References

Baker v. Wade, 553 F. Supp. 1121 (N.D. Tex. 1982), reversed en banc, 769 F.2d 289 (5th Cir. 1985), certiorari denied, 478 U.S. 1022 (1986).

Brown v. Board of Education of Topeka, 347 U.S. 483 (1954)

Carey v. Population Services International, 431 U.S. 678 (1977)

Cruzan v. Director, Missouri Department of Health, 110 S. Ct. 2841 (1990)

Doe v. Commonwealth's Attorney for City of Richmond, 403 F. Supp. 1199 (E.D. Va. 1975), affirmed without opinion, 425 U.S. 901, rehearing denied, 425 U.S. 985 (1976)

Dronenburg v. Zech, 741 F.2d 1388, rehearing en banc denied, 746 F.2d 1579 (D.C. Cir. 1984)

Eisenstadt v. Baird, 405 U.S. 438 (1972)

Griswold v. Connecticut, 381 U.S. 479 (1965)

Katz v. United States, 389 U.S. 347 (1967)

Loving v. Virginia, 388 U.S. 1 (1967)

Moore v. City of East Cleveland, 431 U.S. 494 (1977)

Olmstead v. United States, 277 U.S. 438 (1928)

Palko v. Connecticut, 302 U.S. 319 (1937)

Paris Adult Theatre I v. Slaton, 413 U.S. 49, rehearing denied, 414 U.S. 881 (1973)

People v. Onofre, 51 N.Y.2d 476 (1980), certiorari denied, 451 U.S. 987 (1981)

People v. Uplinger, 467 U.S. 246 (1983), dismissing appeal from 58 N.Y.2d 936 (1983)

Roe v. Wade, 410 U.S. 113, rehearing denied, 410 U.S. 959 (1973)

Stanley v. Georgia, 394 U.S. 557 (1969)

Thornburgh v. American College of Obstetricians and Gynecologists, 476 U.S. 747 (1986)

30. LOOK BUT DON'T TOUCH

State v. Walsh, 713 S.W.2d 508 (Mo. 1986) (en banc).

When the U.S. Supreme Court announced its decision in *Bowers v. Hardwick* on June 30, 1986, holding that the federal constitutional right of privacy was not violated by Georgia's felony sodomy statute, a similar case, *State v. Walsh*, was awaiting decision by the Missouri Supreme Court.

Huber M. Walsh had been arrested at a highway rest stop after he began fondling a fully clothed plainclothes police officer on the morning of April 10, 1985. According to the official charge against him, Walsh "touched Det. Steven Zielinski's genitalia through his clothing and such conduct was a substantial step toward the commission of the crime of sexual misconduct with Det. Zielinski and was done for the purpose of committing such sexual misconduct." Under Missouri law, "sexual misconduct" included "deviate sexual intercourse," which was broadly defined as "any sexual act involving the genitals of one person and the mouth, tongue, hand or anus of another person" when both persons were of the same sex. This definition takes in a wider range of conduct than perhaps any other state sodomy law; usually, such laws pertain just to anal or oral intercourse, and penetration is required for commission of the forbidden act.

When Walsh appeared before St. Louis County Circuit Judge Susan Block, he was in for a pleasant surprise. His attorney, Richard Cooper, of St. Louis, had filed a routine motion to dismiss, claiming the statute facially violated the Equal Protection Clause. Block, who evidently had little regard for the Missouri sodomy law, promptly granted Cooper's motion and dismissed the case against Walsh. In an unpublished memorandum, she accepted the argument that the law, primarily enforced against gay men in situations such as Walsh's, improperly discriminated on the basis of sex. If Walsh had been a woman, he could not have been prosecuted for doing exactly what he had done. Consequently, the law used sex as a classification for determining whether particular conduct was unlawful.

Attorney General William L. Webster appealed Block's ruling directly to the Missouri Supreme Court. Walsh, who craved anonymity in the whole matter, was mortified that his case might be turned into a notorious "gay rights" case, and his attorney, Cooper, expressed initial reluctance about the filing of *amicus* briefs, but finally consented to the filing of briefs from the American Civil Liberties Union (ACLU) of Eastern Missouri, Lambda Legal Defense and Education Fund, and various other groups, urging affirmance of Block's decision. The court heard oral argument from Cooper and Assistant Attorney General Kevin B. Behrndt, and then the case sat, as the court held up its decision to see what the U.S. Supreme Court would do in *Hardwick* . Evidently, the *Hardwick* decision confirmed the disposition of the court, which issued its own decision, reversing Block, about two weeks later.

One of the complications of the case on appeal was that Cooper, who was not a gay law specialist, did not raise at the trial level the wide range of possible constitutional objections to the law, arguing only that it violated equal protection. The *amici* had sought to introduce alternative arguments by brief, including substantive due process (privacy) and state constitutional privacy arguments. Although the court seemed willing to entertain alternative arguments, in the final event it decided the occasion was not right to explore the state constitutional argument, and premised its holding solely on the federal Constitution. This case was distinguishable from *Hardwick*, in that, unlike the Georgia sodomy law, the Missouri law applied only to same-sex couples, and furthermore, Walsh was charged only with fondling the genitals of a fully clothed police officer, not actually committing the more traditional crime of sodomy (in Michael Hardwick's case, oral intercourse). But these distinctions did not seem to make any difference to the majority of the Missouri Supreme Court, whose July 15, 1986, decision by Judge Robert T. Donnelly essentially overlooked the distinctions. (Another distinction, which surely cut against Walsh's appeal, was that his conduct occurred in a public place, although the court did not apparently consider this significant.)

Donnelly framed the issue before the court as "whether the Fourteenth Amendment to the United States Constitution prohibits the states from proscribing homosexual conduct." Donnelly commented that this question could not be answered affirmatively as a matter of the "intent" reflected in the amendment's language and history, but that Walsh and the *amici* were rather arguing that the law "discriminates on the basis of the exercise of a fundamental right to sexual privacy, and is thus a suspect classification under the equal protection clause."

As Cooper argued, the law "prohibits members of the same sex from engaging in certain sexual activities. Thus, a class distinction is presented because it clearly prohibits males from sexual activity with males and females from sexual activity with females, but allows males to engage in sexual activity with females." Behrndt had argued in reply that there was no equal protection issue because the law equally forbade men and women from engaging in sexual activity with members of their own sex. A majority of the court accepted this argument: "We believe it applies equally to men and women because it prohibits both classes from engaging in sexual activity with members of their own sex. Thus, there is no denial of equal protection on that basis." (This, by the way, was virtually the identical argument in support of miscegenation laws that was rejected by the U.S. Supreme Court in *Loving v. Virginia* (1967); Virginia defended its law by pointing out that it equally forbade black people and white people from marrying across the color line.) Furthermore, argued Behrndt, the statute actually made no "classification" as such, but merely prohibited certain homosexual conduct, an interpretation with which Donnelly stated agreement. But, said Donnelly, that did not end the equal protection inquiry, since the statute "embodies a classification based upon sexual preference."

Thus, the court had to determine whether "sexual preference" was a suspect classification, a determination it easily decided in the negative. After reviewing the classifications that the U.S. Supreme Court had deemed suspect or

quasi-suspect, which did not include "sexual preference," the court turned to facing the issue whether it should apply some sort of heightened scrutiny, addressing in turn the factors that the Supreme Court had identified as significant for such a determination in *City of Cleburne v. Cleburne Living Center* (1985).

The ACLU had argued in its *amicus* brief that laws discriminating against homosexuals met the tests set out by the Supreme Court for heightened scrutiny. On the issue of "immutable characteristics," the ACLU had argued that a "homosexual orientation" is something over which "a person has very little control . . . is not acquired voluntarily and is extremely difficult, if not impossible, to change." Donnelly responded that it was not the appropriate role of the court to consider the sort of social science data the ACLU presented in its brief on this point, which he believed called for legislative, not judicial, fact-finding. (This was a strange position for the court to take, in light of the role social science data not presented at trial has played in such significant cases as *Brown v. Board of Education of Topeka* (1954) and *Roe v. Wade* (1973). Furthermore, said Donnelly, the law "does not classify on the basis of a characteristic beyond one's control" because it deals only with activity, not status. "It cannot be said in the usual circumstance that refraining from certain conduct is beyond control. Beyond prohibiting the specified conduct, the state imposes no other burden. Whether the particular burden imposed is impermissible is a separate question."

On another of the equal protection factors, a history of prejudice, Donnelly was unwilling to concede that this could be a basis for requiring heightened scrutiny of the statute. While "it cannot be doubted that historically homosexuals have been subjected to 'antipathy and prejudice,'" so had "other classes whose members have violated society's legal and moral codes of conduct. There is a distinction between classifications that result from prejudice and judgments that result from legitimate classifications. The ACLU's position on this point begs the question of whether the classification is legitimate."

Finally, addressing the claim that gays needed special protection from the courts because of their inability to protect their interests through the democratic political process, Donnelly was "unpersuaded," insisting that "homosexuals, as such, have never been denied the ability to engage in 'political give and take.'"

> That being identified as a homosexual has involved certain political costs does not diminish this ability. The ACLU has again begged the question. If homosexual conduct is properly forbidden, any social stigma attaching to those who violate this proscription cannot be constitutionally suspect. The fact that the democratic process does not respond to those who violate its ordinances is no source of condemnation. Are we to say that drug addicts or pedophiliacs are a powerless class because the democratic process has refused to sanction the activity they seek to have sanctioned? Are we to say the same if society stigmatizes them? We think not. To hold that the losers in a public policy determination constitute a powerless class for purposes of determining the suspectness of the resulting classification is ludicrous on its face.

Thus, concluded the court, the classification embodied in the statute was "neither suspect nor quasi-suspect in relation to the respondent's status as a homosexual." That its suspect classification analysis was totally circular, in essence finding that there was no suspect classification because society had decided to criminalize homosexual activity, seemed to have escaped the attention of the court.

The alternative argument to "suspect class" is "fundamental right." Under the Equal Protection Clause, the courts will apply heightened scrutiny to classifications that deprive some individuals, but not others, of a fundamental right. Here, however, the recent *Hardwick* decision precluded a ruling for Walsh, said Donnelly, because the Supreme Court had held that there was no fundamental right to engage in homosexual sodomy. This meant that in the end the statute would survive if there was a "rational basis" for its enactment.

The state argued that the statute was "a rational exercise of the State's inherent police power to protect and promote public health and morals," while Walsh and the *amici* argued that "the legislation of morality which affects private consensual conduct is not a legitimate state interest" and that the law "fails to bear a rational relation to promotion of public health."

Addressing first the morality issue, Donnelly announced the court's agreement with the pronouncement by Circuit Court of Appeals Judge Robert H. Bork in *Dronenburg v. Zech* (1984), that moral judgments provided the basis "for much of the most valued legislation our society has," including civil rights laws, worker safety laws, and environmental protection laws. Said Bork, "In each of these areas, legislative majorities have made moral choices contrary to the desires of minorities." For this reason, an argument that legislation of morality was unconstitutional could not fly. Donnelly also rejected the precedent of *Commonwealth v. Bonadio*, in which the Pennsylvania Supreme Court had invalidated that state's sodomy law as in excess of the state's police powers by reference not to legal precedent but rather to the writings of English philosopher John Stuart Mill. "We are not bound by the decisions of foreign courts," said Donnelly, "and consider them only for their persuasiveness." Donnelly was not persuaded that statements of political philosophy were an appropriate basis for judicial invalidation of the statute; relief lay with the legislature, not the courts. The court found that punishing "homosexual acts" as a misdemeanor was "rationally related to the State's constitutionally permissible objective of implementing and promoting the public morality."

Furthermore, Donnelly found substantial support for the contention that the statute was a valid public health regulation. The state had raised the spectre of AIDS as a justification for the law; the respondents argued that nobody had ever heard of AIDS when this law was enacted. That did not give Donnelly any pause. He asserted that the statute could be upheld if "any state of facts reasonably can be conceived that would sustain it," citing a 1911 U.S. Supreme Court case as his authority. "That AIDS was not discovered until after the enactment . . . does not affect its present validity. It would be an idle exercise indeed to strike down the statute, upon the grounds urged, only to have it reenacted ostensibly based on current data." Furthermore, AIDS was not the only public health issue presented by homosexuality. Citing a controversial article by the professionally sanctioned and discredited psychiatrist Paul Cameron, which emphasized a claimed "direct oral-fecal link" created by the combination of anal and oral sexual intercourse, Donnelly said, "We need not refer to medical literature to suggest, for example, that there might rationally be health ramifications to anal intercourse and/or oral-genital sex." Donnelly also cited a study about the sex practices of male homosexuals that noted an extremely high number of average lifetime sexual partners for the participants in the study and asserted that "the General Assembly could have reasonably concluded that the general promiscuity characteristic of the homosexual lifestyle made such acts among homosexuals particularly deserving of regulation, thus rationally distinguishing such acts within a heterosexual context."

Finally, Donnelly dismissed the argument that the court should sustain Block's opinion by reliance on the Missouri Constitution. Although it was true that there were cases holding that the Missouri Constitution had its own right of privacy component, they dealt with "protection against publication of private facts." There was no developed Missouri constitutional case law on sexual privacy, and the court was not about to start developing it in this case, where the state constitution had not even been raised before the trial court and the parties had not devoted any substantial effort to developing an argument under the Missouri Constitution. "We will say, however, that whatever justification there may be for a nonoriginalist interpretation of the older United States Constitution, we believe that our Constitution of 1945 must be interpreted according to its plain language."

Donnelly concluded that Block's dismissal of the charges must be reversed and the case remanded for prosecution.

Two judges were moved to dissent from this disposition. Judge Warren D. Welliver believed that the charges against Walsh were not sufficient to sustain a prosecution under the statute. After quoting from *The Rape of the Lock* by Alexander Pope ("I respectfully dissent. What dire offense from amorous causes springs, What mighty contests rise from trivial things!"), he said:

> Just as the theft of a lock of hair created pandemonium in Pope's poem, today a slight

touch through layers of clothing has loosed great ideas and great minds. From the mountain, which I perceive to be a molehill, the principal opinion speaks on the mighty issues of jurisprudence and constitutional law raised primarily by respondent's friends. I fear that respondent is more hurt than helped by his friends, the amici, who I believe are more interested in establishing constitutional protection for homosexuals than in securing the freedom of this individual who is the victim of a woefully insufficient information.

Welliver just could not agree that the slight fondling activity charged in this case could seriously be considered a "substantial step towards the commission of the offense," which was required by Missouri law as a predicate to prosecution. "Without a strict requirement of an overt act, we run the risk of punishing men for mere accidental touchings based upon an officer's translation of a glimmer in the toucher's eye. The simple touch of a fully clothed man is not sufficiently unambiguous to equal 'conduct which is strongly corroborative of the firmness of the actor's purpose to complete the commission of the offense,'" as required by the statute.

> I would not sanction the arrest for attempted sexual misconduct of quarterbacks or wrestlers, nor can I approve the arrest of respondent on this flimsy information. The overt act alleged in this information may be as harmless as a wink or a leer. In this case, the policeman set the hook too soon.

Judge Charles B. Blackmar, joining Welliver's dissent, was also moved to comment that the court was obliged to uphold the trial judge's disposition if there was any basis for doing so, even if it disagreed with her theory of the case. Here, the insufficiency of the charges would suffice to uphold the dismissal. Furthermore, he said, in his view the law went beyond "the limits of state power in defining 'deviate sexual intercourse' as involving the hand."

> This is not the offense of sodomy as discussed in the opinion of the Supreme Court of the United States in *Bowers v. Hardwick* . . . , and it has no long history of legal sanction such as seemed very important to Justice White in that case. Bowers recognizes a right of privacy under the Constitution of the United States, but holds that this right of privacy does not extent to offenses traditionally punished as sodomy. Its rationale is absent here.

Finally, Donnelly himself, despite writing the opinion for the court, wanted to offer some personal comments beyond what his concurring judges would agree to, so he added his own separate postscript, pointing out that the court's opinion did not address the state constitutional argument on the merits and should not be construed as doing so. The Missouri Constitution's right of privacy, he implied, had a firmer basis in that document than did the federal right of privacy, since the 1945 state constitution was enacted after the Missouri Supreme Court had identified a right of privacy in *Barber v. Time, Inc.* (1942), based on language in its predecessor constitution, and the relevant language was repeated in the newer document. Thus, as to the current state constitution, the right of privacy was not merely "judge-made constitutional law," the pejorative phrase used by White in *Hardwick*. Donnelly wrote separately to make clear that in his opinion for the court he intended to "reserve . . . for another day" the question whether the Missouri sodomy law violated a state constitutional right of privacy.

The decision in *State v. Walsh* was a frustrating blow to the gay rights legal movement, coming so soon after *Hardwick* in a case that was so factually distinguishable under a statute that more clearly presented equal protection and overbreadth issues. That the decision's analysis of the equal protection issues was so circular and uncomprehending, and relied on bogus "medical facts" derived from the writings of Paul Cameron, caused particular consternation. But the decision did introduce a new note of realism into the movement's future planning. State court challenges to sodomy laws would have to be carefully planned, with great attention to developing independent state constitutional arguments. Perhaps the movement learned a valuable lesson: that using an existing prosecution as the vehicle for a major state constitutional challenge presented real dangers, especially where an attorney committed to and knowledgeable about gay rights law was not in the saddle during the trial stage to present the appropriate legal theories and, if applicable, to build the appropriate factual record. Subsequent state court challenges to sodomy laws in Michigan, Kentucky, and Texas each drew important lessons from the experience of Walsh.

Case References

Barber v. Time, Inc., 348 Mo. 1199, 159 S.W.2d 291 (1942)

Bowers v. Hardwick, 478 U.S. 186 (1986)

Brown v. Board of Education of Topeka, 347 U.S. 483 (1954)

City of Cleburne v. Cleburne Living Center, 473 U.S. 432 (1985)

Commonwealth v. Bonadio, 415 A.2d 47 (Pa. 1980)

Dronenburg v. Zech, 741 F.2d 1388 (D.C. Cir. 1984)

Loving v. Virginia, 388 U.S. 1 (1967)

Roe v. Wade, 410 U.S. 113 (1973)

31. COMMERCIAL SEX AND THE RIGHT OF PRIVACY

State v. Gray, 413 N.W.2d 107 (Minn. 1987). *Cherry v. Koch*, 129 Misc. 2d 346, 491 N.Y.S.2d 934 (Sup. Ct., Kings County 1985), modified, 126 A.D.2d 346, 514 N.Y.S.2d 30 (App. Div., 2d Dept. 1987).

Although the U.S. Supreme Court recognized a right of privacy inherent in the marital relationship in *Griswold v. Connecticut* (1965), and recognized an extension of that right to unmarried heterosexuals in *Eisenstadt v. Baird* (1972), an attempt to attain recognition for a broader, more general right of privacy under the federal Constitution protecting all consensual activity between adults was rebuffed in *Bowers v. Hardwick* (1986). There, the Court held that homosexuals did not have a fundamental right under the Due Process Clause of the Fourteenth Amendment to engage in consensual sodomy in private, although some lower state courts have ventured beyond *Hardwick* in applying a state constitutional right to private, consensual sodomy between adults. No court, however, seems comfortable with the idea of incorporating prostitution within the zone of conduct protected by a right of privacy. The commercial and public elements of prostitution are repeatedly cited as reason to label such activity other than consensual. The leading post-*Hardwick* case is *State v. Gray*, a 1987 decision by the Minnesota Supreme Court, in which a man accused of sodomy in the context of alleged prostitution sought to challenge the constitutionality of the Minnesota sodomy law applied to his conduct.

According to his later statement to the police, Richard Gordon Gray, Jr., was out driving near Loring Park in Minneapolis one day in May 1986. This was a place where young men hung out looking for sex partners. Gray pulled his car over to the side of the road and asked a man to get in. According to the young man, Gray told him that Gray would pay him to have sex. Gray asked how old the youth was; he answered that he was 18. (The man, who was actually 16 at the time, told police later, "If he was a retard he would believe that.") Gray drove him to Gray's home where they had sex in Gray's bedroom and Gray gave him some money. According to the youth, they had sex on two later occasions, both times with Gray paying. According to Gray, he had sex only once with the young man and made him a loan. The sex involved on all these occasions was apparently fellatio. Gray subsequently suspected that the man had stolen something from him, and contacted the police, who arrested Gray after the man described their sexual activities. Gray had a prior conviction for criminal sexual conduct with a minor, involving a young man under 17 who was Gray's "little brother" in the Big Brother program.

The state filed a charge of sodomy in violation of Minnesota's law penalizing all voluntary sodomy as a misdemeanor. No separate charge of prostitution was filed. Gray's attorney, Peter Thompson, of Minneapolis, moved on September 24, 1986, for dismissal of the charges before Hennepin County District Judge Pamela G. Alexander, claiming that the sodomy law violated the federal and state constitutional rights of privacy. Taking note of *Bowers v. Hardwick*, Judge Alexander held that the federal Constitution was not available for this purpose, but that the Minnesota Constitution did protect personal sexual privacy and that the sodomy statute was unconstitutionally broad and infringed on its face and as applied to Gray on the state constitution's right of privacy.

The state filed for an expedited appeal to the Minnesota Supreme Court, as provided where a trial court declares a state law unconstitutional. Special Assistant Attorney General Robert Stanich appeared for the state on the appeal, and Thompson received *amicus* assistance from civil liberties attorneys in Minneapolis and Washington. In an opinion by Chief Justice Douglas K. Amdahl, the court unanimously reversed on October 2, 1987.

Amdahl's opinion included a lengthy discussion of the *Hardwick* case, concluding that it was "dispositive of and wiped out Gray's argument" that the state sodomy law violated the federal Constitution. Thus, the court had to confront, apparently for the first time, whether its state constitution provided broader rights in matters of personal privacy than the Fourteenth Amendment. Having never previously found a right of privacy under the state constitution, Amdahl noted that the Minnesota Bill of Rights, when compared to the federal constitutional provisions normally cited as the basis for a federal right of privacy, appeared to protect the same rights. Accordingly, the court concluded that "there does exist a right of privacy guaranteed under and protected by the Minnesota Bill of Rights." The scope of protection afforded by that right, however, was described by the court as extending only to fundamental rights, which it defined by quoting the fifth edition of *Black's Law Dictionary*: "those which have their origin in the express terms of the Constitution or which are necessarily to be implied from those terms." Although the court was not limited by U.S. Supreme Court cases in construing its privacy right, and could protect more conduct than the federal courts would protect, it decided not to extend the Minnesota privacy right to Gray's conduct.

Simply put, the court found that Gray lacked standing, as one who was charged with having paid money for sex, to raise the constitutional claims of those who engaged in sexual activity without paying for it. Finding that the trial court had "overextended itself" by allowing Gray to make such a claim, Amdahl disputed Gray's contention that under *Eisenstadt v. Baird* he could claim some sort of derivative standing from those who might be liable for consensual sodomy under the statute. In *Eisenstadt*, said Amdahl, although the Court allowed contraception advocate Bill Baird to challenge his prosecution by asserting the rights of single people to use contraceptives, it did so because single people were not subject to prosecution under the law that was being enforced against Baird; they could not assert those rights directly, but those rights would surely be implicated if the statute was enforced against those who sought to distribute and counsel about contraceptives. Here, there was no basis for finding such a derivative right, said Amdahl, because "persons not currently before this court not only do not stand to lose by the outcome of this case, but they retain an 'effective avenue of preserving their rights themselves.'" Furthermore, Gray could not alternatively ground his standing in a First Amendment overbreadth argument. Although Gray had urged the precedent of *Roberts v. United States Jaycees* (1984), in which the Supreme Court had recognized, albeit in *dicta*, the existence of a "freedom of intimate association" under the First Amendment, Amdahl once again rejected Gray's invocation of an overbreadth basis for standing based on this case, asserting that the court's decision would not affect "persons in situations not before this court."

Amdahl's reasons for construing Gray's standing narrowly became clear as he stated the court's main objection: "our disagreement centers on Gray's attempt to characterize this as a case involving private sexual conduct." To Amdahl, the case was not rendered "private" by the locus of the sex acts, Gray's bedroom. The conduct charged here was "public in every other way: Gray picked up the complainant, who was previously unknown to Gray, at or near a public park recognized as a gathering place of young prostitutes; the sexual contacts between the two were essentially no more than separate 'one night stands' (and if, as Gray stated, the two committed only one sodomous act, our perception of the contact as a one night stand is bol-

stered); and, most importantly, this is a case of sex for compensation."

It was "simply wrong," said Amdahl, "to say that the sexual conduct in this case became private once the bedroom door was closed." The public aspects of the solicitation and the commercial element really made this a case of prostitution, even though Gray was not charged under the prostitution statute. "Were we to draw the line at the bedroom door," said Amdahl, "we would be hard pressed, once presented with the issue, to say that statutes criminalizing prostitution do not violate the right of privacy, and this is something we are quite unwilling to do for reasons well stated by the Iowa Supreme Court in *State v. Price*," a 1976 decision in which that court succinctly summarized the state's interest in penalizing prostitution:

> Prostitution implicates more than private sexual relations between consenting adults. It affects others including the community. Although usually transacted in private, it is nevertheless business which is frequently negotiated in public. Although intimate, it is impersonal. Although involving only consenting adults at the time, it may be a factor in the spread of venereal disease or have a close relationship with other criminal activity.

Although neither Gray nor his young accuser had been charged with prostitution, Amdahl held this no bar to considering the nature of the conduct charged in deciding whether a constitutional right of privacy applied to that conduct. And, so considered, Amdahl found the prospect distinctly unappetizing: "In sum, to say that there exists a fundamental right under our constitution to engage in sodomous acts within a sex for compensation relationship and therefore afford this activity constitutional protection under the right of privacy, is not only to extend that privacy right far beyond constitutional cases, but it is to debase both the Constitution and the concept of fundamental rights." As applied to Gray, the sodomy law did not violate the right of privacy. However, Amdahl cautioned that the court's holding should not be broadly construed, based as it was on the facts of Gray's case. The court's decision "is limited to a holding that any asserted Minnesota constitutional privacy right does not encompass the protection of those who traffic in commercial sexual conduct." Whether the Constitution might be used to invalidate the sodomy law as applied in other factual contexts remained an open question.

The Minnesota case probably presented the worst factual context in which to attack a sodomy law, since the young man was a minor and the sexual activity involved was casual and probably for pay. A more straightforward attempt to attack a prostitution law directly was undertaken by Margo St. James, a prominent female prostitute who organized other prostitutes in attempts to obtain repeal of sexual solicitation and prostitution laws, and Fred Cherry, a man with physical impairments that he claimed prevented him from having sexual relationships outside the context of prostitution. Cherry, a resident of Brooklyn, joined with St. James in a declaratory judgment action in the New York State courts, seeking a judgment that New York's laws penalizing patronizing a prostitute and providing prostitution services could not be enforced against those who discreetly and privately engaged in prostitution. They named as defendants New York City Mayor Edward I. Koch, Brooklyn District Attorney Elizabeth Holtzman, and Police Commissioner Benjamin Ward.

Their attempt was unsuccessful because New York authorities showed little interest in prosecuting those who quietly and discreetly engaged in such activities without incurring the concern of the public. Neither Cherry nor St. James, a "high-class" prostitute who worked out of her home rather than through street solicitation, had ever been arrested or prosecuted. Although they alleged that the existing laws presented the possibility of prosecution and thus "chilled" their constitutional rights of due process, equal protection, and freedom of association, they could do no more than speculate as to the possibility of future prosecutions. Cherry and St. James's first complaint was dismissed by Brooklyn Supreme Court Justice Arthur S. Hirsch on the ground that it included no statement as to where their future acts of prostitution would take place, Hirsch apparently believing that only an allegation of activity to take place in private would present a justiciable issue. In an amended complaint filed on their

behalf by Ronald L. Kuby, an associate of civil rights attorney William Kunstler, they alleged that all the activities would take place in private. The defendants moved for dismissal, arguing that the plaintiffs lacked standing and failed to present a justiciable claim. Justice Gerald Adler, to whom the motion had been assigned, agreed with the public officials. After a lengthy analysis of issues of "law of the case," standing and justiciability, he concluded that the matter should be dismissed. However, he gratuitously proceeded to discuss the merits anyway, "since this matter presents a question of importance to the workings of the criminal justice system and this is a recurring problem."

First discussing the claim that the laws violated St. James's and Cherry's right to privacy, Adler emphasized that the court of appeals' ruling striking down the state sodomy law in *People v. Onofre* (1980) had characterized the protected conduct in that case as "non-commercial." He concluded, "In New York, decisions voluntarily made by adults regarding indulgence in acts of sexual intimacy by unmarried persons are protected under the cloak of the right to privacy only when they are made in a non-commercial private setting." In *People v. Cloud Books* (1985), a case more recent than *Onofre*, a local prosecutor in Buffalo sought to close down an adult bookstore where prostitution allegedly occurred; the court of appeals stated that "prostitution is criminal activity no matter where it occurs." Thus, there was no appellate precedent in New York favoring the challengers of the statute.

Adler took a more analytic approach to the more generalized due process and equal protection claims asserted against the law. For a due process argument to succeed, he concluded, it would have to be shown that prostitution was a fundamental right. He quoted the District of Columbia Court of Appeals' decision in *Lutz v. United States*, a 1981 prosecution for solicitation, holding that "[c]ommercial sex does not concern an intimate relationship of the sort heretofore deemed worthy of constitutional protection." "In the instant case," Adler asserted, "the proscribed activity is not sexual activity but the *business* of engaging in that activity for hire on a regular basis." These statutes were "commercial regulations," which enjoyed a presumption of constitutionality. Since there was no fundamental right to engage in such a business (as opposed to any fundamental right to engage in sexual activity as such), the state need only show a rational basis for seeking to criminalize the conduct. Here, the *Onofre* opinion provided a description of prostitution that served to articulate such interests, quoted from a Pennsylvania decision that had upheld a prostitution statute:

> "Prostitution is an important source of venereal disease. . . . Prostitution is a source of profit and power for criminal groups who commonly combine it with illicit trade in drugs and liquor, illegal gambling and even robbery and extortion. Prostitution is also a corrupt influence on government and law enforcement machinery. Its promoters are willing and able to pay for police protection; and unscrupulous officials and politicians find them an easy mark for extortion. Finally, some view prostitution as a significant factor in social disorganization, encouraging sex, delinquency and undermining marriage, the home, and individual character. (A.L.I. Model Penal Code sec. 207.12 Tent., Draft No. 9, Comment at 171 [1959]). (Footnotes omitted)." *Commonwealth v. Dodge*, 278 Pa. Super. 148, 429 A.2d 1143, 1149.

Left unmentioned, of course, was the degree to which the socially undesirable effects associated with prostitution were due to the criminalization of prostitution, as opposed to prostitution *per se*.

Adler commented that "commercial sex demeans and exploits women, particularly the young and uneducated who require protection of their interests. . . . Another justification for this type of legislation is the need for 'public order.'" Since many in society viewed prostitution as "immoral and degrading," it was appropriate for the state to outlaw it. Since commercial regulations had a strong presumption of constitutionality, these interests were more than sufficient to find such laws constitutional under the police power of the state.

St. James and Cherry had also asserted an equal protection claim. St. James claimed that women within marriage might demand particular compensation for engaging in sex without violating the laws, which thereby discriminated against unmarried women. Recognizing that "a marital exemption exists for the crime of pros-

titution," Adler rejected their argument, based on the special recognition of marriage in constitutional law. Citing *Loving v. Virginia*, in which the Supreme Court invalidated a miscegenation law, Adler asserted that "marriage is a fundamental right where freedom of personal choice is protected to a heightened degree," that it enjoyed "an expanded zone of privacy," and that only a compelling state interest would justify government interference in the sex lives of married people. The legislative objectives of prostitution laws would not be advanced by prosecuting the wife who demanded compensation from her husband. The fears of venereal disease from promiscuity, the public order problems, and the other "attendant evils associated with commercial sex" were just not present, said Adler. Thus, it was rational for the state to treat the prostitute differently from the wife.

Cherry had argued that the law worked an unconstitutional discrimination against persons with disabilities whose sole sexual outlet would be through prostitution. Alder rejected this claim without any analysis, merely asserting that no discrimination on this basis appeared on the face of the statute and neglecting entirely to discuss the issue of disparate impact. (Of course, under U.S. Supreme Court precedents, a disparate impact claim could not be asserted under the Fourteenth Amendment.) Finally, Cherry had argued that men could keep female mistresses without violating the prostitution law, so long as they did not compensate them for individual sex acts. This was discriminatory, said Cherry, who could not afford to keep a mistress. Again, Adler rejected the challenge based on his view that the "attendant evils" of prostitution were not all present when a man kept a mistress. This "distinction" between the cases was sufficient in his view to provide a rational basis for criminalizing the one and not the other.

Cherry and St. James appealed, but the appellate division unanimously rejected their claims to standing and justiciability and asserted in its *per curiam* opinion that the trial court should have declined to reach the merits.

As the Minnesota and New York opinions reveal, and as opinions in other states confirm, judges do not appear ready to give serious consideration to the claim that prostitution is a form of sexual activity that should receive constitutional protection against prosecution. Judges appear willing to accept without much documentation or analysis the arguments that prostitution presents public order problems sufficient to require state intervention (as the American Law Institute concluded during its debates over the Model Penal Code), even when the activity takes place in private between willing adults, nobody is hurt, and there are exigent circumstances, such as Fred Cherry's disabilities. While the courts may be correct in implicitly asserting that the decision whether to penalize such conduct should be left to legislators and, within their discretion, law enforcement authorities, this avoids having to confront the hard political issues, since only one state has seen fit to allow localities to permit heterosexual prostitution in a regulated and taxed form.

Prostitution activities have gone on throughout the world for all of recorded history. Prostitution laws do not apparently deter such activity, but drive it underground, facilitating the sort of organized crime connections that Justice Adler mentioned. Prostitutes are not a significant vector of venereal disease in those Nevada municipalities which regulate and license prostitutes. England has long recognized this; while invoking public order concerns to prohibit street solicitation by prostitutes, the

English penal law traditionally left unpenalized consensual commercial sexual activity in private, on the ground that what adults wanted to do under such circumstances was not the law's business. This conclusion was approved by the Wolfenden Committee, which recommended against proposals to adopt American-style prostitution laws in England. Similar legal toleration for prostitution exists in many other parts of the world. The general lack of legal toleration for sexual diversity in the United States remains a barrier to reform in this area of the law, which would probably enhance public health if tied to appropriate regulation and licensing and enhance the safety of customers and prostitutes by removing some of the motivation for entanglement with organized crime.

Case References

Bowers v. Hardwick, 478 U.S. 186 (1986)
Eisenstadt v. Baird, 405 U.S. 438 (1972)
Griswold v. Connecticut, 381 U.S. 479 (1965)
Loving v. Virginia, 388 U.S. 1 (1967)
Lutz v. United States, 434 A.2d 442 (D.C. App. 1981)
People v. Cloud Books, 65 N.Y.2d 324 (1985)
People v. Onofre, 51 N.Y.2d 476 (1980), certiorari denied, 451 U.S. 987 (1981)
Roberts v. United States Jaycees, 468 U.S. 609 (1984)
State v. Price, 237 N.W. 2d 813 (Iowa), appeal dismissed, 426 U.S. 916 (1976)

32. FINDING FRIENDS IN THE STRANGEST PLACES

People v. Superior Court (Caswell), 46 Cal. 3d 381, 250 Cal. Rptr. 515, 758 P.2d 1046 (1988), affirming 226 Cal. Rptr. 68 (Ct. App., 6th Dist. 1986).

Society's formal disapproval of "deviant" sexuality has led to a variety of tension points between police and those whose sexual tastes vary from the prescribed norm. Few of those tension points have given rise to such frequent confrontation and litigation as public toilets where sexual activity occurs. These are among the few places where the most secretive persons with same-sex attraction (particularly those who otherwise lead conventionally "heterosexual" lives) seek out like-minded partners in

an intense "game" of furtive communication, trying through lingering, discrete signals, and heightened awareness to attempt to make those sexual connections while avoiding offending "innocent" users of the facilities. Others not so "closeted" who find a special sexual charge from making new, anonymous contacts also frequent restrooms intending to initiate sexual activity. Because many of those who engage in this activity have no private place to bring their sexual partners, the sexual acts themselves may be completed on the premises in violation of the laws against public sex acts of virtually every jurisdiction. Even many states that have decriminalized sexual solicitation in public places where the sexual act is to be consummated in private remain concerned about the impact on nonsexual users of the facilities when those seeking sex "hang around" and create a sexual atmosphere at the public toilet.

Law enforcement authorities trying to prevent the use of public toilets for sexual purposes face significant difficulties. Most American public toilets do not have full-time attendants, and most individuals who use public toilets for sexual purposes strive to avoid approaching those who are not interested in their advances, so there are few offended complainants who can identify a potential defendant. While the police might receive complaints that a particular public toilet is becoming a "hangout" for sexual activity, it would be difficult for a uniformed officer actually to catch somebody in the act of solicitation or sexual conduct. Traditionally, law enforcement authorities have dealt with this problem through broad, unspecific laws against vagrancy, loitering, and public lewdness, which authorized police officers to arrest virtually anybody who appeared to be "hanging around" for no good reason. Anybody the police suspected of being present in a restroom for sexual purposes could be arrested under such laws, with no requirement that the arrestee had been observed by the police officer committing any act other than being there.

As the Supreme Court began to develop the concept of due process of law more aggressively beginning in the 1950s, vagrancy and loitering laws came under increasing attack, culminating in *Kolender v. Lawson*, a 1983 Supreme Court decision that invalidated a California law that authorized the police to arrest anyone if he "loiters . . . upon the streets . . . without apparent reason or business and . . . refuses to identify himself or to account for his presence when requested by a peace officer so to do." The Supreme Court held that this sort of law, giving virtually unfettered discretion to police officers to single out anybody they might not like and require identification of indeterminate nature, did not possess the degree of specificity that would put people on notice of what con-

duct was prohibited, and it could lend itself to unequal enforcement against disfavored minorities. Indeed, studies had shown that broad loitering and vagrancy laws tended to be enforced disproportionately against racial and sexual minorities.

As the requirements of due process were tightened, legislators responded with more specific laws, describing the places in which loitering was suspect and requiring that the loitering be for a specific purpose to come within the prohibition of the law. In a companion statute to the one struck down in *Kolender*, the California legislature had imposed misdemeanor penalties on any person "who loiters in or about any toilet open to the public for the purpose of engaging in or soliciting any lewd or lascivious or any unlawful act." The police enforced this law by sending plainclothes police officers to public toilets, trained to act in such a way as to attract solicitations. Since those who frequented public toilets for sexual purposes were aware of the possibility of plainclothes police presence, their elaborate procedures of so-called tea-room "cruising" became ever more intricate, in hopes that they would avoid making any incriminating moves before being absolutely convinced that the object of their intentions was not a police officer. Any miscalculation could be fatal, since the slightest sign of sexual interest, even turning from a urinal with pants unzipped, might lead to arrest. A wink or a raised eyebrow might lead to the cruiser's undoing. Indeed, many men who were present merely to use the facilities, with no intention of "cruising," might be subjected to arrest for so little as smiling or looking "too long" at a plainclothes police officer.

Seizing on the *Kolender* precedent, California lawyers whose practices included representation of many gay and bisexual men caught up in these police enforcement efforts attempted to have the toilet loitering law declared unconstitutional on due process grounds. A series of cases in the mid-1980s led to the California Supreme Court decision in *Caswell*, ending this line of attack. Jay M. Kohorn, of Redondo Beach (who had successfully challenged the law in *People v. Soto*, (1985), mentioned below); Bruce Nickerson, of San Jose; and Fred B. Rosenberg, of San Francisco, joined forces in the *Caswell* litigation to attempt to persuade the court that the toilet loitering statute was being used unfairly in a tense game of "cops" versus "gays" that served no valid public interest. San Jose Deputy District Attorney Joseph Thibodeaux defended the statute.

The *Caswell* case combined several pending prosecutions in which the municipal courts in San Jose had been struggling with this issue, and it decided the matter devoid of reference to the facts of any one case, purely as an abstract proposition of law. This was most unfortunate, since it removed the vivid factual element that could have illuminated for the justices the peculiar sexual underworld that an oppressive society has generated through the perpetuation of stereotyped sex roles and formal disapproval of alternative sexual lifestyles. Conflicting opinions of the courts of appeal in different districts led the California Supreme Court to grant a petition for review in *People v. Superior Court (Caswell)* on July 31, 1986.

The Sixth District Court of Appeal in San Jose had upheld the validity of the toilet loitering law in a unanimous opinion by Presiding Justice Nat A. Agliano on May 16. Agliano's decision had sharply disagreed with a decision of the Second District Court of Appeal (Los Angeles) in *People v. Soto* issued the previous year, which had found the law to be unconstitutional. Ironically, Justice John A. Arguelles, who was to write the California Supreme Court's opinion upholding the law, wrote a concurring opinion in *Soto* holding the law unconstitutional.

The *Soto* court ruled that the law unconstitutionally gave wide discretion to police officers to define for themselves the circumstances under which an individual had crossed the line from innocent presence in a public toilet to loitering with the intent of soliciting unlawful activity. Relying heavily on the U.S. Supreme Court's *Kolender* decision, the court had stated that the loitering statute lacked "objective criteria to guide an officer's decision making process with regard to the criminality of an actor's conduct." As a result, said the court, "discretion to determine the actor's intent or 'purpose' rests solely within the subjective thought processes of police officers who are free at whim to decide in each case whether the requisite

intent to engage in or solicit 'any lewd or lascivious or any unlawful act' accompanies the act of loitering." The court found that this "unfettered discretion" violated both the federal and state due process requirements, "for it permits the criminality of conduct to be measured 'by community or even individual notions of what is distasteful behavior.'"

In *Caswell*, Justice Agliano specifically rejected this reasoning, finding that the statute gave adequate notice to members of the public of the type of conduct that was prohibited (a point not even addressed in the *Soto* opinion but raised by the *Caswell* defendants), and that the statute's requirements were specific enough to avoid the problems of "unfettered discretion" the *Soto* court had identified. The defendants had invoked the U.S. Supreme Court's 1962 decision in *Robinson v. California*, in which the Court had invalidated a California statute that made it a crime, in effect, to be addicted to drugs while in the state of California, regardless whether the individual had actually used drugs in the state. The Court held that punishment of a person because of his "status" as a drug addict was "cruel and unusual punishment" in violation of the Eighth Amendment, applicable to the states through the Due Process Clause of the Fourteenth Amendment. Rejecting the *Caswell* defendants' arguments that, in the absence of overt sexual conduct, hanging around in a public toilet was "entirely innocent activity" for which an arrest would violate the *Robinson* holding, Agliano said that the statute's requirements "that the defendant have knowingly placed himself in the situation and that he or she possess a specified animus, elements which clearly distinguish such a defendant from the passive occupier of a 'status' to which the statute involved in *Robinson* was addressed," took care of any "cruel and unusual punishment" argument. Besides, he said, "The defendants do not argue that there is no valid social purpose to be served by regulating ill-motivated conduct near public toilets: The need is apparent to anyone who, in our increasingly permissive times, has made legitimate use of such a facility."

Agliano also rejected the argument that the crime had not been described with adequate specificity. Applying the normal presumption of constitutionality, it was up to the defendants to show that a person of reasonable intelligence would not know what was prohibited. Since the California Supreme Court had upheld public solicitation statutes with a narrowing construction that they could apply only to the solicitation of unlawful conduct in *Pryor v. Municipal Court* (1979), the inclusion of the term "lewd or lascivious" was not unduly vague, since a statute's meaning was held to be modified by judicial construction as if it had been amended, and it would be clear to any reasonably intelligent person that the act that was forbidden was lingering at a public toilet for the express purpose of soliciting somebody to engage in unlawful activity, either on the premises or elsewhere, or to actually engage in such unlawful activity. Agliano also rejected the idea that the phrase "in or about" made the statute unduly vague. "No reasonable person could fail to understand that the area to be regulated is that within or immediately adjacent to, and thus directly associated with, a public toilet." Of course, Agliano's own decision was implicitly placing a limiting construction on the statute by requiring that the zone of enforcement be delimited to an area "immediately adjacent to" the toilet.

On the more significant issue, on which the *Soto* case turned, Agliano specifically rejected the idea that the statute unconstitutionally gave "unfettered discretion" to police officers. For one thing, he said, many other statutes involved conduct which, although not itself criminal, was made criminal because of the intent of the actor. He cited laws against conspiracy, criminal attempts, and issuance of bad checks with intent to defraud, each of which might be committed by otherwise lawful acts coupled with unlawful intent. To hold that the "loitering with intent" law was unduly vague because it was up to the individual judgment of the police officer, in the first instance, to decide whether an individual's presence, coupled with otherwise lawful conduct, provided sufficient indicia of intent to justify an arrest, could lead to the invalidation of a wide range of statutes, none of which had been questioned or invalidated on such an argument. The argument that this procedure was open to abuse was not a sufficient basis for invalidating it, said Agliano,

because conviction of the offense would require proof beyond a reasonable doubt. All law enforcement activity might risk "harsh and discriminatory enforcement," but that was not a fault of the underlying criminal statutes.

Agliano's opinion showed the dangers of deciding these sorts of issues in a factual vacuum. The underlying facts of the arrests of Caswell and the other defendants were not before him, so he could only speculate about the enforcement methods the police were using and the flimsiness of the evidence on which they might make arrests. Furthermore, the protection of the "proof beyond reasonable doubt" standard did not deal with the reality of this law because few of these cases came to trial. Most of the men caught by plainclothes policemen were not openly gay. They lived closeted lives, many married with children, some employed in jobs they feared losing if litigation brought further exposure to their problems. In most cases, they were terrified of the possibility of a public trial with attendant publicity, and were eager to plead guilty and pay a fine rather than have their problem come to the notice of employers, nongay acquaintances, or family members. In most cases, the quality of the police officer's judgment would never be tested in court. The supreme court's consideration on appeal was similarly devoid of any reference to the actual facts of enforcement practices and consequences of the law. Justice Arguelles's opinion for the court, issued on August 22, 1988, has the same sort of abstract, clinical quality that distinguished Agliano's for the court of appeal.

Arguelles brushed aside the issue of adequate notice in a few brief paragraphs. As far as he was concerned, the "ordinary citizen" knew exactly what was proscribed: lingering for the purpose of soliciting or engaging in lewd and lascivious sexual activity. "Persons of ordinary intelligence need not guess at the applicability of the section," he said; "so long as they do not linger for the proscribed purpose, they have not violated the statute." The specific intent requirement, coupled with the geographic limitation "in or about" a public toilet, saved the law from any vagueness problems, he asserted. And, since *Pryor v. Municipal Court*, everybody knew what "lewd or lascivious" meant, since there the supreme court had adopted a very specific definition, holding that those words "are synonymous, and refer to conduct which involves the touching of the genitals, buttocks, or female breast for the purpose of sexual arousal, gratification, annoyance or offense, if the actor knows or should know of the presence of persons who may be offended by his conduct." This was enough, asserted Arguelles, to satisfy the "fair notice" element of due process.

Turning to whether the law provided adequate guidelines to permit nonarbitrary enforcement, Arguelles recanted his *Soto* opinion. Quoting U.S. Supreme Court Justice Robert H. Jackson, who had stated that "it is embarrassing to confess a blunder," but "it may prove more embarrassing to adhere to it," and Justice Wiley B. Rutledge, who had observed, "Wisdom too often never comes, and so one ought not to reject it merely because it comes late," Arguelles pointedly cited other cases in which members of the California courts had confessed that they were forced by persuasive arguments to contradict their own earlier opinions. He was now persuaded, said Arguelles, that the problems he saw in his *Soto* opinion were not sufficient to justify invalidating the statute. His own opinion in *Soto* had

> failed to take adequate account of the significant differences between the loitering provision at issue in *Kolender* and the provision of [this law,] and also overlooked the significant body of out-of-state decisions which have upheld the constitutionality of loitering statutes . . . that narrow the discretion of enforcing officials by (1) limiting the section's reach to persons who loiter with a specific illicit purpose and (2) confining the statute's operation to defined geographical locations in which loitering for the proscribed purposes has historically been a problem.

Indeed, if truth be told, why would anybody hang around a public toilet any longer than necessary to use the facilities for their intended excretory purposes other than for illicit purposes, Arguelles seemed to be saying. The *Soto* court had ruled that it was enough for the state to punish actual solicitations or performance of sexual acts in a public place; there was no need to criminalize hanging around with intent if no unlawful conduct took place. This was no longer a satisfactory answer for Arguelles. "It is axiomatic," he contended, that

"the Legislature may criminalize the same conduct in different ways." In this context, a prosecutor who might be unable to convince a jury that an actual solicitation took place would want to charge a violation of the loitering statute as well, since the evidence might support a finding of the requisite intent based on otherwise lawful conduct. Furthermore, said Arguelles, neither the statute nor the Constitution required the commission of any criminal act. How could the state deal with complaints by citizens that a particular person was hanging around in the public toilet unless the police were permitted to infer unlawful intent from the fact of suspicious lingering? The police were entitled to infer intent, for example, if they observed somebody known to have solicited unlawful sexual activity in the past lingering suspiciously around a public toilet. The Model Penal Code, not enacted in California, provided further support for his point, he said, since it included a provision similar to the California law, and he commented that law enforcement officials could rely on any "firm indication" that the loitering individual had the requisite intent for a statutory violation.

Arguelles never addressed the issues of plea bargaining surrounding these types of arrests, referring, as did Agliano, to the safeguard provided by the judicial system that innocent persons could rely on the proof requirements at trial for protection against overzealous police officers. Many other laws provided punishments predicated on unlawful intent without unlawful acts, such as the conspiracy statutes, and they had been upheld against constitutional attack.

Responding to the defendants' arguments that these laws all required that some "overt act" have occurred before an arrest could be made, Arguelles contended that lingering in a public toilet was itself an "overt act" and that "mere presence" in a prohibited place appeared as a crime in several provisions of the Criminal Code. Here, the "mere presence" was to be coupled with indicia of prohibited intent, providing more specificity than some of those other sections. The significant number of decisions from other states upholding loitering statutes that incorporated a specific intent requirement indicated at least a majority view among American jurisdictions that such laws were constitutional. The failure of the statute to enumerate the acts that might serve as the basis for inferring forbidden intent was not fatal because the statute as drafted "provides sufficient guidance to police by requiring the loitering be done with a specific intent and within a designated area."

Toward the end of his decision, Arguelles did concede that the law might be used inequitably. The answer to this, evidently, was judicial exhortation, so he provided some: he recognized the possibility that the law "may serve as a vehicle for harassment of citizens based on their unorthodox lifestyles or sexual orientation," noting studies showing how police decoys disappointed in not observing enough conduct to justify an arrest would threaten individuals with arrest in order to get them to leave the area of the toilet.

> Because the potential for discriminatory enforcement is more pronounced in loitering cases than in most other contexts, we stress that a potential suspect's sexual orientation is not, in itself, a sufficient 'articulable fact' to give rise to probable cause and that the police must apply equal standards to both homosexuals and heterosexuals in determining whether an individual's conduct in fact provides probable cause to believe that he is loitering with the proscribed intent. Just as all races have the equal right to use the public streets in all neighborhoods without fear of being arrested on a 'guilt by association' theory . . . both homosexual and heterosexual persons must have the equal right to use public restrooms without fear of police harassment.

Dismissing the defendants' contention that upholding the statute would convert every plainclothes police officer into a "mini-legislature" while on the job, Arguelles concluded that the police officer's discretion went to the issue of probable cause to arrest and was "not a flaw in the definition of the crime itself." He also dismissed the contention that the looseness of the law would result "in a failure to prosecute in some cases where the identical conduct in another part of the state will result in prosecution." This did not strike him as a problem, since, once again, he insisted that the law was specific enough to "avoid any problems under the uniform operation of the law provision" in the California Constitution.

Justices Stanley Mosk and Allen E. Broussard dissented in an opinion by Mosk that was marked by sarcasm at Arguelles's change of heart on the issue. There were other laws that would adequately serve to deal with actual conduct when it occurred, said Mosk. "Justice Arguelles pointed out the adequacy of other laws in his concurring opinion in a decision invalidating this very statute," said Mosk. "It is regrettable that he now disavows his offspring. He was right the first time." Mosk stated alarm with the court's contention that a police officer could base a probable cause determination on no more than an individual's past record for solicitation and the fact of his presence in or around a public toilet. "I need cite no authority for the universally accepted proposition that previous conduct, or even purported propensity to commit crimes, does not justify an arrest when no actual crime is being or has been committed. That the majority would seriously advance a contrary theory is ominous." In this connection, Mosk did not see how the statute could be equitably enforced. How could intent be determined "when there are no accompanying acts or conduct"? "Perhaps [the majority] anticipate[s] a court somehow miraculously peering into the inner recesses of the mind. A crystal ball might be helpful."

Compounding the problem was the phrase "any unlawful act," which might apply to any of literally thousands of provisions and prohibitions in the California Penal Code. "It cannot be seriously contended," he argued, "that 'any unlawful act' places a person on adequate notice as to what laws he may not subjectively intend to violate at some imprecise future time in the course of his dallying." Indeed,

> the statute at issue refers to only one act that constitutes conduct: loitering. Yet loitering— i.e., lingering, dawdling, loafing, tarrying, lazying, lagging, idling, dallying—admittedly is not in itself a criminal offense. That leaves only intent as the prohibited element. Thus to be vulnerable to prosecution, a person must linger near a restroom and think or fantasize about improper sexual acts or any other crime on the books. No overt act. No advances toward any other person. Just thoughts.

This would not do, said Mosk. There were adequate laws on the books to take care of conduct. "But when we invade the thought processes of individuals, we step over the line into a constitutionally impermissible area." In conclusion, Mosk harked back to Justice William O. Douglas's opinion in *Papachristou v. City of Jacksonville* (1972), in which he commented that while vagrancy laws might be "useful" to the police because they made it easy to round up "undesirables," such laws "teach that the scales of justice are so tipped that even-handed administration of the law is not possible. The rule of law," said Douglas, "evenly applied to minorities as well as majorities, to the poor as well as the rich, is the great mucilage that holds society together." This loitering law, Mosk suggested, violated the rule of law by its intrusiveness and potential abuse.

As noted above, the *Caswell* decision illustrates the incompleteness of judicial consideration of issues when viewed in a factual vacuum. Resting on unverified presumptions about the real world in which closeted gay men seek sexual gratification and vice officers look for any excuse to arrest men they suspect of being gay, the court bowed to societal pressure to keep "deviant" sexuality as far away as possible from the sensibilities of those who dislike it. It is probably true that some of those arrested under laws such as the California toilet loitering statute were likely to solicit and engage in sexual activities in and around public toilets, but that is not really the point. As Justice Mosk observed,

if they were caught in an actual solicitation or sexual act, there were adequate laws on the books to deal with them. If they were not caught, who was harmed?

Furthermore, many of those "caught" were not intending to commit any crime and were engaged in totally innocent activity. Indeed, the California Supreme Court's own opinion in *Pryor* had included, as part of the element of a narrowed construction of the term "lewd and lascivious," an element ignored by the court in *Caswell*: that the particular acts take place in the presence of third persons "who might be expected to be offended by them." By its nature, restroom cruising is furtive, the participants seeking to conceal at every turn from unwilling observers that anything sexual is going on. By upholding the application of the law to situations involving no overt solicitation or sexual conduct, the court was violating the principles it had espoused in *Pryor*: that the public's legitimate concern was with what happened in public view under circumstances in which nonconsenting persons would be offended.

Case References

Kolender v. Lawson, 461 U.S. 352 (1983)
Papachristou v. City of Jacksonville, 405 U.S. 156 (1972)
People v. Soto, 171 Cal. App. 3d 1158, 217 Cal. Rptr. 795 (2d Dist. 1985)
Pryor v. Municipal Court, 25 Cal. 3d 238, 158 Cal. Rptr. 330, 599 P.2d 636 (1979)
Robinson v. California, 370 U.S. 660 (1962)

33. WHITHER HETEROSEXUAL "SODOMY"?

Post v. State, 715 P.2d 1105 (Okla. Crim. App.), rehearing denied, 717 P.2d 1151 (Okla. Crim. App. 1986), certiorari denied sub nom. *Oklahoma v. Post*, 479 U.S. 890 (1986). *Schochet v. State*, 320 Md. 714, 580 A.2d 176 (1990), reversing 75 Md. App. 314, 541 A.2d 183 (1988).

In 1986, the U.S. Supreme Court ruled in *Bowers v. Hardwick* that homosexuals did not have a constitutionally protected right to engage in "sodomy," defined in Georgia's sodomy law as including anal or oral sex. The Court did not pass judgment on whether heterosexuals did enjoy such a right, although counsel for the state of Georgia had conceded at oral argument that the statute could probably not be

constitutionally applied to a married heterosexual couple. Just months after announcing the *Hardwick* decision, however, the Court denied a petition for a writ of *certiorari* to the Oklahoma Court of Criminal Appeals in *Oklahoma v. Post*, thus leaving in place a ruling that the Oklahoma sodomy law could not constitutionally be applied to heterosexuals engaging in consensual sodomy in private. Four years later, in *Schochet v. State*, Maryland's highest court narrowly construed a law against fellatio to avoid having to reach the question of its constitutionality. Although some state courts had invalidated heterosexual sodomy prohibitions in earlier years, the rulings in *Post* and, particularly, *Schochet*, are important as possible portents of how this subject might be treated by the U.S. Supreme Court.

The *Post* case dates from January 7, 1983. James Lester Post, Jr., was having a night out on the town, and in the early hours of the morning fell into conversation with a woman while drinking at the Red Eye Saloon in Claremore, Oklahoma. Post invited her to come home with him, and she accepted. They went by way of a convenience store, where they bought some beer. At Post's home, they had sex, including anal and oral intercourse. The woman claimed that Post forced her to have sex; Post claimed that the sexual activity was voluntary. The woman claimed that during the sexual assault, Post repeatedly beat her, resulting in serious eye injury. Post claimed that after their consensual sex, he fell asleep, only to awaken and discover the woman going through his pants pockets and, assuming she was trying to steal his wallet, he struck out and hit her in the eye. They subsequently left the house together. The woman went to a friend's house, called her husband and eventually complained to the police.

Post was charged with rape, crime-against-nature (which the Oklahoma courts construed to include anal and oral intercourse, as well as cunnilingus), and maiming, after former conviction of a felony. Post was defended at trial by Assistant Public Defender Thomas Purcell. Rogers County District Judge Byron Ed Williams presided at the jury trial. Williams instructed the jury that lack of consent was not an element of crime-against-nature, so it could convict even if it believed Post's testimony that the sexual activity was consensual. The jury acquitted Post of the rape charge but convicted on the maiming and crime-against-nature charges.

Post appealed, arguing that consensual sexual activity between adults in private was protected from punishment by the constitutional right of privacy, and that the crime-against-nature law was unconstitutionally vague.

The state, represented on appeal by Assistant Attorney General Robert W. Cole, argued that the Oklahoma Court of Criminal Appeals should stand by its precedent of *Warner v. State* (1971), which had previously upheld the constitutionality of the crime-against-nature statute.

In an opinion by Presiding Judge Ed Parks on February 26, 1986, the court ruled that the federal constitutional right of privacy first identified in *Griswold v. Connecticut* (1965) had been expanded by the U.S. Supreme Court beyond its apparent scope in 1971, so as to encompass consensual heterosexual activity in private. In *Warner*, the Oklahoma court had interpreted the *Griswold* opinion to recognize a right of privacy limited to married persons. Since *Griswold*, however, the Supreme Court had indicated in *Carey v. Population Services International* (1977) that "the outer limits" of the right to privacy "have not been marked by the Court." And, said Parks, the Court's opinion in *Eisenstadt v. Baird* (1972) "indicates to us that the constitutional right to privacy, which at first appeared to be family-based, affords protection to the decisions and actions of individuals outside the marriage union." Parks quoted Justice William J. Brennan's assertion in *Eisenstadt* that while the right of privacy in *Griswold* "inhered in the marital relationship," it was "the right of the *individual*, married or single, to be free from unwarranted governmental intrusion into matters so fundamentally affecting a person as the decision whether to bear or beget a child." Further, said Parks, it would be inappropriate to limit the claimed privacy right to contraception decisions, since in *Stanley v. Georgia* (1969) the Court had found a right of privacy in the ownership and use of pornographic films in the home.

The subsequent Supreme Court decisions led the court to conclude that *Warner v. State* was based on an erroneous reading of *Griswold*. The right to privacy, said Parks, "includes the right to select consensual adult sex partners," and only a compelling governmental interest would justify interfering with their private activities. "We recognize it is the opinion of many that abnormal sexual acts, even those involving consenting adults, are morally reprehensible," said Parks. "However, this natural repugnance does not create a compelling justification for state regulation of these activities." Surely, many found contraceptives and pornography repugnant, but that was not enough to justify the laws struck down in *Eisenstadt* or *Stanley*. The state had not demonstrated that private consensual heterosexual acts "could significantly harm society" so as to provide the necessary compelling interest to sustain the law. However, the court was not willing to invalidate the law, which had been construed to penalize all "unnatural" sex wherever performed, totally. Rather, it was holding that the law could not be used to punish consensual adult sexual activity in private. Bestiality, forced sexual activity, sex with minors, or public or commercial sexual activity were not affected by this opinion, and because "the application of the statute to such conduct is not an issue in this case," the court would not speculate on whether same-sex activity could constitutionally be punished. (The Supreme Court had already granted *certiorari* in *Bowers v. Hardwick* and was to hear oral argument just weeks after this Oklahoma opinion was announced.) Thus, the crime-against-nature convictions against Post were reversed.

Parks announced that the court was also reversing the maiming conviction and remanding for a new trial. Judge Williams had refused to instruct the jury that it could convict Post of the lesser crimes of simple and aggravated assault and battery. Post argued that he was entitled to such an instruction, because he had testified that he struck out in anger and without premeditation, and that the offense depended on his state of mind, not on the degree of injury he inflicted on the woman. The court agreed. Judge Hez J. Bussey dissented, arguing in a brief opinion that it was not a "judicial function" to amend statutes, and that Judge Williams had correctly charged the jury on the maiming issue, given the serious injury the woman had sustained (loss of her eye).

The state filed a motion for stay pending appeal on March 7, and a motion for rehearing on March 16. On April 14, the court denied the motion for rehearing, but granted the stay pending the state's appeal to the U.S. Supreme Court. In his motion for rehearing, Assistant Attorney General David W. Lee argued that the court's opinion was inconsistent with *Doe v.*

Commonwealth's Attorney for City of Richmond (1976) and early cases in which the Supreme Court had upheld sodomy laws similar to Oklahoma's. The court disagreed, pointing out that the prior decisions either had all involved homosexuality or vagueness issues, or had predated the most important privacy decisions on which the court relied in its decision in this case. The court reiterated that "on two occasions before this Court—the brief-in-chief and petition for rehearing—the appellee has utterly failed to prove that private, consensual and non-commercial heterosexual acts between adults could significantly harm society so as to provide a compelling state interest in, or even a rational relationship to support, regulation of these activities."

On June 30, the Supreme Court issued its opinion in *Hardwick*, apparently leaving unsettled the question whether heterosexuals have a right to engage in sodomy. On October 14, the Court denied the state's petition for *certiorari* in *Post*, without comment. Although a denial of *certiorari* denotes no particular opinion on the merits by the Supreme Court, it does give the lower court's opinion the air of finality, and *State v. Post* would subsequently be cited as an invalidation of a sodomy law as applied to heterosexuals which had survived an attempted appeal by the state. It was cited by the defendant-appellant in *Schochet v. State*.

Steven Adam Schochet was charged with rape and anal and oral intercourse after he had sex with Dovie Sullivan, a recently divorced woman, in her home in the early morning hours of October 4, 1986. Sullivan and Schochet told distinctly different stories about what happened that night. According to Sullivan, she was sitting at home with her young daughter sleeping in the next room, listening to music and drinking while celebrating her recent divorce. She responded to a knock on the door by Schochet, whom she did not know, at 12:30 a.m. Schochet claimed to be looking for his friend "Denise" and asked if he could use the telephone to locate her. Sullivan allowed Schochet into her apartment. She claimed that he then forced her to have sex with him, including anal and oral sex, and then went to sleep on the floor of her bedroom. In the morning, Schochet remained in Sullivan's bedroom while she gave her daughter breakfast and sent her off to school. Then Schochet left, and Sullivan went to sleep. As she was getting ready to go to work later on, Schochet knocked on the door again and accused her of having given him "crabs." Schochet demanded that she give him money so he could go to a doctor. Sullivan refused and would not open the door and Schochet went away. When Sullivan returned home from work, she saw Schochet's car parked in the lot. After she got to her apartment, policemen came to question her about an allegation of "child abuse" and left a telephone number to call if she wanted to talk. Later, a female detective visited Sullivan, and Sullivan gave the detective a statement about her encounters with Schochet, which led to the charges against him.

Schochet told a very different story. He had been attending a fraternity party in College Park, and left to visit his friend Denise. When he arrived at her apartment, he was told she was at a party in another building. Looking for the party, he heard loud music from an apartment and thought that was the place. He knocked, Sullivan opened the door, and he asked for Denise. Claiming she could not hear him because the music was too loud, Sullivan asked him in, sat him down, and gave him a drink. While he sat drinking on the sofa, she began to kiss him, unzipped his pants, and performed fellatio. She invited him to the bedroom and they had intercourse, which did not include any anal sex. The next morning Schochet remained quietly in the bedroom while Sullivan got her daughter off to school. He left when she asked him to. When he discovered that she had given him "crabs," he went back to ask if she would take him to a doctor or give him money for treatment. When she refused, he felt "used and angry" and in retaliation called the police with a false report of "child abuse" against Sullivan.

After the close of evidence, Schochet's attorney, Public Defender Alan H. Murrell, of Baltimore, asked Montgomery County Circuit Court Judge Irma S. Raker to instruct the jury that consent was a defense to the charges of sodomy (anal sex) and fellatio (oral sex), which were separate crimes under Maryland law. He also asked for a charge that the law did not apply to consensual sex between adults in private. Raker denied both requests and instructed

the jury, in effect, that Schochet's own testimony showed a violation of the fellatio statute. The jury found Schochet not guilty of every count except fellatio, which was covered by article 27, section 554, of the Maryland Penal Code ("Unnatural and Perverted Sexual Practice"). Judge Raker ultimately sentenced Schochet to five years imprisonment, with the sentence suspended during a five year probation period. Schochet appealed to the Maryland Court of Special Appeals, the intermediate appellate court.

At oral argument, Schochet's appellate counsel, Joseph P. Suntum, of Bethesda, and Assistant Attorney General Gary E. Bair joined issue on the constitutionality of the statute. The American Civil Liberties Union of Maryland filed an *amicus* brief supporting Suntum's position. Suntum argued that section 554 was unconstitutional as applied to adult heterosexuals in private, that Judge Raker had considered improper factors in her sentencing decision, and that the imposition of a five-year sentence for this offense constituted cruel and unusual punishment. Schochet lost his appeal on all counts. In his opinion of May 19, 1988, Judge Charles E. Moylan, Jr., held that the law was constitutional and dismissed the objections with regard to the sentence.

Moylan's opinion was an extended, painstaking examination of the federal privacy precedents up to that time. Although the Maryland Declaration of Human Rights had been held to have a due process component, the court had consistently held it to be no broader than the Due Process Clause of the Fourteenth Amendment, so the court was concerned only with the reach of federal privacy doctrine. And Moylan found, after a careful, selective reading of all the significant federal cases, including *Bowers v. Hardwick*, that the federal right of privacy did not extend to the sexual activities of unmarried heterosexuals.

Following the lead of the Supreme Court's opinion in *Hardwick*, Moylan examined each of the key privacy precedents and found language in each suggesting that the ruling was narrowly focused on the particular issue in the case and, in many cases, asserting that the Court was not deciding broader issues or casting doubt on the validity of laws penalizing various forms of sexual conduct. Beginning with Justice John Marshall Harlan's dissenting opinion in *Poe v. Ullman* (1961), which he identified as the real starting point for the modern constitutional right of privacy, Moylan found a concern with issues of reproductive choice, not sexual activity as such. In *Griswold*, Justice William O. Douglas had framed the Court's opinion in terms of the privacy inhering in the marital relationship. While it was true that Justice Brennan had written in *Eisenstadt* that the right of privacy inhered in the individual, not the marital couple, nonetheless he had gone on to say that it protected the individual's right in fundamental matters such as procreative choice and had denied that the import of this ruling was to invalidate all state regulations of nonmarital heterosexual conduct. Moylan urged great caution in placing reliance on the more far-reaching statements in the Court's opinion in *Eisenstadt*. "Because isolated phrases from *Eisenstadt v. Baird* are frequently lifted out of context, it is important to get a careful handle on precisely what *Eisenstadt v. Baird* has held," he cautioned.

> It is not primarily a due process case at all, although it does stand for the proposition that the decision of whether to beget a child is part of the fundamental right to privacy.... *Eisenstadt v. Baird* is primarily an equal protection case. It strongly suggests that if the purpose of the law were to discourage sexual relations outside of marriage, a legislative discrimination between married persons and unmarried persons would be a rational one and would not offend the equal protection clause.

Finally, Moylan found nothing in *Carey v. Population Services* that would shake the contours of the privacy right identified in *Eisenstadt*. Indeed, the *Carey* opinion had spoken in terms of procreative choice rather than a broader right of privacy, only seven members of the Court participated in the case, and Justice Brennan's famous comment that the Court had not marked the outer limits of the right of privacy was in a portion of the opinion joined by only four Justices.

By contrast, the Court had summarily affirmed in *Doe v. Commonwealth's Attorney* and had articulated a rationale in *Bowers v. Hardwick* that persuaded Moylan that the Court was not ready to find constitutional protection for nonmarital sex, and perhaps not even for marital sodomy. "The failure of homosexuals to qualify for constitutional protection certainly did not seem to be based upon any moral value judgment in favor of heterosexuality over homosexuality," he commented. "The decision either exempted everyone from coverage, or, at most, was based upon the limited coverage of the right to privacy, which would appear to embrace sexual intimacy within marriage but not outside marriage, regardless of whether the extramarital intimacy were heterosexual or homosexual." The Court's "catalogue" of the "limited subject matter" covered by the right to privacy "would seem to have no more place for unmarried heterosexuals than for homosexuals." Indeed, the Court had explicitly rejected the claim that "any kind of private sexual conduct between consenting adults" would be constitutionally protected, citing *Carey* twice on this point.

"The painstaking scrutiny of every word the Supreme Court has written on the subject of the constitutional right to privacy does not yield any evidence that that right covers the type of activity before us in this case," Moylan asserted. Indeed, spread throughout all the Supreme Court's sexual privacy decisions were explicit statements that the right of privacy did not cover a variety of heterosexual activities, including adultery and incest. Justice Harlan had explicitly said that homosexuality was not covered, and Justice Arthur J. Goldberg had reiterated that point in his concurring opinion in *Griswold*. At one time or another in the two decades since *Griswold*, at least eleven Justices had gone on record in one way or another saying either that the right of privacy did not necessarily extend beyond the issues of contraception and abortion, or that it did not necessarily protect from state regulation all consensual sexual activity. "In the absence of any indication from the Supreme Court that a statute such as our Art. 27, sec. 554, at least as applied to unmarried persons, is unconstitutional and in view of numerous indications that such a statute, so applied, is constitutional, we conclude that Judge Raker, in making her ruling upon this issue, was not in error." Just to drive the point home, Moylan devoted several paragraphs to reviewing prior Maryland decisions upholding the constitutionality of section 554.

Amici had strongly argued that changing social mores would justify the court's invalidating the law. Citing studies by the Kinsey Institute and Masters and Johnson, they argued that "modes of sexual expression once thought to be 'unnatural' or 'perverted' are now part of the commonplace experience of a significant majority of Americans, married and unmarried, heterosexual and homosexual." While conceding that this might be true, Moylan said the argument was misdirected and should be made to the legislature. Reviewing the history of sodomy law reform, he asserted that it had been primarily a history of legislative response to changing times rather than judicial fiat. Although the Maryland legislature had rejected a post-*Hardwick* attempt to repeal the state's laws against sodomy and fellatio, there was nothing to prevent reformers from approaching the legislature again. As Justice Hugo L. Black had commented in dissent in *Griswold*, it was up to the legislative branch, not the courts, to reflect current community standards in their criminal code. Unless the Constitution specifically withdrew a subject from legislative consideration, the legislature was where that subject belonged. Finally, since a suspended sentence of five years in prison was far less than the maximum allowed under the statute of ten years, the court concluded that Schochet's sentence was not "cruel or unusual punishment."

Moylan's opinion sparked a lengthy dissent by Judge Alan M. Wilner. While agreeing that the Supreme Court's opinion in *Bowers v. Hardwick* foreclosed constitutional challenge to the law as applied to same-sex couples, he argued that neither the Supreme Court nor the Maryland Court of Appeals, the state's highest court, had directly answered the question whether consensual heterosexual fellatio by adults in private could constitutionally be prohibited. Since there was "a lack of controlling precedent in this State clearly mandating one result or the other," he was inclined to give a more generous reading to the federal privacy precedents and find the statute unconstitutional as applied to this conduct. "Judge Moylan reviews in depth and in some detail pronounce-

ments from the Justices of the Supreme Court since *Poe v. Ullman*, concluding from some grand matrix of all their sayings that this activity is probably not protected, at least when carried on by unmarried couples," he said. "What the majority, in effect, has done is to take a frozen slice of Constitutional history, from 1965 to 1987, and to assume that this steadily emerging Constitutional principle will develop no further. That is a nice conservative view, but it is unrealistic, because it leaves a most fundamental legal principle in a state of absolute illogic."

Wilner argued that "there *is* a Constitutionally protected zone of privacy, ill-defined perhaps but nonetheless existing, that shields certain fundamental personal conduct and expression from substantial governmental interference." Furthermore, he was ready to argue that consensual fellatio fell within the zone, leaving it free from regulation unless the government could advance a compelling interest in regulating it. Reaching back to Justice Louis D. Brandeis's famous dissenting language about "the right to be let alone" in *Olmstead v. United States* (1928), which had been quoted with approval by the Court in *Stanley v. Georgia*, Wilner asserted that the right of privacy predated the contraception cases and had a deeper, broader, more general meaning than a right to procreative choice. Rooted in concepts of personal liberty, he found the privacy right properly to extend to "sexual contact between men and women."

> Throughout history, the subject of sex—i.e., sexual contact and intercourse—has been shrouded in hushed tones and mystery, encrusted with ecclesiastical armor. The whole thrust of society, usually led by old men, has been to place barriers of one kind or another on the expression of this most basic function of all living things, including people. To the extent that these barriers were intended to promote, protect, exalt, and preserve the institution of marriage and with it the nuclear family, they obviously had a significant and useful societal, economic, and therefore political purpose and could reasonably be regarded as within the proper purview of government, even one founded upon notions of social contract, as ours was. But if and to the extent they have no such connection or cease to have any such connection, and simply regulate this

kind of very personal conduct for no apparent reason, the question of authority is legitimately raised.

While the Supreme Court had moved haltingly in this area, said Wilner, it had not limited the privacy protection to married couples, and had not limited it merely to decisions regarding procreation, as *Roe v. Wade* and *Stanley v. Georgia* made clear. "What makes intimate sexual contact between men and women less private because they are not married to one another?" he asked. "What makes the intrusion into the bedroom less repulsive because the occupants are not husband and wife? What makes it less repulsive if the object of the search is not contraceptives but the form of sexual expression?" For Wilner, it was impossible to exclude the conduct at issue from constitutional protection.

Here he again parted company from the court, finding highly relevant the sociological data introduced by the *amicus* brief. In *Hardwick*, the Court had upheld the Georgia sodomy law on the argument that the law expressed the moral view of the citizens of Georgia. Well, the social scientists had proved to Wilner's satisfaction that a law banning heterosexual fellatio in private did not reflect the moral view of the public, since it seemed that a majority of them, perhaps an overwhelming majority, were doing it quite happily. "The majority [of the court], apparently, views this as a matter for the Legislature alone to consider, but I submit that, if the only asserted basis for a criminal statute is a perception of public morality, it is a matter for the courts as well," he asserted. "To hold otherwise would be to allow the power, under the guise of protecting public morality, to impose criminal sanctions on masturbation and all variety of non-coital sexual contact, even down to kissing and hand-holding, when carried on by consenting adults in private. Would the majority commit that authority too to the State Legislature? If not, why not?"

Citing a string of decisions from other states invalidating laws penalizing sodomy or fellatio between heterosexual adults, Wilner asserted that he was not alone in his view, and further asserted that a right of privacy covering this activity was equally well grounded in the Maryland Constitution's due process protection.

Schochet appealed to the Maryland Court of Appeals, which held oral argument on the issue of the constitutionality of the statute. Additional *amicus* briefs were submitted on behalf of various scientific societies in addition to the ACLU of Maryland. After the argument, the court decided to add a new issue to the appeal, and scheduled further argument on the question whether as a matter of statutory interpretation the law could be construed to avoid the constitutional issue by holding it inapplicable to consensual activity in private between heterosexual adults. Having satisfied itself that the statute could be narrowly construed, the court announced on October 9, 1990, that it was reversing Schochet's conviction on that ground, with two dissenting judges voting to affirm the opinion of the lower court and one concurring based on agreement with Judge Wilner's dissent below.

The court's opinion by Judge John C. Eldridge showed great reluctance for the court to get involved in the controversial issue of the right of privacy. It was clear from reviewing reported opinions from other jurisdictions that there was an even split of authority over whether laws penalizing consensual heterosexual activity between unmarried adults were constitutional. Rather than have to interject itself into that quagmire, the court preferred to find some way to construe the Maryland law to avoid the problem. Relying on its prior rulings that substantial constitutional questions should be avoided if at all possible, the court engrafted a limitation on the application of the statute that had no clear basis in its language or legislative history, by emphasizing that none of the reported decisions upholding the law and its application to particular facts involved precisely the kind of conduct charged against Schochet (i.e., consensual heterosexual fellatio between unmarried adults in private).

The state had argued that the statute "makes no reference to the factors of consent-nonconsent, commercial-noncommercial, etc. . . . The provision applies to '[e]very person . . . who shall be convicted of placing his or her sexual organ in the mouth of any other person.'" According to Eldridge, the state's argument overlooked the "very broad and sweeping nature" of the language, which, in the court's view, rendered the statute "reasonably susceptible to different constructions." Since the statute did not say anything specific about consent and the other relevant issues, the court was free to read in whatever limitations it found appropriate to avoid having to pass on the law's constitutionality. Indeed, the Maryland Court of Appeals had done exactly that in the past, imposing narrow constructions on a variety of laws that would have posed substantial constitutional questions had they been strictly construed according to the plain meaning of their broad language.

As to the precise issue in contention, Eldridge cited the Massachusetts Supreme Judicial Court's opinion in *Commonwealth v. Balthazar* (1974), which had imposed a narrow reading on the Massachusetts "unnatural and lascivious acts" law to avoid constitutional problems. Applying the "principle that a statute will be construed so as to avoid a serious constitutional question," Eldridge held that "under that principle, sec. 554 does not encompass consensual, noncommercial, heterosexual activity between adults in the privacy of the home."

Eldridge found his main support for this proposition in the reported decisions of the Maryland courts. Every decision upholding or enforcing section 554 either involved homosexuals, sex with minors, nonconsensual sex, or sex "in places which could not be considered private." "Despite the many cases in this Court involving sections 554 and 553 [the companion sodomy law], none has been a prosecution based on consensual, noncommercial, heterosexual activity between adults in the privacy of the home. This is a strong indication that such conduct is not within the contemplation of sec. 554."

Eldridge rejected the state's argument that such a narrow construction was inconsistent with the law's legislative history. The law had first been enacted in 1916, and there was no recorded legislative history. The state was relying primarily on the reenactment as part of a penal law reform in 1976, when a proposal to repeal the consensual sodomy and fellatio provisions had been removed from the final bill by amendment. Eldridge asserted that the legislative history did not indicate why the legislature

decided to preserve the existing prohibitions. Since construing the statute as Eldridge proposed to do left section 554 "quite viable" in a range of circumstances, he saw no inconsistency with the legislative history.

Chief Judge Robert C. Murphy dissented in an opinion joined by Judge John F. McAuliffe. They argued that the opinion of the Court of Special Appeals was correct and that the court had misapplied the principle of limiting construction to avoid constitutional questions. Since the statute had been unchanged since its 1916 enactment, and it was logical to assume that the 1916 legislature intended to outlaw all fellatio, whether performed consensually or nonconsensually, in public or private, there was no basis in the legislative history for a narrower construction. As to the argument that the broad wording of the statute left room for such construction, Murphy argued just the opposite. The statute's "all-encompassing language was plainly intended to reach those 'unnatural' and 'perverted' sexual practices, therein so vividly described, without exception. No other *reasonable* conclusion is evident."

Since the constitutional issue had to be reached, Murphy would reach it consistently with Judge Moylan's decision below, and he echoed Moylan's comment that if sexual mores had indeed changed to the degree argued by Schochet, the legislature could amend the law to adopt the narrow construction that the court was improperly imposing in this case.

Judge Howard S. Chasanow concurred separately to argue that Judge Wilner had got it right: the constitutional right of privacy extended to this conduct, and the statute could not constitutionally be used to punish Schochet for what the jury concluded had happened in this case.

The decisions in *Post* and *Schochet* may illustrate what will become a new trend in the post-*Hardwick* world. Both cases typify those in which sodomy laws are used against heterosexuals: either forcible sodomy or commercial sodomy is alleged in the complaint, but the jury believes the defendant's argument that the conduct was consensual or that there was no monetary exchange. Nonetheless, the jury is instructed to convict on such a finding, because the law makes no exception for consensual, noncommercial conduct. In these circumstances, the constitutionality of the law is necessarily implicated, and the overwhelming evidence of broad public participation in the kind of activity the law covers makes it very tempting for courts to conclude that there is no longer a rational basis for the law, even if they do not agree that the constitutional right of privacy covers the situation.

Case References

Bowers v. Hardwick, 478 U.S. 186 (1986)

Carey v. Population Services International, 431 U.S. 678 (1977)

Commonwealth v. Balthazar, 366 Mass. 298, 318 N.E.2d 478 (1974)

Doe v. Commonwealth's Attorney for City of Richmond, 403 F. Supp. 1199 (E.D. Va. 1975), affirmed without opinion, 425 U.S. 901 (1976)

Eisenstadt v. Baird, 405 U.S. 438 (1972)

Griswold v. Connecticut, 381 U.S. 479 (1965)

Olmstead v. United States, 277 U.S. 438 (1928)

Poe v. Ullman, 367 U.S. 497 (1961)

Roe v. Wade, 410 U.S. 113 (1973)

Stanley v. Georgia, 394 U.S. 557 (1969)

Warner v. State, 489 P.2d 526 (Okla. Crim. App. 1971)

CHAPTER 3
SPEECH AND ASSOCIATION

The First Amendment of the U.S. Constitution (and its state constitutional analogues) guaranteeing freedom of speech and of the press has come to play a significant role in the interaction of law and sexuality. Especially since the U.S. Supreme Court began to apply the First Amendment to state governments under the theory of incorporation through the Due Process Clause of the Fourteenth Amendment, courts have had to grapple with a variety of arguments about the validity of state and local governmental regulations of communicative activities of a sexual nature, including pornographic books, pictures and films, and public nudity. In addition to questions about the validity of state laws, the federal role in distributing the mail; funding artists and health educators; and regulating interstate telephone, radio, and television communications has increasingly brought federal policies concerning sexually explicit speech under constitutional challenge. While most of the cases on communication in this chapter involve state actions, cases pending as of the beginning of 1992 promised significant federal decisions (perhaps even at the Supreme Court level) soon on the validity of restrictions on sexually explicit art and health education materials.

The First Amendment has also spawned significant decisions about political advocacy of decriminalization of sexual activity and about the rights of persons to associate with others on the basis of their sexual orientation or interests.

Among the cases on associational rights and advocacy considered in this chapter are those dealing with the rights of lesbians and gay men to patronize public accommodations that serve liquor, the right to testify or demonstrate in support of political goals of liberation from oppression for sexual minorities, and the right to form associations to advance such goals.

Cases dealing with communication or associational issues in other chapters include *Eisenstadt v. Baird* (No. 5), the various cases on sexual solicitation discussed in chapter 2 (Nos. 18, 20, 23, 32), *Loving v. Virginia* (No. 48), *Moore v. City of East Cleveland* (No. 53), *Gay Law Students Association v. Pacific Telephone & Telegraph Co.* (No. 77), *BenShalom v. Marsh* (No. 94), and virtually all the cases discussed in chapter 7 (Public Education).

Speech and Association: Readings

Caldwell, G., "The Seventh Circuit in *BenShalom v. Marsh*: Equating Speech With Conduct," 24 *Loyola of Los Angeles Law Review* 421 (Note) (January 1991)

Dee, J.L., "From 'Pure Speech' to Dial-a-Porn: Negligence, First Amendment Law and the Hierarchy of Protected Speech," 13 *Communications & the Law* 27 (Dec. 1991).

Editorial Staff, "The Content Distinction in Free Speech Analysis After *Renton*," 102 *Harvard Law Review* 1904 (June 1989)

Gomez, J., "The Public Expression of Lesbian-Gay Personhood as Protected Speech," 1 *Law & Inequality: A Journal of Theory & Practice* 121 (June 1983)

Karst, K.L., "The Freedom of Intimate Association," 89 *Yale Law Journal* 624 (1980)

McKee, S.H., "Dial-a-Porn: A Private Affair?," 24 *Tulsa Law Journal* 239 (Winter 1988)

34. THE GAY BAR AND THE RIGHT TO HANG OUT TOGETHER

Stoumen v. Reilly, 37 Cal. 2d 713, 234 P.2d 969 (1951) (en banc), reversing 222 P.2d 678 (Cal. App., 1st Dist. 1950). *Vallerga v. Department of Alcoholic Beverage Control*, 53 Cal. 2d 313, 347 P.2d 909, 1 Cal. Rptr. 494 (1959) (en banc), vacating 343 P.2d 54 and 334 P.2d 294 (Cal. App., 1st Dist. 1959).

Before the criminal law reforms sparked by the Model Penal Code and the active lobbying efforts of gay activists during the 1960s and 1970s, "sodomy" and solicitation to commit it were serious felony offenses in virtually every state, and legislators and law enforcement officials in many jurisdictions believed that any assembly of homosexuals in one place was a virtual criminal conspiracy. Restaurants, bars, and social clubs serving a gay clientele were considered "disorderly houses," subject to frequent police raids and shakedowns, occasionally leading to the revocation of liquor licenses or court orders of complete closure of the establishment. Proof that homosexuals were "resorting" to a particular establishment was obtained by sending handsome young plainclothes detectives into the premises on undercover operations. They would note down the stereotypical behaviors of "queers" and "perverts." Responding to the overtures of the gay patrons, they would share drinks, flirt, make dates, and then arrest their unsuspecting victims as soon as they left the premises.

In the immediate post-World War II period, as the first covert gay organizations such as the Mattachine Society were formed in major West and East Coast cities, the first legal challenges arose to these law enforcement practices. It is difficult forty years later for those living in parts of the United States where gay liberation has taken significant hold to appreciate the extraordinary bravery on the part of the litigants and their attorneys, but anyone reading the incredible language in court opinions will begin to appreciate the scorn and opprobrium heaped on homosexuals at that time in language that even the most homophobic judge would today feel compelled to avoid in a published decision. The first major appellate decisions signaling a new freedom of association for gays came from the California courts in the 1950s. The most important cases involved a San Francisco bar, The Black Cat, and an Oakland establishment, The First And Last Chance Bar.

When The Black Cat opened in San Francisco, it quickly became a popular meeting place for gay men and a target for police harassment. While the proprietors and patrons made every attempt to keep the atmosphere in the bar very prim and proper, plainclothes detectives quickly gathered the evidence necessary to convince the State Board of Equalization that the bar had become a "hangout" for homosexuals. Proceedings were initiated to revoke the liquor license of Sol M. Stoumen, proprietor of the bar, pursuant to section 58 of the California Beverage Control Act, and section 61, which prohibited sale of liquor to minors. Section 58 provided that every licensee who permitted his premises to be used as a "disorderly house" or as a place to which people resort for purposes that were injurious to the public morals was guilty of a violation of that section. Among the other charges, the Board asserted that the bartender had sold a beer to a 21-year-old man (the age of majority for liquor purchase in California was 21).

Stoumen was advised by a member of the Board that he should not retain counsel for the hearing, so he represented himself. The hearing officer ruled against Stoumen on both charges and recommended indefinite suspension of the liquor license. The Board voted to accept the findings and recommendation of the hearing officer that during the period between September 3, 1948, and August 15, 1949, the time of the police investigations, Stoumen had permitted his premises "to be used as a disorderly house in that during that period of time persons of known homosexual tendencies patronized said premises and used said premises as a meeting place." The Board also found that he had served beer to a minor. The Board ordered suspension of Stoumen's liquor license.

Stoumen retained counsel, Morris Lowenthal, who filed an action in the Superior Court for San Francisco against Chairman George R. Reilly and the other members of the Board, asking the court to review and reverse the Board's order suspending his license. The government, represented by Deputy Attorney General J. Albert Hutchinson, moved to dismiss the action on the merits. Judge Robert L. McWilliams received the hearing record from the Board and heard oral arguments from both parties before rendering an extensive opinion which was adopted, in full, by the First District Court of Appeal on Stoumen's subsequent appeal. McWilliams rejected all the objections to the procedures used in the Board's hearing process. Then, McWilliams found that the Board had sufficient basis to conclude that The Black Cat had become a hangout for homosexuals, and this finding was adequate under the statute to justify suspending its liquor license. Since this basis was established, McWilliams held that it was unnecessary to rule on the charge of selling liquor to a minor.

McWilliams's opinion is worth quoting, since it colorfully expresses the flavor of the times. After quoting the finding of the Board that Stoumen had allowed homosexuals to patronize The Black Cat and use it as a meeting place, he said:

> It would be a sorry commentary on the law as well as on the morals of the community to find that persons holding liquor licenses could permit their premises to be used month after month as meeting places for persons of known homosexual tendencies with all of the implications that may reasonably be drawn from that last phrase and the people's legal representatives find themselves helpless to take action against the holders of such licenses.
>
> Counsel for Petitioner argue that persons of homosexual tendencies may not lawfully be prohibited from collecting in groups in restaurants for the purpose of securing meals and alcoholic beverages.
>
> An occasional fortuitous meeting of such persons at restaurants for the innocent purpose mentioned is one thing. But for a proprietor of a restaurant knowingly to permit his premises to be regularly used "as a meeting place" by persons of the type mentioned with all of the potentialities for evil and immorality drawing out of such meetings is, in my opinion, conduct

of an entirely different nature which justifies action on the part of the Board of Equalization.

Lowenthal argued in his brief that the recently published "Kinsey Report," which asserted that more than a third of the adult male population had engaged at least once after puberty in some type of same-sex activity leading to orgasm, showed that homosexuality was a commonly occurring phenomenon such that a "social taboo" against homosexuals was unjustified. Commenting that it "will not be necessary to give that phase of Petitioner's argument any extended consideration," McWilliams merely cited the sodomy provisions of the Penal Code and intoned, "Any complaint against those provisions based on the theory that the mores of our times have changed since the enactment of those sections should be directed to the Legislature and not to the courts." Thus began the extended history of judicial unwillingness to consider the findings of social science research in weighing the rationality of laws criminalizing same-sex activity.

McWilliams also sustained the Board on the second count of selling beer to a minor, but found the punishment of suspension of the license was excessive. This was all academic, however, since McWilliams ruled that the first count alone justified suspension of the license. Stoumen's appeal to the First District Court of Appeal was fruitless. In an opinion released October 10, 1950, Presiding Justice John T. Nourse wrote for a unanimous panel that all of Stoumen's procedural objections were without merit, and that "the learned trial judge filed a written opinion correctly disposing of all these issues. This opinion we approve and adopt as our reasons for an affirmance of the judgment." Thus Nourse and his colleagues escaped the distasteful duty of having to write about the merits of the case themselves.

The appellate panel denied a petition for rehearing on November 9, but the California Supreme Court granted a hearing on December 7. In what may have been the first significant appellate victory of the young gay rights movement, Chief Justice Phil S. Gibson's opinion reversed the court of appeal and ordered the trial court to enjoin the Board of Equalization from suspending Stoumen's license.

First taking up the assertion that section 58 justified suspension of a liquor license for allowing gays to congregate at an establishment, Gibson observed:

> There was no evidence of any illegal or immoral conduct on the premises or that the patrons resorted to the restaurant for purposes injurious to public morals.... The terms of the section refer to conduct on the premises or resort thereto for improper purposes, and it is clear that it would be necessary to read something into that section before it could be construed as an attempt to regulate mere patronage by any particular class of persons without regard to their conduct on the premises.... Members of the public of lawful age have a right to patronize a public restaurant and bar so long as they are acting properly and are not committing illegal or immoral acts; the proprietor has no right to exclude or eject a patron "except for good cause," and if he does so without good cause he is liable in damages.

Gibson analogized the case to rulings in New York and Oklahoma holding that a restaurant had not violated the law by serving prostitutes.

> The fact that the Black Cat was reputed to be a "hangout" for homosexuals indicates merely that it was a meeting place for such persons.... Unlike evidence that an establishment is reputed to be a house of prostitution, which means a place where prostitution is practiced and thus necessarily implies the doing of illegal or immoral acts on the premises, testimony that a restaurant and bar is reputed to be a meeting place for a certain class of persons contains no such implication. Even habitual or regular meetings may be for purely social and harmless purposes, such as the consumption of food and drink, and it is to be presumed that a person is innocent of crime or wrong and that the law has been obeyed.

Gibson also rejected the Board's argument that it had an independent basis for closing down The Black Cat in its authorization under the California Constitution, article XX, section 22, giving it "the power, in its discretion, to deny or revoke any specific liquor license if it shall determine for good cause that the granting or continuance of such license would be contrary to public welfare or morals." Stressing that the Board had to have "good cause" to deny or revoke a license, Gibson asserted that "in order to establish 'good cause' for suspension of

plaintiff's license, something more must be shown than that many of his patrons were homosexuals and that they used his restaurant and bar as a meeting place." Without going into any detail, the court was holding that the mere association of homosexuals on the premises, without evidence of unlawful acts, was insufficient justification for denying a liquor license to the proprietor.

Gibson dealt briefly with the allegation of sale of beer to a minor, noting that the young man looked older than his years and, in any event, that the usual punishment in such cases varied from a reprimand to a limited suspension of not more than thirty days. Thus, it was appropriate to send the case back to the Board for an appropriate determination of penalty on this charge, while barring the Board from suspending the license indefinitely on the first charge.

In some respects the court's decision was a major breakthrough. The highest court of a major state had ruled that it could not be assumed that an assembly of homosexuals was unlawful *per se*, and indeed that homosexuals had a right to assemble for lawful purposes of socializing. Unfortunately, the court's opinion was long on factual assertion and short on careful legal analysis. No particular constitutional provision or statute was cited in support of the asserted right of assembly, and the decision was quite narrowly drawn. Its protection for social meeting places for gay people seemed illusory in the years that followed, for two reasons. First, by basing its decision explicitly on the construction of the Alcoholic Beverage Control law and a particular reading of the constitutional authorization for the Board of Equalization, the court was apparently leaving the matter open for simple legislative overruling. Second, and more important, within a legal framework that criminalized same-sex sexual activity and solicitation for same, it would be an easy matter for plainclothes policemen to document the sort of illegal activity that the court had stated could be used to justify a license revocation.

In 1955, the California legislature amended the Business and Professions Code to require the Board of Equalization to suspend the liquor license of any establishment where the licensee had permitted unlawful gambling or the illegal sale of narcotics, or where "the premises of the licensee are a resort for prostitutes, pimps, panderers, or sexual perverts." The new law also provided that "the character of the premises as such a resort may be proved by the general reputation of the premises in the community." The intermediate appellate courts ruled consistently through the mid-1950s that evidence of same-sex dancing, kissing, caressing, or solicitation known to the proprietor or his employees was sufficient under the statute to justify revoking a liquor license under this section. They were careful to state that in no case was the license being revoked merely because homosexuals were congregating in a particular bar, since the California Supreme Court had seemed to indicate by its decision in *Stoumen* that homosexuals had some sort of right, the source of which was unclear, to congregate so long as they did nothing "immoral." It was clear to the courts, however, that affectionate touching and same-sex dancing were immoral.

For example, in *Kershaw v. Department of Alcoholic Beverage Control* (1957), the First District Court of Appeal, noting evidence of this type of conduct, stated that it

> warrants inferences that the place is customarily and regularly used by persons who are prone to and do engage in aberrant sexual conduct to the extent of qualifying as "sex perverts" under the statute, and that they use this public place as a haunt or gathering place for mutual stimulation of their sexually aberrant urges and a place of assignation for the renewal of old and the making of new associations looking toward the consummation of those urges.

Reacting to the state's argument that the legislature intended to overrule *Stoumen* by enacting the new provisions, the *Kershaw* court replied (in the face of plain language to the contrary) that "it would seem a fair inference to conclude that in making that amendment the Legislature acted in light of and consistently with the rule of *Stoumen*, by inference excluding from the coverage of subdivision (e) the type of conduct which the Supreme Court had declared harmless and not inimical to public welfare or morals. The court having so recently and with such clarity said it, why should the Legislature say it again?" Thus, in *Kershaw*, *Nickola v. Munro* (1958), and *Vallerga v. Department of Alcoholic Beverage Control* (1959), the First District Court of Appeal held and reiterated that the new law validly required lifting the liquor license of any establishment where "sex perverts" (which all homosexuals were, by definition) congregated, so long as the police presented evidence of conduct involving open displays of affection. The police raids and license revocations continued unabated.

But the California Supreme Court was apparently dissatisfied with the way things were going, because it agreed to hear an appeal by Albert L. Vallerga and Mary Azar, proprietors of The First And Last Chance Bar, in Oakland, from the court of appeal's decision in their case. Morris Lowenthal, who had developed a specialty of representing the harassed owners of Northern California's gay bars, appeared as *amicus curiae* with his firm in support of Vallerga's trial counsel, J. Bruce Fratis and the firm of Golden and Stefan, of Oakland, against a team of lawyers from the Attorney General's Office. Sitting *en banc*, the supreme court unanimously ruled on December 23, 1959, that the new law did not lend itself to the limiting construction adopted by the lower courts and was unconstitutional because it went beyond the grounds authorized by the people of the state when they adopted the constitutional provision specifying when liquor licenses were to be revoked.

In many of these cases, the proprietors had defended themselves by claiming that their restaurants or bars had not become regular meeting places for homosexuals, that it was merely coincidental that many people who seemed to be homosexuals were observed there by the police, and that in any event the proprietors were unaware of the nature of the crowd or of any improper conduct taking place. In this case, however, there had been no pretenses by the owners of the bar that it was anything other than a business specifically established to serve homosexuals, as they testified. On that basis, and without making any findings about conduct taking place, the hearing officer for the Alcoholic Beverage Control Board found that the literal language of the statute had been satisfied, and that furthermore "it would be contrary to public welfare and morals within the meaning of said words as used in Article XX,

Section 22, of the California Constitution" for the Board to allow the bar to continue serving liquor.

These findings had placed the court of appeal in a dilemma, for it had been holding with monotonous regularity that evidence of immoral conduct (such as two men dancing with each other) was necessary to justify a license revocation, as per the *Stoumen* decision. The state defended the Board's decision by arguing that the legislature had intended to overrule *Stoumen*. The court of appeal took two cracks at the case. In its initial opinion by Presiding Justice Raymond E. Peters issued January 27, 1959, the court reviewed the testimony before the hearing officer and noted that the police officers had reported a few "isolated acts" that might be relied on to justify the license revocation, such as women dancing with and kissing other women and making suggestive remarks to some of the plainclothes women detectives who entered the bar. There was also an incident of two men embracing affectionately, with one commenting to the bartender that "Arley and I are going steady," but this evidently took place out of sight of the employees of the bar. Apart from that, the main evidence from the police was that "the majority of the female customers were dressed in mannish attire, and that the patrons of the bar usually paired off men with men, and women with women."

The hearing officer, perhaps wisely under the circumstances, had not relied on this flimsy evidence to recommend revocation of the license, but instead drew the logical conclusion that gays were regular patrons of the bar and that the explicit language of the statute made that enough for revocation. Reiterating its prior holdings that "illegal or immoral conduct" was a necessary predicate to revocation, Justice Peters concluded:

> At most, the conduct observed indicated that the patrons were homosexuals. But that fact alone will not support the revocation. The conduct observed was not similar to the conduct observed in the *Kershaw* and *Nickola* cases which was held to support revocation orders. There the conduct was disgusting, immoral and illegal. It clearly demonstrated that the continuance of the licenses would be "contrary to public welfare and morals." The same cannot be said of the conduct observed here.

Rejecting all the contentions by the bar owners that the statute was unconstitutional, the court of appeal reversed the superior court's unpublished decision affirming the Board and sent the case back to the Board for consistent proceedings. The state was not satisfied with this result, however, petitioning the court for a rehearing so that it could present a full exposition of the legislative history of the new law in an attempt to persuade the court that *Stoumen* had indeed been overruled. The court granted a new hearing and considered voluminous evidence from the legislative record, but reiterated and adopted its prior decision on July 23, 1959. Vallerga promptly appealed the ruling upholding the constitutionality of the law, and the California Supreme Court granted a hearing on September 16. In a unanimous ruling contained in an opinion by Justice Thomas P. White, the Court held on December 23, 1959, that the new law was unconstitutional.

Noting that the lower courts had construed the 1955 amendment to the Alcoholic Beverage Control Act "in conformity with the holding in the *Stoumen* case" in accord with "the general rule of construction that where possible legislation will be construed to avoid unconstitutional applications," White asserted that such a limited construction was impossible in this case. "The language of that subdivision is too clear and unambiguous to permit any other meaning than that which the literal language conveys."

> Not only does it declare that the grounds for revocation are established if the prohibited classes "resort" on the premises, but it further makes the legislative intent all the more apparent by providing that the character of the premises "as a resort" may be proved by general reputation. To hold that by such language the Legislature intended that grounds for revocation existed only when objectionable conduct took place on the premises would constitute judicial legislation under the guise of interpretation.

However, added the court, this did not mean that *Nickola* and *Kershaw* had been wrongly decided by the First District Court of Appeal, because in both cases there was evidence of the kind of conduct that would justify license revocation under the Board's constitutional authority derived from article XX, section 22 (i.e., "good cause" for suspension to protect the public welfare and morals). Unfortunately for the Board, however, its hearing officer in this case had failed to make the requisite factual findings concerning conduct, basing the suspension entirely on the "inference" from the facts that homosexuals were using the bar as a "resort." For White, the evidence recited in the record would be "sufficient evidence of a display of sexual desires and urges which, when made in a public place as a continuing course of conduct, could reasonably be found by the trier of fact to be 'contrary to public welfare or morals.'" But the evidence had been controverted at the hearing, and the hearing officer made no findings based on it, so the court could not proceed on that basis. Furthermore, the official accusation filed against the bar had not mentioned any of the conduct, but merely invoked the statutory language. Consequently, the supreme court directed that the superior court issue a "peremptory writ of mandate" directing the Board to set aside its revocation order.

On the one hand, *Vallerga* was a victory, but really a pyrrhic victory. While declaring the statute unconstitutional, the court's opinion indicated that the minimal conduct to which police officers testified at trial might, if found to be proven on the record, be justification for revoking the liquor license under constitutional authority. While the decision marked a firm reiteration that the legislature was without constitutional authority to ban gays from congregating in a place regulated by the Alcoholic Beverage Control Board, it also reaffirmed that the Board had authority to revoke a license for "good cause" and that such relatively harmless activities as same-sex dancing and other public displays of affection could constitute "good cause," with no need to show unlawful solicitation or the commission of sodomy on the premises of the bar. This was brought home by the First District Court of Appeal's subsequent decision in *Morell v. Department of Alcoholic Beverage Control* (1962), affirming revocation of a license after undercover police provided evidence that gay people at San Francisco's 585 Club were soliciting each other to go home and have sex (which the law then described as soliciting "to commit a lewd and indecent act").

The California Supreme Court was the first to recognize the right of homosexuals to congregate in bars open to the public, but other jurisdictions soon followed its lead, both in upholding the revocation of liquor licenses when overt displays of affection took place and in requiring evidence that such was occurring before allowing a license to be revoked. Despite the symbolic importance of statements that homosexuals had the same rights as other citizens to congregate in public places for social intercourse and recreation, these decisions did not make the gay bars a safe place in which people could connect with others for romantic purposes, and it was not until the increasingly militant gay rights movement of the 1970s had organized to gain political power (and the state had moved to decriminalize consensual sodomy) that police actions predicated primarily on sexual conduct became a thing of the past. Police continued to carry out plainclothes operations to combat drug trafficking, and bar raids are still a frequent occurrence in some parts of the country, but they focus primarily on allegations (albeit sometimes pretextual) of serving liquor to minors, prostitution, and drug dealing.

The same pattern was followed in New York. The leading case was *Kerma Restaurant Corporation v. State Liquor Authority*, in which the state's highest court, the New York Court of Appeals, voted four to three in 1967 that even where evidence was presented of homosexual solicitation occurring on the premises, the liquor license could not be revoked unless there was evidence that the proprietor knew that the activities were occurring. Shortly thereafter, the court unanimously held in *Becker v. New York State Liquor Authority* that a bar owner who had allowed gay men to dance together in a close, intimate manner (including "embracing one another and gyrating and moving [and] feeling each other's private parts and posteriors") could be held to have the requisite knowledge of the activity to justify revoking his liquor license. In New York, as in California, routine crackdowns on gay bars for sexual activities declined in frequency as gay liberation organizations persuaded politicians that police activities should be directed elsewhere, although raids and prosecutions in response to allegations of drug dealing and prostitution continue to occur from time to time.

Case References

Becker v. New York State Liquor Authority, 21 N.Y.2d 289, 287 N.Y.S.2d 400, 234 N.E.2d 443 (1967)

Kerma Restaurant Corporation v. State Liquor Authority, 21 N.Y.2d 111, 286 N.Y.S. 822, 233 N.E.2d 833 (1967)

Kershaw v. Department of Alcoholic Beverage Control, 155 Cal. App. 2d 544, 318 P.2d 494 (App., 1st Dist. 1957)

Morell v. Department of Alcoholic Beverage Control, 204 Cal. App. 2d 504, 22 Cal. Rptr. 405 (App., 1st Dist. 1962)

Nickola v. Munro, 162 Cal. App. 2d 449, 328 P.2d 271 (App., 1st Dist. 1958)

35. PRURIENCE AND THE SUPREME COURT

Roth v. United States, 354 U.S. 476 (1957), affirming *United States v. Roth*, 237 F.2d 796 (2d Cir. 1956) and *People v. Alberts*, 292 P.2d 90 (Cal. Super., App. Dept., L.A. County 1955).

The expression of sexuality in words, pictures, and other media has been a troublesome issue in America from colonial times. The religious basis for the foundation of some of the colonies led to statutes against profanity and obscenity at an early point, and virtually all of the original states had laws affecting sexually oriented speech at the time the First Amendment was adopted. (The First Amendment provides, of course, that "Congress shall make no law abridging the freedom of speech or of the press.") The first federal obscenity law dates from 1821, and Congress repeatedly passed and recodified laws banning obscene matter from the mails. Surprisingly, however, it was not until 1957, in *Roth v. United States*, that the U.S. Supreme Court gave plenary consideration to the question whether the federal government or the states could punish the sale or distribution of obscene matter either directly or through the mails. Although the Court had stated in many prior cases its assumption that obscenity was not protected from prosecution, it had never previously addressed the issue squarely.

The *Roth* decision actually involved two criminal prosecutions, one under a California statute and the other under the federal postal laws. California authorities prosecuted David S. Alberts, the owner of a mail-order business, on charges that "he had lewdly kept for sale obscene and indecent books, and that he had lewdly written, composed, and published an advertisement of them," all in violation of section 311 of the California Penal Code. Alberts, who waived a jury, was convicted by the trial judge applying the state statutory standard that a book was obscene "if it has a substantial tendency to deprave or corrupt its readers by inciting lascivious thoughts or arousing lustful desire." His attorneys, C. Richard Maddox, of Beverly Hills, and Stanley Fleishman, of Hollywood, appealed the conviction before Judge Charles J. Griffin in the Beverly Hills Municipal Court, to the Appellate Department of the Los Angeles County Superior Court. A unanimous panel of the court ruled on December 29, 1955, that Alberts' conviction should be affirmed, accepting Deputy District Attorney Jere J. Sullivan's argument that the Penal Code provision was constitutional. According to the brief opinion by Judge Edward T. Bishop, the words "obscene or indecent" in the statute were not "unconstitutionally indefinite," having been upheld in criminal statutes by the state and federal courts in "a large number of cases." While it was not always easy to decide "on which side of the line a book should be placed," such problems attached to virtually all criminal statutes. The court also rejected a make-weight argument that the state was preempted from prosecuting Alberts because of the existence of the federal postal laws on obscenity, and said that it saw "no good purpose to be served" by discussing any other issues raised by the appeal. Responding on January 12, 1956, to a motion for rehearing, the court reiterated that it had no obligation to respond to all the issues raised by the parties in writing. Alberts quickly filed a petition with the U.S. Supreme Court seeking review, since there was no state court appellate review of decisions of the Appellate Department of the Superior Court.

The *Roth* prosecution in New York was brought by the U.S. Attorney's Office against another proprietor of a mail-order business. Invoking 18 U.S.C. section 1461, a codification of a law with firm 19th-century roots, the government charged Samuel Roth with twenty-six counts charging "the mailing of books, periodicals, and photographs (and circulars advertising some of them) alleged to be 'obscene, lewd, lascivious, filthy and of an indecent character.'" The case was tried to a jury, which heard the following instructions from District Judge John M. Cashin:

> The test is not whether it would arouse sexual desires or sexually impure thoughts in those comprising a particular segment of the community, the young, the immature or the highly prudish or would leave another segment, the scientific or highly educated or the so-called worldly-wise and sophisticated, indifferent and unmoved. . . .
>
> The test in each case is the effect of the book, picture or publication considered as a whole, not upon any particular class, but upon all those whom it is likely to reach. In other words, you determine its impact upon the average person in the community. The books, pictures and circulars must be judged as a whole, in their entire context, and you are not to consider detached or separate portions in reaching a conclusion. You judge the circulars, pictures and publications which have been put in evidence by present-day standards of the community. You may ask yourselves does it offend the common conscience of the community by present-day standards.
>
> In this case, ladies and gentlemen of the jury, you and you alone are the exclusive judges of what the common conscience of the community is, and in determining that conscience you are to consider the community as a whole, young and old, educated and uneducated, the religious and the irreligious—men, women and children.

The judge had dismissed some counts of the indictment before sending the case to the jury. The jury convicted on four counts and acquitted on nineteen. Judge Cashin sentenced Roth to five years imprisonment and a fine of $5,000 on one count, and a life term of imprisonment for each of the others, to run concurrently, with a $1 fine remitted in each case. Roth appealed, challenging the constitutionality of the statute.

His appeal was argued before the U.S. Court of Appeals for the Second Circuit on June 6, 1956, by Philip Wittenberg, of New York, with Assistant U.S. Attorney George S. Leisure appearing for the government. The Second Circuit panel unanimously sustained his conviction on September 13, but each of the members of the panel produced a separate opinion.

Chief Judge Charles E. Clark, noting the long history of the statute and the many times it had been applied by the Supreme Court in sustaining convictions, said that "we feel it is not the part of responsible judicial administration for an inferior court such as ours, whatever our personal opinions, to initiate a new and uncharted course of overturn of a statute thus long regarded of vital social importance and a public policy of wide general support." Clark said the court was "impressed" by the decision earlier in 1956 by the New York Court of Appeals (which he called "a great court") in *Brown v. Kingsley Books, Inc.*, upholding a prior restraint on sale or distribution of pornographic books, as indicating how little constitutional protection attached to pornography. History showed a "general judicial unanimity in supporting" prosecutions for obscenity. The large mass of state and federal decisions upholding such prosecutions had managed at one time or another to address all the issues they raised, so it was not necessary for the court to go into them in detail. He conceded that there might be problems "when real literature is censored," but asserted that this case involved only "salable pornography," so no literary interests were implicated. Even if the court were free to chart its own course in this area, he said, "we are hardly justified in rejecting out of hand the strongly held views of those with competence in the premises as to the very direct connection of this traffic with the development of juvenile delinquency."

Clark devoted some attention to Roth's argument that the trial judge's description of the word "filthy," contained in the postal statute, resulted in due process problems of constitutional dimensions. Cashin had distinguished "filthy" from "obscene" by stating that the former referred to "that sort of treatment of sexual matters in such a vulgar and indecent way, so that it tends to arouse a feeling of disgust and revulsion," while obscenity referred to material "which tends to promote lust and impure thoughts." This sort of description had been upheld in prior cases, and the court found nothing objectionable in these charges to the jury.

Clark found no problems in sustaining this conviction, "where defendant is an old hand at publishing and surreptitiously mailing to those induced to order them such lurid pictures and material as he can find profitable." There was plenty of evidence before the jury to sustain this conclusion, and under the circumstances the defendant could not be heard to raise arguments about lack of specificity in describing the offense. Neither could he complain that government agents had arrested him after responding to his advertisements, since this method of obtaining evidence had been approved by the Supreme Court in prior cases upholding convictions under the postal laws. Circuit Judge Sterry R. Waterman concurred in a brief paragraph, reiterating Clark's view that the constitutionality of the postal law was so well settled that the issue could be reopened only by the Supreme Court.

Judge Jerome Frank also felt constrained to concur, but not to refrain from writing at length about why, in his view, the postal law was totally insupportable and probably unconstitutional. His opinion, followed by a lengthy appendix, is a bill of particulars as to why obscenity statutes are bad policy and unsound as a matter of constitutional law. The most troublesome issues, for him, were that:

> (a) no one can now show that, with any reasonable probability obscene publications tend to have any effects on the behavior of normal, average adults, and (b) that under that statute, as judicially interpreted, punishment is apparently inflicted for provoking, in such adults, undesirable sexual thoughts, feelings, or desires—not overt dangerous or anti-social conduct, either actual or probable.

He pointed out at length the lack of unanimity among social scientists as to whether either juvenile delinquency or adult sex crimes had any particular relationship to the distribution or use of pornography, and asserted that these "exquisitely vague" statutes, based in "Victorian"

morality of a highly hypocritical sort, lent themselves to oppressive and discriminatory enforcement. It was not enough to say, as Judge Clark had said, that "real literature" was in no danger from these laws, since novels now recognized as "classics" had been prosecuted for obscenity in some jurisdictions at the times of their first publication or distribution. It is impossible to do justice to Judge Frank's extended discussion in the context of this brief essay. The interested reader should consult it in full for an extraordinarily persuasive argument against any attempt by the government to apply penal sanctions to this area of expression.

Roth applied to Justice John Marshall Harlan, the Circuit Justice for the Second Circuit, for permission to stay free on bail while his appeal was pending, which was granted. His petition for *certiorari* was granted and the case was consolidated with *People v. Alberts* for argument. In its January 14, 1957 order granting *certiorari*, the Court specified that three questions would be argued: whether the federal obscenity statute violated the First Amendment, whether the federal obscenity statute violated the Due Process Clause of the Fifth Amendment, and whether the statute violated the First, Ninth, and Tenth amendments by invading "powers reserved to the States and to the people?" The Court had already granted *certiorari* in the *Alberts* case raising similar questions under the Fourteenth Amendment regarding the California statute.

The Court heard argument in both cases on April 22, 1957. As the first case in which the constitutionality of obscenity laws at both the state and federal levels would be directly considered, the case drew wide attention in the legal community, attracting amicus briefs from organizations of authors, publishers, booksellers, and the American and California Civil Liberties Unions. David von G. Albrecht and O. John Rogge argued for Roth, Stanley Fleishman argued for Alberts, Roger D. Fisher appeared for the Solicitor General's Office, and Fred N. Whichello and Clarence A. Linn argued for the State of California. After all this argument, the Court found itself very divided over the case, although a majority was assembled by Justice William J. Brennan, then at the start of his long career on the Court, for a majority opinion. It was an opinion that Justice Brennan would later come to disavow as the consensus behind it began to crumble with the weight of experience, and as Justice Brennan came to reject the theory of "original intent" (basic to this decision) in interpreting constitutional provisions.

Justice Brennan upheld both convictions, finding both the California and federal obscenity statutes constitutional. "The dispositive question," said Brennan, "is whether obscenity is utterance within the area of protected speech and press," and this was "the first time the question has been squarely presented to this Court." Appealing to history, Brennan asserted that those who adopted the First Amendment could not have intended to include obscenity within its protection, since ten of the fourteen states that initially ratified the Bill of Rights "gave no absolute protection for every utterance" and thirteen of them "provided for the prosecution of libel, and all of those States made either blasphemy or profanity, or both, statutory crimes." A Massachusetts obscenity law dated from 1712. "In light of this history," said Brennan, "it is apparent that the unconditional phrasing of the First Amendment was not intended to protect every utterance." Indeed, the Court had held that libel was not protected by the First Amendment in *Beauharnais v. Illinois* (1952). While obscenity law was not as "fully developed" as libel law at the time of enactment, there was enough evidence to show that obscenity was not within the "protection intended for speech and press." Only the communication of ideas with "redeeming social importance" was intended to be protected, and "implicit in the history of the First Amendment is the rejection of obscenity as utterly without redeeming social importance."

Brennan rejected the argument that obscenity laws offended constitutional guarantees "because they punish incitation to impure sexual *thoughts*, not shown to be related to any overt antisocial conduct which is or may be incited in the persons stimulated to such *thoughts*." A complete response to this, said Brennan, was the Court's statement in *Beauharnais* that it was not necessary, in evaluating libelous speech, to consider whether it presented any sort of "clear and present danger," the standard urged by the

defendant there. "Certainly," said the *Beauharnais* court, "no one would contend that obscene speech, for example, may be punished only upon a showing of such circumstances."

Having held that obscenity had no constitutional protection, however, Brennan took pains to state that obscenity and sex were not "synonymous." The depiction of sex was not by itself enough to make a work of art or literature obscene. "Obscene material is material which deals with sex in a manner appealing to prurient interest," said Brennan, noting that the American Law Institute had adopted a definition of obscenity in its Model Penal Code that emphasized prurience as the heart of its definition of obscenity. "Sex, a great and mysterious motive force in human life, has indisputably been a subject of absorbing interest to mankind through the ages; it is one of the vital problems of human interest and public concern." As such, one could speak about it and be within the core of First Amendment protection, so it was important to safeguard speech about sex so long as it "does not treat sex in a manner appealing to prurient interest."

Because of the danger that purported regulation of obscenity might penalize speech that should be protected, the courts had narrowed their definition of obscenity from the English common-law standard, which had centered on the effect of sexually oriented material on the most vulnerable or youthful people. The current test, endorsed by the Court now, was "whether to the average person, applying contemporary community standards, the dominant theme of the material taken as a whole appeals to prurient interest." This description provided "safeguards adequate to withstand the charge of constitutional infirmity," insisted Brennan. Although each of the trial courts in this case had adopted a somewhat different definition of obscenity in determining the fate of the defendants, both had "sufficiently followed the proper standard." In both cases, the emphasis was on the material viewed as a whole and centered on the issue of prurience.

The appellants argued that neither the California nor the federal law provided adequately precise descriptions of the forbidden materials to meet due process requirements. Brennan disagreed, stating that the Court had held in the past that lack of precision was not necessarily fatal to the constitutionality of a statute under the Due Process Clause. It was enough if the language used sufficiently conveyed a warning about the proscribed conduct that would suffice under common understanding. Furthermore, because of the holding that the First Amendment provided no protection for obscenity, Brennan saw little point to Roth's argument that the federal law improperly invaded the province of the states, inasmuch as the Constitution gave Congress plenary power to regulate the mails. On the other hand, Brennan also rejected Alberts's argument that the postal statute preempted state regulation of obscenity sent through the mails. Brennan found that the state law imposed no burden on federal functions, so no preemption issues arose.

Chief Justice Earl Warren concurred in a separate opinion, but felt that Brennan's language was too sweeping and would have limited the decision to the facts in the cases before the Court. While he agreed with Brennan that the long history of obscenity laws generally indicated a consensus that they were necessary and constitutional, he was not ready to issue such blanket statements, preferring to emphasize in the two cases under review the element of scienter (i.e., that each of the statutes the Court was upholding required that the defendant knowingly or intentionally have distributed obscene materials). These convictions did not present a problem for Warren. "[The defendants] were plainly engaged in the commercial exploitation of the morbid and shameful craving for materials with prurient effect," he said. "I believe that the State and Federal Governments can constitutionally punish such conduct. That is all that these cases present to us, and that is all we need to decide."

Justice Harlan parted company from the majority in believing that Congress was precluded from passing the postal obscenity law by the First Amendment, but he agreed that California could pass its obscenity law. At the heart of his differing view was his rejection of the "incorporation concept" by which other members of the Court held that the First Amendment applied to the state governments and the federal government in the same way, and his emphasis on federalism and the restriction of the federal government to dealing with issues of federal importance while letting state governments have significant autonomy in affairs of more local concern. To him, regulation of obscenity was a matter of more local concern because it was the moral standards of the local community that were more directly at stake. Indeed, he was troubled by the Court's apparent lumping together of all obscenity under one broad classification, without acknowledging that each case, each prosecution, presented its distinctive problems requiring the court (and perhaps, ultimately, the Supreme Court) to provide an individualized assessment of the challenged book, picture, or film. It was precisely because individuals could differ so radically as to whether a particular work had a predominant appeal to prurient interest that the Court's scheme was unworkable, in his view, and why the issue of obscenity should be left to the states. It was the genius of the federal system that it provided (then) 48 laboratories in which to experiment. It might be that in some states the people would consider obscene a particular work that would not be considered obscene in other states. For him, it was acceptable that a particular work might be banned in a particular state, but not that a ban should be nationwide by command of federal authorities, since public morality was the type of concern left to the states under the Ninth and Tenth amendments.

Consequently, he was ready to affirm Alberts's conviction but set aside Roth's. The First Amendment, phrased in rather absolute terms, was binding on Congress. There was only an "attenuated federal interest in this field," insisted Harlan, not strong enough to overcome the strong aversion to federal censorship. It was inappropriate for there to be a federal law against inciting particular "thoughts," under a constitution that contained a first amendment aimed at preserving freedom of thought, and the difficulties of defining obscenity in a meaningful way led to problems of statutory overbreadth, a significant danger in the free speech area. It would not be constitutional, asserted Harlan, for the federal statute to reach any material that did not constitute "hard-core" pornography; the current postal statute clearly went beyond that.

On the other hand, the only restriction on the state of California was the Fourteenth Amendment, which posed the question whether regulation of obscenity involved a fundamental right implicit in the concept of ordered liberty. Harlan was persuaded that it did not, leaving California free to carry out its regulation.

Finally, Justice William O. Douglas dissented in an opinion joined by Justice Hugo L. Black. These members of the Court had long opposed any regulation of speech, and they were both ardent "incorporationists" of the First Amendment to apply to the states through the Fourteenth Amendment's Due Process Clause. For them, neither the state nor the federal law could stand against the imperative language of the First Amendment. After reviewing the standards under which the two cases under review were decided at the trial level, Douglas commented: "By these standards punishment is inflicted for thoughts provoked, not for overt acts nor antisocial conduct. This test cannot be squared with our decisions under the First Amendment." The challenged tests involved "the arousing of sexual thoughts. Yet the arousing of sexual thoughts and desires happens every day in normal life in dozens of ways." The Court was giving "the censor free range over a vast domain." This was a drastic curtailment of the First Amendment that was entirely unprecedented and improper.

For one thing, argued Douglas, "it is by no means clear that obscene literature, as so defined, is a significant factor in influencing substantial deviations from the community standards" of conduct. For another, this whole idea of "community standards" conflicts with the clear command of the First Amendment that prohibits the government from prescribing an orthodoxy of thought for the entire population. A test that turned on "offensiveness," as these tests seemed to turn, was "too loose, too capricious, too destructive of freedom of expression to be squared with the First Amendment. . . . It creates a regime where in the battle between the literati and the Philistines, the Philistines are certain to win." Censorship always turned out to be irrational and indiscriminate.

Douglas's views were prescient, and Brennan would come to share them as the Court continued to struggle under the standards endorsed in *Roth* through the next two decades of the Sexual Revolution in manners and communications. By the mid-1960s, the Court was even more fractured in its approach to obscenity, leading to an attempted revision of the Court's standards in the early 1970s in *Miller v. California*, but with only mixed success. Douglas argued that the First Amendment sensibly excluded the government from the field of censorship, and much pain and vain intellectual effort would be spared if only the Court could come to terms with that conclusion.

Case References

Beauharnais v. Illinois, 343 U.S. 250 (1952)
Brown v. Kingsley Books, Inc., 1 N.Y.2d 177, 151 N.Y.S.2d 639, 134 N.E.2d 461 (1956)
Miller v. California, 413 U.S. 15 (1973)

36. THE RIGHT TO MAIL HOMOSEXUALLY ORIENTED PUBLICATIONS

One, Inc. v. Olesen, 355 U.S. 371 (1958), summarily reversing 241 F.2d 772 (9th Cir. 1957). *Manual Enterprises, Inc. v. Day*, 370 U.S. 478 (1962), reversing 289 F.2d 455 (D.C. Cir. 1961).

As a small movement for lesbian and gay rights began to form in a few major cities after World War II, one of the main barriers to concerted action on a national level was the relative isolation of local groups and the lack of a regular means of communication. In an age before easy access to sophisticated telecommunications, and at a time when it was nearly impossible to sell materials explicitly aimed at a lesbian or gay audience on newsstands or in stores serving a general population, distribution of newsletters and magazines through the mails provided the most accessible and affordable means of establishing communications and beginning to build a community of national scope.

Beginning in 1865, Congress had repeatedly passed laws banning obscene, vulgar or indecent materials from being sent through the mails, and imposing criminal penalties on those who tried to mail such articles. In 1950s America, many considered any mention of homosexuality or lesbianism in other than pejorative terms vulgar, indecent, and perhaps even obscene. Thus, battles with the post office were an important feature of the early movement for lesbian and gay rights as the new organizations and businesses attempting to serve the emerging community of homosexuals tried to use the mails to communicate, to solicit business, and to provide goods and services.

One of the first attempts to establish a gay-oriented publication with a national circulation through the mails was made in the early 1950s by a pioneering homophile organization in Los Angeles, One, Inc., which published its magazine, *One*, self-described as "The Homosexual Magazine." *One* included serious discussions about the nature of homosexuality, discrimination, politics, and scientific studies. It also contained true and fictional accounts of the lives of lesbians and gay men and poetry and other literary features, some of which alluded to sexual activity, advertisements by businesses and individuals seeking gay patronage, and occasional sketches and photographs to illustrate the articles.

Litigation arose when the postmaster of Los Angeles, Otto K. Olesen, refused to transmit the October 1954 issue of *One* because he believed that one article and one poem contained obscene material and because the issue contained a notice about a Swiss publication, *The Circle*, that the postmaster considered obscene. Olesen claimed the issue was "non-mailable" under 18 U.S.C. section 1461, the most recent descendant of the post-Civil War statute banning transmission through the mails either of obscene matter or of information about how to obtain obscene matter, as authority for refusing to deliver the magazines. Beverly Hills attorney Eric Julber filed suit on behalf of One, Inc., in the U.S. District Court for the Central District of California in Los Angeles, claiming

that the October 1954 issue of *One* was not "lewd, lascivious, obscene or filthy" (the wording of the statute), and was thus "mailable." The complaint also alleged that Postmaster Olesen's refusal to accept the material for mailing was "arbitrary, capricious and an abuse of discretion," that his determination lacked an evidentiary basis and was erroneous as a matter of law and deprived One, Inc., and its members of due process of law and equal protection of the laws.

Assistant U.S. Attorneys Marvin P. Carlock and Max F. Deutz appeared to defend Postmaster Olesen, as Julber presented his argument before District Judge Benjamin Harrison. In an unpublished opinion, Harrison ruled that the refusal to transmit *One* was proper because it was "non-mailable matter" under section 1461. Julber filed an appeal, which was heard by a three-judge panel of the U.S. Court of Appeals for the Ninth Circuit, consisting of Circuit Judges Stanley N. Barnes and Frederick G. Hamley and District Judge John R. Ross, of Nevada, who wrote the panel's opinion affirming the district court that was released on February 27, 1957.

Ross disclaimed any interest in the court's being "its brother's keeper as to the type of reading to be indulged in," asserting that the court viewed the case as a simple issue of interpretation of a postal regulation, a matter of administrative law in which the role of the court was merely to determine whether the postmaster's action was arbitrary, capricious, or an abuse of discretion, and whether there were reasonable grounds in the record for the district court to have sustained his decision. According to Ross, then, the case turned on whether the Postmaster could reasonably have concluded that the October 1954 issue of *One* was "obscene, lewd, lascivious, filthy or indecent," and this necessarily drew into question "the moral sense of the public," since these terms were, by their nature, somewhat relative. "In approaching the moral side of the issue here presented," wrote Ross, "we are not unmindful of the fact that morals are not static like the everlasting hills, but are like the vagrant breezes to which the mariner must ever trim his sails."

That said, however, Ross and his judicial colleagues were convinced that the October

1954 number was nonmailable. After suggesting that public opinion on what constitutes obscene matter had evolved and in fact loosened up a bit over the years and the law had to take note of such developments, Ross adverted to ancient U.S. Supreme Court decisions for assistance in deciding how to evaluate the issue of *One* in contention. First Ross quoted from the first Justice John Marshall Harlan's decision for the Supreme Court in *Rosen v. United States* (1896), stating:

> The test of obscenity is whether the tendency of the matter is to deprave and corrupt the morals of those whose minds are open to such influence and into whose hands a publication of this sort may fall. . . . Would it . . . suggest or convey lewd thoughts and lascivious thoughts to the young and inexperienced?

Ross then quoted a variety of old cases to similar effect, emphasizing that literature alleged to be obscene should be evaluated based on the effect it might have on children. Further, Ross noted that the Supreme Court, construing a predecessor statute in *United States v. Limehouse* (1932), held that the addition of the word "filthy" to the list of traits making it unlawful to mail an item meant that coarse and vulgar materials that were not necessarily obscene also came under the statutory prohibition. On this basis, "it is apparent that the magazine is obscene and filthy and is therefore nonmailable matter," asserted Ross.

While acknowledging the magazine's stated purpose of "dealing primarily with homosexuality from the scientific, historical and critical point of view—to sponsor educational programs, lectures and concerts for the aid and benefit of social variants and to promote among the general public an interest, knowledge and understanding of the problems of variation," Ross insisted that the article, poem, and advertisement that Olesen had singled out for condemnation "do not comport with the lofty ideals expressed . . . by the publishers."

The article, "Sappho Remembered," concerned the relationship of an adult lesbian and a young girl struggling with her sexuality. The young girl has fallen in love with the lesbian and must decide whether to pursue a "normal married life" or to go with her emotions and live with the lesbian woman. "The climax is reached," said Ross, "when the young girl gives up her chance for a normal married life to live with the lesbian. This article is nothing more than cheap pornography calculated to promote lesbianism. It falls far short of dealing with homosexuality from the scientific, historical and critical point of view." It is not clear from Ross's opinion whether the article was presented as fact or fiction.

The poem, titled "Lord Samuel and Lord Montagu," was about the alleged homosexual activities of Lord Montagu and other British peers, including a warning to all men to steer clear of the public toilets of London when Lord Samuel was "sniffing around the drains." Evidently the innuendos contained in the poem were too much for the judges, who found that "the poem pertains to sexual matters of such a vulgar and indecent nature that it tends to arouse a feeling of disgust and revulsion. It is dirty, vulgar and offensive to the moral senses." All this, although the poem apparently did not contain any explicit descriptions of sexual acts.

Conceding that it was possible that the intended audience of *One* might not find the story or the poem to be vulgar, offensive, or indecent, but merely descriptive of their own lives and standards, Ross contended that this was not the appropriate standard for evaluating the material. "Social standards are fixed by and for the great majority and not by or for a hardened or weakened minority," he stated. He quoted a then-recent Ninth Circuit opinion, *Besig v. United States* (1953), which stated:

> The statute forbidding the importation of obscene books is not designed to fit the normal concept of morality of society's dregs, nor of the different concepts of morality throughout the world, nor for all time past and future, but is designed to fit the normal American concept in the age in which we live. It is no legitimate argument that because there are social groups composed of moral delinquents in this or in other countries, that their language shall be received as legal tender along with the speech of the great masses who trade ideas and information in the honest money of decency.

Thus, because the story and the poem seemed vulgar and offensive to the judges, it did not matter that they might not appear vulgar or offensive in the eyes of their intended readers.

Finally, Ross addressed an item on page 29 of the October 1954 issue under the heading "Foreign Books and Magazines That Will Interest You." It included information about how to obtain copies of the Swiss magazine *The Circle*, which itself contained stories similar to those the court had condemned in *One*. Given the judges' view of the material in *One*, it is not surprising that they found *The Circle* to be similarly obscene, and thus an "advertisement" for it in *One* contributed to the finding that *One* was not mailable.

One, Inc., had argued that the mere inclusion of some items that the court found objectionable was not sufficient to damn the whole publication, since the courts had established the doctrine of judging a work "as a whole" rather than on the basis of particular parts. The test was whether the primary purpose or dominant theme of the work fell within the proscribed categories, and One, Inc., argued that the bulk of the October issue did comport with the publisher's statement of purpose. The judges disagreed. "The magazine under consideration," said Ross, "by reason of the articles referred to, has a primary purpose of exciting lust, lewd and lascivious thoughts and sensual desires in the minds of the persons reading it. Moreover," he insisted, "such articles are morally depraving and debasing." They were sufficient, in the court's view, to label the magazine as a whole "obscene and filthy." Given such a finding, the court rejected as without merit the argument that either the postmaster or the trial judge had erred in finding the October issue to be nonmailable. The court also rejected the contention that the postmaster's actions had deprived One, Inc., of due process of law or equal protection of the laws, asserting that the postal regulation was not intended to single out any class of person but was applied impartially to all "obscene" matter, and that adequate procedural protections had been applied in determining the issue of mailability.

On April 12, 1957, the court denied a petition for rehearing. One, Inc., filed a petition for *certiorari* with the Supreme Court, arguing that the court of appeals had misapplied the Court's precedents in determining that the October issue of *One* was non-mailable based on the three specified items. While the petition

was pending, the Court issued its important decision in *Roth v. United States* (1957), in which it had extended First Amendment protection to sexually explicit materials that previously would have been considered obscene by establishing a two-part test: whether the "dominant theme" of the work appealed to prurient interest, and whether the manner of presentation was "patently offensive" on the basis of community standards, which in the case of material intended for broad national distribution would be a national standard, taking into account the differing acceptability of material in different parts of the country. The Court also indicated that the reaction of the "average person in the community" was the appropriate standard of judging whether particular material was obscene. After issuing the *Roth* opinion, the Court sifted through the backlog of *certiorari* petitions presenting issues of obscenity and the First Amendment, remanded those that required further consideration, and affirmed or reversed without explanation many of those that could be determined based on their existing records to be consistent or inconsistent with *Roth*.

On January 13, 1958, the Court granted the writ of *certiorari* in *One, Inc. v. Olesen*, and announced that it was reversing the Ninth Circuit's opinion, citing *Roth*. The Court offered no explanation for its action. It seems likely that the Ninth Circuit's failing in *One, Inc.*, was to judge the entire October 1954 issue as obscene because one or two articles may have incidentally appealed to prurient interest, when such was not the dominant theme of the issue. Further, the Ninth Circuit's focus on the effect the material might have on "innocent youth" seemed misplaced in light of *Roth*, which required that material be judged in light of its impact on "the average person in the community," not the most vulnerable or impressionable. Additionally, given the Court's subsequent opinion in *Manual Enterprises v. Day*, discussed below, it may be that some members of the Court already doubted whether the postmaster had authority to bar material from the mails in advance of a judicial determination of obscenity. In any event, while the Court's citation of *Roth* indicated that the reasons for its reversal could be found in that opinion, its failure to offer further explanation left some ambiguity for the lower courts.

The Supreme Court's reversal was hailed by the small circle of homophile observers as an important victory. Indeed, it was the first time the Supreme Court had ever decided a case in favor of gay litigants on the merits. Although the lack of an explanation for the Court's opinion left ambiguity about the degree of protection the Court saw for literature on homosexual themes, it was reasonable to look to the *Roth* case as indicating that neither the post office nor the lower federal courts could take the position that mere discussion of homosexuality in a positive light, or even innuendos about homosexual escapades, could automatically render an entire publication obscene and thus nonmailable (and, incidently, subject to prosecution). This was an important breakthrough for a young movement struggling to establish the beginnings of a positive identity.

A further, and more spectacular breakthrough, came in 1962, with the Supreme Court's opinion in *Manual Enterprises v. Day.* Unlike *One, Inc.*, a case which primarily concerned written matter, *Manual Enterprises* involved pictorial depiction of unclothed men under the guise of "physique photography."

Herman L. Womack, the owner of several businesses providing "dirty pictures" to homosexual men, was convicted in the District of Columbia in 1960 of using the mails to solicit orders for "physique pictures" that revealed pubic hair, and in some cases genitals, of the male subjects, and of actually sending less explicit but still sexually oriented pictures of undraped males through the mails in response to orders from postal inspectors. His conviction was affirmed by the court of appeals, and the U.S. Supreme Court had denied *certiorari* in the case in 1961.

Womack was the owner of Manual Enterprises, Inc., which published three magazines, *Manual, Trim,* and *Grecian Guild Pictorial,* all of which were sent through the mails and all of which consisted mainly of pictures of muscular men in various poses in various stages of undress. No pictures in these magazines showed genitals, although there were slight, teasing hints of pubic hair, and the folds of some of the posing garments were arranged in such a way as to suggest that the models might be sporting erections underneath. Some of the pictures included more than one man, and their poses together might suggest erotic attraction to some viewers, but there were no actual depictions of sexual intercourse or contact. The magazines contained little text, beyond brief captions for the pictures and listings of "physique photographers" from whom readers could order photographs directly.

In April 1960, as part of the general crackdown on Womack's businesses by District of Columbia authorities, the local post office withheld copies of his magazines from dispatch and convened an administrative hearing, in which Womack was represented by attorney Stanley M. Dietz, of Washington. At the hearing, the postal inspectors presented psychiatric expert witnesses, who "testified in great detail, explaining how and why the poses used in most of the pictures and the clothing worn by the models would arouse great prurient interest in homosexuals." They also testified that many of the props in the photographs, such as swords and chains, had sexually symbolic meanings for homosexuals. A postal inspector testified that he had placed mail orders for photographs from businesses advertising in these magazines and had received in response photographs showing the pubic area of unclothed men. He also testified that in his past experience, further orders to the same photographers would elicit even more explicit photographs. A raid on one photographer's studio turned up "hard core pornography," depictions of groups of nude males "engaged in homosexual activities." The hearing officer determined that the physique magazines were nonmailable under section 1461, based both on the pictures they contained and on the listings of photographers from whom readers could obtain more explicit pictures.

Manual Enterprises filed suit in the District of Columbia federal district court seeking an injunction against the post office, and sought immediate preliminary injunctive relief, which was denied by District Judge George L. Hart, Jr. On subsequent cross-motions for summary judgment, Hart denied Manual's motion and granted the government's. The U.S. Attorney's Office for the District of Columbia represented the post office, with Donald S. Smith appearing as lead counsel. An appeal to the D.C. Circuit Court of Appeals followed promptly, and was argued on February 13 before a panel of three circuit judges, Charles Fahy, John A. Danaher, and Walter M. Bastian. Bastian wrote the panel's opinion affirming Hart's unpublished disposition of the case, issued March 23, 1961.

After recounting the findings of the administrative hearing, Bastian noted Manual Enterprises's contention that its magazines were "body-building magazines," that it had no idea whether newsstand sales were made to homosexuals as opposed to body-building enthusiasts, and that it could not be held responsible for the photographs that were discovered in the photographers' offices because they were not sent through the mail. Most significantly, Manual disputed the claim that nude photographs of men were necessarily obscene. Manual's arguments were undercut by Womack's admission under cross-examination that the magazines were really intended for the entertainment of homosexual men, but Bastian stated that the court placed more weight on the psychiatrists' testimony about the effect the photographs would have on gay men, and concluded that there was substantial evidence on the administrative record that the magazines were intended for homosexuals.

But were the materials obscene and thus unprotected by the First Amendment? Manual contended that under *Roth* they could not be considered obscene because they would not appeal to the prurient interest of the average member of the public. In *Roth*, the Supreme Court had adopted the "average person in the community" test as the standard, rejecting the idea that allegedly obscene materials should be judged based on the impact they had on the most vulnerable or impressionable people. Now Manual argued that since the "average person in the community" would not be sexually aroused by pictures of almost-naked men, the magazines should not be considered obscene because they appealed to prurient interest.

Bastian rejected this argument, asserting that the Court's purpose in *Roth* was to make clear that obscenity determinations were not to be "predicated on the reaction of the peculiarly prudish or susceptible, and neither is a defense to such a charge to be predicated on the lack of reaction on the part of the peculiarly jaded."

But these magazines were not intended to be read by the "average member of the community," so that person's reactions could not be considered relevant in judging them, he said. "The proper test in this case, we think, is the reaction of the average member of the class for which the magazines were intended, homosexuals." Since the testimony showed that "these magazines would arouse prurient interest in the average homosexual," and that this appeared to be their dominant theme and main purpose, they were clearly obscene. Furthermore, the testimony of the postal inspector about past experience in receiving progressively more explicit photographs when ordering materials from some of the photographers who advertised in the magazines was sufficient to sustain the charge that the magazines provided information about how to get obscene materials, which was also forbidden by the postal regulations. There was no need, consequently, to consider the impact of the photographs that were actually discovered in the photographers' offices, which were like those that had been ruled obscene by the D.C. Circuit during the prosecution of Womack earlier in 1961.

Dietz's petition for *certiorari* on behalf of Manual was granted and the case was argued on February 26 and 27, 1962, with J. William Doolittle, Jr., of Washington, appearing on behalf of the government. The argument occurred before a reduced bench, since Justice Felix Frankfurter was too ill to participate and Justice Byron R. White had not yet taken his seat on the Court. On June 25, the Court announced that six members agreed that the judgment of the court of appeals should be reversed, but no more than three could agree on the same rationale for so holding, so there was neither a written opinion of the Court nor a plurality opinion. Two groups of justices subscribed to separate opinions, Justice Hugo L. Black (who had frequently asserted that there was no exception to First Amendment protection of speech and press for obscenity) joined the judgment without expressing any opinion, and Justice Tom C. Clark dissented.

Writing for himself and Justice Potter Stewart, Justice John Marshall Harlan argued that the magazines were not obscene under the *Roth* test, and that there was no evidence in the record that the publisher knew about the obscene photographs that readers might obtain by placing successive orders to the listed photographers, so the advertisements could not be used to render the magazines nonmailable. Justice Harlan stated that the court of appeals had omitted a crucial step in its consideration whether the photographs in the magazines were obscene: whether they were "so offensive on their face as to affront current community standards of decency," a standard Harlan referred to as "patent offensiveness or indecency." The court of appeals had merely asked whether the photographs appealed to the prurient interest of the homosexual audience for which they were intended. For Harlan, these magazines were not so offensive on their face. They depicted semi-naked men in a variety of poses, but none of the men were actually engaged in any patently offensive conduct. Harlan noted that the American Law Institute, in its Model Penal Code, had embraced the same standard when it defined obscene material as that appealing to prurient interest which "goes substantially beyond customary limits of candor in describing or representing such matters."

To argue, as the government appeared to, that mere nakedness without more could be obscene would be to condemn many universally acknowledged masterpieces of art, some of which could be found hanging in the galleries of the Smithsonian Institute just a short walk from the Court's chambers.

> To consider that the "obscenity" exception in "the area of constitutionally protected speech or press"... does not require any determination as to the patent offensiveness *vel non* of the material itself might well put the American public in jeopardy of being denied access to many worth-while works in literature, science, or art. For one would not have to travel far even among the acknowledged master-pieces in any of these fields to find works whose "dominant theme" might, not beyond reason, be claimed to appeal to the "prurient interest" of the reader or observer.

Such a construction of section 1461, concluded Harlan, would raise serious constitutional questions. Better to construe the statute narrowly so as to avoid that problem and ban from the mails only works that were patently offensive in their explicit depiction of sexual conduct.

Noting that some lower courts had construed *Roth* to protect all but "hard-core pornography," Harlan stated that it was not necessary to go so far in this case, since the materials at issue came nowhere near that point. "Our own independent examination of the magazines leads us to conclude that the most that can be said of them is that they are dismally unpleasant, uncouth, and tawdry. But this is not enough to make them 'obscene.'" Indeed, they were no more objectionable than "many portrayals of the female nude that society tolerates." The depiction of nudity, as such, is not necessarily obscene. Where free expression was concerned, it was better to err on the side against censorship. Since the court of appeals had failed to make this determination, it was unnecessary to deal with the lower court's assertion that the relevant test for prurience should be based on the intended audience rather than on the "average person."

As to the advertising, since there was no indication in the record that Womack or his staff had direct knowledge of the photographs that readers could get by answering advertisements in the magazine, and since it appeared that Womack had deleted advertisements by some photographers after being informed by the post office that those photographers had been convicted of mailing obscene materials to customers, a necessary element of "scienter" was missing. The government had done no more than show that the publisher knew that the photographers would be offering material similar to that which appeared in the magazines, which the Court had just held to be protected by the First Amendment. Consequently, it would be inappropriate to exclude the magazines from the mails based on the advertisements.

Writing for himself, Chief Justice Earl Warren, and Justice William O. Douglas, Justice William J. Brennan, Jr., joined the Court's judgment on the ground that, as he read section 1461, it did not authorize the post office to refuse to mail any magazines based on its decision whether they were obscene. After reviewing the history of section 1461 and its predecessors, Brennan asserted that the questions posed by the case were three: due to the hostility toward prior restraint under the First

Amendment, there was a question whether Congress had the power to "close the mails to obscenity by any means other than prosecution of its sender;" there was a question whether Congress could vest the post office with authority to determine whether particular material was obscene; and there was a question of statutory construction as to whether Congress had indeed delegated such authority to the post office with the intention of achieving such a result.

In the time-honored tradition of avoiding constitutional questions when their determination was unnecessary, Brennan took aim directly at the third question and decided that the procedures used by the post office were not authorized by statute. The post office purported to base its authority on the statutory statement that obscene material was nonmailable matter and that individuals could be prosecuted for attempting to mail it. After a detailed review of the early history of the 1865 predecessor of the current statute, Brennan identified as the understanding of its proponents that the post office "could stop obviously questionable matter for the purpose of transmitting it to prosecuting authorities, could stop matter already held obscene if it were sent again, and could investigate matter sent by persons previously convicted and, if the matter were found violative, could present it to the prosecuting authorities." Asserting that this was the appropriate construction of the original statute, which would avert the need to engage in evaluation of its constitutionality, Brennan traced the subsequent amendments and recodification of the statute, showing to his satisfaction that the legislative history of subsequent enactments leading to the present law evinced no Congressional intent other than what he attributed to the original enactment.

In *Roth*, the Court had upheld the constitutionality of the criminal prosecution provisions of section 1461, as narrowly construed by redefining the scope of obscenity, but cautioned about the necessity of safeguarding material protected by the First Amendment from government censorship. "I imply no doubt," wrote Brennan, "that Congress could constitutionally authorize a noncriminal process in the nature of a judicial proceeding under closely defined procedural safeguards. But the suggestion that Congress may constitutionally authorize any process other than a fully judicial one immediately raises the gravest doubts." Such doubts could be avoided in this case by construing the statute not to authorize a nonjudicial process for excluding materials from the mails as "obscene."

Justice Clark's dissent rejected Brennan's argument that the post office was not authorized to exclude obscene material from the mail. Instead, he argued that it was unnecessary to determine whether the magazines were obscene, since it was clear that they contained advertisements from which readers could obtain indisputably obscene materials. This provided a viable independent ground for denying Manual Enterprises the relief it sought in this case, since the statute also labeled as nonmailable any article that contained information about how to get obscene materials.

Clark's main target was Justice Harlan's contention that there was a scienter element regarding the advertising which the government had failed to prove. Clark stated that he failed to see how the publisher's knowledge was relevant to the issue of mailability under the statute. Since the statute clearly stated that nothing could be mailed which contained information about how to obtain obscene matter, it appeared to Clark that the test under the statute was entirely objective: did the mailed matter contain such information? Quoting the statute, he stated: "Congress could not have made it more clear that the sender's knowledge of the material to be mailed did not determine its mailability but only his responsibility for mailing it." While it might not be appropriate to prosecute somebody for mailing a magazine where the element of scienter was lacking, it was entirely appropriate to keep the magazine out of the mails.

However, even if a scienter requirement existed, Clark scoffed at the contention that it had not been met in this case:

> The content and direction of the magazines themselves are a tip-off as to the nature of the business of those who solicit through them. The magazines have no social, education, or entertainment qualities but are designed solely as sex stimulants for homosexuals. . . . The publishers freely admit that the magazines are

published to appeal to the male homosexual group. The advertisements and photographer lists in such magazines were quite naturally "designed so as to attract the male homosexual and to furnish him with names and addresses where nude male pictures in poses and conditions which would appeal to his prurient interest may be obtained." Moreover, the advertisements themselves could leave no more doubt in the publishers' minds than in those of the solicited purchasers.

Each magazine specifically endorsed the listed photographers and urged readers to patronize them. Some of the magazines asserted that the publisher was familiar with the work of the photographers as a basis for these endorsements. To Clark, this evidence taken together justified at least a remand for further fact-finding. Furthermore, Womack, the owner of the three magazines in question, appeared by his own testimony to have a relatively close relationship with some of the photographers, thus he could be appropriately charged with knowledge about their products, and had himself been convicted of mailing obscene photographs. "How one can fail to see the obvious in this record is beyond my comprehension," wailed Justice Clark.

Manual Enterprises was a significant case in laying the groundwork for the burgeoning gay press that arose during the 1970s. Because of the limited audience at which gay newspapers and magazines was aimed, these publications would not be economically viable unless purveyors of sexually oriented materials (books, photos, and films) could advertise in them, and the publications could not obtain sufficient circulation to attract advertisers unless they could be distributed to a national audience by mail (since the number of those daring enough to subscribe from any one location would not be large enough to support such publications). A national gay newsmagazine like *The Advocate*, which routinely contains articles and other features such as those condemned by the court of appeals in *One, Inc.* and advertisements such as those condemned by the court of appeals in *Manual Enterprises*, would not be economically viable without such advertisements. Thus, the Supreme Court's indication that such materials could not be barred from the mails, however ambiguous and divided the line-up of the Justices in *Manual*, was a crucial step in the process of developing national communication that led, by the early 1970s, to an emerging political movement for civil rights of lesbian and gay people.

Case References

Besig v. United States, 208 F.2d 142 (9th Cir. 1953)

Rosen v. United States, 161 U.S. 29 (1896)

Roth v. United States, 354 U.S. 476 (1957)

United States v. Limehouse, 285 U.S. 424 (1932)

Womack v. United States, 294 F.2d 204 (D.C. Cir.), certiorari denied, 365 U.S. 859 (1961)

37. OBSCENITY IN THE PRIVACY OF THE HOME

Stanley v. Georgia, 394 U.S. 557 (1969), reversing 224 Ga. 259, 161 S.E.2d 309 (1968), opinion on remand, 225 Ga. 273, 167 S.E.2d 756 (1969).

In *Roth v. United States* (1957), the U.S. Supreme Court held that books, pictures, and films that were "obscene" were not protected under the freedom of speech or of the press described in the First Amendment of the Constitution. *Roth* and several subsequent cases dealt with materials that were being held for sale or distribution at the time of their discovery by law enforcement authorities, or with situations where obscene materials were actually being distributed, sold, or exhibited. But what about situations where private citizens were prosecuted for the mere possession of such materials? The 1961 case of *Mapp v. Ohio* raised this question, but the Court focused its opinion instead on the circumstance that the obscene materials had been discovered during a search that failed Fourth Amendment requirements. The Court used the occasion to promulgate a landmark decision extending the existing federal exclusionary rule to the states, barring the introduction at trial of evidence obtained in violation of the Fourth Amendment. Since the obscene material could not be produced at trial, the prosecution of Dollree Mapp for its possession had to be dismissed. Justice Potter Stewart, who dissented from the *Mapp* ruling on extending the exclusionary rule to bind state law enforcement authorities, nonetheless would have upset the conviction on the ground that mere possession of obscenity could not be constitutionally punished, since this was "not consistent with the rights of free thought and expression assured against state action by the Fourteenth Amendment."

The issue next arose from the criminal prosecution of Robert E. Stanley, a Georgia man under investigation for suspected bookmaking activities. Law enforcement authorities assembled several affidavits to support the issuance of a search warrant, authorizing federal Internal Revenue Service agents and an investigator from the Fulton County prosecutor's office to search the house where Stanley rented living quarters for evidence of bookmaking activity. During their search, which yielded no evidence of bookmaking activity, the agents came across three rolls of film in a desk drawer of an upstairs bedroom. They viewed the films using a projector and a screen in an upstairs living room and discovered that the films depicted explicit sexual activity, including sodomy, between men and women. Considering the material obscene, the investigators arrested Stanley under a Georgia law making it a felony for any person to possess "any obscene matter" if the person had "knowledge or reasonably should know of the obscene nature of such matter." Stanley was convicted in a trial before Superior Court Judge Jeptha C. Tanksley, who overruled objections to the constitutionality of the law under which Stanley was prosecuted.

Stanley's lawyer, Wesley R. Asinof, of Atlanta, appealed his conviction to the Georgia Supreme Court, where he was opposed by Fulton County Solicitor General Lewis R. Slaton. The court had no doubts about the constitutionality of the statute and issued a unanimous opinion by Justice John E. Frankum on April 9, 1968, affirming Stanley's conviction.

Stanley had challenged his prosecution on several alternative constitutional grounds. First, he argued that the Georgia Superior Court had improperly allowed introduction of the three rolls of films as evidence against him. The search warrant authorized a search for evidence of bookmaking equipment. Stanley argued that the films clearly were not bookmaking equipment, and thus were not open to seizure under these circumstances. Frankum rejected this argument, asserting that under Georgia law, when a law enforcement officer is conducting a valid search, the officer is authorized to seize any materials the possession of which is unlawful, and that such a search procedure had been specifically approved in the past by the Georgia and federal courts, including the U.S. Supreme Court. The only precedent arguably supporting Stanley's position, *Marcus v. Search Warrants*, a 1961 U.S. Supreme Court ruling contemporaneous with *Mapp v. Ohio*, was not really on point, Frankum argued, because the ruling in that case suppressing the fruits of a search "was made with relation to and in the context of constitutional guarantees of freedom of the press and freedom of speech." Without analysis or explanation, Frankum said, "Here no such question is involved." Presumably, this assertion referred to the obscene character of the film, which, under *Roth*, would apparently have no First Amendment protection.

Next, Stanley argued that his case was distinguishable from past decisions upholding obscenity prosecutions because he possessed the films solely for his own use and had no intent to sell them, to expose them to others, or to circulate them. He contended that mere possession of obscene materials presented no issues of legitimate state concern. Frankum rejected this argument without explanation, merely asserting that "intent to sell, expose or circulate" the obscene matter was not required by the statute. Stanley also made a technical argument related to the sequences of amendments and prior invalidations of portions of the Georgia obscenity laws; the court rejected this argument as well.

Perhaps Stanley's most ingenious constitutional argument was that the law violated the First Amendment because it could be used to prosecute a person who did not even know that the materials in his possession were obscene. By charging a person with a felony if he should "reasonably" have known that a film is obscene, the law dispensed with the element of scienter, which Stanley argued was essential to such a prosecution. Asserting that personal knowledge is "a matter peculiarly within the mind of [the defendant], and it is rarely if ever that the defendant's guilty knowledge is susceptible of direct proof," Frankum said that the court had adhered to the principle that "guilty knowledge may be shown by circumstances as well as by actual and direct proof." Frankum then took off on a convoluted and ultimately illogical train of explanation, asserting, in effect, that anyone who possesses film that turns out to be obscene would meet the scienter requirement in the absence of proof of knowledge of obscenity. He also rejected a subsidiary argument that the obscenity of the films could not be established prior to a judicial review of their contents.

Asinof filed an appeal to the U.S. Supreme Court, which noted probable jurisdiction on October 14, 1968, and heard oral argument from Asinof and Atlanta attorney Robert Sparks, representing Slaton, on January 14 and 15, 1969. The entire Court agreed that Stanley's conviction had to be reversed, but there were two distinct schools of thought as to why. Ironically, it was Justice Potter Stewart, joined by Justices William J. Brennan, Jr., and Byron R. White, who argued that the Court should avoid the pitfalls of a new adventure into the thickets of obscenity law and the First Amendment by resting its decision on the Fourth Amendment exclusionary rule. For Stewart, this was a relatively simple Fourth Amendment case. The warrant authorized a search for evidence of bookmaking. The films were not evidence of bookmaking and did not come within the "plain view" exception, under which a law enforcement officer engaged in a lawful search can seize any contraband within plain view. Thus, the films could not be introduced into evidence against Stanley and the case against him fell apart. Stewart argued that the "plain view" exception did not apply because it was impossible by visual inspection of the rolls of film to determine that they were obscene; only after they were projected were the agents able to make such a determination. Thus, the obscenity was not in plain view of the agents during the course of their lawful search. Presumably, because federal agents were involved in this search, Stewart, who had dissented from the *Mapp* ruling, had no problem applying Fourth Amendment stric-

tures to this case, although he did cite *Mapp* as authority at the end of his opinion.

The opinion for the Court by Justice Thurgood Marshall, representing the views of himself and four other Justices, was rather ambiguous as to its grounding, invoking both First and Fourth amendment principles. Attorney Sparks had argued on behalf of the state that this case was decided by *Roth*, which held that obscene material had no First Amendment protection. As Marshall summarized Sparks's argument, "If the State can protect the body of a citizen, may it not . . . protect his mind?"

Well, no, said Marshall. While *Roth* and subsequent cases had held that obscenity, as such, was not protected by the First Amendment, neither *Roth* nor any subsequent obscenity case decided by the Court was exactly on point. In fact, apart from the *Mapp* case, the Court had been unable to find any prior case involving a prosecution for mere possession of obscene material, so this was very much a case of first impression, and it could not "be decided simply by citing *Roth*." While the Court had recognized a valid governmental interest in "dealing with the problem of obscenity," that did not necessarily mean that any and every state law enacted for that purpose was valid. *Roth* and subsequent cases were concerned with obscenity in a commercial context: selling, distributing, exhibiting. Private possession presented different issues.

"It is now well established," said Marshall, "that the Constitution protects the right to receive information and ideas. . . . Moreover, in the context of this case—a prosecution for mere possession of printed or filmed matter in the privacy of a person's own home—that right takes on an added dimension. For also fundamental is the right to be free, except in very limited circumstances, from unwanted governmental intrusions into one's privacy." Marshall cited a venerable Fourth Amendment argument for this last assertion, Justice Louis D. Brandeis's eloquent dissenting statement in *Olmstead v. United States* (1928), where Brandeis described the right of privacy in terms that the Court had subsequently invoked in *Griswold v. Connecticut* (1965) on the right of married adults to use contraceptives:

The makers of our Constitution undertook to secure conditions favorable to the pursuit of happiness. They recognized the significance of man's spiritual nature, of his feelings and of his intellect. They knew that only a part of the pain, pleasure and satisfactions of life are to be found in material things. They sought to protect Americans in their beliefs, their thoughts, their emotions and their sensations. They conferred, as against the Government, the right to be let alone—the most comprehensive of rights and the right most valued by civilized men.

Marshall said that the rights described by Brandeis were the very rights Stanley was asserting in this case. "He is asserting the right to read or observe what he pleases—the right to satisfy his intellectual and emotional needs in the privacy of his own home." Stanley was asserting "the right to be free from state inquiry into the contents of his library." It was not enough for Georgia to assert that the materials were obscene to overcome Stanley's constitutional rights. "Mere categorization of these films as 'obscene' is insufficient justification for such a drastic invasion of personal liberties guaranteed by the First and Fourteenth Amendments," said Marshall. While there were justifications for obscenity statutes, they did not "reach into the privacy of one's own home." "If the First Amendment means anything, it means that a State has no business telling a man, sitting alone in his own house, what books he may read or what films he may watch. Our whole constitutional heritage rebels at the thought of giving government the power to control men's minds," Marshall opined.

Given this holding, it was clear that Marshall had little sympathy for Georgia's argument that it had to protect its citizens from immoral influences through the criminalization of possession of obscenity. While some might consider the purification of citizens' minds to be a "noble" purpose, it was "wholly inconsistent with the philosophy of the First Amendment." Controlling "a person's private thoughts" was not the business of government. Georgia had also argued that the law was necessary because exposure to obscene materials might lead to deviant sexual behavior or even violent sex crimes. Marshall countered that there was no empirical evidence to support these assertions. While the *Roth* case had accepted such

arguments in justification for laws dealing with the distribution and public exhibition of obscene materials, those commercial contexts raised different issues, such as the danger of distribution to children or exposure of obscene materials to unwilling members of the public. These problems were just not present in a case of private possession, said Marshall, noting that for these very reasons the American Law Institute, in its Model Penal Code, had included a requirement that obscene matter be held for commercial dissemination before its possession could be penalized.

Finally, Marshall rejected the argument that penalizing possession played a necessary part in preventing distribution and sale of obscene materials. It was difficult to prove intent to sell or to distribute when obscene materials were seized in the possession of a possible dealer, argued the state, making such possession laws a critical tool in combating the pornography trade. Such difficulties, if they existed, did not suffice to justify "infringement of the individual's right to read or observe what he pleases," said Marshall. The right involved was "fundamental," so it could not be abridged merely "to ease the administration of otherwise valid criminal laws." Marshall concluded that "the First and Fourteenth Amendments prohibit making mere private possession of obscene material a crime." He noted that because of the fundamental liberties involved in the case by way of the First Amendment, the Court's decision should not be construed to apply to cases involving other items, such as narcotics, firearms, or stolen goods, which did not present such issues, or even to possession of literature or films that were made criminal because they could be used to injure the United States, presumably in terms of internal or external security.

Justice Hugo L. Black concurred separately in a two-sentence statement, relying on his extensive opinions in other cases arguing that there was no exception to the First Amendment, whether binding the federal government or as applied to the states through the Fourteenth Amendment, for "obscenity."

The case was remanded to the Georgia Supreme Court, which ruled on May 8, 1969, that its prior opinion must be vacated and the trial court judgment reversed in light of the Supreme Court's opinion.

Stanley v. Georgia left a constitutional puzzle behind it, because Justice Marshall's opinion for five members of the Court, although expressly invoking the First Amendment as its primary authority, also relied on and quoted from an important Fourth Amendment source, the *Olmstead* dissent, and appeared to premise the protection as much on the location of the films as on their communicative potential. Several commentators and courts have relied on *Stanley* as establishing a concept of "locational" privacy, in contradistinction to the "decisional" privacy exemplified by *Griswold*.

But what exactly was the scope of this privacy of the home described by Marshall? Although his final footnote made clear that "the privacy of the home" would not shelter other forms of contraband materials, might it shelter various forms of conduct, including sexual conduct, which could be validly criminalized if performed in public? Was the First Amendment component of the case so crucial that only materials and activities that carried their own First Amendment "aura" might be protected? If so, would sexual activity be included? Did references in the opinion to Stanley's right to satisfy "emotional" needs by viewing obscene films in private suggest that other activities fulfilling emotional needs might also come within the protected sphere of the privacy of the home?

The ambiguous theoretical basis for Stanley was to become the subject of a heated debate between Justices White and Harry A. Blackmun in their opinions in *Bowers v. Hardwick*, the famous Georgia sodomy case, with Blackmun emphasizing the Fourth Amendment privacy aspect and White emphasizing the First Amendment speech aspect in disagreeing about the applicability of *Stanley* to protect performance of oral sex in the privacy of the home. Perhaps more significantly, in *Osborne v. Ohio*, a 1990 case, the Court would reject one of the fundamental underpinnings of *Stanley*, Justice Marshall's notion that possession could not be criminalized as incidental to attempts to stop production and distribution, at least in the context of so-called kiddie porn. This left the continuing vitality of *Stanley* in some doubt, although it remains one of the most frequently cited opinions of the Supreme Court for the notion that the "privacy of the home" may shield some conduct that could be punished if performed publicly.

Case References

Bowers v. Hardwick, 478 U.S. 186 (1986)
Griswold v. Connecticut, 381 U.S. 479 (1965)
Mapp v. Ohio, 367 U.S. 643 (1961)
Marcus v. Search Warrants, 367 U.S. 717 (1961)
Olmstead v. United States, 277 U.S. 438 (1928)
Osborne v. Ohio, 495 U.S. 103 (1990)
Roth v. United States, 354 U.S. 476 (1957)

38. OBSCENITY AND "COMMUNITY STANDARDS"

Miller v. California, 413 U.S. 15 (1973).

Having decided in *Roth v. United States* (1957) that "obscene" publications were not protected by the First Amendment, the U.S. Supreme Court spent the next fifteen years struggling to agree on some definition of "obscenity" that would be workable enough to provide firm guidance to lower courts for application in individual cases. After a plurality ruled in 1966 in *Memoirs of a Woman of Pleasure v. Massachusetts* that only material that was "utterly without redeeming social value" could be condemned as obscene, the Court gave up for a time the attempt to formulate a majority-backed definition and adopted an *ad hoc* approach. Using its summary affirmance and reversal powers to function as a *de facto* national censorship board, many of the Justices personally reviewed each challenged magazine, book, film, or promotional flyer and personally decided whether the obscenity test had been met. Others, most prominently Justices William O. Douglas and Hugo L. Black, took the absolutist position that the First Amendment protected obscene expression and refused to participate in the censorship process, routinely dissenting from all obscenity conviction affirmances. With the retirements of Justices Black and John Marshall Harlan and the appointment of new Justices Lewis F. Powell, Jr., and William H. Rehnquist by President Richard Nixon, the Court found itself in 1972 with the possibility of forming a new majority around an authoritative legal definition of obscenity, and the *Miller* test resulted.

The case arose from an attempt by a mail-order dealer in "adult" materials to solicit business through blanket mailing of advertisements. One of the advertisements was received by a Newport Beach, California, restaurant owner, who opened the innocent-looking envelope with his mother and, shocked by the sexually explicit contents, contacted the police. The dealer was convicted by a jury under California Penal Code section 311.2(a), which made it a misdemeanor to sell, distribute, or offer to sell or distribute any obscene matter. The California statute defined "obscene" as follows:

> "Obscene" means that to the average person, applying contemporary standards, the predominant appeal of the matter, taken as a whole, is to prurient interest, i.e., a shameful or morbid interest in nudity, sex, or excretion, which goes substantially beyond customary limits of candor in description or representation of such matters and is matter which is utterly without redeeming social importance.

This statute faithfully tracked the current plurality standard of the Supreme Court at the time of its enactment. The Appellate Department of the California Superior Court for Orange County affirmed Marvin Miller's conviction without issuing an opinion, rendering the conviction not further appealable in the California court system.

Claiming that the California law unconstitutionally infringed on protected speech, Miller appealed directly to the U.S. Supreme Court, which noted probable jurisdiction and heard arguments twice, ordering reargument as the new Justices joined the Court for the 1972–73 Term. At the final argument, attorney Burton Marks represented Miller and Michael R. Capizzi represented the state of California. The American Civil Liberties Union filed an *amicus* brief urging reversal of the conviction.

The Court's 5–4 ruling vacating and remanding the case for reconsideration under its new standard was announced by Chief Justice Warren Burger on June 21, 1973. First argued early in the Court's 1971–72 Term, the case had occupied the Justices in internal debate throughout the entire succeeding Term of the Court. The opinion was announced the same day as the Court's ruling in *Paris Adult Theatre I v. Slaton*, in which Justice William J. Brennan, Jr., author of the Court's 1957 *Roth* opinion, partially recanted his original position and, dissenting from the Court's holding that the state could outlaw the exhibition of obscene films by an adult movie theater that restricted admission to consenting adults, adopted the view (which he continued to hold for the remainder of his service on the Court) that the First Amendment protected the exhibition and sale of obscene matter to consenting adults, and that the only legitimate exception to First Amendment protections would be in situations where the state was acting to protect unconsenting adults and minors from exposure to such materials. Justice Douglas, who believed the First Amendment made no exception for obscene materials, dissented separately, also condemning what he saw as serious due process concerns with the operation of the California law and the majority's new obscenity approach.

Burger began the Court's opinion with a brief review of the Court's fifteen years of wandering in the wilderness. He noted that Miller was tried under a state law that attempted to embody the test endorsed by a plurality of the Court in the *Memoirs* case, but now that the Court had summoned a majority around a different test, it was necessary to remand the case for consideration under the new test. The Court now endorsed an approach that based the determination of obscenity on the standards of the community, broadly defined, in which the jury was sitting, and that rejected the notion of the *Memoirs* plurality that material must be utterly without redeeming social value in order to be held obscene, a standard Burger asserted would rarely, if ever, be met.

After asserting that it had "been categorically settled by the Court" (or at least a majority of the Court) that obscene material lacked First Amendment protection, Burger acknowledged "the inherent dangers of undertaking to regulate any form of expression," commenting that state attempts to do so should be "carefully limited."

> As a result, we now confine the permissible scope of such regulation to works which depict or describe sexual conduct. That conduct must be specifically defined by the applicable state law, as written or authoritatively construed. A state offense must also be limited to works which, taken as a whole, appeal to the prurient interest in sex, which portray sexual conduct in a patently offensive way, and which, taken as a whole, do not have serious literary, artistic, political, or scientific value.

A trier of fact in an obscenity prosecution, said Burger, would have to follow certain "basic guidelines":

> (a) whether "the average person, applying contemporary community standards" would find that the work, taken as a whole, appeals to the prurient interest ... ; (b) whether the work depicts or describes, in a patently offensive way, sexual conduct specifically defined by the applicable law; and (c) whether the work, taken as a whole, lacks serious literary, artistic, political, or scientific value.

While Burger disclaimed any attempt by the Court to write obscenity laws for the states, he did give "a few plain examples of what a state statute could define for regulation" under part (b) of the standard the Court had announced: "(a) Patently offensive representations or descriptions of ultimate sexual acts, normal or perverted, actual or simulated. (b) Patently offensive representations or descriptions of masturbation, excretory functions, and lewd exhibition of the genitals."

"Sex and nudity may not be exploited without limit by films or pictures exhibited or sold in places of public accommodation any more than live sex and nudity can be exhibited or sold without limit in such public places," Burger argued. By protecting material that had serious literary, artistic, political, or scientific value, the Court majority believed it would be able to shield from prosecution such otherwise potentially obscene materials as illustrated medical texts. Burger contended that the panoply of due process rights attendant on all criminal pros-

ecutions would ensure that only truly "hard core" obscene pornography was likely to lead to a conviction.

Objecting to Justice Brennan's arguments in his *Paris Adult Theater I* dissent, Burger asked how Brennan could on the one hand uphold the right of the state to punish distribution of obscene materials to unconsenting adults or minors and on the other hand contend that it was impossible for the Court to come up with a definition of obscenity specific enough to withstand constitutional challenge. While it was true that obscenity prosecutions presented difficult issues of proof to the courts, that "this may not be an easy road, free from difficulty," still Burger was not willing to concede that any "amount of 'fatigue' should lead us to adopt a convenient 'institutional' rationale—an absolutist, 'anything goes' view of the First Amendment—because it will lighten our burdens." This would be an "abnegation" of the Court's duty to uphold constitutional guarantees, Burger insisted, quoting Brennan's own opinion for a plurality of the Court in an earlier obscenity case.

Burger then turned to defending the majority's decision that "community standards," rather than some national standard, should be applied in obscenity prosecutions. Burger insisted that "our Nation is simply too big and diverse for this Court to reasonably expect that such standards could be articulated for all 50 States in a single formulation, even assuming the prerequisite consensus exists." He contended that it would be "unrealistic" to expect jurors to be able to apply such a hypothetical national standard. They could be expected to reflect only the standards of the community in which they lived. Under the California statute applied in this case, the jury had been charged to consider the standards of the state of California in deciding whether Miller was attempting to sell obscene materials through his mail circulars. This was not a constitutional error, insisted Burger, despite Miller's attempt on appeal to argue that only a national standard would be consistent with a national constitutional protection for freedom of the press. "Nothing in the First Amendment requires that a jury must consider hypothetical and unascertainable 'national standards' when attempting to determine whether certain materials are obscene as a matter of fact," held Burger.

> It is neither realistic nor constitutionally sound to read the First Amendment as requiring that the people of Maine or Mississippi accept public depiction of conduct found tolerable in Las Vegas, or New York City. . . . People in different States vary in their tastes and attitudes, and this diversity is not to be strangled by the absolutism of imposed uniformity. . . . [The] primary concern with requiring a jury to apply the standard of 'the average person, applying contemporary community standards' is to be certain that, so far as material is not aimed at a deviant group, it will be judged by its impact on an average person, rather than a particularly susceptible or sensitive person—or indeed a totally insensitive one. . . . We hold that the requirement that the jury evaluate the materials with reference to 'contemporary standards of the State of California' serves this protective purpose and is constitutionally adequate.

Burger dismissed the arguments by Douglas and Brennan that the Court's decision would lead to repression of free expression, insisting that equating obscenity with "the free and robust exchange of ideas and political debate" would demean the "grand conception of the First Amendment and its high purposes in the historic struggle for freedom." So long as the First Amendment protected works with serious literary, artistic, political, or scientific value, Burger did not see how free expression was seriously abridged under the Court's new rules. After all, he argued, the purpose of the First Amendment was to protect expression of ideas, and, as far as he could see, protecting portrayal of "hard-core sexual conduct" hardly qualified under that purpose. He argued that 19th-century America, which vigorously prosecuted sexually explicit publications, was not a place known for suppression of diversity in ideas, whether in economics, politics, literature or "the outlying fields of social and political philosophies." Censorship of ideas was not what this decision was about, he insisted.

> One can concede that the "sexual revolution" of recent years may have had useful byproducts in striking layers of prudery from a subject long irrationally kept from needed ventilation. But it does not follow that no regulation of patently offensive "hard core" materials is needed or permissible; civilized people do not allow unregulated access to heroin because it

is a derivative of medicinal morphine.

Justice Douglas was clearly incensed by the Court's decision, and his vigorous dissent takes on both the newly articulated rules and the procedures California used to prosecute Miller. "Today we leave open the way for California to send a man to prison for distributing brochures that advertise books and movies under freshly written standards defining obscenity which until today's decision were never the part of any law," Douglas exclaimed, commenting that the Court had "worked hard to define obscenity and concededly has failed." After rehashing the lengthy history of unsuccessful attempts by the Court to do more than engage in *ad hoc* adjudication as to the status of particular prosecuted materials, he characterized all the proposed tests, including the new tests the Court was now articulating, as "vague tests" under which it would be improper to sustain convictions "for the sale of an article prior to the time when some court has declared it to be obscene." Even conceding, for argument's sake, that a state could prosecute for the sale of obscene materials, Douglas would want a judicial determination of obscenity to precede any threatened prosecution. Given his view that the Court had failed to adopt a definition of obscenity that would give the reasonable person fair notice of what materials were obscene, Douglas would want to reserve prosecution to those cases where somebody sold material which had previously been adjudged obscene. Otherwise, he observed, "the criminal law becomes a trap. . . . My contention is that until a civil proceeding has placed a tract beyond the pale, no criminal prosecution should be sustained."

But, of course, this due process concern was advanced for argument's sake, for Douglas next reiterated his longstanding argument that the First Amendment contained no "implied exception in the case of obscenity."

> The idea that the First Amendment permits government to ban publications that are "offensive" to some people puts an ominous gloss on freedom of the press. That test would make it possible to ban any paper or any journal or magazine in some benighted place. The First Amendment was designed "to invite dispute," to induce "a condition of unrest," to "create dissatisfaction with conditions as they are," and even to stir "people to anger." . . .

The idea that the First Amendment permits punishment for ideas that are "offensive" to the particular judge or jury sitting in judgment is astounding. No greater leveler of speech or literature has ever been designed. To give the power to the censor, as we do today, is to make a sharp and radical break with the traditions of a free society. The First Amendment was not fashioned as a vehicle for dispensing tranquilizers to the people. Its prime function was to keep debate open to "offensive" as well as to "staid" people.

Noting that the Court had intimated that the material Miller advertised was "garbage," Douglas insisted that "so is much of what is said in political campaigns, in the daily press, on TV, or over the radio. By reason of the First Amendment—and solely because of it—speakers and publishers have not been threatened or subdued because their thoughts and ideas may be 'offensive' to some."

After noting that the Court had struck down criminal laws in other contexts when "offensiveness" was the defining element of the crime, Douglas contended that if "offensive" sexual materials were to be criminalized, it should be up to the people to decide by constitutional amendment what the standard was to be. So long as the First Amendment contained no express exception for any form of communication, he was not ready to invent one as a matter of "interpretation."

We deal with highly emotional, not rational, questions. To many the Song of Solomon is obscene. I do not think we, the judges, were ever given the constitutional power to make definitions of obscenity. If it is to be defined, let the people debate and decide by constitutional amendment what they want to ban as obscene and what standards they want the legislatures and the courts to apply. Perhaps the people will decide that the path towards a mature, integrated society requires that all ideas competing for acceptance must have no censor. Perhaps they will decide otherwise. Whatever the choice, the courts will have some guidelines. Now we have none except our own predilections.

Finally, Justice Brennan dissented briefly in an opinion joined by Justices Potter Stewart and Thurgood Marshall. Referring to his newly articulated position on obscenity expressed in dissent in *Paris Adult Theatre I*, Brennan argued that the California statute was unconstitutionally overbroad, since it would punish distribution of "obscene" materials to consenting adults. "Since my view in *Paris Adult Theatre I* represents a substantial departure from the course of our prior decisions," said Brennan, "and since the state courts have as yet had no opportunity to consider whether a 'readily apparent construction suggests itself as a vehicle for rehabilitating the statute in a single prosecution, . . . , I would reverse the judgment" and remand for new proceedings.

The new *Miller* standard marked, at one and the same time, an advance and a retreat for the protection of sexually oriented materials. The Court had finally summoned a majority in support of a standard which, at least some thought, could provide sufficient guidance to lower courts and juries that it would no longer be necessary for the Court to continue on its course of *ad hoc*, fact specific determinations. The Justices could thus abandon the distasteful duty of having to review personally all the challenged films and other publications, so long as they were satisfied that the *Miller* requirements had been applied in the proceedings below. In this sense, no sexually oriented material would be judged on the basis of the reactions of the nine individuals who sat on the Court at any one time. On the other hand, the Court had rejected the quite plausible argument that the difficulties inherent in defining obscenity were such that no matter what it held, people were being put at risk for prosecution in cases where they could never really be sure prior to adjudication whether what they were doing was illegal. This was dramatically illustrated during the 1990s with the prosecution of rap song writers for sexually "offensive" lyrics, where the same song and lyrics were found obscene by one judge and not obscene by a jury sitting in a different district in the same state.

On the other hand, the *Miller* test was calculated to be reasonably flexible in accommodating changing community standards. While some argued that in a nation with national media and book and magazine distribution it was unfair to subject publishers and producers to a "community standards" test, on the other hand a national standard might impose on the more sexually liberated regions the lowest common denominator of prudery. In exchange for having to watch their step in the "Bible belt," producers of sexually oriented materials were almost guaranteed the ability to carry their products to the margins of outrageousness in those parts of the country where a typical jury was unlikely to condemn anything as being too "far out."

Relieved at having apparently rid itself of this recurring problem, the Court refused to reconsider the *Miller* test in any significant way for the next two decades, resisting all attempts by Justices Brennan and Marshall to prod it toward fashioning a narrower exception to First Amendment protection as described in Brennan's *Paris Adult Theatre I* dissent. Under the *Miller* regime, sexually oriented materials of unprecedented explicitness appeared on the newsstands of many large American cities without serious threat of prosecution, and the mails now carry materials that would even, to quote an old saw, "make a sailor blush." Media depiction of heterosexual (and to a much lesser extent, homosexual) activity has become relatively commonplace, and public standards for discussion of sexuality, fueled by the epidemic of sexually transmitted herpes in the 1970s and AIDS in the 1980s, have broadened so far that few juries in the nation's major urban areas could possibly find offensive the kinds of materials that preoccupied the Court in 1957 when it decided *Roth*.

On the other hand, the *Miller* approach lent itself to new dangers to freedom of sexual speech in the 1990s, as antipornography zealots found a new strategy to prosecute those who produced and distributed sexually explicit materials. Local officials in more conservative parts of the country, working together with the federal Justice Department's antipornography specialists, have begun to target national distributors of pornographic material for prosecution in the most conservative jurisdictions where their materials can be found. Thus, producers who make sexually explicit videotapes in Los Angeles or San Francisco will be subject to the judgments of rural juries in Alabama and Mississippi by responding to mail-order requests from those jurisdictions, or even by the happenstance of one of their products being purchased in California and then resold by the purchaser in a different state. As the Justice Department accelerated its antipornography activities during the administrations of Ronald Reagan and George Bush, it appeared that federal authorities were successfully exploiting the *Miller* "community standards" approach to impose a new "lowest common denominator" for tolerance of sexually explicit materials in the United States.

Case References

A Book Named *"John Cleland's Memoirs of a Woman of Pleasure" v. Massachusetts*, 383 U.S. 413 (1966)
Paris Adult Theatre I v. Slaton, 413 U.S. 49 (1973)
Roth v. United States, 354 U.S. 476 (1957)

39. STATES CAN CLOSE DOWN "PORN" THEATERS

Paris Adult Theatre I v. Slaton, 413 U.S. 49 (1973), remanding *Slaton v. Paris Adult Theatre I*, 228 Ga. 343, 185 So. 2d 768 (1971); decision on remand, 231 Ga. 312, 201 So. 2d 456 (1973), certiorari denied, 418 U.S. 939 (1974).

Paris Adult Theatres I and II on Peachtree Street in Atlanta, Georgia, specialized in showing sexually oriented films for adults. Attempting to avoid offending passersby, the commonly owned and operated theaters refrained from exhibiting pictorial advertising on their exteriors. Apart from the titles of the films and the name of the Theatres, the exterior of the building carried only a sign stating "Atlanta's Finest Mature Feature Films" and a notice on the entry stating: "Adult Theatre—You must be 21 and able to prove it. If viewing the nude body offends you, Please Do Not Enter." While this notice indicated that the films contained nudity, it did not indicate that they depicted scenes of simulated fellatio, cunnilingus, vaginal intercourse, and group sex. Admission was $3.

On December 12, 1970, as the theaters were preparing to show two new features, *It All Comes Out in the End* and *Magic Mirror*, Atlanta Judicial Circuit District Attorney Lewis R. Slaton and Solicitor General of the Criminal Court of Fulton County Hinson McAuliffe were filing a petition with the Fulton County Superior Court, seeking a temporary injunction against exhibition of the films on grounds that they were obscene. Superior Court Judge Jack Etheridge refused to grant the temporary restraining order, but did issue an order to the theater owners requiring them to produce the films for examination by the court to determine whether their showing should be permanently enjoined. Meanwhile, the theaters could continue to show the films and were barred from destroying them or shipping them out of the jurisdiction of the court.

Judge Etheridge held a hearing on January 13, 1971. The parties waived a jury trial. After viewing the films, Etheridge issued his opinion on April 12. "Assuming that obscenity is established by a finding that the actors cavorted about in the nude indiscriminately, then these films may fairly be considered obscene," he decided.

> Both films are clearly designed to entertain the spectator and perhaps, depending on the viewer, to appeal to his or her prurient interest. The portrayal of the sex act is undertaken; but the act itself is consistently only a simulated one if, indeed, the viewer can assume an act of intercourse or of fellatio is occurring from the machinations which are portrayed on the screen. Each of the films is childish, unimaginative, and altogether boring in its sameness.

Despite these findings, Etheridge denied the state's demand for an injunction against exhibition of the films. "It appears to the court that the display of these films in a commercial theater, when surrounded by requisite notice and by reasonable protection against the exposure of these films to minors, is constitutionally permissible."

Solicitor General McAuliffe appealed this ruling to the Georgia Supreme Court. D. Freeman Hutton of Atlanta defended the theaters. The court reversed Etheridge's opinion on November 5, holding that the state could ban the showing of a film deemed to be obscene. Writing for the unanimous court, Justice Peyton S. Hawes held that the U.S. Supreme Court's decision in *Stanley v. Georgia* (1969), upon which the theater owners apparently relied, did not support Judge Etheridge's decision. In *Stanley*, the Court held unconstitutional a Georgia law penalizing the private possession and use of obscene materials (in that case, sexually oriented films). Although accepting that the films seized in *Stanley* were obscene under then-prevailing First Amendment doctrine, the Court ruled that First Amendment protection for freedom of thought, especially within the privacy of the home, overcame any interest the state might have in promoting morality by suppressing obscenity. This case was different, wrote Hawes. Furthermore, the Court had recently ruled in *United States v. Reidel* (1971) that the federal government could prohibit distribution of obscene publications through the mails. Even though the materials were being mailed in an inoffensive wrapper to a private home, the Court had held that the rule of *Stanley* did not reach that case. The Georgia Supreme Court found *Reidel* to be "dispositive" of the constitutional issues. "The defendants in this case were making sales and delivery of the films involved in the only practical way in which it could be done, that is, by selling to the public the right to come into their theater and view the showing of such films." The court found no reason to grant immunity from prosecution to such exhibitions when the Supreme Court had upheld prosecution of those who sold obscene materials through the mails. "[*Reidel*] clearly establishes once and for all that the sale and delivery of obscene material to willing adults is not protected under the First Amendment," Hawes asserted.

Hawes also rejected the make-weight argument that the films were not obscene under prevailing standards. "The films in this case leave little to the imagination. It is plain what they purport to depict, that is, conduct of the most salacious character." To Hawes, these films were "hard core pornography" with no First Amendment protection.

The theater owners petitioned the U.S. Supreme Court to review the decision, and their petition was granted on June 26, 1972. The Court heard oral arguments early in its October 1972 Term, with Robert E. Smith, of Maryland, representing the petitioners and Thomas E. Moran representing the state of Georgia. The Court had received an *amicus* brief urging affirmance by Charles H. Keating (who later became infamous for his role in a savings and loan scandal) and others on their own behalf. The case was caught up with a general reconsideration of First Amendment obscenity law in which the Court was then engaged, and the opinion was not issued until the end of the Term, on June 21, 1973, together with the Court's reformulation of its obscenity test in *Miller v. California.* Since the Court had adopted a new standard for determining whether material was obscene, it vacated the decision of the Georgia Supreme Court and remanded the case for reconsideration whether the two films in question were entitled to First Amendment protection. Differences within the Court over the proper approach to obscenity and the degree to which a state might constitutionally regulate the exhibition of sexually oriented films resulted in a lengthy opinion for the Court by Chief Justice Warren E. Burger and dissenting opinions by Justices William O. Douglas and William J. Brennan, Jr., the latter joined by Justices Thurgood Marshall and John Paul Stevens.

"It should be clear from the outset," wrote Burger, "that we do not undertake to tell the States what they must do, but rather to define the area in which they may chart their own course in dealing with obscene material." A Georgia statute penalized the exhibition of obscene materials, and Georgia case law authorized issuance of an injunction against exhibition after a judicial determination of obscenity. The Court had that day announced a new standard for determining obscenity, so the case had to be remanded for reconsideration in light of that new standard. But the remand was not to be taken as "disapproval" of Georgia's procedures, which supplied all appropriate due process protection. Furthermore, it was not required that the trial court receive "expert" testimony on whether the material was obscene. "Expert" testimony was not necessary to determining obscenity, and the films themselves were "the best evidence of what they represent."

Having said this, however, Burger moved on to comment on the other part of the holding below, stating that "we categorically disapprove the theory, apparently adopted by the trial judge, that obscene, pornographic films acquire constitutional immunity from state regulation simply because they are exhibited for consenting adults only." Rejecting any extension of *Stanley v. Georgia* from the privacy of the home to a "public accommodation" such as a commercial motion picture theater, Burger rejected the idea that warning potential customers about "nudity" and posting an age restriction on admission were sufficient to make this a "private" showing. The commercial element made this a fit subject for state regulation. "The States have a long-recognized legitimate interest in regulating the use of obscene material in local commerce and in all places of public accommodation, so long as these regulations do not run afoul of specific constitutional prohibitions," he asserted. In this case, "we hold that there are legitimate state interests at stake in stemming the tide of commercialized obscenity, even assuming it is feasible to enforce effective safeguards against exposure to juveniles and to passersby." What was at stake were "the interest of the public in the quality of life and the total community environment, the tone of commerce in the great city centers, and, possibly, the public safety itself." Burger based this assertion on studies and reports purporting to show that commercialized obscenity might stimulate unlawful conduct by the viewer, producing "at least an arguable correlation between obscene material and crime." Invoking former Chief Justice Earl Warren's comment about the "right of the Nation and of the States to maintain a decent society," Burger said it was best left to state legislatures to determine how that decent society was to be maintained.

Replying to arguments that the state had proceeded on unproven assumptions about the negative effects of obscenity on society, Burger responded that a wide range of legislation rested on such assumptions, in areas ranging from securities regulation to antitrust policy. While First Amendment values demanded more than assumptions when speech was at issue, the long-established exemption of obscenity from First Amendment protection yielded a lesser standard for state justification of regulation. Burger asserted:

> The sum of experience, including that of the past two decades, affords an ample basis for legislatures to conclude that a sensitive, key relationship of human existence, central to family life, community welfare, and the development of human personality, can be debased and distorted by crass commercial exploitation of sex. Nothing in the Constitution prohibits a State from reaching such a conclusion and acting on it legislatively simply because there is no conclusive evidence or empirical data.

While the states could decide to adopt a *laissez-faire* attitude and drop regulations on obscenity, the Constitution did not compel them to do so.

Burger specifically rejected the argument that the right of privacy recognized in *Stanley* and *Griswold v. Connecticut* (1965) had anything to do with this case. The Court had never recognized commercial movie theaters as being "private" places, and they were specifically included in the definition of public accommodations under the Civil Rights Act of 1964. Prior decisions had spoken of the right of privacy in terms of "fundamental rights" under the Due Process Clause, but nothing in those decisions had ever intimated any "fundamental privacy right implicit in the concept of ordered liberty to watch obscene movies in places of public accommodation." The privacy of the home concept, relied on in *Stanley*, did not create a zone of privacy "that follows a distributor or a consumer of obscene materials wherever he goes," asserted Burger. Indeed, privacy and public accommodations were "mutually exclusive" concepts. Furthermore, as opposed to the situation in *Stanley*, here the state of Georgia was not primarily concerned with attempting to "control the minds" of theater patrons. Under the new obscenity test set out in *Miller v. California*, obscenity was material that lacked *any* "serious literary, artistic, political, or scientific value as communication." Nobody was being deprived of communication of "ideas" when its exhibition was banned.

Finally, Burger rejected the argument that exhibition to "consenting adults" was somehow beyond state regulation, once again reiterating that Georgia's concern here was with the "tendency" of such exhibitions "to injure the community as a whole, to endanger the public safety, or to jeopardize, in Mr. Chief Justice Warren's words, the States' 'right to maintain a decent society.'"

Justice Douglas, who believed that the First Amendment should be interpreted to bar any prosecution or injunction against obscenity, wrote a brief dissenting opinion, congratulating Justice Brennan for having seen the light and abandoned his former position that some forms of sexually oriented material could be banned under the rubric of "obscenity." Disagreeing as he did with the new *Miller* tests, Justice Douglas would have reversed the Georgia Supreme Court's decision and denied any injunction against exhibition of the films. For Douglas, the issue of obscenity was one of personal taste, and the lack of obscenity laws at the time of the adoption of the First Amendment persuaded him that the First Amendment itself was not adopted with the intent or understanding that obscene materials were exempt from its protection. "The list of activities and publications and pronouncements that offend someone is endless," he lamented, but that did not justify censorship. While he might find offensive material that the Court deemed obscene, he did not even bother viewing the books and films that came before the Court for determination, because he felt that the First Amendment barred him acting as a "censor."

While he applauded the effort of Brennan "to forsake the low road which the Court has followed in this field," he felt Brennan had not gone far enough. "I see no constitutional basis for fashioning a rule that makes a publisher, producer, bookseller, librarian, or movie house operator criminally responsible, when he fails to take affirmative steps to protect the consumer against literature, books, or movies offensive to those who temporarily occupy the seats of the mighty," he railed.

> When man was first in the jungle he took care of himself. When he entered a societal group, controls were necessarily imposed. But our society—unlike most in the world—presupposes that freedom and liberty are in a frame of reference that makes the individual, not government, the keeper of his tastes, beliefs, and ideas. That is the philosophy of the First

Amendment; and it is the article of faith that sets us apart from most nations in the world.

Justice Brennan's opinion is an extended consideration of the pros and cons of the Court's attempt to define obscenity and guide lower courts, legislatures, and common citizens in determining when materials are obscene and subject to regulation. He provided a history of the Court's struggle in this area, from *Roth v. United States* (1957), when it first attempted a comprehensive definition, through the multitude of obscenity rulings during the 1960s, which Brennan characterized as falling far short of "agreement on a workable definition of the term." The "essence" of the problem, said Brennan, was that the Court had been unable to provide "sensitive tools" to "separate obscenity from other sexually oriented but constitutionally protected speech, so that efforts to suppress the former do not spill over into the suppression of the latter." Indeed, the Court had been so frustrated in trying to articulate the difference between protected and unprotected sexually oriented speech, that it had fallen into a practice of issuing brief *per curiam* opinions in a string of cases involving individual films and other articles, offering no reasoned explanation for its decisions. One Justice, Potter Stewart, had exclaimed that he could not describe pornography any better than that he knew it when he saw it. The Justices could not even agree on what was or was not pornographic, some finding that protection extended to anything that was not "hard core" pornography, others finding a wider range of material unprotected.

As far as Brennan was concerned, the opinion issued the same day in *Miller* did not solve the problem because it continued in the same process, merely adjusting the tests slightly to emphasize that a local rather than a national standard of acceptability was to be used while requiring evidence that the material had no "serious" communicative value of a type protected by the First Amendment. Said Brennan:

Our experience with the *Roth* approach has certainly taught us that the outright suppression of obscenity cannot be reconciled with the fundamental principles of the First and Fourteenth Amendments. For we have failed to formulate a standard that sharply distinguishes protected from unprotected speech, and out of necessity, we have resorted to the [summary affirmance or denial of *certiorari*] approach, which resolves cases as between the parties, but offers only the most obscure guidance to legislation, adjudication by other courts, and primary conduct.

In short, almost any approach the Court might adopt would verge on the unconstitutionally vague. It was not enough for the Court to use a standard based on the personal perceptions of the Justices; that way, nobody could be sure whether his or her film or book was constitutionally protected until five members of the Supreme Court had reached agreement on the matter.

Vagueness in this area produced a variety of problems of constitutional dimensions. First, a vague approach provided inadequate notice of what conduct an obscenity law proscribed. This made various artistic and literary professions "hazardous," and invited "arbitrary and erratic enforcement of the law," leaving great discretion to local authorities. A vague statute in the area of speech or press created special problems, however, because of the probability that it would deter "free dissemination of ideas" that might be protected. It was this very concern that had led the Court in *Roth* to reject the old English cases that underlay previous American obscenity law, that "judged obscenity by the effect of isolated passages upon the most susceptible persons." The U.S. courts had used this standard in the 19th century in enforcing postal regulations against mailing of obscene matter. The problems of inadequate notice and chilling effect were bad enough, but they were compounded by the "institutional stresses" that the current approach stimulated in the judicial system. Almost every new case presented "a constitutional question of exceptional difficulty." As a result of the Court's failure "to define standards with predictable application," there was "no probability of regularity in obscenity decisions by state and lower federal courts." Furthermore, this approach was subjecting judges at all levels to the offensive task of having to view all the material claimed to be obscene and to make a judgment. "While the material may have varying degrees of social importance, it is hardly a source of edification to the members of this Court who are compelled to view it before passing on its obscenity," said Brennan.

What alternatives were available to the Court to escape the vagueness problem? One approach would be to specify that any "depiction or description of human sexual organs" was outside First Amendment protection. That would provide a bright line test that would solve the institutional difficulties, but "would be appallingly overbroad, permitting the suppression of a vast range of literary, scientific, and artistic masterpieces." The second approach, that of the Court in *Miller*, was to refine the *Roth* test to make it somewhat more descriptive. For Brennan, however, the *Miller* test made changes that were, "for the most part, academic." The approach remained the same. Indeed, said Brennan, the likely effect of *Miller* would be "permitting far more sweeping suppression of sexually oriented expression, including expression that would almost surely be held protected under [the pre-*Miller*] formulation." The test remained too subjective; deciding whether a challenged work had "serious" value called for personal judgments that should not be the basis of constitutional protection. This approach would have "no ameliorative effect" on the "cluster of problems" that Brennan had identified.

A third approach might have the judges throw up their hands and transfer the whole problem to juries. As long as community standards were supposed to prevail, why not let a jury of members of the community decide and treat their holding as the kind of factual determination that was normally not subject to judicial review unless totally out of line with the evidence? This would reduce the institutional problem but, Brennan concluded, would do nothing to create a more predictable and consistent standard. In fact, it would probably make that problem worse.

Another alternative would take the views of Justices Douglas and Black seriously. These Justices had long argued that the First Amendment, written in absolute terms ("Congress shall make no law . . ."), should be taken at its word. There should be no exception for obscenity. This was a tempting way to solve the vagueness problem, but Brennan felt it was not yet justified. He stated:

I am convinced that it would achieve that desirable goal only by stripping the States of power to an extent that cannot be justified by the commands of the Constitution, at least so long as there is available an alternative approach that strikes a better balance between the guarantee of free expression and the States' legitimate interests.

For Brennan, this alternative was to refrain from regulating the exhibition or distribution of obscenity to consenting adults under circumstances where minors were excluded and the public promotion of the material was discrete. Brennan reached this result by shifting the focus from the inherent nature of the material to the state's interest in suppressing it. And here, he found that the state interests carrying the most weight and empirical support were those in protecting minors from premature exposure to such material, and in protecting the sensibilities of passersby who might be offended by blatant pandering.

[T]he state interests in protecting children and in protecting unconsenting adults may stand on a different footing from the other asserted state interests. It may well be, as one commentator has argued, that "exposure to [erotic material] is for some persons an intense emotional experience. A communication of this nature, imposed upon a person contrary to his wishes, has all the characteristics of a physical assault. . . . [And it] constitutes an invasion of his privacy."

Once the focus switched to the state interests, it was clear that the Georgia Supreme Court's holding in this case had to be reversed. The theater restricted admission to those over age 21, and warned potential patrons that they were entering an "adult theater" where they could expect to confront "nudity." If there was any justification for banning this operation, it "must be found, therefore, in some independent interest in regulating the reading and viewing habits of consenting adults," and here *Stanley v. Georgia* provided the answer: the state has no valid interest in doing that. In *Stanley*, the Court had rejected as "wholly inconsistent with the philosophy of the First Amendment" a state interest predicated on "control of the moral content of a person's thoughts." While the state had a legitimate concern in promoting public morality, the "interest in regulating morality by suppressing obscenity, while often asserted, remains essentially unfocused and ill defined. And, since the attempt to curtail unprotected speech necessarily spills over into the area of protected speech," asserted Brennan, "the effort to serve this speculative interest through the suppression of obscene material must tread heavily on rights protected by the First Amendment."

Chief Justice Burger had written for the Court that the legislature was authorized to act on the basis of its assumptions about the harmful effects of obscenity on the community. If that was so, said Brennan, "it is hard to see how state-ordered regimentation of our minds can ever be forestalled." If the state could tell citizens what they cannot read or view, it was a short step to telling them what they must read or view. This would be clearly unconstitutional. Although the interests of the state in promoting morality could not be said to be "trivial or nonexistent," they could not "justify the substantial damage to constitutional rights and to this Nation's judicial machinery that inevitably results from state efforts to bar the distribution even of unprotected material to consenting adults." Realizing that his opinion would leave difficult questions regarding the state's authority to protect minors and unconsenting adults, nonetheless Brennan concluded that the approach he was advocating would "introduce a measure of clarity to this troubled area, would reduce the institutional pressure on this Court and the rest of the State and Federal Judiciary, and would guarantee fuller freedom of expression while leaving room for the protection of legitimate governmental interests." Nonetheless, it was Burger's view rather than Brennan's that won the endorsement of the Court.

On remand, the Georgia Supreme Court gave the attorneys for the city and state and the theaters an opportunity for supplemental briefing to determine whether the contested films were obscene under the *Miller* test. In its new opinion of October 30, 1973, by Justice G. Conley Ingram, the court decided to reaffirm its prior ruling, finding that the obscenity test set out in Georgia statutes was sufficiently similar to that in *Miller* so that a *de novo* determination of obscenity was not necessary. Since the Georgia law was intended to reach only "hard core pornography" in any event, the prior determination that the films were obscene was well within the area charted by *Miller*. Ingram

saw no due process problem with proceeding in this manner, since in his view Judge Etheridge had been applying a constitutionally acceptable standard when he made his initial obscenity determination. Since Burger's opinion for the Supreme Court had expressly rejected the notion that obscene material was still protected if only exhibited to "consenting adults," there was nothing more for the Georgia court to do than to reaffirm its ruling. The court had arranged for another showing of the films so that its newer members would be in a position to cast their votes, and they all concurred that the films were obscene under the new standards.

Justice William B. Gunter concurred separately. He was convinced by Brennan's argument that this game was not worth the candle, and if it were up to him the theater would be allowed to exhibit the films. But, being bound by the Supreme Court's decision, he was "required" to hold that the Georgia statute, which fell within the boundaries marked out by the Supreme Court, was not unduly vague, and to concur in the result.

The theater again petitioned for *certiorari*, which was denied on July 25, 1974. Justice Douglas predictably dissented, arguing that the films had First Amendment protection and the decision below should be reversed. Justices Brennan, Stewart, and Marshall also dissented, arguing that under the Court's rulings in *Miller* and this case, it was inappropriate for the Court to have decided the *certiorari* petition without viewing the films in question and subjecting them to the new standard. Justice Brennan, author of their brief dissent, reiterated his arguments in support of a revised approach. Although normally four votes are all that is needed to grant *certiorari*, in this instance Justices Stewart and Marshall were not urging decision of the case on the merits. The Court put a final end to the case when it denied a petition for rehearing on October 15, 1974.

The Court's decision in *Paris Adult Theater I* gave the green light to states and localities to proceed against "adult" movie theaters. However, by adopting a test in *Miller* that provided protection when a work had *any* serious literary, artistic, political, or scientific content, the Court may have unwittingly carved out a greater degree of protection for pornography, at least in those parts of the country where a fairly representative jury or reasonably sophisticated judge might be open to expert opinions on literary and artistic quality. As standards of acceptability in the depiction of sex broadened during the 1970s and 1980s, it became much more difficult to get a jury or judge to find that a film depicting sexual activity was obscene, and municipal governments began to turn to zoning regulations to try to relocate adult movie theaters away from central business districts or residential areas, rather than to ban them entirely. This was borne out by a jury verdict rendered in 1990 in Cincinnati in an obscenity prosecution against an art museum and its director for the exhibition of Robert Mapplethorpe's photographs that depicted homosexuality and sado-masochistic conduct, as well as nude children. The jury was persuaded by art experts that the photographs had serious artistic value, despite their offensiveness to many. Jurors were quoted after the case as saying they did not want Cincinnati to appear in the eyes of the world to be an unduly puritanical or unsophisticated community when it came to art.

The Court's rejection of Justice Brennan's "consenting adults" approach to the issue, however, had serious doctrinal consequences because it confirmed a narrow interpretation of *Stanley v. Georgia* that left plenty of room for the antipornography campaigns of Attorney General Ed Meese during the Reagan Administration. *Paris Adult Theatre I* was cited by the Court as subsequent authority in cases upholding criminal penalties for distribution and private possession of sexually oriented depictions of minors, and by the opponents of sexually oriented telephone message services. It was also cited by the Court in holding that a state could prohibit nude barroom or theater dancing. Taken together with *Reidel*, this opinion stopped short the developing notion of sexual freedom as including an almost absolute liberty for consenting adults to consume sexually oriented materials in places where minors and unconsenting adults were excluded.

Case References

Griswold v. Connecticut, 381 U.S. 479 (1965)
Miller v. California, 413 U.S. 15 (1973)
Roth v. United States, 354 U.S. 476 (1957)
Stanley v. Georgia, 394 U.S. 557 (1969)
United States v. Reidel, 402 U.S. 351 (1971)

40. HIPPIES AND THE CONSTITUTION

United States Department of Agriculture v. Moreno, 413 U.S. 528 (1973), affirming 345 F. Supp. 310 (D.D.C. 1972).

One of the more colorful flowerings of the countercultural revolution of the 1960s was the emergence of the hippies—lifestyle radicals who advocated "dropping out" of the mainstream culture to form free-living, free-loving communes, where unrelated adults and children could live together without the hierarchial constraints of traditional family structures. The hippies made their greatest impact on the national consciousness by participation in the tumultuous protests at the Democratic National Convention during the summer of 1968, but the establishment of hippie communes in rural areas and a few cities continued as the focus of ire for conservative legislators into the 1970s. Much of that ire was aroused by the free and

easy group sexuality reported to be central to hippie communal life.

Hippies remained newsworthy, and some of the news reports highlighted the economic arrangements that made hippie communes possible. Chief among them was the federal food stamp program, begun in 1964 as part of President Lyndon B. Johnson's "War on Poverty," and renewed periodically by Congress as a centerpiece of the national welfare system and an important stimulus for the sale of American agricultural produce. As originally enacted, the food stamp program authorized the purchase of food stamps at great discounts from face value by low income "households." A "household" was originally defined as "a group of related or non-related individuals, who are not residents of an institution or a boarding house, but are living as one economic unit sharing common cooking facilities and for whom food is customarily purchased in common." This definition seemed tailor-made for the countercultural hippie communes, in which adult members held down low-paying or part-time unskilled work or, due to their unconventional appearance and mannerisms, could register with unemployment offices confident of being rejected for any well-paying work that might come along.

News reports about food stamp purchases by hippie communes stimulated calls by some conservative legislators to amend the food stamp program so as to exclude hippies from participation. In January 1971, as a congressional conference committee met to reconcile differing versions of the Department of Agriculture appropriations bill, the committee agreed to amend the definition of an eligible "household" by removing the word "unrelated," with an indication that this was intended to eliminate hippies and hippie communes from the food stamp program. The appropriations bill passed Congress in this form, with little further discussion. Evidently, the conference committee members gave no thought to the untoward consequences this amendment would have for poor Americans, many of whom pooled expenses in shared living situations, although they did recognize that it might adversely affect the elderly (about whose sex lives they cared little) whom they exempted from the relatedness requirement.

As soon as the new law became effective, the Secretary of Labor adopted a new regulation defining eligible households, and many food stamp recipients received notices that they would be cut off from the program because of the presence of unrelated persons in their households. Suddenly, the living arrangements of the urban poor loomed as an obstacle to accomplishing the purposes of the food stamp program, which had been declared by Congress in 1964 to be "to safeguard the health and well-being of the Nation's population and raise levels of nutrition among low-income households." Organizations representing needy individuals found several typical examples of injustice caused by the new definition and filed a class action suit in the U.S. District Court for the

District of Columbia, seeking to enjoin operation of the new definition. Represented by Ronald F. Pollack and Roger Schwartz, of New York City, and John R. Kramer, of Washington, D.C., they persuaded a federal district judge temporarily to enjoin the Agriculture Department from terminating food stamp eligibility for households containing unrelated persons until a three-judge district court could assemble to consider the validity of the new regulation, which the plaintiffs claimed was both unauthorized by the statute and unconstitutional.

It was not difficult for the plaintiffs to make an overwhelmingly compelling argument that the new definition was having adverse consequences far beyond the "hippie" sphere of concern to members of Congress. They had merely to tell their stories. Lead plaintiff Jacinta Moreno was a 56-year-old diabetic who lived with Ermina Sanchez and Ermina's three children. They lived together because they needed to pool their public assistance payments in order to afford to keep a roof over their heads and food on the table. Their joint income barely covered rent, gas, and electricity, leaving a pittance for monthly living expenses (including food). Without food stamps, the two women and the three children would have to move to less suitable quarters, drastically reduce their food intake, or resort to crime to obtain enough money for a subsistence diet. They were clearly not hippies. Another named plaintiff, Sheilah Hejny, lived with her husband and three children. They were an indigent family, dependent on food stamps to stretch their public assistance payments. They had taken in a 20-year-old neighbor with emotional problems who had been thrown out of her home by her mother. They had been notified that because she was not related to them, they would lose their food stamp eligibility. Another plaintiff was Victoria Keppler, a poor woman whose daughter had a hearing deficiency. To afford to send her to a special school, Victoria had to become a boarder in the apartment of another woman who was also on public assistance and who lived near the school. However, she was threatened with loss of her food stamp eligibility, a key element of her tenuous financial circumstances, because she was not related to the woman whose apartment she was sharing.

The government assembled a legal team from the Justice Department and the U.S. Attorney's Office in the District of Columbia to defend the anti-hippie amendment, made up of Assistant Attorney General L. Patrick Gray, III, U.S. Attorney Harold H. Titus, Jr., and Justice Department staff attorneys Harland F. Leathers and Peter J. P. Brickfield. This assemblage of high-powered legal talent appeared before the three-judge district court of Circuit Judge Carl McGowan and District Judges John Lewis Smith, Jr., and Aubrey E. Robinson, Jr., for a hearing on the plaintiffs' motion for a preliminary injunction and the government's motion for summary judgment. At the hearing, attorneys for the plaintiffs indicated that they would also ask the court to grant summary judgment in their favor, since as far as they could see there were no factual disputes requiring trial. The case struck them as focusing entirely on the legal questions of whether the regulation was an appropriate effectuation of the statute, and whether the statute itself was constitutional. Counsel for the government, however, argued that if the government's motion for summary judgment was denied, the government wanted to present evidence at trial, although they could not specify which factual issues had to be developed at trial.

The three-judge panel decided that there were no issues requiring fact-finding, and it issued its unanimous decision granting the plaintiffs' motion for summary judgment on May 26, 1972. The government argued that the restriction of food stamp eligibility was justified by Congress's concern to bolster public morality by excluding the immoral "hippie communes" from participation in the program. The court rejected this as a legitimate justification for a provision that excluded so many otherwise eligible persons from participating in the program, in a unanimous opinion by Judge McGowan.

After rejecting the government's contention that the three-judge court lacked jurisdiction to consider the constitutionality of the regulation and the statute, McGowan turned first to the plaintiffs' suggestion that the regulation was beyond the authority of the Secretary of Agriculture. The regulation provided, with some exceptions, that households would be ineligible for food stamps unless the group of persons living in the household "are all related to each other." The plaintiffs had argued that it was possible to construe the statute in such a way as to avoid the hardships to them by recognizing that several "households" could simultaneously exist in the same living quarters. While this was possible, the Secretary's definition seemed to McGowan to be "well within the bounds of the legislative plan," and consequently not really subject to challenge as a departure from the policy announced by Congress in its 1971 amendment.

The constitutional challenge was more successful, however. McGowan found that the case was appropriate "for the application of traditional equal protection analysis." The statute created a classification, "households of related persons versus households with one or more unrelated persons." This classification seemed to McGowan to be "irrelevant" to the overall purposes Congress had articulated for the food stamp program: "the improvement of the agricultural economy, and the alleviation of hunger and malnutrition." Said McGowan, "The relationships among persons constituting one economic unit and sharing cooking facilities have nothing to do with their abilities to stimulate the agricultural economy by purchasing farm surpluses, or with their personal nutritional requirements."

Since the classification was irrelevant to the statutorily identified goals of the food stamp program, it could be sustained only if there was some other legitimate governmental purpose that could be imputed to Congress in adopting this provision. The only purpose that appeared in the legislative history was the desire to exclude hippies from the program. A bare desire to "harm a politically unpopular group" would not suffice to sustain legislation, so now the government was arguing that the exclusion of households with unrelated persons was necessary to promote "morality." While it was normal, in equal protection cases not involving "suspect classifications," for courts to give great deference to Congress and to embrace just about any rational explanation that might be contrived to support a statute that could be labeled "commercial or social regulation," the court was unwilling to do that in this case for two reasons.

First, said McGowan, "interpreting the amendment as an attempt to regulate morality would raise serious constitutional questions." In recent years, the U.S. Supreme Court had decided several cases concerning the "rights to privacy and freedom of association in the home," including such leading cases as *Griswold v. Connecticut* (1965), *Stanley v. Georgia* (1969), and *Eisenstadt v. Baird* (1972), in each of which the Court had at least implicitly rejected regulation of morality as a legitimate justification for government dictation of private lifestyle choices. Given these cases, the power of Congress to "legislate against its conception of immorality" was "doubtful at best" in the context of home living arrangements. "The visible conflict with fundamental personal freedoms operates to remove this case from the reach of the general rule regarding economic and social legislation," McGowan argued. Although the Food Stamp Act was legislation of that type, the particular amendment challenged in this case "directly impinges on First Amendment freedoms" of association, "and the hypothesized purpose—the fostering of morality—is not 'social and economic' in the traditional sense." Where hypothesizing a particular justification for a statute created such a heavy constitutional issue, the court was relieved of its normal obligation to do so.

Furthermore, even if the court indulged in hypothesizing such a purpose, the result would be an overbroad regulation, since, as demonstrated by the circumstances of the plaintiffs in this case, the household amendment "in terms disqualifies all households of unrelated individuals, without reference to whether a particular group contains both sexes," which was presumably the basis for Congress's concerns about the immorality of the hippie lifestyle. For the statute to survive scrutiny by the court, it would be necessary to read into it a vague requirement that the Secretary find a particular household to be immoral due to a sexual relationship between persons of the opposite sex, according to the unimaginative Judge McGowan. His opinion totally ignores the possibility that some congressmen might also have objected to food stamps going to homosexual households—a

possibility amply confirmed by subsequent bills in which legislators attempted to restrict access to federal welfare and public assistance programs on the basis of the sexual orientation of recipients. McGowan stated:

> In such circumstances, courts are not obliged to stretch their imaginations to the furthest limits in order to save a statute. When a court conceives a purpose neither declared in the statute itself nor explicitly identified in the legislative history, and then rewrites the statute so that it is precise with respect to that purpose, it treads perilously close to the congressional domain, since the definition of societal goals, and the choice of the regulatory classifications through which to achieve them, are normally determinations to be made in the first instance by the legislature. The doctrine that courts should endeavor to save the constitutionality of a statute was formulated in deference to the principle of separation of powers. We decline to follow that doctrine past the point at which it threatens to compromise the principle itself.

The fact was that the court was confronted with "hasty, last-minute congressional action," an "obvious afterthought" to Congress's "reexamination of the food stamp program." "Congress apparently thought it prudent to exclude what it assumed to be an easily identifiable and easily separable group," hippies, but the group "has proven to be not so facilely ascertainable; and the classification has achieved results which were apparently unintended." It was up to Congress to repair the damage, but the court was not about to maintain a classification that appeared so patently unconstitutional.

Finally, McGowan rejected the government's "startling" proposition at oral argument that if the hippie exclusion was not maintained the whole food stamp program should be enjoined until Congress could reconsider the matter. McGowan insisted that there was no indication that Congress considered this particular restriction to be the keystone of the program, such that the whole program was invalid if households with unrelated persons were to be included. After all, the program had been operating since 1964 with payments going to such households, and it was only a conference amendment, not a well-considered change emerging from hearings and careful consideration, that was at issue here. Congress apparently still regarded as essential the stated goals of the program, which had not been amended in 1971, and those would not be advanced by enjoining operation of the whole program.

The government appealed to the U.S. Supreme Court, which noted probable jurisdiction on December 4, 1972, and scheduled oral argument for April 23, 1973. A. Raymond Randolph, Jr., argued for the government on appeal and Ronald F. Pollack argued for the class plaintiffs. By now, the government had concluded that the "morality" argument would not work in light of the district court's opinion, so it had come up with a new argument: that the exclusion of households with unrelated persons was an antifraud measure, an argument not even discussed in the district court's opinion and apparently dreamed up in a last-ditch effort to save the antihippie amendment. Only two members of the Court were willing to buy such an argument: Justice William H. Rehnquist and Chief Justice Warren E. Burger, neither of whom was customarily inclined to view constitutional challenges to federal legislation with much favor.

In his opinion for the Court, issued June 25, 1973, Justice William J. Brennan, Jr., made short work of the only congressional purpose to be found in the legislative history, "to prevent so-called 'hippies' and 'hippie communes' from participating in the food stamp program." Brennan stated: "The challenged classification clearly cannot be sustained by reference to this congressional purpose. For if the constitutional conception of 'equal protection of the laws' means anything, it must at the very least mean that a bare congressional desire to harm a politically unpopular group cannot constitute a *legitimate* governmental interest." Thus, as McGowan had stated in a footnote, a "purpose to discriminate against hippies" could not, in and of itself, justify the household amendment. After noting that in the district court the government said that the congressional purpose was really regulation of morality but that the government "has now abandoned the 'morality' argument," Brennan turned to the government's new argument, that Congress might have thought that households with unrelated persons "are more likely than 'fully-related' households to contain individuals who

abuse the program by fraudulently failing to report sources of income or by voluntarily remaining poor" and that such households are "relatively unstable," thus complicating detection of fraud.

> But even if we were to accept as rational the Government's wholly unsubstantiated assumptions concerning the differences between "related" and "unrelated" households, we still could not agree with the Government's conclusion that the denial of essential federal food assistance to *all* otherwise eligible households containing unrelated members constitutes a rational effort to deal with these concerns.

For one thing, the Food Stamp Act had more direct antifraud provisions, including requirements that recipients register with employment services and accept offered employment, and imposing criminal penalties on anyone who obtained or used food stamps fraudulently. "The existence of these provisions necessarily casts considerable doubt upon the proposition that the 1971 amendment could rationally have been intended to prevent those very same abuses," said Brennan.

More to the point, the 1971 amendment provided its own incentive for fraud, since two unrelated individuals could "legally avoid the 'unrelated person' exclusion simply by altering their living arrangements so as to eliminate any one of the three conditions" provided by the amendment's definition of a household. For example, they could arrange to use separate kitchen facilities, thus escaping the definition of a household and not having to pool their income for eligibility purposes. In one of the affidavits included in the record, the California Director of Social Welfare explained that in fact "hippies" were most likely to be able to "alter their living arrangements" to retain eligibility for food stamps, but "the AFDC mothers [i.e., mothers on public assistance] who try to raise their standard of living by sharing households will be affected. They will not be able to utilize the altered living patterns in order to continue to be eligible without giving up their advantage of shared housing costs." Ironically, the antihippie amendment was easily thwarted by hippies but would end up excluding large numbers of people whom Congress had not intended to exclude. Thus, concluded Brennan, the regulation was "wholly without any rational basis" and could not even survive the most deferential equal protection scrutiny.

Justice William O. Douglas concurred in an unduly lengthy opinion that restated all the factual matter from Justice Brennan's opinion but then placed its focus almost entirely on the First Amendment, thus bringing the case solidly within the "fundamental rights" branch of equal protection analysis.

> This case involves desperately poor people with acute problems who, though unrelated, come together for mutual help and assistance. The choice of one's associates for social, political, race, or religious purposes is basic in our constitutional scheme. . . . I suppose no one would doubt that an association of people working in the poverty field would be entitled to the same constitutional protection as those working in the racial, banking, or agricultural field. I suppose poor people holding a meeting or convention would be under the same constitutional umbrella as others. The dimensions of the "unrelated" person problem under the Food Stamp Act are in that category. As the facts of this case show, the poor are congregating in households where they can better meet the adversities of poverty. This banding together is an expression of the right of freedom of association that is very deep in our traditions.

Douglas, like Brennan, conceded that the detection of fraud might be a legitimate goal of the government, but could find no rational relationship between that goal and the exclusion of "unrelated" households. "Problems of the fisc . . . are legitimate concerns of government. But government 'may not accomplish such a purpose by invidious distinctions between classes of its citizens,'" said Douglas, who insisted that the "right of association, the right to invite the stranger into one's home is too basic in our constitutional regime to deal with roughshod."

Justice Rehnquist's dissent, joined by the Chief Justice, criticized the Court for being concerned with issues more properly the province of the legislature, in his view. Although Congress had attacked a problem with "a rather blunt instrument" and "persuasive arguments may be made that what we conceive to be its purpose will not be significantly advanced by the enactment of the limitation," Rehnquist

insisted that such policy questions were for Congress, not the Court. He did not believe that the "asserted congressional concern with the fraudulent use of food stamps" (asserted, of course, only by the Justice Department lawyers before the Supreme Court, where the argument was first advanced, and never by members of Congress during consideration or debate on the amendment) "is, when interpreted in the light most favorable to sustaining the limitation, quite as irrational as the Court seems to believe." Rehnquist argued that it was a rational policy choice for Congress to have determined that it wanted to support with food stamps traditional family units of related individuals. "This unit provides a guarantee which is not provided by households containing unrelated individuals that the household exists for some purpose other than to collect federal food stamps." Since equal protection analysis did not require Congress to draw lines with "mathematical precision," in his view it was not unconstitutional to draw this particular line just because some hardships would result. The line Congress drew did achieve the result it intended—to "deny food stamps to members of households which have been formed solely for the purpose of taking advantage of the food stamp program." Since it was achieving this purpose, it could hardly be criticized as lacking all rationality.

The Court's decision in *Moreno* had an importance that transcended the particular dispute, because it picked up from McGowan's footnote and enshrined in the majority text the proposition that active congressional dislike for a particular unpopular group—a group characterized by some as flaunting sexual immorality—could not provide a legitimate basis for constructing a legislative scheme intended to deny that group a benefit generally made available to others. The notion that mere dislike for a group is not a legitimate basis for legislation disadvantaging that group could be a powerful tool for challenging a variety of legislative disabilities imposed on sexual minorities, although the Court has generally not seen fit to embrace that idea when such cases have later surfaced on its docket. The concept nonetheless has significant merit and power, and has proved useful at times in the lower courts.

Case References

Eisenstadt v. Baird, 405 U.S. 438 (1972)

Griswold v. Connecticut, 381 U.S. 479 (1965)
Stanley v. Georgia, 394 U.S. 557 (1969)

41. EMPOWERING SEXUAL MINORITIES THROUGH LEGAL ORGANIZATION

In re Thom, 33 N.Y.2d 609, 347 N.Y.S.2d 571 (1973), reversing 40 A.D.2d 787, 337 N.Y.S.2d 588 (1st Dept. 1972), decision on remand, 42 A.D.2d 353, 350 N.Y.S.2d 1 (1st Dept. 1973)

Lesbians and gay men began to form organizations to advance their civil rights shortly after World War II. These organizations tended to be small and secretive, although by the early 1960s they were becoming more visible, occasionally picketing in public and even filing *amicus* briefs in significant court cases, such as the U.S. Supreme Court's consideration of immigration law provisions barring homosexuals from immigrating to the United States. By the late 1960s the pressure for larger scale action was building among this sexual minority, as the example of spectacular gains for racial minorities and women spurred homosexuals into new activism. The Stonewall Riots of June and July 1969 in New York's Greenwich Village demonstrated a new willingness to take direct action, and led to the formation of the Gay Activists Alliance and, within a few years, the National Gay Task Force. Meahwhile, however, some lawyers involved with GAA in New York conceived the idea of forming a public interest law firm to advance gay rights.

Led by William J. Thom, a young associate at a small, prestigious midtown law firm, the group drew up articles of incorporation for Lambda Legal Defense and Education Fund. They modeled their articles on those of the Puerto Rican Legal Defense and Education Fund, whose formation as a not-for-profit organization had been approved by the State Commissioner of Education and whose application to practice law in corporate form had been approved by the Appellate Division, First Department, in Manhattan. Lambda adopted the following statement of purpose: "The Corporation is organized to seek, through the legal process, to insure equal protection of the laws and the protection of civil rights of homosexu-

als." As its mission, Lambda specified the following:

> (a) to initiate or join in judicial and administrative proceedings whenever legal rights and interests of significant numbers of homosexuals may be affected; (b) to provide to homosexuals information which will broaden their awareness of their legal rights and obligations; (c) to inform the legal community and the public of the goals, methods and accomplishments of the Corporation.

In his application to the appellate division for approval, Thom described Lambda's proposed activities:

> These activities include providing without charge legal services in those situations which give rise to legal issues having a substantial effect on the legal rights of homosexuals; to promote the availability of legal services to homosexuals by encouraging and attracting homosexuals into the legal profession; to disseminate to homosexuals general information concerning their legal rights and obligations, and to render technical assistance to any legal services corporation or agency in regard to legal issues affecting homosexuals.

Having received approval of his application from the relevant committees of the Association of the Bar of the City of New York and the New York County Lawyers Association, as required by the appellate division's rules, Thom filed his petition with the court hopeful for a quick resolution so the new organization could be promptly launched. His hopes were dashed, however, when a five-member panel of the court issued a *per curiam* opinion on November 9, 1972, denying his application and dismissing his petition.

The court did not provide much explanation for its decision. Asserting in conclusory fashion that the "stated purposes" for Lambda's formation were "on their face neither benevolent nor charitable" as required by the judiciary law for this type of law practice by a corporation, the court contended that there was no demonstrated need for this corporation. "It is not shown that the private sector of the profession is not available to serve this clientele, nor that, as to indigents, the existing legal assistance corporations are not available." Acknowledging an affidavit accompanying the application asserting that there was a "lack of desire on the part of some attorneys who work pro bono publico to take the cases of homosexuals," the court sniffed that "this appears to be no more than a matter of taste," and, after all, the affidavit did not state that lawyers "are completely lacking." As far as the court was concerned, homosexuals could find attorneys without this organization's assistance. Modeling the application on that of the Puerto Rican Legal Defense and Education Fund carried no weight with the judges; "The latter's application demonstrated clearly that indigence is rife amongst the intended clientele. It does not appear that discrimination against homosexuals, which undoubtedly exists, operates to deprive them of legal representation."

The court concluded that there had been a proliferation of these legal defense fund types of organizations and asserted that more guidance from the legislature would be helpful in determining how to evaluate these sorts of applications. In any event, it was not enough to justify approval that Lambda sought to advance the interests of a "minority."

Thom appealed the ruling to the court of appeals, with civil rights attorneys Victor Rabinowitz and Herbert Jordan taking over the appellate argument. Attorneys Daniel M. Cohen and Samuel A. Hirshowitz, of New York City, appeared on behalf of Attorney General Louis J. Lefkowitz, as required by statute, to defend the laws governing approval of law corporations, as required by the judiciary law. All but one of the members of the court of appeals agreed that the appellate division's determination should be reversed. In their opinion of July 3, 1973, Judges Charles D. Breitel, Matthew J. Jasen, Hugh R. Jones, and Sol M. Wachtler were content to rule *per curiam* that the appel-

late division's decision was "unsupportable in finding that the Lambda Corporation was neither benevolent nor charitable in ostensible purpose and that there was no demonstrated need for the corporation." At the same time, however, they rejected the argument that the appellate division was without discretion in deciding whether to grant such applications. Suggesting that the "responsibility of the sponsors, the method of financing, the scope of activities proposed, and still others not predictable or definable in advance, any or all of which may affect the public interest" were among the factors the appellate division could consider within its discretion, the majority remanded the matter to the appellate division for further consideration.

The argument about the degree of the appellate division's discretion was responsive to a separate opinion by Court of Appeals Judge Adrian P. Burke, which was joined by Chief Judge Stanley M. Fuld. By contrast to the brief, one-paragraph *per curiam* opinion, Burke wrote a lengthy concurring opinion pointing out the specific failings of the appellate division's factual assertions concerning the Lambda petition, and arguing that in fact the appellate division had little discretion to reject such petitions apart from technical problems of compliance with the relevant statutes. To rule otherwise, Burke suggested, might violate constitutional requirements of equal protection or First Amendment rights of speech and association.

Reviewing the rules the appellate division had adopted for considering and approving applications to practice law from public interest corporations such as Lambda, Burke noted that they appropriately required a demonstration that the organization would be structured in such a way that lay persons would not dominate their operations, that there would be adequate financing to provide high-quality legal representation, and that the lawyers employed would maintain an appropriately professional relationship with their clients. As to all the requirements of the rules, "it is not disputed that Lambda's petition complied in all respects." The key difficulty was the appellate division's conclusion, which the four other members of the court of appeals called "unsupportable," that Lambda's stated corporate purposes were neither benevolent nor charitable as required by statute. Here, said Burke, Lambda had correctly argued that this conclusion was inconsistent with the appellate division's approval of the Puerto Rican legal group and raised equal protection issues. The Puerto Rican group was not planning to limit its operation to represent indigent persons. Its stated purposes were to participate in cases where the legal interests of Puerto Ricans were affected, without limitation based on the indigency of clients. Apparently, the appellate division had considered such activities benevolent or charitable purposes within the meaning of the judiciary law. In fact, there was case law upholding such a determination in other circumstances. Since Lambda's stated purpose was "substantially identical," merely substituting homosexuals for Puerto Ricans, there was "no justification for a finding that one was motivated by charitable goals while the other was not."

Since Lambda was a benevolent or charitable organization and was appropriately organized according to the technical rules governing such organizations, the question remained whether the appellate division had any discretion to deny the application. "We think not," said Burke and Fuld, parting company from the majority of the Court, for to accord discretion, without any articulated standards, might raise First Amendment issues of the type addressed by the Supreme Court in *NAACP v. Button* (1963) and similar cases. Clearly, homosexuals had a First Amendment right to retain attorneys and pursue their civil rights through the courts. The Supreme Court had stated in *United Transportation Union v. Michigan Bar* (1971), a case presenting the issue whether a union could itself practice law through employed counsel rather than by retaining the services of an independent contractor attorney in private practice, "The common thread running through our decisions . . . is that collective activity undertaken to obtain meaningful access to the courts is a fundamental right within the protection of the First Amendment." Thus, Lambda had a First Amendment right to employ attorneys to advance the cause of gay rights.

However, said Burke, there was more involved here than merely the right of Lambda to retain counsel, since Lambda was seeking permission to practice law as a corporate entity. The Supreme Court had recognized the right of the states to regulate law practice in order to protect the public. There was a legitimate concern that a corporation practicing law might not provide appropriate representation if nonlawyers played too great a role in its legal decisionmaking or, more significantly, if its attorneys did not provide adequate representation to individual clients because of their primary responsibility to the corporation that employed them. The appellate division could appropriately require, through its rules, that these concerns be satisfied. However, it would violate equal protection to let the appellate division deny an application from a group that had met the requirements of the rules based solely on the appellate division's opinion as to whether the group's services were needed by members of the public. Such a "subjective determination" without objective standards would lead to a discriminatory result. "We can perceive no rational distinction in the need for group legal services as between Puerto Ricans and homosexuals," said Burke. "Both groups are minorities subject to varied discriminations and in need of legal services. Absent evidence to the contrary, it must be assumed that the services of private attorneys are equally available or unavailable to both groups." The appellate division's determination had no rational basis.

Judge Domenick L. Gabrielli was the lone dissenter. He asserted that the appellate division had adequately explained its reasons for dismissing the petition by its unanimous determination that Lambda's stated purposes were neither benevolent nor charitable. He felt this was fully supported by the record, since the Puerto Rican Legal Defense Fund's application emphasized the indigency of many to be served by that organization, and Lambda's application made no such showing. He would leave such determinations to the discretion of the appellate division. He particularly criticized the concurrers, Judges Burke and Fuld, for "substituting their judgment in the matter for the judgment of those to whom the responsibility was delegated." He asserted that the *per curiam* opinion left the appellate division "very little to consider" on remand.

The appellate division did not feel itself totally limited, however. If the court of appeals had virtually held that the application must be approved, nonetheless the court had stated that the appellate division retained discretion to assure compliance with all legal requirements, including that the proposed activities comport with the judiciary law provision describing the circumstances under which corporations could be allowed to practice law. To the appellate division, which produced a *per curiam* opinion on remand on October 18, 1973, one of Lambda's stated purposes did not comport with the statutory limitations: the proposal to "promote legal education among homosexuals by recruiting and encouraging potential law students who are homosexuals and by providing assistance to such students after admission to law school." This had nothing to do with practicing law, so far as the appellate division was concerned. "We do not deem it appropriate to lend our approval to" this purpose, they harrumphed, otherwise finally granting Thom's petition.

Thus was born the first public interest law firm exclusively dedicated to advancing the legal rights of lesbians and gay men. From the modest beginnings of a few friends gathered in Bill Thom's living room, Lambda grew slowly and steadily until the mid-1980s, when the combined challenges of the emerging AIDS epidemic and increasing national reputation prompted a dramatic spurt in growth leaving Lambda by 1990 one of the largest and best known and respected lesbian and gay rights organizations in the United States. After Lambda's successful launch, lesbian and gay attorneys in other parts of the country followed suit, forming Gay Rights Advocates in California and Gay and Lesbian Advocates and Defenders in Boston. Lambda remained preeminent, however, and by 1991 was the largest such organization operating on a national scale.

Case References

NAACP v. Button, 371 U.S. 415 (1963)

United Transportation Union v. Michigan Bar, 401 U.S. 576 (1971)

42. PUBLIC EMPLOYEES MAY ADVOCATE FOR GAY RIGHTS

Van Ooteghem v. Gray, 628 F.2d 488 (5th Cir. 1980), vacated for hearing en banc, 640 F.2d 12 (5th Cir.), certiorari dismissed without prejudice, 451 U.S. 935 (1981), affirmed in part, vacated and remanded, 654 F.2d 304 (5th Cir. 1981), certiorari denied, 455 U.S. 909 (1982), decision on remand, 584 F. Supp. 897 (S.D. Tex. 1984), affirmed as modified, 774 F.2d 1332 (5th Cir. 1985).

It took an unconscionably long time, but after ten years of legal struggle, Gary John Van Ooteghem finally won at least partial vindication for his discharge from public employment for being a gay rights advocate. Harris County, Texas, Treasurer Hartsell Gray hired Van Ooteghem in the category "Cashier/Assistant County Treasurer" in January 1975. Van Ooteghem's worked was so exemplary that he was quickly promoted to assistant country treasurer, and accorded the professional privilege of setting his own hours and taking time off as needed. Van Ooteghem, a gay man with a mission, decided that he would testify before the Commissioners Court of Harris County, which

was considering a gay rights issue. On July 28, he informed his boss that he was gay and that he planned to testify in favor of a gay rights measure. Gray flew into a panic and came up with a stratagem to prevent the testimony: he would adopt a new policy on office hours, requiring the assistant county treasurer to remain in the office during business hours when the Commissioners Court would be meeting. On July 31, Gray gave Van Ooteghem a letter setting forth this new policy and requiring him to acknowledge his agreement with the new schedule by signing the letter. When Van Ooteghem refused to sign the letter, he was discharged.

Van Ooteghem found some local activist attorneys, Larry Sauer and J. Patrick Wiseman, who were willing to represent him, and filed suit against Gray in the U.S. District Court for the Southern District of Texas on August 29, 1975, asserting that the discharge violated his right of free speech under the First Amendment and demanding reinstatement and back pay. County attorneys appeared to defend Gray. After the usual pretrial dueling, there was a trial before District Judge Ross N. Sterling, who concluded that the discharge did violate the First Amendment and ordered Gray on March 20, 1978, to offer Van Ooteghem reinstatement with back pay. Sterling also concluded that Van Ooteghem's attorneys were entitled to $7,500 for their work on the case and awarded that amount in costs and attorneys fees.

Gray appealed to the U.S. Court of Appeals for the Fifth Circuit, where he was represented by county attorneys Joe Resweber and Billy E. Lee, and Wiseman presented oral argument for Van Ooteghem. A unanimous panel agreed that Sterling's decision was correct on the outcome of the merits, but that more work had to be done to justify the attorney's fee award. There was less unanimity, however, over the correct First Amendment standard to apply to the case, generating majority and concurring opinions on October 22, 1980.

Circuit Judge Irving L. Goldberg, author of the panel's majority opinion, was evidently amused with Gray's attempts to escape personal liability and to protect the county treasury from Sterling's monetary awards. To Goldberg, the whole case had such a dramatic quality that he cast his opinion in theatrical terms, describing Gray as being "featured in several roles" and characterizing Van Ooteghem as Gray's "co-star." Behind the levity, however, was a serious attempt to grapple with the First Amendment free speech rights of public employees who want to advocate on behalf of gay rights.

As a nontenured political appointee, Van Ooteghem could have been fired for any or no reason, so long as the reason for discharge was not "constitutionally infirm," said Goldberg. Invoking such familiar Supreme Court precedents as *Perry v. Sindermann* (1972) and *Pickering v. Board of Education* (1968), he asserted: "No governmental benefit can be denied for a rea-son that infringes constitutionally protected interests, including freedom of speech." The Supreme Court's decisions left three questions for the court to answer: whether Van Ooteghem's proposed exercise of free speech was a "substantial" or "motivating" factor in the discharge, whether the speech was constitutionally protected, and whether Van Ooteghem would have been discharged in the absence of his decision to testify for gay rights. The last test was required by the Supreme Court's decision in *Mt. Healthy City School District v. Doyle* (1977), which held that when government action was taken for several reasons, including an unconstitutional one, the action would be upheld if the untainted reasons would have been sufficient to sustain the action.

Whether the answers to these questions were issues of fact or law would be significant for purposes of reviewing Sterling's rulings, since a district court's factual findings would be set aside only if clearly erroneous, but questions of law were subject to more searching review. Goldberg concluded that in trying to determine the motivation for Van Ooteghem's discharge, Sterling confronted a "clear factual choice: was Van Ooteghem fired for his mere absence from work regardless of the purpose of this absence, making this a simple insubordination case as claimed by Gray, or, alternatively, was the establishment of set working hours and the dismissal for their violation an attempt to prevent and punish his decision to speak to a political body on a controversial, political issue?" Since this was essentially a factual determination, Sterling's findings could only be rejected if clearly erroneous, and Goldberg found that they were not. The coincidence of timing between Van Ooteghem's "coming out" speech to Gray and the promulgation of the new attendance rule, which was completely inconsistent with the past professional standard under which Van Ooteghem was working, provided a firm basis in the record for Sterling's conclusion that Van Ooteghem's speech was the motivation for the discharge. "The stipulated facts provide no basis from which any justification for the new schedule can be reasonably inferred," said Goldberg, "other than the desire to thwart Van Ooteghem's lobbying on behalf of homosexuals."

The question of whether Van Ooteghem's speech was constitutionally protected in this context was somewhat more difficult and divided the panel as to analytical approach. Sterling had found that Van Ooteghem's speech "did not significantly interfere with the operation of the Treasury nor did it impede Van Ooteghem's performance of his daily duties." These were factual determinations that were not clearly erroneous based on the trial record, but by what constitutional standard were they to be judged? Reviewing the Supreme Court's decisions on public employee speech and other First Amendment activities, Goldberg concluded that where the public employee sought to speak on a matter of public interest, the state was put to the burden of demonstrating a compelling interest in preventing the speech, which could be satisfied only by a showing of "material and substantial interference" with the operation of a government department. "It may be true that some treasury workers, or Gray himself, found the prospect of an employee addressing the Commissioners Court on homosexual rights to be distressing," commented Goldberg. "However, the ability of a member of a disfavored class to express his views on civil rights publicly and without hesitation—no matter how personally offensive to his employer or a majority of his coemployees—lies at the core of the Free Speech Clause of the First Amendment." Any disturbance that might arise in this case, said Goldberg, as a matter of law would not present a "substantial and material disturbance."

Finally, the court had to apply the *Mt. Healthy* test to determine whether the unconstitutional motivation was outweighed by other justifications for discharge. Gray had claimed to have discovered various other reasons to discharge Van Ooteghem, but these were all raised after the event. At the time, Van Ooteghem's record was considered excellent; as Goldberg said, he "was shown to be brilliant and hard working." When Gray made his discharge decision, there was no "collateral justification" for the discharge.

Having concluded that the discharge violated Van Ooteghem's constitutional rights, Goldberg turned to the issue of remedy. A reinstatement order was *pro forma* in such cases,

but there was considerable controversy about the back pay remedy—not as to amount, but as to who should pay it. Here, Gray tried to do some fancy steps, asserting that he should not be personally liable (even though at trial the county had argued that the discharge decision was a personal decision of Gray, not an official decision for which county liability should apply), and that the county, as a subdivision of the state, also should escape liability through immunity under the Eleventh Amendment. Goldberg worked his way carefully through this minefield, noting precedents finding that Texas counties were not entitled to such immunity from damage suits and that Gray's acts could best be characterized as being undertaken in an official character. On another aspect of Sterling's determination, however, Goldberg was not so easily persuaded. The costs and attorney's fees figure was arrived at without any discernible calculation based on the factors required by federal precedents, so Goldberg concluded that the case should be remanded for the limited purpose of having the judge retry the attorney's fees issue in order to make a calculation with a firm factual basis.

Circuit Judge Thomas M. Reavley filed a concurring opinion. He agreed with Goldberg that the discharge was unconstitutional, that the damages were properly awarded against Harris County, and that a further hearing was needed prior to determining attorney's fees. Where he parted company was on the standard to be used in evaluating the degree of protection afforded Van Ooteghem's speech. He argued that Goldberg had drawn the wrong conclusion from the Supreme Court cases. While the Court had held that the state must satisfy the "compelling interest" standard in cases involving belief and association, Reavley contended that the Court had not gone so far in cases involving public employee speech, for the simple reason that speech was likely to be more disruptive or have a more direct impact on the ability of a government office to operate, particularly when directed to politically controversial issues. Rather, said Reavley, the Court had endorsed using a balancing test to deal with public employee speech issues. The compelling interest test would be too onerous for public employers, because it was so difficult to meet.

This did not change the outcome, however, for Reavley agreed that in this case the balance should be struck in favor of Van Ooteghem's free speech rights. Sterling had found that Van Ooteghem's "temporary absence to address the Commissioners Court could not have substantially impeded the functioning of the Treasury," and Reavley did not find this conclusion clearly erroneous.

Gray was so eager to appeal this ruling that he apparently filed overlapping petitions for rehearing with the Fifth Circuit and for *certiorari* with the Supreme Court. The Fifth Circuit acted first, voting on February 26, 1981, to schedule the case for reconsideration on written briefs by the full circuit; in light of this, the Supreme Court dismissed the *certiorari* petition without prejudice on April 27, 1981. The *en banc* circuit received briefs from the attorneys, as well as an *amicus* brief drawn up on behalf of the counties of Texas by University of Houston Law School Professor David Crump, attacking the conclusion that individual Texas counties could be held liable for damages in this kind of case. The *en banc* court issued a *per curiam* opinion on August 24, 1981, finding no fault with the ultimate disposition of the case on the merits. The court asserted that there was no reason to decide between Goldberg and Reavley regarding the standard to be applied: under either standard, Van Ooteghem's speech was protected and no more need be said on that matter.

The *en banc* court found more troubling the detailed arguments concerning the county's liability, which had not been treated at any length by the district court, and decided it would be prudent to vacate the remedial portion of Sterling's order and remand the matter for a more detailed consideration of these issues at the trial level. The court also agreed with the panel that the attorneys fees issue required retrial as well. By now, Gray had been succeeded in office by a new treasurer, who renewed the petition for *certiorari* in the Supreme Court, which was again denied, this time unconditionally, on January 18, 1982.

The case went back to District Judge Sterling, who accepted briefs from the parties and ruled on May 11, 1984, on Van Ooteghem's motion for summary judgment. Sterling decided

every point in Van Ooteghem's favor, holding that Gray's discharge of Van Ooteghem had been an expression of official policy, subjecting the government to liability, and that existing Fifth Circuit precedents made clear that Harris County was not an "agency of the state of Texas" and thus was not shielded by the state's Eleventh Amendment immunity against damage suits in the federal courts. Sterling again reviewed the attorney's fees issue, this time itemizing his calculations based on time expended and normal fees. Given the risk and novelty of the case, he decided to double the original fee award for the first trial, and then added on substantial sums to compensate Van Ooteghem's lawyers for the appellate work and retrial of the damages and fees issues, yielding a final figure of almost $90,000.

There was no way Harris County was going to pay that amount of money without a further appeal to the Fifth Circuit, and, indeed, a three-judge panel of the circuit did find this sum excessive in an opinion by Circuit Judge Patrick E. Higginbotham issued on October 29, 1985. While endorsing Sterling's conclusions that the county was liable to Van Ooteghem and his attorneys, the panel significantly recrafted the remedy in the case. First, it found that Van Ooteghem, a political appointee of Gray, would not necessarily have expected to continue in office after Gray's successor was elected, putting a natural ending point on the calculation of back pay and making a reinstatement remedy inappropriate. At this point, said Higginbotham, it would be inequitable to require the new county treasurer to rehire Van Ooteghem solely as a remedy against the act of his predecessor. Rather, Van Ooteghem was "entitled to be considered for employment free of any prejudice stemming from his earlier termination." If he applied and was rejected for that reason, he "will be free to pursue that claim." Most of Higginbotham's opinion was devoted to reviewing and affirming Sterling's finding that the discharge was an official act of the county, and that the county, not the state, was liable for damages and fees. Having disposed of that matter, and having rejected the defendants' continuing argument that they were entitled to yet further retrial of the case on the merits, Higginbotham focused on the attorney's fees award. He found Sterling's action in doubling the fees for the original trial to be inappropriate, yielding as it would a $300 an hour fee. "That lions at the bar may command such fees is not the measure," he said; $150 an hour was "fair compensation" for the services rendered and risks taken in this kind of litigation, which had been taken on a contingency basis. Higginbotham recalculated the fee award at just under $50,000.

What was most interesting about the whole extended saga of Van Ooteghem's case was the relatively noncontroversial conclusion, which achieved unanimous endorsement from the *en banc* court of appeals and no dissent from any judge at any level of the case, that open advocacy of gay rights by a public employee enjoyed sufficient First Amendment protection to overcome whatever embarrassment or disruption that might arise from it. While this proposition may seem obvious, it was not obvious to courts not so long ago.

During the 1960s, some federal courts accepted the argument that only the model, closeted gay public employee need be retained in service. Anyone who might make a public issue of his homosexuality or his endorsement of gay rights was fated for quick, nonredressable termination. Indeed, the Supreme Court itself

deadlocked at about the same time as the *Van Ooteghem* case was finally decided over the question whether an Oklahoma law authorizing the discharge of public school teachers who advocated gay rights violated the First Amendment. In that case, a dissenting circuit judge had argued that since sodomy was a crime *malum in se* (i.e., intrinsically criminal in nature), a school board would be fully justified in discharging any school teacher who publicly argued that gay people should be free from legal prosecution or discrimination due to their sex lives. And the Supreme Court ruled in 1986 that sodomy laws themselves did not violate the due process clause, thus allowing states to impose penal sanctions on gay people for their sex lives.

Viewed in this light, Van Ooteghem's case is an important victory for the right of sexual minorities to seek liberation through active engagement in the political process at a time when the federal courts have proved generally inhospitable to claims of constitutional entitlement to first-class citizenship for gays.

Case References

Mt. Healthy City School District v. Doyle, 429 U.S. 274 (1977)
Perry v. Sindermann, 408 U.S. 593 (1972)
Pickering v. Board of Education, 391 U.S. 563 (1968)

43. STANDING ON THE CORNER, WATCHING THE PARADE GO BY

Olivieri v. Ward, 613 F. Supp. 616 (S.D.N.Y. 1985) (application for preliminary injunction granted), reversed and remanded, 766 F.2d 690 (2d Cir. 1985), 637 F. Supp. 851 (S.D.N.Y. 1986) (permanent injunction granted), affirmed, 795 F.2d 1005, affirmed as modified, 801 F.2d 602 (2d Cir. 1986), certiorari denied, 480 U.S. 917 (1987). Ruling on attorney's fee application, 1986 Westlaw 11451 (S.D.N.Y. 1986) (not officially reported).

In June 1970, on the first anniversary of the Stonewall protests that helped launch the modern lesbian and gay rights movement, gay activists in New York organized a commemorative march on the last Sunday of the month, beginning in Greenwich Village and heading north toward Central Park. Refusal by the police department to grant a permit for the march meant that the marchers were relegated to the sidewalks for most of the route, but the event

was cheerful and peaceful. Over the course of the 1970s, the annual Gay Pride March became an accepted part of the New York "parade season." Bending the rules against issuing permits for new annual parades in Manhattan, the politicians prevailed on the police department to issue a permit for a march on Sixth Avenue and, eventually, to the main route for major parades, Fifth Avenue. By the early 1980s, the march organizers had decided to change directions, beginning the march at Columbus Circle (the southwest corner of Central Park) and marching down Fifth Avenue to Greenwich Village, where the march would empty into a large street fair on Christopher Street, eventually culminating in a rally on West Street, dancing on the Hudson River piers, and fireworks.

Once the march was permanently moved to Fifth Avenue, it would annually pass St. Patrick's Cathedral, seat of the Archdiocese of New York. The Archdiocese was a noted opponent of gay rights legislation introduced in the City Council early in the 1970s. Lesbian and gay Catholics, organized as Dignity, New York, participated in the annual march, and sought to communicate their views about their own identity as Catholics and about the Church's opposition to lesbian and gay rights, by demonstrating at the Cathedral during the march. From 1976 through 1982, Dignity marchers would leave the main body of the march upon reaching the Cathedral, stream across the sidewalk and on to the Cathedral steps, and hold a demonstration and religious service as the rest of the marchers passed up (or later, down) the avenue. The only untoward incident in connection with this annual demonstration occurred in 1981, when two St. Patrick's parishioners, who had formed a committee for the "defense" of the Cathedral, physically attacked some of the Dignity demonstrators and had to be restrained by the police. Sobered by their experience, the two attackers restricted themselves in the future to nonviolent protest against the march, and Dignity's regular annual demonstration in 1982 encountered no problems. But the two attackers filed suit against the city of New York in 1983, seeking to prevent issuance of the permit for the march. When their suit was unsuccessful, they contacted the police department, warning that there would be a large turnout of protesters and that it would be best for public safety if Dignity were prohibited from demonstrating at the Cathedral. The antimarch organizers claimed to have undertaken a campaign to recruit protesters that would bring thousands of angry Catholics to protect the Cathedral from the sacrilege wrought by the Dignity demonstration.

Police authorities responded to these threats by closing off all access to the sidewalk and steps in front of the Cathedral for the 1983 march. Despite the predictions of the antimarch protesters, fewer than a hundred demonstrators materialized and there was no violence during the march. Although the police barred Dignity from holding its usual demonstration on the Cathedral steps, Dignity did pause in front of the Cathedral and conducted a brief ceremony on the street, after which police allowed two Dignity officers to walk on to the sidewalk and place a wreath on the Cathedral steps. The police had erected barriers along both sides of the street, keeping antimarch demonstrators back from the line of march. When the police proposed the same arrangement for the 1984 march, Dignity members filed a last-minute challenge in the U.S. district court, claiming that the restriction on access to the public sidewalk violated their First Amendment rights, but District Judge Kevin Duffy dismissed the case, ruling that the Dignity members (led by their president, Michael Olivieri), had waited too long after learning of the police department's intentions, thus leaving the court inadequate time to consider the case.

Having learned that lesson, Olivieri and other Dignity plaintiffs filed suit against Police Commissioner Benjamin Ward and his department and Mayor Edward I. Koch with regard to the 1985 march as soon as the police department made clear that it would bar access to the sidewalk and steps of the Cathedral again and would entertain no proposals for alternative ways of dealing with the issue. This time, the antimarch leaders, better organized than in the past, had approached the police department demanding the right to demonstrate against the gay pride march on the sidewalk in front of the Cathedral. Seeking what they viewed as a "compromise," the police offered to let Dignity hold a wreath-laying ceremony involving a limited number of its members, which would be seen primarily by other Dignity members at the march. Dignity rejected this compromise, arguing that it should be entitled to demonstrate in a way effective to communicate its views to all the other marchers who would pass the Cathedral during the march. Dignity proposed two alternatives, which the police department rejected out of hand: first, Dignity proposed allowing each group of demonstrators, pro and con, to take up stations at each end of the sidewalk with a police-patrolled buffer zone in between; alternatively, Dignity proposed (and the march committee agreed) that it hold its parade-long service and demonstration in the eastern-most lane of Fifth Avenue as the rest of the march continued down the remaining lanes. The police department countered by offering to set up demonstration areas around the corner from the Cathedral's Fifth Avenue facade, on Fiftieth and Fifty-First streets, with each group of demonstrators occupying space out of sight of the other, but both being able to see the vacant sidewalk in front of the Cathedral. Dignity rejected this proposal, which would blunt the symbolism of protesting at the Cathedral and would relegate their demonstration to an area out of sight and hearing of many of the marchers.

The matter came before Chief Judge Constance Baker Motley, with Assistant Corporation Counsels David D. Drueding and Jonathan L. Pines representing the city and attorneys Stuart W. Gold, Ann E. Verdon, and Valerie Caproni representing Dignity and its officers. Judge Motley first urged Dignity to seek an internal resolution by appealing the police department's decision to the mayor, but the matter was thrown back into her court when Mayor Koch said he would back the police department in this dispute. Motley then scheduled a hearing and called Police Commissioner Ward as a witness, since neither Dignity nor the city proposed to call any witnesses and she felt it necessary to hear first hand the police department's justification for restricting access to what was, after all, the quintessential public forum. After hearing Commissioner Ward's testimony and arguments from attorneys for both sides, Motley issued her order on June 13, 1985, just two weeks before the scheduled march, granting a preliminary injunction and ordering the parties to come back within a few days with a suitable plan for allowing Dignity to demonstrate. When the city's attorneys failed to submit a plan on schedule, Motley issued a brief order enjoining the city from interfering with Dignity's right to have a reasonable num-

ber of members demonstrate on the sidewalk in front of the Cathedral.

Noting that public sidewalks were a traditional "public forum" for political discussion and protest, Motley found that Dignity's First Amendment rights would be irreparably injured if the police department was allowed to exclude Dignity from access to the steps before the Cathedral. The government's right to limit access to a public forum was very limited. According to a then-recent decision by the Supreme Court, *Clark v. Community for Creative Non-Violence* (1984), the government could "enforce reasonable time, place, and manner restrictions as long as the restrictions are 'content-neutral, are narrowly tailored to serve a significant government interest, and leave open ample alternative channels of communication.'" Motley found that the police department's position failed all of these tests.

First, as to content-neutrality, she found that "the sidewalk in front of St. Patrick's has been made available to other demonstrators and parade participants in the past, and that both plaintiffs and their opponents are being removed because their speech is controversial and thought likely to cause a disturbance." This was, in effect, a restriction on a particular subject of speech, and as such content-based. It did not matter that the police department was excluding both the pros and the antis from the space, if the reason for the exclusion was the subject matter of their protest. "Therefore," concluded Motley, "defendants' attempt to ban all speech from the front of St. Patrick's Cathedral only on the day when the dominant subject matter will be gay rights is suspect as a subject matter distinction." Even if the police were correct in arguing that the content-neutrality requirement had been met by excluding both sides of the controversy from access, however, Motley concluded that the other prongs of the time, place, and manner test had not been met.

Turning next to the "important governmental interest" apart from suppression of speech that had to be present for the government to impose its restrictions, Motley cast considerable doubt on the fears Ward expressed about potential violence should Dignity be allowed to conduct the type of demonstration it had presented from 1976 through 1982. While conceding that "maintaining public order" was an important governmental interest, Motley insisted that the government could not curtail speech unless it showed that there was "a significant basis in fact for its prediction of *disorder*." Here, Motley found the police commissioner's predictions that allowing a Dignity demonstration on the Cathedral sidewalk would lead to significant disorder was not much more than "a speculative fear of unrest."

> The seven year experience of plaintiffs' full-scale demonstrations provides defendants with an unusually detailed and consistent factual record to serve as a basis for prediction. Although there was a minor scuffle caused by anti-gay activists in 1981, plaintiffs held their usual demonstration in front of the Cathedral in 1982 without incident—belying defendants' assertion that it is only the "freezing" of the sidewalk in 1983 and 1984 which has maintained order. Other than the 1981 incident, and despite veiled threats and annual predictions of mass demonstrations by anti-gay groups, there has been no other violence and no more than 100 demonstrators have ever appeared in opposition to Dignity. There is no rational basis for assuming that this year will be any different, or that anti-gay demonstrators will appear in front of the Cathedral in such numbers as would cause a major threat to public safety.

Furthermore, Motley found even more constitutional support for Dignity's free speech rights in the very speculation by Ward that the controversial nature of Dignity's message might provoke a response from counter-demonstrators. "It is precisely when speech in the public forum is provocative, challenging, and hotly contested that the core values of the First Amendment concerning the free exchange of ideas are most directly implicated," she said, "and that the state's duty to protect the speaker's right to speak is most pointedly called into play." While the police department was not proposing complete suppression of Dignity's speech, the court would have to "examine closely any assertion by the government that peaceful speech by peaceful demonstrators on a controversial public issue in a classic public forum must be curtailed even by a time, place, and manner restriction because of the hostile, angry reaction of others." In this case, given the historic peacefulness of Dignity's past demonstrations, the government's interest struck

Motley as "comparatively weak," and past Second Circuit precedent upholding restrictions on demonstrators on public sidewalks were clearly distinguishable. In *Concerned Jewish Youth v. McGuire* (1980), the circuit court had upheld restrictions on Jewish Defense League demonstrations at the Russian Embassy. To Motley, this case was not comparable, since the JDL was a militant protest organization that had been implicated in violent protest, unlike Dignity, and there were significant foreign policy implications attendant on allowing them to demonstrate at the embassy of a foreign power antagonistic to the United States. Similarly, in *International Society for Krishna Consciousness v. City of New York* (1979), her own prior decision allowing the police to restrict a religious society from carrying on street activities at the entrance to the United Nations, concerns about international terrorism and safety issues were credible and paramount. Furthermore, in those cases, the city had a legitimate interest in keeping all demonstrators away from the designated areas, apart from the content of their particular messages. In this case, the restriction seemed purely content-driven, given the lack of serious support for the city's speculations about potential violence.

Motley turned last to the requirement that any restriction be narrowly tailored to meet a compelling governmental interest. Here again, she found the defendants' case to be "problematic," since the police had rejected out of hand all attempts by Dignity to come up with alternative schemes to allow a demonstration without imperiling public safety. Motley was attracted by Dignity's proposal to let each group of demonstrators occupy a different part of the sidewalk, which she had embraced during the hearing. The police department had claimed that it had a regular "policy" of keeping potentially disruptive protesters as far apart as possible, and that none of Dignity's proposed compromises would accomplish this. Furthermore, argued the city, since it was also denying the antigay protesters' demand to use the sidewalk, Dignity was not being subjected to any sort of unequal treatment.

Motley was not taken in by this ploy. "The issue is not whether, given the specific facts of this case, there is justification for granting a *preference* to plaintiffs in the use of the forum. The question is whether there is a content-neutral reason to deny access for either or both groups to a public forum that is otherwise open to *everyone*." Regardless of Dignity's intentions, the police policy would preclude allowing the antigay protesters to assemble near the parade on Fifth Avenue, Motley observed. "Once this group, which has a history of harassing and attacking pro-gay demonstrators, is removed, so is the potential for any conflict with Dignity demonstrators. The accompanying state interest in maintaining order would thereby be satisfied in full, since there is no reason to expect conflict between plaintiffs and the rest of the marchers, whose organizers support the Dignity demonstration." Thus, the solution to the whole problem was simple, Motley concluded: "Simply keep the anti-gay demonstrators at a reasonable distance from the parade and otherwise leave the public forum undisturbed." Although she had taken the long way around to get there, Motley had arrived at the crux of the case: the problem was not caused by Dignity, but by the hostile reactions of a handful of troublemakers. The solution was to remove the troublemakers if they threatened to go beyond words in their antigay protest. Since the city's alleged policy was to keep *hostile* demonstrators away from those against whom they were demonstrating, the only demonstrators who needed to be restricted or restrained were the antigay demonstrators. Motley stated:

> This conclusion is bolstered by plaintiffs' undisputed observation that the primary agenda of the anti-gay demonstrators is to *prevent* plaintiffs' speech. To remove Dignity from its preferred public forum because of fear of disruption by its opponents would be, as plaintiffs have suggested, to provide a blueprint for a modified heckler's veto: Any group seeking to keep another group from using a particularly evocative public forum need only threaten to appear with a sufficiently large, disruptive group of counterdemonstrators and the entire area will be "frozen."

Since this was not, contrary to the police department's assertions, a situation involving "mutually hostile" groups, "it is the anti-gay demonstrators and not Dignity's members who present the threat of violence. In that context, defendants' decision to prevent both Dignity and the antigay groups from demonstrating in front of St. Patrick's Cathedral is not a narrowly tailored means of serving the legitimate governmental ends at stake."

Finally, the restrictions did not leave Dignity with an adequate alternative channel of communication for its message, since the very location of the planned demonstration was a significant component of the message. Even if it could be concluded that a demonstration someplace other than the sidewalk would be sufficient, Motley suggested, the need for alternative channels arose only if the other prongs of the test were met, which they were not in this case. Thus, because she had found the police department's predictions of violence to be merely speculative and the department's reaction to the situation to be excessive, she was inclined to grant a preliminary injunction barring the police from excluding Dignity from demonstrating on the sidewalk. However, she indicated that her order would also recognize the right of the police to use their professional discretion in maintaining order during the march, and granted the defendants ninety-six hours to come up with a plan that would permit a reasonable number of Dignity members to demonstrate at the Cathedral during the march, which she ordered presented to the court by 5:30 P.M. on Monday, June 17. When the attorneys for the city failed to submit a proposed order on time, Motley issued a brief order embodying the general terms of the concluding paragraphs of her opinion.

The city immediately appealed her decision, obtaining an emergency hearing at the Second Circuit on June 25. On June 28, the circuit panel issued a brief decision reversing Motley, over the strong dissent of Circuit Judge Amalya Kearse. Writing for a majority of the panel, Circuit Judge Richard J. Cardamone asserted that, based on an "independent" review of the record, he found Motley's conclusion that the police department's fears of violence were merely speculative to be "clearly erroneous." He found that the record provided the following reasons to credit the police department's fears: lawsuits had been filed by "groups" seeking to stop the march, and conservative Catholic organizations had "expressed strong opposition to gays gathering near the

Cathedral" and had participated with the newly formed "Committee to Defend the Cathedral" in a mail campaign to recruit counter-protesters. Cardamone also found testimony that some members of these groups "overran police barriers" at the prior parade, protesting that the police had "double-crossed" them by letting Dignity hold a brief service in the street in front of the Cathedral. Cardamone also relied on the Archdiocese's strong opposition to gay rights manifested in recent litigation over a mayoral executive order that would have compelled social service agencies operated by church-related groups not to discriminate in employment against gays. Cardamone also found significant that Dignity members had reportedly demonstrated at the Cathedral "more than once" during the past year, and that parade organizers had informed the police of threats of disruption against the parade by a group of Orthodox Jews, planned for the point where the march would go through the "diamond district" a few blocks south of the Cathedral. Cardamone found that all these factors, taken together, provided a reasonable basis for the police department to conclude, in an exercise of professional judgment, that it would be safer not to allow Dignity to demonstrate on the sidewalk before the Cathedral.

Since Cardamone was unwilling to credit Motley's finding that fears of violence were purely speculative, he rejected the notion that the police department's "solution" to the "problem" was not "narrowly tailored" to accomplish the government's legitimate interest. Rejecting the "heckler's veto" argument, Cardamone wrote that the police department was merely following its "established policy" to "keep demonstrators away from the line of march of a parade, and to keep demonstrators and counter-demonstrators away from each other," which he characterized as a "common sense" policy that was even-handedly applied here by excluding both pro and anti demonstrators. He also asserted that letting Dignity demonstrate briefly on the street or off to the side provided an adequate alternative means of communicating its message. Speaking in terms of bowing to the "Police Department's expertise" in deciding how to maintain order, Cardamone stated that Motley's order should be reversed and the po-

lice department left, in effect, to exercise its own discretion on how to deal with the potential situation.

Judge Kearse sharply disagreed, although she would have modified Motley's order to specify the exact maximum number of demonstrators Dignity could bring onto the sidewalk, for the sake of clarity. Agreeing with Motley, Kearse contended that implementation of the police department's alleged policies would not require clearing the sidewalk. Rather, as Motley had observed, the policies could be implemented by removing the group that threatened violence from the area of the other group's demonstration.

> It is clear from the record . . . that if it were not for the threats of certain anti-gay Catholic groups, plaintiffs' group would be permitted to use the Cathedral sidewalk. Further, according to a Department official, the Catholic anti-gay groups would be perfectly satisfied with the Department plan to bar everyone from the Cathedral sidewalk since their primary goal is to prevent plaintiffs' group from occupying that location. The latter fact confirms plaintiffs' contention that the Cathedral sidewalk is a forum of especial symbolic significance for their message.

This was, to Kearse, a "classic heckler's veto" situation, of a type that the courts had consistently rejected in the past, and that Motley had properly rejected. She characterized as "an untoward ironic twist" the police department's argument that it was merely being even-handed in excluding both sides of the controversy from the sidewalk.

Furthermore, having reviewed the record, she saw no basis for labeling Motley's factual findings "clearly erroneous." As far as she could see, the march had been held every year since 1970 without any significant incident, Dignity had conducted its service on the steps of the Cathedral every year from 1976 to 1982 without serious incident, and the only exceptions were "two isolated instances of violence in 1981, each instigated by and involving a single anti-gay individual" and that these incidents did not recur when Dignity conducted its usual demonstration in 1982. Furthermore, the police department's subsequent predictions concerning this march had always been wrong: there had been no violence and no significant number of counter-demonstrators in recent years.

In the event, the 1985 parade went off without incident, although Dignity was restricted to its more recent practice of the brief ceremony in the street followed by the wreath-laying ceremony. In the fall of 1985, Dignity renewed its efforts to resume its former practice of demonstrating on the sidewalk, petitioning Judge Motley to issue a permanent injunction this time. Apparently stung by the Second Circuit's rather bizarre characterization of the facts in its June 1985 decision, this time Motley held several days of hearings, listening to eleven witnesses (including several police officers), and made detailed factual findings in her lengthy opinion of June 13. Her findings refuted virtually every factual allegation on which Cardamone had relied in his 1985 opinion, and exposed the close collaboration between Catholic Church officials and police. Indeed, it appeared that a police officer had actually telephoned a variety of potential antigay groups to solicit them to appear at the parade to justify the department's restrictions on Dignity! A police official had also suggested to the Archdiocese that some religious event should be scheduled at the Cathedral that afternoon to provide a reason for the police to keep the sidewalk clear. To Motley, all of this evidence, taken together with the police department's notably poor record of prognostication, provided ample basis for finding the department's fears to be totally speculative:

> Upon careful evaluation of the voluminous evidence in this case the court concludes that police predictions of a significant potential for violence from counter-demonstrators at the 1986 Gay Pride Parade are incredible. Even were the court untroubled by the credibility of police assertions, however, it would find their predictions irrational in view of the negligible support that has been offered for them. The court also finds that any potential for violence at the 1986 Parade will not be significantly affected by the presence of Dignity on the Cathedral sidewalk. Rather, the court concludes that in light of the absence of any heightened potential for violence caused by Dignity's presence on the sidewalk, a more convincing explanation for the police decision . . . is discomfort with the content of Dignity's message. Police sensitivity to the discomfort

of counter-demonstrators and the Catholic Church, as well perhaps, as discomfort within the Police Department, itself, with Dignity's message, are more credible explanations for the challenged restriction than any serious concern on the part of the police with an increased potential for violence rising from the mere presence of Dignity on the sidewalk.

Concluding that the stretch of sidewalk on Fifth Avenue in front of the Cathedral was a "classic public forum for the exercise of First Amendment rights," Motley now issued a permanent injunction requiring the police department to allow up to one hundred Dignity members to demonstrate on the sidewalk in front of the Cathedral for so long as the march continued to be held in that area in 1986 and the future.

Again the city rushed to appeal, arguing before a panel of Second Circuit judges on June 26, just days before the march, that Judge Motley's injunction would lead to significant disorder and that the police could not guarantee the safety of the public as a consequence. In light of Motley's detailed factual findings, however, even Cardamone had to agree that the police department's fears were woefully exaggerated. Deciding that there was not adequate time to issue an opinion, the panel engaged in unusual negotiation of a settlement of the dispute with counsel for the parties from the bench. The agreement hammered out was that both Dignity and the counter-demonstrators would be allowed to demonstrate on the sidewalk, in penned-in areas patrolled by the police, with Dignity providing twenty-five demonstrators who would be allowed thirty minutes for their demonstration. Then, after a thirty-minute period for emptying the demonstration area, twenty-five antigay demonstrators would be allowed to occupy the same space. The judges insisted that this was necessary in order to be "fair" to the counter-demonstrators.

On September 16, the panel issued its unanimous decision embodying this "compromise" and avoiding mention of the most embarrassing facts uncovered in the trial before Judge Motley, but agreeing that the police department appeared to have been motivated by interests other than public safety in seeking to exclude Dignity from the Cathedral sidewalk.

As an apparent political sop to the police department, wounded by Motley's derogatory comments, the new decision by Cardamone commended the police "who over the years have guarded successfully the safety of demonstrators and the public during this parade." In light of the factual record that only once in the history of the parade had there been the slightest disruption by the two antigay bigots who had organized the committee to "defend" the Cathedral, this comment was itself bizarre, highlighting the intensely political nature of the litigation.

Dissolving Motley's permanent injunction, Cardamone stated that the compromise agreed upon by the parties in June 1986 would henceforth stand as the *modus operandi* for this march. Since so much judicial time had now been spent on the problem, "We do not think therefore that our order should be modified readily or that this litigation should—like the Gay Rights Parade—become an annual event." On March 9, 1987, the Supreme Court refused requests by both the city and Dignity to review this final resolution, the city having claimed that it should not have been ordered to let anyone demonstrate on the sidewalk and Dignity claiming that the resulting restricted demonstration remained a violation of its First Amendment rights. The final word, however, had already been spoken by Judge Motley. She had initially refused to grant attorney's fees to the plaintiffs, observing that although they had prevailed before her there was no statutory basis for awarding fees. Responding on October 7, 1986, to a renewed motion for fees, Motley went on at length about the plaintiffs' technical failure in failing to include an alleged violation of 42 U.S.C. section 1983 in their final pre-trial papers, but then agreed that their claim did sound under section 1983, and, since the City was no longer contesting the fee demand, she would allow the plaintiffs to collect reasonable attorney's fees.

The litigation over Dignity's right to continue demonstrating on the public sidewalk in front of St. Patrick's Cathedral demonstrates, more than anything else, the way well-established constitutional doctrine may fall by the wayside when religious conservatives exert themselves to block the activities of sexual minorities. As Judge Kearse tellingly observed in her dissent from the Second Circuit's first opinion in the case, there was no basis in the record for finding Judge Motley's initial conclusions "clearly erroneous," and as Judge Motley amply demonstrated in her second opinion, most of the factual assertions upon which Judge Cardamone purportedly relied in his first opinion were totally specious, fabricated by the defendants or not even supported by the record on which Cardamone purportedly relied. What was going on in this case, at least at the circuit court level, was not legal reasoning, but rather power politics. Although the Catholic Church was not formally a party to the proceedings, as Judge Motley's second opinion revealed, the Church was intimately involved with the police department in attempting to thwart Dignity's First Amendment rights, and the circuit court was not about to cross the Church in this regard unless starkly confronted with a detailed factual record clearly refuting the police department's position.

Ironically, in subsequent Gay Pride Marches, Dignity has continued to occupy its demonstration area, but the interest of the antigay demonstrators has apparently melted away. Within a few years, the antigay demonstrators could summon no more than a few dozen individuals to appear and spout venom at the marchers from their holding area across Fifth Avenue from the Cathedral, and the antigay demonstrators have been hard-pressed to find even twenty-five who want to occupy the designated area on the sidewalk. Perhaps some of the wind was taken out of the demonstrators' sails when the city enacted a gay rights ordinance in 1986, and half-hearted attempts to place a repeal referendum on the ballot were unsuccessful. Dignity's expulsion from its meeting place at a Jesuit Church by order of the Archdiocese may also have affected subsequent demonstrations, since Dignity suffered a schism over how to respond to the expulsion, with the more politically activist members undertaking monthly protest demonstrations at the Cathedral, while the remaining nonactivists largely refrained from protest activity. By the early 1990s, Dignity's interest in demonstrating on the sidewalk during the march had waned, and the whole issue, so hotly fought during the 1980s, seemed largely moot, although echoes of this case would be heard when the Irish Lesbian and Gay Organization demanded during the 1990s a place in the St. Patrick's Day Parade run by the Ancient Order of Hibernians, a conservative Irish-Catholic group.

Case References

Clark v. Community for Creative Non-Violence, 468 U.S. 288 (1984)

Concerned Jewish Youth v. McGuire, 621 F.2d 471 (2d Cir. 1980), certiorari denied, 450 U.S. 913 (1981)

International Society for Krishna Consciousness v. City of New York, 484 F. Supp. 966 (S.D.N.Y. 1979)

44. WHERE CAN YOU WATCH A SEXY FILM?

City of Renton v. Playtime Theatres, Inc., 475 U.S. 41 (1986), reversing 748 F.2d 527 (9th Cir. 1984), on remand, 789 F.2d 804 (9th Cir. 1986).

For decades the U.S. Supreme Court had struggled with the problems of reconciling restrictions on "obscenity" with First Amendment strictures against content-based censorship. On the one hand, most of the Justices believed that obscene messages in any medium did not enjoy First Amendment protection; on the other, it was hard to define "obscenity" or to grapple with speech that was considered "indecent" or "offensive" by many but that fell short of any definition precise enough to avoid constitutional vagueness problems. The result has been a confusing history of litigation over attempts by cities, states, and the federal government to place restrictions on sexually oriented communications. Few such issues were as heavily litigated during the 1970s and 1980s as attempts by municipalities to exclude from all or part of their areas "adult" theaters that exhibited sexually explicit movies.

In *Paris Adult Theatre I v. Slaton* (1973), the Supreme Court held that a city or state could pass a law forbidding the exhibition of obscene motion pictures in a commercial theater. Could a city take the next step and ban the theater entirely, or require that such theaters be located away from residential areas, churches, parks, or prime business districts, without a specific finding that every film exhibited at the theater is obscene (as opposed to merely "indecent" or "offensive" to some people)? Or would a presumption of First Amendment protection apply to the operation of the theater and be overcome only in the case of individual films? The Court began to answer these questions in *Young v. American Mini Theatres, Inc.*, a 1976

case in which no five Justices could agree on the same rationale for upholding a Detroit zoning ordinance that tried to avoid the creation of a "porn district" by requiring that adult theaters be no closer to each other than 1,000 feet, and in any event be located no closer than within 500 feet of any residential zone. The lack of a single opinion commanding a majority of the Court left the issue somewhat in doubt, as did the particular nature of Detroit's approach to the issue, which left open the constitutionality of other approaches. Ultimately, the zoning ordinance of the small city of Renton in the state of Washington provided the Court with a vehicle for appraising a broader approach and issuing an opinion commanding the support of a clear majority of the Court.

Ironically, at the time Renton passed its ordinance, there were no businesses within the city to which it would apply. Renton was a suburb of Seattle, which had passed a zoning ordinance aimed at adult theaters that was then under attack in the Washington State courts. Although Renton did not have any adult theaters, it did have some motion picture theaters located downtown that were the subject of speculation. The mayor, concerned about the possibility that these theaters might be acquired by somebody interested in using them to show sexually oriented films, suggested to the City Council that it consider enacting an ordinance that would ensure that these downtown theaters could not be used for that purpose. The Council's Planning and Development Committee held public hearings, reviewed the experiences of other cities with adult theaters and zoning laws, and received a report from the City Attorney's Office on the legal issues that such ordinances might raise. While the Committee was studying the issue, the Council passed a resolution imposing a moratorium on the licensing of "any business . . . which . . . has as its primary purpose the selling, renting or showing of sexually explicit materials," because such uses "would have a severe impact upon surrounding businesses and residences."

Finally the Committee completed its work, recommending adoption of an ordinance that would prohibit operation of any adult motion picture theater within 1,000 feet of any residential zone, single- or multiple-family dwelling, church, or park, and within one mile of any school. The ordinance did not require any finding that the theater was showing or intending to show obscene films, merely that it show any of a variety of sexual activities or exhibit any of a variety of "specified anatomical areas." Early in 1982, the mayor's fears came true. An investor, operating as Playtime Theatres, Inc., signed an agreement to buy two downtown theaters in Renton with the plan of operating them as adult theaters. At least one of the theaters was in an area excluded from such activities by the city ordinance. Before finally closing on the purchase of that theater, Playtime filed an action in the U.S. district court, seeking a declaration that the ordinance was unconstitutional and a permanent injunction against its enforcement.

Reacting to Playtime's suit, the city filed an action in state court, seeking its own declaratory judgment as to both the facial constitutionality of the ordinance and its application to the theater in question, and igniting a procedural jumble of removals to federal court and remands to state court that ultimately boiled down to a federal magistrate's recommendation to enjoin operation of the ordinance followed by the federal district court's decision to uphold it. These differences of opinion showed the complexities in an area where the Supreme Court had yet to speak in a reasonably unified voice.

During the litigation, Renton amended its ordinance to include a list of purported justifications for its enactment, and to reduce the minimum distance between adult theaters and schools from one mile to 1,000 feet. The list of reasons reflected a mix of concerns about the impact of adult theaters on property values of the surrounding community and the atmosphere of the community, unhappiness with the nature of films to be exhibited at the theaters, alarm at the effects of "pornography" on the morals of the community, and citation of experiences in other cities where adult theaters had operated. (The Council specifically cited a 1978 decision by the Washington Supreme Court, *Northend Cinema, Inc. v. Seattle*, which had described the impact on particular Seattle neighborhoods of the operation of adult theaters.) The amended ordinance also amplified the definition of adult theaters to require that the exhibited films appeal to prurient interest, apparently attempting to track some of the language of Supreme Court obscenity decisions, although the ordinance still did not limit its operation to obscene films.

After the magistrate issued his initial opinion finding the ordinance unconstitutional, Playtime closed on the theater and began showing adult films. The Renton authorities then initiated an obscenity hearing in the state court, which determined that some, but not all, of the films exhibited were obscene. All this seemed to be academic, however, because the district court ruled on February 17, 1983, that the ordinance was constitutional. Contradicting the magistrate, who had found that the ordinance left only 200 undesirable acres within the city limits for the operation of adult theaters, the court found that there were 520 acres where such theaters could be operated, and, relying on the Supreme Court's decision in *Young*, held that the ordinance did not totally prevent Playtime from operating in Renton. The district court rejected Playtime's argument that Renton had to demonstrate adverse impacts in its own city rather than relying on studies from Seattle or Detroit, and found that the purposes of the ordinance were unrelated to the suppression of speech, being based primarily on concerns about property values and the other effects of adult theaters on the surrounding areas.

The district court's decision set loose a new wave of litigation, with the city attempting to get the theaters closed by judicial order while Playtime appealed the decision. The U.S. Court of Appeals for the Ninth Circuit heard oral argument in the case on May 9, 1984, with Robert Eugene Smith, of Encino, California, appearing for Playtime, and Lawrence J. Warren and Daniel Kellogg, of Renton, appearing for the city. On November 28, 1984, a unanimous three-judge panel issued its decision holding that the magistrate had been correct, the city had not met its burden of showing adequate justification for the ordinance, and remanding the case to give the city further opportunity to make such a showing.

The court's opinion by Circuit Judge Betty B. Fletcher proceeded from the premise that because the city was seeking to restrict the location of theaters showing all sexually oriented films, not only obscene films, there was a requirement to subject the city's justifications to strict scrutiny because the ordinance would reach constitutionally protected speech under the First Amendment. How restrictive was the ordinance? It was not enough to say that 520 acres were free for adult theater use in Renton under the ordinance, said Fletcher, because the land was not really "available" for that use. "A substantial part of the 520 acres is occupied by: (1) a sewage disposal site and treatment plant; (2) a horseracing track and environs; (3) a business park containing buildings suitable only for industrial use; (4) a warehouse and manufacturing facilities; (5) a Mobil Oil tank farm; and, (6) a fully-developed shopping center." In other words, if Playtime wanted to operate an adult theater in Renton, it had either to find space in the few remaining vacant acres not restricted by the ordinance, or it would have to acquire one of these five existing structures and convert it to theater use.

Fletcher found that the district court's reliance on *Young* was inappropriate, given these facts. In *Young*, the Detroit zoning ordinance provided for dispersal of adult theaters throughout the metropolitan area to avoid the creation of a single porn district. There was no issue in *Young* about the availability of sites, but the limitations of the Renton ordinance, by contrast, worked "a substantial restriction on speech."

Finding that *Young* was not helpful in resolving the problem, Fletcher based her analysis on *United States v. O'Brien*, a 1968 case in which the U.S. Supreme Court dealt with a federal law penalizing the destruction of draft cards. The Court upheld the law, even though it had been applied to punish individuals who burned their draft cards as a form of political protest. The Court held that it was possible to separate out the speech and nonspeech issues, where a law was enacted for a purpose that did not directly relate to regulating the content of speech. In *O'Brien*, the Court found that there were administrative reasons to require that all adults subject to the military draft have draft cards, and these reasons had nothing to do with regulating speech as such, but rather with administrative necessity. Under the Court's analysis in *O'Brien*, which was frequently cited and applied in a wide range of circumstances, a law that has the effect of restricting protected speech will be valid only if the regulation is within the constitutional power of the government, it furthers an important or substantial governmental interest that is unrelated to the suppression of free speech, and the incidental restriction on free speech is no greater than essential to further the government interest. While these constitutional tests were less demanding than those applied to a direct regulation of speech, they were sufficiently stringent, in Fletcher's view, to doom the Renton ordinance.

Before applying the *O'Brien* test to the Renton ordinance, however, Fletcher considered the standard of review the court should use, particularly with regard to the key factual finding about the effect of the ordinance on Playtime's ability to operate an adult theater somewhere within the city limits of Renton. The district court had found that 520 acres were available. The court of appeals felt that the 520 acres were not really available, and the magistrate had found that only 200 acres were available. Whose finding would count? Fletcher held that this issue presented a mixed question of fact and law in a First Amendment context, justifying *de novo* review by the circuit court of the factual findings below. This meant that the court could set aside the district court's conclusion that the 520 acres were available.

Applying the *O'Brien* test, Fletcher concluded that Renton's "asserted interest in enacting the zoning ordinance is very thin" based on the record on appeal. Although city officials testified that a public hearing preceded enactment of the ordinance, there was no record of the hearing, and it was not until the amended ordinance, which responded to Playtime's initiating legal proceedings, that the city actually adopted a list of explicit reasons for the ordinance. Fletcher was not impressed with the list. While purporting to rely on the experiences of Detroit and Seattle to justify its approach, Renton had taken an approach that was different from that of either of those cities. Detroit required dispersal of adult theaters; Seattle restricted them to a tightly defined district. By contrast, Renton's approach was mixed. The 520 or fewer acres where an adult theater might be located were not concentrated as in Seattle or dispersed leaving many options for theater locations as in Detroit. There was no record that the Council had made findings specific to Renton.

As to the other justifications recited in the amended ordinance, they were "conclusory and speculative," said Fletcher. Furthermore, Renton's justifications did not show that the ordinance was unrelated to the suppression of speech. While some of the listed justifications went to issues such as property values and the impact on surrounding areas, some of them were directly concerned with the content of the films to be exhibited at adult theaters. The district court had found that the former concerns predominated, but that was not the test that the Ninth Circuit had applied in prior litigation. Rather, the circuit's 1983 decision in *Tovar v. Billmeyer* required that "where mixed motives are apparent, as they are here, . . . the court [must] determine whether 'a motivating factor in the zoning decision was to restrict plaintiffs' exercise of first amendment rights.'" Here it was clear that such restriction was a motivating factor, especially when there was little evidence on the record supporting the nonspeech factors cited in the amended ordinance. Finally, Fletcher rejected the city's argument that it was constitutional effectively to ban adult theaters from the tiny Renton community, because Seattle, with its concentrated adult theater area, was within an easy drive. She quoted the Supreme Court's statement in another case that "[o]ne is not to have the exercise of his liberty of expression in appropriate places abridged on

the plea that it may be exercised in some other place." Because the district court had applied the wrong standard to evaluate Renton's justifications for the law, the case would have to be remanded for further hearings.

The city of Renton appealed for U.S. Supreme Court review, under federal rules providing for a direct appeal of a case in which a federal court holds a state or local law unconstitutional. Although the federal rule normally requires that the federal appellate decision have been a final order, a condition not satisfied in this case, the Supreme Court, eager to take another crack at putting together a solid majority on this issue, noted probable jurisdiction on April 15, 1985, and indicated in its opinion that it was treating Renton's appeal papers as a petition for writ of *certiorari* and exercising its discretion to grant the writ. The case immediately became a *cause célèbre* for the opposing forces of the civil liberties proponents and the antipornography groups. Heavy-weight litigators were retained by both sides, with E. Barrett Prettyman, Jr., arguing the case for Renton and Jack R. Burns retained to represent Playtime. The Court received *amicus* briefs in support of the ordinance from the Freedom Council Foundation, the National Institute of Municipal Law Officers, the National League of Cities, and Jackson County, Missouri. Opponents submitting *amicus* briefs included the American Civil Liberties Union, the American Booksellers Association, and the Outdoor Advertising Association of America. All were concerned with the degree of autonomy the Court might find for localities in using zoning laws to restrict sexually oriented businesses.

The Court heard oral argument on November 12, 1985, and announced its decision, in an opinion by Justice William H. Rehnquist, on February 25, 1986. Rehnquist's opinion commanded a solid majority of the Court. Justices William J. Brennan, Jr., and Thurgood Marshall dissented, and Justice Harry A. Blackmun concurred in the result without endorsing Rehnquist's opinion.

Rehnquist held that the Ninth Circuit had misconceived the reach of *Young v. American Mini Theatres*. The key point in *Young* was that a city could use zoning rules that did not altogether ban the operation of an adult theater. If the zoning rules left open the possibility that such a theater could operate within the city limits, it was to be evaluated as "a form of time, place, and manner regulation" rather than as a content-based regulation of speech. Under such an analysis, the burden on the city was much lighter than if the regulation were found to be content-based. Such regulations would be "acceptable so long as they are designed to serve a substantial governmental interest and do not unreasonably limit alternative avenues of communication."

While the Renton ordinance might not "at first glance" fit neatly in either the "content-based" or "content-neutral" category, said Rehnquist, the district court had found that the ordinance was aimed at the "secondary effects" of adult movie theaters "on the surrounding community." Although the court of appeals had rejected this finding based on its prior opinion in *Tovar*, *Tovar* was inconsistent with the approach of *United States v. O'Brien*, said Rehnquist, "the very case that the Court of Appeals said it was applying." It was enough that the "secondary effects" issue predominated among the city's reasons for enacting the ordinance. That some legislator might have been concerned also about the content of the films was not enough to invoke a full-fledged First Amendment "content-based" analysis. This, in Rehnquist's view, was the relevant holding to be derived from *Young*: that a zoning ordinance intended to deal with the secondary effects of adult theaters was to be evaluated under the less demanding "time, place and manner" analysis. That left a two-stage inquiry for the Court: was the Renton ordinance "designed to serve a substantial governmental interest," and did it allow "for reasonable alternative avenues of communication." Rehnquist answered both questions affirmatively.

First, Rehnquist insisted that Renton did not have to make particularized studies of its own problems but could rely on studies elsewhere showing the effects of adult theaters on the surrounding community. Renton could reasonably believe that the conclusions drawn from Seattle, described in the Washington Supreme Court's decision in *Northend Cinema*, were equally valid if applied to Renton (even though Renton was a relatively small town by comparison with Seattle). That Seattle decided to deal with the problem differently did not affect this issue. Furthermore, said Rehnquist, Renton's approach to dealing with the issue was well within the realm of reasonableness. There was nothing to the quasi-equal protection theory Playtime had raised at oral argument: that singling out movie theaters from all possible sexually oriented businesses was unfair. There was no other adult business in Renton, so one would not expect the city to have any concerns sufficient to generate legislation.

Finally, on the issue of reasonable alternatives, Rehnquist pointed out that the court of appeals had not differed with the district court's finding that the ordinance left 520 acres as a possible location. Although the court of appeals had asserted that much of those 520 acres were not available due to other uses, this argument cut little ice with Rehnquist. "That respondents must fend for themselves in the real estate market, on an equal footing with other prospective purchasers and lessees, does not give rise to a First Amendment violation," he said, asserting that the First Amendment gave theaters no guarantee that they "will be able to obtain sites at bargain prices." The First Amendment required Renton only to give Playtime a reasonable opportunity to open and operate an adult theater, and to Rehnquist the situation found by the district court was such a reasonable opportunity.

Justice Brennan's dissenting opinion disputed Rehnquist on virtually every point. First, he found that the limitations imposed by Renton were "based exclusively on the content of the films" to be shown at the theater. As such, there was no way to conclude that this was a "content-neutral" regulation. But even if it could be characterized as content-neutral, it was "plainly unconstitutional" under the Court's precedents on these issues. On the issue of content-neutrality, Brennan argued at length that the singling out of adult movie theaters by the regulation belied the contention that Renton was primarily concerned with secondary effects rather than with the content of the films. "Other motion picture theaters, and other forms of 'adult entertainment,' such as bars, massage parlors, and adult bookstores, are not subject to the same regulations," he pointed out. This was "selective treatment," which strongly suggested that Renton was interested in "discriminating against adult theaters based on the content of the films they exhibit." While the Court's response might be appropriate if this were merely a commercial regulation with no First Amendment implications, it was not appropriate where the regulation had this kind of direct effect on protected speech.

As further proof, if any were needed, that the secondary effects arguments were makeweights, the city had not even adopted its "justification" provisions until after the lawsuit was filed. Before that amendment, there was "no indication that the ordinance was designed to address any 'secondary effects.'" Indeed, even the district court had observed that many of the stated justifications "were no more than expressions of dislike for the subject matter." As to those justifications that did relate to secondary effects, "the Court cannot, as it does, merely accept these *post hoc* statements at face value." The normal presumption of validity for legislative findings does not apply in the First Amendment area, insisted Brennan. There was not an adequate record here of specific findings on secondary effects in Renton to meet the First Amendment standard. Indeed, while the Court said that Renton could rely on studies at other cities, there was no indication in the record that Renton was relying on anything more than prior court decisions concerning the constitutionality of those cities' efforts to restrict adult theaters. There was no indication that anybody in Renton had actually reviewed any studies of the situation in those cities directly. Since Renton adopted a zoning ordinance different in its approach, there was even less reason to credit reliance on the Seattle and Detroit experiences. All of the circumstances surrounding adoption of the ordinance suggested that content regulation was intended.

Furthermore, said Brennan, even if he agreed that the regulation was intended primarily to deal with secondary effects rather than to regulate speech, he would not agree with the Court's subsequent disposition of the case, because the Court was unduly deferential on a record that provided no justification for such deference. "The city made no showing as to how uses 'protected' by the ordinance would

be affected by the presence of an adult movie theater," he said. This was clearly distinguishable from the Detroit case, where there was testimony on the legislative record from urban planners and real estate experts on which the Detroit City Council could rely in crafting an approach to the problem for that city. "Here, the Renton Council was aware only that some residents had complained about adult movie theaters, and that other localities had adopted special zoning regulations for such establishments. These are not 'facts' sufficient to justify the burdens the ordinance imposed upon constitutionally protected expression."

Finally, said Brennan, the Court's resolution of the issue of "reasonable alternative avenues for communication" was inappropriate as well. The court of appeals' findings that most of the 520 acres were not available for adult theater use should not have been dealt with so lightly. Rehnquist said that the theater owners had to fend for themselves equally in the real estate market. That was not an accurate statement here because they were not equal: they were restricted to only 520 acres, a restriction not imposed on their competitors for real estate. The theaters were not asking for a low price guarantee, only a reasonable opportunity to locate in a viable place to operate their theaters. Because the ordinance was greatly restrictive, it was plainly unconstitutional.

The Court remanded the case for consistent proceedings. On May 13, the Ninth Circuit panel vacated its prior decision and announced that the district court's decision, denying Playtime an injunction against the ordinance, was affirmed. Playtime had to stop operating at the sites it had purchased.

The Court's decision in *Renton* became the firm precedent that the antipornography forces were seeking. Although there would be subsequent litigation over the reasonableness of particular restrictions, the Court's opinion effectively instructed state and local legislators on how to adopt a zoning regulation that would withstand constitutional review. Adult theaters could be restricted as to location with relative impunity and without any need for a showing of secondary harms specific to that community. The decision provided a powerful tool for the restriction of cinema depictions of sexual activity in American cities.

Case References

Northend Cinema, Inc. v. Seattle, 90 Wash. 2d 709, 585 P.2d 1153 (1978)

Paris Adult Theatre I v. Slaton, 413 U.S. 49 (1973)
Tovar v. Billmeyer, 721 F.2d 1260 (9th Cir. 1983)
United States v. O'Brien, 391 U.S. 367 (1968)
Young v. American Mini Theatres, Inc., 427 U.S. 50 (1976)

45. DOES SEXUAL ACTIVITY IN BOOKSTORES HAVE FIRST AMENDMENT PROTECTION?

Arcara v. Cloud Books, Inc., 478 U.S. 697 (1986), reversing *People v. Cloud Books, Inc.*, 65 N.Y.2d 324 (1985), which reversed in pertinent part 101 App. Div. 2d 163 (1984), which had affirmed in pertinent part 119 Misc. 2d 505 (1983). Decision on remand from the Supreme Court: 68 N.Y.2d 553 (1986).

From the beginnings of recorded history, civil and religious authorities have tried to prevent unmarried consenting adults (whether heterosexual or homosexual) from getting together for sexual activity outside of their homes. Whether explained as promoting morality, protecting public health, or bolstering preferred social institutions such as the family, laws forbidding sexual contact in public places have a long tradition. When the sexual contact involves monetary exchange, the law is even more forbidding.

The existence of such laws has not, however, prevented people from seeking out public venues for sex with strangers, nor has it prevented entrepreneurs from providing such venues, in the form of bathhouses, theaters, and "adult" bookstores. During the Sexual Revolution of the 1960s and 1970s, adult bookstores became particularly notorious locations for anonymous sexual encounters both heterosexual and homosexual. Outside of the large cities, adult bookstores were among the few places where gay men could seek sexual partners protected from the elements and the unfriendly reactions of nongay people that would be risked in parks or on public thoroughfares.

In *Arcara v. Cloud Books, Inc.*, the U.S. Supreme Court considered a First Amendment challenge to regulation of public sex in adult bookstores, involving a New York public health law dating from 1914, which was originally titled "Suppression of Certain Nuisances." The New York law was one of a type enacted in several states modeled on a 1909 Iowa law that sought to prevent the occurrence of illicit sex in public

places by authorizing the confiscation and closing of such places as a sanitary measure. This went beyond the normal remedy for such activities, which might involve prosecution of the persons involved and injunctions against future violations.

The New York law, amended over the years and most recently codified as "Houses of Prostitution: Injunction and Abatement" in article 23, title II, of the New York Public Health Law, designated as a "nuisance" "any building, erection, or place used for the purpose of lewdness, assignation, or prostitution." When a court found that such a nuisance existed, it was mandatorily directed by the statute to order the removal and sale of all fixtures or movable property used in conducting the nuisance and to "direct the effectual closing of the [premises] against its use for any purpose, and so keeping it closed for a period of one year," unless the owner paid all costs of the proceeding and filed a bond for the full value of the property. In addition, of course, the statute authorized injunctive relief against continuation of unlawful conduct on the premises.

Richard J. Arcara, the District Attorney of Erie County, New York, had a particular interest in the suppression of vice. He was noted for vigorous prosecution of sex crimes laws (especially during election years), and his office was prominently involved in Supreme Court litigation concerning New York laws on sodomy, loitering for the purpose of sexual solicitation, and sale of pornography. He was constantly engaged in campaigns to "clean up" Erie County (including the city of Buffalo and surrounding suburbs), and one of his targets in this campaign was an adult bookstore in the suburban town of Kenmore, Village Book and News Store (Village News).

Village News, operated by a corporation named Cloud Books, Inc., was reputed to be a gathering place for men to meet for anonymous sex. The front portion of the building was given over to the display and sale of sexually oriented books, magazines, and films. In a room toward the back of the building were several coin-operated movie booths. The back room was entered through a swinging half door, so that activity in the back room was visible to the proprietor from the front counter area. An undercover deputy sheriff visited the store several times between September 13 and October 1, 1982, seeking evidence of illicit sexual activity. The officer claimed to have witnessed acts of public masturbation and fellatio, and he claimed to have been propositioned by several men to engage in sexual activity for pay.

Based on the agent's report, District Attorney Arcara filed suit in the New York Supreme Court for Erie County, seeking to have the "nuisance" permanently enjoined and abated. He based his action on two theories: common-law nuisance (subsequently dismissed by the court) and violation of the Public Health Law. Arcara immediately applied for a temporary restraining order, authorizing seizure and closure of the premises, but the application was denied by Justice John C. Broughton, who commented that he saw no hurry to close down the store, since Arcara had not attempted to prosecute any of the individuals alleged to have engaged in illegal sexual activity or shown that such a remedy would be inadequate.

Justice Broughton also denied Arcara's subsequent application for preliminary injunctive relief, noting that a grant of such relief would effectively decide the case. Village News filed an answer by its attorney, Paul J. Cambria, Jr., of Buffalo, denying that it was allowing illicit sexual activity to occur on the premises, or that it had established the store for the purpose of providing a venue for such activities. Consequently, there were factual issues requiring a trial before the store could be seized and shut. Village News filed a motion for summary judgment on the Public Health Law claim,

making two arguments: first, the law in question was not applicable to a bookstore, since it was clearly labeled as a law for the enjoining and abatement of houses of prostitution, and second that closing a bookstore in order to prevent illicit sex from taking place on the premises would violate the First Amendment rights of the operator as a prior restraint on speech.

The motion was argued before Justice Thomas P. Flaherty, who denied it on May 31, 1983, and set the case for trial. Justice Flaherty (and all succeeding appellate judges writing opinions in this case) considered the argument that the law did not apply to Village News flimsy and unpersuasive. It was clear from the language of the statute that *any* building where prostitution allegedly took place was within the reach of the law, regardless whether prostitution was the main function of the business or merely an activity incidental to lawful functions. In fact, the 1914 predecessor statute did not specify applicability to houses of prostitution in its title, and subsequent amendments of the statutory language had broadened rather than narrowed its scope. On appeal, the only substantive embellishment on this point was to require that the district attorney show a pattern of prostitution activity rather than rely on a single documented incident.

Justice Flaherty was equally dismissive of the prior restraint argument. Attorney Cambria argued that closing the store would prevent the exhibition and sale of books and films that were not obscene under current First Amendment standards, thus constituting a prior restraint of a type that the Supreme Court had held inappropriate unless there was no less restrictive way to achieve the legitimate non-speech-related purpose of the statute. Village News was not conceding that the alleged sexual activity had actually taken place, but in order to challenge the constitutionality of the statute's application had to argue as if the conduct had taken place and was entitled, at least derivatively, to constitutional protection. Arcara replied that he was not seeking to close the store in order to prevent the exhibition and sale of constitutionally protected movies and books; he was seeking to close the store to prevent its operation as a nuisance under the Public Health Law.

Justice Flaherty, relying on cases from other jurisdictions upholding the application of similar laws to businesses of varying kinds where illicit sexual activity was said to have occurred, agreed with the district attorney that the case had nothing to do with First Amendment issues. He asserted that Village News was trying to use the First Amendment as "a curtain behind which illegal activity can be freely conducted," and concluded that the "protections afforded by the laws and constitutions of the United States and the State of New York are designed to enhance the full exercise of the freedoms we enjoy and are not to be subverted as shields for illegal conduct."

Village News promptly appealed to the Appellate Division, Fourth Department, which announced its decision on April 12, 1984, affirming Justice Flaherty in all respects. Justice Reid Moule, writing for a unanimous five-judge panel, found that the closure of the bookstore, if ordered after trial, would be based not on the content of the movies and books, but rather on the nature of the behavior of patrons on the premises. According to Justice Moule, "closure of the bookstore . . . would not constitute a prior restraint on protected First Amendment speech since the People seek only to employ the statute to enjoin illegal conduct occurring on the premises, not to regulate the content of the materials disseminated by the store."

Cambria had argued for Village News that the case was controlled by the Supreme Court's decision in *United States v. O'Brien* (1968), the prosecution of a draft-card burner protesting the Vietnam War. In *O'Brien*, the Court had held that when speech and nonspeech elements were combined in the same course of conduct, a law aimed at the nonspeech elements but having an incidental effect on the speech elements would be justified if it met a three-part test: (1) Was the regulation of the nonspeech element within the constitutional power of the government? (2) Did it further an important or substantial government interest? (3) Was the incidental restriction of First Amendment freedom no greater than essential to the furtherance of that interest? Cambria argued that the Public Health Law provision failed the third part of the test, since the goal of preventing illicit sex at the Village News bookstore could be satis-

fied in the first instance by issuing an injunction requiring the owner to prevent such conduct from occurring in the future. It was not essential to seize the store and its contents and close the place down for a year to achieve this result.

The Fourth Department held that *O'Brien* was inapplicable. *O'Brien* had involved the destruction of a draft card as a form of political protest, conduct which had an expressive element. The conduct the government sought to prevent at Village News had no expressive element, according to Justice Moule, and so the *O'Brien* test did not apply. Moule did not consider the possibility that the sexual activity undertaken by the men in the back room might itself constitute expressive conduct under the First Amendment, at least to the extent that prostitution was not involved. It is unlikely that Cambria would have argued this point, since a direct attack on the constitutionality of regulating the sexual conduct was not necessary to win the case on the theory he was advancing.

Justice Moule also rejected Cambria's argument that shutting down the bookstore would violate the First Amendment overbreadth doctrine. In addition to preventing illicit sex, a shutdown would also prevent the constitutionally protected activities of exhibiting and selling nonobscene movies and books. Moule concluded, without further explanation, that "[s]ince the conduct sought to be enjoined in this case is not 'constitutionally preferred activity,' the overbreadth doctrine is inapplicable."

Even though the appellate division justices were in unanimous agreement on the merits, they must have felt some uncertainty about the result, since they granted Village News's motion for leave to appeal to the court of appeals, New York's highest court, certifying the questions whether the statute could be applied to a bookstore and whether the mandatory closure provisions of the law constituted an impermissible prior restraint.

Six members of the court of appeals sat on the case. They all agreed in their June 13, 1985, opinion that the statute, even though titled as a law concerning "Houses of Prostitution," could be applied to any building in which prostitution was alleged to occur, including a bookstore. But five members of the court agreed to take a broad view of the First Amendment doctrine of prior restraint and voted to reverse the lower courts on that issue.

Writing for the court, Chief Judge Sol M. Wachtler disagreed with the appellate division that First Amendment issues were irrelevant to the case. He asserted: "It is beyond dispute that the activity of selling books is entitled to the protections of the First Amendment . . . and any limitation by a State of First Amendment freedoms must be premised upon 'a compelling state interest in the regulation of a subject within the State's constitutional power to regulate.'" Wachtler cited a long list of cases from other jurisdictions holding that laws authorizing the closure of bookstores and theaters after they sold or exhibited obscene materials violated First Amendment rights against prior restraint. Acknowledging Arcara's contention that these cases were irrelevant because he was not premising his request for closure on the content of books and movies sold at Village News, Wachtler insisted nonetheless that "[a]n ordinance which prohibited all exercise of First Amendment rights in all public areas would be just as unconstitutional as one barring only expression with some particular content." In this case, the closure order would prevent First Amendment activity at the store for a period of one year, regardless of the content of books and films exhibited and sold there. Because book stores are engaged in protected activity under the First Amendment, they "may not simply be equated with ordinary nuisances or with personal property subject to forfeiture." Thus, the motivation of the district attorney in seeking closure was not dispositive of the constitutional issues.

The court accepted Cambria's argument that the *O'Brien* case provided the required analytical method for evaluating Village News's defense. As Cambria had contended, the last part of the *O'Brien* test (whether abridgment of First Amendment rights was necessary to achieve the state's legitimate interest in curtailing illicit sexual activity) was fatal to Arcara's case. A more narrowly tailored injunction aimed at specific unlawful sexual activity could meet the state's interest. If such relief proved ineffective, the district attorney could make a later application for broader relief. Wachtler concluded that "closure of defendant's bookstore is not essential to the furtherance of the purposes underlying title II, and is thus an unconstitutional restraint on defendant's First Amendment rights. While closure might be the most efficient remedy, 'considerations of this sort do not empower a [State] to abridge freedom of speech.'"

Judge Matthew J. Jasen dissented from this portion of the ruling on prudential grounds, arguing that it was unnecessary for the court to address the constitutional issues, since the trial court had not yet actually ordered seizure and closure of the store. In his view, the matter should have been remanded for trial, which might have obviated the need for a ruling on the constitutional issues. In this, Judge Jasen echoed the views of concurring Justice Samuel Green in the appellate division.

Arcara applied for and obtained a writ of *certiorari* from the U.S. Supreme Court to review whether enforcement of the statute against a bookstore "found to be used as a place for prostitution and lewdness" violated the First Amendment. The Supreme Court heard oral argument on April 29, 1986, with Cambria again representing Village News and Attorney John J. DeFranks representing Arcara. By now the case had attained some notoriety, attracting *amicus* briefs from the City of New York urging reversal of the court of appeals and from the American Civil Liberties Union urging affirmance. The city of Santa Ana, California, also filed a brief which the Court did not characterize with regard to its position on the merits.

The Supreme Court announced its decision on July 7, 1986, at the end of its 1985 Term. Little attention was paid to the decision, since the Court's decision upholding Georgia's sodomy law in *Bowers v. Hardwick*, issued late in June, was the focus of attention from most commentators. The Court divided 6–3 on the merits of the case, with Chief Justice Warren E. Burger writing the opinion of the Court reversing the New York Court of Appeals. Chief Justice Burger insisted that the appellate division rather than the court of appeals had taken the appropriate view of the *O'Brien* decision and its impact on the case. He said that the "court ignored a crucial distinction between the circumstances presented in *O'Brien* and the circumstances of this case: unlike the symbolic draft card burning in *O'Brien*, the sexual activity carried on in this case manifests absolutely no element of protected expression." Burger relied for this proposition on *Paris Adult Theatre I v. Slaton*, a 1973 case in which the Court had held that the constitutional right of privacy did not extend to persons engaging in sexual activity in an "adult" movie theater open to the public. "First Amendment values may not be invoked by merely linking the words 'sex' and 'books.'" Furthermore, the Public Health Law was not concerned with regulating bookstores, as such, but rather was a law of general applicability to all places where illicit sexual activity occurred. If the state wished to close the bookstore for violations of the fire code or for other health hazards to patrons, the First Amendment would not provide a defense for the owner, so why should it provide one in this case?

Burger also observed that any burden on First Amendment activities was dissipated because the operators of Village News would be free under the closure order to reestablish their business at another location; the order ran against the premises, not the business. The Court had not in the past subjected every criminal or civil penalty to the "least restrictive means" analysis merely because the penalty would have an incidental effect on First Amendment rights. For the Chief Justice, the key to invocation of that stringent test was that arguably protected First Amendment activity was the "element that drew the legal remedy in the first place, as in *O'Brien*," or that the statute was drawn in a way that inevitably singled out those engaged in protected activity. This was not such a statute, since it was concerned only with the location of the illicit sexual activity, not with the other activities that might occur at the location.

Justice Sandra Day O'Connor concurred in a brief opinion joined by Justice John Paul Stevens, noting that Cambria's argument under *O'Brien* could lead to the absurd result of denying the right of the state to arrest a journalist for violating traffic laws due to the incidental burden on First Amendment media rights. She did observe, however, that if the statute was invoked as a pretext for closing down a bookstore selling sexually oriented materials

that had First Amendment protection, the *O'Brien* test might become relevant.

Justice Harry A. Blackmun dissented in an opinion joined by Justices William J. Brennan, Jr., and Thurgood Marshall. He insisted that "generally applicable statutes that purport to regulate non-speech repeatedly have been struck down if they unduly penalize speech, political or otherwise," citing cases concerning trespass, breach of peace, littering, and excessive noise. Acknowledging that "at some point . . . the impact of state regulation on First Amendment rights becomes so attenuated that it is easily outweighed by the state interest," Blackmun argued that shutting down a bookstore "substantially impairs First Amendment activities" in a way that "can no more be compared to a traffic arrest of a reporter . . . than the closure of a church could be compared to the traffic arrest of a clergyman."

For Blackmun, the issue was really one of overbreadth. The state could achieve its purpose by arresting the patrons who commit unlawful acts or by enjoining their future occurrence on the premises. "But the statute in issue does not provide for that. Instead, it imposes absolute liability on the bookstore simply because the activity occurs on the premises. And the penalty—a mandatory 1–year closure—imposes an unnecessary burden on speech." Noting the frequency of cases generated by Arcara from Erie County concerned with sexual behavior and erotic literature that had come before the Supreme Court in recent years, Blackmun insisted that the Court's decision created a loophole in First Amendment law through which officials like Arcara could "suppress 'undesirable,' protected speech without confronting the protections of the First Amendment." Only by proving selective prosecution could a bookstore hope to obtain First Amendment protection, and this could be quite difficult.

The Supreme Court had noted in granting review of the case that the New York decision appeared to conflict with decisions from Virginia and Pennsylvania, thus justifying consideration of the issue at the national level. The Court's decision resolves this conflict by holding that states may resort to the closure of adult bookstores, even where their wares have not been adjudged unprotected by the First Amendment, under public health nuisance statutes based on illicit sexual activities on the premises. The Court's decision thus endangers the continued existence of adult bookstores as one of the few outlets for gay men outside of large cities as places to meet for sexual contact. In addition, adult bookstores may be the only source of gay-oriented literature in such areas and, due to the notoriety attending enforcement proceedings, their operators may find it difficult if not impossible to rent alternative quarters for operations.

However, the decision will not have that effect in New York, because the state's court of appeals decided to take another look at the case. Treating the Supreme Court's decision as a remand for redetermination consistent with the opinion, the court of appeals scheduled argument for November 12, 1986, and took little time determining that it could not agree with the result dictated by the Supreme Court. In a new opinion issued on December 18, 1986, the court of appeals resorted to article I, section 8 of the New York State Constitution, which states in pertinent part: "Every citizen may freely speak, write and publish his sentiments on all subjects, being responsible for the abuse of that right; and no law shall be passed to restrain or abridge the liberty of speech or of the press."

Chief Judge Wachtler, writing for a unanimous court, insisted that the Supreme Court's construction of First Amendment rights merely prescribed the minimum floor of protection for speech throughout the country, leaving the states free to provide greater protection, which he concluded New York had done.

> Freedom of expression in books, movies and the arts, generally, is one of those areas in which there is great diversity among the States. Thus it is an area in which the Supreme Court has displayed great reluctance to expand Federal constitutional protections, holding instead that this is a matter essentially governed by community standards. . . . However, New York has a long history and tradition of fostering freedom of expression, often tolerating and supporting works which in other States would be found offensive to the community.

Wachtler then found that New York courts had actually been more critical of those nonspeech regulations that incidentally burdened speech than had been the Supreme Court, and concluded that despite the Supreme Court's holding it would violate the New York Constitution to grant Arcara's request for an order closing down Village News. "Of course," he continued, "a bookstore cannot claim an exemption from statutes of general operation aimed at preventing nuisances or hazards to the public health and safety. It is, however, entitled to special protection, and no undue burden is placed on the State by requiring it to prove that in seeking to close the store it has chosen a course no broader than necessary to accomplish its purpose. If other sanctions, such as arresting the offenders or injunctive relief, prove unavailing, then its burden would be met."

Judge Wachtler concluded by asserting that Justice O'Connor's illustration of the reporter arrested for a traffic violation was inappropriate, since "closing a bookstore for a year, as is required by this statute, cannot be said to have such a slight and indirect impact on free expression as to have no significance constitutionally." Consequently, Arcara's petition was to be denied on state constitutional grounds, and Village News would not have to stand trial faced with the prospect of forfeiture and closure under the Public Health Law.

Case References

Bowers v. Hardwick, 478 U.S. 186 (1986)
Paris Adult Theatre I v. Slaton, 413 U.S. 49 (1973)
United States v. O'Brien, 391 U.S. 367 (1968)

46. REFUSING ADVERTISING FROM GAY BUSINESSES

Hatheway v. Gannett Satellite Information Network, Inc., 157 Wis. 2d 395, 459 N.W.2d 873 (App.), review denied, 461 N.W.2d 445 (Wis. 1990).

In 1982, Wisconsin became the first state in the United States to amend its civil rights laws to provide that "sexual orientation" could not be the basis for discrimination in employment, housing, and public places of accommodation. Few cases have arisen testing the application of this law, particularly in the area of public accommodations. One such case began, however, when the *Green Bay Press Gazette*, a newspaper published by Gannett Satellite Information Network, Inc., refused to accept classified business advertisements from two gay-owned and -oriented organizations.

One organization was Among Friends, a gay and lesbian membership organization directed by Jay Hatheway, which published a magazine for gay people living in rural Wisconsin and offered to provide information and referrals for people seeking medical, legal, or other professional assistance. Hatheway submitted two advertisements, both of which were rejected by the newspaper. The first stated: "Gay/lesbian resources, referrals, networks for rural Wisconsin. Write to Among Friends, Box 881, Madison, Wisconsin 53701." The second, in addition to the Among Friends address, stated: "Gay/lesbian referrals for medical, legal and professional assistance for rural Wisconsin." The newspaper told Hatheway that it would not run the advertisements because they included the words "lesbian" and "gay" and that the paper would not, in any event, run advertising for a gay and lesbian organization as a matter of policy.

The other organization was a business owned by two lesbians, Peggy and Tracey Vandeveer, who were marketing sweatshirts and submitted an advertisement reading: "Unique, hand-painted sweatshirts for lesbians. Very affordable. For info, write to P.O. Box 10522, Green Bay, WI 54307–0522." When this ad was rejected, they submitted a second, slightly modified to say "Unique, screen-painted sweatshirts with gay/lesbian slogans," but this was also rejected. The newspaper's stated reason for rejecting the advertisement was that it believed the Vandeveers were lesbians providing services primarily to a gay and lesbian clientele, and "we just don't print those kinds of ads."

Hatheway retained Madison attorney Mark F. Borns, and the Vandeveers found their way to Paula Ettelbrick, legal director at Lambda Legal Defense and Education Fund. Charges filed at the Wisconsin Human Rights Commission, alleging discrimination in public accommodations on the basis of sexual orientation, produced no resolution of the matter, so a joint suit was filed by Hatheway and the Vandeveers in Brown County Circuit Court. Judge Vivi L. Dilweg granted the newspaper's motion for summary judgment, and the plaintiffs appealed. Oral argument was held before the Court of Appeals of Wisconsin on June 14, 1990.

The theory of the suit was that the newspaper was a "public place of accommodation" which was prohibited from discriminating on the basis of sexual orientation in the provision of goods and services. The *Green Bay Press Gazette* was the largest newspaper serving four counties in northeastern Wisconsin, and published a large classified advertising section separate from its editorial and news pages, captioned as "Northeastern Wisconsin's Complete Shopping Center in Print." In publicizing its advertising section, the *Gazette* described it as a "classified mall" and a "shopping center under one roof," claiming that "one phone call will get your message in over 79,000 homes Sunday, and over 56,000 daily." The Wisconsin civil rights law defined "place of public accommodation" as follows:

> "Public place of accommodation or amusement" shall be interpreted broadly to include, but not be limited to, places of business or recreation, hotels, motels, resorts, restaurants, taverns, barber or cosmetologist,

aesthetician, electrologist or manicuring establishments, nursing homes, clinics, hospitals, cemeteries, and any place where accommodations, amusement, goods or services are available either free or for a consideration except where provided by bona fide private, nonprofit organizations or institutions.

Hatheway and the Vandeveers reasoned that the *Press Gazette*'s classified advertising operation was surely a "place of business" where "goods or services are available . . . for a consideration." The newspaper argued, through its attorneys David Lucey, John R. Dawson, and Michael L. Silhol, of Milwaukee, that the legislature did not intend to include newspapers in the coverage of the statute, which would, in their view, raise serious First Amendment issues. In many other contexts, courts had ruled the government could not compel newspapers to publish particular articles or advertising, although the Supreme Court had ruled in *Pittsburgh Press Co. v. Pittsburgh Commission on Human Relations* (1973) that a state could prohibit newspapers from publishing employment advertisements that stated a preference for men or women as applicants as part of enforcement of an employment discrimination statute.

The Wisconsin Court of Appeals apparently decided that the First Amendment was an issue it wanted to avoid, because the appellate panel unanimously decided to ignore the plain meaning of the statute and to construe it to exempt newspapers from coverage. In its opinion of July 10, 1990, by Judge Gordon Myse, the court held that a "literal" interpretation of the statute was not appropriate.

Although the definition provision stated that it was to be "interpreted broadly," Myse reasoned that certain venerable rules of statutory construction should be applied which, taken together with legislative history, indicated that in fact the legislature really intended a rather narrow interpretation of the statute, under which only businesses like those actually listed would be covered. "We are aware that the plain language of the act makes clear that the businesses subject to the act are not limited to those identified," he conceded, but "[n]onetheless we do not conclude that the legislature by adopting this language intended to subject every place of business where goods and services are pro-

vided to the provisions of the public accommodations act." This was because, when a legislature includes an illustrative list in a statutory definition, the list should be given some meaning in interpreting the statute, otherwise it would be "superfluous," and legislatures are presumed to intend that all statutory language be included for a reason. If the general provision really covered all businesses, then there would be no need for the list, said Myse. "We decline to read the statute so as to render the entire listing irrelevant to the statute's meaning."

Another old rule of statutory construction, *ejusdem generis*, also came into play. Myse described this as holding that "where a general term is preceded or followed by a series of specific terms, the general term is viewed as being limited to an item of the same type or nature as those specifically enumerated." He also characterized this rule as *noscitur a sociis*, or "a word is known by the company it keeps."

Applying these "principles of statutory construction," Myse found that newspapers should not be included in the act's coverage because they were not "comparable to or consistent with the businesses enumerated in the statute itself." Even though the statute itself called for a "broad" interpretation, Myse felt that newspapers were too "dissimilar" to the other listed types of businesses to be included.

Myse found support for this interpretation in the legislature's action over the years of adding specific new types of businesses to the statutory list. For example, where the original statute had listed "barbershops," the legislature had amended the law specifically to list "cosmetologist, aesthetician, electrologist or manicuring establishments." If the law already covered all businesses providing services to the public, why would the legislature feel any need to supplement the existing list? And, the legislature had "twice specifically rejected a proposed amendment that would delete the businesses listed and apply a broader definition" that was more generally inclusive of all businesses. To Myse, this signaled a legislative intention that the law be construed to cover only businesses similar to those listed.

Breathing a sigh of relief, Myse explained: "This conclusion makes it unnecessary for us to examine the constitutional implications that a contrary decision would have involved. We specifically refrain from addressing the constitutionality of any act, rule or order requiring a newspaper to publish any specific item." At the same time, realizing that its construction of the statute could be further construed as sharply limiting its reach due to the peculiar list of specific businesses in the statute, Myse insisted that "we have not limited the scope of the act beyond the specific holding in this case."

> We also do not wish this holding to imply that we endorse Gannett's decision not to run these classified ads. While we have determined that the refusal to print the proffered ads is not a violation of the public accommodations acts, the wisdom of a policy that refuses to accept an ad designed to offer medical and other assistance to those engaged in an alternative lifestyle is not within our power to review.

This expression of judicial disclaimer of what Gannett had done was all well and good, but the decision, despite all disavowals, had adopted a method of construction that rendered ineffectual certain clear wording, including the phrase "any place where accommodations, amusement, goods or services are available," as well as the phrase "shall be interpreted broadly to include, *but not limited to*, places of business." In applying for review to the Wisconsin Supreme Court, the plaintiffs argued that the court of appeals' construction was clearly wrong and adopted solely to avoid having to grapple with the more difficult constitutional issues presented by the case. But the Wisconsin Supreme Court was no more willing to tackle those issues than the court of appeals, denying review without explanation on September 6, 1990, with only one justice, Louis S. Ceci, dissenting without opinion.

The decision in the *Hatheway* case avoided one of the most difficult, recurring issues faced by lesbian and gay organizations and businesses: how to make their existence and services known to large numbers of people through the existing mass media. So long as newspapers (and radio and television stations) are free to reject gay advertising on grounds of "taste" or "policy," and the lesbian and gay press remains small and of limited circulation, such organizations and businesses face severe limitations on their ability to survive and serve the communities they were designed to serve.

At about the same time that the Wisconsin case was being considered by the courts, a similar controversy arose in New York City over the refusal by the publisher of the Yellowpages telephone directory to create a special category of "Gay and Lesbian Organizations," so that users of the directory seeking to find and contact such organizations could find them without necessarily knowing their exact names, under which they were listed in the general alphabetical listings in the white pages. The phone company took the position that no other ethnic, racial, or religious group had a separate listing. For example, there was no specific category of Jewish organizations or Irish organizations. The Gay and Lesbian Alliance Against Defamation, in consort with several other gay and lesbian community and service organizations, filed a complaint in the New York City Commission on Human Rights, asserting that the Yellowpages was a "place of public accommodation" under the city's human rights ordinance forbidding discrimination on the basis of sexual orientation. Settlement talks ensued, resulting in the creation of a "Gay and Lesbian Organizations" subcategory within a broader category of Social and Service Organizations.

Case Reference

Pittsburgh Press Co. v. Pittsburgh Commission on Human Relations, 413 U.S. 376 (1973)

47. WHEN CAN A STATE PROHIBIT DANCING IN THE NUDE?

Barnes v. Glen Theatre, Inc., 111 S. Ct. 2456 (1991), reversing *Miller v. Civil City of South Bend*, 904 F.2d 1081 (7th Cir. 1990) (en banc). Cases below: *Glen Theatre, Inc. v. Civil City of South Bend*, 726 F. Supp. 728 (N.D. Ind. 1985), reversed and remanded sub nom. *Glen Theatre, Inc. v. Pearson*, 802 F.2d 287 (7th Cir. 1986), decision on remand, 695 F. Supp. 414 (N.D. Ind. 1988), reversed, 887 F. 2d 826 (7th Cir. 1989), reversed en banc sub nom. *Miller v. Civil City of South Bend*, 904 F.2d 1081 (7th Cir. 1990).

Erotic nude dancing ranks very high among media for the expression of sexuality. Serge Diaghilev's Ballet Russe created a scandal before World War I in Paris when the lead dancer, Vaslav Nijinsky, wearing a tight body stocking simulating the nude figure, enacted a masturbation fantasy on stage to the sensuous strains of Debussy's tone poem, *Prelude to the Afternoon of a Faun*. But this use of nudity (or simulated nudity) as a form of erotic expression came very late in the game, for erotic dancing as an artistic medium has ancient roots in various world cultures.

This form of expression comes into conflict, however, with the prudery of American society, long dominated by the Puritan ethos that banned public expressions of sexuality as unsuitable to "public morality" or a "decent society." During the 19th century, many states, including Indiana, passed laws prohibiting public nudity of any kind. These laws were used by law enforcement authorities to prosecute nude dancers and the proprietors of establishments in which they performed. Although such laws became the subject of much litigation in the 1970s and 1980s as changing sexual mores and the demands of customers led to more nude dancing in bars and "adult" theaters and bookstores, it was not until 1991, in the Indiana case of *Barnes v. Glen Theatre, Inc.*, that the U.S. Supreme Court directly addressed the constitutional merits of laws used to penalize such activity.

Indiana's law, frequently rephrased and reenacted, was most recently embodied in a 1976 "public indecency" law, which made it a misdemeanor for any person to "knowingly or intentionally, in a public place" engage in sexual intercourse, deviate sexual conduct, appear in a "state of nudity," or fondle the genitals of himself or another person. The law defined nudity to mean "the showing of the human male or female genitals, pubic area, or buttocks with less than a fully opaque covering, the showing of the female breast with less than a fully opaque covering or any part of the nipple, or the showing of covered male genitals in a discernibly turgid state." As interpreted by the Indiana courts, this meant that female dancers who wished to appear nude had to wear, at a minimum, "pasties" fully covering their nipples and a "G-string" covering the pubic area and anus.

Initial attempts to challenge the statute as unconstitutionally overbroad in reaching protected expression were apparently met by a limiting construction in the Indiana Supreme Court, which held in *State v. Baysinger* (1979) that the law might be construed to "allow some nudity as a part of some larger form of expression meriting protection, when the communication of ideas is involved" if necessary to avoid constitutional concerns. The U.S. Supreme Court summarily dismissed an appeal from this decision, apparently agreeing that the statute, as construed, was not overbroad, but issuing no written opinion. In a subsequent case, however, the Indiana Supreme Court cast some doubt on whether it had actually limited the application of the law, when it ruled in 1984 in *Erhardt v. State* that the law could penalize a partially nude dance in the "Miss Erotica of Fort Wayne" competition.

In 1985 and 1986, several cases arose in South Bend, Indiana, out of attempts by local law enforcement officials to enforce the public nudity law against some adult bookstores, theaters, and bars. Two specialty dancers and the proprietor of the Chippewa Bookstore, Glen Theatres, Inc., filed suit in the federal district court, seeking a declaration that the nudity law was unconstitutional and an injunction against its operation against them. The bookstore had been raided by the police several times, resulting in eleven arrests of dancers and various prosecutions, although at the time the complaint was filed there were no prosecutions ongoing. The bookstore was constructed in such a way that passersby could not see what was happening inside, and customers who wished to view nude dancing would not be in the same room as the dancers, but rather would view them through glass panels from another room. All customers were over age 18, paid admission, and were advised prior to their admission that they would be seeing nude dancing. Liquor was not sold on the premises. Charles A. Asher, of South Bend, and Lee J. Klein, of Okemos, Michigan, appeared on behalf of the bookstore and the dancers. Deputy City Attorney Robert C. Rosenfeld, of South Bend, and Assistant Attorney General William E. Daily, of Indianapolis, appeared on behalf of the city and the state, respectively.

Chief Judge Allen Sharp decided on July 26, 1985, that a preliminary injunction should be issued barring the police department from enforcing the law against the Chippewa or its dancers. Sharp concluded that the public nudity statute was overbroad on its face, since there were a variety of contexts in which public nudity might be part of constitutionally protected expression. Recognizing that the Indiana Supreme Court had upheld the statute against an overbreadth challenge in *Baysinger*, Sharp observed that a subsequent ruling by the U.S. Supreme Court, *Schad v. Mount Ephraim* (1981), had appeared to recognize that nude dancing had some First Amendment protection, a point that the Indiana Supreme Court had not conceded in its *Baysinger* ruling. Consequently, one of the premises underlying that ruling had been superseded by a later development. Also, Sharp noted that the Indiana court's *Erhardt* decision seemed to extend the law's reach to circumstances that might have been excluded by *Baysinger*'s alleged "narrow" construction, thus casting doubt on the continued vitality of that narrowing. Thus, he concluded that the petitioners had a reasonable likelihood of prevailing on the merits.

He found little difficulty in concluding that enforcement of the statute pending a final decision on the merits would impose irreparable harm on the petitioners, which would be greater than any harm imposed on the state or city. He also found that there was a strong public interest in protecting First Amendment rights, while, given the factual context (nude dancing in an enclosed structure to which only consenting adults were admitted), the state's interest in preventing "public indecency" would not be "undermined" by preliminarily enjoining enforcement of the law. After further argument and consideration, Sharp substituted a permanent injunction for his preliminary injunction on October 10, 1985, and the state appealed to the U.S. Court of Appeals for the Seventh Circuit, which heard oral argument from Daily and Asher on April 18, 1986. Meanwhile, emboldened by Sharp's order, other adult-oriented businesses in South Bend that wanted to present nude dancing in their establishments made preparations to do so, but were warned off by the local police. Several dancers and proprietors then filed suit in the federal court seeking injunctive relief similar to that awarded Glen Theatres. A hearing was held by District Judge Robert L. Miller, Jr., on May 5, 1986. Those cases were pending when the Seventh Circuit issued its judgment in the state's appeal.

A unanimous Seventh Circuit panel ruled on September 30 that Sharp had misconstrued his authority with regard to the overbreadth issue. Chief Judge Walter Cummings devoted much of his opinion to determining the effect of *Baysinger* and the Supreme Court's dismissal without opinion of the appeal in that case. He concluded that the Supreme Court's dismissal was in effect a ruling on the merits of the issue whether the Indiana law, as construed by the state's supreme court, was overbroad in violation of the First Amendment, thus Sharp was precluded from reconsidering that issue. Cummings found no support for the argument that the Supreme Court's subsequent opinion in *Schad*, a zoning case, had changed matters any. While the Supreme Court had commented in *Schad* that a state could not prohibit an entertainment program "solely because it displays the nude human figure," and had commented that "nude dancing is not without its First

Amendment protections from official regulations," this did not mean that the Court had in any way upset the overbreadth ruling in *Baysinger*. "*Schad* is consistent with *Baysinger*'s decision that nudity needs to be combined with some sort of expressive activity before it falls within First Amendment protection," said Cummings. This means that the issue for Sharp was not whether the statute was overbroad, but rather whether its application to the nude dancing performance proposed by the petitioners in this case was unconstitutional. Given the Supreme Court's approval of *Baysinger*, the only issue left open here was whether the law was unconstitutional "as applied;" a facial challenge was precluded by binding precedent. The court remanded the case to Sharp for further factual findings.

On remand, Sharp consolidated the Glen Theatre case with the two cases pending before Judge Miller, *Miller v. Civil City of South Bend* and *Diamond v. Civil City of South Bend*, and held a new hearing on January 11, 1988, at which he set deadlines for the submission of briefs and proposed findings of fact. Oral argument was held July 15, 1988. Among the materials submitted by the petitioners was a videotape of nude dancing of the type they proposed to present, which was subsequently described by Sharp in his opinion:

> The tape consists of four separate performances. The performances are basically identical. They consist of a female, fully clothed initially, who dances to one or more songs as she proceeds to remove her clothing. Each dance ends with the dancer totally nude or nearly nude. The dances are done on a stage or on a bar and are not a part of any type of play or dramatic performance. They are simply what are commonly referred to as "striptease" acts.

Adopting Judge Miller's factual findings in the *Miller* and *Diamond* cases and his own findings in the *Glen Theatre* case, supplemented by the new stipulations and the videotape, Judge Sharp ruled on September 9, 1988, that the Indiana law could constitutionally be applied to the nude dancing performances that were proposed by the petitioners. He concluded that "the type of dancing these plaintiffs wish to perform is not expressive activity protected by the United States Constitution. These strip tease dances

are not performed in any theatrical or dramatic context," he asserted, and "their conduct falls squarely within the prohibitions of Indiana's Public Indecency statute, which has been found constitutional. This court cannot find any constitutionally protected expression in these performances, and must conclude that the dances are mere conduct." Sharp dismissed the petitions and levied costs against the petitioners.

A new appeal to the Seventh Circuit was much more successful than the first had been. The petitioners drew an entirely different panel of judges the second time around, which unanimously endorsed an opinion by Circuit Judge Joel M. Flaum, issued October 19, 1989, finding that Sharp had again missed the point. While conceding that the circuit's first opinion might have left some ambiguity as to what the district court was supposed to do on remand, Flaum contended that it was clearly not supposed to decide anything about "the degree of expression embodied in a particular dance routine." Rather, taking as a given that "non-obscene nude dancing as entertainment is a form of expression entitled to limited first amendment protection," the district court was supposed to determine as a factual matter whether the state of Indiana was using its public indecency statute "to prohibit nude dancing as entertainment, and thus limit plaintiffs' expression." The circuit court had not intended to have Sharp make an individual judgment about "aesthetic appeal or artistic merit."

Thus Sharp's findings were "clearly erroneous." The evidence on remand showed that the plaintiffs wanted to present a nonobscene striptease routine of a type that federal courts in several circuits had recognized as having some First Amendment protection. After briefly noting earlier cases in which the Supreme Court had suggested or intimated that such nude dancing had some First Amendment protection, Flaum stated, "Our reading of these precedents constrains us to conclude that the Supreme Court would not permit Indiana to apply its public nudity statute to the activity these plaintiffs wish to engage in," even though the activity might have only minimal artistic value. While the government could impose reasonable time, place, or manner restrictions on the activity, or, under the Twenty-first Amendment, prohibit it entirely in establishments serving liquor (which was not the case here), or of course ban obscene dances, the broad, undifferentiated ban in this statute was not narrowly tailored as required when First Amendment interests were at stake. The panel reversed Sharp's ruling and ordered the cases remanded for entry of injunctive relief. The panel's opinion was not the last word for the circuit, however, since enough judges were upset with the opinion to result in granting the state's motion for rehearing *en banc* in an order of January 8, 1990, and the entire circuit sat to hear a new oral argument on January 31, 1990.

The argument within the circuit over how to handle the case must have been quite heated, as the resulting opinions issued on May 24, 1990, run for more than fifty pages in the *Federal Reporter*. The *en banc* reconsideration produced the same result as the panel, with the circuit splitting seven to four in upholding the panel's determination that the Public Indecency law could not constitutionally be applied to the type of nude dancing the various plaintiffs sought to perform. Judge Flaum again delivered the view of the circuit, but his lengthy opinion was supplemented by a brief concurring opinion by Circuit Judge Richard D. Cudahy, and an extensive treatise by Circuit Judge Richard A. Posner, which expanded upon almost every point made in the court's opinion. There were three dissenting opinions, by Circuit Judges John L. Coffey, Frank H. Easterbrook, and Daniel A. Manion.

Flaum's opinion, while reiterating the points made in the panel opinion, expanded on some of them. As he conceptualized the case, the question presented was "whether non-obscene nude dancing of the barroom variety, performed as entertainment, is expression and thus entitled to protection under the first amendment." Flaum reviewed the numerous cases in which the Supreme Court had either commented or implied that nude dancing had some First Amendment protection, although it had never confronted the issue head-on in a case requiring such a determination in the absence of obscenity or other complicating factors. Then he set out a brief history of dancing as an expressive art, characterizing "dance as entertainment" as "one of the earliest forms of expression known to man," and insisting that "inherently, it is the communication of emotion or ideas."

Flaum dismissed as unworthy the state's contention that "the dance involved loses its expressive qualities as the dancers lose their clothing." The Supreme Court had held in *Schad* that "nudity alone does not place otherwise protected material outside the mantle of the first amendment;" if dance was expressive, it did not become less so because the striptease terminated in nudity. Indeed, nudity heightened the expressive quality. Flaum went on in this vein much longer than really necessary, probably to counter the extended dissenting opinion by Judge Easterbrook, who argued at great length that what was being penalized was not First Amendment "speech."

Having concluded that the nude dancing was protected expressive activity, Flaum conceded that the state could regulate its presentation in various ways, such as forbidding obscene dancing, restricting it to enclosed areas where unsuspecting members of the public would not be offended by it, or forbidding it in places that served liquor. However, concluded Flaum, "the total ban at issue here does not fall within any of these constitutionally permissible areas of legislation," so the statute was unconstitutional as applied to nude barroom-type dancing.

Judge Cudahy's brief concurrence added nothing substantive to the court's opinion, but expressed the judge's reluctance to treat the whole issue of nude dancing as one worthy of First Amendment concern. While finding that the application of the First Amendment to this case was "correct as a matter of law," he lamented that "the high purposes of the Amendment seem, in these circumstances, in some danger of being lost." Asserting that it was "clear" that "the message of the striptease is not a subject that the Founding Fathers had in mind in drafting the First Amendment," he suggested that the court should exercise "caution in making the Amendment do service in situations as improbable as this one seems to me."

The lengthy concurring opinion by Judge Posner is a rhetorical masterpiece. If not for the practical considerations of length in a work such as this, it would be worth even more extended quotation and review than the following, not least for its literary qualities and eloquent exploration of the difficult questions posed by nonspeech forms of artistic expression in First Amendment jurisprudence.

Despite its fascinating length, Posner's opinion might be summed up by quoting one decisive paragraph early on:

> *De gustibus non est disputandum*; but whether one has a taste or a distaste for erotic dance in general or striptease dances in particular, to say as the district judge did in this case that a striptease dance is not "expressive activity," but "mere conduct," is indefensible and a threat to artistic freedom. This is not to suggest that the State of Indiana has no power to regulate nude striptease dancing; it has ample power. But to try to justify that power, as the district judge in this case tried, on the ground that such dancing is not expression is misguided.

Characterizing the case as a "fascinating freak" because Indiana's public nudity statute was far more absolute than those in most other states and, unusually, did not rely on the Twenty-first Amendment's reservation to the states of total regulatory authority in connection with sale and service of liquor in public places as its source of authority, Posner proceeded to toy at some length with the issues posed by changing public tastes in matters sexual, speculating that what would have been considered obscene thirty years ago was no longer so.

Posner then developed at length his rejoinder to four basic arguments raised by the various dissenters. First, he rejected the argument that treating nude dancing as First Amendment expression meant that virtually any conduct could qualify for such protection, arguing that in order for conduct to be "expressive" as such, it required some sort of communication between the person performing the conduct and others perceiving it. This was the distinction he found between nude dancing for an audience and social dancing, which the Supreme Court had held lacked First Amendment protection in *City of Dallas v. Stanglin* in 1989.

Posner next took on the argument that even if nude dancing is expressive, it is not the type of expression the First Amendment protects, which must be limited to the communication of ideas and opinions. Clearly, said Posner, this could not be the case, otherwise virtually all nonverbal art would lose First Amendment protection. He found the implications of this contention for nonvocal music to be "particularly arresting." Most nonvocal music, he said, with perhaps the limited exception of "program music" intended to illustrate a story, was concerned with emotions and feelings rather than ideas or opinions. If the nude dancing at the Kitty Kat Lounge, one of the plaintiffs in the consolidated case, was not "expression," then neither were "Mozart's piano concertos and Balanchine's most famous ballets." By the same token, he argued, some of the greatest pictorial art found in leading museums had more to do with emotions than ideas, but was nonetheless surely protected. He sarcastically suggested that "the reason we think that art is an intellectual medium and therefore has nothing important in common with striptease is that most of us obtain no enjoyment from art."

> It requires an educated taste to distinguish *Venus With a Mirror* [by Titian] from a camp photo of a fat woman. Knowing that it is a cultural monument we assume that its significance must be intellectual, since it is dead to most of us emotionally. But the painting is not an intellectual statement; there are no ideas in the painting. There is pattern, design, harmony, and color in abstract painting, and these attributes evoke pleasure and other emotions in an appreciative viewer. But there is no story, no articulable idea, no verbal meaning. The notion that all art worthy of the name has a "message" is philistine, and leads to the weird conclusion that nonrepresentational art and nonprogrammatic, nonvocal music are entitled to less protection under the First Amendment than striptease dancing because the latter has a more distinct, articulable message. And likewise that Beethoven's string quartets are entitled to less protection than *Peter and the Wolf*.

Dismissing the contention that "the Founding Fathers would writhe in their graves if they knew that the nude dancers of the Kitty Kat Lounge could unwrap themselves with the First Amendment," Posner replied that "such arguments merely demonstrate the inadequacy of original understanding as a guide to constitutional interpretation" and that such arguments would if accepted change the Constitution from a living document into a petrified reminder of the limits of human foresight; that a conception of free speech which privileges the burning of the American flag but permits government to ban performances of twelve-tone music is more absurd than one that protects flag burning, twelve-tone music and striptease; and that if the purpose and scope of the First Amendment's speech and press clauses are exhausted in the protection of political speech, because freedom of political speech is all that is necessary to preserve our democratic political system, this implies the exclusion from the amendment's protections not only of all art (other than the political) but also of science. For one can have democracy without science, just as one can have democracy without art.

Concluding on the point, Posner asserted that if only the expression of ideas and opinions was protected by the Constitution, then "most music and visual art, and much of literature are unprotected," which would be a "shocking contraction" of the accepted understanding of constitutional protection for expression in modern times.

Posner next addressed the argument that "mere entertainment" was not entitled to constitutional protection. This, of course, was a variety of the earlier argument seeming to differentiate high art from low by virtue of its "intellectual" content. Posner was not buying. "Art is entertainment." Indeed, for those who love art, "it is primarily as a superior form of entertainment and consolation" rather than "as a source of insight or edification, although it often is that as well." Posner referred to a hypothetical that must have been the subject of much discussion between himself and Easterbrook, at whose dissenting views it is aimed: bullfighting. Commenting that bullfighting was "more expressive, more artistic, culturally richer than most popular American sports," Posner asked why it was not constitutionally protected and concluded this was due to aspects of its performance having nothing to do with its expressive qualities but rather because of "its harmful consequences," including cruelty to animals.

Posner, prime exponent of the "law and economics" approach to law, then resorted to his most frequent metaphor, almost regardless of the area of law involved: the marketplace.

He found erotic performances to be "a major component of the First Amendment marketplace," unlike ballroom dancing, social conversation, and other "audience of one" activities, that he labeled "minor" by comparison. He asserted that there was no principled ground for distinguishing Shakespeare's plays, created as entertainment, from the nude dancing at the Kitty Kat Lounge. State's attorney Daily had argued that only "established" works of art could be seen as protected by the First Amendment. This was nonsense, said Posner, since many great works of art were controversial and far from established when first presented to the public. "The Constitution does not look down its nose at popular culture even if its framers would have done so," insisted Posner, noting that the "line between expressive (in the sense of communicative) and nonexpressive activity" was not distinct. There was a substantial "gray area" which entertainment, among other things, occupied, and where government had greater scope for regulation, and it was necessary for the courts to derive some general rules by which government could be guided in its regulatory activities, but he found "indefensible" the argument that putting the label "entertainment" on certain conduct clearly rendered it unprotected.

Finally, Posner rejected the argument that there was some sharp distinction between speech and conduct, as suggested by the trial judge and the dissenters. Finding the case "a symphony of sterile dichotomies," Posner asserted:

the medium in which experience is encoded is [normally] irrelevant to its expressive character and social consequences. The pitter-patter of raindrops does not become expressive activity by being recorded, and a recording of Beethoven's Ninth Symphony is not entitled to more constitutional protection than the live performance from which the recording was made. The government could not shut down the theaters on the ground that what actors do is conduct, not speech, with the result that a production of *King Lear* by the Royal Shakespeare Company would be outside the scope of the First Amendment but a nonobscene pornographic movie within it.

Attempting to distinguish in First Amendment cases between "speech" and "conduct" was specious. What explained the hostility of some of the judges in dissent (and even Judge Cudahy, in concurrence) to using the First Amendment to protect this activity? Posner's reply:

> It is a feeling that the proposition, "the First Amendment forbids the State of Indiana to require striptease dancers to cover their nipples," is ridiculous. It strikes judges as ridiculous in part because most of us are either middle-aged or elderly men, in part because we tend to be snooty about popular culture, in part because as public officials we have a natural tendency to think political expression more important than artistic expression, in part because we are Americans—which means that we have been raised in a culture in which puritanism, philistinism, and promiscuity are complexly and often incongruously interwoven—and in part because like all lawyers we are formalists who believe deep down that the words in statutes and the Constitution mean what they say, and a striptease is not a speech. But the element of the ridiculous is not all on one side. Censorship of erotica is pretty ridiculous too. What kind of people make a career of checking to see whether the covering of a woman's nipples is fully opaque, as the statute requires? . . . Most of us do not admire the Islamic clergy for their meticulous insistency on modesty in female dress. Many of us do not admire busybodies who want to bring the force of law down on the heads of adults whose harmless private pleasures the busybodies find revolting. The history of censorship is a history of folly and cruelty.

Posner apparently found the state's brief to be a pathetic attempt to justify application of the law to nude dancing, and the response of the state's lawyer at oral argument to questions from the bench little better; Posner characterized part of the argument as "far-fetched." He noted the failure of the state to present the kind of evidence that might sustain the regulation as necessary to combat prostitution or violence against women, points raised too late in the case to be argued validly for the first time on appeal, or its failure to frame a statute soundly based on its Twenty-first Amendment authority.

Posner suggested that a local ordinance might even have withstood review better than a statewide statute, questioning whether the state could justify banning all nude dancing while conceding that a particular municipality might have a sound justification to do so as a "place,

time or manner" regulation so long as its citizens could obtain such entertainment outside the city limits. Posner found particularly telling the Indiana Supreme Court's own ambiguous attempt to limit the statute from being applied to "art" of the theatrical variety. If Indiana had an important purpose in preventing nude performances, why allow a theater to present a virtual striptease, as the Lyric Opera of Chicago had done in a recent performance of Richard Strauss's opera *Salome*, while banning nude dancing in a theater aimed at "adult" entertainment. Where was the credible intellectual distinction based in constitutional doctrine? So long as the Indiana Supreme Court had purported to carve out an exception of the public nudity statute for "expressive" nudity, it was inappropriate for the district judge to have interpreted this narrowly to exclude nude dancing from its compass when nude dancing was obviously expressive.

Posner ended a concluding diatribe with the comment that if the state was really serious about banning nude dancing, rather than leaving the matter to its municipalities, which could pass appropriate ordinances, then it should resort to its Twenty-first Amendment powers to avoid this sort of constitutional mess.

The dissenters were fully as sarcastic and heated as Posner. Coffey, for example, saw the law as a legitimate regulation of the "manner" of expressive conduct, consistent with the Supreme Court's First Amendment cases. He placed particular weight on the Court's 1986 decision in *Bowers v. Hardwick*, the Georgia sodomy law case, in which the Court had premised the validity of the statute regulating a so-called victimless crime committed in private on grounds of morality. Decrying a climate of "moral permissiveness" that the founders who drafted the First Amendment "certainly never contemplated," Coffey argued that the state was fully within its constitutional authority to legislate a ban on public nudity, and it was not the proper role of a federal court to interpose itself in that process. People who sought sexual permissiveness "are free to live in areas that cater to this moral climate," he said. "But many states, such as the State of Indiana, obviously wish a more wholesome lifestyle" and had a right to reflect their own "community standards" in legislation such as the public indecency law.

Coffey was particularly offended by Posner's characterization of those supporting the law as "busybodies." "Judge Posner's statement merely reflects differences in moral values among the population," Coffey insisted. "Conduct that a more vocal minority considers to be the work of 'busybodies' reflects the implementation of the less vocal majority's deeply held concerns and should be respected." In fact, Coffey did not mind being called a "busybody" as he wrote "to uphold the moral ethics, ideals and principles of the majority of the people of the State of Indiana speaking through their legislative representatives."

Advancing past the argument that the law was intended solely to uphold morality in the abstract, Coffey insisted that it was also intended to protect women from exploitation and possible violence that might result from the "lustful male sexual passions and appetites" that might be stimulated by viewing nude dancing exhibitions. He also asserted that the sexual exploitation of nude dancing could have a psychologically harmful effect on the dancers, drawing an analogy from the Supreme Court's decision in *Osborne v. Ohio* (1990), which upheld a law penalizing private possession of "kiddie-porn" on grounds of the harm to young children used to produce those materials. "I see no reason why the will of the people, expressed in the legislative branch, should not be permitted to prohibit this activity and overcome an alleged First Amendment right that is based on a foundation of quicksand." As if to crown his argument, Coffey then asserted the "close association" of nude dancing with prostitution, noting recent Seventh Circuit cases in which that link had been established. This was accompanied by a lengthy quotation from Attorney General Edwin Meese's Commission on Pornography's Final Report of 1986, which had controversially asserted a direct link between erotic expression and violence.

Coffey asserted that it was by no means too late for Indiana to have raised some of these issues for the first time at oral argument before the court of appeals, contrary to Posner's suggestion, because all of these particular arguments were just more aspects of the general argument regarding protecting public morality that the state had been articulating all through the litigation. For Coffey, the state's interest in public morality provided ample justification for regulating conduct that barely qualified for any First Amendment protection at all, and he devoted the balance of his opinion to showing that there was little if any basis for finding any First Amendment expression to protect. Coffey invoked the Supreme Court's recent opinion in *Employment Division v. Smith* (1990), where the Court upheld the application of a law criminalizing use of peyote by Native Americans who used the drug for religious purposes. Coffey argued that the case provided a suitable analogy to the nudity statute, which he asserted served public purposes unrelated to the suppression of speech. Just as the Native Americans did not have an exemption from such a law because of its incidental burden on free exercise of religion, those who sought to dance nude did not have a special exemption from the legitimate ban on public nudity.

Finally, Coffey noted that full nudity was not really necessary to the dancers' performances; dancers wearing the minimal coverings required by the statute "have long conveyed the alleged message of 'eroticism and sensuality,' that the majority has divined in the plaintiffs' conduct," he asserted. Thus, there were "alternative channels" for communicating their message, which was all the Supreme Court had required in cases involving time, place, and manner regulation. In this case, the "relevant substantive evil" was "the damage to public morality resulting from the violation of Indiana's well-drafted statute barring public nudity," not the expressive content, if any, of the plaintiffs' performances. As such, there was no real content-based regulation, and expression was "hardly impeded."

Easterbrook wrote an even more elaborate dissenting opinion, joined in whole or in part by each of the other three dissenting judges. He concentrated his firepower on what he saw as a basic mischaracterization of the statute and the issues it presented. "Indiana does not regulate dancing," he insisted, "it regulates public nudity." For him, the case was decided by the Supreme Court's famous draft-card burning case, *United States v. O'Brien* (1968), in which the Court had adopted a test for determining whether a regulation of conduct that had an incidental effect on protected speech was nonetheless constitutionally valid.

> Conduct that plays a role in expression is not exempt from neutral regulation. Persons sought to sleep in the park [in *Clark v. Community for Creative Non-Violence* (1984)] to convey a message about homelessness. Nonetheless, the Court held, the Park Service may apply its regulation forbidding camping. Regulation of conduct is acceptable if it furthers an important interest that is "unrelated to the suppression of free expression." *United States v. O'Brien* ... Burning a draft card in *O'Brien*, sleeping in [*Community for Creative Non-Violence*], entering a military reservation ..., boycotting criminal defense work. . . , all were done to send a political message; although politics are the heart of the First Amendment, all of these messages were held subject to viewpoint-neutral regulation of the conduct.

The lengthy recitations of the history of dance as expressive conduct were beside the point, argued Easterbrook. Even conceding that the nude dancing in this case had some level of First Amendment protection—a point he would dispute later in this opinion—that did not render the law unconstitutional because this regulation was not motivated by or focused on that expressive aspect of the dancing. The state allowed erotic dancing without full nudity; it was clearly the nudity, not the erotic nature of the dance, that was the evil the state sought to combat. "If Indiana forbade nudity *only* when employed in dance, then it would have a tough row to hoe," said Easterbrook. "A dance-only law would be a regulation *of expression* if, as my colleagues believe, dance is speech. Regulation of expression faces high hurdles." He disputed Posner's assertion that a local ordinance aimed directly at nude dancing would be easier to sustain; it was precisely the lack of a focus on dancing that made the Indiana law so defensible in his view. However, "Indiana didn't try to clamp down on dancing because of what it expresses," he asserted. Nudity was the state's only concern. He agreed with Coffey that the rationale of *Employment Division v. Smith* was very telling in this case; the state could legislate against "socially harmful conduct" without reference to whether that conduct might, in some circumstances, carry constitutional protection because

of its context, whether it be expressive conduct or religious conduct. "Neutrality" was a "sufficient" condition to save such a law from invalidation.

Furthermore, Easterbrook strongly contested the conclusion that nude dancing of the type described in this case could be characterized as "speech" for First Amendment purposes. He found that the majority's approach would, in effect, find that "all purposive conduct is speech," a conclusion he was not willing to embrace. He suggested that "James Madison would have guffawed had anyone suggested public nudity as an example of 'freedom of speech,'—or of anything that could be derived from the Framers' conception by a series of plausible interpretations. Parading in a state of undress is conduct, not speech." To drive home his point, Easterbrook quoted a dissenting opinion by Justice William O. Douglas, in which Justice Hugo L. Black had concurred, in which these First Amendment "absolutists" had stated that "no one would suggest that the First Amendment permits nudity in public places." "What these absolutists gave as a *reductio ad absurdum*," he said, "the court today holds the First Amendment commands."

Easterbrook contended that his colleagues had taken "a wrong turn" by devoting so much attention to discussing music and literature; what was at issue in this case was conduct, plain and simple, and no amount of rationalization would make it otherwise. To compare the dancing in this case to real artistic expression was absurd. "Barroom displays are to ballet as white noise is to music," he asserted. Real art involved the application of a creative intelligence that he did not see in the jerks and grinds of a striptease. "Sex may be entertaining and is at least as expressive as nude go-go dancing," but the Court had allowed the states to forbid sexual activity in public places, even though such activity was "expressive" in some sense. Easterbrook challenged Posner's bullfighting hypothetical, saying that under Posner's approach, bullfighting had to be characterized as expressive conduct protected by the First Amendment, and that a minor concern about cruelty to animals would not withstand the kind of strict scrutiny that would have to be applied to it. Clearly, bullfighting could be regulated because it was conduct, and it was the conduct, not the expressive elements, that was being regulated. Finally, Easterbrook devoted some attention to the *Schad* case, claiming that it had been misconstrued and misapplied by the majority.

Easterbrook then resorted to a more process-oriented objection to the majority opinion. Since "people act for reasons," under the majority's approach all conduct could be called expressive, and all of a sudden the courts would have to subject virtually all regulation of conduct to First Amendment scrutiny, evaluating the intentions of the legislators and the relative "importance" of the state interests they were trying to promote. This was akin to the "substantive due process" approach that had long been discredited in constitutional jurisprudence as an inappropriate substitution of the court's judgment about the wisdom of laws for the legislature's judgment. Judges should not be taking on this role themselves.

"If nude dancing is 'speech' it is so by the barest margin," Easterbrook asserted; "someone standing at the center of the First Amendment (political speech) would need binoculars to see this far into the periphery." It was important to democratic self-governance that courts not interfere with legislative judgments when they were dealing with conduct that had such peripheral First Amendment ties. Unduly expanding the limits of protected "speech" would transfer "the locus of power" to judges from legislators, who were entitled to express the community's views on these matters.

Invoking the Supreme Court's *Hardwick* opinion, Easterbrook noted that "much law is based on nothing other than moral views. Sometimes morality combines with instrumental concerns." Perhaps the Supreme Court's decision was a "rationalization of a law that has no effects beyond depriving *hoi polloi* of a harmless pastime."

> Maybe not. Ours is not the decision. States may offer different social climates from which the people may select. Indiana has one, Illinois another. Society is the richer when choices increase. . . . We may doubt the wisdom of requiring women to wear more clothing in the bars of South Bend than in the *Folies Bergère* or on the beaches of Rio de Janeiro without

concluding that Indiana has exceeded its powers under the Constitution.

Finally, there was a dissenting opinion by Circuit Judge Daniel Manion, in which Coffey and Easterbrook both joined. Manion emphasized District Judge Sharp's finding that there was no "expressive activity" involved in the nude dancing and argued that even if some expressive element was found, the statute was valid because "the state interest in preventing public nudity—an interest unrelated to the suppression of speech—outweighs whatever expressive elements are contained in a striptease." Like Easterbrook, Manion argued that the majority's emphasis on the expressive qualities of dance was really beside the point, since the challenged statute was not concerned with dance as such, but rather with public nudity; there was only an incidental effect on arguably protected expressive activity. Manion noted that even Asher had not argued that any particular expression was being promoted by the nude dancing. Manion reiterated the separation of powers and federalism arguments found in Coffey's and Easterbrook's dissents and emphasized what to him seemed the impropriety of taking out of the hands of elected legislators the decisions about the tone they wanted to set for their community. "This court's decision stands for the proposition that we know better than the people of Indiana," he asserted. While Posner had characterized those who championed "censorship" as busybodies, at least those busybodies could be thrown out at the next election if the people disagreed with what they had done, unlike life-tenured federal judges.

Manion then recited chapter and verse from the Supreme Court's opinions to illustrate that conduct and even speech had been held superseded by public interests in a variety of cases; characterizing the dancing to have an expressive component was just the beginning of the analysis. He asserted that Indiana was entitled to rely on the evidence generated in other jurisdictions and by various studies to conclude that allowing public nudity, including nude dancing, could have deleterious effects on the public, including prostitution, violence against women, and the like. The Supreme Court had acknowledged as much in its decisions upholding zoning restrictions on the location of theaters where pornographic films or erotic performances were to take place. Although the record was not entirely clear about it, it was likely that these cases really involved an attempt by South Bend police officials to deal with the crime problems generated by a red light district, and the local officials were in a better position than the circuit court of appeals to know whether there was a problem and how to deal with it.

Manion concluded that since the district court found and counsel for the plaintiffs had conceded that the nude dancing involved in this case "does not express anything," there was no basis for finding that it was protected by the First Amendment. And even if nude dancing was to be considered "inherently expressive," as the majority held, it could be regulated through a content-neutral statute such as Indiana's consistently with the Supreme Court's existing precedents.

The Supreme Court was eager to get its hands on this case, granting certiorari on the first day of its October 1990 Term and setting oral argument for January. The case had become something of a *cause célèbre* by this point in its history. Indiana Deputy Attorney General Wayne E. Uhl argued for the state, and prominent civil liberties attorney Bruce J. Ennis, Jr., argued the case for the dancers and their employers.

Although the case was argued relatively early in the Term, it consumed the Court's attention until almost the end of the Term, with the 5–4 decision announced on June 21, 1991. It was indicative of the divisiveness of the issue that no one opinion represented the views of the entire five-member majority. Chief Justice William H. Rehnquist's opinion reversing the Seventh Circuit was joined by Justices Sandra Day O'Connor and Anthony M. Kennedy. The necessary votes to make a majority for reversal of the court of appeals came from Justices Antonin Scalia and David Souter, each of whom stated entirely separate grounds for their conclusions. The dissenters united behind a single opinion by Justice Byron White.

Rehnquist's brief opinion placed the greatest weight on *United States v. O'Brien*. Noting that the Court's prior decisions had intimated that nude dancing had some constitutional pro-

tection, he grudgingly conceded that it is "expressive conduct within the outer perimeters of the First Amendment, though we view it as only marginally so." But, of course, this did not end the inquiry, for the Court had frequently upheld regulation of speech or other expressive materials or conduct subject to First Amendment protection when the reason for the regulation could be distinguished from the content of the expression. This was a "time, place or manner" case, he concluded, and Indiana had legitimately sought to regulate public nudity in a way that only incidentally, and constitutionally, burdened whatever protected expression there was.

Rather mechanically applying the *O'Brien* tests, Rehnquist found first that it was "clearly within the constitutional power of a State" to pass a public indecency statute, and served a "substantial" government interest. Although there was no legislative history on which to rely for an indication of legislative intent, the law on its face was meant to deal with "societal order and morality," and similar statutes existed in virtually all the other states. "Public indecency, including nudity, was a criminal offense at common law, and this court recognized the common-law roots of the offense of 'gross and open indecency' [in 1948 in *Winters v. New York*]." English sources showed that public nudity was considered an act "*malum in se*," that is, one that is intrinsically wrong, not just wrong because the subject of negative legislation. The law in Indiana had a long history dating to 1831, when the whole idea of nude dancing was not even imagined by lawmakers. The concern of legislatures in passing these laws was with public morals and order; they had no particular content-based intention to ban particular expressive messages. The concern with order and morality was "unrelated to the suppression of free expression," as required by *O'Brien*.

While "people who go about in the nude in public may be expressing something about themselves by so doing," Rehnquist conceded, the Court in *O'Brien* had rejected the contention that an expansive notion of "expressive conduct" could trump a content-neutral statute. Rehnquist disputed the argument that the state of Indiana was seeking through this law to prevent the erotic message intended by the nude dancing. "Presumably numerous other erotic performances are presented at these establishments and similar clubs without any interference from the state, so long as the performers wear a scant amount of clothing." Furthermore, Rehnquist did not believe that the minimal clothing requirement of the statute would deprive the dancing of "whatever erotic message it conveys; it simply makes the message slightly less graphic." The evil with which Indiana was concerned in this statute was not eroticism, it was nudity. The two could be distinguished, and the mere fact that the nudity was combined with an expressive dance activity did not change this basic intention of the state or render the law unconstitutional.

Analogizing to the *O'Brien* case, it was clear that burning a draft card to protest the Vietnam War was an expressive act, but the Court upheld criminal punishment for that act because of the noncommunicative element in it: the destruction of a public document. So here, "it was not the dancing that was prohibited, but simply its being done in the nude," said Rehnquist. "The statutory prohibition is not a means to some greater end, but an end in itself." The fourth *O'Brien* test required that where there is some regulation of speech, it be no greater than essential to the furtherance of the government's interest. Rehnquist asserted that this test also had been met. The public indecency statute was indeed "narrowly tailored," since it required a bare minimum of coverage by pasties and a G-string, a state of undress that was "the bare minimum necessary to achieve the state's purposes." Accordingly, the court of appeals' decision was reversed.

Justice Scalia joined in the result, but eschewed the First Amendment analysis. For him, this was not a First Amendment case because he saw the Indiana law as purely a regulation of conduct. "On its face," he insisted, "this law is not directed at expression in particular." The dancer's intention to convey a "message of eroticism" was not an element of the statutory offense, and even the "most explicit" such message would not incur a penalty, so long as the dancer did not perform any of the prohibited actions. Furthermore, the enforcement history of the statute showed that it was targeted on nudity, not "expressive" conduct, since there

was a substantial load of reported cases which mainly involved nonexpressive conduct. He disputed the dissent's argument that because nude dancing performed within an enclosed room for paying adult customers could hardly give "offense" to unsuspecting members of the general public, the only remaining—and illegitimate—purpose of the law as applied to nude barroom dancing related to its expressive content. "Perhaps the dissenters believe that 'offense to others' *ought* to be the only reason for restricting nudity in public places generally," he commented, "but there is no basis for thinking that our society has ever shared that Thoreauvian 'you-may-do-what-you-like-so-long-as-it-does-not-injure-someone-else beau ideal—much less for thinking that it was written into the Constitution." To illustrate his point, Scalia argued that the law's purpose would be violated if "60,000 fully consenting adults crowded into the Hoosierdome to display their genitals to one another, even if there were not an offended innocent in the crowd." This was because society could pass laws against conduct that did no harm to any one person in particular, because such conduct was considered immoral by society. He noted laws against sadomasochism, cockfighting, bestiality, suicide, drug use, prostitution, and sodomy as examples. Citing *Bowers v. Hardwick*, he asserted that while there was a diversity of views as to whether any or all of those activities should be penalized, it was well established that the state had the power to do so. The purpose of the Indiana statute, said Scalia, was not to protect people from being offended; rather, it was "to enforce the traditional moral belief that people should not expose their private parts indiscriminately, regardless of whether those who see them are disedified." Thus, the dissent had no basis for arguing that "the purpose must be repression of communication."

After noting that the Court had recognized in other contexts the validity of general content-neutral regulations that might incidentally burden speech, Scalia pointed out that "virtually *every* law restricts conduct, and virtually *any* prohibited conduct can be performed for an expressive purpose—if only expressive of the fact that the actor disagrees with the prohibition." Carrying the dissent's arguments to their logical conclusion, virtually every general law might be subject to First Amendment scrutiny, a result neither compelled by the Court's First Amendment precedents nor justified in this case. When government tried to prohibit conduct because of its expressive content, there was a sound basis for applying First Amendment standards, but this was not so when government's interest in the conduct had nothing to do with expressive content. Only if suppression of protected First Amendment activity was a *purpose* of a law were First Amendment concerns properly raised, insisted Scalia, referring to his opinion in *Employment Division v. Smith*. In that case, he had found no free exercise problem with a general penal law ban on use of peyote that had been contested by Native Americans who sought to use the drug in religious ceremonies. Here, he asserted that there was "even greater reason to apply this approach to the regulation of expressive conduct," since this sort of problem was likely to arise more frequently in the area of speech than religious practice.

Scalia found himself unable to join in the plurality opinion's rationale for the case because he disagreed with the premise of *O'Brien* that a general, content-neutral law had to be tested by some lowered First Amendment standard when it incidentally burdened free expression. "I think we should avoid wherever possible . . . a method of analysis that requires judicial assessment of the 'importance' of government interests—and especially of government interests in various aspects of morality," he said. As in *Bowers v. Hardwick*, where the Court held that a state's concern with morality was sufficient to sustain a felony sodomy statute, concern with morality should be enough to sustain Indiana's public indecency statute, with no need to weigh the "importance" of that interest against First Amendment concerns, since a content-neutral law raised no such concerns. Since the state was regulating conduct, not expression, "those who choose to employ conduct as a means of expression must make sure that the conduct they select is not generally forbidden."

Justice Souter, while agreeing with the plurality that the Indiana law was constitutional as applied to nude barroom dancing, also placed his agreement on a different rationale from

Rehnquist's. He agreed that nude dancing "is inherently expressive," but asserted that "nudity per se is not." It was, in his view, a "condition, not an activity, and the voluntary assumption of that condition, without more, apparently expresses nothing beyond the view that the condition is somehow appropriate to the circumstances." In nude dancing, however, the combination of nudity with the expressive activity of dancing produced something more by enhancing the force of the expression. Thus, forbidding nudity in this context did raise First Amendment issues.

Souter also agreed with Rehnquist that the *O'Brien* case was the appropriate precedent to apply, but he would take a slightly different route to sustain the statute's application by emphasizing not the purpose of protecting morality in general but rather a purpose to avoid the specific ills that had been shown to accompany nude dancing, which he referred to as "the secondary effects of adult entertainment establishments of the sort typified by respondents' establishments." Such effects included prostitution, sexual assaults, and other criminal activity, all of which had been shown to follow upon the operation of establishments presenting nude erotic dancing. While it was true that neither the Indiana legislature nor its courts had specifically identified preventing such effects as the purpose of the law, he felt it was appropriate to acknowledge these justifications that the state was now urging on appeal. While these concerns might not be sufficient to sustain all applications of the statute, they would surely sustain its application to the plaintiffs' activities.

When this justification was considered, the *O'Brien* analysis fell neatly into place. It was clear that the "prevention of such evils" was within the power of the state, and that the statute would substantially further this important governmental interest, which involved protecting third parties from harm. Indeed, the Court had upheld restrictive zoning ordinances based on evidence of such secondary effects and the important state interest in preventing them. As to the third prong of *O'Brien*, that the governmental interest be "unrelated to the suppression of free expression," he felt, contrary to the dissent, that this test was also satisfied. While some might argue that it was the expressive power of nude dancing that led to the "second-ary effects," and thus the law was concerned with the content of expression, Souter was not willing to make this connection; for him, all that had been shown was that "the effects are correlated with the existence of establishments offering such dancing," which did not consti-tute proof of a causal relationship based on the content of expression rather than the fact of nudity. For him, the "concentration of crowds of men predisposed to such activities" attracted by the offer of nude dancing may in itself be the source of the secondary effects, and the attrac-tion could well be the nudity rather than the dancing as such. "In neither case would the chain of causation run through the persuasive effect of the expressive component of nude dancing," he asserted. Finally, Souter found that the re-striction on the expressive activity was slight. "Pasties and a G-string moderate the expres-sion to some degree, to be sure, but only to a degree. Dropping the final stitch is prohibited, but the limitation is minor when measured against the dancer's remaining capacity and opportunity to express the erotic message." He noted that one of the plaintiffs was featured in a sexually explicit film being shown at a theater in South Bend; clearly her ability to express her erotic message had not been totally stifled by prohibiting her from dancing totally nude.

Justice White's dissenting opinion, joined by Justices Thurgood Marshall, Harry A. Blackmun, and John Paul Stevens, rested on an analysis of statutory purpose by process of elimi-nation. Having found first that nude dancing possessed expressive content that entitled it to some First Amendment protection (a point on which eight of the nine justices agreed to some extent), and that *O'Brien* was the appropriate precedent, White argued that the majority of the Court had gone wrong in its consideration of the third prong of the *O'Brien* test: whether the law related to a regulation of speech. Ac-cording to White, all the cases relied on by Rehnquist and Scalia had in common that the laws sustained involved "truly *general* proscrip-tion on individual conduct." In *Hardwick*, for example, sodomy was prohibited wherever and by whomever performed, and in *Smith* peyote consumption was similarly proscribed across the board. "By contrast, in this case Indiana does

not suggest that its statute applies to, or could be applied to, nudity wherever it occurs, in-cluding the home," and indeed, if Indiana tried to apply it in the home, it would run into con-stitutional trouble under *Stanley v. Georgia* (1969), in which the Court had held that states could not punish the mere possession of ob-scene material in the privacy of the home.

Further cutting against viewing the law as one of general application was the narrowing construction suggested by the Indiana Supreme Court, under which the law would not be used against nudity "as a part of some larger form of expression meriting protection when the com-munication of ideas is involved." The state was taking the position, for example, that the law would not be used to shut down a production of *Salome* that involved a real striptease, or a production of the rock musical *Hair*, or indeed any legitimate play or ballet performance. Since all these "exceptions" were being carved out, the law could hardly be called a general prohi-bition of all nudity to promote social order and morality, and an inaccurate description of it as a general prohibition could not justify applying it to "a significant amount of protected expres-sive activity," including nude dancing. Clearly, the purpose of the statute could not be deter-mined from its face, but had to take into ac-count its judicial interpretation and actual ap-plication by the police.

For White, when the statute was evaluated in light of its actual application, it appeared that the main purpose of forbidding public nu-dity was to protect people who did not want to view others in the nude from being offended. But that could not be the purpose of forbidding nude dancing, since it was taking place under circumstances where nobody who viewed it could be offended, since they had paid admis-sion specifically to see it. Thus, the purpose of forbidding nude dancing in this context must be "to protect the viewers from what the State believes is the harmful message that nude danc-ing communicates." The perceived harm was the very communicative aspect of the perfor-mance. White characterized as "transparently erroneous" the Court's assertion that it could separate out the nudity from the communica-tion in its analysis. The element of nudity was an important part of the message, since it intensified the emotional or erotic impact of the performance, and thus was an "expressive component of the dance, not merely incidental 'conduct.'" Consequently, the statutory purpose could not be characterized as "unrelated to expressive conduct." Since this was so, the law had to be subjected to the stringent requirement in the fourth prong of *O'Brien*, that it be upheld "only if narrowly drawn to accomplish a compelling governmental interest."

While conceding that some of the interests identified by the Court and Justice Souter might be seen as "important and substantial," White nonetheless contended that the statute was not "narrowly drawn." "If the State is genuinely concerned with prostitution and associated evils," he argued, "it can adopt restrictions that do not interfere with the expressiveness of nonobscene nude dancing performances." For example, the state could legislate on the distance required between performers and audience members, it could restrict hours of operation, and it could use zoning laws either to avoid the creation of red light districts or, conversely, to concentrate such activities in such districts, depending on the policy preferences of local legislators. Furthermore, it was clear that the state could bar prostitution outright, as well as obscene performances. But "banning an entire category of expressive activity" was not consistent with the narrow tailoring requirement of First Amendment doctrine.

White next turned to refuting Scalia's arguments in support of the statute's constitutionality. Regardless whether he agreed with Scalia's argument that only conduct was being regulated, he found the major premise that the Indiana law was a "general" law to be flawed, and it lay at the heart of Scalia's argument. Scalia's own hypothetical of the 60,000 nude Hoosiers was now turned against him by White, who contended, "No one can doubt, however, that those same 60,000 Hoosiers would be perfectly free to drive to their respective homes all across Indiana and, once there, to parade around, cavort, and revel in the nude for hours in front of relatives and friends. It is difficult to see why the State's interest in morality is any less in that situation, especially if, as Justice Scalia seems to suggest, nudity is inherently evil, but clearly the statute does not reach such

activity." Since the law clearly did not treat nudity as itself inherently evil, it seemed that it was being used against nude dancing because of its expressive effect. White also contested Scalia's reliance on the theory of *Smith*:

> The Indiana law, as applied to nude dancing, targets the expressive activity itself; in Indiana nudity in a dancing performance is a crime because of the message such dancing communicates. In Smith, the use of drugs was not criminal because the use was part of or occurred within the course of an otherwise protected religious ceremony, but because a general law made it so and was supported by the same interests in the religious context as in others.

The Court finally confronted the issue of a non-liquor-related ban on nude dancing in *Barnes v. Glen Theatre*, but the result could not be comforting to those concerned about the continued erosion of constitutional protection for nonobscene erotic expression in the United States. Although the majority of the Court could not agree on a single rationale for upholding the Indiana public indecency law's ban on public nudity, their combination of views was likely to sustain a wide variety of state prohibitions on erotic expression, and did not bode well for the survival of other forms of sexual expression. In particular, Justice Souter's use of the "secondary effects" argument might justify significant incursions on traditionally protected territory, and Justice Scalia's "general law" approach appeared to create an enormous loophole through which a state could drive wide-ranging prohibitions if the majority of its citizens (as represented in the legislature) were so minded.

By embracing this restrictive view of First Amendment protection in the context of sexual expression, the Court was reinforcing America's puritanical tradition, a tradition that many believe places this country at odds with itself, for another venerable American tradition, recognized by the Court in other contexts, is the guarantee of individual liberty.

Case References

Bowers v. Hardwick, 478 U.S. 186 (1986)

City of Dallas v. Stanglin, 490 U.S. 19 (1989)

Employment Division v. Smith, 110 S. Ct. 1595 (1990)

Erhardt v. State, 468 N.E.2d 224 (Ind. 1984)

Osborne v. Ohio, 495 U.S. 103 (1990)

Schad v. Mount Ephraim, 452 U.S. 61 (1981)

Stanley v. Georgia, 394 U.S. 557 (1969)

State v. Baysinger, 272 Ind. 236, 397 N.E.2d 580 (1979), appeals dismissed sub nom. *Clark v. Indiana*, 446 U.S. 931 (1980) and *Dove v. Indiana*, 449 U.S. 806 (1980)

United States v. O'Brien, 391 U.S. 367 (1968)

Winters v. New York, 333 U.S. 507 (1948)

CHAPTER 4
THE FAMILY

The "approved" form for sexual expression in American society, at least if one judges based on laws and public opinion polls, is within the context of the heterosexual marital relationship. Same-sex couples are excluded from marriage, laws in many jurisdictions criminalize all nonmarital sexual activity, and civil laws may impose a variety of disabilities on those who wish to carry on their reproductive and parenting activities outside the context of traditional, heterosexual marriage. This chapter is about the relationship of law with fundamental issues about families: how they are constituted, how they are recognized (or not recognized) by the state, and particularly how the state defines the rights of parents and children in the context of parental sexual diversity.

In 1967, the U.S. Supreme Court recognized in *Loving v. Virginia* that the choice of a marital partner has fundamental significance for the individual, but the cases discussed in this chapter indicate that lesbian and gay litigants have not been successful in translating this holding into a same-sex marriage option. On the other hand, some more recent cases show the new willingness of courts to recognize that nonmarital partners may be entitled to recognition as families, and municipal legislators (as well as some private employers) have begun to accommodate family diversity by recognizing domestic partners as, in some sense, spousal equivalents.

The Supreme Court ruled in 1971, in *Stanley v. Illinois*, the case of an unwed father, that the biological progenitor of a child has certain fundamental rights as a parent to maintain custody or contact with the child, which may be overcome only by an individualized demonstration of unfitness. Parents who do not fit the "traditional" mold, whether due to homosexual orientation, transvestism, transsexualism, or active extra-marital sexuality, have not always succeeded in convincing courts that sexual diversity should not be a disqualification for parenting, as cases discussed

herein illustrate, although there appears to be a trend of greater acceptance of the claims of lesbian and gay parents. In addition, several cases in this chapter explore issues of adoption, foster care, and guardianship where the sexuality of the parties has played a significant role.

This chapter discusses leading cases involving family issues raised by sexual diversity. Related cases discussed in other chapters include *Jhordan C. v. Mary K.* (No. 9), *Adams v. Howerton* (No. 115), *In re Kaufmann's Will* (No. 117), *In re Bacot* (No. 118), and *Estate of Cooper* (No. 119).

The Family: Readings

Ali, S.-P., "Homosexual Parenting: Child Custody and Adoption," 22 *University of California at Davis Law Review* 1009 (Spring 1989)

Berger, V., "Domestic Partnership Initiatives," 40 *DePaul Law Review* 417 (Winter 1991)

Bozett, F.W. (ed.), *Gay and Lesbian Parents* (1987)

Brantner, P.A., "When Mommy or Daddy is Gay: Developing Constitutional Standards for Custody Decisions," 3 *Hastings Women's Law Journal* 97 (1992)

Delaney, E.A., "Statutory Protection of the Other Mother: Legally Recognizing the Relationship Between the Nonbiological Lesbian Parent and Her Child," 43 *Hastings Law Journal* 177 (November 1991)

Eblin, R.L., "Domestic Partnership Recognition in the Workplace: Equitable Employee Benefits for Gay Couples (and Others)," 51 *Ohio State Law Journal* 1067 (October 1990)

Editorial Staff, "Custody Denials to Parents in Same-Sex Relationships: An Equal Protection Analysis," 102 *Harvard Law Review* 617 (January 1989)

Editorial Staff, "Joint Adoption: A Queer Option?" 15 *Vermont Law Review* 197 (Summer 1990)

Engleman, M.R., "*Bowers v. Hardwick*: The Right of Privacy — Only Within the Traditional Family?" 26 *Journal of Family Law* 373 (Winter 1987)

Gray, D., "Marriage: Homosexual Couples Need Not Apply," 23 *New England Law Review* 515 (Autumn 1988)

Hammer, S., "The Role of Sexual Preference in Custody Disputes," 1986 *Annual Survey of American Law* 685 (November 1987)

Katz, K.D., "Majoritarian Morality and Parental Rights," 52 *Albany Law Review* 405 (Winter 1988)

Lewis, C.A., "From This Day Forward: A Feminine Moral Discourse on Homosexual Marriage," 97 *Yale Law Journal* 1783 (July 1988)

Link, D., "The Tie That Binds: Recognizing Privacy and the Family Commitments of Same-Sex Couples," 23 *Loyola of Los Angeles Law Review* 1055 (April 1990)

Loomis, J.S., "Opening the Doors of Ohio Adoption Law," 17 *Ohio Northern University Law Review* 361 (Spring 1990)

Melton, R.L., "Legal Rights of Unmarried Heterosexual and Homosexual Couples and Evolving Definitions of Family," 29 *Journal of Family Law* 497 (February 1991)

Polikoff, N.D., "This Child Does Have Two Mothers: Redefining Parenthood to Meet the Needs of Children in Lesbian-Mother and Other Nontraditional Families," 78 *Georgetown Law Journal* 459 (February 1990)

Shapiro, E.D. & Schultz, S., "Single-Sex Families: The Impact of Birth Innovations Upon Traditional Family Notions," 24 *Journal of Family Law* 271 (1985–86)

Stein, R., "The Gay Divorcee: Unconventional Relationships Require Unconventional Contracts," 9 *California Lawyer* 22(2) (April 1989)

Stone, D.H., "The Moral Dilemma: Child Custody When One Parent is Homosexual or Lesbian—An Empirical Study," 23 *Suffolk University Law Review* 711 (Fall 1989)

Strasser, M., "Family, Definitions, and the Constitution: On the Antimiscegenation Analogy," 25 *Suffolk University Law Review* 981 (Winter 1991)

Walker, L.D., "Problem Parents and Child Custody," 4 *American Journal of Family Law* 155 (Summer 1990)

Watson, C.K., "Transsexual Marriages: Are They Valid Under California Law?" 16 *Southwestern University Law Review* 505 (Spring 1986)

Wishard, D.R., "Out of the Closet and Into the Courts: Homosexual Fathers and Child Custody," 93 *Dickinson Law Review* 401 (Winter 1989)

48. THE RIGHT OF MARITAL CHOICE

Loving v. Virginia, 388 U.S. 1 (1967), reversing 206 Va. 924, 147 S.E.2d 78 (1966).

The Civil Rights revolution ignited by the U.S. Supreme Court's 1954 decision in *Brown v. Board of Education of Topeka* met significant resistance in the states of the old Confederacy. The High Court had declared racial segregation in public schools unconstitutional under the Equal Protection Clause of the Fourteenth Amendment, but some state governments persisted in enforcing the so-called Jim Crow laws that had been adopted after Reconstruction to preserve separation of the races, including laws requiring segregation in hotels, theaters, restaurants, and other public places.

Perhaps the strongest resistance to abandonment of such laws came in the area of sexual relations and marriage. Southern legislators frequently based their opposition to public school integration on fears of racial mixing leading to intermarriage and "mongrelization." When the Court heard *Brown v. Board of Education* in 1953 and 1954, a majority of the states had statutes outlawing interracial marriages. Many states outside the South repealed those laws over the next fifteen years, responding to the clear message of *Brown* that the days of Jim Crow were over, but "miscegenation" laws, as they were called, remained in effect in all the southern states.

Some of these laws dated from the pre-Civil War days of legal slavery, although many were revised and reenacted earlier in the 20th century. "An Act to Preserve Racial Integrity" was passed in Virginia in 1924. The Act made it a felony (a crime punishable by at least a year in prison) for "any white person" to "marry any save a white person." For purposes of the law, white persons were persons who had "no trace whatever of any blood other than Caucasian." Non-white persons were "every person in whom there is ascertainable any Negro blood." The law declared void any marriage between a white person and a non-white person, and also made it a crime for Virginians to leave the state to contract an interracial marriage with the intention of returning as a married couple.

The law was also concerned with the marital activities of American Indians. A person with one great-great-grandparent of American Indian descent was allowed to marry a white person (in fond memory of the cohabitation of John Rolfe and the Indian princess, Pocahontas, revered figures in Virginia's early history), but otherwise Indians were also denied the right to intermarry with whites. The law was not concerned with intermarriage between colored persons and Indians, or with intermarriage between persons both of whom had racially mixed ancestry.

Richard Loving, a white man, and Mildred Jeter, a black woman, both Virginia residents, fell in love and determined to marry. Because they could not contract a legal marriage in Virginia, they went to the District of Columbia in June 1958 to tie the knot. They returned to Caroline County, Virginia, to set up their marital home. Local consternation ensued, and a grand jury indicted them for violating the miscegenation law. On January 6, 1959, they pleaded guilty and were each sentenced to one year in jail, but the judge announced he would suspend their sentences if they would leave the state and not return to Virginia together for twenty-five years. The judge explained his decision with the following statement: "Almighty God created the races white, black, yellow, malay and red, and He placed them on separate continents. And but for the interference with His arrangement there would be no cause for such marriages. The fact that He separated the races shows that He did not intend for the races to mix."

Following the judge's orders, the Lovings left for the District of Columbia, but their hearts yearned for the Old Dominion and they filed a motion with the Virginia courts in 1963, seeking to have their sentences set aside on constitutional grounds. They also filed a lawsuit in the federal district court asking for a declaration that the Virginia law was unconstitutional. State Circuit Judge Leon M. Bazile denied their state court motion, and they appealed to the Virginia Supreme Court, which issued its unanimous decision on March 7, 1966.

The Virginia court's opinion exemplifies the approach of many southern courts after *Brown v. Board of Education*. The court rejected the Lovings' challenge without undertaking any legal analysis. The Virginia Supreme Court had dealt with a challenge to the state's miscegenation law a decade earlier, in *Naim v. Naim* (1955), when the court concluded that the law was justified "to preserve the racial integrity" of Virginia citizens, and to prevent "the corruption of blood," "a mongrel breed of citizens," and "the obliteration of racial pride." The court also relied on old precedents holding that

regulation of marriage was inherently a state prerogative.

In rejecting *Brown v. Board of Education*'s precedential relevance to the miscegenation issue, the court relied on a literal reading of Chief Justice Earl Warren's opinion, which by its terms dealt only with school segregation. Justice Carrico asserted that no federal court, and only one state court, had indicated any doubt about the constitutionality of miscegenation laws after *Brown* was decided. However, the court considered the conditions placed on the suspended sentence too severe. According to the court, the reason for a suspended sentence is to achieve the "rehabilitation" of the offender, and this could be achieved quite simply by forbidding the Lovings from living together as husband and wife in the Commonwealth of Virginia.

Richard and Mildred Loving promptly appealed to the U.S. Supreme Court. They were joined in the appeal by the Japanese American Citizens League. The Court heard argument in their case on April 10, 1967, and promptly and unanimously reversed the state court's decision on June 12, in any opinion by Chief Justice Warren.

Before the Supreme Court, Virginia argued that there was no equal protection violation because both white and colored citizens were equally guilty of an interracial marriage and were subject to equal punishment. Indeed, Richard and Mildred Loving were both sentenced to the same one-year imprisonment and subjected to identical conditions for suspension of their sentences. In addition, the state argued that there might be an as-yet undiscovered scientific basis for finding that interracial marriage was harmful; pending such a discovery, it was better to be safe than sorry.

Warren rejected both prongs of Virginia's argument. First, it was clear from *Brown v. Board of Education* that "equal treatment" was not the issue when laws containing racial classifications were subjected to constitutional scrutiny. Any laws containing racial classifications would place a "very heavy burden of justification" on the state, and the state's only real justification was that articulated by its supreme court in *Naim v. Naim*, which Warren characterized as maintaining white supremacy. Although the law prohibited both whites and blacks from marrying each other with strict impartiality, Warren observed that the law placed no restrictions on marriages between blacks and those of Asian descent or other racial groups. Clearly, Virginia's concern was not for "racial purity" as such, but actually rather for the purity of the "white race."

The Court found an alternative basis for its holding in the Due Process Clause of the Fourteenth Amendment, which provides that the states may not deprive any person of life, liberty, or property without due process of law. The right to marry "has long been recognized as one of the vital personal rights essential to the orderly pursuit of happiness by free men." Since the right to marry was so basic and fundamental to human freedom, the state could not abridge that right without legitimate justification. Since the state's only justification for the law was one contrary to "the principle of equality at the heart of the Fourteenth Amendment," that justification could not serve to shelter the law from attack under the Due Process Clause. Although the Court did not state precisely the test by which it would evaluate state laws regulating marital choice, its description of that choice as a "fundamental freedom," viewed in the light of cases involving other identified fundamental freedoms, suggested that such laws would receive the same strict scrutiny that was applied to racial classifications under the Equal Protection Clause.

The Court's opinion was unanimous, but Justice Potter Stewart wrote a brief separate concurring opinion indicating his view that "it is simply not possible for a state law to be valid under our Constitution which makes the criminality of an act depend upon the race of the actor." This was significant, because Justice Stewart later dissented in cases extending the due process analysis of *Loving* to other sexual issues.

Most of Chief Justice Warren's opinion in *Loving* dealt with the equal protection argument, but his brief treatment (just two paragraphs) of the due process analysis was more significant in the long term. By the time the Court spoke in *Loving*, a series of cases going back two decades had established the basic principles of equal protection that made the outcome of any case involving racial classifications used to perpetuate white supremacy virtually a foregone conclusion in the Supreme Court. Racial classifications are inherently suspect under the Constitution. Only a compelling governmental justification will be accepted as a defense of such classifications, and even then the state law must be narrowly tailored to achieve the government's legitimate purpose. Under such a test, virtually all governmental classifications based on race must fall in the absence of a compelling remedial justification (such as taking race into account to redress past racial discrimination).

But Warren's analysis of the due process argument was something quite new. Although his opinion does not explicitly mention privacy or sex, the final two paragraphs of *Loving v. Virginia* became an important part of the foundation for later decisions of the Supreme Court concerning sexual freedom and sexual choice, frequently characterized collectively as the law of sexual privacy.

The characterization of the right to marry as fundamental placed marital choice and the marital relation within a newly emerging body of substantive law, which would eventually lead to wholesale invalidation of many state laws governing contraception, abortion, fornication (sexual relations outside of marriage), and sexual practices other than procreative vaginal intercourse, and it would raise serious constitutional doubts about other customary restrictions on the right to marry. Before *Loving*, the Court's concern with personal sexuality had been quite limited. After *Loving*, serious constitutional questions could be raised about any state law regulating sexual activities that might fall within the broad sphere of marriage and reproduction.

Case References:

Brown v. Board of Education of Topeka, 347 U.S. 483 (1954)

Naim v. Naim, 197 Va. 80, 87 S.E.2d 749 (1955)

49. JUDICIAL DISCRETION AND THE LESBIAN MOTHER

Nadler v. Superior Court, Sacramento County, 63 Cal. Rptr. 352 (App., 3d Dist. 1967).

One of the most important consequences for lesbian and gay people of the ferment over questions of human sexuality during the 1960s was a new willingness by courts to consider allowing homosexuals to retain custody of their children in divorce proceedings. For much of the 20th century, the weight of psychiatric opinion holding that homosexuality was a form of mental illness had led courts to hold, as a matter of law, that homosexuals were unfit to raise their own children. One of the first decisions to reject that view was *Nadler v. Superior Court,* a 1967 ruling by the California Court of Appeal in a contested custody action involving the 5-year-old daughter of a lesbian. The court's decision reveals little about the facts of the case, and says almost nothing about homosexuality and its relevance to a custody decision. Nonetheless, in historical context it is a legal landmark that deserves at least brief mention.

Ellen Doreene Nadler filed suit in the Superior Court in Sacramento County, seeking a divorce from Walter Robert Nadler and custody of the couple's daughter. During the divorce proceeding before Judge Joseph Babich, Walter's attorney, Ernest F. Winters, introduced evidence that Ellen was a lesbian who was engaged in sexual activity with other women. Persuaded of the truth of the evidence on Ellen's sexuality, Babich ruled on October 5, 1967, that "the homosexuality of the plaintiff as a matter of law constitutes her not a fit or proper person to have the care, custody and control of . . . the minor child of the parties hereto, therefore it will be for the best interest and welfare of said minor child to now place her in the custody of her father." During the court proceeding, he stated that he was not engaging in an exercise of discretion in this case, because he believed he was required as a matter of law to award custody to the father. Indeed, apart from the issue of Ellen's homosexuality, both parties had stipulated that Ellen and Walter were equally able and willing to provide physical care and support for the child. At the time, it was a criminal offense in California to engage in homosexual conduct, which may have decisively influenced Babich in his conclusion.

Ellen, represented by Clyde M. Blackmon of the Legal Aid Society of Sacramento County, petitioned the court of appeal for a writ of mandate to order Judge Babich to take additional evidence on the issue of the effect of Ellen's homosexual conduct on her daughter's well-being. Ellen argued that her fitness could not be determined as a matter of law solely because she was a lesbian, but rather that the court was required to explore the issue of the effect of her homosexuality and exercise its discretion in determining custody.

The court of appeal agreed with Ellen's argument. Justices Fred R. Pierce, Leonard M. Friedman, and Edwin J. Regan issued a *per curiam* opinion on October 30, 1967, rejecting Babich's approach to the case. California statutes and court rulings provided substantial support for the proposition that the trial judge was supposed to exercise discretion in making a child custody determination, giving primary consideration to the welfare of the child. The court quoted the leading California Supreme Court custody decision, *Taber v. Taber* (1930):

> The trial court is necessarily allowed a wide latitude in the exercise of its discretion. In the first instance it is for the trial court to determine, after considering all the evidence, how the best interests of the child will be preserved. The question of [best interest is] to be determined solely from the standpoint of the child, and the feelings and desires of the contesting parties are not to be considered, except in so far as they affect the best interests of the child.

To the court of appeal, this pronouncement suggested that treating a parent as unqualified for custody on the basis solely of sexual orientation was an evasion of the trial court's responsibility to exercise discretion. The court of appeal said that "it is not until the trial court has considered *all the evidence* that it may exercise its discretion as to how the welfare of the child will best be served." Consequently, the court held that the trial court "erred in failing to exercise its discretion and ruling as a matter of law that petitioner was an unfit mother," and ordered the trial court to reopen the matter and make a decision informed by consideration of the evidence. The court did not express any view about what that decision should be, or indeed to what extent Ellen's sexuality should be considered in making the determination, although it seems clear that the court of appeal expected her sexuality to remain an issue.

The *Nadler* decision marked a major step forward for the parental rights of lesbians and gay men by rejecting the reflexive sort of action taken by Judge Babich and requiring, in effect, that homosexuality be only one element among many in determining parental fitness, rather than the only and decisive negative element. As such, it was consistent with the emerging view of the American medical establishment that human sexuality was a much more complicated matter than had previously been thought, and that homosexuality, in particular, might well be an example of sexual diversity rather than sexual pathology. This emerging view, which captured majority support early in the 1970s in resolutions adopted by professional organizations of psychiatrists and psychologists, proved controversial in the courts. Even in the 1990s there were some state courts that persisted in holding parental sexual orientation to be dispositive in child custody disputes, but a majority of the state courts to rule on the matter would eventually embrace the *Nadler* court's approach, relegating parental sexuality to a less important consideration in focusing on the best interest of the child.

Case Reference

Taber v. Taber, 209 Cal. 755, 290 P. 36 (1930)

50. CONSTITUTIONAL RIGHTS OF THE UNWED FATHER

Stanley v. Illinois, 405 U.S. 645 (1972), reversing 45 Ill. 2d 132, 256 N.E.2d 814 (1970).

The Supreme Court has long recognized that the biological progenitors of children have certain constitutional protections for their autonomous role as parents. As early as 1923, in *Meyer v. Nebraska*, the Court deemed the right to conceive and raise one's children as "essential." The Court had characterized reproduction as one of the "basic civil rights of man" in *Skinner v. Oklahoma* in 1942, and stated in *Prince v. Massachusetts* in 1944: "It is cardinal with us that the custody, care and nurture of the child reside first in the parents, whose primary function and freedom include preparation for obligations the state can neither supply nor hinder." In each of these cases, a state sought to interfere with the natural parent's autonomy in making fundamental decisions related to the conception and rearing of children. Whether found to be rooted in the Due Process Clause, the Equal Protection Clause, or the Ninth Amendment, the Court had perceived that there was something fundamentally important about the relationship of parent and offspring that raised a significant barrier against state intervention. In *Stanley v. Illinois*, the Court had to determine whether the same considerations applied to the custodial claims of an unwed father who had never taken any action to establish a legally recognized bond with his children.

Peter and Joan Stanley lived together off and on for eighteen years, never marrying, but producing three children together. Peter, who was a poor man without significant marketable job skills, contributed what little he could to the maintenance of the household, and established a continuing parental relationship with the children. When Joan died, two of the children were still minors. Being poor and a single man, Peter felt he could not adequately provide for their upbringing by himself and arranged for some friends, the Nesses, to take the children in. An Illinois state social worker checking on the children's status after the death of their mother determined that they were living with the Nesses under circumstances where nobody had any legal obligation to provide for their care. The state initiated a child dependency proceeding before Cook County Circuit Court Judge John P. McGury under the state's Juvenile Court Act, seeking to have the children declared wards of the state and placed with court-appointed guardians. Stanley protested that the children should not be declared wards of the state nor their guardianship awarded to anybody other than him.

The Juvenile Court Act provided: "Those who are dependent include any minor under 18 years of age who is without a parent, guardian or legal custodian." The law defined "parents" as "the father and mother of a legitimate child, or the survivor of them, or the natural mother of an illegitimate child, and includes any adoptive parent. It does not include a parent whose rights in respect of the minor have been terminated in any manner provided by law." Applying these provisions to the petition before him, Judge McGury found that the two minor children had no legal parent, guardian, or custodian and were thus dependent within the meaning of the statute, compelling a ruling that they be designated wards of the state and that guardians be appointed for them. When Stanley protested this decision, McGury indicated that he would be willing to entertain a future petition by Stanley to be appointed guardian of his children.

Stanley's attorney, Patrick T. Murphy of Chicago, appealed this ruling on his behalf to the Illinois Supreme Court, opposed by Chicago State's Attorney Edward V. Hanrahan's office, represented by Assistant State Attorneys Thomas E. Brannigan and James A. Rooney. Stanley argued that by automatically according recognition and parental rights to married couples and unwed mothers but denying them to unwed fathers, the state violated his right to equal protection of the laws under the Fourteenth Amendment of the U.S. Constitution. He contended that as the actual guardian and

parent of the children he should be entitled to the same presumption of fitness accorded other parents, so that the state could deprive him of parental rights only on an affirmative showing of neglect or disability to fulfill the parental role. He also argued that the state's Paternity Act, which provided that unwed fathers had "no right to custody or control of the child except such custody as may be granted pursuant to an adoption proceeding" additionally violated his constitutional rights. The Illinois Supreme Court was unpersuaded, ruling unanimously on March 24, 1970, that the Illinois statutes were valid and affirming Judge McGury's decision.

Writing for the court, Chief Justice Robert C. Underwood asserted without explanation that "[t]he distinction between the class of mothers and the class of fathers is rationally related to the purposes of the Juvenile Court Act" and "thus it is not constitutionally mandated that Stanley be accorded the rights which accrue to the class of natural mothers of illegitimate children." Underwood offered no further explanation or analysis of the constitutional claim or the reasons for denying it, merely citing without comment a 1957 decision by the U.S. Supreme Court, *Morey v. Doud*, which struck down as violative of equal protection a state commercial regulation that gave American Express Company an exclusive monopoly on money exchange business in the state, on the ground that discrimination against other financial services companies did not reasonably further the articulated purpose of the state law.

Underwood dismissed Stanley's argument that Illinois laws prevented the state from interfering with his relationship with his children absent a showing of neglect or disability, pointing out that the children were literally "dependent minors" under the statutory definition and that the law gave the court "continuing jurisdiction" over them, including the right to transfer custody to a court-appointed guardian. In any event, by failing while Joan was alive to establish any legal ties to the children, Stanley had apparently forfeited any argument that he had the legal rights afforded by Illinois law to "parents" within the meaning of the statute. As to Stanley's final argument, that the Paternity Act also imposed an unconstitutional disability on him, Underwood observed that the claim was premature, since Stanley had as yet made no attempt to establish a legal bond with the children, and Judge McGury had indicated that he would be willing to entertain a petition to that effect in the future.

Murphy assisted Stanley in filing a petition with the U.S. Supreme Court, seeking review of this decision and moving the Court for permission to proceed *in forma pauperis*, which meant that the Court, if it granted the petition, would appoint an attorney to argue Stanley's case. The Court granted both requests on January 25, 1971, designating Murphy to argue the case on Stanley's behalf. Illinois Assistant Attorney General Morton E. Friedman appeared to present the state's case at the oral argument held October 19, 1971. Jonathan Weiss and E. Judson Jennings of the Center on Social Welfare Policy and Law filed an *amicus curiae* brief urging reversal of the Illinois decision. Calvin Sawyer and Richard L. Mandel of the Child Care Association of Illinois, Inc., filed an *amicus curiae* brief providing social science materials relevant to the case but taking no position on the ultimate outcome. The case was heard by a seven-member court, Justices Lewis F. Powell, Jr., and William H. Rehnquist not yet having taken their seats in succession to the recently departed Justices Hugo L. Black and John Marshall Harlan.

The Court split five to two over the decision, announced April 3, 1972, to reverse the Illinois Supreme Court. Justice Byron R. White wrote an opinion for a majority of the seven-member court, with Justice William O. Douglas joining in all but the final portion in which White summarized his holding. Chief Justice Warren E. Burger dissented in an opinion joined by Justice Harry A. Blackmun. White characterized the case as being at heart about a "presumption" enacted by Illinois in its Juvenile Court Act that unwed fathers were "unfit" parents unless proved otherwise, and held that such a presumption could not be applied to an unwed father while the opposite presumption applied to unwed mothers and married parents without violating the Equal Protection Clause.

After summarizing the facts of the case, White devoted the first substantive part of his opinion to developing the idea of the adverse presumption the statute imposed on Stanley. At the outset, White rejected the notion that any difference in treatment accorded unwed fathers under the statute was "immaterial and not legally cognizable for the purposes of the Fourteenth Amendment," commenting that "if there is delay between the doing and the undoing petitioner suffers from the deprivation of his children, and the children suffer from uncertainty and dislocation" as a result. Recognizing that a poor man like Stanley might not have "the means at hand" to "erase the adverse consequences of the proceeding in the course of which his children were declared wards of the state," White declared that it was necessary to focus on that initial dependency proceeding to effectuate Stanley's constitutional rights as a father.

The state argued that Stanley was free to petition for adoption of the children, but White found this an unsatisfactory solution to the problem, since the Illinois law treated Stanley as a "stranger" to his own children, with no priority in adoption proceedings and without the presumption of fitness that the law apparently attached to unwed mothers and married parents. White took a somewhat different view from the Illinois Supreme Court on the likelihood that Stanley would be successful in an adoption proceeding, given his single state and his poor economic situation, and also dismissed the argument that Stanley's interests were adequately protected because he could petition the state court for "custody and control" of his children. "Passing the obvious issue whether it would be futile or burdensome for an unmarried father—without funds and already once presumed unfit—to petition for custody, this suggestion overlooks the fact that legal custody is not parenthood or adoption," White asserted. A court-appointed custodian could be removed at any time without cause under Illinois law, and would be under constant, perhaps intrusive, supervision of the court. "Obviously, then," concluded White, "even if Stanley were a mere step away from 'custody and control,' to give an unwed father only 'custody and control' would still be to leave him seriously prejudiced by reason of his status." Consequently, there was a real constitutional issue that the Court had to address.

Curiously, however, White stated his conclusion in a confusing blend of due process and equal protection:

> We conclude that, as a matter of due process of law, Stanley was entitled to a hearing on his fitness as a parent before his children were taken from him and that, by denying him a hearing and extending it to all other parents whose custody of their children is challenged, the State denied Stanley the equal protection of the laws guaranteed by the Fourteenth Amendment.

This summary was curious because Stanley had not framed his appeal in terms of "due process," but solely in terms of "equal protection." This provided a basis for the dissenters to assert that the Court had improperly decided the case on the basis of a constitutional argument not raised before the lower court or in the petition for *certiorari*.

White began to explain his ruling by describing the procedures Illinois used to remove "non-delinquent children from the homes of their parents." There were two types of proceedings: neglect proceedings, in which the State had to show that the parents were unfit or providing an unsuitable environment, and dependency proceedings, in which the State merely had to show that the children were without a parent legally responsible for their care and upbringing. In this case, the state proceeded under the dependency route, making no attempt to show that Stanley was an unfit parent or unable to provide for the care of his children, resting solely on the statutory definition of "parents," which excluded unwed fathers. Alone among all parents, unwed fathers in Illinois were subject to a "simplistic" proceeding in which their fitness was essentially "irrelevant" to the outcome. "Unfitness" was tacitly presumed by the law, and the unwed father was not even afforded the opportunity to rebut this presumption in the course of the dependency proceeding, being relegated to a subsequent attempt to gain custody through a separate proceeding while, in the interim, being deprived of custody of his children.

"In considering this procedure under the Due Process Clause," said White, it is necessary to recognize that due process does not require a hearing every time the government impairs a private interest of a citizen. The Court must weigh the interests of the individual and the state in determining whether the individual's interest is significant enough, compared to the state's interest, to justify interposing the hearing requirement. In this case, White found it easy to justify the hearing, because if a particular unwed father was indeed fit to assert parental control over his children, the state's primary interest in the welfare of the children was not advanced by applying a presumption of unfitness. Indeed, given the more general policy of preventing the breakup and dislocation of intact families upon the death of a parent, the Illinois statute would prove detrimental to the best interest of the children in cases where an unwed mother died leaving the children under the care of a fit unwed father.

After briefly quoting key phrases from the body of Supreme Court precedent on the constitutional protection afforded to parental autonomy in decisions of conception and child rearing, White asserted that this case fit squarely within the same concerns. Particularly significant was *Levy v. Louisiana*, a 1968 case in which the Court had recognized that some constitutional protection should extend to "family relationships unlegitimized by a marriage ceremony," invalidating a state law depriving illegitimate children of standing to bring wrongful death actions for the deaths of their parents. It was clear to White that Stanley's "interest in retaining custody of his children is cognizable and substantial." As against Stanley's interest, the state's interest in protecting the welfare of minors within its jurisdiction was also substantial. "We do not question the assertion that neglectful parents may be separated from their children," conceded White, but that was not really this case, because the state had made no argument that Stanley was unfit to have control of his children due to neglect. Indeed, White questioned whether there was any state interest in separating a fit unwed father from his children, since the state "registers no gain toward its declared goals when it separates children from the custody of fit parents," and, if Stanley was indeed fit as he claimed, "the State spites its own articulated goals when it needlessly separates him from his family."

White analogized the situation to that where a state imposed a presumption that any driver involved in a traffic accident could be deprived of his license on a tacit presumption that he must have been at least partially at fault in the accident. In *Bell v. Burson*, a 1971 case decided shortly before *Stanley v. Illinois*, the Court had held this law unconstitutional on due process grounds because the state was depriving an individual of a significant interest "without reference to the very factor (there fault in driving, here fitness as a parent) that the State itself deemed fundamental to its statutory scheme." In this case, Illinois argued that in most cases it was likely that unwed fathers were unfit, having abandoned the mother and child or, in some cases, even being unaware that they were fathers. While that might be true, White said, as long as all unwed fathers could not be placed in such a neglectful category, it was inappropriate for the state to apply an adverse presumption when such important interests were at stake.

White posed another analogy, this time to *Carrington v. Rash*, a 1965 case in which the Court had invalidated a Texas law that prevented military service members stationed in Texas from voting in Texas state and local elections unless they were Texas residents prior to entering the service. The right to vote is quite important, and the Court ruled that Texas could not imply a nonrebuttable adverse presumption that all service members stationed in Texas had no intention to become and remain Texans. While it might be administratively convenient to apply such a presumption, the significance of the right denied was too great to give way to mere administrative convenience.

Similarly, while it might further administrative convenience to presume that unwed fathers were unfit or unattached to their children, the interests of those fathers who had maintained a continuing relationship with their children were too important to be outweighed by such administrative convenience. "The Constitution recognizes higher values than speed and efficiency," White asserted. "Indeed, one might fairly say of the Bill of Rights in general, and the Due Process Clause in particular, that they were designed to protect the fragile values

of a vulnerable citizenry from the overbearing concern for efficiency and efficacy that may characterize praiseworthy government officials no less, and perhaps more, than mediocre ones." Using presumptions "is always cheaper and easier than individualized determination," said White, "but when, as here, the procedure forecloses the determinative issues of competence and care, when it explicitly disdains present realities in deference to past formalities, it needlessly risks running roughshod over the important interests of both parent and child" and thus could not stand. Indeed, the state's interest "in caring for Stanley's children is *de minimis* if Stanley is shown to be a fit father," White asserted. While it was "more convenient to presume than to prove," that was "insufficient" advantage to "refuse a father a hearing when the issue at stake is the dismemberment of his family."

Chief Justice Burger argued in dissent that Stanley had never posed the Due Process Clause as a source of his rights in this situation, relying solely on the Equal Protection Clause, which disappeared from White's analysis until the very end of the opinion, when White reintroduced it in his final section by asserting without any extended discussion that if parents generally had a due process right with regard to continuing custody of their children, then unwed fathers could not be deprived of this right while it was accorded to unwed mothers without offending the Equal Protection Clause. To Burger, this distorted the issue before the Court, which was solely whether the Illinois definition of "parents" standing by itself violated the Equal Protection Clause, without any reference to substantive due process. Here, he said, the Court held "*sua sponte*" that the Due Process Clause required Stanley to have an opportunity to demonstrate his parental fitness before being deprived of his children, and then premised its equal protection holding on this due process holding.

This "method of analysis" is, of course, no more or less than the use of the Equal Protection Clause as a shorthand condensation of the entire Constitution: a State may not deny *any* constitutional right to some of its citizens without violating the Equal Protection Clause through its failure to deny such rights to *all* of its citizens. The limits on this Court's jurisdiction are not properly expandable by the use of such semantic devices as that.

Burger also disputed White's characterization of the Illinois law as containing a presumption of unwed father "unfitness." He found no such presumption in the law, and asserted that the Court's opinion totally overlooked, and never came to grips with, several arguments by Illinois in its brief and at oral argument, most significantly that it was rational to distinguish between the father and the mother, and certainly to distinguish between an unwed father and a married couple, when the state's purpose was to provide for the welfare of the child. A married couple had signified its willingness, by the very act of marrying, to incur the legal obligations imposed on married couples, including legal obligations with regard to the care and raising of any children of the marriage. Unwed parents had not undertaken any such obligations. Furthermore, if the state was concerned with locating responsibility for the care of illegitimate children, it was rational to focus on the mother, who could easily be identified at the time of birth, as opposed to the father, who had no legal relation to the child and who might not even be present or aware of the birth, or might disavow the child entirely. Noting that the Illinois laws afforded Stanley many opportunities to establish a legal tie to his children, Burger asserted that his failure to take advantage of any of them, and indeed, his action in turning over the children to the Nesses, cut against the Court's opinion in the case. Had Stanley prevailed in the Illinois courts, observed Burger, "the *status quo* would have obtained: the Nesses would have continued to play the role of actual custodians until either they or Stanley acted to alter the informal arrangement, and there would still have been no living adult with any legally enforceable obligation for the care and support of the infant children." Thus, *Stanley* did not present a particularly sympathetic case on the facts, when weighed against the state's interest in ensuring that every child have a legally responsible custodian.

While it was true that Stanley might have been among the minority of unwed fathers who did acknowledge his paternity, live with his children's mother, and contribute to their raising and support, Burger asserted that Illinois was not constitutionally obligated "to tailor its statutory definition of 'parents' so meticulously as to include such unusual unwed fathers, while at the same time excluding those unwed, and generally unidentified, biological fathers who in no way share Stanley's professed desires." Invalidating a state law on constitutional grounds was serious business, and Burger felt that the Court had expanded "its legitimate jurisdiction" in this case beyond the limits contemplated by Congress when it reached out to strike down the law on a ground not properly argued in the state courts.

Despite Burger's dissent, the decision in *Stanley* quickly became established as a bedrock of constitutional family law, being frequently cited as a bulwark of the constitutional rights of biological parents. As such, it has proven particularly useful in child custody and visitation disputes involving lesbian and gay parents, providing the basis for courts requiring states to come up with substantial evidence of unfitness and danger to the children before depriving natural parents of a continuing custodial role. While some courts find that burden easily met by accepting stereotypical views of lesbian and gay people, or by giving inordinate weight to the presumed hostility of society against children raised in a homosexual household, others have conscientiously studied the scientific evidence of the impact (or lack of impact) of parental sexuality on child development and ruled accordingly, citing *Stanley* as their basic text.

Case References

Bell v. Burson, 402 U.S. 535 (1971)

Carrington v. Rash, 380 U.S. 89 (1965)

Levy v. Louisiana, 391 U.S. 68 (1968)

Meyer v. Nebraska, 262 U.S. 390 (1923)

Morey v. Doud, 354 U.S. 457 (1957), overruled by *City of New Orleans v. Dunes*, 427 U.S. 297 (1976)

Prince v. Massachusetts, 321 U.S. 158 (1944)

Skinner v. Oklahoma, 316 U.S. 535 (1942)

51. MUST THE STATE AUTHORIZE SAME-SEX MARRIAGE?

Baker v. Nelson, 291 Minn. 310, 191 N.W.2d 185 (1971), appeal dismissed, 409 U.S. 810 (1972).
Singer v. Hara, 11 Wash. App. 247, 522 P.2d 1187 (Div. 1, 1974).

As agitation for the right to marry increased in the lesbian and gay community during the late 1980s, a pair of appellate rulings from the early 1970s concerning same-sex marriage loomed ever larger in the research of lawyers in this area. The two cases, *Baker v. Nelson* and *Singer v. Hara*, had long been regarded as posing insurmountable barriers to same-sex marriage, responding negatively to the argument that gender-neutral marriage laws should be construed to allow persons of the same sex to marry, that the federal constitution required the state to authorize same-sex marriage, or that a state equal rights amendment in Washington would have that effect. These two decisions are remarkable for the factual assumptions on which they rest—assumptions that appear even less tenable two decades later than they did at the time, due to significant changes in the lives of lesbians and gay men in the intervening decades.

Richard John Baker and James Michael McConnell applied to Gerald R. Nelson, the clerk of the Hennepin County, Minnesota, District Court, for a marriage license. Nelson declined to issue the license because the applicants were both men. Although the relevant Minnesota statute did not expressly forbid same-sex marriage, there were various references throughout the state's laws on domestic relations to "husband" and "wife." Neither Baker nor McConnell failed to qualify for issuance of a marriage license on grounds other than being of the same sex. They retained Minneapolis attorney R. Michael Wetherbee, who filed a lawsuit against Nelson in the Hennepin County District Court, seeking a writ of *mandamus* ordering Nelson to issue them the marriage license. County Attorney George Scott and Assistant County Attorney David E. Mikkelson appeared in opposition. District Judge Tom Bergin backed up his clerk, ruling that Nelson was not required to issue a marriage license to the two men and specifically directing that

Nelson not issue a license. They appealed to the Minnesota Supreme Court. The supreme court unanimously rejected their petition in an opinion by Justice C. Donald Peterson issued October 15, 1971.

Baker and McConnell based their case on two alternative theories. The first was based on statutory construction. They contended that it was possible to interpret the Minnesota marriage statute to allow same-sex marriages. Their alternative theory was that if the marriage law could not be interpreted to authorize same-sex marriage, the law was unconstitutional by virtue of the First, Eighth, Ninth, and Fourteenth amendments of the federal constitution.

The court made short work of their first argument. Although the Minnesota statute did not specifically prohibit same-sex marriage and, in fact, the operative language of the law did not specify the gender of the parties, Peterson stated that a "sensible interpretation" of the law required restricting marriages to opposite-sex couples because the legislature should be presumed to have used the term "marriage" in its common, everyday meaning. "It is unrealistic to think that the original draftsmen of our marriage statutes, which date from territorial days, would have used the term in any different sense," said Peterson, quoting entries from *Webster's Third New International Dictionary* of 1969 and *Black's Law Dictionary* (4th edition) defining marriage as involving persons of the opposite sex and resulting in a relation of husband and wife. The references to "husband" and "wife" and "groom" and "bride" elsewhere in the statute as the result of a 1969 amendment made even clearer the legislature's understanding that it was not authorizing same-sex marriage.

Turning to the alternative constitutional arguments, the court did not even find worthy of discussion the assertion that the First Amendment's right of freedom of association or the Eighth Amendment's prohibition of cruel or unusual punishment had anything to do with the case, dismissing them in a brief footnote. Instead, the court focused on the argument that the right to marry was a "fundamental right" and that restricting that right to opposite-sex couples was "irrational and invidiously discriminatory." While conceding that in such cases as *Skinner v. Oklahoma* (1942) and *Griswold v. Connecticut* (1965), the U.S. Supreme Court had used language identifying the institution of marriage as holding a central place in society, Peterson pointed out that in both cases marriage was tied to procreation in a way that suggested again the restriction of that right to opposite-sex couples. In *Skinner*, the Court had stated, "Marriage and procreation are fundamental to the very existence and survival of the race." This association of marriage with procreation, said Peterson, "manifestly is more deeply founded than the asserted contemporary concept of marriage and societal interests for which petitioners contend," and the Fourteenth Amendment was not "a charter for restructuring it by judicial legislation." Similarly, in *Griswold* the Court had emphasized the privacy inherent in "an intimate relation of husband and wife." Justice Arthur J. Goldberg's concurring opinion, resting on the Ninth Amendment, also emphasized "the traditional relation of the family—a relation as old and as fundamental as our entire civilization." (Incredibly, Peterson asserted in a footnote that Goldberg's opinion "stopped short . . . of an implication that the Ninth Amendment was made applicable against the states by the Fourteenth Amendment." Peterson's assertion is incredible because, of course, Goldberg was invoking the Ninth Amendment as a source of an unenumerated right of privacy to be the basis for striking down a birth control statute enacted by the state of Connecticut.) Thus, the "right to marry" that Baker and McConnell advanced was not freely available to all persons, but only to persons of the opposite sex.

The court also rejected an alternative argument based on the Equal Protection Clause, asserting that "there is no irrational or invidious discrimination" in denying same-sex couples the right to marry. Baker and McConnell had pointed out that the state did not require opposite-sex couples to prove their capacity to produce children or their willingness to do so as a prerequisite for marriage, countering the notion that marriage was reserved for the purpose of procreation. No matter, said Peterson, "the classification is no more than theoretically imperfect," and "abstract symmetry" is not required under the Fourteenth Amendment.

The petitioners had relied heavily on the Supreme Court's 1967 decision, *Loving v. Virginia*, which held unconstitutional laws forbidding interracial marriages. In the course of that opinion, Chief Justice Earl Warren had written:

> Marriage is one of the "basic civil rights of man," fundamental to our very existence and survival. . . . To deny this fundamental freedom on so unsupportable a basis as the racial classifications embodied in these statutes, classifications so directly subversive of the principle of equality at the heart of the Fourteenth Amendment, is surely to deprive all the State's citizens of liberty without due process of law. The Fourteenth Amendment requires that the freedom of choice to marry not be restricted by invidious racial discrimination.

To Baker and McConnell, this language indicated that the right to marry was "fundamental," which meant that the state would have a heavy burden of justifying the use of any sexual classification in denying that right to two people. To Peterson, however, the references to racial classifications made clear that the *Loving* opinion was primarily about race discrimination rather than any fundamental right to marry. "*Loving* does indicate," he said, "that not all state restrictions upon the right to marry are beyond reach of the Fourteenth Amendment. But in commonsense and in a constitutional sense, there is a clear distinction between a marital restriction based merely upon race and one based upon the fundamental difference in sex."

This opinion, not ideally developed in its reasoning, was to stand without review, since the U.S. Supreme Court announced on October 10, 1972, that it was dismissing Baker and McConnell's appeal "for want of substantial federal question." To the Justices, no significant constitutional issue had even been raised by the case. Ironically, McConnell and Baker had found a county clerk willing to issue them a marriage license and were "wed" in a ceremony in Blue Earth County, Minnesota, on September 3, 1971, just weeks before the Minnesota Supreme Court denied their appeal. However, when Baker, a military veteran, then applied to the Veterans Administration for increased benefits, claiming that McConnell was his dependent spouse, he was turned down, and the federal courts affirmed the VA's decision in the case of *McConnell v. Nooner.*

An additional element initially provided some hope for a different outcome when John F. Singer and Paul C. Barwick instigated litigation in the state courts of Washington seeking a marriage license: a recently adopted amendment to the Washington Constitution that absolutely banned sex discrimination by the state. On September 20, 1971, just a few weeks before the Minnesota Supreme Court ruled in *Baker v. Nelson*, Singer and Barwick applied for a marriage license at the office of King County, Washington, Auditor Lloyd Hara. Hara refused to grant the license. Retaining attorney Michael E. Withey, of Seattle, the two men filed suit against Hara in King County Superior Court on April 27, 1972, petitioning for immediate injunctive relief on the alternative theories that the Washington marriage law allowed same-sex marriage or that denial of their application violated rights protected by the Washington and federal constitutions. King County Prosecuting Attorney Christopher T. Bayley and Deputy Prosecuting Attorney Richard D. Eadie appeared in opposition. Superior Court Judge Frank Roberts, Jr., denied the application for relief in an order of August 9, 1972, holding that the plaintiffs had not stated a *prima facie* case for the relief they sought.

Singer and Barwick brought their case to the Court of Appeals of Washington, Division 1, which unanimously denied their appeal on May 20, 1974, in an opinion by Chief Judge Herbert A. Swanson. Their petition alleged that Judge Roberts had erred by assuming that same-sex marriages would be destructive to society, and included forty pages of argument in the fields of sociology, theology, science, and medicine, which they argued were a necessary background for intelligent consideration of their claim. Swanson noted that "we deem it appropriate to observe that appellants' discussion in that regard does not present a legal argument,

nor is there any evidence in the record to suggest that the trial court in fact based its order on the 'erroneous and fallacious conclusion' to which the appellants take exception." Although acknowledging the usefulness of this nonlegal material to the discussion, "we have endeavored to confine this opinion to discussion of the legal issues presented without attempting to present our views on matters of sociology, theology, science and medicine." Thus, Swanson's opinion makes no further mention of any nonlegal arguments.

The legal theories of the appeal were the same as those advanced in *Baker v. Nelson*, with the critical addition of the Washington Equal Rights Amendment (ERA), which became effective December 7, 1972, as the new article 31 of the state's constitution. The amendment provides: "Equality of rights and responsibility under the law shall not be denied or abridged on account of sex." Having concluded, without much discussion, that the existing marriage law did not authorize same-sex marriage, Swanson addressed the claim that his construction of the law set up a classification based on sex that was unconstitutional as a result of this amendment. Singer and Barwick argued that during the fiercely waged ratification campaign, opponents of the amendment repeatedly stated that it would require the state to allow same-sex marriages. Since the voters approved it in the face of those assertions, they argued, the voters were authorizing same-sex marriage. Swanson rejected this argument, noting that the proponents of the amendment had strongly countered the proposition that the ERA would require same-sex marriages to be approved by the state. Furthermore, public opinion polls coincident with the voting indicated that most voters did not believe the ERA would have any effect on the marriage laws.

More fundamental for the court was its view that restriction of the right to marry to opposite-sex couples was not sex discrimination. As the state argued, "all same-sex marriages are deemed illegal by the state," regardless whether they involved all men or all women. There would be no violation of the ERA "so long as marriage licenses are denied equally to both male and female pairs." Singer had argued that *Loving v. Virginia* compelled rejection of this argument. In that case, Virginia had argued that so long as both races were equally forbidden to marry members of the other race, there was no discrimination, since the restriction applied equally to both races. The U.S. Supreme Court had rejected that argument because the Fourteenth Amendment imposed a "very heavy burden of justification" on "state statutes drawn according to race," said Swanson, but the analogy to this case just did not hold. "The operative distinction," Swanson wrote, "lies in the relationship which is described by the term 'marriage' itself, and that relationship is the legal union of one man and one woman." Regardless of the apparent gender-neutrality of the statute, it was clearly founded on the "presumption that marriage, as a legal relationship, may exist only between one man and one woman who are otherwise qualified to enter that relationship." Numerous Washington cases involving a wide variety of marital issues had incorporated this assumption, as had courts in other jurisdictions confronted with the issue of same-sex marriage, including the Minnesota Supreme Court in *Baker v. Nelson.*

Given this definition of marriage, it was apparent to the court that *Loving* provided no precedent for this case. "There is no analogous sexual classification in the instant case because appellants are not being denied entry into the marriage relationship because of their sex; rather, they are being denied entry into the marriage relationship because of the recognized definition of that relationship as one which may be entered into only by two persons who are members of the opposite sex." As the Kentucky Court of Appeals had stated in 1973 in *Jones v. Hallahan*, a marriage license denial case involving a lesbian couple, a marriage license was not authorized for the applicants "because what they propose is not a marriage." Since marriage was, by definition (and the Kentucky court quoted three dictionary definitions), the union of a man and a woman, it was impossible for two persons of the same sex to marry: "A license to enter a status or a relationship which the parties are incapable of achieving is a nullity," said the Kentucky court. By contrast, the union of a black person and a white person of the opposite sex was a marriage, so there was no definitional barrier to the result in *Loving v. Virginia.*

The same sort of analysis, asserted the court, was applicable to the argument under the state's ERA. This was not discrimination on the basis of sex, because what the applicants sought was an impossibility: by definition, a marriage is a union of a man and a woman. The court stated:

> The ERA does not create any new rights or responsibilities, such as the conceivable right of persons of the same sex to marry one another; rather, it merely insures that existing rights and responsibilities, or such rights and responsibilities as may be created in the future, which previously might have been wholly or partially denied to one sex or to the other, will be equally available to members of either sex. . . . A generally recognized "corollary" or exception to even an "absolute" interpretation of the ERA is the proposition that laws which differentiate between the sexes are permissible so long as they are based upon the unique physical characteristics of a particular sex, rather than upon a person's membership in a particular sex per se.

Access to marriage, and the rights and responsibilities of marriage, "is based upon the state's recognition that our society as a whole views marriage as the appropriate and desirable forum for procreation and the rearing of children," said Swanson, even though there was no requirement that married couples have or raise children. Since "no same-sex couple offers the possibility of birth of children by their union," the state's refusal to recognize that union is based on the physical limitations associated with sex (i.e., that same-sex couples were incapable of reproduction), rather than upon a classification on the basis of sex that would offend the ERA.

The same analysis was applicable under the Fourteenth Amendment's Equal Protection Clause, said Swanson. Since this was not a case of sex discrimination, the case law on how sex discrimination should be treated under the Equal Protection Clause was essentially irrelevant. As to the alternative argument that this interpretation of the marriage laws was discrimination against homosexuals as such, the court would not apply strict scrutiny (although disclaiming taking any position on the question whether "homosexuals constitute a class having characteristics making any legislative classification applicable to them one having common denominators of suspectability"). For the reasons already articulated regarding conception and child rearing, the court held that the exclusion of same-sex couples from the institution of marriage had a rational basis. The restriction of marriage to opposite-sex couples served "interests of basic importance" to society, said Swanson, although the court would not seek to define them in detail, insisting that this was a matter of legislative judgment. "For constitutional purposes," he said, "it is enough to recognize that marriage as now defined is deeply rooted in our society. . . . [M]arriage is so clearly related to the public interest in affording a favorable environment for the growth of children that we are unable to say that there is not a rational basis upon which the state may limit the protection of its marriage laws to the legal union of one man and one woman."

Having disposed of all other constitutional claims in a brief footnote with no substantive discussion, Swanson concluded that the trial court had correctly refused to order Hara to issue a marriage license. The court rejected a petition for rehearing two months later, and the Washington Supreme Court declined to review the case.

Both James McConnell and John Singer suffered adverse consequences from filing their lawsuits. McConnell's notoriety led to him being denied employment as a librarian at the University of Minnesota, which in turn led to a federal lawsuit alleging improper discrimination. As for Singer, the notoriety generated by his case, together with other peculiarities of his workplace dress and conduct, led the Equal Employment Opportunity Commission's Seattle office to discharge him from his clerical job, which also led to federal litigation that helped spur new federal civil service regulations providing, for the first time, explicit job protection for homosexuals in the federal service. (See *Singer v. U.S. Civil Service Commission* [No. 73.])

The factual premise of these marriage decisions that those familiar with the lesbian and gay community of twenty years later would most readily reject is the notion that it is rational for society to restrict the institution of marriage to opposite-sex couples because of a concern with creating a supportive environment for child rearing. Between those who retain custody or have extended visitation rights with their children from opposite-sex marriages, those who serve as adoptive or foster parents, and those who reproduce using donor insemination techniques, a significant number of lesbian and gay people are now raising children, many in the context of coupled relationships with others of the same sex. If the state's main purpose in creating and reinforcing the marriage relationship is to assist in the rearing of children, that purpose is being severely undercut by denying access to marriage for the thousands of lesbian and gay couples who are raising children. This is illustrated by the unfortunate litigation, discussed elsewhere in this book, where disputes threatening the well-being of the children are not simply dealt with under existing family law doctrines based on the best interest of the child, due to the ambiguity in the relationship of the "parents" created by denial of the right to marry.

The *Baker* and *Singer* decisions are also noteworthy for their total lack of discussion of all the other aspects of marriage that have little or nothing to do with child rearing but would seem to have everything to do with an equal protection analysis of the exclusion of same-sex couples. The demand for legal recognition of same-sex relationships has become so strong that new marriage challenges are beginning to be filed, and it is likely that they will reach appellate courts during the 1990s. Although *Baker* and *Singer* stand as precedents that will surely be invoked by government attorneys and judges in opposing these suits, the new demographics of lesbian and gay life present cogent reasons for a fresh examination of the issues.

Case References

Griswold v. Connecticut, 381 U.S. 479 (1965)

Jones v. Hallahan, 501 S.W.2d 588 (Ky. 1973)

Loving v. Virginia, 388 U.S. 1 (1967)

McConnell v. Anderson, 451 F.2d 193 (8th Cir. 1971), certiorari denied, 405 U.S. 1046 (1972)

McConnell v. Nooner, 547 F.2d 54 (8th Cir. 1976)

Singer v. United States Civil Service Commission, 530 F.2d 247 (9th Cir. 1976), vacated, 429 U.S. 1034 (1977)

Skinner v. Oklahoma ex rel. Williamson, 316 U.S. 535 (1942)

52. "PALIMONY" AND THE COHABITING COUPLE

Marvin v. Marvin, 18 Cal. 3d 660, 134 Cal. Rptr. 815, 557 P.2d 106 (1976) (en banc); appeal after remand, 172 Cal. App. 3d 871, 176 Cal. Rptr. 555 (2d Dist. 1981).

Changing sexual mores have led to changing living arrangements. As societal disapproval of sexual cohabitation has declined, the number of those living in unmarried sexual relationships, whether heterosexual or homosexual, has risen sharply. When such relationships persist for many years and then dissolve, the parties are frequently left with significant financial disputes. The abolition of common-law marriage by statute in many jurisdictions, and the universal refusal of states to sanction homosexual marriage, mean that the normal processes of domestic relations law are not available to separating cohabitants to resolve their disputes. They must fall back on the common law, with the financially disadvantaged partner hoping that the law will provide an equitable remedy while the financially advantaged partner hopes that the law will refuse to order any transfer of wealth. The almost universal criminalizing of prostitution long provided the theoretical basis for refusing recovery in such cases, the courts holding that a "meretricious" sexual relationship could not be part of the consideration for any sort of contractual or equitable recovery.

In this, as in many other areas of the law, the California courts became the foremost pioneers, holding as early as 1932, in *Trutalli v. Meraviglia*, that sexual cohabitants could lawfully contract concerning the ownership of property acquired during their relationship, and that such contracts would not be held unenforceable as tainted by the meretricious sexual relationship. The California Supreme Court reiterated this principle in 1943, in *Vallera v. Vallera*, where the court stated: "If a man and a woman [who are not married] live together as husband and wife under an agreement to pool their earnings and share equally in their joint accumulations, equity will protect the interests of each in such property." All well and good, if the less economically advantaged party could prove an actual agreement, but the relative in-

formality of many such relationships could make it quite difficult to provide such proof. The way out of such a dilemma was provided in the most attention-getting way by the California Supreme Court in 1976, when it heard the appeal of Michelle Triola, the longtime cohabitant of Hollywood movie star Lee Marvin, and decided that the courts could find contracts implied in fact or law in the absence of proof of an express agreement in order to make an equitable division of property acquired during a cohabitation relationship.

Michelle and Lee met in 1964. He was a film actor and she was an aspiring singer. He was married to Betty, but their marriage was on the rocks. In October of that year, Michelle and Lee began to live together. She later claimed that they had an understanding (not written) that while they lived together they would combine their efforts and earnings and share equally any property acquired during their relationship. As part of this relationship, claimed Michelle, they agreed to hold themselves out to society generally as spouses and Michelle would perform the "normal" role of wife, including being Lee's homemaker, housekeeper, cook, and companion. Michelle claimed that she agreed, at Lee's request, to give up her singing career and devote herself full-time to him, in exchange for which he agreed to provide financial support for the rest of her life. They could not actually marry, of course, because Lee's divorce from Betty was not final until two years later. Michelle claimed that after the divorce was final, she and Lee reaffirmed their oral agreement.

Michelle and Lee lived together until 1970, during which time his acting career became quite lucrative and considerable property was acquired, all in his name. In 1970, Lee told Michelle to move out because he wanted to end the relationship. He continued to send her monthly support payments for a while, but then stopped and claimed he had no further obligation to her. Michelle retained the services of prominent Los Angeles domestic relations attorney Marvin M. Mitchelson, and filed suit in Los Angeles County Superior Court, seeking a declaration of her contractual and property rights and requesting the court to impose a constructive trust on half the property acquired by Lee during the course of their relationship. Lee retained the Los Angeles firm of Goldman and Kagon, which filed a demurrer to the complaint, asserting that Michelle's claims had no legal basis. Superior Court Judge William A. Munnell refused to dismiss the complaint at that point, and ordered discovery and preparation for trial. At trial, Lee's attorneys again moved to dismiss the case, claiming that the pre-trial discovery confirmed that there was no express agreement to enforce, and even if there were such an agreement, its enforcement would be contrary to public policy, since Lee was still married to Betty when the alleged agreement was made and such agreement would violate Betty's rights under California's community property laws governing property acquired during a marriage.

Judge Munnell granted Lee's motion to dismiss the case. When he suggested at the hearing that he agreed with the public policy argument, Michelle's lawyer offered to amend the complaint to allege that the parties had reaffirmed their agreement after the divorce, but the judge refused to allow such an amendment. Munnell also refused to allow an amendment adding additional claims against Santa Ana Records, a company that Michelle claimed was owned by Lee and similarly obligated to her as part of Lee's alleged promise, early in their relationship, to assist Michelle in developing a career as a recording artist.

When the Court of Appeal for the Second District refused to revive the suit, Michelle appealed to the California Supreme Court, which set the case for *en banc* review. Given Lee's prominence as a Hollywood star, the case gained considerable notoriety, attracting *amicus* briefs from attorneys and organizations in San Francisco, Berkeley, and Oakland. Since the case had not actually been tried prior to Munnell's dismissal order, the supreme court confronted the dispute solely as a matter of legal theory,

addressing the question whether Michelle's allegations, as yet untested at trial, would be sufficient to support a claim for legal relief. With only one member of the court, Justice William P. Clark, Jr., partially dissenting, the court held that Michelle was entitled to a trial of her claims. The December 27, 1976, opinion of the court was written by Justice Mathew O. Tobriner.

Tobriner first addressed the theoretical issues raised by Michelle's allegations of an express, albeit unwritten, agreement between herself and Lee. Rehearsing the older California precedents holding that cohabitants were not barred from making enforceable agreements about property merely due to their having a nonmarital sexual relationship, Tobriner considered and dismissed each of the theories Lee raised in opposition to the enforceability of such an agreement.

Lee's first argument was that enforcing the agreement would violate public policy. Not only was he still married to Betty when the relationship with Michelle began, but several of the California courts of appeal had ruled in recent years that if the sexual component in the relationship was "illicit" or the agreement depended on the sexual relationship in any way, it was not enforceable. Tobriner rejected this interpretation of prior California cases, asserting that close scrutiny of those decisions showed "a narrower and more precise standard: a contract between nonmarital partners is unenforceable only *to the extent* that it *explicitly* rests upon the immoral and illicit consideration of meretricious sexual services." While the court would not enforce an agreement to commit prostitution, it would enforce an agreement where there was significant nonsexual consideration on the part of the parties underlying their relationship. Given Michelle's allegations about the nature of her agreement with Lee, it was clear that the standard for enforcement would be met here if those allegations stood up at trial, because much more was involved in this relationship than sex. It was a living-together agreement under which Michelle provided the services of homemaker, housekeeper, and cook, not just sexual partner, and Tobriner observed that numerous cases had upheld enforcement of agreements between nonmarital partners in virtually indistinguishable factual settings.

Although the past decisions hover over the issue in the somewhat wispy form of the figures of a Chagall painting, we can abstract from those decisions a clear and simple rule. The fact that a man and woman live together without marriage, and engage in a sexual relationship, does not in itself invalidate agreements between them relating to their earnings, property, or expenses. Neither is such an agreement invalid merely because the parties may have contemplated the creation or continuation of a nonmarital relationship when they entered into it. Agreements between nonmarital partners fail only to the extent that they rest upon a consideration of meretricious sexual services. Thus the rule asserted by defendant, that a contract fails if it is "involved in" or made "in contemplation" of a nonmarital relationship, cannot be reconciled with the decisions.

By contrast, the only cases that appeared superficially to support Lee's arguments were those in which consideration was expressly founded on sexual services, and even there Tobriner stated on behalf of the court that some of those decisions, being inconsistent with the court's current approach, were now disapproved. He derived from those cases, viewed in the light of others supporting Michelle's claim, the rule that only where the "sexual consideration" was inseparable from the overall consideration of the contract would the whole agreement be unenforceable. Limitations of language made it difficult to articulate precisely what Tobriner was getting at, but it was clear that the court wanted to distinguish between the "kept woman" situation and the situation where two adults jointly agreed to live together in a nonmarital relationship as equal partners, each contributing services of value to the relationship in her or his own way.

Tobriner also rejected the argument that enforcing the alleged agreement would violate California's community property laws. At the time of Betty's divorce from Lee, the court had fixed her rights with regard to community property of their marriage, and nothing Lee might have promised to Michelle could supersede that. Enforcement of any agreement between Michelle and Lee would obviously not be allowed to impair any of Betty's rights, but that did not make their agreement entirely unenforceable; Betty's rights would just have to be taken into

account by the trial court in devising an appropriate remedy for Michelle. Tobriner also dismissed Lee's argument, based on a Civil Code provision requiring that contracts for "marriage settlements" be in writing, that Michelle's claim must fail because it was based on an alleged oral agreement. This was not a marriage settlement case, said Tobriner, since Michelle was not claiming that she was married to Lee, merely that they had an agreement to hold themselves out to others as being married. Tobriner also rejected Lee's argument based on another Civil Code section barring actions for breach of promises to marry, pointing out that this was also inapplicable to the current situation. Clearly, Lee's lawyer had grasped at any possible straw in the sprawling and complex California Civil Code that might plausibly be raised in his client's behalf, but these theories were quite strained.

Tobriner concluded this part of the opinion by reiterating that "adults who voluntarily live together and engage in sexual relations are nonetheless as competent as any other persons to contract respecting their earnings and property rights."

> Of course, they cannot lawfully contract to pay for the performance of sexual services, for such a contract is, in essence, an agreement for prostitution and unlawful for that reason. But they may agree to pool their earnings and to hold all property acquired during the relationship in accord with the laws governing community property; conversely they may agree that each partner's earnings and the property acquired from those earnings remains the separate property of the earning partner.

As long as the agreement did not rest solely on "illicit meretricious consideration," concluded Tobriner, the parties were free to "order their economic affairs as they choose, and no policy precludes the courts from enforcing such agreements." In this case, given her factual allegations, Michelle was entitled to a trial of her claim.

Of course, it was possible that at trial Michelle would be unable to prove any express agreement, the most common evidentiary difficulty in cases of this type being the failure of the parties to make their agreement more concrete than general oral expressions of good will and "don't worry about it." Anticipating this contingency, Tobriner next examined the possibility that Michelle could assert legal claims based on implied contract theories. Here prior California law provided a variety of theories, all complicated by the enactment of the Family Law Act in 1970, intended to replace prior common-law rules governing the dissolution of marriage and specifically to separate out issues of fault and community property rights. At least two prominent court of appeal decisions, *In re Marriage of Cary* (1973) and *Estate of Atherley* (1974), had held that the Family Law Act required courts to apply community property principles in dividing up property after nonmarried cohabitants parted ways, regardless of any agreements between the parties, while one court of appeal decision, *Beckman v. Mayhew* (1974), rejected that view.

Tobriner stated that the Family Law Act had no application to this issue and common-law rules must prevail in determining property disputes between separating cohabitants. California cases predating the Family Law Act, such as *Vallera*, had rested on alleged express agreements, but Tobriner saw no reason, the court having decided that express agreements could be enforced, to deny enforcement of implied agreements, based either on the actual conduct of the parties (implied in fact contracts) or on equitable principles (implied in law contracts). The theoretical basis for contracts implied in fact rests on the common understanding that people may, by their conduct, manifest the intention to make agreements, even though they do not put such agreements into words. While the precise details of those agreements may seem unclear, it is nonetheless obvious to the intelligent observer that the parties do have an agreement, and if the requisites of consideration are present, such an agreement should be enforced. By contrast, implied in law contracts rest on the view that public policy should impose a requirement of payment for benefits willingly received, in the absence of an express agreement to pay, under circumstances where it seems fair to impose such a requirement. The law's goal in such cases is to avoid unjust enrichment of the recipient of a benefit under circumstances where it is clear that the recipient desired to receive the benefit (or at least had no objection to receiving it) under circumstances where the person conferring the benefit could reasonably expect something in return.

Reviewing the pre-*Cary* cases, Tobriner noted that they "exhibited a schizophrenic inconsistency." They would enforce express contracts unless they believed the contracts "rested upon an unlawful consideration," so they were clearly applying "common law principle as to contracts" in those cases. At the same time, the courts were, in many cases, disregarding "the common law principle that implied contracts can arise from the conduct of the parties." In at least one case, a court of appeal had spoken of leaving the parties "in the position in which they had placed themselves," as if this sort of abstention from decisionmaking was not, in itself, a decision, since it normally left the economically less advantaged party out in the cold. Furthermore, prior cases had erected a distinction even in enforcing express agreements, placing virtually no value on the services a woman typically contributed to a cohabiting relationship, while placing value on money or property contributed by the man, and then holding that each would be compensated based on their contribution; given such a valuation approach, the woman was typically entitled to little or nothing. One judge, dissenting in the *Vallera* case, which had taken this approach, pointed out the unreality of such a valuation method: "Unless it can be argued that a woman's services as cook, housekeeper, and homemaker are valueless, it would seem logical that if, when she contributes money to the purchase of property, her interest will be protected, then when she contributes her services in the home, her interest in property accumulated should be protected." Indeed, such was really the theory of community property law, under which each partner has an equal share in all property acquired, in recognition of the nonmonetary but nonetheless valuable services performed by the woman that frees the man to earn tangible assets outside of the home.

While Tobriner rejected the holdings in *Cary* and *Atherley* that the Family Law Act required application of community property principles to cases involving dissolution of nonmarital partnerships, nonetheless he agreed with those decisions that prior case law upholding a valuation scheme that gave no credit for the woman's homemaking contribution was unfair. "The principal reason why the pre-*Cary* decisions result in an unfair distribution of property," asserted Tobriner, "inheres in the court's refusal to permit a nonmarital partner to assert rights based upon accepted principles of implied contract or equity." The court now decided that all the reasons formerly advanced in support of this approach lacked merit. California law had moved beyond the point of using "guilt" as a factor in dividing property acquired during a relationship, and social changes had left far behind the outmoded notion that a person could have no reasonable expectation of equitable treatment when entering into a nonmarital cohabitation situation. There was no reason to presume that the services typically rendered by a woman as a homemaker were intended as a "gift" to her partner, and Tobriner also rejected the most obstinately recited old chestnut—that fairness in this situation would "discourage marriage." Indeed, the pre-*Cary* rule, as Tobriner pointed out, might discourage a wealthy person from marrying a poor one out of fear that the wealthy person would immediately be subject to a significant transfer of wealth upon dissolution of the relationship. "Although we recognize the well-established public policy to foster and promote the institution of marriage, perpetuation of judicial rules which result in an inequitable distribution of property accumulated during a nonmarital relationship is neither a just nor an effective way of carrying out that policy," Tobriner sensibly intoned.

> In summary, we believe that the prevalence of nonmarital relationships in modern society and the social acceptance of them, marks this as a time when our courts should by no means apply the doctrine of unlawfulness of the so-called meretricious relationship to the instant case. As we have explained, the nonenforceability of agreements expressly providing for meretricious conduct rested upon the fact that such conduct, as the word suggests, pertained to and encompassed prostitution. To equate the nonmarital relationship of today to such a subject matter is to do violence to an accepted and wholly different practice.

Tobriner noted that many young couples now cohabited prior to marriage "to make sure that they can successfully later undertake marriage"

and that nonmarital relationships were also pervasive in other situations, including those where poor people whose actual relationships ceased could not afford to pay for legal divorces but wished to establish a new relationship with somebody else. "The mores of the society have indeed changed so radically in regard to cohabitation," he insisted, "that we cannot impose a standard based on alleged moral considerations that have apparently been so widely abandoned by so many." Of course, Tobriner felt it necessary at this point, to avoid criticism from "traditionalists," to append language about marriage being "at once the most socially productive and individually fulfilling relationship that one can enjoy in the course of a lifetime," but the sentences stand out as a *pro forma apologia* in the context of the court's recognition of nontraditional lifestyles.

Tobriner concluded that in addition to enforcing express property agreements between cohabitants, the courts "may look to a variety of other remedies in order to protect the parties' lawful expectations" by examining their conduct toward each other. He specifically mentioned using the theory of "constructive trust," as urged by Michelle in this case, or the old implied in law theory of *quantum meruit*, under which the person rendering services is entitled to compensation for their fair value. On remand, he said, Michelle should be allowed to amend her complaint to allege implied contract theories as well as her original express contract theory, and that the court's opinion did not "preclude the evolution of additional equitable remedies to protect the expectations of the parties to a nonmarital relationship in cases in which existing remedies prove inadequate; the suitability of such remedies may be determined in later cases in light of the factual setting in which they arise." He also noted that the court had not taken any position on whether a party was entitled to "support payments from the other party after the relationship terminated."

Justice Clark partially dissented to express dismay with the wide-ranging discussion of equitable remedies. He agreed with the court that a person in Michelle's situation could assert both express and implied in fact contract claims, but he was opposed to the broad extension to the implied in law contract realm, with its expansive theories of equitable principles and *quantum meruit* imposing duties to pay for services where there was no agreement, either express or implied. To Clark, this approach left open altogether too many questions about the limits of liability. While courts should enforce agreements, said Clark, "in the absence of agreement, we should stop and consider the ramifications before creating economic obligations which may violate legislative intent, contravene the intention of the parties, and surely generate undue burdens on our trial courts."

The case was remanded for trial. On the second go-round, Superior Court Judge Arthur K. Marshall specifically found that there was no agreement, express or implied, between Michelle and Lee. However, looking to Tobriner's final comments about the range of equitable remedies that could be imposed depending on the facts of particular cases, he did exactly what Clark feared might happen in his partial dissenting opinion. Marshall found, as an equitable matter, that Michelle, who had put off her singing career to be Lee's companion, was entitled to "rehabilitation" payments from Lee sufficient to sustain her through two years of attempting to reestablish her career, payments which he calculated at $1,000 per week, for a total of $104,000. Lee appealed this ruling, which was overturned by the Court of Appeal for the Second District in an opinion of August 11, 1981, by Associate Justice James A. Cobey.

As a preliminary matter, Cobey pointed out, neither Michelle's original complaint nor her amended complaint had made any claim for "rehabilitation" payments, as such. She was claiming a right founded on an agreement, which the trial court expressly found did not exist. Thus, unless her complaint was further amended to present such a claim, which did not appear on the record, it was inappropriate for the trial judge to award damages on a claim never asserted. Furthermore, while Tobriner's opinion did suggest that the lower courts could develop appropriate equitable remedies to protect the expectations of the parties, Cobey believed that Marshall had roamed far beyond even this liberal remedial approach. Since the trial court expressly found "that defendant never had

any obligation to pay plaintiff a reasonable sum as and for her maintenance and that defendant had not been unjustly enriched by reason of the relationship or its termination and that defendant had never acquired anything of value from plaintiff by any wrongful act," it was inappropriate to use equitable powers in support of a transfer of wealth from the defendant to the plaintiff. As far as Cobey could see, the trial court's factual findings may have established Michelle's need for financial assistance and Lee's ability to provide it, but did not establish that Lee had any legal duty to provide it. "The award, being nonconsensual in nature, must be supported by some recognized underlying obligation in law or in equity," Cobey insisted. "A court of equity admittedly has broad powers, but it may not create totally new substantive rights under the guise of doing equity."

Presiding Justice Joan Dempsey Klein dissented from this disposition, pointing out that the trial court had found that Lee continued to pay support to Michelle for several months after their breakup under some sort of "arrangement," which could well have provided the basis for a finding of obligation. Klein observed that Tobriner's opinion encouraged the trial court to use equitable principles to achieve a just result between the parties. Because of the way the case came up on appeal, lacking a full record of the proceedings in the trial court, it may have been that there was a factual basis for the award of damages here, and the trial judge merely neglected to include a clear finding of fact supporting the award in his brief memorandum disposition. Rather than reverse the damage award without possibility of further relief, Klein would have remanded the case to the trial court to give Marshall a second chance to specify an appropriate factual basis for the damage award to Michelle. There is no indication in published court opinions that Michelle took the case any further.

The California Supreme Court's opinion in *Marvin v. Marvin*, unanimously holding that property disputes between separating cohabitants could be determined by reference to express or implied contract theory, and concluding with only one dissenting vote that even equitable implied in law contract theories were available in such cases, quickly became a focus of media and courtroom attention. While few other states were willing to follow California all the way, especially with regard to equitable remedies, some other state courts subsequently embraced the notion that changing social conditions and attitudes toward sex and sexuality made it appropriate to use express and implied contract theories to govern property dispositions, provided there was some factual basis for finding an agreement. While the refusal of most other jurisdictions to adopt the implied in law branch of *Marvin* still leaves many cohabitants without legal redress, nonetheless the law has come a significant way from the prior absolute refusal to provide any assistance to the economically disadvantaged party in such circumstances.

Case References

Atherley, Estate of, 44 Cal. App. 3d 758, 119 Cal. Rptr. 41 (1975)

Beckman v. Mayhew, 49 Cal. App. 3d 529, 122 Cal. Rptr. 604 (1974)

Cary, In re Marriage of, 34 Cal. App. 3d 345, 109 Cal. Rptr. 862 (1973)

Trutalli v. Meraviglia, 215 Cal. 698, 12 P.2d 430 (1932)

Vallera v. Vallera, 21 Cal. 2d 681, 134 P.2d 761 (1943)

53. FAMILY DIVERSITY AND THE SINGLE-FAMILY ZONING LAW

Moore v. City of East Cleveland, 431 U.S. 494 (1977).

The U.S. Supreme Court ruled in *Village of Belle Terre v. Boraas* (1974) that a municipality could restrict occupancy of residential housing to "single families" for the purpose of preserving the particular residential character of a neighborhood. Rejecting claims that such a restriction violated individual liberties protected by the Fourteenth Amendment, the Court applied the lenient standard for review of land-use regulations that had been adopted in 1926 in *Euclid v. Ambler Realty Co.*, under which the government had merely to show a rational basis for a properly enacted zoning ordinance for the measure to survive judicial scrutiny. The Belle Terre ordinance was not particularly restrictive, however, since it placed no limit on the number of related persons who could reside in the same house, and even allowed up to three unrelated persons to live together. Thus, that decision left unanswered important questions about how the Court might treat more intrusive zoning laws that sought to enforce "traditional" family values by defining the "single family" more narrowly. Such an ordinance was challenged successfully in *Moore v. City of East Cleveland*, a case that forced the Court to confront a variety of constitutional issues that would later prove significant in cases implicating a host of liberty interests.

Inez Moore owned a two and one-half story house in the small suburb of East Cleveland, Ohio, population roughly 40,000. Her house was divided into two apartments. In one lived Mrs. Moore with her son and two grandsons, Dale and John. Dale was the son of her resident son. John, the offspring of Mrs. Moore's other son, had come to live in the house at the age of one when his mother died and his father felt incapable of caring for him. The two grandsons of Mrs. Moore developed a quasi-sibling relationship, and Mrs. Moore served as a maternal figure for both young boys.

In 1973, when John was about 7 years old, a city housing inspector making a routine inspection issued a violation notice to Mrs. Moore. It seemed that under East Cleveland's single-family zoning law, a homeowner was restricted from living with grandchildren who were offspring of more than one of the homeowner's children. Either Dale and his father would have to leave, or John would have to leave. Mrs. Moore protested the notice and refused to move John out of her home. Contending that she had a constitutional right to live with any member of her family, she refused to apply for a variance and defied the city housing department. The city then filed criminal charges against her. Mrs. Moore moved to dismiss the charges, claiming that a restriction against her living with both of her grandsons in her own home violated her constitutional rights. The trial judge overruled her motion and convicted her, sentencing her to five days in jail and a $25 fine, as well as an order to remove John from the house. Mrs. Moore appealed to the Ohio Court of Appeals, which affirmed the conviction on the authority of the recently decided *Belle Terre* case in an unpublished memorandum. The Ohio Supreme Court refused to review this decision, and Mrs. Moore appealed to the U.S. Supreme Court, which granted review and heard oral argument on November 2, 1976, from Moore's attorney, Edward R. Stege, Jr., of Cleveland, and the city's attorney, Leonard Young, also of Cleveland.

The Court was sharply divided about the proper disposition of the case, as reflected in its 5–4 vote and the multiplicity of decisions filed by the Justices. Writing for a plurality of the Court, Justice Lewis F. Powell, Jr., held that the East Cleveland zoning ordinance's definition of "single family" violated the Due Process Clause because it invaded the sanctity of family life without any substantial justification. While joining the plurality opinion, Justice William J. Brennan, Jr., wrote separately for himself and Justice Thurgood Marshall to emphasize how East Cleveland's zoning ordinance ignored the reality of family diversity in America by adopting an excessively narrow view of "the family." Justice John Paul Stevens, concurring, believed that the decision was more properly rooted in Mrs. Moore's rights, as a property owner, to determine who would reside on her property. Chief Justice Warren E. Burger filed a lengthy dissent, arguing that Mrs. Moore's failure to apply for a zoning variance under existing East Cleveland procedures should lead the Court to exercise discretion not to assert jurisdiction to decide Mrs. Moore's constitutional claims; he would hold that in such disputes the individual citizen should be required to exhaust available administrative remedies. Justice Potter Stewart, joined by Justice William H. Rehnquist, argued in dissent that the Court had failed to apply the *Belle Terre* decision properly; having determined that local governments had the power to impose single-family zoning restrictions on residential

homeowners, he would give those governments wide latitude to define the concept of "single family" in accord with their local interests. Finally, Justice Byron R. White, using language he would re-use in numerous dissenting and majority opinions on the subject of substantive due process, cautioned against the wanton recognition of new rights under the Due Process Clause and argued that this regulation, which he described as "commercial," be given the full deference normally accorded commercial regulations, since he doubted that the right of a grandmother to live with her grandchildren carried much weight.

Justice Powell's opinion for the plurality particularly emphasized the long American tradition of the extended residential family, in which several related generations would live together, providing mutual support and nurturance. For him, the factor that set this case apart from *Belle Terre* was that the Belle Terre zoning ordinance affected only unrelated individuals, allowing all those related by blood, adoption, or marriage to live together. "East Cleveland, in contrast, has chosen to regulate the occupancy of its housing by slicing deeply into the family itself," he observed. "This is no mere incidental result of the ordinance. On its face it selects certain categories of relatives who may live together and declares that others may not. In particular, it makes a crime of a grandmother's choice to live with her grandson in circumstances like those presented here."

Under the circumstances, Powell believed that neither *Belle Terre* nor *Euclid* provided the appropriate standard of judicial review, for he saw the right of family members to live together coming within the "privacy" realm protecting choice in marriage, reproduction, and other aspects of family life, characterized by the Court in many cases as "fundamental rights" that could not be abridged without a showing of compelling state interest. He asserted that "when the government intrudes on choices concerning family living arrangements, this Court must examine carefully the importance of the governmental interests advanced and the extent to which they are served by the challenged regulation." East Cleveland flunked this test, he concluded, because it could not show how excluding particular relatives from residing in Mrs.

Moore's home served any of the interests generally advanced in support of single-family zoning ordinances. While he conceded that the goals of "preventing overcrowding, minimizing traffic and parking congestion, and avoiding an undue financial burden on East Cleveland's school system" were all "legitimate," he could not see how the definition of "single family" in the zoning ordinance served them more than "marginally." A homeowner could live with six teen-age children, all licensed drivers, while Mrs. Moore could not live with her son and two young grandchildren (two licensed drivers at most). If her son had two sons, rather than a son and a nephew, living with her, they could both attend the city schools. Drawing the distinctions that East Cleveland drew seemed to do little to serve the interests it had identified as justifying the ordinance.

When the city sought to distinguish most of the prior family privacy cases by arguing that they had nothing to do with the rights of grandparents, Powell drew on his understanding of due process derived from the late Justice John Marshall Harlan's influential dissenting opinion in *Poe v. Ullman* (1961) describing the substantive scope of the concept of "liberty" under the Due Process Clause as bearing an important relation to the "traditions" of American life. In arguing that the power of judges to give substantive content to the Due Process Clause was not totally unguided or unrestricted, Harlan had asserted that the conscientious judge was seeking a "balance" based in history:

> The balance of which I speak is the balance struck by this country, having regard to what history teaches are the traditions from which it developed as well as the traditions from which it broke. That tradition is a living thing. A decision of this Court which radically departs from it could not long survive, while a decision which builds on what has survived is likely to be sound. No formula could serve as a substitute, in this area, for judgment and restraint.

Powell noted, in illustration of this point, that many substantive due process decisions of the first third of the century dealing with commercial regulation had been overturned, but that those dealing with the sanctity of family life had survived as precedents, particularly citing *Meyer v. Nebraska* (1923) and *Pierce v. Society of*

Sisters (1925), cases in which the Court held that the Due Process Clause protected the rights of parents to make fundamental choices about the education and raising of their children. Both *Meyer* and *Pierce* were frequently cited by the Court as part of the precedential foundation for the individual rights revolution of post-World War II jurisprudence, and had been cited particularly by Justice Harlan in his *Poe* dissent and Justice William O. Douglas in his opinion for the Court in *Griswold v. Connecticut*, the 1965 decision generally recognized as the fountainhead of modern family privacy law.

Now, said Powell, it was well established that long-held traditions of American life should be consulted in giving substantive content to the guarantee of liberty in the Fourteenth Amendment, and that American tradition included a "traditional" family that went beyond the confines of the nuclear family. "The tradition of uncles, aunts, cousins, and especially grandparents sharing a household along with parents and children has roots equally venerable and equally deserving of constitutional recognition," he asserted. "Out of choice, necessity, or a sense of family responsibility, it has been common for close relatives to draw together and participate in the duties and the satisfactions of a common home." Indeed, this case illustrated the phenomenon of family closeness in times of trouble. John Moore's wife died when their infant son was one year old, and Inez Moore took in young John Jr. in this familial crisis. Powell asked: What could be more traditional than that?

> Whether or not such a household is established because of personal tragedy, the choice of relatives in this degree of kinship to live together may not lightly be denied by the State. *Pierce* struck down an Oregon law requiring all children to attend the State's public schools, holding that the Constitution "excludes any general power of the State to standardize its children by forcing them to accept instruction from public teachers only." By the same token the Constitution prevents East Cleveland from standardizing its children—and its adults—by forcing all to live in certain narrowly defined family patterns.

In his concurring opinion, Justice Brennan immediately picked up on Justice Powell's theme, emphasizing that not only were extended, nonnuclear family living arrangements quite traditional, but that they continued to make up a substantial proportion of the American population, and particularly poor and minority populations in the nation's overcrowded cities. He characterized the prescribed single-family limits of East Cleveland as reflecting a white, middle-class suburban view of life, and insisted that a municipality could not adopt that culturally and economically defined standard and try to impose it on all its residents. While agreeing with Powell's decision in full, Brennan wrote separately "to underscore the cultural myopia of the arbitrary boundary drawn by the East Cleveland ordinance in the light of the tradition of the American home that has been a feature of our society since our beginning as a Nation . . . ." Reciting statistics showing how black and white households were substantially differently constituted in ways that would result in significant unfairness were the East Cleveland model to be widely adopted, Brennan argued:

> [T]he prominence of other than nuclear families among ethnic and racial minority groups, including our black citizens, surely demonstrates that the "extended family" pattern remains a vital tenet of our society. It suffices that in prohibiting this pattern of family living as a means of achieving its objectives, appellee city has chosen a device that deeply intrudes into family associational rights that historically have been central, and today remain central, to a large proportion of our population.

Justice Brennan also addressed the variance issue, arguing that "the matter of a variance is irrelevant also because the municipality is constitutionally powerless to abridge, as East Cleveland has done, the freedom of personal choice of related members of a family to live together." The existence of the variance procedure did not make the ordinance any less irrational along the lines Justice Powell had identified, and gave local authorities all too much discretion to decide which nonnuclear families they would permit to live in East Cleveland. Such a procedure was subject to altogether too much discretion when it came to issues so important as the right to select one's living companions. "We have now passed well beyond the day when illusory escape hatches could justify the imposition of

burdens on fundamental rights," Brennan asserted.

Justice Stevens joined in striking down East Cleveland's definition of "single family," but on an entirely different ground. For him, it was unnecessary to wander into the quagmire of substantive due process that had so divided the rest of the Court. Better to focus on the rights of property owners and the very tests established in the *Euclid* and *Belle Terre* cases. Turning to the *Euclid* case, he noted that the Court had held that a zoning ordinance could be declared unconstitutional if it was shown that it had "no substantial relation to the public health, safety, morals, or general welfare." Stevens argued that the particular restriction that was applied to Inez Moore failed to meet even this lenient test.

While the Supreme Court had not had much occasion to deal with the single-family zoning issue apart from *Belle Terre*, the highest courts of many states had grappled with the issue, and had been almost unanimous in holding that "attempts to limit occupancy to related persons" were unconstitutional. While recognizing "a valid community interest in preserving the stable character of residential neighborhoods" as justifying "a prohibition against transient occupancy," the courts of many states, "in well-reasoned opinions," had "permitted unrelated persons to occupy single-family residences notwithstanding an ordinance prohibiting, either expressly or implicitly, such occupancy." And, of course, even the Belle Terre ordinance upheld by the Court permitted up to three unrelated persons to live together in a single-family zone. It was clear that the legitimate concern of local governments was with the issues of transience and population density, and that these issues did not necessarily correlate with the degrees of relatedness of housing occupants. Said Stevens:

> There appears to be no precedent for an ordinance which excludes any of an owner's relatives from the group of persons who may occupy his residence on a permanent basis. Nor does there appear to be any justification for such a restriction on an owner's use of his property. The city has failed totally to explain the need for a rule which would allow a homeowner to have two grandchildren live

with her if they are brothers, but not if they are cousins. Since this ordinance has not been shown to have any "substantial relation to the public health, safety, morals, or general welfare" of the city of East Cleveland, and since it cuts so deeply into a fundamental right normally associated with the ownership of residential property—that of an owner to decide who may reside on his or her property—it must fall under the limited standard of review of zoning decisions which this Court preserved in *Euclid*. . . . Under that standard, East Cleveland's unprecedented ordinance constitutes a taking of property without due process and without just compensation.

Chief Justice Burger's dissent is of little substantive interest for this discussion, since it focuses entirely on the issue of the availability of the variance as a basis of avoiding deciding the case on the merits. Justice Stewart, however, provides a provocative argument against the plurality's approach, arguing that the *Belle Terre* decision stood for a much broader proposition than either Powell or Brennan would acknowledge. Noting that the Court in *Belle Terre* had asserted that the right of individuals to live together was not a fundamental right under the Due Process Clause, Stewart argued that the *Belle Terre* decision "thus disposes of the appellant's contentions to the extent they focus not on her blood relationships with her sons and grandsons but on more general notions about the 'privacy of the home,'" notions that Justice Powell had invoked by citing *Meyer* and *Pierce* as principal authorities for the plurality's holding.

Furthermore, he rejected the argument that the result should be any different because of Mrs. Moore's blood relation to John, Jr. "To suggest that the biological fact of common ancestry necessarily gives related persons constitutional rights of association superior to those of unrelated persons is to misunderstand the nature of the associational freedoms that the Constitution has been understood to protect," Stewart argued, embracing a view of associational rights premised on concerns about ideological freedom rather than family ties. Neither would Stewart credit the claim that the Court's "family" decisions compelled a conclusion that a grandmother had a fundamental right to live with her grandchildren, arguing that none of the long line of cases cited by Powell on

family rights could be "equated" with this situation. Stewart contended that the Court had recognized only fundamental rights that were "implicit in the concept of ordered liberty," and that "the interest that the appellant may have in permanently sharing a single kitchen and a suite of contiguous rooms with some of her relatives simply does not rise to that level. To equate this interest with the fundamental decisions to marry and to bear and raise children," insisted Stewart, "is to extend the limited substantive contours of the Due Process Clause beyond recognition." Stewart's argument had disturbing implications; what if a state decided to prohibit children over the age of 21 from living with their parents in order to prevent "undue density" in a family residential neighborhood?

Stewart also rejected the contention that the ordinance violated the Equal Protection Clause, which Powell refrained from addressing since he was invalidating the statute under due process. Characterizing a residential zoning ordinance as "economic and social legislation" of the type that merited great judicial deference to legislative judgments, he argued that the ordinance must be upheld if it bears a rational relationship to a permissible state objective. In *Belle Terre*, the Court had held that a local government could legitimately seek to preserve the residential, low-density character of a neighborhood by adopting restrictions on residential occupancy. Given this precedent, Stewart found that the East Cleveland ordinance did not lack rationality. "Obviously, East Cleveland might have as easily and perhaps as effectively hit upon a different definition of 'family.' But a line could hardly be drawn that would not sooner or later become the target of a challenge like the appellant's." Consequently, since a line had to be drawn somewhere if the city was to achieve its objective, and any definition would produce some "hardship" in a particular case, the Court should allow the city to draw the line, "unless we are to use our power to interpret the United States Constitution as a sort of generalized authority to correct seeming inequity wherever it surfaces." In this case, said Stewart, he saw no warrant for the Court to second-guess the city or the local prosecutor over where to draw the line or when to enforce the ordinance. Finally, the existence of a variance provision struck Stewart as further demonstration of the reasonableness of the ordinance overall. The city recognized that hardships could occur and provided a mechanism for those suffering hardships to receive permission to house persons who fell outside the definition. More could not be asked, in his view.

Justice White, an ardent foe of substantive due process, used the occasion of his dissent to state many views he would carry verbatim into other opinions, both dissenting and for the Court, on a range of issues. In language identical to his majority opinion for the Court in *Bowers v. Hardwick* (1986), a decision sustaining the constitutionality of a state sodomy law, White cautioned against identifying new "rights" in the Due Process Clause, asserting that the Court's legitimacy was most questionable when it purported to identify rights that could not be fairly derived from the actual language of the Constitution. While he was willing to concede that the concept of "liberty" in the Fourteenth Amendment would surely extend to an individual's selection of living companions, he was not willing to label that liberty as "fundamental," thus subjecting it to demanding judicial review.

Like Justice Stewart, White was dismissive of the notion that the right to live with one's grandchild was "implicit in the concept of ordered liberty." He also rejected Justice Powell's contention that the country's traditions could serve as an appropriate source of identifying fundamental rights. "What the deeply rooted traditions of the country are is arguable," he insisted, and "which of them deserve the protection of the Due Process Clause is even more debatable."

> The suggested view would broaden enormously the horizons of the Clause; and, if the interest involved here is any measure of what the States would be forbidden to regulate, the courts would be substantively weighing and very likely invalidating a wide range of measures that Congress and state legislatures think appropriate to respond to a changing economic and social order.

In other words, tradition could be a dead hand on the ability of the government to respond to a changing world. Interestingly, Justice White used almost exactly the opposite argument in

sustaining the sodomy law in *Bowers v. Hardwick*, where he rested his decision largely on the "tradition" branch of fundamental rights jurisprudence, paying little attention to the argument that the private choice of sexual partners by consenting adults might be "implicit in the concept of ordered liberty" despite a long history of outlawing such behavior.

White just did not see that the East Cleveland ordinance imposed such an onerous restriction as to rise to levels of constitutional import. He pointed out that East Cleveland was a relatively small suburb; its restrictive language was not necessarily embraced by other suburbs of Cleveland, so Mrs. Moore could move if she wanted to live with both of her grandchildren.

> If there is power to maintain the character of a single-family neighborhood, as there surely is, some limit must be placed on the reach of the 'family.' Had it been our task to legislate, we might have approached the problem in a different manner than did the drafters of this ordinance; but I have no trouble in concluding that the normal goals of zoning regulation are present here and that the ordinance serves these goals by limiting, in identifiable circumstances, the number of people who can occupy a single household.

Furthermore, since no fundamental interest was involved, Justice White would also evaluate the ordinance under the limited rationality test for purposes of equal protection, and reach the same result.

The Court's decision in *Moore v. East Cleveland*, whether premised on Justice Powell's view of the sanctity of family living arrangements under the Due Process Clause's protection of liberty or under Justice Stevens' view of the rights of an owner of residential property to decide who can live there, marked an important departure from the existing precedents on family privacy, in that it recognized constitutional protection extending beyond the narrow issues of nuclear family life (the husband and wife or parent and child relation) to recognize that other forms of family life play fundamental roles in American society deserving of protection from irrational governmental restrictions. Whether the concept of this case can be extended to unrelated persons, of either sex, who seek to live together in sexual relationships in residential neighborhoods, has not yet been faced by the Supreme Court, since the Belle Terre ordinance upheld by the Court allowed up to three unrelated persons to live together. What would the Court say to a case brought by cohabiting homosexuals or heterosexuals fighting such a restriction? If Justice Stevens prevailed in the argument, the Court might hold that the owner of occupancy rights in residential property has a right to select a living companion regardless of biological or marital relation, and that the government's only legitimate concern is with issues of transience and population density. But Justice Stevens was a lone voice in *Moore*, and the constituents of the plurality have been much diminished by changes on the Court calculated to undermine support for a broad reading of the constitutional right of privacy on which Justice Powell's opinion relied.

Case References

Bowers v. Hardwick, 478 U.S. 186 (1986)
Euclid v. Ambler Realty Co., 272 U.S. 365 (1926)
Griswold v. Connecticut, 381 U.S. 479 (1965)
Meyer v. Nebraska, 262 U.S. 390 (1923)
Pierce v. Society of Sisters, 268 U.S. 510 (1925)
Poe v. Ullman, 367 U.S. 497 (1961)
Village of Belle Terre v. Boraas, 416 U.S. 1 (1974)

54. VISITATION WITH LOVER PRESENT?

DiStefano v. DiStefano, 60 App. Div. 2d 976, 401 N.Y.S.2d 636 (4th Dept. 1978); earlier decision, 51 App. Div. 2d 885, 380 N.Y.S.2d 394 (4th Dept. 1976). *Gottlieb v. Gottlieb*, 108 App. Div. 2d 120, 488 N.Y.S.2d 180 (1st Dept. 1985).

Divorces sparked by the homosexuality of a wife or a husband can lead to bitter disputes about the custody of the children, with the parties trading allegations about what will be in the best interest of the children. The nongay spouse, bitter about the "alienation of affections" he or she believes has been encouraged by the gay spouse's sexual partner, can usually find a psychiatric expert to testify that the gay spouse's sexual partner will have an adverse effect on the welfare of the children, justifying vesting sole custody in the nongay spouse, even in circumstances where the court finds no basis for holding that the gay spouse is unfit to be a custodian for the children. Sometimes, courts are even persuaded that the gay spouse's rights to visitation with the children should be specially limited to exclude the gay spouse's sexual partners from contact with the children—a limitation that can put an enormous strain on the gay spouse's relationship with his or her partner. Two significant New York appellate rulings, spaced a decade apart, addressed this sort of limitation.

James and Maureen DiStefano were married in 1964 and had three children together. Maureen developed a sexual relationship with Nancy Wilson, which led to the breakup of her marriage with James. They signed a separation agreement in 1973, later incorporated into the divorce decree of January 25, 1974, which provided for joint custody of the children. This agreement rapidly broke down, and James filed suit on May 15, 1974, in New York State Supreme Court, Erie County, seeking sole custody and exclusion of Nancy Wilson from any contact with his children. James claimed that Wilson had made repeated efforts to alienate the children from their father. Attorney David J. Kulick, of Buffalo, New York, represented James, and Paul I. Birzon, of Buffalo, represented Maureen. The supreme court referred the case to the Erie County Family Court for hearing before Judge J. Douglas Trost.

At the hearing, Trost heard testimony by James and Maureen, as well as several clergymen, two psychiatrists, two psychologists, an anthropologist, a probation officer, and a psychiatric social worker. Nancy Wilson was not called as a witness. With the consent of the parties, Trost had ordered an investigation by the Probation Division of the Family Court and psychiatric evaluations by the Family Court Clinic. After considering all the evidence and reports, he decided to grant sole custody to James and limited visitation for Maureen, excluding Wilson from contact with the children. Trost's unpublished opinion did not make any mention of the contents of the probation report or psychiatric evaluations, which evidently had not been shown to the attorneys for the parties and were not subject to any questioning or examination during the hearing.

Maureen appealed to the Appellate Division, Fourth Department, which concluded that the record was incomplete, since there was nothing in the record to indicate that Trost had received or acted on the probation and psychiatric reports. Assuming that Trost had relied on these reports, the appeals court felt that it would be inappropriate for it to rule on the merits, since this would involve deciding the case "on the basis of different factors from those which the trial court had before it." Thus, it was necessary to remand the case, with orders that the reports relied on be made the subject of a further hearing in which the parties would have an opportunity to challenge their accuracy and examine those who had prepared them. The court's *per curiam* opinion of February 24, 1976, stressed that this was especially important where, as here, "respondent is an admitted lesbian actively engaged in an intimate relationship with another of the female sex."

Trost reopened the case for further hearing on the reports and issued a new order confirming custody for James and specifying that Maureen would have visitation rights at her home from 10 A.M. each Saturday until 7 P.M. each Sunday, conditioned on the exclusion from her home of Nancy Wilson during these visitation periods. Maureen objected that the custody award and the limitations on visitation violated her constitutional rights of due process, equal protection, and sexual privacy, but on further appeal, the appellate division made light of these constitutional arguments. In its *per curiam* opinion of January 20, 1978, the court asserted that no constitutional issue was presented for review. "Although she is an admitted practicing homosexual," said the court, "the trial court found that homosexuality, per se, did not render her unfit as a parent. The court made no effort to restrict her preferred sexual activity, although deviate sexual intercourse remains

a crime in this state and similar statutes have been held to be free of constitutional infirmity." (It was not until 1980 that New York's highest court declared the state's law against consensual sodomy unconstitutional.)

Turning to the merits, the court said that "while the sexual life style of a parent may properly be considered in determining what is best for the children, its consideration must be limited to its present or reasonably predictable effect upon the children's welfare." In reviewing the trial court's decision, the appeals court's role was rather limited, since it was the trial court that had seen the witnesses, evaluated their credibility, and most importantly in a custody and visitation dispute, been in a position to form a personal impression of the parties. Consequently, the appeals court would only modify or overturn the trial court's decision if it found no support in the official record of the proceeding.

After noting the large body of expert professional testimony considered by the judge, little of which was explicitly recounted in Trost's unpublished opinion and order, the court concluded that Trost's decision "reasonably may be read to conclude that the wife's conduct in failing to keep her lesbian relationship with Nancy Wilson separate from her role as a mother has had, and predictably will have, a detrimental effect upon the children. That conclusion is amply supported in the record." Unfortunately, the court said nothing further about what there was in the record that specifically supported these conclusions, but appeared to find them sufficient to deny sole or joint custody to Maureen.

That the testifying experts consisted of pairs of psychiatrists and psychologists suggests that each party brought its expert in each discipline, that the experts gave conflicting opinions about the likely impact on the children of allowing further contact with Nancy Wilson, and that Trost chose to believe the husband's experts. The court's opinion does not reveal the identity of the experts, but it is well known that there are a handful of experts who tended to show up on either side of lesbian or gay parent custody and visitation cases, and who predictably gave their long-held opinions. At that time, objective research on the psychological impact on children of being raised by a lesbian or gay parent was just beginning to be published, but these "expert" opinions appeared to be based largely on theory, or, in the case of practicing psychologists and psychiatrists, theory flavored by the individual cases in which they had served as practitioners. Unfortunately, the appellate opinion gives nothing of the flavor of this testimony, although it does indicate that there was testimony from which Trost could conclude that Wilson "made repeated efforts to alienate the children from their father," thus supporting the exclusion of Wilson from further contact with them.

The court did, however, agree with Maureen that her visitation rights had been unduly restricted. "It appears that aside from the effect upon the children of the life style of the wife in her relationship with Nancy Wilson, she is otherwise a fit parent," said the court, which decided to amend the visitation award "to provide that the wife shall have no visitation rights during the month of August each year, but shall have full visitation with the children during the entire month of July each year, not limited to her own home, but conditioned upon the total exclusion of Nancy Wilson from any contact with the wife and children during such visitation." Thus, Maureen could have the children for a solid month each summer, but the price for this precious continuity in maintaining her relationship with her children was that she had to be separated from her lover for an entire month, a circumstance that could predictably cause a severe strain on that relationship.

A decade later, the tables were turned when a New York court considered the case of a marriage that collapsed when the husband turned out to be gay. Richard and Linda Gottlieb lived together with their young daughter in a house they had purchased in Manhattan. Richard began to feel stirrings of discomfort with his sexual situation, and placed a "personal" classified advertisement in the *Village Voice*, a weekly newspaper, seeking a male sex partner. He incautiously put his home telephone number in the advertisement and kept correspondence with those who replied to his advertisement in a desk drawer at home. His wife became suspicious that something was awry when calls began to come in and had her suspicions confirmed when she discovered some of the correspondence.

The subsequent divorce proceedings that Linda initiated were quite bitter. As the litigation dragged on, Richard acquired a lover who moved in with him. Their Manhattan building had several apartments; Richard and his lover lived in one, Linda and their daughter in another on a different floor. The daughter began to develop a friendly relationship with Richard's partner and his partner's family members, which was suddenly threatened when New York Supreme Court Justice Henry R. Williams ruled that Linda should have sole custody, with Richard's visitation rights limited to alternate weekends. The decision conditioned Richard's visitation rights on "the total exclusion of his lover or any other homosexuals during such visitation periods" and provided that "the child will not be taken to any place where known homosexuals are present nor will defendant involve the child in any homosexual activities or publicity." This last restriction was responsive to Richard's burgeoning activities as a gay rights spokesperson in the press, in part stimulated by this litigation, and his active participation in a gay fathers group that included social events involving the fathers and their children. Justice Williams retired while the case was pending, but Justice Hortense Gabel, to whom the case was reassigned, rejected Richard's objections to the decision and entered an order embodying Williams's custody award and visitation restrictions.

Richard appealed to the Appellate Division, First Department, which heard argument from New York City attorney Iris Darvin on his behalf, and Rita Warner representing Linda. A joint *amicus* brief from the Lambda Legal Defense and Education Fund and the National Organization for Women (NOW) Legal Defense and Education Fund was submitted to the court, supporting Richard's contention that the custody and visitation determinations were inappropriate. Richard argued that his wife's sexual affairs themselves created ongoing problems for his daughter, and that he should be granted either joint or sole custody. He also contended that the restrictions on the presence of his lover were not in his daughter's best interests, and that the last restriction, regarding "homosexual activities or publicity" was unnecessary. Indeed, participation in the gay fathers group could have a beneficial effect for his daughter in adjusting to the situation by bringing her into contact with other children of gay dads and sharing experiences with them.

The appeals panel was sharply divided over the last restriction in its decision of April 30, 1985, although it unanimously agreed to confirm the award of custody to Linda without any substantive discussion in the opinions issued by the justices, and to strike down the exclusion of Richard's lover from being present during visitation with the daughter. In his opinion for the majority of the five-member panel, Justice Arnold L. Fein rejected the dissent's objection that this restriction had an unnecessary "unpleasant connotation." "The crucial criterion to be applied," said Fein, "is not a critique of the morality of defendant's lifestyle, but what is best for the child's welfare."

> Plainly this seven year old child should not be involved in homosexual activities or publicity. So long as the defendant acts with discretion and the child is not in any way involved in or exposed to defendant's sexual conduct, this restriction should present no problem, in what the dissent characterizes as a "close" case. The evidence in the record was sufficient to sustain this limited restriction imposed by the trial court. It would serve no useful purpose to outline the evidence here. It is more than adequate to indicate the possibility that the child might be involved in "homosexual activities or publicity."

Justice Leonard H. Sandler's dissent, joined by Justice John Carro, had suggested that this restriction was not appropriate in the absence of a parallel restriction on Linda. Fein rejected this approach. "The appropriate guide is set forth in *Guinan v. Guinan*," a 1984 ruling by the Appellate Division, Third Department, on a father's demand for change of custody, alleging that his wife had "engaged in homosexual relations with other women during the marriage, at times in the presence of the children," an allegation she firmly denied. In that case, the court had stated: "Sexual conduct between a parent and a stranger to the marriage, whether homosexual or heterosexual, which takes place in the presence of the children of the marriage can certainly be held to have an adverse effect on the children." Without further discussion, Fein indicated that the record did not support any restriction on Linda but did support the restriction on Richard, presumably because the record showed Richard was engaged in a sexual relationship. Was he indicating that he considered it likely that Richard, now settled in an established relationship of several years duration with his lover, might expose his daughter to a succession of transient relationships in the future? Or that he considered Richard's relationship with his lover to be a negative factor, as compared with any relationships Linda might have in the future with men?

Presiding Justice Theodore R. Kupferman concurred, explaining the rationale for dropping the restriction on the presence of Richard's lover during visitation: "Inasmuch as the parties live in the same building, albeit on different floors, the daughter must be fully conversant with the fact that her father has a live-in male lover, and that excluding the lover as a condition of visitation serves no real purpose other than as a punitive measure against the father." As to the restriction on exposing the child to "homosexual activities or publicity," said Kupferman, "[t]he father having advertised in the *Village Voice* for a homosexual relationship, there can be no gainsaying the fact that he may very well be involved in other homosexual activities. It is not proper to subject this child to that possibility. It is one thing for a girl of this tender age to know of her father's proclivities, and even to adjust to it, it is quite another thing to be part of it." Finally, Kupferman suggested that despite the signature of NOW Legal Defense Fund on the *amicus* brief in support of Richard, he doubted that the majority of NOW's members would object to this restriction.

Justice Bentley Kassal's brief concurring opinion came the closest to identifying with some frankness the reason why the majority favored keeping the restriction:

> The father has demonstrated by his past conduct that his sense of values and discretion in regard to his daughter is questionable. It cannot be disputed that a child's sexual maturation and sense of sexual security must be safeguarded so that the child will have a proper identification as to what the parents' role model should be.

The child should not be subjected to experiences which will unduly complicate or distort her understanding of her relationship to her parents and others. This applies equally to heterosexual or homosexual activity. She should not be involved in or exposed to any sexual conduct which might affect her emotionally.

Now things were out in the open, but the reasoning does not inspire confidence that the justices in the majority had any real notion of what the case was about or what the real issues confronting Richard Gottlieb's daughter were, or about the competence of the legal system to resolve these sorts of disputes in a way helpful to the future well-being of all concerned. That Gottlieb had placed a personals advertisement during his confused period of trying to come to terms with his homosexuality and, inexperienced in such things, had given out his home telephone number and kept correspondence at home, said little about how he was conducting his life by the time of the appellate consideration of the case. Further, the effective ban on involving his daughter in the gay fathers group activities with other children was likely to deprive her of one of the best ways of making a satisfactory adjustment to the fact that her father was a gay man living in a relationship with another gay man. It was in the daughter's psychological interest to come to understand her father's lifestyle, not to be shielded from it.

This was the implicit message of Sandler's dissent, although, as with most of the other justices, his opinion is frustratingly opaque.

> It of course goes without saying that a small child should not be involved in sexual activities or publicity of any character, homosexual or heterosexual. We are unable to discern from the record a basis for the assumption that the defendant would expose his child to such inappropriate activities sufficient to justify such a direction. We acknowledge that it was poor judgment for defendant to advertise for a male companion during the last stages of his cohabitation with plaintiff as husband and wife, leaving the apartment phone number as one to be called. This questionable action must be measured against the record as a whole, which is convincing that the defendant

is an intelligent, responsible person, devoted to his child, who would not expose her to inappropriate, destructive behavior. The same, of course, is equally true of the plaintiff wife.

While conceding that it might be a "close" issue whether the appeals court should set aside the trial judge's restriction on the basis of the record, Sandler called for some realism on the part of the court:

> Nonetheless, given the central reality that we are considering an issue between two worthwhile, responsible, moral people, one of them a homosexual and the other a heterosexual, the unpleasant connotation inherent in the special restriction on one and not on the other seems to us sufficient to justify our deleting this particular restriction precisely as we have all agreed to strike the other restrictions.

The opinions by the justices in the majority indicated a discomfort with and ignorance about homosexual relationships and their impact on the children of gay people that were surprising, given the array of professional authority marshalled in the briefs by Gottlieb's attorney and Lambda and NOW. While the case may have been complicated by their perceptions of Richard's behavior during his initial period of sexual exploration, the question before the court concerned the present and the future, not the past, and having settled down into a stable relationship, it seemed unlikely that Richard's future conduct would bear any resemblance to the past, crediting him at least with the capacity to learn from his past mistakes. While the court took a progressive step in striking down the restriction on the presence of Richard's lover (who testified at the trial hearing) during visitation with the daughter, its retention of the prejudicial and insulting restriction regarding "homosexual activity and publicity" revealed the sort of biases gay parents have come to expect from a largely uncomprehending judicial system.

Case Reference

Guinan v. Guinan, 102 App. Div. 2d 963, 477 N.Y.S.2d 830 (3d Dept. 1984)

55. MERGING LESBIAN HOUSEHOLDS?

Schuster v. Schuster, 90 Wash. 2d 626, 585 P.2d 130 (1978).

Perhaps the most celebrated lesbian child custody dispute of the 1970s was that between Sandra Lee Schuster and Madeleine Cecil Isaacson and their ex-husbands, James and Jerry. Neither woman began as a gay rights activist, but their frustrations with the judicial system led them to active media work, culminating in their joint appearance with their children in the documentary film *Word Is Out* while their case was still pending in the courts of the state of Washington. Although each woman had been able to retain custody of her children, they were thwarted by the courts and their ex-husbands' opposition from merging the two households under one roof.

Each of the women had children from their marriages. Good friends as housewives, they gradually fell in love with each other and out of love with their husbands. They separated from their husbands and moved in together with their children, creating one big household in which all the children considered themselves siblings and each woman shared parenting roles for all the children. Each woman was granted custody of her own children during divorce proceedings, but the court ordered the women to live separate and apart from each other, finding that the mothers living together in a lesbian relationship created an unsuitable environment for raising their children. The court also ordered the women not to take their children out of state. Desperate to stay together and not to break up the joint family they had created, the two women rented separate apartments in the same building and continued, in effect, to maintain a common household.

The two husbands then filed a petition seeking modification of the original custody decrees, alleging that the mothers' new living arrangements violated the original decree and that they had violated the court's order by taking the children out of state in connection with a speaking engagement in San Francisco. The fathers moved that the mothers be held in contempt for their alleged violations of the decrees. The

mothers filed counter-petitions seeking an end to the restrictions in the original custody decrees. By this time, the mothers had begun to publicize the case, emphasizing the unnecessary expense to which they were subjected by having to rent two apartments and maintain two households where, in their opinion, one would do.

The modification petitions were consolidated in one proceeding before King County Superior Court Judge Norman Ackley. The husbands hired a team of lawyers from Seattle, the Washington State branch of the American Civil Liberties Union (ACLU) provided representation to the mothers, and the court appointed a guardian *ad litem* to represent the interests of the children. The upshot of the hearing before Judge Ackley was a complete victory for the mothers. Ackley found that the restrictions were no longer necessary; so long as the mothers were in effect maintaining one household and it was working out, he saw no need to impose the financial burden of renting two separate apartments. He also saw no reason to impose a contempt finding on the mothers.

The fathers appealed to the Washington Supreme Court, which heard the case *en banc* and was sharply split over how to handle it. The judges split three ways in the decision issued October 5, 1978. A plurality of the court agreed with Ackley that the original custody awards should not be modified, but believed that sufficient changed circumstances had not been shown to justify modifying the original custody decrees in any way. When their votes were added to those of three dissenting judges who favored overturning the original custody decrees and awarding custody to the now-remarried fathers, the result was a reversal of Ackley's decision to remove the restrictions. However, two members of the court believed Ackley's decision was justified in all respects, and their votes ensured that the mothers would at least retain custody, albeit with the original restrictions intact.

The plurality opinion by Justice Robert F. Brachtenbach took the view that the original decree should not have been modified because neither the mothers nor the fathers had demonstrated the kind of change in circumstances that was necessary to modify a custody decree. "We have long held that a modification will not be granted unless there has been a subsequent substantial change in circumstances which requires a modification of custody in the best interests of the child," he asserted. The policy behind this rule, which he deemed "obvious," was to avoid instability in children's lives that would arise from relitigation of their custody upon every minor change in circumstances. Under this rule, he said, "the fathers must lose their modification decrees." They had relied, at least in part, on their own remarriages as a change of circumstances now rendering their households superior for raising the children. This was essentially irrelevant in Brachtenbach's view, however, because the statute governing child custody required "a change in the circumstances of either the child or the custodian, the mothers in this case," not a change involving the noncustodial parent.

Neither did Brachtenbach consider the "changes" in the mothers' living arrangements sufficient to justify removal of the prior restrictions. While the mothers had shown that it would be preferable for them to be able to share one household "both financially and in pursuit of their own relationship," Brachtenbach asserted that this issue had been settled in the original divorce cases, from which the mothers had not directly appealed. Thus, it was to be considered settled under the policy of stability in custody determinations, and the plurality staunchly resisted the temptation posed by *amicus* briefs to delve into constitutional challenges to the original decree at this remove.

Finally, the plurality rejected the attempt by the fathers to use the mothers' alleged violation of the original decrees as a basis of modifying custody. "Punishment of the parent for contempt may not be visited upon the child in custody cases," intoned Brachtenbach. "The custody of a child is not to be used as a reward or punishment for the conduct of the parents," since it is the best interest of the child that is to control.

Justice James M. Dolliver concurred in the decision to leave custody with the mothers, but dissented from the decision to reverse Ackley's order lifting the living restrictions, in an opinion joined by Justice Robert F. Utter. Dolliver argued that the plurality had missed an important point in Ackley's factual findings: there had indeed been a change of circumstances. Ackley found that "since the time of the Divorce Decree the respondents at first lived separate and apart and then moved into adjoining apartments where they in fact lived together as one household and that the living arrangement did not prove to be against the best interests of the children, except it added a financial burden" that would not be there if they could all move together into one apartment or house. Since Ackley had made a finding of changed circumstances, argued Dolliver, "the crucial question . . . is not whether the trial court made a finding of changed circumstances but whether there is evidence in the record to support the findings." Dolliver noted that there was "voluminous testimony" about the living environment for the children, including expert testimony about the functioning of the joint Schuster-Isaacson household. "This development of a family unit and the strengthening of the relationships among the eight family members presents a significant change of circumstances which may appropriately be recognized and was recognized by the trial court in its findings," Dolliver argued.

In addition, Ackley had found that the original living restrictions now posed a financial burden that was detrimental to the children, since extra resources devoted to housing might better be devoted to the children's other needs. Since a trial court should be given "broad discretion" on these sorts of matters, Dolliver argued that it was error for the supreme court to reverse the trial court's decision, given this factual support in the record. While it was true that the changed circumstances resulted from the mothers' decision to defy the original decree, Dolliver agreed with the plurality that the parties should not be "punished" by imposing a contempt citation that would be of no benefit to the children.

Justice Hugh J. Rosellini dissented in a sharply worded opinion that was joined by Chief

Justice Charles T. Wright and Justice Orris L. Hamilton. Rosellini argued that the court's disposition of the case contradicted its recent ruling in *Gaylord v. Tacoma School District No. 10* (1977), in which the court had upheld the dismissal of a high school teacher found "guilty" of "immorality" because of his status of being a "homosexual." According to the court's opinion in that case, a school district would be justified in excluding from the classroom such a person, who would be an unsuitable role model for young children. Rosellini found the *Gaylord* opinion dispositive of the question whether open lesbians should be awarded custody of their children. In his view, the problem was compounded by the women's decision to become activists and involve their children in publicizing their custody dispute in newspaper interviews, television and radio shows, and the documentary movie.

> From such publicizing it can be readily seen that they are not content to pursue their lifestyle but are also using their children for the purpose of advocating and proselytizing that style. I am unable to understand how the court can declare that a school teacher who only admitted to his preference as a homosexual and did not engage in any overt act, is guilty of immorality, and yet, in the instant case, can find perfectly moral the conduct of the respondents.

Rosellini reproduced a lengthy quotation from a then-recent law review article, arguing that the state had a strong interest in maintaining prohibitions on homosexual activity and avoiding any endorsement of such activity as a matter of preserving the traditional structure of society. He also cited some intermediate appellate decisions from other jurisdictions in which similar views had been endorsed in the context of denying custody or limiting visitation rights of gay or lesbian parents. Endorsing these views, Rosellini argued that the change in the fathers' circumstances (i.e., remarriage), justified rethinking the original custody awards.

> In this case the trial court found, in the original trial, that both parents were fit and proper persons to have the custody of the children. The fathers have since remarried and have established good homes. Where should the scales of justice be tipped? In favor of the mothers who are living in a lesbian relationship? Or on the side of the fathers whose lifestyles and relationships are considered normal and moral? On the state of this record, the primary and paramount consideration in awarding the children to a parent is the welfare of the children. I would hold that the mothers are not morally fit to have the custody of the children, and I would award the children to the fathers.

The plurality opinion is so oblique that it is difficult to discern exactly what was going on in the Washington Supreme Court in deciding this case. One has to draw inferences from the concurring and dissenting opinions to form a view about the topics of discussion among the judges. It seems likely that the plurality's refusal to lift the living restrictions may have had something to do with the mothers' activities in publicizing the case, although they would certainly disavow that motivation on the record. Otherwise, the plurality's decision on this point makes little sense, given the explicit findings of changed circumstances by Judge Ackley, documented by direct quotation from Ackley's decree in Dolliver's concurring and dissenting opinion. While in one sense the court's opinion might be said to stand for the proposition that lesbian mothers do not lose custody just because their ex-husbands remarry and form "traditional" heterosexual households, thus rendering them more "attractive" as custodial parents, it may be seen as having a broader significance in light of Rosellini's angry dissent. For the plurality sent a clear message that a custody award, even to (in effect) a lesbian household, is not to be upset without some significant evidence of change *in that household* that is detrimental to the children.

Case Reference

Gaylord v. Tacoma School District No. 10, 88 Wash. 2d 286, 559 P.2d 1340, certiorari denied, 434 U.S. 879 (1977)

56. CHILD CUSTODY AND THE FORNICATING MOTHER

Jarrett v. Jarrett, 78 Ill. 2d 337, 36 Ill. Dec. 1, 400 N.E.2d 421 (1979), reversing 64 Ill. App. 3d 932, 21 Ill. Dec. 718, 382 N.E.2d 12 (1st Dist. 1978), certiorari denied, 449 U.S. 927, rehearing denied, 449 U.S. 1067 (1980).

The U.S. Supreme Court ruled in 1972 in *Stanley v. Illinois* that a state could not impose a conclusive presumption that an unwed father was unfit to have custody of his children after the death of their mother. The case was quickly interpreted by many as standing for the proposition that conclusive presumptions about the unfitness of natural parents to retain custody of their children violated the Due Process Clause of the Fourteenth Amendment. This holding would have important ramifications for the custodial rights of parents whose sex lives deviated from the "straight and narrow," as courts in many states embraced the proposition that the sex lives of parents should be considered in custody disputes only if they directly affected the children in a detrimental way. Of course, even that formulation left plenty of room for a court to deny custody to a parent whose lifestyle was considered to present a danger to the moral welfare of the children, as illustrated in the leading (and much litigated) Illinois case of *Jarrett v. Jarrett*.

On December 6, 1976, Judge Marion E. Burks of Cook County, Illinois, Circuit Court, ended the marriage of Jacqueline and Walter Jarrett on Jacqueline's petition alleging extreme and repeated mental cruelty by Walter. At the time, the couple had three daughters, ages 12, 10, and 7. Judge Burks awarded Jacqueline custody of the children, subject to Walter's right to visitation at reasonable times. They quickly settled into a routine where Jacqueline would take the children to religious school on Saturday mornings, and Walter would pick them up later on Saturday evening to take them to church. The children would sleep over at Walter's home and would be returned to Jacqueline on Sunday evening.

In April 1977, Jacqueline informed Walter that her new boyfriend, Wayne Hammon, would be moving in with her and the girls. Walter, a devout Catholic, protested vocifer- ously, arguing that this would set a terrible moral example for the girls, but Jacqueline disagreed and allowed Wayne to move in. The girls were "not thrilled" with this development, but quickly came to regard Wayne as a parent and friend. He helped transporting them about, paid them allowances out of his own income, and played with them and their friends. Wayne, Jacqueline, and the girls quickly formed a well-functioning household. When Jacqueline first told the girls that Wayne would be moving in, they asked whether she would be getting married to him. Jacqueline said it was too soon after the divorce to consider remarriage. In addition, under the divorce decree she would have to sell the family house and split the proceeds with Walter within six months of any remarriage, and finances were not such that she and Wayne would be able to afford to purchase an appropriate new home for themselves and the girls under the circumstances. Jacqueline explained to the girls that some people, including their father, had moral objections to unmarried adults living together, but that she did not think it was a problem as long as they genuinely loved each other. The girls came to accept the arrangement.

Walter did not, however, and filed suit in the circuit court seeking a change of custody, alleging that the open cohabitation of Jacqueline and Wayne was harmful to the moral welfare of his daughters. At the trial before Judge Burks, Jacqueline, Walter, and Wayne all testified at length. Jacqueline related how she, Wayne, and the children had cohered into a stable family unit, and explained the emotional and financial reasons for her decision not to marry Wayne for the time being. Wayne testified about the nature of his relationship with the children, including discussions that he and Jacqueline had jointly held with the children about their relationship and the differing views that various people might have about the propriety of it.

Wayne testified that he was acquainted with the Jarretts' neighbors, who had learned about his presence from Jacqueline.

Walter testified that Jacqueline's living arrangements contravened his moral beliefs, and that he did not want his children raised in that atmosphere, which he characterized as an "improper moral climate." Walter insisted that he had certain moral ideals that he wanted to instill in his children, but that Jacqueline's example would make this difficult. On cross-examination, he conceded that when he picked up the children on Saturday evenings they had always been clean, healthy, well-dressed, and well-nourished, and that his conversations with the oldest daughter had revealed no serious objections by the children to Wayne's presence in the home, although they complained that he sometimes yelled at them when they were rowdy.

Judge Burks did not find any evidence that Jacqueline was an unfit mother, but he concluded that Wayne's moving into the family home was a change of circumstances that affected the moral climate of the home. He granted Walter's petition for a change of custody to him with visitation rights for Jacqueline, stating that it was "necessary for the moral and spiritual well-being and development" of the children that they live with their father. Burks's amended custody decree was filed on July 19, 1977. Jacqueline petitioned for a rehearing and to stay the order pending appeal, but Burks denied both motions and the girls moved to Walter's home.

Jacqueline's appeal was promptly heard by the First District Appellate Court of Illinois, with Chicago attorneys Michael W. Verzatt arguing for Jacqueline and Louis A. Solomon and Arthur M. Solomon arguing for Walter. The appeals court panel was divided over the proper outcome, but a majority agreed that Burks had abused his discretion in ordering removal of the children from Jacqueline's home without having found either that she was an unfit parent or that the children were suffering some serious present harm. Each of the justices wrote a separate opinion announced on September 13, 1978.

Presiding Justice Mel R. Jiganti emphasized that Illinois law sought stability in child custody determinations, such that an initial determination of custody could not be upset without evidence either that the custodial parent was unfit, which Burks had not found, or that a change in conditions affected the welfare of the children detrimentally.

> The original judgment order found Jacqueline to be a fit and proper person to have sole responsibility for the care, custody, control and education of the children. Such an award must be viewed as embracing all the ramifications of those terms, including the development of a person by fostering to varying degrees the growth or expansion of knowledge, wisdom, desirable qualities of mind or character, physical health, or general competence. Evidence in the instant case raised no question of Jacqueline's fitness as a good mother who properly cared for the physical and emotional needs of her daughters. The question raised by the defendant is whether her open relationship with Hammon constitutes such a disregard for community standards as to endanger her children's moral well-being.

As to this question, Jiganti asserted that Illinois courts had "often allowed women whose behavior society may have considered to be questionable to retain custody of their children or have refused to change custody in the absence of any evidence that the 'imprudence' was detrimental to the child's welfare." This was such a case, as far as he was concerned. Jacqueline's qualities as a caring parent were evident on the record. No fault could be found with the appearance, health, or stability of the children or the condition of the home, he said, and Jacqueline and Walter between them were seeing that the children regularly attended religious school and church. Jiganti observed:

> It is evident that Jacqueline Jarrett, Wayne Hammon, and the three Jarrett children function as a family unit. . . . There was no noticeable disruption of the children's routine by Hammon's entry into their lives, nor were they subject to the vagaries of an unstable relationship, shuttled back and forth between residences, or given cause to suspect that anything of an improper nature was transpiring. There was no evidence of any feelings of guilt or fears aroused in the children. Jacqueline and Hammon were open in their feelings for each other, open in their relationship to the children and to their community. From the evidence in the record before us, they are mature adults and their relationship is not

relevant here unless it is shown as having a negative effect on the children.

Jiganti refused to "indulge in speculation as to what effects might possibly 'raise their ugly heads' at some future time." He insisted that it was an abuse of discretion for the trial court to "impose its own standard in this regard and infer, without any evidence in the record, that Jacqueline's conduct in living with a man to whom she was not married was detrimental to the welfare of the children and in and of itself sufficient to disqualify her as the custodian of the children." Interestingly, however, although Jiganti cited various prior Illinois decisions as authority for general propositions earlier in the opinion, for this conclusion his only cited authority was an intermediate appellate decision from Colorado, *In re Marriage of Moore* (1975).

Justice Seymour F. Simon wrote a separate concurring opinion, adding his view that the change in custody would not have accomplished what Walter wanted, since it still involved liberal visitation rights for Jacqueline with no limitation on the presence of Wayne while the girls stayed over at her house. Consequently, "the children continued to be exposed to the same relationship between Jacqueline and Wayne that prompted the trial judge to grant a change of custody." Simon contended that living arrangements like Jacqueline's were increasingly common. Despite criminal fornication laws, prosecution of such situations "today is extremely unusual," he observed.

> Realistically, if a divorced parent chooses to enter into such a living arrangement, there is no way to insulate his or her children from knowledge of and exposure to the relationship the parent is maintaining, unless, perhaps, a court is willing to go to the extreme and unusual length of terminating the parent's visitation privileges. No one in this case has even suggested such a drastic and cruel approach. Here, living with their mother and Wayne on a permanent basis could not affect the children appreciably differently than spending weekends with their mother and Wayne after their custody was changed. In either case the children were fully exposed to their mother's relationship with Wayne and, therefore, that relationship in itself did not warrant a change in custody.

Justice Daniel J. McNamara dissented, emphasizing the criminal fornication law of Illinois, which had been relied on in earlier decisions of the First District Appellate Court, such as *Hahn v. Hahn* (1966) and *Gehn v. Gehn* (1977), to justify denying an adulterous or fornicating mother continued custody of her children. Quoting from the *Gehn* decision, McNamara argued that this very court had decided just the previous year that it might be "not only difficult but impossible to present evidence showing objective effects that such conduct would have on minor children," but that "[t]he effects may well be subjective ones that will raise their ugly heads and make their presence known at some future time." For McNamara, Jacqueline's own testimony that she had sought to justify her situation to her children as not being "wrong" provided a basis for a change in custody. "When a mother teaches children that her own criminal conduct is proper, it is unlikely that she will be able to proscribe any future illegal activities of the children," insisted McNamara, who found ample basis in the record for Burks to have concluded that there was "a material change of circumstances affecting the welfare of the children."

The court ordered that custody be returned to Jacqueline and denied Walter's petition for rehearing on November 1, 1978. Walter then appealed to the Illinois Supreme Court, which heard argument on his behalf from the Solomons and from Jacqueline's new attorney, Michael H. Minton, of Arlington Heights. The court also received an *amicus* brief from the Illinois Chapter of the American Academy of Matrimonial Lawyers. On December 20, 1979, a sharply divided court reversed the appellate court and ordered that custody be returned to Walter. Chief Justice Joseph H. Goldenhersh and Justice Thomas J. Moran dissented.

The majority opinion by Justice Robert C. Underwood embraced the reasoning of dissenting Appellate Justice McNamara. "The relevant standards of conduct are expressed in the statutes of this State," said Underwood, citing the Penal Code provisions holding that "any person who cohabits or has sexual intercourse with another not his spouse commits fornication if the behavior is open and notorious." While the Illinois courts had held that "essentially private and discreet" fornication was not to be prosecuted, this was not Jacqueline's situation. She had told her neighbors that Wayne was living with her, the relationship was open to the children, and so forth. Furthermore, Underwood was unimpressed by the statistics cited in Appellate Justice Simon's opinion about the frequency of cohabitation in the United States. While the absolute number of 1.1 million households nationwide with cohabiting adults and at least one child sounded large in isolation, this formed "only a small percentage of the adult population." More to the point, he felt that such an argument "simply nullifies the fornication statute."

> The logical conclusion of [Jacqueline's] argument is that the statutory prohibitions are void as to those who believe the proscribed acts are not immoral, or, for one reason or another, need not be heeded. So stated, of course, the argument defeats itself. The rules which our society enacts for the governance of its members are not limited to those who agree with those rules—they are equally binding on the dissenters.

In this case, the sex crimes laws and the adultery laws evidenced "the relevant moral standards" of the state of Illinois, and since the laws governing child custody instructed the courts to consider the moral welfare of children, it was appropriate for the court to take into account an open violation of those laws as relevant to the children's welfare. "Conduct of that nature, when it is open, not only violates the statutorily expressed moral standards of the State," insisted Underwood, "but also encourages others to violate those standards, and debases public morality. . . . Jacqueline's disregard for existing standards of conduct instructs her children, by example, that they, too, may ignore them. . ., and could well encourage the children to engage in similar activity in the future." Thus, the record supported Circuit Judge Burks's conclusion "that their daily presence in that environment was injurious to the moral well-being and development of the children."

Underwood denied that the court was mechanically applying a conclusive presumption of unfitness due to cohabitation, emphasizing that Jacqueline had a full hearing and that the evidence showed open and notorious cohabitation rather than a discreet and private sexual relationship between her and Wayne. Although there were several recent Illinois appellate decisions that Jacqueline had cited in her support, the court was now overruling them. Underwood specifically rejected Jiganti's statement that Burks had applied his own moral standards, asserting that Burks was applying the moral standards of Illinois as established by the legislature. As to the issue of actual harm to the children, Underwood refuted the appellate court's declaration that such harm was merely speculative.

> At the time of the hearing the three Jarrett children, who were then 12, 10 and 7 years old, were obviously incapable of emulating their mother's moral indiscretions. To wait until later years to determine whether Jacqueline had inculcated her moral values in the children would be to await a demonstration that the very harm which the statute seeks to avoid had occurred. Measures to safeguard the moral well-being of the children, whose lives have already been disrupted by the divorce of their parents, cannot have been intended to be delayed until there are tangible manifestations of damage to their character.

Underwood also noted his view that the "open cohabitation" of Jacqueline and Wayne could "also affect the mental and emotional health of the children," asserting that it was difficult to predict "what psychological effects or problems may later develop from their efforts to overcome the disparity between their concepts of propriety and their mother's conduct." Underwood denied that the U.S. Supreme Court's opinion in *Stanley v. Illinois* compelled any different result, arguing that the Jarretts' case was "fundamentally different."

> The trial court did not presume that Jacqueline was not an adequate parent, as the juvenile court in effect did in *Stanley*. Rather the trial court recognized that the affection and care of a parent do not alone assure the welfare of the child if other conduct of the parent threatens the child's moral development. Since the evidence indicated that Jacqueline had not terminated the troublesome relationship and would probably continue it in the future, the trial court transferred custody to Walter Jarrett, an equally caring and affectionate parent whose conduct did not contravene the standards established by the General Assembly and earlier judicial decisions.

The two dissenters vociferously disagreed with the majority's reasoning. Chief Justice Goldenhersh, noting the failure of the trial court to find Jacqueline unfit or to find any tangible harm to the children, insisted that the majority was ruling that a cohabiting parent was unfit *per se*, and that the court had no factual basis for asserting that a cohabiting parent would inevitably raise immoral children. "I question that any competent sociologist would attribute the increase of 'live in' unmarried couples to parental example," he scoffed. Noting that the majority had cited cases dating from the 19th century to World War II, Goldenhersh argued that the cases did not reflect "prevailing public policy" but rather "the prejudice extant in that period." "Courts are uniquely equipped to decide legal issues and are well advised to leave to the theologians the question of the morality of the living arrangement into which the plaintiff had entered," he insisted. He found no basis in the record for finding that it was in the interest of these girls to go live with their father.

Justice Moran also joined in dissent, emphasizing that the majority appeared to be imposing a conclusive presumption regarding cohabiting parents, for which he found no factual support in the record. "In this case, not one scintilla of actual or statistical evidence of harm or danger to the children has been presented," he said, noting that the only testimony in the record, by Walter, was that the children appeared healthy, well-adjusted, and so forth. He accused the majority of using child custody as a method of punishing Jacqueline for fornication, a crime for which she was neither prosecuted nor convicted (itself indicating something about the prevailing standards of the community). To Moran, what the majority was doing was a blatant violation of the *Stanley* decision.

Despite the strength of the dissenting views, the court rejected Jacqueline's petition for rehearing on February 1, 1980. Later that year, on October 20, the U.S. Supreme Court announced its refusal to consider the case, but three members of the Court, Justices William J. Brennan, Jr., Thurgood Marshall, and Harry A. Blackmun, dissented. Brennan wrote a brief opinion, joined by Justice Marshall, taking up the argument from Justice Moran's dissent below. "The decision of the Illinois Supreme Court that, in effect, a divorced woman's ostensible violation of the Illinois fornication statute presumptively harmed the best interests of the children and that this was conclusive for purposes of custody presents a serious question under the Fourteenth Amendment," Brennan asserted.

I had supposed that *Stanley* established the proposition that "the interest of a parent in the companionship, care, custody, and management of his or her children" cannot be determined by the evidentiary shortcut of a conclusive presumption. Thus, for purposes of this case, *Stanley* would seem to foreclose custody modification on the basis of a similar conclusive presumption of serious adverse effect on the children's best interests despite whatever contrary evidence may have been or might be adduced. This is particularly true since there is no rational basis for the conclusive presumption actually utilized, whether Jacqueline is viewed as having violated the fornication statute only or as being a lawbreaker generally.

Noting that Illinois rarely, if ever, enforced its fornication statute, Brennan observed that Illinois "can hardly contend that there is a rational correlation between divorced parents who fornicate and divorced parents who impair the healthy development of their children." He pointed out that other Illinois criminal statutes, including traffic laws, were much more frequently enforced, but that nobody would argue that Jacqueline should lose custody if she violated the traffic laws. Since the only record evidence about the children's condition showed that condition to be good while they were living with her, he could see no basis for imposing a presumption to remove them from her home.

Finally, Brennan argued that the Court should have granted *certiorari* in the case because it was clear from census data that this was a widespread situation, and could prove a constantly recurring question in the state courts. If the Fourteenth Amendment indeed barred the sort of presumption imposed by the Illinois Supreme Court in this case, the Court should address the issue directly.

Encouraged by the three dissenting votes, Jacqueline petitioned the Court to reconsider its decision not to hear the case, but the dissenters could not muster a fourth vote for *certiorari* and her petition was denied on December 15, 1980.

The many judicial opinions in *Jarrett v. Jarrett* recapitulate the variety of arguments on the issue whether a cohabiting divorced parent should be able to retain custody of his or her children. The approach of the Illinois court has been widely followed, although there have been many dissenting courts that have allowed such living arrangements to continue.

Perhaps the most extreme example of a court following the Illinois rule to its logical extreme came in Rhode Island in 1989, when that state's supreme court ruled in *Parrillo v. Parrillo* that the mother would not only lose custody but that her boyfriend could not be present at any time when she was exercising the limited visitation rights the court was willing to award her. (This sort of restriction is very common in custody decisions involving lesbian and gay parents.) The U.S. Supreme Court also denied review in this case.

These decisions are ironic in light of the accelerating trend of unmarried parental cohabitation in the United States, well documented in the 1980 Census and reaffirmed in the 1990 Census, showing that nontraditional family living situations are becoming so pervasive in American life that some courts have begun to rethink the very definition of "family" for a variety of purposes. If these trends continue, it seems unlikely that the approach of the court in *Jarrett v. Jarrett* can persist much longer.

Case References

Gehn v. Gehn, 51 Ill. App. 3d 946, 10 Ill. Dec. 120, 367 N.E.2d 508 (1st Dist. 1977)

Hahn v. Hahn, 69 Ill. App. 2d 302, 216 N.E.2d 229 (2d Dist. 1966)

Moore, In re Marriage of, 35 Colo. App. 280, 531 P.2d 995 (1975)

Parrillo v. Parrillo, 554 A.2d 1043 (R.I.), certiorari denied, 110 S. Ct. 364 (1989)

Stanley v. Illinois, 405 U.S. 645 (1972)

57. SEXUAL ORIENTATION AND MATERNAL FITNESS

Bezio v. Patenaude, 381 Mass. 563, 410 N.E.2d 1207 (1980).

Can the "natural" mother of a child be deprived of custody on the basis of her sexual orientation, or the presumed impact of her sexual orientation on the development and welfare of her children? Until the medical profession's views of sexual orientation began to evolve away from a "sickness" model during the 1960s, this question would not even be deemed worthy of debate by most courts. Of course, any deviation from the social norm, such as homosexuality, would be considered a disqualifying factor in a custody dispute. But court proceedings soon came to reflect changes in medical orthodoxy in the 1960s and 1970s. By 1980, a unanimous decision of the Supreme Judicial Court of Massachusetts became the leading appellate precedent for the proposition that maternal sexual orientation and the mother's involvement in a

lesbian relationship, without particular evidence of adverse effects, were not a sufficient basis for denying child custody.

Brenda A. King, a Massachusetts resident, bore a daughter out of wedlock in 1972, when she was about 19 years old. At the time, Brenda was close friends with Magdalena Patenaude, a woman almost ten years older than she, to whom she had been introduced by her pastor at a time when Brenda was experiencing emotional difficulties. The pastor thought that Magdalena, who had been through similar emotional problems, could be a good friend to Brenda, and so it developed. (Much later, the Franklin County probate judge suggested that the early, close friendship of Brenda and Magdalena might have had a "homosexual basis.") From the time her daughter was born until she married James L.

Bezio in April 1974, Brenda entrusted the care of her child to Magdalena on many occasions. After the marriage, Brenda, her daughter, and James all lived with Magdalena for three weeks until James, an Army member, had to return to his posting in North Carolina, and Brenda moved there with James.

Brenda became pregnant and began to experience medical difficulties, which soon became severe. Dissatisfied with the medical care available through the Army, Brenda returned to Massachusetts in August 1974 with her daughter, whose care she entrusted to Magdalena while she returned to North Carolina for about a month. Brenda then developed pregnancy complications and potentially fatal, deep thrombophlebitis, necessitating hospitalization in Massachusetts. Her daughter continued in Magdalena's care. Brenda's second daughter was delivered by Caesarean section. Brenda continued to suffer medical complications, and was in and out of the hospital, with her children staying in Magdalena's care most of the time. Brenda's parents, with whom she evidently did not get along, seem to have played little if any role through this time in caring for the children. Brenda was moving back and forth between Massachusetts and North Carolina to be with her husband at the Army posting and with her children, who were living with Magdalena.

In October 1975, Magdalena called Brenda and asked her to hurry back to Massachusetts. One of the children was sick, and Magdalena said she was having trouble securing medical care because she did not have any legal relationship to the children. Brenda met with the attending physician and discussed the possibility of having Magdalena appointed guardian of the children so she would have legal authority to secure medical treatment for them in an emergency. On November 21, 1975, Magdalena filed a petition for temporary and permanent guardianship in the Franklin County Probate and Family Court with Brenda's assent. The court appointed Magdalena temporary guardian with custody of the two children, but problems developed when Magdalena subsequently sought to limit Brenda's visitation with the children. In February 1976, Brenda requested temporary custody, to which Magdalena agreed, an

arrangement that was continued by the Probate Court in May 1976. However, further conversations between the women led to Brenda's decision to leave the children with Magdalena after all, since she became convinced that she was not sure of her ability to provide proper care for them. The probation officer assigned to the case notified the court, which ordered a change of custody back to Magdalena.

Later that year, Brenda assented to Magdalena's appointment as permanent guardian with custody. The same attorney represented both women. The judge granted Brenda virtually unlimited visitation rights "at all reasonable times and occasions." At the time of this order, Brenda was still experiencing both financial hardship and medical problems. Brenda wrote to the court that Magdalena was "the only one fully qualified to raise my children in a manner which I myself would do if I could." As before, however, disputes arose about Brenda's visitation rights, and in February 1977, Brenda and her husband, James, filed a petition to vacate the guardianship and return custody to Brenda. (They were soon divorced, and James dropped out of the case.) At the same time, Brenda filed a motion to compel visitation. The Franklin County Probate Court ordered that Brenda be allowed at least three hours of visitation every other Saturday afternoon until the matter was resolved. In April 1977, Brenda's parents filed a petition for guardianship, and the judge appointed a guardian *ad litem* to investigate the whole situation. The guardian *ad litem*'s report included the following:

> Ms. Bezio lives in what she describes as a "lesbian relationship" with a young woman. At this time she is not seeking custody of her children feeling that her chosen life style could cause problems for the children. Having battled with her own inner conflicts of gender identification for years, she does not wish to in any way influence her children. . . . Of striking concern to Ms. Bezio is the feeling that Mrs. Patnode [*sic*] is depriving her children of their identity and family heritage. . . . Ms. Bezio is anxious for her children to be placed in the custody of their grandparents and feels that her previous conflicts with them have been resolved.

This sounds a bit like a "put-up job," with Brenda's parents prevailing on her at a time of financial, physical, and emotional weakness to take the children away from Magdalena and give them to their grandparents. In any event, Brenda's parents soon dropped their petition. The children continued in Magdalena's custody, with Brenda exercising her court-ordered visitation rights, while the case dragged on without a hearing due to the illness of the probation officer who had rendered the report and Brenda's inability to pay her lawyer, who thus exerted little effort to secure a hearing. At last, Brenda decided that enough was enough: she wanted her children back and she would take them. On July 22, 1978, after picking up her children for the scheduled Saturday afternoon visitation, Brenda disappeared with them. She took them to Vermont, where she rented an apartment and enrolled them in school. At the ultimate trial of the case, the first grade teacher of the older child testified that she made rapid progress in picking up educational skills she lacked at the start of the year, attributing the progress to Brenda's work with the child at home. Brenda's landlady, who happened also to be a social worker, testified positively about the quality of home life Brenda provided for the children, as did a Vermont Department of Public Health supervisor who had visited the home, who saw "good rapport" between Brenda and her children, "a good strong relationship." However, Magdalena had initiated proceedings in Massachusetts to secure return of the children. Brenda and the children were tracked down and Brenda was arrested on a Massachusetts warrant for "kidnapping" her own children, since Magdalena was the legal guardian with custody. According to the Vermont police officer who executed the warrant, the children said at the time that they loved their mother and did not want to go back to Magdalena. When the police returned the children to Magdalena, the complaint against Brenda was dismissed.

Brenda moved back to Massachusetts and filed a "care and protection" complaint in Franklin County District Court, making allegations of neglect and child abuse against Magdalena, which caused the court to move the children in mid-December to a neutral foster home, with each woman being granted visitation rights during alternate weeks. A Department of Social Welfare investigator reported to the court that the charges against Magdalena were not valid and recommended returning the children to Magdalena, which the district court judge did, denying all visitation rights to Brenda for a period of three months. The probate judge later found that Brenda's allegation against Magdalena "was engendered by the bitterness caused by this litigation."

Brenda, distraught at what was happening to her relationship with her children, checked into a rehabilitation residential program for persons dealing with stressful situations, where she received continuing therapy from March through June of 1979, and continued to receive therapy there on an out-patient basis after leaving the program. Her psychologist later testified that she did not suffer from any mental illness, that her mental health was good, and that she was a "very capable and competent mother."

In May 1979, Brenda petitioned the court for restoration of her visitation rights, which were granted but placed under supervision by a counselor due to her past abduction of the children. The counselor would later testify at a custody hearing that she "saw an increasing exchange of love displayed in hugs and kisses, a sharing of their past experiences that they would recall and laugh about." Others involved in the supervision also testified about the high quality of Brenda's relationship with her children. At the hearing before Probate Judge Keedy to determine custody, Brenda testified that she wanted to have the children live with her in her apartment, where she was living in a homosexual relationship with a young school teacher.

Brenda's attorney presented expert testimony regarding the impact of parental sexual orientation on the children. Dr. Alexandra Kaplan, a clinical psychologist and professor of psychology at the University of Massachusetts, testified as follows: "There is no evidence at all that sexual preference of adults in the home has any detrimental impact on children. . . . Many other issues influence child rearing. Sexual preference per se is typically not one of them." When Magdalena's attorney asked further whether there was "nothing to prove that a homosexual relationship would make or in any way influence a child to be a homosexual rather than a heterosexual," Dr. Kaplan responded:

> Quite to the contrary. . . . Most children raised in homosexual situations become heterosexual as adults. . . . There is no evidence that children who are raised with a loving couple of the same sex are any more disturbed, unhealthy, maladjusted than children raised with a loving couple of mixed sex. It is irrelevant to their mental health.

Magdalena's attorney had called as an expert witness psychologist David Johnson, who had seen the children in play therapy, and who concurred with Dr. Kaplan's opinion that parental homosexuality *per se* is "irrelevant to parenting ability."

This testimony evidently did not persuade Judge Keedy, however, for he concluded that Brenda's homosexual relationship, taken together with the superior situation provided by Magdalena, justified denying her custody petition. Keedy stated that the "environment in which she proposes to raise the children, namely, a Lesbian household, creates an element of instability that would adversely affect the welfare of the children." When this was considered together with Brenda's "unwillingness or inability in the past to assume the responsibility of their care," the judge concluded that the children should remain with Magdalena, allowing Brenda two hours each week of supervised visitation. Keedy noted that Magdalena "has provided an excellent home and care for these children. She loves the children and they love her. The children love their natural mother and desire to visit with her but they regard the defendant [Magdalena] as their real mother. . . . It would cause great trauma with the children to remove them from a home where they are happy and secure and from the custody of one who loves them and has their welfare at heart. Their best interest requires that they remain with the defendant."

Brenda applied for direct review in the Massachusetts Supreme Judicial Court, which was granted. At the oral argument on June 9, 1980, she was represented by Northampton attorneys William C. Newman and Wendy Sibbison, with Geoffrey A. Wilson, of Greenfield, representing Magdalena. The court received *amicus* briefs urging reversal from the Civil Liberties Union of Massachusetts and Gay and Lesbian Advocates and Defenders, a Boston-based lesbian and gay rights litigation organization. Brenda argued that the probate judge had inappropriately deprived a natural mother, who had never been determined to be an unfit parent, of the custody of her children in violation of Massachusetts law and her constitutional rights as a parent. She further challenged the judge's conclusion, contrary to all the expert testimony, that placement of the children in a "Lesbian household" would necessarily cause an adverse impact on their development.

The supreme judicial court announced its decision on September 22, 1980, unanimously reversing the probate court in a decision by Justice Paul J. Liacos. As argued by Brenda, Liacos asserted that the probate court had gotten the law totally wrong. In 1979, the supreme judicial court had ruled in a case titled *Custody of a Minor* that "a finding of current parental unfitness is required in a proceeding which results in a parent's loss of child custody," an assertion that "derives from the substantial respect we accord family autonomy." The court had cited the U.S. Supreme Court's 1944 decision in *Prince v. Massachusetts*, where the Supreme Court described a "private realm of family life which the state cannot enter," which the supreme judicial court called "a cardinal precept of our jurisprudence."

Magdalena had argued that the appropriate approach was to apply the standard "best interest of the child" test, asserting that she would provide the superior setting for raising the children, and that the probate court had correctly applied the standard in this case. Since Brenda had assented to the award of permanent guardianship and custody to Magdalena in October 1976, she argued, there was no issue in this case of the court invading the private family realm against the will of a natural parent. Once the guardianship and custody were vested in Magdalena, the burden should be on Brenda to show that Magdalena was unfit before a change could be ordered. Liacos rejected this approach, harking back to several Massachusetts decisions in which parents were seeking to regain custody from guardians. For example, in *Duclos v. Edwards*, a 1962 case, the supreme judicial court had affirmed a probate judge's order to return three children to the custody of their natural father when they had been living with a guardian for nine years while the natural parents went through various marital difficulties, divorced, and the father remarried. The court emphasized the importance of keeping a natural family unit together, even though it might be distressing for the guardian, who had formed a strong attachment to the children, as well as, initially, for the children, who would have to readjust to life with their father and stepmother after a long period of living with the guardian. Said Liacos, "We conclude that *Duclos* stands for the following proposition: Where a natural parent is fit to further the best interests of the child, the natural bond between that parent and child normally would render an otherwise suitable guardian an 'unsuitable' custodian" within the meaning of the Massachusetts statutes.

Magdalena had cited another case, *Wilkins v. Wilkins*, a 1949 decision in which the supreme judicial court approved awarding custody to a guardian based on evidence that the children strongly resisted placement with their natural parents, experiencing nightmares at the prospect. This was an instance of applying the "best interests of the child" test in an appropriate manner, given the facts of the case, said Liacos, but the evidence in this case was that the children had a good relationship with Brenda, despite all the interruptions and ups and downs along the way. As Judge Keedy had found, "the children love their natural mother and desire to visit with her." Said Liacos, "Natural parents should be denied custody only if they are unfit to further the welfare of their children." There was no reason even to reach Brenda's constitutional arguments, since one could reach this conclusion based on applying Massachusetts statutory precedents to this case.

Judge Keedy had made no finding that Brenda was currently unfit. His determination seemed to rest largely on the past rather than on present circumstances. Furthermore, said Liacos, Keedy's statements about the negative impact of a "Lesbian household" on the children were "insufficient to support the judge's conclusion that custody should remain in the guardian." Reviewing the expert testimony in

the record, Liacos concluded that it "does not support an inference that the mother's lesbianism would render her unfit to further her children's welfare." Experts for both sides had stated that "a mother's sexual preference *per se* is irrelevant to a consideration of her parenting skills." Liacos, who was co-author of the leading treatise on Massachusetts rules of evidence, objected to Keedy's apparent decision to take "judicial notice" of an "adverse effect" that had no support in the record:

> A finding that a parent is unfit to further the welfare of the child must be predicated upon parental behavior which adversely affects the child. The State may not deprive parents of custody of their children "simply because their households fail to meet the ideals approved by the community . . . [or] simply because the parents embrace ideologies or pursue lifestyles at odds with the average." . . . In the total absence of evidence suggesting a correlation between the mother's homosexuality and her fitness as a parent, we believe the judge's finding that a lesbian household would adversely affect the children to be without basis in the record. This is not a matter about which the judge could take judicial notice. "Matters are judicially noticed only when they are indisputably true. . . . Judicial notice is not to be extended to personal observations of the judge."

In this case, Judge Keedy found that "although the plaintiff's psychological and emotional condition has improved, the elements of instability that have plagued the plaintiff's relationship with her children are still present." To the extent this finding was based on the judge's personal views about homosexuality, there would have to be a new hearing where competent evidence could be evaluated relating to Brenda's current ability to provide an appropriate home for the children. A year had passed since the first hearing, said Liacos, "and new evidence may be required to determine the issues," so the case was remanded to the probate court for further hearings. Liacos noted that there was no indication in the record whether James Bezio, natural father of the younger child, had assented to being dropped from the case after the divorce. As a natural father, he was entitled to participate in any proceeding that might deny him custody of his daughter, said Liacos, citing the U.S. Supreme Court's decision in *Stanley v. Illinois* (1972). There is no indication in subsequently published Massachusetts decisions as to how this custody dispute was resolved on remand.

Bezio v. Patenaude turned out to be a highly influential case for the proposition that lesbian mothers could not be presumed to be unfit parents for their natural children, particularly when expert opinions, and the studies that have been undertaken in recent years, concur that parental sexual orientation, *per se*, does not contribute any adverse effect to the psychological development of children. Although some courts in other jurisdictions refused to follow this holding, most of the decisions that have cited *Bezio v. Patenaude* (which, in the ten years following

its announcement, was cited in more than a dozen other jurisdictions) have followed it. As such, it marked an important breakthrough for lesbian and gay parents as one of the first opinions by the highest court of a state to reject the former, commonly held and followed presumption that homosexuals were unfit parents for their natural children.

Case References

Custody of a Minor, 377 Mass. 876, 389 N.E.2d 68 (Mass. 1979)

Duclos v. Edwards, 344 Mass. 544, 183 N.E.2d 708 (1962)

Prince v. Massachusetts, 321 U.S. 158 (1944)

Stanley v. Illinois, 405 U.S. 645 (1972)

Wilkins v. Wilkins, 324 Mass. 261, 85 N.E.2d 768 (1949)

58. INTERRACIAL COUPLES AND CHILD CUSTODY

Palmore v. Sidoti, 466 U.S. 429 (1984), reversing 426 So. 2d 34 (Fla. App. 1982); further decision denying jurisdiction, 472 So. 2d 843 (Fla. App. 1985).

The U.S. Supreme Court held in 1967 in *Loving v. Virginia* that a state law forbidding interracial marriages violated the Equal Protection and Due Process clauses of the Fourteenth Amendment. Any use of a racial classification by the government in a legislative enactment was held to be inherently suspect, due to the likelihood that prejudice and stereotypes, rather than legitimate reasons, underlay the classification. Furthermore, freedom of choice in marriage was held to be a fundamental right, premised on the guarantee that no person could be deprived of liberty without due process of law. The state's interest in maintaining the "purity of the races" was held to provide insufficient justification for abridging this liberty.

Having required the states to drop bans on interracial marriage, the Court inevitably had to confront the question whether the social stigma attaching to such marriages could be a legitimate factor in child custody disputes. The traditional standard for determining which parent will be granted legal custody of a minor child is the "best interest of the child." Could a court legitimately find that a parent's remar-

riage to a person of a different race would so endanger the child's best interest as to justify a change in custody?

Linda and Anthony J. Sidoti, a Caucasian couple living in Florida, divorced in May 1980 when their daughter Melanie was about 3 years old. Under the terms of the divorce decree, Linda had custody of Melanie. Anthony remarried several months after the divorce. He petitioned the Hillsborough County (Florida) Circuit Court in September 1981 for a change of custody. In the petition, he alleged that Linda was not properly caring for Melanie, and that there had been a change in circumstances: he was now remarried and Linda was cohabiting with a black man, Charles Palmore, Jr., whom she married two months after the petition was filed.

The court ordered that an investigation be made by a court counselor. The counselor, who had previously recommended against an award of custody where an interracial couple was involved in a prior case, again recommended in this case that Linda be denied continued custody because of her cohabitation and subsequent marriage to a black man. Asserting that Linda had "chosen for herself and her child, a life-style unacceptable to the father and to society," the counselor concluded that Melanie would be "subject to environmental pressures not of choice," particularly when she began to attend school. The circuit court judge heard testimony from the parties about the quality of care Melanie had been receiving from her mother. Although there was testimony from Anthony about personal hygiene issues, the court made no findings on the issue, finding instead that "there is no issue as to either party's devotion to the child, adequacy of housing facilities, or respectability of the new spouse of either parent."

Despite the lack of any finding that Linda was unfit to continue as Melanie's custodian, the circuit court granted Anthony's custody petition. While asserting that Anthony's unhappiness about Linda's choice of a new sexual and marital partner was not sufficient reason to change custody, the judge indicated his own disapproval of the situation, and based the decision on the social disapproval which he considered bound to prove upsetting to Melanie.

> The father's evident resentment of the mother's choice of a black partner is not sufficient to wrest custody from the mother. It is of some significance, however, that the mother did see fit to bring a man into her home and carry on a sexual relationship with him without being married to him. Such action tended to place gratification of her own desires ahead of her concern for the child's future welfare. This Court feels that despite the strides that have been made in bettering relations between the races in this country, it is inevitable that Melanie will, if allowed to remain in her present situation and attains school age and thus more vulnerable to peer pressures, suffer from the social stigmatization that is sure to come.

Linda appealed the circuit court's unpublished decision to the Second District Court of Appeal, which affirmed on December 8, 1982, without opinion. Under Florida procedures, an affirmance without opinion is final and not subject to appeal to the Florida Supreme Court. Thus, Linda's next step was direct appeal to the U.S. Supreme Court. Her attorney, Robert J. Shapiro, filed a petition for *certiorari*, arguing that the custody decision had been impermissi-

bly tainted by consideration of the race of Linda's husband. Anthony's attorney, John E. Hawtrey, argued that the Florida courts had correctly determined that the best interest of the child would require the more conventional setting of a same-race family. The Court granted *certiorari* on October 17, 1983, and set the case for argument on February 22, 1984. The case attracted *amicus* briefs from the federal government, the American Civil Liberties Union, the Women's Legal Defense Fund, and others, all urging reversal of any custody determination that took race into account.

The Supreme Court unanimously reversed the Florida decision, in an opinion by Chief Justice Warren E. Burger issued on April 25, 1984. Observing that it was unusual for the Supreme Court to involve itself in a child custody dispute, Burger asserted that the case raised "important federal concerns arising from the Constitution's commitment to eradicating discrimination based on race." Finding that the trial court's unpublished decision apparently placed no credence on Anthony's allegations going to Linda's fitness as a parental custodian, Burger observed that the trial court "was entirely candid and made no effort to place its holding on any ground other than race." It was clear that had Charles Palmore been "a Caucasian of similar respectability," there would have been no change in custody ordered by the court.

This was impermissible under the Equal Protection Clause, since it was an instance of "governmentally imposed discrimination based on race." Burger invoked the Court's precedent in *Shelley v. Kraemer*, a 1948 case in which the Court held that judicial enforcement of a private agreement to discriminate on the basis of race in the sale of private property constituted "government action" and was not allowed under the Equal Protection Clause. Similarly, while the Florida courts were using the facially neutral standard of best interest of the child, to give any weight to the race of the stepfather was an instance of "state action" raising Fourteenth Amendment concerns. "Classifying persons according to their race is more likely to reflect racial prejudice than legitimate public concerns," said Burger; "the race, not the person, dictates the category." The trial court's use of race in making this decision was subject to "strict scrutiny." For the decision to survive, it must be shown that it was justified "by a compelling governmental interest and must be 'necessary . . . to the accomplishment'" of a "legitimate purpose."

Here the government did have a substantial interest, "a duty of the highest order to protect the interests of minor children, particularly those of tender years." But, said Burger, that did not justify basing the decision on the race of the stepfather.

> It would ignore reality to suggest that racial and ethnic prejudices do not exist or that all manifestations of those prejudices have been eliminated. There is a risk that a child living with a stepparent of a different race may be subject to a variety of pressures and stresses not present if the child were living with parents of the same racial or ethnic origin. The question, however, is whether the reality of private biases and the possible injury they might inflict are permissible considerations for removal of an infant child from the custody of its natural mother. We have little difficulty concluding that they are not. The Constitution cannot control such prejudices but neither can it tolerate them. Private biases may be outside the reach of the law, but the law cannot, directly or indirectly, give them effect.

Burger concluded his opinion by noting that long ago, in cases involving racial segregation in housing, the Court had indicated that private racial prejudices could not be the basis of government policies. In *Buchanan v. Warley*, a 1917 case, the Court had invalidated a Kentucky law forbidding black people from buying homes in "white" neighborhoods, commenting that a plan "to promote public peace by preventing race conflicts," while "desirable," could not be achieved by "laws or ordinances which deny rights created or protected by the Federal Constitution." Burger concluded that whatever problems a child might encounter from living in a racially mixed household in 1984 provided no more basis for sustaining discriminatory government action than the problems, if any, a black family would have experienced living in a "white" neighborhood in 1917. The Court ordered the Florida custody decision reversed.

That did not end the matter for Linda Palmore, however, for Anthony Sidoti had moved with his wife and Melanie to Texas, and the Florida courts denied her subsequent attempts to regain custody of the child, holding that Melanie's custody should now be determined by the Texas courts. No published Texas decision exists to reveal the outcome of Linda's quest.

The Supreme Court's decision in *Palmore v. Sidoti* was a significant landmark in providing that free-floating societal racial prejudice should not be considered by courts as a factor in making child custody determinations. The decision was firmly grounded in the Court's equal protection jurisprudence in race cases, under which government classifications or policies based on race almost never survive "strict scrutiny," since most of the Justices have consistently held that government may not take race into account for purposes of discriminating against racial minorities. Left open, and somewhat more controversial, was whether the case provided a precedent for cases involving other forms of prejudice.

Most particularly, parents of diverse sexuality have sought to invoke the principles established in *Palmore v. Sidoti* with mixed success. Some courts have accepted a broad reading of *Palmore* and held that social prejudice against homosexuals should not be used as a basis for denying custody or visitation rights to a homosexual parent. Others, however, have rejected the precedent of *Palmore*, contending that sexual orientation was not a "suspect classification" on a par with race, so that a lower level of judicial "scrutiny" need be given to the resulting discrimination. Indeed, some courts have held that societal prejudice was a sufficient reason to deny custody to homosexual or transsexual parents, because the state needed only a "rational basis" to discriminate on the basis of sexual orientation, and the conceded difficulties that a child might encounter, such as the teasing of schoolmates and disapproval of teachers and other adults in positions of authority, provided sufficient reason for the state rationally to conclude that a child would be better off in a nongay household. Final disposition of this issue awaits a definite resolution by the Supreme Court of whether sexual orientation classifications used by the state require heightened scrutiny when challenged in the courts.

Case References

Buchanan v. Warley, 245 U.S. 60 (1917)

Loving v. Virginia, 388 U.S. 1 (1967)
Shelley v. Kraemer, 334 U.S. 1 (1948)

59. CREATING "GAY FAMILIES" THROUGH ADULT ADOPTIONS

In re the Adoption of Robert Paul P., 63 N.Y.2d 233, 471 N.E.2d 424, 481 N.Y.S.2d 652 (1984), affirming 97 A.D.2d 991, 469 N.Y.S.2d 833 (1st Dept. 1983), affirming 117 Misc. 2d 279, 458 N.Y.S.2d 178 (Fam. Ct., N.Y. County 1983). *In re Adult Anonymous II*, 88 A.D.2d 30, 452 N.Y.S.2d 198 (1st Dept. 1982), reversing 111 Misc. 2d 320, 443 N.Y.S.2d 1008 (N.Y. Fam. Ct., N.Y. County 1981).

American society has traditionally recognized two methods for the creation of family relationships: marriage and adoption. Under the common law, a marital relationship could be created by a man and a woman living together and holding themselves forth as a married couple, but gradually most of the states have moved to statutory regulation of marriage, under which the prospective marital couple must obtain a license from the state and have a ceremony performed by a person authorized by statute to perform such ceremonies, during which they exchange vows pertinent to the legally defined relationship they are forming. No state authorizes same-sex couples to enter marital relationships under the common law or by statute, and litigation has been unsuccessful seeking to obtain same-sex marriage through clever statutory interpretation of domestic relations statutes or constitutional challenges.

Access to a family relationship through adoption has been even more sharply circumscribed, since the English common law appropriated for American purposes under the Constitution did not recognize adoption, and this institution has been established only by statute in the various states. (Continental European countries deriving their legal systems from Roman law, by contrast, have always recognized the concept of adoption.) When the states began to pass their adoption laws during the 19th century, they tended to follow the pattern of European statutes, which authorized the legal creation of a family relationship that was held to "imitate nature" in the sense of being legally

recognized as equal to a natural familial relationship. Adopted persons take on all the legal attributes of a family member of the adopter, including rights of inheritance.

For same-sex couples, the possibility of using adoption as a device to create legally recognized families arose as the natural consequence of unavailability of marriage or other legal alternatives. Although the main reasons for seeking such status had been emotional or symbolic, there were also strong economic incentives. These became more pressing for many same-sex couples in New York City in the early 1980s as the severe shortage of adequate rental housing under a strict rent regulation regime led landlords to adopt a new strategy for obtaining apartment vacancies and accompanying rent increases: strict enforcement of the provisions limiting occupancy to signatory tenants and members of "their immediate family," provisions found in the form leases in universal use in rent-stabilized apartments in the city. A strong trend of conversion from rental to cooperative apartments, also fueled by the combination of housing shortage and rent regulation, contributed as well to landlords' motivations to achieve evictions in order to reduce the number of apartments that had to be offered to existing tenants at reduced "insider" prices in order to reach the percentage threshold of sales needed under New York real estate law to effect such a conversion. Particularly in the crowded residential areas of Manhattan (New York County) and Brooklyn (Kings County), lesbian and gay tenants began to receive eviction notices alleging that they had violated their leases through the occupancy of their sexual partners.

While some tried the strategy of alleging that their partners should be considered "family members" for purposes of the lease, others sought the apparent "quick-fix" remedy of adult adoption, creating a legal family relationship between adopter and adoptee that would effectively bar an eviction. Petitions for such adoptions were filed in the family courts with mixed success. Two became the subject of sufficient controversy to generate appellate opinions.

In the first case, called *In re Adult Anonymous II* (because a prior opinion using a similar caption had previously been published), William J. Thom, a New York attorney who had founded the Lambda Legal Defense and Education Fund in 1973 to bring test case litigation on behalf of lesbian and gay people, filed a petition on behalf of two gay men, ages 32 and 43, who sought to form a family through adoption. The older man's parents were deceased, so the younger man was petitioning to be the adoptive "parent." Had the younger man been the adoptee, the adoption would have formally dissolved his legal relationship with his own parents, a result he wished to avoid. In his petition to adopt the partner with whom he had been living in his apartment for over two years, the younger man, identified as "Mr. S," asserted that he and "Mr. H" had a sexual relationship, and sought to formalize their relationship for emotional and symbolic reasons and to preserve their right to live together, since some other tenants in his building had already been threatened with eviction for violation of the "immediate family" clause in their leases.

As required by statute, the men had submitted their relationship to inspection by the county probation department, which had recommended approving the petition, finding that the younger man had assumed a protective posture toward the older one, taking the more active leadership role in the relationship. "Mr. S had indicated that despite the fact that Mr. H is older by some 9 years, that he feels that Mr. H's parents have been dead for a considerable number of years, and that Mr. H has a slight speech impediment, stuttering, and that he needs more looking after," said the probation department report. "There is no question that the two adults have made a commitment at least for the past 2–1/2 years." The probation report concluded that the men's motivation for the adoption "primarily appeared to be a desire on the part of two adult males to maintain a lifestyle without being subject to discrimination and possible eviction from their rental home."

New York County Family Court Judge Mortimer Getzels denied their application, in an opinion issued on November 4, 1981. Noting the history of New York's adoption statute, dating back to 1873, and the 1915 amendment that had authorized the adoption of one adult by another, Getzels stated that adoption in New York was purely a matter of statute and that the court "may not create a right to adopt not bestowed by the legislature." Although the statute stated no requirement that the adopter be older than the adoptee, and placed no other express limitation on the relationship of the parties who could adopt, Getzels concluded that approval of the petition "would violate the legislative intent of the Domestic Relations Law and do violence to the public policy that generates this state's laws on adoption." Quoting a 1952 opinion by the state's court of appeals in *In re Upjohn*, Getzels found that "embodied in our adoption statute is the fundamental social concept that the relationship of parent and child . . . may be established, independently of blood ties, by operation of law." To Getzels, whatever relationship the petitioner sought here, it was not one of "parent and child." Since this adoption would not, in Getzels's view, result in a parent-child relationship, but rather would serve as a substitute for marriage, disapproval of the petition was required.

The Court is most sympathetic to the yearning of two decent people living exemplary, productive lives who are seeking to obtain some legal recognition of the bond that exists between them. It is mindful that what consenting adults do sexually in private has been decriminalized on constitutional grounds. The relationship is no longer what it was for Oscar Wilde and Lord Alfred Douglas—the love that dares not speak its name. But a statutory mechanism for conferring status on the relationship, with concomitant rights and obligations, is yet to be devised. It would pose a formidable problem on draftsmanship, if indeed it was determined that such legislation would serve some societal purpose.

The petitioners appealed to the Appellate Division, First Department, where Assistant New York City Corporation Counsel Trudi Mara Schleifer appeared for the City Law Department to argue in opposition to the petition. On July 8, 1982, the five-judge appellate division panel reversed and granted the adoption petition. The panel opinion, by Justice Sidney H. Asch, emphasized the lack of particular restrictions in the adoption law and changing social realities in arguing that the statute could be interpreted to permit this adoption. Citing and quoting with approval the first *Adult Anonymous* adoption opinion by Brooklyn (Kings County) Family Court Judge Leon Deutsch, Asch agreed that New York, unlike some other jurisdictions that specifically required that the older party adopt the younger, had created an open adult adoption mechanism that could be used for a variety of purposes in the interests of the parties, not limited to creating a parent and child relationship. In this case, there was a significant economic incentive in the apartment where the men resided. Since the landlord had been evicting tenants "with minor violations of their leases" in anticipation of a co-op conversion, the couple's desire to avoid eviction from their home and purchase it when it went co-op was "not a frivolous consideration." Justice Asch wrote, "Historically, more frequently than not, adoption has served as a legal mechanism for achieving economic, political and social objectives rather than the stereotype parent-child relationship." Adults had used adoption in the past to achieve "strictly economic purposes," including inheritance and tax consequences. The right to stay in the apartment was a similar motivation. "Such a material concern is one of sober life reality," Asch commented, "and should not be regarded as a cynical device to evade the strictures of the parties' leases or the policy of the adoption law." Inheritance concerns had stimulated the decision to let the younger man adopt the older, but this was entirely legitimate, since inheritance concerns had traditionally been implicated in adult adoptions.

These parties, advised by counsel, had made "a well-thought out decision," had considered the legal consequences, and appeared to be proceeding in their mutual interest with no fraud or deception. Although there was a sexual relationship between the parties, that should be no impediment, since incest taboos applied only to persons related by blood and there was precedent in New York and other jurisdictions allowing persons in a sexual relationship to adopt each other for economic reasons. Now that the court of appeals had struck down the state's sodomy law in 1980 in *People v. Onofre*, there was no public policy reason based on the sexual relationship to deny the adoption petition. Besides, there were practical reasons to approve the petition apart from the issue of the apartment. "One of these parties may become ill or hospitalized," said Asch. "At many institutions only family members can visit. Consent for medical or other procedures may be required. Again, only a family member has authority to give such consent."

Asch concluded that social change made it necessary for the court to be more flexible in applying the statute to this situation:

> The "nuclear family" arrangement is no longer the only model of family life in America. The realities of present day urban life allow many different types of non-traditional families. The statutes involved do not permit this Court to deny a petition for adoption on the basis of this court's view of what is the nature of a family. In any event, the best description of a family is a continuing relationship of love and care, and an assumption of responsibility for some other person. Certainly that is present in the instant case.

This opinion drew a sharp dissent from Justice Joseph P. Sullivan, who characterized the result as "a subversion of the adoption process." Reiterating Judge Getzels's assertion that the purpose of the statute was to create a parent and child relationship, Sullivan observed,

> Petitioners do not make even a pretense of any intention to establish a parent-child relationship. Adoption is for them a means of obtaining a legal status for their homosexual relationship. While there is no pre-adoption litmus test to assess whether any prospective adoptive parent is capable of accepting the rights and assuming the responsibilities of a parent, an adoption petition should be rejected where, as here, no showing is made that a parent-child relationship, even in the broadest sense, is intended.

Indeed, the statute itself used the terms "parent" and "child" to refer to the adopter and adoptee in various provisions, evincing a legislative intent that a parent-child relationship result from an adoption.

As to the argument that the *Onofre* decision had removed any public policy objection to approving the adoption, Sullivan noted that *Onofre* had been decided in 1980 while the adoption statute was passed in 1873. It could hardly be argued, he said, that a legislature could have intended to authorize legal recognition for a sexual relationship that was unlawful when the adoption provision was passed. To Sullivan, the court was intruding in the legislative sphere. If homosexuals were to obtain legal recognition for their relationships, they would have to obtain it from the legislature.

The appellate division's decision, which was not appealed further, did not end the matter however, since some family court judges insisted that it be narrowly construed to apply to situations where the probation department found at least a simulation of a "parent and child" situation and a strong and realistic fear of eviction. (Mr. S had alleged that the landlord was in the process of evicting people prior to a planned co-op conversion.) Furthermore, the First Department's jurisdiction did not extend to Brooklyn, where a large lesbian and gay population had similar concerns about their housing security. (The first *Adult Anonymous* decision arose in Brooklyn.)

In a subsequent Manhattan case where Jack Mitchell petitioned to adopt his younger life partner and business associate of 25 years, Robert Paul Pavlik, Family Court Judge Leah R. Marks denied the petition in the face of apparently controlling appellate precedent. Michael J. Lavery, then general counsel of Lambda Legal Defense and Education Fund, who had represented the petitioners on appeal in *Adult Anonymous I*, represented Mitchell in his fight to obtain approval of the adoption petition.

Mitchell, who was age 57 at the time of the petition, sought to adopt Pavlik, who was age 50, for four specified reasons, as summarized by the court:

1. The prospective adoptive parent wishes to prevent his family from interfering in the distribution of his estate.

2. The parties wish to fully protect their work product which has been growing and represents a body of art work that should neither be separated nor destroyed.

3. The parties wish to continue residing in their present apartment without interference.

4. The parties wish to have the psychological and personal satisfaction that would result from a legal status for their relationship.

Judge Marks found this list of reasons inadequate to justify granting the petition. Although estate contests were a major preoccupation of gay people with assets in a state where contested probates were known to drag on for many years as assets wasted and their surviving partners were delayed (and not infrequently denied) inheritances due them, Marks was unwilling to recognize this as a legitimate problem to be solved through adoption. She concluded, disapprovingly, that "the evasion of existing inheritance laws is a main purpose of this adoption." She was similarly dismissive of the contention that adoption was an appropriate means to safeguard the art collection the men had jointly acquired. "The parties have never negotiated partnership agreements, incorporated, or developed any other business contract to give special protection to their business relationship or their work product." While it was true that adoption might achieve the desired results much more cheaply than having a lawyer put together and file the complex of legal documents necessary to achieve the same result, adoption was not intended for that purpose, she asserted. She noted that the petitioner had supplied no evidence of any serious threat to their joint residence, and that the appellate term had recently recognized a long-term gay male relationship as creating an "immediate family" for lease purposes in *420 East 80th Co. v. Chin* (1982), lessening the likelihood of a serious threat of eviction on these grounds. (The protection of the *Chin* decision, which was affirmed by the appellate division, proved evanescent, since the court of appeals effectively overruled that decision in 1983 in *Hudson View Properties v. Weiss*, discussed below.)

Finally, Marks felt it was not the role of the family court to approve adoptions as a substitute for "gay marriage." "The Legislature has not granted homosexuals the right to marry, a right that would seem more suitable to the circumstances of these parties," she commented. If a marriage went sour, divorce was available. On the other hand, she said, "Parties to an adoption cannot revoke their actions; all results are permanent because this is the establishment of a parent-child relationship with the ongoing responsibilities and rights. Adoption is not merely to satisfy the desires of the parties, but the establishment of a special relationship."

As to the precedential weight of *Adult Anonymous II*, Marks asserted that the cases were factually distinguishable. The appellate division had

> discussed the relationship of the two men involved at length and described the adoptive father as having acted for years in a parental role whatever their ages might have been and whatever their sexual preferences. The Appellate Division did not say that the adoption process was properly utilized to formalize homosexual activities in a legal bond, but upheld that particular homosexual adoption as a legal proceeding whereby one person took the other into the relation of a child and acquired the rights and responsibilities of a parent.

This case was different because the parties made no pretense of establishing a parent and child relationship, and the law provided suitable mechanisms through wills, contracts and incorporation to achieve their economic purposes.

Reversal appeared certain to the parties, since Judge Marks's understanding of *Adult Anonymous II* seemed quite backwards. Justice Asch had emphasized that creation of a parent-child relationship was *not* the only purpose of the law authorizing adult adoption, and had emphasized the traditional use of adult adoption to accomplish other ends in granting the adoption in that case. Thus it was quite surprising that an appellate division panel (all five members of which had not participated in the *Adult Anonymous* case) unanimously affirmed Judge Marks's ruling, without even publishing an opinion, on November 15, 1983. Perhaps it was not so surprising, however, when the same panel unanimously granted a motion for leave to appeal to the court of appeals on January 5, 1984. (Under New York law then prevailing, a unanimous decision of the appellate division could be appealed only by permission of either

the appellate division or the court of appeals; where there was a dissent in the appellate division, an appeal could be taken as of right. This was subsequently changed to give the court of appeals sole control over its docket.) Clearly, the appellate division, faced with contrary results in gay adult adoption cases, foresaw a stream of unproductive and repetitive cases that could be forestalled by a definitive ruling from the court of appeals.

When the case was argued to the court of appeals by Michael Lavery, he faced no opposition, since City Corporation Counsel Frederick A. O. Schwarz had decided not to oppose the concept of gay adult adoptions. Lambda Legal Defense filed an *amicus* brief in support of the adoption petition, written by staff attorney Abby R. Rubenfeld and cooperating attorneys Craig J. Davidson and M. Ricardo Dubriel. The court split five to two, with a majority voting to affirm denial of the adoption petition. Judge Matthew J. Jasen's opinion for the court, published October 16, 1984, harked back to Judge Getzel's original petition denial in *Adult Anonymous II* and Justice Sullivan's dissent in the appellate division in that case, holding that granting a same-sex adult adoption petition in a case where the parties made no pretense of establishing a parent-child relationship was a misuse of the statute.

"Our adoption statute embodies the fundamental social concept that the relationship of parent and child may be established by operation of law," wrote Jasen. In this, the New York laws "reflect the general acceptance of the ancient principle of *adoptio naturam imitatur*," that the purpose of the adoption statute was to "imitate nature" in creating a parent-child relationship where none had existed previously. Since "imitating nature" required that a parent adopt a child, it was "plainly not a quasi-matrimonial vehicle to provide nonmarried partners with a legal imprimatur for their sexual relationship, be it heterosexual or homosexual." Indeed, it would be "utterly repugnant to the relationship between child and parent in our society," and "a patently incongruous application of our adoption laws" to approve such an adoption. This was confirmed by various provisions of the adoption laws that provided, for example, that the adoption be "in the best interest of the [adoptive] child," and made other references to "parent" and "child." Since adoption was unknown at common law, the statute should be interpreted in line with this "narrow legislative purpose."

Did this mean that adult adoptions for reasons other than child rearing were inappropriate? Not necessarily. "There are many reasons why one adult might wish to adopt another that would be entirely consistent with the basic nature of adoption," said Jasen,

> including the following: a childless individual might wish to perpetuate a family name; two individuals might develop a strong *filial* affection for one another; a stepparent might wish to adopt the spouse's adult children; or adoption may have been forgone, for whatever reason, at an earlier date. . . . But where the relationship between the adult parties is utterly incompatible with the creation of a parent-child relationship between them, the adoption process is certainly not the proper vehicle by which to formalize their partnership in the eyes of the law. Indeed, it would be unreasonable and disingenuous for us to attribute a contrary intent to the legislature.

Asserting that the court of appeal's decision in *Onofre* had nothing to with this decision, Jasen concluded that it was for the legislature, not the courts, to decide whether New York would change its laws "so as to permit sexual lovers, homosexual or heterosexual, to adopt one another for the purpose of giving a matrimonial legal status to their relationship" or alternatively to establish "a separate institution" for the same purpose.

Judge Bernard Meyer dissented, in an opinion joined by Chief Judge Lawrence H. Cooke. Meyer insisted that the court's decision was inconsistent with *Onofre*. Resting on Justice Asch's decision in *Adult Anonymous II* and Family Court Judge Deutsch's opinion in *Adult Anonymous I* for legal analysis, Meyer contended that the majority of the court "misconceives the meaning and purpose" of the adoption laws. In Meyer's view, the majority had inappropriately concluded that "the relationship of parent and child" is a "*condition* precedent to adoption." Rather, he argued, adoption created a parent and child relationship where one had not previously existed, and there was nothing about such a relationship that required the par-

ties to be any particular age. "[T]he Legislature has not conditioned adult adoption upon there being a parent-child relationship, but rather has stated that relationship to be the result of adoption." If the legislature wanted to place limitations or conditions on adult adoption, it could have done so, but it had not done so expressly in the statute.

Furthermore, argued Meyer, contrary to the majority, the adoption statute had always been "most liberally and beneficially applied." While it was true that there was appellate division precedent in New York denying an adult adoption where the parties had a sexual relationship (a case cited by the majority and in Justice Sullivan's dissent in *Adult Anonymous II*), that case had involved an adulterous relationship and an attempt to commit fraud in violation of the inheritance laws. "Here, however, there is no suggestion of undue influence and the relationship, which by the present decision is excised from the adoption statute's broad wording, has, since the *Onofre* decision, been subject to no legal impediment. That it remains morally offensive to many cannot justify imposing upon the statute a limitation not imposed by the Legislature." The majority's objection that it would be inappropriate to sanction a sexual relationship through the adoption process was also not persuasive to Meyer, who argued that the adoption statute required no inquiry into the possible sexual relationship of the adoptive parties. "It is enough that they are two adults who freely desire the legal status of parent and child," he asserted. The motives they listed for wanting to adopt were "perfectly proper," and the lower court rulings should be reversed to grant the adoption.

The court's ruling came as a disappointment to those involved in the case, and received considerable media attention, but it did not put an end to the struggle to obtain family-type status for same-sex adult couples. For one thing, attorneys discovered that they could still get gay adult adoption petitions approved by some family court judges by artfully drafting their petitions to avoid the points found objectionable by the court of appeals, particularly any mention of a sexual relationship between the adopter and the adoptee. Indeed, Judge Jasen's opinion had specified various acceptable motivations, and suddenly some gay men and lesbian women found an urgent necessity to perpetuate their family names or cement their "filial" bonds by adopting their "roomates"!

For another, the apartment eviction problem had previously come to a boil when the court of appeals ruled in 1983 in *Hudson View Properties v. Weiss* that a woman and her child could be evicted from an apartment because she had allowed her boyfriend to move in before they were formally married. Julia Weiss had argued that the landlord was discriminating against her on the basis of marital status. Not so, ruled the court; the landlord was merely attempting to enforce an immediate-family lease provision which the tenant had freely signed. Within weeks, the legislature had amended the Real Property Law to provide that tenants were entitled to have one unrelated adult roommate, regardless of any lease restrictions to the contrary, although the roommate would not acquire any rights to the apartment independent of the tenant's residence there.

Furthermore, the disappointment over the court's ruling was tempered by disagreement within the gay community over the acceptability of adoption as a substitute for gay marriage. Adoption did not create an equal partnership, but rather a parent-child relationship. It would cut off the legal relationship of parent and child between the adoptee and his or her natural parents, if still living, and it could not easily be terminated if the couple decided to break up. The adoptee would be forever the legal child of the adopter, entitled to inherit a portion of the adopter's estate under laws of intestate succession and perhaps to assert other claims based on the family relationship, unless, of course, the adoptee was subsequently adopted by somebody else. Something different needed to be found, and either despairing of attaining judicial or legislative approval for gay marriage or rejecting marriage as an appropriate model for gay adult relationships due to its patriarchal and heterosexual trappings, some gay advocates began arguing for an entirely different institution of "domestic partnership," which became a major legislative goal of the late 1980s.

Case References

Adult Anonymous, In re, 106 Misc. 2d 792, 435 N.Y.S.2d 527 (Fam. Ct., Kings County 1981)

420 East 80th Co. v. Chin, 115 Misc. 2d 195, 455 N.Y.S.2d 42 (App. Term, 1st Dept. 1982), affirmed, 97 A.D.2d 390, 488 N.Y.S.2d 9 (1st Dept. 1983)

Hudson View Properties v. Weiss, 59 N.Y.2d 733, 450 N.E.2d 234, 463 N.Y.S.2d 428 (1983)

People v. Onofre, 51 N.Y.2d 476, 434 N.Y.S.2d 947, 415 N.E.2d 297, certiorari denied, 451 U.S. 987 (1980)

Upjohn, In re, 304 N.Y. 366, 107 N.E.2d 492 (1952)

60. CUSTODY RIGHTS OF GAY FATHERS IN RELATIONSHIPS

Roe v. Roe, 324 S.E.2d 691 (Va. 1985).

When the "natural parents" of a child battle over custody and visitation rights, courts normally state that they are deciding the issue by reference to the "best interests of the child." When one of the parents is gay, the court must determine whether sexual orientation is a relevant factor, how to weigh it as a factor, and whether the way in which the parent expresses his or her sexual orientation renders that parent either "unfit" or less desirable than the other parent as a custodian of the child. These questions are particularly complicated in those jurisdictions where sexual activity between persons of the same sex is condemned by the criminal law, even when consensual, private adult conduct is involved.

The Virginia Supreme Court's 1985 *Roe v. Roe* decision is perhaps the harshest categorical rejection of gay men involved in cohabitation relationships with their sexual partners as suitable custodians of their children. The court's substitution of its judgment for that of the trial judge, who observed the parties, interviewed the child, and concluded that it would be appropriate to award joint custody and extended residence during a part of the year with each parent, is particularly remarkable in an area of the law where so much turns on judicial judgments about the character of the contestants. Also remarkable is the total lack of consideration of expert testimony or other evidence on the impact on a child of living in a homosexual household.

David and Catherine Roe (fictitious surname) married in 1971. Their daughter was born in 1974. The Roes separated in 1975 and agreed amicably that Catherine would have full custody over the child. In 1976, a Virginia court entered a final decree of divorce confirming and incorporating the custody agreement. In 1978, Catherine developed cancer, requiring extensive surgery and medical treatment that made it impossible for her to take care of the daughter, who went to live with David. David petitioned the court for a change of custody to him in the fall of 1979, which Catherine initially opposed on the ground that she expected to be able to care for her daughter again on a full-time basis by March 1980. But Catherine apparently changed her mind, because the parties presented a consent decree to the court in October 1979, stating that custody should be awarded to David with reasonable visitation rights for Catherine, in light of her physical inability to care for the daughter.

In 1983, Catherine learned from their daughter that a man had moved into David's house, and that the two were living together as lovers. Catherine filed a petition in July with the circuit court in Fairfax County, seeking a temporary restraining order returning her daughter to her custody pending a hearing on Catherine's request for a change of custody back to her. Catherine's petition alleged that David and his lover shared the same bed in a bedroom of the house where the daughter lived, that the daughter had seen the two men "hugging and kissing and sleeping in bed together," and that other gay people had visited the house and exhibited similar behavior in the child's presence. Catherine also alleged that her daughter, then 9 years old, was unhappy living with David and wanted to return to Catherine, and that Catherine was now well enough to care for her daughter full time. Circuit Judge Richard J. Jamborsky issued an order that the child stay

with her mother until a hearing could be held on August 25, 1983.

At the hearing, Jamborsky heard testimony from both parents and David's lover, but apparently heard no expert testimony regarding homosexuality or the impact on a child of living with a homosexual parent. David and his lover testified that they did not "flaunt" their homosexuality. Jamborsky also interviewed the daughter in chambers. He concluded that the girl was a "very lovely, outgoing, bright and intelligent child . . . a very happy child [who] seemed to be well adjusted and outgoing." Jamborsky found no evidence that David's conduct had any adverse effect on the child, but that she preferred to live with her mother.

Jamborsky, who ruled from the bench, concluded that both David and Catherine were fit parents, and that they were equally capable of serving as custodians for their daughter. He found that there was little animosity between David and Catherine, and that each had been a fit, devoted, and competent custodian when they had custody of their daughter. He was concerned about the conduct to which the child was exposed in David's home, however. Rejecting the men's testimony about the degree of discretion they practiced, he stated that "this relationship of sharing the same bed or bedroom with the child being in the home would be one of the greatest degrees of flaunting that one could imagine. It flies in the face of *Brown v. Brown*, and it flies in the face of society's mores anyway." (*Brown v. Brown* was a 1977 decision of the Virginia Supreme Court that upheld termination of a mother's custody over her two young sons after she began living in an adulterous relationship with a male lover.) He also expressed concern about the child seeing males hugging and "patting each other on the behind," although he conceded that football players are seen doing that sort of thing all the time. "Whether the Court would find them distasteful or not, it is simply not something that the Court is competent to get involved in . . . all of these things require such judgment as to appropriateness or inappropriateness that the Court is simply not going to try and get involved." While expressing concern that the daughter might find the situation awkward when she got into the teen years, the judge opined that a further petition for change of custody could be entertained at that time. He concluded, however, that for now a joint custody award would be the most appropriate measure, with the daughter living with David during the school year and Catherine during vacation periods, with liberal visitation rights for each parent when the child was in the custody of the other. However, he conditioned David's custody upon his "not sharing the same bed or bedroom with any male lover or friend while the child is present in the home."

Catherine immediately appealed to the Virginia Supreme Court, alleging that Jamborsky had abused his discretion in concluding that it was in the best interest of the daughter for David to have custody, even on a joint basis. At the hearing before the supreme court, Catherine was represented by Richard J. Byrd, of Fairfax, and David was represented by James M. Lowe, of Alexandria. The court received a joint *amicus* brief from the American Civil Liberties Union of Northern Virginia, the Center for Constitutional Rights, the Lesbian Rights Project, and the Women's Legal Defense Fund, attempting to present the kind of evidence that would have been adduced had expert witnesses testified at the hearing, to the effect that all studies had shown that being raised in a gay household is not harmful to children. The Virginia Supreme Court was not buying this argument, however. Without any discussion of the authorities and references cited in the *amicus* brief, the court unanimously ruled on January 18, 1985, that Catherine should have sole custody of her daughter.

Justice Charles S. Russell's opinion for the court found the precedent of *Brown v. Brown* to be dispositive of the merits of the case. The court had commented in *Brown*:

> In all custody cases the controlling consideration is always the child's welfare and, in determining the best interest of the child, the court must decide by considering all the facts, including what effect a nonmarital relationship by a parent has on a child. The moral climate in which children are to be raised is an important consideration for the court in determining custody, and adultery is a reflection of a mother's moral values. An illicit relationship to which minor children

are exposed cannot be condoned. Such a relationship must necessarily be given the most careful consideration in a custody proceeding.

In *Brown*, the court had quoted with approval from a 1977 Louisiana decision, *Beck v. Beck*, where the court had held that a mother engaged in an adulterous relationship "in total disregard of the moral principles of our society . . . is generally held morally unfit for custody." The decision in *Brown*, said Russell, was not premised on the existence of the adulterous relationship, as such, but rather on "Mrs. Brown's exposure of the children to an immoral and illicit relationship."

David's chief precedent was a *Doe v. Doe* decision, in which the Virginia Supreme Court had refused to allow the father and stepmother to adopt a child over the protest of the child's lesbian mother, who lived in another state with her lover where the child would visit from time to time. In that case, said Russell, the court had emphasized that adoption was a final and irrevocable step cutting off all parental rights. "Although we declined to hold that every lesbian mother or homosexual father is *per se* an unfit *parent*, we were not presented, in *Doe*, with the question of the impact of a homosexual relationship upon a child in the context of day-to-day custody." Now that question was before the court, and the court found *Brown* to be controlling.

> The father's continuous exposure of the child to his immoral and illicit relationship renders him an unfit and improper custodian as a matter of law. Indeed, the mother contends that the influences to which the child is exposed here are far more deleterious than those in *Brown*. She points out, as an illustration of the relative degree of abhorrence by which our society regards such conduct, that adultery is a class four misdemeanor in Virginia . . . which is seldom prosecuted, while the conduct inherent in the father's relationship is punishable as a class six felony . . . which is prosecuted with considerable frequency and vigor, as evidenced by the decided cases annotated under those respective sections of the Code. However that may be, we have no hesitancy in saying that the conditions under which this child must live daily are not only unlawful but also impose an intolerable burden upon her by reason of the social condemnation attached to them, which will inevitably afflict

her relationships with her peers and with the community at large. . . The father's unfitness is manifested by his willingness to impose this burden upon her in exchange for his own gratification.

The court made no mention of the U.S. Supreme Court's April 1984 decision in *Palmore v. Sidoti*, in which the High Court had rejected a very similar argument in a case involving the custody rights of a white mother who, after divorce, had married a black man.

While Judge Jamborsky had believed that "ordering [David] out of his lover's bedroom" took care of the worst problems involved in continuing custody for David, the supreme court was "not so persuaded." The daughter remained aware of her father's relationship, and it was likely that "the open behavior of the father and his friends in the home can only be expected to continue." Russell found that "the impact of such behavior upon the child, and upon any of her peers who may visit the home, is inevitable." It was in the daughter's best interest, said Russell, to "protect" her from the "burdens imposed by such behavior, insofar as practicable," which could best be done by giving Catherine sole custody and denying David any visitation rights in his home or in the presence of his lover so long as his current living arrangements continued. Consequently, the court reversed Jamborsky's order and remanded the case for a redetermination of the conditions under which David might visit with his daughter.

Russell's decision was shocking on several grounds. For one thing, it showed how criminal sodomy laws can be twisted around to support conclusions that are entirely insupportable in fact. There was no evidence before the court that David and his lover were violating the Virginia sodomy law, which pertains to oral and anal intercourse (and which might be violated by a heterosexual couple just as easily),

and the comment about the sodomy law being "prosecuted with considerable frequency and vigor" was also a distortion, since examination of the reported cases would show that the prosecutions virtually all involved conduct in public places (usually vice squad officers luring gay men into sexual activity before arresting them). By characterizing any gay relationship as automatically "illicit," the court was virtually creating a status offense of being in a gay relationship, regardless of the conduct of the parties in that relationship. The court cited no authority for the proposition that two men hugging and kissing, or even sharing a bed, is illegal in Virginia.

More seriously, perhaps, the court drew conclusions with no foundation in competent evidence about the "impact" on the daughter of remaining in David's home. Russell did not even feel it necessary to specify what that impact would be; he concluded that an "impact"—type not specified—would be inevitable, without citation to any testimony or published authority. He did not even discuss pertinent decisions by appellate courts in other states that have considered, at length, the conflicting testimony of experts on this subject, or the recent U.S. Supreme Court decision holding that a court deciding a custody dispute could not be party to societal discrimination. Russell's opinion dealt with the issue of custody by a gay male parent engaged in a relationship with another man as if it were a totally unprecedented incident in American law. The decision was made in a factual vacuum, relying solely on the prejudices of the judges masquerading as "common knowledge."

Case References

Beck v. Beck, 341 So. 2d 580 (La. App. 1977)
Brown v. Brown, 218 Va. 196, 237 S.E.2d 89 (1977)
Doe v. Doe, 222 Va. 736, 284 S.E. 2d 799 (1981)
Palmore v. Sidoti, 466 U.S. 429 (1984)

61. WHEN MOTHER LIVES A "HOMOSEXUAL LIFESTYLE"

S.N.E. v. R.L.B., 699 P.2d 875 (Alaska 1985).

In 1984, the U.S. Supreme Court decided *Palmore v. Sidoti*, holding that a white woman who had married a black man did not thereby forfeit the right to continued custody of her child from a previous marriage with a white man. While the mother's entering into an interracial marriage might subject the family (including the child) to societal bias and prejudice, such prejudices could not be the basis on which a court would modify a prior custody arrangement due to "changed circumstances," for to do so would be to lend the support of the government to private race discrimination. Soon after the Court's decision, the Alaska Supreme Court cited *Palmore* as authority against a change of child custody away from a lesbian mother.

R.L.B., previously married and divorced, was in his early thirties when he met S.N.E., who was also divorced. She was one year younger than he, and uncertain about her sexuality. They began living together in a sexual relationship. They married after she became pregnant, but the marriage did not work out and they divorced after three months. She was still pregnant at the time. They made a voluntary agreement under which their child would be in her custody after birth, but the father would have reasonable visitation rights. After the child was born, S.N.E. moved from Alaska to the state of Washington, where she lived in a sexual relationship with a female companion and attended graduate school on leave from her regular job.

Three years after having signed the original separation and custody agreement, R.L.B. (who had since remarried) filed suit in Alaska Superior Court in Anchorage, represented by Robert H. Wagstaff, of Anchorage, seeking legal custody of his son. Claiming that it was in the child's best interest to live with R.L.B.'s wife and R.L.B., the husband contended that S.N.E. was now a lesbian with radical political views, that she was emotionally unstable, and that he was actually the "primary" parent of the

child. S.N.E. was represented by Charlene A. Lichtman and Sandra K. Saville, of Anchorage. Superior Court Judge J. Justin Ripley appointed Vincent Vitale, of Anchorage, to be guardian *ad litem* for the child, and designated Andrew M. Brown as master to hold a hearing and establish a factual record for decision. The hearing was held on July 14, 1983, in Anchorage.

After receiving Brown's recommendations and the hearing record, Ripley issued a protective order, barring any of the parties or their attorneys from talking about the case with anybody who was not a party or a potential witness. Ripley then issued an order granting custody of the child to the father, R.L.B., finding that there had been a change of circumstances justifying modification of the original custody agreement. Specifically, Ripley found:

There has been a change of circumstances in the parties' lives since the original decree sufficient to warrant a review and change of custody to plaintiff as follows:

(a) At the time of the earlier decree [the child] was unborn and custody in the plaintiff was physically impossible;

(b) A child has an overriding need to be with its mother during the first days and months of its life, if possible, and that phase of [the child's] life has passed;

(c) Plaintiff and [his current wife] have become at least equal caretakers of [the child] and defendant has relinquished that authority in [the child's] life to them;

(d) Defendant has since the original decree significantly changed personally including a choice to live a homosexual lifestyle;

(e) Defendant has moved her residence to Seattle, Washington, and has left her profession, perhaps permanently, so that [the child's] household, community and contact with his father and most appropriate male role model will be significantly altered unless custody is changed to plaintiff;

(f) Defendant has demonstrated an inability at times to cope with child rearing without significant support from plaintiff or others;

(g) Defendant has actively interfered with the development of an open, frequent and loving relationship between plaintiff and their son.

S.N.E. promptly appealed this ruling to the Alaska Supreme Court, which reversed Ripley's custody award by a 4–1 vote in a decision announced on May 10, 1985, holding that the decision was tainted by Ripley's consideration and comments about S.N.E.'s sexual orientation and lifestyle.

Justice Allen T. Compton's decision began by noting that the standard in all child custody cases in Alaska was, by statute, the best interests of the child, but that this standard was applied somewhat differently as between original custody decrees and petitions to modify custody. Whether the original custody arrangement was made by order of a court in a contested case or by agreement of the parties, in a subsequent action to modify a decree, the burden was on the party seeking the modification to show that a change in circumstances since the time of the original arrangement made it necessary for the court to reconsider the issue of best interests of the child. In looking at allegations of changed circumstances, the court had to restrict its consideration to "facts directly affecting the child's well-being," said Compton. "We have often endorsed the requirement that there be a nexus between the conduct of the parent relied on by the court and the parent-child relationship."

In this connection, Compton made clear, sexual activity by the parent was not to be a consideration unless it could be shown that such activity had a negative effect on the child's welfare, citing *Bonjour v. Bonjour* (1977), a case involving a mother living with "another man in an adulterous relationship" where the Alaska Supreme Court had held that such activity did not justify a denial of custody to the mother without evidence of such an adverse effect. He also cited cases involving out-of-wedlock birth, unstable relationships of the mother, and mental health problems of the mother, in each of which the Alaska court had restricted its consideration to factors adversely affecting the child. In this case, Compton asserted, although R.L.B. denied that he was pinning the modification petition on the mother's sexual orientation, it seemed clear from the record that this is what was going on. Not only was homosexuality the subject of testimony by most of the twenty-two witnesses at the hearing, but it was mentioned numerous times in the trial court's factual findings and conclusions of law, and was cited by Ripley in his ultimate factual finding as a changed circumstance justifying modification of custody. That particular finding, said Compton, "reflects the taint apparent throughout the record."

> In marked contrast to the wealth of testimony that Mother is a lesbian, there is no suggestion that this has or is likely to affect the child adversely. The record contains evidence that the child's development to date has been excellent, that Mother has not neglected him, and that there is no increased likelihood that a male child raised by a lesbian would be homosexual. Simply put, it is impermissible to rely on any real or imagined social stigma attaching to Mother's status as a lesbian.

Compton cited, for his last assertion, *Palmore v. Sidoti*. He noted that the only finding by Ripley that could plausibly bear on the impact of S.N.E.'s homosexuality on the child was "a possible adverse effect . . . related to the likely duration of Mother's current relationship." Compton dismissed this factor, arguing that it was essentially based on "conjecture," since there was "no evidence Mother's relationship was not committed. Instead," remarked Compton, "the court relied on its own unsupported opinion that homosexual relationships are unstable and usually of short duration."

Concluding that Ripley's decision had been "impermissibly tainted by reliance in part on the fact that Mother is a lesbian," the court decided to remand the case for reconsideration, instructing that "consideration of a parent's conduct is appropriate only when the evidence supports a finding that a parent's conduct has or reasonably will have an adverse impact on the child and his best interests." The court also decided that Judge Ripley's "gag order" had been too broad and, responding to S.N.E.'s petition, held it unconstitutional. While it is true that an Alaska statute authorized closing a child custody proceeding to the public when it was necessary "in the best interests of the child" to do so, the Alaska Constitution's guarantee of freedom of speech meant that this could only be done out of absolute necessity. Ripley's order was so broadly drawn that neither parent would be able to discuss the case and their reactions to it with a professional counselor or a family member who was not expected to serve as a witness. The court left in place Ripley's decision to seal the records and close the hearings to the public, but struck the portion of the order barring the parties and their attorneys from talking with anybody about the case.

Justice Edmond W. Burke filed a brief dissenting opinion, disagreeing that Ripley's custody ruling was "fatally flawed by references to the matter of Mother's sexual orientation." Burke contended that the references had been "taken entirely out of context," and that Ripley's detailed factual findings and legal conclusions showed "a careful analysis of the difficult issue to be decided, and a thorough understanding of the proper weight to be given to the matter of Mother's sexual preference." However, he did not explain what the weight was, merely asserting that the custody order should have been affirmed.

The Alaska Supreme Court's decision in *S.N.E. v. R.L.B.* marked a significant extension of the *Palmore* principle to lesbian and gay child custody disputes. Contrary to some courts that have held *Palmore* essentially irrelevant because it was premised largely on the strong public policy against race discrimination, the Alaska court recognized that *Palmore* stands for a broader proposition: that societal bias and prejudice against a parent should not be embraced by a court to determine a child custody contest, regardless of the personal characteristic or trait that is the occasion of the bias. The *S.N.E.* decision was not an unmixed blessing, however, for even as Justice Compton was applying *Palmore* to overturn the lower court's decision, he stated, at least by implication, that it would be a negative consequence if the son were to be gay. Thus, even the court that was rejecting homophobia as a basis for determining child custody was itself, perhaps unconsciously, incorporating homophobic judgments into its decision.

Case References

Bonjour v. Bonjour, 566 P.2d 667 (Alaska 1977), appeal after remand, 592 P.2d 1233 (Alaska 1979)

Palmore v. Sidoti, 466 U.S. 429 (1984)

62. THE RIGHTS OF THE TRANSSEXUAL PARENT

Daly v. Daly, 102 Nev. 66, 715 P.2d 56, certiorari denied, 479 U.S. 876 (1986).

Has a man ceased to be a father when he becomes a woman? The Nevada Supreme Court confronted this question in *Daly v. Daly*, and decided, by a 3–2 vote, that the father's parental rights should be terminated in such a situation, despite the lack of any evidence that he was not fit to continue in a parental role. The court premised its decision solely on the alleged emotional impact of the father's sex change on his young daughter.

Tim Daly and Nan Toews married in 1969, and their daughter, Mary, was born in 1973. Tim and Nan separated in 1979, and Nan, who retained custody of Mary, moved with her to Reno, Nevada. Nan's mother resided with Nan and Mary. Tim continued to live in Oakland, California, where he was employed as a research scientist at the Lawrence Berkeley Laboratory of the University of California. The Nevada Second Judicial District Court entered a divorce decree on February 17, 1981, giving Nan custody and according Tim visitation rights. Under the court's decree, Tim was required to provide child support and health insurance for Mary.

Tim, who felt insecure about his sexual identity, consulted Lynn Frazier, a psychotherapist who specialized in the treatment of transsexuals. Frazier subjected Tim to the extended process that medical professionals use to determine whether an individual is a true transsexual before recommending sex reassignment surgery. This included a lengthy period of psychological evaluation, followed by hormonal therapy to produce female secondary sexual characteristics and by a period of living as a woman to determine whether the individual is psychologically capable of making the change. When Tim had completed the evaluation process, Frazier diagnosed him as a transsexual and recommended the surgery. Tim decided that he had to prepare Mary for what was going to happen. While she was visiting with him on her summer vacation, he told her all about the process, and asked her to keep it a secret from her mother and grandmother.

Here the accounts of the mother and the father sharply diverge. According to the mother, Mary returned from this visit with her father a changed person. As summarized subsequently by the Nevada Supreme Court's majority opinion:

> Respondent testified that when Mary returned from the August visitation with her father, she would vacillate from being wide awake to being very sluggish. A certified academically talented child since seven years of age, she would sit at the kitchen table for hours cutting a large piece of paper into small pieces. She would take a pencil and trace the grain of the oak floor for hours. She wet the bed and, in fact, was incontinent in class a week prior to trial. Mary had not wet the bed since she was two years old. She had a short attention span and could not follow instructions, nor perform simple tasks. She also became inattentive and her handwriting degenerated into a scrawl. In addition, Mary became quiet and withdrawn.

However, the dissenters on the supreme court drew a different picture from the testimony, noting that Nan had recalled these things only in retrospect. Indeed, nothing about Mary's conduct after returning from her summer visit with her father led Nan to suspect that anything was wrong, they asserted, until Mary told her on February 14, 1982, that her father was having a sex-change operation. Nan promptly took her to a child psychologist, who advised Nan that it was "very dangerous to allow Mary to be in the company of her father again." But a neighbor and a school teacher, both of whom knew Mary, testified that they did not notice any particular problems with

Mary during the period between her return home and when she told her mother about the impending operation.

The majority opinion paints a picture of Nan concerned about Mary's disturbed mental state, seeking to shield her from further upset to her normal development by exposure to a father who was, in her opinion, no longer a father. The dissent paints a picture of an outraged, tradition-minded mother immediately consulting a lawyer and unilaterally denying the father his legal visitation rights. When Tim, now known as Suzanne Lindley Daly, tried to visit Mary in Reno in 1982, Nan obtained assistance from law enforcement authorities to keep him away from the house, pretending that she had a court order authorizing police assistance. In August 1982, Nan refused to pick up Suzanne's birthday present for Mary at the post office, and asked Suzanne not to telephone any more. When Suzanne tried to visit in January 1983, she was "deterred by Mary's gun-wielding grandmother, who would not permit him [her] to enter the premises," according to the dissenting judges.

Nan sought a court order barring Suzanne from contacting Mary, and had originally initiated proceedings in May 1982 to terminate Suzanne's parental rights permanently. The trial judge of the Second Judicial District, Washoe County, John E. Gabrielli, heard testimony from the parties, neighbors and friends, and experts for both sides, and concluded in an unpublished order of April 11, 1983, that Suzanne's parental rights should be terminated.

Under Nevada law, a decision to terminate parental rights requires a finding of both jurisdictional and dispositional grounds for the court to act. A statute lists jurisdictional grounds, which include abandonment, neglect, unfitness, or "risk of serious physical, mental or emotional injury to the child if he were returned to, or remains in, the home of his parent or parents," as well as "only token efforts" by the parent "to support or communicate with the child," to prevent neglect, to avoid being unfit, or to eliminate the risks identified above. At the trial, Nan's expert witness testified that there would be a serious risk of emotional or mental injury to Mary if she had further contact with her father, and that there was no guarantee that this risk could be avoided by exposing Mary to psychological or psychiatric treatment. Suzanne also presented an expert witness, who conceded on cross-examination that "there are children who are not able to accept a parent as a transsexual," but that it was possible that proper treatment could help Mary to adjust to the situation. Mary also testified at the trial, stating that she had no wish to see her father any more. She said it would be disturbing to her to see him again after what had happened. By the time of the trial, through Nan's efforts, Mary had not had any direct contact with her father for more than six months, although Suzanne attempted to maintain communication with her and maintained her insurance coverage.

Judge Gabrielli concluded that there were jurisdictional grounds to terminate Suzanne's parental rights, based on the testimony about risk of harm and Nan's expressed desire to sever all ties with her former husband. As to the "dispositional" grounds, Gabrielli found that Nan was a good mother who was sincerely concerned about Mary's best interests, while Suzanne was "a selfish person whose own needs, desires and wishes were paramount and were indulged without regard to their impact on the life and psyche of the daughter, Mary." Gabrielli found not only the risk of serious harm, but also concluded that the extended period without direct contact between father and daughter could be considered "abandonment" under the termination statute (even though some of that period was attributable to efforts by Nan and her mother to keep Suzanne away). Consequently, he issued an order terminating Suzanne's parental rights.

Suzanne appealed to the Nevada Supreme Court, which heard argument from Ann Casamajor, of Albany, California, representing Suzanne, and Nada Novakovich, of Reno, representing Nan. The court was sharply split over the case, upholding Gabrielli's decision in its March 6 ruling, but producing a sharp dissent from two of the justices. Justice Thomas L. Steffen's opinion for the court found that there was substantial evidence in the record to support Gabrielli's findings about risk of harm to Mary from further exposure to her father. He found that "Suzanne's efforts to regain visitation rights are shown to be a continuing source of apprehension to the child." Finding that Mary's reaction to Suzanne was one of "revulsion," and that it was uncertain whether psychological treatment for Mary could change this reaction, Steffen supported Gabrielli's decision. He seized on Suzanne's testimony at trial that "Mary should know lesbians, homosexuals and transsexuals and 'be a part of their lives' if 'they are my friends.'" Steffen found that this would create a posture of "recurring conflict with the child's mother and the 'traditional' upbringing enjoyed by Mary during her formative years," and that "the resulting equation does not bode well for the emotional health and well-being of the child."

Steffen insisted that the court saw no basis for "such disruption of Mary's life" and that there was no need to inflict "a continuing sense of instability and uneasiness on this child." Of course, when Mary reached the age of majority and was out of the control of her mother, she was free to seek out a relationship of some sort with her father. Steffen stated:

> In the meantime, given the circumstances concerning Mary's view of Suzanne and the extent of her opposition to further ties with a vestigial parent, it can be said that Suzanne, in a very real sense, has terminated her own parental rights as a father. It was strictly Tim Daly's choice to discard his fatherhood and assume the role of a female who could never be either mother or sister to his daughter.

Suzanne had clearly made some errors that contributed to the defeat. She had stopped paying child support when she was denied visitation, and had not herself resorted to litigation to secure her visitation rights, which the court seized on as support for the finding of "abandonment," despite her repeated efforts to visit and communicate with Mary. Interestingly, the court's opinion omits any discussion of various legal arguments advanced by Suzanne, who had premised her case in part on *Palmore v. Sidoti*, the 1984 case in which the U.S. Supreme Court stated that private prejudices could not be the basis for decision in a matter involving the best interest of a child. Concluding that none of Suzanne's arguments had any merit or would require reversal, the court affirmed Gabrielli's decision.

Justice Elmer M. Gunderson dissented, in an opinion joined by Justice Charles E. Springer.

Gunderson claimed that the majority had mischaracterized the case entirely. Suzanne was not seeking any right of visitation at this time, merely to preserve her parental tie to Mary. Suzanne was perfectly willing to forego direct contact until such time as Mary was willing to allow contact to resume. Suzanne just wanted to assure that her status as a parent would continue. Gunderson saw no basis for severing the parental relationship.

Gunderson asserted that none of the grounds for terminating parental rights required by Nevada statutes had been met in this case. There was no risk of serious harm to Mary in a situation where Suzanne was willing to refrain from exercising any visitation rights. Furthermore, Nan's actions had contributed greatly to the factual basis for finding "abandonment," since she blocked all access and communication, and there was evidence that Suzanne's attorney had been ineffective in assisting him during the period of contention leading up to the trial. Gunderson asserted that Gabrielli's findings about Suzanne's "selfishness" were not supported by the evidence, since it appeared that, having been informed that visitation would present a serious risk to Mary, Suzanne had agreed not to press any visitation rights.

Gunderson also rejected Gabrielli's findings regarding "Mary's anxieties over the dispute between her parents" as a basis for terminating parental rights, asserting that "no judicial resolution of the instant appeal can stop any hostilities that exist between the parties. With the father foregoing any contact with Mary, little else can be done to resolve Mary's anxieties." While recognizing Mary's desire to avoid future contact with her father, Gunderson asserted that the court should

> also recognize the importance of not severing a parent's rights where a less restrictive alternative exists to permit preservation of a family tie. . . . While Mary may no longer have a father figure, she still has a second parent who desires to contribute to her financial support, and who might someday in the future provide her with needed comfort, affection, and help.

Gunderson pointed out that the majority opinion was premised on the issue of visitation, and thus was rather beside the point, given Suzanne's willingness to forego visitation in order to preserve her family tie with Mary.

> As previously noted, the appellant father in this matter is a well educated person, long employed by one of this nation's eminent academic institutions. He served this country honorably in its armed forces, and, the record indicates, has never been known to violate any of our country's laws. Appellant fathered Mary Daly in wedlock, and, since divorce, has maintained an interest in her and has continued attempts to provide for her, even though the respondent has improperly impeded those legitimate efforts.

Gunderson indicated his doubts about the legitimacy of a diagnosis of transsexuality and the whole process of sex reassignment surgery and sex change generally, but said that Suzanne should not be blamed for following the advice of highly credentialed medical professionals, no matter how misguided that advice might turn out to be in the long view of history.

> As I assess the record, the fact that the appellant father has suffered emotional problems which are foreign to the experience of this court's members, and has followed the possibly poor advice of eminent medical authorities in his attempt to relieve them, does not justify a total and irrevocable severance of appellant's formal legal tie to a child he obviously cares about and desires to help nurture. By holding that such a severance is justified in these facts, it seems to me, we are being unnecessarily and impermissibly punitive to the exercise of a medical option we personally find offensive, thereby depriving a child of a legal relationship which might well be to the child's advantage in the future.

Suzanne petitioned the U.S. Supreme Court for *certiorari*, contending that her parental rights had been unconstitutionally terminated in violation of the principles of *Palmore v. Sidoti*, but the Court denied review on October 6, 1986.

The decision in *Daly v. Daly*, virtually the only one of its kind to be reported by an appellate court, stands as a sad reminder of the difficulties courts encounter when dealing with new phenomena for which there is little or no precedent. From the sharply contrasting presentation of the facts by the majority and dissenting opinions, one concludes that this might well have been a case where young Mary, puzzled and confused by what was happening with her father, tried to work things out in her own mind over a period of many months and finally confided in her mother, whose instant outrage and shock ultimately poisoned Mary's attitudes toward her father. The "revulsion" seen by the majority of the court may well have sprung from Mary's anxieties—not necessarily anxieties about her father's sex change, but more likely anxieties about the war being waged by her mother and the resulting termination of contact with her father. Of course, it is also possible that Judge Gabrielli was correct, that it was not in Mary's interest to see her father any more, but, as Justice Gunderson pointed out, by the time the case got to the Nevada Supreme Court, Suzanne was no longer pressing for visitation.

The resulting decision might be held to stand for the proposition that the *Palmore* principles do not apply outside the realm of race discrimination, but the lack of any discussion by the court of the relevance or irrelevance of *Palmore* makes it difficult to draw any such conclusion with confidence. Perhaps the main distinction between the two cases was that in *Palmore* any contention about psychological or emotional harm to a child growing up in a mixed-race home was purely speculative, whereas Judge Gabrielli heard expert testimony from a mental health professional who had examined Mary that the young girl had been emotionally scarred by her father's revelation and the subsequent developments. Perhaps *Daly v. Daly* should be regarded as such a fact-specific ruling that no general legal principle can be extracted from it: certainly not that all transsexuals may automatically be deprived of continued contact and parental ties with their children.

Case Reference

Palmore v. Sidoti, 466 U.S. 429 (1984)

63. SOCIETAL PREJUDICE AND THE LESBIAN MOTHER

S.E.G. v. R.A.G., 735 S.W.2d 164 (Mo. App., E.D. 1987).

In few states have the courts been so unremittingly and publicly hostile to the custody and visitation claims of lesbian and gay parents as in Missouri, whose state supreme court was the first in the nation to uphold the constitutionality of a sodomy law *after* the U.S. Supreme Court's 1986 decision in *Bowers v. Hardwick*. Although litigators belatedly raised state constitutional claims in *State v. Walsh* (1986), hoping to salvage a lower court victory that predated the U.S. Supreme Court ruling, the Missouri Supreme Court refused to take the bait. It affirmed the constitutionality of Missouri's law on the authority of the *Hardwick* decision, even though the Missouri law was much broader than Georgia's. The Missouri law encompassed conduct that had not traditionally been considered sodomous under either the common law or the criminal statutes of most states that regulated consensual adult conduct, while the Georgia law only applied to anal or oral intercourse. With this strong statutory and judicial disapproval of homosexual conduct, it was not surprising that at the first opportunity the Missouri courts also refused to apply the principle of *Palmore v. Sidoti* (1984)—that private prejudices may not inform child custody decisions—to a contested custody case involving a gay parent.

S.E.G. (wife) and R.A.G. (husband) married in 1973, when wife was age 16 and pregnant (husband was then age 20). Their first child, a son, was born later in 1973, followed by three daughters born in 1975, 1979, and 1982. The Missouri Division of Family Services employed husband as a caseworker. Wife taught natural child birth classes and did baby-sitting jobs out of the family home in Union, Missouri. Husband had a drinking problem, and wife threatened to divorce him if he did not seek treatment. Husband entered the White Deer Alcoholic Treatment Center in 1984 for a month-long course of treatment, and later claimed that he had not drunk alcoholic beverages since May 1984. Despite the treatment, wife determined to end the marriage, and the parties separated in June 1984, both continuing to reside in Union. In November 1984, wife met Kitty Ann Shelby, known by the nickname of Airrow, at an Adult Children of Alcoholics meeting. The two women became close friends and by February 1985, had begun a sexual relationship. Airrow continued to reside in St. Louis, but would drive to Union several times a week to sleep over at wife's home. Airrow became friendly with the children, who were then living in the family home with wife. The two women were open with the children about their sexual relationship (including expressing affection for each other, and hugging and kissing in view of the children), which the children apparently accepted. The youngest child, then about 2½ years old, occasionally slept in the same bed with the women. Wife also occasionally drove with the children to St. Louis to visit with Airrow, and they would all sleep over at Airrow's home. Husband, who had moved out of the family home upon separation from wife, was apparently unaware of the nature of the relationship between his wife and Airrow.

On April 19, 1985, Franklin County Circuit Court Judge Ralph Voss entered a decree of dissolution of the marriage, granting custody of the children, the family home, maintenance, and child support to wife. Once the decree was entered, wife became less secretive with husband, who discovered the nature of her living situation and relationship with Airrow, and promptly filed a motion on May 3, 1985, for a new trial or amended judgment. Voss responded by amending the custody award to grant primary custody and the family home to husband, removing the award of maintenance and child support to wife, and restricting wife's visitation so as to exclude the children from any exposure to Airrow or to wife's homosexual "lifestyle" or activities. Voss's decision was consistent with the few relevant Missouri precedents predating *Hardwick* and *Palmore*, all of which rejected custody and unrestricted visitation claims from gay or lesbian parents. Wife, represented by

Gale L. Toko, of St. Louis, appealed the amended award to the Missouri Court of Appeals, Eastern Division. Husband was represented by Prudence L. Fink, of Union, Missouri.

The appeals court took two years to decide the case, but unanimously affirmed Voss's amended order on July 21, 1987. Presiding Judge Gary M. Gaertner's opinion makes clear that there is little that a homosexual parent could do in Missouri to retain custody of his or her children, short of staying entirely in the closet, hiding all traces of homosexual orientation, and avoiding all sexual activity that might come to the attention of the children, the other spouse, or the court. Voss had received evidence, in the form of published articles in professional journals, indicating that studies of children raised by gay parents had shown "no significant differences among heterosexual and homosexual divorced parents and their children," according to Gaertner. (This one-sentence summary does not really do justice to the cited articles, which went much further in indicating that children raised by gay parents do not differ on any statistically significant measure of psychological and physical growth and adjustment, including sexual development.) Voss had found these studies not to be credible, and Gaertner indicated that such a decision was within the trial court's discretion.

But the true focus of the appeals court's decision became evident when Gaertner ventured to discuss the merits of the case as he saw them:

> Since it is our duty to protect the moral growth and the best interests of the minor children, we find wife's arguments lacking. Union, Missouri, is a small, conservative community with a population of about 5,500. Homosexuality is not openly accepted or widespread. We wish to protect the children from peer pressure, teasing, and possible ostracizing they may encounter as a result of the "alternative life style" their mother has chosen.

Gaertner was not persuaded that *Palmore v. Sidoti* required a different result. In that case, involving a custody dispute after the divorced white mother remarried to a black man, the Florida courts had changed custody from the mother to the father on the principal ground that the courts believed that living in an interracial household would impose significant stigma and psychological harm on the children due to societal prejudice. The U.S. Supreme Court rejected this basis for modifying custody, asserting that "the Constitution cannot control such prejudices but neither can it tolerate them." The Court relied on the Equal Protection Clause of the Fourteenth Amendment, holding that the Florida decision was impermissibly tainted by racial prejudice.

Gaertner asserted that *Palmore* did not apply to "the situation at hand" because "homosexuals are not offered the constitutional protection that race, national origin, and alienage have been afforded." He cited in support of this proposition cases holding that race, national origin, and alienage were "suspect" classifications under the Equal Protection Clause, and then cited, without discussion or further comment, the *Hardwick* and *Walsh* decisions upholding the constitutionality of sodomy laws.

Wife had also advanced a due process argument, contending that homosexuals had the same fundamental parenting rights as heterosexuals, which could not be abridged in the absence of evidence of a nexus between harm to the child and the parent's homosexuality. Gaertner was not persuaded, noting that Missouri courts had held that parental rights could be abridged "in the face of evidence that their exercise will result in emotional harm to a child or will be detrimental to the child's welfare." Having rejected published studies showing that parental homosexuality had no such necessary consequences, the court decided this issue on the basis of its own uninformed suppositions. After rehashing the facts about how the children were exposed to the relationship between wife and Airrow, the court asserted without citation of expert opinion: "[A]ll of these factors present an unhealthy environment for minor children. Such conduct can never be kept private enough to be a neutral factor in the development of a child's values and character. We will not ignore such conduct by a parent which may have an effect on the children's moral development." Gaertner asserted that this "analysis" was sufficient to answer all the constitutional arguments raised by wife and by the American Civil Liberties Union in an *amicus* brief, and that citation of cases from other jurisdictions holding to the contrary were not persuasive.

The court also rejected wife's allegations that husband's alcoholism should weigh against the custody change, or allegations (perhaps motivated by desperation given the poor state of Missouri precedents) that husband had sexually molested the children. Voss had resolved these factual issues against wife, and Gaertner saw no basis for rejecting Voss's conclusions based on the trial record.

Finally, wife had challenged the restrictions on her visitation rights. After noting that all prior Missouri decisions had restricted the visitation rights of homosexual parents, Gaertner refused to depart from this practice.

> We are not presuming that wife is an uncaring mother. The environment, however, that she would choose to rear her children in is unhealthy for their growth. She has chosen not to make her sexual preference private but invites acknowledgement and imposes her preferences upon her children and her community. The purpose of restricting visitation is to prevent extreme exposure of the situation to the minor children. We are not forbidding wife from being a homosexual, from having a lesbian relationship, or from attending gay activist or overt homosexual outings. We are restricting her from exposing these elements of her "alternative life style" to her minor children. We fail to see how these restrictions impose or restrict her equal protection or privacy rights where these restrictions serve the best interest of the child.

Given these rulings, it was not surprising that the court also upheld Voss's decision to award the family home to husband and cancel the maintenance award. Gaertner asserted that husband's modest salary would be significantly stretched in caring for four minor children, whereas there was no evidence wife could not obtain full-time employment and support herself, since she had experience and training in natural childbirth teaching and daycare, which were saleable job skills. Wife filed a motion for rehearing or to transfer the case to the state's supreme court, which was denied on August 27, 1987.

S.E.G. v. R.A.G. is one of about half a dozen similar Missouri appellate decisions concerning custody and visitation rights of homosexual parents. Both before and after *Palmore*, Missouri courts, when not asserting without proof that children would actually be harmed by living with a gay parent or being exposed to any aspect of the gay lifestyle, would alternatively rest their decision on the argument that societal bias against homosexuals (usually amply reflected in the courts' own opinions) justified sheltering children to the extent possible from any public identification with a homosexual person. From reading these cases, one concludes that the courts would even cut off all visitation rights if they could, based primarily on the view, all contrary evidence being dismissed without any serious evaluation as not "credible," that

the best interests of a child require minimizing to the extent possible any contact with or exposure to homosexuals. The Missouri cases are evidence of discretionary judging at its worst, and of the long road ahead for those trying through public education to extend rational approaches to gay family issues beyond the more receptive courts of such states as Alaska, California, Iowa, Massachusetts, and New York.

Case References

Bowers v. Hardwick, 478 U.S. 186 (1986)
Palmore v. Sidoti, 466 U.S. 429 (1984)
State v. Walsh, 713 S.W.2d 508 (Mo.1986) (en banc)

64. "SEXUAL MISCONDUCT," CHILD CUSTODY, AND THE PRIMARY CARETAKER

David M. v. Margaret M., 385 S.E.2d 912 (W. Va. 1989).

Allegations of "sexual misconduct" are common in child custody disputes, particularly when one parent is trying to extract a favorable settlement from another and using child custody as a "bargaining chip." Many court rulings on custody have placed significant emphasis on the sexual conduct of parents, finding unfitness on the basis of allegations of adultery, homosexuality, or cohabitation. Counter to this is a trend by some courts to view parental sexuality as relevant in custody disputes only to the extent that it can be shown to have an adverse impact on the child, eschewing any automatic conclusions that conduct which society might deem immoral should play a role in the custody determination in the absence of such impact evidence. A prime example of this approach is the West Virginia Supreme Court of Appeals' decision in *David M. v. Margaret M.*, which provides a detailed policy discussion of West Virginia's "primary caretaker" presumption in custody disputes in the context of "sexual misconduct" by the primary caretaker.

David and Margaret were married on August 4, 1979, and lived together in Wood County, West Virginia, until September 7, 1988. David sought the divorce, alleging that

his wife had engaged in adulterous conduct and subjected him to cruel and inhuman treatment. David sought custody of the couple's then 5-year-old son. Margaret responded to David's divorce petition by denying the allegations of cruel and inhuman treatment, but also sought divorce, arguing that there were irreconcilable differences between the couple. Margaret also sought sole custody of her son, arguing that as the child's primary caretaker she should be entitled to the benefit of the primary caretaker presumption previously adopted by West Virginia's courts as a substitute for the traditional maternal preference when children are of "tender years," which had been legislatively abolished in the state.

The Wood County Circuit Court referred the matter to a family law master, who held a fact-finding hearing. Margaret testified that she had adulterous sex three times during her marriage to David. Two times the sexual activity occurred late at night when the child was asleep. The third time she had sex during the day, but when the child was not at home. There was no evidence that the child knew about this sexual activity or was affected by it. Margaret and David testified about their parental roles, and testimony was also heard from others familiar with the couple. The master concluded that Margaret was the primary caretaker, that there were irreconcilable differences between the parties, that Margaret had committed adultery at least twice during the previous two years, and that due to her sexual immorality Margaret was not a fit and suitable person to have custody of her son. The circuit court accepted the master's findings, granted a divorce, and awarded custody to David, with liberal visitation rights for Margaret.

Margaret appealed this ruling to the West Virginia Supreme Court of Appeals, represented by attorneys Patrick E. McFarland and Eugene T. Hague, of Parkersburg. David was represented by Philip E. D'Orazio. The supreme court of appeals issued its decision on October 19, 1989, reversing the circuit court's decision on the custody issue and instructing the court to award custody to Margaret. The decision by Chief Justice Richard Neely included a lengthy discussion of the policy determinations behind the primary caretaker presumption and the reasons for narrow application of the parental unfitness exception.

Neely began his decision with a brief history of American law on child custody. Nineteenth-century courts almost always awarded custody to fathers, especially when the divorce could be attributed to some misconduct or fault of the mother. "That rule was a logical extension of the inferior legal status of women, the husband's property right in his family's labor, and the husband's absolute obligation to support his children," commented Neely, but by the end of the century it had become increasingly clear that the preference for fathers "made little sense in light of human emotions and society's expectation that children would be raised by women." As a result, the rule began to be eroded by common-law development and statutory enactments, until by the mid-20th century it was "almost always the rule that a mother was the preferred custodian of young children if she was a fit parent." However, courts could differ widely in their determination of maternal fitness, many placing significant stress on maternal sexual activity as a disqualifying factor, and, as Neely noted, giving women "the short end of the double standard" when com-

paring the sexual peccadillos of mothers and fathers. During the second half of the 20th century, the law began to evolve toward a gender-neutral standard, which focused on the "best interest of the child" rather than the interests or conduct of the parents. At the same time, notions of sexual equality made it appear improper, if not actually unconstitutional, for there to be any formal gender preference in child custody determinations. In 1980, the West Virginia legislature, following the new trend, abolished gender preferences and provided that custody determinations be made "for the best interest of the children based upon the merits of each case."

The West Virginia Supreme Court of Appeals interpreted this legislative command broadly, however, to authorize it to adopt evidentiary presumptions that would serve the best interest of the child while simplifying the fact-finding process. The most important of these was the presumption that the primary caretaker of the child should be awarded custody if that parent was considered fit, regardless of the fitness of the other parent. The court also would not order joint custody in any contested case, although it would honor the voluntary agreement by the parents to assume the burden of joint custody.

Neely explained why West Virginia had departed from a presumptionless, gender-neutral approach, which might seem to make sense "at first glance." An individualized, gender-neutral approach "poses serious problems," he asserted, "because the welfare of the child is often lost by the distorted incentives created by the divorce settlement." Research had shown that children formed a special bond with their primary caretaker, usually their mother, and that "this unique attachment to a primary caretaker is an essential cornerstone of a child's sense of security and healthy emotional development." Thus, it was normally in the child's best interest to remain in the custody of the primary caretaker. "Without a presumption in favor of the primary caretaker parent," said Neely, "the process—or even the prospect—of sorting out custody problems in court affects those problems, usually for the worse," especially because the "unpredictability of courts in divorce matters offers many opportunities for a parent (generally the father) to minimize support payments and to gain leverage in settlement negotiations" by threatening a custody fight with an indeterminate outcome. Because research had also shown that women were disproportionately concerned to maintain custody of their children, it was clear that such tactics by men could force women into accepting divorce settlement terms that were not only economically unfavorable to them, but also quite disadvantageous to their children.

Neely pointed out that presumptions about equality of treatment on the basis of sex broke down in such situations. It was rare for alimony or child support payments to leave a divorced woman with children in the same economic position after her divorce, since the level of payments rarely reflected the true costs of being a custodial parent. Among other things, Neely noted the persistent differential in men's and women's pay, due partially to the segregation of women, especially custodial working mothers, into lower paying occupations due to their need for more time for parental duties. Studies showed that working women with children put in several fewer hundred hours at the workplace each year than working women without children, thus exacerbating the income gap. When the costs of litigating custody disputes requiring individualized determinations of fitness without any evidentiary presumptions were factored in, the result would likely be even worse for the children. Since the presumption itself was gender-neutral, it would not work against a father who was truly the primary caretaker.

One of the great benefits of the primary caretaker presumption, said Neely, was that it dispensed with the need for hired experts, whose testimony he tended to regard with considerable scorn.

> Expert witnesses are, after all, very much like lawyers. They are paid to take a set of facts from which different inferences may be drawn and to characterize those facts so that a particular conclusion follows. There are indeed cases in which a mother or father may appear competent on the surface, only to be exposed after perfunctory inquiry as a child abuser. Under truly careful inquiry, such discoveries might be made more often. Such careful inquiry, however, is almost impossible in the real world because it requires experts who combine

competence and integrity in a way that is seldom found, at least in courtrooms. The side with the stronger case can afford to hire only competent experts with profound integrity; the side with the weaker case, on the other hand, wants impressively glib experts who are utterly devoid of principles. When both parents are good parents, the battle of the experts can result only in gibberish.

Any procedure that required a court to decide which parent was "better qualified" for sole custody would be subject to considerable personal bias by the judge. Even when the judge strove to avoid bias, the hearing process itself would be detrimental to the best interest of the child, stretching out the proceedings, introducing a note of uncertainty in the child's life, and draining the resources of both sides to pay their attorneys for trial time as well as experts' fees. The very process of having their parents' personalities and merits debated by "experts" in court could be damaging to the children. "In much the same way that an artillery battery can 'liberate the hell out of' a peaceful hamlet," said Neely, "experts can create emotional imbalances in the very children they are trying to protect." Consequently, a process that reduced the relevance of experts and the length of the proceedings could only be salutary for the best interest of the child.

Neely noted that the West Virginia courts had viewed children as falling into three groups, justifying three different procedures. The youngest children, up to about age 6, were deemed incapable of expressing a firm preference, and thus custody should be awarded to the primary caretaker without exception if found to be fit. Children from age 6 through the early teen years might be consulted as to a preference, but only in a close case where some factor was needed as a tie-breaker in the decision. Children of that age should not be routinely consulted, said Neely, due to the likelihood that they would be inclined to select the parent who produced the most "pleasant" (i.e., least demanding) environment for them, rather than the one who would do the best job in raising them. Children 14 and older should routinely be consulted and their wishes followed in almost all cases, said Neely, because if they were dissatisfied with the placement they were capable of causing considerable problems. Neely reviewed the substantial literature about how children suffer in child custody battles, further supporting the idea that the primary caretaker presumption, if properly interpreted and applied, could serve the interest of children by truncating proceedings, reducing the role of experts, and reinforcing existing relationships that were a cornerstone of the child's emotional security. Of course, the presumption allowed for liberal visitation for the noncustodial parent unless that parent were somehow unfit to maintain a continuing role in the child's life.

Asserting that not litigating the issue of child custody was the best thing for the parent, Neely asserted that the primary caretaker presumption would help to deter litigation and protect the caretaker parent from unfair settlement maneuvers. When the outcome of any litigation was entirely predictable, there would be a strong incentive for the parties to settle any differences over custody in a more equitable manner. While admitting that this presumption "inevitably involves some injustice to fathers who, as a group, are usually not primary caretakers," Neely argued that this was justified by the many advantages of the presumption. "Any rule concerning custody matters will be gender-biased, in effect if not in form," he said. "An allegedly gender-neutral rule that permits exhaustive inquiry into relative degrees of [parental] fitness is inevitably going to favor men in most instances."

> This bias follows from the observed pattern that in consensual divorces where there is no fight over money—either because there isn't any or because there is enough to go around— women overwhelmingly receive custody through the willing acquiescence of their husbands. Experience teaches that if there is any chance that the average mother will lose her children at divorce, she will either stay married under oppressive conditions or trade away valuable economic rights to ensure that she will be given custody.

Under such circumstances, it was appropriate to adopt a rule that greatly reduced the possibility that this would happen, and the primary caretaker rule was seen as providing this benefit.

That left the important question, however, of determining the fitness of the primary care-

taker. The rule would not work, said Neely, if the standard of fitness was interpreted too strictly. The relative "fitness" of the two parents was not the issue; only whether the primary caretaker was fit. Here, the court had previously adopted a five-part test.

> To be a fit parent, a person must: (1) feed and clothe the child appropriately; (2) adequately supervise the child and protect him or her from harm; (3) provide habitable housing; (4) avoid extreme discipline, child abuse, and other similar vices; and (5) refrain from immoral behavior under circumstances that would affect the child.

The last category is the most important for this study of sexuality and the law. Said Neely, "[R]estrained normal sexual behavior does not make a parent unfit. The law does not attend to traditional concepts of immorality in the abstract, but only to whether the child is a party to, or is influenced by, such behavior." Neely asserted that under this five-part test, the question whether a primary caretaker was a fit parent could be determined on the basis of testimony by neighbors, school teachers, and other lay witnesses, without any need to emphasize psychological "experts" who were largely "hired guns" in such contests. Given the court's breakdown of children into three age groups in which the primary caretaker rule was relevant only to the two younger groups, and fully dispositive only in the youngest, the presumption worked together with the fitness requirement to reduce substantially the litigation burden accompanying a contested custody issue in a divorce.

Before attempting to apply these rules to the dispute between David and Margaret, Neely noted that the West Virginia Supreme Court's approach, which was rather new and untested when first adopted, had gathered support from the appellate courts of other states, and it was fast displacing both the "maternal preference" rule and the "gender-neutral presumptionless" approach requiring individualized determinations of which parent was better suited for custody. Courts in Oregon and Minnesota had adopted the West Virginia approach outright, and courts in many other states had gone so far as to recognize primary caretaker status as a significant factor, if not totally dispositive, in child custody disputes. While some states showed a disposition to favor joint custody, Neely downplayed this as an inadequate solution to the custody problem, noting the difficulties for a child of having to adjust to two different households, especially when there was geographical separation, and the difficulties of having two equal decisionmakers about every significant aspect of the child's life, especially when they were people who might harbor negative feelings about each other from their terminated marriage. While West Virginia would honor a voluntary joint-custody agreement, its courts would not order joint custody in a contested case.

Finally turning to the matter of David and Margaret, Neely found that there was inadequate support for the conclusion that Margaret was unfit because of her adulterous activities. Quoting prior West Virginia cases, he noted:

> Acts of sexual misconduct by a [primary caretaker], albeit wrongs against an innocent spouse, may not be considered as evidence going to the fitness of the [caretaker] for child custody unless [his or] her conduct is so aggravated, given contemporary moral standards, that reasonable men would find that [his or] her immorality, *per se*, warranted a finding of unfitness because of the deleterious effect upon the child of being raised by a [primary caretaker] with such a defective character.

In this case, there was evidence of a few acts of adultery, but there was no evidence that Margaret's "marital misconduct was known to the child or damaged the child." Sexual misconduct, standing alone, was not sufficient basis for a finding of unfitness. Neely characterized what Margaret had done as "restrained normal sexual behavior" that did not render her an "unfit parent."

> The circuit court was clearly wrong in its position that the three instances of sexual misconduct, occurring over two years, warranted a finding of unfitness, without evidence establishing that the child was harmed or that the conduct *per se* was so outrageous, given contemporary moral standards, as to call into question her fitness as a parent. The absence of such evidence requires reversal.

The West Virginia Supreme Court of Appeals' decision in *David M. v. Margaret M.* adopted a strong reformist vision of child custody decisionmaking. By focusing on the child's relationship with a primary caretaker, and rejecting the significance of parental sexual activity that is not clearly shown to injure the child, the court sought to eliminate the sort of biased views of parental sexuality that taint the child custody and visitation determinations of many state courts. In a footnote, Chief Justice Neely noted a string of earlier West Virginia decisions in which trial courts had "erroneously applied a broad interpretation of the fitness requirement" in the context of deciding a primary caretaker custody case. Among them were those in which the trial courts relied on a finding of an "immoral atmosphere" in the home, or the "speculative harm of a mother's friendship with another woman who was a lesbian" as a basis for finding maternal unfitness. If the Court's approach is followed diligently in the spirit indicated by Neely's opinion and these footnote references, it would provide a strong basis for protecting the legitimate parental interests of parents of diverse sexual orientations and practices, consistent with the best interest of their children.

65. GAYS AS ADOPTIVE OR FOSTER PARENTS

Babets v. Dukakis, No. 81083 (Mass. Super. Ct. 1986) (unpublished); *Babets v. Secretary of the Executive Office of Human Services*, 403 Mass. 230, 526 N.E.2d 1261 (1988). *Opinion of the Justices*, 525 A.2d 1095 (N.H. 1987). *In re Adoption of Charles B.*, 50 Ohio St. 3d 88, 552 N.E.2d 884 (1990).

Many courts have viewed the combination of homosexual adults and minor children as volatile and fraught with danger. Mythology about human sexuality suggests that "impressionable" children may be harmed by exposure to paren-tal figures whose sexuality is "deviant" in any way, and many courts appear to accept, without question, that it is against the best interest of the child to be raised under any circumstances presenting even the slightest risk that the child will "become" gay. Studies of the development of children raised by homosexual parents belie the mythology and suggest the irrelevance of these courts' concerns. The sexual orientation of children raised by lesbian or gay parents does not correlate with the sexual orientation of the parents. And, it seems that children do not "become" gay; rather, they discover their sexual orientation at some time during the transition from childhood to sexual maturity.

Furthermore, studies have shown that children raised by lesbian or gay male parents are no more likely to have psychological adjustment problems than children raised in "heterosexual" homes. Experts on child development are increasingly willing to testify on behalf of lesbian or gay male parents who seek to retain custody or preserve visitation rights as such studies become more widely disseminated.

When the parent is a "biological" parent, constitutional protections for family relationships weigh heavily on any court asked to sever such relationships. The U.S. Supreme Court has held that the Due Process Clause prevents the state from intervening in family relationships without compelling justification. The constitutional protections for family relationships are less relevant when the issue is adoption or foster care. While courts are willing to tolerate some "imperfection" in a family that is biologically constituted, they may be reluctant to create an "imperfect" family *ab initio* by approving adoption by an adult who presents what the judges would consider a "flaw" in parental qualifications, since the standard used in such cases emphasizes the interests of the child rather than the interests of the potential foster or adoptive parent. Two states, New Hampshire and Florida, legislatively ban adoptions of children by lesbians and gay men, and New Hampshire's ban also extends to foster placements. (The Florida ban has been declared unconstitutional by at least one trial judge in an unpublished decision that the state did not appeal.) The New Hampshire legislation grew directly out of a foster care controversy in neighboring Massachusetts, which resulted in lengthy litigation.

In 1985, the Massachusetts Department of Social Services approved the foster placement of a pair of young brothers with Donald C. Babets and David Jean, a gay male couple living in Boston. The youngsters had experienced several unsuccessful foster placements, Babets and Jean had been approved after investigation for foster placement, and the youngsters' mother, who could not herself care for the children, had agreed to the placement. Within days of the placement, a reporter for *The Boston Globe* went around the neighborhood interviewing people about what they thought of the placement of two young boys with a gay male couple.

The resulting newspaper article caused a furor, to which state social services officials reacted by immediately removing the boys from the home and by promulgating a new set of regulations that effectively precluded lesbians and gay men from being foster parents. The gay press reported that the regulations, announced by Secretary of the Executive Office of Human Services Philip W. Johnston, had originated in the office of Governor Michael Dukakis. The new regulations were announced in July 1985 to become effective February 1, 1986. They began by stating that the "best interests of the child" should govern all out-of-home placements, but then created a hierarchy of desirability for foster placements which placed married heterosexual couples at the top and single people or unmarried couples at the bottom, and required written approval from the head of the agency before placing a child with a single person. Prior parenting experience was not a factor: a single person or a gay couple with significant experience would be rated below a married couple with no parenting experience in terms of desirability. The state announced that this hierarchy was based on its view that a "traditional" heterosexual family setting was the most desirable within which to raise children.

The new policy generated immediate opposition from professional social workers within the state's Executive Office of Human Services and massive protests by lesbian and gay community activists. A class action lawsuit was constructed by Gay and Lesbian Advocates and Defenders, a public interest law firm based in Boston, and its cooperating attorney, Anthony Doniger, challenging the new regulations as violative of equal protection of the laws, due process, federal and state civil rights laws, federal and state privacy and association rights, and the requirements of state laws governing the professional practice of social work and the rights of children under such laws. Babets and Jean were the lead plaintiffs, joined by Reverend Kathryn Piccard, a single foster parent; Catherine Braydon, a divorced mother and foster parent; and the National Association of Social Workers.

The state promptly moved to dismiss the suit on standing and substantive grounds. Chief Justice Thomas R. Morse, Jr., of the Massachusetts Superior Court ruled on September 8, 1986, that the lawsuit could proceed against Philip Johnston, secretary of Human Services, although he dismissed the social workers association as a plaintiff party for lack of standing, dismissed the complaint against Governor Michael Dukakis as not a proper party defendant, and dismissed some of the state law claims.

Justice Morse began his decision by considering the equal protection allegations. He found that the system of hierarchies of preference for foster placements created a classification system based on marital status, which must be evaluated under the Equal Protection Clause. However, he found that marital status was not a "suspect classification" requiring heightened or strict scrutiny under the Equal Protection Clause, relying on the U.S. Supreme Court's decision in *Village of Belle Terre v. Boraas* (1974), and that becoming a foster parent was not a "fundamental interest," relying on the U.S. Supreme Court's decision in *Smith v. Organization of Foster Families* (1977). Consequently, the regulation had to be sustained if there was some rational basis for it.

Rational basis analysis, as developed by the U.S. Supreme Court during the New Deal years for review of challenged economic regulations, did not place many justification demands on government defendants. However, in *City of Cleburne v. Cleburne Living Center* (1985), the Supreme Court had articulated a somewhat more demanding rational basis test for equal protection cases involving regulations that disadvantaged groups that are feared or unpopular, such as the mentally ill. Justice Morse also noted that the Court had disapproved the "bare desire to harm a politically unpopular group" as a legitimate basis for legislation in *U.S. Department of Agriculture v. Moreno* (1973), a case

in which the Court struck down food stamp regulations intended to disqualify "hippie communes" from receiving public assistance.

Justice Morse concluded that the complaint stated a claim under the Equal Protection Clause, asserting that the classification scheme appeared to have no rational basis. Noting the policy statement in the state's child welfare law, which identified the purpose "to assure good substitute parental care" through foster placements, Morse commented that "it is anomalous that the Commonwealth should concoct a classification so disadvantageous to a class of persons—single parents—who may well be as good as or better at parenting than some married couples." He characterized as "perplexing" the Department of Social Service's actions in approving Babets and Jean as foster parents, placing children with them, initially finding that they gave excellent care to the children, and then arguing that a preference for a married couple "is rationally related to a legitimate purpose." If the best interests of the child were to govern foster placement decisions, he opined, "then any distinction between married couples and single persons is wholly arbitrary and capricious and adverse to the needs of children," and "prospective foster parents should be selected on the basis of their ability to provide temporary care and support for children, not on the basis of an arbitrary factor such as marital status."

Justice Morse noted further that although the regulations did not discriminate against homosexuals on their face, since homosexuals were "single persons" (even when living as couples, due to the state's refusal to allow homosexual marriage), they were necessarily disadvantaged by the regulation. Furthermore, the commissioner had made public statements making quite clear that homosexuals would not be approved by him for foster placements. Morse found this no more defensible than a preference for married foster parents: "Any exclusion of homosexuals from consideration as foster parents, all things being equal, is blatantly irrational." Morse cited Massachusetts decisions finding that "sexual preference per se is irrelevant to a consideration of parenting skills" in the context of custody and visitation disputes, and concluded that the lesbian and gay plaintiffs were entitled to prove at trial that the motivation for the regulations, which was relevant to the equal protection issue, was a desire to harm an unpopular group rather than a legitimate concern for the best interests of children to be placed in foster care.

Morse then concluded that the plaintiffs had also stated a claim under the state due process clause, which in Massachusetts requires "that legislation bear a *real* and *substantial* relation to the public health, safety, morals or some other phase of general welfare," relying on *Leigh v. Board of Registration of Nursing*, a 1985 Massachusetts Supreme Judicial Court decision. Given his prior conclusion on the lack of a rational basis for the law, Justice Morse found it easy to conclude that the plaintiffs had stated a substantive due process claim. Morse also found it easy to conclude that a viable claim had been stated under 42 U.S.C. section 1983, a federal statute authorizing suits for violations of civil rights by state officials acting under color of state law, but found that the allegations of the complaint did not measure up under a state civil rights statute dealing with coercive action by state officials.

Morse next turned to the regulatory requirement that applicants for approval as foster parents indicate their sexual orientation on the application form. Morse decided that because the decision to apply for consideration as a foster parent is voluntary, and because the sexual orientation of an applicant might be a relevant consideration in deciding on a placement, no constitutional privacy or associational rights were violated by the regulation. Morse noted that the application form contained other inquiries, equally if not more personal in nature, about health and medical and criminal records that were not challenged by the plaintiffs. Since it was necessary in the interests of the child to conduct an extensive background check on all applicants to be foster parents, Morse believed that questioning about sexual orientation was not unduly intrusive or unrelated to a legitimate government interest in this connection.

Finally, Justice Morse considered the particular claims asserted by the National Association of Social Workers, and found them insufficient to confer standing to sue, since in his opinion none of the allegations of the complaint indicated that the Association or its members were threatened with individual harm by the regulation.

Morse's decision to allow the lawsuit to go to trial threw the whole matter into discovery, where the plaintiffs fought an extensive battle, taking them to the Massachusetts Supreme Judicial Court, to secure from the Dukakis administration internal documents that would show the motivation of officials in drafting and promulgating the challenged regulations. The high court ruled that the Dukakis administration's claims of executive privilege had no basis in state law and ordered production of the documents. The Massachusetts legislature, reacting to publicity surrounding the regulations and the ensuing litigation, twice passed amendments to budget bills requiring the Department of Social Services to comply with the antigay foster care regulations. The first such amendment received a line-item veto from Governor Dukakis, who insisted that the regulation was sufficient standing by itself. As the litigation over discovery heated up, however, the governor signed the second amendment, which had passed during the summer of 1988 while he was campaigning for the office of President of the United States.

Meanwhile, media attention focused on the case throughout New England was having repercussions in neighboring New Hampshire, where conservative legislators had introduced a bill in the state House of Representatives to ban adoption or foster care placement involving homosexual parents, or operation of any licensed child care agency by homosexuals. Opponents of the bill claimed that it would be unconstitutional, bolstered by Justice Morse's decision. The House certified to the New Hampshire Supreme Court the question whether the proposed ban would violate the federal or state constitutions. The court first sent the questions back to the House, stating that it was uncertain how to construe the term "homosexual" in the proposed bill. The House passed an additional resolution, adopting a definition based on the commission of anal or oral sex with a person of the same gender. Observers did not miss the irony that New Hampshire had repealed its sodomy law a decade earlier: the proposed law would disqualify people from being foster or adoptive parents or running child care agencies solely because they engaged in conduct the state considered legal.

The court issued its opinion on May 5, 1987. Without any mention of the prior Massachusetts Superior Court ruling, which was not officially published, the court concluded that the proposed law would not offend the federal or state constitutions. The court had to do quite a bit of twisting and turning to reach its result, however. For one thing, the definition of "homosexual" adopted by the legislature was so poorly drafted that it would have produced absurd results had it been interpreted literally. The court decided to adopt a narrow construction for purposes of its constitutional analysis, to exclude from the definition of "homosexual" those who were unwilling participants in the defined sexual activities, or those who had some homosexual experiences in their youth but were exclusively heterosexual in their sexual activities as adults. Further, the court assumed that the law would be applied only prospectively, so that it would not have to consider the rationality of terminating successful existing foster placements or adoptions solely because the parents were homosexual within the meaning of the statute.

The court concluded that the rational basis test was the only applicable test for an equal protection analysis of this question, and that the question to be decided was whether "a blanket exclusion of homosexuals from adoption, foster parentage, or child care agency licensure is rationally related" to the legislative purposes of promoting "the provision of a healthy environment, . . . role models and positive nurturing" to children involved in such settings. Noting that "the source of sexual orientation is still inadequately understood and is thought to be a combination of genetic and environmental influences," the court concluded that the state could legitimately conclude that having a homosexual parent as a role model might be detrimental to a foster child. (Ironically, the court's source for this assertion about the nature of human sexuality was a footnote in a law review article which argued for a more liberal standard in child custody and visitation cases involving claims by lesbian and gay parents.) The court sought to bolster this conclusion by invoking "the State's especially great responsibility in the foster care and adoption contexts to provide for the welfare of the children affected by placement decisions." By contrast, parents bore most of the responsibility in deciding on day care placement. Consequently, the court concluded that the portion of the proposed law banning homosexuals as licensed operators of day care centers would not be rational, but that the ban on homosexuals as foster or adoptive parents would be.

The court also rejected a due process challenge, holding that since there was no fundamental interest in being an adoptive or foster parent and that since "the classification created here embodies a prediction of a risk not immediately disprovable by contrary evidence," there was no basis for asserting that the bill would deprive "homosexuals" of due process of law under the federal or state constitutions. Finally, the court rejected the notion that the bill might violate a right of privacy, citing *Bowers v. Hardwick* (1986), in which the U.S. Supreme Court had ruled that the federal constitutional right of privacy did not extend to consensual homosexual anal or oral sex, and rejected the argument that the bill might affect protected associational rights.

Justice William F. Batchelder vigorously dissented from the court's opinion, pointing out the irony that homosexual sodomy was not a crime in New Hampshire but heterosexual sodomy was a crime, and that the legislature was moving to disqualify homosexuals while allowing heterosexual adulterers to serve as role models for adoptive or foster children. "The State is never less humanitarian," he asserted, "than when it denies public benefits to a group of its citizens because of ancient prejudices against that group."

Batchelder argued that the legislature had received no evidence that homosexuals as a group were deficient in any of the characteristics required for successful foster or adoptive parenting, and cited a long string of journal articles documenting that "the overwhelming weight of professional study on the subject concludes that no difference in psychological and psychosexual development can be discerned between children raised by heterosexual parents and children raised by homosexual parents." He further noted New Hampshire precedents on due process that would support finding that the deprivation of the opportunity to be a foster or adoptive parent was serious enough to invoke due process concern, and argued that a less categorical approach could be used to determine whether a particular homosexual applicant was fit to be a foster or adoptive parent.

Shortly after the advisory opinion was issued, the legislature passed the bill, which was signed by the governor. Lesbian and gay rights advocates considered bringing a challenge against the law as enforced, but decided that the existing advisory opinion and the conservative cast of the post-*Hardwick* federal courts might yield even worse opinions, regardless of forum, so they decided to leave things as they were.

Meanwhile, a new dispute over the adoption rights of gay people was brewing in Ohio. An unfortunate youngster named Charles who suffered from learning disabilities and acute lymphocytic leukemia was in the custody of the Licking County Department of Human Services, having suffered from parental neglect and abuse. He had been placed in a series of foster homes beginning in 1985, while his name was placed with several different exchanges for a permanent adoption placement. However, no placement had been effected by the end of 1987.

In 1986, the agency assigned Mr. B, a psychological assistant, to counsel Charles. They developed a warm personal relationship, and the agency allowed Charles, who was apparently otherwise institutionalized, to visit in Mr. B's home, including unsupervised weekend and holiday visits. Mr. B and Charles developed a strong affectionate bond. During the developing relationship between Charles and Mr. B, Mr. B, who is gay, started a relationship with Mr. K, who moved in with him, becoming his domestic partner. Mr. K and Charles also developed a friendly relationship. Charles also developed a friendly relationship with Mr. B's mother and sister.

On January 15, 1988, Mr. B filed a petition to adopt Charles, who was then 7 years old, and a "consent to adoption" form was sent to the supervisor of adoptions of the Licking County agency, as required by statute, since Charles

was in the legal custody of the agency. Almost three months later, Executive Director Russell Payne sent back a four-page notarized reply denying assent to the adoption. Payne indicated that Mr. B did not meet the preferred profile for an adoptive parent, and that the agency believed that adoption into a homosexual household had no practical precedent regarding potential risks to Charles. However, it appears that this notice from Payne was late under Ohio rules on the time within which an agency can object to an adoption and a trial judge ruled it untimely and approved the adoption. The agency appealed.

The Court of Appeals of Ohio for Licking County reversed the trial judge's decision, in an opinion by Judge Ira G. Turpin. Turpin noted that the trial court had made no detailed findings of fact, making it impossible for the appellate court to determine whether the trial court's factual findings were supported by evidence in the record. Judge Turpin surmised that the trial court believed that after three years without a successful placement "this child needed a loving home and that this one was the only one he would ever get." Given the trial court's determination, Judge Turpin concluded that its decision could be reversed only if "as an unexceptional matter of absolute per se law, homosexuals are ineligible to adopt in Ohio." Turpin concluded for the court that this, indeed, was the case.

Although the legislature had not adopted any express ban on homosexuals adopting children, Turpin asserted that imputing to the legislature an intention to allow such adoptions was "inappropriate and unwarranted." "The so-called 'gay lifestyle' is patently incompatible with the manifest spirit, purpose and goals of adoption," he wrote. "Homosexuality negates procreation. Announced homosexuality defeats the goals of adoption. It will be impossible for the child to pass as the natural child of the adoptive 'family' or to adapt to the community by quietly blending in free from controversy and stigma."

It was clear that the majority had not considered the case law on interracial adoption, which addresses exactly these concerns. In a lengthy dissenting opinion, Judge Earle E. Wise reviewed the Ohio statute and case law developments on interracial adoption and concluded that the ability of the adoptive child to "pose" as the natural child of the adoptive parents was irrelevant. Ohio had amended its adoption laws in 1977 to remove the requirement that racial, religious, and cultural backgrounds be taken into account in adoption. In 1974, the Ohio Supreme Court had overruled the Portage County Welfare Department's objection to an interracial adoption, holding that a "permanent placement in a judicially approved home environment . . . is clearly preferable to confining the child in an institution or relegating the child to a life of transience, from one foster home to another" until an agency found an ideal placement. Furthermore, the legislative history of the 1977 amendments showed legislative awareness of gay adults adopting each other to create family units and sought to express disapproval of that, but at the same time said nothing one way or the other about homosexuals adopting children; at the same time, the statute allowed single adults to adopt.

Judge Wise concluded that the rhetorical pronouncements of the majority were contradictory and unconvincing. Rather than precluding adoptions by adult homosexuals because of some belief that the "gay lifestyle" would be harmful to a child, he would have the trial court determine whether a particular applicant, regardless of sexual orientation, lived in a way that would be detrimental to the child. Even assuming that "homosexuality negates procreation," wrote Judge Wise,

> so also do many physical defects in heterosexuals, but that furnishes one of the reasons for adoption, i.e., the inability to have children by a person or persons who love children and desire to be a parent or parents may fulfill that love and desire by adoption of a child. Therefore, announced homosexuality per se does not defeat the goals of adoption anymore than physical defects in heterosexuals.

Judge Wise further noted that the obligation incumbent on Ohio, under the Adoption Assistance and Child Welfare Act of 1980, was to guarantee to children needing homes the earliest possible suitable permanent placement. National policy dictated avoidance of institutionalization or transient foster care to the extent possible, so that rejecting a homosexual

applicant on a *per se* basis because he or she did not fit some ideal parental profile was inconsistent with this policy. "Charles, with all his problems, especially deserves a chance to be someone's child forever. The petitioner, Mr. B, offers that chance. . . . I agree with the trial court that Charlie should get Mr. B."

Mr. B petitioned the Ohio Supreme Court for review, which was quickly granted. The supreme court heard oral argument from both Robin Lyn Green, Mr. B's attorney, and C. William Rickrich, who had been appointed as guardian *ad litem* for Charles, as well as William B. Sewards, Jr., assistant country prosecutor from Licking County, on behalf of the agency. The supreme court issued its *per curiam* opinion reversing the court of appeals on March 28, 1990.

The supreme court rejected the view of the court of appeals "that it could never be in the child's best interest to be adopted by a person such as Mr. B." Noting first that Ohio law specifically authorized adoption by unmarried adults, the court insisted that adoption decisions must be made on a case-by-case basis in the best interest of the child to be adopted. Reviewing the facts and case law, the court concluded that the trial court's decision approving the adoption was not an abuse of discretion. The agency had drawn up a list of qualifications for an ideal placement for Charles that had proven virtually impossible to fulfill over the three years of his foster care, despite several attempts to place Charles permanently. Several witnesses at the trial level had testified to the suitability of Mr. B and to the availability of other role models, including Mr. B's mother and sister. The guardian *ad litem* appointed by the court to represent Charles's interests had concluded that the adoption should be approved.

The court then reviewed a variety of past cases in which custody or adoption issues had been played out against a background of parental sexual "misconduct," such as adultery or promiscuity, and found that these decisions had never been made on a *per se* basis, but rather after careful scrutiny of the individual cases concerning possible adverse impact on the child. The court pointedly noted that only one witness at the trial had opposed the adoption of

Charles by Mr. B: the administrator of social services for the agency, who "had no formal education in either social work or psychology" and whose personal contact with Charles had been brief. Her testimony went not to the specifics of Mr. B's credentials, but rather to the ways in which he failed to meet the agency's ideal profile of an adoptive parent. By contrast, Mr. B had presented professional witnesses who had testified to the suitability of the placement in some detail, as well as family members who testified in detail about the home life Charles would have with Mr. B. Given this record, the court concluded that there was no abuse of discretion by the trial court to find Mr. B qualified to adopt Charles. The court also agreed that the agency's objections had been untimely in any event, since the statute required an agency having custody to file its objections within thirty days of notice that an adoption petition had been filed.

Justice Alice Robie Resnick dissented. Although she agreed with the majority of the court that the court of appeals had been incorrect in holding homosexuality a *per se* basis for exclusion, she felt there was a nexus between Mr. B's homosexuality and adverse impact on Charles. Noting Charles's various physical and mental problems, she felt that placing an 8 year old with those problems "in an environment with a homosexual who is engaged in a homosexual relationship is not in the best interest of the child." As her opinion unfolds, it becomes clear that her main concern rests on misinformation about acquired immune deficiency syndrome (AIDS) and how AIDS is spread. A doctor at Children's Hospital, Ohio State University, had sent an unsolicited *ex parte* letter to the court insisting that Charles would be at risk for Human Immunodeficiency Virus (HIV) infection if placed with Mr. B. Although Mr. B had tested negative for HIV antibodies, Justice Resnick expressed concern that he might become infected in the future because he "falls within a high-risk population for AIDS. Why place a child whose immune system has already been altered [by leukemia] in such an environment?" she asked.

In addition, Justice Resnick expressed concern about placing a developmentally disabled child in a "homosexual environment." While

acknowledging "research on this issue which shows that homosexuals can be effective parents," she believed that Charles presented special issues due to his physical and mental problems. Although Charles could use a permanent home, as far as she was concerned it should not be in a "homosexual environment."

The decision in *Adoption of Charles B.* was issued just weeks before Massachusetts announced that it was changing its foster care regulations in a way that would allow the plaintiffs in the *Babets* case to withdraw their lawsuit. The secretary of the state's Executive Office of Human Services announced that under new regulations the hierarchy of preferential placements would be abandoned. Applicants for approval as foster parents would be evaluated on an individual basis without regard to marital status or sexual orientation. Those applicants with past parenting experience who were found qualified to be foster parents by social workers could be certified without further approval from the agency. Applicants with no past child care experience would require permission from a supervisor, regardless of their marital status. The head of the agency would no longer be involved in making these decision on a case-by-case basis.

The decisions by the Ohio Supreme Court and the New Hampshire Supreme Court, taken together with the decision by Superior Court Justice Morse in Massachusetts, show the diversity of views regarding the eligibility of lesbians and gay men to adopt children. Neither of the appellate decisions was unanimous. Opposition to allowing such adoptions seems based on a view that homosexuals differ from heterosexuals in some way relevant to the ability to raise stable, well-adjusted children. Studies of children raised by homosexual parents refute such beliefs, but are sometimes discredited by courts, mainly because they run against "common sense," which in this context usually means judicial prejudice. The continued unwillingness of most courts to apply any test more stringent than "rational basis" to classifications that directly or indirectly disadvantage lesbian and gay people makes it more difficult to attack exclusionary policies. However, the Ohio Supreme Court decision shows how the persuasive facts of an individual case may overcome judicial reluctance to recognize the legitimate claims of lesbian and gay litigants.

The *Charles B.* dissent introduces the new factor of AIDS into the equation. There is virtually no risk that a homosexual parent will transmit AIDS to an adoptive or foster child because the virus implicated in AIDS is not spread by even close contact between parents and children, as illustrated by careful studies of hundreds of homes in which persons infected with the virus have lived with family members for long periods of time. If a person who actually had AIDS sought to adopt a child, a court might be concerned with the ability of such an individual to provide the level of care and attention a young child needs. Raising the issue

of AIDS in a case where the adoptive parent is not even infected with the virus appears a pretext for discrimination against gay men, given the real lack of risk that an infected parent might present to the health of an adoptive child.

Case References

Bowers v. Hardwick, 478 U.S. 186 (1986)

Burrell, In re, 388 N.E.2d 738 (Ohio 1979)

City of Cleburne v. Cleburne Living Center, 473 U.S. 432 (1985)

Leigh v. Board of Registration of Nursing, 395 Mass. 670 (1985)

Smith v. Organization of Foster Families, 431 U.S. 816 (1977)

United States Department of Agriculture v. Moreno, 413 U.S. 528 (1973)

Village of Belle Terre v. Boraas, 416 U.S. 1 (1974)

66. NO RECOVERY FOR COHABITANTS

Elden v. Sheldon, 46 Cal. 3d 267, 250 Cal. Rptr. 254, 758 P.2d 582 (1988), vacating 164 Cal. App. 3d 745, 210 Cal. Rptr. 755 (2d Dist. 1985).

One of the most frequently remarked phenomena of American society in the wake of the Sexual Revolution of the 1960s is the increasing number of heterosexual adults who cohabit without contracting a marriage, as well as the increasing number of homosexual couples who live openly together in a quasi-marital relationship. Among heterosexuals, the incidence of such cohabitation increased 800 percent between 1960 and 1970. Would the common law respond to this social change by modifying doctrines premised on the marital relationship? Two such doctrines, allowing causes of action for loss of consortium or for the negligent infliction of emotional distress upon the death or severe injury of a spouse, were at issue in *Elden v. Sheldon*, in which the California Supreme Court refused to modify existing doctrine to take account of new social realities.

Richard C. Elden and Linda Eberling lived together for several years in a close and loving relationship, but were not married to each other. In December 1982, Eberling was driving her car with Elden as a passenger when the car was struck by a car driven by Robert Louis Sheldon. Eberling was thrown from the car and died at

the scene. Elden sustained serious physical injuries, as well as severe emotional distress from observing Eberling's death and, of course, the permanent loss of her companionship as his domestic partner. Elden filed suit against Sheldon and the owner of the car, claiming damages for his physical injuries as well as loss of consortium and negligent infliction of emotional distress for the loss of Eberling. Seeking the benefit of California Court of Appeal decisions that appeared to create consortium and emotional distress actions in situations where unmarried cohabitants could show the requisite "close" relationship, Elden alleged that his relationship with Eberling had been both "stable and significant" and possessed the characteristics of a marriage.

The action was brought in Superior Court, Los Angeles County, before Judge George Xanthos, with Los Angeles attorney Michael L. Robins representing Elden, Patrick A. Messica, Jr., of Los Angeles, representing Sheldon, and Peter J. Godfrey, of Santa Ana, representing the owner of the car Sheldon was driving, not named in the reported opinions of the case. The defendants moved to dismiss the claims for loss of consortium and emotional distress. Xanthos granted the motion in an unpublished order, which led to settlement of the claim for physical injuries. Elden appealed the dismissal to the Court of Appeal for the Second District, which ruled on February 15, 1985, that the claims had properly been dismissed. The unanimous three-judge panel held, in an opinion by Justice Lynn D. Compton, that despite the sympathetic factual situation, the court should not expand liability to reach this situation without action by the legislature, and it specifically declined to follow decisions by other courts of appeal that might have led to a different result.

Compton's opinion first addressed the issue of loss of consortium. Elden had relied heavily on *Butcher v. Superior Court*, a 1983 decision by the Fourth District Court of Appeal, where the court held that an unmarried cohabitant could state a cause of action for loss of consortium by demonstrating that the nonmarital relationship was both "stable and significant" and possessed the characteristics of a marriage. The cohabitants in that case had children together, held themselves out in their community as spouses, and lived together with merged finances over many years. Compton rejected *Butcher* as a precedent, not because of the factual distinctions with Elden's case, but on grounds of policy.

The loss of consortium action was originally grounded in the old common-law concept that upon marriage the wife became a single legal entity with the husband, so that a husband could sue for loss of consortium in the sense that he suffered a personal physical injury when his wife was seriously injured or killed. Interestingly, the wife could not sue for loss of consortium, since she was not seen as an independent legal entity having a right to sue and, under the inequality pertaining in the old common law, she did not have a reciprocal claim on the economic and sexual services of her husband. The loss of consortium action had a checkered past in California, where it had even been abolished by the California Supreme Court for a period of time, then revived on an equal and reciprocal basis in *Rodriquez v. Bethlehem Steel Corp.* (1974), which held that either spouse had a right to recover for an injury to the "marital entity." "The law is concerned with the protection of the 'relational' interests of married persons and recognizes as an actional tort any interference, intentional or negligent, with the continuation of the relation of husband and wife," said Compton. "The right of consortium therefore parallels the existence of the marital relationship and terminates at its dissolution by death or divorce."

Given this basis of the action in the marital relation, a claim of loss of consortium by an unmarried cohabitant of the deceased lacked a firm foundation, insisted Compton, noting that the policy of the law was to continue "to grant preferential status to the relationship of husband and wife," as legislatively reflected in the statutes governing the rights and responsibilities of married persons. Compton found support for this holding in the legislature's "continuing refusal to recognize unmarried cohabitants as 'heirs' under the wrongful death statutes," noting that "loss of consortium is, of course, recoverable in a wrongful death action." Thus, if the court were to recognize a loss of consortium action involving unmarried cohabitants, it would be "circumventing the Legislature's clearly expressed intent to exclude unmarried cohabitants from the class of persons entitled to sue for wrongful death," an exclusion that had been upheld by the overwhelming majority of courts faced with the issue. The decision to extend such a cause of action "would necessitate identifying and weighing competing notions of public policy, social mores, and moral values," said Compton. "Such a decision is best left to the Legislature."

One reason for refraining from extending the cause of action was that "marriage is the only dependable means by which a relationship may be legally defined for purposes of determining loss of consortium." The *Butcher* court's approach did not create the kind of "bright line test" that could be easily applied by the courts, calling instead for an intrusive fact-finding process with unpredictable results. "It is not the function of this or any other court to sift through the myriad relationships of an injured party in order to determine which of those 'near and dear' to the victim have suffered an injury proximately caused by tortious conduct," she insisted.

The same reasoning drove the decision on the emotional distress claim. The California Supreme Court had first recognized such a claim in *Dillon v. Legg*, a 1968 case where a mother was allowed to recover damages for emotional distress caused when she witnessed a car strike and kill her minor child. The *Dillon* court established a three-part test for determining the appropriate circumstances for allowing such a cause of action upon satisfactory proof of actual emotional distress:

> (1) Whether plaintiff was located near the scene of the accident as contrasted with one who was a distance away from it. (2) Whether the shock resulted from a direct emotional impact upon plaintiff from the sensory and contemporaneous observance of the accident, as contrasted with learning of the accident from others after its occurrence. (3) Whether plaintiff and the victim were closely related, as contrasted with an absence of any relationship or the presence of only a distant relationship.

The *Dillon* court stressed that "foreseeability" was the key concern in establishing these tests. In order to keep liability for accidents within manageable limits, it was willing to recognize only a cause of action for emotional distress to observers in circumstances where it would be highly foreseeable to the tortfeasor that his negligence could cause such injury (i.e., where the injury was suffered by a close relative present at the scene of the accident who witnessed the accident as it was happening). In subsequent cases, the lower courts developed an elaborate body of doctrine concerning all three tests.

In this case, Elden clearly met the first two tests, being present in the car at the time of the accident and actually seeing Eberling thrown from the car and killed. However, as far as Compton was concerned, Elden failed the third test because he had no "legal" relation to Eberling. Compton noted the holdings in *Trapp v. Schuyler Construction*, a 1983 Second District Court of Appeal decision stating that "close relationship" did not include "friends, housemates, or those engaged in a 'meaningful relationship,'" and *Drew v. Drake*, a 1980 decision directly on point where the court denied recovery for emotional distress where the victim was a three-year cohabitant and lover of the plaintiff. The *Drew* court said that "to allow

persons standing in a 'meaningful relationship' (to use a contemporary colloquialism) to recover for emotional distress resulting in physical injury would abandon the *Dillon* requirement that '[the] courts . . . mark out the areas of liability, excluding the remote and unexpected.'" Compton stated agreement with this view, noting that the most prominent case going the other way, *Mobaldi v. Board of Regents of University of California* (1976), involved a foster mother whose relationship to the injured child was known to the hospital staff at the time the injury occurred, thus removing the foreseeability problem. Compton insisted that *Dillon*'s relationship requirement be construed to cover only relationships that are "legally cognizable." A contrary ruling would open up liability too widely to "every conceivable type of relationship," a result that "neither law nor logic would countenance."

> In every automobile accident it might be said that it is foreseeable that there would be a person in the vicinity who cared for the injured party and would be distressed at seeing him or her injured or killed. On the other hand, an ever increasing scope of liability based on tenuous and inventive theories tends to drive up the cost of insurance and thus frustrate the salutary policy of the law of encouraging all drivers to carry liability insurance in order to compensate truly deserving victims of automobile accidents.

The insurance point was no small consideration in California, a state heavily dependent on automobile transport where insurance rates continued to climb to such a great extent that voter initiatives on the subject of limiting rates were successful by the end of the decade.

Elden appealed this decision to the California Supreme Court, which announced on April 25, 1985, that it had granted a hearing in the case. The potential impact on the state's liability insurance system if the decision were overturned drew wide interest in the case and *amicus* participation on behalf of insurance consumers and insurance companies. On August 18, 1988, after long consideration and a considerable change in the membership of the court due to a voter revolt against the perceived ultra-liberalism of its prior decisions, the court announced that it was affirming the decision of the court of appeal, with only one dissenting vote. The court's opinion by Justice Stanley Mosk grounded the affirmance solidly on considerations of policy and precedent, admitting that pure logic would have led to a different result. Dissenting Justice Allen E. Broussard argued that the changing social climate required a change in the law.

Mosk first addressed the infliction of mental distress claim. Mosk recounted the *Dillon* holding and the relatively strict construction it had received by most of the lower courts, and expressed disapproval of some of the court of appeal decisions to the extent they had strayed beyond the "close relationship" test in *Dillon*. As Mosk characterized Elden's case,

> [Elden] asserts that he should have been allowed the opportunity to show that he met the "closely related" prong of the *Dillon* test by proof that he and his partner had a de facto marriage. The basis of his claim of foreseeability is that in recent years there has been a marked increase in the number of unmarried cohabitants, and therefore it is foreseeable that two persons occupying the same vehicle may be unmarried cohabitants whose relationship parallels that of a legally married couple.

> We have no quarrel with the factual premise of plaintiff's position. There can be no doubt that the last two decades have seen a dramatic increase in the number of couples who live together without formal marriage, that some of these couples are bound by emotional ties as strong as those that bind formally married partners, and that they may share financial resources and expenses in the same manner as married couples. It may well be also that the number of such households has increased to the point that emotional trauma suffered by a partner in such an arrangement from injury to his companion cannot be characterized as "unexpected or remote." Nevertheless, we conclude, for the reasons stated below, that an unmarried cohabitant may not recover damages for emotional distress based on such injury.

Mosk contended that although the *Dillon* court had stressed foreseeability, it had rested its decision on other policy considerations as well. The three-part test, in fact, confounded recovery for foreseeable injuries if the plaintiff was not present physically at the time of the accident, even though it was foreseeable when a child was injured in an accident that the mother would suffer emotional distress, even if she was not present and learned of the accident from others. Recovery should be denied in such cases "for the sound reason that the consequences of a negligent act must be limited in order to avoid an intolerable burden on society."

Mosk identified several "policy reasons" for rejecting Elden's claim. First, he asserted, was the state's "strong interest in the marriage relationship." If unmarried cohabitants were granted a right previously restricted to married persons, the interest in "promoting marriage" would be "inhibited." Inasmuch as marriage had a special, protected status under California law, it would not do to wipe away important legal distinctions between married and unmarried relationships. "Our emphasis on the state's interest in promoting the marriage relationship is not based on anachronistic notions of morality," he insisted. "The policy favoring marriage is 'rooted in the necessity of providing an institutional basis for defining the fundamental relational rights and responsibilities of persons in organized society.'" Marriage was defined by the law as carrying both rights and responsibilities, and Mosk could see no "convincing reason" why plaintiffs who were not under such legal obligations should be permitted to "recover for injuries to their partners to the same extent as those who undertake these responsibilities."

The second basis Mosk identified was the presumed "burden" that extending liability would place on the courts, which would have to inquire on a case-by-case basis into the nature of the relationship to determine whether it met the "foreseeability" test.

> A determination whether a partner in an unmarried cohabitation relationship may recover damages for emotional distress based on such matters as the sexual fidelity of the parties and their emotional and economic ties would require a court to undertake a massive intrusion into the private life of the partners. Further, application of these factors would not provide a sufficiently definite and predictable test to allow for consistent application from case to case.

Finally, Mosk contended that there was a "need to limit the number of persons to whom a negligent defendant owes a duty of care" as a practical matter, citing with approval a New York case, *Tobin v. Grossman* (1969), where that state's highest court had commented: "Every injury has ramifying consequences, like the ripplings of the waters, without end. The problem for the law is to limit the legal consequences of wrongs to a controllable degree." To Mosk, this problem became particularly acute when the claim was for negligent infliction of emotional distress resulting from injury to another, since the range of people who could suffer from mental distress as a result of witnessing or learning about an accident suffered by somebody they knew was potentially quite large. Every distant relative and friend might be able to maintain a plausible claim for some degree of mental injury. It was necessary for the courts to draw a line as a practical matter. The few cases which extended liability to the "functional and emotional equivalent" of family members might have had sympathetic facts, but the result was bad law.

> We decline to follow the rationale of those decisions for to do so would result in the unreasonable extension of the scope of liability of a negligent actor. The need to draw a bright line in this area of the law is essential. . . . The temptation to give legal effect to close emotional ties between unrelated or distantly related persons is often strong, for it cannot be denied that in some cases such relationships offer as much affection, support and solace as is provided by immediate family members, and that the emotional trauma suffered as the result of injury to a person in such a relationship may be as devastating as that suffered by a member of the immediate family. Yet we cannot draw a principled distinction between an unmarried cohabitant who claims to have a de facto marriage relationship with his partner and de facto siblings, parents, grandparents or children. The "problems of multiplication of actions and damages" that would result from such an extension of liability . . . would place an intolerable burden on society.

Mosk reached a similar result considering the loss of consortium claim. Although the Supreme Court had revived the consortium cause of action in *Rodriquez*, it had subsequently cautioned that such claims must be "narrowly circumscribed" due to "the intangible nature of the loss, the difficulty of measuring damages,

and the possibility of an unreasonable increase in the number of persons who would be entitled to sue for the loss of a loved one." As with the emotional distress action, there was a significant interest, in terms of predictability and avoiding undue burden on the courts, in having a bright line test based on legal relationships. The only real exception Mosk found to the solid body of precedent was the *Butcher* case. "We disapprove *Butcher*," said Mosk, "insofar as it is contrary to our conclusion." Mosk also rejected the argument that *Marvin v. Marvin*, a 1974 case in which the California Supreme Court had allowed a woman to sue the man with whom she had been cohabiting for "breach of contract" based on their living-together arrangements, dictated a different result.

> In overruling prior decisions which denied even contract recovery to a partner in a cohabitation relationship on the ground that such an arrangement was immoral, we commented on the increase in the number of cohabiting couples and the change in society's perception of their status. We concluded, "we cannot impose a standard based on alleged moral considerations that have apparently been so widely abandoned by so many." It is evident from what we say above that our determination here is not based on a value judgment regarding the morality of unmarried cohabitation relationships.

Justice Broussard's dissent was scornful of the policy arguments Mosk had advanced, commenting that the majority

> concede that this artificial limitation has no relationship to the nature or foreseeability of the plaintiff's injury, factors usually considered important in defining the perimeters of tort liability. Rather, they posit that the "no marriage—no recovery" rule is justified for policy reasons. One need barely scratch the surface of these purported policies to discover their hollowness. The convenience and certainty of a fool-proof bright line is not sufficient to justify denying recovery to an entire class of deserving plaintiffs on the arbitrary ground of marital status.

Broussard took a decidedly different view from Mosk of the policy underlying the *Dillon* rules. "Recognizing the need for a principled yet flexible framework for limiting liability, we offered guidelines for determining foreseeability in a given case," he said. "These guidelines were based on the plaintiff's physical, temporal and relational proximity to the primary victim at the time of the accident. It is in the context of defining foreseeability that the relationship between the primary victim and the plaintiff is relevant." In *Dillon*, the court observed that the defendant was more likely to foresee injury to a person closely related to the victim, but that did not rule out the distinct possibility that the victim might have a close relationship with a person not "legally" related to him or her.

> The majority do not conclude that the plaintiff was unrelated or distantly related to his injured lover. Nor do they challenge the general proposition that the sheer number of unmarried cohabitants in our society makes it foreseeable that injury of an adult will result in emotional suffering by his or her intimate partner. Given the wide-spread reality and acceptance of unmarried cohabitation, a reasonable person would not find the plaintiff's emotional trauma to be "remote and unexpected." This should end the inquiry. The parties' closeness is only pertinent to foreseeability; once foreseeability is established, the nature of their relationship has no logical connection to the plaintiff's legal standing.

Broussard concluded that there was no rational basis to "limit recovery to married persons," and he characterized as "boilerplate" the policy arguments that the majority "dredge up" to bolster the court's holding.

First, as to the state's interest in marriage, Broussard ridiculed the proposition that this rule would play any role in promoting marriage, sarcastically noting it was unlikely that people would take any account of the need to marry in order to ensure that they could collect for emotional distress if they happened to witness a serious accident involving injury to their lover. Furthermore, Elden's claim would not in any way diminish the right of recovery of married couples, and marriage would retain its "preferential status," since married couples would automatically meet the third *Dillon* test while unmarried couples would be put to some proof regarding their close relationship. While it was true that society fostered marriage for a variety of reasons, extending liability in this case would not undermine marriage in any way Broussard could see, and it would be consistent with other instances in which the law now ex-

tended protection to unmarried cohabitants in such areas as housing, credit, and family relations. Furthermore, Broussard noted, this holding was particularly unfair to lesbian and gay couples, who were precluded by law from marrying but could suffer serious emotional injury upon witnessing injury or death of a life partner, as had been the case in *Coon v. Joseph*, a 1987 court of appeal decision denying recovery to a gay life partner in such a situation.

Broussard also dismissed the "burden on the courts" argument, noting that the court had itself dismissed such arguments in the past as a basis for denying relief to deserving plaintiffs, most pertinently in *Rodriquez* and *Dillon*. "The capability of courts and juries to make sensitive factual determinations is regularly demonstrated in cases, like this one, in which loss of consortium is alleged," he commented. The factual determinations in such cases frequently required "consideration of evidence concerning the quality and nature of the plaintiff's relationship with his or her partner before and after the partner's injury. . . . Whether the purpose is to determine legal standing or to assess the measure of damages, the same inquiry concerning the plaintiff's relationship is made and the same kind of evidence is properly considered." Furthermore, as the *Butcher* court had noted, one could derive a list of objective factors to be measured, such as "the duration of the relationship; whether the parties have a mutual contract; the degree of economic cooperation and entanglement; exclusivity of sexual relations; and whether there is a 'family' relationship with children." Such an "objective" approach would cut down on the possibility of inconsistent application and simplify the fact-finding task.

Broussard labeled "misplaced" the court's concern with invasion of privacy as a part of the factual inquiry. After all, it was the plaintiff's privacy that was being invaded, not the defendant's, and the plaintiff voluntarily placed the nature of his relationship in issue by bringing suit in the first place. The court could devise an appropriate protective order, if necessary, to protect sensitive information from unnecessary public disclosure.

Finally, Broussard rejected the court's contention that this was necessarily the appropriate place to "stop" liability for the consequences of an accident, stating that he did not share the court's "enthusiasm for crude, bright lines." He found this approach "arbitrary," and preferred that the law use "functional grounds that correspond with real loss," the approach the court had taken in *Dillon*.

> Only tortfeasors lucky enough to have injured a de facto rather than a de jure spouse benefit from a bright line based on marriage. An approach that grants recovery to those plaintiffs foreseeably and genuinely injured by a negligent defendant's acts both advances the goals of tort compensation and sufficiently limits liability. To that end, a standard based on the significance and stability of the plaintiff's relationship is workable and fair.

Turning to the loss of consortium claim, Broussard once again found the policy considerations cited by the majority to be unconvincing, particularly its reliance on the "lack of precedent" for such an action, chiding the majority for ignoring "the lesson of *Rodriquez*" and retreating "to the unfortunate pattern of refusing to acknowledge the obsolescence of assumptions upon which existing law is based."

> The modern view regards consortium as a package of relational interests, including love, companionship, emotional support, and sexual relations. The marital status of the plaintiff has no more bearing on his or her standing to claim injury to these interests than does age or socioeconomic status. Accordingly, there is no principled reason to perpetuate the fiction that only marital partners suffer compensable loss of consortium.

Broussard charged the court with abdicating its responsibility for "the upkeep of the common law," asserting, in a quote from the court's opinion in *Rodriquez*, that the vitality of the common law "can flourish only so long as the courts remain alert to their obligation and opportunity to change the common law when reason and equity demand it."

The California Supreme Court's decision in *Elden v. Sheldon* marked an abrupt halt to the attempt by some lower California courts to take account of social realities in determining whether actual injuries to individuals should be recompensed. It was a particularly unfortunate decision for sexual minorities who might be barred from marriage, such as same-sex couples and trans-gender persons, as shown by the decision in *Coon v. Joseph*. In the name of judicial economy, the court adopted an arbitrary, tradition-based bright line that provides protection to an ever decreasing portion of the adult population.

Case References

Butcher v. Superior Court, 139 Cal. App. 3d 58, 188 Cal. Rptr. 503 (4th Dist. 1983)

Coon v. Joseph, 192 Cal. App. 3d 1269, 237 Cal. Rptr. 873 (1987)

Dillon v. Legg, 68 Cal. 2d 728, 69 Cal. Rptr. 72, 441 P.2d 912 (1968)

Drew v. Drake, 110 Cal. App. 3d 555, 168 Cal. Rptr. 65 (1980)

Marvin v. Marvin, 18 Cal. 3d 660, 134 Cal. Rptr. 815, 557 P.2d 106 (1976)

Mobaldi v. Board of Regents of University of California, 55 Cal. App. 3d 573, 127 Cal. Rptr. 720 (1976), overruled, 138 Cal. Rptr. 315 (1977)

Rodriquez v. Bethlehem Steel Corp., 12 Cal. 3d 382, 115 Cal. Rptr. 765, 525 P.2d 669 (1974)

Tobin v. Grossman, 24 N.Y.2d 609, 301 N.Y.S.2d 554, 249 N.E.2d 419 (1969)

Trapp v. Schuyler Construction, 149 Cal. App. 3d 1140, 197 Cal. Rptr. 411 (2d Dist. 1983)

67. DEFINING NEW FAMILY FORMS

Braschi v. Stahl Associates Co., 74 N.Y.2d 201, 543 N.E.2d 49, 544 N.Y.S.2d 784 (1989), reversing 143 A.D.2d 44, 531 N.Y.S.2d 562 (1st Dept. 1988).

The Sexual Revolution of the 1970s began to take new forms in the 1980s, as epidemics of herpes, hepatitis, and finally, Acquired Immune Deficiency Syndrome (AIDS) led to changes in the free and easy sexuality of the prior decade. Monogamy regained a new acceptability, and coupling became the order of the day, even among those who could not formally marry due to the restrictions of marriage laws. Lesbian and gay people, people who were separated but not divorced, and people whose economic dependence on public benefits programs provided strong disincentives to marriage nonetheless settled into couple relationships, and the legal system began to face questions about how and whether to accord recognition to these nontraditional families.

In New York City, one of the earliest battles about this issue occurred in the housing courts, and a major stimulus for the problem was the AIDS epidemic among gay men. The overwhelming majority of New York City residents were apartment renters. The terms of rentals were governed by a bewildering variety of regulatory laws and codes. About 100,000 apartments in the city were covered by the state Rent Control Law, which forbade evictions of tenants who paid their rents and did not damage the landlord's property. Upon the death of tenants, their apartments could become decontrolled and rents would be allowed to rise to market levels (usually five to ten times their controlled levels) and pass into the Rent Stabilization System based on the state's Rent Stabilization Law. (About a million apartments in the city were governed by rent stabilization.) Apartments would not become decontrolled, however, if a deceased tenant was survived by a member of his or her family who had resided with the tenant. Under a regulation promulgated by the rent control administrators, resident members of the tenant's family would have a right to succeed to the statutory tenancy and the rent would remain controlled.

As gay men began to die from AIDS, many left survivors who were threatened with eviction by landlords who did not consider the survivors members of the deceased tenants' families. A small portion of these cases arose in rent-controlled apartments. The first such case to go to trial, *Gelman v. Castaneda*, was decided in favor of the surviving life partner of the deceased tenant. A housing judge ruled in 1986 that the surviving partner was a family member. The landlord did not appeal the ruling and the case went no further.

In the following few years, *Gelman* was treated as the housing court precedent on the issue. Meanwhile, many more of these cases arose in the more numerous rent-stabilized apartments, and litigation raged at various levels of the state court system over whether gay life partner survivors of stabilized tenants should have succession rights. The issues under stabilization were somewhat different, since the Rent Stabilization Law did not explicitly embrace the concept of survivorship rights to apartments. In 1985, the highest New York court, the court of appeals, ruled that an informal policy of rent administrators according survivorship rights to family members of rent stabilized tenants was invalid in the absence of express statutory language or a validly promulgated regulation. Rent administrators quickly responded with an "emergency bulletin" promulgating such a policy, which was subsequently declared invalid by intermediate appellate courts within days of the promulgation of a valid Rent Stabilization Code containing such provisions. Despite heavy lobbying by members of the gay and lesbian community, the administrators included a succession provision in the 1987 Code that defined "family" in traditional terms of marriage, blood relationship, or adoption.

Thus, succession rights issues were quite unsettled when Leslie Blanchard, a prosperous gay man, died from AIDS on September 14, 1986, leaving his life partner of ten years, Miguel

Braschi, to do battle with his landlord over their residence in a rent-controlled apartment. Braschi retained Owen Wincig, a solo practitioner, to represent his interest in the dispute. Stahl Associates Company, the landlord, argued that *Gelman* was of dubious validity, and ordered Braschi to vacate the premises.

Braschi filed suit in New York State Supreme Court, New York County, requesting injunctive relief to prevent his eviction. Stahl Associates retained Shea and Gould, a large New York City law firm, to defend the case. The matter came before Justice Harold Baer, Jr., on a motion for a preliminary injunction. Justice Baer granted the injunction on March 18, 1987, concluding that the facts before him showed "a nontraditional unit that had existed for over ten years and fulfills any definitional criteria of the term 'family.'" He observed that they "were economically, socially and physically a couple like any traditional couple except their relationship could not be legally consummated. The mere non-existence of a legal piece of paper," observed Baer, "should not erase the time, love and commitment given by Braschi and Blanchard to each other." Because Baer's decision broke no new ground in light of *Gelman*, it was not selected for publication.

Stahl Associates decided to challenge the ruling. Its appeal was heard by a panel of four appellate division justices, who issued their unanimous ruling reversing Justice Baer on August 18, 1988. Despite the importance of the case as a matter of first impression at the appellate level, none of the four wanted to be individually identified with the ruling, which was released as an unsigned memorandum. They argued that at common law there was no legal right for anybody to succeed to the leasehold of a deceased tenant. Consequently, any rights in the situation must be based on the statute, which did not contain any definition of the term "family." "The plaintiff has not persuasively demonstrated that in enacting Section 2204.6(d) to protect spouses and family members from eviction, the Legislature was also including and granting legal status and recognition to nontraditional family relationships." After observing that the court of appeals had previously denied a gay man the right to adopt his life partner in order to create family ties between

them, the court concluded that it was up to the legislature, not the courts, to decide whether nontraditional families were to be accorded any official status.

Braschi decided to appeal the decision and moved the court for a stay of his eviction pending appeal. Since the decision was unanimously against him, his chances of getting the court of appeals to hear the appeal were slim. The court controls its docket tightly, and normally does not grant review of unanimous appellate division cases. However, the appellate division is itself authorized under New York law to certify questions to the court of appeals. The appellate division justices who had heard the case decided that the matter was important enough to justify review, but they deadlocked on how long a stay to grant. A fifth justice was added to the panel to break the tie, and the majority decreed a stay until the court of appeals announced its opinion in the case.

By this time, the case had attracted wide attention. The Lesbian and Gay Rights Project of the American Civil Liberties Union (ACLU), based in New York, agreed to take responsibility for arguing the appeal and collaborating with Wincig on the brief. Nan Hunter, director of the Project, and the two staff attorneys, William Rubenstein and Judith Levin, wrote a brief arguing the case two ways: they contended that the court either should adopt a broader understanding of the term "family," as had Justice Baer, or alternatively that the court should rule that the equal protection clauses of the federal and state constitutions would be offended by a succession rule that excluded gay couples from its protection. The latter argument was advanced with high hopes, for a constitutionally based decision by the court would not only reverse the appellate division's construction of the Rent Control Law but would also open up the Rent Stabilization Code to broader construction, and might even provide a vehicle for attacking other government policies that treated gay couples unfavorably by comparison with traditional families.

The possibility of a wider impact for the decision attracted seven *amicus* briefs in support of Braschi's quest to keep his apartment. The lesbian and gay community weighed in with a brief by the Lambda Legal Defense and

Education Fund. The particular impact of the tenant succession issue on persons struggling with the AIDS epidemic was addressed by a brief from the Gay Men's Health Crisis legal services department. The Association of the Bar of the City of New York focused on the constitutional issues in its *amicus* brief. The burden of a narrow, traditional "family" definition on the poor and minorities was the subject of briefs from Community Action for Legal Services and the Legal Aid Society of New York City. A coalition of social service and religious groups, joined by New York's lesbian and gay bar association, the Bar Association for Human Rights, filed an *amicus* brief written by West Coast family diversity specialist Thomas F. Coleman.

Perhaps the most dramatic intervention came from New York City. As the *Braschi* case became the subject of community attention, another succession struggle began involving a community celebrity, Everett Quinton, the surviving life partner of actor Charles Ludlam. At the dedication of "Ludlam Place," a stretch of street in front of Ludlam and Quinton's "Ridiculous Theater Company" in Greenwich Village, Mayor Edward I. Koch publicly vowed solidarity with surviving life partners of persons with AIDS who were struggling to keep their apartments. Given the mayor's position, it seemed inevitable that the city would also file an *amicus* brief, and the Human Rights Commission began work on a draft, only to learn that the Corporation Counsel's office was opposed to filing such a brief, fearing that a constitutional holding for Braschi would damage the city's defensive position in a lawsuit initiated by lesbian and gay schoolteachers to protest the exclusion of their life partners from eligibility for inclusion as family members under health insurance benefit plans. A representative of the mayor's office intervened, brought together community representatives and the corporation counsel, Peter Zimroth, and a compromise was reached by which the city filed a brief urging the court of appeals to reverse the appellate division solely by resort to broad construction of the Rent Control Law without reaching constitutional issues.

The case was argued on April 26, 1989. William Rubenstein of the ACLU represented Braschi, and found a mostly sympathetic bench

deeply concerned over how one might define who would be entitled to protection from eviction so as to distinguish mere roommates from family members. Dean Yuzek, of Shea and Gould, argued for the landlord that the notion of "family" should be treated consistently under all the laws of the state, including the laws on intestacy and a wide variety of property rights, none of which had been construed by the court to veer from the traditional. In addition, he noted, as had the lower court, that the court of appeals had recently held in the "gay adoption" case, *In re Adoption of Robert Paul P.* (1984), that the issue of adopting nontraditional definitions of family was properly one for the legislature.

The court issued its decision on July 6, 1989. The chief judge had recused himself from the case without explanation. The six remaining judges divided three ways on the issue. Judges Richard Simons and Stewart Hancock would have affirmed the appellate division and dismissed the appeal, agreeing with Yuzek that the issue of redefining family structures was properly for the legislature. Judge Vito Titone, in a plurality decision joined by Judges Judith Kaye and Fritz Alexander, accepted Rubenstein's argument that the court should recognize a broader concept of "family" along the lines suggested by Justice Baer and other lower court decisions on tenant succession. Judge Joseph Bellacosa, providing the necessary vote for Braschi to carry the day, held back from endorsing a judicially inspired redefinition of "family" while agreeing that Braschi should be given the protection of the succession regulation.

Because his was the necessary majority vote to decide the case, Bellacosa's decision describes the scope of its precedential value. Noting the ambiguity of the statute and its remedial nature, "intended as a protection against one of the harshest remedies known to the law—eviction from one's home," he opted for a "generous construction." "The best guidance available to the regulatory agency for correctly applying the rule in such circumstances," he insisted, "is that it would be irrational not to include this petitioner and it is a more reasonable reflection of the intention behind the regulation to protect a person such as petitioner as within the regulation's class of 'family.'" Consequently, since it would be irrational to exclude Braschi, a ten-year emotional and economic domestic partner of Blanchard, he was included. Since four judges of the court of appeals agreed that Braschi should be protected if his allegations could be substantiated at trial, a preliminary injunction should be available to prevent the irreparable injury of eviction from his apartment.

Judge Titone took a broader view in his plurality opinion, employing language that provoked fascinated media attention due to its suggestion of a major change in legal concept. He argued that the term "family . . . should not be rigidly restricted to those people who have formalized their relationship by obtaining, for instance, a marriage certificate or an adoption order. The intended protection against sudden eviction should not rest on fictitious legal distinctions or genetic history, but instead should find its foundation in the reality of family life." For purposes of applying the rent control succession rules, Titone would include in the concept of family "two adult lifetime partners whose relationship is long-term and characterized by an emotional and financial commitment and interdependence." He asserted that "it is reasonable to conclude that, in using the term 'family,' the Legislature intended to extend protection to those who reside in households having all of the normally familial characteristics." In a footnote, he hopefully observed that "the concurrer apparently agrees with our view of the purposes of the non-eviction ordinance, and the impact this purpose should have on the way in which this and future cases should be decided." Judge Titone referred to a variety of lower court decisions setting out guidelines for determining whether two unrelated persons should be considered family members, implicitly adopting them on behalf of the plurality.

Titone's opinion embraced a broader concept of family than was necessary to decide Braschi's petition for preliminary injunctive relief. Not until later in the opinion, when he came to analyze the particular facts of the case, did he indicate that Braschi's claims rested on a relationship between two men. The view of family adopted by the plurality extended beyond same-sex couples and, significantly, did not seem to emphasize or rest upon a sexual relationship. An emotional relationship, coupled with financial interdependence, was the focus of the opinion, evidenced by citation to lower court opinions dealing with a variety of sexual and nonsexual living arrangements as sources for guidance on the issue before the court.

The court of appeals' opinion in *Braschi* was among the first by a state court of last resort to recognize, at least implicitly, the concept of legal recognition of nontraditional families in the context of a homosexual relationship. Due to the facts of the case and the fragmenting of the majority, however, the impact of the decision outside the narrow realm of rent control tenant succession issues was unclear. Would the court adopt a similarly fluid concept of family if presented with a rent-stabilization case, or a demand by lesbian and gay teachers to have their partners treated as family members under employee benefit plans? In a different sphere of decisionmaking, the court had decided a series of cases recognizing nontraditional family structures on constitutional grounds in challenges to municipal single-family zoning laws. By avoiding the constitutional issues in *Braschi* as suggested by the city of New York's *amicus* brief, the court refrained from joining the debate, raging in the federal courts of appeals, over the status of sexual orientation as a "suspect classification" in equal protection jurisprudence, leaving to another day the resolution of numerous issues pending in the lower courts of the state.

Case References

Gelman v. Castaneda, New York Law Journal, October 22, 1986 (N.Y. City Civil Ct.)

Robert Paul P., In re Adoption of, 63 N.Y.2d 233 (1984)

68. LINGERING SUSPICION OF LESBIAN MOTHERS

White v. Thompson, 569 So. 2d 1181 (Miss. 1990).

Despite the impressive gains lesbian mothers have made in custody and visitation contests in some states, reluctance to allow lesbians to retain custody of their children is still the rule in many parts of the country. Although many courts now appear reluctant to reveal openly that parental homosexuality is at the heart of their decisions, passionate dissenting opinions make clear exactly what is happening. A prime example of this phenomenon is the Mississippi Supreme Court's 1990 decision in *White v. Thompson.*

David and Andrean (An) White, both teenagers, were married in December 1983 in McComb, Mississippi. They had two children, David and Joseph, who were still preschoolers in 1987 when their parents' marriage finally fell apart. The marriage had been marked by frequent moves (including to Texas and California), separations, father's drinking problems, and sexual infidelities by both parents. Late in 1987, while living in a trailer bought by An's father on property owned by David's parents, Elva and Ed Thompson, the couple finally came to a parting of the ways. At the time, Phyllis Hasberger, a co-worker of An's at a local store, and her son Joshua were living with the Whites in the trailer. An asked David to move out, which he did, going back to his parents' home, and a few weeks later An and Phyllis began a sexual relationship. Both women needed to work to support themselves and their children, but the demands of childcare interfered and both eventually lost their jobs.

Although neither David nor An had filed any kind of divorce proceeding, it was clear that the marriage was over. David's parents, believing that the current living situation was bad for their children, persuaded David to join them in filing a complaint in the Pike County Chancery Court, alleging that An had used marijuana in the children's presence, neglected their health and well-being, and conducted herself in an immoral manner with Phyllis so that

An was now unfit to retain custody of the children. Considering that their own son was incapable of taking care of the children, the Thompsons requested that they be given custody and that An be ordered to contribute to the children's financial support. They also asked the court to restrain An from removing the children from the jurisdiction. Shortly after the complaint was filed, David abducted the children while ostensibly taking them out to dinner, and delivered them to his parents. An then answered the complaint, denying the allegations and counterclaiming against the Thompsons, demanding return of the children and payment of child support by David. At about this time, An and Phyllis moved out of the trailer and went to live with Phyllis's uncle in a neighboring town.

Chancery Judge R. B. Reeves held hearings on the complaints and motions on June 29 and August 11, 1988, at which An was represented by Elizabeth L. Gilchrist, of Jackson, Mississippi, and the Thompsons by John Gordon Roach, Jr., of McComb. At the hearing, An testified about her current living conditions, admitted to having used marijuana in the trailer while the children were outside or in their room, and admitted that sometimes she slept late in the morning while the children were outside playing. An admitted that she had some affairs with other men during her marriage. She testified that her relationship with Phyllis was very good and she did not believe it was harmful to her children or that her in-laws' opposition to it required her to terminate it. An asserted, with corroboration from other witnesses, that the children's behavior had deteriorated while they were living with the Thompsons. An claimed that after David left, the living conditions for the children in the trailer had improved. She also claimed that nobody had ever complained about her performance as a parent until she began her relationship with Phyllis, and she argued that her children could not be taken from her unless it could be shown that her living arrangement was detrimental to them.

The Thompsons claimed that while in An's care the children's health and welfare were being neglected, that they went hungry and were inadequately clothed, and that living with An and Phyllis was not a stable environment for the children. The Thompsons emphasized that they were able to provide a stable, traditional home for the children, and claimed that the children's behavior actually improved after they began living with the Thompsons. They admitted that their son should not have custody due to his poor financial condition and drinking problems.

Chancellor Reeves found that An was "unfit, morally and otherwise" to have custody of her children and ordered that custody be given to the Thompsons. He also ordered An to pay the Thompsons $150 each month toward support of the children, beginning thirty days after she found a new job. Reeves also ordered David to pay $150 a month to his parents for support of the children. Reeves granted An limited visitation rights and ordered that Phyllis not be present during such visitation. Reeves also ordered An not to take the children out of state without written permission from the Thompsons. An promptly appealed the order, claiming that Reeves had impermissibly premised the change in custody on her lesbian relationship, without any evidence that the relationship had a detrimental effect on the children. She also challenged the restrictions on her visitation rights.

A three-judge panel of the Mississippi Supreme Court heard the case on appeal and unanimously determined to affirm Reeves's order. The opinion by Justice Edwin Lloyd Pittman, issued on October 17, 1990, went to great lengths to deny that Reeves's order was premised solely on the lesbian relationship. According to Pittman, Reeves had relied on An's "financial situation, her past adulterous behavior, her marijuana use, and the lesbian relationship. He did not mention the allegations concerning the children's health, their going hungry, and lack of parental supervision."

According to Pittman, the Mississippi courts had in the past adopted a strong presumption in favor of natural parents in custody contests with grandparents. Indeed, in 1968 the court had ruled that as against the mother, paternal grandparents had no right to custody of a grandson "until they have charged and proved that she has forfeited her natural right to the custody of her minor son by abandonment or by immoral conduct, or other circumstances which clearly indicate that the best interest of the child will be served in the custody of another." Custody was not to be changed merely because a nonparent was in a better financial position to provide care, or because the mother wished to take the child out of the jurisdiction.

Given this strong case law, An argued that an inadequate factual basis had been established to deprive her of custody. There was no evidence, she claimed, to show that her living situation had the kind of detrimental effect on her children described in prior Mississippi cases as necessary to overcome the strong presumption of parental rights for a natural parent.

Pittman disagreed. While conceding that "the predominant issue in this case seems to have been Mrs. White's lesbian relationship, and the chancellor may have relied almost entirely on this," an independent review of the record by the supreme court panel showed that there was sufficient evidence from which the chancellor could have concluded that An was unfit.

> There was credible evidence, discounting the morality aspects of this case, that the children had not been properly supervised, and that they had not been adequately clothed or fed, and there had been a resulting deleterious effect on their health. A parent's chosen manner of living may not take precedence over the well-being of the children involved.

An had cited cases from other jurisdictions holding that homosexuality *per se* should not by itself determine a custody dispute. Pittman claimed that factors other than homosexuality were present in this case to justify the chancellor's result, so the court did not have to deal with the issue of homosexuality. Also, noting that visitation terms were within the discretion of the chancery court, he argued that there was no abuse of discretion on Reeves's part in restricting An's visitation rights. Citing without any analytic discussion several cases from other jurisdictions which had upheld similar restrictive visitation orders in cases involving homosexual parents (*L. v. D.* [Missouri, 1982], *Irish v. Irish* [Michigan, 1980], *J.L.P.(H.) v. D.J.P.* [Missouri, 1982], *In re J.S. & C.* [New Jersey, 1984], *In re Jane B.* [New York, 1976], *DiStefano v. DiStefano* [New York, 1978]), Pittman asserted that there was a "majority rule" that such restrictions were proper. What Pittman's uncritical citations omitted were subsequent decisions from some of the same jurisdictions taking different positions, such as *Gottlieb v. Gottlieb* (1985) in New York.

On petition for rehearing, which was denied on November 28, 1990, all the other justices of the full court concurred with the panel except for Justice James L. Robertson, who filed a blistering dissent, making quite clear that the supreme court's decision was inconsistent with prior Mississippi case law and clearly motivated by An's lesbian relationship. "Of course there is evidence that three and a half year old David and seventeen month old Joseph have been neglected," he admitted, "but no more than one would expect to find in any case where a twenty-four year old mother with but a high school diploma and no independent means has been in effect deserted by a drunken husband who has provided not a penny in support. The poor are much with us, and sadly many of these are young women with children and without support. I had not thought heretofore we regarded this grounds for taking these children from their mothers," he asserted, citing several prior Mississippi cases on point. "If the neglect found here is to become the standard, I dare say few of our economically disadvantaged citizens will find their children secure from grandparents who engage skilled counsel."

As far as Robertson was concerned, this case began because Elva and Ed Thompson objected to having their grandsons raised in a lesbian household. "I trust no one will seriously suggest this a per se basis for stripping An of custody of her two minor children," Robertson asserted, citing more than a dozen cases from other jurisdictions holding that parental homosexuality was not a *per se* basis for finding parental unfitness. "At most it is a factor to be considered," he argued, "and to inform adjudication only when there is a demonstrable present adverse effect upon the children or a substan-

tial likelihood of such effect in the future. Such effect must be predicated upon positive proof and not prudish prejudice."

In this case, said Robertson, the standard for changing custody had clearly not been met. He saw no basis in the record for distinguishing this case from others in which the Mississippi courts had refused to change custody when the main complaint against the custodial parent was sexual indiscretion. "It is important that An's estranged husband makes no claim to custody," Robertson observed. "His closet is filled with as many skeletons as hers, if not more. David White is a career drunk who, after An threw him out, took up with a live-in girlfriend of his own. His financial neglect of his children has been massive. Indeed, most of An's neglect is attributable to the employment she has been forced to pursue because of David's irresponsibility."

Robertson pointed out that there was no basis in Mississippi law for applying the routine best interest of the child standard when grandparents were contesting custody. In such a case, he asserted, the law required a ruling in favor of the natural parent, even if the grandparents could theoretically provide a better home, unless the natural parent was shown to be "totally unfit." The law presumed that natural parents were fit, and that the best interests of children were served by leaving them in the custody of natural parents. "Grandparents demanding custody are held to the same standard as public welfare authorities," he asserted; "that is, they must show by clear and convincing evidence that the theretofore custodial parent (1) has abandoned the child or (2) practices gross and depraved immorality to the demonstrable detriment of the child or (3) is mentally or otherwise unfit to have custody."

> I have read this record and do not find proof even approaching these standards. If Phyllis Hasberger were a man to whom An was married and, if the facts of this case were otherwise wholly identical, I dare say that no court would dream of placing custody with these children's grandmother and step-grandfather.

While it was true that on appeal of such cases, findings of ultimate fact were to be reviewed on a "clearly erroneous" standard, said Robertson, the appellate court was only so limited in its factual review when the trial court had applied the correct legal standard. Here, the trial court had failed to apply the "clear and convincing evidence standard" required for termination of custody of a natural parent, so the supreme court should have imposed a close scrutiny on the factual record. In addition, it was clear to Robertson that the court had applied the wrong legal standard. "The test is abandonment, not neglect," he asserted, and there was no evidence to suggest that An had abandoned her children. "The test for unfitness is moral depravity, not unconventionality, and in any event actual or probable substantial adverse impact must be shown." The chancellor and the supreme court had, in Robertson's view, applied much too relaxed a standard in this case. "I see no evidence remotely suggesting An's conduct has the actual or potential effect our law deems necessary to take her children from her. What evidence there may be is certainly not clear and convincing."

The Mississippi Supreme Court's decision in *White v. Thompson* shows how all too many courts have handled custody disputes involving gay parents. While either shying away from discussing the issue of homosexuality on the merits, or asserting that they are basing their decision on factors other than parental sexuality, the courts bend evidentiary and substantive rules to ensure that the children are removed from the custody of the homosexual parent. In most jurisdictions, the time is long past when a court would actually assert that parental homosexuality is evidence of unfitness *per se*, but this "progress" is cold comfort for the homosexual parent when the courts allow stereotypical views of homosexuality to color their evidentiary findings, and tacitly depart from established precedents to reach their results.

Furthermore, the body of court decisions supporting restrictions on the visitation rights of noncustodial homosexual parents, much of it based on unsubstantiated judicial conclusions that exposure to a parent's loving homosexual partner would be harmful to the child, is readily invoked to rub salt in the wound of the custody determination. While some judges stand ready to reject such unsubstantiated conclusions, reliance on them remains the rule rather than the exception in many parts of the United States.

Case References

DiStefano v. DiStefano, 60 A.D.2d 976, 401 N.Y.S.2d 636 (1978)

Gottlieb v. Gottlieb, 108 A.D.2d 120, 488 N.Y.S.2d 180 (1st Dept. 1985)

Irish v. Irish, 102 Mich. App. 75, 300 N.W.2d 739 (1980)

Jane B., In re, 85 Misc. 2d 515, 380 N.Y.S.2d 848 (1976)

J.L.P.(H.) v. D.J.P., 643 S.W.2d 865 (Mo. Ct. App. 1982)

J.S. & C., In re, 129 N.J. Super. 486, 324 A.2d 90 (1984)

L. v. D., 630 S.W.2d 240 (Mo. Ct. App. 1982)

69. CAN YOU STILL BE MY "MOMMY"?: VISITATION AND THE LESBIAN CO-PARENT

Alison D. v. Virginia M., 77 N.Y.2d 651, 569 N.Y.S.2d 586, 572 N.E.2d 27 (1991), affirming 155 A.D.2d 11, 552 N.Y.S.2d 321 (2d Dept. 1990).

In 1984, Lambda Legal Defense and Education Fund presented a conference at New York University Law School titled "Lesbians Choosing Motherhood." The event drew over three hundred women eager to learn about new reproductive technologies through which they could conceive children without engaging in heterosexual activity. This event was very much a sign of the times, as more and more female couples planned for and raised children independent from men. It was only a matter of time before these new, nontraditional families would raise legal issues.

Indeed, even as Lambda's conference was taking place, a court in California was struggling with the first dispute about child visitation to receive national media attention between former lesbian partners. *Loftin v. Flournoy* did not result in a published opinion, but it stimulated the writing of a law review article that quotes extensively from the judge's bench ruling. The couple involved in that case planned to have a child related to both of them by obtaining sperm from Loftin's brother to inseminate Flournoy, thus making Loftin an aunt of Flournoy's child. They raised the child together for a time, but then their relationship fractured, and Flournoy would not allow Loftin to continue seeing the child. Building on the existing biological relationships, the judge ruled that as an aunt who had taken an active role in raising the child, Loftin was entitled to seek visitation rights in the best interest of the child despite Flournoy's opposition.

Things were not so simple in the cluster of cases that arose toward the end of the 1980s and generated a series of appellate decisions within the space of one year beginning in the summer of 1990. The first to reach a state's highest court was *Alison D. v. Virginia M.*, decided by the New York Court of Appeals in May 1991. The result in *Alison D.* was forecast by two California appellate decisions, *Curiale v. Reagan*, decided by the Third District Court of Appeal in August 1990, and *Nancy S. v. Michele G.*, decided by the First District Court of Appeal on March 20, 1991, the same day that *Alison D.* was being argued before New York's high court. In all three cases, the courts ruled that the former lesbian partner of the child's mother did not have standing to pursue visitation, so the best interests of the child were not pertinent to the lawsuits. Within weeks of the *Alison D.* ruling, similar rulings were issued by the Wisconsin Supreme Court in *Sporleder v. Hermes* and in the Minnesota Court of Appeals in *Kulla v. McNulty*. It appeared that the state courts were not willing to accept the argument that these parenting arrangements created any new legal rights to visitation.

Although some of the facts differed among these cases, there were basic similarities. In all of them, the couple planned to have a child and raise that child together, with or without making a written agreement describing their decision. In some, the "co-parent" carried out the act of inseminating her partner. One of the cases involved an adoption that had been planned by the couple, although it had been carried out in the name of one of them. In all of these cases, both women played parenting roles, and the "nonbiological" mother apparently played a greater parenting role in some of them. After the relationship broke up, the "natural" mother may have allowed visitation to continue for some time, but in each case she eventually refused to allow her former partner to maintain contact with the child.

The case of Alison D. and Virginia M. was typical. The women began their relationship in 1977, moved in together in 1978, and decided to start a family in 1980. They began with Virginia M. becoming pregnant and giving birth in 1981 to a son, A.D.M., who was given Alison's surname as his middle name. Next Alison became pregnant. Alison played the greater parenting role of the two, since Virginia was working outside the home during Alison's pregnancy while A.D.M. was an infant. A.D.M. referred to Alison as his "mommy" and treated both women equally as his parents. When A.D.M. was 2½ years old, the relationship between the women terminated. Alison moved out of the home, but Virginia allowed her generous visitation rights. However, when Virginia was able to buy out Alison's share of their jointly purchased home a few years later, she began to cut back on visitation. Alison moved to Ireland to pursue a career opportunity in 1987 after securing Virginia's promise that she could maintain contact with A.D.M. Virginia reneged on her promise, blocking phone calls, returning letters and gifts, and eventually relocating. Alison needed an investigator's assistance to locate Virginia, and filed suit in the New York State Supreme Court, Dutchess County, seeking a writ of *habeas corpus* under the Domestic Relations Law for a determination of visitation rights.

Alison was proceeding under section 70 of the Domestic Relations Law, which authorized granting the writ at the request of "either parent" to determine custody. Treating visitation as a minor form of custody, the courts had construed this provision to authorize the writ for visitation determinations as well. Alleging that she was a "parent" of A.D.M., in fact if not in law, Alison argued that it was in A.D.M.'s best interest to continue some relationship with the woman he thought of as his other "mommy."

Virginia's attorney, Anthony G. Maccarini, moved to dismiss the case for lack of jurisdiction, arguing that Alison was not a parent and thus the court was not authorized to issue the writ or to entertain the suit on the merits. Without denying any of the factual allegations of Alison's complaint, Maccarini argued that the court was not authorized even to hear the case.

Supreme Court Justice James D. Benson agreed with Maccarini, granting the motion to dismiss from the bench on July 18, 1988. Benson said that "the biological parent of the child is the parent within the meaning of the statute. The court declines to adopt the definition of a parent as someone standing in loco parentis." Alison took her case to Lambda Legal Defense and Education Fund, where Legal Director Paula Ettelbrick, who had been consulting on several such cases around the country, agreed to represent her on appeal. In addition, the American and New York Civil Liberties Unions and an organization of lesbian and gay parents filed *amicus* briefs urging the Appellate Division for the Second Department to reverse Justice Benson's determination and order a consideration of the merits of Alison's visitation claim.

The appellate division panel ruled on March 2, 1990, in a *per curiam* opinion. Ironically, the subsequent ruling by the court of appeals would also be announced in a *per curiam* opinion. Perhaps realizing how harshly formalistic their rulings were, none of the judges who joined in them wished to be personally associated with either the reasoning or the results. By a vote of three to one, the panel agreed with Justice Benson that the case should be dismissed for lack of jurisdiction.

The court relied primarily on a 1987 decision by the court of appeals, *In re Ronald FF. v. Cindy GG.* Ronald was Cindy's boyfriend. He moved in with her when she became pregnant, although it turned out later that he was not the father. However, he helped to raise the child, although he did not live with Cindy and the child continuously. At a time when they were not living together, Ronald learned that Cindy was planning to move to Mexico. He brought an action in supreme court seeking a declaration of his right to continued visitation, which was granted when a social worker testified that

it would be in the boy's best interests to continue a relationship with the person he regarded as his father.

The court of appeals reversed, holding that the lower courts had incorrectly relied on its 1976 ruling in *Bennett v. Jeffreys*, in which it had held that a third party might be awarded custody under "extraordinary circumstances." This extraordinary circumstances doctrine, which the lower courts thought applicable in Ronald's case, was to be used only for custody determinations, said the court. When a child was in the custody of its natural parent, the extraordinary circumstances doctrine had no place, since the legal parent of a child had a right to determine with whom the child would associate.

Now, following *Ronald FF.*, the appellate division ruled that this precedent applied to deprive Alison of standing to sue for visitation. If Ronald was not entitled to sue, neither could Alison, since they were similarly situated. Rejecting all arguments as to differences between the two cases (most significantly, that Alison and Virginia had together planned to have A.D.M. and raise him, unlike Ronald and Cindy), the *per curiam* opinion held that Alison's "*in loco parentis*" theory had to be rejected.

The court also rejected the argument that it should follow the methodology of the court of appeals in *Braschi v. Stahl Associates Co.*, a 1989 case in which that court had defined the term "family" broadly to include a same-sex couple. The surviving partner was seeking protection from eviction under a rent control regulation that accorded protection to members of a deceased tenant's family. In both cases, the key words in the statutes, "family" and "parent," were not statutorily defined. In *Braschi*, the court of appeals opted for a broad definition that reflected the "reality" of family life in New York, asserting that this would best effectuate the statutory purpose of avoiding disruption of families after the death of a tenant. Without discussing the court's methodology, the *per curiam* opinion merely asserted that "the underlying circumstances in *Braschi* . . . , including the definition of the word 'family' used in the regulations, are totally inapposite to those at bar."

Trying to soften the blow of their decision, the *per curiam* judges concluded that they did not want it to be interpreted as minimizing "the close and loving relationship that the petitioner has apparently developed with the child," and speculated that if she had standing under the Domestic Relations Law "her claim for visitation would have been worthy of serious consideration." Small comfort! This comment exacerbated the perceived unfairness of the decision.

Justice Sybil Hart Kooper was furious in dissent, pointing out that this was a situation where the court should be considering the best interests of the child and that the case called for a "realistic" interpretation of the term "parent" "within the context of the circumstances presented." Under the particular facts Alison alleged in her complaint, said Kooper, she had established standing.

Kooper based her dissent heavily on the court of appeals' decision in *Braschi*, pointing out how in both cases a formalistic approach to legal analysis would fail to come to grips with the real-world problem presented to the court. Even had Alison lived for ten years with Virginia and A.D.M., she would have no standing to contest visitation under the court's ruling, a result unacceptable to Kooper. "It need hardly be emphasized," she said, "that when the courts become involved in family matters concerning relationships between parent and child, simplistic analysis and the strict application of absolute legal principles should be avoided. The governing criterion, as always, is the best interests of the child." The *Braschi* approach was instructive on how the court should proceed, looking to the reality of the situation rather than using "rigid analysis." In *Braschi*, the court of appeals said it would eschew "fictitious legal distinctions or genetic history" in deciding what constituted a family. The same approach should be applied here.

Kooper argued that recognizing Alison as having some rights as a parent would be less of a departure from tradition than the court's *Braschi* opinion, because there was "ample authority" in other jurisdictions supporting the parental rights of third parties under a variety of circumstances. In fact, she argued, far from serving A.D.M.'s best interests, the *per curiam*'s

approach might prove "detrimental," since biological relationships had nothing to do with the quality of the parent-child relationship. The purpose of visitation, after all, was to serve the interests of the child, which should be foremost in the court's consideration. Kooper argued that a parent's right to control her child's association should not be regarded as absolute, but should be weighed together with the child's interest in reaching a determination on visitation.

Kooper also rejected the court's holding that "the absence of explicit statutory authority" ended the matter. Courts in other jurisdictions had used equitable theories, such as *in loco parentis*, to overcome apparent statutory barriers in cases involving stepparents who had formed close relationships with their former spouses' children. The "significant question" in these cases, said Kooper, was not the biological or legal relationship, but the "underlying nature" of the actual relationship between the child and the adult. The concept of a biological "stranger," cited by the court as precluding a determination on the merits in this case, "neither accords with reality nor furthers the best interests of the child."

In this regard, the court's reliance on *Ronald FF.* seemed to her misplaced. That case merely stood for the proposition that the "extraordinary circumstances" doctrine was not appropriate for visitation cases, not that a parent had an absolute right to control her child's associations. The court of appeals had not discussed such alternative theories as *in loco parentis* in that case.

Although a majority of the court seemed to think that the matter was easily disposed of, perhaps their decision to issue a *per curiam* opinion reflected some uncertainty about the correctness of their course, for the panel voted to give Alison permission to bring her case to the court of appeals, which scheduled argument for March 20, 1991. As the first such case to go to a state's highest court, Alison's quest attracted national media attention and additional *amicus* support. The appellate division level *amici* were joined on appeal by the Association of the Bar of the City of New York, the NOW Legal Defense and Education Fund, a coalition of concerned family law professors, and the Youth

Law Center. Taken together, these *amicus* briefs presented a strong plea for realism as against formalism, for recognition of the interests of children to maintain ties with those who nurtured them early in life. These pleas were unavailing, however, since the court's opinion, issued *per curiam* on May 2, approved the appellate division's reasoning and upheld dismissal of Alison's suit. Again, the only woman on the court, Judge Judith Kaye, turned out to be the only dissenter.

The court's *per curiam* opinion was curiously brief and opaque, given the factual novelty of the issue it was considering. After briefly summarizing the facts, the court devoted only three paragraphs to disposing of the matter. The statute authorized "either parent" to bring an action seeking visitation rights. Although the court recognized Alison's "understandable concern for and interest in the child and of her expectation and desire that her contact with the child would continue," the court could not help her out because she was not a parent "within the meaning" of the statute. Why not? "Traditionally, in this State it is the child's mother and father who, assuming fitness, have the right to the care and custody of their child, even in situations where the nonparent has exercised some control over the child with the parents' consent." Letting a "third person" assert visitation rights "would necessarily impair the parents' right to custody and control." Since Alison was not claiming that Virginia was unfit for custody, she had "no right to petition the court to displace the choice made by this fit parent in deciding what is in the child's best interests." In other words, by conceding that Virginia was a fit parent, Alison was also conceding that Virginia's decision about what was in A.D.M.'s best interests was not subject to judicial review.

The court concluded by invoking the *Ronald FF.* decision, pointing out that some other states had explicitly authorized awarding visitation rights to third persons but that New York's legislature had not (with the narrow exception of grandparents and siblings in extraordinary circumstances involving parental unfitness). If Alison sought a remedy, she should go to the legislature.

As had Justice Kooper in the appellate division, Judge Kaye in her dissent emphasized the unreality of the court's opinion, disposing of a visitation controversy without reference to the best interests of the child. "The Court's decision, fixing biology as the key to visitation rights, has impact far beyond this particular controversy," she said, "one that may affect a wide spectrum of relationships—including those of longtime heterosexual stepparents, 'common-law' and nonheterosexual partners such as involved here, and even participants in scientific reproduction procedures." Noting estimates that 15.5 million children in the United States did not live with two biological parents and that as many as eight to ten million were born into families with gay or lesbian parents, Kaye asserted that the impact of the holding would fall "hardest on the children of those relationships, limiting their opportunity to maintain bonds that may be crucial to their development." The court had retreated from its "proper role" by tightening standing rules in this case, because it was the best interests of the child, not the "standing" of the contestant, that should be foremost in importance.

Kaye observed that this appeal dealt solely with whether Alison should have the opportunity to persuade the trial court in the first instance that she had the type of relationship with A.D.M. that could be characterized as "parental." Only then would the court even proceed to the issue of best interests. In light of this posture, Kaye disagreed with the *per curiam* court's assertion that it was "powerless" to proceed without express statutory authorization. The lack of a statutory definition of "parent" left the court free to interpret that term broadly to effectuate the statutory purpose. Kaye found the court's narrow approach inconsistent with its past practice: "We have not previously taken such a hard line in these matters," she said, "but in the absence of express legislative direction have attempted to read otherwise undefined words of the statute so as to effectuate the legislative purposes." And the main purpose of these provisions of the Domestic Relations Law was to promote the best interest of the child and the child's welfare and happiness. Surely, a decision that precluded consideration of those factors was inappropriate.

The legislative history of the Domestic Relations Law showed that the *habeas corpus* provision was not intended to displace the court's traditional equitable authority in domestic relations cases, but rather to make clear that, contrary to older doctrine, "either parent" could bring a visitation proceeding. Indeed, there was even New York precedent for the proposition that a petitioner could seek equitable relief in a visitation case when he or she did not qualify under the *habeas* statute. In *Bennett v. Jeffreys,* the court had recognized that in cases of conflict over custody or visitation, the best interests of the child were to determine the outcome. While it was true that in *Ronald FF.* the court had held that custody and visitation presented distinct issues meriting distinct treatment, at the same time the *per curiam* in this case had characterized visitation as a "limited form of custody." Custody of a fit parent could not lightly be interfered with, thus the extraordinary circumstances doctrine of *Bennett.* A different standard was appropriate for visitation cases, but Kaye doubted that it should be an absolute right in the fit parent to dictate whom the child could see. Kaye asserted that the refusal to extend the *Bennett* doctrine to visitation disputes in *Ronald FF.* was premised on the court's view that the fitness of the parent, a key issue in a custody case, was not relevant to visitation determinations. By citing *Ronald FF.* as an absolute bar to Alison's standing, the court was taking the law "a step beyond *Ronald FF.* by establishing the *Bennett* 'extraordinary circumstances' test as the only way to reach the child's best interest in a section 70 proceeding." This was too high a barrier.

Kaye recognized that there had to be some limits on who can petition for custody, but she disputed the argument, accepted below by the appellate division, that defining "parent" more broadly would throw open the door to "every dedicated caretaker." The court knew how to create workable definitions for broad, statutorily undefined terms, as it had shown in *Braschi* when it adopted a realistic definition of "family." Without suggesting her own definition, Kaye argued that the court should have taken this opportunity to fashion a definition that would have made it possible for third parties in genuine parent-child relationships to have access to the court for purposes of presenting evidence of the best interests of the child.

The court of appeals' decision in *Alison D. v. Virginia M.* was within the mainstream of judicial thinking on this issue, as demonstrated by the appellate decisions in California that came before it and the appellate decisions in Wisconsin and Minnesota that followed it. Yet these decisions created a real tension with the growing body of precedent involving stepparents, since same-sex domestic partners were fully analogous to stepparents. They were people who had no biological or legal relationship with the child but who served in the role of parent through their relationship with the child's "natural" parent. Although the law did not recognize same-sex marriage, this was just the type of "artificial" or "fictitious" distinction that the New York Court of Appeals had cast aside in *Braschi,* when it needed to adopt a definition of "family" that would serve the ultimate purpose of the rent control law. The ultimate purpose of laws on child custody and visitation is to advance society's interest in the care and nurturing of children by advancing the best interest of the child. Formalistic barriers to considering those interests do not serve society's interest. More of these cases are pending. Perhaps *Alison D.* will not become the "leading case" that its first-in-time status suggests.

Case References

Bennett v. Jeffreys, 40 N.Y.2d 543 (1976)

Braschi v. Stahl Associates Co., 74 N.Y.2d 201 (1989)

Curiale v. Reagan, 222 Cal. App. 3d 1597, 272 Cal. Rptr. 520 (3d Dist. 1990)

Kulla v. McNulty, N.W.2d (Minn. App. 1991)

Loftin v. Flournoy, No. 569630–7 (Cal. Super., Alameda Co., 11/2/84) (unpublished disposition); see Shapiro & Schultz, *Single-Sex Families: The Impact of Birth Innovations Upon Traditional Family Notions,* 24 Journal of Family Law 271 (1985–86)

Nancy S. v. Michele G., 279 Cal. Rptr. 212 (App., 1st Dist. 1991)

Ronald FF. v. Cindy GG., 70 N.Y.2d 141 (1987)

Sporleder v. Hermes, 162 Wis. 2d 1001, 471 N.W.2d 202 (1991), Wis. 2d, N.W.2d (1991), affirming 157 Wis. 2d 431, 459 N.W.2d 602 (App. 1990)

70. A LESBIAN COUPLE AS A "FAMILY OF AFFINITY"

In re Guardianship of Sharon Kowalski, 478 N.W.2d 790 (Minn. App. 1991), review denied, February 10, 1992. Prior decisions: *In re Guardianship of Kowalski*, 382 N.W.2d 861 (Minn. App.), certiorari denied, 475 U.S. 1085 (1986), review denied, April 18, 1986; 392 N.W.2d 310 (Minn. App. 1986).

Sharon Kowalski and Karen Thompson came to symbolize the desire of many in the lesbian and gay community for societal recognition of their relationships, as Karen waged a six-year battle to be reunited with her partner after a tragic automobile accident and the intervention of Sharon's parents separated them for four years. This struggle at one and the same time dramatically illustrated how existing legal arrangements failed to reflect the changing reality of lesbian and gay lives in the final decades of the 20th century, while also providing an opportunity for the legal system to adjust to these changes. In the end, the Minnesota Court of Appeals' recognition of their "family of affinity" triumphed over the persistent attempts by Sharon's parents to keep the two women apart.

Sharon and Karen met about four years before the accident that was to change their lives. They exchanged rings, named each other as insurance beneficiaries, and considered themselves the equivalent of a "married couple." Secure in their joint home in St. Cloud, Minnesota, they never revealed the nature of their relationship to Sharon's parents, who lived in the rural, culturally isolated "Iron Range" region of northern Minnesota where Sharon was born, because they assumed that the Kowalskis would not understand or approve of their relationship. Neither did they join in the growing trend among lesbian and gay couples to produce documentary evidence of their relationship, in the form of powers of attorney, partnership contracts, or joint wills. Indeed, the two women were not part of any organized "gay community" in St. Cloud, but kept very much to themselves.

On November 13, 1983, a serious automobile accident left Sharon brain-damaged and paralyzed. Confined in St. Cloud Hospital and unable to speak, she could not communicate to her doctors or parents the nature of her rela-

tionship to Karen Thompson, the woman known to her parents only as a "roommate" who persisted in coming to the hospital and showing physical affection for Sharon. Disturbed by the Kowalskis' coldness to her, Karen finally decided to tell them the nature of her relationship with their daughter. They refused to believe her, and apparently came to view her as a "predatory lesbian" who had an unnatural interest in their daughter. When the Kowalskis sought to restrict Karen's visits to Sharon, Karen obtained the assistance of Minneapolis attorney M. Sue Wilson and filed a petition in state court seeking appointment as Sharon's guardian. Donald Kowalski, Sharon's father, retained Jack Fena, a Hibbing, Minnesota, lawyer, and cross-petitioned for guardianship, which was awarded to him on April 25, 1984, by District Judge Bruce R. Douglas, of Sherburne County. However, the court credited Karen's assertions that the women were lesbian partners and directed that Donald Kowalski afford Karen Thompson equal visitation rights and access to medical and financial information and personnel. Judge Douglas specifically refused to appoint joint guardians because of "the difficulties existing between" Thompson and the Kowalskis. Karen agreed not to appeal this ruling, since her visitation rights were made specific and, she thought, binding on Donald Kowalski.

A period of tense relations between the Kowalskis and Thompson ensued, as the Kowalskis transferred Sharon to a series of nursing homes and sought to restrict Karen's visitation. Karen, an expert in physical therapy, complained that the Kowalskis were not providing adequate rehabilitative care to Sharon. She argued that they were trying to keep Sharon in a relatively helpless state to avoid her achieving the ability to demand a permanent reunification with Karen. Claiming that Karen's visits were not in Sharon's best interests because Sharon appeared depressed after those visits, Donald Kowalski secured the support of Sharon's doctors for the total exclusion of Karen. Early in 1985, Kowalski moved the court to amend its original order and support his exclusion of Karen from further contact with Sharon. After hearing from several members of the staff of the nursing home in the Iron Range to which Kowalski had moved his daughter, the court concluded that the ongoing conflict between Karen and the Kowalskis created a tense situation that was not in Sharon's best interests. On July 23, 1985, the court confirmed Donald Kowalski's appointment as sole guardian and ended Karen's legal rights to visitation and consultation. Kowalski was given sole authority to determine who should visit Sharon in the nursing home. Kowalski then ordered the nursing home to bar Karen from visiting his daughter.

Thus began five years of desperate appeals by Karen to achieve reunification with her lover. Karen had begun to publicize her problem in 1984 as a way of seeking financial assistance from members of the gay community for her legal struggle, and she was able to attract the Minnesota Civil Liberties Union's interest. In 1985, she hit the road in earnest, beginning to speak around the country and appearing on radio and television. Karen's legal appeals had little success at first. On March 4, 1986, the Minnesota Court of Appeals, in a unanimous decision by Chief Judge Peter S. Popovich, confirmed the trial court's decision to give Donald Kowalski sole authority over Sharon. Karen's desperate attempt to get the U.S. Supreme Court involved in the case was rejected by that court on March 24, 1986, and the Minnesota Supreme Court refused to review the court of appeals' decision on April 18, 1986. Other motions by Karen for further relief were rejected by the court of appeals on August 19, 1986. And there the matter rested for several years, as Karen sought to build support for her efforts at reunion with Sharon and found herself becoming a nationally prominent gay movement activist.

Karen finally found a legal loophole that allowed her to revive the matter in 1988. The original guardianship order by Judge Douglas required an annual physical and mental evaluation of Sharon to determine whether she was

capable of expressing her wishes regarding the guardianship and visitation issues. Karen suspected that these annual reviews were not being done, and even if they were, that the nursing home staff, sympathetic to the Kowalski family, was not providing an adequately "neutral" evaluation. Since Donald Kowalski had moved Sharon to a nursing home in the Iron Range, out of the jurisdiction of the original trial court, Karen took a desperate stab at getting another judge involved, and her attorney was able in May 1988 to persuade District Judge Robert V. Campbell, of St. Louis County, to order specialists at a neutral facility to evaluate Sharon. The doctors concluded that Sharon was capable of expressing her wishes and that she desired to be visited by Karen. The doctors also recommended that Sharon be transferred to a facility that was better equipped to provide the rehabilitative services she required. In January 1989, Campbell responded to these recommendations by ordering that Karen be allowed to visit, and Sharon was transferred to a new facility near Karen's home in St. Cloud. Not only was contact restored between the two women, but Karen, who had specially equipped her home to be wheelchair accessible, was able to bring Sharon home for weekend visits.

Late in 1988, Donald Kowalski, sick and wearied from the long legal battle with Karen Thompson, notified Judge Campbell that he wished to be removed as Sharon's guardian. This sparked the last battle for the guardianship. Karen filed a petition on August 7, 1989, seeking appointment as Sharon's sole guardian. No competing petition was filed, and the court held a series of hearings in Duluth and Minneapolis during August and September of 1990. The purpose of the hearings was to evaluate Karen's petition. The task for Campbell was to determine whether appointment of Karen as guardian would be in the best interest of Sharon. Although the Kowalskis had officially dropped out of the battle, a surprise champion for their efforts to keep Sharon out of Karen's control emerged: Karen Tomberlin, a friend of the Kowalski family, wrote to the attorney appointed by the court to represent Sharon and suggested that she be considered an alternative guardian. The attorney wrote to Campbell, suggesting Tomberlin as an alternative to Karen.

The evidence at the hearing was focused on Sharon's condition and Karen Thompson's suitability as a guardian. Karen produced sixteen medical witnesses, all of whom had treated Sharon and had personal knowledge of her condition. Virtually all the professionals who were in recent contact with Sharon were called as witnesses. Their testimony indicated Sharon's enthusiasm for continued contact with Karen and her desire to live with Karen, as well as Karen's ability to care for Sharon in an appropriate manner. Three witnesses appeared in opposition to Thompson's petition: Debra Kowalski, Sharon's sister; Kathy Schroeder, a friend of Sharon and the Kowalskis; and Karen Tomberlin. Each stated their opposition based on their opinions as to Sharon's true wishes. None of them had been frequent visitors during Sharon's extended confinement, and none had accompanied Sharon on any of her more recent outings from the rehabilitation center where she was confined. Sharon's parents did not attend the hearings.

Convinced that she had built an overwhelming trial record in support of her guardianship petition, Karen was shocked when Judge Campbell issued an opinion on April 23, 1991, appointing Karen Tomberlin to be the guardian. There had been no evidence at the hearing of Tomberlin's qualifications, if any, for such an appointment, and in fact Tomberlin had testified that she would not be able to care for Sharon in her home, but instead would have to leave her in an institution. Campbell's decision, which was not officially published, seemed to be based more on a political reaction to the history of the case than on the testimony presented at the hearing.

Campbell rejected the testimony of the medical experts and accepted the opinion of the adverse lay witnesses that Sharon was not able to express a reliable preference concerning her guardianship. He rejected the medical testimony that Sharon would do better on an outpatient basis and found that "constant, long-term medical supervision in a neutral setting, such as a nursing home . . . is the ideal for Sharon's long-term care." He also concluded that Thompson was "incapable of providing, as a single caretaker, the necessary health care to Sharon at Thompson's home in St. Cloud."

Finally, bowing to the history of contention between the Kowalskis and Thompsons, and Debra Kowalski's testimony that her parents would never visit Sharon if she was living in Thompson's home, Campbell concluded that the only way to preserve Sharon's family ties was to appoint a "neutral" guardian. Although he recognized that Karen and Sharon were a "family of affinity," he asserted that the situation was actually like a "family torn asunder into opposing camps" requiring neutral intervention. Finally, Campbell asserted that Thompson's activities in publicizing the case, fundraising, and even involving Sharon during some of her outings in lesbian and gay community appearances, were contrary to Sharon's best interest. Reaching back to the earliest period after the accident when Karen told the Kowalskis that she and Sharon were lesbian lovers, Campbell asserted that Karen had committed an "invasion of privacy" by "outing" Sharon to her family and to the world. This, in his view, showed that Karen was acting in her own interest rather than in the best interest of Sharon.

News of Campbell's decision sparked outrage in the lesbian and gay community nationwide, leading to petitions, fundraising rallies, and hundreds of newspaper editorials calling for a reversal on appeal. Karen approached the appeal with some trepidation, having lost two prior rounds before the Minnesota Court of Appeals in her continuing struggle. *Amicus* briefs were filed on her behalf by the American Civil Liberties Union, Lambda Legal Defense and Education Fund, and the National Organization for Women. Thomas F. Sjogren, a Duluth attorney, represented Tomberlin in arguing for affirmance of Campbell's decision. A unanimous panel of the court of appeals ruled on December 17, 1991, that Campbell's decision was totally unsupported by the trial record, and ordered that Karen Thompson be appointed sole guardian of Sharon.

Judge Jack Davies's opinion was a detailed, point-by-point refutation of each aspect of Campbell's decision, beginning with a total rejection of the concept of a "neutral" guardian. "There is no language in the statute specifically directing that a guardian be a neutral, detached party," asserted Davies.

To the contrary, when taken as a whole, the statute's enumerated factors direct that a guardian be someone who is preferred by the ward if possible, has a positive interaction with the ward, and has high involvement with, and commitment to, promoting the ward's welfare. This necessarily entails a guardian with demonstrated understanding and knowledge of the ward's physical and emotional needs.

Whereas Judge Campbell seemed to be seeking a guardian who would be a "mediator" between the Kowalskis and Thompson, the statute, according to Davies, favored appointment of a guardian who would be an advocate for Sharon, and the best advocate for Sharon in this situation was Karen, who had battled since 1983 to preserve her relationship with her life partner.

Turning to the issue of Sharon's preference, Davies quoted the written report from the medical evaluation team at Miller-Dwan Medical Center, the neutral facility appointed by Campbell in 1989 to evaluate Sharon's ability to express her preferences:

> We believe Sharon Kowalski has shown areas of potential and ability to make rational choices in many areas of her life and she has consistently indicated a desire to return home. And by that, she means to St. Cloud to live with Karen Thompson again. Whether this is possible is still uncertain as her care will be difficult and burdensome. We think she deserves the opportunity to try.

"All the professional witnesses concurred in this conclusion," said Davies, "including Sharon's current treating physician." There was no competent medical testimony to contradict the Miller-Dwan team's recommendation. The lay witnesses expressed skepticism about Sharon's ability to express her wishes reliably, pointing to her impaired short-term memory as a result of brain damage from the accident, but Davies dismissed their testimony as not carrying the weight of the unanimous view of the doctors who had testified. For Campbell to have rejected unanimous medical expert testimony was clearly erroneous, he asserted. Under the statute, a "ward with sufficient capacity may express a wish as to a guardian," and that choice "may only be denied by the court if found not

to be in the ward's best interests." In this case, Sharon's wishes should be considered.

As to Thompson's qualifications for appointment, Davies noted that all the medical professionals who had worked with Sharon in her most recent residences consistently testified that Karen achieved outstanding interaction with Sharon, was strongly equipped to attend to her social and emotional needs, and was exceptionally qualified to provide support for her continued rehabilitation. The doctors stated that their long-term goal for Sharon was to assist her in returning to life outside an institution, and that Thompson was "the only person willing or able to care for Sharon outside an institution." While Sharon's relatives and Karen Tomberlin were not equipped to provide noninstitutional housing and care, Karen Thompson had built a "fully handicap-accessible home near St. Cloud" in the hope that Sharon could come to live there. Noted Davies, "Tomberlin testified that she is not willing or able to care for Sharon at home and is in a position only to supervise Sharon's needs in an institution." Contrary to Campbell's conclusions, Sharon's doctors and therapists had testified that a highly motivated person such as Thompson could provide adequate care for Sharon on outings and in a home setting. Although Thompson would need some assistance for bathing, therapy and medical care, this could be provided by a home health care organization.

More importantly, the doctors testified that Karen Thompson appeared to be the person best able to motivate Sharon to participate in her rehabilitation, and that Karen's interaction with the medical staff had been cooperative and supportive. "The court-appointed social worker also testified that Thompson was attentive to Sharon's needs, and would be a forceful advocate for Sharon's rehabilitation," said Davies. In light of all this testimony, the court of appeals found that Campbell's conclusions about Sharon's need for further institutionalization and Thompson's incapacity as a guardian were "without evidentiary support and clearly erroneous" since they were contradicted by the testimony of "Sharon's doctors and other care providers." Davies asserted that the trial court "is not in a position to make independent medical determinations without support in the record," which Campbell had clearly done in this case.

Davies also specifically rejected Campbell's finding that it would be in the best interest of Sharon to appoint a "neutral" guardian, and that Tomberlin could provide such neutrality. First of all, Campbell had never considered any other arrangement to help maintain contact between Sharon and her parents while Sharon lived with Thompson. Why not consider using Tomberlin as an intermediary in such circumstances, as a "neutral driver" who could transport Sharon to her parents' home for visits? Davies pointed out that placement of Sharon with Karen Thompson would not bar the Kowalskis from visiting their daughter. "It is not the court's role to accommodate one side's threatened intransigence," he asserted, "where to do so would deprive the ward of an otherwise suitable and preferred guardian."

Furthermore, Tomberlin was hardly "neutral" in this matter, and there was inadequate evidence in the trial record to evaluate her qualifications to be a guardian for Sharon. The trial had focused solely on Thompson's petition for appointment, and thus on Thompson's qualifications. Tomberlin's contacts with Sharon under circumstances where her abilities to provide care and support could be evaluated by the medical staff had been minimal, and the expert witnesses were not even questioned during the hearing about Tomberlin's qualifications in that regard. Only Debra Kowalski and Kathy Schroeder were questioned about Tomberlin. And it appeared that Tomberlin was actually allied with the Kowalskis, not a neutral party.

> Tomberlin testified that all her information about Sharon's situation has come directly from the Kowalskis and that she talks with them weekly. Tomberlin lives near the Kowalskis and helped facilitate the appearance at the hearing of Schroeder and Debra Kowalski in opposition to Thompson. Both in her deposition and at the hearing, Tomberlin testified that her first and primary goal was to relocate Sharon to the Iron Range, close to her family. This testimony undermines the one "qualification" relied on by the trial court

in appointing Tomberlin—her role as an impartial mediator.

Finally, Davies addressed Campbell's attempts to picture Thompson as an opportunistic political activist who was more interested in herself and "gay rights" than in Sharon's welfare. Davies found that the record did not support Campbell's findings on this score, either. "Since the accident, Sharon's doctors and therapists testified that Sharon has voluntarily told them of her relationship with Thompson," so the issue of "outing" raised by Campbell was "no longer relevant." Furthermore, Sharon's doctor testified that it was actually in Sharon's best interest for the nature of her relationship with Thompson to be revealed, "because it is crucial for doctors to understand who their patient was prior to the accident, including that patient's sexuality," in order to accomplish effective rehabilitation. There was no evidence in the record to show any harm to Sharon from her attendance at public events with Karen. A medical staff person who accompanied Sharon to an event where she and Karen received an award from the National Organization for Women had testified that Sharon "had a great time" and "interacted well with other people." The only negative testimony about these events came from Schroeder and Debra Kowalski, who asserted their own beliefs that Sharon did not want to attend events of a gay or lesbian nature, but they had not been in attendance at such events to observe Sharon's reactions. Davies also rejected the implication that Karen Thompson's fundraising activities had been self-serving. He noted that the uncontradicted testimony was that all funds raised went to the litigation, and anything left over was being spent on special equipment for Sharon.

In their attempt to discredit Karen, the adverse witnesses had also raised the issue of Karen's social life since the accident. Separated from her lover for years, Karen had not remained totally isolated and celibate. Campbell had seized on this as further evidence that Karen was not totally devoted to Sharon. Karen had testified, however, that "anyone who is involved in her life understands that she and Sharon are 'a package deal,' and that nothing would interfere with her commitment to Sharon's well-being." Concluded Davies: "The other witnesses who testified about Thompson's interaction with Sharon over the past seven years could find no reason to question Thompson's commitment to Sharon's best interests." Finally, Davies noted that Tomberlin and Campbell had not complied with the formal requisites for appointment of a guardian, since Tomberlin had not formally petitioned for appointment and the statutory opportunity for comment on the appointment had not been afforded to the other petitioner, Thompson.

Davies concluded that the trial court "clearly abused its discretion in denying Thompson's petition and naming Tomberlin guardian instead." All the testimony in the case from medical experts supported Thompson's petition. "This choice is further supported by the fact that Thompson and Sharon are a family of affinity, which ought to be accorded respect," asserted Davies. In reversing the lower court's decision, said Davies, "it should be made clear that this court is also reversing specific restrictions on the guardian's decisionmaking power that might be read into the trial court order. She is free to make whatever decisions she and the doctors feel are necessary to achieve Sharon's best interests, including decisions regarding Sharon's location." At the same time, however, Davies directed Thompson to "con-tinue efforts at accommodating visitation between Sharon and the Kowalskis, without unreasonable restrictions."

Karen Tomberlin filed a motion seeking review of this decision by the Minnesota Supreme Court, but her motion was promptly denied on February 10, 1992, and Karen and Sharon's long legal struggle was at an end.

The *Guardianship of Kowalski* case marked an important development in the emerging movement for recognition of lesbian and gay families by the courts. Coming on the heels of the New York Court of Appeals' 1989 decision in *Braschi v. Stahl Associates Co.*, holding that a gay male couple could be considered a "family" for purposes of a residential rent regulation protecting succession rights, the *Kowalski* ruling showed a new willingness by appellate courts to abandon formalistic legal distinctions based on blood ties and marriage laws and to recognize the reality of modern family life, which can take many nontraditional forms. The case was also important in providing a dramatic illustration for lesbian and gay couples that they had to take legal steps if they wanted to preserve their families from this sort of drawn-out litigation in the event of an emergency.

Case Reference

Braschi v. Stahl Associates Co., 74 N.Y.2d 201, 544 N.Y.S.2d 784, 543 N.E.2d 49 (1989)

CHAPTER 5
DISCRIMINATION: THE CIVILIAN SECTOR

The issue of discrimination among persons on the basis of their sexuality is logically subdivided between the civilian and military sectors. Chapter 5 concerns both governmental and private-sector discrimination on the basis of sexuality and sexual orientation in civilian (i.e., nonmilitary or national security) occupations. Chapter 6 deals with military and national security issues.

In the public sector, most of the issues litigated in these cases concern the constitutionality of decisions by a governmental agency to refuse employment, services, or benefits to a particular individual because of that individual's sexuality. These cases normally arise under the Fourteenth Amendment, either through the Due Process or Equal Protection clauses. Some of the earliest victories for attorneys litigating on behalf of lesbian and gay clients came in establishing that governmental bodies may not engage in unreasoning or reflexive discrimination on the basis of sexual orientation. While, as the military cases discussed in the next chapter show, the equal protection rights of sexual minorities are not yet firmly established in constitutional precedent, there is a growing body of judicial decisions recognizing that differences in treatment, lacking a basis other than active dislike or fear, offend constitutional principles of due process and equal treatment.

The issues become more complex in the nongovernmental sector. In the absence of statutory protection, sexual minorities are subject to unequal treatment without legal redress by private actors, since constitutional rights do not normally bind private actors. Cases in this chapter discuss theories, mainly rejected by the courts, to apply existing federal antidiscrimination laws to the plight of sexual minorities. Although the federal government has not seen fit to protect lesbians, gay men, transvestites, or transsexuals against such discrimination, some states and municipalities have been moved by the abundant evidence of discrimination to pass local laws on the subject. By the end of 1992, such laws had taken effect in Wisconsin, Massachusetts, Hawaii, Connecticut, New Jersey, Vermont, and California. In addition, more than one hundred cities or counties had enacted similar protection. Cases in this chapter explore some of the difficulties of interpretation and application that such laws may present.

This chapter includes discussion of many leading cases on private- and public-sector discrimination on the basis of sexuality in a civilian (i.e., non-military, non-intelligence agencies) context. Cases discussed in other chapters relating to these issues include *Van Ooteghem v. Gray* (No. 42), *High Tech Gays v. Defense Industrial Security Clearance Office* (No. 97), and the cases concerning teachers and other public school employees (Nos. 99, 100, 102, 104, 105, 108, 109).

Discrimination—The Civilian Sector: Readings

Arriola, E.R., "Sexual Identity and the Constitution: Homosexual Persons as a Discrete and Insular Minority," 10 *Women's Rights Law Reporter* 143 (Winter 1988)

Capers, I.B., "Sexual Orientation and Title VII," 91 *Columbia Law Review* 1158 (June 1991)

Case, B., "Repealable Rights: Municipal Civil Rights Protection for Lesbians and Gays," 7 *Law & Inequality: A Journal of Theory and Practice* 441 (July 1989)

Cotton, D.D., "Title VII and Transsexualism," 80 *Northwestern University Law Review* 1037 (Winter 1986)

Douglas, J.A., "I Sit and Look Out: Employment Discrimination Against Homosexuals and the New Law of Unjust Dismissal," 33 *Washington University Journal of Urban and Contemporary Law* 73 (Summer 1988)

Green, R., "Spelling Relief for Transsexuals: Employment Discrimination and the Criteria of Sex," 4 *Yale Law & Policy Review* 125 (Fall-Winter 1985)

Halley, J.E., "The Politics of the Closet: Towards Equal Protection for Gay, Lesbian, and Bisexual Identity," 36 *University of California at Los Angeles Law Review* 915 (June 1989)

Heatherly, G.E., "Gay and Lesbian Rights: Employment Discrimination," 1985 *Annual Survey of American Law* 901 (October 1986)

Hoerrner, M.D., "Fire At Will: The CIA Director's Ability to Dismiss Homosexual Employees as National Security Risks," 31 *Boston College Law Review* 699 (May 1990)

Jones, M., "When Private Morality Becomes Public Concern: Homosexuality and Public Employment," 24 *Houston Law Review* 519 (May 1987)

Simon, H.A., & Daly, E., "Sexual Orientation and Workplace Rights: A Potential Land Mine for Employers?," 18 *Employee Relations Law Journal* 29 (Summer 1992)

Stinson, J.M., "Who's Been Sleeping In Your Bed? An Analysis of the Government's Approach to the Sexual Orientation of Its Employees," 30 *Arizona Law Review* 155 (Winter 1988)

Strasser, M., "Suspect Classes and Suspect Classifications: On Discrimination, Unwittingly or Otherwise," 64 *Temple Law Quarterly* 937 (Winter 1991)

Sunstein, C.R., "Sexual Orientation and the Constitution: A Note on the Relationship Between Due Process and Equal Protection," 55 *University of Chicago Law Review* 1161 (Fall 1988)

Taitz, J., "Judicial Determination of the Sexual Identity of Post-Operative Transsexuals: A New Form of Sex Discrimination," 13 *American Journal of Law & Medicine* 53 (Spring 1987)

71. BASIC PROTECTION FOR GAY FEDERAL EMPLOYEES

Norton v. Macy, 417 F.2d 1161 (D.C. Cir. 1969).

The Stonewall Riots, which occurred in New York during the last weekend of June 1969, are frequently said to mark the beginning of the modern gay rights movement. Such assertions, however, tend to overlook the important groundwork laid by an earlier generation of advocates for the equal civil rights of homosexuals. The early advocates began forming organizations for that purpose almost two decades earlier in cities where an active gay community had reached a certain critical mass, such as Los Angeles, San Francisco, New York, and Washington. Spurred by Frank Kameny, a federal civil servant who was discharged during the 1950s because of his homosexuality (and was denied judicial review of his claim of unconstitutional discrimination on procedural grounds), the Mattachine Society of Washington, D.C., became an insistent force for reform of the discriminatory practices of the U.S. Civil Service Commission, which consistently took the position that homosexuals were "unsuitable" for federal employment. Ironically, the opinion that marked Mattachine's most important appellate victory was rendered by a panel of the U.S. Court of Appeals for the District of Columbia Circuit just days after the outbreak of the Stonewall Riots. *Norton v. Macy* was one of the first cases in which the federal courts rejected the argument that the government could freely discriminate against gays in its employment practices.

Clifford Norton, a military veteran, was a budget analyst at the National Aeronautics and Space Administration (NASA) in Washington, D.C. He was also a homosexual, but extremely secretive. He was well-regarded at the agency, considered a "competent employee" by his superiors, doing "very good work," as one of them later testified. Apparently, nobody at the agency knew that he was gay until the off-duty incident that led to his discharge. Norton was driving around Lafayette Square on the evening of October 22, 1963, just in front of the White House, an area where gay men would "cruise" in the evening. He spotted somebody interesting and pulled over to the curb. The object of his attentions, one Madison Monroe Procter (appropriately named for two former presidents of the United States, given the location!), got into his car and they drove once around the Square, during which time Procter later claimed that Norton touched his knee and invited him to come to Norton's home "for a drink." Norton stopped his car, Procter got out and went to his own car, and the two men drove away from the Square toward Norton's home in a Southwest Washington apartment building. Police officers who had staked out the Square and noticed this activity followed in their cars. In the parking lot of Norton's building, the police questioned the two men and, after Procter told them about what happened while driving around the Square in Norton's car, the officers arrested both men and brought them in to the police station, where they interrogated them about what had happened that evening and about their prior sexual histories.

When the police learned that Norton worked at NASA, they telephoned NASA Security Chief Fuger and invited him to join the interrogation of Norton. Fuger arrived at 3 A.M., as the interrogation was continuing. Without letting Norton know who Fuger was, the police allowed Fuger to monitor an extended bit of interrogation conducted for his benefit. Throughout the interrogation, Norton insisted that he had not made any sexual pass at Procter. The police concluded the interrogation by giving Norton a traffic summons. Then Fuger identified himself to Norton and asked him to come directly to NASA to continue talking. At NASA, Fuger and a colleague continued to interrogate Norton in an office of the otherwise-deserted building until after 6 A.M. Tired and worried, Norton finally admitted that he had engaged in homosexual activity while in high school and college, that he occasionally experienced homosexual desires when drinking, and that at such times he occasionally had "blackouts" during which he engaged in homosexual activity, but that he could not recall the details of what happened during the blackouts. Norton said he experienced a blackout when he met Procter, and could only remember inviting him home for a drink.

On the basis of Norton's statements, and a later written statement obtained from Procter confirming that Norton had made a pass at him (Procter said it would "take an idiot" not to be able to figure out that Norton had made a sexual pass at him), NASA officials concluded that Norton should be discharged on two grounds: his conduct the evening of October 22 was, in NASA's words, "immoral, indecent, and disgraceful conduct" meriting discharge; his past sexual history indicated that he possessed "traits of character and personality which render him . . . unsuitable for further Government employment." Norton's superior, one Mr. Garbarini, apparently took this action reluc-

tantly. He later testified that he was "not worried" about any possible effect of this incident on Norton's job performance, and even asked the personnel department of the agency whether there was some way things could be worked out to keep Norton employed, since he did not feel Norton presented any security problems for the agency. Higher officials told Garbarini that discharge in such cases was a "custom within the agency," so Garbarini stated that Norton was discharged not due to any real concerns about security or Norton's ability to get along and work competently, but solely due to the possibility that his continued employment might "turn out to be embarrassing to the agency" if a similar incident in the future became a "public scandal."

Norton protested the discharge decision, insisting that he was not homosexual, had not made any pass at Procter, and that he had not knowingly engaged in any homosexual activity in his life. Both a Civil Service appeals examiner and the Board of Appeals and Review concluded that Norton's protests were unsupported by the evidence, which they held justified the Agency's decision that Norton must be discharged to further the "efficiency of the service," the applicable standard for federal civil servants who were "veterans preference eligible" under then-pertinent federal statutes.

Norton obtained legal counsel from Glenn R. Graves and John W. Karr, of Washington, and the moral support of the Mattachine Society, which wrote on his behalf to John W. Macy, Jr., chairman of the Civil Service Commission, protesting what had happened to Norton. Macy sent Mattachine a written reply on February 25, 1966, asserting that the agency was merely enforcing "the prevailing mores of our society," as it felt required to do under federal law.

Norton filed suit against Macy, seeking a determination that his discharge was unlawful, in the federal district court, where his case was assigned to Judge John J. Sirica, later to become world-famous as the presiding judge at the Watergate trials. In addition to attacking the substantive discharge decisions, Norton asserted that the evidence used by the Agency was tainted by an illegal arrest, illegal detention for interrogation, and the sort of "third degree inquisition" that had long been held illegal in criminal cases. Sirica granted a motion to dismiss by the government in an unpublished order, and Norton appealed to the D.C. Circuit, which held oral argument on January 13, 1969. Graves represented Norton, and a recent addition to the U.S. Department of Justice staff, James G. Greilsheimer, appeared for the government, which assumed this would be an easy case because the circuit had previously upheld the discharge of a homosexual air traffic controller in *Dew v. Halaby* (1963), and the U.S. Court of Appeals for the Fifth Circuit had also very recently sustained the discharge of a gay federal civil servant, holding that the Commission had wide discretion to decide such a person was unsuitable for federal employment, in *Anonymous v. Macy* (1968).

Norton was lucky to draw a three-judge panel that included the two leading liberal lights of the court of appeals, Chief Judge David L. Bazelon and Circuit Judge J. Skelly Wright, who agreed, in an opinion by Bazelon, that the discharge could not stand. Circuit Judge Edward A. Tamm dissented from the July 1, 1969, ruling.

Reviewing the facts, Bazelon found that the evidence on the record was sufficient for the Commission to have rejected Norton's denial that he made a homosexual advance to Procter. The question presented, said Bazelon, was whether an employee who had made an off-duty homosexual advance, and whose past history indicated the "personality traits" revealed by the interrogation, was properly discharged under the applicable statutory standard. Under 5 U.S.C. section 7512(a), one with veterans' preference could be dismissed only for "such cause as will promote the efficiency of the service." Furthermore, the U.S. constitution itself placed some limits on the government's personnel decisions, which had to accord with the requirements of due process of law. "The Government's obligation to accord due process sets at least minimal substantive limits on its prerogative to dismiss its employees," said Bazelon: "it forbids all dismissals which are arbitrary and capricious." Furthermore, a dismissal under these circumstances should receive greater constitutional scrutiny than the norm, not only because Norton was a veteran but, more importantly, because this kind of discharge

would attach a particular stigma on him, since it would "disqualify the victim from any other Federal employment, damaging his prospects for private employ, and fixing upon him the stigma of an official defamation of character." Bazelon was very careful in his choice of words here, not saying that branding Norton a homosexual was defamatory, but clearly implying that branding him as "unsuitable" for federal employment was.

Bazelon also noted in passing that such decisions as *Griswold v. Connecticut* (1965) and *Stanley v. Georgia* (1969), then very recent, had created an "ill-defined area of privacy which is increasingly if indistinctly recognized as a foundation of several specific constitutional protections." Without carrying this point further, he intimated that the privacy concept might apply to disciplinary action against federal civil servants for off-duty private sexual conduct.

Given these constitutional and statutory considerations, said Bazelon, there was a burden on the employer agency to show some "rational basis" for concluding that the discharge of a civil servant such as Norton would "promote the efficiency of the service." Stated otherwise, the Civil Service Commission had to act "reasonably" under all the circumstances presented by the case. In this connection, Bazelon rejected as unreasonable that labeling Norton's conduct on October 22, 1963, as "immoral" ended the need for further analysis. Bazelon stated:

> A pronouncement of "immorality" tends to discourage careful analysis because it unavoidably connotes a violation of divine, Olympian, or otherwise universal standards of rectitude. However, the Civil Service Commission has neither the expertise nor the requisite anointment to make or enforce absolute moral judgments, and we do not understand that it purports to do so. Its jurisdiction is at least confined to the things which are Caesar's, and its avowed standard of "immorality" is no more than "the prevailing mores of our society."

If the Civil Service Commission was to find unsuitable any person it deemed to have engaged in "immoral" activity, Bazelon suspected that the ranks of federal civil servants would be seriously reduced. "Indeed," he commented, "it may be doubted whether there are in the entire

Civil Service many persons so saintly as never to have done any act which is disapproved by the 'prevailing mores of our society.'" Disqualifying anybody who ever engaged in homosexual conduct, for example, might disqualify more than a third of all adult males, according to the 1948 Kinsey study, which Bazelon cited as "the most widely accepted study of American sexual practices."

While the court was not ready to say that the Commission could not label Norton's conduct on October 22 as "immoral," "indecent," or "notoriously disgraceful," tracking the language of statutes and regulations, to discharge an employee solely on the basis of such labels raised serious constitutional issues. Bazelon asserted that "the notion that it could be an appropriate function of the federal bureaucracy to enforce the majority's conventional codes of conduct in the private lives of its employees is at war with elementary concepts of liberty, privacy, and diversity." Only off-duty conduct that would have "some ascertainable deleterious effect on the efficiency of the service" could properly serve as the basis for a discharge. In *Dew v. Halaby*, the circuit court had upheld a discharge of a homosexual employee, but the circumstances were different. There, a relatively new and untried federal employee in a sensitive position calling for excellent judgment and reliability—air traffic controller—had admitted past marijuana use as well as having engaged in gay sex for pay in the past. Moreover, Bazelon pointed out, there was a strong dissent in that case, the U.S. Supreme Court granted *certiorari*, and the case was settled and withdrawn from Supreme Court consideration by offering the appellant reinstatement with back pay, indicating that even in such a strong case for discharge the agency had finally come to the conclusion that discharge was not warranted.

Bazelon conceded that homosexual conduct might provide an appropriate basis for discharge in some circumstances, repeating the folk wisdom about the vulnerability of gays to blackmail and "unstable personality" characterizations based on the type of activity. He also noted that a homosexual employee who made passes at other employees at work would provide an obvious example of someone meriting discharge due to the deleterious effect of such conduct.

But none of these cases seemed relevant to Norton, since his own supervisor had testified that he did not have any real concern about security or inability to work effectively in Norton's case.

The only concern really asserted by the Commission here was the potential for future embarrassment. Said Bazelon:

> The assertion of such a nebulous "cause" poses perplexing problems for a review proceeding which must accord broad discretion to the Commission. We do not doubt that NASA blushes whenever one of its own is caught *in flagrante delicto*; but if the possibility of such transitory institutional discomfiture must be uncritically accepted as a cause for discharge which will "promote the efficiency of the service," we might as well abandon all pretense that the statute provides any substantive security for its supposed beneficiaries.

A charge of potential embarrassment, said Bazelon, might well be a "smokescreen" covering "personal antipathies or moral judgments" which should not be the basis for a discharge decision under the Veterans Preference Act. In this case, neither NASA nor the Civil Service Commission could show any "specific connection" between Norton's off-duty conduct and the efficiency of NASA. Norton was apparently a very quiet, discrete man who could not be accused of flaunting or "carelessly" displaying "his unorthodox sexual conduct in public," so the potential for future embarrassment was really minimal. "We think the unparticularized and unsubstantiated conclusion that such possible embarrassment threatens the quality of the agency's performance is an arbitrary ground for dismissal," said Bazelon. While it was true that the circuit court had in the past upheld dismissals where the financial peccadillos of federal employees were the basis on grounds that included "embarrassment" to the agency, Bazelon asserted that in those cases a real connection had been made between the employees' financial difficulties and the efficiency of their agencies. No such showing had been made here.

Finally, Bazelon sought to clarify the limits of the court's holding. "Lest there be any doubt," he said, "we emphasize that we do not hold that homosexual conduct may never be cause for dismissal of a protected federal employee." Even potential embarrassment from an employee's off-duty conduct was not totally ruled out as a basis for discharge, depending on the circumstances of the individual case. "What we do say is that, if the statute is to have any force, an agency cannot support a dismissal as promoting the efficiency of the service merely by turning its head and crying 'shame.'"

Judge Tamm was outraged at the majority's intrusion on agency discretion in this case, feeling as he did that the Commission's decision was fully supported by the record. "Sensitive to phantom defects in administrative action but insensitive to reality," he charged, "they turn *their* heads and cry 'shame' at the same time avoiding the calling of the chorus of cases outlining the proper scope of judicial review of agency determinations." Tamm insisted that federal agencies were given wide discretion to make personnel decisions, essentially free from substantive review. Tamm could not agree with the setting of a precedent that "off-duty homosexual conduct, coupled with a capacity for "blackingout" while intoxicated, bears no real relationship to the functioning of an efficient service within a government agency."

> Homosexuals, sadly enough, do not leave their emotions at Lafayette Square and regardless of their spiritual destinies they still present targets for public reproach and private extortion. I believe this record supports the finding that this individual presents more than a potential risk in this regard and that his termination will serve the efficiency of the service. Despite the billows of puffery that continue to float out of recent opinions on this subject, I believe that the theory that homosexual conduct is not in any way related to the efficiency and effectiveness of governmental business is not an evil theory—just a very unrealistic one.

Tamm's arguments failed to persuade his colleagues, either on the panel or the full circuit, since the government's subsequent petition for rehearing was denied on October 20, 1969, just two days before the sixth anniversary of Norton's late night encounter with the Washington vice squad. The government did not attempt further appeal.

Norton v. Macy marked a historic breakthrough in the law governing the rights of lesbians and gay men. For the first time, a federal appellate panel had held, in effect, that prejudicial labels, such as "immoral" or "disgusting," were not sufficient to terminate the federal employment of lesbians and gay men. At the very least, an agency would have to show that the employee's behavior (not mere "personality traits" or "homosexual conduct" as such) significantly affected the ability of that agency to continue to carry out its functions efficiently and credibly. While it would turn out that this standard was not particularly high, and seemed to protect only the most secretive and conformity-minded gays in federal service, it was a start. The principles established in *Norton v. Macy* were haltingly developed in other cases, until the Civil Service Commission finally was compelled to revise its policies and affirmatively state that homosexuality and private homosexual conduct were not, as such, disqualifiers for federal employment. This conclusion was virtually compelled by the Civil Service Reform Act of 1978, which established a statutory requirement that employees in the protected civil service not be disciplined or terminated except for legitimate, work-related cause.

Case References

Anonymous v. Macy, 398 F.2d 317 (5th Cir. 1968), certiorari denied, 393 U.S. 1041 (1969)

Dew v. Halaby, 317 F.2d 582 (D.C. Cir. 1963), certiorari granted, 376 U.S. 904, certiorari dismissed by agreement of the parties, 379 U.S. 951 (1964)

Griswold v. Connecticut, 381 U.S. 479 (1965)

Kameny v. Brucker, 282 F.2d 823 (D.C. Cir. 1960), certiorari denied, 365 U.S. 843 (1961)

Stanley v. Georgia, 394 U.S. 557 (1969)

72. A HOMOSEXUAL'S FITNESS TO PRACTICE LAW

In re Kimball, 33 N.Y.2d 586, 347 N.Y.S.2d 453 (1973), reversing 40 App. Div. 2d 252, 339 N.Y.S. 2d 302 (2d Dept. 1973). See also *State ex rel. Florida Bar v. Kimball*, 96 So. 2d 825 (1957).

Harris L. Kimball was admitted to the Florida Bar in 1953 and established himself in law practice. In 1955, police officers accused him of engaging in oral sex with another man on the beach at Orlando in violation of a city ordinance concerning sodomy. They arrested Kimball, and he was released on bond. Kimball forfeited the bond, which, he claimed, was equivalent under local law to a plea of *nolo contendere*.

The Florida Bar conducted a hearing, at which the police officers, the other participant in the beach incident, Kimball, and his witnesses all testified. The Florida Bar satisfied itself that there was cause to initiate a formal disbarment proceeding, in which Kimball represented himself before a referee. There were several sessions before the referee, at which Kimball presented different explanations of what happened. At the first, he testified that the two men had only been swimming; at the second, that the other had made unwelcome advances to Kimball, which Kimball had rejected; at the third, he asserted that the other participant had forced him into a position which led the police officers incorrectly to believe he was engaging in sexual activity. Kimball denied throughout the proceedings having actually engaged in conduct forbidden by the law. The other participant also presented inconsistent accounts of the incident at the two hearings at which he appeared, but essentially charged that Kimball had been the instigator of their activities. The referee found that Kimball "had committed an act contrary to good morals and the law of this state" and recommended disbarment. The Florida Bar Board of Governors concurred with the referee's report and referred the matter to the Florida Supreme Court. At this point, Kimball did not bother to argue the matter further, and the supreme court adopted the report and ordered that Kimball be disbarred.

Kimball eventually left Florida and pursued other lines of work. Over the next few years, the issue of homosexuality received considerable public debate, as states began to repeal or modify their sodomy laws in response either to the general wave of penal law reform stimulated by the American Law Institute's recommended Model Penal Code or to the sexual revolution that began in the late 1960s, including the newly visible gay liberation movement that erupted in some major cities after the June 1969 Stonewall Riots in New York. Kimball, who had by the 1970s moved to New York and become caught up in the new struggles for gay liberation, decided to apply for admission to the New York Bar in 1972, taking and passing the bar examination and receiving a favorable report from the Committee on Character and Fitness of the Appellate Division, Second Department, "notwithstanding the admission of the applicant to being a homosexual and having engaged in homosexual acts."

At the time Kimball applied for admission to the bar, the New York courts had presumably not knowingly admitted any practicing homosexuals to the practice of law. As part of its Model Penal Code reform, New York had reformed its old felony sodomy law so as to impose a misdemeanor penalty for anal or oral sex between unmarried persons. In Florida, too, sodomy had recently been downgraded from a felony to a misdemeanor offense by the state supreme court's decision in *Franklin v. State* (1971). Thus, the crime of which Kimball was accused in Florida was no longer a felony either in Florida or in New York. This was significant because New York law required automatic disbarment for commission of a felony, but the courts had greater discretion to determine whether an applicant who had committed a misdemeanor was fit to practice law. Kimball urged the character committee to take note of these developments and to recommend his admission.

The Character Committee felt stymied, however, by an old New York Court of Appeals decision, *In re Peters* (1927), which the Committee felt precluded a positive recommendation until Kimball could get himself readmitted to the Florida bar. The Committee issued its report without making a recommendation and referred Kimball's application to the justices of the Appellate Division in the Second Department. A five-judge panel voted three to two to deny the application, in a *per curiam* opinion issued January 3, 1973, in which Justices James D. Hopkins, Fred J. Munder, and Henry J. Latham joined. Justices M. Henry Martuscello and J. Irwin Shapiro dissented.

All five judges agreed that the Character Committee had misconstrued the *Peters* precedent, since that case had concerned peculiar facts and the court of appeals was merely responding to a certified question that did not bear directly on Kimball's situation. Although the Florida disbarment and the incidents that led up to it were facts to be considered, it was up to the New York court to satisfy itself independently as to Kimball's fitness to practice law. From there, however, the majority and dissenters diverged sharply.

The majority rejected Kimball's argument that the Florida Supreme Court's then-recent decision finding the sodomy law of that state unconstitutionally vague (and thus leaving in place only a misdemeanor law involving "unnatural and lascivious acts") made the Florida disbarment now irrelevant to his New York bar application. Assuming Kimball engaged in the conduct alleged in the criminal prosecution, it would still be a crime in Florida, albeit a misdemeanor, and thus relevant. Furthermore, the court observed, sodomy was a felony in New York at the time of Kimball's Florida disbarment, so had Kimball committed the offense in New York at that time, he would have been subject to automatic disbarment, and later changes in the law did not detract from the validity of the original disbarment proceeding. Lectured the majority, "Moreover, we cannot overlook as trifling the conduct of the applicant in attempting to mislead the authorities in Florida by giving false testimony in the disbarment proceeding."

Kimball next argued that the Florida prosecution had been a set up. He alleged that he had been entrapped by an Air Force sergeant because he was representing a client who had been assaulted by an Air Force enlistee. The majority held these allegations to be irrelevant because Kimball had neither raised them before the Character Committee nor before the Florida Bar authorities at the time of his disbarment.

Finally, although Kimball did not explicitly make this argument, the majority found implicit in his application for admission the contention that social change in the intervening years justified overlooking his Florida bar history and evaluating him afresh. The majority rejected this approach, and gratuitously remarked that so long as sodomy remained a crime in New York (albeit a misdemeanor), "homosexuality, which, in its fulfillment, usually entails commission of such a statutorily proscribed act, is a factor which could militate against the eligibility of an applicant for admission to the Bar who proposes to pursue this way of life in disregard of the statute." But, said the majority, there was no need to pronounce definitively on this contention, since Kimball's behavior in connection with the Florida disbarment provided sufficient grounds to deny his application. The majority also expressly refrained from dealing with the question whether the New York sodomy law might itself be unconstitutional.

Justices Martuscello and Shapiro penned a spirited dissenting opinion, which would ultimately be adopted by the court of appeals. Observing that the Character Committee had unanimously found that Kimball had "the character and fitness required for admission to the Bar, even though he was and is a homosexual; and, so finding, it said it did not consider his homosexuality indicative of unfitness to practice law," the dissenters could not agree with the majority that the old Florida disbarment should stand in Kimball's way. For the dissenters, the implicit contention of Kimball's application that social changes concerning homosexuality should be considered by the court were the central issue:

To us it seems clear that the social and moral climate in New York (and probably throughout the Western World) has in recent years changed dramatically with respect to homosexuality and consensual homosexual acts. . . . In our opinion, an applicant for admission to the Bar in New York in 1972 cannot be considered unfit or lacking the requisite character to practice law, merely because he is an avowed homosexual; and we agree with the Character Committee's finding that this applicant is fit for admission to the Bar.

Thus, the dissenters accepted Kimball's argument, and would have held that the past Florida conviction was not a bar to Kimball's present admission to practice law.

Taking apart the majority's reasoning piece by piece, the dissenters began with the contention that because sodomy was a felony in New York in 1955, Kimball would have been subject to an automatic disbarment in New York whose validity was not affected by subsequent law reform developments. For one thing, Kimball's effective *nolo* plea in Florida should not be considered binding in any other proceeding, said the dissenters, because *nolo* pleas are generally treated as not binding on the merits in any other proceeding as against the defendant. More significantly, however, the dissenters insisted that the issue for the New York courts in 1972 was Kimball's present fitness to practice, not his fitness almost two decades before, and they believed him to be fit in 1972 "even though he is a conceded homosexual."

As their parting shot, the dissenters observed that New York's consensual sodomy misdemeanor statute "may well be unconstitutional, as unreasonably discriminatory, because it makes it a crime when committed by unmarried persons but not when committed by married persons." (This observation by the dissenters was the likely cause for the majority's statement that it would not consider the constitutionality of New York's sodomy law in this case.)

The dissenters also rejected the majority's characterization of Kimball's behavior in connection with the Florida disbarment proceedings as a basis for denying his admission in 1972. Although there were discrepancies in Kimball's testimony at the various hearings, the dissenters felt that the New York courts were not bound to accept the findings of guilt in those

proceedings, and, furthermore, "when we consider the applicant's youth at the time of the disbarment proceeding, the nature of the charge against him, the social and moral climate then prevailing with respect to such acts, the predicament he was in, and what must have been his then distraught emotional and mental state, we cannot view his attempts to exculpate himself as establishing a basic lack of good character." Kimball's exemplary conduct for the fifteen years since his disbarment should be taken into account in determining whether he was presently fit to practice law in New York.

Kimball's attorney, Jeremiah S. Gutman, presented his arguments for reversal to the court of appeals, with *amicus* assistance from E. Carrington Boggan, a young gay rights attorney representing the Gay Activists Alliance. Gay attorneys in New York were particularly alarmed by the *dicta* in the appellate division's decision, which might imply that practicing homosexuals could be considered unfit to practice law in New York, an attitude that underlay the almost contemporaneous refusal by the Appellate Division in the First Department to approve the certificate of incorporation of the Lambda Legal Defense and Education Fund, a public interest law firm organized to advance gay rights. Daniel M. Cohen and Samuel A. Hirshowitz argued on behalf of the state's Law Department in opposition to the appeal.

The court of appeals reversed the appellate division in a brief *per curiam* opinion issued July 3, 1973. According to the court, while Kimball's conduct "may be now and has been in the past violative of accepted norms, they are not controlling, albeit relevant, in assessing character bearing on the right to practice law in this State. Notably, the Committee on Character and Fitness found appellant to be of good character and qualified at this time." Concerning the effect of the Florida disbarment, the court stated its acceptance of the dissenting opinion in the appellate division and sent the case back to the appellate division for reconsideration.

Judge Domenick L. Gabrielli wrote a lengthy dissent. After arguing that the Florida disbarment provided an adequate basis to deny Kimball's application, Gabrielli endorsed the most frightening aspect of the appellate division's decision, its *dicta* about the qualifications of homosexuals to practice law. Relating that attorney Gutman had stated at oral argument that "the applicant is and has been in violation of section 130.38 of the Penal Law, which he considers to be an unconstitutional provision," Gabrielli contended that this should in itself be sufficient to bar admission to law practice, so long as the law itself was not declared unconstitutional by the court. "It cannot be denied," insisted Gabrielli, "that the Appellate Division has full and complete authority to deny admission to the Bar, to one who is an avowed and admitted persistent violator of any criminal statute. No less authority surrounds the present case." But, of course, the court had implicitly denied that by its cryptic *per curiam* opinion, which began "There should be a reversal. . . ." And certainly this was the appellate division's construction of the court's opinion, since it admitted Kimball to practice without further difficulty.

The legal controversy of Kimball's New York Bar admission marked the first time that an openly gay attorney whose sexuality was a matter of record during the admission process was finally allowed to engage in law practice, despite the existence of a sodomy law. The court

of appeals' almost unanimous decision in the case presaged future significant New York victories, including the eventual approval of the corporate charter for Lambda Legal Defense and ultimately the declaration of unconstitutionality of New York's sodomy law and law against loitering for the purpose of soliciting deviate sexual intercourse, all of which followed within ten years of the *Kimball* decision. By its decision in *Kimball* (and its prior decisions striking down state regulations that in effect outlawed gay bars), the Court of Appeals of New York played a significant role in the gradual recognition that lesbian and gay people were entitled to full citizenship rights in a diverse society. The court's decision also paved the way for other states, including, ironically, Florida, whose supreme court, following the New York lead, ruled in *Florida Board of Bar Examiners re N.R.S.* (1981) that the private, consensual sexual conduct of bar applicants was not relevant to fitness to practice law.

Case References

Florida Board of Bar Examiners re N.R.S., 403 So. 2d 1315 (Fla. 1981)
Franklin v. State, 257 So. 2d 21 (Fla. 1971)
Peters, In Re, 250 N.Y. 595, 225 N.Y.S. 144 (1927)

73. GOVERNMENT "ABOUT-FACE" ON SEXUAL ORIENTATION DISCRIMINATION

Singer v. United States Civil Service Commission, 530 F.2d 247 (9th Cir. 1976), vacated and remanded, 429 U.S. 1034 (1977).

The McCarthy witch-hunts of the early 1950s resulted in official policies of employment discrimination against "sexual deviants" by agencies of the federal government. By the early 1970s, the government had abandoned the argument that homosexuals in the government presented a significant risk of subversion, but the exclusionary policies continued. They were to be officially abandoned only when the federal courts began to take seriously the notion that due process of law required that there be some rational basis for exclusion, and that mere

embarrassment by puritanical government supervisors over the off-duty sexual activities of their employees, or unsubstantiated fears that the public would lose confidence in a public service that employed gay people, did not provide such a basis. In *Singer v. United States Civil Service Commission*, a federal appeals court faced the tension between due process requirements and the embarrassment factor and gave greater weight to embarrassment.

If anyone were to present an embarrassment problem to a federal agency, it was John

F. Singer, who was not only the plaintiff in this case but also the plaintiff in *Singer v. Hara* (1974), a famous suit seeking a marriage license for Singer and his male lover. Singer was a loud, proud gay man at a time when such were unusual. In the true spirit of liberation, he was determined to be absolutely open about who and what he was, and let the chips fall where they may. Certainly, he thought, one place where he could be open and not encounter discrimination was the Equal Employment Opportunity Commission (EEOC), the nation's chief enforcement agency against employment discrimination. John Singer was wrong.

Singer had previously lived and worked in San Francisco, the gay mecca where liberation efforts had begun well before New York's famous Stonewall Riots of 1969. Even in that city, Singer had stood out for his uninhibited insistence on equal treatment for homosexuals, kissing other men in public and generally proclaiming his sexuality at work and in the street. He moved to Seattle and took a clerical job at the EEOC on August 2, 1971, on a one-year probationary term. Of course, Singer let his boss know from day one that he was gay. And Singer did not wait long to stir things up, applying for a marriage license with his boyfriend at the King County Auditor's Office on September 20, 1971, with full press attention for his efforts. The newspaper accounts the next day identified Singer as an employee of the EEOC. Singer also quickly became involved with local gay community organizations in Seattle, serving on the board of directors of the Seattle Gay Alliance and working on public programs dealing with gay issues. In most of these contexts, Singer identified himself as an EEOC employee.

Gay liberation was not advanced enough in Seattle, at the EEOC, or at the U.S. Civil Service Commission for Singer's activities to go on unpunished for very long. On May 12, 1972, a Civil Service investigator sent Singer a letter, inviting him to an interview "to comment upon, explain or rebut adverse information which has come to the attention of the Commission." Singer attended the May 19 interview with an attorney, Christopher E. Young. At that meeting, a Civil Service official advised Singer that the Commission had determined

that "you are homosexual. You openly profess that you are homosexual and you have received wide-spread publicity in this respect in at least two states." The official cited a bill of particulars that began with Singer's openness about his sexuality while living in San Francisco, and included clippings from various newspapers in which Singer had been interviewed or quoted, appearances on radio programs, gay rights stickers on his car windows, and his use of his EEOC affiliation "for identification purposes" in a host of gay rights settings. Singer refused to comment on these matters.

On May 22, Singer's attorney wrote to the Civil Service Commission, asking to know which Civil Service regulations authorized this investigation of Singer or provided any basis for deeming him unsuitable for employment. The Commission responded the next day, citing a regulation that characterized as disqualifying factors for federal employment: "Criminal, infamous, dishonest, immoral, or notoriously disgraceful conduct." At that time, the Federal Personnel Manual Supplement published by the Commission provided that "[p]ersons about whom there is evidence that they have engaged in or solicited others to engage in homosexual or sexually perverted acts with them, without evidence of rehabilitation, are not suitable for Federal employment."

Singer and his lawyer passed up an opportunity to appear before the Commission for further conversation on May 24, instead submitting an affidavit from Singer on May 26. It stated that Singer had read the investigative report, that his identification as an EEOC employee in newspaper accounts of the marriage license case had been made by the reporter without his "specific authorization," similarly that his identification with the EEOC in other gay rights contexts had not been done with his knowledge or consent, and that he saw nothing in the Civil Service report "which in any way indicates that my conduct has been in violation of regulations pertaining to federal employees."

These responses did not satisfy the Civil Service Commission, which instructed the EEOC on June 26 to discharge Singer. In a letter to Singer, the Commission set forth its reasons at length. It first indicated that the investigation had revealed that Singer had "flaunted and broadcast [his] homosexual activities and [had] sought and obtained publicity in various media" and that his activities "are those of an advocate for a socially repugnant concept." The Commission then asserted that Singer's continued employment "will not promote the efficiency of the service" because of

> the possible revulsion of other employees to homosexual conduct and/or their apprehension of homosexual advances and solicitations, the hazard that the prestige and authority of a Government position will be used to foster homosexual activity, particularly among youth; the possible use of Government funds and authority in furtherance of conduct offensive to the mores and law of our society; and the possible embarrassment to, and loss of public confidence in, your agency and the Federal civil service.

Singer appealed this decision, but a Civil Service hearing examiner upheld the decision in a September 14 opinion rendered after considering briefs from Singer's attorney and the Commission's staff. The examiner's unpublished decision (later quoted extensively in the court of appeals' opinion) noted that while Singer's supervisor and co-workers at the EEOC had made no complaint about his activities or behavior in the office (and, indeed, had praised his work in evaluation reports and letters), "there is more to the 'efficiency of the service' than the proper performance of assigned duties."

> The immoral and notoriously disgraceful conduct which is established by the evidence in your case, in our view, does have a direct and material bearing upon your fitness for Federal employment. Activities of the type you have engaged in, which has not been limited to activity conducted in private, are such that general public knowledge thereof would reflect discredit upon the Federal government as your employer, impeding the efficiency of the service by lessening general public confidence in the fitness of the government to conduct the public business with which it is entrusted. The federal government, like any employer, may be judged by the character and conduct of the persons in its employ, and it will promote the efficiency of the service to remove from its employ any individual whose detrimental influence will detract from that efficiency.

What is particularly notable about this recitation is that none of the public activity in the record compiled against Singer by the Commission related to unlawful public sexual conduct. Virtually all of the activity related to public education and debate about homosexuality, or casual public displays of affection that were no different in type from what heterosexual couples casually did on a daily basis. The Civil Service Commission was not hounding Singer out of the federal service for having sex in public; rather, it was pursuing him for being an openly gay political activist.

Singer decided to appeal the decision further, taking his case to the Commission's central Board of Appeals and Review in Washington, D.C., which issued its decision and order on December 1, 1972, affirming the regional office's decision against him. The Board stated that the evidence in the case "indicated that appellant's actions establish that he has engaged in immoral and notoriously disgraceful conduct, openly and publicly flaunting his homosexual way of life and indicating further continuance of such activities." This required his discharge, because it would "reflect discredit" on the government and impede the efficiency of the service by "lessening general public confidence in the fitness of the Government to conduct the public business with which it is entrusted."

Having exhausted his administrative appeals, Singer filed a class action suit, on behalf of himself and others similarly situated, in the U.S. District Court for the Western District of Washington on December 29, 1972. Assistant U.S. Attorney Charles Mansfield, of Seattle, moved the court to dismiss Singer's complaint, arguing that the record before the Civil Service Commission showed that Singer had received full due process rights and that the evidence supported the Commission's conclusions. Chief Judge Walter T. McGovern agreed and granted summary judgment to the government on March 29, 1974.

Singer appealed to the U.S. Court of Appeals for the Ninth Circuit, where his appellate attorney, Lawrence F. Baker, of Seattle, argued that his dismissal violated the Fifth Amendment's requirement of due process because there was no "rational nexus" between Singer's gay rights activities and public conduct and the efficiency of the service, and also the First Amendment's protection of free expression and the right to petition the government for redress of grievances. Most of the activities cited by the Civil Service Commission as justification for discharge involved comments by Singer on issues of public debate, or his active participation in such debate. Government attorney Mansfield argued that the record fully supported the Commission's conclusion as to "possible embarrassment to, and loss of public confidence in the agency and the Federal Civil Service," emphasizing Singer's probationary status and the court's limited scope of review for federal personnel actions.

Singer's was not the only case being litigated against the federal government questioning its employment policies with respect to homosexuals. While Singer's case was pending, the Civil Service Commission was responding to an opinion from the U.S. District Court for the Northern District of California in *Society for Individual Rights v. Hampton* (1973) by significantly revising its policy. In that case, the court had ruled that the Commission could order the discharge of a federal employee only if it could show that his or her conduct had actually impaired the efficiency of the civil service; mere speculation about potential embarrassment or unhappiness by co-workers was not sufficient to meet the requirements of due process of law. The *Hampton* court recognized that there might be circumstances where the conduct of a particular homosexual employee would justify discharge, but the Commission would have to compile a record sufficient to show that "more is involved than the Commission's unparticularized and unsubstantiated conclusion that possible embarrassment about an employee's homosexual conduct threatens the quality of the government's performance."

Reacting to *Hampton*, the Commission issued a bulletin on December 21, 1973, announcing a proposal to adopt new regulations, which became final on July 2, 1975, changing the Commission's policy on employment of homosexuals in the public service. The pertinent change in the regulations was the removal of the word "immoral" from the factors to be considered in suitability determinations. The De-

cember 1973 bulletin, after reviewing the *Hampton* opinion, instructed Civil Service investigators and decisionmakers as follows:

> Accordingly, you may not find a person unsuitable for Federal employment merely because that person is a homosexual or has engaged in homosexual acts, nor may such exclusion be based on a conclusion that a homosexual person might bring the public service into public contempt. You are, however, permitted to dismiss a person or find him or her unsuitable for Federal employment where the evidence establishes that such person's homosexual conduct affects job fitness— excluding from such consideration, however, unsubstantiated conclusions concerning possible embarrassment to the Federal service.

These instructions were amplified when the Commission published new "guidelines" for making suitability determinations to accompany its new regulations. The amended guidelines for determining "infamous or notoriously disgraceful conduct," which remained as a suitability factor, now said in part:

> Individual sexual conduct will be considered under the guides discussed above. Court decisions require that persons not be disqualified from Federal employment solely on the basis of homosexual conduct. The Commission and agencies have been enjoined not to find a person unsuitable for Federal employment solely because that person is homosexual or has engaged in homosexual acts. Based upon these court decisions and outstanding injunction, while a person may not be found unsuitable based on unsubstantiated conclusions concerning possible embarrassment to the Federal service, a person may be dismissed or found unsuitable for Federal employment where the evidence establishes that such person's sexual conduct affects job fitness.

What did this all mean? These regulations and guidelines had been published by the time attorneys Baker and Mansfield appeared to argue before the Ninth Circuit panel for Singer's case, which consisted of Circuit Judges Richard H. Chambers and Anthony M. Kennedy (later to be elevated to the U.S. Supreme Court by President Ronald Reagan) and Senior District Judge William J. Jameson, of Montana. Would the new policies be applied to Singer's case, and would they make a difference if so applied? Or would the court decide that Singer's 1972 discharge was not affected by these 1973 regulations? The answer was not long in coming. On January 12, 1976, in an opinion by Jameson, the court upheld the discharge, asserting that the new regulation and guidelines had no application to Singer's case and stating that the court's decision to treat the new rules as inapplicable did not "imply that the amended regulations and guidelines would require a different result under the facts of this case." To the court, Singer's activities provided ample justification for discharge, apparently even under the new guidelines, which it was assertedly not applying.

After noting the rather limited scope of judicial review of agency personnel decisions and the essential irrelevance of Singer's probationary status to the issue whether his discharge violated protected substantive constitutional rights, especially First Amendment rights, Jameson reviewed the existing federal decisions on employment rights of homosexual employees. The leading case was *Norton v. Macy*, in which a divided panel of the U.S. Court of Appeals for the District of Columbia Circuit had ruled in 1969 that a federal agency could not dismiss an employee for homosexual conduct without showing "some reasonably foreseeable, specific connection between an employee's potentially embarrassing conduct and the efficiency of the service." Norton had been caught in a police entrapment action targeted at suspected homosexuals, which the circuit court described in its opinion as "of at least questionable legality." Apart from his arrest, his homosexual activities had been totally private. Norton was, apparently, the model of a "closeted" federal employee, secretive about his homosexuality, concealing it to the extent possible from his supervisors and co-workers and members of the public. Under those circumstances, the D.C. Circuit had found the Commission's decision to discharge Norton untenable. The *Norton* decision had been hailed by the newly emerging gay rights movement as a major breakthrough: a federal appeals court had implicitly rejected the Civil Service Commission's rule that any evidence that an individual engaged in homosexual conduct, even in private, marked the individual as "unsuitable."

Subsequent decisions, however, had given *Norton* a rather narrow reading, emphasizing, as had the *Norton* court, that the public exposure of Norton's homosexuality had occurred under questionable circumstances and was an isolated instance. *Norton* could be interpreted, and was by many courts, as providing protection only for the most secretive and "closeted" homosexuals. This was reflected in the district court's opinion in *Hampton*, when the court commented that it was "unsubstantiated" conclusions about agency embarrassment that could not be the basis for a discharge decision. If the Commission could demonstrate that the employee did not fit the *Norton* stereotype of the "good gay," the existing cases would not appear to provide protection for that person.

Jameson concluded that Singer did not fit the *Norton* mold. "We conclude from a review of the record in its entirety," he said, "that appellant's employment was not terminated because of his status as a homosexual or because of private acts of sexual preference. . . . [The] discharge was the result of appellant's 'openly and publicly flaunting his homosexual way of life and indicating further continuance of such activities,' while identifying himself as a member of a federal agency." This distinguished Singer's case from Norton's. Said Jameson, "*Norton v. Macy* recognized that notorious conduct and open flaunting and careless display of unorthodox sexual conduct in public might be relevant to the efficiency of the service." This provided the necessary "rational connection" between Singer's conduct and the "efficiency of the service" to meet the tests of prior cases.

Turning to Singer's First Amendment arguments, Jameson had to deal with two recent appellate precedents from other circuits holding that advocacy of gay rights was protected activity under the First Amendment. In *Gay Students Organization of University of New Hampshire v. Bonner* (1974), the First Circuit had rejected efforts by public university officials to end certain gay student association activities on campus. The officials had been reacting to public embarrassment and criticism from Governor Meldrim Thomson, Jr., and various state legislators. The court had concluded that the student activities, meant to educate the community and obtain better treatment for gays, were of a type specifically protected by the First Amendment. In *Acanfora v. Board of Education of Montgomery County* (1974), the Fourth Circuit had ruled that a gay public school teacher's statements in support of gay rights were also protected and could not provide a basis for his removal from classroom teaching, although the court ultimately sustained Joseph Acanfora's removal from the classroom for other, unrelated reasons.

Jameson concluded that *Bonner* and *Acanfora* were "factually distinguishable" because "neither involved the open and public flaunting or advocacy of homosexual conduct." Among the activities involved in *Bonner* was a gay dance on campus that involved same-sex dancing and received sensational newspaper coverage in the daily press in New Hampshire; in *Acanfora*, newspaper and national television interviews with the teacher that made his case the subject of national discussion. While there were factual distinctions between these cases and Singer's, the analogies to the types of activities involved were much more striking and relevant. Singer was advocating equal rights for gays in the same ways as Acanfora and the New Hampshire gay students organization, although he may have been a bit more personally flamboyant than they in doing so. But literally without any further analysis or explanation, Jameson concluded that applying the balancing test that the U.S. Supreme Court had adopted in *Pickering v. Board of Education* (1968) for determining whether the government's "efficiency" needs outweighed a public employee's right to engage in First Amendment protected activities, the Commission could "properly conclude" that the EEOC's needs outweighed Singer's interest in "exercising his First Amendment Rights through publicly flaunting and broadcasting his homosexual activities." The opinion contained no discussion of why Singer's activities were more objectionable than Acanfora's or the New Hampshire gay students', but flatly asserted that they were.

Singer filed a petition for *certiorari* with the U.S. Supreme Court. The Civil Service Commission, evidently now somewhat embarrassed by the case, had the solicitor general file a letter with the Court, indicating that it had changed its policies regarding homosexuals in the Civil Service. The Court voted six to three to grant the petition, vacate the Ninth Circuit's judgment, and remand the case for reconsideration "in light of the position now asserted" by the government. Chief Justice Warren E. Burger and Justices Byron R. White and William H. Rehnquist dissented without opinion. For anyone conversant with the Supreme Court's opinions on homosexual rights during the 1970s and 1980s, no explanation for these dissents would be needed, however. (Chief Justice Burger and Justice White wrote opinions upholding Georgia's sodomy law, and then-Justice Rehnquist dissented from the Court's denial of review of a circuit court decision ordering the University of Missouri to recognize a lesbian and gay student groups.) The *Singer* case was eventually settled without further judicial proceedings.

Singer v. U.S. Civil Service Commission was important not as a leading precedent, for the Ninth Circuit's decision was vacated on review by the Supreme Court, but rather for the significant policy questions it raised about the degree of protection for the employment rights of lesbian and gay public employees, and indeed all those supposedly protected from discrimination on the basis of sexual orientation. Shortly after the Supreme Court took its action in the case, Congress passed the Civil Service Reform Act of 1978, which, with its accompanying regulations, reorganized federal employment under the supervision of the new Office of Personnel Management and adopted into federal statutory law many of the due process requirements articulated in cases such as *Norton v. Macy*. In particular, the new law and regulations made clear that only conduct that actually impaired the efficiency of the service could be used to find a federal employee "unsuitable." But what did this mean in the context of active gay rights advocacy in the style of John Singer? Was protection to be afforded only to the closeted homosexual employee, who keeps his sexual orientation a deep secret, or were homosexual federal employees to have the same rights as all other employees to participate openly in society as a lesbian or gay person? Would there continue to be a double standard of the type implicitly adopted by the Ninth Circuit in

Singer's case, or would gay federal employees be able to conduct their lives in the same open, casual manner as heterosexual employees without the fear of repressive "investigations" and judgments of "unsuitability"?

Perhaps the advance of the gay liberation movement, and increasing public willingness to let gay people lead their lives without blatant employment discrimination, have made the facts of Singer's case seem anachronistic to some. However, the same public opinion polls that show widespread support for statutory bans on sexual orientation discrimination in some parts of the country show significant minority endorsement of such discrimination, and referenda instituted by opponents to repeal such laws still pass with alarming frequency, fueled by hate campaigns based on the most vicious stereotypes. Singer's case shows that the formal status protection of gay rights laws and regulations are essentially meaningless for gay people who seek to live their lives on an open and equal basis with their nongay colleagues, unless those laws are read liberally to include protection for people like Singer.

Case References

Acanfora v. Board of Education of Montgomery County, 491 F.2d 498 (4th Cir.), certiorari denied, 419 U.S. 836 (1974)

Gay Students Organization of the University of New Hampshire v. Bonner, 509 F.2d 652 (1st Cir. 1974)

Norton v. Macy, 417 F.2d 1161 (D.C. Cir. 1969)

Pickering v. Board of Education, 391 U.S. 563 (1968)

Singer v. Hara, 522 P.2d 1187 (Wash. App. 1974)

Society for Individual Rights v. Hampton, 63 F.R.D. 399 (N.D. Cal. 1973), affirmed, 528 F.2d 905 (9th Cir. 1975)

74. A TRANSSEXUAL IN A TENNIS TOURNAMENT

Richards v. United States Tennis Association, 93 Misc. 2d 713, 400 N.Y.S.2d 267 (Sup. Ct., N.Y. County 1977).

Dr. Richard H. Raskind, a New York ophthalmologist, felt uncomfortable in his body. Although born male, Dr. Raskind believed that he was actually a woman trapped in a man's body. After many years of consultation with doctors and considerable agonizing, Dr. Raskind, diagnosed as a transsexual, decided in 1975 at the age of 41 to undergo sex reassignment surgery and hormonal therapy, to conform his body to his emotional and psychological makeup.

A surgeon experienced in sex-reassignment surgery, Dr. Roberto Granato, removed Raskind's genitals, constructed a vagina through plastic surgery, and left Dr. Raskind with an "internal sexual structure [that] is anatomically similar to a biological woman who underwent a total hysterectomy and ovariectomy." Throughout the process of sex change, Raskind underwent endocrinological testing and administration of female hormones to change the endocrinological hormonal balance to that of a woman. Removal of the testes led to a tremendous decrease in the level of male hormones in Raskind's blood, producing decreased muscular mass, a change in the muscle-fat ratio to that characteristic of a woman, and development of female breast structure.

Raskind began the process as a highly fit male athlete, having competed successfully in major tennis tournaments and being the third-ranked male player in the Eastern United States in the age 35–and–over category. The sex-reassignment surgery and hormonal changes could not change his 6'2" height, but did lead to a weight reduction to 147 pounds. Experts asserted that by 1977, Raskind, who had changed her name to Renee Richards, had muscle development, weight, height, and physique within the female norm for her age.

Despite her sex change, Richards retained her interest in and devotion to tennis, and she wanted to continue competing at the tournament level. This posed a problem, however, since the changes in her musculature and hormonal balance made it unlikely she could compete at her former level against male athletes. Besides, she now identified as a woman and desired to compete as such. Richards began applying to compete as a woman and encountered serious opposition from administrators and fellow players.

Richards applied to compete as a woman in the 1976 U.S. Open Tennis Tournament, to be held in July of that year at the West Side Tennis Club, in Forest Hills, New York, under the sponsorship of the U.S. Tennis Association (USTA), the U.S. Open Committee (USOC), and the Women's Tennis Association (WTA). In a letter to the chairman of the USOC, explaining her decision to apply as a woman although ranked by USTA as a man, Richards related the details of her sex change process and asserted that she was now physically, emotionally, and psychologically a woman and thus qualified to compete as such. Responding to her application, the USTA instituted a requirement that all women competitors undergo the Barr body test, a sex-chromatin test that had been used since 1968 by the International Olympic Committee to determine whether women competitors had the normal female genetic makeup of two x chromosomes. The Olympics had instituted the test in response to allegations that certain competitors from Eastern Bloc countries were actually either men disguised as women or genetically deviant persons with two x chromosomes and a y chromosome. In either case, proponents of the testing argued that the masculine-appearing women had an undue advantage in height, weight, and musculature that was unfair to the "normal" women in the competition. The USTA made a similar argument in requiring the Barr body test for the first time in 1976 for the U.S. Open and restricting the women's competition to competitors who had two x chromosomes and no y chromosomes as measured by that test.

Richards demanded that USTA waive the test requirement in her case, based on her doctors' statements that she was now physically and hormonally female, in addition to being psychologically and emotionally female as before her sex change. USTA refused to waive the requirement, and Richards never showed up at the qualifying site, thus effectively withdrawing her application to compete that year. The lack of a competitive ranking as a woman by the WTA was another barrier to her competing, since such was required by USTA of all women competitors.

Richards applied again in 1977 to compete in the tournament scheduled to take place on August 25, 1977, at Forest Hills. Meanwhile, she had played competitively in other tournaments as a woman, including the Mutual Benefit Life Open on August 7 at the Orange Town Tennis Club, in South Orange, New Jersey, in which she reached the final rounds. Eugene Scott, the tournament chairman for that competition, had not required any chromosomal testing, although he did require the Phenotype test, which involved observation of primary and secondary sexual characteristics, which Dr. Richards could easily pass due to her reconstructive surgery and the anatomical results of her hormone therapy. However, because the WTA refused to compute competitive ranks based on any tournament in which the Barr body test was not used to qualify the women competitors, Richards still did not have a WTA rank, and once again USTA refused to waive the Barr body test in her case.

On June 27 and July 1, 1977, Richards went to the Institute of Sports Medicine and Athletic Trauma at Lenox Hill Hospital in New York, which had been designated by the USOC to perform the sex-chromatin test for women applicants to the tournament. Because Richards had an active Herpes infection at that time, the procedures for testing were modified slightly, and the resulting test was characterized as "ambiguous." Dr. George Veras, assistant director of the Institute, requested that Richards come in for a second test or for a more definitive and elaborate Karyotype test (which is ten to twenty times more expensive), but Richards refused.

Richards filed suit against USTA, WTA, and the USOC, which directly administers the U.S. Open at Forest Hills, claiming that their refusal to rank her as a woman and allow her to compete in the Women's Division of the tournament violated the New York State Human Rights Law and the Fourteenth Amendment of the U.S. Constitution. Charging that the Barr body test "is recognized to be insufficient, grossly unfair, inaccurate, faulty and inequitable by the medical community in the United States for purposes of excluding individuals from sports events on the basis of gender," Richards asked Justice Alfred M. Ascione, of the New York Supreme Court, New York County, to grant a preliminary injunction ordering USTA and USOC to drop the Barr body test requirement and allow her to compete based on the Phenotype test, which she knew she could pass. Attorneys Michael Rosen and Edward Heller of the politically well-connected firm of Saxe, Bacon & Bolan, represented Richards. Peter K. Leisure, of Curtis, Mallet, Prevost, Colt & Mosle, represented the USTA and the USOC, and Laurence Aufmutn represented the WTA.

Both sides submitted affidavits and oral testimony at the hearing before Justice Ascione, arguing about the reliability of the Barr body test as a determinant of genetic gender, the broader question of whether a postoperative transsexual is really a woman, and the highly specific issue of whether a postoperative transsexual would have an unfair advantage in women's tennis competition. Experts were found to testify on both sides of these questions.

On the issue of unfair advantage, Eugene Scott, of the Mutual Benefit Life Open, in which Richards had just competed, submitted an affidavit indicating that he had invited Richards to compete in his tournament as a woman "because as a tennis tournament chairman based on the information afforded to me, I recognize her as a woman" based on the Phenotype test of primary and secondary sexual characteristics. George W. Gowen testified for the USTA that the tournament sponsors did not intend to discriminate, but were concerned that the large amounts of prize money now awarded in professional tennis competition, as well as the nationalistic zeal demonstrated in international competition, had provided a strong temptation for impostors. Alluding to "world-wide experiments, especially in the iron curtain countries, to produce athletic stars by means undreamed of a few years ago," Gowen asserted that USTA believed the Olympic standard for determining gender was "a reasonable way to assure fairness and equality of competition" and that "the ques-

tion at issue transcends the factual background or medical history of one applicant."

USTA's medical expert, Dr. Daniel Federman, a professor and chairman of the Department of Medicine at Stanford Medical School, submitted an affidavit asserting that the Barr body test reliably and inexpensively determined the presence of a second x chromosome in "normal" women. Federman contended that the y chromosome, the determinant of male gender, controlled the production beginning at puberty of male sex hormones, which resulted "on average, in greater height, different body proportions, and a higher muscle mass than in the female." Although the removal of testes and treatment with female hormones during the sex-reassignment procedure could "reduce male strength," Federman contended that they could not "affect the individual's achieved height or skeletal structure." Federman asserted that certain aspects of sexual identity are immutable; despite all the efforts of sex-reassignment specialists, there remain differences between women and postoperative transsexuals. Federman described the Barr body test, conceding that individuals with chromosomal defects might not be definitively classified by that test alone, and indicated that the Karyotype test, which could give a definitive answer, was also available in appropriate cases, although it took a least a week to obtain results and was much more expensive.

The WTA submitted affidavits from its executive director, Jerry Diamond, and from professional tennis players Francoise Durr, Janet Newberry, Kristien K. Shaw, and Vicki Berner, all arguing that it would be unfair to allow Richards to compete as a woman. Diamond indicated that WTA would continue to refuse to rank as a woman any player who could not pass the Barr body test. Durr, Newberry, and Shaw, all active tennis competitors, indicated that height and strength were factors of advantage in tennis competition; given players of equal skill, the taller and stronger player was more likely to win. Berner, director of women's tennis for USTA and formerly a highly ranked women's singles player, claimed that Richards's competition record since her sex change was unmatched by any "normal" woman in her age range in the history of professional women's tennis.

In addition to her physician, Dr. Granato, who testified that except for reproductive capacity, Richards should be considered a woman, classified as a female, and allowed to compete as such, Richards presented as experts Dr. Leo Wollman, Dr. Donald Rubbell, and Dr. John Money. Wollman, a specialist in sex-reassignment procedures who had treated over 1,700 transsexual patients, argued that even though Richards would fail the Barr body test, she should be classified as female because she had the external genital appearance, the internal organ appearance, the gonadal identity, the endocrinological makeup, and the psychological and social development of a woman. Dr. Rubbell, Richards's gynecologist, asserted that his medical examinations revealed Richards to be physically a woman, and that Richards's perception of herself was entirely as a woman.

Perhaps the most weighty testimony came from Dr. Money, a nationally known psychologist who had written extensively on the subject of transsexualism and who had consulted professionally with Richards. Money stated that "for all intents and purposes, Dr. Richards functions as a woman." Money criticized the Barr body test as creating an irrebuttable presumption as to gender based on a single factor and asserted that it was erroneous to assume that the test would accurately determine the sex of all individuals, since chromosome patterns differed among individuals. The determination of sex required consideration of a wide variety of factors—external genital appearance, internal anatomy, psychology, endocrine balance, somatic structure (i.e., muscular tone, height, weight, breasts, physique), and chromosome makeup—without giving undue weight to chromosomes. Based on his twenty-six years of experience as a psychoendocrinologist, Money asserted that Richards should be classified as female and that there was no justification in law or medicine to classify her as other than female. He also said that her participation at Forest Hills would create no undue advantage in competing against other women because her muscle development, weight, height, and physique fit within the female norm.

Finally, Richards presented an affidavit from woman tennis star Billie Jean King, whose experience included playing against men and playing against and as a doubles partner with Richards in tournament competition since her sex change. King asserted, based on these experiences, that Richards "does not enjoy physical superiority or strength so as to have an advantage over women competitors in the sport of tennis."

Ascione found Richards's experts more convincing than those of the tennis establishment. Summarizing the technical testimony on transsexuality, he stated:

> A transsexual is an individual anatomically of one sex who firmly believes he belongs to the other sex. This belief is so strong that the transsexual is obsessed with the desire to have his body, appearance and social status altered to conform to that of his "rightful" gender. They are not homosexual. They consider themselves to be members of the opposite sex cursed with the wrong sexual apparatus. They desire the removal of this apparatus and further surgical assistance in order that they may enter into normal heterosexual relationships. On the contrary, a homosexual enjoys and uses his genitalia with members of his own anatomical sex. Medical Science has not found any organic cause or cure (other than sex reassignment surgery and hormone therapy) for transsexualism, nor has psychotherapy been successful in altering the transsexual's identification with the other sex or his desire for change.

Thus, it was clear that differential treatment for Richards, or for transsexuals in general, was not discrimination on the basis of sexual orientation, since transsexualism is not about sexual orientation as such, but rather gender identity. "In this court's view," wrote Ascione in his August 16 ruling in favor of Richards, "the requirement of the defendants that this plaintiff pass the Barr body test in order to be eligible to participate in the women's singles of the U.S. Open is grossly unfair, discriminatory and inequitable, and violative of her rights under the Human Rights Law of this state." Opining that "the only justification for using a sex-determination test in athletic competition is to prevent fraud," Ascione asserted that Richards was not trying to defraud the defendants. Furthermore, Ascione was "totally convinced that there are very few biological males, who are accomplished tennis players, who are also either preoperative or post-operative transsexuals," so this was a very individualized problem presented by Richards, not calling for the kind of categorical response mounted by the defendants.

Given the rigors of surgery and hormone therapy that a transsexual had to endure to achieve her "true" sex, Ascione asserted, "the unfounded fears and misconceptions of defendants must give way to the overwhelming medical evidence that this person is now female." Without ruling that the Barr body test could not be used, Ascione asserted that it could not be used as the sole determinant of gender for purposes of sports competition. After summarizing the preamble of the New York Human Rights Law, with its rhetoric of equal opportunity and its importance to a "free democratic state," Ascione recited the list of forbidden categories of discrimination and, without singling out or discussing how any one of them might apply to this case, concluded that the defendants' actions had violated the law and granted Richards's prayer for preliminary injunctive relief.

It is unfortunate that Ascione did not set out his analysis in determining that the law had been violated. It is one thing to determine that

Richards was "female," quite another to determine that her exclusion based on the Barr body test was sex discrimination. Clearly, it is a form of discrimination based on gender, in the sense that women who were born as men cannot pass the test while women who were born as women can. On the other hand, since some other courts have rejected the contention that discrimination against transsexuals is "sex discrimination" as that term was intended by legislators in civil rights laws, the lack of further explanation from Ascione renders his decision less than fully persuasive as a precedent. There is no discussion of the legislative history of the addition of "sex" to the human rights law and the possible meanings that term might have in the minds of legislators, or of the theoretical problems presented by decisions in other cases rejecting sex discrimination charges from homosexuals or transvestites. Thus, the case is more significant as an example of judicial willingness to credit the testimony of the sex change advocates than as a reasoned exposition of the status of their handiwork under civil rights laws.

Renee Richards was subsequently able to compete as a woman in tennis tournaments. Contrary to the fervent allegations of women tennis professionals who opposed her case, she did not emerge as an unbeatable tower of strength.

75. DOES TITLE VII PROTECT "EFFEMINATE" MEN?

Smith v. Liberty Mutual Insurance Co., 569 F.2d 325 (5th Cir. 1978), affirming 395 F. Supp. 1098 (N.D. Ga. 1975).

In 1975 and 1976, the Equal Employment Opportunity Commission (EEOC) ruled in two cases that Title VII of the Civil Rights Act of 1964, which prohibits employment discrimination on the basis of sex, was not intended by Congress to prohibit discrimination against homosexuals. The legislative history of the inclusion of "sex" in Title VII provided no direct explanation of Congress's intent, because "sex" was added by a floor amendment in the House of Representatives without explication through

legislative hearings, committee reports, or substantive debate. The EEOC used the well-accepted canon of statutory construction that when words in a statute are not specially defined, they should be given the common, everyday meaning one would expect legislators would have intended had they thought about the matter. Given the state of the world in 1964, it was implausible to believe that members of Congress intended to pass a national law prohibiting discrimination against homosexuals, a group whose sexual activities were considered manifestations of mental illness by most of society and some of which were subject to criminal sanction in almost every state. At least, it is unlikely they would have passed such a law without talking explicitly about its intended effect.

But what about situations where men were rejected for employment opportunities because they were perceived by potential employers as insufficiently masculine? Was conformity to stereotypes about sex roles and masculine behavior a legitimate job requirement in a country that prohibited discrimination on the basis of sex? Were courts willing to entertain the possibility that discrimination on the basis of perceived sexual orientation (i.e., the stereotype that gay men are effeminate) was in fact a form of sex discrimination that should be cognizable under Title VII? Bennie Smith decided to find out after being turned down on that basis for a mail room job at Liberty Mutual Insurance Company.

Smith, a black man, applied for an administrative job as a mail clerk at Liberty Mutual on February 11, 1969. He was interviewed by the mail room supervisor, Nathaniel Nash, also a black man. According to later testimony by Weldon Cole, Liberty Mutual's administrative manager for its southern division, Nash indicated to him that Smith was qualified, indeed "over qualified," for the job, but that Nash recommended against hiring him because he found him to be effeminate. After learning that he would not be hired and the reason why, Smith filed a charge with the EEOC, charging race discrimination and, in an amended charge, sex discrimination.

When the EEOC had not acted on his complaint within the statutory time limit, Smith received a right-to-sue letter and filed suit in the U.S. District Court for the Northern District of Georgia, seeking class action certification for his claim that Liberty Mutual discriminated against applicants on the basis of race and sex. District Judge Sidney O. Smith denied a motion to add a claim for punitive damages on December 4, 1973, and ruled on March 4, 1974, against Smith's request for class certification of his claim. Smith's allegations relating to his sex discrimination claim were not factually controverted by Liberty Mutual, and he

moved for summary judgment on that claim, with Liberty Mutual filing a cross-motion to dismiss. Judge Smith stayed any ruling on the motions pending *en banc* reconsideration by the U.S. Court of Appeals for the Fifth Circuit of its decision in *Willingham v. Macon Telegraph Publishing Co.* (1975), a case that appeared to present similar issues in a different context.

In *Willingham*, a panel of the Fifth Circuit had ruled on June 12, 1973, that an employer's different grooming standards for men and women with regard to hair length constituted *prima facie* sex discrimination, putting a burden on the employer to show that the different standards were a bona fide occupational requirement reasonably necessary for the conduct of the employer's business. The circuit voted to reconsider the case *en banc* and issued its opinion on February 12, 1975, vacating the panel decision and holding that discrimination on the basis of grooming standards was not sex discrimination.

By now, Smith's case had been reassigned to District Judge James C. Hill, who heard arguments on the motion from Atlanta attorneys E. Lundy Baety, representing Smith, and Melburne D. McLendon, representing Liberty Mutual. Baety pointed out that Liberty Mutual had subsequently hired a female black applicant for the mail room clerk position; thus, the employer was willing to employ a person with feminine characteristics in that position (i.e., masculinity was not a required job attribute) and was discriminating against Smith because he was a man with such characteristics as opposed to a woman. Consequently, argued Baety, this was clearly a case of sex discrimination. McLendon countered that Liberty was merely requiring that applicants of each sex display characteristics appropriate to their sex, relying on *Willingham*.

Judge Hill treated the motions as cross-motions for summary judgment and ruled in favor of Liberty Mutual, holding that the claim for sex discrimination was not available to Smith under Title VII in an order of June 3, 1975. Hill accepted Liberty Mutual's argument that it had not established a rule imposing differential requirements on the basis of sex. "It appears," he wrote, "that the defendant concluded that the plaintiff, a male, displayed characteristics inappropriate to his sex, the counterpart being a female applicant displaying inappropriate masculine attributes."

Hill's order, adopting a somewhat patronizing tone, was substantially devoted to a civics lecture on freedom and restraint in society. He asserted that "at the beginning point" in American history, "the presumption in this nation was that individual citizens are free to make such transactions as they chose to make—advised or ill-advised; wise or foolish; morally right or morally wrong; indeed, prejudiced or unprejudiced." Having rejected a monarchical or dictatorial system under which everything is forbidden unless it is prohibited, Hill stated, "In our main pursuits, we suffer our fellows to commit their blunders while they helplessly watch us do ours." This basic freedom had been abridged only to the extent that the Constitution, and legislation enacted within the authorization of the Constitution, had specifically abridged it. The freedom to discriminate, except as so modified, has "equal standing and dignity with law, and this Court must act so as to secure [it]," said Hill, "whether the person acting as judge of the Court approves of or denounces the law and whether or not he personally feels that the freedom is wisely retained or ought to be limited or proscribed."

With this as prelude, he considered the Civil Rights Act of 1964 and its prohibition on sex discrimination in employment. After musing about the relative merits of "strict" and "liberal" construction of the law, he continued:

No matter how ingeniously contrived, action which accomplishes the forbidden result will be declared illegal. Some may say that this is "liberal construction."

Rights not forbidden are reserved to the individual. The courts know, from these laws, not only what is forbidden but, by absence of proscription, what is not forbidden. If the law making process has yet reserved freedom of action (by not forbidding it) to an employer, it is the duty of the courts to protect it. Thus, beyond the outer edge of the law; that is, in areas where freedom has not been constitutionally restricted; the courts firmly secure the freedom. Some may here find "strict construction" or, perchance, "liberal construction" of a freedom.

This brought Hill face to face with the problem presented by Smith and his denial of employment. "Much has been written upon the subject of so-called 'sex plus' discrimination," he said. "In the final analysis, isn't this but a 'shorthand' way of saying that the national purpose cannot be circumvented by lip service adherence to the Civil Rights Act while thwarting its purpose through the application of employment standards, to male and female alike, which, in application, deny employment to one sex or the other?"

Having asked the question, Hill answered it by affirming that this was not the problem in Smith's case. The employer was not requiring all employees to have masculine characteristics, as a result disadvantaging women, or feminine characteristics, as a result disadvantaging men. Rather, the employer was requiring that employees conform to the characteristics appropriate to their sex. What Smith was complaining about, thus, was not sex discrimination, but discrimination on the basis of "affectional or sexual preference," which Congress had not prohibited. Legislation was pending in Congress to cover this, but it had not been enacted. "The Civil Rights Act is not just the 'starting point' for this Court's extension of limitations upon employers; it is both the starting point and the ending point," declared Hill, who noted that he was not about to enact the pending gay rights legislation in his chambers. Thus, he granted Liberty Mutual's motion to dismiss the sex discrimination allegations. Ironically, Hill's opinion does not indicate whether Smith was gay; the unspoken assumption of the opinion is that Liberty Mutual perceived him to be gay because he was effeminate.

Judge Hill then proceeded to try the case on the race discrimination charges, receiving adverse testimony against Smith and documentary evidence, although Smith decided not to appear in person at the trial. Statistical evidence introduced during the trial indicated that the percentage of black clerical employees at Liberty Mutual went from 5.8 percent in 1966, shortly after Title VII went into effect, to 66.9 percent in 1974. Cole testified at the trial that the decision not to hire Smith was made by Nash, who objected to Smith's effeminacy, not his race. Said Cole, questioned about Nash's reasons for turning down Smith, "Well, I know what he told me when I discussed it with him when I got the notice from the EEOC. He said that there was no question the man was qualified for the particular position that was open at the time, but that frankly he thought he was effeminate." What effeminacy had to do with sorting and delivering mail was apparently not discussed.

Hill admitted over objection a report by the EEOC's investigator, Jean Levine, indicating, in Hill's words,

> that this man was not turned down for race, but that he was denied employment for effeminate characteristics, and there has not been a scintilla of evidence to the contrary.... He wasn't employed because the interviewer didn't like this particular person, white, black, male or female, he just didn't like him because he was, in his view, gave evidence of the characteristics of sexual aberration.

After the brief trial, Hill ruled on July 31, 1975, in an unpublished opinion, that Smith's remaining race discrimination claim should also be dismissed.

Smith appealed to the Fifth Circuit, where a three-judge panel unanimously affirmed Hill's rulings in an opinion by Chief Judge John R. Brown on March 13, 1978. Since Brown's opinion is probably among the most frequently cited appellate rulings for the proposition that Title VII does not protect homosexuals from employment discrimination, it is curious that the opinion has so little to say on the subject in terms of legal analysis. Unfortunately, the law of sex discrimination under Title VII was not well advanced at that time. The concept that "sexual stereotyping" might be a form of sex discrimination was in its infancy and was not even mentioned in the court's opinion (since it had barely been alluded to, as a concept, in Hill's opinion). At that time, the federal appeals courts were just beginning to think through the concept of sexual harassment as a form of sex discrimination under Title VII, an issue that the U.S. Supreme Court would not address on the merits until the mid-1980s. Consequently, the case was argued as a "sexual preference" discrimination case, even though it was more properly conceptualized as a "sexual stereotyping" case.

District Judge Hill had premised his rejection of Smith's sex discrimination claim on *Willingham*, in which the court rejected a claim of sex discrimination from a young man who was denied employment because of his long hair. For the Fifth Circuit, *Willingham* had raised the more general question "whether Congress intended to include *all* sexual distinctions in its prohibition of discrimination (based solely on sex or on 'sex plus') or whether a line can legitimately be drawn beyond which employer conduct is no longer within the reach of the statute." The court concluded in *Willingham* that Congress intended to create a guarantee of "equal job opportunities for males and females," but that lack of express congressional guidance as to what that meant should deter the courts from adopting "questionable application" of the law without further legislative guidance.

Applying *Willingham* to this case, Judge Brown stated, "Here the claim is not that Smith was discriminated against because he was a male, but because as a male, he was thought to have those attributes more generally characteristic of females and epitomized by the descriptive 'effeminate.'" It was not until his trial that Smith's counsel raised the claim that "the employer discriminated against him, not because he was too womanly, but because he simply was a male and females were given preference," a claim the court evidently found unsubstantiated. Without further explanation, Brown said that the court adhered to its conclusion in *Willingham* and that "Title VII cannot be strained to reach the conduct complained of here." In a footnote, Brown cited cases from other circuits following *Willingham*'s reasoning, the EEOC's earlier decisions on discrimination against homosexuals, and two district court decisions holding that Title VII did not protect transsexuals, *Powell v. Read's Inc.* (1977), and *Voyles v. Ralph K. Davies Medical Center* (1975). None of these cases directly related to Smith's inadequately articulated claim of "sexual stereotyping." And none of the cited court decisions dealt with homosexuality, *per se*, although some reflected, as did this court's (and Smith's counsel's), basic confusion between sexual orientation and gender behavior stereotypes.

Most of the substance of Brown's opinion dealt with Smith's charge of race discrimination, which carried little weight given the statistics at Liberty Mutual and the fact that the recommendation against hiring Smith was made by a black supervisor whose only negative concerns related to Smith's alleged effeminacy. The court concluded as well that Hill had correctly rejected Smith's request to certify a class action. "There was no showing that Smith was a member of any class beyond the 'effeminate' group, or who or how many were in such class or classes or whether as an individual Smith had been or was in a position to sustain the same injury which would thereby qualify him as a class plaintiff," said Brown. Indeed, Smith did not even appear at his own trial. "As a champion," observed Brown, "he could hardly enter the lists in absentia."

The Fifth Circuit rejected, perhaps without even knowing what it was doing, a theory of Title VII protection that would—in the opposite context involving a "masculine" woman that had been off-handedly mentioned by Judge Hill—be adopted by the U.S. Supreme Court in 1989 in *Price Waterhouse v. Hopkins*. In that case, the Court held that when an employer fails to promote a woman because her behavior is considered excessively masculine, the employer has discriminated on the basis of sex in violation of Title VII. Would the Court follow that logic to its ultimate conclusion if a case such as Bennie Smith's was presented today? At heart, discrimination on the basis of sexual orientation might be said to operate on the same theory that the Court adopted in *Hopkins*: discrimination due to an employee's failure to conform to gender stereotypes is "sex discrimination."

Case References

EEOC Dec. 76–75, CCH Emp. Prac. para. 6495 (1976)

Powell v. Read's, Inc., 436 F. Supp. 369 (D. Md. 1977)

Price Waterhouse v. Hopkins, 490 U.S. 228 (1989)

Voyles v. Ralph K. Davies Medical Center, 403 F. Supp. 456 (N.D. Cal. 1975)

Willingham v. Macon Telegraph Publishing Co., 507 F.2d 1084 (5th Cir. 1975) (en banc), vacating 482 F.2d 535 (5th Cir. 1973)

76. DISCRIMINATION AGAINST GAYS IS NOT "SEX DISCRIMINATION"

DeSantis v. Pacific Telephone & Telegraph Co., 608 F.2d 327 (9th Cir. 1979).

As the movement for lesbian and gay rights gathered increased visibility during the 1970s, openly lesbian and gay attorneys began to challenge discriminatory practices in the courts. The budding movement had succeeded in getting some politicians to introduce proposals to expand existing civil rights laws to forbid discrimination on the basis of "sexual preference," but they were realistic enough to conclude that enactment of federal legislation was far off and, apart from isolated state or municipal victories, it was unlikely that most lesbian and gay people would be working under such legislative protections any time soon. Meanwhile, attempts were made to find protection under existing civil rights laws. Perhaps the most comprehensive attempt, and most decisive judicial repudiation, came in *DeSantis v. Pacific Telephone & Telegraph Co.*, a 1979 decision by the U.S. Court of Appeals for the Ninth Circuit in San Francisco.

The Ninth Circuit's decision in *DeSantis* actually involved the consolidated appeal of three separate cases, two against Pacific Telephone and Telegraph Company (PacTel) and one against the Happy Times Nursery School. Each of the three cases presented a slightly different factual predicate and legal theory.

Robert DeSantis, Bernard Boyle, and another gay man, identified in the court's opinion only as Simard, all encountered difficulties with Pacific Telephone because of their homosexuality. DeSantis alleged that he was not hired because a PacTel supervisor concluded that he was gay. Boyle, an employee, claimed that after co-workers discovered that he was gay, they subjected him to continual harassment that forced him to resign to preserve his health.

Boyle claimed that supervisors knew of the harassment but did nothing to stop it. Simard made similar claims, adding that in his case the supervisors had joined in the harassment and marked his file as not eligible for rehire, resulting in rejections of applications from him in 1974 and 1976. DeSantis, Boyle, and Simard, who jointly filed a class action suit against PacTel in the U.S. District Court for the Northern District of California after the Equal Employment Opportunity Commission (EEOC) rejected their sex discrimination complaints on jurisdictional grounds, alleged that company officials had stated publicly that they would not knowingly hire homosexuals. They alleged that PacTel's policies and practices were unlawful sex discrimination under Title VII of the Civil Rights Act of 1964, and also violated the post-Civil War Ku Klux Klan Act, 42 U.S.C. section 1985(3), which outlaws conspiracies to deprive individuals of their civil rights.

In another complaint against PacTel, Judy Lundin and Barbara Buckley, employed as telephone exchange operators by PacTel, claimed that they suffered insults and harassment and were eventually discharged after PacTel co-employees and supervisors learned that they were engaged in a lesbian relationship with each other. Lundin also charged that the union failed to represent her properly. Lundin and Buckley sued PacTel under Title VII in the district court in San Francisco.

The complaints against PacTel were consolidated with a case against another employer. Donald Strailey, a teacher at the Happy Times Nursery School, claimed that he was discharged because he wore a small gold ear-loop to school before the commencement of the school year. He alleged that the school concluded from this that he was gay and fired him on that basis. After the EEOC rejected his sex discrimination charge, Strailey filed suit in federal court under Title VII and 42 U.S.C. section 1985(3).

In all three cases, the federal district judges agreed with the EEOC that discrimination against homosexuals was not encompassed within the sex discrimination prohibition of Title VII, and that a valid claim had not been stated under section 1985(3) in the cases where that was alleged. Consequently, all three lawsuits were dismissed in response to pretrial motions by the defendants, without benefit of testimony or factual findings.

On appeal, all plaintiffs were represented by Richard Gayer, then one of a handful of openly gay attorneys in San Francisco, who was beginning a distinguished career as a litigator of gay rights cases. The defendants were represented by Harold R. Crookes, of San Francisco, and William H. Ng, of Washington, D.C. A three-judge panel consisting of two circuit judges, Herbert Y.C. Choy and Joseph T. Sneed, and visiting Senior U.S. District Judge Dudley B. Bonsal of the Southern District of New York, issued its decision affirming the various district courts on all counts on May 31, 1979, in an opinion by Judge Choy, and denied a petition for rehearing on July 12, 1979.

Gayer had posed a variety of Title VII sex discrimination theories for the consideration of the court, all but one of which were unanimously rejected by the three-judge panel. First, Gayer argued that the inclusion of "sex" in Title VII encompassed all sex-related discrimination, including discrimination on the basis of sexual orientation or preference, and that such a construction would be within the admittedly ambiguous intention of Congress. "Sex" was added to the list of prohibited reasons for discrimination in a floor amendment offered in the House of Representatives by opponents of the legislation, who were surprised that the House voted to approve their amendment and then passed the legislation. There were no committee hearings or legislative findings related to sex discrimination. The bill then went to the Senate, where a floor amendment was added to clarify how the prohibition of sex discrimination under Title VII would mesh with the prohibition of sex discrimination in pay, which had been enacted the previous year as an amendment to the Fair Labor Standards Act. Discussion of this amendment did not include any consideration of what "sex" should be construed to mean in the context of Title VII.

Because the legislative history sheds no light on the meaning of the term, federal courts follow the normal rule of statutory construction of giving the term its most common, everyday meaning which one presumes was the meaning intended by legislators when they used the word. Following earlier decisions such as *Holloway v.*

Arthur Andersen & Co. (1977), a Ninth Circuit case involving discrimination against a transsexual, and *Smith v. Liberty Mutual Insurance Co.* (1978), a Fifth Circuit case in which the plaintiff was discharged because of his "effeminate" appearance and behavior, the *DeSantis* panel held that the plain meaning of "sex," as understood by Congress, would not have included sexual orientation. The court concluded that Congress was concerned, plain and simply, with discrimination against women.

Gayer then posed an alternative argument, based on the "disparate impact" theory of discrimination that the U.S. Supreme Court had articulated in 1971 in *Griggs v. Duke Power Co.* In *Griggs*, the Court held unlawful under Title VII various hiring qualifications that had the tendency to screen out applicants disproportionately on the basis of race. The Court stated that apparently neutral employment practices that disproportionately disadvantage a protected group under Title VII can be used only if the employer shows that they are necessary for the conduct of its business. Gayer argued that this theory applied at least to his male homosexual clients because a policy of refusing to hire or employ homosexuals would have a disproportionate impact on men. Gayer contended that a greater percentage of men than women were homosexual, a claim supported by the so-called Kinsey Report and the work of subsequent sex researchers.

Choy characterized this argument as "an artifice to 'bootstrap' Title VII protection for homosexuals under the guise of protecting men generally" and asserted that "[t]his we are not free to do," since it would "frustrate congressional objectives" as they had been identified in prior cases holding that Title VII did not protect homosexuals from discrimination. None of the proposals to amend Title VII to add sexual orientation had yet achieved floor consideration or a vote in Congress, a state of affairs that Choy mischaracterized as consistent refusal by Congress "on many occasions" to extend protection to homosexuals. Concluding that accepting Gayer's argument would violate the court's mandate to "give effect to the legislative will," Choy and Bonsal rejected this argument. Sneed disagreed, in a partial concurring opinion, arguing that the suits by the gay men should

be allowed to proceed solely on the disparate impact theory.

While conceding that it might be difficult for them to prove liability on that basis, Sneed asserted that it was not impossible. "[I]t will be necessary to establish that the use of homosexuality as a bar to employment disproportionately impacts on *males*, a class that enjoys Title VII protection," he said. "Such a showing perhaps could be made were male homosexuals a very large proportion of the total applicable male population." (Kinsey had asserted in 1948 that more than a third of the adult male population had engaged in some degree of homosexual activity.) Rejecting the charge of "bootstrapping," Sneed said: "Their claim, if established properly, would in fact protect males generally. I would permit them to try to make their case and not dismiss it on the pleadings."

Gayer also advanced a variety of other sex discrimination arguments, all rejected by the court. One was that the employers had unlawfully imposed different employment criteria on the basis of sex. If a male employee preferred males as sexual partners, he was subject to discharge, while a female employee who desired male sexual partners was not subject to discharge, and vice versa. The court dismissed this argument cursorily as more bootstrapping, pointing out that "whether dealing with men or women the employer is using the same criterion: it will not hire or promote a person who prefers sexual partners of the same sex." The court also rejected the idea that this case should be covered by EEOC rulings involving discrimination against employees who associated with black people. Choy countered that the complaint in this case was not that the defendants discriminated against the plaintiffs because of their choice of friends but rather because of the nature of the sexual relationship with their friends. Even if it would violate Title VII for an employer to discriminate on the basis of the gender of an employee's friends, it would not constitute a violation to discriminate because of the nature of that relationship.

Finally, Straileyhad argued that his case actually involved sexual stereotyping. Because he wore an ear-loop to work one day (at a time before the school year began when children were not present), he had failed to conform to the School's stereotype of appropriate male attire and behavior. Strailey argued that this constituted sex discrimination, a claim that the Fifth Circuit had previously denied in *Smith v. Liberty Mutual Insurance Co.* Following *Smith* without any substantive discussion or analysis, Choy rejected this argument. (A decade later, the U.S. Supreme Court held, without much substantive discussion, that sexual stereotyping was a violation of Title VII in *Price Waterhouse v. Hopkins*, a 1989 case involving a woman passed over for partnership in an accounting firm because she did not conform in appearance and behavior with the firm's image of femininity.)

Gayer had alternatively argued that the harassment and subsequent discharges of the plaintiffs had violated their civil rights under section 1985(3), which forbids conspiracies "for the purpose of depriving, either directly or indirectly, any person or class of persons of the equal protection of the laws, or of equal privileges and immunities under the laws," and giving a right of action to anyone injured by such a conspiracy. This law had originally been passed to give a cause of action to southern blacks who were injured by the concerted actions of white racists during the height of Ku Klux Klan activity in the late 19th century. In *Griffin v. Breckenridge* (1971), the U.S. Supreme Court had held that this provision applied where there is "some racial, or perhaps otherwise class based, invidiously discriminatory animus behind the conspirators' action." The Ninth Circuit had held in 1979 in *Life Insurance Co. of North America v. Reichardt* that sex discrimination fell within the ambit of section 1985(3). Gayer argued that sexual orientation discrimination should also be covered under this theory.

The court rejected this argument as well. While conceding that the provision had been "liberated from the now anachronistic historical circumstances of reconstruction America," it asserted that the "underlying principle" of expanded coverage was a "governmental determination that some groups require and warrant special federal assistance in protecting their civil rights." The court saw no evidence of any such governmental determination in the case of gays. Indeed, quite the opposite, gays were the targets of official government discrimination, including criminalization [which, Choy noted, had been upheld in *Doe v. Commonwealth's Attorney*

for the City of Richmond* (1976)] and, as Choy had previously stated, Congress had "repeatedly refused" to amend Title VII to add sexual orientation. At that time, no appellate court had identified sexual orientation as a "suspect classification" under the Equal Protection Clause. Consequently, said Choy, "we conclude that homosexuals are not a 'class' within the meaning of section 1985(3)." Judge Sneed, in his concurring opinion, reiterated the point, producing a lengthy footnote citing other groups that had been denied protection under this provision and asserting: "This section is not a writ by which the judiciary can provide comfort and succor to all groups, large and small, who feel social disapproval from time to time."

The *DeSantis* opinion is the most decisive, sweeping repudiation of the contention that discrimination on the basis of sexual orientation, either actual or presumed (in the case of Strailey), is forbidden either by the federal Civil Rights Act or the so-called Ku Klux Klan Act. Viewed in light of subsequent Supreme Court decisions and the growing body of commentary asserting that sexual orientation should be treated as a suspect classification under the Equal Protection Clause, significant portions of the court's analysis appear questionable now. But the lower federal courts have continued to cite *DeSantis* as precedent without any further substantive analysis or consideration of intervening developments, and most gay rights litigators have given up trying to persuade the EEOC or the federal courts that existing laws forbid discrimination against homosexuals, focusing attention instead on achieving express legislative protections at the state and municipal levels.

Case References

Doe v. Commonwealth's Attorney for the City of Richmond, 403 F. Supp. 1199 (E.D. Va. 1975), affirmed, 425 U.S. 901, rehearing denied, 425 U.S. 985 (1976)

Griffin v. Breckenridge, 403 U.S. 88 (1971)

Griggs v. Duke Power Co., 401 U.S. 424 (1971)

Holloway v. Arthur Andersen & Co., 566 F.2d 659 (9th Cir. 1977)

Life Insurance Co. of North America v. Reichardt, 591 F.2d 499 (9th Cir. 1979)

Price Waterhouse v. Hopkins, 490 U.S. 228 75 (1989)

Smith v. Liberty Mutual Insurance Co., 569 F.2d 325 (5th Cir. 1978)

77. PROTECTING "OPENLY GAY" CALIFORNIANS

Gay Law Students Association v. Pacific Telephone & Telegraph Co., 24 Cal. 3d 458, 156 Cal. Rptr. 14, 595 P.2d 592 (1979), reversing in part, 65 Cal. App. 3d 608, 135 Cal. Rptr. 465 (1st Dist. 1977).

When gay legal activists in California decided to take on the notorious antigay employment practices of Pacific Telephone and Telegraph Company (PacTel), one of California's largest employers, they decided to pursue alternative federal and state remedies simultaneously, arguing that antigay discrimination was "sex discrimination" under federal and state employment discrimination statutes and, as well, that it violated the duties of a heavily regulated public utility under California constitutional and statutory provisions. What they did not expect was that the California Supreme Court would, *sua sponte*, declare that the very act of being openly gay was a political act that would specifically protect the actor from discrimination by any California employer. This declaration was based on California statutes protecting the political freedoms of citizens of that state. The activists also prevailed on some of their other state constitutional and statutory claims, but were unsuccessful, either in state or federal court, in establishing that antigay discrimination was covered by existing employment discrimination laws. (Their federal action, *DeSantis v. Pacific Telephone and Telegraph Co.*, is discussed in essay No. 76.)

The state court action was initially quite unsuccessful. Attorneys David C. Moon, of the San Francisco Neighborhood Legal Assistance Foundation, and Robert E. Mann, Richard Gayer, and John Eshleman Wahl joined together on behalf of their various individual and organizational clients, including some individuals claiming to have been refused employment or discharged by PacTel because of their homosexuality, the Society for Individual Rights (a San Francisco Bay Area organization with roots in the early gay rights movement of the 1950s), and a newly formed organization of lesbian and gay students at the Hastings College of the Law and the Boalt Hall Law School. They first attempted to get the California Fair

Employment Practices Commission (FEPC) interested in their case, but the FEPC consistently took the position that it had no jurisdiction to investigate or decide cases of alleged antigay discrimination. Then they filed suit in the California Superior Court in San Francisco against both PacTel and the FEPC, seeking a declaration that antigay discrimination, whether specifically by the telephone company or in general, violated California constitutional and statutory requirements. They sought an order requiring the FEPC to accept jurisdiction over their case, as well as an order requiring the telephone company to cease its alleged discriminatory policies. They also sought money damages for those who had been denied employment or discharged due to their sexual orientation, on a class action basis.

Representatives of the California Attorney General's Office, as well as attorneys for PacTel, moved to dismiss the complaints as failing to state a cause of action against either of them. Assistant Attorney General Warren J. Abbott and Deputy Attorney General Richard N. Light appeared for the FEPC, and San Francisco attorneys Alan C. Nelson and Calvin A. Mendonca appeared for PacTel. After oral argument, Superior Court Judge Byron Arnold dismissed the complaint without leave to amend, agreeing with the defendants' arguments. The plaintiffs appealed to the California Court of Appeal, where they drew a polyglot panel made up of retired Superior Court Judge Emerson, who wrote the court's opinion, Acting Presiding Justice James B. Scott, and Justice Norman Elkington, from a different division of the court of appeal, sitting by designation. The court of appeal sustained Arnold's dismissal on all counts.

Emerson first rejected the argument that the Fair Employment Practices Act, first passed by the California legislature in 1959, prohibited employment discrimination on the basis of sexual orientation, either directly or through its ban on sex discrimination. The plaintiffs had argued that the act should be construed to ban *all* unjustified employment discrimination, regardless of "category," by analogy to the state's Unruh Civil Rights Act, which had been broadly construed by the California Supreme Court in *In re Cox* (1970) to forbid all discrimination in public accommodations. Emerson asserted that this analogy was not appropriate.

Under the common law, there had been a well-established principle that operators of businesses that provided goods and services to the public should not engage in arbitrary discrimination in dealings with their customers or potential customers. The Unruh Act, said Emerson, was "an articulation of a long-standing common law doctrine," not really a creator of new law. While the state's supreme court had declared in *Cox* that it covered all forms of public accommodation discrimination, even though it contained a list of categories of prohibited bases of discrimination, the court had never made a similar declaration regarding the FEP law, and for good reason: the common-law rules regarding employment were exactly the opposite. The "American rule" was that employment was presumed to be at will, and that employers had free reign to hire and fire as they liked. While it was true that the California Supreme Court had in one case prior to the adoption of the FEP Act, *James v. Marinship Corp.* (1944), applied common-law principles to the issue of employment discrimination, that case had dealt with the state-recognized monopoly over labor supply exercised by a labor union, not with the decision by an employer whether to hire or fire an employee. When the legislature passed the FEP Act, it was carving out an exception to the common-law rule, and statutes in derogation of the common law were normally narrowly construed.

Furthermore, Emerson found no support for the contention that the FEP's ban on sex discrimination could be construed to include sexual orientation discrimination. For one thing, the allegation that this could be achieved through a "disparate impact" analysis (i.e., that antigay policies disparately excluded men from employment opportunities) lacked empirical support. For another, this interpretation had clearly not been within the contemplation of

the legislature when it amended the FEP Act to add "sex" to the list of categories, and it had been rejected by a variety of federal courts and the Equal Employment Opportunity Commission when advanced in the context of Title VII of the Civil Rights Act, which also banned sex discrimination. Emerson also rejected without any separate discussion the contention that discrimination against gays was sexual stereotyping; this was a theory that would gain U.S. Supreme Court endorsement only a decade later, in *Price Waterhouse v. Hopkins*, a case involving a woman denied a partnership at an accounting firm for being inadequately "feminine" in demeanor and personal style, and has yet to succeed in a gay-related case.

Emerson also rejected the more imaginative and exotic theories advanced by the plaintiffs. For one, the plaintiffs had argued that antigay policies violated rights of free association, drawing analogies to cases involving interracial marriage and other cases where associational rights were held to have statutory or constitutional protection. Emerson found that "the rationale under which those cases were decided is that an employee should not be penalized for associating with members of a different race or of the opposite sex," which was clearly not the issue here. "It is apparent that a classification along the lines of sexual preference creates no barriers to association between the sexes, nor does it penalize either sex for being members of that sex," he concluded.

Neither did Emerson find any basis for liability by the FEPC for refusing to assert jurisdiction on an equal protection theory. The plaintiffs had argued that since employment had been identified in California cases as a fundamental right, the failure to prohibit antigay discrimination denied gays the "equal protection of the laws," a right specifically guaranteed in the California Constitution. Emerson claimed that this "right to work" was not necessarily a "right to work for a particular employer, public or private." "There is simply no constitutional right to work for an unwilling employer," he said, and furthermore, it was not the state that was denying gays the right to work for PacTel. "It has simply remained neutral," he said, so California equal protection precedents were "inapplicable." Furthermore, he found no class-based discrimination here by the government that would call for a "suspect class" analysis urged by the plaintiffs. Emerson also rejected the argument that the FEPC must be made available to combat antigay discrimination, holding that denial of such a forum would not offend due process of law.

Finally, addressing one of the arguments that would provide victory for the plaintiffs at the state supreme court level, Emerson rejected the contention that PacTel's status as a heavily-regulated utility subjected it to any special obligations not to engage in employment discrimination. While it was true that *James v. Marinship* had used language suggesting that "monopolies" had certain common-law responsibilities not to engage in arbitrary discrimination, Emerson noted that the case had been decided long before passage of the FEP Act, and it involved racial discrimination, a topic as to which there was little doubt of a firm state policy. "No such policy with reference to homosexuals has been enunciated," asserted Emerson, mentioning that the legislature had recently rejected an attempt to amend the FEP Act to include sexual orientation. Until the legislature amended the statute, said Emerson, "we do not feel impelled to change, or to add to the legislative scheme."

The plaintiffs appealed to the California Supreme Court, which was sharply divided over the case. At the supreme court level, the case attracted *amicus* participation from many of California's leading gay rights attorneys and advocates, as well as clinical faculty at the Stanford Law School. While the supreme court unanimously agreed with the lower court that the FEP Act did not confer jurisdiction on the FEPC to deal with charges of antigay discrimination, it voted by the narrowest margin to accept the plaintiffs' theory about the special responsibilities of PacTel as a "monopoly," and, as noted at the outset, the majority spontaneously advanced its own theory based on the political freedom of the individual. The court's decision was announced on May 31, 1979.

The opinion for the court by Justice Matthew O. Tobriner first dealt with the California constitutional arguments. Article I, section 7 of the California Constitution contained a general equal protection clause, which Tobriner

asserted could be interpreted to impose on the state and its instrumentalities the obligation not to engage in arbitrary employment discrimination, which would include discrimination against homosexuals. Citing the California Supreme Court's prior decision in *Morrison v. Board of Education*, a 1969 case involving a schoolteacher discharged for engaging in off-duty homosexual activity, Tobriner asserted that "under California law, the state may not exclude homosexuals as a class from employment opportunities without a showing that an individual's homosexuality renders him unfit for the job from which he has been excluded." The problem in this case, of course, was whether a "private" employer, PacTel, qualified as an instrumentality of the state for purposes of this constitutional requirement.

Characterizing PacTel as "a public utility to whom the state has granted a monopoly over a significant segment of the telephonic communications industry in California," Tobriner held that it was appropriate to impose this constitutional requirement on the corporate defendant. Although the California courts had held that the constitutional provision required "state action" before a violation could be found, they had also established that they were not bound by the definition of state action adopted in the federal courts. California state action doctrine had developed separately and was broader in its scope. Thus, Tobriner framed the question to be decided rather broadly to match the California approach to the issue: "Is the California constitutional equal protection guarantee violated when a privately owned public utility, which enjoys a state-protected monopoly or quasi-monopoly, utilizes its authority arbitrarily to exclude a class of individuals from employment opportunities?" When so phrased, the question appeared to Tobriner virtually to answer itself.

"In California," asserted Tobriner, "a public utility is in many respects more akin to a governmental entity than to a purely private employer." Public utilities were so heavily regulated as to their policies and practices that members of the public inevitably identified them closely with the government. Prices and standards were closely regulated by statute and public service commission rulings, and the government dictated bookkeeping and accounting methods, and even awarded PacTel the power of eminent domain in support of its public service obligations. "Under these circumstances," said Tobriner, "we believe that the state cannot avoid responsibility for a utility's systematic business practices and that a public utility may not properly claim prerogatives of 'private autonomy' that may possibly attach to a purely private business enterprise."

Tobriner found PacTel's claim to enjoy free reign in employment policies particularly untenable for several reasons, not least of them the fundamental rights in employment previously recognized by the California courts. He stated:

> Protection against the arbitrary foreclosing of employment opportunities lies close to the heart of the protection against "second-class citizenship" which the equal protection clause was intended to guarantee. An individual's freedom of opportunity to work and earn a living has long been recognized as one of the fundamental and most cherished liberties enjoyed by members of our society . . . , and, as one jurist has aptly noted, "discrimination in employment is one of the most deplorable forms of discrimination known to our society, for it deals not with just an individual's sharing in the 'outer benefits' of being an American citizen, but rather the ability to provide decently for [oneself and] one's family in a job or profession for which he qualifies and chooses."

Tobriner specified three particular reasons for concluding that "arbitrary discrimination in employment particularly flouts constitutional principles when it is practiced by a state-protected public utility." First, due to the utility's virtual monopoly position over jobs in its particular sphere of operation, its discriminatory practices would impose a special burden on those individuals seeking employment in that industry. Arbitrary rejection by PacTel would leave someone with particular skills in telephonic communications with no other California employment opportunity. Second, "employment discrimination by a public utility can be particularly pernicious because, in light of the utility's position, the general public cannot avoid giving indirect support to such discriminatory practices." Those who disapproved PacTel's employment policies and wished not to support them with their patronage would have to forego using the telephone, since there was no free market competitor to provide an alternative to PacTel's service. Finally, because PacTel's monopoly position derived from state franchise, allowing it to discriminate would be "particularly incompatible with the values underlying our constitutional equal protection guarantee." The state had "immunized PacTel from many of the checks of free market competition and [had] placed the utility in a position from which it [could] wield enormous power over an individual's employment opportunities." Consequently, PacTel could not be heard to complain if the state required it to use that power fairly, not arbitrarily.

Tobriner found support for this last contention in a U.S. Supreme Court case, *Steele v. Louisville & Nashville Railroad Co.* (1944), a landmark decision imposing on labor unions a duty of fair representation of all employees they represented, whether or not members, regardless of race. This obligation was premised by the Court on the union's monopoly position as exclusive representative of all the workers, which was conferred on it by virtue of federal legislation requiring the employer to negotiate with the representative designated by a majority of the workers. By analogy, Tobriner found that PacTel had been accorded a virtual monopoly by the state over employment opportunities in telephone communications. It similarly should have a duty not to engage in arbitrary discrimination. Tobriner saw no reason to distinguish PacTel from the defendants in *Steele* merely because one was a private employer and the other was a labor union. "An individual who is arbitrarily excluded from a job suffers no less detriment, and no less 'second class' treatment, when that discrimination is effected by the invidious practice of a state-protected employer than when it is implemented by a state-protected union," he asserted.

Concluding that the California Constitution's equal protection guarantee did extend to PacTel's employment policies, Tobriner disclaimed any attempt by the court "to abridge a public utility's right to prefer the best qualified persons in reaching its hiring or promotion decisions." Rather, the court's ruling required PacTel not to "automatically" exclude homosexuals from consideration, just as it could not arbitrarily exclude any particular class of persons from consideration under this decision. While PacTel officially disclaimed having a discriminatory policy, the plaintiffs were entitled to attempt to prove discrimination at trial, so the decision to dismiss this part of the complaint had to be reversed.

Tobriner concluded that there was also statutory authority in the Public Utilities Code to support the plaintiffs' position. Section 453 forbade public utilities from subjecting "any corporation or person to any prejudice or disadvantage." While some, including the dissenters, argued that this merely applied to the regulated utility's provision of services to the public, not its employment policies, Tobriner rejected such a limited view of the statutory obligation. He pointed out that while the earliest statutory predecessor of the current Section 453, enacted in 1878, had expressly applied solely to the rates and services of the regulated companies (primarily railroads), subsequent enactments had broadened the language to its present form, which clearly indicated that more than rates and services were now covered. In this regard, Tobriner found support in the common-law traditions that underlay the Unruh Civil Rights Act. Public utilities in California, as had already been noted, were granted monopoly power in their particular sphere. "In order to retain the delegated right to exercise such power [under the common law], monopolists were obligated to comply with an implied covenant that such authority be utilized for the good of the public weal and not be abused for personal motives or prejudices." To Tobriner, it seemed that "in contemporary times a public utility, such as PacTel, undoubtedly constitutes a paradigm example of an enterprise 'affected with the public interest,'" so it seemed appropriate to find that it had a general obligation not to engage in arbitrary discrimination. Not only did the statutory language, legislative history, and common-law derivations of section 453 support such a conclusion, he insisted, it was also supported by the constitutional principles already discussed.

Tobriner specifically rejected the argument that to impose this obligation would violate another well-established public policy of "em-

ployment at will." That was a policy applied in the private sector, but PacTel, as already shown, did not stand in the position of a purely private employer. By virtue of "its public service status," said Tobriner, a public utility such as PacTel had to give up some of the privileges it might have as a purely private-sector actor. Thus, contrary to the lower court, Tobriner thought that the California Supreme Court's earlier decision in *Marinship* did support the plaintiffs' case. Since section 453 provided a basis for the court's decision regarding PacTel, it was not necessary for the court to decide whether California common law, standing alone, would forbid a public utility from engaging in employment discrimination, but *Marinship* certainly provided a theoretical basis for making such an argument.

But Tobriner then suggested an alternative theory for the plaintiffs' case, which had not been argued or briefed by the parties, but which potentially had much broader application than merely to regulated public utilities. He observed that Labor Code sections 1101 and 1102 had been passed to ensure that California employers, whether public or private, not "misuse their economic power to interfere with the political activities of their employees." Section 1101 provided that no "employer shall make, adopt, or enforce any rule, regulation, or policy: (a) Forbidding or preventing employees from engaging or participating in politics. . . . (b) Controlling or directing, or tending to control or direct the political activities or affiliations of employees." Similarly, section 1102 stated: "No employer shall coerce or influence or attempt to coerce or influence his employees through or by means of threat of discharge or loss of employment to adopt or follow or to refrain from adopting or following any particular course or line of political action or political activities." "These statutes cannot be narrowly confined to partisan activity," said Tobriner, but must be broadly applied to all character of political activities, expressions, and associations.

> Measured by these standards, the struggle of the homosexual community for equal rights, particularly in the field of employment, must be recognized as a political activity. Indeed

the subject of the rights of homosexuals incites heated political debate today, and the "gay liberation movement" encourages its homosexual members to attempt to convince other members of society that homosexuals should be accorded the same fundamental rights as heterosexuals. The aims of the struggle for homosexual rights, and the tactics employed, bear a close analogy to the continuing struggle for civil rights waged by blacks, women, and other minorities. . . .

A principal barrier to homosexual equality is the common feeling that homosexuality is an affliction which the homosexual worker must conceal from his employer and his fellow workers. Consequently one important aspect of the struggle for equal rights is to induce homosexual individuals to "come out of the closet," acknowledge their sexual preferences, and to associate with others in working for equal rights.

Thus, the allegation in the complaint that PacTel's policy was directed at any homosexuals who could be identified as such took on "a special significance." Specifically, the plaintiffs had alleged that PacTel discriminated against "manifest" homosexuals and against those who "make 'an issue of their homosexuality.'" PacTel allegedly would not accept employment referrals from a homosexual organization. Essentially, the complaint charged PacTel with adopting a "policy . . . tending to control or direct the political activities or affiliations of employees" in violation of section 1101, and was coercing them in their political activities in violation of section 1102, although that claim had not been expressly articulated. The California court had previously recognized a private right of action for violations of those sections, so Tobriner concluded that the complaint also stated a cause of action under that theory.

However, Tobriner agreed with the dissenters and the courts below that the FEP Act did not ban antigay discrimination. Unlike the Unruh Act, the FEP Act did not merely codify existing common-law requirements, but modified the employment-at-will rule to specify particular forbidden motivations for employment discrimination. Sexual orientation was not on the list, and its inclusion had been specifically rejected by the legislature. Neither was there any validity to the argument that sexual orientation discrimination was already covered as a

species of sex discrimination, although "as a semantic argument, the contention may have some appeal." It was just not consistent with the legislative intent, and parallel cases under Title VII in the federal courts had unanimously rejected the claim.

While sympathetic to the plight of gays, Tobriner could not agree that the equal protection clause required an extension of the FEP Act to gays through judicial interpretation. The plaintiffs' could not cite any authority "in support of the proposition that a remedial statute which affords a benefit to one or a number of historically aggrieved groups is unconstitutional if the same benefit is not afforded to all historically aggrieved groups," because there was none. The U.S. Supreme Court had made the point emphatically in *Katzenbach v. Morgan* (1966), when it stated that "a legislature need not 'strike at all evils at the same time,'" but could pick and choose by advancing reform "one step at a time."

Tobriner concluded that if the court exempted PacTel from an obligation not to engage in arbitrary employment policies, the result could disadvantage more groups than just homosexuals. He stated:

We would necessarily empower any public utility to engage in an infinity of arbitrary employment practices. To cite only a few examples, the utility could refuse to employ a person because he read books prohibited by the utility, visited countries disapproved by the utility, or simply exhibited irrelevant characteristics of personal appearance or background disliked by the utility. Such possible arbitrary discrimination, casting upon the community the shadow of totalitarianism, becomes crucial when asserted by an institution that exerts the vast powers of a monopoly sanctioned by government itself. We do not believe a public utility can assert such prerogatives in a free society dedicated to the protection of individual rights.

Justice Frank K. Richardson and his two dissenting colleagues were not persuaded by this argument. The dissenters maintained that PacTel was a private employer entitled to the same privilege as all other private employers under the well-established employment-at-will rule to make personnel decisions free of government intervention, except for the specific forms of discrimination proscribed by the FEP Act. According to their view, the other various constitutional and statutory provisions cited by the majority had "no bearing whatever on the subject of the employment of homosexuals."

First, on the equal protection point, without disputing the argument that a state actor might be bound not to discriminate arbitrarily against homosexuals, Richardson argued that PacTel was a purely private actor that incurred no obligations by virtue of the equal protection clause. More importantly, he noted, article I, section 8 of the California Constitution, which directly followed the equal protection provision, specified the right to be free of employment discrimination for all Californians based on a list of specific factors that did not include sexual orientation. As to Section 453 of the Public Utilities Code, it was clear to Richardson that it had nothing to do with the employment policies of utilities, and had never been so applied. The Public Utilities Commission had recently construed the Code not to apply to employment in a case involving racial discrimination, and the supreme court had denied review of that decision. While it had, in another case, extended its jurisdiction to some scrutiny of employment policies, that was done in the context of an investigation into a utility's "efficiency or rates," not its employment policies in general.

As did the lower court, Richardson rejected the contention that section 453's codification of common-law requirements in the area of public services had any employment component. *Marinship* greatly postdated the enactment of section 453, and that section was not deemed relevant to the court's holding. The established common-law principle governing employment in California was employment at will, and this principle should be applied except to the extent expressly overridden by statutory enactment, not through a strained interpretation of general policies. Indeed, Richardson maintained that the majority's approach to section 453 was no less than "judicial legislation."

Finally, as to the Labor Code provisions, "The majority's reliance on these sections is invalid, and the very fact that it makes the attempt betrays the fundamental weakness of its legal position," Richardson asserted. There was nothing in the complaints in this case having to do with PacTel trying to control its employees' political activities, and the plaintiffs had never raised that issue at any point in the case. "I fully concur in the majority's concern toward homosexuals who have suffered the detriment, trauma, or indignity of employment discrimination," said Richardson.

> They are entitled to all of the rights, protections, and privileges of other citizens, no less and no more. In the contemplation of the law, homosexuals stand neither burdened by prejudice nor blessed with preference. Nonetheless, it is not our function to tell employers, large or small, whom to employ. Courts should not attempt to police general employment practices in the absence of some clear constitutional or statutory authority. Neither exists in the matter before us.

Seizing upon Richardson's dissent, PacTel petitioned the court for rehearing, but the petition was denied July 25, 1979.

The California Supreme Court's decision in *Pacific Telephone* was one of the first significant decisions by any appellate court to extend substantive protection against employment discrimination to gay people in any context, at a time when no state had legislated directly against such discrimination and there were but a handful of municipal ordinances and executive orders on the subject. By invoking the Labor Code political freedom provisions, the court recognized a theory of wider application that provided the basis for a subsequent formal opinion by California Attorney General John Van De Kamp in 1986, taking the position that any employment discrimination against openly gay applicants or employees by private sector employers in California was unlawful.

The court's opinion may also have provided some of the basis for Governor George Deukmejian's subsequent veto of a legislative amendment to the Fair Employment and Housing Code adding "sexual orientation" to the enumerated categories of discrimination. This addition was unnecessary, said Deukmejian, arguing that there was no documented evidence of widespread discrimination against gays, who already had adequate protection under existing laws.

The case against PacTel, remanded for trial, dragged on for a decade of interminable discovery tactics, as PacTel attorneys buried the plaintiffs in mountains of paper, continuing to deny any policy of discrimination. Finally, toward the end of the 1980s, an alert attorney looking through the voluminous employment records turned over in discovery uncovered a pattern: PacTel interviewers used a particular letter code to identify applications from suspected homosexuals. When the plaintiffs' attorneys presented this evidence to PacTel, the company realized that it would likely lose the case in a superior court trial in San Francisco, and agreed to settle for approximately $5 million, providing financial damages for class members and compensating the attorneys and public interest firms that had assumed the burden of preparing the case for trial. PacTel also agreed as part of the settlement to adopt an express nondiscrimination policy.

More than a decade after the California Supreme Court's *Pacific Telephone* decision, Governor Pete Wilson also asserted that the addition of "sexual orientation" to the Code was unnecessary when he vetoed a bill similar to the one previously vetoed by Governor Deukmejian. Just days after Wilson announced his veto, the California Court of Appeal for the First District ruled in *Soroka v. Dayton-Hudson Corp.* that the *Pacific Telephone* case and subsequent developments made clear that the Labor Code political freedom provision protected gay employees from employment discrimination in the private sector. Wilson, who had encountered massive protests from gay rights demonstrators during public appearances following his veto, promptly announced that he would instruct the state Labor Department to accept and investigate claims of discrimination in violation of the Labor Code provisions and pursue appropriate enforcement. State gay rights leaders, who had sharply criticized Wilson for the veto, argued that the Labor Code route was cumbersome, and that explicit statutory protection against discrimination on the basis of sexual orientation would provide firmer grounding for employment rights than would judicial interpretation of the Labor Code provisions. Meanwhile, Dayton-Hudson Corporation had appealed the *Soroka* decision to the state supreme court. In 1992, the state amended the Labor Code provisions to expressly ban employment discrimination on the basis of sexual orientation.

Although few other states have the kind of express protection for the political rights of private-sector employees found in the California Labor Code, the *Pacific Telephone* decision by the California Supreme Court has nonetheless played an important role in focusing the legal debate over the employment rights of homosexuals, while providing a basis for California courts to construct a legal theory for protection of private-sector employees from sexual orientation discrimination. While the case has yet to be cited as persuasive precedent in a similar case in any other jurisdiction, it is the subject of extended comment in law reviews and illustrates the importance of ingenuity in framing legal arguments as a technique to gain recognition for previously unrecognized rights.

Case References

Cox, In re, 3 Cal. 3d 205, 90 Cal. Rptr. 24, 474 P.2d 992 (1970)

DeSantis v. Pacific Telephone & Telegraph Co., 608 F.2d 327 (9th Cir. 1979)

James v. Marinship Corp., 25 Cal. 2d 721, 155 P.2d 329 (1944)

Katzenbach v. Morgan, 384 U.S. 641 (1966)

Morrison v. State Board of Education, 1 Cal. 3d 214, 461 P.2d 375 (1969)

Opinion of Attorney General John Van De Kamp, 69 Ops. Att'y Gen. 80 (Cal. 1986)

Price Waterhouse v. Hopkins, 490 U.S. 228 (1989)

Steele v. Louisville & Nashville Railroad Co., 323 U.S. 192 (1944)

Soroka v. Dayton Hudson Corp., 235 Cal. App. 3d 654, 1 Cal. Rptr. 2d 77 (1st Dist. 1991), appeal pending

78. DUE PROCESS RIGHTS FOR GAY FBI EMPLOYEES

Ashton v. Civiletti, 613 F.2d 923 (D.C. Cir. 1979).

Few agencies of the federal government have been more consistent in rooting out and removing their lesbian and gay employees than the Federal Bureau of Investigation (FBI), a law enforcement agency of the U.S. Department of Justice. At the same time, few agencies have been more publicly evasive about their personnel policies concerning homosexuality. This paradox is well illustrated by the case of Donald Ashton, an employee in the Bureau's mail room whose lawsuit upon constructive discharge from the agency brought the paradox to light in the pages of the *Federal Reporter*, while establishing that nonprobationary employees of the Bureau are entitled to due process hearings before being deprived of their jobs.

After graduating from high school in 1973, Donald Ashton applied to the FBI for an entry-level job as a mail sorter at the Bureau's headquarters in the J. Edgar Hoover Building in Washington, D.C. After undergoing the Bureau's routine security check, during which the issue of Ashton's sexual orientation never came up, he was offered an appointment as a clerk in Civil Service pay grade GS 2. The appointment letter from Director Clarence Kelley, dated September 5, 1973, specified that the appointment was for a one-year probationary period, and that the position was not covered by the competitive Civil Service system. Ashton's position was described to him as a "temporary indefinite" appointment. In the FBI's employee's handbook that he received, this type of appointment was described as follows: "If you have a 'temporary indefinite' appointment, this does not mean that your position has any limited duration. You may assume that your position is secure." Ashton began working on October 3 in the Messenger Unit of the Files and Communications Division, more commonly referred to as the mail room. He passed his probationary year without incident and was subsequently promoted two pay grades, to GS 4.

Early in 1975, the FBI received a report from the Naval Investigative Service, which stated that a person under investigation for homosexual activities had named Ashton as one of his sexual contacts. On January 10, Special Agent Paul F. Shea called Ashton into his office together with Ashton's boss, Special Agent Richard White, who was then chief of the Mail Processing Unit, and confronted Ashton with this report. After some confusion about the name of the person under investigation, Ashton recalled that he had met him some months earlier at a Washington restaurant and gone with him to his apartment in Quantico, Virginia. Responding to specific questions from Shea, Ashton denied engaging in oral intercourse with this person but said they had fondled each other. Ashton also indicated that he had known of his own homosexuality since his junior year in high school three years earlier. Ashton rejected Shea's suggestion that he seek psychiatric help. (Ashton later stated during his court proceeding, "I accepted my status and trusted the conclusions of the American Psychiatric Association that homosexuality is not a mental disorder.") Ashton also stated that nobody at the FBI knew about his homosexuality, because he conducted himself with discretion. In fact, said Ashton, even his roommate, a fellow FBI employee, was unaware of Ashton's sexual orientation.

What happened next was the subject of some dispute. Shea left the room briefly to consult with an officer in the Bureau's Administrative Division who was familiar with the Naval report. According to Ashton, when Shea returned to the room he told Ashton that he could either resign immediately or be discharged, and that resignation would be preferable for him because the Bureau would give him good job references that would avoid mention of his homosexuality. Shea also allegedly told Ashton that if he did not resign, "everyone would know of [his] homosexuality," which Ashton later said was a matter of indifference to him. Shea and

White had a different recollection of that part of the meeting, insisting that Shea merely told Ashton he had the right to resign to avoid disciplinary action, which might include censure, censure and probation, or dismissal, and that although Shea would recommend dismissal, his recommendation might or might not be followed by higher-ups in the Bureau.

Confused and frightened, unhappy at the prospect of resigning a job in which he had been doing well, and lacking any legal counsel or advice as to his rights in the situation apart from what Shea had told him, Ashton concluded that he had no possible alternative to resignation, and signed a handwritten statement resigning immediately. The whole meeting lasted about ninety minutes. Ashton had second thoughts about his resignation when he was unsuccessful finding new work. He suspected that the Bureau's references had something to do with this, and hired Washington attorney Steven Rosenthal to represent him in seeking reinstatement at the FBI. Rosenthal wrote to Director Kelley on January 24, asserting that Ashton's resignation was involuntary and requesting reinstatement. Kelley denied the request in a letter dated February 5.

Ashton filed suit against the attorney general, Benjamin R. Civiletti, and other officials in the chain of command at the FBI, on May 9, asserting that his resignation had been coerced, his rights of property and liberty had been denied without the hearing required by the Due Process Clause, and that substantively his First and Fifth amendment rights had been violated by terminating him for a reason bearing no rational relationship to his job duties. The government, represented by Assistant U.S. Attorney Constantine J. Gekas, answered denying the allegations of the complaint and moved for summary judgment. Arguing that the Bureau's exemption from coverage under the competitive Civil Service effectively rendered Ashton an "at-will" employee, the government argued that he could be dismissed at any time for any or no reason. The government also argued that his resignation had been voluntary, submitting affidavits by Shea and White affirming that Ashton was given a choice and was not coerced.

District Judge Thomas A. Flannery granted the government's motion for summary judg-ment in an unpublished memorandum. Rejecting Ashton's arguments that the FBI's handbook and statements made to him in writing on his initial appointment created a property interest in continued employment sufficient to trigger due process protections, Flannery ruled that Ashton had failed to allege sufficient facts to show any sort of "tenure" system at the FBI, which would, in any event, be inconsistent with the Bureau's mission. "If anything," Flannery concluded, "the practical realities of job security at the Bureau are the opposite of the conditions analyzed by the [Supreme] Court in [*Perry v.*] *Sindermann,*" a leading case establishing that federal employees with a reasonable expectation of continued employment generated by Civil Service regulations or other policy statements were entitled to due process protection in their jobs. Flannery did not address the factual disparities concerning the January 10 meeting or the substance of Ashton's First and Fifth amendment claims.

Ashton's appeal was argued before the U.S. Court of Appeals for the District of Columbia Circuit on February 21. At oral argument, the appellate panel of Chief Judge J. Skelly Wright and Circuit Judges Carl McGowan and Harold Leventhal tried to pin down Gekas on exactly what was the FBI's policy on the employment of homosexuals. Published policies of the Bureau made no mention of homosexuality or sexual deviation as such. The FBI handbook did state that employees should not engage in "criminal, infamous, dishonest, immoral, or notoriously disgraceful conduct, neglect of duty, or other conduct prejudicial to the Government," and elsewhere referred to the duty of FBI employees to restrict themselves to conduct that was not only proper but always appeared proper, so as to avoid shaking the public's confidence in the agency. Gekas relied on this in his argument to the court, but Rosenthal argued that there was a factual issue whether Ashton's discreet behavior presented any problems under these standards. Gekas insisted that Ashton's homosexuality, "without further inquiry of any kind and particularly with respect to job-relatedness," justified termination of employment. The court asked him to supply a more definitive statement of the agency's policy after the hearing. On March 2, 1979, Gekas filed a supplemental memorandum with the court, containing the following statement: "The Federal Bureau of Investigation has always had an absolute policy of dismissing proven or admitted homosexuals from its employ."

This firm statement seemed contradictory to the members of the court with what was being stated publicly by the current director of the Bureau. While the panel was working on its decision, Director William H. Webster appeared on a broadcast of *Face the Nation* on July 22, 1979, during which he was questioned about the pending cases of "file clerks who were dismissed from the bureau because they were homosexuals." Responding to questions, Webster stated:

All of our employees at FBI headquarters have top secret clearance, and therefore presumably have access anywhere in the building, although we have internal restrictions that would protect the most sensitive material from any employee who just happened to come along. Law enforcement generally has been troubled by this problem. Tradition in law enforcement— and I've checked around all the different federal agencies and I know the posture in state and local law enforcement—has been that there is a potential for compromise for those who engage in such conduct which is generally not approved by society, and in some places, illegal. Now, we treat it as a factor, and I must say in candor, it's a significant factor. It's a troublesome thing; I hope that the particular case will be handled with fairness and justice and I hope that at some point we will have a better understanding of the problem and the policy that should be addressed to it.

Follow-up questioning by correspondent Fred Graham probed whether the Bureau disciplined employees for engaging in illicit opposite-sex relationships: "No," said Webster, "that's not the rule. We're trying to stay out of people's private lives unless their conduct, and the emphasis is always on conduct, not personal beliefs, impacts upon the effectiveness of that individual and the Bureau and the area in which—" "So an agent can live with a person of the opposite sex?" asked Graham. "Well, I don't have a policy for or against that conduct but how the Bureau is seen is important in our effectiveness." There was also the conflict revealed by Shea's affidavit, which indicated that when he consulted with the Administrative Division

about how to proceed on Ashton's case, he was told that the possible actions were "censure, censure and probation, or dismissal"—not that there was an absolute policy of dismissing all homosexuals.

The unanimous court of appeals panel issued its decision October 4, 1979, in an opinion by Judge McGowan, reversing the district court and remanding the case for proceedings on the merits. Although the court did not rule on the substantive constitutional questions surrounding the FBI's alleged "policy" on homosexuals, it did note the confusion and contradiction over what those policies were, as well as the stark contrast with a policy directive the Civil Service Commission had released in 1973, which the court quoted in full:

You may not find a person unsuitable for Federal employment merely because that person is a homosexual or has engaged in homosexual acts, nor may such exclusion be based on a conclusion that a homosexual person might bring the public service into public contempt. You are, however, permitted to dismiss a person or find him or her unsuitable for Federal employment where the evidence establishes that such person's homosexual conduct affects job fitness—excluding from such consideration, however, unsubstantiated conclusions concerning possible embarrassment to the Federal Service.

The clear implication of the remand was that the Bureau could not take action without developing some evidence that Ashton's conduct actually affected his ability to do the job.

In his argument to the court for Ashton, Rosenthal had stressed three grounds for challenging the Bureau's action: that it was arbitrary and capricious in violation of the Administrative Procedure Act, that it violated substantive constitutional protections against dismissal under the circumstances involved in the case, and that the FBI's own regulations, properly construed, did not extend to Ashton's dismissal. The court determined that the only issue it really had to decide at this point in the litigation was whether Ashton had a due process entitlement to a pretermination hearing, at which the other issues (and factual controversies) could be explored and resolved in the first instance. As to that issue, the court entertained few doubts that the combination of the handbook and

Ashton's circumstances sufficed to create such an entitlement.

Although the Bureau emphasized on appeal that it was exempt from the Civil Service rules that normally required pretermination hearings for nonprobationary employees, the court held that this was not determinative, since it was mandated by the *Perry v. Sindermann* precedent to look to the "rules or understandings" that define the terms of an individual's employment. "We are convinced," said McGowan, that the FBI has fostered rules and understandings that, by entitling appellant to believe that he would lose his job only for a job-related reason, gave him a property interest in his position such that he could be fired only under the procedural protections of the Due Process Clause." The basis for this conclusion included Ashton's initial appointment letter, indicating that his appointment was probationary for one year. From this, Ashton could reasonably deduce that after one year his status would change to nonprobationary, placing some sort of constraint on agency personnel actions. Further, the handbook's definition of "temporary indefinite" appointments made clear that "your position is secure, if you continue to do satisfactory work," and there was no allegation that Ashton's work had been unsatisfactory. Finally, all the provisions on which the Bureau relied for condemning Ashton's alleged "behavior" appeared to require some sort of link to job performance before conduct would provide a basis for discipline, and there had been no factual determination at any level, whether within the Bureau or before the district court, that Ashton's homosexuality had any relation to his job performance. "[A]ll the rules," wrote McGowan, may be seen as attempts to regulate job-related behavior and thus as giving employees no notice that they may be fired at will, without warning, for any or no reason." Quoting the U.S. Supreme Court's decision in *Board of Regents v. Roth* (1972), McGowan asserted that the Bureau had made to Ashton "a clearly implied promise of continued employment" which created a protected property interest in such continued employment.

Of course, the court was not in a position to resolve the factual controversies, such as whether Ashton resigned or was constructively discharged. Furthermore, it would be have been premature to decide the ultimate questions of substantive constitutional law regarding the permissibility of the FBI's asserted "absolute policy" of dismissing all homosexuals discovered in its ranks without proving some relation between their sexuality and their job performance. The court ordered that the case go back to the district court for further consistent proceedings. On January 4, 1980, the court denied the government's petition for rehearing.

Ashton v. Civiletti was an important assertion of the due process rights of gay employees at the nation's preeminent law enforcement agency. While the court did not decide whether the agency could maintain an "absolute policy" of removing all gay employees, it did raise doubts about the public statements that Director Webster had been making concerning the agency's policies, which became relevant in subsequent litigation and controversy about the Bureau's ability to recruit at the nation's leading law schools. Furthermore, the decision interpreted relatively innocuous statements in the FBI's handbook as binding the agency not to discharge nonprobationary employees without some plausible determination that their conduct negatively affected their ability to perform their assigned tasks and implicitly scolded the agency for apparently maintaining such a harsh and inflexible approach to homosexuality by comparison with the Civil Service Commission. (The opinion also gave passing notice to the situation in the armed forces, where the new, mandatory discharge regulations that were later adopted by the Reagan Administration were not yet on the horizon, and existing regulations had been interpreted by the D.C. Circuit in prior litigation to have a degree of discretionary flexibility in dealing with homosexuality that differed substantially from the FBI's articulated "absolute policy.") The *Ashton* decision also incidentally gave publicity and a permanent reference source for the otherwise not easily obtainable text of the Civil Service Commission's December 21, 1973 bulletin, announcing the government's new policy regarding homosexuality in federal employment.

Case References

Board of Regents v. Roth, 408 U.S. 564 (1972)
Perry v. Sindermann, 408 U.S. 593 (1972)

79. "WHICH RESTROOM SHOULD PLAINTIFF USE?"

Sommers v. Budget Marketing, Inc., 667 F.2d 748 (8th Cir. 1982). *Sommers v. Iowa Civil Rights Commission*, 337 N.W.2d 470 (Iowa 1983).

Few cases better illustrate the plight of transsexuals in an uncomprehending society than that of Audra Sommers, born Timothy Kevin Cornish, who lost a job over the issue of which restroom she could use at the office. Neither the federal nor Iowa state court judges who considered her case deemed it necessary to offer more than a superficial analysis of her legal claims.

Cornish, believing himself to be psychologically female, placed himself under the care of a physician for diagnosis and performance of sex-reassignment treatment, expected to culminate in sex-reassignment surgery. At the earliest stages, such treatment includes hormonal therapy to recast body shape and weight, and cross-dressing to simulate a female appearance and facilitate the transformation of sex and gender. On April 22, 1980, dressed and acting as a woman although not yet having undergone sex-reassignment surgery, Cornish began working as a clerical employee of Budget Marketing, Inc., in Polk County, Iowa, under the name Audra Sommers. After Sommers had worked without complaint about her performance for two days, she was recognized by an old acquaintance who also worked at Budget Marketing and her employment troubles began. Other women employed at the company complained that they did not want Sommers to use the women's restroom, and she insisted she would not use the men's room. The company discharged her the next day, April 25.

Sommers filed charges against the company with the Equal Employment Opportunity Commission (EEOC), alleging that her discharge violated Title VII of the Civil Rights Act of 1964, which forbids employment discrimination on the basis of sex. The EEOC provided no relief, but issued Sommers a letter authorizing suit in the federal district court. Represented by Des Moines attorneys Linda S. Pettit and Anthony J. Touschner, Sommers filed suit in the U.S. District Court for the Southern District of Iowa. Richard L. Pick, of Des Moines, filed a motion to dismiss for failure to state a claim or lack of subject matter jurisdiction on behalf of the company. Pick also requested in the alternative that Sommers provide a more definite statement as to the basis of her claim.

On January 20, 1981, Chief Judge William C. Stuart of the district court ordered Sommers to submit an amended complaint spelling out the basis of her claim in more detail. Stuart asked that Sommers specify whether she was claiming she had been discriminated against because she was male, female, or transsexual, and whether she had actually undergone sex-reassignment surgery. Sommers filed an amended complaint, claiming that she was discriminated against because she was a female person, that is, a woman with the anatomical body of a man, and revealing that she had not yet had surgery. In support of her claim, Sommers argued that the term "sex" in Title VII should be expansively interpreted to protect from discrimination someone who was anatomically male but psychologically female. Budget Marketing reaffirmed its motion to dismiss, introducing an affidavit by a physician stating that the medical profession regarded persons like Sommers to be males. Sommers countered the motion with affidavits from two physicians stating that the medical profession currently regarded persons like Sommers to be female.

Judge Stuart treated the motion to dismiss as a motion for summary judgment on the merits and granted the motion. Noting that at least one federal court had already refused to grant relief to a transsexual plaintiff under Title VII in *Voyles v. Ralph K. Davies Medical Center* (1975), Stuart agreed with that decision that "sex" could not be stretched to cover this situation:

> The plaintiff's own medical affidavit defines the condition of the plaintiff as one form of transsexualism. Irrespective of the plaintiff's manipulation of semantics, the Court finds no genuine issue of fact as to the plaintiff's sex at

the time of discharge from employment. Although the Court is aware of the plaintiff's personal dilemma, the Court does not believe that Congress intended by its laws prohibiting sex discrimination to require the courts to ignore anatomical classification and determine a person's sex according to the psychological makeup of that individual. The problems of such an approach are limitless. One example is the simple practical problem that arose here—which restroom should plaintiff use?

Plaintiff, for the purposes of Title VII, is male because she is an anatomical male. This fact is not disputed. As the Court accepts the biological fact as the basis for determining sex, the Court finds that entry of summary judgment is appropriate.

Sommers appealed to the U.S. Court of Appeals for the Eighth Circuit, where she found no more kindly a reception for her claim. The court unanimously ruled that Sommers was not protected from discharge by Title VII. The January 8, 1982, *per curiam* opinion rested solely on the lack of any legislative history supporting an expansive definition of "sex." That term had been added to Title VII by a floor amendment in the House of Representatives one day before the House passed the bill, without benefit of committee hearings and reports that might have provided some background on Congress's intent in adding it to the statute. However, said the court, it is "generally recognized that the major thrust of the 'sex' amendment was towards providing equal opportunities for women." Furthermore, attempts to amend Title VII to provide a more expansive definition by adding the term "sexual preference" had been unsuccessful. While the court recognized that Sommers's claim was not of sexual preference discrimination, the court believed that the lack of subsequent legislative amendment indicated Congress was content to give "sex" the narrow meaning of male or female. "Because Congress has not shown an intention to protect transsexuals, we hold that discrimination based on one's transsexualism does not fall within the protective purview of the Act."

In common with other courts that had considered the problem, the court expressed sympathy for Sommers's situation, but asserted that it was powerless to act. "According to affidavits submitted to the district court, even medical experts disagree as to whether Sommers is prop-

erly classified as male or female," the court commented. "Budget faces a problem in protecting the privacy interests of its female employees. . . . The appropriate remedy is not immediately apparent to this court. Should Budget allow Sommers to use the female restroom, the male restroom, or one for Sommers' own use?" The court suggested that "some reasonable accommodation" might be worked out by the parties, but that such an issue was not before the court. "Rather, the issue is whether Congress intended Title VII of the Civil Rights Act to protect transsexuals from discrimination," and the court found that Congress had no such intention.

Sommers had not put all her eggs in one basket, however, having also filed charges against Budget Marketing before the Iowa Civil Rights Commission. Unlike Title VII, the Iowa Civil Rights Act prohibited discrimination not just on the basis of sex but also on the basis of disability. After the Commission dismissed her initial complaint of sex discrimination, Sommers returned with a new complaint of disability discrimination, but the Commission refused to entertain the charge, asserting that "her file had been closed due to lack of jurisdiction." Sommers sought review of this ruling in the Polk County District Court, but Judge Richard Strickler denied review, upholding the Commission's decision that it lacked jurisdiction in her case. Sommers appealed to the Supreme Court of Iowa, where her attorneys, Pettit and Touschner, were opposed by Assistant Attorney General Scott H. Nichols for the Commission.

Writing for a unanimous court, Justice Louis W. Schultz announced on May 18, 1983, that dismissal of Sommers's claims was proper on both theories. Although recognizing that the Civil Rights Act was remedial legislation that should be given a broad, liberal interpretation to further its overall goal of eliminating unjustified employment discrimination, the court apparently could not bring itself to treat Sommers's claim seriously. Particularly ironic is the court's declaration that a transsexual is "a person with a serious problem of gender disorientation [which] often begins early in life and may be due to medical, in addition to psychological, disturbances," but that such a person was not a person with a "disability" for purposes of the Civil Rights Act. Indeed, the court seemed to have a reasonably sophisticated view of transsexuality:

> Transsexualism differs from homosexuality or transvestism. Homosexuals do not suffer from gender identity disturbances as do transsexuals and transvestites. Homosexuals accept their anatomical structure and the male or female role, except with regard to sexual preference. A transvestite represents a status between the homosexual and the transsexual and obtains satisfaction by dressing or masquerading in clothing of the opposite sex.

> It is generally agreed that transsexualism is irreversible and can only be treated with surgery to remove some of the transsexual feelings of psychological distress; psychotherapy is ineffective. Generally, the surgery involves sexual reassignment which involves removing the male sex organs and constructing female sex organs. It apparently has proven psychological, but not physical, benefits for its recipients.

Turning to the question whether Sommers might be protected by the ban on "sex" discrimination in Iowa law, Schultz noted that Strickler had found neither the plain meaning of the statute nor legislative intent to support Sommers's claim. Sommers had argued that transsexualism had "all the characteristics of the other impermissible classifications," and that because the legislature had not specifically stated that it was banning discrimination on the basis of "male or female sex" but rather had used the broad term "sex," it was possible to reach all sexually based forms of discrimination. Schultz rejected her argument, stating first that there was no specific mention of transsexuals in the law, and second that there was no basis in legislative intent for extending protection to transsexuals. He stated:

> As Sommers admits, the legislature's primary concern was a desire to place women on an equal footing with men in the workplace. We also believe that the legislature's purpose in banning discrimination based on sex was to prohibit conduct which, had the victim been a member of the opposite sex, would not have otherwise occurred.

Of course, had Sommers been born female, the employer's conduct that she attacked in this case "would not have otherwise occurred."

This was a case of first impression in Iowa, but there was adequate federal precedent for giving "sex" a narrow construction in the absence of legislative history indicating a contrary intent. In addition to *Voyles*, the Eighth Circuit had issued its decision upholding dismissal of Sommers's federal charges by the time the Iowa Supreme Court ruled. Given the administrative posture of the case, it was a simple matter for the court, without engaging in any more subtle analysis, to hold that the Commission's determination that it did not have jurisdiction "was not unreasonable, arbitrary, or capricious."

Turning to the disability claim, the court had a more difficult task, since it had seemed, in its initial discussion of transsexuality, virtually to concede that this was some form of impairment by labeling it a "disturbance" with "medical" and "psychological" roots. However, the court was unwilling to take the next step and recognize that the employment difficulties faced by people like Sommers brought her situation within the protection of the statute. Iowa had adopted a definition for its disability provision modeled on the statutory and regulatory framework of the federal Rehabilitation Act, defining disabilities as physical or mental impairments that limit one or more major life activities of an individual, and extending protection to those who suffer discrimination because they are "regarded as having such an impairment" even though they might not be actually impaired. The Iowa Civil Rights Commission, adopting regulations literally tracking the federal regulations, defined "major life activities" to include "working." Sommers argued that she was clearly covered by the statutory and regulatory frameworks. She had a condition that the court itself had seemed to describe as an impairment, either medical or mental, and that impairment was preventing her from working because of the attitudes of fellow employees and her employer.

Schultz rejected her claim. For one thing, he said, "a physical impairment relates to an organic disorder of the body. No claim is made that a transsexual has an abnormal or unhealthy body. The commission could reasonably conclude that under its rule Sommers had no physical impairment." As to the claim of mental impairment, Schultz pointed to the illustrative regulation, asserting that a "psychological disorder is a substantial handicap if it is a mental impairment 'such as mental retardation, organic brain syndrome, emotional or mental illness, and specific learning disabilities.'" To Schultz, Sommers's condition was nothing like those described in the regulation.

> A person who is anatomically of one sex but psychologically and emotionally of the other sex obviously has a grave problem, but that problem does not necessarily constitute the kind of mental condition that the legislature intended be treated as a substantial handicap to employment under the statute. The commission could reasonably conclude that to be covered the disorder must fall into the class of psychological disorders delineated in the rule.

For Schultz, the distinguishing factor between the "delineated" disorders and transsexuality was that they "are inherently likely to have a limiting effect on one or more major life activities," but that transsexuality did not have that inherent effect. While transsexuals might have problems due to the attitudes of others, this did not mean, according to Schultz, that "the condition meets the rule definition of impairment."

> The condition must independently come within the definition of impairment before attitudes of others can be said to make the condition a substantial handicap. Because transsexualism lacks the inherent propensity to limit major life activities of the listed examples of mental impairment, the commission could reasonably conclude it is not a mental impairment under the statute or rule.

Indeed, Schultz indicated that an "adverse societal attitude" toward transsexuals did not necessarily mean that they were perceived as having a "physical or mental impairment." They might face discrimination because they were considered "undesirable" rather than because they were considered "impaired." "While we do not approve of such discrimination," Schultz piously proclaimed, "we do not believe it is prohibited by the Iowa Civil Rights Act. The court is not a super-legislature, and we will not extend the provisions of the Act."

The Iowa Supreme Court's decision, based on such subtle distinctions, might make a logical case for not protecting transsexuals from discrimination on the basis of "sex" or "disability." But, in common with the Eighth Circuit, it seemed to overlook the broad remedial goals of civil rights law to end categorical discrimination that was unjustified. Although the state court did not seem to have the same preoccupation with toilets as the federal court, the result was the same. An individual's sexuality was the cause of the loss of her job, but the courts were unwilling to entertain the notion that this was precisely the type of discrimination that the legislatures were prohibiting when they included "sex" in their statutory schemes. The very notion that transsexuals are "undesirable" should not disqualify them from protection. After all, the other categories of discrimination (race or color, religion, national origin) were all included because various groups suffered discrimination due to their status as social "undesirables."

The antipathy of legislators for transsexuals argues even more strongly for the need to provide protection. When Congress passed the Americans With Disabilities Act in 1990, this antipathy was reflected in amendments to the original bill explicitly excluding from protection all transsexuals, transvestites, and homosexuals who might encounter discrimination due to their sexuality. While one might understand the fine logical distinctions drawn by Schultz and his colleagues on the Iowa Supreme Court to distinguish transsexuality from other "impairments" covered under disability law, it is difficult to understand the logic of passing civil rights laws to protect the disenfranchised and despised from discrimination, but specifically omitting protection for one of the of the most discriminated-against groups in American society.

Case Reference

Voyles v. Ralph K. Davies Medical Center, 403 F. Supp. 456 (N.D. Cal. 1975), affirmed without opinion, 570 F.2d 354 (9th Cir. 1978)

80. SAME-SEX HARASSMENT AND THE MALE EMPLOYEE

Joyner v. AAA Cooper Transportation, 597 F. Supp. 537 (M.D. Ala. 1983), affirmed without published opinion, 749 F.2d 732 (11th Cir. 1984); later opinion, 41 Fair Empl. Prac. Cas. (BNA) 492 (M.D. Ala. 1984). *Wright v. Methodist Youth Services*, 511 F. Supp. 307 (N.D. Ill. 1981). *Carreno v. Local Union No. 226*, 54 Fair Empl. Prac. Cas. (BNA) 81, 55 Empl. Prac. Dec. (CCH) para. 40,412 (D. Kan. 1990).

In 1986, the U.S. Supreme Court endorsed the trend of decisions in the lower federal courts concerning sexual harassment as a violation of the prohibition against employment discrimination on the basis of sex under Title VII of the Civil Rights Act of 1964. In *Meritor Savings Bank v. Vinson*, the Court found that both strands of sexual harassment theory—*quid pro quo* and hostile atmosphere—could be actionable under Title VII where it was established that a particular employee was adversely affected due to her sex. In his opinion for the Court, Justice William H. Rehnquist said, "Without question, when a supervisor sexually harasses a subordinate because of the subordinate's sex, that supervisor 'discriminates' on the basis of sex." Rejecting the defendant's argument that only harassment shown to have a tangible effect on an employee's terms and conditions of employment would violate Title VII, Rehnquist remarked that Title VII was not limited in its impact to "economic" or "tangible" discrimination, but extended to all "terms, conditions, or privileges of employment," and endorsed the Equal Employment Opportunity Commission's regulations on the subject, which provide that each employee is entitled to an environment free of hostility motivated by the employee's sex.

How might this theory translate when the employee is subjected to sexual harassment by a supervisor of the same sex, or subjected to a hostile atmosphere because he maintains a homosexual lifestyle? To date, no federal appeals court has published an opinion on the subject, but three district court decisions (one affirmed without opinion by an appellate court) suggest that the outcome would be different depending on which strand of sexual harassment theory was involved in the case.

In *Wright v. Methodist Youth Services* and *Joyner v. AAA Cooper Transportation*, federal trial judges ruled that *quid-pro-quo*-type sexual harassment, where an employee suffers adverse consequences after rejecting the sexual advances of a supervisor of the same sex, is actionable under Title VII. But in *Carreno v. Local Union No. 226*, the court rejected the argument that a hostile environment, including both verbal and physical harassment, violates Title VII when motivated by the employee's sexual orientation rather than his sex *per se*. (Early in 1992, the U.S. Court of Appeals for the Sixth Circuit took the same position as the *Carreno* court in *Dillon v. Frank*, an unofficially published decision.)

The earliest case, *Wright*, arose in 1979 when Donald Wright, a young man terminated as an employee of Methodist Youth Services (a nonprofit private agency providing social services to minors who are wards of the state of Illinois), filed charges with the Equal Employment Opportunity Commission (EEOC), alleging that his supervisor, Dale Hillerman, made sexual advances toward him. Wright claimed that he had rebuffed these overtures and been terminated as a consequence. After exhausting administrative remedies against Methodist Youth Services at the EEOC without result, Wright obtained a right-to-sue letter and filed suit in the U.S. District Court in Chicago represented by Chicago attorneys Ivan Rittenberg and Robert S. Harlib. The suit named as defendants Hillerman and another Methodist Youth Services employee, as well as Methodist Youth Services. In addition to alleging a violation of Title VII, Wright claimed that his discharge violated 42 U.S.C. sections 1983 and 1985, which prohibit unconstitutional discrimination under color of state law and provide remedies for governmental violation of constitutional rights. The defendants, who moved to dismiss the complaint for failure to state a claim, were represented by Chicago attorney Richard N. Janney.

For purposes of deciding the motion, District Judge Milton I. Shadur treated as true Wright's allegations of sexual harassment. He quickly disposed of the section 1983 and 1985 claims, holding that Methodist Youth Services, despite its close relationship with the state government and extensive state funding, was not itself a government actor or acting under color of state law with respect to Wright's allegations. Turning to the Title VII claim; however, Shadur found no problem in asserting jurisdiction. Although there was no direct precedent for holding that an employee discharged for refusing sexual advances from a same-sex supervisor had a right to assert a Title VII claim, Shadur said that "Title VII should clearly encompass it." At this time, the theory of sexual harassment under Title VII was just beginning to win acceptance in the lower federal courts. Shadur relied primarily on a 1977 decision by the U.S. Court of Appeals for the District of Columbia Circuit, *Barnes v. Costle*, which upheld the validity of a *quid pro quo* sexual harassment claim (i.e., that an employee was discharged unlawfully for rejecting the sexual advances of a supervisor). The *Barnes* court stated:

> It is no answer to say that a similar condition could be imposed on a male subordinate by a heterosexual female superior, or upon a subordinate of either gender by a homosexual superior of the same gender. In each instance, the legal problem would be identical to that confronting us now—the exaction of a condition which, but for his or her sex, the employee would not have faced.

However, Shadur found that Wright's failure to name Hillerman or the other defendant employee in his charges filed with the EEOC precluded him from suing them as individual defendants under Title VII, since exhaustion of administrative remedies against each named defendant was a jurisdictional prerequisite to such a suit. Consequently, Shadur dismissed Wright's lawsuit as against the individual defendants and ordered Methodist Youth Services to serve an answer to the complaint as the sole remaining defendant. There is no further reported opinion in the case, suggesting that the defendant probably settled the case before trial.

The *Joyner* case presented a more complicated factual situation. Timothy L. Joyner was employed as a shop mechanic by AAA Cooper Transportation, an interstate motor carrier, in March 1980, at $7.45 an hour. After working as a mechanic for some time at AAA's Montgomery, Alabama, terminal, Joyner applied for a transfer from shop mechanic to the employment classification of pick-up and delivery driver, which would involve loading and unloading trucks and making short-distance delivery runs in the Montgomery metropolitan area.

While his application for transfer was pending late in 1980, Joyner claimed that he was approached by the terminal manager at a local drive-in restaurant and invited to join the manager in his car. When Joyner got in the car, he claimed that the manager started to fondle him and asked him to have sex. Joyner claimed that he "emphatically refused to accede to the requests and left the automobile." Some time after this incident, Joyner encountered the chairman of the board of AAA, Earl Dove, who was visiting the Montgomery terminal, and, in response to Dove's question about how his work was going, told him of the incident with the terminal manager. Professing shock and disbelief, Dove promised to investigate the matter and, on returning to company headquarters in Dothan, Alabama, summoned the general manager of the company, William Buntin, and told Buntin the story. The terminal manager was contacted and denied that the incident had occurred. Buntin, who did not believe Joyner's charges, nevertheless told the terminal manager that such activity would be a serious violation of company policy and that he would be suspended pending investigation if any similar charges were made in the future. Buntin then called Joyner and told him the problem would not recur.

The terminal manager sought out Joyner, however, and told him that he had heard about Joyner's charges. Joyner concluded from the conversation that the manager would find some way to exact revenge against him. About a year later, Joyner was told that his transfer request had been approved. Joyner objected to the assistant terminal manager, Everett Norris, that now he did not want to transfer because he would have to work under the direct supervision of the terminal manager, who had it in for him. Nonetheless, Joyner was transferred on October 19, 1981. Under company rules, he went to the bottom of the seniority list for pick-up and delivery drivers, forfeiting his seniority from the mechanic list, but received a substantial hourly wage increase.

Joyner's work as a driver did not last long, since a general business slowdown reduced his hours in the first half of December and led to a layoff on December 18. Several other drivers with more seniority, as well as a less senior part-time man, were all laid off at the same time due to lack of available work. Under company rules, an employee lost "regular status" if he worked short hours or was on layoff status for six consecutive weeks. Joyner lost his regular status and was considered terminated effective January 29, 1982. After he was laid off on December 18, Joyner asked Norris whether he could have his old mechanic job back, but the job had been filled and, having forfeited his mechanic seniority as a result of the transfer, Joyner was not entitled to "bump" the new mechanic. Joyner called the terminal manager regularly to inquire about recall possibilities, but he was repeatedly told there was no work for him, even though other drivers had told Joyner that business was picking up, and some of the other laid-off drivers were recalled. Despite this, the terminal manager told Joyner that he could not come back to work and that the manager did not owe him "a damn thing." Joyner contacted Buntin at company headquarters and asked for employment as a line haul driver, but Buntin told him that he was not qualified for that work, based on his personnel records. Eventually, AAA recalled all the drivers who were laid off in December 1981 except Joyner, including the less senior part-time man, and even hired a new driver in March 1982 at a time when Joyner was still available and eager for recall.

Concluding that he was not recalled because of the terminal manager's personal grudge against him, Joyner found a job with another company and filed charges against AAA at the EEOC on April 28, 1982. The EEOC determined after investigation that there was no violation of Title VII, but issued Joyner the required right-to-sue letter. Joyner, represented by Montgomery attorneys L. Gilbert Kendrick and R.B. Moore, filed suit in the U.S. District Court for the Middle District of Alabama on December 20, 1982. The company was represented by Birmingham attorneys Peyton Lacy, Jr., and Harry L. Hopkins. District Judge Truman M. Hobbs conducted a nonjury trial on September 14, 1983, and issued his opinion finding for Joyner on November 18, 1983.

Perhaps the key testimony was provided by two other AAA employees, Danny Wyatt and Thomas Earl Hall, who both testified that the terminal manager had made sexual advances toward them. In light of that testimony, the company did not seriously contest Joyner's claim that he had also been the target of unwelcome sexual advances by the terminal manager. Rather, the company focused its case on attempting to show that Joyner's discharge resulted from an impartial application of seniority rules, having nothing to do with the sexual issue. Judge Hobbs agreed with this argument, but found that the failure to recall Joyner violated Title VII. He was a qualified short-haul driver with a good work record, ready and willing to be recalled when work picked up, but was bypassed in favor of a less senior man and a new employee. While it was true that his regular status had terminated on January 29, the company could not credibly rely on this technicality as a defense, since it had recalled all the other drivers except Joyner when work picked up, and the terminal manager's grudge against Joyner for rebuffing his advances, and, more seriously, for reporting the incident to higher management, provided the best credible explanation.

In the years since *Wright v. Methodist Youth Services* had been decided, the sexual harassment cause of action had grown in acceptance in the federal courts, and the EEOC had issued guidelines in 1982 recognizing this theory. "While the decisions holding that unwelcome sexual harassment violates Section 703 [Title VII's prohibition on sex discrimination] have dealt with harassment in the *heterosexual* context," said Hobbs, noting without discussion the *Wright* decision as an exception, "this Court determines that unwelcome *homosexual* harassment also states a violation of Title VII."

Relying on the recent decision by the U.S. Court of Appeals for the Eleventh Circuit in *Henson v. City of Dundee* (1982), Hobbs observed that the courts had approved two strands of sexual harassment theory: *quid pro quo* and hostile environment. Hobbs did not believe that the hostile environment theory applied to this case. There was only one incident of "unwelcome and unsolicited sexual harassment involving plaintiff," said Hobbs, so the court would consider only the *quid pro quo* theory. Joyner met all the requirements of establishing a *prima facie* case, said Hobbs.

> Unquestionably, plaintiff satisfied the first three elements; viz., he was a male, he was subjected to unwelcome sexual harassment, and since the evidence established the terminal manager's homosexual proclivities, the harassment to which plaintiff complained was based upon sex. The Court also finds that plaintiff satisfied the fourth element in that the evidence was sufficient to show that plaintiff's rejection of the homosexual overtures ultimately caused a tangible job detriment. Finally, employer liability by virtue of respondeat superior naturally follows from a finding that the other four elements are present.

Since Joyner had repeatedly requested recall after December 18, but was passed over for recall when business picked up while a part-time employee and a new employee were hired, and there was no evidence that these individuals were more qualified than Joyner, his burden of establishing a *prima facie* case of discrimination was easily met.

However, Hobbs also found that AAA had met its burden of showing a "legitimate, non-discriminatory reason" for failing to recall Joyner from layoff. That reason was that Joyner lost his employment status with the company pursuant to an objective company rule regarding number of hours worked. By failing to work the minimum number of specified hours for six consecutive weeks, Joyner, in common with more senior drivers, lost his employee status, and thus had no particular call on a job when business picked up. Conceding this was true, however, Hobbs further found that Joyner met his rebuttal burden of showing that this reason for failing to recall him was pretextual. In common with Joyner, the other drivers had also lost their regular employee status and had no par-ticular call on a job when business picked up, yet Joyner was the only one of the whole crew who was not rehired. Hobbs found no discriminatory intent on the part of the company when it rehired more senior drivers, but found that a violation did occur when the company rehired the less senior part-time man and the new employee in preference to Joyner. When this was coupled with evidence of the terminal manager's antagonistic attitude to Joyner, it became clear why he was not recalled. Hobbs stated:

> The Court finds that this refusal to recall plaintiff when a position became available on March 1, 1982, was contaminated by plaintiff's earlier refusal to succumb to the terminal manager's homosexual advances and by the terminal manager's anger at plaintiff's report of that incident to the president of the company. The terminal manager's homosexual overtures to plaintiff and his angry reaction to plaintiff's reporting the encounter were significant factors in the decision of the terminal manager not to recall plaintiff from layoff. In the view of the Court, plaintiff's bid to return to work would not have been rejected *but for* plaintiff's refusal to cooperate with the terminal manager's homosexual demands and his action of reporting the incident to Mr. Dove. In other words, in the Court's opinion there is a clear nexus between the rejection of the sexual harassment and the tangible job detriment.

So finding, Hobbs ruled that Joyner was entitled to reinstatement with back pay, in an amount reduced by his interim earnings at the other company. This came to a total of almost $5,000. The company appealed to the Eleventh Circuit, which heard oral argument on the appeal but affirmed Hobbs's ruling without publishing an opinion on December 4, 1984. Meanwhile, Hobbs had granted a petition for attorney's fees for Joyner's lawyers on the trial, which was later supplemented with an award of fees for the appeal work.

Taken together, the *Wright* and *Joyner* opinions provide solid precedent for the proposition that unwelcome sexual propositions in the workplace, regardless of the genders of the proposers and the recipients of those propositions, have no place and are actionable under Title VII. However, attempts to extend the other prong of the sexual harassment theory to a gay employee who suffered abuse because of his sexual orientation were unsuccessful.

J. Mario Carreno, a journeyman electrician and member of Local 226 of the International Brotherhood of Electrical Workers, divorced his wife and began to live as a gay man in a relationship with another man in 1980. Beginning in July 1986, Carreno began to experience harassment from fellow employees who had learned about his off-duty lifestyle. The incidents included verbal abuse for a period of a year while Carreno worked on various jobs obtained through the union's hiring hall. On October 20, 1987, Carreno was referred by the hiring hall to Shelley Electric Company, for work at a construction site in Fort Riley, Kansas. Carreno suffered continuous harassment from fellow employees, who used antigay slurs and even physically assaulted him. As the harassment mounted, Carreno could no longer function in the workplace and walked off the job on December 8, 1987. He called the union and asked that a grievance hearing be held on the failure of the company to do anything about the harassment, which he claimed was carried on openly while a supervisor looked on and did nothing to help him. The union refused to hold a hearing, despite repeated requests from Carreno. Carreno filed two separate complaints of discrimination with the Kansas Civil Rights Commission against the union, and finally filed suit against both Shelley Electric and the union under Title VII in the U.S. District Court, represented by Pantaleon Florez, Jr., alleging sexual harassment on the basis of sex in violation of Title VII. The union was defended by attorney Jerry R. Shelor of Topeka. William H. Dye, of Wichita, represented Shelley Electric. Both defendants moved for summary judgment, alleging that there were no material facts in dispute and that the harassment of Carreno was not actionable under Title VII. District Judge Dale E. Saffels agreed and dismissed the case on September 27, 1990.

Carreno emphasized in his complaint, and was very insistent about it, that he was charging discrimination on the basis of sex, not sexual orientation, but Saffels was not buying this argument. "The issue before the court," he said, "is whether a homosexual male may recover under Title VII of the Civil Rights Act of 1964 . . . and the Kansas Act Against Discrimination, for constructive discharge as a result of verbal and physical harassment directed at him by co-workers who disapprove of his homosexual lifestyle." Since Carreno was not asked for sexual favors, Saffels concluded that this was a "hostile and offensive working environment" case, and the issue under the established doctrines was whether Carreno suffered from this environment because of his sex. To Saffels, the answer was clearly negative.

> In this case, the harassment suffered by the plaintiff was not encountered because of his sex; rather this harassment was encountered because of his sexual preference. While the plaintiff has expressly stated that he is not asserting discrimination based on sexual preference, the undisputed facts indicate that the plaintiff was not harassed because he is a male, but rather because he is a homosexual male. Every derogatory comment made to the plaintiff related to his homosexuality.

Saffels noted that several courts of appeals, most notably the Ninth Circuit in *DeSantis v. Pacific Telephone & Telegraph Co.* (1979), had held that discrimination based on sexual preference was not covered by Title VII. He found the rationale of these cases (i.e., that Congress had no intention of adopting a broad definition of "sex" in Title VII) to be persuasive, given the lack of substantive legislative history and the unlikelihood that Congress in 1964 contemplated or intended adopting a national gay rights law. Saffels acknowledged the *Wright* and *Joyner* decisions, but found them to be irrelevant to Carreno's case, holding that the *quid pro quo* "paradigm" was distinguishable from the hostile environment "paradigm." Both defendants' motions to dismiss the case were granted.

In 1992, the Sixth Circuit quoted extensively from the *Carreno* decision in *Dillon v. Frank*, an unofficially published decision presenting quite similar facts. Although the court expressed sympathy for the plaintiff, it reiterated that Congress had no apparent intention to protect homosexuals from any form of workplace discrimination based on their sexual orientation. The court did suggest, however, that the harassment described in Dillon's complaint could provide grounds for a variety of state law tort actions, so the gay employee subjected to serious harassment that includes extreme cruelty and physical assaults is not without some recourse at law.

Thus, while employees appear to be protected by Title VII against *quid pro quo* sexual harassment of a homosexual nature, they may not be protected by Title VII against "hostile environment" harassment that arises because of antigay prejudice by fellow employees. Either way, the federal judiciary has ensured that the homosexual employee is without protection (unless, of course, the plaintiff in a *quid pro quo* case is a gay employee who is rejecting the sexual advances of a supervisor). The *Carreno* and *Dillon* cases provide additional evidence, if evidence be needed, that an amendment of Title VII to extend to sexual orientation discrimination would add an important element of protection for lesbian and gay employees, apart from issues of hiring, assignment, promotion, or discharge, since on-the-job harassment by antigay employees remains a major concern for those lesbian and gay people who decide not to remain in the closet at work.

Case References

Barnes v. Costle, 561 F.2d 983 (D.C. Cir. 1977)

DeSantis v. Pacific Telephone & Telegraph Co., 608 F.2d 327 (9th Cir. 1979)

Dillon v. Frank, 952 F.2d 403 (6th Cir. 1992) (table), unofficially reported at 58 Fair Empl. Prac. Dec. (BNA) 144, 58 Empl. Prac. Dec. para. 41,332

Henson v. City of Dundee, 682 F.2d 897 (11th Cir. 1982)

Meritor Savings Bank v. Vinson, 477 U.S. 57 (1986)

81. A TRANSSEXUAL AIRLINE PILOT FIGHTS FOR HER JOB

Ulane v. Eastern Airlines, Inc., 742 F.2d 1081 (7th Cir. 1984), certiorari denied, 471 U.S. 1017 (1985), reversing 581 F. Supp. 821 (N.D. Ill. 1984). Interim ruling on motion to dismiss unofficially reported at 28 Fair Empl. Prac. Cas. (BNA) 1438.

Kenneth Ulane joined the U.S. Army in 1964, earned his pilot's wings, and served as a fighter pilot until 1968. He successfully flew combat missions in the Vietnam War, earning the Air Medal with eight clusters. Honorably discharged in 1968, Ulane joined Eastern Airlines as a second officer, and over the next decade logged over 8,000 air hours as he progressed to first officer and also served as a flight instructor.

Ulane's record as a pilot was excellent on all counts, but he felt that something was wrong. Since childhood, Ulane had felt uncomfortable in his own body, believing that his physical gender was out of sync with his emotional identity. This disjunction never affected his work, and nobody around him suspected any problem. He did not behave in an effeminate manner or express any unusual stress on the job, but by the late 1960s Ulane found the situation intolerable and sought professional help. While still in the Army, he sought psychiatric and medical assistance for this problem, but was unable to persuade the relevant medical authorities to approve a sex change procedure for him. Ulane struggled in therapy seeking some solution to his psychological difficulties. He went through two marriages and had children, but things just did not somehow seem right. Finally, early in 1979, while a patient of one Dr. Berger, Ulane was diagnosed as a transsexual, and he was able to convince his physicians to initiate the procedures for a sex change.

The normal procedure for a transsexual who desires a sex change is a course of hormonal therapy and some time spent living as a woman prior to the actual operation so that the individual can be as sure as possible that the sex change is the right thing for him to do. Because he feared that he would lose his job with Eastern if he reported for work dressed as a woman, Ulane confined his preparatory cross-dressing to off-duty times and did his best to conceal the physical changes resulting from his hormonal therapy from his superiors and co-workers. This took a great effort of will, and Ulane was unable to spend the full time period that would normally be required carrying on this deception. He was able to convince the Gender Identity Board at the University of Chicago Medical School that he should be allowed to undergo the sex change operation, and the remainder of the procedure was performed during 1980.

Ulane's deception had been most successful. Eastern Airlines officials were astonished when Ulane, who had obtained a new birth certificate from the state of Illinois identifying himself as female and changed his name legally to Karen Ulane, reported for work and sought reinstatement as a pilot. Ulane, anticipating problems, had approached the Federal Aviation Administration (FAA), presented it with his sex change situation, and obtained a new flight license in the name of Karen Ulane. Since it had no prior experience with sex change operations, the FAA issued Ulane a conditional medical certificate, pending further developments, which was later upgraded to an unconditional certificate.

Eastern's response to Ulane's request to resume his work was immediately negative. Eastern officials immediately involved their legal department, which anticipated possible litigation and attempted to frame a plausible basis for Ulane's discharge in a detailed letter released to Ulane on April 24, 1981. Eastern asserted in the letter that continued employment of Ulane as a pilot was inconsistent with the safety considerations underlying Eastern's "coordinated crew concept"; that the first-class medical certificate issued to Ulane by the FAA was conditional; that the sex change surgery, which was "unproven" and "experimental," had not solved Ulane's "underlying psychological problem;" that Ulane's continued presence in the cockpit would counteract Eastern's efforts to assure the public of the safety of airline travel; and, finally, that if the sex change operation had been successful in changing Ulane from a male to a female, it had "changed [him] from the person Eastern has hired into a different person. Eastern would not have hired [him] had it known [he] contemplated or might in the future contemplate such an action." The letter concluded that each of the stated grounds for discharge "represents an independent ground."

Ulane filed suit in federal district court in Chicago, alleging that his discharge violated Title VII of the Civil Rights Act of 1964 and other federal statutes (including the post-Civil War Civil Rights Acts and the Railway Labor Act, which governs airline labor relations) and state common-law doctrines governing defamation and intentional or reckless infliction of emotional and mental distress. Ulane also sought relief through arbitration unsuccessfully. Ulane was represented by Dean Dickie, Brian D. Roche, and Fay Clayton, of the Chicago firm of Sachnoff, Weaver & Rubenstein. Eastern retained Chicago attorney Catherine Tinker, of Conlin & Adler, as local counsel, with the litigation being directed by Eastern's regular Atlanta counsel, David M. Brown, of Gambell & Russell.

Eastern responded to the filing of the lawsuit with a second letter to Ulane, dated March 25, 1982, asserting as additional grounds for the discharge that Ulane had failed to disclose to the company the medication and the psychiatric and medical treatment she had been receiving over the past several years, showing "a gross disregard for the safety of . . . fellow employees and the public at large and a consistent lack of sound judgment." It also asserted that Ulane had failed to reveal the full scope of medications and psychiatric treatments to the FAA in the certificate she submitted for medical certification, again showing "a consistent pattern of poor judgment and willingness to endanger . . . fellow crew members and passengers for [his] own benefit." Eastern also charged in this letter that Ulane had instigated publicity accompanying the filing of the lawsuit that was designed to embarrass Eastern Airlines, and that "this notoriety would undermine Eastern's efforts to reassure passengers of the safety of airline transportation."

Ulane's case was assigned to District Court Judge John F. Grady, Jr. Eastern promptly moved to dismiss the first two counts of the lawsuit under Title VII, which alleged that Ulane was discriminated against on the basis of sex as a female in Count I and as a transsexual in Count II. Ruling orally on the motion, Judge Grady refused to dismiss it. Admitting that he really did not understand much about transsexuality at this early stage of the proceedings, Grady insisted that despite the accumulating case law in the lower federal courts holding that discrimination against transsexuals was not covered by Title VII, there was no binding precedent in the U.S. Court of Appeals for the Seventh Circuit. "What does seem to me apparent," he said, "is that there is no way out of the conclusion that whatever the physiology may be, it has something to do with sex as that term is constantly understood."

The trial before Grady was a battle of the experts. In the end, Grady was more persuaded by Ulane's experts and physician (who was called as a witness by Eastern but whose testimony overall favored Ulane's case) than by Eastern's experts, who expressed total hostility to transsexuals and total disagreement with the accumulating literature on transsexuality. According to Grady, the key issues in trying the first two Counts (which were all he intended to try at the initial stage of the litigation) were whether Ulane was now a woman who had suffered discrimination on account of sex, and whether discrimination on account of transsexuality was a violation of Title VII.

Grady gave an extended decision from the bench on December 28, 1983, finding that Ulane was a transsexual, that she had been discharged for being a transsexual, and that the discharge violated Title VII, but expressing some reservation as to whether the record would support a finding that Ulane was now a woman who had suffered from sex discrimination on that basis. However, given the state of the case law and the possibility that the court of appeals would reverse his determination under Count II for lack of jurisdiction, Grady indicated he would grant judgment for plaintiff on both Counts I and II, ordering reinstatement with full seniority, benefits, back pay, and reasonable attorney's fees, and certifying the judgment under Rule 54(b) of the Federal Rules of Civil Procedure so that Eastern could appeal the judgment while the other counts of Ulane's complaint remained in abeyance.

Grady's extended comments of December 28, edited for grammar and continuity, are published in *Federal Supplement* and provide entertaining and enlightening reading, for they show how a judge's thinking on a matter can be utterly transformed by the process of hearing witnesses and giving deep study and consideration to a case presenting novel issues. Grady

takes on each ground of defense asserted in Eastern's two letters to Ulane and demolishes each one, as well as refuting the existing case law withholding the protection of Title VII from transsexuals.

Grady began with a discussion of the jurisdictional issue. He started by noting that the case law cited to him focused primarily on homosexuality and transvestism, and insisted that it was irrelevant for that reason.

> There is in the record before us evidence which makes quite clear that there is a distinction between homosexuals and transvestites on the one hand and transsexuals on the other. Homosexuals and transvestites are not persons who have sexual identity problems. They are content with the sex into which they were born. Transsexuals, on the other hand, are persons with a problem relating to their very sexual identity as a man or a woman. I believe on that basis the situation of a homosexual is distinguishable.

Conceding that Title VII was "not intended and cannot reasonably be argued to have been intended to cover the matter of sexual preference, the preference of a sexual partner, or the matter of sexual gratification from wearing the clothes of the oppositive sex," Grady asserted that it was "an altogether different question" whether the issue of "sexual identity" was covered by the law.

> Prior to my participation in this case, I would have had no doubt that the question of sex was a very straightforward matter of whether you are male or female. That there could be any doubt about that question had simply never occurred to me. I had never been exposed to the arguments or to the problem. After listening to the evidence in this case, it is clear to me that there is no settled definition in the medical community as to what we mean by sex.

Adverting to *Carrillo v. Illinois Bell Telephone Co.* (1982), in which the issue was whether discrimination against a Hispanic person was race discrimination within the meaning of 42 U.S.C. section 1981, a post-Civil War statute making race discrimination a federal offense for which compensatory and punitive damages were awardable to the discriminatee, Grady insisted that the disputes over that issue were "illustrative of the fact that the things we think we know we do not necessarily know and that people sometimes react to other people according to stereotypes, misperceptions, and other motivations which are arguably discriminatory and are arguably redressable under statutes which might not be thought ordinarily to apply to those situations."

Rejecting the testimony of one expert, Dr. Wise, that sexual identity was entirely a matter of chromosomes and that Ulane was "beyond a shadow of a doubt a transvestite" because the whole idea of transsexuals was incorrect, Grady commented that "I have never heard an expert witness state that he was sure of anything beyond a shadow of a doubt." Consequently, he placed no weight on Wise's testimony, stating that he "would be inclined to believe that the opposite of anything he testified to would be more probably true than not true." Grady found by the greater weight of the evidence that "sex is not a cut-and-dried matter of chromosomes, and that while there may be some argument about the matter in the medical community, the evidence in this record satisfies me that the term, 'sex,' as used in any scientific sense and as used in the statute can be and should be reasonably interpreted to include among its denotations the question of sexual identity." Thus, he held that Title VII would forbid discrimination on the basis of sexual identity against transsexuals. While the legislative history of Title VII was devoid of any discussion by Congress as to the meaning of "sex" as used in the statute, Grady believed that it was appropriate to give the word a meaning consistent with the weight of current medical opinion.

Eastern argued that Ulane was not really a transsexual, since it presented experts who disputed the whole existence of the phenomenon of transsexuality. In essence, Eastern's experts argued, Ulane was a transvestite who sought to enhance her sexual gratification by shedding the outward, physical manifestation of the male sex, but that the whole thing was a psychological delusion or a deliberate deception. Grady totally rejected this argument, noting that the third edition of the *Diagnostic and Statistical Manual*, then in use by the psychiatric profession, clearly provided definitional recognition of transsexuality, and that the unanimous decision of the Gender Identity Board at the University of Chicago Medical School constituted

suitably "prestigious auspices" on which to base a finding that Ulane was, indeed, a transsexual. Grady found it incredible to assert that somebody with Ulane's history, an airline pilot who had been through two unsuccessful marriages and had spent more than a decade struggling with sexual identity while urgently seeking a sex change procedure, was anything other than totally serious in believing she was a transsexual and seeking out and submitting to these procedures. Furthermore, Eastern's arguments about Ulane's judgment in keeping the situation secret from the company were totally mistaken; Ulane had shown excellent understanding of the situation, since she correctly predicted how Eastern would react if it knew what was going on, and since, by the great weight of the expert testimony, the therapy she was receiving bore no relevance to her continued competence to serve safely as an airline pilot. Grady was unpersuaded by Eastern's argument that Ulane had not gone through the full year or two of "life experience" as a female prior to the surgery and thus was clearly faking things:

> It seems to me that one of the many unreasonable positions Eastern takes in this case is that plaintiff did not try to live as a woman in her job. She had been fired from her job just as soon as she had surgery. Apparently Eastern would have me believe that if Ken Ulane had shown up for work in a dress and boarded the plane that there would have been no problem at Eastern. Now, if Eastern means, well, she should have done it in some other job, she did do it in whatever other job she could find. How much that proved I do not know because it was not the job that she hopes to regain. Where she could have found a job as an airline pilot cross-dressing as a woman and maintain that job for a period of a year is something which leaves me totally mystified.

Pointing to Ulane's experience for the three years after the operation, Grady observed that she seemed to have made a good adjustment to living as a woman. While she was not currently flying airplanes, "Eastern will not let her fly an air liner, nor will anybody else in the present circumstance." Summarizing the evidence about Ulane's appearance and manner as observed in the courtroom and by various witnesses, he indicated that she gave every appearance of being a woman. "It would take an extremely practiced eye, it seems to me, to detect any difference between the plaintiff and the biological woman. My observation of her in this courtroom and on the witness stand leads me to concur with those witnesses who have said that she appears to be a biological woman."

On the question whether Ulane was discharged because of transsexuality, Grady concluded that this was obvious. There had never been any criticism of Ulane's performance before Eastern learned about the sex change operation, and Eastern made no pretense that the discharge was for any other reason. Unlike the usual run of Title VII cases, where defendants asserted a wide array of reasons having nothing to do with the basis for discharge asserted in the plaintiff's complaint, in this case Eastern's conduct left no doubt.

Having found all the requisites for a *prima facie* case under Title VII, Grady proceeded to deal methodically with the defenses Eastern articulated in its letters to Ulane and disposed of all of them. He concluded that the assertions about lack of judgment, safety concerns, and the impact on the public were all unavailing. Grady asserted that Ulane had been astute in realizing that she must not let Eastern know what was going on until the sex change had occurred, and that she had taken all proper steps to assure herself that her situation presented no safety issues. Grady observed that it was well established under Title VII that the preferences of customers and co-workers could not be used as a basis for discriminating, reciting the cases in which employers asserted that blacks or women could not perform certain jobs because of anticipated rejection by customers. Grady noted that the conditional medical certificate issued to Ulane by the FAA after her operation was no different from the conditional medical certificate issued to pilots with alcoholism problems who have emerged from rehabilitation programs, which Eastern normally accepted as a suitable basis for returning those pilots to the cockpit. To Eastern's contention that the surgery had not resolved the "underlying psychological problem," Grady retorted that the surgery was not intended to solve that "problem," but rather to alleviate its symptoms by conforming the plaintiff's appearance to her inner perceived identity. Ulane had presented no

safety problems prior to his operation, while operating Eastern's planes for twelve years as a person disturbed about personal sexual identity. Surely, now that the surgery had taken place and she could live in a way that was consonant with that identity, her psychological situation would present less basis, not more, for being concerned about safety.

At bottom, Grady concluded, Eastern's main concern in the case was with public relations and personnel problems with other pilots who were prejudiced against Ulane. This was not a valid basis for defending a Title VII lawsuit. "Now, why was the plaintiff really fired?" Grady asked. "What was the real reason?

> I conclude from the evidence I have heard in this case that Eastern thought it had a real image problem: A transsexual in the cockpit. How is that for you? What are we going to do about that? The public will not accept it. We will be the laughing stock of the airline industry. We have got to do something about it. Without giving it very much mature thought, Eastern went into action to sever itself from this problem. It probably thought this was the way to solve it, but they took the wrong course in my view. The legal department did the directing, and the medical department did the casting and provided the props. There has been some testimony about the plaintiff's facade and her dissembling, her manipulation. I find that the real facade and the real dissembling and the real manipulation has been on the part of Eastern Airlines.

Having become well-versed in the difficulties and misunderstandings transsexuals encounter in everyday life, Grady had been convinced that this form of mistreatment was totally unjustified. His opinion at times reads as a diatribe against Eastern for reacting to the situation out of prejudice and ignorance rather than taking the time, as Grady had done, to learn about transsexuality and make informed judgments accordingly. Grady concluded that all of Eastern's articulated defenses were unreasoning, unjustified by the evidence, and in the end pretextual, since public relations was consistently the concern underlying all of them. Grady was particularly scornful of Eastern's position that the discharge was justified by Ulane's failure to disclose her medication and psychiatric counseling on her application to the FAA for medical certification. "If Eastern Airlines decides to fire pilots who are untruthful concerning relevant medical information on their FAA applications, it must fire them without regard to sex," he stated. "It did not do so in the case of male pilots." There was testimony concerning a male pilot who had failed to disclose medical information on an FAA application, but Eastern took no action against that pilot.

Grady seemed particularly incensed by Eastern's argument that Ulane had deliberately generated negative publicity for the airline after filing suit. He noted that the filing of a lawsuit is a public matter, and that the media coverage that flowed from that was natural. Grady had read the newspaper articles and viewed recordings of the television programs, and he concluded that Ulane conducted herself with dignity, responded truthfully to questions, and did not venture in her comments beyond factual assertions. Grady noted that Eastern had taken no action against an Eastern pilot who appeared in *Playboy Magazine* with a nude photograph of his wife, and that Eastern had failed to present anything other than wild speculation that employment of Ulane as a pilot would have a negative impact on Eastern or on airline passengers' perceptions about airline safety.

Although Grady entered judgment for Ulane on both Counts I and II, Ulane's attorneys were concerned that his concluding remarks that Ulane had made out the better case under Count I, alleging discrimination as a transsexual, left them vulnerable to misunderstanding on appeal. They applied to Grady for a clarification on the record that he also had found Ulane to have suffered discrimination as a woman. On February 8, 1984, Grady issued a brief memorandum, citing cases and law review articles to support his statement that "plaintiff may have made an equally good case on Count I. . . . She has prevailed on her Title VII claim and should not be burdened with having to appeal the rejection of an alternative theory to support the relief granted," he concluded, entering judgment on both counts.

Ulane's attorneys were still not satisfied, fearing that neither the oral opinion from the bench nor the brief memorandum had laid an adequate basis in factual findings to defend Grady's judgment, so they applied for further clarification, which came in another memoran-

dum of supplemental findings issued March 6. Insisting that he had clearly found for plaintiff on both counts, Grady added, "As an alternative to my finding that plaintiff is a transsexual, I find that plaintiff's post-operative legal status is that of a female. If on the evidence presented in this case the choices were limited to male or female, I would and do find that the evidence clearly predominates in favor of the conclusion that plaintiff is a female, not a male." Grady concluded summarily that all the evidence supporting his judgment on Count I also supported his judgment on Count II.

The Seventh Circuit heard argument on Eastern's appeal, certified under Rule 54(b), on June 5, 1984, from Brown for Eastern and Dickie for Ulane. The three-judge panel issued its unanimous decision reversing the district court in an opinion by Circuit Judge Harlington Wood, Jr., on August 29. Claiming that "we do not condone discrimination in any form," Wood insisted that the holding on Count II must be reversed because "Title VII does not protect transsexuals." Rejecting Grady's assertion that "sexual identity" could reasonably be construed as comprehended within the term "sex" found in Title VII, Wood insisted that the lack of any legislative history or definitional discussion by Congress about the meaning of sex meant that the courts must give that term the narrowest, most commonplace and everyday meaning. "While we recognize distinctions among homosexuals, transvestites, and transsexuals, we believe that the same reasons for holding that the first two groups do not enjoy Title VII coverage apply with equal force to deny protection for transsexuals."

The court asserted that the lack of discussion by Congress "clearly indicates that Congress never considered nor intended that this 1964 legislation apply to anything other than the traditional concept of sex." If Congress had intended a broader meaning, insisted Wood, the idea of protecting homosexuals and the like "would no doubt have sparked an interesting debate." Furthermore, subsequent attempts to amend Title VII to extend protection on the basis of "affectational or sexual orientation" had been unavailing, which indicated to Wood that Congress preferred to retain a narrow prohibition under Title VII. Wood observed that Congress had failed to act in the face of a rapidly accumulating body of cases in the lower federal courts according such a narrow meaning to "sex" under Title VII. For the court to adopt a broader meaning would be judicial legislation, beyond the proper rule of the courts. Expert medical testimony was not a basis for usurping Congress's prerogative to make the policy decision whether Title VII should be expanded to protect additional groups.

As to the ruling on Count I, Wood found Grady's supplemental memorandum insufficient to support his finding that Ulane was a woman who had suffered discrimination on that basis. According to Wood, "the district judge's previous findings all centered around his conclusion that Eastern did not want '[a] *transsexual* in the cockpit (emphasis added).'

> Ulane is entitled to any personal belief about her sexual identity she desires. After the surgery, hormones, appearance changes, and a new Illinois birth certificate and FAA pilot's certification, it may be that society, as the trial judge found, considers Ulane to be female. But even if one believes that a woman can be so easily created from what remains of a man, that does not decide this case. If Eastern had considered Ulane to be female and had discriminated against her because she was female (i.e., Eastern treated females less favorably than males), then the argument might be made that Title VII applied . . . but that is not this case.

It was clear to Wood that Eastern discriminated against Ulane solely because she was a transsexual. Thus, the court entered judgment for Eastern on Count I, and dismissed Count II as being without jurisdictional basis. Ulane petitioned the court for rehearing and rehearing *en banc*, but both petitions were denied on November 16, and the following year the U.S. Supreme Court denied her petition for *certiorari*.

Ulane's case is one of many in which the federal courts have held that transsexuals are not protected from discrimination under Title VII. It is a particularly frustrating case to consider, because it seems clear that the trial judge made an extraordinary and successful effort to understand the intricacies of the issue, but the court of appeals was not willing to make a simi-

lar effort. While the court of appeals was correct in its conclusion that the weight of twenty years of adverse precedent provided little direct basis for recognizing Title VII protection for transsexuals as such, it was inappropriate for the appellate court to have totally rejected Judge Grady's conclusion, based on hearing extensive expert testimony and reviewing numerous authorities, that Ulane had successfully become a woman and encountered discrimination on that basis as alleged in Count I of her complaint.

Grady's opinion noted the disparate treatment of Ulane and male pilots in a number of instances. Had the court of appeals taken Ulane's case seriously, rather than in the jaunty or light-hearted manner indicated by some of its language, it would have remanded the matter for further findings on the claim that Ulane had suffered discrimination because she had become a woman. Certainly, the scarcity of women as pilots on major airlines would provide the statistical underpinnings for the claim that gender-based prejudice exists in the industry. Women with pilot licenses from the FAA have been largely confined to flying smaller commuter aircraft and have made little progress in winning positions with the major airlines.

The main problem Ulane's case illustrates, however, is the failure of the federal appellate courts to take seriously the discrimination and misunderstanding transsexuals suffer. While the U.S. Supreme Court's more recent opinion in *Price Waterhouse v. Hopkins* (1989), holding that discrimination on the basis of sexual stereotyping is actionable under Title VII, may provide some hope for more receptivity by the federal courts for such claims, Congress's action in 1990 specifically exempting transsexuals, transvestites, and homosexuals from protection under the newly enacted Americans With Disabilities Act might well persuade the courts that Congress has no intention of throwing the weight of federal protection behind sexual minorities.

Case References

Carrillo v. Illinois Bell Telephone Co., 538 F. Supp. 793 (N.D. Ill. 1982)

Price Waterhouse v. Hopkins, 490 U.S. 228 (1989)

82. PRIVILEGED DISCRIMINATION OR COMMON-LAW RIGHT?

Madsen v. Erwin, 395 Mass. 715, 481 N.E.2d 1160 (1985).

The United States is a religiously pluralistic society, with a long tradition of steering clear of governmental intervention in religious matters. One important aspect of this tradition is the wide leeway accorded religious institutions in their personnel practices as a matter of interpretation of the First Amendment protection for "free exercise" of religion. This situation has proved frustrating to sexual minorities who experience discrimination at the hands of religious authorities and discover that their attempts to invoke legal process are defeated by the qualified immunity from suit enjoyed by religious bodies. The situation is particularly frustrating when the employer's claim to religious status is made in the context of an apparently secular business activity. Such was the case when *The Christian Science Monitor* (a general circulation newspaper of international reputation published under the auspices of the First Church of Christ, Scientist, in Boston) dismissed a star sports reporter, Christine Madsen, when it discovered that she was a lesbian.

The *Monitor* is published under the direct supervision of the Christian Science Church, which controls its hiring and personnel policies. All those employed at the newspaper are required to be members in good standing of the Church and are considered its employees by the Church, down to the requirement that they wear Church employee identification badges while in the newspaper's offices. As such, the Church consistently took the position that it could discharge employees who failed to carry out their lives in accord with the precepts of Christian Science religious teachings.

Madsen began working for the *Monitor* as a "copygirl" in June 1974. She received numerous promotions and salary increases as she advanced into the ranks of *Monitor* reporters. Madsen developed a specialty writing about women's sports activities, and in 1982 was awarded first place honors in the best sportswriter category of the New England Women's Press Association for a four-part series entitled "Women in Sports" that appeared in the *Monitor* in May 1981. Madsen did not write about religious or moral topics.

Early in December 1981, *Monitor* officials began to hear rumors that Madsen had either asked a manager's wife to attend a lesbian meeting or had enticed a manager's wife into a lesbian relationship. Among those discussing the rumors with each other were Earl W. Foell, the editor; Pamela O. Marsh, the quality control editor; and J. Anthony Periton, manager of the Christian Science Publishing Society, which publishes the newspaper. On December 14, Marsh approached Madsen to discuss the rumor. Madsen denied the rumor, but told Marsh that she was a lesbian. Marsh indicated she would have to report this to the editor, who had been asked to check out the rumors by the publisher. Marsh and Madsen discussed the situation the next day, when Marsh relayed to Madsen that complaints had been received from other editors about rumors suggesting Madsen was gay or had entered into a homosexual marriage with another woman. Again, Madsen denied the specific rumors about her conduct, while admitting that she was gay.

Madsen's sexual orientation and behavior were the subject of a meeting on December 16 of Foell, Periton, and Marsh. At that meeting, Periton stated that he would have to find out if Madsen went to gay meetings, since that would indicate whether she was gay. Madsen later complained that about this time she had the feeling she was being followed. On December 18, Madsen met with Periton and complained about what had been happening. Periton repeated the various rumors to Madsen, who refused to discuss their substance. When Periton demanded to know whether the rumors were accurate, Madsen again denied rumors about her behavior (including the story, evidently becoming widespread among *Monitor* staff, that she had tried to seduce a manager's wife), but confirmed that she was gay. Periton thanked Madsen for being honest and told her that it was Church policy to "let the employee go in cases like this." On December 23, Periton gave Madsen a booklet published by the Church titled *Morals of Today*, and asked Madsen to "heal herself" of homosexuality so that she could continue working for the *Monitor*. Madsen refused, and Periton told her that he would have to bring the matter to the attention of the Church's personnel manager, Warren D. Silvernail.

On December 29, Madsen met with Karen Gould, the Church's employee relations manager who dealt with "employee problems." Gould again recited all the rumors about Madsen, which Madsen denied. Gould indicated that it was Madsen's sexual orientation, not the rumors, that were the cause of the "problem." Gould asked Madsen if she was "seeking healing" to end her homosexuality. Madsen replied that she was not. Gould then gave Madsen an ultimatum: if she did not resign her job by December 31, she would be discharged for "religious differences." Madsen's boss, Special Sections Editor Curtis J. Sitomer, who wanted to keep her on the staff, told Madsen he would talk to Gould about arranging a leave of absence to straighten things out, but Gould insisted that a leave of absence would be possible only if it was expressly for the purpose of Madsen seeking healing to cure herself of homosexuality. When Madsen was unwilling to undertake such action, Gould told Madsen on January 4 that she was discharged immediately and would be sent her severance and accrued vacation pay. Gould put a memorandum in Madsen's personnel file, stating that she was "not recommended for rehire unless a radical change in views on homosexuality takes place."

Madsen went to activist attorney Katherine Triantafillou, of Boston, for legal representation. Triantafillou confronted a difficult legal problem. At that time, neither Boston nor the state of Massachusetts had any legislation expressly prohibiting employment discrimination on the basis of sexual orientation (although both the city and state would subsequently enact such laws, too late to benefit Madsen). Furthermore, although the Massachusetts courts had recognized some exceptions to the common-law presumption of employment at will, under which

an employer was immune from suit for discharging an employee in the absence of express statutory prohibitions, those exceptions were limited in ways that made it unlikely that a "wrongful discharge" claim could be made out. Massachusetts did have theoretically strong statutory protections for employee privacy, although they had not been much interpreted by the courts. Triantafillou used her imagination and constructed a catch-all legal complaint that asserted almost every conceivable constitutional, statutory, and common-law argument, hoping that at least some of these arguments would withstand the inevitable motion to dismiss the litigation. As filed in the Massachusetts Superior Court, Suffolk County, the complaint alleged violations of the federal and state constitutions, Massachusetts civil rights statutes, and the state privacy statute. It also asserted common-law claims of wrongful discharge, defamation, intentional infliction of emotional distress, sexual and affectional preference discrimination, and "breach of fiduciary responsibilities under deeds of trust," a claim specifically asserted against the trustees of the Church. The Church's attorney, Theodore E. Dinsmoor, filed a motion to dismiss, which was denied on all counts by Superior Court Judge George N. Asack without any written or oral explanation.

The Church appealed to the Massachusetts Supreme Judicial Court, arguing that its First Amendment free exercise rights would be irreparably impaired by having to litigate the case at trial. It secured a hearing from the court, with oral argument held on October 4, 1984. The court struggled for more than ten months with the complicated and imaginative legal theories Triantafillou had presented, announcing its decision on August 21, 1985. In an opinion focusing mainly on the Church's First Amendment claims, Justice Joseph R. Nolan held that summary judgment should be granted on the constitutional, statutory, and contractual claims, and dismissal for failure to state a claim should be granted without prejudice on the torts claims, with leave to replead them. Justice Francis P. O'Connor partially dissented, asserting that the court had improperly reached the First Amendment issues inasmuch as, in his view, Madsen as an at-will employee had stated no legal basis for contesting her discharge, making the First

Amendment analysis (with which he had some problems) irrelevant.

Nolan turned first to the most disputed issue in the case: was the *Christian Science Monitor* a "religious activity of the Christian Science Church," such that its personnel policies were shielded from judicial review by the First Amendment's Free Exercise Clause. Madsen had introduced an affidavit from a friend who had received a direct mail subscription solicitation from the *Monitor*, in which the newspaper was described as "not a church organ, . . . but rather an international daily newspaper that touches on all the vital issues of the day." Nolan considered this hearsay and not sufficient to overcome the many indicia of how closely intertwined were the Church and the newspaper. Silvernail had filed an affidavit stating that the Church's personnel office was "in charge of the personnel functions at the Church and its religious activities including The Christian Science Publishing Society which publishes the *Christian Science Monitor*." Silvernail asserted that a memorandum regarding Christian Science principles of sexual morality had been distributed to the staff of the newspaper, and that staff members were required to wear badges identifying them as Church employees while at work. Prospective employees filled out applications for employment by the Church, and the employee handbook specified that "the policy of The Mother Church [is] to employ only members of the Church in all of its activities, including The Christian Science Publishing Society." All of this evidence was self-serving (i.e., saying that Madsen was a Church employee did not really make it so if she was not), and in some sense beside the point, since the real question under First Amendment case law was not whether Madsen was employed by the Church, but rather whether she was employed in a religious or a secular capacity. (A church, after all, is no less bound than any other person or organization to abide by the rules of civil society, but the First Amendment creates an exception to those rules, in some circumstances, for practices required by the religious teachings of the church.) Nolan concluded that Madsen was an employee of the Church, an apparently inescapable conclusion, given the state of the record.

As to whether the newspaper was a "church organ" or a religious activity of the Church, after ruling out the affidavit based on the direct mail solicitation as "hearsay" that was "unacceptable to defeat summary judgment," Nolan said that even if it was taken into account, "a vague statement that the *Monitor* is 'not an organ' of the Church was insufficient to rebut the clear inference created by Silvernail's affidavit that the *Monitor* is a religious activity of the Church." Nolan did not, however, discuss any of the details of Silvernail's affidavit that led him to that conclusion. Instead, he asserted that the issue for the court was whether a dispute centered on the Church's refusal to employ a homosexual in one of its "religious activities" was one in which a court could intervene.

"Courts cannot question the verity of religious doctrines or beliefs," asserted Nolan. "Beyond that, a court must defer to the Church in matters of ecclesiastical decisions. . . . On the affidavits, the decision to fire Madsen because of her sexual preference can only be construed as a religious one, made by a Church as employer. Thus, we must defer to that decision." Nolan drew support from two trial court decisions in other jurisdictions, holding that religious employers were exempt from complying with municipal ordinances forbidding discrimination on the basis of sexual orientation. Both of those cases involved positions that were unequivocally religious in nature. In *Walker v. First Presbyterian Church* (1980), the discharged homosexual was the organist who performed at church services. In *Lewis ex rel. Murphy v. Buchanan* (1979), the plaintiff was a disappointed applicant for a teaching position at a parochial school. Unlike Madsen, both of those plaintiffs would clearly have been involved in a religious activity of the church, but Nolan made no mention of the factual distinctions, merely quoting from those decisions to support the notion that requiring a church to pay damages to a wrongfully discharged employee would be like taxing the free exercise of religion, and that "the desire of a city government to protect the employability of homosexuals is not such a clear and present danger to a 'substantial interest of the state' as to justify the invasion of an individual's freedom of conscience which is proposed here." Nolan's main reliance, apparently, was on a then-recent law review article by Professor Douglas Laycock on the difficulties of reconciling civil rights laws with free exercise in the context of church employment, in which Laycock argued that it would interfere with the constitutional free exercise rights of churches to require them to employ persons who did not owe them a strict duty of loyalty and theological conformity.

Nolan concluded that in light of the deference compelled by the Free Exercise Clause, "Madsen's asserted rights must yield," and her constitutional claims as well as her state statutory privacy claim and breach of contract claims "must fall." Nolan concluded that "entanglement of the defendants in such litigation would involve the court in a review of an essentially ecclesiastical procedure whereby the Church reviews its employees' spiritual suitability for continued employment," which Nolan deemed "impermissible under the First Amendment." He also agreed with the San Francisco Superior Court in *Walker* that requiring the Church to pay damages to Madsen would be "penalizing" the Church for its religious beliefs.

> The *Monitor*, as Madsen's employer, had the right to terminate Madsen's employment. Nothing in the United States Constitution, the Massachusetts Constitution, or Federal or State statutes prohibits the *Monitor* from doing this on the facts in this case. She had no written employment contract. She received severance and vacation pay. There has been no showing of bad faith. . . . There is no suggestion that Madsen's discharge deprived her of future compensation for past service. . . . There is no legal basis then for Madsen's claim of wrongful discharge, breach of contract, and deprivation of constitutional rights by her termination.

In a footnote, Nolan also indicated that no claim had been made out under Massachusetts civil rights laws banning sex discrimination in employment, citing federal precedents holding that sexual orientation discrimination did not violate the sex discrimination prohibition of Title VII of the federal civil rights act. Nolan also asserted that the facts alleged in Madsen's complaint, which were apparently not addressed in the affidavits submitted by the Church on its motion to dismiss, would not support the remaining torts claims that the court had dis-

posed of through the motion for summary judgment. "However," he said, "we think that the plaintiff should be given the opportunity to replead her claims for the above recited torts in the light of the following principles":

> Without retreating for a moment from the foundational rule "that the First Amendment prohibits civil courts from intervening in disputes concerning religious doctrine, discipline, faith, or internal organization, . . . we restate the equally important rule that the rights of religion are not beyond the reach of the civil law. Under the banner of the First Amendment provisions on religion, a clergyman may not with impunity defame a person, intentionally inflict serious emotional harm on a parishioner, or commit other torts. . . . The torts of which Madsen complains are conduct and hence, they are subject to regulation. We recognize that the defendant may be able to interpose defenses or qualified privileges, but these are generally not raised by motion to dismiss [for failure to state a legal claim].

Thus, although the court was for now either denying or dismissing all of Madsen's claims, she could continue the lawsuit by reframing her factual claims to raise more clearly the various issues of tortious behavior by the Church.

Justice O'Connor took exception to much of Nolan's opinion. His main argument was that the agonizing over the First Amendment was all unnecessary because, as far as he could see, the factual allegations in Madsen's complaint did not support any legal theories on which she might prevail under state or federal law. Only if a plaintiff could state a valid theory of recovery would it become necessary for the court to decide whether the defendant was immune from suit under the First Amendment. And Madsen had not, so far as O'Connor was concerned, stated any valid theories:

> The court rightly states that, because Madsen was an employee at will, the *Monitor* lawfully fired her, because nothing in the Federal or State Constitutions, in Federal or State statutes, or in public policy, prohibits an employer from firing an at will employee on the facts of this case. Therefore, the court rightly concludes that there is no legal basis for Madsen's claims of wrongful discharge, breach of contract, deprivation of constitutional rights, or deprivation of civil rights. . . . The correctness of these conclusions, however, does not in any

way depend on the First Amendment. Those conclusions would be correct if the controversy were entirely unrelated to a church or to church personnel. For that reason alone, the court's discussion of the First Amendment is inappropriate. The court's analysis may be incorrect as well.

O'Connor observed that Madsen was employed as a sportswriter and did not write on religious or moral subjects. To O'Connor, whether Madsen could continue to be employed as a sportswriter for the *Monitor* "does not appear to be a dispute about religious doctrine, discipline, faith, or internal organization, within the decided cases." Although the U.S. Supreme Court had upheld the autonomy of church authorities in appointing ministers, it had "never held that civil courts cannot intervene in similar matters involving lay church employees." Grasping the distinction that Nolan had seemingly overlooked in his opinion for the court, O'Connor observed:

> While the beliefs and practices of a minister are of critical importance to the church in which the minister functions, making judicial involvement in decisions affecting a minister's tenure inappropriate, it is far from clear that the same is true with respect to a sportswriter on the staff of a church-affiliated newspaper.

O'Connor cited as support *EEOC v. Southwestern Baptist Theological Seminary* (1981), in which the Fifth Circuit had held that the exemption from Title VII requirements for churches in their employment of religious personnel did not extend to the nonministerial employees of a religious seminary. Thus, O'Connor was not ready to agree with the court that the decision to fire Madsen was essentially a religious one requiring judicial deference: "Rather, I tend to think that the First Amendment would not preclude judicial intervention in this matter and that whether the First Amendment would protect the employer in this case requires a judicial balancing of the competing Church and State interests." Indeed, O'Connor noted that both cases cited by Nolan as authority had involved application of balancing tests rather than a strictly deferential approach.

O'Connor said he would not go further on this subject, since, as he had stated at the outset, it was not necessary for the court to reach

the First Amendment issues because there was no legal claim stated in Madsen's complaint. But O'Connor did go further in another direction, also dissenting from the court's refusal to dismiss Madsen's torts claims with prejudice. He could find no basis in the complaint for allowing Madsen to "replead" those claims. First, he found that the court's approach here was inconsistent with its First Amendment discussion. If it would place an undue burden on free exercise to require a church to pay damages to a wrongfully discharged employee, why would it not also raise free exercise concerns to require a church to pay damages when it committed torts in the course of enforcing its doctrinal views? But more to the point, O'Connor found that the factual allegations just did not support any of the torts claims. There could be no defamation, he asserted, when the discussions about Madsen's lesbianism were all confined, at least so far as the complaint alleged, within the top ranks of employees with personnel responsibilities. Neither was there a valid emotional distress claim, since, said O'Connor, nothing alleged in the complaint rose to the level of outrageousness that the courts required before damages could be awarded for purely mental distress.

Finally, on Madsen's privacy claim, O'Connor asserted that all of the defendants' inquiries into her sexual orientation were undertaken within the scope of an employment investigation. "Because the defendants could lawfully have discharged Madsen on the basis of her sexual preference, when allegations surfaced about Madsen's sexual preference the defendants had a right to question her about it." O'Connor did not find the questioning described in the complaint to amount to an "unreasonable, substantial or serious interference" with Madsen's privacy, as would be required to state a claim under the Massachusetts privacy statute. Neither did he find the limited disclosure among *Monitor* managerial employees to constitute the kind of "public" disclosure that would be a necessary element for such a claim.

Since Madsen had stated in her complaint that she was alleging there all the facts on which she relied, O'Connor saw no reason to allow repleading of the torts claims. Presumably, there were no other facts not already pled that were relevant to Madsen's case.

The *Madsen* case had an important impact on the development of lesbian and gay rights law in Massachusetts, for gay political groups were engaged in ongoing struggles to enact affirmative statutory protections for lesbian and gay employees, and the attention the case received in the press both highlighted the problem of discrimination and alerted religious groups of the need to protect their "rights" to discriminate on the basis of theological doctrine. When Massachusetts finally enacted a gay rights law years later, it contained a specific exemption for religious organizations, not only from the sexual orientation provisions but also from other provisions of the Massachusetts Law Against Discrimination. These exemptions, insisted on by religious lobbyists, ironically proved crucial in staving off a subsequent attempt by religious conservatives to mount a referendum to repeal the law, since a provision of the Massachusetts Constitution barred referenda on issues relating to religion, and the Supreme Judi-

cial Court held in *Collins v. Secretary of Commonwealth* (1990) that the provisions broadening existing religious exemptions in the state discrimination law rendered the gay rights law immune from referendum repeal on this basis!

The long-running *Madsen* case, which once again became bogged down at the trial level after the supreme judicial court's opinion, was only one in many conflicts arising between religious organizations and gay rights advocates over the fundamental question whether the First Amendment should be able to shield virtually all activities that have some religious connection or connotation from the workings of gay rights legislation.

Case References

Collins v. Secretary of Commonwealth, 407 Mass. 837, 556 N.E.2d 348 (1990)

EEOC v. Southwestern Baptist Theological Seminary, 651 F.2d 277 (5th Cir. 1981)

Lewis ex rel. Murphy v. Buchanan, 21 Fair Empl. Prac. Cas. (BNA) 696 (Minn. Dist. Ct. 1979)

Walker v. First Presbyterian Church, 22 Fair Empl. Prac. Cas. (BNA) 762 (Cal. Super. Ct. 1980)

83. CAN LOCAL LAWS BAN FEDERAL DISCRIMINATION?

United States v. City of Philadelphia, 798 F.2d 81 (3d Cir. 1986).

Federal courts assessing challenges to antigay federal policies under the Equal Protection Clause have to determine the level of scrutiny to apply to those policies. Heightened scrutiny will apply to any categorical discrimination that uses a "suspect" classification (i.e., one that is likely to reflect bias rather than reasoned policymaking). In determining whether a particular classification is suspect, the U.S. Supreme Court has evaluated various factors, among them whether the classification describes a group that is unable to participate and to represent effectively its interests in the legislative process. In evaluating this factor, lower federal courts confronting equal protection arguments from gay rights advocates have differed in how they evaluate the ability of sexual minorities to represent themselves in the political process.

Some courts, noting the steady increase in municipal gay rights ordinances, and the more limited success in obtaining statewide antidiscrimination laws, executive orders, and election of openly gay officials, have asserted that gays are now able to take care of themselves politically and do not need the extra assistance of heightened judicial scrutiny of laws that deliberately discriminate against them. As one example, the U.S. Court of Appeals for the Seventh Circuit found it significant in *BenShalom v. Marsh* (1989), a case challenging the U.S. Department of Defense's antigay policies, that many large cities have gay rights laws, there are openly gay members of Congress, and the mayor of Chicago had recently participated in a gay rights parade. To this court, such facts meant that gays were not politically powerless for purposes of equal protection analysis. By contrast, and applying a more careful and sophisticated analysis, a Ninth Circuit judge contended in *Watkins v. United States Army* (1989) that gay political power at the local, and sometimes state, level did not translate into effective representation at the national level, where federal policy decisions are made. While gays had proven able to organize politically in some localities and states, all efforts to enact substantive protection for the civil rights of gay people at the federal level had been unsuccessful because continued societal prejudice against gay people made it difficult for them to construct the political coalitions and sympathetic support that are necessary to enact federal legislation protecting minorities.

This disparity in political power was forcefully illustrated in the confrontation between the Philadelphia Commission on Human Relations and the Department of Defense over military recruiting at Temple University Law School. Philadelphia had enacted a municipal ordinance that banned discrimination on the basis of sexual orientation in various ways, including employment agency policies, and further banned any person from aiding, abetting, inciting, compelling, or coercing the doing of any unfair employment practice, as defined in the ordinance. Lesbian and gay students at Temple Law School decided to try to use the ordinance to attack the Defense Department's exclusionary policies.

In the fall of 1982, two openly gay law students, Richard Brown and Loretta DeLoggio, applied at the Temple Placement Office for interviews with the Judge Advocate General (JAG) Corps, the military unit that employs lawyers within the uniformed services to prosecute and defend in court martial proceedings. Under Temple's policies, employers that used the Placement Office selected whom they wanted to interview to fill 75 percent of the interview time slots, but the remaining 25 percent of the slots were filled at random by the Placement Office from among those who applied. Neither Brown nor DeLoggio was selected for an interview. Both of them filed complaints with the Philadelphia Commission on Human Relations, alleging that the Temple Placement Office was an "employment agency"

under the ordinance, and that by providing interviewing facilities and cooperating with the JAG Corps, Temple had violated the ban against sexual orientation discrimination. After conducting its own investigation, which revealed that the Temple Placement Office was aware of the Defense Department's exclusionary policies, the Commission initiated its own complaint against Temple, supplementing the individual complaints of the two law students.

The Commission held a public hearing on the complaints, at which the U.S. Justice Department appeared as *amicus curiae*, arguing that enforcing the ordinance against the law school placement office in this context would violate the Supremacy Clause of the U.S. Constitution. In effect, the federal government argued that the Defense Department's antigay exclusion was a federal policy that would override any local policy to the contrary. The Commission rejected this view and found that Temple had violated the ordinance in three ways: by allowing the JAG Corps to interview at the school, by referring candidates to the JAG Corps, and by "aiding and abetting" the JAG Corps in carrying out its discriminatory policy. While the Commission could not order the federal government to stop discriminating, it held that it could order a nongovernmental entity in Philadelphia to avoid any complicity with such discrimination.

Both the federal government and Temple University filed complaints in the U.S. District Court for the Eastern District of Pennsylvania, alleging that the Commission's action was invalid and should be enjoined on supremacy grounds. Meanwhile, the Commission had received similar charges against the University of Pennsylvania, which it held in abeyance pending the outcome of the federal litigation. The Philadelphia Lesbian and Gay Task Force and a student organization, Lesbians and Gays at Penn, sought leave to intervene in the litigation before District Judge James T. Giles. The plaintiffs filed motions for summary judgment. Giles held a hearing in which all parties and potential parties participated. He concluded at the end of the hearing that the Supremacy Clause did preclude the Commission from interfering with military recruitment at Temple or anywhere else. He found that the Commission was attempting "to regulate . . . indirectly through Temple University the conduct of the United States, insofar as it adheres to its policy of discrimination against homosexuals." All parties had conceded that the issue of the constitutionality of the Defense Department's policies was not before the court in this case, so Giles had to consider those policies valid and unchallenged in the context of the litigation.

Holding that the Supremacy Clause forbids any state or local agency "from interfering with or attempting to frustrate the willingness of private citizens or entities or public entities from participating with the United States to carry out a joint effort protected under the constitution," Giles issued an order forbidding the Commission from "adjudicating any complaint or taking any adverse action under the [ordinance] against any person, corporation, association or group based on the Commission's objection to the policy of the United States in discriminating on the basis of sexual orientation in its military recruitment efforts." He also found that the Commission had adequate legal representation from the city of Philadelphia and did not need the litigation assistance of the Philadelphia Lesbian and Gay Task Force, whose interests it would adequately represent, so he denied the Task Force's motion for intervenor status.

Both the city and the Task Force appealed these decisions and orders to the Third Circuit, which heard oral argument on June 16, 1986. Deputy City Solicitor Susan Shinkman appeared on behalf of the Commission, and Philadelphia attorney David W. Webber argued on behalf of the Task Force. Temple was represented by Robert J. Reinstein and the federal government by Robert V. Zener from the Justice Department's Civil Division Appellate Staff. The case attracted *amicus* briefs from the American Civil Liberties Union of Greater Philadelphia, the American Council on Education, and the Lambda Legal Defense and Education Fund. Lambda was the only participant in the appeal that argued that the Defense Department's policy was unconstitutional, a point that the appellate panel noted was not preserved for appeal, having been conceded away by the Commission before the district court. The three-judge appellate panel issued

its unanimous decision in an opinion by Circuit Judge Collins J. Seitz, affirming Giles in all respects, on August 1, 1986.

The first step of the Supremacy Clause analysis was to determine whether the Commission's application of the ordinance to bar military recruiting at Temple "conflicts with Congressional legislation or with any discernible Congressional policy." It was not enough, apparently, for the Defense Department to adopt regulations banning gays from uniformed military service, since the U.S. Supreme Court had framed Supremacy Clause analysis in terms of congressional policy in *Penn Dairies v. Milk Control Commission* (1943). Congress had not directly forbidden gays to serve, although it had enacted, through its approval of the Uniform Code of Military Justice, a law against anal or oral sex by military members regardless of gender. A local law would be held to "conflict" with congressional legislation or policy if it stood "as an obstacle to the accomplishment and execution of the full purposes and objectives of Congress," according to another World War II-era Supreme Court opinion, *Hines v. Davidowitz* (1946).

Seitz found that Congress had expressed itself on the subject of military recruiting along two distinct lines. First, it had directed the military branches to conduct "intensive recruiting campaigns to obtain enlistments" as part of the legislation establishing the all-volunteer armed forces when the military draft ceased operations. Second, during the Vietnam War era, Congress had repeatedly included in military appropriations bills (as well as in other appropriations measures providing funds that might go to educational institutions) provisions forbidding expenditure of any of the appropriated funds at schools that barred military recruitment or had a policy against the operation of Reserve Officer Training Corps (ROTC) units on campus. Seitz asserted that "only one reasonable conclusion" could be drawn from these two lines of legislation: "Congress considers access to college and university employment facilities by military recruiters to be a matter of paramount importance." The legislative history of the appropriations bills provided ample statements from committee reports to support this conclusion. It was "obvious" to Seitz that the

Commission's order to Temple thus conflicted with a "discernible Congressional policy," as specified in the *Penn Dairies* case.

But that was not enough to resolve the case, since the Supreme Court had also held in *McCarty v. McCarty* (1981) that a mere verbal conflict would not lead to federal preemption unless the consequences of the state or local regulation "sufficiently injure the objectives of the federal program to require nonrecognition" of the local policy. Seitz interpreted this to mean that the Commission's order would be displaced by federal law only if it would "significantly impair the military's ability to recruit doctors, lawyers, and other skilled personnel." This was adequately demonstrated, he believed, by affidavits in the record from Lieutenant General Edgar A. Chavarrie, the deputy assistant secretary of defense for military personnel and force management, showing that a substantial proportion of the skilled recruits for military services from the Philadelphia area came from on-campus college and university recruiting. Indeed, for some skills, on-campus recruiting was virtually the entire source. While the order against Temple's Placement Office might not by itself have a significant effect, the possibility of similar orders against all college and university placement offices in the Philadelphia area would (and there was that complaint against Penn still pending before the Commission). It was clear that a general policy against on-campus recruiting in the Philadelphia area had "the potential to frustrate effective recruiting of skilled personnel" in that area.

Seitz asserted that the court could not turn a blind eye to the possible consequences of upholding the Commission's order, rejecting the argument from the Commission and *amici* that the court should be concerned only with the specific order against the Temple Law School Placement Office. "We cannot conceive of any reason why the Commission would prohibit the military from recruiting lawyers at Temple, yet permit it to recruit doctors or engineers at the University of Pennsylvania." Lambda's *amicus* brief had brought to the court's attention that as of then 48 municipalities, eleven counties, and seven states had adopted policies prohibiting employment discrimination on the basis of sexual orientation. (The state policies at that time were executive orders in all but one state, Wisconsin, which then had the only statewide gay rights ordinance.) This led Seitz to comment that it was also likely that enforcement agencies in other jurisdictions would likely adopt the same interpretations of their civil rights laws. If local jurisdictions were allowed to interfere in military recruiting in this manner, recruitment could be frustrated throughout the nation, not just in Philadelphia. Ironically, the more successful gay groups were in obtaining local and state ordinances, the stronger was the argument for preempting the effect of those ordinances against discrimination by a federal agency.

Consequently, the court concluded that Giles' injunction against the Commission should be upheld in all its broad sweep, even though the injunction was not narrowly focused on Temple. Given the possibility that the Commission might proceed against landlords who rented space to military recruiters, or businesses that provided them with supplies or other services, it was appropriate to ban any "adjudication" by the Commission that might interfere with military recruiting, even though the Commission had given no indication that it would pursue anything other than on-campus recruiting at the present time. Thus, Seitz rejected the contention that Giles' order was too broad, exceeding the appropriate discretion to award equitable relief, even though he conceded that there was "some merit" to the Commission's argument that the case should be remanded for a more narrowly focused order. He asserted that the court's opinion, in any case, would limit the scope of interpretation of the order, so a remand for that purpose was not required.

Finally, dealing with the Task Force's appeal, Seitz upheld Giles' decision to deny the Task Force intervenor status. Normally, when the defendant in a case is a governmental unit, there is a strong presumption that the governmental unit is capable of presenting its side of the case. Seitz said that the Task Force had not shown that the city attorneys had failed to provide adequate representation to the interests of the gay community. The Task Force had argued that it would not have stipulated, as had the city, to the constitutionality of the Defense Department's policies. This did not persuade

Seitz, who asserted that differences over tactics did not overcome the "presumption of adequate representation" in such cases. Besides, by appealing Giles's order and filing a brief on appeal, the Task Force had been able to make its arguments to the court, which were taken into account and referred to in its opinion.

Thus ended the brief, but valiant, attempt by some activist law students to take on the Defense Department by capitalizing on local success in obtaining a gay rights ordinance. As noted at the outset, the case forcefully indicates the limitations of such local political power in dealing with the most pervasively antigay regime in the country, the Department of De-fense, and the essential irrelevance of local gay political power to the determination whether heightened scrutiny under the Equal Protection Clause should be given to such nationwide antigay policies.

Case References

BenShalom v. Marsh, 881 F.2d 454 (7th Cir. 1989), certiorari denied, 110 S. Ct. 1296 (1990)

Hines v. Davidowitz, 312 U.S. 52 (1941)

McCarty v. McCarty, 453 U.S. 210 (1981)

Penn Dairies v. Milk Control Commission, 318 U.S. 261 (1943)

Watkins v. United States Army, 875 F.2d 699 (9th Cir. 1989) (en banc) (Norris, Cir. J., concurring), certiorari denied, 111 S. Ct. 384 (1990)

84. CAN GAYS BE FBI AGENTS?

Padula v. Webster, 822 F.2d 97 (D.C. Cir. 1987).

The Federal Bureau of Investigation (FBI), a national law enforcement agency within the U.S. Department of Justice, had a problem. The law schools and other graduate schools from which it recruited its agents were taking a stand against discrimination on the basis of sexual orientation, and many were forbidding employers that discriminated on that basis from using their placement facilities. In 1979, the FBI told the U.S. Circuit Court of Appeals for the District of Columbia, in no uncertain terms, that it "has always had an absolute policy of dismissing proven or admitted homosexuals from its employ." But when law schools began to question the Bureau's policies, they started to receive more equivocal responses.

FBI Director William H. Webster, for example, stated in a press conference about the Bureau's position toward homosexuality:

> Now we treat it as a factor, and I must say in candor, it's a significant factor. It's a troublesome thing; I hope that the particular case will be handled with fairness and justice and I hope that at some point we will have a better understanding of the problem and the policy that should be addressed to it.

This statement did not satisfy some of the law schools, however. At Temple University Law School in Philadelphia, Professor Marina Angel wrote to the Bureau seeking a statement of its policy in compliance with the school's nondiscrimination policy, and received the following reply in a letter from FBI Legal Counsel and Assistant Director John Mintz, dated July 31, 1980: "The FBI's focus in personnel matters has been and continues to be on conduct rather than status or preference and we carefully consider the facts in each case to determine whether the conduct may affect the employment. At the same time, we recognize individual privacy rights of applicants and employees." In letters that he sent to other law schools inquiring about the Bureau's policies, Mintz made a variety of statements that led some schools to believe they could allow the Bureau to recruit without violating their nondiscrimination policies. He stated that "individual sexual orientation, whether homosexual or heterosexual, may involve secret conduct that is relevant to employment in the FBI in that it increases employee susceptibility to compromise or breach of trust." While stating his confidence that the Bureau had not engaged in "improper discrimination regarding sexual orientation," Mintz wrote to one law dean that homosexual conduct was a significant factor in

FBI hiring decisions, but that such decisions were not taken "simply because of . . . sexual orientation." When these sorts of non-committal statements inspired requests for further clarification from one dean, Mintz replied:

> In fairness . . . based upon experience, I can offer no specific encouragement that a homosexual applicant will be found who satisfies all of the requirements. . . . In any event, each case is reviewed independently for an objective determination of suitability.

It was in this climate of ambiguity—assurances of no improper discrimination or no categorical discrimination coupled with assertions that it was unlikely a homosexual applicant would meet the Bureau's requirements—that Margaret Padula, a recent law graduate, decided to apply for a position as an FBI agent in the summer of 1982. She took the Bureau's written examination and submitted to the standard hiring interview. On the basis of these selection devices, she was ranked 39 out of 303 qualified female applicants and 279 out of 1,273 male and female applicants combined. The next step in the Bureau's hiring process was a routine background check, that involved contacting references and reviewing documentary records on the applicant. During this routine process, the Bureau uncovered evidence that Padula was a lesbian, information that she freely confirmed when questioned about it. Padula stated that she was unembarrassed and open with family, friends, and co-workers about being a lesbian, although she did not "flaunt" that fact. In short, she was a perfectly normal, relaxed person who happened to be sexually attracted to women rather than men.

Padula's application sat and sat and sat, until finally on October 19, 1983, the Bureau sent her a notice that she would not be offered a position. She asked for reconsideration, but was turned down, ostensibly due to the intense competition for the position. No mention was made of her homosexuality in these communications from the Bureau. Early in 1985, after much soul-searching, Padula decided that she had been turned down because of her sexual orientation, and that this discrimination must be challenged. She filed suit against FBI Director Webster in the U.S. District Court for the District of Columbia, where her case was assigned

to District Judge Gerhard A. Gesell, a veteran district judge who seems to have drawn more than his share of cases challenging the government's discriminatory policies against homosexuals. Represented by Washington lawyers Jeffrey J. Kanne and Susan W. Shaffer, Padula alleged that her denial of employment by the FBI was subject to judicial review based on the Bureau's stated policy of nondiscrimination solely on the basis of sexual orientation. She alleged that as an openly lesbian person, she was not engaged in any conduct that would make her employment detrimental to national security. She also alleged that the FBI's conduct in her case violated her rights to privacy, equal protection, and due process under the First, Fourth, Fifth, and Ninth amendments to the U.S. Constitution.

The FBI moved for summary judgment, alleging that there was no factual dispute, that, as a matter of law, its hiring decisions were not subject to judicial review, and that no constitutional violations had occurred because there was a rational basis for rejecting Padula's application. Judge Gesell was convinced by the Bureau's arguments and, in an unpublished memorandum and order issued November 15, 1985, granted the motion. Gesell found that the FBI's various statements and communications, uncovered by Padula's discovery requests, did not amount to a binding policy statement on which judicial review could be premised. As to the constitutional provisions cited by Padula, Gesell found that they did not require the Bureau to do more than articulate a rational basis for its decision. Even if one concluded that the Bureau was discriminating on the basis of sexual orientation, Gesell believed that the "minimum rationality standard" which the Bureau would have to meet in this case was "clearly met."

Padula promptly appealed this decision, focusing her appeal on two claims: first, that the Bureau's hiring decision in her case was subject to judicial review because of the "policy" of nondiscrimination it had publicly embraced, and second, that consideration of her sexual orientation violated her right to equal protection of the laws. On March 16, 1987, a three-judge panel heard oral argument in the case from Kanne and Department of Justice attorney Freddi Lipstein. The members of the panel were Circuit Judges Robert H. Bork (later that summer to be nominated unsuccessfully to the Supreme Court by President Ronald Reagan), Laurence H. Silberman, and Chief Judge Howard T. Markey of the U.S. Court of Appeals for the Federal Circuit, sitting by designation. This panel reached a decision relatively quickly, issuing an opinion by Silberman on June 26, 1987. Ominously, the opinion was issued just days short of the first anniversary of the U.S. Supreme Court's decision in *Bowers v. Hardwick*, a decision that Silberman accorded decisive weight in determining that dismissal of Padula's claim was appropriate. Indeed, by accident of timing, Padula's appeal was the vehicle for the first federal appellate ruling to determine the impact of *Hardwick* on equal protection rights of lesbians and gay men.

Silberman began with a discussion of the question of judicial review. Because FBI hiring decisions were committed to agency discretion by law pursuant to 5 U.S.C. section 701(a)(2), they were generally sheltered from judicial review, unless it could be found that the agency had voluntarily bound itself to a particular policy, in which case a court could review whether the agency had violated its own articulated policy. Padula argued that the FBI had done this in order to gain access to university placement offices. Reciting the various statements by Director Webster and Counsel Mintz, Padula claimed that the Bureau had clearly indicated that it would not base hiring decisions solely on sexual orientation, but would evaluate personal conduct and lifestyle, whether homosexual or heterosexual, in light of its personnel and security needs. Holding up her own, openly lesbian lifestyle as the subject of scrutiny, Padula argued that the FBI's application of its policy had been faulty in her case.

Silberman never got that far, however, because he agreed with Gesell that the FBI had not actually bound itself in any way by the statements and letters on homosexuality uncovered by Padula's discovery requests. For Silberman, the main issue was apparently whether these statements purported to diminish agency discretion, or whether they left the Bureau essentially free to apply its judgment on a case-by-case basis. "Pronouncements that impose no significant restraints on the agency's discretion

are not regarded as binding norms," he commented. While internal rules or guidelines adopted by an agency "have occasionally been held to bind agency conduct," and "[the] more than a dozen FBI letters to law schools involved here might well be sufficient to establish a binding policy if they in fact limited the Bureau's discretion," Silberman asserted that they did not do so. Contrary to Padula's claim, said Silberman, while "the pronouncements reaffirm the Bureau's traditional pledge not to improperly discriminate against any applicant" and to focus on conduct rather than status, they "quite explicitly" stated that "individual sexual orientation may involve conduct that is relevant to employment in the FBI in that it increases employee susceptibility to compromise or breach of trust." Thus, the Bureau's stated policy made clear that sexual orientation and conduct were relevant factors. Even though the FBI made these statements as part of a concerted campaign to avoid being barred from law school placement offices, that did not affect the meaning of the statements. "Indeed," said Silberman, "the FBI was very careful—if a bit clever—not to tie its hands in any way." By producing innocuous statements about not discriminating "improperly," the Bureau had actually tried to gain access without making any real nondiscrimination commitment, found Silberman. The best that could be concluded in support of Padula's position was that "the FBI has committed itself not to consider the sexual orientation of an applicant who can show he does not engage in sex, but it clearly has done no more."

Turning to the equal protection issue, Silberman dealt first with the question whether the FBI's policies should be subjected to heightened or strict scrutiny. The requirement of equal protection of the laws, as applied to the federal government and its agencies by the Due Process Clause of the Fifth Amendment in the same manner that the requirement applies to the states through the express Equal Protection Clause of the Fourteenth Amendment, would subject a government policy to heightened scrutiny only if the policy disadvantaged a "suspect" or "quasi-suspect" class or implicated a fundamental right. Silberman concentrated his analysis on the suspect class question. Here, there was initial disagreement over defining the class. The FBI had reiterated throughout the controversy over on-campus recruitment that it did not discriminate on the basis of sexual orientation, but that conduct was the basis for its decisions. "By that," said Silberman, "we understand the government to be saying that it would not consider relevant for employment purposes homosexual orientation that did *not* result in conduct." Padula had argued against accepting this status-versus-conduct distinction, asserting that in fact the Bureau considered a homosexual a person who engaged in homosexual conduct, and that the fine distinction the Bureau sought to draw was clearly intended to exclude homosexuals as such from employment. Silberman concluded that it was not really necessary to get into this dispute, because Padula was not claiming to be a celibate homosexual, and it was her denial of employment that was at stake in the case. Consequently, for purposes of his analysis, he would assume that the class involved consisted of people who engaged in homosexual conduct. As thus defined, he argued that it would be impossible for the resulting class to be "suspect" because of the *Hardwick* decision, as well as the District of Columbia Circuit's prior decision in *Dronenburg v. Zech* (1984), in which his colleague on the panel, Judge Bork, had thoroughly trashed the U.S. Supreme Court's privacy jurisprudence in a way that substantially contributed to his failure of confirmation for the Supreme Court just months after the *Padula* opinion was issued.

In *Dronenburg* and *Hardwick*, the D.C. Circuit Court and the Supreme Court had rejected the argument that consensual homosexual conduct was sheltered from government restriction by the right of privacy under the Due Process Clause. In *Hardwick*, the Supreme Court had gone further, ruling broadly that criminal penalties for consensual sodomy did not implicate a fundamental right under the Due Process Clause, and that the presumed moral preferences of a state's electorate provided sufficient justification to meet the test of minimum rationality imposed on all government policies that restrict personal liberty. What did these decisions mean for equal protection analysis? "Although the [*Dronenburg*] court's opinion focused primarily on whether the constitutional right of privacy protected homosexual conduct,"

said Silberman, "the court reasoned that if the right to privacy did not provide protection, 'then appellant's right to equal protection is not infringed unless the Navy's policy is not rationally related to a permissible end.'" In other words, once the court determined that the rationality test was the appropriate test for due process purposes, it followed that it was also the appropriate test for equal protection purposes.

Similarly, in *Hardwick*, the Court had used the rational basis test to uphold a statute that clearly restricted personal liberty. "We therefore think the courts' reasoning in *Hardwick* and *Dronenburg* forecloses appellant's efforts to gain suspect class status for practicing homosexuals," said Silberman.

> It would be quite anomalous, on its face, to declare status defined by conduct that states may constitutionally criminalize as deserving of strict scrutiny under the equal protection clause. More importantly, in all those cases in which the Supreme Court has accorded suspect or quasi-suspect status to a class, the Court's holding was predicated on an unarticulated, but necessarily implicit, notion that it is plainly unjustifiable (in accordance with standards not altogether clear to us) to discriminate invidiously against the particular class. . . . If the Court was unwilling to object to state laws that criminalize the behavior that defines the class, it is hardly open to a lower court to conclude that state sponsored discrimination against the class is invidious. After all, there can hardly be more palpable discrimination against a class than making the conduct that defines the class criminal.

In other words, Silberman was saying that in *Hardwick* the Supreme Court had implicitly ruled that discrimination against gay people was normally justifiable, since it sustained the ultimate discrimination against them: outlawing the conduct that "defined" them as a class.

This did not mean, of course, that all discrimination of any kind whatsoever against gay people by the government was always justifiable, said Silberman. There was still the rational basis test to be met. If, indeed, the FBI had discriminated against Padula because she was a lesbian, it could do so only if there was a rational basis for believing that a lesbian could not be an acceptable FBI agent. Silberman found support for the FBI's decision in the circuit court's prior decision in *Dronenburg*, where it had accepted the argument that the Navy's exclusion of homosexuals was rational on the premise that homosexual conduct was "detrimental to the maintenance of morale and discipline." The court there had observed, apparently as a matter of judicial notice, that homosexuality "generates dislike and disapproval among many . . . who find it morally offensive" and was criminalized by about half the states. "The FBI," said Silberman, "is a national law enforcement agency whose agents must be able to work in all the states of the nation." How could it be asked to employ somebody in that position whose normal sexual conduct was outlawed by half the states? To do so would "undermine the law enforcement credibility of the Bureau." Even more importantly, in the course of their work FBI agents performed duties "that involve highly classified matters relating to national security." Silberman asserted, "It is not irrational for the Bureau to conclude that the criminalization of homosexual conduct coupled with the general public opprobrium toward homosexuality exposes many homosexuals, even 'open' homosexuals, to the risk of possible blackmail to protect their partners, if not themselves." Thus, the Bureau's particular needs justified this discrimination, as did the Navy's in *Dronenburg*.

Of course, the FBI had presented no evidence in support of these claims. The case was being decided on a motion for summary judgment, without benefit of trial. Under "rational basis" jurisprudence, however, this did not really matter, since the Supreme Court has traditionally been willing to indulge in imagining a rational basis for legislation without requiring the legislature or other government body to show that it had actually adopted the policy on that basis after a consideration of evidence. District Judge Thelton Henderson of the Northern District of California, who heard *High Tech Gays v. Defense Industrial Security Clearance Office* (1990), did review such evidence. He concluded that the Department of Defense's reasons for subjecting gay applicants for security clearances to heightened investigation had no merit, noting especially that the long-held theory of gays as security risks not only lacked any empirical basis but had even been rejected in internal Defense Department studies. But

Henderson's conclusions were subsequently set aside by the Ninth Circuit, which in adopting Silberman's approach to the issue also seemed to adopt the bizarre theory that in imagining a justification for a policy under the rationality test, a court was apparently free to reject contrary empirical evidence!

While Silberman's equal protection analysis seemed fully congruent with the implicit homophobia of the Supreme Court's decision in *Hardwick* (i.e., that societal hatred of homosexuals provides a constitutionally valid justification for outlawing their conduct), many commentators reacted quite heatedly to Silberman's assertion that the equal protection analysis could be performed in this cursory fashion without reference to the various factors that the Supreme Court had traditionally used to determine whether a particular classification unconstitutionally disadvantaged specific groups. In particular, commentators argued that the Equal Protection Clause and the Due Process Clause were intended to serve different purposes, and an undifferentiated use of the rational basis test undermined that distinction. By importing into equal protection analysis the Supreme Court's fundamental rights analysis from *Hardwick*, Silberman had effectively relegated gay people to a perpetual second-class citizenship similar to that suffered by black Americans before the Supreme Court's implicit assertion in *Brown v. Board of Education of Topeka* (1954) that second-class citizenship was not consistent with a constitutional guarantee of equal protection of the laws to all citizens. That is, in order to sustain discrimination against gay people, all the government had to show was that gay people were generally disliked by many members of society. Prejudice was sufficient to justify prejudice.

Despite the controversy it generated among legal commentators, Silberman's opinion on the equal protection issue, the first on the subject after *Hardwick*, proved highly influential. It has been accepted by every subsequent federal court of appeals panel called to rule on an equal protection challenge to an antigay federal government policy, with one exception: the three-judge panel in *Watkins v. United States Army* (1989), whose opinion rejecting this analysis was subsequently vacated by the *en banc* Ninth Circuit, which disposed of the case on other grounds.

The Ninth Circuit subsequently accepted this reasoning, however, in *High Tech Gays*. Thus, for now at least, Silberman's rationalization that a class of homosexuals, defined by conduct subject to criminalization, is not entitled to any real substantive protection under the Equal Protection Clause, is the orthodox view in the federal appeals courts, although not without its detractors in some of the federal district courts. Since the Supreme Court has never directly addressed this peculiar theory, its future viability is subject to continuing speculation.

Case References

Bowers v. Hardwick, 478 U.S. 186 (1986)

Brown v. Board of Education of Topeka, 347 U.S. 483 (1954)

Dronenburg v. Zech, 741 F.2d 1388 (D.C. Cir. 1984)

High Tech Gays v. Defense Industrial Security Clearance Office, 895 F.2d 563, rehearing en banc denied, 909 F.2d 375 (9th Cir. 1990)

Watkins v. United States Army, 875 F.2d 699 (9th Cir. 1989), certiorari denied, 111 S. Ct. 384 (1990)

85. ARE TRANSVESTITES "DISABLED"?

Blackwell v. United States Department of the Treasury, 830 F.2d 1183 (D.C. Cir. 1987), affirming dismissal but vacating decision, 656 F. Supp. 713 (D.D.C. 1986). Prior trial decision on motion to dismiss: 639 F. Supp. 289 (D.D.C. 1986).

Courts faced with legal issues concerning transvestites have a particularly difficult task, since transvestism is little understood by the lay public and frequently confused with homosexuality or transsexuality. An understanding of these different facets of human sexuality is necessary before one can adequately analyze the legal issues they present.

Sexologists (scientific students of human sexuality) recognize five main classifications, acknowledging that the lines between them may be blurred in actual cases: heterosexuals, homosexuals, bisexuals, cross-dressers (including transvestites), and transsexuals. Individuals are placed in a category based on a particular combination of the three components of gender identity: core gender identity (the individual's inner perception of him or herself as male or female); gender role (the individual's manifestation of gender identity through dress and behavior); and sexual orientation (the individual's disposition of erotic attachment toward others of a particular gender). Each of the components is subject to transposition independently of the other components. That is, people may experience a transposition of core gender identity (e.g., be born biologically male but feel themselves to be essentially female) without being transposed with regard to sexual orientation, or may similarly be transposed with regard to gender role (e.g., desire to dress in the garb of the opposite sex) without any transposition of sexual orientation.

Cross-dressers are transposed on gender role, with an emphasis on physical appearance and clothing. They may be heterosexual, bisexual, or homosexual, and they may or may not be transposed on core gender identity. Some cross-dressers are sexually aroused by wearing clothes normally worn by persons of the opposite sex; for others, cross-dressing is not particularly sexual, but has to do with other aspects of their self-image. When sexologists speak of transvestites, they are normally speaking of those for whom cross-dressing has an aspect of sexual arousal. Thus, transvestites are defined as a subset of the group of cross-dressers.

The federal courts in the District of Columbia had to cope with this complicated situation when William A. Blackwell filed suit against the Treasury Department. Blackwell, a homosexual cross-dresser who normally presented himself in clothing of ambiguous but somewhat feminine character, had been employed by the Treasury Department for about ten years when he was laid off in a force reduction in February 1982. Under the Department's personnel rules, individuals on layoff were accorded priority consideration for reemployment and were informed of all job openings in the Department. Shortly after his layoff, Blackwell learned of a clerical position open in the Department's Bureau of Public Debt for which he was qualified. The job involved making ledger entries and included no public contact.

Blackwell applied and presented himself for an interview with the unit supervisor on May 6, 1982. He presented himself as he normally had for ten years at his other Treasury jobs: hair in long braids, pants of a feminine style with a broad stretch belt, shirt-blouse, but obviously a male. Blackwell's gestures were "slightly effeminate," and his figure was affected by foam implants in his breasts. To anyone with eyes to see, he was clearly a cross-dressing male.

The unit supervisor was not fazed by his appearance. The interview centered on Blackwell's experience and credentials. Blackwell asked whether there was any objection to his lifestyle and was told there was none. Blackwell said nothing more definite to explain his manner of dress and appearance, and the unit supervisor believed that he was a homosexual. She recommended that he be hired for the position, and Blackwell was passed on to the first-level supervisor for further interviewing.

The first-level supervisor was not free to see him and suggested that the second-level supervisor, one Mr. Strange, undertake the interview. Strange spoke with Blackwell for ten or fifteen minutes and advised him that he "would be in touch." When Blackwell left the office, one of Strange's associates commented on his appearance and said she couldn't stand it. Blackwell had said nothing during the interview about being a transvestite, and Strange made no inquiries as to the reason for Blackwell's mode of dress and behavior.

Within a few hours after interviewing Blackwell, Strange cancelled the vacancy for the clerical position by oral instruction to a subordinate and had the position relisted at a higher level for which Blackwell would not have been qualified. Strange never discussed Blackwell's application with the unit supervisor who had recommended hiring him. After learning that he would not be hired, Blackwell initiated an appeal of the decision within the Department. The appeal dragged on for more than three years. Finally, impatient for some resolution, Blackwell filed suit against the Department in the U.S. District Court for the District of Columbia. The case was assigned to Judge Gerhard A. Gesell, a veteran of the bench who had been serving since his appointment by President Lyndon Baines Johnson in 1967.

Blackwell based his lawsuit on three separate theories. First, he invoked a 19th-century civil rights law that forbids conspiracies to deprive persons of equal protection of the laws. He charged that officials at the Treasury had conspired to reclassify the clerical openings in order to deprive him of employment. Then, he asserted that he had suffered discrimination on the basis of a handicap, within the meaning of the Rehabilitation Act of 1973, which forbids the federal government from depriving persons of employment opportunities on the basis of mental or physical handicaps. Blackwell alleged that transvestism was a mental impairment within the meaning of the Act. Finally, he asserted that the Treasury Department, a governmental employer, had violated his right to equal protection of the laws under the Fifth Amendment's Due Process Clause, which, among other things, requires the government to refrain from unjustified categorical discrimination in its employment policies.

The Treasury Department quickly moved to dismiss the case, arguing that the conspiracy claim was not supported by Blackwell's allegations, since Strange had acted individually in denying him employment, that the constitutional claim was time-barred, and that the Rehabilitation Act did not apply because Blackwell was not a "handicapped individual" within the meaning of the Act. Judge Gesell, ruling on the motion on May 27, 1986, agreed to dismiss the conspiracy claim and the constitutional claim. However, he allowed Blackwell to proceed to trial on the handicap discrimination claim.

The Rehabilitation Act broadly defines a "handicapped individual" as "any person who (i) has a physical or mental impairment which substantially limits such person's functioning or one or more of such person's major life activities, (ii) has a record of such an impairment, or (iii) is regarded as having such an impairment." Judge Gesell observed that the American Psychiatric Association's diagnostic manual classified transvestism as a mental disorder. Although Blackwell was not physically or mentally incapable of undertaking major life activities (such as taking care of himself, walking, seeing, hearing, speaking, breathing, learning, or working), he alleged that he was denied employment because he was regarded as being mentally impaired due to his transvestism. Consequently, Gesell found that Blackwell had alleged a *prima facie* case of handicap discrimination and was entitled to a trial of his claim.

A hearing was quickly scheduled. After Blackwell repeated the allegations of his complaint and described his interview and denial of employment, Strange took the stand. He said that he had no recollection of the interview, which had occurred more than four years previously, but he did recall Blackwell's long braided hair and a negative comment by one of Strange's associates after Blackwell left the office. Strange asserted that he had received several applications from laid-off Treasury employees for the vacancies that had been posted, but that he was not satisfied with the quality of the applicants, and had decided to upgrade the position in order to attract a better quality of applicants who would, if hired, be probationary employees, unlike the priority applicants who would immediately have protected status under Civil Service regulations. Strange insisted that Blackwell never told him that he was a transvestite, and that Blackwell's lifestyle had nothing to do with the decision to upgrade the position.

Judge Gesell issued his ruling after trial on September 19. The judge concluded that Strange had refused to hire Blackwell because he perceived Blackwell to be a homosexual. Gesell commented:

> There is nothing to suggest that Mr. Strange had any understanding one way or the other as to the difference between a homosexual and a transvestite or that he focused on the fact that plaintiff's dress was somewhat more feminine than that of many homosexuals. To make matters more difficult, some transvestites are homosexuals. Yet, as a matter of statutory analysis, while homosexuals are not handicapped it is clear that transvestites are, because many experience strong social rejection

in the work place as a result of their mental ailment made blatantly apparent by their cross-dressing life-style.

Thus, Judge Gesell concluded that the Treasury's defense was pretextual, but that did not end the matter because of the judge's finding regarding Strange's motivation. Since Strange thought Blackwell was a homosexual and seemed unaware of the difference between homosexuality and transvestism, how could he be said to have discriminated against Blackwell because he regarded him as having a mental impairment (i.e., transvestism)? To Gesell, this seemed an insurmountable difficulty and required dismissing the case. Gesell asserted that Blackwell's "handicap was not automatically apparent as is gender." Since the Rehabilitation Act forbids employers from directly inquiring about handicaps that are not job-related, the burden should not be placed on the employer to inquire as to whether a handicap "not automatically apparent" actually exists. Since Blackwell never affirmatively told either the unit supervisor or Strange that he was a transvestite, they could not be charged with that knowledge, or with failing to hire him because they thought he was impaired due to transvestism.

Imagine how Blackwell felt about all this. On the one hand, the court had ruled that a transvestite is a handicapped person within the meaning of the Rehabilitation Act. Since transvestism manifests itself in cross-dressing behavior, it would seem quite apparent to any reasonable person who observes a transvestite "in action." But the judge was holding that even though Strange seemed to have denied Blackwell employment because of conclusions he drew as to Blackwell's sexuality based on his appearance, Blackwell was out of luck because Strange seemed not to know the difference between homosexuality and transvestism!

Blackwell appealed to the U.S. Court of Appeals for the District of Columbia Circuit, where a panel consisting of Circuit Judges Ruth Bader Ginsburg and Kenneth W. Starr and Judge Helen W. Nies of the Federal Circuit heard arguments on September 22, 1987, and issued its opinion on October 16. Judge Ginsburg, writing for the court, indicated that they were affirming Judge Gesell's decision to dismiss. Since there was no precedent for holding that homosexuality was a handicap under the Rehabilitation Act, and Gesell had found that Strange "perceived Blackwell to be a homosexual," the court agreed that Strange could not have been guilty of discrimination on the basis of transvestism.

But the appeals court disagreed strongly with Gesell's apparent ruling that protection under the Rehabilitation Act would depend on a job applicant giving the employer "precise notice of a handicap that is not 'automatically apparent.'" Noting regulations that forbid asking a prospective employee whether he or she is handicapped, Ginsburg insisted that the court could not require Blackwell to have explained his condition in order to invoke the protection of the Act. On the other hand, Ginsburg asserted that the liability of the government should not turn on "the level of sophistication or ability to classify of the particular interviewing officer—in this case, on whether that officer knows that homosexuality and transvestism are not one and the same." Thus, the court vacated Judge Gesell's decision.

However, Judge Ginsburg never expressly stated why the case should be dismissed if Rehabilitation Act coverage did not depend on Blackwell having expressly informed Strange about the reason for his appearance. The logical implication of Ginsburg's statement was that if a reasonable person would have concluded from his appearance that Blackwell suffered from a mental impairment (i.e., transvestism) within the meaning of the Act and went on to deny him employment because of that conclusion, the Act would apply and the issue would be whether Blackwell, the applicant, was qualified for the job for which he had applied. Ginsburg seems to have concluded that persons presenting themselves for a job interview dressed as a member of the opposite sex do not necessarily put the employer on notice by their appearance that they are transvestites, having a condition that qualifies for Rehabilitation Act protection. It is hard to know what she might have been thinking about why someone who is not a transvestite would wear sexually ambiguous clothing to a job interview, and what conclusions a reasonable person might draw from being faced by such a job applicant.

Seeking to clarify the court's holding, Judge Nies wrote a concurring opinion, the premise of which was that a person could not have suffered discrimination on account of a particular handicapping condition if "that handicapping condition is unknowable without violating the regulations against asking questions concerning a person's handicaps." Nies would have found the Act to apply if "a reasonable interviewer would or should have known or been aware of the applicant's handicap." Nies then attempted to explain why the case had to be dismissed, asserting that nothing in Blackwell's past record or present appearance would have led Strange to conclude that Blackwell was a transvestite. Nies noted that Blackwell had described his manner of dress that day as "unisex" style, and that Gesell had characterized it as only "somewhat more feminine than that of many homosexuals." (This remark itself betrays confusion on the part of Judge Gesell as to the difference between sexual orientation and gender role identity, concepts as to which he as well as Nies may have been uninformed.) She concluded that, in any event, Blackwell was not arguing that Strange should have concluded he was a transvestite based on his appearance but rather that Strange's knowledge with regard to this was not pertinent to making out a *prima facie* case.

For the appeals court, the crucial issue was the motivation for the decision to deny Blackwell the position. It seemed clear, from Judge Gesell's characterization of the evidence, that Blackwell's presentation of himself as a somewhat effeminate man dressed in feminine garb was the reason for the decision, since Gesell found that Blackwell was qualified and had been found suitable by the "experienced Unit Supervisor." Blackwell's presentation of himself was the outward manifestation of his transvestism. It is hard to know how a transvestite could be more open about his or her condition than to appear in public dressed and groomed in a manner appropriate to a member of the opposite sex. Yet both Judge Gesell and the appeals court seemed to agree that such open and blatant cross-dressing does not make the condition of transvestism "automatically apparent," since, as far as they were concerned, some homosexuals dress that way and a typical person might conclude that somebody thus dressed is a homosexual.

This line of reasoning conflates sexual orientation and gender role identity and does exactly what the appeals court says should not be done. It allows the "level of sophistication or ability to classify" of the typical person to deprive transvestites (who may not be aware of the necessity to tell an interviewer what to the transvestite seems obvious) of the protections of the Rehabilitation Act. But perhaps the court took this route because it did not share Judge Gesell's opinion that transvestism is a handicapping condition within the meaning of the Act. Nowhere in the opinions does either appellate judge actually express agreement with Judge Gesell's holding; and, although the appeals court affirmed the dismissal of the case, it vacated Gesell's opinion. While the premise (especially of the concurring opinion) seems to

be that a refusal to hire an applicant because of perceived transvestism would violate the Act if the employer knew the applicant was a transvestite, the opinions are ambiguous.

Blackwell's case was something of a *cause célèbre* in the District of Columbia, and was undoubtedly largely responsible for Congress's decision while considering the Americans With Disabilities Act (ADA) to expressly exclude transvestism from inclusion as a "disability." Along with "homosexuality" and "transsexuality," transvestism was the subject of a special provision of the law, applying both to the new ADA (which was signed into law in July 1990) and the Rehabilitation Act. Regardless of the judgments of medical professionals that transvestites are suffering from a mental impairment, Congress has declared that they are not to receive any protection against discrimination in employment or public accommodations under federal law.

86. DOES TITLE VII PROTECT "MASCULINE" WOMEN?

Price Waterhouse v. Hopkins, 490 U.S. 228 (1989), reversing 825 F.2d 458 (D.C. Cir. 1987), modifying 618 F. Supp. 1109 (D.D.C. 1985); on remand: 1989 WL 105318 (D.C. Cir.); 737 F. Supp. 1202 (D.D.C.), affirmed, 920 F.2d 967 (D.C. Cir. 1990).

Can evidence of sexual stereotyping be used to establish that an employer or other person covered by civil rights laws (such as Title VII of the federal Civil Rights Act of 1964) has engaged in unlawful discrimination on the basis of sex? The U.S. Court of Appeals for the Fifth Circuit implicitly answered this question in the negative in *Smith v. Liberty Mutual Insurance Co.* (1978), when it denied relief to a man rejected for employment because the interviewer considered him "effeminate." What about the converse, a woman rejected for partnership at a major national accounting and consulting firm because some partners of the firm considered her behavior inadequately feminine?

In *Price Waterhouse v. Hopkins*, the U.S. Supreme Court approved using evidence of such sexual stereotyping in establishing a violation

of Title VII. The *Price Waterhouse* litigation was an extended saga stretching over almost six years, producing two published opinions on the merits by the U.S. District Court for the District of Columbia and two published opinions on the merits by the U.S. Court of Appeals for the District of Columbia Circuit, in addition to a lengthy set of opinions in the U.S. Supreme Court from plurality, concurrers, and dissenters. These opinions range widely over a variety of significant issues of proof and remedy under Title VII, in addition to the merits of the argument that sexual stereotyping may be evidence of sex discrimination. This consideration of the case focuses on the sexual stereotyping issue, with brief summary treatment of the complex Title VII proof and remedy issues more appropriately dealt with in a treatise on employment discrimination law.

Ann Hopkins and her husband were both employed at Touche Ross, a major national accounting firm, when her husband was made a partner there. Because of Touche Ross policies against considering spouses of partners for partnership, Hopkins resigned and obtained a position at Price Waterhouse in 1978. She was told a few years later that she could not be considered for partner at Price Waterhouse because her husband was a partner at a leading competitor. She threatened to resign as a result, but the problem was resolved when her husband left Touche Ross to form his own consulting firm. In 1982, the partners in Price Waterhouse's Office of Government Services (OGS), where Hopkins worked, unanimously voted to recommend her for partnership. Viewed on objective business-related evidence, Hopkins was a top candidate for partnership. She had played a major role in obtaining two significant contracts for the partnership involving very large sums of money and seemed to command high regard from the firm's clients. One of her contracts was credited by a senior partner, Joseph Connor, with establishing Price Waterhouse's credibility in an important new government market, leading to many other important contracts for the firm. Hopkins was responsible for more new business and worked longer hours than any of the 87 men nominated by their offices for partnership that year.

Price Waterhouse had a highly formalized procedure for considering applicants for partnership, necessitated by its large size and geographic dispersion. At the time Hopkins filed suit in 1984, the firm had 662 partners stationed in 90 offices scattered across the United States, of whom seven were women. In 1982, 88 senior managers were proposed for partnership; Hopkins was the only woman nominee. Price Waterhouse was governed by a Senior Partner and Policy Board, which delegated the initial screening of partnership applicants to an Admissions Committee. The Committee circulated evaluation forms to all partners of the firm. Partners who had extensive working contact with a candidate completed a "long-form" evaluation calling for detailed comment and analysis; partners who had only casual knowledge of the candidate completed a "short form" calling for more general comment. The forms called

for ratings in 48 categories of relevant skills and accomplishment, as well as more subjective statements about the candidates' suitability. After considering the responses to the evaluation forms and performing follow-up interviews to clear up ambiguities, the Admissions Committee would vote on its recommendations to the Policy Board. The Committee could make one of three recommendations: approve a candidate for placement on the ballot, turn down a candidate, or place a candidate on "hold" for reconsideration in a later round. Most of those placed on hold would normally come up for consideration in a later year, and most of those would eventually be approved for partnership. The Policy Board had discretion to accept or reject decisions by the Admissions Committee, sometimes making such decisions based on business considerations outside the Committee's purview. Finally, the entire partnership would vote on the candidacies of those recommended for approval by the Policy Board. This process left much room for the subjective judgments of individual partners to play a significant role in the process. There was no established mechanism by which the firm systematically instructed partners on the requirements of civil rights laws or the appropriate factors to consider in making comments about candidates. Review of the evaluation forms completed by partners over a period of several years during the litigation revealed a variety of remarks about women candidates that could be interpreted as singling them out for different treatment and standards. At least one partner had stated unequivocally on an evaluation form that he did not believe women capable of serving as partners at Price Waterhouse, and even had doubts about their ability to be senior managers. (No such direct statement was found on any evaluation form for Hopkins, however.)

Hopkins's candidacy proved controversial, despite her unanimous endorsement by the partners in her office. She was an aggressive person, by all accounts very demanding to work with and for. She was known to swear when angry, and apparently made little effort to cultivate a traditionally feminine appearance and demeanor. Her personality, style, and appearance made a decisive impression on many of the partners who filled out evaluation forms, whether they endorsed or opposed her candidacy. Some of those who endorsed her candidacy noted that other partners might feel uncomfortable with her masculine style, but that this discomfort could be due to their own prejudices, and that she was no more aggressive or foul-mouthed than many male partners of the firm. Some of those who advised placing her candidacy on hold or who voted no considered these "interpersonal skills" problems to be decisive. One partner commented that she needed a course in "charm school," another suggested that "she may have overcompensated for being a woman" by maintaining this aggressive posture. Of the thirty-two partners who submitted evaluations, eight recommended denial of partnership, three favored putting her on hold, and eight indicated insufficient basis for an opinion; the remaining thirteen recommended an affirmative vote. This division put Hopkins toward the bottom of the list of 88 candidates, and led the Admissions Committee to recommend putting her candidacy on hold. The Policy Board concurred with this recommendation, which was communicated to Hopkins.

Under Price Waterhouse policies, Thomas Beyer, as the chief partner in Hopkins's office, was the one who met with Hopkins to discuss the decision and the reasons for it. Beyer had been Hopkins's leading proponent in the partnership process. The main purpose of their meeting was to figure out how to proceed in making Hopkins a more attractive candidate for the following year. Beyer advised Hopkins "to walk more femininely, talk more femininely, dress more femininely, wear make-up, have her hair styled, and wear jewelry," according to the district court's summary of that conversation. Apparently Beyer believed that Hopkins's failure to conform to society's view of appropriate feminine behavior and appearance was a substantial factor in the decisions by the Admissions Committee and the Policy Board not to recommend her for partnership that year. Hopkins subsequently met with Joseph Connor, a senior partner, who urged her to undertake a Quality Control Review to allow her to work with more partners so she could demonstrate her skills and "allay concerns about her ability to deal with staff." Connor made no direct mention of the "femininity" issue.

Shortly after her meeting with Connor, Hopkins arranged a lunch meeting with Donald Epelbaum, one of the OGS partners who had supported her candidacy. At that meeting, Hopkins described her conversation with Connor in a way that led Epelbaum to reconsider his support for her candidacy, since he felt Hopkins had misrepresented what Connor told her. Another OGS partner, who had at first supported her candidacy and then urged putting it on hold, also soured on Hopkins in the following months. When it came time four months later for the OGS partners to decide on recommendations for the next partnership cycle, this opposition led them to decide against proposing Hopkins again. When she learned of this, Hopkins spent a few months considering her options and then decided to reject the advice of those OGS partners who urged her to remain at Price Waterhouse as a senior manager. In the national accounting firms, being passed over as partner signals the end of the career track; Hopkins decided to take the advice of one OGS partner who urged her to quit and seek employment elsewhere. However, she still wanted to become a Price Waterhouse partner and decided to sue the firm for sex discrimination. After an interview with Touche Ross, where she was offered a senior manager position with assurance of a "fast track" review for partnership, she decided to go it alone as a consultant while pursuing her remedy. She established her own consulting business, which was moderately successful for several years, and then obtained a managerial position in a governmental agency, which she held at the time the litigation finally concluded in 1990. She never earned as much while self-employed or working for the government as she would have earned as a Price Waterhouse partner, or even as much as in the positions she might have obtained with other major accounting firms after leaving Price Waterhouse.

After exhausting administrative requirements under Title VII by filing a charge with the Equal Employment Opportunity Commission and obtaining a right-to-sue letter, Hopkins filed suit in the federal district court in Washington, D.C. Represented by Washington attorneys Douglas B. Huron and James H. Heller, her case was assigned to Judge Gerhard A.

Gesell, one of the longest-serving judges on that bench. Price Waterhouse fielded a team of three attorneys, Stephen E. Tallent, Wayne A. Schrader, and Kathy Davidson Ireland, in defense. Claiming that her resignation from Price Waterhouse was actually a "constructive discharge" and that she had been denied promotion due to her sex in violation of Title VII, Hopkins sought a court order making her a partner at Price Waterhouse, together with back pay and other monetary relief. Discovery dragged on for many months, as Hopkins's attorneys demanded, obtained, and reviewed every evaluation form and other document generated during the Price Waterhouse partnership process for the years 1982, 1983, and 1984.

Judge Gesell conducted almost five full days of hearings in the trial of the case. In addition to the extensive documentary evidence, Hopkins's attorneys presented an expert witness, Dr. Susan Fiske, a social psychologist and associate professor of psychology at Carnegie-Mellon University, who was presented as an expert and academic scholar in the area of sexual stereotyping. Price Waterhouse's attorneys raised no objections to her qualifications. Fiske, who had never met with Hopkins or observed her at work, testified about the latent sexism she saw reflected in both obviously sex-linked comments in the evaluation forms and gender-neutral comments that made criticisms about Hopkins's interpersonal skills and business style. According to Fiske, some of the strongly negative comments made by partners who had little personal contact with Hopkins provided evidence of sexual stereotyping. While she could not necessarily point to any particular such comment as being the direct result of stereotyping, she asserted that she could draw conclusions from the totality of the comments that the process was affected by the stereotyping views of some of the partners, both proponents and opponents of Hopkins' candidacy. She based her conclusions not only on the Hopkins evaluations but also on comments found in the evaluation forms for other women candidates in other years.

Price Waterhouse did not offer any expert to rebut Fiske's testimony. Its trial strategy instead focused on showing that Hopkins's personality made working with her difficult and

justified the negative comments she had generated, and that the nature of the business required a degree of collegiality in working with partners and staff that she had not achieved. Although various objective factors might appear to qualify Hopkins for partnership, argued Price Waterhouse's attorneys, the subjective factors were of equal importance and justified the decision by the Policy Committee to put her on hold and the subsequent decision by the OGS partners not to recommend her for reconsideration the next year.

After concluding the trial, Judge Gesell issued his first opinion in the case on September 20, 1985. He noted that Hopkins had advanced three arguments for finding the partnership decision discriminatory: first, that criticisms of her interpersonal skills were "fabricated"; second, that male candidates with equal or worse interpersonal problems were made partners; and third, that the criticisms of her were a product of sexual stereotyping by certain partners, whose views were improperly given full weight in Price Waterhouse's partnership selection process. While denying Hopkins's allegations, Price Waterhouse argued that it had a legitimate business justification for the partnership decisions, founded in the collegial nature of the business and the negative impact on morale if Hopkins, as a partner, were set over a significant number of staff.

Gesell found Hopkins's first two argument unconvincing. Concerns about Hopkins's interpersonal skills surfaced throughout the evaluations, from supporters and opponents alike. Clearly, these concerns had not been fabricated; she was an aggressive personality, difficult to work with, occasionally disruptive, and foul-mouthed. Furthermore, he concluded, the Admissions Committee appropriately took into account the issue of interpersonal skills when it decided to recommend putting her candidacy on hold. While it was true that Price Waterhouse had elevated two men to partnership who had also inspired negative comments about their interpersonal skills, in both cases the Policy Board had decided to advance them for particular business reasons that did not pertain to Hopkins' case. Clearly, interpersonal skills issues were taken seriously by the Admissions Committee and Policy Board with justification. While Hopkins presented strong "objective" credentials in terms of effort and success with clients, she had received more "no" votes in the evaluations than almost all the other candidates for partnership in 1982, and looking at Price Waterhouse's overall record with women as partnership candidates, the differences in rates of approval between women and men were not statistically significant. Although the actual number of women partners at Price Waterhouse was small, this did not strike Gesell as significant where women made up only a small portion of the pool of qualified persons for consideration.

However, Gesell was persuaded by Hopkins's argument that sexual stereotyping had infected the partnership process and that Price Waterhouse had knowingly allowed it to do so without taking any steps to deal with the problem. Finding that both the comments about Hopkins and about other women candidates supported this conclusion, Gesell especially noted Fiske's testimony that "unfavorable comments by male partners, slanted in a negative direction by operation of male stereotyping, were a major factor in the firm's evaluation" of Hopkins.

> That deep within males and females there exist sexually based reactions to the personal characteristics of one of the opposite sex should come as no surprise [said Gesell]. It is well documented that men evaluating women in managerial occupations sometimes apply stereotypes which discriminate against women. Indeed, the subtle and unconscious discrimination created by sex stereotyping appears to be a major impediment to Title VII's goal of ensuring equal employment opportunities. . . . One common form of stereotyping is that women engaged in assertive behavior are judged more critically because aggressive conduct is viewed as a masculine characteristic.

Gesell concluded that "while stereotyping played an undefined role in blocking plaintiff's admission to the partnership in this instance, it was unconscious on the part of the partners who submitted comments." The evidence offered by Fiske did not prove intentional stereotyping. Much the opposite, the whole point of her testimony was that such stereotyping is an unconscious process. This posed problems under Title VII because Hopkins's claim was ap-

propriately analyzed as a mixed-motive disparate-treatment claim, under which the plaintiff's initial burden was to show intentional discrimination. However, Hopkins argued that the Price Waterhouse partnership selection system "permitted negative comments tainted by stereotyping to defeat her candidacy, despite clear indications that the evaluations were tainted by discriminatory stereotyping. All the evaluators were men." Although it would be clear to any objective reader of the evaluations, even without the expertise of Fiske, that at least some of the evaluations bore the taint of stereotyped responses to Hopkins's personality traits, "the Policy Board never addressed the problem," concluded Gesell. "The firm never took any steps in its partnership policy statement or in the evaluation forms submitted to partners to articulate a policy against discrimination or to discourage sexual bias. The Admissions Committee never attempted to investigate whether any of the negative comments concerning the plaintiff were based on a discriminatory double standard." These failures sufficed, in Gesell's view, to meet the requirements of a *prima facie* case of sex discrimination. "Although the stereotyping by individual partners may have been unconscious on their part, the maintenance of a system that gave weight to such biased criticisms was a conscious act of the partnership as a whole."

Gesell acknowledged the particular difficulties of applying Title VII nondiscrimination requirements to the heavily subjective process of partnership decisions, but noted that the U.S. Supreme Court had recently ruled in *Hishon v. King and Spaulding* (1984) that such decisions were subject to Title VII, since policies governing promotion to partnership were terms or conditions of employment. Although partnerships must be given freedom "to evaluate the qualifications of employees who seek to become partners, they are not free to inject stereotyped assumptions about women into the selection process," he asserted. Price Waterhouse's failure to deal with the problems of sexism in its evaluation process suggested a "double standard" that violated Title VII. Although Price Waterhouse had a legitimate concern with "abrasive conduct in men or women seeking partnership," it could not prevail where "discriminatory stereotyping of females was permitted to play a part." Gesell stated:

> Comments influenced by sex stereotypes were made by partners; the firm's evaluation process gave substantial weight to these comments; and the partnership failed to address the conspicuous problem of stereotyping in partnership evaluations. While these three factors might have been innocent alone, they combined to produce discrimination in the case of this plaintiff.

Having found that Hopkins had established that sexual stereotyping had improperly tainted the partnership process in her place, Gesell held that the burden was on Price Waterhouse to show by "clear and convincing evidence" that it would not have offered partnership to Hopkins even in the absence of such impermissible motivation. Gesell concluded that Price Waterhouse had failed this test. While it had shown that there were genuine concerns about Hopkins's interpersonal skills, it had not shown that she would not have been offered partnership even had the stereotyped remarks been removed from the record, although Gesell also could not say with certainty that she would have been offered partnership. Given the allocation of burden of proof at this point, however, such an ambiguous conclusion went against Price Waterhouse, which had the burden of persuasion on this point.

Having found that Hopkins's rights had been violated, however, Gesell was unwilling to provide any remedy other than her legal fees. This was because he did not believe that the situation at Price Waterhouse was such that Hopkins was compelled to resign. The law governing "constructive discharge" requires that the employer has created such intolerable circumstances that the employee could do nothing other than resign. "Plaintiff has not shown any history of discrimination, humiliation or other aggravating factors that would have compelled her to resign," Gesell concluded. Indeed, her experience at the firm "appears to have been quite normal and amicable." She may have wanted to leave with the idea of pursuing partnership elsewhere, but she was not compelled to do so, and she was encouraged by many in the OGS to continue as a senior manager there. Consequently, she was not entitled to an order

making her a partner, or even for compensation since her resignation. Her only relief would normally be the difference between partner-level compensation and her actual compensation from the time she was denied partnership until her resignation. Even this, Gesell said, would not be awarded, because the attorneys, thinking to simplify the trial of the case and avoid unnecessary trial time, had agreed without consulting him to omit any proof on the issue of damages from the trial, pending a decision on liability. Gesell asserted that the parties did not have the authority to control the litigation in that manner, and one who determined not to present evidence without first consulting the court proceeded "at his own peril." Consequently, Gesell ordered Hopkins's claims dismissed while awarding her reasonable attorney's fees and costs.

Having thus won a pyrrhic victory, Hopkins determined to appeal the decision. Of course, Price Waterhouse also appealed the decision on the merits. The case was argued in the D.C. Circuit on October 23, 1986, with James H. Heller arguing for Hopkins and Stephen R. Tallent arguing for Price Waterhouse. For the first time on appeal, Price Waterhouse attacked the testimony of Hopkins's expert, Dr. Fiske, and argued that the record evidence did not support Gesell's conclusions about sexual stereotyping.

The panel split over the case in its opinions issued August 4, 1987, almost a year after the argument. Circuit Judge Harry T. Edwards and District Judge Joyce Hens Green, sitting by designation, agreed with Gesell that Hopkins had adequately demonstrated a violation of Title VII, in an opinion by Judge Green. They parted company from him in finding, however, that Hopkins had been constructively discharged and ordered the case remanded for reconsideration of remedies, including the possibility of ordering that Hopkins be made a partner of Price Waterhouse. Circuit Judge Stephen F. Williams dissented, accepting Price Waterhouse's argument that sexual stereotyping was not a valid basis for finding a Title VII violation, although he agreed with his colleagues that if a Title VII violation were found in this case, the district court should consider the remedies of awarding partnership or offering significant back pay.

Price Waterhouse had attacked Gesell's ruling directly on two grounds, arguing that evidence in the record did not support the finding of stereotyping and that Gesell's findings regarding the legitimacy of complaints about Hopkins's behavior constituted "a legitimate nondiscriminatory business reason" for the decision on Hopkins's partnership candidacy. Noting that in challenging a factual finding by the district court Price Waterhouse would have to show that the finding was "clearly erroneous," Green concluded that Price Waterhouse failed in its burden, since there was competent evidence in the record from which Gesell could draw his factual conclusions. Gesell had based his conclusion on the actual comments partners made on the evaluation sheets, Fiske's testimony about the significance of those comments, and the comments made about other women in previous years.

Green rejected Price Waterhouse's argument that the stereotyping comments made by Hopkins's proponents should be disregarded in determining whether stereotyping had led to her candidacy being placed on hold. "Characterizing a female candidate as 'macho' and 'masculine' is certainly one way of qualifying, thereby diluting, an endorsement," she commented. "Supporters of a male candidate are very unlikely to describe that candidate in sexual terms, i.e., as 'masculine,' or to excuse character flaws as merely the result of 'overcompensating for being a man.'" Fiske had testified that such comments by Hopkins' supporters reflected "a conscious effort on the part of the commenters to overcome their stereotypical attitudes and vote for Hopkins despite their disdain for her behavior." They were echoing the complaints of Hopkins's critics, "thereby lending credence to those complaints and unwittingly undermining the support they sought to provide." Green also rejected Price Waterhouse's contention that the reference to "charm school" was a harmless, gender-neutral comment. "'Charm school' is a somewhat derogatory colloquialism for an institution formally known as a 'finishing school'" and had a specifically feminine connotation, said Green, citing *Webster's Third New International Dictionary*.

She also found unavailing Price Waterhouse's attempts to downplay Beyer's comments to Hopkins about acting more "femininely." There was testimony from a member of the Policy Board and the Admissions Committee, Roger Marcellin, that he had "no doubt that Tom Beyer would be the one that would have to talk with her" about what had happened, and that "he knew exactly where the problems were." Clearly, Gesell could conclude that Beyer's comments represented more than his own opinions and were meant to convey the basis for the firm's action in her case.

Price Waterhouse tried on appeal to discredit Fiske's testimony by describing it as "sheer speculation" of "no evidentiary value." Price Waterhouse characterized the quality of information available to Fiske as insufficient for the conclusions she was drawing. "To the extent that Price Waterhouse believes Dr. Fiske lacked necessary information," concluded Green, "the firm is in fact quarreling with her field of practice and the methodology it employs," because Fiske had testified that experts in her field could draw such conclusions on the basis of what she had seen. Since Price Waterhouse had not raised such objections at trial, it was too late to do so now.

Green also rejected Price Waterhouse's argument that evaluations of other candidates containing statements about women should be disregarded, concluding that such evidence could be appropriately considered as supporting Gesell's conclusion that Price Waterhouse was aware that partners of the firm had evaluated women candidates "in terms of their sex." This was the sole purpose for that evidence.

Turning to Price Waterhouse's challenge of Gesell's legal theory of the case, Green noted that the U.S. Supreme Court had held in *International Brotherhood of Teamsters v. United States* (1977) that the necessary intent or motivation for a disparate treatment case could be drawn by inference from "the mere fact of differences in treatment." Thus, it did not matter that the evidence may have shown "unconscious" stereotyping on the part of individual partners. Said Green, "[T]he Supreme Court has never applied the concept of intent so as to excuse an artificial, gender-based employment barrier simply because the employer involved did not harbor the requisite degree of ill-will towards the person in question." It was enough that the employer followed a practice that treated men and women differently. It would be rare to find a bigot as honest as the Price Waterhouse partner who had actually written on an evaluation form that he "objected to all female candidates as a matter of principle." It was a practical necessity in cases such as this to draw inferences rather than seek an explicit avowal of discriminatory intent.

It was true that under controlling Supreme Court and D.C. Circuit precedents it was inappropriate to require the defendant, "simply on the basis of the inference of discrimination raised by plaintiff's *prima facie* case, to prove that discrimination was not the but for cause of the challenged employment decision," conceded Green. "Here, however, Hopkins has offered direct evidence that her gender was a significant motivating factor in her failure to make partner, and Price Waterhouse's claim that it had other legitimate reasons for its decision in no way negates her showing." Once a plaintiff had made out the *prima facie* case in this kind of "mixed-motive" situation, the burden would shift to the employer to show by clear and convincing evidence that "the unlawful factor was not the determinative one," as the D.C. Circuit had ruled in 1983 in *Toney v. Block*, its leading case on the issue. To Price Waterhouse's argument that Gesell had himself found that Hopkins's personality provided a legitimate justification for the partnership decision, Green rejoined that Price Waterhouse had failed to show that Hopkins's personality, as distinct from the stereotyped reactions to it, was "the determinative factor."

Where Green parted company from Gesell was in his analysis of the relief available to Hopkins. This was an industry where somebody would have to quit if they did not become a partner and wanted to achieve the status and rewards of partnership. Hopkins had made clear that a partnership opportunity was an absolute prerequisite for any job to be satisfactory for her. She quit Touche Ross because her partnership there was blocked, and she threatened to quit Price Waterhouse when she was told her husband's position would block her partnership there. Green found that "the custom-ary and nearly unanimous practice at Price Waterhouse, as at most other accounting firms, is for senior managers who have been passed over for partnership to resign, and one of the OGS partners who strongly opposed Hopkins' candidacy advised her to do just that." In light of all this, Green asserted that Gesell had adopted a "literal interpretation" of the circuit court's precedents on "constructive discharge" that was "misplaced" here. It was enough, said Green, "if the employer simply tolerates discriminatory working conditions that would drive a reasonable person to resign." While the mere fact of discrimination, without more, was not enough to find constructive discharge, what happened to Hopkins "would have been viewed by any reasonable senior manager in her position as a career-ending action." Thus, it was a constructive discharge situation, and Gesell should reconsider the remedy available to Hopkins. Since there would be a new trial on damages, the grounds on which Gesell had refused to order back pay were now "moot," and it was appropriate for him to hear testimony on money damages as well.

Circuit Judge Stephen F. Williams dissented, accusing the majority of adopting "a novel theory of liability under Title VII" without adequate discussion or consideration of its consequences and boundaries. "An analysis grounding Title VII liability in such stereotypes may well be meritorious," he said, "but its articulation would require care." What boundaries should be set in this area? "Dismissal of a male employee because he routinely appeared for work in skirts and dresses would surely reflect a form of sexual stereotyping, but it would not, merely on that account, support Title VII liability," asserted Williams. Furthermore, as far as he was concerned, the record in this case "provided no causal connection between Hopkins' fate and such stereotyping as went on among Price Waterhouse's 662 partners." The evidence of stereotyping came from isolated comments picked up from a small percentage of the large number of evaluation forms reviewed, not all those seized on by Fiske and Gesell were clearly evidence of stereotyping, and many of the comments came from Hopkins's supporters.

Under the precedents of *Texas Department of Community Affairs v. Burdine* (1981) and *Toney v. Block*(1983), the Supreme Court and the D.C. Circuit had recognized that in a case such as this the employer's burden was to show that its action was not "pretextual." Well, here Gesell had found that the concerns about Hopkins were not pretextual, but on the contrary that Price Waterhouse had "legitimate, nondiscriminatory reasons for distinguishing between plaintiff and the male partners with whom she compares herself." That should be sufficient to end the matter. Williams proceeded to evaluate the testimony at length, discounting the significance of many of the comments and concluding that "the only remark by a Hopkins opponent that can be characterized as manifesting sexual stereotyping is the facetious suggestion that she should take a 'course at charm school.' The smoke from this gun seems to me rather wispy," said Williams, noting that it was pulled from the context of a lengthy commentary including substantive comments about Hopkins's character. Williams spent the better part of a page of his opinion discounting the significance of the reference.

He also took on the testimony of Fiske, in a paragraph dripping with sarcasm, concluding, "To an expert of Fiske's qualifications, it seems plain that no woman could *be* overbearing, arrogant or abrasive: any observations to that effect would necessarily be discounted as the product of stereotyping. If analysis like this is to prevail in federal courts, no employer can base any adverse action as to a woman on such attributes."

Williams was particularly critical of the theory that Price Waterhouse's liability could be premised on its failure to take steps to eradicate sexual stereotyping from its partnership selection process. Commenting on Gesell's holding to this effect, he said, "It breaks new ground, blithely free of any effort to link it to any established legal principles." He argued that this new theory of liability had not been carefully defined and gave no indication of when such an employer duty would arise. "The rule turns Title VII from a prohibition of discriminatory conduct into an engine for rooting out sexist thoughts." He also found incredible Gesell's assertion that "[i]nnocent alone, the

three factors combined to produce discrimination in the case of this plaintiff," cracking that "such alchemy is mysterious." To Williams, the evidence in the record might show some sexist attitudes, but that such "generalized discrimination" was not sufficient to prove unlawful discrimination, especially when the defendant had come forth with non-pretextual grounds for its decision, as Gesell had found in this case.

The Supreme Court granted Price Waterhouse's *certiorari* petition on March 7, 1988, and heard argument on October 31 from attorneys Kathryn A. Oberly, of Washington, for Price Waterhouse and James H. Heller, again appearing for Hopkins. A majority of the Court was unable to agree on a single opinion in the case. On May 1, a majority of the Court announced that it agreed with the D.C. Circuit that sexual stereotyping could be used as evidence of sex discrimination, but different Justices had different conceptions of where that left the plaintiff and defendant with regard to their respective burdens of proof. A plurality opinion by Justice William J. Brennan, Jr., representing the views of Justices Thurgood Marshall, Harry A. Blackmun, and John Paul Stevens, took the position that the lower courts had erected too high a burden for the employer to meet in rebutting the *prima facie* case. For this sort of mixed-motive case, they argued, an employer had to establish that it would have made the disputed decision in the absence of discrimination by a preponderance of the evidence. Justices Byron R. White and Sandra Day O'Connor wrote separate opinions, concurring in the result (i.e., a remand to the lower courts for reconsideration in light of the reversal on the burden of proof issue) but each differing slightly from the plurality in describing the employer's burden in this sort of case. Justice Anthony M. Kennedy dissented, in an opinion joined by Chief Justice William H. Rehnquist and Justice Antonin Scalia, arguing that the Court had improperly created a new standard of proof in mixed-motive cases that was unnecessary and confusing in light of the Court's existing precedents in this area.

Justice Brennan's discussion of the legal theory of the case concentrates on rejecting the concept of "but-for" discrimination as a *sine qua non* in a mixed-motive case. The lower federal courts had become caught up in a semantic game, trying to characterize their appropriate role in cases where more than one motivation for an employment decision appeared in the record. Brennan argued that the issue under Title VII was not whether the discriminatory motive was the but-for cause of the decision, but rather whether it was a substantial factor. It was entirely possible, he said, that no one motive was the but-for cause. So long as the discriminatory motive played a part in the decision, however, the decision was tainted, and the requirements to make a *prima facie* case were met. That was significant in this case, because Judge Gesell had not found that sexual stereotyping was the but-for cause of the decision to place Hopkins's partnership on hold, but he had found that it was a "significant" factor. Reviewing the text and legislative history of Title VII, Brennan concluded that the statute was intended to strike a balance between the employer's freedom to make personnel decisions based on the merits and the strong national interest in eradicating discriminatory decisionmaking. "We conclude that the preservation of this freedom means that an employer shall not be liable if it can prove that, even if it had not taken gender into account, it would have come to the same decision regarding a particular person." In terms of proof, however, this showing should be treated as an affirmative defense, which in this context of civil litigation, would require the employer to persuade the fact-finder by the preponderance of the evidence, not by the more demanding "clear and convincing" evidence test imposed by the lower courts in this case.

Turning to the specific issue of sexual stereotyping as evidence of gender discrimination, Brennan said that "an employer who acts on the basis of a belief that a woman cannot be aggressive, or that she must not be, has acted on the basis of gender." Noting that Price Waterhouse had referred to "sex stereotyping" in quotation marks throughout its brief, as if to insinuate either that such stereotyping had not occurred in this case or that it lacked "legal relevance," Brennan rejected both possibilities. As to the second, "we are beyond the day when an employer could evaluate employees by assuming or insisting that they matched the ste-

reotype associated with their group," since, as the Court had stated in *Los Angeles Department of Water & Power v. Manhart* (1978) quoting from an earlier Seventh Circuit opinion, "'Congress intended to strike at the entire spectrum of disparate treatment of men and women resulting from sex stereotypes.'" Brennan stated: "An employer who objects to aggressiveness in women but whose positions require this trait places women in an intolerable and impermissible Catch-22: out of a job if they behave aggressively and out of a job if they don't. Title VII lifts women out of this bind."

While stereotyped remarks by themselves could not constitute a Title VII violation, said Brennan, they could certainly be evidence that "gender played a part" in making an employment decision. Here, the stereotyping did not just consist of "stray remarks." The Price Waterhouse situation did not just present discrimination "in the air," but rather evidenced discrimination focused on Hopkins and her partnership application. As to the objection that Price Waterhouse had demonstrated a legitimate reason for its decision, Brennan said it was not enough for Price Waterhouse to show that "it was motivated only in part by a legitimate reason." The premise of mixed-motive cases was that more than one reason played a part in the contested decision. "The employer instead must show that its legitimate reason, standing alone, would have induced it to make the same decision," concluded Brennan.

After discussing why the appropriate standard for making that determination was the "preponderance of the evidence" standard, Brennan turned to Price Waterhouse's attack on Fiske's testimony. Agreeing with the court of appeals that objection to Fiske's credentials and methods came too late in the game, Brennan commented,

> We are tempted to say that Dr. Fiske's expert testimony was merely icing on Hopkins' cake. It takes no special training to discern sex stereotyping in a description of an aggressive female employee as requiring "a course at charm school." Nor, turning to Thomas Beyer's memorable advice to Hopkins, does it require expertise in psychology to know that, if an employee's flawed "interpersonal skills" can be corrected by a soft-hued suit or a new shade of lipstick, perhaps it is the employee's sex and

not her interpersonal skills that has drawn the criticism.

Brennan also rejected the argument, embraced by dissenting Circuit Judge Williams, that stereotyping comments made by Hopkins's supporters should not be considered as evidence against the defendant. "A negative comment, even when made in the context of a generally favorable review, nevertheless may influence the decision-maker to think less highly of the candidate." The Policy Board had reviewed all the comments, and was undoubtedly influenced by negative comments which tended to corroborate those made by opponents. Finally, Brennan observed that Price Waterhouse seemed to believe that the Supreme Court could not affirm the ruling against it without deciding that Hopkins was actually not as described by her critics. "The District Judge acknowledged that Hopkins' conduct justified complaints about her behavior as a senior manager," said Brennan. But Brennan also concluded that the reactions of at least some of the partners were reactions to Hopkins as a *woman* manager.

> Where an evaluation is based on a subjective assessment of a person's strengths and weaknesses, it is simply not true that each evaluator will focus on, or even mention, the same weaknesses. Thus, even if we knew that Hopkins had "personality problems," this would not tell us that the partners who cast their evaluations of Hopkins in sex-based terms would have criticized her as sharply (or criticized her at all) if she had been a man.

Making such a determination was not the Court's function. "We sit not to determine whether Ms. Hopkins is nice, but to decide whether the partners reacted negatively to her personality because she is a woman."

Justice White's brief concurring opinion emphasized slight differences with the plurality as to the burdens of making out a *prima facie* case and rebutting it, although he agreed in essence with the result in this case because he felt that the record satisfied his view of the applicable tests. He asserted that Hopkins's initial burden had been to show that gender considerations were a substantial factor in the adverse employment decision. He differed from the plurality, which had apparently required the employer to produce "objective" evidence in meeting its rebuttal burden. "In a mixed mo-

tive case, where the legitimate motive found would have been ample grounds for the action taken," said White, "and the employer credibly testifies that the action would have been taken for the legitimate reasons alone, this should be ample proof." He asserted that this would "even more plainly be the case" when the employer had not conceded the existence of the illegitimate motive.

Justice O'Connor wrote a lengthy opinion, concurring in the judgment but focusing almost entirely on the issues of proof. She argued strongly that it was appropriate, as the plurality held, to put the burden on the employer to rebut the *prima facie* case by the preponderance of the evidence:

> At this point [after making out a *prima facie* case] Ann Hopkins had taken her proof as far as it could go. She had proved discriminatory input into the decisional process, and had proved that participants in the process considered her failure to conform to the stereotypes credited by a number of the decisionmakers had been a substantial factor in the decision. It is as if Ann Hopkins were sitting in the hall outside the room where partnership decisions were being made. As the partners filed in to consider her candidacy, she heard several of them make sexist remarks in discussing her suitability for partnership. As the decisionmakers exited the room, she was *told* by one of those privy to the decisionmaking process that her gender was a major reason for the rejection of her partnership bid. If, as we noted in *Teamsters*, "presumptions shifting the burden of proof are often created to reflect judicial evaluations of probabilities and to conform with a party's superior access to the proof," one would be hard pressed to think of a situation where it would be more appropriate to require the defendant to show that its decision would have been justified by wholly legitimate concerns.

However, O'Connor emphasized that she would erect a higher initial burden for the plaintiff to meet in making out a *prima facie* case, because she disagreed with Justice Brennan's rejection of the but-for standard. "The plurality proceeds from the premise that the words 'because of' in the statute do not embody any causal requirement at all. Under my approach," she said, "the plaintiff must produce evidence sufficient to show that an illegitimate criterion was a substantial factor in the particular employment decision such that a reasonable factfinder could draw an inference that the decision was made 'because of' the plaintiff's protected status." This would shift the burden of proof to the employer to show by a preponderance of the evidence that the same decision would have been made in the absence of discrimination for other reasons.

Justice Kennedy's dissent disputed the Court's apparent construction of a new, distinct evidentiary framework for analyzing mixed-motive disparate-treatment cases. He argued that the existing framework, set forth in *Burdine*, was totally adequate to deal with these cases. Under *Burdine*, the Court had made clear that the burden of proof in a Title VII case never shifts to the defendant. Contrary to O'Connor, Kennedy would not place on the employer a burden of proving by a preponderance of the evidence that the same decision would have been taken in the absence of the discriminatory motive. The burden would always stay with the plaintiff in proving that discriminatory motivation had caused the disputed decision. While in some senses the Court's opinion (with the plurality view being tempered by the moderating views expressed by Justice O'Connor) marked only a "minor refinement in Title VII procedures," it was nonetheless confusing and unnecessary to depart from the established tests familiar to the lower courts for this particular kind of case.

Furthermore, Kennedy wanted to "stress that Title VII creates no independent cause of action for sex stereotyping." Evidence of such stereotyping "is, of course, quite relevant to the question of discriminatory intent," he conceded, but the "ultimate question" was "whether discrimination caused the plaintiff's harm." Price Waterhouse's failure to address alleged stereotyping in its partnership selection process could not serve as an independent basis for finding a Title VII violation, said Kennedy, agreeing with dissenting Circuit Judge Williams's comment that imposing such an obligation would turn Title VII into "an engine for rooting out sexist thoughts." He also echoed Williams's sarcasm toward Hopkins's expert witness, Dr. Fiske. "The plaintiff who engages the services of Dr. Fiske should have no trouble showing that sex discrimination played a part in any decision," said Kennedy, who found the plurality's "enthusiasm for Fiske's conclusions unwarranted." Quoting Williams's sarcastic description of Fiske's conclusions, Kennedy commented: "Today's opinions cannot be read as requiring factfinders to credit testimony based on this type of analysis," citing O'Connor's concurring opinion.

On August 1, 1989, the D.C. Circuit panel (including District Judge Green) reconvened to order a remand of the case back to Judge Gesell for consistent proceedings in light of the Supreme Court's decision. Gesell offered the parties (and particularly Price Waterhouse) the opportunity to offer more testimony before he considered the issue of the defendant's liability anew under the less demanding test adopted by the Supreme Court, but Price Waterhouse declined to present anything new, apart from participating in litigation over the proposed remedy. This issue was vigorously contested, with Price Waterhouse mounting a full-scale attack on the issue of awarding Hopkins a partnership as a remedy in the case. It argued, among other things, that this would violate the firm's constitutional free association rights.

In his opinion of May 25, however, Gesell rejected Price Waterhouse's arguments. First, on the issue of liability, he held that the existing record, which had not been supplemented, still supported his original conclusions, despite the weaker evidentiary burden placed on Price Waterhouse. The first time around, he had concluded that the record was about evenly balanced as to whether Hopkins would have made partner in the absence of stereotyping remarks in her evaluations, since her objective accomplishments were balanced by the legitimate concerns about her abrasive personality. Since Price Waterhouse had a burden, in the nature of an affirmative defense, to show by a preponderance of the evidence that Hopkins would not have been made a partner, Gesell concluded that the defendant must still lose with the evidence in such equipoise.

On the issue of remedy, Gesell concluded that, consistent with *Hishon* and the Supreme Court's holding there that partnership decisions were subject to Title VII challenge, it was not plausible to conclude that the court lacked equitable power to order that Hopkins be made a partner. Price Waterhouse had argued that Gesell should exercise his discretion, in light of the prolonged controversy, to restrict her recovery to monetary damages. But the remedial purposes of Title VII included making the plaintiff whole, and the only way to make Hopkins whole was to make her a Price Waterhouse partner. Gesell dismissed as an empty gesture the notion of merely ordering Price Waterhouse to consider her for partnership or to put her up to a vote, since he could predict what the outcome of that would be. On the issue of monetary relief, however, Gesell was persuaded by Price Waterhouse's argument that Hopkins had not fully satisfied her obligation to mitigate damages. Normally, a back pay claim is reduced by the amount that the plaintiff earned or could, with reasonable effort, have earned since the discharge. In this case, Hopkins had not only taken steps that further alienated an OGS partner, resulting in the vote not to present her for reconsideration, but she had failed to pursue career opportunities with other major accounting firms, presumably in hopes of winning the litigation and coming back to Price Waterhouse as a partner. In any event, she had actually earned less than she could have earned through reasonable attempts to secure employment in the industry, so Gesell reduced her damage award accordingly from her claim of over $475,000 to $371,000.

Once again the case was appealed to the D.C. Circuit, which this time upheld Gesell's rulings in all respects in an opinion by Circuit Judge Harry T. Edwards of December 4, 1990. Agreeing with Gesell's analysis of the partnership issue, Edwards commented that it would be "inconceivable . . . that the Supreme Court intended to open up a partnership's admission decisions to judicial scrutiny while placing them beyond effective judicial remedy," and agreed with Gesell that Price Waterhouse's large size and geographic dispersion rendered essentially irrelevant the kinds of considerations that had led common-law courts routinely to refuse specific enforcement of employment agreements. Edwards noted that the Equal Employment Opportunity Commission had filed an *amicus* brief with the court urging it to uphold Gesell's remedial order, and this lent further weight to the conclusion that the court was authorized to

award partnership as a remedy. Edwards rejected the constitutional free association claim, pointing to decisions in which the Supreme Court rejected such defenses when raised in other business contexts. He also held that Gesell had properly calculated the back pay due to Hopkins, rejecting Price Waterhouse's argument that Hopkins's shortcomings in mitigation would justify denying her any recovery. After all, she had not sat on her hands all those years, but did undertake gainful employment, and Gesell had found that she would not, even with proper mitigation, have earned as much as if she had been a partner at Price Waterhouse. Under the circumstances, the back pay award was appropriate. There was a brief concurring opinion by Circuit Judge Karen L. Henderson, expressing some reluctance in joining the court's opinion, especially on the issue of awarding partnership, expressing reluctance to resort to a forced partnership situation as a remedy in a Title VII case, but concluding that there had been no clear error or abuse of discretion in Gesell's final opinion.

Thus ended the long saga of Hopkins's quest for partnership at Price Waterhouse. The litigation was significant for producing agreement among virtually all of the judges who had anything to do with the case at any level that sexual stereotyping could provide the evidentiary basis for a Title VII violation. Since state courts routinely adopt Title VII federal case law in interpreting their own state fair employment laws, the opinion may have an impact beyond federal litigation.

Accepting the theory that gender nonconforming appearance and behavior might have some protection marked a significant advance in sex discrimination theory, even though many of the courts acted as if they were unaware of the significance of what they were doing. The Supreme Court, in particular, seemed largely distracted by the allocation of proof issues, almost treating the sex stereotyping issues as incidental to the significance of the case. Congress also focused on the proof issues in its subsequent reaction to the case, amending Title VII in the 1991 Civil Rights Act to provide that the law is violated whenever an impermissible consideration is "a motivating factor for any employment practice, even though other factors also motivated the practice."

But *Price Waterhouse v. Hopkins* might open a new door to theories of Title VII liability, such as that rejected by the lower courts in *Smith v. Liberty Mutual Insurance*. Changes on the Supreme Court since *Price Waterhouse*, particularly the retirements of two members of the plurality, Justices Brennan and Marshall, might portend a less expansive interpretation of Title VII in future cases, but even the dissenters agreed that evidence of sexual stereotyping was relevant to a Title VII determination, suggesting that this theory will continue to play some role in civil rights jurisprudence.

At the same time, however, it would not be appropriate to treat this precedent too expansively and see it as an automatic extension of protection against discrimination for homosexuals, transsexuals, and transvestites, all of whom might theoretically be seen to qualify as manifesting nongender conforming behaviors or appearances. There was no suggestion in any of the opinions that Hopkins was perceived to be a lesbian, for example, or that if she suffered discrimination solely on account of such a perception, she would be protected under Title VII. The reach of this decision might be to a case like *Smith v. Liberty Mutual*, where the denial of employment turned entirely on a perception of effeminacy, and where homosexuality was never explicitly cited by the employer as the justification for its decision. Smith's sexual orientation was at bottom irrelevant in that case, just as Hopkins's was in her case.

Thus, it would be surprising if a conservative Supreme Court, or lower federal courts, interpreted nonconformity in matters of sexual orientation, as such, to be within the mandate of *Price Waterhouse v. Hopkins*, even though strong arguments might be made that the discomfort with gender nonconformity that played such a significant role in Hopkins's rejection for partnership is at the heart of much discrimination on the basis of sexual orientation.

Case References

Hishon v. King & Spaulding, 467 U.S. 69 (1984)

International Brotherhood of Teamsters v. United States, 431 U.S. 324 (1977)

Los Angeles Department of Water & Power v. Manhart, 435 U.S. 702 (1978)

Smith v. Liberty Mutual Insurance Co., 569 F.2d 325 (5th Cir. 1978)

Texas Department of Community Affairs v. Burdine, 450 U.S. 248 (1981)

Toney v. Block, 705 F.2d 1364 (D.C. Cir. 1983)

87. THE NOT-SO-PRIVATE FEDERAL CIVIL SERVANT

Schowengerdt v. United States, 944 F.2d 483 (9th Cir. 1991), certiorari denied, 112 U.S. 1514 (1992); earlier decision, sub nom. *Schowengerdt v. General Dynamics Corp.*, 823 F.2d 1328 (9th Cir. 1987).

Various forms of privacy are protected under the U.S. Constitution from intrusion by the government or its agents. The U.S. Supreme Court has recognized a right of privacy under the Due Process clauses of the Fifth and Fourteenth amendments protecting personal liberties, such as procreative decisions, although the Court has held that this right does not extend to private consensual sexual activity between adults, at least in a same-sex context. A right of privacy based in more explicit constitutional language is the right of the people to be free from unreasonable searches and seizures, specified in the Fourth Amendment of the Bill of Rights. To what extent is a civil servant protected by this latter privacy right from searches aimed at uncovering information concerning his private, off-duty consensual sexual activities? That question received at least a partial answer from the U.S. Court of Appeals for the Ninth Circuit in *Schowengerdt v. United States*.

Richard Neal Schowengerdt had been employed by the U.S. Navy as a civilian engineer working on secret weapons-related projects at the Naval Industrial Ordinance Plant in Pomona, California, for more than thirteen years. He had a "secret" security clearance because of the nature of his work. He was also a chief warrant officer in the Naval Reserve, assigned to a missile test center. Security services at the Ordinance Plant were provided to the Navy under contract by General Dynamics Corporation.

Schowengerdt had a private office at the plant. His office door, his desk, and his credenza each had a lock, and, due to the secret nature of papers with which he was dealing, Schowengerdt was supposed to keep the door, desk, and credenza locked when he was not in the office. Security guards, who had passkeys to all offices, desks, and other furniture, made regular checks, known to Schowengerdt and all other employees, to ensure that locks were secure and confidential information properly stored. In addition, special security investigators might search private offices and furniture under various circumstances.

Schowengerdt, a married man, had responded to advertisements in "swingers" magazines, and kept copies of his letters and related materials (including photographs of himself both in uniform and nude) in a manila envelope in his credenza. The letters referred to his own sexual interests and activities. A reader of these materials might conclude that Schowengerdt engaged in extra-marital activity, including bisexual activity, and had sent copies of the photographs to his correspondents and sexual contacts, along with information about where he worked and how to contact him at work. On the outside of the envelope, Schowengerdt had written, "Strictly Personal and Private. In the event of my death, please destroy this material as I do not want my grieving widow to read it."

Early in August 1982, Charles Kessel, a security investigator for General Dynamics, received an anonymous telephone call concerning Schowengerdt. The caller indicated that there was material in Schowengerdt's credenza that would be "of interest to the security department." Following up on the tip, Kessel entered Schowengerdt's office on August 9 after Schowengerdt had left the office for the day. Later testimony conflicted as to whether the credenza was locked or open, but Kessel had a passkey in any event. He found the manila envelope and examined the contents. The next day, while Schowengerdt was out of his office,

Kessel returned with two Navy officials, Special Agent Carl Jensen of the Naval Investigative Service, and K.D. Tillotson, the commanding officer for the Navy at the plant. They searched the office more thoroughly, removing a variety of personal items. Jensen's supervisor, the security chief at the plant, had authorized this further search, agreeing with Jensen that they did not need a search warrant.

Based on his review of the documents and other materials from Schowengerdt's office, Jensen launched a security investigation. He interviewed Schowengerdt, and later claimed that Schowengerdt admitted to him that he was "bisexual." Jensen also searched Schowengerdt's home with his permission. Jensen concluded that there was no evidence Schowengerdt had been contacted by "hostile agents" or that he was the "target of blackmail." Jensen wrote up his findings and sent them to various federal security officials and Schowengerdt's Naval Reserve commander. He also notified the U.S. Postal Service that Schowengerdt had been receiving pornographic materials through the mail. Schowengerdt's commander instituted discharge proceedings, under a naval regulation mandating discharge for any personnel who were homosexual or bisexual, and despite his repeated denials that he was bisexual or had made any such admission to Jensen, Schowengerdt was honorably discharged. A letter to this effect was sent to his home by regular mail and opened by members of his family, who had apparently been unaware up to that time of the nature of Schowengerdt's problems at work. He was not, however, dismissed from his position at the plant.

Five months after the search took place, Schowengerdt resigned his position at the plant and obtained related employment in private industry, for which he would need a security clearance. His application was stalled for sixteen months when the Navy security personnel responded to a questionnaire from the Defense Industrial Security Clearance Office with a full account of the search of his office and his discharge from the Naval Reserve.

Schowengerdt filed suit in federal district court in Los Angeles against General Dynamics and Kessel, the Navy, his commander, and security officers, alleging that his constitutional rights and several federal statutes had been violated by this sequence of events. The heart of Schowengerdt's claim was that the seizure of the manila envelope and its contents, and the further investigation of his office, violated his privacy rights because this material had no relationship to security concerns or workplace misconduct. Relying on cases holding that the government normally had limited, if any, legitimate concern with off-duty sexual conduct by its civilian employees, Schowengerdt alleged that in this case, at the very least, the search should have ceased as soon as Kessel learned that the material in the envelope was purely personal and had no relationship to his work. Schowengerdt claimed that the subsequent activities of the General Dynamics and federal officials violated a panoply of federal procedural rules and statutes, including the Privacy Act. He also claimed violations of his First Amendment right to freedom of association and speech, and challenged his Naval Reserve discharge based on Fifth Amendment due process and Ninth Amendment privacy arguments.

All defendants moved to dismiss the complaint. On July 20, 1984, District Judge A. Andrew Hauk granted the motions in full in an unpublished order. Hauk found that Schowengerdt failed to allege facts that established that he had "any reasonable expectation of privacy in the desk as part of an investigation into his job performance." He also found that Schowengerdt had not yet exhausted administrative remedies of internal military appeal of his discharge from the Reserve, thus depriving the court of jurisdiction to address that claim. Hauk found that his other constitutional and statutory claims were without merit and did not warrant discussion.

Schowengerdt appealed to the U.S. Court of Appeals for the Ninth Circuit, which heard argument on February 6, 1986. Carl B. Pearlston, Jr., of Torrence, California, represented him in the oral argument. The defendants were represented by Stephen E. O'Neal for the government and Nancy P. McClelland, of the Los Angeles firm of Gibson, Dunn & Crutcher for General Dynamics and its employee Kessel. The court of appeals ruled on July 30, 1987, having apparently held up its consideration of the case pending a ruling by

the U.S. Supreme Court in *O'Connor v. Ortega*, a case presenting similar issues. The appeals court held that Hauk had properly dismissed Schowengerdt's statutory claims, but that dismissal had been inappropriate on the central claim in the case (i.e., that the search of the credenza and subsequent search of the office violated his rights under the Fourth Amendment). The court also held that, since Schowengerdt had by now exhausted his administrative remedies on the naval discharge, it was appropriate for the district court to consider his constitutional challenge to that action.

In her opinion for the court, Circuit Judge Betty B. Fletcher began her discussion by noting that the U.S. Supreme Court had established in *Bivens v. Six Unknown Agents of the Federal Bureau of Narcotics* (1971) that the victim of a constitutional violation by a federal agent had a right to recover damages against the agent, even though there might not be any particular federal statute authorizing such a recovery. The Supreme Court had specifically approved a *Bivens*-type action for a Fourth Amendment violation, and the Ninth Circuit had recognized *Bivens*-type jurisdiction for First Amendment violations in *Gibson v. United States* (1986). Of course, a *Bivens*-type action could be brought only for a constitutional violation, which required, in this case, that the search have constituted "state action." General Dynamics and Kessel had defended on the theory that they were private actors. Fletcher rejected this contention, finding that General Dynamics, as a government contractor, and Kessel, as the employee charged with carrying out security searches on behalf of the government, were actually involved in "state action" when they carried out a search at the Navy-owned plant of the office of a naval employee. In the second search, Kessel was joined by two Naval agents, and the results of the search had been used by the government. Thus, the "private" status of Kessel and General Dynamics was not a valid defense in this case.

More difficult was the question whether there had been any Fourth Amendment violation at all. District Judge Hauk contended that the office, the desk, and the credenza were all the property of the government, which it was entitled to search at any time. "Fourth Amendment privacy interests do not, however, turn on property interests," asserted Fletcher. Indeed, in *Katz v. United States*, a 1967 case involving government electronic eavesdropping on a telephone call placed from a phone booth, the Supreme Court had held that the key inquiry was whether the individual had "a reasonable expectation of freedom from government intrusion" under the particular circumstances.

In *O'Connor v. Ortega*, public hospital officials had searched the desk and files of Dr. Ortega while he was on an administrative leave, looking for evidence of work-related improprieties. Several personal items of Ortega were seized during the search. Ortega brought a *Bivens*-type action, claiming that his Fourth Amendment rights were violated. The Ninth Circuit had upheld his claim, reversing a grant of summary judgment by the trial court, opining that Ortega had a reasonable expectation of privacy with respect to the contents of his desk and files, even though they were technically hospital property. The Supreme Court reversed on other grounds, finding that in the particular posture of the case the Ninth Circuit should not have reached the ultimate constitutional question. However, every member of the Supreme Court appeared to agree that Ortega did have a reasonable expectation of privacy in his desk and filing cabinets, although they did not agree on how such a determination should be made or where it leads.

In particular, the Court had clearly held that a person's Fourth Amendment rights were not terminated by government employment, but at least eight of the Justices agreed that the "operational realities of the workplace" might lead to a conclusion in a particular case that the employee had no reasonable expectation of privacy. For example, said Justice Sandra Day O'Connor, writing for a plurality of the Court, if an employee's office is generally open to fellow employees or members of the public, it would not be reasonable for the employee to expect the contents of the office to be private in the same way that a home is private. A majority of the Court went even further in finding protection, however. Justice Antonin Scalia, concurring in the Court's judgment, asserted that "constitutional protection against unreasonable

searches by the government does not disappear merely because the government has the right to make reasonable intrusions in its capacity as an employer." This statement was picked up approvingly by Justice Harry A. Blackmun in his dissenting opinion. Scalia and Blackmun differed on the circumstances when such an intrusion could be deemed "reasonable."

Reviewing prior circuit court decisions, Fletcher found conflicting authority in a variety of circumstances where government employers had searched employees' desks and lockers. She noted that a majority of the *Ortega* court had indicated that some offices were so open to members of the public that no reasonable expectation of privacy could possibly exist, but since Schowengerdt's office was at a "secure" facility and he had confidential documents, his office "was obviously not so open to the public as to render his expectation of privacy unreasonable on this basis." Fletcher concluded that "Schowengerdt would enjoy a reasonable expectation of privacy in areas given over to his exclusive use, unless he was on notice from his employer that searches of the type to which he was subjected might occur from time to time for work-related purposes." Since Schowengerdt had alleged in his complaint that there were "no regulations providing for searches of employees' office furnishing," there was a factual dispute between Schowengerdt and the government as to the basis for concluding whether his expectation of privacy was reasonable. In those circumstances, the case should be sent back for fact-finding on this question, using the *Ortega* decision for guidance as to the factors to be considered. Fletcher quoted approvingly from Justice Scalia's concurring opinion, which provided the necessary fifth vote for the *Ortega* ruling. Scalia had asserted that in order to be "reasonable," both "the inception and the scope of the intrusion must be reasonable."

Ordinarily [wrote Scalia], a search of an employee's office by a supervisor will be "justified at its inception" when there are reasonable grounds for suspecting that the search will turn up evidence that the employee is guilty of work-related misconduct, or that the search is necessary for a noninvestigatory work-related purpose such as to retrieve a needed file. . . . The search will be permissible in its scope when "the measures adopted are reasonably related to the objectives of the search and not excessively intrusive in light of . . . the nature of the [misconduct]."

Fletcher then turned to the reason for the search. Schowengerdt had alleged that the purpose of the search was to investigate his sexual conduct and that this was not a legitimate objective. The Ninth Circuit had previously ruled in *Thorne v. El Segundo* (1983) that "the Constitution prohibits unregulated, unrestrained employer inquiries into personal sexual matters that have no bearing on job performance." Fletcher asserted that a search of Schowengerdt's desk and credenza "to find and seize materials relating to such matters would be reasonable only if relevant to his job as a naval engineer," and that the "scope of the inquiry must be no broader than necessary." Thus, it would be necessary on remand for the parties to develop the reason for the search, and the necessity, if any, for a search and seizure of this scope. Since it was not clear from the allegations of Schowengerdt's complaint that it would be impossible for him to show facts supporting a conclusion that the search was unconstitutional, Hauk should not have prematurely ended the case by dismissing his claim prior to discovery.

On remand, the parties commenced discovery, and Schowengerdt essentially defeated himself by the admissions he made. Most of the factual descriptions at the beginning of this essay about the security and search practices at the plant are taken from the factual summary of the Ninth Circuit's later decision and are based on statements Schowengerdt made at his deposition. When it became clear to the defense attorneys that these statements provided a firm basis for arguing that Schowengerdt had no reasonable expectation of privacy under the circumstances, they moved for summary judgment, which was granted by the district court, which also held that Schowengerdt's challenge to his discharge from the Naval Reserve was without merit. Schowengerdt had argued that the evidence did not support the conclusion that he was bisexual, and thus he should not have been discharged. The district court found that there was sufficient evidence in the record, including Schowengerdt's "admission" to Jensen during

the investigation and the contents of the materials seized from his credenza, to support the Navy's conclusion that he was bisexual or at least had desires in that direction, covered by the Navy's discharge directive. Since the Ninth Circuit had upheld the Navy's discharge policies based on sexual orientation against a variety of constitutional attacks over the years, the district court concluded it was appropriate to grant summary judgment on this part of the case as well.

Schowengerdt again appealed to the Ninth Circuit, which heard argument on March 8, 1991. Schowengerdt represented himself at the oral argument. Assistant U.S. Attorney Donna R. Eide represented the government, and Nancy P. McClelland again represented the private defendants. The circuit court panel unanimously concluded that Schowengerdt's appeal was without merit, affirming the summary judgment in an opinion by Circuit Judge William C. Canby, Jr., on September 6, 1991. (Ironically, only weeks earlier in *Pruitt v. Cheney*, Canby had written an opinion for another circuit panel reversing the summary judgment of another challenge to the Department of Defense's sexual orientation policies, but on equal protection grounds.)

Canby found, as expected, that Schowengerdt's admissions during fact-finding about the search and investigative policies at the plant fully supported a conclusion that a reasonable plant employee would not have expected his desk and credenza to be immune from search. Indeed, knowing that security guards had passkeys and conducted regular searches for security reasons, Schowengerdt must have expected that a manila envelope dramatically annotated would at some point attract attention. "Schowengerdt and his fellow employees were well aware that the Navy was extremely concerned about the variety of ways by which classified information could be divulged to inappropriate sources," said Canby, "other than through the loss or theft of inadequately secured documents."

Given that peculiar environment, Schowengerdt did not have a reasonable expectation of privacy in his office or in his locked credenza, or in a manila envelope stored in the credenza which indicated on its exterior that it contained information which he wanted kept secret from his wife. He should have known that his credenza, even if locked, was subject to search, and that the inscription on the manila envelope would serve only to trigger the curiosity of an investigator, or any fellow employee, trained to be alert to possibilities of blackmail.

As to the discharge, Canby found Schowengerdt's claim of a First Amendment violation (i.e., that he was discharged because of what he wrote in the materials seized during the search) to be without merit. Canby had, in fact, rejected a similar sort of First Amendment claim in *Pruitt v. Cheney*. It was clear that when the Defense Department discharged somebody after that individual said or wrote something revealing their sexual orientation, the Department's action was not because of the content of the speech, as such, but because of what the speech revealed about the speaker. In this case, Schowengerdt "was not discharged for writing about bisexuality but rather for being a bisexual, of which his purely private correspondence was evidence." There was no procedural due process violation either, since Schowengerdt was afforded full procedural rights and a hearing on his discharge. As to substantive due process, Canby noted that the Ninth Circuit had repeatedly upheld the Defense Department's regulations against procedural due process attack in such cases as *Beller v. Middendorf* (1980) and *High Tech Gays v. Defense Industrial Security Clearance Office* (1990). In *High Tech Gays*, the circuit court held that the Supreme Court's 1986 decision in *Bowers v. Hardwick* had, in effect, overruled the *Beller* court's alternative application of "heightened scrutiny" under the Due Process Clause to the Department's antigay policies; since homosexual conduct enjoyed no due process protection, heightened scrutiny was not available to a military policy requiring discharges in cases of homosexual conduct that was at issue in *Beller*. "Thus," concluded Canby, "Schowengerdt's argument for a substantive due process violation here is precluded by *Beller, Hardwick*, and *High Tech Gays*."

Schowengerdt had argued that his discharge was "arbitrary and capricious" because he had never been proven to be bisexual. Here, Canby was faced with factual findings by the Navy dis-

charge board that appeared to be based on testimony about Schowengerdt's own admission of bisexuality to Jensen, which the board apparently found credible. The seized correspondence also supported the conclusion that he was bisexual. A conclusion for which there was support in the record could not be set aside as arbitrary and capricious. Furthermore, Schowengerdt had never raised any equal protection challenge prior to his oral argument before the circuit court, thus waiving any right to consideration of an equal protection challenge to the Defense Department's actions in his case. This was significant, given Canby's recent opinion in *Pruitt*, but Canby did not make the connection explicit in his opinion.

Schowengerdt, now unrepresented by counsel, filed a petition for *certiorari* with the Supreme Court on December 2, 1991, but it was denied on March 23, 1992.

The Schowengerdt opinions by the Ninth Circuit, taken together with the Supreme Court's decision in *Ortega*, make clear that government employees do have a right of privacy on the job to be free from searches or seizures that do not concern work-related issues, but that this general right might disappear to the extent that a particular workplace makes such an expectation unreasonable. Particularly in the context of military-related work that carries security clearance requirements, there seems to be a relatively low degree of reasonable expectation of privacy when the employer, whether the government or a defense contractor, carries on a regular policy of security-related inspections and investigations. Thus, employees who wish to preserve the confidentiality of their sexual activities assume the burden in such employment to leave no incriminating evidence at the office, even under lock and key.

Case References

Beller v. Middendorf, 632 F.2d 788 (9th Cir. 1980), certiorari denied, 454 U.S. 855 (1981)

Bivens v. Six Unknown Agents of the Federal Bureau of Narcotics, 403 U.S. 388 (1971)

Bowers v. Hardwick, 478 U.S. 186 (1986)

Gibson v. United States, 781 F.2d 1334 (9th Cir. 1986), certiorari denied, 479 U.S. 1054 (1987)

High Tech Gays v. Defense Industrial Security Clearance Office, 895 F.2d 563 (9th Cir. 1990)

Katz v. United States, 389 U.S. 347 (1967)

O'Connor v. Ortega, 480 U.S. 709 (1987)

Pruitt v. Cheney, 943 F.2d 989 (9th Cir. 1991), amended, 963 F.2d 1160 (9th Cir. 1992), cert. denied, — S. Ct. — (1992)

Thorne v. El Segundo, 726 F.2d 459 (9th Cir. 1983), certiorari denied, 469 U.S. 979 (1984); later decision, 802 F.2d 1131 (9th Cir. 1986)

88. SEXUAL PRIVACY IN THE PRIVATE-SECTOR WORKPLACE

Soroka v. Dayton Hudson Corp., 235 Cal. App. 3d 654, 1 Cal. Rptr. 2d 77 (1st Dist. 1991), review granted, 4 Cal. Rptr. 2d 180, 822 P.2d 1327 (1992).

The federal Constitution provides limited protection for the privacy interests of public employees by requiring, at minimum, that there be some rational nexus between a particular invasion of privacy by a public employer and the job duties of the employee. Thus, for example, the U.S. Supreme Court held in *National Treasury Employees Union v. Von Raab* (1989) that routine drug testing of public employees requires, at minimum, some showing that being free of drugs has a rational connection with the particular job functions of that employee. Some states have gone further in protecting privacy, however, extending guarantees against intrusive employer searches into the private sector. California is one such state.

In 1972, California voters amended that state's constitution to provide that "privacy" is among the inalienable rights of all the state's residents. According to the ballot pamphlet circulated among voters prior to the election, the amendment was intended to limit both government and businesses in the collection of information about individuals. The ballot argument noted that "each time we . . . interview for a job . . . , a dossier is opened and an informational profile is sketched." Arguing that "the ability to control circulation of personal information" is "fundamental to our privacy," the ballot argument stated that one purpose of the amendment was to prevent government and businesses "from collecting . . . unnecessary information about us." Since the ballot argument provided the only explicit legislative history for the amendment, California courts relied on it as an authoritative source for construction of the amendment and concluded soon after it was passed that the amendment was intended, among other things, to prevent California employers, whether public or private, from unjustifiably invading the privacy of their employees.

In *Soroka v. Dayton Hudson Corp.*, one California appellate court concluded that the amendment's reach went even further, protecting job applicants (not just present employees) from intrusive preemployment testing calculated, among other things, to reveal the sexual orientation and practices of employees as part of an effort to screen out those whose sexuality the employer believed to indicate emotional instability and unreliability. The court bolstered its conclusions on this count by referring to political freedom provisions of the state's Labor Code that had been construed more than a decade earlier by a narrow majority vote of the state's supreme court to protect openly gay job applicants from discrimination in hiring by a highly regulated state utility.

Dayton Hudson Corporation, owner and operator of Target Stores, retained a psychological consulting firm, Martin-McAllister, to score and evaluate a written psychological test of applicants for positions as store security officers (referred to as SSOs) at Target's retail outlets. The test, referred to as the "Psychscreen," was a combination of two well-known psychological tests, the Minnesota Multiphasic Personality Inventory and the California Psychological Inventory. These tests were originally developed to diagnose persons with psychological problems, but had been adopted by various employers concerned with screening out unstable applicants for jobs with significant public safety implications, such as police and correctional officers, pilots and air traffic controllers, and nuclear plant operators. Target concluded that this test might be useful in preventing the hiring of unstable or undependable characters as store guards. Although store guards were not armed, they were in a position to threaten public safety in their interactions with customers and store employees, thought Target executives. No formal validation study was performed before Target adopted the test, but it was administered to some of Target's most highly rated store guards, who received excellent scores.

Under Target's arrangement with Martin-McAllister, job applicants would fill out the written test form which would be submitted to Martin-McAllister without having been reviewed by any Target official. Martin-McAllister would score the examination and make a recommendation to Target based on numerical scores in five categories: emotional stability, interpersonal style, addiction potential, dependability, and reliability. Target did not review or receive answers to any of the individual test questions.

The Psychscreen consisted of 704 true-false questions, inquiring about the test-takers' attitudes and beliefs on a wide range of subjects, some very personal. Included among the questions were some about specific religious beliefs, such as whether the test-taker believed in "the second coming of Christ" or whether the test-taker's "sins are unpardonable." As to sex, the test inquired whether the test-taker was "strongly attracted by members of my own sex," whether the test-taker had "been in trouble one or more times because of my sex behavior," and whether male test-takers "often wished I were a girl." In scoring such questions, Martin-McAllister was looking for signs of social nonconformity that would affect its evaluations of a job applicant's "emotional stability," "dependability and reliability," or "socialization." Several applicants, some of whom were rejected for security officer jobs, believed that these questions were unnecessarily intrusive, and a group of them filed suit against the company in 1989, led by Sibi Soroka, who had been hired by Target as a security guard but who was personally offended, particularly by questions about religion and sexuality. Representing them were Oakland attorneys Brad Seligman and Elaine B. Feingold. San Francisco attorney Nancy L. Ober represented Target.

In the suit filed in Alameda County Superior Court in September 1989, Soroka and his co-plaintiffs sought class certification and moved at an early point for preliminary injunctive relief, barring Target from using the Psychscreen while the litigation was pending. Their theory of attack relied on a wide-ranging laundry list of asserted causes of action, including the state constitutional privacy provision, the Fair Employment and Housing Code (which banned discrimination on the basis of religious belief and practice), the Labor Code, and a range of tort theories, including invasion of privacy, disclosure of confidential medical information, fraud, negligent misrepresentation, and intentional and negligent infliction of emotional distress.

In moving for preliminary injunctive relief, Soroka submitted an affidavit from a professional psychologist who contended that the Psychscreen was not justified or proper as an employment screening device, because, the expert claimed, it generated a majority of false-positive results. In other words, the expert asserted that most of those whose employment Martin-McAllister recommended against based on the Psychscreen were actually qualified for employment and falsely labeled as unstable or unreliable. Soroka also claimed in support of the motion that Target's own experts deposed during initial discovery had admitted that at least one of the source tests, the Minnesota Multiphasic, was "virtually useless" as a preemployment screening test.

Opposing the motion, Target submitted affidavits from its own experts claiming that the test was valid. Target's vice president of loss prevention swore that using the test had increased the quality and performance of the security officers, but, as Soroka pointed out in rebuttal, Target had been unable to document any changes in "asset protection" specifically linked to use of the test. Indeed, it appeared that the test itself had been revised at some point to delete some of the most intrusive, non-job-related questions.

In deciding whether to order preliminary relief pending trial, Superior Court Judge Joanne Parrilli had to determine whether Soroka was likely to prevail on the merits after trial and whether the interim harm that might be suffered by job applicants if Target continued to use the test outweighed the harm Target might suffer if deprived of the use of this screening device. She never reached the second question, however, because she determined that Soroka was unlikely to prevail on the first. Parrilli based her conclusion heavily on a recent court of appeal decision, *Wilkinson v. Times Mirror Corp.* (1989), holding that the California constitutional right of privacy did not bar a legal publisher, Matthew Bender, from requiring job applicants to submit to urinalysis for drug and alcohol use. The *Wilkinson* court reasoned that job applicants had a lesser degree of protection than employees, because of the "voluntary" nature of their submission to testing; they were free to seek employment from a company that did not do such testing if they did not want to be tested, said the court, so the degree of intrusiveness was low enough to impose a relatively low level of justification on the employer. According to the *Wilkinson* court, an employer need merely show that it had a legitimate interest for conducting preemployment screening that was not unreasonable. The California Supreme Court denied review in the *Wilkinson* case in March 1990. Soroka moved for preliminary relief in September of that year.

Both parties had moved for summary adjudication, and Soroka had also pressed for a ruling certifying the case as a class action. Judge Parrilli ruled against Soroka on all motions and also denied the company's motion for summary adjudication, thus setting the matter for trial without preliminarily barring continued use of the tests. Soroka appealed to the First District Court of Appeal. A panel of that court unanimously reversed the trial court on October 25, 1991, as to preliminary relief and class certification, sending the case back to the superior court for reconsideration of both of those issues. In so doing, the court rendered the first appellate decision in California specifically holding that a private-sector employer's inquiries into the sexual orientation of job applicants violated both the state constitution and the Labor Code.

In his opinion for the unanimous panel, Judge Timothy Reardon sharply disputed the *Wilkinson* court's embrace of a lesser degree of protection for the privacy rights of job appli-

cants than for employees. (The *Wilkinson* court panel was drawn from a different geographical "division" of the First District, so the *Soroka* court panel was not strictly bound to follow it.) "Our review of the ballot argument satisfies us that the voters did not intend to grant less privacy protection to job applicants than to employees," he asserted. The ballot argument had specifically mentioned, in support of the privacy amendment, that job applicants were subjected to requests for "unnecessary" information, so clearly this was one of the phenomena at which the amendment was aimed. Consequently, said Reardon, the same "compelling interest" test should be used in requiring employers to justify intrusive preemployment screening as would be used to evaluate privacy invasions against employees.

In addition to disputing *Wilkinson*'s construction of legislative history, Reardon found unpersuasive the earlier court's reliance on a recent California Supreme Court decision in *Schmidt v. Superior Court* (1989) dealing with a ban on residents under the age of 25 imposed by a trailer court. Although the supreme court had rejected a constitutional privacy challenge mounted against that rule, on the ground that the age-based regulation, in the court's view, was "neither irrational nor arbitrary or otherwise vulnerable to constitutional attack," Reardon was unpersuaded that this had established a more general relaxation of privacy protection for those who could be conceptualized as "applicants" for some right or benefit. Reardon believed that the *Schmidt* decision dealt with property rights that might not conceptually come within the privacy amendment. More significantly, the ballot argument had specifically mentioned job application situations as coming within its purview, so Reardon did not believe that the supreme court could have intended its decision in *Schmidt* "to constitute such a major change in the law" without having expressly "articulated that change in an unmistakable manner." He also rejected the argument that a previous decision by the same division of the district court of appeal in a drug testing case had adopted the *Wilkinson* distinction, pointing out that comments in the opinion that might suggest that results were merely *dicta*.

Thus, the *Soroka* court was satisfied that job applicants enjoyed the same level of protection as employees, and that both under the federal Fourth Amendment in the public sector and the California constitution in both sectors, the protection for job applicants required the employer to show a compelling interest to use a particular invasive screening device. In this context, that meant that Target would have the burden at trial of showing a specific nexus between invasive questions about religious and sexual beliefs and practices and the job requirements of store security officers. Since Judge Parrilli had applied the wrong test, the court proceeded to apply the compelling interest test, and found it likely that Soroka would prevail on the merits:

> In its opposition to Soroka's motion for preliminary injunction, Target made no showing that a person's religious beliefs or sexual orientation have any bearing on the emotional stability or on the ability to perform an SSO's job responsibilities. It did no more than to make generalized claims about the Psychscreen's relationship to emotional fitness and to assert that it has seen an overall improvement in SSO quality and performance since it implemented the Psychscreen. This is not sufficient to constitute a compelling interest, nor does it satisfy the nexus requirement. Therefore, Target's inquiry into the religious beliefs and sexual orientation of SSO applicants unjustifiably violates the state constitutional right to privacy.

Consequently, Soroka had met the initial burden of showing a likelihood of success on the merits of his constitutional claim.

Reardon then turned to the statutory claims, although it was not strictly necessary for the court to deal with them on this appeal, since likelihood of success on the constitutional claim would be sufficient to support the grant of preliminary relief if Soroka also came out ahead on the "balance of harms" test. Nonetheless, evidently anticipating the possibility of appeal by Target and hoping to protect Soroka's right to interim relief if the Supreme Court disagreed with his analysis of the constitutional issues, Reardon went ahead to explain how the tests also violated the Fair Employment and Housing Act and the Labor Code.

California's Fair Employment and Housing Act prohibits employment discrimination on the basis of religion. In her decision denying preliminary relief, Parrilli found that Soroka was not likely to prevail on the claim that Target's hiring decisions were made on the basis of religious beliefs, or that the questions asked in the Psychscreen inventory were designed to reveal such beliefs. This result was rather incredible, in light of the provision in the Act that an employer was prohibited from making any non-job-related inquiry that expresses "directly or indirectly, any limitation, specification, or discrimination as to . . . religious creed," and the provision that any attempt to identify an individual on the basis of religious creed had to be justified by a showing of job-relatedness. Adverting to the Psychscreen questions about the applicant's beliefs with regard to Christian doctrine, Reardon asserted that "these questions were intended to—and did—inquire about the religious beliefs of Target's SSO applicants," and thus constituted an "inquiry that expresses a 'specification [of a] religious creed'" within the meaning of the Act. Since Target had not even addressed the question of the job-relatedness of such specific religious inquiries in its opposition to the motion for preliminary relief, it seemed quite likely that Soroka would prevail at trial in showing that such inquiries violated the Act.

Turning next to the Labor Code, Reardon also found clearly incorrect the trial judge's conclusion that the Psychscreen was not designed to "reveal an applicant's sexual orientation." Labor Code sections 1101 and 1102 provide that California employers are barred from "making, adopting or enforcing any policy that tends to control or direct the political activities or affiliations of employees," or from "coercing, influencing, or attempting to coerce or influence employees to adopt or follow or refrain from adopting or following any particular line of political activity by threatening a loss of employment," said Reardon, and these prohibitions applied to a situation where an employer inquired into the sexual orientation of job applicants with the intent of using such information as a basis for a hiring decision. In 1979, the California Supreme Court had ruled in *Gay Law Students Association v. Pacific Telephone and Telegraph Co.* that these provisions made it unlawful for a heavily regulated public utility, such as the telephone company, to maintain a policy against employing persons known to be gay. The "struggle of the homosexual community for equal rights, particularly in the field of employment, must be recognized as a political activity," said the *Pacific Telephone* court, and the very status of being openly gay in the workplace could be construed as a political act. Relying on this opinion, California Attorney General John Van de Kamp issued a formal opinion ruling in 1986 that the Labor Code provisions barred private employers in California from discriminating on the basis of sexual orientation. Just a few weeks prior to the announcement of the *Soroka* court's opinion, Governor Pete Wilson had vetoed a bill intended to add "sexual orientation" to the enumerated unlawful bases for discrimination under the Fair Employment and Housing Act. Wilson cited the *Pacific Telephone* decision and the attorney general's opinion ruling in support of his conclusion that the amendment was unnecessary because discrimination on the basis of sexual orientation was already unlawful in California. Now Reardon and his colleagues on the *Soroka* panel were ready to back up the governor's assertion, stating without equivocation: "These statutes also prohibit a private employer from discriminating against an employee on the basis of his or her sexual orientation."

The Psychscreen included at least one question which, on its face, asked the applicant to reveal his or her sexual orientation. Said Reardon:

> One of the five traits that Target uses the Psychscreen to determine is "socialization," which it defines as "the extent to which an individual subscribes to traditional values and mores and feels an obligation to act in accordance with them." Persons who identify themselves as homosexual may be stigmatized as "willing to defy or violate" these norms, which may in turn result in an invalid test. As a matter of law, this practice tends to discriminate against those who express a homosexual orientation. (See Lab.Code, sec. 1101.) It also constitutes an attempt to coerce an applicant to refrain from expressing a homosexual orientation by threat of loss of employment. (See id., sec. 1102.)

Clearly, Soroka had met the burden of showing likelihood of success on his claim that use of the Psychscreen violated the Labor Code provisions.

Having disposed of the issue of "likelihood of success on the merits," Reardon turned to the issue of "interim harm," which Parrilli had never reached. He found that the interim harm to job applicants was "clear," since they would suffer a deprivation of constitutionally protected privacy rights as well as statutory rights to be free of discrimination on the basis of religion and sexual orientation as long as Target continued to use the Psychscreen. On the other hand, Reardon found that any interim harm to Target if it were deprived of use of these tests was at best "minimal and speculative," since Target had presented no direct evidence that the challenged test questions were job-related. Noting that the injunction would run only against "Target's use of the Psychscreen in its present form and only during the pendency of the trial," Reardon observed that Target was "free to use other, legally proper methods to determine the emotional stability of its SSO applicants," presumably without inquiring into their religious beliefs or sexual orientations. Thus, the balance of harms supported awarding preliminary injunctive relief to Soroka.

The court also devoted a section of its decision to the issue of class certification, concluding that Judge Parrilli had applied incorrect standards in denying certification of the class, but withheld that portion of the opinion from publication. Reardon concluded that the case should be remanded, with instructions to grant the preliminary injunction and reconsider the issue of class certification prior to trial.

As soon as the decision was made public, attorneys for Target indicated that the company intended to appeal the ruling. The employer bar was concerned that the broad-ranging language of the opinion might be construed to ban a wide range of preemployment testing practices as violative of the state constitution, and hoped to limit the effect of the decision, even if it did not achieve a full overruling. Gay rights advocates hailed the decision as the first appellate ruling to recognize the application of the *Pacific Telephone* construction of the Labor Code provisions to a general, nonpervasively regulated private employer.

The governor claimed vindication for his veto of the gay rights law, which had turned into a source of considerable embarrassment when a public opinion poll released the day after the veto showed that the bill enjoyed the support of a substantial majority of Californians from both major political parties, and angry protesters from the gay community began to disrupt the governor's every public appearance with loud protests. However, few would speculate with confidence about the ultimate fate of the decision on appeal to the conservative state supreme court, although it was widely noted that two of the unanimous court of appeal panel members were appointees of Wilson's conservative predecessor. In January 1992, the California Supreme Court announced that it would review the *Soroka* decision. Later in 1992, Wilson signed legislation amending the Labor Code provisions to ban antigay employment discrimination expressly.

Case References

Gay Law Students Association v. Pacific Telephone and Telegraph Co., 24 Cal. 3d 458 (1979)

National Treasury Employees Union v. Von Raab, 109 S. Ct. 1384 (1989)

Schmidt v. Superior Court, 48 Cal. 3d 370 (1989)

Wilkinson v. Times Mirror Corp., 215 Cal. App. 3d 1034, 264 Cal. Rptr. 194 (1st Dist. 1989), review denied, 3/15/90

CHAPTER 6
DISCRIMINATION: MILITARY AND NATIONAL SECURITY ISSUES

The Uniform Code of Military Justice, and predecessor regulations governing the conduct of military personnel, have long included prohibitions of sodomy (oral and anal sex). During World War II, psychiatrists persuaded military leaders that the armed forces should go beyond banning particular sexual behavior and attempt to identify and screen out all personnel with a homosexual orientation. As recounted by Allan Berube in *Coming Out Under Fire: The History of Gay Men and Women in World War Two,* the psychiatrists argued that homosexuals did not have suitable personalities for military service and that they would be disruptive to military order and harmful to the morale of the troops.

Despite the efforts of military doctors to discover homosexuals and obtain their exclusion from the ranks, however, thousands of lesbians and gay men served with distinction in the armed forces during the war as attested by the many military veterans who made up the leadership of early homophile organizations during the 1950s. Indeed, among the first activities of these organizations were protests and lobbying to change military policies, under which those discharged for "homosexuality" could be permanently stigmatized by the codes placed on their discharge papers. Internal controversy at the Pentagon over the justifications for excluding homosexuals from the uniformed services led to establishment of an internal study committee, which produced a report concluding that the purported justifications for excluding gays were not supported by objective evidence. This "Crittendon Committee Report" was buried by the military leaders, however, who were not willing to provoke public controversy at a time when reactionary forces in Congress and the media had raised the spectre of subversion of national security by homosexuals.

The postwar national security program, initiated by President Harry S. Truman in response to concerns about internal Communist subversion after the fall of the Chiang-kai Shek government in China and the domination of eastern Europe by Soviet Russian occupation forces, also came to target lesbians and gay men who worked for the government or government contractors. The Red Scare of the late 1940s and early 1950s led to the identification and exclusion of many gay government employees, and the institution of a security clearance program limited employment opportunities for gay scientists and technicians seeking employment with defense contractors. Senator Joseph McCarthy, a leader of anti-Communist forces in Congress, charged that the U.S. State Department employed scores of subversive homosexuals, and the Department subsequently discharged several career employees as part of the antigay "witchhunt."

In addition to protesting military policies, the early homophile organizations (especially the Washington, D.C., chapter of the Mattachine Society) targeted the security clearance program as a major source of unfair oppression. Perhaps the most vocal leader in this fight was Franklin Kameny, an Army employee who lost his job in the Army Map Service and had the temerity to file suit against the government questioning the constitutionality of the targeting of gays in the "loyalty" program. Although the U.S. Court of Appeals for the District of Columbia Circuit dismissed his case on procedural grounds in a 1960 decision that avoided discussing the merits, and the U.S. Supreme Court refused Kameny's petition for review, he did not give up his struggle against discrimination, and decided to devote his life to opposing the federal government's policy of discharging gay employees. He lobbied the American Civil Liberties Union (ACLU) to take up the cause of homosexuals as a basic civil liberties issue and provided nonlegal representation to numerous civil servants battling discharges or refusals of security clearances. (A first-person account of Kameny's story can be found in Part Two of Marcus, *Making History* (1992), an oral history of the modern lesbian and gay rights movement.) Kameny's persistent lobbying finally paid off, as the ACLU began, at first hesitantly during the 1960s, and then more boldly during the 1970s, to champion an end to the antigay military and national security policies. In the mid-1980s, the ACLU started the Lesbian and Gay Rights Project in its national office to coordinate efforts by its state affiliates on these and other gay rights issues.

Challenges to the military and national security exclusions of gays reached a new stage of visibility during the 1970s when Sergeant Leonard Matlovich, a highly decorated veteran of the Vietnam War, publicly declared his homosexuality and sued the U.S. Department of Defense after his subsequent discharge. Matlovich's case was the first in a series of challenges to question the constitutionality of these exclusionary policies under the Fifth Amendment's Due Process Clause (which includes a requirement that the government abide by principles of equal protection derived from the Fourteenth Amendment) and the First Amendment's freedoms of speech and association. The lawsuits led to considerable public discussion. Although Defense Department leaders continued to argue that the exclusionary policy was necessary to accomplish the military's national defense goals, studies commissioned by the Defense Department and Congress's General Accounting Office suggested otherwise, and it appeared that either Congress or the White House was likely to end (or significantly modify) the policy during the 1990s.

The most significant such challenges to produce appellate decisions are discussed in this chapter. Related cases concerning discrimination by the federal government against its les-bian and gay employees discussed in other chapters include *Norton v. Macy* (No. 71), *Ashton v. Civiletti* (No. 78), *Padula v. Webster* (No. 84), and *Schowengerdt v. United States* (No. 87).

Military and National Security Issues: Readings

Benecke, M.M., and Dodge, K.S., "Military Women in Nontraditional Job Fields: Casualties of the Armed Forces' War on Homosexuals," 13 *Harvard Women's Law Journal* 215 (Spring 1990)

Berube, A., *Coming Out Under Fire: The History of Gay Men and Women in World War Two* (New York: Free Press, 1990)

Davis, J.S., "Military Policy Toward Homosexuals: Scientific, Historical, and Legal Perspectives," 131 *Military Law Review* 55 (Winter 1991)

Editorial Staff, "A Judicial Blow to the Military's Anti-Gay Policies—*Pruitt v. Cheney*," 27 *Harvard Civil Rights—Civil Liberties Law Review* 244 (Winter 1992)

Editorial Staff, "Mounting a Constitutional Challenge on Article 125," *Army Lawyer* 18–19 (August 1989)

Gibson, E.L., *Get Off My Ship: Ensign Berg v. the U.S. Navy* (New York: Avon Books, 1978)

Harris, S., "Permitting Prejudice to Govern: Equal Protection, Military Deference, and the Exclusion of Lesbians and Gay Men From the Military," 17 *New York University Review of Law & Social Change* 171 (March 1989)

Hippler, M., *Matlovich: The Good Soldier* (Boston: Alyson Publications, 1989)

Leonard, A.S., "*Watkins v. United States Army* and the Employment Rights of Lesbians and Gay Men," 40 *Labor Law Journal* 438 (July 1989)

Lewis, M.H., "Unacceptable Risk or Unacceptable Rhetoric? An Argument for a Quasi-Suspect Classification for Gays Based on Current Government Security Clearance Procedures," 7 *Journal of Law & Politics* 133 (Fall 1990)

Lewis, R.W., "*Watkins v. U.S. Army* and *Bowers v. Hardwick*: Are Homosexuals a Suspect Class or Second Class Citizens?" 68 *Nebraska Law Review* 851 (Fall 1989)

Marcus, E. *Making History* (New York: HarperCollins, 1992)

Sunstein, C.R., "Sexual Orientation and the Constitution: A Note on the Relationship Between Due Process and Equal Protection," 55 *University of Chicago Law Review* 1161 (Fall 1988)

89. ARE ALL GAYS "SECURITY RISKS"?

Adams v. Laird, 420 F.2d 230 (D.C. Cir. 1969), certiorari denied, 397 U.S. 1039 (1970).

After World War II, the perceived threat of Communist subversion in the U.S. government led to the adoption of stricter procedures for determining which government employees, and employees of government contractors, would be entitled to see information that was considered significant for purposes of national security. Spurred by the activities of investigatory committees of the House of Representatives and the Senate, and particularly Senator Joseph McCarthy, to uncover Communists throughout American society, the U.S. Department of Defense adopted a security clearance program that provided few procedural rights to applicants. In 1959, the U.S. Supreme Court ruled in *Greene v. McElroy* that existing procedures failed to meet the requirements of the Fifth Amendment's Due Process Clause. President Dwight D. Eisenhower issued an Executive Order on February 20, 1960, directing the Defense Department to adopt new procedures in compliance with the Court's opinion. Under the resulting program, applicants seeking security clearances for employment in defense industries were entitled to a hearing before a field board and an appellate determination by a central industrial personnel access authorization board.

Under the Executive Order, the procedures were "to insure that no person is granted, or is allowed to retain, an authorization for access to classified information unless the available information justifies a finding that such access authorization . . . is clearly consistent with the national interest." The Defense department directive establishing the program provided that decisions on security clearances should be made "in the light of all the surrounding circumstances" and emphasized that a clearance decision "must be an over-all commonsense one."

Underlying these broad general standards was an attitude toward diverse sexuality that ensured that homosexuals would have a difficult time obtaining such clearances. Senator McCarthy had railed against homosexuals as "subversives" during his investigations of the State and Defense departments in the early 1950s, and the Defense department had itself adopted a general policy shortly prior to World War II of removing all identified homosexuals from active duty, although enforcement of that policy had been erratic due to wartime manpower needs.

During the 1950s, the Defense Department ordered an internal study, which became known within the Department as the Crittenden Committee Report. It concluded that homosexual service members did not present any greater risk of subversion than nonhomosexual members. Due to the controversy about homosexuality generated by Senator McCarthy's investigations, the continuing views of the American medical establishment that homosexuality was a sign of mental illness and instability, and the existence of laws penalizing some forms of homosexual conduct in every state, the Department never accepted the recommendations of the Crittenden Committee Report and buried it deep in classified files, not to emerge until freedom of information requests filed by legal researchers thirty years later brought it to light.

One of the earliest cases in which a "practicing homosexual" challenged the denial of a security clearance and tried to pursue his case to the U.S. Supreme Court was *Adams v. Laird,*. It arose at a time when all but a handful of states outlawed many forms of homosexual conduct. Robert Larry Adams, employed as an electronic technician by Melpar, Inc., a defense contractor located in the so-called Research Triangle area in North Carolina, obtained a secret-access authorization from the Defense Department in 1957 as required by his job. Adams worked with this level of security clearance for five years without incident, then left to take a job in private industry. In 1962, his new employer, National Scientific Laboratories, Inc., asked him to apply for a top-secret authorization, which he would need for certain work it wanted him to perform. Adams made the application and waited while the Screening

Board for the Defense Department undertook its investigation.

Adams waited and waited and waited. Finally, during the summer of 1964, the Screening Board contacted Adams and invited him to come to the Office of Naval Intelligence at the Potomac Naval Command Center for an interview to clear up some issues raised by his application. Adams reported for the interview at 9 A.M. on July 30, 1964, and was met by two investigators. They advised him at the beginning of the interview that he had a right to refrain from answering questions and that any answers he gave might be used against him. Adams indicated his eagerness to obtain the authorization and willingness to answer all questions. The first part of the interview dealt with some errors in Adams's written application. Then the agents raised the issue of homosexuality. Adams was open and forthright. He admitted that he had engaged in homosexual activity since the age of 14, including with fellow employees, whose names he refused to reveal. He also admitted that about two and one-half years earlier he had once solicited a young man (since enrolled as a student at Duke University) with whom he was working on a science fair project to engage in homosexual activity with him. At that time, he had told the young man that he, Adams, was actively homosexual. The agents also confirmed that Adams patronized a restaurant popular with gay people. The interview lasted the entire day, with a lunch break and some rest breaks. The agents let Adams call his employer to say he would be late getting back to work. Adams agreed to come back for another interview on August 5, and appeared at that time to answer more questions.

No further action was taken for almost a year, when his secret clearance was suspended and he received a notice that his application had been denied. The notice, as required by Defense Department policy, specified reasons for the denial, which were as follows:

1. Criterion 16: Information available to the Screening Board indicates that you have engaged in criminal and immoral conduct and acts of sexual perversion and may continue to do so. This information is:

a. On July 30, 1964, you acknowledged to several persons that you had engaged in numerous acts of sexual perversion, beginning when you were 14 years of age and continuing up to that date.

b. In 1962, while you and [Mr. "X"] were working jointly on a local science fair project, you solicited the said ["X"] to engage in unlawful and immoral acts of sexual perversion.

(Further details with respect to the matters alleged in this paragraph will be furnished to you upon your written request and will in any event be included in the record on which the determination in your case will be made.)

2. Criterion 14: The information set forth in paragraph 1, above, and the subparagraphs thereunder, reflects behavior, activities, and associations which tend to show that you are not reliable or trustworthy.

3. Criterion 17: The information set forth in paragraph 1, above, and the subparagraphs thereunder, reflects acts of a reckless, irresponsible, or wanton nature which indicate such poor judgment and instability as to suggest that you might disclose classified information to unauthorized persons, or otherwise assist such persons, whether deliberately or inadvertently, in activities inimical to the national interest.

4. Criterion 19: The information set forth in paragraph 1, above, and the subparagraphs thereunder, furnishes reason to believe that you may be subjected to coercion, influence, or pressure which may be likely to cause you to act contrary to the national interest.

Adams replied seeking more particulars about why or how his conduct was considered incompatible with getting the security clearance, as suggested by the parenthetical statement in the first notice. He received a second letter, dated June 30, with a list of what the Screening Board characterized as "further details." Adams responded with a letter admitting some of the factual allegations, denying others, and contending that some of the things he said at the interview were mainly for the purpose of ending the interview and might not be particularly reliable. Adams requested a hearing, which took place before the Field Board in Washington. He retained a lawyer to represent him, a Mr. Graves, whose strategy at the hearing appeared to be minimizing Adams's homosexual activity. One of the agents testified about what

Adams said during the interview the previous year, and the government placed in evidence an affidavit from "Mr. X," recounting the solicitation incident. The government's attorney, a Mr. Tilton, indicated that Mr. X was willing to testify personally but was unavailable at that time, but that Mr. X could reply to interrogatories. Graves indicated that this was adequate, but never submitted interrogatories after the hearing. Graves indicated that he also had affidavit testimony to submit in support of Adams's loyalty and trustworthiness, which Tilton accepted on the same basis. After the hearing, Tilton submitted interrogatories, which elicited a response favorable to Adams. Adams also testified in his own behalf. Cross-examination of witnesses was allowed.

The field examiner submitted a report to the Central Board for review based on the hearing record and posthearing submissions. The Central Board notified Adams by letter dated April 7, 1966, almost two years after the initial interview and four years after his application, that it had tentatively decided to deny his application. The Board offered the opportunity for an oral argument, at which Adams's attorney argued in his behalf that his conduct did not justify suspending or denying his clearance, which effectively made him unemployable in a defense industry job. Nevertheless, the Board confirmed its tentative conclusion and notified Adams that it had concluded that authorizing him access to any classified information "is not clearly consistent with the national interest." The Board indicated that it had based its conclusion on three factors, which were subsequently summarized by the federal appeals court as follows:

> (1) homosexual acts engaged in with two fellow employees at Melpar, Inc., whom [Adams] would identify only as Messrs. "A" and "B",
>
> (2) a homosexual act with one "Y" in 1963, and
>
> (3) the solicitation of "X" in 1962, when they were working jointly on a science fair project, to engage in homosexual acts.

The Board specifically stated that it "attributed no adverse significance" to the other allegations made by the investigators, including Adams's patronage of a gay-oriented restaurant, his engaging in homosexual acts as a teenager, and his refusal to answer more detailed questions about his homosexual acts with one of his fellow employees at Melpar. Thus, the Board was denying Adams a security clearance based on a handful of homosexual acts and one solicitation occurring over a period of a few years prior to Adams's application for the clearance.

Adams filed suit in the U.S. District Court for the District of Columbia against Secretary of Defense Melvin Laird, alleging that the procedures under which he was denied a clearance were constitutionally defective and asking the court to order Laird to grant him the security clearance he needed to continue working in the defense industry. The government promptly moved for summary judgment, which was granted by District Judge Howard F. Corcoran without written opinion or statement of reasons. Adams's attorneys, William M. Barnard and Ralph J. Temple, appealed this decision to the U.S. Court of Appeals for the District of Columbia Circuit, which scheduled argument for June 5, 1969. Justice Department attorney H. Yale Gutnick appeared for the government at the argument before a three-judge panel of the circuit. Barnard argued that the evidence obtained by the government was defective in two respects. First, by reference to the U.S. Supreme Court's decision in *Miranda v. Arizona* (1966), he argued that the "police interrogation" tactics used by the Defense investigative agents merited the protection of presence of counsel, so that information obtained in that interview should not be used in making the security clearance determination. He also argued that no weight should have been given to the affidavit by Mr. X, who was not subject to cross-examination. Barnard also argued that the procedures for making the security determination were constitutionally flawed, in that the standards for decision were not articulated with adequate specificity, and that no findings were made that the clearance denials were "required in the national interest." Gutnick responded that this was not a criminal proceeding, so *Miranda* was irrelevant, Adams had apparently waived his opportunity to send interrogatories to Mr. X, and the security procedures were adequate to meet the requirements of due process. Further, Gutnick emphasized that the president's Executive Order did not require a finding that denying a clearance was "required in the national interest," but rather that a clearance was to be issued only if the secretary found that it was "consistent" with the national interest to do so.

The panel announced its decision denying Adams's appeal on December 12, 1969, in an opinion by Circuit Judge Carl McGowan, with Circuit Judge J. Skelly Wright dissenting. While expressing sympathy for Adams, McGowan concluded that the government's arguments were correct on all counts.

First, as to the investigative interrogation back in the summer of 1964, McGowan said that the decision by the Screening Board to request an interview with Adams was sparked by statements Adams voluntarily made in his application and the resulting investigation of his application. Adams was not commanded to appear, but had done so voluntarily. He was not "in custody," a requirement for *Miranda* rights to arise. He was not subjected to onerous conditions, since he was given rest and restroom breaks and allowed to leave the premises for an hour lunch break. He had been advised of his right not to answer questions but had voluntarily agreed to do so. While "the agents were persistent, as professional investigators have a way of being," they did not engage in coercive tactics. McGowan stated:

> Appellant was obviously torn between distaste for revealing highly intimate details of his personal life, on the one hand, and, on the other, his desire not to endanger the success of his application by seeming to be uncooperative or to be concealing matters which inferentially might be regarded as much worse than they were in fact. His lot, in short, was an unhappy and uncomfortable one, as is true of anyone who occupies as ambivalent a position as does the homosexual in the contemporary social order. It was not, in our view, significantly worse than would normally obtain if it be thought that he was properly subject to questioning at all on this subject.

Given the criteria under which the clearance decision would be made, it was not surprising that the agents were engaging in this line of questioning. "The moment that appellant decided to press his application in the face of investigation and to submit himself for that purpose to interrogation," asserted McGowan,

"pressure upon him was inevitable." It was understandable that in retrospect Adams was unhappy about those interviews, when he may have approached them thinking that nothing much was wrong. "We are not unsympathetic" to Adams's feelings, said McGowan, but "we do not find in the record anything so shocking about it as to transgress the limits of due process or to render wholly unreliable the statements attributed to appellant in the course of that interview."

McGowan also made short work of the contention that the Mr. X affidavit should be excluded from consideration. Graves had not objected at the hearing to the introduction of the affidavit, probably because he intended to submit an affidavit on behalf of Adams under a similar arrangement for the other side to submit interrogatories. McGowan found that this objection "borders on the frivolous" under the circumstances.

Turning to the substance of the case, McGowan rejected the argument that the government could deny a clearance only if it clearly found that the applicant would use secret information to the nation's detriment. That was not the test, he said. While Adams was alleging that the standards under which these decisions were made were not sufficiently articulated, he was really contending that the standard adopted was inappropriate. The president had clearly articulated a standard in his Executive Order: that clearances be given only on a finding that "it is clearly consistent with the national interest to do so." Said McGowan, "We know of no constitutional requirement that the President must, in seeking to safeguard the integrity of classified information, provide that a security clearance must be granted unless it be affirmatively proven that the applicant 'would use' it improperly." Asserting that the decision to whom to grant such clearances was "an inexact science at best," McGowan found that it would be inappropriate to cabin the discretion of the decisionmakers to the degree argued by Adams. Besides, "[a]ppellant is not being sent to jail; he is being told rather that, on the information developed and the facts found after hearing, [the government] cannot make a finding that giving him access to secret information is 'clearly consistent with the national interest.'" Since this was "within the range of rational choice" as a standard for the president to adopt, the Due Process Clause did not require judicial intervention.

McGowan believed that the Defense Department directives establishing the security clearance program

> include ample indications that a practicing homosexual may pose serious problems for the Defense Department in making the requisite finding for security clearance. They refer expressly to the factors of emotional instability and possible subjection to sinister pressures and influences which have traditionally been the lot of homosexuals living in what is, for better or worse, a society still strongly oriented toward heterosexuality.

Of course, as was typical at the time and still to a great extent among the conservative members of the federal appeals courts, McGowan cited no authority for these propositions, and was apparently unaware of the Crittenden Committee Report or the increasing arguments within American psychiatry (highlighted in a report issued about the same time by a task force of the National Institutes of Health chaired by Dr. Evelyn Hooker) about the proper description of homosexuality and other forms of sexual diversity on the continuum of mental health, which by 1969 had advanced rather far toward the eventual decision by the American Psychiatric Association in 1973 to remove homosexuality from its official list of mental disorders. For McGowan, at that time and place, it was sufficient to assert that issues of "instability" and "possible subjection to sinister pressures and influences" were enough to justify the Defense Department's virtual exclusion of acknowledged homosexuals from employment by defense contractors.

Picking up on Adams's argument that a security clearance had apparently been granted to another applicant who had admitted committing homosexual acts while stationed on Army duty in Korea, McGowan noted that the security clearance people were persuaded by evidence that this homosexual interest was situational and had ceased upon return to civilian life. By contrast, Adams was a practicing homosexual by his own statements. Would Adams want the Defense Department to adopt an ex-

press policy of excluding anybody with a history of homosexuality from receiving a clearance for the sake of consistency with his case? Surely this was inconsistent with the kind of case-by-case "commonsense" determination that the Defense Department directive and the situation called for.

Finally, McGowan rejected the contention that the Central Board had failed to make findings that would support its conclusion. The Board had clearly found that Adams had engaged in homosexual acts while an adult and an employee of defense contractors, and had solicited Mr. X. The Board had expressly based its decision on these findings, finding that they provided reason to believe that Adams might be subject to coercion, influence, or pressure that would cause him to act contrary to the national interest. This was stated in a letter to Adams about the reason for declining his application and suspending his existing clearance. There was no procedural default, and, said McGowan, "appellant does not really urge upon us an abuse of discretion in any substantive sense," noting that at the Field Board hearing Adams had not attempted to present any evidence going to the issue whether his homosexuality had any relationship to his eligibility for a security clearance; rather, Adams had concentrated at the hearing on contesting the validity of the investigators' factual allegations about his conduct. Without stating any view as to whether there was any question of substantive due process lurking in the case, McGowan concluded that on the record before the court, he could find no constitutional violation or abridgement of Adams's procedural rights under the Executive Order.

Dissenting Judge Wright, while agreeing there had been no procedural irregularities of constitutional dimension in the case, was unwilling to let the substantive issue drop so quickly. He would have remanded the case to the Central Board "for a determination of the relationship between the alleged homosexual conduct and the ability of appellant to protect classified information." He took this position in light of Adams's record of eight years between the time he received a secret clearance and the time his clearance was suspended, during which there was not a hint of any security problem. Although there was evidence in the record that he had been homosexually active during the relevant period, there was no evidence he had ever betrayed his country. Indeed, even though the Defense Department uncovered information about Adams's homosexuality prior to the investigative interview (as indicated by the Mr. X affidavit, which was dated more than a month before that interview), it had not done anything about suspending Adams's security clearance until almost a year later. "The Defense Department's lassitude was justified," said Wright. "But despite this record of reliability, the Board made no real effort to show why its factual findings relating to homosexuality precluded continued security clearance in this case."

Wright invoked his own opinion for the D.C. Circuit in *Norton v. Macy*, decided earlier that year, holding that a federal employee could not be discharged for homosexual conduct unless the government could show a specific nexus between that off-duty conduct and fitness to work for the government. Even before the Supreme Court criticized existing security clearance procedures in *Greene v. McElroy*, said Wright, it was "firmly established that the due process clause of the Fifth Amendment encompasses the 'right to hold specific private employment and to follow a chosen profession free from unreasonable governmental interference,'" quoting the Court's opinion in *Greene*. Lifting Adams's clearance "at least seriously impaired" him from gaining employment in his chosen profession, and to do that without some sort of nexus finding offended due process. "Assumptions predicated on appellant's unfortunate affliction unrelated to the facts of this case cannot provide a legal basis for effectively denying him access to his livelihood." As this quote, and similar language in *Norton* indicated, Judge Wright, a committed humanitarian, had not quite absorbed or accepted the newly surfacing contention that homosexuality was not an illness, but for him, it offended due process for the government to base conclusions about loyalty and reliability on assumptions about an illness.

Responding to McGowan's finding that the government had adequately articulated factual findings supporting its decision, Wright asserted that the quoted "reasons . . . were merely one-sentence recitations checked off from a list previously prepared for denying security clearances generally." They were not demonstrated to have any direct connection to the facts of Adams's case, including his many years of service with security authorization. For example, as to the finding that Adams's homosexuality affected his reliability or trustworthiness, "no rational connection between isolated homosexual activity and reliability is demonstrated by *facts* as distinguished from unsupported assumptions. If the Board has any evidence indicating either that this appellant specifically, or that homosexuals taken as a group, are not trustworthy or reliable, it ought to include that evidence in this record."

Wright also rejected the contention that anything in the record documented that Adams was "reckless." "The conclusion is simply baldly stated as though no facts were necessary to support it," he commented, "and the central, uncontested fact in this case—that in appellant's eight years of handling classified materials the Board has been unable to point to a single breach of security—is simply ignored." While the Board's fears of blackmail might have some basis "in common experience," it was hard to see how they were relevant to Adams's case, since he was open about his homosexuality. Surely, after these proceedings, a threat to reveal his homosexuality could have no detrimental effect on his reliability! Wright concluded:

> In sum, the clear impression left by reading the record in this case is that appellant was denied his clearance simply because of homosexual acts, without any effort to determine whether his status as a homosexual related to his ability to protect classified information. The Board's ruling is in effect a bill of attainder against all homosexuals, at least insofar as obtaining security clearances is concerned.

To Wright, this was unacceptable. While the Defense Department needed to exercise discretion in deciding to whom to award security clearances, "there must in all cases be some rational relationship between the facts found and the actions of the Board." The "least he should be able to expect" before his livelihood is taken away is "a decision in which there is a rational nexus between the facts and the conclusions drawn therefrom." Since there was none in this case, the decision should have been reversed.

Adams petitioned the U.S. Supreme Court to review the case with the assistance of the American Civil Liberties Union, but the petition was denied on April 20, 1970.

Adams v. Laird is notable for several things. It is frequently cited by federal courts in security clearance and military litigation to support the proposition that the Defense Department and other agencies concerned with security may deny employment or clearances to homosexuals without finding any rational nexus of the type suggested by Wright, since the court apparently approved a virtual blanket rule that practicing homosexuals could be presumed to present security risks. This citation continues despite the absence of any recognition in either the majority or dissenting opinions of the changing scientific views about human sexuality, or any awareness of military studies such as the Crittenden Committee Report, which signifi-

cantly undermined assumptions about the security risks posed by homosexuals.

More notable, however, is the dissent by Skelly Wright, and the short shrift given his arguments by McGowan or subsequent courts. When compared to other cases in which government discrimination on bases other than sexual orientation or conduct is challenged, it becomes clear that Wright's description of the requirements of due process is generally followed. Something about sexuality, however, diverts the courts from their normal path. Something about sexuality leads them to indulge in assumptions about one group that would normally be considered inappropriate if indulged in about other groups (e.g., an assumption that members of a particular racial or ethnic group are lazy, irresponsible, or less intelligent than others).

Case References

Greene v. McElroy, 360 U.S. 474 (1959)
Miranda v. Arizona, 384 U.S. 436 (1966)
Norton v. Macy, 417 F.2d 1161 (D.C. Cir. 1969)

90. CHALLENGES TO UNBRIDLED MILITARY DISCRETION

Matlovich v. Secretary of the Air Force, 591 F.2d 852 (D.C. Cir. 1978), vacating and remanding D.C. Civil Action No. 75–1750 (D.D.C. 1977) (oral opinion); decision on remand, 23 Fair Empl. Prac. Cas. (BNA) 1251 (D.D.C. 1980); ruling on motion to stay proceedings pending administrative review, 414 F. Supp. 690 (D.D.C. 1976). *Berg v. Claytor*, 591 F.2d 849 (D.C. Cir. 1978), vacating and remanding 436 F. Supp. 76 (D.D.C. 1977).

Leonard Matlovich was an airman with a problem. A politically conservative military volunteer who had risen to the rank of technical sergeant while serving several tours of duty in Vietnam, winning the Bronze Star, Purple Heart, two Air Force commendation medals, and a meritorious service medal, Matlovich had been the ideal Air Force volunteer. He had always achieved the highest service ratings from his superiors, and he was highly esteemed by enlisted personnel and officers as a human relations instructor at the Tactical Air Command at Langley Air Force Base in Virginia. He planned a career in the military and had re-

ceived encouragement for his plans from superior officers. But by 1973 Matlovich had come to realize that his sexual orientation might be homosexual, and this was a problem because, as he knew, military regulations specified that homosexuals should be separated from the service.

Always cautious when faced with novel issues, Matlovich decided that he could not firmly conclude he was homosexual without getting some sexual experience. He discreetly found a gay bar off base and had some sexual experiences, including some with other service members who were not in his unit. Finally convinced that he was indeed gay, Matlovich confronted his ethical duty to reveal this to his commander, since he knew of the regulations mandating discharge. Matlovich was convinced that the problem was not as bad as he thought, however, because Air Force Manual 39–12, which contained the Air Force's policy regarding separation of homosexuals, also provided that exceptions could be made if "the most unusual circumstances exist and provided the airman's ability to perform military service has not been compromised." Surely this was his situation, thought Matlovich, since he had the highest possible ratings, had never engaged in sexual activity on base, with minors, or with anyone either under his command or in a position of command authority over him.

Believing that the exception would surely be made in his case, Matlovich went to his commanding officer early in 1975 and disclosed that he had concluded that his "sexual preferences are homosexual as opposed to heterosexual." Matlovich also wrote to the secretary of the Air Force, announcing his homosexuality and urging that the exception to normal policy be made in his case due to his superior record and his firm resolve not to engage in sexual activity with any service members working under his command. The Secretary directed the Air Force's Office of Special Investigation to look into Matlovich's case. After questioning Matlovich, the Office recommended administrative discharge proceedings be commenced.

An administrative discharge board met for four days in September 1975. Washington attorneys David F. Addelstone, Susan H. Herman, and Barton F. Stichman assisted Matlovich in the hearing, presenting expert testimony on homosexuality and its lack of relevance to fitness to serve in the Air Force. Matlovich also testified about his ability to continue to serve effectively. He also testified truthfully about his limited sexual experiences since 1973. The board concluded that Matlovich had engaged in conduct forbidden by the Uniform Code of Military Justice and recommended a general discharge for unfitness.

Matlovich's commanding officer at Langley decided to accept the board's recommendation of discharge, but upgraded it to an honorable discharge in light of Matlovich's sterling service record. Matlovich appealed to the secretary of the Air Force, urging that the secretary exercise the discretion allowed by the regulations to keep him in the service. Learning that the secretary had rejected his appeal, Matlovich filed suit against the secretary and his commanding officer, Colonel Alton J. Thogersen, on October 21, 1975, asking the federal district court to declare his discharge invalid and enjoin it from taking place. District Judge Gerhard A. Gesell denied the request for temporary relief, and the next day Matlovich was honorably discharged from the Air Force.

Matlovich immediately moved to exhaust administrative remedies, applying to the Air Force Board for the Correction of Military Records to overturn his discharge. He also amended his federal court complaint to seek reinstatement in addition to a declaration that the discharge was invalid. The government obtained a stay of the federal court proceedings from Judge Gesell by promising that the Board would have authority to consider the constitutionality of the regulation. The Board denied Matlovich's appeal, and the secretary adopted the Board's findings and recommendations without further comment.

Both Matlovich and the Air Force applied to Judge Gesell for summary judgment. Among the facts stipulated in the cross-motions were that Matlovich had engaged in consensual sexual conduct with other male adults several times since 1973, and that there were past instances in which the Air Force had retained members discovered to be homosexual. After hearing oral argument from Matlovich's new attorney, E. Carrington Boggan of New York, a board member of Lambda Legal Defense & Education Fund, and Royce B. Lamberth, from the U.S. Department of Justice's Civil Division, Judge Gesell ruled from the bench, granting the Air Force's motion in an oral opinion.

Matlovich had argued that the regulation requiring separation of homosexuals was unconstitutional, as a violation of the constitutional right of privacy derived from *Griswold v. Connecticut* (1965), an argument that had recently been rejected by a three-judge district court considering a challenge to the constitutionality of Virginia's sodomy statute in *Doe v. Commonwealth's Attorney for City of Richmond*

(1975). Judge Gesell agreed with the *Doe* ruling, finding that there was no constitutional right to engage in homosexual conduct. He found further that the Air Force policy of discharging homosexuals was rational, and that the burden of proving that an exception should be made in his case had not been met by Matlovich. Gesell accepted at face value the government's argument that an excellent service record was not by itself the sort of "exceptional circumstance" contemplated by the regulation as justifying retaining a homosexual service member.

However, Gesell was clearly bothered by the treatment Matlovich had received from the Air Force. After summarizing his excellent service record, stressing Matlovich's valiant conduct under fire in Vietnam, Gesell urged that "it would appear that the Armed Forces might well be advised to move toward a more discriminatory and informed approach" to the problem of homosexuality: "to approach it in perhaps a more sensitive and precise way."

While Matlovich's case was pending, another challenge to the military's policies was brewing in the U.S. Navy. Ensign Vernon E. Berg, III, an Annapolis graduate on active duty as an ensign attached to the admiral's staff as information officer on the USS *Little Rock*, based in Gaeta, Italy, was subjected to a Naval Investigative Service inquiry after an enlisted man serving on the *Little Rock* alleged that Ensign Berg attempted to engage him in sexual activity while he was on shore. Although Berg denied the allegations, he did admit to naval investigators that he considered himself bisexual and had engaged in sexual activity with other men before and during his service in the Navy. The Navy notified Berg on July 24, 1975, that it was initiating administrative proceedings for his discharge. Berg, the son of a retired naval officer, immediately submitted his resignation and, within a few weeks, was transferred to the Norfolk (Virginia) Naval Base in anticipation of dismissal.

After thinking over his situation, however, Berg decided he wanted to continue his naval career. He contacted Boggan, who was already involved with Matlovich's appeal. Boggan's research revealed that the apparent harshness of naval regulations requiring discharge of homosexuals had been interpreted by the service to authorize exceptions in some cases, or at least it had been so represented to a federal court in *Champagne v. Schlesinger* (1974). Maintaining that he had never engaged in any activity that would detract from his ability to fulfill his naval commitments, Berg wrote to naval authorities on November 4, requesting that his prior resignation be withdrawn. The Navy convened an administrative discharge board on January 19, 1976, to consider Berg's case. Berg presented expert testimony challenging the Navy's assertion in its regulation, SECNAVIST 1909.A, that "[m]embers involved in homosexuality are military liabilities who cannot be tolerated in a military organization." Among those who testified in Berg's defense was his father.

Berg's case seemed doomed from the outset, however, since his discharge board was clearly predisposed against him. When questioned at the outset of the hearing, three of the five members stated that they could envision no circumstances under which it would be advisable to retain a homosexual in the service; the other two stated they could foresee a recommendation of retention only if the homosexual officer were confined to shore duty. All five officers insisted that they could keep an open mind and were willing to consider expert testimony that might contradict their views. Berg requested that the discharge board be replaced with officers who did not hold firm views on the issue of homosexuality, but his request was denied.

The board determined, based on Berg's admissions, that he had engaged in homosexual conduct while in the service and should be discharged under other than honorable conditions. Since Berg's commanding officer, Admiral Rumble, disqualified himself from participating in the case, presumably due to the personal antagonism that had developed between himself and Berg, the matter was referred to the commander of the Sixth Naval District, who endorsed the board's recommendation. On April 12, 1976, the chief of naval personnel forwarded the recommendation for discharge to the assistant secretary of the Navy, who approved it on May 20. Berg filed suit in the federal district court in Washington on May 28, seeking a temporary restraining order against his discharge. It was denied by Judge Gesell, and the Navy discharged Berg under other than honorable circumstances on June 3. Berg pursued his lawsuit, seeking a declaration that his discharge was unlawful and requesting reinstatement and back pay. While the case was pending before Judge Gesell, the Navy sought to blunt Berg's constitutional claims by upgrading his discharge to honorable. Stipulating the administrative hearing record as the basis for suit, both parties moved for summary judgment.

On May 27, 1977, Gesell issued a written opinion in Berg's case that echoed his opinion in Matlovich's case but amplified his reasoning. First rejecting Berg's challenge to the constitutionality of the discharge regulation, Gesell broadly characterized the developing sexual privacy case law of *Griswold v. Connecticut* (1965), *Eisenstadt v. Baird* (1972), and *Roe v. Wade* (1973), as "prohibiting interference by the state with relationships between men and women," and concluded that he was "constrained" by the precedent of *Doe v. Commonwealth's Attorney* from extending the sexual privacy cases to homosexual conduct.

Gesell also rejected Berg's contention that the Navy's policy failed to meet the test of minimal rationality. Noting that the Navy did not contend its policy was necessary to enforce "morality" or even to protect security, Gesell accepted the argument articulated by naval officers at Berg's discharge hearing that a known homosexual officer could not function effectively aboard ship because enlisted men and fellow officers would subject him to ridicule and lack of respect, undermining his ability to provide leadership and compounding the "already severe pressures faced by all officers aboard ship." Essentially, the Navy was arguing that homosexual officers must be removed not because of any failings on their part, but because the prejudices of others would make it difficult for them to serve effectively. Gesell dismissed the argument that discrimination to accommodate the prejudices of nongay service members was inappropriate. While acknowledging that "there are problems inherent in burdening a class of people because of the reactions they engender," he asserted that "where the class that is burdened is neither 'suspect,' nor engaged in constitutionally protected be-

havior, the Government may take the reactions of third parties into account in setting its policy." Gesell cited no authority for the proposition that sexual orientation is not a "suspect" classification under the Equal Protection Clause, and engaged in no discussion of the question.

Berg had argued that there was no evidence in the discharge record that his own ability to serve had been undermined when his homosexuality became known. In fact, he had introduced testimony showing that enlisted men and fellow officers in his command supported his effort to remain in the service. Gesell rejected such evidence as irrelevant to the issue of the policy's constitutionality. "The issue," he wrote, "is whether the concerns expressed by the Navy would apply to so few officers that a general policy against homosexuality is irrational." Claiming that the burden was on Berg to show such was the case, Gesell rejected Berg's argument that the Navy's failure to document its concerns with actual studies was fatal to its policy. It was enough for Gesell that some naval officers had testified that incidents had occurred where homosexual officers had become ineffective, especially given the "extreme deference appellate courts have steadfastly given military procedures which were subject to constitutional attack."

Gesell also rejected Berg's challenges to the procedures that had been used in his case. Finding that Berg's admission of engaging in homosexual conduct effectively eliminated the need for various procedural protections that are normally required to ensure accurate fact-finding, Gesell concluded that none of Berg's procedural objections to the nature of the hearing were significant enough to warrant reversal of the Navy's actions. Because Berg's discharge had been upgraded to honorable, Gesell found that the liberty interest that might require a more formal hearing procedure was no longer present.

Gesell rejected as well Berg's charge that the discharge board was biased based on the five officers' statements about their attitudes toward homosexual officers. Finding that the regulations implicitly required an impartial hearing board, Gesell nonetheless determined that the decision of naval authorities to reject Berg's challenge to the impartiality of the board was neither arbitrary nor capricious. Because Berg had admitted engaging in homosexual acts, Gesell concluded that any alleged bias was irrelevant to the board's fact-finding function in determining whether Berg had violated regulations. As to Berg's allegations that the board was partial on the issue of discretion to recommend retention, Gesell noted that each board member had stated that he could keep an open mind on the ultimate question in the case. Gesell also commented that it was not inappropriate for the hearing officers to bring preconceived policy notions to their task: "In this discretionary area the experience and views of members of the board may be an important factor in reaching the final policy determination." Besides, Gesell asserted, the reviewing authorities had the board members' statement in the record, and so could suitably discount their recommendations if need be.

Acknowledging that it was "clear that the plaintiff was a fine officer," nonetheless Gesell asserted that "there is nothing in his record that marks him as being highly unusual or especially valuable to the Navy," which Gesell evidently considered the test for a discretionary retention decision. Gesell concluded that there was "no legal basis" for setting aside Berg's discharge and dismissed his complaint. However, as in Matlovich's case, Gesell ended his opinion by voicing disquiet at the Navy's continuing antigay policies. "[T]he records in recent homosexual cases demonstrate that physicians and psychologists differ widely concerning the causes and varied manifestations of homosexuality," he stated. "Thus there is also a continuing need for the military establishment to be aware of further investigation in this area. In the final analysis there is, after all, an obligation to accommodate personnel policy to changing scientific knowledge and social standards to the fullest extent so long as conduct which threatens to interfere with defense objectives can be avoided."

Matlovich and Berg appealed the dismissals of their cases to the U.S. Court of Appeals for the District of Columbia Circuit, which consolidated the two cases and heard oral argument on May 15, 1978. The three-judge panel included Chief Judge J. Skelly Wright, Circuit Judge Spottswood W. Robinson, III, and Judge

Oscar H. Davis of the U.S. Court of Claims, sitting by designation. Judge Davis wrote the opinions for the unanimous panel, which were announced December 6, 1978, vacating Judge Gesell's opinions and ordering that the cases ultimately be sent back for further proceedings. The panel issued a separate opinion in each case.

In *Matlovich*, Judge Davis concluded that there was no need for the panel to determine whether the Air Force's regulation providing for discharge of homosexuals was constitutional, because the Air Force had failed to meet the burden that the court held, contrary to Gesell, was on the Air Force; that is, to explain why an exception to the normal rule had not been made in Matlovich's case. Davis reviewed the Air Force regulations and the proceedings in Matlovich's case and concluded that it would be impossible for the court to review whether the Air Force had acted in an arbitrary or capricious manner in this case because the Air Force had never really explained the basis for its actions. All along the line, officials had merely stated in conclusory terms that there were no exceptional circumstances in Matlovich's case justifying retention. Although the Air Force had stipulated during consideration of the cross-motions for summary judgment that other homosexual airmen had been retained, it had never explained what the difference was between Matlovich and those other airmen.

"What we have, then," said the court, "is a serviceman with an admittedly outstanding record of considerable duration, with minimal sexual involvement with Air Force personnel and none with those with whom he worked and with substantial testimony that the Air Force community would be able to accept his homosexuality." Although the Air Force maintained that there were no "exceptional circumstances" to warrant retention, "what are 'exceptional circumstances,' or what they have been in the past, is left uncertain and unknown."

Actually, the court hinted at its suspicions that the Air Force's stubborn refusal to articulate the reasons for not keeping Matlovich related to his decision to be open about his homosexuality, commenting that "the almost-total lack of specificity in the Air Force's determinations leads one to consider the possibility, for instance, whether Matlovich's failure of retention may have been affected by his 'going public' with his homosexuality and the publicity surrounding his case, and that if his homosexuality had been discovered and handled by the Air Force, without public notice, the result might have been different." The court intimated that if this was the case, it might provide an independent ground for challenging the discharge, and the court was entitled to know about it.

The court backed up its conclusion that the Air Force was required to explain why it was not making an exception in Matlovich's case with an extended, detailed analysis of the general principles in administrative law requiring that agencies provide reasoned explanations for their actions in order to make possible a meaningful judicial review. Indeed, the court found that the very regulations and directives on which the government was relying appeared to contemplate reasoned explanations at each decisionmaking step. Rejecting the government's argument that "it is impossible for the Service to specify 'where the most unusual circumstances exist' and what constitutes a compromise of the airman's 'ability to perform military service,'" the court held that similar sorts of explanations were routinely demanded in cases involving conscientious objectors requesting release from service, on which it was basing much of its analysis. The court concluded that the Air Force might proceed in one of two ways: (1) it could publish detailed rules specifying the exceptional circumstances under which homosexual service members might be retained or (2) it could engage in meaningful case-by-case adjudication, explaining in each case the reasons for its decision so that meaningful judicial review could be afforded to service members who believed they had been treated unfairly.

In Berg's case, the panel issued a brief opinion incorporating by reference much of the analysis from the *Matlovich* opinion. "As in *Matlovich*," wrote Davis," we cannot tell why Berg failed of retention or appraise that exercise of discretion. The Administrative Discharge Board found that his record in the service did not reflect such an outstanding potential as a naval officer as to militate against separation. . . . But we have nothing to show or indicate

that these very general and very imprecise standards represent Navy policy, or that they have been applied in the past or are being applied currently, or that they sum up the actual considerations which went into the Navy's ultimate decision not to retain Berg."

The court of appeals sent the cases back to Judge Gesell with orders that they be remanded to the Air Force and the Navy, and noted that Matlovich and Berg would be free to come back to federal court to seek "judicial relief from any adverse determination made on this remand." On September 10, 1980, Judge Gesell concluded Matlovich's case by ruling that his discharge had been "unlawful *ab initio*." and ordered reinstatement with full back pay. The military brass decided to buy their way out of their immediate problem by offering Matlovich a large monetary settlement which, after some deliberation, he accepted. Similarly, in Berg's case the Navy offered a settlement to end the litigation, which Berg accepted. Thus, neither case generated an appellate decision on whether the regulations were constitutional.

But the *Matlovich* and *Berg* cases did provide an occasion for the U.S. Department of Defense to reconsider its policies on homosexuals. The resulting reconsideration, however, went in the opposite direction from that recommended by Judge Gesell. Instead of updating its policies to reflect the recent conclusions of sex researchers and mental health experts and exercising greater discretion so as to retain homosexuals with good service records whose conduct did not appear likely to disrupt the service, the Defense Department eliminated the suggestion from existing regulations and policies that exceptions would be made to the general rule requiring discharge of homosexuals. By the time this review of the rules was completed, the conservative Reagan Administration had taken office, and the new civilian leaders of the Department willingly promulgated the new rules mandating the discharge of all homosexuals without exception, a policy that became increasingly controversial through the 1980s as service members with excellent records continued to file challenges to the constitutionality of the policy and the Department's own consultants submitted reports indicating that there was no rational basis for it.

Case References

Champagne v. Schlesinger, 506 F.2d 979 (7th Cir. 1974)

Doe v. Commonwealth's Attorney of City of Richmond, 425 U.S. 901 (1976), summarily affirming 403 F. Supp. 1199 (E.D. Va. 1975)

Eisenstadt v. Baird, 405 U.S. 438 (1972)

Griswold v. Connecticut, 381 U.S. 479 (1965)

Roe v. Wade, 410 U.S. 113 (1973)

91. FINDING A RATIONAL BASIS FOR NAVAL DISCRIMINATION

Beller v. Middendorf, 632 F.2d 788 (9th Cir. 1980), certiorari denied, 452 U.S. 905, rehearing denied, 454 U.S. 1069 (1981), reversing *Saal v. Middendorf*, 427 F. Supp. 192 (N.D. Cal. 1977), affirming *Beller v. Middendorf* and *Miller v. Rumsfeld* (N.D. Cal.) (unpublished rulings); certiorari denied, sub nom. *Beller v. Lehman*, 425 U.S. 905 (1981).

The U.S. Court of Appeals for the Ninth Circuit in San Francisco ruled in October 1980, more than two years after hearing oral arguments, that in three cases involving the discharge of enlisted personnel who had admitted engaging in homosexual activity, the U.S. Navy had acted rationally by refusing to consider their individual fitness to serve the defense needs of the United States. According to the court, the possibility that retention of a homosexual service member might lead to particular problems provided a rational basis for a policy mandating the discharge of all homosexual service members, regardless of the quality of their individual service records. In so ruling, the court rejected a strongly argued contrary opinion by District Judge William W. Schwarzer in one of the underlying cases. The Ninth Circuit's opinion in *Beller v. Middendorf* disposed of three separate cases that had worked their way through the federal court system over a period of about five years.

The first involved Dennis Beller, who had enlisted in the Navy in 1960 and, most recently, reenlisted for a six-year term in 1972. His good record resulted in frequent advancement, to the point where he was subjected to a background investigation in 1975 in order to obtain a top-secret clearance for high-level work. The investigation showed that he had frequented some gay bars during shore leave and had served for two years as president of a predominantly gay motorcycle club in Monterey, California. Naval Investigative Service members interrogated Beller, during which he revealed that he first engaged in sexual activity with males after enlisting in the Navy and had continued to engage in sexual activities during his enlistment, but Beller refused to reveal the names of his sexual contacts. Beller was called before an administrative discharge board, which recommended an honorable discharge by reason of unfitness. The chief of naval personnel accepted the recommendation and ordered Beller discharged on December 18, 1975.

Retaining Los Angeles attorney Richard P. Fox, Beller filed suit against the Navy, seeking an injunction against his discharge, expungement of any mention of homosexuality from his service records, a declaratory judgment on his service contract rights, and damages for an alleged violation of the federal Privacy Act when the investigators communicated information about his sexual activities to his commanding officers. Senior District Judge George B. Harris stayed the discharge pending disposition, but subsequently ruled in favor of the Navy. Beller was honorably discharged, but classified as ineligible for enlistment. During the entire proceeding, no argument was made that anything other than his private homosexual activities were the basis for his discharge.

The second case involved Yeoman Second Class James Miller, who had enlisted in 1965 and reenlisted twice, most recently in 1972 for a six-year term. A Naval Investigative Service inquiry of an unrelated incident in 1975 brought to light that Miller had gay sex with two Taiwanese natives while stationed in Taiwan. Prior to the investigation, Miller had received reassignment orders to the USS *Oriskany*, based in Alameda, California, where he successfully served for over a year prior to the convening of a hearing board to consider his discharge. In fact, his commanding officer, who had been informed that Miller confessed to the investigators about his homosexual activities, gave him a secret clearance needed for some of his assignments. The hearing board, which met on April 12, 1976, heard from several witnesses who testified as to Miller's good character and exemplary naval service, and was persuaded to recommend his retention by a vote of two to one, even though he had engaged in homosexual activity on two occasions. Miller insisted that he was not "a homosexual," but had merely "slipped" on those two occasions. The dissenting board member recommended an administrative discharge under honorable conditions. After the board vote, the senior medical officer at the naval base examined Miller and concluded that he was not a homosexual and showed no evidence of psychosis or neurosis. Miller's commanding officer forwarded the hearing board's recommendation, together with his personal recommendation for retention of Miller, to the chief of naval personnel. The assistant director of the Enlisted Performance Division rejected these recommendations, however, urging that because Miller had admittedly engaged in homosexual acts (conduct prohibited by the Uniform Code of Military Justice), he should be given a general discharge under honorable conditions by reason of misconduct. The assistant secretary of the Navy approved this recommendation and scheduled Miller to be discharged on June 23, 1976.

Miller had retained John Vaisey, of San Francisco, as his legal counsel, and filed suit that same day asking the federal district court in San Francisco either to stay his discharge or order that it be upgraded to an honorable discharge. In response, the chief of naval personnel upgraded the discharge to honorable, but the discharge was stayed briefly by Judge Harris until he dismissed the case, based on his prior ruling in Beller's case. Miller immediately applied to the Ninth Circuit to extend the stay pending appeal, which the court did. While the case was pending, Miller was assigned to work for the commanding officer of enlisted personnel at Treasure Island in San Francisco Bay. His commanding officer requested that the Navy retain him, but the Navy denied all Miller's efforts to reenlist.

Finally, there was the case of Mary Roseann Saal, who enlisted in 1971 and trained to be an air traffic controller. She was assigned to the Alameda Naval Air Station, where she received extraordinarily positive performance ratings and renewed her enlistment in January 1972 for a three-year term. The Naval Investigative Service launched an investigation of alleged homosexual activity, during which Saal admitted being engaged in a lesbian relationship with another service member in March 1973. She indicated that she intended to continue the relationship. An administrative discharge board was scheduled for July 6, 1973.

Prior to the board hearing, Saal obtained the services of Equal Rights Advocates, Inc., of San Francisco (which later became the National Center for Lesbian Rights), with Mary C. Dunlap as lead counsel, and filed suit in the federal district court seeking injunctive relief. The board met as scheduled on July 6 and recommended a general discharge for Saal. The board was instructed that her individual fitness was irrelevant; if it was found that she had engaged and was continuing to engage in homosexual activities, discharge was mandated. In August 1973, District Judge Oliver J. Carter granted a preliminary injunction, requiring the Navy to retain Saal while the case proceeded. In November, the chief of naval personnel notified Saal that he had accepted the recommendation of the board to discharge her. In January 1974, the Navy moved to dismiss Saal's lawsuit, but Judge Carter denied the motion as premature. Pursuant to his earlier order, Saal was continuing to serve and received an exuberantly supportive performance rating from her commanding officer, concluding that "she is recommended for reenlistment and for advancement."

Realizing that her enlistment term would soon run out, Saal requested an extension so that she could continue to work as a naval air traffic controller while her lawsuit was pending. Her commander, not wanting to affect the lawsuit, forwarded her request to the chief of naval personnel without recommendation, requesting advice on how to proceed. The chief replied on December 12 that Saal should be separated with an honorable discharge when her enlistment expired in January, and ordered the prior directive for a general discharge by reason of unfitness to be canceled because of "the average performance evaluation marks which have been earned during her period of service." (The district court reproduced Saal's performance evaluations as an appendix to its opinion. If these were "average," then the standard of performance by naval enlisted personnel is truly extraordinary, since there is no negative comment whatsoever among the string of superlative evaluations.)

After Saal's enlistment term ran out, she continued to work pursuant to the preliminary injunction issued by Judge Carter. The Navy moved to dismiss the action as moot. Carter granted the motion on August 19 and lifted his stay, allowing the Navy to discharge Saal, which it did on August 22. Within a few weeks, Saal filed an amended complaint, contending that she had been deprived of due process of law by reason of having been denied reenlistment and labeled as ineligible for reenlistment.

On May 5, 1976, Saal moved for summary judgment, claiming that the Navy's policy was facially unconstitutional because it presumed irrebuttably that every person involved in homosexual conduct was unfit to serve, and that the policy was unconstitutional as applied to her denial of reenlistment despite her demonstrated fitness to serve, as evidenced by her performance ratings. Right up to her discharge in August, she continued to receive superior ratings on her work. Her final rating, covering the period from March through July, concluded: "Highly recommended for advancement and reenlistment." Clearly, actual performance fitness had nothing to do with the discharge or denial of reenlistment. The Navy had lost the services of a highly trained and skilled air traffic controller (a difficult, stress-filled occupation calling for highly specialized skills) by discharging Saal. The Navy filed a cross-motion for summary judgment on June 24, claiming that the action was moot, that the court lacked jurisdiction, that Saal had failed to exhaust administrative remedies, that Saal had no continued right to employment, and that the discharge of homosexuals as "military liabilities" was a rational policy.

Saal's case was reassigned in August to District Judge Schwarzer, who promptly heard arguments and issued his decision on the cross-motions on February 8, 1977. He ruled against the Navy on all its procedural arguments and held the Navy's policy was arbitrary and capricious in presuming that all homosexuals were unfit to serve regardless of their individual records. Finding that Saal had a liberty interest that had been unjustifiably violated by the Navy's actions in her case, he granted Saal's motion for declaratory and injunctive relief, ordering the Navy to consider any application for reenlistment in light of all relevant factors, including her demonstrated fitness. Ruling that further factual findings were necessary before he could order damages, he reserved ruling on that question pending further proceedings. The Navy promptly appealed the decision, which was consolidated with the pending *Beller* and *Miller* appeals for argument before a Ninth Circuit panel on November 8, 1978.

Schwarzer's opinion is worth some examination, because it is an extraordinary exception to the general run of judicial opinions about the military's homosexual exclusion policies. For one thing, Schwarzer cut through the Defense Department's customary dissembling about the exact nature of its policies. As it had successfully argued in *Champagne v. Schlesinger* (1974) in persuading the Seventh Circuit to dismiss a suit by a discharged gay sailor, the Navy argued in Saal's case that the court lacked jurisdiction until such time as the discharged enlisted person had exhausted administrative remedies by seeking review before the Board for Correction of Naval Records, which was authorized to recommend to the secretary of the Navy correction of military records if it found "the existence of any error or an injustice." The secretary had full discretion to act on such recommendations. Taking the position that its formal policy did not mandate discharge for homosexuality because the secretary retained discretion under these appeal procedures, the Navy argued that Saal had to apply to the Board and to pursue her case to the secretary before filing suit.

Schwarzer dismissed this argument. It was clear that there was no basis for Saal to pursue such an appeal. She had received an honorable discharge, so there was nothing to "correct" in her record. There was no indication that the Board had any jurisdiction to recommend changes in the classification of "ineligible for reenlistment" that had been imposed on Saal. Most significantly, the various policy statements submitted by the Navy indicated quite clearly that the merits of Saal's service record had been considered "irrelevant" at every stage of the proceedings.

Schwarzer analyzed Saal's claim as presenting an issue of deprivation of liberty without due process of law under the Fifth Amendment of the U.S. Constitution. He relied on *Board of Regents v. Roth* (1972), in which the U.S. Supreme Court had ruled that such a claim would arise if the state, in declining to rehire a person, made a charge "that might seriously damage his standing and associations in his community" or "imposed . . . a stigma or other disability that foreclosed his freedom to take advantage of other employment opportunities." "The stigmatizing effects of defendant's actions are indisputable," said Schwarzer, concluding that the cumulative actions of the Navy in Saal's case

> plainly fell within the concept of stigma under *Roth*. . . . The Navy's own position as reflected in its instructions and regulations and its actions in this case, and the continuing existence of criminal statutes proscribing certain homosexual activities, compel the conclusion that, rightly or wrongly, a disclosure of homosexual activity will tend to stigmatize a person, particularly when coupled with an involuntary separation from military service.

Conceding that the Navy had a right to exercise discretion in decisions about enlistment, reenlistment, and discharge of personnel, Schwarzer insisted that such decisions had to take into account the constitutional rights of military personnel. Schwarzer acknowledged numerous decisions of the Supreme Court and lower courts holding that those constitutional rights had to be applied "in light of the 'unique military exigencies' that necessarily govern many aspects of military service," as Justice Lewis F. Powell had commented in his concurring opinion in *Middendorf v. Henry* (1976). This meant Saal had the burden to show that there was "no rational connection" between the Navy's regulations and the "unique military exigencies" in order to prevail. Schwarzer held that Saal had met this burden.

The Navy regulation required mandatory processing for discharge in only three circumstances: homosexual activity; sale or trafficking in drugs; fraudulent concealment of preservice homosexuality or drug trafficking. All other forms of "misconduct" were subject to warnings, lesser types of discipline, and rehabilitative efforts before a discharge proceeding must be initiated. While it was true that the regulation merely mandated "processing" for discharge, Schwarzer rejected the Navy's argument that this allowed discretion to retain homosexuals, since the Navy had stated a policy in its Instruction 1900.9Aa to commanding officers as follows: "Members involved in homosexuality are military liabilities who cannot be tolerated in a military organization. . . . Their prompt separation is essential." Little room for discretion there!

What were the Navy's justifications, based on "exigencies," for mandating discharge? Schwarzer received in evidence an affidavit of the assistant chief of naval personnel for performance and security, which recited a list of problems that "would certainly" arise if homosexuals were retained: "tensions and hostilities would certainly exist between homosexuals and the great majority of naval personnel," "an individual's performance of duties could be unduly influenced by emotional relationships with other homosexuals," chain of command problems might arise from romantic involvements between gay officers and enlisted personnel, if parents became concerned about exposing their children to homosexuals recruitment would be adversely affected, homosexuals might be sexually aggressive in a disruptive way, closeted homosexuals might be less productive or effective due to fears of prosecution and stigmatization. Noting that the Navy was no longer claiming that gays were special security risks, Schwarzer commented that "the problems which the Navy enumerates to support blanket exclusion of persons who engage in homosexual acts are problems which are endemic to a heterogeneous society such as the Navy and with which it deals in the ordinary course of its operations on a case by case basis." The flaw with the Navy's rationale was that any member, regardless of sexual orientation, might cause any of the problems on the list, and there was no warrant for presuming that any given homosexual member would cause any of these problems. Only homosexuals were classified as "intolerable" and singled out for "prompt separation," regardless of their service records.

Accepting that "persons who engage in homosexual acts may be a source of the listed problems," Schwarzer rejected the argument that it was thus rational to single out homosexuals for mandatory exclusion, "regardless of the fitness of the particular individual." Saal had continued to receive superior ratings without any adverse criticism, even during the long pendency of her service under the injunction issued by Judge Carter. Even when her homosexuality was known to her commanders and fellow service members, none of the problems listed by the Navy had occurred and she had even been recommended for promotion and reenlistment by her commander. Clearly, Schwarzer stated,

> as applied to her, the mandatory exclusion policies and regulations are irrational and capricious. Due process requires that plaintiff's application for extension of service or reenlistment receive the same consideration as that of other Navy personnel similarly situated, without reference to policies or regulations substantially mandating exclusion or processing for discharge of persons who engage in homosexual activity.

Schwarzer stressed that he was not ruling in general that the Navy was mandated to enlist or to retain homosexuals. Rather, he was mandating that enlistment and retention decisions had to be based rationally on the qualifications of an individual. Noting that the military services had "been in the vanguard in providing equal opportunities to segments of our society that have long suffered discrimination," and indeed had accomplished this without any evidence of impairment of "efficiency or effectiveness," he held that the Navy's failure to accord Saal the same kind of treatment was "irrational and capricious and thus in violation of the Fifth Amendment."

The Ninth Circuit panel heard oral argument on the combined appeals involving Beller, Miller, and Saal on November 8, 1978, but took almost two years to reach its decision, announced October 23, 1980 in an opinion by Circuit Judge (later U.S. Supreme Court Justice) Anthony M. Kennedy. The panel unanimously affirmed the decisions regarding Beller and Miller, and reversed Schwarzer's decision in Saal's case. While expressing some reservations about the Navy's policies and refraining from substantive comment on whether homosexual activities by military personnel were protected from adverse action by the constitutional right of privacy, the court held that it was rational for the Navy to apply a general presumption that homosexual members would pose one or more of the problems listed in the assistant chief of naval personnel's affidavit rather than have to make a case-by-case determination regarding each homosexual service member.

Kennedy agreed with Schwarzer and Harris, the district judges in the three cases, that the matters were not moot, that attempts to exhaust administrative remedies in these cases would be futile gestures, given the Navy's policy statements, and that the federal courts had jurisdiction to hear their cases. He also agreed that, regardless of the Seventh Circuit's ruling in *Champagne v. Schlesinger*, it was clear that the Navy's policy mandated discharge of homosexuals in every case regardless of their individual fitness apart from their sexual conduct.

Noting that each of these cases involved admitted homosexual conduct, Kennedy said that neither a property nor a liberty interest protected by the Due Process Clause was implicated in these cases. The regulations and policies mandating discharge themselves defeated any contention that a homosexual member would have a reasonable expectation of continued employment in the military, he held, thus vitiating any property interest claim. As to the issue of a liberty interest, in the end each of the litigants before the court had received an honorable discharge, so Kennedy failed to see how the test of *Board of Regents v. Roth* had been met. "If the Navy's charges of homosexuality were false, made public, and followed by discharge, we can assume a deprivation of liberty would occur," he said, but in these cases the plaintiffs admitted or were found to have engaged in homosexual activity and were afforded hearings in which to argue that they should be retained. The only publicity about their homosexuality to occur outside the military was due to their filing suit. Furthermore, their classification as ineligible for reenlistment could not be considered a "stigma" of the type referred to in *Roth*. Their discharge papers did not reflect this classification, and "the real stigma imposed by the Navy's action, moreover, is the charge of homosexuality, not the fact of discharge or some implied statement that the individual is not sufficiently needed to be retained," this being "especially true since the regulations do not make fitness of the particular individual a factor in the decision to discharge." In other words, since a discharge for homosexuality said nothing about a person's individual fitness, that person was not being labeled "unfit" by the government, and his or her liberty interest had not been impaired through any procedural failing of the government.

The substantive due process issue was somewhat different. Here, Kennedy had to deal with the question whether it was rational for the government to have adopted its policy. "When conduct, either by virtue of its inadequate foundation in the continuing traditions of our society or for some other reason, such as lack of connection with interests recognized as private and protected, is subject to some government regulation, then analysis under the substantive due process clause proceeds in much the same way as analysis under the lowest tier of equal protection scrutiny," said Kennedy, invoking the minimal rationality standard under which the Supreme Court almost always defers to legislative or executive judgments. At the other extreme, of course, would be situations where the government "seriously intrudes into matters which lie at the core of interests which deserve due process protection," in which case a compelling state interest test is applied, putting a high burden on the government and frequently leading to invalidation of the government's actions or policies. Kennedy asserted that the issue of the Navy regulations

"lies somewhere between these two standards." Noting that there was "substantial argument" on both sides of the question whether private, consensual homosexual conduct was protected by the Constitution, including the Supreme Court's summary affirmance in *Doe v. Commonwealth's Attorney for City of Richmond* (1976), upholding the validity of Virginia's sodomy law, Kennedy stated that "we can concede *arguendo*" that the reasons underlying some of the Supreme Court's privacy cases "suggest that some kinds of government regulation of private consensual homosexual behavior may face substantial constitutional challenge." But in this case the Navy was not seeking to impose criminal penalties; rather, it was seeking to exclude homosexuals from service due to its judgment that their retention would create certain kinds of problems that would detract from the military mission. "We conclude," he wrote, "in these cases, that the importance of the governmental interests furthered, and to some extent the relative impracticality at this time of achieving the Government's goals by regulations which turn more precisely on the facts of an individual case, outweigh whatever heightened solicitude is appropriate for consensual private homosexual conduct."

In other words, the court recognized that something more stringent than the test of mere rationality might be applicable to a situation where government was interfering with private, consensual homosexual conduct between adults. However, the court found that the test of heightened scrutiny was adequately met by the Navy's contention that its need to prevent the sorts of disruptions that might occur from the retention of some homosexuals justified excluding all homosexuals because it was impractical to determine in each case whether the particular homosexual would cause the enumerated problems.

Kennedy emphasized that "[t]he nature of the employer—the Navy—is crucial to our decision." Reiterating the long-established doctrine that constitutional rights had to be weighed in light of the special nature of the military mission, he commented:

> Regulations which might infringe constitutional rights in other contexts may survive scrutiny because of military necessities.

...Despite the evidence that attitudes towards homosexual conduct have changed among some groups in society, the Navy could conclude that a substantial number of naval personnel have feelings regarding homosexuality, based upon moral precepts recognized by many in our society as legitimate, which would create tensions and hostilities, and that these feelings might undermine the ability of a homosexual to command the respect necessary to perform supervisory duties.

Even the witnesses who testified on behalf of Miller, Beller, and Saal had conceded under questioning that it was possible that "a member's homosexual conduct might in other circumstances cause difficulties, especially aboard a ship."

While the Navy's "blanket rule requiring discharge ... is perhaps broader than necessary to accomplish some of its goals," said Kennedy, it was sustainable in view of the importance of the Navy's role and special needs for order and discipline. This did not mean that the court thought the policy was "wise," but rather that in the particular sphere of the military it was not deemed totally irrational. (Kennedy's opinion was thus somewhat unusual among the post-*Matlovich* military cases in its formalistic, unenthusiastic upholding of the antigay policies.) The appeals by Beller and Miller were denied, and the Navy's appeal of Saal's case was granted. The court subsequently denied a petition for rehearing filed by Beller, and the Supreme Court announced its refusal to review the case on June 1, 1981.

Reaction to the Ninth Circuit's opinion was mixed. The court had upheld the Navy's continued reliance on a theory that would have been rejected out of hand had it been advanced to justify discrimination on the basis of race or sex: that discrimination against homosexuals was justified not primarily because of any failings by homosexuals, but rather because of adverse effects due to the bias of others (other sailors,

parents of potential sailors, civilian law enforcement authorities, etc.). On the other hand, the court had done what no other federal appellate court had previously done: it suggested that government policies that discriminate against homosexuals might be subject to a test of heightened scrutiny, that government intrusion into the private, consensual activities of homosexuals presented serious constitutional questions, and that the court was upholding the Navy's policy quite narrowly on the basis of special needs of the military. Kennedy had stated that a policy of discriminating against homosexuals, while justified by military necessity, might be unconstitutional in nonmilitary spheres. He had also pointedly stated that the court was not passing on the wisdom of the policy.

This tempered approach led gay rights groups to refrain from actively opposing Kennedy's appointment to the Supreme Court by Ronald Reagan, since it seemed to reflect an openness to the argument that societal prejudice against homosexuals may be unconstitutional in some circumstances. (This optimism was yet to be tested at the time of this writing.)

On the other hand, all was not silver lining, since the *Beller* opinion was frequently cited in subsequent cases challenging the antigay policies of the Defense Department as a definitive ruling that the policies were not irrational. The Defense Department continued to cite the *Beller* decision as late as 1991, at a time when internal recommendations to abandon the policy were in fact asserting that it was not rational and was rapidly becoming indefensible.

Case References

Board of Regents v. Roth, 408 U.S. 564 (1972)

Champagne v. Schlesinger, 506 F.2d 979 (7th Cir. 1974)

Doe v. Commonwealth's Attorney for City of Richmond, 425 U.S. 901, rehearing denied, 425 U.S. 985 (1976), affirming 403 F. Supp. 1199 (E.D. Va. 1975)

Middendorf v. Henry, 425 U.S. 25 (1976)

92. REVISITING GAY SEX IN THE NAVY

Dronenburg v. Zech, 741 F.2d 1388, rehearing en banc denied, 746 F.2d 1579 (D.C. Cir. 1984).

Naval Petty Officer James L. Dronenburg's lawsuit challenging the U.S. Navy's discharge of him for engaging in sexual activity with an enlisted man in a Navy barracks seemed to have little great significance in itself. Ultimately, however, it loomed large in the developing law of privacy and sexuality because it provided a vehicle for Circuit Judge Robert Bork, a former Yale Law School professor and outspoken opponent of "unenumerated rights" jurisprudence, to place in the official reports of the federal courts his view that the Supreme Court's privacy cases contained no common thread applicable to homosexual conduct. Bork's methodology sparked a heated debated within the U.S. Court of Appeals for the District of Columbia Circuit, reflected in the dissenting and concurring opinions responding to Dronenburg's petition for rehearing *en banc*. The debate carried on further when Justice Lewis F. Powell announced his retirement from the Supreme Court in 1987 and President Ronald Reagan designated Judge Bork to be his successor.

Jim Dronenburg enlisted in the Navy right after graduating high school. He had a talent for languages, becoming fluent in Korean and serving for nine years as a Navy linguist and cryptographer with a top-security clearance and "an unblemished service record." He "earned many citations praising his job performance." Dronenburg was assigned to the Defense Language Institute, in Monterey, California, to advance his skills in service to the defense of his country. While assigned in Monterey, Dronenburg became sexually involved with a 19–year-old seaman recruit at the base, and they had sex together in the barracks. The young seaman told naval investigators about this, and the Navy instituted an investigation of Dronenburg in August 1980. At first Dronenburg denied he had engaged in gay sex, but after repeated questioning he finally admitted that he was a homosexual and had engaged in gay sex repeatedly in the barracks. On September 18, 1980, Dronenburg received formal notice that the Navy was considering discharging him for this activity.

A Navy administrative board convened January 20 and 22, 1981, to consider whether Dronenburg should be recommended for discharge. Dronenburg testified on his own behalf, admitting he had engaged in homosexual conduct but insisting that it was not relevant to his qualifications and would not affect his performance as a linguist and cryptographer. The board disagreed, voting unanimously that he should be discharged. The board was split, however, on the characterization for the discharge, two voting to recommend a general discharge and one voting to recommend an honorable one, in light of Dronenburg's long, previously unblemished record. Dronenburg's commander accepted the board's recommendation, but on appeal to the secretary of the Navy Dronenburg secured an honorable discharge. As soon as he had been discharged, Dronenburg filed suit in the U.S. District Court for the District of Columbia against the chief of naval personnel, Vice Admiral Lando Zech, asserting that the Navy's regulation providing that members of the Navy who engage in homosexual conduct "shall normally be separated from the naval service" was an unconstitutional violation of his right of privacy. Dronenburg sought declaratory and injunctive relief, restoring him to his position with back pay and benefits. (He later dropped the monetary claims, restricting his requested relief to reinstatement.)

The case was assigned to District Judge Oliver Gasch, who promptly granted a motion to dismiss filed by the U.S. Justice Department. Dronenburg appealed to the D.C. Circuit Court of Appeals, which heard argument on September 29, 1983. Dronenburg was represented on appeal by San Francisco attorney Stephen V. Bomse on behalf of Gay Rights Advocates, a public interest law firm. The government was represented by William G. Cole from the Justice Department. Attorneys for the Washington office of the American Civil Liberties Union filed a brief supporting Dronenburg's case.

The court of appeals announced its opinion denying Dronenburg's appeal on August 17, 1984. Judge Bork's opinion for the court found that the right of privacy mentioned in the U.S. Supreme Court's prior opinions did not apply to homosexual conduct, and that the appeals court had no "warrant" to recognize a new right of privacy applicable to homosexual conduct.

Bork began his opinion by disposing of various procedural objections that the government had raised. Noting that the D.C. Circuit had asserted subject matter jurisdiction over a prior similar lawsuit by Air Force Sergeant Leonard Matlovich in 1978, Bork held that the law of the circuit seemed to provide for jurisdiction. As Dronenburg had dropped his claim for damages, Bork held that sovereign immunity principles were not applicable, since the D.C. Circuit had previously held that the federal government had effectively waived its sovereign immunity defense to lawsuits seeking injunctive relief by the enactment of 5 U.S.C. section 702, the legislative history of which indicated Congress's intent to waive sovereign immunity where damages were not claimed.

Bork then proceeded to consider Dronenburg's constitutional claims. Dronenburg asserted that the Navy's policy of discharging those who engaged in homosexual conduct violated the rights of privacy and of equal protection, the former based on the case law stemming from *Griswold v. Connecticut* (1965), the latter because the Navy allegedly did not prohibit nonmarital heterosexual contact between service members or discharge enlisted personnel for engaging in such conduct. (Dronenburg's discharge had preceded the adoption of new regulations early in the Reagan Administration that mandated discharge of all homosexuals, regardless whether they engaged in sexual activity in the service.) Even if the court did not find that due process or equal protection principles required strict or heightened scrutiny of the Navy's policy, Dronenburg argued that the Navy's policy did not meet the test of rationality required of all government actions under the Due Process Clause of the Fifth Amendment.

The argument that the Supreme Court's privacy cases had a common thread that extended to homosexual conduct did not impress Bork. First, he noted that the Supreme Court had in fact apparently decided the precise ques-

tion of homosexual conduct by summarily affirming a federal district court's decision upholding the constitutionality of Virginia's sodomy law in *Doe v. Commonwealth's Attorney for City of Richmond* in 1976. While some had argued that the summary affirmance should not be considered binding on the constitutional question, Bork disagreed, explaining that the district court had not dismissed the test case on procedural grounds. In any event, insisted Bork, a lower federal court was not in the position to speculate about what the Supreme Court meant, since the Supreme Court had itself said in *Hicks v. Miranda* (1975) that a summary disposition was a decision on the merits binding on lower courts.

However, even if *Doe v. Commonwealth's Attorney* could be narrowly construed as a decision on the standing of the test-case plaintiffs to challenge the sodomy law, Bork asserted that the Supreme Court's privacy precedents would not support an extension of the right of privacy to homosexual conduct. Beginning his review of those cases with *Griswold*, Bork found that the Court's opinion "stressed the sanctity of marriage" in striking down a state ban on marital couples' use of contraceptives to prevent pregnancy. "It did not indicate what other activities might be protected by the new right of privacy," said Bork, "and did not provide any guidance for reasoning about future claims laid under that right."

Proceeding through the other major privacy opinions, Bork found each one to be narrowly focused on particular conduct rather than serving as expressive of some more theoretical right. *Loving v. Virginia* (1967), in which the Court struck down a Virginia statute penalizing interracial marriage, was, for Bork, an opinion about race discrimination. After quoting the final operative paragraph of the opinion, identifying marital choice as a constitutional right, Bork commented, "[t]here is in this passage no mode of analysis that suggests an answer to the present case, certainly none that favors" Dronenburg. Bork found *Eisenstadt v. Baird* (1972) similarly uninstructive. In *Eisenstadt*, the Court had struck down a Massachusetts law that in effect criminalized the sale of contraceptives to unmarried persons. "If the right of privacy means anything," wrote Justice William J.

Brennan, Jr., for the Court, "it is the right of the *individual*, married or single, to be free from unwarranted governmental intrusion into matters so fundamentally affecting a person as the decision whether to bear or beget a child." Bork found this unenlightening when applied to Dronenburg's challenge to the Navy regulations. How was the court of appeals to know whether the Navy's regulation was "unwarranted," or whether homosexual conduct was a matter "so fundamentally affecting a person as the decision whether to bear or beget a child." "*Eisenstadt* itself does not provide any criteria by which either of those decisions can be made," commented Bork.

Bork came to *Roe v. Wade* (1973), the Supreme Court's landmark decision on abortion. Quoting a lengthy paragraph from Justice Harry A. Blackmun's decision, which Bork characterized as "the pivotal legal discussion," Bork emphasized Blackmun's statement that the right to privacy was not "absolute." Indeed, Blackmun said "it is not clear to us that the claim asserted by some *amici* that one has an unlimited right to do with one's body as one pleases bears a close relationship to the right of privacy previously articulated in this Court's decisions. The Court has refused to recognize an unlimited right of this kind in the past." Blackmun then cited *Jacobson v. Massachusetts*, a 1905 case holding that a state could require vaccinations under its police powers to protect public health, and *Buck v. Bell*, a 1927 case upholding compelled sterilization of a woman determined to be mentally defective under procedures the Court believed satisfied the procedural requirements of the Due Process Clause. Once again, Bork insisted, the Court had alluded to a limited right of privacy, listed illustrative cases of situations covered or not covered by it, but failed to provide an "explanatory principle that informs a lower court how to reason about what is and what is not encompassed by the right of privacy." Bork similarly found no enlightenment in *Carey v. Population Services International* (1977), in which the Supreme Court held that adolescents were entitled to have access to birth control under the right of privacy.

These cases posed a peculiar jurisprudential problem, said Bork. Since the Court had not rooted its privacy decisions in the text of the Constitution itself, it was difficult for a lower court to perceive a reasoned basis for deciding whether to extend the "right of privacy" to new factual situations. Said Bork, "In this group of cases . . . we do not find any principle articulated even approaching in breadth that which appellant seeks to have us adopt," which Bork summarized as a right to do with one's body what one likes without government interference. Not only had the Supreme Court disclaimed such a fundamental right in *Roe v. Wade*, but it seemed to Bork inconsistent with the Court's description of fundamental rights as "implicit in the concept of ordered liberty." "We would find it impossible to conclude that a right to homosexual conduct is 'fundamental' or 'implicit in the concept of ordered liberty,'" said Bork, "unless any and all private sexual behavior falls within those categories, a conclusion we are unwilling to draw." Without any discussion, Bork implicitly presumed that there was no constitutionally significant distinction to be drawn between consensual homosexual conduct in private between adults and other types of sexual activity forbidden by state laws, such as heterosexual fornication, prostitution, adultery, incest, forcible sex, or sex with minors. Only if all those kinds of sexual activity were held protected by a constitutional right of privacy could Bork see protecting consensual homosexual activity. Bork sealed his discussion by quoting Justice Byron R. White's assertion in dissent in *Moore v. City of East Cleveland* (1977) that the Court strains its legitimacy when it creates new rights not founded in constitutional text. Whatever the meaning of this comment for the Supreme Court, said Bork, it certainly suggested that lower federal courts should refrain from recognizing new constitutional rights. In a footnote, Bork revealed that he had previously published his view that the Supreme Court did not have the power to recognize rights not based on constitutional text, but insisted that this was beside the point in his role as a judge of the court of appeals.

Bork also gave short shrift to Dronenburg's alternative argument that, to the extent the naval regulation was based solely on some view of morality, it lacked a reasonable justification, and that the Constitution mandated that the courts protect minorities from repressive majoritarian enactments founded on majoritarian moral views. Bork rejected this contention as contrary to the whole concept of representative democracy. According to Bork, majoritarian decisions in a constitutional democracy are presumptively valid unless the Constitution has specifically taken away the government's authority to make such decisions. Arguing that Dronenburg's theory would undermine the wide range of social legislation that imposed majoritarian moral views on dissenting minorities, such as civil rights and environmental protection laws, Bork asserted that Dronenburg's argument on this would not "withstand examination."

Since Bork could find no constitutionally protected right implicated in Dronenburg's case, he proceeded to evaluate the Navy's policy under the rationality test required by the Due Process Clause. He concluded that the regulation "bears a rational relationship to a permissible end," accepting the proposition that banning homosexual conduct in the Navy was "a rational means of advancing a legitimate, indeed a crucial, interest common to all our armed forces." The Navy need not provide studies or statistics to prove the harmful effects to morale or discipline if such conduct were tolerated, asserted Bork. Indeed, Dronenburg's own case, in which a 27–year-old petty officer had sexual relations with a 19–year-old seaman, illustrated the kind of problems the regulation was intended to prevent; sexual relations across military ranks would make "personal dealings uncomfortable." The special needs of the military made it rational, said Bork, for the Navy to conclude that such a ban was necessary to carry out its mission.

Apart from a passing remark early in the opinion that resolution of Dronenburg's equal protection claim was "to some extent dependent" on resolution of his due process privacy claim, Bork made no further mention of equal protection in his opinion.

Dronenburg petitioned for rehearing by the full D.C. Circuit. The petition was denied on November 14, 1984, but not without considerable public debate by the circuit's judges.

In a dissenting opinion joined by three other members of the court, Judge Spottswood W. Robinson, III, chided the three-judge panel and the majority of the circuit for allowing to stand in the federal reports "a revisionist view of constitutional jurisprudence." He argued that the wide-ranging discussion of constitutional privacy was "wholly unnecessary to decide the case before the court," that opinions of the courts of appeals were not a proper vehicle to "throw down gauntlets to the Supreme Court," and that it was not the function of a court of appeals to "conduct a general spring cleaning of constitutional law." "Judicial restraint begins at home," protested Judge Robinson. Getting closer to the merits, Robinson stated disagreement with Bork's method of interpreting *Doe v. Commonwealth's Attorney*, and even stronger disagreement with Bork's summary acceptance of the Navy's justification for its regulation without considering the equal protection considerations such a justification would raise, in light of the Navy's apparent lack of concern about the possibly similar disruptive effects on discipline or morale of heterosexual sexual relationships in the military. The dissenters refrained from stating a view as to whether the right of privacy extended to homosexual conduct, merely asserting that the panel's decision was unsatisfactory in failing to apply faithfully the Supreme Court's privacy jurisprudence to the case before it.

This attack by the dissenters brought additional opinions in support of denying rehearing from Judges Ruth Bader Ginsburg and Kenneth Starr, and a further opinion in justification of his prior opinion by Judge Bork. Judge Ginsburg argued that *Doe v. Commonwealth's Attorney* provided sufficient basis for the panel's decision. Acknowledging that the panel's opinion "airs a good deal more than disposition of the appeal required," she dismissed the fears of Dronenburg and the *amici* who supported his petition that the panel's discussion of constitutional rights could be construed as speaking for the entire circuit. "I read the opinion's extended remarks on constitutional interpretation as a commentarial exposition of the opinion writer's viewpoint," she said, "a personal statement that does not carry or purport to carry the approbation of 'the court.'" Judge Starr briefly stated his agreement that the courts of appeals should not be chiding the Supreme Court, but asserted that this is not what the panel had done. He agreed with the panel that the existing privacy case law did not extend to homosexual conduct, which, he emphasized, had been prohibited by the federal or state governments in some form "for two centuries in a variety of ways" that had never been questioned until recent years. He also commented that Bork had reached this conclusion without having to rely on any dissenting opinions from the Supreme Court.

Finally, Bork wrote in his own defense, joined by Circuit Judge Antonin Scalia, who was shortly to take a seat on the Supreme Court. Bork absolutely rejected the criticisms of the dissenters. It was necessary for him to review all the Supreme Court's privacy decisions, he said, because Dronenburg had based his argument on them. As to the charge that he had improperly criticized the Supreme Court for creating doctrinal confusion in its privacy cases, he was in good company, insisted Bork, noting that other highly respected courts of appeals had criticized Supreme Court precedents in their opinions, citing examples of Henry J. Friendly, Learned Hand, and Jerome Frank, none of whom, he asserted, "could be characterized as lacking judicial restraint." It was not the role of the courts of appeals to unquestioningly or uncritically react to Supreme Court rulings like military inferiors to the commanding officer's orders. Unlike the military, said Bork, the judicial system is based on reasoned consideration and criticism of judicial opinions. While the court of appeals would be bound to follow a Supreme Court ruling on point, it was not bound to refrain from expressing its unhappiness or dissatisfaction with that precedent. In this case, indeed, the dissent may have been reading "criticisms" into the panel opinion when all that was there were observations about the lack of doctrinal guidance provided by those decisions.

Dronenburg was eager to appeal the decision further to the Supreme Court. However, at a meeting of attorneys from various lesbian and gay rights legal organizations, there was strong agreement that a military case was not the appropriate vehicle for a challenge to sodomy laws in the Supreme Court, and attorneys

from Gay Rights Advocates agreed to ask Dronenburg to forego further appeals on prudential grounds. After some initial reluctance, he finally agreed.

Bork's opinion proved highly influential among other court of appeals judges, particularly those appointed by President Reagan, to judge by its frequency of approving citation. Both before and after the Supreme Court's opinion in *Bowers v. Hardwick* (1986), in which Justice White's opinion for the Court essentially adopted Bork's privacy analysis, setting off the firestorm that eventually sank Bork's Supreme Court nomination, the lower federal courts have cited *Dronenburg v. Zech* as authority for the proposition not only that the right of privacy cannot be used to invalidate the military's exclusion of homosexuals, but also as dispositive of equal protection issues Bork never explicitly addressed. Those appeals courts that determined that sexual orientation was not a suspect classification would evaluate the military regulations under a minimum rationality test, and would quote Bork's assertion that "common sense and common experience" demonstrated the rationality of the Navy's policy. Thus, *Dronenburg v. Zech* stands as one of the most influential federal appellate opinions upholding the authority of the Defense Department to discharge personnel found to have engaged in homosexual activity.

Case References

Bowers v. Hardwick, 478 U.S. 186 (1986)

Carey v. Population Services International, 431 U.S. 678 (1977)

Doe v. Commonwealth's Attorney for City of Richmond, 403 F. Supp. 1199 (E.D. Va. 1975), affirmed, 425 U.S. 901 (1976)

Eisenstadt v. Baird, 405 U.S. 438 (1972)

Griswold v. Connecticut, 381 U.S. 479 (1965)

Hicks v. Miranda, 422 U.S. 332 (1975)

Jacobson v. Massachusetts, 197 U.S. 11 (1905)

Loving v. Virginia, 388 U.S. 1 (1967)

Matlovich v. Secretary of the Air Force, 591 F.2d 852 (D.C. Cir. 1978)

Moore v. City of East Cleveland, 431 U.S. 494 (1977)

Roe v. Wade, 410 U.S. 113, rehearing denied, 410 U.S. 959 (1973)

93. THE CASE OF THE "MODEL GAY SOLDIER"

Watkins v. United States Army, 875 F.2d 699 (9th Cir. 1989) (en banc), certiorari denied, 111 S. Ct. 384 (1990). Cases below: 541 F. Supp. 249 (W.D. Wash. 1982); 551 F. Supp. 212 (W.D. Wash. 1982), reversed and remanded, 721 F.2d 687 (9th Cir. 1983). Unpublished disposition on remand, reversed and remanded, 837 F.2d 1428 (9th Cir.), amended, 847 F.2d 1329 (9th Cir.), order for rehearing en banc, 847 F.2d 1362 (1988).

As in so many cases challenging the U.S. Department of Defense's policies barring homosexuals from military service, *Watkins v. United States Army* provided an incongruous example of the government litigating for eight years, at great expense, to rid itself of an exemplary soldier whose immediate supervising officers testified solidly in favor of keeping him in the service. Although the case ultimately resulted in no direct determination of the constitutional issues raised by the military policies, it not only vindicated Watkins's own service record but also established that the retention of an openly gay soldier in the ranks was not inimical to the national interest. Thus, although the U.S. Court of Appeals for the Ninth Circuit (and the Supreme Court by refusing to review the case) did not directly address the constitutional issues raised by Perry Watkins, they implicitly rejected the Defense Department's asserted reasons for seeking to exclude lesbians and gay men from the uniformed services.

Watkins was a Vietnam-era draftee. He reported for his preinduction physical examination on August 27, 1967, at which time he indicated on the Report of Medical History that he had homosexual tendencies or had experienced such tendencies in the past. He was referred for psychiatric evaluation. At that time, Army psychiatrists routinely rejected claims of homosexuality unless the claimant could prove that he had engaged in homosexual activity, which Watkins could not. Watkins was inducted and served in the United States and Korea as a chaplain's assistant, personnel specialist, and company clerk. He was investigated for homosexual activities during his initial enlistment, and told an Army Criminal Investigation Division (CID) agent that he had been gay since the age of 13 and had engaged in sex with two other soldiers since enlisting. CID could not develop sufficient independent evidence to pursue the

case, and Watkins was retained in the service until honorably discharged on May 8, 1970.

Watkins had found a real home in the Army. He enjoyed his assigned activities and the egalitarian atmosphere which, as a black man, he had not experienced in the civilian world. After much thought, Watkins decided to pursue a career as a professional Army man. Due to the CID investigation and its inconclusive nature, his discharge papers had been marked "Unknown" as to reenlistment eligibility. Watkins decided to pursue re-enlistment, and applied in May 1971 to have that designation corrected. On June 3, the Army notified him that he was now considered "eligible for reentry on active duty," and on June 18 he re-enlisted for a three-year term. This three-year term was quite successful, since Watkins seemed to have established a solid relationship with his commanding officers through his excellent work and good humor. He also got to indulge his penchant for cross-dressing, participating with his commanders' permission in a variety of drag shows, some in military and some in civilian contexts. However, when Watkins applied for a security clearance in connection with a proposed assignment, the clearance was denied in January 1972, based on his 1968 statements in the CID investigation.

Watkins reenlisted for a six-year-term on March 21, 1974, and was reassigned to South Korea as a company clerk. Now his troubles began, for his commanding officer, Captain Albert J. Bast, III, was evidently a "by-the-book" type who was not inclined to "look the other way" in the matter of an openly gay soldier. Bast initiated proceedings to dismiss Watkins as unsuitable for service due to his homosexuality. On October 14, 1975, a four-member board convened at Camp Mercer, South Korea, to hear testimony and argument in the case. Bast testified that he had discovered Watkins's

507

homosexuality through examination of his service records, and that Watkins had confirmed personally to Bast that he was gay. Bast also testified, however, that Watkins was "the best clerk I have known," and that his homosexuality did not affect the company. Watkins's immediate superior, First Sergeant Owen Johnson, testified that everybody in the company knew Watkins was gay but that it posed no problem. The board unanimously concluded that Watkins was "suitable for retention in the military service," as it had the discretion to do under the regulations in effect at that time, which authorized, but did not require, discharge of known homosexual soldiers.

Watkins was rotated to a stateside assignment and then to Germany as a clerk and personnel specialist with the Fifth U.S. Army Artillery Group, whose commander granted him a "secret" security clearance in November 1977. Watkins applied for a position in the Nuclear Surety Personnel Reliability Program, which required a further background check and reconfirmation of his security clearance. At first, Watkins was rejected by the program because of the notations in his service record regarding his homosexuality, but his commander, Captain Dale E. Pastian, insisted that Watkins's application be reconsidered because of his "outstanding professional attitude, integrity, and suitability for assignment" in the program, and also because the 1975 board decision had indicated that Watkins should be retained in the service and allowed to advance in the military. After a military doctor reviewed Watkins's record and interviewed him, the problem was resolved, Watkins retained his clearance and was assigned to the program in July 1978.

This did not end Watkins's travails, however. Accusations by some soldiers, one of whom had been disciplined by a board on which Watkins sat, sparked another investigation in 1979. As a result of this investigation, the commander of the U.S. Army Personnel Clearance Facility revoked Watkins's clearance because he honestly admitted to the new round of investigators that he was gay. Proceedings were initiated to discharge Watkins. He appealed the clearance ruling, which was referred to the Army's deputy chief of staff for personnel. Watkins, now serving in the Pacific Northwest,

filed suit in federal district court with the assistance of American Civil Liberties Union (ACLU) cooperating attorney James Lobsenz of Seattle, challenging the revocation of his security clearance and seeking an order barring his discharge. The judge advocate general cleared the matter for a discharge disposition, and Watkins was informed on September 17, 1981, that a discharge board would be convened to consider terminating his enlistment. Watkins amended his complaint in the federal district court on October 12, and sought a temporary restraining order against the discharge board convening. District Judge Barbara J. Rothstein, to whom the case had been assigned, denied the request for temporary relief, allowing military procedures to run their course.

The discharge board convened on October 28, and divided two to one on what to recommend. The majority believed that Watkins should be dismissed from the service on an honorable basis, based on his statements that he was gay. The dissenter argued that Watkins's homosexuality had not been proved within the meaning of Army regulations, so he should be retained in the service. Watkins's commanding officer, Major General Robert M. Elton of the Ninth Infantry Division, adopted the recommendation of the majority of the board, making his own additional "finding" that Watkins "has engaged in homosexual acts with other soldiers." Elton directed that Watkins be discharged on April 19, 1982. Judge Rothstein entered an injunction at Watkins's request, barring his discharge until the court could adjudicate the merits of his challenge to the Army's actions. The Army quickly appealed, but Rothstein concluded that she could continue with adjudication of the case while the appeal for interlocutory relief was pending. So Watkins remained enrolled in the Army while the case proceeded, with Department of Justice attorney Stanley E. Alderson and Assistant U.S. Attorney Christopher L. Pickrell, of Seattle, representing the government.

Lobsenz had framed Watkins's case on several alternative theories. First, he argued, revocation of Watkins's security clearance was unconstitutional based on procedural and substantive arguments deriving from the Fifth Amendment's Due Process Clause and the First

Amendment. Alternatively, Lobsenz argued that the military regulations were unconstitutional facially and as applied to Watkins as violative of due process, privacy, the First Amendment, and estoppel principles. The estoppel argument was essentially that the military had allowed Watkins to enlist and serve for fourteen years and could not now raise his homosexuality, about which it had known from the beginning, as a basis for discharge without any evidence of actual misconduct. There was an Army regulation against "double jeopardy" that Watkins contended would apply in his case, since a prior discharge board had considered his homosexuality and recommended in favor of retaining him in the Army without restriction. Watkins sought an injunction against revocation of his security clearance and his discharge, and an order requiring the Army effectively to ignore its regulations on homosexuality in any future personnel decisions regarding him.

The case was complicated somewhat by a change in military regulations, adopted in response to rulings by the U.S. Court of Appeals for the District of Columbia Circuit, making homosexuality a mandatory basis of discharge, rather than merely authorizing the discharge of homosexuals at the recommendation and discretion of commanders. The government argued that these regulations were constitutional and allowed for no discretion; if Watkins admitted being gay, he was subject to discharge. As to the estoppel argument, the government contended that the federal district court lacked authority to order the Army to violate its own regulations, regardless of its past actions.

Judge Rothstein issued her order on May 18, 1982, concluding that the Army was precluded by its past conduct and proceedings with regard to Watkins from now relying on his homosexuality as a basis for discharge, but reserving any determination on the issue of the security clearance because Watkins's appeal as to that was still pending within the Defense Department. At the heart of Rothstein's decision was the 1975 discharge board decision to retain Watkins in the service and the failure of subsequent investigations to uncover any actual violations by him of military conduct codes. The only thing "new" since the prior discharge board had been additional admissions by

Watkins that he was gay. The Army's own regulations prohibited taking disciplinary or discharge action against a soldier on the basis of conduct that had already been the subject of a prior adjudication. Rothstein concluded that the issue of reenlistment required further argument because Watkins's current enlistment term would not expire until October of 1982, and set a schedule for briefs on that question. Because she was deciding the matter on grounds of estoppel, she did not have to consider the due process and equal protection issues raised by Watkins's complaint. This was just as well, since the Ninth Circuit, to which any order she issued might be appealed, had relatively recently upheld several discharges of gay service members for engaging in homosexual activity while enlisted.

After considering briefs and further argument, Rothstein issued an additional decision on October 5, 1982, finding that the Army was precluded from considering Watkins's homosexuality in deciding whether to allow him to reenlist. The Army had made an initial determination, purportedly because Watkins had "refused" to answer further questions about his conduct. Rothstein found this to be bogus. Although Watkins had refused to answer questions without his counsel being present, Rothstein found that he had the right to counsel, since the questions might involve issues that would bear on the lawsuit or possible violations of military law, as to which Watkins was entitled to assistance, and the Army had suggested a date for an interview when Lobsenz was unavoidably unavailable. After reviewing the precedents on sovereign immunity and estoppel, Rothstein concluded that it was appropriate to apply the estoppel theory against the Army's use of Watkins's homosexuality as a basis for denying reenlistment.

The estoppel determination required findings on several distinct issues. Did the Army know that Watkins was gay when it had previously allowed him to reenlist? Clearly, yes. Did the Army intend that Watkins rely on its conduct in allowing him to reenlist, or did the Army at least act in a way so that Watkins had a right to think that the Army intended his reliance? Rothstein found that the Army's actions clearly led to an affirmative response, since it had allowed him to reenlist in 1971 despite his past admissions of homosexuality and had "corrected" his discharge record to reflect "suitability for reenlistment." On the basis of this and the subsequent resolution of all questions about his homosexuality in favor of retention over many years, Rothstein found that the Army had engaged in affirmative conduct that would appropriately form the basis for reliance on which to ground the estoppel theory. Finally, Rothstein found that Watkins could reasonably have concluded, as a result of his experience, that the Army was willing to interpret its rules on homosexuality flexibly in order to retain a good soldier, and that discharge for homosexuality was not mandatory: "Had plaintiff known the true facts (i.e., that discharge for homosexuality was mandatory), it is highly unlikely that he would have invested twelve additional years in the Army." Now he was "tied up in litigation, less than six years from retirement, having invested more than 14 years in the Army," so it was clear that Watkins had relied to his detriment on the Army's willingness to allow him to pursue a career. If he could not reenlist, he would not be entitled to the military pension he would have earned had a six-year reenlistment term been fulfilled by him. He also would have to retrain for civilian employment skills and was unlikely to be able to attain the kind of pension security he would need in the civilian sector, having lost fourteen prime employment years to military service.

Rothstein concluded that the injury to Watkins from having "relied on the Army's approval of his military career—and being denied it now—is the loss of his career." On the other hand, any injury to the public from retaining him in the service was "non-existent," because he had "demonstrated that he is an excellent soldier. His contribution to this Nation's security is of obvious benefit to the public." Consequently, there was no weighty countervailing reason to deny his application for reenlistment.

On the same day as Rothstein's new order, the Army summoned Watkins and his attorney to a "hearing" on his application for reenlistment, conducted by a military attorney, Captain Russell D. Johnson of the judge advocate general's staff, and the commander of Watkins's

battalion, Captain Thomas Landwermeyer. This hearing was apparently held solely for the purpose of posing to Watkins the same questions about his homosexuality that the Army wanted to pose over the summer of 1982 when Lobsenz was unavailable. Now Lobsenz was available and advised Watkins to answer none of the questions, since they were all, in his view, irrelevant or prejudicial. There was no new information that would provide a basis for a new "investigation" of Watkins's sexual activities, and the court had precluded reliance on his past statements or conduct considered by early investigations and "boards." The transcript of this strange proceeding was published by Judge Rothstein along with a supplementary opinion she issued on October 28, in response to a new motion for summary judgment by the government. She was scornful of the Army's motives and conduct in holding this hearing, and of its argument that Watkins's refusal to answer questions should now become the basis of dismissing his case and his application for reenlistment: "The Army cannot now avoid the estoppel by characterizing homosexual acts as military crimes and by pretending to investigate such crimes. Not only is the attempt transparent, the consequences are unjust." Watkins had not been properly notified that the October 5 hearing was to "investigate" his conduct, and Rothstein believed that fundamental due process rights would be violated were the Army to gain some tactical advantage by its conduct on October 5. The Army reenlisted Watkins on November 1, 1982, with the understanding that the reenlistment would be voided if the court of appeals reversed Rothstein's order.

While the Army's appeal was pending, Watkins received a new performance evaluation, in which he scored a perfect 85 out of 85 possible points. He received perfect scores in every category, and earned an endorsement for promotion. The written evaluation included the following statements:

> SSG Watkins is without exception, one of the finest Personnel Action Center Supervisors I have encountered. . . . He requires no supervision, and with his "can do" attitude, always exceeds the requirements and demands placed upon him. I would gladly welcome another opportunity to serve with him, and

firmly believe that he will be an asset to any unit to which he is assigned.... SSG Watkins' potential is unlimited. He has consistently demonstrated the capacity to manage numerous complex responsibilities concurrently. He is qualified for promotion now....

The Army's appeal from Rothstein's orders was heard by a Ninth Circuit panel on September 12, 1983, with Justice Department attorney Alfred R. Mollin presenting the government's argument. The panel's decision of December 9 was a limited victory for the government. Circuit Judge Herbert Y. C. Choy wrote for the unanimous panel that the estoppel theory could not be used to order the Army to ignore or disobey its own valid regulation. Judge Rothstein could only order Watkins' reenlistment on an estoppel theory if the regulation was itself found to be unconstitutional. Concurring, Circuit Judge William A. Norris cast considerable doubt on the constitutionality of the regulation:

> The Army rewarded Sgt. Watkins' years of outstanding service by destroying his chosen career. When he needed only five more years to qualify for retirement benefits, he was discharged solely because the Army decided to purge all homosexuals from its ranks by changing its regulations to make discharge of homosexuals mandatory rather than discretionary. In my view, this regressive policy demonstrates a callous disregard for the progress American law and society have made toward acknowledging that an individual's choice of life style is not the concern of government, but a fundamental aspect of personal liberty. . . . After the change in regulations, Sgt. Watkins' superior officers could not save his military career, despite his exemplary record. As a consequence, our nation has lost a fine soldier, and Sgt. Watkins has suffered a manifest injustice.

But, given the procedural posture of the case, Norris felt compelled to concur, because he believed that the three-judge panel was bound by the circuit's prior decision in *Beller v. Middendorf*, a 1980 ruling upholding the constitutionality of "similar regulations adopted by the Navy." He was critical of the *Beller* decision, as he indicated in a dissent from the circuit's denial of a petition to reconsider that case *en banc*, but Watkins's case had to be remanded now so that the district judge could

take a first crack at the constitutional question. Norris would be heard from again, however.

The case went back to Judge Rothstein, who, finding herself bound by prior Ninth Circuit rulings, issued an unpublished order dismissing Watkins's case and allowing the Army to end his new enlistment, which had been entered conditioned on the disposition of his case. Now it was Watkins's turn to appeal, and Norris's turn to express his views on the unconstitutionality of the Army's policies. But consideration of the appeal was delayed significantly, since the argument of the case was put off pending the Supreme Court's decision of *Bowers v. Hardwick*, in which it was anticipated that many of the constitutional issues might be addressed. In the event, however, the *Hardwick* decision directly addressed only the constitutional right of privacy as it might apply to consensual sodomy between homosexuals, leaving other constitutional questions open. The Ninth Circuit heard argument on Watkins's appeal on April 22, 1987, and issued its opinion on February 10, 1988, reversing Rothstein's unpublished order and remanding the case to Rothstein with orders to enter an appropriate injunction, requiring reinstatement of Watkins.

The court of appeals panel was split, however. All three judges agreed that Watkins should be entitled to reinstatement and that the Army's regulation should be found unconstitutional, but only two members of the panel, Norris and Circuit Judge William C. Canby, Jr., felt able to take this course. Circuit Judge Stephen Reinhardt published a dissenting opinion, blasting the *Hardwick* decision but concluding that it provided a binding precedent that compelled dismissal of Watkins's suit.

In his earlier concurring opinion, Norris had cast doubt on the constitutionality of the Army's regulations by invoking the Supreme Court's privacy cases. Now that was no longer possible; *Hardwick* made it clear that a privacy theory could not be used to challenge a government policy that discriminated on the basis of sexual orientation. So Norris changed his tack; quickly dismissing all other constitutional claims asserted by Watkins, Norris focused in on the equal protection requirement binding on the federal government through the Fifth Amendment's Due Process Clause and determined that the Army's policy deprived Watkins of equal protection of the laws. Norris's opinion, the first by a circuit court of appeals to take on directly and thoroughly the issue of sexual orientation and equal protection, was a methodical treatment that carefully described and considered all existing authority on the issues.

First, and crucially, Norris had to determine whether the Army's policy even presented an equal protection issue. The Uniform Code of Military Justice banned all sodomy, whether heterosexual or homosexual. Watkins had been investigated from time to time regarding allegations of engaging in homosexual conduct. In the proceedings that led up to the discharge decision and the initiation of this litigation, Major General Elton had supplemented the discharge board's findings with his own independent finding that Watkins had engaged in homosexual conduct with other soldiers during the period of service in the Army. If this factual finding was accepted, then the case might well be controlled by the Ninth Circuit's prior decisions upholding the discharge of gay service members for engaging in homosexual conduct. But Judge Rothstein, confronted by this record, had concluded, among other things, in reaching her initial estoppel decision, that Elton was not authorized to make such independent findings. The discharge board, which heard the evidence, had made no finding regarding Watkins's engaging in homosexual activity; the board majority premised its recommendation for discharge solely on Watkins's statements that he was gay, and the dissenter found that no homosexual conduct had been proved. Said Norris, "The Army has not contested . . . these rulings and, on appeal, relies solely on Watkins' 1968 statement as evidence of homosexual conduct."

For Norris, it was clear that the regulations being applied in this case were not concerned primarily with conduct, except as conduct became evidence of status. Norris accepted the argument that sexual orientation, rather than conduct, was at the heart of the regulation.

> Under the regulations any homosexual act or statement of homosexuality gives rise to a presumption of homosexual orientation, and anyone who fails to rebut that presumption is conclusively barred from Army service. In

other words, the regulations target homosexual orientation itself. The homosexual acts and statements are merely relevant, and rebuttable, indicators of that orientation.

Norris concluded that "the discrimination against homosexual orientation under these regulations is about as complete as one could imagine."

Next, Norris addressed the issue of what level of judicial scrutiny to use in evaluating the regulation. In its equal protection jurisprudence, the Supreme Court had devised a multitiered system depending on the nature of the issues and the parties. If unequal treatment by the government related to a fundamental right or interest of the individual, or if the classification on which the government discriminated was "suspect," then the court would find the government's policy unconstitutional unless it was supported by a compelling governmental interest and narrowly tailored to advance that interest, the so-called strict scrutiny standard. Important rights or interests or quasi-suspect classifications would receive heightened but less searching scrutiny; otherwise, a government policy imposing unequal treatment would be sustained if it had some rational basis, which could normally be presumed in the case of properly enacted legislation or regulations.

Norris concluded that government discrimination on the basis of sexual orientation involved a "suspect" classification, so that the policy had to be tested by the strict scrutiny standard. Before he got to this conclusion, however, he had to deal with *Hardwick* and the prior Ninth Circuit military cases, especially since they formed the heart of Judge Reinhardt's dissenting opinion. Norris contended that *Hardwick* had little if anything to do with this case. Seeking to restrict *Hardwick*, of which he obviously disapproved, to the narrowest possible precedential weight, Norris emphasized that the Supreme Court in *Hardwick* purported to decide only whether the constitutional right of privacy barred states from penalizing consensual sodomy between homosexuals. He argued that *Hardwick* had nothing to say, either expressly or by implication, on the issue of equal protection, apart perhaps from that branch of equal protection analysis dealing with fundamental rights. If Watkins was claiming that the military regulations violated equal protection because they deprived him of a fundamental right to engage in homosexual sodomy, he would be out of court. But that was not Watkins's claim; he was claiming that by discriminating on the basis of homosexual *orientation*, the regulations improperly used a suspect classification. *Hardwick* had nothing to say about "suspect classification" analysis.

The same was true of the prior Ninth Circuit cases, *Beller v. Middendorf* and *Hatheway v. Secretary of the Army* (1981), both of which were decided on grounds not relevant to Watkins's case. In *Beller*, the discharged sailors challenged the Navy's policy on the theory that the constitutional right of privacy made the military sodomy law unconstitutional. In *Hatheway*, the discharged soldier contended that the "fundamental rights" branch of equal protection theory could similarly be used to strike down the Army's regulations. In neither case was the circuit focusing on the "suspect classification" branch of equal protection analysis when it upheld the military policies. Although *Hardwick* now precluded the arguments advanced by the plaintiffs in *Beller* and *Hatheway*, it did not similarly preclude Watkins's suspect classification argument.

Norris also rejected the Army's argument that the circuit court's decision in *DeSantis v. Pacific Telephone and Telegraph Co.* (1979) precluded Watkins's argument. In *DeSantis*, the circuit court had rejected an argument by gay plaintiffs premised on 42 U.S.C. section 1985(3), a post-Civil War statute intended to let former slaves bring federal lawsuits against private individuals who conspired to deprive the plaintiffs of "equal protection of the laws." The court concluded that a violation of section 1985(3) could not be found where "the courts have not designated homosexuals a 'suspect' or 'quasi-suspect' class." However, the *DeSantis* court had not engaged in any analysis of the question whether homosexuals should be so designated, merely dropping the issue to focus on Title VII of the Civil Rights Act, the plaintiff's alternative source of authority. So, Norris said, *DeSantis* was not binding on the suspect class issue because it was not a "holding" on that issue.

At the same time, Norris rejected the authority of *Padula v. Webster* (1987), a D.C. Circuit case rejecting a challenge to the Federal Bureau of Investigation's policy against hiring homosexuals. In *Padula*, the court was focusing on a policy that emphasized homosexual conduct, and held that since the Supreme Court had upheld sodomy laws from constitutional attack in *Hardwick*, an equal protection challenge to a policy discriminating on the basis of homosexual conduct must fail. "*Padula*'s reasoning, echoed in Judge Reinhardt's dissent, rests on the false premise that *Hardwick* approves discrimination against homosexuals," Norris asserted. "To repeat what we said above, *Hardwick* held only that the constitutionally protected right to privacy does not extend to homosexual sodomy. But we see no principled way to transmogrify the Court's holding that the state may criminalize specific sexual conduct commonly engaged in by homosexuals into a state license to pass 'homosexual laws'—laws imposing special restrictions on gays because they are gay."

Turning to the merits of the suspect classification issue, Norris concluded that gays meet all the tests normally imposed by the Supreme Court in designating suspect classifications. The first test—a history of purposeful discrimination—was evidently met with little discussion; the military's own regulation was "Exhibit A."

The second factor, a stumbling point for many courts, is more difficult to articulate. As summarized by Norris, it "may in fact represent a cluster of factors grouped around a central idea—whether the discrimination embodies a gross unfairness that is sufficiently inconsistent with the ideals of equal protection to term it invidious." In evaluating this factor, the Supreme Court had considered different things in different cases: "(1) whether the disadvantaged class is defined by a trait that 'frequently bears no relation to ability to perform or contribute to society,' (2) whether the class has been saddled with unique disabilities because of prejudice or inaccurate stereotypes; and (3) whether the trait defining the class is immutable." Norris believed that gays would qualify under any of these tests.

Indeed, as he noted, the Army conceded that its policy reflected prejudice against gays because several of the reasons it normally recited in support of the policy had to do with the presumed prejudice against gays from other members of the service as a potential source of disruption and bad morale if gays were allowed to serve. But the Army argued that "the public opprobrium directed towards gays does not constitute prejudice in the pejorative sense of the word, but rather represents appropriate public disapproval of persons who engage in immoral behavior." This went too far, said Norris, because the regulations focused on status; a celibate homosexual would be subject to discharge under the regulation, while a heterosexual who engaged in an isolated instance of situational homosexual conduct might be retained. Furthermore, as Norris observed, all homosexuals, regardless of their conduct, were subject to mandatory discharge, but military regulations prohibited only certain sexual conduct, oral or anal sex, while apparently permitting (by omission) other forms of homosexual conduct, such as mutual masturbation, handholding, kissing, and other pleasurable sexual touching. In this case, the Army had no evidence that Watkins ever engaged in acts defined as "sodomy." Finally, Norris believed that for purposes of this analysis, homosexual orientation should be considered an immutable trait. Even though the Supreme Court had never indicated that "immutability" of the defining trait was a necessary prerequisite to finding a suspect class, it had given this factor weight in some contexts, and Norris considered sexual orientation in the same class as race in this regard. If a medication were available to change skin color, that would not make discrimination on the basis of race less suspect, Norris asserted; similarly, he contended, if through therapy some homosexuals might be deterred from homosexual conduct, that did not make discrimination on the basis of sexual orientation less suspect.

The final factor normally considered by the Supreme Court was whether those in the suspect classification were disempowered from achieving adequate consideration of their interests in the normal political process. A group that could protect its interests in the legislature hardly needed the special assistance of the courts to protect its rights. Gays did not have such

power, concluded Norris. While it was true that a few states had passed laws banning antigay discrimination, the relevant focus of attention in a challenge to military policy was national politics, and there gays had been singularly unsuccessful up to that time. There was not one piece of federal legislation providing affirmative protection for gays, and there were specific laws imposing unequal or discriminatory treatment, including immigration laws, penal laws governing federal property (including sodomy laws), and the military regulations. Gays were particularly disabled from effective political participation because prejudice against them was so great that many, perhaps most, hid their sexual orientation in order to get by in their everyday life without having to experience discrimination first-hand. As a result, public officials were reluctant to take up their cause, seeing it as a political liability.

Summarizing, Norris concluded that analysis of the relevant factors "ineluctably leads us to the conclusion that homosexuals constitute such a suspect class." Applying strict scrutiny to the Army's regulations, then, Norris found that the Army had failed to show that the exclusion of gays was "necessary to promote a compelling government interest," even when one took into account the special deference that the courts were supposed to accord to the military in running its own affairs. The Army's standard arguments in support of its policies sounded suspiciously to Norris like the arguments the Army had used in support of racial segregation until it was ordered by President Truman to integrate its forces in the 1940s. "Today it is unthinkable that the judiciary would defer to the Army's prior 'professional' judgment that black and white soldiers had to be segregated to avoid interracial tensions," Norris stated. In fact, in a recent case involving an interracial child custody dispute, *Palmore v. Sidoti*, the Supreme Court had held that the courts could not be complicit in enforcing private prejudices.

But the Army's defense of its regulation went further than resting on prejudice or fears of disruption if homosexuals were to serve. "Apparently, the Army believes that its regulations rooting out persons with certain sexual tendencies are not merely a response to prejudice, but are also grounded in legitimate moral norms."

In other words, the Army believes that its ban against homosexuals simply codifies society's moral consensus that homosexuality is evil. Yet, even accepting arguendo this proposition that anti-homosexual animus is grounded in morality (as opposed to prejudice masking as morality), equal protection doctrine does not permit notions of majoritarian morality to serve as compelling justification for laws that discriminate against suspect classes.

This was so by analogy from *Loving v. Virginia*, a 1967 case in which the Supreme Court struck down as violative of equal protection a Virginia miscegenation statute that was claimed to properly represent the moral views of a majority of Virginians concerning interracial marriage. Said Norris:

> Although courts may sometimes have to accept society's moral condemnation as a justification even when the morally condemned activity causes no harm to interests outside notions of morality [e.g., *Hardwick*], our deference to majoritarian notions of morality must be tempered by equal protection principles which require that those notions be applied evenhandedly. Laws that limit the acceptable focus of one's sexual desires to members of the opposite sex, like laws that limit one's choice of spouse (or sexual partner) to members of the same race, cannot withstand constitutional scrutiny absent a compelling governmental justification. This requirement would be reduced to a nullity if the government's assertion of moral objections only to interracial couples or only to homosexual couples could itself serve as a tautological basis for the challenged classification.

As to the Army's other objections to employing homosexuals in the ranks, Norris found them to be overbroad factors that could be addressed by more narrowly focused regulations. He had particular scorn for the security concerns the Army expressed; it was the Army's policy that made closeted gays a target for blackmail and subversion, said Norris. An openly gay man like Watkins posed no more security risk than a sexually active nongay service member. Concluding that the Army's policy was unconstitutional, Norris and Canby voted to remand the case to Rothstein for an order that the Army offer Watkins reinstatement, and to consider what other relief he might merit as a result of his situation since his discharge.

Reinhardt dissented, but "with great reluctance," since he stated his disagreement with the *Hardwick* decision. But he found that decision dispositive of the equal protection issue because he would not accept Norris's status-versus-conduct distinction in dealing with the issue of homosexuality. Homosexuals were people who desired to have sex with others of their sex, and usually engaged in such conduct. In his view, to define the class in a way that ignored its sexual activity was unrealistic. Furthermore, he found no basis for Norris's conclusion that the *Hardwick* decision did not authorize discrimination against homosexuals. He felt that it was an antihomosexual decision; why would the Court single out "homosexual sodomy" for condemnation when the challenged statute banned all sodomy, heterosexual or homosexual, unless the decision was solely concerned with the homosexual aspect of the penalized sexual conduct? Indeed, contended Reinhardt, Norris's decision was dangerous for promoting a view of *Hardwick* that would further erode the privacy rights of all Americans; by saying *Hardwick* was not an antihomosexual decision, Norris was in effect saying that the Court would allow the state to ban heterosexual sodomy on the basis of majoritarian moral views, a result Reinhardt believed the Court had not intended.

Reinhardt said that he would agree with Norris that homosexuals are a "suspect class" were it not for the *Hardwick* decision, but *Hardwick* precluded that conclusion.

> The majority opinion treats as a suspect class a group of persons whose defining characteristic is their desire, predisposition, or propensity to engage in conduct that the Supreme Court has held to be constitutionally unprotected, an act that the states can—and approximately half the states have—criminalized. Homosexuals are different from groups previously afforded protection under the equal protection clause in that homosexuals are defined by their conduct—or, at the least, by their desire to engage in certain conduct. With other groups, such as blacks or women, there is no connection between particular conduct and the definition of the group. When conduct that plays a central role in defining a group may be prohibited by the state, it cannot be asserted with any legitimacy that the group is specially protected by the Constitution.

Contending that "sodomy is an act basic to homosexuality," Reinhardt concluded that a decision upholding the constitutionality of a sodomy statute must preclude a finding that homosexuals are a suspect class. He devoted extended discussion to explaining further his view that Norris was misinterpreting the holding and scope of *Hardwick*, and was building his theory on sand. But he did not want to leave anybody with the idea that he approved of the *Hardwick* decision:

> [As] I understand our Constitution, a state simply has no business treating any group of persons as the State of Georgia and other states with sodomy statutes treat homosexuals. In my opinion, invidious discrimination against a group of persons with immutable characteristics can never be justified on the grounds of society's moral disapproval. No lesson regarding the meaning of our Constitution could be more important for us as a nation to learn. I believe that the Supreme Court egregiously misinterpreted the Constitution in *Hardwick*. In my view, *Hardwick* improperly condones official bias and prejudice against homosexuals, and authorizes the criminalization of conduct that is an essential part of the intimate sexual life of our many homosexual citizens, a group that has historically been the victim of unfair and irrational treatment.

Although Reinhardt personally believed that gays were entitled to heightened scrutiny of antigay laws and regulations, "it is my obligation to follow *Hardwick* as long as it has precedential force—and for now it does."

Besides that, however, Reinhardt was bothered by the panel's willingness to ignore Ninth Circuit precedent upholding the military policies against gays. He felt that *Hatheway*, in particular, represented a binding precedent on the Army's policies that could not be ignored. And, if a rationality test were to be applied under the equal protection theory, the Army's justifications for its policies would clearly suffice. Norris's distinction between homosexuals and those who engaged in homosexual acts just would not do because the members of the class would "consist principally of active, practicing homosexuals," and one could not justify striking down the Army's policy on the theory that it was unfairly applied to a handful of homosexual celibates. Furthermore, since Watkins

did not deny that he had engaged in homosexual conduct at some time, there was some question in Reinhardt's mind whether he had standing to challenge the Army regulation on the status theory; his case could well be controlled by *Hatheway*, which a three-judge panel of the Ninth Circuit must treat as a binding precedent in a homosexual conduct case. Reinhardt asserted that "the majority's status/conduct distinction does not advance its cause."

Reinhardt concluded that only three bodies could provide relief to Watkins: the Supreme Court, the Army (by changing its regulations), or Congress (by overruling the regulations legislatively). While he understood that his conclusion provided "little solace" to Watkins, he did not believe that a Ninth Circuit panel, bound by *Hardwick*, *Hatheway*, and *Beller*, was in a position to do any more.

The government petitioned for rehearing and rehearing *en banc*. Picking up an argument from Reinhardt's dissent, the government argued that Norris's opinion was inappropriately premised on the view that Watkins had not engaged in any homosexual conduct. On the broader question of constitutionality, the government argued that *Hardwick* and other precedents precluded the conclusion that the Army regulations were unconstitutional. On June 8, Norris issued a revised opinion, incorporating references to Watkins's alleged homosexual conduct (which had apparently played no role in the Army's decision to proceed against Watkins) but not altering the substance of his opinion. At the same time, the circuit announced that it would consider the case *en banc*, and set it down for argument on October 12, 1988, when the Justice Department sent out E. Roy Hawkens to confront Lobsenz at the oral argument.

In the huge Ninth Circuit, an initial *en banc* hearing takes place before a panel of eleven judges. In this case, the eleven were sharply split over how to handle it. Although the majority of the active judges in the circuit had voted for an *en banc* argument to consider the equal protection claim, after hearing the arguments, five of the judges decided it would be better to avoid the constitutional issues altogether by revisiting, and reversing, the original three-judge panel decision on the issue of estoppel. Led by Circuit Judge Harry Pregerson, this group concluded that the Army should be held, as per Judge Rothstein's original decision, to be precluded from relying on Watkins's homosexuality as a basis for denying reenlistment, in light of the record of fourteen years service during which his homosexuality was known to the Army from the time of his initial induction. Judges Norris and Canby from the second three-judge panel, who had voted to find the Army's regulation unconstitutional under equal protection, still clung to that view, but differed as between themselves on the estoppel issue. Thus, Norris wrote separately to reiterate his view from the first three-judge panel that the estoppel argument was not available in this case, and from the second three-judge panel that the regulation was unconstitutional, while Canby joined in Pregerson's estoppel decision, but wrote a one-paragraph opinion indicating his continued agreement with Norris on the constitutional issue. Circuit Judge Cynthia Holcomb Hall wrote a dissenting opinion, arguing that estoppel was not available but taking no position on the constitutional issue, although arguing strongly that the court should not be substituting its judgment for the Defense Department on what impact reinstatement of Watkins could have on national defense, which suggested how she might come out on the constitutional issue. The opinions were announced on May 3, 1989.

Pregerson's opinion, a complicated argument on the issue of estoppel against the government, is noteworthy in this context primarily for his consideration of one factor: whether ruling for Watkins on estoppel grounds would work a significant enough harm on the government to justify denying Watkins the relief he sought (i.e., reinstatement). As to this, Pregerson said:

> The record in the instant case shows that Sgt. Watkins has greatly benefitted the Army, and therefore the country, by his military service. Even the Army's most recent written evaluation of Watkins, completed during the course of this legal action, contains nothing but the highest praise, describing Watkins' duty performance as "outstanding in every regard" and his potential as "unlimited." In addition, Watkins' homosexuality clearly has not hurt the Army in any way. In the words of an Army review board, "there is no evidence suggesting that [Watkins's] behavior has had either a degrading effect upon unit performance, morale or discipline, or upon his own job performance."

Pregerson then quoted a similar conclusion from Judge Rothstein's initial opinion in the case. After reviewing the traditional estoppel elements and determining, in a manner similar to Rothstein, that they had been met in this case, Pregerson concluded: "This is a case where equity cries out and demands that the Army be estopped from refusing to enlist Watkins on the basis of his homosexuality." The majority of the *en banc* panel thus voted to reinstate Rothstein's original court order of October 5, 1982.

In his separate opinion concurring in the result, Norris revived substantial portions of his prior opinion on the constitutional issue, preceded by a paragraph reiterating his view that there were significant doubts whether estoppel could be invoked against the government in this context and that there was no justification for invoking the doctrine in this case. Although Norris's argument was substantively identical to that made in his prior opinion, he was bolstered this time by favorable scholarly commentary published in response to the panel opinion, most prominently by University of Chicago Professor Cass R. Sunstein. Norris quoted liberally from Sunstein's article, arguing strongly that the distinction between status and conduct Norris had embraced in the panel decision was crucial to understanding the case. Sunstein had argued that the panel majority correctly interpreted *Hardwick* not to implicate the equal protection analysis, pointing out that due process and equal protection serve analytically distinct purposes that would be undermined were a purely due process decision like *Hardwick* held to decide the kind of equal protection issues raised by Watkins. Judge Canby, in his single-paragraph opinion, stated concurrence with the majority, but insisted that he intended "no retreat, however, from my conviction that the Army's discrimination against Watkins because of his homosexual orientation denies him equal protection of the laws." In addition, "I agree with everything Judge Norris says today on the equal protection point," and because the circuit was sitting *en banc*, he felt it was appropriate to reach the constitutional issues.

Judge Hall's dissent avoided the constitutional issues, arguing instead that estoppel was inappropriately invoked, and even if it were properly considered here, in this case the judiciary's appropriate deference to military judgments should dictate abstention from interfering in a military personnel matter. Hall was particularly scornful of the majority's attempt to marshall the facts to support the traditional "estoppel" factor of showing "affirmative misconduct" on the part of the government on which the plaintiff had relied. She argued that all the so-called misconduct (i.e., failure to follow its own regulations authorizing discharge) was negative, not affirmative, in character. While most of her dissent is a technical discussion of the estoppel issues, she also disputed the majority's contention that the harm to the Army and the public of reinstating Watkins was "nonexistent":

> The majority does not justify the ability of judges to substitute their assessment of a homosexual's impact on military preparedness for the Army's absent substantial federal interests. Courts are not particularly well-suited to determine whether individual homosexual servicemen bring more to the Army than they take from it. In any event, the majority fails even to undertake this task, relying solely upon the undisputed fact that Watkins is an excellent soldier. The Army has concluded that having homosexual soldiers in the Army, even good soldiers like Watkins, interferes with the Army's mission. The majority does not challenge this assessment.

> Furthermore, the majority fails to acknowledge the ramifications of its holding. We simply have no idea how many "known" homosexuals the Army has reenlisted in years past. By ignoring the ability of other homosexuals to invoke the equitable estoppel rationale advanced by the majority, it greatly minimizes the probable damage to the public interest, as judged by the Army.

Since the majority had determined that ordering reinstatement of Watkins posed no appreciable "damage to the public interest," this argument carried little weight.

The Army was quite disturbed by the result in this *en banc* ruling, immediately petitioning for reconsideration by the full circuit and,

at the same time, initiating negotiations with Lobsenz and Watkins to attempt a monetary settlement without reinstatement. When the circuit court refused to consider the matter further and negotiations with Watkins had proved fruitless by the deadline for seeking Supreme Court review, the government filed a *certiorari* petition, asking the Supreme Court to hold that estoppel could not be invoked against the Army in a personnel decision. But the Supreme Court was not interested in getting involved in the ongoing dispute between gays and the military, having denied *certiorari* earlier in 1990 in several cases presenting the substantive issues on the merits, and the Court announced on November 5, 1990, that it would not review the case. Only when his victory was final and complete would Perry Watkins agree at last to settle with the Army, based on the reasonable expectation of pension rights he would have earned had his reenlistment in 1981 been accepted, as well as back pay to cover the intervening years, during which his background and skills had relegated him to relatively low-paying work.

Although the final outcome of Watkins's challenge was not a precedential appellate decision on the unconstitutionality of the Defense Department's policy excluding gays from uniformed service, his case was very important for several reasons. Due to his exceptional performance record and the media attention the case received, Watkins was able to put a face on the previously somewhat "faceless" issue of antigay discrimination. This was heightened because he was a charming and articulate black man, confounding in one person many of the stereotypes about homosexuals carried by the general public. Furthermore, Watkins's challenge provoked the writing of an opinion by Circuit Judge Norris for the three-judge panel that was one of the strongest endorsements of equal protection rights of homosexuals ever published by a federal appeals court. Although Norris's panel opinion was vacated by the subsequent *en banc* review, it was published and then republished in the form of his concurring opinion, remaining in the law books to be discussed and cited by scholars and judges. Norris's extensive quotation of the strongly positive comments and recommendations for retention by Watkins's superior officers helped give the lie to the

Army's contention that homosexuality was inevitably "incompatible" with military service.

Finally, of course, there was the *en banc* court's conclusion that Watkins's homosexuality, *per se*, presented virtually no detriment to the Army, a finding it had to make in order to invoke estoppel to require Watkins's reenlistment, and which the Supreme Court implicitly accepted by refusing to review the case. While not a decision on the constitutional merits, it was a strong blow against the Army's unsubstantiated justifications for excluding gays from the uniformed services, and seemed typical of what more sensitive and thoughtful Americans were beginning to say about the military exclusion, as reflected in public commentaries and opinion polls.

Case References

Beller v. Middendorf, 632 F.2d 788 (9th Cir. 1980), petition for rehearing en banc denied sub nom. *Miller v. Rumsfeld*, 647 F.2d 80 (9th Cir.), certiorari denied, 452 U.S. 905 (1981)

Bowers v. Hardwick, 478 U.S. 186 (1986)

DeSantis v. Pacific Telephone and Telegraph Co., 608 F.2d 327 (9th Cir. 1979)

Hatheway v. Secretary of the Army, 641 F.2d 1376 (9th Cir.), certiorari denied, 454 U.S. 864 (1981)

Loving v. Virginia, 388 U.S. 1 (1967)

Padula v. Webster, 822 F.2d 97 (D.C. Cir. 1987)

Palmore v. Sidoti, 466 U.S. 429 (1984)

94. CAN WE TALK ABOUT IT?: DISCHARGE FOR SPEAKING OUT

BenShalom v. Marsh, 881 F.2d 454 (7th Cir. 1989), certiorari denied, 110 S. Ct. 1296 (1990), reversing 703 F. Supp. 1372 (E.D. Wis. 1989). Prior decisions included: *BenShalom v. Secretary of the Army*, 489 F. Supp. 964 (E.D. Wis. 1980), settlement enforced, 826 F.2d 722 (7th Cir. 1987).

When the U.S. Supreme Court decided on February 26, 1990, to deny review in Miriam BenShalom's challenge to the exclusion of gay people from military service, it put an end to a fourteen-year struggle by a determined lesbian woman who was eager to serve her country. The Supreme Court's abstention left unresolved the fate of thousands of lesbian and gay career service members who might be summarily removed from their jobs if their sexual orientations were discovered.

Miriam BenShalom enlisted in the U.S. Army Reserve for a three-year term in 1974. She had been active in the lesbian and gay community in Milwaukee, and made no secret about it. At her graduation ceremony from a Reserve officer training program, she spoke with a reporter who asked how it felt for a lesbian activist to be an officer in the Reserve. BenShalom truthfully related her gratification at the recognition of her accomplishments. When the interview was published, BenShalom was discharged, even though there had been no complaints about her work and she was highly regarded by subordinates, colleagues, and immediate supervisors.

At that time, military regulations authorized the discharge of any soldier who "evidenced homosexual tendencies, desire or interest, but is without overt homosexual acts." Commanding officers had discretion not to discharge a particular soldier in the national interest. BenShalom demanded a hearing on her discharge, arguing that she should not be removed from the Reserve because there was no connection between her sexual orientation and her ability to serve. However, a hearing board determined that she should be honorably discharged as "unsuitable" for military service. BenShalom wrote to her commanding officer, requesting that the board's recommendation be rejected. She was unsuccessful and was discharged on December 1, 1976, with eleven months left to run on her enlistment.

BenShalom filed a petition in the U.S. District Court for the Eastern District of Wisconsin, seeking an order reinstating her with her Reserve unit. Both sides filed motions for summary judgment, and the U.S. Department of Defense moved in the alternative to dismiss the case for failure to state a claim. After long pondering, District Judge Terence T. Evans issued his decision on May 20, 1980, ordering that the Army reinstate BenShalom for the duration of her enlistment period.

BenShalom had challenged her discharge on several grounds. Noting that she was never charged with any violation of military rules forbidding homosexual conduct, but merely for stating that she was a lesbian, BenShalom contended that the discharge violated her First Amendment rights of free speech and association. She also alleged violation of due process under the Fifth Amendment.

Judge Evans agreed that the First and Fifth amendments had been violated in her case. Acknowledging that the judiciary normally defers to military judgments about the suitability of individuals for service, he concluded nonetheless that the rules under which BenShalom was discharged were too broad to withstand First Amendment review. He found that BenShalom had "engaged in no known homosexual activity. She did not advocate homosexuality to anyone while on duty. Her homosexuality caused no disturbances except in the minds of those who chose to prosecute her. In fact, the record is clear that her sexual preferences made no differences to her immediate superiors or her students." (At the time of her discharge, BenShalom was an instructor for the Reserve.) Although Judge Evans conceded that the military would have grounds for discharging anyone whose sexuality was disruptive or expressed in *conduct* violating military codes, he concluded that the rule was not tailored narrowly enough to accommodate First Amendment concerns.

Judge Evans found an alternative basis for his ruling in the right of privacy under the Fifth Amendment's due process clause. The judge found a basis in *Roe v. Wade* (1973) and *Griswold v. Connecticut* (1965) to hold that "[t]he privacy of the integral components of one's personality—the essence of one's identity—this court believes, is an interest so fundamental or 'implicit in the concept of ordered liberty' as to merit constitutional protection." Because the regulation chilled free association with known

homosexuals, it violated First Amendment associational rights regarding intimate association, and by intruding into an individual's personality raised Fifth Amendment concerns as well. Judge Evans commented that "the law remains unsettled as to whether private sexual *conduct* between consenting adults is protected by the right of privacy," but asserted that "the court believes that constitutional privacy principles clearly protect one's sexual *preferences* in and of themselves from government regulation." Because the military had shown no nexus between her status as a lesbian and her fitness for service, "due process will not countenance her discharge which so clearly invaded interests protected by the Constitution," which Evans held "outweigh any interest presented in support of the Army's action."

Although the Army did not appeal Evans's decision due to ongoing settlement negotiations, it eventually refused to reinstate BenShalom when the negotiations collapsed without agreement. BenShalom reapplied to the district court for enforcement of its order. The court ordered the Army to give BenShalom back pay for the eleven months remaining on her initial enlistment. She preferred service to lucre, however, and appealed this decision to the U.S. Court of Appeals for the Seventh Circuit, which remanded the case, holding that the court had improperly reconsidered the remedy. The district court then ordered reinstatement again, and was backed up on appeal by the circuit. By the time BenShalom was reinstated (after contempt proceedings against the Army), it was 1987.

As her eleven months of reinstatement neared their end in the summer of 1988, BenShalom indicated her intention to reenlist, and the Army indicated its intention to forbid her from doing so. Unlike her earlier litigation, new litigation would focus on new regulations adopted by the Defense Department early in the 1980s in response to court decisions finding fault with discharge decisions under the old regulations. The new Army Reserve regulation, AR 140–111, Table 4–2, mandated discharge of anyone who was an "admitted homosexual," which clearly applied to BenShalom.

BenShalom filed suit again, seeking an order that the Army allow her to reenlist. This time, in addition to her First Amendment argument, BenShalom alleged that the regulation violated the equal protection requirements of the Fifth Amendment. (The 1986 *Hardwick* decision had severely undermined the privacy argument which had been successful in her previous litigation.) BenShalom sought temporary relief pending trial, and District Judge Myron Gordon granted a temporary injunction ordering her reenlistment. The Army, finding BenShalom otherwise qualified to serve, decided to extend her enlistment until the litigation was resolved. While the case was pending, BenShalom's immediate commander promoted her, and she ended up being the commanding officer of her own unit before the case was finally resolved.

On January 10, 1989, Judge Gordon issued his decision, finding that the Army's new rules violated the First Amendment and equal protection, and ordering BenShalom's reenlistment. After careful scrutiny of the new rules, Gordon decided that they focused purely on status. Engaging in homosexual acts (which could be forbidden under *Hardwick*) was not the basis for exclusion. The military was solely interested in excluding persons of a homosexual *orientation*, who might engage in homosexual activity in the future even if they had not done so in the past.

Quoting liberally from Judge Evans's earlier opinion, Judge Gordon opined that nothing had changed with regard to the First Amendment analysis. Gordon concluded, as had Evans, that homosexual status did not equate with homosexual conduct. The Army asserted that "common sense" dictated making the equation. Gordon disagreed: "In this context, 'common sense' amounts to little more than a euphemism for prejudice. The court must decline to give such bias a sanctuary in our constitutional jurisprudence."

As for equal protection, Judge Gordon emphasized the distinction between status and conduct, insisting that "the debate over whether sexual orientation constitutes a suspect or quasi-suspect classification has been blurred by a failure adequately to differentiate between classifications based on conduct and those based on status." For Gordon, sexual orientation was a status, not a behavior, and thus *Hardwick* was not relevant to the equal protection analysis. Gordon noted the history of purposeful discrimination against homosexuals, asserted that the trait of homosexual orientation "bears no relationship to an individual's ability to contribute to the good of society" and that "in only a very few communities do homosexuals possess the political power effectively to obtain redress from invidious discriminations in the political arena," and concluded that homosexuals "constitute a discrete and insular group subject to potential prejudicial political power." Gordon found support for his conclusions in a three-judge panel decision written by Judge Norris of the Ninth Circuit in *Watkins v. United States Army* (1989), a decision that was subsequently vacated for *en banc* reconsideration. (By the time Gordon's decision was appealed to the Seventh Circuit, Norris's opinion had become a concurring opinion to the Ninth Circuit's *en banc* decision, stating alternative grounds for ordering the reinstatement of an openly gay Army staff sergeant.)

Such a conclusion would normally lead to strict scrutiny of any governmental policy using sexual orientation as a discriminatory classification, but Gordon stated that this was not necessary to challenge the exclusion of homosexuals from military service because he found that "the classification fails even the most deferential standard of review. The classification is not rationally related to any articulated legitimate government interest."

"The elimination of all soldiers with homosexual orientation from the ranks of the Army is not rationally related to the advancement of any compelling government interest," asserted Gordon. Although the military had a legitimate interest in regulating sexual conduct between soldiers, Gordon concluded that "such regulation must be targeted at the conduct itself and cannot be based on prejudicial stereotypes of what people with certain orientations are like." Gordon rejected the assertion that the challenged regulation was based on constitutionally unprotected conduct, and he declared the regulation unconstitutional on its face.

The Army immediately appealed to the Seventh Circuit, which heard argument on May 18, 1989, and quickly announced its decision reversing the district court on August 7, denying rehearing on October 11. Judge Harlington Wood, Jr., wrote for a unanimous three-judge panel.

The court first rejected Gordon's First Amendment analysis on grounds of deference to military judgments. Wood cited *Brown v. Glines*, a 1980 decision in which the U.S. Supreme Court upheld a regulation requiring military personnel to obtain advance approval from a base commander before circulating a petition on a military base, and *Goldman v. Weinberger*, a 1986 decision in which the Supreme Court upheld a military regulation that directly infringed otherwise protected religious practice. Although acknowledging that "Judge Gordon's analysis is, as customary, thoughtful and articulate" and finding support in Justice William J. Brennan's dissenting opinion in *Brown*, Wood asserted that *Brown*'s requirement of extreme deference to the military was binding on lower courts and required normal First Amendment analysis to give way to military discretion over disciplinary matters.

This conclusion was reinforced by *Goldman*, where the Court held that activity historically protected by the First Amendment could be abridged within the military. Conceding that the Army had presented no direct evidence that retaining BenShalom would undermine discipline or morale or endanger national security, nonetheless the court was unwilling to require the Army "to take the risk that an admitted homosexual will not commit homosexual acts which may be detrimental to its assigned mission," asserting that judges did not have the expertise to second-guess the judgments of military experts on this issue.

Besides, Wood insisted, BenShalom was not discharged for speech, as such, but for what she revealed about herself by her speech. "BenShalom is free under the regulation to say anything she pleases *about* homosexuality and about the Army's policy toward homosexuality. She is free to advocate that the Army change its stance; she is free to know and talk to homosexuals if she wishes. What BenShalom cannot do, and remain in the Army, is to declare herself to *be* a homosexual." Consequently, in the court's view there really was no First Amendment issue to consider.

As to equal protection, the court rejected Gordon's conceptualization of the issue. Because the military regulation defined a homosexual as one "who desires bodily contact between persons of the same sex . . . with the intent of obtaining or giving sexual gratification," any military personnel who declared themselves to be homosexual would, by definition, be declaring their intent to engage in conduct that was deemed criminal under the Uniform Code of Military Justice. "Homosexual" as conceptualized by the military was not a status, but rather an anticipation of conduct. A person who described him or herself as a celibate homosexual has no special claim to equal protection of the laws, under this view, because such a self-description "can rationally and reasonably be viewed as reliable evidence of a desire and propensity to engage in homosexual conduct." As far as the court was concerned, the military could draw a "reasonable inference" from the admission of being homosexual that an individual would engage in homosexual activity at some time. "The Army need not try to fine tune a regulation to fit a particular lesbian's subjective thoughts and propensities," concluded Wood. Such reasoning underlies much discrimination, of course. For example, some employers refused to employ women of child bearing capability in jobs involving exposure to chemicals that might cause birth defects, assuming that all women of child bearing capability would have children. The Supreme Court held such employment policies unlawful under Title VII of the Civil Rights Act of 1964 in *United Auto Workers v. Johnson Controls, Inc.* (1991).

Having satisfied itself that "homosexual" is a category defined by conduct rather than by status, the court made the inevitable connection to *Hardwick*, asserting that "[i]f homosexual conduct may constitutionally be criminalized, then homosexuals do not constitute a suspect or quasi-suspect class entitled to greater than rational basis scrutiny for equal protection. The Constitution, in light of *Hardwick*, cannot otherwise be rationally applied, lest an unjustified and indefensible inconsistency result." If classifications based on sexual orientation are not suspect, then the most deferential rational basis review is all that is called for under equal protection theory. The court relied on *Padula v. Webster*, a 1987 decision in which the D.C. Circuit Court of Appeals rejected a challenge to the antigay hiring policy of the Federal Bureau of Investigation, accepting the FBI's characterization of homosexuality as a classification defined by conduct.

The court had little difficulty concluding that the military's exclusionary policy was rational. Although Judge Gordon had found that even the most deferential review failed to save the Army's exclusionary policy, the circuit court disagreed. In the military context, there was a "compelling interest" in maintaining discipline and morale in the nation's defense forces. The contention that antigay policies were founded solely on prejudice carried no weight with the court, which disavowed the assertion by Ninth Circuit Judge Norris in *Watkins v. U.S. Army* that the only justification for the military's policy was antigay prejudice. Said Wood, "Homosexuals have suffered a history of discrimination and still do, though possibly now in less degree. We do not see, however, that the new regulation embodies a gross unfairness in the military context so inconsistent with equal protection as to be termed 'invidious.'" The court also asserted that there was evidence that homosexuals "are not without political power," noting the existence of an openly gay congressman and the appearance of Chicago's mayor at a "gay rights parade."

Few judicial decisions better illustrate how differing conceptions of sexuality and sexual orientation underlie much of the debate over the constitutional status of homosexuals. In a sense, the Defense Department's approach in *BenShalom*, as accepted by the Seventh Circuit, involved a basic semantic confusion. Is it possible to speak of sexual orientation or other aspects of sexuality in isolation from actual physical conduct? BenShalom argued that sexual orientation can be so distinguished, and as such marks a status as to which discrimination should be judged apart from conduct. Her basic contention was that by identifying herself as a lesbian she was indicating the orientation of her emotional life, apart from any physical activity. The Defense Department's regulation, as construed by the court, refuses to accept the possibility that a person could have a "sexual orientation" that does not express itself in specifically sexual conduct of a type that can be criminalized.

That the dispute had to be decided in the context of military service was unfortunate, since a court that did not feel the obligation to extend great deference to the asserted "expertise" of the military might have given more serious consideration to the asserted justifications for the policy and held it unconstitutional under a "rational basis" approach. As it was, however, and acknowledging that the military's policy probably rested on prejudice, the court was unwilling to require the military to deal with society's antigay prejudices at the same time as the military has to carry out the mission of defending national security.

Case References

Bowers v. Hardwick, 478 U.S. 186 (1986)

Brown v. Glines, 444 U.S. 348 (1980)

Goldman v. Weinberger, 475 U.S. 503 (1986)

Griswold v. Connecticut, 381 U.S. 479 (1965)

Padula v. Webster, 822 F.2d 97 (D.C. Cir. 1987)

Roe v. Wade, 410 U.S. 113, rehearing denied, 410 U.S. 959 (1973)

United Auto Workers v. Johnson Controls, Inc., 111 S. Ct. 1196 (1991)

Watkins v. United States Army, 875 F.2d 699 (9th Cir. 1989)

95. PURE AND SIMPLE STATUS DISCRIMINATION?

Woodward v. United States, 871 F.2d 1068 (Fed. Cir. 1989), certiorari denied, 110 S. Ct. 1295 (1990). Proceedings below: *Woodward v. Moore*, 451 F. Supp. 346 (D.D.C. 1978); 25 Fair Empl. Proc. Cas. (BNA) 695 (D.D.C. 1981), vacated, 684 F.2d 1033 (D.C. Cir. 1982).

In the continuing litigation over discharges of gay people from the military services, the distinction between status and conduct has loomed ever larger as a focus for analysis and attack of government regulations. Prior to World War II, the military's concerns had solely been with sexual conduct by gays; those who refrained from any homosexual conduct were not considered a problem. Preparing for wartime mobilization, the U.S. Department of Defense was convinced by apparently well-meaning psychiatrists that homosexuals had personality traits that made them unsuitable for military service, and undertook an effort to identify homosexual draftees and enlistees to prevent their assignment to active duty. Those already on duty discovered to be gay might be processed for discharge, depending on the attitudes of their commanding officers.

Official policies went through alternating periods of more or less strictness, depending on personnel needs. During the 1950s, an internal report within the U.S. Navy concluded that many of the concerns about homosexuals in service were unfounded, but this result was politically unsatisfying to Defense Department policymakers, and the report was suppressed. (Although never officially released, this Crittenden Committee Report was substantially disclosed during the 1980s in response to a Freedom of Information Act request by Professor Rhonda Rivera of Ohio State University.) During the 1970s, with the flowering of an active movement for gay rights in civilian society, discharged homosexuals began to mount court challenges. In some cases, they won on the technical argument that existing regulations allowed military commanders the discretion to retain gay personnel with superior records, making the discharge of exemplary gays unfathomable. The military "corrected" this problem early in the 1980s by revising its regulations to require discharge of all homosexuals, regardless whether

they had engaged in any sexual activity prior to or during their military service, thus shifting the official focus completely from conduct to status in discriminating against gays. However, the record of the military's actual enforcement activities during the 1970s indicated that the concern with homosexual identity as a disqualification for military service long predated the new regulations. The case of James Mark Woodward illustrates this.

Woodward enlisted in the U.S. Naval Reserve in 1972, a time when the Navy's stated policy was to separate any known homosexuals or "members involved in homosexuality" from the service. Naval regulations defined "homosexuality" to include "the expressed desire, tendency, or proclivity toward such acts whether or not such acts are committed." However, the Navy took the position that in extraordinary circumstances it retained the discretion not to separate particular homosexual members, based on service personnel needs and individual performance records. At the time of his enlistment, Woodward completed a "fitness questionnaire" in which he indicated his sexual attraction and desire for sexual activity with "members of his own sex," but also noted that he had never actually engaged in homosexual conduct. Despite this open admission of his sexual orientation, Woodward was accepted for naval flight school in June 1972. This was, of course, during the period when the United States was engaged militarily in Vietnam and had a significant need for naval pilots that outstripped the pool of satisfactory volunteers.

After completing flight school successfully, Woodward was assigned to a fleet operational squadron based in the Philippine Islands, Carrier Airborne Early Warning Squadron 116 under Commander A. J. Moore. Woodward did not know any other gay officers, but he did make the acquaintance of some gay enlisted men, with whom he socialized. Questions about

Woodward arose when he visited the Subic Bay Officers' Club in 1974 "in the company of an enlisted man who was awaiting discharge from the Navy because of homosexuality." When word of this got back to Commander Moore, he questioned Woodward directly. Consistent with his enlistment papers, Woodward stated quite openly that he had "homosexual tendencies" and that, because he did not know any gay officers, he socialized with gay enlisted men. Moore immediately demanded Woodward's resignation. Woodward refused, and Moore then sent a recommendation to the chief of naval personnel that Woodward be discharged.

Woodward wrote to the chief of naval personnel, transmitting the letter through Commander Moore, stating:

> I am, and have been, since I became sexually aware, primarily homosexually oriented. . . . I do, and will continue to, associate with other homosexuals. . . . I am well aware of the problems of social acceptance and special problems of leadership with which I will be confronted as my associates become aware of my homosexuality. . . . For the good of both the Navy and myself, I respectfully request the chance to contribute to the defense of the United States as an honest, open, "gay" officer. I recommend that the matter of my homosexuality be dropped as a matter of official concern.

Woodward's file was reviewed by an assignment officer in the chief's office, and a decision was made to reject Moore's discharge recommendation. Instead, since Woodward's Reserve active duty obligation had some time yet to run, the chief decided to exercise his regulatory discretion to assign Woodward to inactive duty for the balance of his obligation period. Woodward's fitness ratings were not outstanding, although they were not worse than those of many other Reserve officers who were retained for active service. When the factor of acknowledged homosexuality was added in, Woodward appeared "noncompetitive" with other Reserve officers available for reassignment or release. At that time, as the U.S. participation in the Vietnam War ended, the Navy was reducing the number of Reserve officers on active duty, and Woodward's reassignment to inactive duty would be consistent with that policy.

On October 22, 1974, the chief of naval personnel released Woodward from active duty and reassigned him to Reserve Staff in San Diego without pay. He received a *pro forma* promotion to lieutenant, junior grade. Later, the Navy released him from further reserve status at his request. During his time on inactive status, Woodward was twice passed over for promotions that he would normally have earned.

At the end of his six-year Reserve obligation, the Navy discharged Woodward, but prior to his discharge he brought suit in June 1976 in the federal district court in Washington, D.C., seeking reinstatement to active duty and back pay. He was represented in the action before District Judge Barrington D. Parker by David Gespass, of Washington. Special Assistant U.S. Attorney Patricia J. Kenney represented the Navy. Ruling on cross-motions for summary judgment, Parker held on May 31, 1978, that there appeared to be no abuse of discretion in Woodward's case, which he believed to be the relevant standard for adjudicating Woodward's complaint. Without analysis or discussion, Parker stated that "the use of Woodward's admission of homosexual tendencies and his association with homosexuals as a basis for the exercise of that discretion did not result in invidious discrimination in violation of due process, nor in violation of his right to freedom of association," citing the recent district court decision upholding the discharge of Navy Ensign Vernon Berg, then pending on appeal to the U.S. Court of Appeals for the D.C. Circuit. Parker also dismissed claims that Woodward had been deprived of appropriate procedural protection, noting that the manuals and regulations relied on by Woodward were applicable only to disciplinary proceedings, and that Woodward, as to whom there was no evidence of any actual violation of military sodomy laws, had not been subjected to any "discipline" as such.

Woodward appealed this determination to the D.C. Circuit, which remanded his case to the district court on March 26, 1979, for reconsideration in light of the circuit court's decisions in the cases of Berg and Sergeant Leonard Matlovich. The circuit court had held that the Navy and the Air Force could not dismiss these excellent officers without articulating some basis from which the court could determine whether the discharges were an abuse of discretion. Since the military services were taking the position that current regulations and policies allowed discretion to retain gay officers in the service under appropriate conditions, the court reasoned that the service should be required to explain why a particular homosexual member should not be retained.

On remand, Judge Parker ruled in 1981 that the secretary of the Navy should be required in Woodward's case to come up with a suitable explanation as to why Woodward had not been retained (other than a mere assertion that he was gay and thus "unsuitable" for military service). Parker rejected the Navy's argument that a release of a Reserve officer from active duty was not comparable to an outright discharge from the service, and thus that the *Berg* and *Matlovich* decisions were not controlling. This victory for Woodward, the high point of his extended litigation, was achieved after Washington attorney Dan Schember had joined his legal team as lead counsel. The Navy appealed Parker's order to the D.C. Circuit, which suddenly developed jurisdictional qualms about the case. As time had passed, Woodward's back pay claim had become sufficiently large to exceed the jurisdictional limit for damage claims against the federal government in the district courts, so the circuit court vacated Parker's opinion and transferred the case to the U.S. Court of Claims, which has exclusive jurisdiction of claims for damages against the government exceeding $10,000, for a *de novo* consideration of the merits. The transfer of the case to the Court of Claims brought new government counsel, John S. Groat, of the Commercial Litigation Branch of the U.S. Justice Department.

Before Court of Claims Judge Lawrence S. Margolis, Woodward claimed that his release from active duty due to his admitted homosexual orientation violated his First and Fifth amendment rights of freedom of speech, due process (privacy), and equal protection. The Navy contended that the court lacked jurisdiction to review this decision which was confided to the Navy's discretion, and that in any event Woodward's service record, apart from any consideration of his homosexuality, justified the chief of naval personnel's decision to reassign

him to inactive duty. Margolis rejected the claim that the reassignment decision was not subject to judicial review; although the decision was confided to naval discretion, that did not preclude a consideration of whether the Navy had violated Woodward's constitutional rights. However, even assuming that "homosexual conduct" as such was constitutionally protected (which in this pre-*Hardwick* time was still a possible assumption for a federal trial judge), Margolis found that the Navy had enough independent justification for its decision to meet the test set out by the Supreme Court in *Mt. Healthy City School District v. Doyle* (1977) because his performance was apparently below the level necessary to be retained on active duty. Said Margolis, "The Navy has introduced credible evidence by personnel officers who regularly review files that even without consideration of Woodward's homosexual tendencies, he would have been recommended for release at the time his record was reviewed. In other words, a Navy Ensign with a similar record to his would have been released if his file had reached the reviewing office at the same time Woodward's file did."

Woodward appealed to the U.S. Court of Appeals for the Federal Circuit, which hears appeals from decisions of the Court of Claims. In the interim, however, the U.S. Supreme Court issued two significant decisions bearing on the merits of his case. In one, *Bowers v. Hardwick*, the Court held in 1986 that the constitutional right of privacy did not extend to the sort of homosexual conduct (oral or anal intercourse) forbidden by a Georgia sodomy statute. In the other, *Webster v. Doe*, a challenge to the discharge of a gay Central Intelligence Agency employee, the Court had held in 1988 that hiring decisions confided to agency discretion, even very broad discretion, were still subject to judicial review of "colorable" constitutional claims. So, on the one hand, *Webster v. Doe* vindicated Margolis's holding that the Navy's reassignment decision was subject to judicial review of constitutional claims. On the other, however, the Federal Circuit panel unanimously held in a March 29, 1989, opinion by Circuit Judge Glenn L. Archer, Jr., that the *Hardwick* decision essentially foreclosed Woodward's equal protection challenge. (The court dismissed in a footnote as clearly without merit his First Amendment claim.)

Archer disagreed with Margolis, at the outset, that application of the *Mt. Healthy* test clearly disposed of the case. In *Mt. Healthy*, the Supreme Court had held that where a government action was challenged as violating a constitutional right, the government action could be upheld if the government could show that it would have taken the same action without regard to the constitutional issue. In this case, that meant that Woodward's reassignment would not be subject to constitutional challenge if the Navy could show that it would have reassigned him without regard to his homosexuality. Archer said that Margolis' reasoning on this was off because "Woodward's file would not have reached the reviewing office at all had he not been homosexual and admitted it to his commanding officer." Other ensigns with similar service records were not routinely referred to the chief of naval personnel for reassignment; this more frequently happened at the lieutenant, j.g. (junior grade), level. The record showed, in fact, that a large number of ensigns with service records less good than Woodward's had not been reassigned off active duty in the relevant time period.

This meant that the *Mt. Healthy* defense was not available to the Navy in Woodward's case, and the court would have to consider his due process and equal protection challenges. Here, the status and conduct business became rather confused. Woodward had never admitted to having engaged in homosexual conduct, but he had stated in his enlistment papers that he "was attracted sexually to, or desired sexual activity with, members of his own sex." (Actually, he probably had not stated that as such but rather checked off a box on a form with this wording.) He had told his commanding officer that he was gay, and he had written to the chief of naval personnel that he wished to be retained as an openly gay officer. Said Archer, "There is no claim by Woodward that he is celibate. Nevertheless, Woodward's counsel, in his briefs, attempted to characterize Woodward as having only homosexual tendencies. While acts of sodomy have not been expressly admitted by Woodward," in view of his statements and associating with gay sailors "we need not address

the factual situation where there is action based *solely* on 'status as a person with a homosexual orientation.'" This was quite a logical leap for Archer to take, given the lack of any positive evidence that Woodward had ever engaged in sexual activity with another man, either in or outside the Navy.

After reviewing the *Hardwick* ruling, and treating it as in effect validating D.C. Circuit Judge Robert Bork's assertion in *Dronenburg v. Zech* (1984) that the constitutional privacy doctrine did not provide a coherent theory for application to circumstances outside those specifically deemed covered by the Supreme Court, Archer asserted, "Protection of homosexuality as a private right, therefore, is not an apparent or necessary result that can be reached from the Supreme Court's precedent. We must therefore reject Woodward's claim that homosexuality is constitutionally protected under the right of privacy." This was a radically broad use of *Hardwick*, which had dealt only with the constitutionality of a law penalizing specific homosexual acts: anal or oral sex. But it was the same radically broad use that was being made by circuit courts in other parts of the country considering challenges to the military policy against homosexuals. It was stretched even more egregiously when Archer turned to the equal protection claim, where he found *Hardwick* to be "equally persuasive, if not dispositive, of this argument as well."

In an equal protection challenge, the court would have to determine what level of "scrutiny" to apply to discriminatory governmental actions. Since Archer had already determined that there was no fundamental right to engage in homosexual conduct, the question would center on whether homosexuals as a "suspect" class merited heightened protection under traditional equal protection theory, similar to that extended to racial minorities. Archer said that the court would "decline" to add homosexuals to the list of suspect or quasi-suspect classes (such as gender and illegitimacy).

> Homosexuality, as a definitive trait, differs fundamentally from those defining any of the recognized suspect or quasi-suspect classes. Members of recognized suspect or quasi-suspect classes, e.g., blacks or women, exhibit immutable characteristics, whereas homosexuality is primarily behavioral in nature....

The conduct or behavior of the members of a recognized suspect or quasi-suspect class has no relevance to the identification of those groups.

Furthermore, after *Hardwick*, it could hardly be argued that discrimination against homosexuals was constitutionally infirm, said Archer, relying on D.C. Circuit Judge Laurence Silberman's pronouncement in *Padula v. Webster* (1987) that "there can hardly be more palpable discrimination against a class than making the conduct that defines the class criminal" and noting that the Supreme Court had upheld a state's ability to do that. Thus, blurring the distinction between status and conduct, or defining status solely in terms of conduct, produced a constitutional dead end for gays; even those as to whom there was no evidence of conduct could be discriminated against because their status was being defined by the courts in terms of their presumed desire to engage in such conduct.

Without heightened scrutiny, mere rationality would suffice to uphold the Navy's policy of discrimination against homosexuals. Here, there were ample court of appeals cases to cite holding that it was "obvious" that the military would be better off without gays, and no evidence was needed on the point. These cases never relied on empirical evidence, because the Supreme Court had never demanded empirical evidence in a "rationality" case, presuming that legislators and other government policymakers were rational unless shown otherwise. If evidence were required, the military would be in trouble, since every study it had commissioned on the subject had concluded that the military policy was questionable.

Intoning the standard litany that professional military judgments were entitled to "special deference" from the courts, Archer concluded that the secretary of the Navy's broad grant of discretion from Congress to make naval personnel decisions was sufficient to shield Woodward's reassignment from further challenge.

Woodward petitioned the Federal Circuit for rehearing or rehearing *en banc*, but in vain. He petitioned the U.S. Supreme Court to review the case, but his petition was denied on February 26, 1990. *Woodward*, taken together with the decision in Miriam BenShalom's similar challenge in the Seventh Circuit (denied Supreme Court review at the same time), showed how the blurring of status and conduct in conceptualizing sexual orientation (a concept that some federal judges purport not to understand, to judge by what they write in their published opinions) has continued to impede efforts to get the Defense Department to evaluate even-handedly the issue of homosexual members in the military.

Case References

BenShalom v. Marsh, 881 F.2d 454 (7th Cir. 1989), certiorari denied, 110 S. Ct. 1296 (1990)

Berg v. Claytor, 591 F.2d 849 (D.C. Cir. 1978), vacating and remanding 436 F. Supp. 76 (D.D.C. 1977)

Bowers v. Hardwick, 478 U.S. 186 (1986)

Dronenburg v. Zech, 741 F.2d 1388, rehearing en banc denied, 746 F.2d 1579 (D.C. Cir. 1984)

Matlovich v. Secretary of the Air Force, 591 F.2d 852 (D.C. Cir. 1978)

Mt. Healthy City School District v. Doyle, 429 U.S. 274 (1977)

Padula v. Webster, 822 F.2d 97 (D.C. Cir. 1987)

Webster v. Doe, 486 U.S. 592 (1988)

96. SECURITY CLEARANCES FOR CIA CONTRACTOR EMPLOYEES

Dubbs v. Central Intelligence Agency, 866 F.2d 1114 (9th Cir. 1989), decision on remand, 769 F. Supp. 1113 (N.D. Cal. 1990).

Government agencies concerned with national security or law enforcement have long resisted granting security clearances to individuals they know to be lesbian or gay. When the modern security establishment was formed after World War II, homosexuals were widely considered subversives whose reliability was inherently questionable. These attitudes were reinforced by the position of most psychiatrists and psychologists, who labeled homosexuals as "sexual deviants" with unstable personalities. As further research in human sexuality and the birth of a gay liberation movement in the 1960s led the medical community to alter its views, this rationale for exclusion from access to classified information lost its viability.

Still reluctant to grant clearances to gays, the security establishment seized on a new rationale: foreign agents would target gays for blackmail, thus making them unacceptable security risks. The agencies clung to this rationale even though there was no objective evidence for it. A secret Pentagon study during the 1950s finding no evidence that gays were more susceptible than others to security breaches was suppressed by officials of the U.S. Department of Defense.

Despite the lack of evidence to support the security risk rationale, courts proved extremely reluctant to challenge the security arguments, holding that such judgments by security officials were either totally discretionary and not subject to judicial review or were consistent with "common sense." In cases such as *Padula v. Webster* (1987) and *High Tech Gays v. Defense Industrial Security Clearance Office* (1990), federal courts of appeals refused to question such arguments made by the Federal Bureau of Investigation (FBI) or the Defense Department. Their decisions were partially premised on the U.S. Supreme Court's decision in *Bowers v. Hardwick* (1986), holding that a state's felony sodomy law did not violate the constitutional privacy rights of gays and was subject only to the relatively undemanding rational basis review under the Fourteenth Amendment. From *Hardwick*, the federal circuit courts concluded that equal protection claims asserted by gays were also to be decided by reference to the rationality test, and that evidence that foreign agents might target gays for subversion provided a rational basis for the security agencies to treat gays differently from other security clearance applicants.

One court bucked this tide, however. On January 25, 1989, a panel of the U.S. Court of Appeals for the Ninth Circuit, refusing to indulge the espionage fantasies of the Central Intelligence Agency (CIA) without more solid

evidence, reinstated a lawsuit by a lesbian employee of an agency contractor who had been denied a security clearance. It thus contributed to the growing tide of criticism of a theory that was later described by the secretary of defense as an "old chestnut" not worthy of further credence.

Julie Dubbs was employed by SRI International, a defense contractor, as a technical illustrator during the 1970s. She was openly gay, but managed to obtain Defense Department security clearances needed for her work. In January 1981, SRI requested that Dubbs be granted security approval for access to information on a CIA contract concerning "sophisticated technical systems for collecting intelligence and the information collected by those systems." Dubbs and her partner submitted to interviews with CIA investigators, during which questions about her sexuality and sexual conduct were asked. On March 9, 1981, the CIA's director of security, William Kopatish, wrote to Dubbs notifying her that the agency would not grant her approval for access to the information:

> In evaluating your case, we have taken into account the strict standards of personal conduct which must be met if an individual is to have access to SCI, and we have noted the recency and persistence of the pattern of your homosexual activity. Our concern about homosexual activity is that such activity may be exploitable in a manner which may put sensitive intelligence information at risk. For example, hostile intelligence services target on employees of firms doing classified work for the U.S. Government and, more specifically, on employees with access to sensitive information. Certain hostile intelligence services regard homosexual behavior as a vulnerability which can be used to their advantage. Employees of such firms engaging in homosexual activity, thus, would be doubly targeted. Such targeting might include surveillance of them and their associates. In addition, efforts would be made to place them in circumstances in which their conduct could lead to arrest or other sanctions or otherwise influence their actions through direct or indirect pressure on them or their partners. You have acknowledged that you have been an active homosexual since your teenage years and that you have had relationships with various women lasting from four months to two years. However, this information does not appear to have been volunteered or in any way acknowledged by

yourself, or your partner, during the course of your initial security investigation. Only during the course of another security investigation was this information disclosed by you. The initial silence of both you and your partner regarding such highly significant security information indicates a perception of vulnerability, on your part and a willingness to engage in deceptive behavior in order to prevent the disclosure of possibly damaging personal information. These factors raise serious doubts about your reliability and your susceptibility to compromise by a hostile intelligence service. When these factors are considered in light of the clear possibility that any future relationships that you establish may involve a partner who is not an open homosexual and who fears public exposure, the risk to the national security is significantly increased.

Kopatish cited Director of Central Intelligence Directive No. 1/14 (1984), which established minimum standards for access to the information and provided that any "doubt concerning personnel having access" should be "resolved in favor of the national security." Kopatish asserted that granting Dubbs access would not be "clearly consistent with the interests of national security." Appeals of this decision proving fruitless, Dubbs eventually determined to file suit against the agency.

She obtained legal representation from Richard Gayer, a San Francisco attorney who specialized in cases challenging denial of clearances to gay people, filing suit against the CIA, its director, and Kopatish in July 1985 in the U.S. District Court for the Northern District of California. Dubbs claimed that she is an "openly Gay woman" who "is stable, is not subject to undue influence or duress through exploitable personal conduct, and meets all other constitutional requirements" of the agency. She pointed out that lacking the appropriate clearance from the CIA had caused her to lose at least one good job assignment at SRI and would reduce the company's flexibility in assigning her, thus blocking good assignments and possible promotions, substantially limiting her chances of advancement. She claimed that the agency had a blanket policy of denying security clearances to all persons who engaged in homosexual conduct, or alternatively that the CIA considered homosexual conduct a negative factor without subjecting heterosexual conduct to equal

scrutiny, resulting in impermissible discrimination on the basis of sexual orientation. She also alleged that the CIA's refusal to grant her a clearance was "arbitrary and capricious" in violation of the Administrative Procedure Act, and asked that her suit be certified as a class action on behalf of "all Gay women and men who apply for, have applied for, and may in future apply for" security clearances from the CIA needed for work in private industry, as well as all current holders of clearances.

The case was assigned to District Judge Eugene F. Lynch. The government moved to dismiss the case for failure to state a claim. Lynch denied this motion in a memorandum opinion dated November 27, 1985. Both parties then filed motions for summary judgment, and Lynch scheduled arguments on the questions whether the CIA had a blanket policy of denying clearances to gays, whether such a policy was unconstitutional, and whether, if CIA did not have a blanket policy, the way it took homosexuality into account nonetheless violated the Constitution. In an unpublished opinion dated September 3, 1986, Lynch found that there was no blanket policy, thus avoiding the question whether such a policy would be constitutional. Lynch also ruled for the CIA on the question whether its consideration of homosexuality as a negative factor was unconstitutional. He held that "individualized consideration of sexual orientation is not unconstitutional," and implicitly denied Dubbs's Administrative Procedure Act claims as well when he observed that a court could not "require the CIA to articulate precisely how the decision to grant or deny clearances in individual cases is made."

Dubbs appealed this ruling to the Ninth Circuit, which heard argument on August 13, 1987. A few weeks later, the judges decided to put off considering the case until after the U.S. Supreme Court had ruled in *Webster v. Doe*, a pending case against the CIA presenting similar issues in the case of a gay CIA employee. After the Supreme Court ruled in *Webster* in 1988, the court had the parties submit new briefs on the impact of *Webster*, and finally issued its ruling on January 25, 1989, partially affirming and partially reversing Lynch's decision. The unanimous panel decision held that the CIA's policy, at least as described in Dubbs's complaint and the communications in the record, might be found to be a blanket policy, thus requiring a decision by the trial court on its constitutionality. While agreeing that the Administrative Procedure Act claim was probably invalid in light of *Webster v. Doe*, the panel also held that Lynch had improperly dismissed Dubbs's claim that the manner in which the CIA took account of homosexuality in its decisionmaking process was subject to constitutional challenge.

The opinion by Circuit Judge William A. Norris quickly reviewed the evidence before the trial judge on this motion, which consisted of factual allegations of the parties in their papers, deposition testimony by a former CIA security director, Robert Gambino, and some documents (including Kopatish's letter to Dubbs denying her application). Norris agreed with Dubbs "that the evidence would support a finding that the CIA in fact denies security clearances to all persons known to commit homosexual acts."

> While it is true that Gambino testified that the CIA did not follow a *per se* policy of discriminating against gays, but rather followed a "total person" approach of deciding each case on its individual merits, he also testified in a way that gives rise to a permissible inference that the CIA in fact considers all those who engage in homosexual conduct to be unacceptable security risks. Gambino testified that in his view the medical and psychiatric professions were in "disarray as to whether or not homosexuality is an outward manifestation of a deeper psychological problem," and that "[homosexuality] raises a considerable doubt, a risk, and a risk which *has* to be resolved in favor of the agency." It is important to note what Gambino did not say: he did not say that homosexuality *could* raise a risk; he testified that it necessarily *does* raise a risk—a risk which is resolved against the homosexual applicant.

Norris also found support for the "blanket policy" theory in Kopatish's letter to Dubbs. "For evidentiary purposes, it is important that the Kopatish letter expresses security concerns that apply to all, not just some homosexuals. Even persons such as Dubbs who are openly gay fall under the CIA's dark cloud of suspicion because of 'the clear possibility that any future

relationships that [they] establish may involve a partner who is not an open homosexual and who fears public exposure, the risk to national security [being] significantly increased.'" Thus, it was a reasonable inference that the CIA viewed all "persons who engage in homosexual activity to be unacceptable security risks." Thus, ruled Norris, Lynch was clearly wrong in holding that there was no blanket policy for him to subject to constitutional scrutiny, and his summary judgment ruling to that effect had to be reversed.

Without intimating any view as to the constitutionality of a blanket policy, Norris noted that in *Webster v. Doe* the Supreme Court had "intimated that only colorable constitutional claims are judicially reviewable in the context of CIA employment terminations, and because we see no reason why the same rule should not apply to SCI clearance denials, we necessarily decide that a blanket policy of security clearance denials to all persons who engage in homosexual conduct would give rise to a colorable equal protection claim." Norris further noted that the impact of *Bowers v. Hardwick* on this ruling had not been addressed by the Supreme Court in *Webster v. Doe* because the CIA had not raised the issue in its petition for *certiorari*; the Ninth Circuit panel would similarly refrain from considering the potential impact of *Hardwick* "at this stage of the litigation," said Norris, without further explanation.

Norris then turned to Dubbs's equal protection challenge to the CIA's alleged "case-by-case" consideration of the homosexuality of applicants. Dubbs claimed that the CIA treated homosexuality and heterosexuality differently in this regard. Lynch had granted summary judgment on two grounds: first, he held that Dubbs had "conceded that there is no constitutional infirmity to allowing an individualized consideration of sexual orientation," and second, that inquiring into the CIA's decision process for security clearances would be "excessively intrusive into the sensitive operations" of the agency. The circuit court disagreed with both rationales.

First, Lynch had clearly missed the point of Dubbs's equal treatment argument. While she had conceded that the CIA might take homosexual conduct into account as one factor in deciding whether to grant a clearance, she had argued that it would violate constitutional requirements for the CIA to treat homosexual conduct differently from heterosexual conduct in this regard. Dubbs had argued that the CIA "may base a denial only upon factual evidence showing susceptibility to blackmail based on threatened disclosure of orientation or practice." "In other words," said Norris

> Dubbs argues that the CIA may deny a security clearance to a person whose sexuality makes him/her susceptible to blackmail, but that the CIA must apply the same standards to homosexuals and heterosexuals in making that determination. Thus, the only concession Dubbs made is that the CIA may treat homosexual behavior as it treats heterosexual behavior. This is hardly surprising since Dubbs has no colorable equal protection argument in the absence of disparate treatment.

As to Lynch's second ground, it was clear in light of the Supreme Court's decision in *Webster v. Doe* (which was rendered after Lynch's ruling) that constitutional review of CIA clearance denials could not be denied solely on the argument that the court could not inquire into the reasons for a security clearance denial. Writing for the Court in *Webster*, Chief Justice William H. Rehnquist had expressly rejected the CIA's claim that having to explain its decisions would "entail extensive 'rummaging around' in the Agency's affairs to the detriment of national security." Rehnquist observed that the CIA had been held answerable to employment discrimination claims under Title VII of the Civil Rights Act of 1964, which would require just as much "rummaging around," and that the district court could control the discovery process as needed to protect confidential information.

However, Norris agreed with Lynch that Dubbs could not challenge denial of her clearance under the arbitrary and capricious standard of the Administrative Procedure Act (APA). In *Webster*, the Supreme Court had held that decisions confided to the "discretion" of the director of the CIA were not subject to such review, and could be challenged only on the basis of the Constitution or the failure of the director to follow rules and procedures he had himself established as an exercise of his discre-

tion. Because security clearance decisions were also statutorily vested in the discretion of the director, the APA standard would not apply.

After the court of appeals' decision was issued, Dubbs filed an amended complaint seeking to cure this defect in the APA pleading by alleging that her clearance denial violated the director's own procedures and making other adjustments to conform the complaint more closely to the court of appeals' ruling. The agency again filed a motion to dismiss, which Judge Lynch granted in part and denied in part on August 20, 1990. The agency was relying heavily on the recent decision of the Ninth Circuit in *High Tech Gays*, which came down earlier in 1990, but Lynch was unwilling to treat *High Tech Gays* as dispositive of the constitutional issues before him concerning the blanket policy or the claims of unequal treatment.

The CIA argued that, based on *High Tech Gays*' holding that equal protection claims by gays did not invoke any "heightened scrutiny" of governmental policies, the agency was entitled to complete deference from the court to its determination that gays presented an unacceptable security risk. Lynch was unwilling to indulge an irrebuttable presumption that the agency acted rationally in considering all sexually active gay people to present unacceptable security risks. Since the circuit panel had found that Dubbs stated a constitutionally colorable claim, it would render her constitutional rights meaningless to credit the agency's assertions without any meaningful fact-finding on the court's part. In *High Tech Gays*, said Lynch, the Defense Department had actually presented evidence to document its assertions about the need to engage in extra scrutiny of security clearance applications from gays. The Defense Department did not in that case claim that all gays must inevitably be denied clearances; the contested issue in that case related to higher standards for such clearances, not blanket denials. In this case, the CIA would have the burden of showing that its more stringent requirements bore some rational relation to facts. Lynch asserted:

> If defendants' argument that this Court may properly decide the constitutionality of a blanket policy of denying all homosexual persons access . . . upon a motion to dismiss were correct,

then the *High Tech Gays* court should not have proceeded to examine the evidence adduced by the parties. Rather, after having decided the appropriate level of scrutiny, it should have presumed, as defendants ask this Court to do, that the Department of Defense acted rationally in subjecting all persons who engage in homosexual conduct to an expanded security clearance check. The fact that the court in *High Tech Gays* did not adopt this approach indicates that it necessarily assumed that government had to articulate a rational relationship between their policy and the ends which it is designed to serve.

Furthermore, even the *Padula* court, while dismissing the claims of a disappointed lesbian job applicant against the FBI, had asserted that not all antigay discrimination by the government was automatically constitutional, stating that the discriminating agency "must justify that discrimination in terms of some government purpose. . . . None of these courts found it proper to imagine that a legitimate government interest would necessarily be served by denying a security clearance to a homosexual and then summarily uphold this denial, as defendants invite this Court to do." Furthermore, rejecting the CIA's belated attempt to base its policy on *Bowers v. Hardwick*, Lynch asserted that "no court, so far as this Court is aware, has interpreted *Bowers* to allow for the elimination of the equal protection rights of homosexuals."

Lynch proceeded to spell out how he thought the equal protection claim should be decided. First, the court would have to determine what the CIA's policy actually was with regard to gay security clearance applicants and what the government's reasons were for maintaining the policy. Then, the court would have to determine whether the policy was rationally related to the interests to be served. Finally, the court would have to reach some conclusion as to whether the policy as a whole was rational. Lynch suggested that a trial would probably have to be held for him to make appropriate factual findings.

Turning to the APA claim, Lynch agreed with the CIA that the amended complaint was no more successful than the original complaint in stating a justiciable claim under the Act. While Dubbs had amended her complaint to allege that the director had violated his own policies in denying her clearance, it was clear to Lynch from a review of the policy statements issued by the director that the policy itself was ultimately a discretionary one. Lynch saw a clear analogy to the decision in *Padula v. Webster*, where Padula had argued that the FBI's responses to law school placement office inquiries about its policies had indicated a policy of nondiscrimination on the basis of sexual orientation. The court had found that the FBI had craftily worded its responses to be essentially meaningless in this regard by stating merely that it would not engage in "improper" discrimination on the basis of sexual orientation, thus reserving to itself discretion to decide what sort of discrimination might be improper. The same had occurred here, held Lynch, when the directives actually instructed CIA officials to do what they thought "necessary" in making security clearance determinations; there was no legal constraint imposed by the directive, and thus nothing to be reviewed under the APA.

Having clearly signaled the likelihood that he might find the CIA's policies to raise serious constitutional issues of equal protection, Lynch provided the impetus for settlement of the case. Within a few weeks after he issued his opinion, the government initiated settlement negotiations, which resulted in a written agreement in June 1991, under which Dubbs dropped her suit and the agency agreed to reevaluate her application for a security clearance along the lines suggested in her complaint. According to the settlement agreement:

> Reprocessing plaintiff for access . . . will be carried out pursuant to the whole person concept, and without reference to defendants' previous denial of access. Defendants agree that the adjudicative standards applied to plaintiff will not differ from those applied to heterosexual individuals considered for SCI access. Defendants further agree that plaintiff's homosexual conduct and associations will be considered in the same manner as heterosexual conduct and associations in defendants' security determinations. However, information about specific incidents of homosexual conduct, like information about specific incidents of equivalent heterosexual conduct, may be cause for denial.

While *Dubbs* did not result in a constitutional ruling on the merits of Dubbs's claim, the willingness of the Ninth Circuit to put the CIA to some proof of the need to exclude gays from access to sensitive information marked a major break from the tradition of extreme judicial deference to the judgments of national security agencies. *Webster v. Doe*, and the subsequent statement by Secretary of Defense Richard Cheney during a congressional oversight hearing that the security risk rationale was "an old chestnut" of doubtful validity, suggested that

the security establishment would have to undertake a serious rethinking of reflexive policies that had been applied for half a century.

Case References

Bowers v. Hardwick, 478 U.S. 186 (1986)

High Tech Gays v. Defense Industrial Security Clearance Office, 895 F.2d 563 (9th Cir. 1990)

Padula v. Webster, 822 F.2d 97 (D.C. Cir. 1987)

Webster v. Doe, 486 U.S. 592 (1988)

97. HEIGHTENED SCRUTINY OF GAY SECURITY CLEARANCES

High Tech Gays v. Defense Industrial Security Clearance Office, 895 F.2d 563, rehearing en banc denied, 909 F.2d 375 (9th Cir. 1990), reversing 668 F. Supp. 1361 (N.D. Cal. 1987).

The U.S. military and security establishment has long believed that "sexual deviants" pose severe risks to national security. While these institutions have never been able to present evidence substantiating this belief, and some studies commissioned by the U.S. Department of Defense have even reached conclusions to the contrary, they have persistently relied on these beliefs in their policies concerning homosexuality. One example is the process by which the Defense Department decides whether to grant security clearances for access to information classified "secret" or "top secret" for employees of defense contractors.

Under the system in effect during the 1980s, the Defense establishment accepted the possibility that some lesbian and gay people might be considered eligible for security clearances, but that only an intensified investigation could make such a determination. If a defense contractor wanted to hire somebody for a position requiring access to confidential information or to assign a current employee to such a position, the contractor had to submit an application for a clearance completed by the individual. The application would trigger scrutiny by the Defense Industrial Security Clearance Office (DISCO).

In the case of applications for a secret clearance, DISCO would conduct a quick canvas of

federal law enforcement and security agencies to determine whether there was any "adverse" information about an individual. Applicants for top-secret clearances would receive more extensive scrutiny from DISCO; the Defense Investigative Service would conduct checks of state and local records and interview individuals who might have knowledge about the individual. Under its procedures, DISCO would consider adverse or "questionable" any information that the applicant might be a homosexual, regardless of that individual's behavior or degree of openness about his or her sexual orientation, would conduct an intensive investigation into the person's activities and associations, and would normally transmit the application to the Directorate for Security Clearance Review (DISCR) with a negative recommendation. By contrast, if no "adverse" or "questionable" information developed, DISCO was authorized to grant the clearance. Evidence of homosexuality was one on a list of types of evidence that would trigger extended consideration and negative recommendations to DISCR. DISCO did not consider adverse evidence of nonmarital heterosexual activity unless it involved aggravating factors that might subject the individual to blackmail. DISCR would then consider the application and make a determination whether to grant a security clearance. If it denied a clearance, it would send a written reason for the denial to the applicant, who had an opportunity to apply in writing and to demand a hearing. The Defense Department maintained a central index record of all security clearance cases, including an indication whether the Investigative Service had investigated the applicant.

This system had significant negative consequences for lesbians and gay men whose professional training involved science and technology. Since many of the best-paying and most intellectually challenging positions in science and industry included some work on Defense Department contracts, the need for a security clearance was virtually a routine job qualification. Any government procedure that would subject lesbian and gay applicants to extended investigations, frequently culminating in denial of clearances for reasons that would strike most people outside the security establishment as absurd, could have a major adverse effect on job opportunities and career advancement. While the typical security clearance procedure that did not involve adverse evidence could be concluded successfully in a few months, applications from gay people could drag on for many months longer, and might not be resolved for more than a year. While some gay people did get the top-secret clearances necessary for the most challenging and well-paying work, they tended to be limited to those so deeply closeted and secretive about their sex lives that no trace of their homosexuality would come to the attention of investigators, or, alternatively, to those whose openness, combined with a strong reputation for technical excellence and a "straight and narrow" (i.e., either monogamously coupled or virtually celibate) lifestyle, gave so little ground for criticism that eventually the security establishment, usually at an advanced appeal stage, would give in and issue the clearance rather than be embarrassed by court proceedings.

Many gay people who worked in science and industry considered this situation intolerable. The medical profession had long since disavowed the attitudes about homosexuality that provided the foundation for these policies, having approved resolutions during the 1970s indicating that homosexuality was not a mental illness, and that gay people were not as such any less stable or responsible than heterosexuals. It was time for gay people to challenge the lingering prejudices. They formed an organization called "High Tech Gays" to advance the scientific and career interests of gay people in high technology fields, and called on veteran gay rights attorney Richard Gayer to initiate litigation challenging the current procedures.

The resulting suit was brought in the name of the organization and three of its members, Timothy Dooling, Joel Crawford, and Robert Weston, all of whom had individually tangled with the clearance system.

Dooling had accepted a job offer at Lockheed Missiles and Space Company, and applied for a secret clearance on May 2, 1983. On March 22, 1984, almost eleven months later, DISCO sent a memorandum to DISCR recommending that Dooling be denied a clearance. The memo by G. M. Crane, director of DISCO, indicated that DISCO was recommending denial of the clearance because of a "pattern of sexual perversion" as follows: "SUBJECT disclosed that he visits gay bathhouses, belongs to a gay organization and has homosexual activity with casual acquaintances. SUBJECT claims that he intends to inform his employer of his homosexuality and stated that he intends to continue his homosexual lifestyle in the future." On this basis, DISCO concluded that granting a clearance to Dooling "is not considered to be clearly consistent with the national interest." No other basis for denying the clearance was cited. Despite the recommendation, DISCR granted the clearance in May, about one year after Dooling's initial application. This process substantially delayed Dooling's ability to begin working.

Crawford had applied for a clearance in December 1981. After DISCO recommended that the clearance be denied, DISCR denied the clearance based on "homosexual activity and susceptibility to coercion." Crawford retained a lawyer to write to DISCR on his behalf, protesting the denial. DISCR initiated further investigations and uncovered a history of past drug use that it could use to justify the denial without reference to homosexuality.

Weston, also a Lockheed employee, applied in 1984 for a top-secret clearance required for a new job assignment. Because he indicated on his application that he was a member of High Tech Gays, Lockheed did not forward his application to DISCO, because Defense Department guidelines at that time indicated that an employer should not bother forwarding applications containing information about the applicant that would result in lengthy processing delays and the possibility that the clearance would be denied. The guidelines specified membership in homosexual organizations as the type of information that would have such a result. (Weston actually ended up suing Lockheed for refusing to pursue his application, but that suit was dismissed after the Defense Department changed its guidelines to avoid discouraging the submission of applications.)

The case was filed against DISCO in the federal district court in San Francisco, where it was assigned to Judge Thelton E. Henderson, who granted a motion to certify the case as a class action on July 3, 1985. The class was to consist of

> All gay persons who, since January 1982, have applied for, are now applying for, or may in the future apply for Secret or Top Secret industrial clearances from DISCO, in any of the eight DIS regions in the country, and all gay persons who, since January, 1982, have held, now hold, or may in the future hold such clearances.

The last portion of the certification was necessary because the lawsuit attacked not only the procedures under which DISCO allegedly subjected gay people to unequal procedures but also the Defense Department's retention of a central index identifying all those security applicants who had been subjected to a DIS investigation, which would include many members of the class. However, the plaintiffs dropped their demands regarding the central index issue in a subsequent amended complaint.

DISCO was represented at the trial stage by Assistant U.S. Attorney Stephen Schirle, of San Francisco. The parties filed cross-motions for summary judgment, submitting affidavits and making oral arguments. On August 19, 1987, Judge Henderson released a lengthy opinion, granting most of the plaintiffs' motions and denying most of the defendants' motions. In effect, Henderson held that DISCO's pro-

cedures violated the plaintiffs' rights to equal protection under the Due Process Clause of the Fifth Amendment and their rights of freedom of association under the First Amendment. He ordered DISCO to deal with applications from gays on an individualized basis instead of automatically subjecting them to DIS investigations and adverse recommendations to DISCR.

Henderson began his opinion by quickly dispatching the defendants' arguments that the named plaintiffs lacked standing to bring suit. DISCO claimed that none of them had suffered the distinct and tangible personal injury required to present a case or controversy to the court. Henderson strongly disagreed, noting that not only did the lengthy process that DISCO unequally imposed on homosexuals subject them to employment disadvantages, but the very fact of unequal treatment had been identified by the U.S. Supreme Court in *Heckler v. Matthews* (1984) as being adequate by itself to create standing. "Plaintiffs have shown distinct and tangible personal injury caused by the stigma of unequal treatment," said Henderson.

The equal protection challenge presented the immediate question of the level of judicial review of DISCO's policies. Henderson reviewed the Supreme Court's three-tiered approach to equal protection analysis, most recently summarized by the Court in *City of Cleburne v. Cleburne Living Center* (1985). Where the equal protection challenge involves a "fundamental right" or a policy that uses a "suspect classification," the Court would apply strict scrutiny, requiring that the policy be "precisely tailored to serve a compelling governmental interest." If the challenge involved a policy that used a "quasi-suspect classification," heightened scrutiny was appropriate to determine whether the policy was "substantially related to a legitimate state interest." In the absence of a fundamental right or a suspect or quasi-suspect classification, the government was still required to provide some justification for a policy that treated similarly situated identifiable groups of people differently; such a policy had to be "rationally related to a legitimate state interest." Although governmental policies normally passed the rationality test without much trouble, in *Cleburne* the Court had indicated that this test was not without teeth. A policy solely motivated by prejudice or bias would not survive; there had to be some other, objective basis of support for the challenged discriminatory policy.

The continuing issue in litigation initiated by gays to redress discrimination was which tier of scrutiny would apply to their claims, a question the Supreme Court had not directly addressed. Henderson, focusing on DISCO's guidelines that treated as adverse any indication of homosexuality, contended that the policy used a "quasi-suspect classification," so that heightened scrutiny should apply. In *Cleburne*, the Court had identified the factors that would go into determining whether a particular policy affected a "suspect class." Henderson believed that applying these factors yielded a conclusion that gays should at least receive the level of constitutional protection provided in cases of gender discrimination: heightened scrutiny to determine whether the policy substantially advanced a legitimate state interest.

The Supreme Court's first factor was whether the classification involved an identifiable group that had been the subject of discrimination in the past. "Lesbians and gay men have been the object of some of the deepest prejudice and hatred in American society," asserted Henderson. "Some people's hatred for gay people is so deep that many gay people face the threat of physical violence on American streets today." Justice William J. Brennan, Jr., had concluded as much in his dissent from the Court's denial of *certiorari* in *Rowland v. Mad River Local School District* (1985), where he concluded that "discrimination against homosexuals is 'likely . . . to reflect deep-seated prejudice rather than . . . rationality,'" invoking the standard set by the Court in *Plyler v. Doe* (1982).

Wholly unfounded, degrading stereotypes about lesbians and gay men abound in American society [wrote Henderson]. Examples of such stereotypes include that gay people desire and attempt to molest young children, that gay people attempt to recruit and convert other people, and that gay people inevitably engage in promiscuous sexual activity. Many people erroneously believe that the sexual experience of lesbians and gay men represents the gratification of purely prurient interests, not the expression of mutual affection and love. They fail to recognize that gay people seek and engage in stable, monogamous relationships. Instead, to many, the very existence of lesbians and gay men is inimical to the family. For years, many people have branded gay people as abominations to nature and considered lesbians and gay men mentally ill and psychologically unstable.

Concluding that these "stereotypes have no basis in reality and represent outmoded notions about homosexuality," Henderson asserted that "the fact that a person is lesbian or gay bears no relation to the person's ability to contribute to society," thus making policies that discriminate against gay people suspect.

Furthermore, this "pervasive discrimination" made it very difficult for gays to achieve equal treatment through the political process. The very real fear of discrimination against them deterred large numbers of gay people from joining political movements to advance their rights, so they had to depend on the courts to protect them from discriminatory governmental policies.

Another reason for applying strict scrutiny to DISCO's policies, said Henderson, was that they "impinge upon the right of lesbians and gay men to engage in any homosexual activity, not merely sodomy, and thus impinge upon their exercise of a fundamental right." Arguing that the Supreme Court's 1986 opinion in *Bowers v. Hardwick* upholding the constitutionality of the Georgia sodomy law was concerned only with actual acts of sodomy covered by that law, anal or oral intercourse, Henderson argued that DISCO's broader concern with any "homosexual activity" went far beyond the issues decided in *Hardwick*. Indeed, the Defense Department's policy treated concealment of "sexual preference" in itself to be a "disqualifying factor," thus placing homosexual status at the center of its policy. *Hardwick* was about penalizing certain conduct, which only half the states now penalized, not about discriminating against people because of who they are. For Henderson, people retained a fundamental right to engage in acts of affection and human contact, even if the state could penalize "sodomy":

Hardwick does not hold, for example, that two gay people have no right to touch each other in a way that expresses their affection and love for each other. Nor does *Hardwick* address such issues as whether lesbians and gay men have a fundamental right to engage in homosexual activity such as kissing, holding hands, caressing, or any number of other sexual acts that do not constitute sodomy under the Georgia statute.

Henderson noted that the D.C. Circuit had recently held that *Hardwick* did not decide the equal protection question, in *Doe v. Cheney* (1989), and that a trial court in that circuit had applied heightened scrutiny to a discriminatory government decision involving a gay employee in *Swift v. United States* (1987). Insisted Henderson, "[I]t appears to this Court that the proper interpretation of *Hardwick* is that under the Constitution no person has a fundamental right to engage in sodomy, not that lesbians and gay men have no fundamental right to engage in other types of affectional or sexual activity." Indeed, since "the Constitution protects an individual's right to express attraction, affection or love for another human being through sexual activity that does not constitute the specific acts that the Supreme Court in *Hardwick* held are not entitled to Constitutional protection," DISCO's policy did invade the fundamental rights of gay security clearance applicants by premising adverse determinations on their engaging in such activities.

Realizing that he was bucking the trend of the circuits in taking the view that the case required heightened scrutiny, Henderson alternatively held that DISCO's policies did not even meet the rationality test. Invoking *Cleburne*'s requirement that the government provide some justification for unequal treatment even when no suspect classification or fundamental right was involved, Henderson held that "there is no rational basis for defendants' subjecting all gay applicants to expanded investigations and mandatory adjudications while not doing the same for all straight applicants." This unequal treatment reflected "irrational prejudice and outmoded stereotypes and notions . . . , not rational considerations." Henderson systematically rejected each of the government's arguments to justify automatic expanded investigations of gay applicants. First, contrary to the government's argument that gay people should be generally considered unwilling to obey the

law because of their sexual activities, Henderson noted that much of the activity in question was outlawed nowhere, and in half the states sodomy was legal.

All of the other government arguments centered in some way on the old notion that gays were inherently less reliable or were more vulnerable to subversion. Henderson held that these arguments were not sufficient because there was no proof to back them up. For example, he rejected the notion that homosexuals necessarily suffered "emotional tension, instability or other difficulties" due to societal discrimination, making them categorically more risky than others, invoking the resolutions passed by the medical professional associations refuting these views. That some gays might have these problems did not justify subjecting all gays to expanded investigations. Similarly, the blackmail arguments did not persuade Henderson, who noted that congressional investigations had not revealed any objective basis for the view that gay government employees were more susceptible to blackmail than heterosexuals. Henderson was particularly dismissive of the argument that gays should be singled out because, in at least half the states, their sex lives were subject to criminal prosecution. Pointing out that most sodomy law jurisdictions did not discriminate between heterosexual and homosexual sodomy, he contended that DISCO's policy of ignoring the sexual activities of consenting heterosexuals while scrutinizing gays was irrational, since sodomy was unlawful in either case. As he had previously noted, gays might engage in a wide range of lawful sexual activities, but the policy presumed they were vulnerable to blackmail regardless of the nature of their activities. "Defendants' policy represents a simplistic approach to complex issues regarding national security and potential blackmail and is not founded on any rational basis," he insisted. "All people have aspects of their lives, often private consensual sexual activities, that they prefer to keep private. This fact does not mean that those people would be susceptible to blackmail if someone were to learn of the private information." Finally, it was not adequate to point out that DIS investigates some allegations of heterosexual misconduct, since DISCO considered all homosexual activity to be "misconduct," quite a different standard. Henderson concluded that no matter what standard of review was used, DISCO's policy failed the equal protection test.

Throwing a bone to DISCO, however, he granted summary judgment against the plaintiffs on the theory that DISCO's policy also violated procedural due process rights. Since rejected gay applications had a right to appeal, have their cases heard, and examine witnesses, Henderson found no procedural defect.

Finally, as to the First Amendment claim, Henderson found that DISCO's policy of considering membership in a gay organization adverse information that would trigger an expanded investigation to constitute a distinct violation of constitutional rights of association. "All citizens have first amendment rights to belong to lawful associations," he asserted. Any governmental actions that would "impair" such rights must survive "exacting" scrutiny. Henderson found that DISCO's use of gay organization membership as a triggering mechanism could not survive such scrutiny, since it was "clearly not the least restrictive means to achieving the governmental interests in protecting national security." No inference as to an individual's trustworthiness or loyalty to the United States could be drawn from mere organizational membership.

As to the individual claims of plaintiffs, Henderson granted summary judgment to Dooling and Crawford with respect to their claims of sexual orientation discrimination, but granted judgment to DISCO regarding Crawford's disqualification for drug use. Henderson issued injunctive relief ordering DISCO to stop subjecting gay applicants to expanded security investigations. The government promptly petitioned for a rehearing to introduce new evidence it claimed had developed between the oral argument and Henderson's decision. In the interim, a sex and espionage scandal at the U.S. Embassy in Moscow involving heterosexual marine guards had produced testimony verifying that the KGB, the Soviet Union's leading spy agency, targeted gay American government employees for subversive activities. One of the marines testified at his court martial that a Russian agent asked whether any of his colleagues were homosexu-

als. Henderson rejected the motion, but agreed to grant a stay of his opinion while the case went to the Ninth Circuit on appeal. The appeal was argued on December 16, 1988, with Jay S. Bybee of the Justice Department's appellate staff arguing for the government and Gayer representing High Tech Gays and the plaintiff class. The court received amicus briefs in support of High Tech Gays from Matthew A. Coles for the American Civil Liberties Union of Northern California and Stephen V. Bomse as cooperating attorney for National Gay Rights Advocates, a San Francisco-based public interest law firm.

The Ninth Circuit announced its decision reversing Henderson's decisions in favor of High Tech Gays on February 2, 1990. In an opinion by Circuit Judge Melvin Brunetti, the court held that the only correct standard of judicial review here was the rationality standard, which it believed that the government had clearly met, and that there was no unconstitutional burden on the association rights of gay security clearance applicants.

Brunetti reached these conclusions by adhering to the interpretation of *Hardwick* that had been followed in recent cases by the Seventh and D.C. circuits, with an additional twist that subsequently earned a pointed rebuke from another member of the Ninth Circuit, Judge William C. Canby, Jr., who dissented from the circuit's refusal to grant *en banc* rehearing. Noting that this was a case brought under the Fifth Amendment Due Process Clause rather than the Fourteenth Amendment Equal Protection Clause, which was applicable only to actions by the individual states, Brunetti argued that *Hardwick* was totally controlling. *Hardwick* was a "due process" case, in that the asserted right of privacy by which *Hardwick* sought to challenge the Georgia sodomy law was based on the Fourteenth Amendment's Due Process Clause. In this case, High Tech Gays was challenging DISCO's policy based on the Fifth Amendment Due Process Clause. Since the Court had held that there was a rational basis to criminalize "homosexual activity," no due process argument could be used to attack any government policy that imposed adverse consequences on "homosexual activity." "If for federal analysis we must reach equal protection of the Fourteenth Amendment by the Due Process Clause of the Fifth Amendment," said Brunetti, "and if there is no fundamental right to engage in homosexual sodomy under the Due Process Clause of the Fifth Amendment, it would be incongruous to expand the reach of equal protection to find a fundamental right of homosexual conduct under the equal protection component of the Due Process Clause of the Fifth Amendment." This tortured reasoning totally neglected the Supreme Court's own statement in *Hardwick* that it was not deciding any equal protection issues in the case, as well as casting aside without any substantive discussion all distinctions between equal protection and due process jurisprudence.

As to the Supreme Court's factors for determining whether a legislative classification was suspect, the court disagreed with Henderson on two out of the three factors. While conceding that homosexuals had been subjected to a long history of discrimination, Brunetti said they would not qualify for heightened protection under equal protection theory because "homosexuality is not an immutable characteristic; it is behavioral and hence is fundamentally different from traits such as race, gender, or alienage, which define already existing suspect and quasi-suspect classes." Furthermore, noting that gays had achieved some victories in recent years in getting cities and states to ban sexual orientation discrimination, Brunetti dismissed the contention that gays constituted a politically powerless minority that was not capable of defending its interests through the normal rough and tumble of representative democracy.

Since rationality review was to be used, said Brunetti, and government actions are presumed rational unless shown otherwise, the burden was on High Tech Gays to show that DISCO's policies were irrational, and the burden had not been met. Brunetti appeared to base this assertion heavily on the evidence that Henderson had refused to receive when he denied the government's motion to reopen the case as a result of the revelations from the Moscow Embassy scandal. Now that there was "credible" evidence to back up the view that the Russians targeted gays as people who might be subverted to gain intelligence information, there

was a rational basis for subjecting gay security clearance applicants to more searching scrutiny. Given the allocation of proof, he said, it was not determinative that the government could not present firm evidence that gay employees had been blackmailed into subversive activities in the past. It was enough for the Defense Department to show that it had a rational basis for believing there might be a problem in the future. For this, the government had only to show that gays were targeted, not that they were targeted successfully.

> The [Defense Department] has determined what groups are targeted by hostile intelligence efforts. If an appellant falls within a targeted group—like homosexuals—the [Defense Department] subjects the applicant to an expanded investigation. The expanded investigation determines whether the applicant is susceptible to coercion or otherwise vulnerable to hostile intelligence efforts.

All quite rational, asserted Brunetti. The government was not discriminating against gays, rather it was using its discretionary judgment to protect national security. "No one has the 'right' to a security clearance," said Brunetti. "Inexact science or not the [Defense Department] has articulated a rational relationship between their [sic] policy of subjecting homosexual applicants to expanded investigations and its compelling interest in national security." This was enough to justify the policy, and the court did not need to get into the question whether gays were emotionally more vulnerable than others; it was enough that they were targeted, and "the counterintelligence agencies' reasons for targeting homosexuals—even if based on continuing ignorance and prejudice— are irrelevant." If gays were targeted, the Defense Department "must be assured that because of the targeting, the individual will not compromise national secrets."

The challenge based on the First Amendment was equally unavailing. DISCO was not basing its decisions "solely" on membership in gay organizations, said Brunetti. Membership in a homosexual organization was merely one factor on the list of factors that might lead to an expanded investigation to determine whether the individual merited a security clearance. Since High Tech Gays had not "shown membership in a gay organization to be a distinct, separate, abstract ground for denying security clearances," its claim in this regard was baseless.

Noting that Dooling had eventually been awarded his clearance and Crawford's had ultimately been denied for reasons not having to do with his sexuality, the court concluded that neither man was entitled to individual relief. The court reversed the portions of Henderson's decision finding for High Tech Gays, and remanded the case for further proceedings consistent with its decision. Gayer filed a petition for rehearing and rehearing *en banc*, which was denied by the panel and the circuit. However, two members of the circuit, Judges William A. Norris and William C. Canby, Jr., dissented from the denial of rehearing *en banc* in a lengthy opinion by Judge Canby arguing that sexual orientation should be treated as a suspect classification for equal protection analysis under the Fifth Amendment.

Norris and Canby made up the majority of the three-judge panel that had ruled the Defense Department's antigay policies unconstitutional in *Watkins v. United States Army* (1989), and they had concurred separately in the *en banc* circuit decision to order Watkins's reinstatement, continuing to argue that the case should be disposed of on the merits rather than by the merits-avoiding strategem of estoppel that the circuit had used in that case. They reiterated the same arguments here, aiming their fire particularly at the overly generalized assertions in Brunetti's panel opinion about the precedential effect of *Hardwick* and DISCO's national security rationale for treating gays differently from other applicants.

"The class of 'homosexuals' clearly qualifies as a suspect category, triggering strict judicial scrutiny of any governmental discrimination against them," insisted Canby, charging that the panel had improperly applied the Supreme Court's second and third criteria for identifying suspect classifications.

For one thing, the Supreme Court had never specified "immutability" as a defining characteristic of a suspect classification. Rather, the Court had specified that a class, to be suspect, must "exhibit obvious, immutable, or distinguishing characteristics that define [it] as a discrete group." "The real question," said Canby, "is whether discrimination on the basis of the class's distinguishing characteristic amounts to an unfair branding or resort to prejudice, not necessarily whether the characteristic is immutable." In any event, for purposes of this analysis it was appropriate to consider homosexuality immutable. "It is not enough to say that the category is 'behavioral.' . . . The question is, what causes the behavior? Does it arise from the kind of a characteristic that belongs peculiarly to a group that the equal protection clause should specially protect?" For Canby, the answer was clearly yes, since sexual identity is, in his view, "not a matter of conscious or controllable choice," and for all practical purposes not changeable through voluntary effort.

Canby also disputed the panel's assertion that homosexuals had adequate access to the political process. Despite isolated legislative victories on the state and local levels, gays were politically powerless, particularly compared with blacks or women, as to whom the Court was willing to apply heightened scrutiny despite their success in achieving federal and state civil rights protection and winning elections to thousands of legislative positions at all levels of government.

"Homosexuals, then, are exactly the kind of class that should trigger strict scrutiny," said Canby, arguing that the panel's decision, by denying that protection, "creates the opportunity for immense abuse." He also found most unfortunate the panel's misconstruction of *Hardwick* and its impact on the equal protection issue. Observing that the panel's analysis of the equal protection question seemed to "collapse" the fundamental rights and suspect class issues into one issue because the equal protection claim was being asserted as against the federal government through the Fifth Amendment's Due Process Clause rather than through the Fourteenth Amendment's Equal Protection Clause, Canby argued that the constitutional textual source "makes no difference." The Supreme Court had made clear that equal protection rights under the Fifth Amendment were identical to those derived from the Fourteenth in *Weinberger v. Wiesenfeld* (1975). He also rejected the panel's contention that because it was constitutional to criminalize sodomy, it was constitutional to discriminate against homosexuals. This relied on an improper reading of *Hardwick*, which had held that it was constitutional for a state to ban sodomy and to prosecute homosexuals for violating that ban. The Court had held that homosexuals did not have a fundamental right to engage in anal or oral sex. For Canby, "All *Hardwick* established was that a homosexual had no fundamental right to violate the sodomy laws—laws that presumably apply (as they are written) to others not protected by the marital right [of privacy]." He analogized to the Court's recent decision in *Employment Division v. Smith* (1990), holding that a state law criminalizing the use of peyote did not violate the free exercise rights of Native Americans who wished to use peyote in religious ceremonies, pointing out that in neither instance did the Court's opinion give government free license to legislate against homosexuals or Native Americans as such. "The equal protection question of a suspect classification cannot be answered by the mere absence of a fundamental right," he insisted; "they are different issues. The equal protection issue can be fully addressed only by examining the class discriminated against, to see whether it bears the traditional indicia of suspectness," which, for him, homosexuals clearly do.

Finally, Canby pointed out the panel's failure to grasp Judge Henderson's distinction between "homosexual acts" and "sodomy." The Supreme Court had upheld criminal penalties only with regard to anal and oral intercourse, but had not ruled on the wide variety of other sexual activities in which homosexuals might engage. "It is an error of massive proportions to define the entire class of homosexuals by sodomy," he declared. While it was probably true that homosexuals, as a group, were more likely than not to engage in sodomy, "homosexuality, like heterosexuality, is a status. As an amicus [National Gay Rights Advocates] points out, one is a homosexual or a heterosexual while playing bridge just as much as while engaging in sexual activity." The Defense Department was not aiming its policy solely at persons who committed sodomy. Rather, it was "making the unsupported assumption that homosexuals are more likely to betray their country than other classes of persons," and was discriminating against them on that basis.

Even if one were left to review this policy under the rationality test, however, Canby would disagree with the panel's result, since he saw nothing in the record to suggest that a policy subjecting all homosexuals to expanded investigations had any rational justification. The government's argument really boiled down to its contention that the targeting of homosexuals for exploitation by agents of hostile nations (because the foreign agents perceived homosexuals to be vulnerable to blackmail due to prejudice against them in American society) meant that they should not be granted clearances until after an exhaustive special investigation. Or, as Canby rephrased it, "if our society treats a group unfairly, then our government is justified in treating that group even more unfairly because the KGB will seek to exploit the 'outcast' feelings of that group." Asked Canby, "Who is going to break the discriminatory cycle if we don't?" This was the height of irrationality, said Canby: "Thus, even if the KGB's policy *never works*, gays and lesbians may be subjected to stricter standards of examination for security clearances than other groups, just because the KGB (perhaps indulging in some stereo-typical prejudices of its own) incorrectly assumes homosexuals to be less loyal than other citizens."

The historical record showed that it was irrational for the KGB to target gays, since there was little evidence that gays in any numbers had betrayed their country at the urging of foreign agents. The Defense Department's own Crittendon Committee Report from the 1950s, at the height of Red Hysteria and McCarthyism, had concluded that gays as such were not greater security risks than heterosexuals. Besides, said Canby, the government's argument was an afterthought, since it was first made in detail on the motion to Judge Henderson to reopen the case.

For Canby, the active rationality review established in *Cleburne* would clearly overcome this governmental justification. In that case, the Supreme Court had rejected fear and conjecture as a basis for imposing special barriers for a license to open a group home for the mentally retarded, even though it held that the mentally retarded were not a suspect class. Similarly here, said Canby, the real basis for

DISCO's policy seemed to be fear and conjecture with little support in reality.

The Ninth Circuit's opinion in *High Tech Gays* was not appealed to the Supreme Court. By 1990, the Court had become so conservative that legal advocates for lesbian and gay rights were avoiding at all costs getting the Supreme Court involved in their cases. But there were signs that the public scolding the Defense Department had received from Henderson, Canby, and Norris was having some effect on the security establishment. In 1991, the CIA settled a pending suit by a lesbian on the basis that it would not make categorical judgments based on an applicant's homosexuality, and an internal memorandum from the Army surfaced during discovery in a case challenging the Naval Academy's expulsion of a gay midshipman, indicating that the Defense Department had already undertaken contingency planning for a policy change should it eventually lose a federal court challenge. Testifying before the House Budget Committee on July 31, 1991, Secretary of Defense Dick Cheney responded to questioning about the Defense Department's policies on homosexuality by saying that he had "inherited" these policies, and described as "a bit of an old chestnut" the notion that gays presented any sort of special security risk. (He virtually had to say this, since it was revealed at about the same time that one of the top officials in the Defense Department, with the highest security clearance, was gay and known to be so by most of his top-level colleagues.) It seemed only a matter of time before the security establishment might realize that the continuing legal battles were not worth the effort, particularly in light of a historic record that provided no tangible support for the policy it was exhaustingly defending at taxpayer expense.

Case References

Bowers v. Hardwick, 478 U.S. 186 (1986)

City of Cleburne v. Cleburne Living Center, 473 U.S. 432 (1985)

Doe v. Casey, 796 F.2d 1508 (D.C. Cir. 1986), certiorari denied, 487 U.S. 1223 (1988)

Doe v. Cheney, 885 F.2d 898 (D.C. Cir. 1989)

Employment Division v. Smith, 110 S. Ct. 1595 (1990)

Heckler v. Matthews, 465 U.S. 728 (1984)

Plyler v. Doe, 457 U.S. 202, rehearing denied, 458 U.S. 1131 (1982)

Rowland v. Mad River Local School District, 470 U.S. 1009 (1985)

Swift v. United States, 42 Fair Empl. Prac. Cas. (BNA) 787 (D.D.C. 1987)

Watkins v. United States Army, 875 F.2d 699 (9th Cir. 1989) (en banc), certiorari denied, 111 S. Ct. 384 (1990)

Weinberger v. Wiesenfeld, 420 U.S. 636 (1975)

Weston v. Lockheed Missiles & Space Co., 881 F.2d 814 (9th Cir. 1989)

98. WHAT IS THE ARMY'S RATIONALE FOR DISCRIMINATION?

Pruitt v. Cheney, 943 F.2d 989 (9th Cir. 1991), certiorari denied, — S. Ct. — (1992), reversing *Pruitt v. Weinberger*, 659 F. Supp. 625 (C.D. Cal. 1987).

The Reverend Dusty Pruitt's fight to win reinstatement in the U.S. Army Reserve, which continues at this writing, may provide a new opportunity for serious judicial scrutiny of the U.S. Department of Defense's policy of discharging all personnel discovered to be homosexual. Although a three-judge panel of the Ninth Circuit Court of Appeals had concluded by a vote of two to one in *Watkins v. United States Army* (1989) that the Defense Department policy violated the equal protection requirement of the Fifth Amendment of the Bill of Rights, a larger panel of Ninth Circuit judges had vacated that decision in 1989, ruling instead that Sergeant Perry Watkins was entitled to reinstatement because the Army had allowed him to reenlist several times during the 1970s despite his open and candid admission of his homosexuality on numerous occasions. The U.S. Supreme Court had refused to review that decision, but it was a decision that did not go to the underlying validity of the exclusionary policy, so *Pruitt*, held in abeyance by the court until the *Watkins* case could be resolved, won renewed attention, together with a case pending before the District of Columbia Circuit Court of Appeals challenging similar naval regulations.

Dusty Pruitt served with distinction in the U.S. Army during the final years of the Vietnam War, from January 1971 through July 1975, rising to the rank of captain. She left the active service to seek ordination as a Methodist minister, but remained an officer in the Army Reserve. In recognition of her continuing excellent service, the Army notified Pruitt on May 25, 1982, that she had been selected for promotion to the rank of major effective February 6, 1983. That promotion would not occur, however, because Pruitt's private life was becoming more and more public and would finally come to the Army's attention just days prior to the scheduled promotion.

Pruitt's ministry at an independent Christian church was not of a conventional sort. Most of the church's members were lesbian or gay, as was Pruitt herself. She had participated in religious marriage ceremonies with two women over the course of recent years, and she had become more outspoken about the rights of lesbians and gay men. On January 27, 1983, the *Los Angeles Times* published an interview with Pruitt headlined "Pastor Resolves Gay, God Conflict" in which she discussed the difficulties of reconciling her private and public lives as a lesbian, a military reserve officer, and a religious pastor. In the course of the interview, Pruitt mentioned her two marriage ceremonies and her military service.

The Army's reaction to this news was swift. Pruitt's promotion was promptly canceled and an investigation launched. Pruitt's reaction to these events was also swift. Contacting the Southern California branch of the American Civil Liberties Union (ACLU), Pruitt obtained legal representation and filed suit in the federal district court in Los Angeles, seeking injunctive relief against the Army's actions. Conceding in her complaint that she was a lesbian and that military regulations apparently required her discharge, Pruitt alleged that the Army was barred by the First Amendment from discharging her solely on the basis of her admissions in a newspaper article that she was a lesbian. The article did not state that she had engaged in any sexual activity, so she argued that the suspension of her promotion and the threatened discharge must be directed solely at her statements, and constituted an impermissible restriction on free speech. Pruitt's lawyers felt she was on strong ground here, since a federal district court in Wisconsin had ruled in 1980 in *BenShalom v. Marsh* that the discharge of an Army Reserve officer solely because she told a newspaper that she was a lesbian violated the First Amendment.

The Army moved to dismiss the case for failure to state a claim. District Judge William Gray denied the motion without prejudice, and stayed the action pending the Army's completion of its investigation, which had barely gotten under way. On April 17, 1984, the Army advised Pruitt that it would revoke her security clearance because it had developed "substantial evidence" that she was a "practicing homosexual" within the meaning of the Army regulation, which defined a homosexual as "a person, regardless of sex, who engages in, desires to engage in, or intends to engage in homosexual acts." Pruitt contested the decision to suspend her security clearance, writing to the Army on May 16, 1984, that she was "a homosexual," but that she did not believe that she was a security risk. "I cannot see what the matter of my being a homosexual has to do with my security clearance," she wrote.

The Army convened an administrative board for a hearing on September 7, 1985. The evidence received by the board included a copy of the *Los Angeles Times* article; Pruitt's federal court complaint (in which she stated that she was a homosexual); her letter of May 16, 1984, in which she reiterated that she was a homosexual; and a copy of her military record, which of course contained no information about her sexual orientation or activities but documented her excellent service record extending over more than ten years. Although Pruitt attended the hearing with her ACLU lawyer, she refused to testify. The board reached the only conclusion possible given the state of the record: Pruitt was a homosexual. Under the regulation, discharge was mandatory, and the board recommended that in light of the lack of any evidence of sexual conduct, Pruitt be honorably discharged. The Army Department accepted the board's recommendation and discharged Pruitt honorably on July 9, 1986.

Pruitt immediately revived her federal lawsuit and moved for summary judgment, arguing that there were no disputed facts and that the Army's action was illegal. The Army responded by moving again to dismiss the case for failure to state a claim. After considering the arguments from a team of ACLU attorneys on behalf of Pruitt and from a team of Justice Department lawyers on behalf of the Army, Judge Gray issued his decision dismissing the case on April 17, 1987. Without discussing the analysis of the First Amendment claim that had led District Judge Terence T. Evans to rule against the Army in *BenShalom*, Gray simply asserted that he was "unable to accept such an argument." After quoting in full the Army's official statement of reasons for its policy, which claimed that homosexuality "is incompatible with military service" and asserted without proof that the presence of homosexuals in the service would impair "the accomplishment of the military mission" by adversely affecting the maintenance of "discipline, good order, and morale," undermining "mutual trust and confidence among members" and so forth, Gray stated that "it makes little difference whether a person has committed homosexual acts, or would like to do so, or intends to do so" in light of the Army's policy statement.

> A person in one of the last two categories could reasonably be deemed to be just as incompatible with military service as one who engages in homosexual acts. Certainly, the morale factor could reasonably be considered to be the same, and the Army understandably would be apprehensive of the prospect that desire or intent would ripen into attempt or actual performance. The acknowledgement by the plaintiff that she is a homosexual is simply an admission that she comes within a classification of people whose presence in the Army is deemed by the Army to be incompatible with its above expressed goals.

Relying on the *BenShalom* decision and the absence of any evidence that she had engaged in actual homosexual conduct, Pruitt's lawyers had decided explicitly to raise only First Amendment issues in their complaint, although they also made a Fifth Amendment due process claim, asserting that the Army's action failed to

follow its own regulations. Gray did not expressly consider any other possible constitutional arguments in his decision. After quoting an excerpt from Judge Evans's *BenShalom* decision concerning the ability of the military to adjust to life without an antigay exclusionary policy, with which Gray stated some agreement, he asserted that the regulation held invalid by Evans was somewhat broader than the redrafted regulation that was being applied to Pruitt, thus distinguishing the cases. He concluded that "it is not for this Court to assess the wisdom of the Army's policy here concerned."

Pruitt appealed the dismissal, but her case quickly became entangled with the other litigation pending in the Ninth Circuit on this issue. The court of appeals heard oral arguments from ACLU cooperating attorney Mary Newcombe and Justice Department attorney E. Roy Hawkens and then placed the case on the shelf for several years as the circuit struggled first with *Watkins* and then with *High Tech Gays v. Defense Industrial Security Clearance Office* (1990), in which a three-judge panel upheld the Defense Department's practice of subjecting gay security clearance applicants to protracted investigations of their sexual activities. In *High Tech Gays*, the court rejected the argument that discrimination on the basis of sexual orientation warranted strict or heightened scrutiny under the equal protection doctrine. Referring to the Supreme Court's 1985 decision in *City of Cleburne v. Cleburne Living Center, Inc.*, the Ninth Circuit held that in the case of a classification that was not constitutionally "suspect," the Defense Department's policy could be upheld if there was a rational basis for it. The circuit court found such a rational basis in evidence that agents of foreign governments seeking disclosure of American military secrets targeted homosexual military personnel and contractor employees.

The Ninth Circuit panel in Pruitt's case called for reargument and new briefing in light of the circuit's decisions in *Watkins* and *High Tech Gays*, and finally rendered its decision on August 19, 1991. In a unanimous ruling, the court held that Judge Gray had correctly dismissed Pruitt's First Amendment claim, but that it was not proper to have dismissed the case entirely because the Army's policy raised equal protection problems that could not be resolved on a motion to dismiss in the absence of an evidentiary record. The court's opinion, by Circuit Judge William C. Canby (who had concurred with Circuit Judge William A. Norris's conclusion in *Watkins* that the Army's policy violated equal protection), suggested that the Army would have to come up with more than the unsubstantiated assertions in its regulations that homosexuality was "incompatible with military service" in order to defend its policy from constitutional attack.

Canby first addressed Pruitt's free speech argument. He found it to have been effectively refuted by the Seventh Circuit in its 1989 decision in *BenShalom*, which rejected District Judge Evans's 1980 holding that the policy violated the First Amendment. The problem, said Canby, was that Pruitt's denial of promotion and eventual discharge was not because of her speech, as such, but rather because of what her speech revealed about her. "Pruitt was discharged not for the content of her speech," said Canby, "but for being a homosexual." Canby found a "classical dichotomy between the punishment of speech and the punishment of conduct."

> Because she was not discharged for her conduct, Pruitt concludes that she was discharged for her speech. The Army, however, is not discharging members just for homosexual conduct, or even primarily for homosexual conduct. It is discharging members because of their *status* as homosexuals. The pertinent portion of the regulation is entitled "Separation for Homosexuality." A homosexual is defined not only as a person who commits homosexual acts, but as one who "desires to engage" in them. ... The Army did not discharge Pruitt because she spoke candidly about her sexuality to a newspaper. Nor did it discharge her for publicly expressing her views on a timely and controversial subject, or for demonstrating compassion for and association with homosexuals. The Army discharged Pruitt because she admitted to being homosexual, and [the regulations] require separation of homosexuals from the armed forces. That it was her homosexuality, and not her speech, that caused Pruitt to be discharged is apparent.

Thus, for Canby, the question was not whether the Army was free to discharge Pruitt for her speech, but rather whether it was free to discharge her solely because she was a lesbian.

Gray had not considered this issue. While it was true that Pruitt's complaint had not expressly raised any issue other than the speech issue, Canby asserted that it was improper for Gray to dismiss the case without considering alternative grounds for challenging the military's policy. Searching the complaint, Canby found that Pruitt had in effect made a claim that she was being discharged because of her status when she alleged that "the defendants do systematically remove homosexuals who are similarly situated to the plaintiff from the Armed Services of the United States and the United States Army on the basis of thoughts, speech and status." This was sufficient, in Canby's view, to satisfy the "notice pleading" policy of the Federal Rules of Civil Procedure, under which the defendant need merely be put on notice of the possible variety of claims that could be raised by the complaint. At a minimum, said Canby, Pruitt should be allowed to amend her complaint to state more fully an equal protection claim and then pursue such a claim at trial.

Turning to such a claim, Canby found that the Army had never denied that it discriminated on the basis of sexual orientation. Rather, the Army's claim had been that such discrimination was fully and conclusively supported by existing court decisions, such that the district court could dispose of the claim by granting a motion to dismiss. The matter had been so hashed over by the courts for the past twenty years that there was nothing more to argue about. But Canby did not accept this view. Looking back at the Ninth Circuit's leading precedents, he found that they either involved actual homosexual conduct by service members, as in *Beller v. Middendorf* (1980), the circuit's leading case on the issue, or had avoided the equal protection issue completely, as in *Watkins*. Furthermore, Canby asserted that *Beller* and related cases predated significant developments at the level of the Supreme Court in equal protection theory, which made it necessary to revisit the issue.

In 1984, the U.S. Supreme Court had ruled in *Palmore v. Sidoti*, a case concerning child custody in the context of an interracial marriage, that although the Constitution could not control the prejudices of private citizens, it could not tolerate such biases as sources of public policy and decisionmaking. "Private biases may be outside the reach of the law," said the Court, "but the law cannot, directly or indirectly, give them effect." In 1985, when it was considering the constitutionality of a zoning regulation that discriminated against group homes for the mentally retarded, the Court recalled this statement from *Palmore* and struck down the regulation (even though the Court did not consider mental retardation a "suspect classification") because it appeared that the regulation was motivated solely by biases and prejudices against mentally retarded people. In so doing, the Court in *City of Cleburne* gave new meaning to the traditional "rational basis test" used to evaluate situations where the government treated groups of people differently based on particular characteristics or classifications. The government would have to come up with some objective justification for differential treatment; it could not rest mainly on dislike or fear of the disadvantaged group.

Canby noted that it was this new "rational basis" approach that the Ninth Circuit had recently followed in *High Tech Gays*. Whereas earlier cases had accepted without much question the assertion by national security authorities that it was necessary to deny security clearances to homosexuals, the Ninth Circuit had relied in that case on factual testimony about the criteria used by foreign agents to target security clearance holders for attempted subversion. Canby saw an important distinction in this new approach when applied to the Army's regulation. It meant, at least, that the Army's policy could not be sustained merely by quoting the regulation, which asserted that homosexuals must be excluded because of a string of conclusory statements about the negative effect their inclusion would have. "We have before us only a complaint that has been dismissed for failure to state a claim," said Canby. "After *Palmore, Cleburne* and *High Tech Gays*, we cannot say that the complaint is insufficient on its face. Assuming that Pruitt supports her allegations with evidence, we will not spare the Army the task, which those cases imposed, of offering a rational basis for its regulation, nor will we deprive Pruitt of the opportunity to contest that basis."

The traditional doctrine of deferring to military judgments would not suffice to dispose of this case, either, said Canby. While it was true that the Supreme Court had directed the lower federal courts to defer to expert military judgments, it was impossible to determine whether deference was warranted in the absence of any factual record detailing the basis for the military judgment. "If we now deferred, on this appeal, to the military judgment by affirming the dismissal of the action in the absence of any supporting factual record," said Canby, "we would come close to denying reviewability at all." The past record of litigation over discharges of homosexuals made clear that such decisions were subject to judicial review, so the court would decline to engage in absolute deference as demanded by the Army.

The Army petitioned for rehearing and rehearing *en banc*, but both petitions were rejected by the Ninth Circuit on May 8, 1992. The circuit court noted that no member of the circuit had voted to request rehearing in the case, and issued a slightly revised version of its opinion, clarifying the prior opinion to make clear that the burden on the Army was to show a rational basis for its policy that is not based on the prejudice of others toward lesbians and gay men.

Thus, Dusty Pruitt's challenge was sent back to the federal district court for the development of a factual record on which a ruling as to the constitutionality of the Army's regulation could be based. The timing of this was crucial. A few months later in Washington, the federal district court dismissed a challenge to a similar naval regulation brought by Joseph Steffan, who had been expelled from the Naval Academy and drummed out of the service just weeks before his scheduled graduation after admitting that he was gay. While Steffan's attorneys perfected their appeal to the District of Columbia Circuit Court of Appeals, events were unfolding that would bring the Defense Department's policy into active disrepute. National media attention to the *Pruitt* and *Steffan* cases had contributed to a shift in public opinion, as leading pollsters now asserted that a clear majority of the public opposed the military exclusion. More significantly, internal Defense Department studies, disclosed in the course of discovery in the *Steffan* case, indicated that the sole basis for the continued exclusion was the military's fear that antigay defense personnel would not get along with gay personnel. Secretary of Defense Dick Cheney admitted as much in a congressional oversight hearing when he characterized the traditional suspicion of gays as "security risks" as an "old chestnut" that carried little weight. In public statements, both Cheney and General Colin Powell, chairman of the Joint Chiefs of Staff, indicated that the security concerns were no longer significant, but that they feared morale problems among prejudiced service members if openly gay people were allowed to remain in the service. If this became the Defense Department's only ground for defending the policy, however, it was clear from *Palmore* and *Cleburne* that the policy must fall because although the Constitution could not force individuals to abandon their personal prejudices, it could not, in the Supreme Court's words "tolerate them" or "give them effect" as a matter of government policy. In December 1992, the Supreme Court denied the government's petition for review, making it likely that Pruitt's case would be the vehicle for declaring the Defense Department's policy unconstitutional if the political branches did not moot the question first.

As the *Pruitt* case headed back to trial and the *Steffan* case headed to the court of appeals, the question was not whether the military policy would be declared unconstitutional, but rather when and by whom it would be ended: by the D.C. Circuit, by the Ninth Circuit, or by the political branches of government in response to the changing attitudes of the public? As Judge Evans had declared in *BenShalom* more than a decade earlier, comparing the current exclusion of gays to prior policies excluding or segregating women and members of racial minority groups: "The vital mission of the Army has withstood these changes in racial and heterosexual standards. It should be able to similarly withstand any changes necessary to live without the regulation found to be offensive by the court."

Case References

Beller v. Middendorf, 632 F.2d 788 (9th Cir. 1980), certiorari denied, 452 U.S. 905, 454 U.S. 855 (1981)

BenShalom v. Marsh, 881 F.2d 454 (7th Cir. 1989), certiorari denied, 110 S. Ct. 1296 (1990), reversing 489 F. Supp. 964 (E.D. Wis. 1980)

City of Cleburne v. Cleburne Living Center, Inc., 473 U.S. 432 (1985)

High Tech Gays v. Defense Industrial Security Clearance Office, 895 F.2d 563 (9th Cir. 1990)

Palmore v. Sidoti, 466 U.S. 429 (1984)

Steffan v. Cheney, 780 F. Supp. 1 (D.D.C. 1991), appeal pending

Watkins v. United States Army, 875 F.2d 699 (9th Cir. 1989), certiorari denied, 111 S. Ct. 384 (1990)

CHAPTER 7
EDUCATIONAL INSTITUTIONS

Sexuality and schools are a volatile combination. Few subjects are more likely to spark controversy than lesbian, gay, or transsexual teachers; lesbian and gay student groups; or sex education. Such issues have convulsed the entire nation (after Surgeon General C. Everett Koop recommended in 1986 that explicit education about homosexual practices be incorporated in the elementary school curriculum as part of AIDS education efforts), as well as entire states (when California voters were asked in 1980 to vote on a ballot proposition mandating the discharge of openly gay schoolteachers, and Oklahoma legislators subsequently passed such a law) and, of course, those communities where the activities of teachers or students have brought the issue to the fore.

Core constitutional questions under the First and Fourteenth amendments are addressed in the cases in this chapter. In the cases presented, the courts have had to balance the goals of public education with the constitutional claims of teachers and students who encounter disparate treatment based on their sexuality. Indeed, because the U.S. Supreme Court has been hesitant to address these questions in definitive rulings on the merits, the same issues seem to be litigated over and over again in different judicial circuits, and many of the most apparently solid and well-established principles do not appear to deter school administrators and government officials from reiterating discriminatory policies. In 1992, Alabama enacted a law mandating its state universities to deny recognition and financial support to lesbian and gay student groups and requiring the state's public schools to instruct their students that homosexuality is morally wrong and perverted behavior. The resulting lawsuit, immediately threatened by the American Civil Liberties Union, may prove the vehicle to bring many of these issues to the Supreme Court for a definitive ruling.

Educational Institutions: Readings

Dennis, D.I., and Harlow, R.E., "Gay Youth and the Right to Education," 4 *Yale Law & Policy Review* 446 (Spring-Summer 1986)

Editorial Staff, "On Toleration (Mandatory High School Assembly on Eradicating Prejudice Against Sexual Deviants)," 2 *Benchmark* 31–32 (January-February 1986)

Schneider-Vogel, M., "Gay Teachers in the Classroom: A Continuing Constitutional Debate," 15 *Journal of Law & Education* 285 (Summer 1986)

99. PUBLIC SCHOOLTEACHERS AND HOMOSEXUAL ACTS

Morrison v. State Board of Education, 1 Cal. 3d 214, 82 Cal. Rptr. 175, 461 P.2d 375 (1969), reversing 74 Cal. Rptr. 116 (App., 2d Dist. 1969).

Few cases involving homosexuality and employment have so perturbed the courts as those in which public schoolteachers challenge the efforts of administrators to remove them from the teaching profession for engaging in homosexual activity. In most such cases, regardless of the niceties of legal doctrine and theory, the teachers lose. However, in one of the early reported appellate decisions on the subject, *Morrison v. State Board of Education*, a teacher achieved landmark recognition by the closely divided California Supreme Court of the principle that teachers who engage in homosexual activity should not automatically be considered disqualified for employment in that profession.

Marc S. Morrison began experiencing homosexual feelings at the age of 13. These feelings persisted through his college years. He sought psychotherapy to cure this condition, and, feeling that he had it "under control," he obtained a teaching position during the 1950s. According to Morrison, he was able to suppress homosexual impulses and engaged in no homosexual activity until the spring of 1963. Then, at the age of 37, in the context of a long-standing friendship with a fellow male teacher in the Lowell Joint School District, these urges resurfaced at a moment of extreme tension.

Morrison had become quite friendly with Fred Schneringer and Schneringer's wife, who were going through significant marital and financial difficulties. Schneringer frequently stopped by Morrison's apartment to discuss his problems. These sessions apparently became quite emotional and for about a week in April 1963, became physical, although apparently the sexual activity did not go beyond cuddling and, perhaps, mutual masturbation, which was not a criminal offense in California at that time. In short, at a point of high emotional tension in his life, Fred Schneringer found consolation in the arms of Marc Morrison. The physical relationship never recurred after those few occa-sions during the one week in April, but apparently the memory of it continued to bother Schneringer, since a year later he went to the school authorities and told them about it. On being confronted with Schneringer's statements, Morrison resigned his position at Lowell on May 4, 1964. There the matter might have ended, but the Lowell school superintendent informed the California State Board of Education, which set in motion procedures to revoke Morrison's teaching license in August 1965.

A hearing officer for the board conducted an evidentiary hearing at which Morrison represented himself and candidly admitted the truth of Schneringer's allegations, while maintaining that under the circumstances he did not consider that he had done anything wrong. An investigator for the board testified that he found no evidence that Morrison had engaged in any homosexual activity after the brief episode with Schneringer, or that the episode had affected Morrison's ability to teach. Nonetheless, relying on the California Education Code, which authorized the state board to revoke the license of a teacher for "immoral or unprofessional conduct," the hearing officer found that Morrison's conduct with Schneringer was "immoral," despite Morrison's contention to the contrary, and recommend that his certification be revoked. The state board accepted this recommendation on March 11, 1966.

Morrison stewed about the matter for a while, and then decided to seek vindication. He retained Los Angeles attorney Melville B. Nimmer, who filed suit on his behalf in the Superior Court of Los Angeles County on February 14, 1967, seeking a writ of mandamus to compel the board of education to reinstate Morrison as a licensed teacher in the state of California. Deputy Attorney General Edward M. Belasco appeared on behalf of the board at the hearing before Superior Court Judge Ralph H. Nutter. The parties stipulated that the administrative hearing record be accepted by the court in lieu of a new factual hearing, and argued as to the significance of the factual findings. Nimmer contended that the Education Code provisions were unduly vague and that, in any event, it would offend due process to allow revocation of Morrison's license without a finding that his ability to teach had been impaired by the brief, private, consensual incident with Schneringer. Belasco argued that the hearing record supported the officer's findings of immoral conduct, which was all that was necessary under the Code to support revocation of a license, and that the California courts had not previously questioned the operation of the Education Code in like cases.

Nutter was persuaded by Belasco's arguments and denied the writ. He found that the record contained undisputed evidence of acts that "involved moral turpitude and constituted unprofessional conduct." Therefore, the board's action was correct "in that petitioner demonstrated he was unfit for service as a teacher in the California public school system" within the meaning of the Code.

Morrison appealed to the Second District Court of Appeal without success. In a decision issued on January 6, 1969, a three-judge panel of the court unanimously affirmed the trial judge. Presiding Justice Lester William Roth rejected the argument that the privacy of the acts in question, or their legality, bore any significance for the outcome of the case, since what was in question was "morality," not "legality." The Education Code specifically mandated the immediate discharge and license revocation of any schoolteacher convicted of a variety of crimes, including sodomy, apart from the provision on "immoral and unprofessional conduct." This must mean that the broader provision included conduct that was not criminal but nonetheless considered immoral. There could be little doubt, asserted Roth, that homosexual conduct was immoral. It was irrelevant that the record contained no evidence "that the homosexual character of petitioner did in any manner affect petitioner's capacity, ability and willingness to perform in a satisfactory manner as a teacher or had any effect at any time on any pupils taught by him." The board had a "legitimate interest in maintaining the integrity of the schools and protection against potential influences on impressionable pupils who may be affected by the conduct of its teachers outside of the classroom."

Morrison had argued that implicit in the board's action was its belief that a homosexual teacher, as such, could not be trusted with children and was inherently more "dangerous" than a heterosexual. In his brief, Nimmer cited numerous medical and sociological authorities to support the argument that a homosexual teacher did not necessarily present any more danger in that connection than a heterosexual one. Roth said the court would refrain from getting into that issue, since on the face of the record there was no evidence that the trial court had relied on any such factual assumption. Indeed, "we think that one can properly assume that if appellant were a heterosexual and that if the conduct here complained of and made public were committed with the wife of some member of the faculty, that the right of the State Board to proceed and act would be no different."

Morrison appealed to the California Supreme Court, which granted review on March 12, 1969. The court divided sharply over the proper disposition of the case, voting four to three to remand the matter to the trial court for further proceedings, after narrowly redefining the operation of the Education Code provision on "immoral or unprofessional conduct." The court's opinion of November 20, 1969, by Justice Mathew Tobriner, concluded that the Code could be applied to revoke the license of a homosexual teacher, but only on a showing that he had actually engaged in conduct that rendered him unfit to teach, and that the evidence in the record was insufficient to meet the board's burden of proof on this issue.

Tobriner began his analysis of the case by focusing on an appropriate interpretation of the phrases "immoral conduct," "unprofessional conduct," and "acts involving moral turpitude," the last of which appeared in a separate provision of the Education Code authorizing local school boards to discharge teachers. He noted that similar language was strewn through California statutes dealing with the licensing or employment of a wide range of professionals, including lawyers, doctors and other personal service providers, and teachers and other government employees. Surely, the legislature could not have meant exactly the same thing when it used these words in the vast array of licensing statutes, since each profession presented different issues with regard to moral fitness depending on the manner in which the practitioner served clients, patients, or the public.

Reviewing cases involving lawyers, for example, it appeared that not every action that might be deemed "immoral" in the abstract had been held relevant to fitness to practice law, since the main concern of the legislature there must be with conduct reflecting on honesty as opposed to sexual probity. Similarly, referring to the 1969 U.S. court of appeals' decision in *Norton v. Macy*, involving a homosexual federal civil servant in the District of Columbia, Tobriner described the approach of the California courts as similar to that of the federal court, which had asserted that labeling particular conduct as "immoral" was not determinative of the ultimate question whether the employee was unfit for continued employment. Said Tobriner:

> Terms such as "immoral or unprofessional conduct" or "moral turpitude" stretch over so wide a range that they embrace an unlimited area of conduct. In using them, the Legislature surely did not mean to endow the employing agency with the power to dismiss any employee whose personal, private conduct incurred its disapproval. Hence the courts have consistently related the terms to the issue of whether, when applied to the performance of the employee on the job, the employee has disqualified himself.

In this case, therefore, those terms must be construed in light of the issue whether the teacher was unfit to teach. "Without such a reasonable interpretation," Tobriner said, "the terms would be susceptible to so broad an application as possibly to subject to discipline virtually every teacher in the state," since some people considered "laziness, gluttony, vanity, selfishness, avarice, and cowardice" to be "immoral conduct." Recent studies undertaken by the state legislature had uncovered widely differing opinions among educators themselves as to what conduct might come within the description of the Education Code. "We cannot believe that the Legislature intended to compel

disciplinary measures against teachers who committed such peccadillos if such passing conduct did not affect students or fellow teachers," Tobriner asserted, implicitly rejecting Court of Appeal Judge Roth's contention that Morrison would necessarily have been subject to the same license revocation had he engaged in a brief petting affair with the wife of a faculty colleague. "One could expect a reasonably stable consensus within the teaching profession as to what conduct adversely affects students and fellow teachers," contended Tobriner, but "no such consensus can be presumed about 'morality,'" since moral standards were shifting and evolving phenomena. Giving too broad a reading to the authorization of discipline, discharge, or license revocation for immoral conduct vested altogether too much unbridled discretion in local school boards and the state board, and might, at the local level, lead to significantly different standards being imposed from one district to the next.

> We therefore conclude [said Tobriner] that the Board of Education cannot abstractly characterize the conduct in this case as "immoral," "unprofessional," or "involving moral turpitude" within the meaning of . . . the Education Code unless that conduct indicates that the petitioner is unfit to teach. In determining whether the teacher's conduct thus indicates unfitness to teach the board may consider such matters as the likelihood that the conduct may have adversely affected students or fellow teachers, the degree of such adversity anticipated, the proximity or remoteness in time of the conduct, the type of teaching certificate held by the party involved, the extenuating or aggravating circumstances, if any, surrounding the conduct, the praiseworthiness or blameworthiness of the motives resulting in the conduct, the likelihood of the recurrence of the questioned conduct, and the extent to which disciplinary action may inflict an adverse impact or chilling effect upon the constitutional rights of the teacher involved or other teachers.

These factors were held to be relevant only to the extent that they ultimately bore on the question of fitness to teach ("i.e., in determining whether the teacher's future classroom performance and overall impact on his students are likely to meet the board's standards").

Tobriner turned briefly to the question whether the statute, as construed, could be "constitutionally applied" to Morrison's case. While the statute as broadly construed by the board of education and the lower courts raised serious constitutional concerns, Tobriner found them to be totally vitiated by the narrowing construction he had adopted in this opinion. By requiring a specific showing that particular conduct had rendered a teacher unfit based on evidence of actual harm to students and colleagues, he believed that problems of vagueness or other due process concerns were eliminated. It was true that courts and commentators had contended in many cases and articles that the terms "immoral" or "unprofessional" or "moral turpitude" were in themselves void for vagueness. Just the same, once such terms received a limiting and narrowing construction from the state's highest court, they must be read so as to integrate that interpretation into their meaning. Thus, the question became whether the statute "as construed" was unduly vague or imprecise in giving too much discretion to its enforcers, in this case the local and state boards of education. Tobriner found that the new, narrow construction adequately reigned in the discretion of these authorities.

Tobriner last considered whether the hearing record supported the revocation of Morrison's license, in light of this limiting construction of the statute. He noted:

> [A]n individual can be removed from the teaching profession only upon a showing that his retention in the profession poses a significant danger of harm to either students, school employees, or others who might be affected by his actions as a teacher. . . . Accordingly, we must inquire whether any adverse inferences can be drawn from that past conduct as to petitioner's teaching ability, or as to the possibility that publicity surrounding past conduct may in and of itself substantially impair his function as a teacher.

Turning to the hearing record, Tobriner found virtually no negative evidence bearing on this question. The board had not presented any "medical, psychological, or psychiatric experts to testify as to whether a man who had had a single, isolated, and limited homosexual contact would be likely to repeat such conduct in the future." Furthermore, there was no evidence in the record on the question whether somebody of Morrison's "background" presented

more danger of "untoward conduct with a student" than would a heterosexual teacher. There was no evidence that Morrison was publicly promoting "improper conduct." In short, "the board failed to show that petitioner's conduct in any manner affected his performance as a teacher." As such, the hearing record could not possibly support the board's action or the action of the lower courts in upholding the board's action.

Furthermore, the board took its action years after the incident with Schneringer. Morrison's motivations "at the time of the incident involved neither dishonesty nor viciousness, and the emotional pressures on both petitioner and Schneringer suggest the presence of extenuating circumstances." There was also no evidence that the events of April 1963 had become so "notorious" that they would impair Morrison's ability to teach at Lowell six years later.

Referring again to *Norton v. Macy*, Tobriner asserted that there were significant factual similarities in the two cases, inasmuch as the "immoral" conduct alleged against Norton was conceded by his federal employer to have caused no difficulties in the work place or with fellow employees. "The employee had neither openly flaunted nor carelessly displayed his unorthodox sexual conduct in public," commented Tobriner, and the agency sought to justify its action against him only based on its fear of future "embarrassment." The U.S. court of appeals had held that this was not enough to sustain a discharge; competent evidence of unfitness for the job was necessary.

In this case, the board of education was relying heavily on a court of appeal decision in *Sarac v. State Board of Education*, a 1957 case in which the court upheld the discharge of a public schoolteacher who had pleaded guilty to a criminal charge of disorderly conduct "arising from his homosexual advances toward a police officer at a public beach." In that case, the teacher had "admitted a recent history of homosexual activities," which the court found sufficient to justify the discharge. "The court's discussion in that case includes unnecessarily broad language suggesting that all homosexual conduct, even though not shown to relate to fitness to teach, warrants disciplinary action. The proper construction of [the Education

Code], however, as we have demonstrated, is more restricted than indicated by this dicta in *Sarac*, and to the extent that *Sarac* conflicts with this opinion it must be disapproved," said Tobriner.

Although the superior court in this case had "found" that Morrison was "unfit," that finding might well be based on the "erroneous dicta" from *Sarac*. It should not be considered final, particularly in light of the factual hearing record. That record, as Tobriner had shown, contained virtually no evidence by the board of education going to the issue of fitness, unless one concluded that any conduct that might be labeled "immoral" was sufficient to find "unfitness."

Tobriner concluded his opinion with a brief apologia about the importance of eliminating "unfit elementary and secondary teachers," insisting that this opinion would not stand in the way of that process. But "the power of the state to regulate professions and conditions of government employment must not arbitrarily impair the right of the individual to live his private life, apart from his job, as he deems fit," asserted Tobriner.

> Moreover, since modern hiring practices purport to rest on scientific judgments of fitness for the job involved, a government decision clothed in such terms can seriously inhibit the possibility of the dismissed employee thereafter successfully seeking non-government positions. . . . That danger becomes especially acute under circumstances such as the present case in which loss of certification will impose upon petitioner "a 'badge of infamy,' . . . fixing upon him the stigma of an official defamation of character." [Quoting *Norton v. Macy*.]

This opinion did not mean that Morrison was necessarily entitled to receive his license back, said Tobriner. If the board felt that the necessary evidence existed on the crucial question, it could reopen the hearing and attempt to show that Morrison was actually unfit to teach, and, if Morrison were to be reinstated as a teacher, "the board also has at its disposal ample means to discipline petitioner for future misconduct."

> Finally, we do not, of course, hold that homosexuals must be permitted to teach in the public schools of California. As we have explained, the relevant statutes, as well as the applicable principles of constitutional law, require only that the board properly find, pursuant to the precepts set forth in this opinion, that an individual is not fit to teach. Whenever disciplinary action rests upon such grounds and has been confirmed by the judgment of a superior court following an independent review of the evidence, this court will uphold the result.

Tobriner's opinion drew two dissenting opinions, by Justices Raymond L. Sullivan and Louis H. Burke, in each of which Justice Marshall F. McComb concurred.

Sullivan argued strenuously that the lower courts and the board of education had done no more or less than was exactly required by the language of the Education Code, which he did not find vague or otherwise offensive to due process. As far as he was concerned, the legislature could properly condition a teaching license on moral conduct, regardless whether public or private, and there was ample basis in law and custom for the hearing officer to find that Morrison's conduct in April 1963 was immoral. Sullivan found the 1957 court of appeal decision in *Sarac* to be valid and on point, quoting from the *Sarac* opinion:

> Homosexual behavior has long been contrary and abhorrent to the social mores and moral standards of the people of California as it has been since antiquity to those of many other peoples. It is clearly, therefor, immoral conduct within the meaning of [the Education Code]. It may also constitute unprofessional conduct within the meaning of that same statute as such conduct is not limited to classroom misconduct or misconduct with children. . . . It certainly constitutes evident unfitness for service in the public school system within the meaning of that statute. . . . In view of appellant's statutory duty as a teacher to "endeavor to impress upon the minds of the pupils the principles of morality," and his necessarily close association with children in the discharge of his professional duties as a teacher, there is to our minds an obvious rational connection between his homosexual conduct on the beach and the consequent action of respondent in revoking his secondary teaching credential on the statutory grounds of immoral and unprofessional conduct and evident unfitness for service in the public school system of this State.

Sullivan rejected all attempts by the majority to distinguish the facts in *Sarac*. For Sullivan, the issue was not whether the acts took place in public or in private, consensually or otherwise. On the issue of morality, the question was whether they were "homosexual acts." "It would be fatuous to assume," he argued, "that such acts became reprehensible only if committed in public. One would not expect petitioner and Schneringer to commit the acts here involved . . . in full view of the citizenry." Sullivan also found no significant distinction in the criminal prosecution of *Sarac*, since it was clear that the Education Code applied to "immoral" acts, regardless whether they were also criminal.

Sullivan also found convincing the *Sarac* court's determination that homosexual acts involved "moral turpitude," which was authorized as a ground for discharge in the Education Code. Sullivan noted that the court had sustained disbarment of an attorney for acts of "moral turpitude" in *In re Boyd* (1957), and, compared with an attorney, whose work would not necessarily bring him into contact with impressionable children, a teacher should be held to, if anything, a higher standard of conduct.

> Quite apart from [the] statutory mandate [to teach students good morals], petitioner stood *in loco parentis*; his young charges looked to him as the person taking the place of their parents during school hours. They looked to him not only for explicit words of guidance but as an example of good conduct. Nevertheless, as the Board and the trial court determined, he not only was a potential danger to them because of his immoral acts but especially so because of his insistence that such acts which he frankly admitted, were not in his view immoral at all.

Pointing to these distinctions between the role of a teacher and the other professional and governmental roles that were the subject of cases discussed by Tobriner, Sullivan argued that those cases, such as *Norton v. Macy*, were essentially irrelevant. Here, the court was dealing with a teacher, and with a board of education that had exercised its professional expertise to determine that the conduct in question rendered Morrison unfit to teach. A reviewing court should not lightly intrude into such professional discretion, especially when the hearing record

"vividly" disclosed the performance of homosexual acts by the petitioner.

Sullivan could find no requirement in the Education Code for the kind of evidence that Tobriner demanded in his opinion for the court, and he felt that the court was stepping beyond its role as a reviewing body in demanding such evidence. He pointed out that neither Morrison nor his attorney had challenged the hearing record as insufficient, actually stipulating that it be introduced as the factual basis for the superior court's review, and that they made no attempt to introduce at the hearing level the kind of evidence Tobriner now required. (Sullivan deemed it irrelevant that Morrison was not represented by counsel at the hearing, since he could have exercised a right to counsel and freely chose to proceed without representation.) Sullivan was himself satisfied that the hearing record supported the factual findings of the hearing officer and the board of education.

Burke's dissent focused mainly on the procedural issues addressed by Sullivan. He concluded that the court's opinion was rendering a "ruling on a question of law" that "it was error to conclude that immoral or unprofessional acts were committed or that the acts that were committed involved moral turpitude." He could not agree with this result, finding that the board of education has "properly exercised the statutory discretion vested in it in this case and that its decision should be sustained on judicial review in any court of law." But the main focus of his attention was the rather active judicial review exercised by the majority, which he deemed neither constitutionally required nor appropriate. The trial courts were authorized to engage in the normal sort of "substantial evidence" reviews when considering administrative rulings, and this standard did not vary based on the particular agency whose acts were being reviewed. Such a standard was quite deferential to the agency, and ordinarily did not require the kind of searching, *de novo* review of the record that Tobriner seemed to be imposing here on the superior court. Burke could not agree that this was constitutionally required or appropriate.

The *Morrison* case was a significant victory for the right of homosexual persons, as such, to teach in California schools (despite Tobriner's express disclaimer of having ruled on that precise question). It was at the same time, however, a very limited victory, for there was considerable language in the opinion to suggest that it might be narrowly construed by subsequent courts, as indeed turned out to be the case. Morrison himself was a person who had struggled to contain his homosexual impulses and, to believe his testimony, allowed them to break through these restraints only once in all his years of teaching, for the relatively brief, and apparently quite innocuous, physical relationship with Schneringer. Reviewing the factors that Tobriner mentioned as being within the reasonable inquiry of the board of education in determining fitness, it was unclear that the Morrison decision would provide any assistance to a teacher such as Sarac, a "practicing homosexual" apprehended in a public solicitation incident. Since many such arrests occur on the flimsiest of evidence (often as little as the word of an undercover police officer eager to effect an arrest at the slightest sign of sexual interest from another man or even on the mere suspicion of such interest), and many of those arrested are so fearful of publicity that they plead guilty to avoid a trial, later California courts

frequently departed from the "spirit" of Morrison to emphasize the letter, limiting the case to its peculiar facts and arguing that any public homosexual conduct by a schoolteacher is sufficient basis to find unfitness.

On the other hand, the Morrison decision has been quite influential, both in California and in other jurisdictions, as a principled statement that affixing the label "homosexual" to a person does not end the inquiry or give rise to an automatic determination that the individual, as such, must be separated from government service, even when that service involves daily contact with elementary school age children. Together with Norton v. Macy, Morrison v. State Board of Education has become a leading case for the proposition that a government employer must show a rational basis for concluding that an employee's conduct has rendered that employee unfit to perform his or her job functions before the employee can be excluded from the job.

Case References

Boyd, In re, 48 Cal. 2d 69, 307 P.2d 625 (1957)

Norton v. Macy, 417 F.2d 1161 (D.C. Cir. 1969)

Sarac v. State Board of Education, 249 Cal. App. 2d 58, 57 Cal. Rptr. 69 (1967)

100. THE "CATCH-22" FOR GAY TEACHERS

Acanfora v. Board of Education of Montgomery County, 359 F. Supp. 843 (D. Md. 1973), affirmed, 491 F.2d 498 (4th Cir.), certiorari denied, 419 U.S. 836 (1974).

Joseph Acanfora, III, enrolled at Penn State University in the fall of 1968. He loved science and determined to pursue a career in meteorology. By his junior year, he decided he would prefer to pursue his scientific interest in a career where he could work with people, and switched to an education major. At the same time, gay students at Penn State responded to the 1969 Stonewall Riots in New York and subsequent rise of a movement for gay rights by forming a student gay rights organization in the fall of 1970. Acanfora joined the group and became its treasurer.

In January 1971, the gay students petitioned the university for official recognition. Although the student government voted affirmatively, the university administration refused to extend official recognition. The gay students filed suit, with Acanfora as a named plaintiff. Acanfora participated in publicity for the suit, announcing he was gay and arguing that the state university's refusal to extend recognition was unconstitutional. During the spring term of 1972, Acanfora's senior year, he was suspended from a student teaching assignment by the dean of the College of Education expressly because he had publicly announced his homosexuality. Acanfora filed a lawsuit against the dean and was reinstated, receiving a satisfactory evaluation for his student teaching. Acanfora maintained, as he did throughout his subsequent ordeals, that he never discussed his homosexuality with his students or teaching colleagues, inside or outside the classroom.

Acanfora applied for teaching positions in several school systems. Recalling the difficulties he had encountered with the dean by being open about his homosexuality, he decided not to list his membership in Homophiles of Penn State on employment application forms, which routinely included a space for listing extracurricular activities and organization memberships. Acanfora was offered employment as a junior high school science teacher at Parkland Junior High School by the Montgomery County, Maryland, school district for the 1972–73 school year.

Because he had applied for teaching positions in both Pennsylvania and Maryland, Acanfora applied for teaching certification in both states. There was no problem with the Maryland certification process, but the Pennsylvania board that was to determine whether an applicant had the "good moral character" necessary for certification was evenly split on Acanfora due to his openness about being gay, and the matter was referred to John Pittenger, the Pennsylvania secretary of education, for final decision. Meanwhile, Acanfora began teaching eighth grade earth science classes in the Montgomery County junior high school, and early reports on his teaching were positive.

On September 22, 1972, Secretary Pittenger called a news conference to announce that he would grant certification to Acanfora. The newsworthy event led to articles in the *New York Times* and the *Washington Post*, which brought the fact of Acanfora's sexual orientation to the attention of Montgomery County school officials for the first time. Deputy Superintendent Donald Miedema, after consulting some colleagues and board of education members, transferred Acanfora to a nonteaching position with no reduction in salary, pending an investigation, which apparently consisted of a brief discussion with the school system's psychiatrist. As Miedema later testified, the board

of education would not "knowingly hire a homosexual." Although there were no complaints about his classroom performance and no allegation that he had said anything about homosexuality to students or to colleagues, Acanfora was denied reinstatement to the classroom. Some students and faculty rallied in support of Acanfora, signing petitions calling for his reinstatement, and newspaper and television reporters called him for interviews. Stories appeared in many newspapers, and Acanfora submitted to interviews that ran on public television, local news programs, and the national news broadcast of *60 Minutes*. The substance of the media reporting focused on Acanfora's statements that he did not discuss homosexuality with his students or colleagues and believed that his removal from the classroom violated his constitutional rights. The school board refused to reinstate him and refused to renew his contract at the end of the school year.

Acanfora filed suit against the school board and the top administrators of the Montgomery County school district under 42 U.S.C. section 1983, claiming that the school board's actions violated his rights to freedom of speech, due process, and equal protection. The case was assigned to District Judge Joseph H. Young, who issued a wide-ranging opinion on May 31, 1973, finding that the school board's policy of refusing to employ homosexuals was unconstitutional, but that Acanfora should not be reinstated because of the notoriety generated by his media appearances. Attorneys Michael H. Gottesman and Darryl J. Anderson, of Washington, and Rob Ross Hendrickson, of Baltimore, represented Acanfora, while Robert S. Bourbon, of Rockville, and Alan I. Baron, of Baltimore, represented the defendants.

The central factual issue that concerned Judge Young was whether Acanfora's employment as a junior high school earth science teacher was likely to have a deleterious impact on the students attending Parkland Junior High. The school district produced two expert witnesses, both professors of pediatrics, who testified that the presence of a known homosexual teacher in a classroom of impressionable students could sway students with bisexual tendencies, or whose sexuality was not yet firmly established, to become gay. These experts testified that the school's goal should be to prevent students from becoming homosexual if at all possible, since the stigma imposed on homosexuals by society might lead to mental and emotional problems for the individual. Acanfora's experts, who included a professor of pediatrics, an instructor in family psychology, and one of the nation's leading sex researchers, Dr. John Money of Johns Hopkins University, sharply contradicted the district's experts, arguing that sexual orientation is determined in the first five or six years of life and that an eighth grade teacher's "role model" effect would be negligible in the determination of students' sexual orientation. On the contrary, argued Money and Acanfora's other expert witnesses, the presence of an openly gay teacher might be beneficial to gay and bisexual students, since he might serve the function of showing students that a homosexual can meaningfully participate in society.

Judge Young also received in evidence a copy of the 1972 Final Report and Background Papers produced by the National Institute of Mental Health Task Force on Homosexuality, under the leadership of Dr. Evelyn Hooker, one of the first social scientists to attempt unbiased scientific study of homosexuals outside the context of mental institutions or the clients of mental health professionals. The Task Force's report stressed a multifactorial model for the etiology of human sexuality, under which no one factor was accorded decisive weight. The report recommended a reassessment of antigay employment policies, although it did not specifically address the issue of public schoolteachers. There were some dissenting votes on the Task Force from those who asserted that existing scientific evidence did not provide a firm enough basis to support the Task Force's conclusions.

Young concluded from this conflicting expert testimony that "it would be premature to state definitively that Acanfora's presence in the classroom will have no deleterious effect. . . . A finding that sexual orientation is in large part predisposed by age five or six does not preclude an incremental effect of a teacher on a bisexual adolescent." Finding that the "danger" to students was probably much less than the defendants contended, Young nonetheless believed

it was "not illusory," and that Acanfora's employment as an eighth grade earth science teacher would pose "sensitive problems, both for relationships among students and between students and parents."

Nonetheless, Young determined that a policy forbidding employment of homosexuals as schoolteachers would be unconstitutional, because, in his view, it would violate important rights of due process and equal protection.

The Due Process Clause of the Fourteenth Amendment requires that the states not deprive their residents of liberty without due process of law. After reviewing the U.S. Supreme Court's leading cases on protection of individual liberty under the Due Process Clause, Young asserted:

> As autonomous and rational beings, individuals are capable of reasoned decisions in pursuit of chosen goals. Given man's imperfect knowledge, full freedom of thought and association is imperative for individual self-development and social progress. So long as the freedoms of others are not affected, a government intended to promote the life, liberty and happiness of its citizens must abstain from interference with individual pursuits, no matter how unorthodox or repulsive to the majority.

Invoking the then-recent sexual privacy decisions concerning contraception and abortion, Young proclaimed, "In this context, the time has come today for private, consenting adult homosexuality to enter the sphere of constitutionally protectable interests. Intolerance of the unconventional halts the growth of liberty." While acknowledging that scientific debate continued about how to characterize homosexuality, Young concluded that "it is undisputed, however, that homosexuality *per se* does not preclude successful job performance."

Invoking the Wolfenden Report from England and the American Law Institute's Model Penal Code, both of which recommended legalizing consensual sodomy, and recounting the lack of any reported prosecution under Maryland's sodomy law of adults engaged in consensual sex in private, Young argued that the persistence of sodomy laws probably violated the constitutional guarantees of liberty and privacy. For Young, mere nonenforcement of the law was not the answer, however.

It is no less true now than when written in 1859 [by John Stuart Mill] that although society no longer puts heretics and sinners to death, nor does it act so vigorously as to stamp them out, it cannot flatter itself as free from the stain of legal persecution. The *chief* harm in these laws is the perpetuation of social stigma, cramping mental development, cowing reason, and repressing human expression for fear of social disfavor.

Young concluded this section of his opinion with a call for tolerance of diversity. He then briefly argued that discrimination against homosexuals should be considered "suspect" under the Equal Protection Clause, relying principally on the then-recent opinion by Justice William J. Brennan, Jr., for a plurality of the Supreme Court in *Frontiero v. Richardson*, asserting that sex was a suspect classification. Recognizing that "from this, it does not necessarily follow that sexual preference is similarly 'suspect' as a classification," Young argued that "the broad thrust of the opinion of the Court substantially supports extrapolation." But recognizing that Justice Brennan's opinion might not provide enough grounding for applying strict scrutiny to the school board's policy, Young decided to evaluate it under the rational basis test, under which society's interest "in protecting children from themselves as they develop their ability to think and act independently in the surrounding culture" must be weighed against the principles of individual liberty he had just expounded. Here, Acanfora's claim ran up against the U.S. Supreme Court's recognition of the authority of school boards to require some restriction on the personal rights of teachers in achieving their important social function.

Young asserted that "if Acanfora had admitted confidentially on his application that he is a homosexual, but that he had no intention of publicizing the fact, denial of employment for that reason would be unconstitutional. In this context, the Board of Education's policy of not knowingly employing any homosexuals is objectionable." Indeed, even when Acanfora's homosexuality became known due to the press conference held by Pennsylvania officials to announce his certification and the subsequent news coverage, because this publicity was not instigated by Acanfora, Young felt that Acanfora should not be taxed with responsibility for that publicity. "The cause of the publicity was, in the immediate sense, independent of plaintiff's speech and action. There is no evidence that during the period of his employment prior to transfer, Acanfora made his homosexuality known to the school community." Furthermore, as a public employee with a one-year contract to teach eighth grade earth science, Acanfora was entitled to a hearing prior to any deprivation of his contractual rights. This had not been afforded by the school district in this case. Thus, at the time Acanfora was transferred the decision was probably unconstitutional.

But at this point the case was not really about the constitutionality of the transfer and subsequent nonrenewal of Acanfora's contract, according to Judge Young, but rather about whether Acanfora was now entitled to reinstatement as an eighth grade earth science teacher at Parkland Junior High. Young found that Acanfora's activities after his transfer were relevant to this issue, and here Young found that Acanfora's media activities to publicize his case had rendered him unemployable in his former teaching position. Although the Supreme Court had held in a variety of cases that public employees enjoy the same First Amendment rights as other citizens to participate in the public discussion of issues of public importance, the government may remove a public employee whose First Amendment activities impair his ability to fulfill his public employment effectively.

Young asserted:

The instruction of children carries with it special responsibilities, whether a teacher be heterosexual or homosexual. The conduct of private life necessarily reflects on the life in public. There exists then not only a right of privacy, so strongly urged by the plaintiff, but also a duty of privacy. It is conceded that it would be improper for any teacher to discuss his sex life in the school environment. Plaintiff has taken the position that he has not engaged, and will not engage, in such a discussion. The more difficult question is the limitation on the outside activities of the plaintiff.

Finding that "the subject of homosexuality is peculiarly sensitive and of special concern to the American family," and that the "consensus of experts . . . is that prevention of homosexuality is a desirable goal, essentially because of the cultural stigma and repression for which it is the target," Young held that a teacher who seeks to make a public issue of his homosexuality has forfeited the right to continue to teach. Rebuffing Acanfora's argument that his media appearances were a necessary part of his legal strategy to persuade the school board to change its position and to reinstate him, Young decided that the appearances did not serve that goal:

> As indicated earlier, mere knowledge that a teacher is homosexual is not sufficient to justify transfer or dismissal. In addition, the homosexual teacher need not become a recluse, nor need he lie about himself. Like any other teacher, he may attend public gatherings and associate with whomever he chooses. But a sense of discretion and self-restraint must guide him to avoid speech or activity likely to spark the added public controversy which detracts from the educational purpose. . . . The point is that to some extent every teacher has to go out of his way to hide his private life, and that a homosexual teacher is not at liberty to ignore or hold in contempt the sensitivity of the subject to the school community.

Consequently, Young refused to order the school board to reinstate Acanfora to the classroom. Although he determined that the transfer of September 26 was "without legal justification as matters then stood," Acanfora had forfeited the assistance of the court by failing to exercise "discretion in his public life" after the transfer. So the school board's subsequent refusal to renew his contract and return him to the classroom was not "arbitrary or capricious under either the First Amendment or the Equal Protection Clause of the Fourteenth Amendment," and Acanfora was without a remedy for the initial wrongful transfer.

Acanfora refused to accept this decision by the court, filing an appeal with the U.S. Court of Appeals for the Fourth Circuit. His case was argued on November 6, 1973, by Michael Gottesman before a three-judge panel, consisting of retired Supreme Court Justice Tom C. Clark, Senior Circuit Judge Herbert S. Boreman, and Circuit Judge John D. Butzner, Jr. Robert Bourbon argued for the school board. The court received *amicus* briefs in support of Acanfora's case from the American Civil Lib-

erties Union and the National Education Association and its local Maryland affiliate.

Writing for the unanimous panel in its February 7, 1974, opinion, Judge Butzner totally rejected Young's analysis of the First Amendment issues attendant on Acanfora's post-transfer media appearances. According to Butzner, the Supreme Court's key precedent of *Pickering v. Board of Education* (1968) provided that "a teacher's comments on public issues concerning schools that are neither knowingly false nor made in reckless disregard of the truth afford no ground for dismissal when they do not impair the teacher's performance of his duties or interfere with the operation of the schools." Analyzing Acanfora's media appearances by this standard, the court found that Acanfora had not crossed the line Judge Young drew on acceptable public comment by a teacher.

> In short, the record discloses that press, radio, and television commentators considered homosexuality in general, and Acanfora's plight in particular, to be a matter of public interest about which reasonable people could differ, and Acanfora responded to their inquiries in a rational manner. There is no evidence that the interviews disrupted the school, substantially impaired his capacity as a teacher, or gave the school officials reasonable grounds to forecast that these results would flow from what he said.

The court concluded that Acanfora's post-transfer publicity did not provide any justification either for the school board's actions or the dismissal of his lawsuit.

The court concluded, however, that it could not order Acanfora's reinstatement, because he omitted to mention his membership in Homophiles of Penn State on his employment application. The record showed that the school district would not have hired him had he revealed his homosexuality during the hiring process. The application form concluded with a sworn statement that it was "accurate" and that falsification would be "cause for dismissal from service." The omission was not inadvertent; Acanfora testified at trial (and Judge Young found) that he deliberately excluded this organizational affiliation to avoid the discrimination he anticipated had he been open about his sexuality. Consequently, this was deliberate falsification for which he could be dismissed.

Acanfora attacked this reasoning on two grounds: first, that the school board's policy of not hiring homosexuals was nonetheless unconstitutional, so he could not be faulted for failing to supply that information; and, second, that the school board had fired him because he was homosexual, not because he failed to list Homophiles of Penn State on his employment application. The court rejected both arguments. Relying on several U.S. Supreme Court cases, most notably *Dennis v. United States* (1966) and *Bryson v. United States* (1969), the court found that the unconstitutionality of an underlying government policy did not give an individual the right to refuse to answer questions truthfully or to attack the underlying policy when his untruthfulness was revealed. In *Bryson*, the Supreme Court had stated that

> it cannot be thought as a general principle of our law a citizen has a privilege to answer fraudulently a question that the Government should not have asked. Our legal system provides methods for challenging the Government's right to ask questions—lying is not one of them. A citizen may decline to answer the question, or answer it honestly, but he cannot with impunity knowingly and willfully answer with a falsehood.

As to Acanfora's second argument, the court noted that the school board was unaware of the omission from Acanfora's application prior to Acanfora's testimony before the district court, so it could not be expected to have raised that as grounds for its prior actions. However, based on the testimony of the deputy superintendent, it was clear that the omission was a reason for refusing to renew his contract at the end of the year, and it was considered grounds for dismissal by the school board, as indicated on the form itself. "Acanfora purposely misled the school officials so he could circumvent, not challenge, what he considers to be their unconstitutional employment practices."

Thus, the court concluded that Acanfora was not entitled to reinstatement because the school board had an independent ground for his dismissal that was not based directly on its challenged employment policy. Without approving or disapproving Judge Young's conclusions about whether the policy itself was constitutional, the court held that the school board was entitled to dismiss Acanfora for his omission. Acanfora petitioned the U.S. Supreme Court to review the case, but was turned down later in 1974.

The *Acanfora* case was among the first in which an openly gay schoolteacher challenged his dismissal without the complicating factor of an arrest for engaging in public sexual activity. Acanfora's removal from the classroom was initially based solely on the fact of his sexual orientation. Judge Young's ruling that a *per se* exclusion of gays, even open gays, from teaching would be unconstitutional was novel for that time, but his decision posed the ultimate catch-22 for an openly gay teacher: he can be gay, even openly gay, and be a public teacher so long as he avoids any activity that might bring his sexual orientation to the attention of students or their parents. The court of appeals' response to this ruling pointed out its absurd disjunction with First Amendment precedents, but that court imposed its own dilemma on the gay teaching applicant: even if it would violate the Constitution for the school board to refuse to hire him solely due to his sexual orientation, he must reveal his sexual orientation during the application process if the form he files includes questions that will elicit that information, even though he knows it will probably result in his not receiving an offer of employment. Of course, it would be difficult for a denied applicant to prove that the denial was due to a policy of systematic discrimination against gays, since the school board could easily hide behind a bland statement about the superior qualifications of other candidates and deny discriminating on that basis. The most effective way to challenge the policy is to be hired on the merits and then challenge a transfer or dismissal following upon revelation of the teacher's sexual orientation, since no questions of qualifications to teach will arise. But this more direct method of challenge is denied by the court of appeals' opinion.

Due to the publicity it received, *Acanfora* made a major contribution to the public debate about homosexuality. However, it also set the unfortunate pattern seen in many later cases. While piously proclaiming that discrimination on the basis of sexual orientation *per se* in public education is of questionable constitutionality, courts almost always find a way to deny the discharged school teacher reinstatement. While many of these cases arise where teachers are discharged after being arrested for engaging in sexual activities in violating of criminal statues (usually in quasi-public places), in some cases the only "offense" is either being gay or being perceived to be gay.

The best explanation for these outcomes is that courts continue to believe those "experts" who maintain that the presence of openly gay teachers will result in students who would not otherwise become gay being influenced to be gay, and that there is a valid public interest in "preventing homosexuality." While judges state that homosexuality should be "prevented" because homosexuals suffer discrimination in society, the suspicion lingers that many judges themselves view homosexuality as an undesirable trait worth preventing in the interest of the individual. In this, judges likely reflect the views of many in our society.

Case References

Bryson v. United States, 396 U.S. 64 (1969)
Dennis v. United States, 384 U.S. 855 (1966)
Frontiero v. Richardson, 411 U.S. 677 (1973)
Pickering v. Board of Education, 391 U.S. 563 (1968)

101. GAY STUDENTS HAVE A RIGHT TO "PARTY"

Gay Students Organization of the University of New Hampshire v. Bonner, 509 F.2d 652 (1st Cir. 1974), modifying 367 F. Supp. 1088 (D.N.H. 1974).

The birth of the modern gay liberation movement in the late 1960s quickly sparked organizational activity at colleges and universities. The earliest lesbian and gay student groups arose at "liberal" major universities, such as Columbia and Cornell, but soon activity spread to less likely venues, such as the University of New Hampshire (UNH). There, adverse reaction by university and government officials generated the first important appellate ruling on the associational rights of lesbian and gay students at public universities.

In the spring of 1973, some gay students at the UNH organized their group and petitioned the university for official recognition, which was readily granted. In their statement of purpose filed with UNH, the students asserted that their primary purpose in forming the UNH Gay Students Organization (GSO) was "to promote the recognition of gay people on campus and to form a viable organization through which bisexual and homosexual people may express themselves." To this end, the organization planned to hold "social functions . . . in which both gay and straight people can learn about the others' thoughts and feelings concerning sexuality and sexual roles." The statement of purpose also spoke of educational and public relations activities and about providing "a place to communicate with each other and form discussion groups so that a healthy gay consciousness can evolve among students."

Early in the fall term of 1973, the students began planning their first major event, a dance on campus scheduled for November 9. Although UNH officials gave permission for the event, which went off smoothly with no disruption, resulting media attention stirred negative comments in the conservative New Hampshire political community, especially from Governor Meldrim Thomson, Jr., who complained directly to UNH officials about allowing such a "spectacle" as a gay dance to occur on the campus. The UNH board of trustees met immediately to consider this "problem," and issued a statement on November 10, noting the "continuing public and [executive] committee concern" about the GSO. The trustees voted to obtain a judicial determination of the "legality and appropriateness of scheduling social functions by the Gay Student Organization" and "directed that in the interim the University administration would schedule no further social functions by the Gay Students Organization until the matter is legally resolved." Pursuing this strategy, UNH filed a declaratory judgment lawsuit on November 21 in the Strafford County Superior Court, and served a copy of the complaint on GSO officers on November 28. GSO President Wayne April had requested permission for the organization to present a play on December 7 followed by a social event. Responding to April on November 21, the same day the state court suit was filed, Michael O'Neil, director of recreation and student activities at UNH, indicated that the play could be presented but that after-play activities must be limited to a "meeting" rather than a "social event."

GSO had been conferring with the New Hampshire Civil Liberties Union, in Concord, which agreed to provide representation. Attorney Richard S. Kohn filed a complaint on behalf of GSO in the federal district court on November 29, seeking declaratory and injunctive relief regarding the right of GSO to hold social events on campus. Responding specifically to the refusal to allow a social event on December 7, Kohn filed a petition for a temporary restraining order on December 3, but District Judge Hugh H. Bownes decided that there would be no irreparable injury sufficient to require such temporary relief and denied the petition, while setting the matter for a hearing on request for preliminary injunctive relief on December 10.

The struggles of UNH GSO had captured the attention of gay activists throughout New England, including the staff of a radical gay liberation newspaper published in Boston, *Fag Rag*. The *Fag Rag* staff decided to show their support by coming *en masse* to the GSO event on December 7, with copies of their latest issues to distribute. *Fag Rag* was a deliberately "outrageous" publication, featuring radical commentary and advocacy of uninhibited gay sexuality. Although the play presented on December 7 aroused little reaction or adverse comment from UNH officials, they were very upset about the distribution of *Fag Rag*. According to O'Neil, the GSO asked for permission to sell

copies of the publication to members of the audience, which was denied on the ground that GSO did not have a permit to sell publications as required by the student handbook. April then asked O'Neil for permission to distribute free copies to audience members. After examining the publication, which he deemed obscene, O'Neil denied permission for distribution and requested that copies of the magazine be removed from the table at the entrance to the theater where they were stacked by *Fag Rag* staff. April complied promptly, but it seems that some *Fag Rag* staff, undeterred by this hostile reaction to their handiwork, distributed some copies on their own, which ended up in the hands of a student university trustee and others. At least one copy may have eventually found its way to the governor's office. In any event, the *Fag Rag* issue came to dominate UNH's subsequent actions.

Manchester attorney Joseph A. Milliment represented UNH at the federal court hearing on December 10, during which the court heard testimony and argument about the GSO's request for a preliminary injunction. The parties agreed at the close of the hearing that it could serve as a final hearing on the merits. But that was before the governor dropped a bombshell on the university in an "open letter" to the board of trustees, dated December 15. Governor Thomson, expressing the expected political outrage, fulminated as follows:

> Therefore, after very careful consideration, I must inform you the trustees and administration that indecency and moral filth will no longer be allowed on our campuses. I am not interested in legalistic hairsplitting that begs these important issues. Either you take firm, fair and positive action to rid your campuses of socially abhorrent activities or I, as governor, will stand solidly against the expenditure of one more cent of taxpayers' money for your institutions.

> Translated simply, that means that unless you take successful corrective action before the capital budget is reconsidered, I shall oppose the inclusion of any money therein for the University and will veto that budget, if necessary.

University President Thomas N. Bonner reacted to the governor's letter and accompanying media commentary by issuing a public statement condemning the distribution of *Fag Rag* at the play and ordering an "immediate investigation" to determine who was responsible for that. In addition, he declared:

I am today serving notice on the Gay Students Organization that any repetition of the offending behavior of December 7, 1973, will result in my seeking its immediate suspension as a student organization until the courts have acted on the several issues involving GSO now before them. The organizations will be held fully responsible for any ancillary activities carried on by those attracted from other places to a GSO event.

I have ordered that the current Trustee ban on GSO social functions be interpreted more strictly by administrative authorities than had been the case before December 7, 1973.

These developments prompted Milliment to request that the hearing be reopened for new evidence, including testimony about the *Fag Rag* distribution, the governor's letter, and the university's subsequent actions, so an additional hearing was held on December 28. On January 16, Judge Bownes issued his opinion, granting GSO the injunctive relief it sought and giving the university a thorough lecture on the First Amendment and equal protection rights of student activists.

The gay student activists were lucky in having had a constitutional path blazed for them by the antiwar activists of the 1960s. Their confrontations with university officials and public authorities had produced a series of important U.S. Supreme Court decisions protecting the rights of protesters and political agitators on the nation's campuses. *Tinker v. Des Moines Independent Community School District* was the seminal case, in which the Court ruled in 1969 that high school students had a First Amendment right to wear black armbands in protest of the Vietnam War, commenting, "[t]he vigilant protection of constitutional freedoms is nowhere more vital than in the community of American schools." In *Healy v. James* (1972), the Court ruled that a university could not refuse to extend official campus organization recognition to a proposed chapter of Students for a Democratic Society (SDS), a radical protest group whose very name struck fear in the hearts of university administrators from coast to coast. The Court said: "The primary impediment to

free association flowing from nonrecognition is the denial of use of campus facilities for meetings and other appropriate purposes." Reviewing these precedents, Bownes concluded they meant that, "absent justification, a student organization may not be denied those rights which are necessary to its maintenance and orderly growth."

Given such precedents, it was easy for Bownes to conclude that the GSO and its members had significant First Amendment rights to obtain official recognition, to associate, and to present their views on the UNH campus. GSO had not been denied recognition or access to campus facilities for educational programs, so Bownes concluded that more "traditional" First Amendment rights had not been violated. Of more immediate concern was the university's ban on social functions by GSO. Could social functions also be covered by the First Amendment? Bownes certainly thought so, holding that among the rights to which GSO and its members were entitled was "the right to sponsor and participate in social functions." Noting that a federal district court in Georgia had recently reached a similar conclusion, based on the precedent of *Healy v. James*, Bownes asserted that "support for this position lies in the pervasive importance of social functions in the university setting," which he found to be "particularly true for minority groups."

Not content to rest his decision solely on the First Amendment, however, Bownes also accepted the argument that the university's actions had violated GSO members' right to equal protection of the laws under the Fourteenth Amendment. Equal protection doctrine, as developed by the Supreme Court, focuses different levels of judicial scrutiny on governmental policies depending on the nature of the right at stake or the identity of the groups affected. The question whether government policies disadvantaging gays should receive "strict scrutiny" has become the subject of heated debate in the federal circuit courts of appeals over the past twenty years, but Bownes did not have to initiate such a debate because in this case the university's policy decision implicated fundamental rights of association protected by the First Amendment; the Supreme Court has used "strict scrutiny" to evaluate policies, even if the classification involved is not labeled "suspect," when fundamental rights are implicated. In such cases, government policies must be narrowly tailored to serve a substantial governmental interest.

Bownes found support in many federal cases for the proposition that public universities and other government-funded or -operated forums for expressive activities had to be made available on an "evenhanded" basis. At UNH, various student organizations formed around particular political causes, including the Black Student Union, WOMEN!, SDS, and Young Alliance for Freedom. University officials had never forbidden any of these groups from holding social events on campus. If the government wanted to restrict GSO from holding social events, there had to be some substantial justification for treating it differently, and it could not be that the university disliked the message of support for lesbian and gay rights that the student group was advocating. Turning to the scope of permissible regulation of GSO functions by the university, Bownes commented that "recent trends in the Supreme Court indicate that a state university regulation challenged solely on Equal Protection grounds should be judged in the light of a relatively vigorous standard: 'that [University] means must substantially further [University] ends.'"

Given these constitutional requirements, Bownes found that there would be "only three circumstances under which a university may deny or withdraw recognition or the rights and privileges flowing therefrom from a student organization: (1) failure or refusal to abide by reasonable housekeeping rules; (2) 'demonstrated danger of violence' or disruption of the university's educational mission; and (3) violation of the criminal law by the organization or by its members at a function sponsored by the organization." He found no basis for regulation in the first "circumstances," since there was no allegation by the university that GSO had failed to comply with any rules. Even in the *Fag Rag* matter, Bownes found that outsiders were responsible for the ultimate distribution, and UNH officials had conceded on cross-examination that GSO President April had acted "responsibly" in obeying O'Neil's instructions

regarding distribution of the newspaper. Neither was there any evidence of "disruption" or "violence" at GSO events.

The university tried to argue, however, that the governor's threat of cutting off state funding for the UNH system if GSO was allowed to continue holding events on campus provided a justification for limiting GSO. This, said UNH, presented a "clear and present danger to its educational mission." Bownes was unwilling to accord constitutional weight to such threats, however:

> I am not blind to the reality of these threats. However, financial retaliation against the University for maintaining a system mandated by the First and Fourteenth Amendments would be in reality an attempt to abridge the rights guaranteed by those Amendments. The basic purpose of the Bill of Rights is to protect the people against arbitrary and discriminatory use of political power. . . . A state university may not be blackmailed into depriving its students of their constitutional rights.

Finally, as to the third "circumstance," the university had pointed to the New Hampshire criminal laws forbidding consensual sodomy and solicitation to commit sodomy. It claimed that "GSO social functions are tantamount to criminal solicitation of deviate sexual relations." Also, pointing to the *Fag Rag* incident, UNH officials noted state laws forbidding distribution of obscene materials. However, Bownes found, there was no serious allegation that any unlawful conduct was engaged in by UNH students at any GSO function. "In fact," said Bownes, "Kelly, an officer of the GSO, testified that the GSO did not advocate public homosexual acts." Bownes had found that *Fag Rag* staff, not GSO members, were responsible for distributing copies of that publication, and Kelly had testified that GSO considered *Fag Rag* an "extremist shock paper" whose distribution GSO did not advocate. In short, Bownes rejected the contention that forbidding GSO social events was necessary to prevent future violations of New Hampshire laws. He said it was time enough to enforce the laws if actual violations occurred.

"In essence," Bownes concluded, "this case is quite simple. The First Amendment guarantees all individuals, including university students, the right to organize and associate 'to further their personal beliefs.'" That was precisely what GSO wanted to do through its social activities. Unless UNH could come up with more substantial arguments than it had presented at the two hearings, there seemed to be no justification for allowing it to restrict GSO's activities. "Minority groups, as well as majority groups, must be given an opportunity to express themselves; for only in this way can our system of peaceful social change be maintained." The university was entitled to take steps to prevent violence or other disruptions of school activities, but "the University must respect the rights of the GSO." Bownes permanently enjoined UNH from "prohibiting or restricting the sponsorship of social functions or use of the University facilities for such functions by the Gay Students Organization." He further enjoined UNH from "treating the Gay Students Organization differently than other University student organizations."

Governor Thomson and the university administration were not about to take this rebuff lying down! At a meeting of the trustees held shortly after the injunction was issued, the trustees discussed various ways of trying to get the injunction vacated, including challenges to the jurisdiction of the court based on the lack of personal service of the complaint on various trustees and the governor. They filed an appeal in the U.S. Court of Appeals for the First Circuit. An attorney for the governor intervened in the case, seeking dismissal of the injunction against him, since although he had been named as a defendant he had never been personally served with a complaint. The gay students' cause attracted an *amicus* brief from the recently formed Lambda Legal Defense and Education Fund in New York.

In its decision issued December 30, 1974, the U.S. Court of Appeals for the First Circuit unanimously affirmed Judge Bownes's decision on the merits, although it concluded that the injunction had to be slightly modified, since it should not run personally against the governor or various trustees who had not been served with complaints. After devoting much of his decision to disposing of the various technical objections to personal liability by particular defendants, Chief Judge Frank M. Coffin turned to the substance of the case, finding such a firm

basis in the First Amendment for ordering injunctive relief that it was unnecessary to consider the alternative Equal Protection Clause theory at any length. In a brief footnote, Coffin commented, "The equal protection challenge to the university strikes us as substantial in its own right, . . . and our First Amendment analysis draws heavily upon the conclusions which must be drawn from the fact that only the GSO among campus groups has been forbidden to hold social events."

Coffin prefaced his decision on the merits of the First Amendment challenge with a brief apologia regarding the sensitive nature of the case. He said, "[w]e are conscious of the tension between deeply felt, conflicting values or moral judgments, and the traditional legal method of extracting and applying principles from decided cases."

> The underlying question, usually not articulated, is whether, whatever may be Supreme Court precedent in the First Amendment area, group activity promoting values so far beyond the pale of the wider community's values is also beyond the boundaries of the First Amendment, at least to the extent that university facilities may not be used by the group to flaunt its credo. If visceral reactions suggest an affirmative answer, the next task for judges is to devise a standard which, while damping down the First Amendment on a university campus, is generally applicable and free from the dangers of arbitrariness. At this point troubles arise. How are the deeply felt values of the community to be identified?

Coffin described a series of emotionally charged issues, such as abortion, socialism, conscientious objection to military service, and the like, on which community opinion was likely to be sharply divided. He concluded that "we are unable to devise a tolerable standard exempting this case at the threshold from general First Amendment precedents" that would work appropriately with regard to all such controversial issues. The Supreme Court had already answered negatively, in cases such as *Healy*, the question whether there was something "different about a university that makes it an enclave sheltered from the full play of the First Amendment." Indeed, the Court had emphasized the importance of preserving First Amendment values in the academic setting.

What it came down to, said Coffin, was whether, despite university recognition and permission to hold some kinds of meetings on campus, the GSO's members' rights of association were being abridged by the restriction on social events. While it was true that the *Healy* precedent went to the issue of recognition, "the Court's analysis in *Healy* focused not on the technical point of recognition or non-recognition, but on the practicalities of human interaction." The Court's conclusion that nonrecognition violated First Amendment rights was premised on the accompanying denial of access to university facilities. "The ultimate issue at which inquiry must be directed," said Coffin, "is the effect which a regulation has on organizational and associational activity, not the isolated and for the most part irrelevant issue of recognition *per se.*"

Rejecting UNH's argument that the ban on social events was permissible because other kinds of events were allowed, Coffin noted the comment in *Healy* that "[t]he Constitution's protection is not limited to direct interference with fundamental rights." Social events were an important mechanism for an organization to attract members and facilitate interaction among them. *Healy* had previously been construed by other courts as supporting a conclusion that universities must allow student groups to hold social events on campus. "We are also led to this conclusion by the realization that efforts by a state to restrict groups other than GSO to gatherings that were in no sense 'social events' would be rejected out of hand."

> Even a lecture or discussion, which appear to be the only types of meetings which the appellants would allow the GSO to hold, becomes a social event if beer is served beforehand or coffee afterward. Teas, coffees and dinners form the backbone of many a political candidate's campaign, and yet these activities would seemingly be subject to prohibition. While a university may have some latitude in regulating organizations such as fraternities or sororities which can be purely social, its efforts to restrict the activities of a cause-oriented group like the GSO stand on a different footing. . . . Considering the important role that social events can play in individuals' efforts to associate to further their common beliefs, the prohibition of all social events must be taken to be a substantial

abridgement of associational rights, even if assumed to be an indirect one.

Since GSO was a "political action organization," UNH's argument that its social events were not "speech" was unavailing. "The GSO's efforts to organize the homosexual minority, 'educate' the public as to its plight, and obtain for it better treatment from individuals and from the government thus represent but another example of the associational activity unequivocally singled out for protection in the very 'core' of association cases decided by the Supreme Court," Coffin asserted. Even if it were not "so intimately bound up with the political process," GSO's social activities would be protected because beliefs did not have to be "political" to be protected; the Supreme Court had recognized protection for economic, religious, or cultural beliefs as well.

In fact, said Coffin, the district court was incorrect in asserting that GSO had not been deprived of any "more traditional First Amendment rights" just because it was officially recognized and allowed to hold meetings. Coffin found that GSO social events had their own "communicative content" that made them protected First Amendment expression. "There can be no doubt that expression, assembly and petition constitute significant aspects of the GSO's conduct in holding social events," he asserted. Because of the particular nature of the sexual minorities involved, social events were at the heart of an ability to attract members, organize, and allow the kind of exchange of ideas for which GSO was formed. "And beyond the specific communications at such events is the basic 'message' GSO seeks to convey that homosexuals exist, that they feel repressed by existing laws and attitudes, that they wish to emerge from their isolation, and that public understanding of their attitudes and problems is desirable for society."

Indeed, the outside community's reaction to GSO's two events (the dance and the play), including the governor's letter to the university administration, underscored the communicative element in all GSO's activities, whether or not social. And it was clear, in light of Thomson's and Bonner's statements, that "the regulation imposed was based in large measure, if not exclusively, on the content of GSO's expression." The reaction to the dance was not due to any "violence" or "disruption," it was "precipitated by the GSO's program and the fact that the organization was aggressively presenting it to the public."

Because of the expressive nature of GSO's activities, the appropriate test for determining the degree of permissible governmental regulation was that established in *United States v. O'Brien* (1968), the famous case in which the U.S. Supreme Court considered whether the federal government could prosecute a person who burned his draft card in protest of the Vietnam War. The Court upheld the defendant's conviction on the ground that the government was entitled, for administrative purposes, to require individuals to preserve their draft cards, that this furthered an important or substantial governmental interest that was unrelated to the suppression of speech, and that the incidental burden on free expression was no greater than necessary to accomplish the legitimate purpose. War protesters could find ways to make their statement other than burning draft cards. It was clear, however, from reviewing the *O'Brien* tests, that UNH's regulation here failed to meet the tests, because its opposition to GSO's events was "content-related, the curtailing of expression which they find abhorrent or offensive." In the same vein, Coffin found, in agreement with Bownes, that UNH's purported interest in preventing the commission of sex crimes could not justify the restrictions, since there were no serious allegations that any crimes had been committed by GSO students at their events. While the university had the authority to prevent "imminent lawlessness," it would have to come up with more solid evidence than was presented in the record before it could use that basis to justify a ban on GSO social events.

Finally, Coffin noted that UNH could take action, if necessary, to prevent disruption of its educational activities. Again, however, since the district court had found no improper conduct by GSO members, it did not appear that UNH's real motivation had anything to do with disruption. "Defendants sought to cut back GSO's social activities simply because of the activities sponsored by that group. The ban was not justified by any evidence of misconduct attributable to GSO," concluded Coffin, "and it was altogether too sweeping."

The First Circuit's decision was a historic validation of the free speech and association rights of sexual minorities in the public sphere. The state decided not to appeal the case to the Supreme Court, and GSO was allowed to hold social events without further university interference. The court's decision became the leading precedent on the issue, serving as an important basis for decisions in support of the rights of gay student groups at public universities in several other federal circuits. In light of its strong wording and the unanimous agreement of the First Circuit judges, most public university administrators, when confronted with this opinion, quickly dropped their opposition and agreed voluntarily to recognize gay student groups and to allow them to engage in the full range of campus activities accorded other groups. Even some private school administrators, imbued with the necessity to meet the requirements of academic freedom and free inquiry suggested by accrediting organizations, gave great weight to the *Bonner* case in deciding how to deal with on-campus gay student groups.

Case References

Healy v. James, 408 U.S. 169 (1972)

Tinker v. Des Moines Independent Community School District, 393 U.S. 503 (1969)

United States v. O'Brien, 391 U.S. 367 (1968)

102. CAN A TEACHER CHANGE HIS SEX (AND STILL BE A TEACHER)?

In re Grossman, 127 N.J. Super. 13, 316 A.2d 39 (App.), petition denied, 65 N.J. 292, 321 A.2d 253 (1974); *Grossman v. Bernards Township Board of Education*, 11 Fair Empl. Prac. Cas. (BNA) 1196, 11 Empl. Prac. Dec. (CCH) para. 10,686 (U.S. Dist. Ct., D.N.J. 1975), affirmed without opinion, 538 F.2d 319 (3d Cir.), certiorari denied, 429 U.S. 897 (1976). Related decision on pension: *In re Grossman*, 157 N.J. Super. 165, 384 A.2d 855 (App. 1978).

On March 5, 1971, Paul Grossman, a married (father of three) 54–year-old tenured elementary school music teacher with fourteen years of service in Bernards Township, New Jersey, resolved his long-standing gender discomfort problems by submitting to sex-reassignment surgery on the advice of competent medical professionals. He then presented himself to the school district as Paula Grossman and sought to return to classroom teaching. After a summer of turmoil and anguish involving protests and arguments among administrators, teachers and parents (during which Grossman rejected a compromise offer from the school board to take a one-year probationary contract and teach an elective music course at the high school level), the board of education voted on August 19, 1971, to suspend Grossman without pay and to file charges with the state's commissioner of education seeking approval for dismissal, posing the difficult question whether somebody acknowledged to be fully competent, both physically and mentally, to teach music to elementary school students could be denied employment solely because of a sex change.

The question was novel. While the concept of severe gender discomfort leading to a diagnosis of transsexualism was long known to psychiatry, it was only with the relatively recent development of plastic and reconstructive surgery that sex change operations had become possible, and they were still a rare phenomenon when Grossman submitted to the process. There was no empirical evidence based on past experiences about the effect of such a situation on elementary school age children who would have to confront in the classroom as a woman a teacher they had previously known as a man. There were no statutes or adjudicated cases on record to guide the consideration of the commissioner of education or subsequent

courts called on to deal with the matter. There was, however, a New Jersey statute governing the circumstances under which a tenured elementary school teacher might be discharged. It provided that no tenured teacher could be dismissed "during good behavior and efficiency" except "for inefficiency, incapacity, unbecoming conduct, or other just cause."

The board of education had voted five charges against Grossman. As later summarized by the New Jersey courts, they alleged first that her presence as a teacher "had created and would continue to create a degree of sensation and notoriety within the system and the community which would severely impair the Board's ability to conduct an efficient and orderly school system." The second specification was that Grossman had, in violation of the tenure statute, exhibited conduct "unbecoming a teacher" by failing to disclose his gender discomfort situation to the school district prior to the surgery, so that the matter was presented as a complete surprise when "Paula Grossman" showed up asking to continue teaching. The third was that as a result of the sex change, Grossman was no longer capable of acting as the "Paul Grossman" who was engaged as a teacher by the school district. The fourth specification charged Grossman with engaging in behavior that was "deviant from the accepted standards of the community." Finally, the board charged that she exhibited "abnormality." In summary, the board alleged that each of these charges, individually, would constitute "just cause" as required by the tenure statute for dismissal.

New Jersey's assistant commissioner of education, William A. Shine, held a hearing to make a factual record on the charges. In addition to Grossman and various school district administrators and employees, Shine heard, either by testimony or deposition, from four "expert" witnesses, two presented by each side. The board's experts were Dr. Charles W. Socarides and Dr. Harvey Martin Hammer, while Grossman presented testimony from Dr. Charles L. Ihlenfeld and Dr. Robert W. Laidlaw. Most of the expert testimony went to questions about the nature of transsexualism, the legitimacy of a diagnosis of transsexualism, and the degree of acceptance in the medical community for the concept of sex-reassignment surgery as a treatment for that condition. This testimony was presented primarily in response to the fourth and fifth charges filed by the board, alleging "deviant" and "abnormal" behavior. However, the issue that emerged at the hearing and loomed much larger in the testimony and the ultimate findings and disposition by the commissioner concerned the psychological impact on elementary school children ages 10 through 12 of having Paula Grossman teach them after they had previously known her as Paul Grossman.

The expert witnesses were sharply split on the issue of psychological harm. Socarides, whose views on sexual abnormality and deviancy were by 1974 somewhat outside the mainstream of American psychiatry, as evidenced by a then-recent vote of American Psychiatric Association members to remove homosexuality from the Association's list of psychiatric illnesses, asserted that transsexualism was a psychiatric syndrome, and that the presence of Grossman in the classroom could create "some anxieties among those already predisposed due to their own inter-emotional conflicts over their castration fears and so forth." Asserting that "sexual gender role is of paramount significance in life, and its formation and helping it and its growth is so important," he concluded that "such things could cause disturbance" that would be difficult for school authorities to measure and identify, since the impact on children might not express itself for many years. Socarides presented a view of the teacher as a "role model" for children, and contended that presenting Grossman as such a role model could be "very disruptive" of the process by which children, especially young boys, "learn how to be men from their teachers."

Hammer's testimony largely echoed Socarides's. He asserted that "such an individual would have a very negative effect on the mental health of the children in the classroom." He noted that it had already been reported that a 14-year-old boy in the school system who had been experiencing a severe "self-image problem" but had been responding to treatment had suffered a "set-back" after learning about Grossman's sex change operation.

As expected, Grossman's experts took a contrary position. Ihlenfeld testified that children's sense of gender identity was well established before the age when they would confront Grossman in the classroom, and her teaching would have no adverse effect on them. Ihlenfeld asserted that "if a child should be so upset by the thought that Mrs. Grossman had surgery, then this may be the child who has a potential for developing a problem and should have counselling anyway." Laidlaw agreed, acknowledging that although there might be initial "snickering or gossiping or wise-cracking" among the ten to twelve year olds, it would be "transitory" and would not detract from Grossman's "effectiveness as a teacher on the children."

After hearing the testimony, Shine modified the third charge against Grossman and accepted it as dispositive of the case. As modified, the third charge specified:

> Paul Monroe Grossman knowingly and voluntarily underwent a sex-reassignment from male to female. By doing so, he underwent a fundamental and complete change in his role and identification in society, thereby rendering himself incapable to teach children in Bernards Township because of the potential her (Grossman's) presence in the classroom presents for psychological harm to the students of Bernards Township. Therefore, Paula a/k/a Paul Monroe Grossman should be dismissed from the system by reason of just cause due to incapacity.

The commissioner rejected all the other charges. He found that the board's own offer to Grossman to teach music at the high school level significantly undercut the contention that her presence in the system would inevitably impair the Board's ability to run the system, and, while acknowledging that Grossman might better have kept the school authorities informed of what was happening with his medical situation, the evidence did not support any implication that Grossman was trying to deceive the school officials about what was going on. The record evidence also included a report from three psychiatrists retained by the board during the summer of 1971 to examine Grossman, and their unanimous view confirmed the diagnosis of Grossman's physicians that he/she was a genuine transsexual for whom gender-reassignment surgery was an indicated treatment. On this basis, the commissioner dismissed the allegation that Grossman's behavior was "deviant" or "abnormal" in a sense that would justify dismissal.

But the commissioner did conclude that the weight of the expert testimony supported a finding that Grossman, now as Paula rather than as Paul, could have a negative impact on the psychological health and development of elementary school students. He found on that basis that Grossman was no longer "capable" of fulfilling the classroom teacher role for which she had originally been hired. However, the commissioner found that this was not a case of "moral turpitude." He concluded that while the board was no longer required to employ Grossman as an elementary school teacher, it should be required to apply on her behalf to the Teachers' Pension and Annuity Fund to obtain a disability pension, and that Grossman should receive back pay pursuant to a recently passed state law which he interpreted to authorize back pay in these circumstances.

Both sides appealed to the state's board of education, which affirmed the commissioner in all respects except one; the state board found that the back-pay order represented an incorrect interpretation of the recently enacted statute on the subject, which the board contended was not intended to apply to already-ending cases such as Grossman's. Both sides then appealed the state board of education's ruling to the appellate division of the superior court, Grossman rejecting the idea that the testimony of the psychiatric experts about hypothetical psychological impact on the students provided a sufficient basis to terminate her tenured appointment, and the board resisting both the dismissal of its other charges and the order regarding pension and back pay.

A three-judge panel heard arguments on January 14, 1974, from Grossman's lawyer, Richard J. Schachter, of Newark, attorney Gordon A. Millspaugh, Jr., of Newark, for the school board, and Deputy Attorney General Erminie L. Conley on behalf of the state board of education.

The appellate division panel disposed of the case quickly, issuing an opinion on February 20, 1974, by Judge Baruch S. Seidman, upholding the commissioner on all grounds and reversing the state board of education's denial of back pay. For the court, of course, this was a case of review of the determination of administrative bodies (the commissioner and the state board of education) whose factual determinations were normally to be treated as final if supported by evidence on the record. This placed a significant burden on the appealing parties, who must show not that a new decisionmaker could reach a different decision from that of the commissioner of the state board, but rather that neither the commissioner nor the state board could have reasonably reached the conclusions they reached based on the evidence in the record.

For Seidman, the issue boiled down to the potential impact of Grossman on the students, as it had for the commissioner. Given the record evidence, it was virtually impossible for the Bernards Township school board to win the argument that there was no basis in the record for the commissioner's dismissal of their other charges, since the appellate court was not supposed to make an independent determination on those issues. And, with the expert testimony so evenly split, it was also virtually impossible for Grossman to win the argument that a rational decisionmaker could not have come to the commissioner's conclusion, unless the court could be persuaded that the "expert" testimony supporting that conclusion was not worthy of credence. Given the sharply conflicting testimony of the experts, the court had necessarily to rely heavily on the determination of the commissioner, who had heard the experts testify personally. Grossman argued that there was little or no empirical data to indicate that psychological or emotional harm would necessarily result from her continued employment as an elementary school music teacher at Bernards Township. This argument did not persuade the court:

It is not within our competency to balance the persuasiveness of the evidence on one side as against the other. The choice of accepting or rejecting the testimony of the witnesses rests with the administrative agency subject to our oversight of whether there was substantial, legal evidence to support the conclusions reached. . . . The issue was thoroughly presented and argued by both sides. The Commissioner resolved the conflicting medical evidence in favor of the board. Understandably, in a case of this nature, most of the supporting evidence was in the form of opinions given by medical experts, as, indeed, was the opposing evidence. We do not believe that those opinions were based on conjecture or speculation. We are convinced that the evidence adduced sustained as reasonably probable the board's hypothesis that there would be emotional harm to the students if Mrs. Grossman were retained in the school system.

Having approved the commissioner's factual findings, the court had to determine whether they supported the legal conclusion that Grossman was "incapable" of teaching, as specified in the tenure statute. Grossman had argued that "incapacity" should be given a technical interpretation as indicating solely the mental or physical capacity of the teacher. There was no dispute that Grossman was mentally and physically capable of teaching music, so the "incapacity" provision could not provide justification for her discharge. Seidman characterized this view of the statute as "too narrow," citing past New Jersey court decisions that made clear that the statute operated in a broader factual context. From his reading of the cases, he concluded that "the touchstone is fitness to discharge the duties and functions of one's office or position." This issue of fitness was not restricted to issues of "misconduct" or to actual physical or mental incapacity. "The problem to be resolved," said Seidman, "is whether 'incapacity' of a teacher, as that term is used in the statute, can be established solely by a finding that the teacher will have an adverse effect upon the students in the classroom." (It is interesting to note how the "factual finding" in this regard is transmuted through the proceeding. The experts had, in essence, predicted that Grossman *could* have a harmful impact on some students. The commissioner found that she would probably have such an impact. Now, Seidman was saying that she "will have an adverse effect.")

Further reviewing teacher discharge cases from New Jersey and other jurisdictions, Seidman found that the courts had accepted the argument in the past that the "impact and effect upon his or her students" had been accepted as a basis for discharging an otherwise qualified teacher. In a New York City discharge case that was appealed to the U.S. Supreme Court, *Adler v. Board of Education* (1952), that Court had stated:

A teacher works in a sensitive area in a schoolroom. There he shapes the attitude of young minds toward the society in which they live. In this, the state has a vital concern. That the school authorities have the right and the duty to screen the officials, teachers, and employees as to their fitness to maintain the integrity of the schools as a part of ordered society, cannot be doubted.

In a 1967 case, *In re Fulcomer*, the appellate division had instructed the commissioner in making a personnel decision to "take into consideration any harm or injurious effect which the teacher's conduct may have had on the maintenance of discipline and the proper administration of the school system." In a case decided by the chancery division in 1973, *Kochman v. Keansburg Board of Education*, the court had upheld a requirement that teachers undergo annual physical examinations by observing that the legislature "is concerned with protecting school children from the influence of unfit teachers."

Seidman placed particular emphasis on the California Supreme Court's decision in *Morrison v. State Board of Education* (1969), where the court stated that a homosexual teacher who had been involved in an "isolated, noncriminal, homosexual relationship" could be disciplined or discharged by the school board on a showing that the teacher's conduct would have a negative effect on students—a showing, by the way, that the court held had not been made in that case. The court commented that the issue was whether "his retention in the profession poses a significant danger of harm to either students, school employees, or others who might be affected by his actions as a teacher." In a subsequent California Court of Appeal case, *Board of Trustees v. Stubblefield*, the court had described "the calling" of a teacher as "so intimate, its duties so delicate, the things in which a teacher might prove unworthy or would fail are so numerous that they are incapable of enumeration in any legislative enactment."

> His habits, his speech, his good name, his cleanliness, the wisdom and propriety of his official utterances, his associations, all are involved. His ability to inspire children and to govern them, his power as a teacher, and the character for which he stands are matters of major concern in a teacher's selection and retention.

Based on all these New Jersey and foreign authorities, Seidman concluded that the commissioner's finding on harm justified the discharge of Grossman from teaching at Bernards Township:

> We think it would be wrong to measure a teacher's fitness solely by his or her ability to perform the teaching function and to ignore the fact that the teacher's presence in the classroom might, nevertheless, pose a danger of harm to the students for a reason not related to academic proficiency. We are convinced that where, as has been found in this case, a teacher's presence in the classroom would create a potential for psychological harm to the students, the teacher is unable properly to fulfill his or her role and his or her incapacity has been established within the purview of the statute.

Seidman did indicate, however, that the court's ruling should not be construed as holding that Grossman was not qualified to teach. The issue was whether she could teach at Bernards Township, where the students in question had previously known her as a man. Different circumstances might present different issues. Seidman dismissed with little discussion Grossman's contention that this result violated her rights to equal protection of the laws, since there was no indication that the school board would not dismiss other teachers if it concluded that their presence presented a risk of psychological harm to students. He also rejected the argument by the board that it was improper for the commissioner to order the school board to apply for a disability pension for Grossman. Seidman asserted that it was up to the Pension Board, upon receiving the application, to determine whether Grossman had a "disability" sufficient to merit awarding the pension. (In later litigation, an appellate divison panel unanimously overruled the Pension Board's decision that Grossman was not entitled to a disability pension.)

The issue of back pay turned on a question of statutory construction, as to which there was no presumption that the state board of education had any special competence. After reviewing past statutes and legislative history, Seidman concluded that the new law on back pay during the pendency of disciplinary proceedings was intended to be remedial and should apply to this situation, so the state board's decision was reversed on this point, and the whole case was remanded back to the commissioner with instructions to determine the amount of back pay to award. In all other respects, the decision of the state board of education was affirmed by the court. Grossman sought review in the state supreme court, which denied a petition to hear the case on May 29, 1974.

She then took her case to a federal forum, filing charges with the Equal Employment Opportunity Commission (EEOC) alleging that her discharge violated Title VII of the Civil Rights Act, which prohibits "sex discrimination." The EEOC, which had consistently taken the position that discrimination against transsexuals is not covered by Title VII, dismissed her complaint. She then filed suit in the federal district court, alleging both a violation of Title VII and violations of her constitutional and statutory civil rights under a variety of federal statutes and constitutional provisions, but all to no avail. On September 10, 1975, U.S. District Judge George H. Barlow dismissed her complaint in a brief memorandum opinion, noting that virtually none of the grounds stated in the complaint would constitute a legal cause of action in light of the facts in her case. In particular, Barlow found it unnecessary to get into the argument whether a postoperative transsexual was a man or a woman, because, as far as he was concerned, she was not discharged because of her gender, but rather because she changed it. While there was a "scarcity" of legislative history about the meaning of "sex" as used in Title VII, Barlow found no basis to conclude that Congress ever intended to provide protection against discrimination for transsexuals, and drew support from the EEOC's similar conclusion in this case. The U.S. Court of Appeals for the Third Circuit affirmed Barlow's disposition of the case in an unpublished order of June 8, 1976, and the U.S. Supreme Court denied a petition for *certiorari* on October 18, 1976.

The *Grossman* case illustrates the extraordinary way some courts treat expert testimony in cases requiring factual findings about human sexuality. Here was a virtually unprecedented situation, where there was no empirical data on which to draw any conclusion about whether a postoperative transsexual would cause psychological harm to students by her mere presence, when they had previously known her as a man. The commissioner, and ultimately the court, claimed to base their determinations solely on the word of two psychiatrists who had undertaken no systematic study of the issue, but were rather giving their opinions based on their own theories.

There was no reference in the court's opinion to whether the views of these psychiatrists necessarily reflected a consensus of American or world psychiatry, and the experts presented by Grossman sharply controverted their testimony. Yet the court, perhaps baffled by sharply controverted testimony from "experts," decided to play safe by avoiding any possibility, however hypothetical, of risk to students through further exposure to Grossman. The case raises serious questions about the competency of such a system of fact-finding to dispose of these sorts of issues in a rational manner. While it is undeniable that the school authorities have a heavy burden to avoid any situation in which students may be harmed, it is also undeniable that the livelihood of an individual presents a fundamental interest that ordinarily cannot be abridged by government agencies without a substantial showing of rational justification. In this case, the system imposed a severe sanction with little such basis.

Case References

Adler v. Board of Education, 342 U.S. 485 (1952)

Board of Trustees v. Stubblefield, 16 Cal. App. 3d 820, 94 Cal. Rptr. 318 (App. 1971)

Fulcomer, In re, 226 A.2d 30 (N.J. Super. Ct., App. Div. 1967)

Kochman v. Keansburg Board of Education, 305 A.2d 807 (N.J. Super., Ch. Div. 1973)

Morrison v. State Board of Education, 1 Cal. 3d 214, 82 Cal. Rptr. 175, 461 P.2d 375 (1969)

103. COMMUNICATING THROUGH THE CAMPUS PRESS: GAY ADVERTISING

Mississippi Gay Alliance v. Goudelock, 536 F.2d 1073 (5th Cir. 1976), certiorari denied, 430 U.S. 982 (1977).

The First Amendment of the U.S. Constitution protects freedom of speech and the press in the abstract, but the precise freedom that is protected varies with the context and the source of possible suppression. In particular, the protected freedom has always been identified as acting against governmental, as opposed to private, regulation. Furthermore, by specifically mentioning freedom of "the press," the amendment also appears to provide protection to the press to make editorial decisions without governmental interference. Effective freedom of speech depends, of course, on the speaker's access to a medium of communication that can convey the speaker's message to those who may have an interest in hearing it. If the government has no involvement in providing the medium of communication, can the government be enlisted in an effort to make a medium available for a speaker whose views are unpopular? In *Miami Herald Publishing Co. v. Tornillo* (1974), the U.S. Supreme Court made abundantly clear that a privately owned medium of communication, such as a newspaper, may not be compelled by the government to afford access to any particular speaker, since this would violate the freedom of the press guaranteed by the First Amendment. This decision built on the Court's previous ruling in *Columbia Broadcasting System v. Democratic National Committee* (1973), in which the Court held that the television networks were not required to accept paid political advertising.

The First Amendment has played an important part in the movement for lesbian and gay rights in instances where the government provides the medium for communication, because having provided a forum for public communication, the government may not censor that forum on the basis of the content of speech. The right of public forum access has been invoked to protect the rights of lesbian and gay people to demonstrate and to communicate with each other on matters of mutual concern in parks, streets, and other public places without government interference, subject, of course, to reasonable time, place, and manner regulations that are not content-based. But the First Amendment has been invoked in support of the right of privately owned media to refuse to publish information of interest or concern to gay people, and to reject advertising from gay organizations.

Attempts by gay people to build their movement and organizations by using the press to spread the message about their existence and availability have been sporadic as a result of the nongay media's reluctance to carry a gay message. While the nongay, privately owned press in some parts of the country has been receptive to advertising from gay organizations, in other areas, where hostility to homosexuals is greatest and the need for such communication is consequently heightened, the privately owned nongay media are least likely to allow access. This is particularly true in those parts of the country most resistent to repeal of sodomy laws. Failing to achieve access to the privately owned press, some gay organizations have attempted to communicate to their potential audience through the government-subsidized press on college and university campuses. The most celebrated attempt was made in 1973, at an early point in the modern gay rights movement when small gay organizations were making their first real bid for public visibility. The attempt was made by the Mississippi Gay Alliance, an orga-

nization whose very struggle to incorporate as an openly gay organization had been the subject of a separate court battle.

In August 1973, a woman identified in the court's opinion only as Ms. DeBary, an officer of the Mississippi Gay Alliance, appeared at the offices of the *Reflector*, the campus newspaper at Mississippi State University (MSU), to submit a paid advertisement for publication. The advertisement read, in full:

Gay Center — open 6:00 to 9:00 Monday, Wednesday and Friday nights.
We offer— counseling, legal aid and a library of homosexual literature.
Write to— The Mississippi Gay Alliance P.O. Box 1328 Mississippi State University, MS 39762

Bill Goudelock, the student editor of the *Reflector*, refused to accept the advertisement, although the *Reflector* printed paid and unpaid advertisements from businesses and political, social, and religious organizations, both from the surrounding community and from campus groups. The Alliance was not an official campus group, but some of its members were students at MSU. In February 1974, the Alliance submitted material for an announcement in the *Reflector*'s "Briefs" column, which printed free announcements of campus and local organizations, but the Alliance's announcement was never printed. The following month, the Alliance and some of its individual members filed suit against Goudelock and several university officials, alleging unconstitutional censorship of their attempts to communicate with the public through the pages of the *Reflector*. They alleged that because the *Reflector* was the official newspaper on the MSU campus and received funding through student activity fees assessed against all students at the state university, the *Reflector* was a governmentally operated forum that could not censor or exclude submitted materials on the basis of their content. The university officials, claiming that they exercised no editorial control over the *Reflector*, moved to dismiss the case against themselves. Goudelock asserted the First Amendment rights of a newspaper editor to make editorial decisions free of governmental supervision.

At a hearing to consider the defendants' motions to dismiss, Chief Judge William C. Keady, of the U.S. District Court for the Northern District of Mississippi at Oxford, encouraged the parties to arrive at a factual stipulation that he could use as a basis for a ruling on the legal issues. The Alliance was represented by Mark Shenfield, a Jackson, Mississippi, attorney. Travis H. Clark, Jr., of Greenwood, represented Goudelock. Lawyers from the Mississippi Attorney General's Office appeared on behalf of the university officials. The parties eventually stipulated to the following facts: that the named plaintiffs were not MSU students and the Alliance was not a recognized student organization (although some of its members were students); that Goudelock had been elected editor of the *Reflector* by the student body; that funds supporting the *Reflector* were derived, in part, from a nonwaivable fee charged to all MSU students; and that the university officials named as defendants did not give Goudelock any instructions not to accept for publication the Alliance's advertisement or notice. Keady concluded, based on the stipulated facts, that the *Reflector*'s editorial decisions were made independently of university officials or policies, so those decisions could not be seen as "state action." Indeed, there was precedent for the view that student editors who were given editorial autonomy were themselves protected by the First Amendment's free press guarantee. The state officials, ruled Keady, could neither require Goudelock to print the advertisements nor require him not to do so. Keady dismissed the complaint, and the Alliance appealed to the U.S. Court of Appeals for the Fifth Circuit.

The Fifth Circuit panel was unable to agree on a unanimous ruling for its August 12, 1976, decision. Two if its members, Circuit Judges James P. Coleman and Walter Pettus Gewin, joined in a brief opinion by Coleman affirming Keady's dismissal of the complaint. Circuit Judge Irving L. Goldberg dissented in a lengthy opinion arguing that an appropriate compromise of the First Amendment rights of the various parties would provide access for the Alliance to the advertising columns of the *Reflector*.

For Coleman, it was dispositive of the case that the university officials did not "supervise or control what is to be published or not pub-

lished in the newspaper." As such, even though the newspaper did receive funding through student activity fees, it was to be treated just like a privately owned newspaper for First Amendment purposes. Coleman quoted from the Supreme Court's opinion in *Tornillo*: "The choice of material to go into a newspaper . . . constitutes the exercise of editorial control and judgment. It has yet to be demonstrated how governmental regulation of this crucial process can be exercised consistent with First Amendment guarantees of a free press as they have evolved to this time."

While this finding, debatable as it was, would have been sufficient for a "principled" decision, Coleman revealed the true biases of the majority of the panel by the language he used (characterizing the Alliance as "this off-campus cell of homosexuals"), and by dredging up the irrelevant issue of the Mississippi sodomy law, which he characterized as a "special" reason for holding that Goudelock had not committed an "abuse of discretion" by rejecting the Alliance's advertisement. After quoting the full text of the sodomy law, which had survived with no change of language from its initial enactment in 1848 and had recently been upheld against constitutional challenge by the Mississippi Supreme Court in *State v. Mays* (1976), he asserted, "The editor of the *Reflector* had a right to take the position that the newspaper would not be involved, even peripherally, with this off-campus homosexually-related activity." In a footnote, he commented further:

> One may not be prosecuted for being a homosexual, but he may be prosecuted for the commission of homosexual acts. Taking into consideration the laws of Mississippi on the subject, speaking as only one member of the panel, Judge Coleman is of the opinion that *no* newspaper in the State may be required to advertise solicitations for homosexual contacts, any more than a paper could be expected to advertise solicitations for contacts with prostitutes. The advertisement tendered by the Gay Alliance offered *legal aid*. Such an offer is open to various interpretations, one of which is that criminal activity is contemplated, necessitating the aid of counsel.

Judge Goldberg was outraged by the insinuations contained in Coleman's concluding remarks. Before addressing the important First

Amendment conflicts he found in the case, he insisted that any "alternative holding" reflected in those remarks "is clearly and absolutely wrong." Coleman seemed to be saying that any notice placed by a homosexual organization was inevitably a solicitation to engage in unlawful sexual conduct and thus had no First Amendment protection. "Such a holding obviously would be fallacious," insisted Goldberg. "The ad directly solicits nothing approaching criminal activity, and the publication of the ad would not have involved the *Reflector*, 'even peripherally,' in the proscribed activities described in the majority opinion." Since no statute of Mississippi did or could make criminal the status of being a homosexual, and "none of the services listed in the advertisement could conceivably be characterized as illegal," the exception to First Amendment protection "whereby statements which propose illegal transactions are rendered valueless for first amendment purposes cannot be applied to this advertisement." Noting that there was no allegation that the advertisement was obscene, or that the books in the Alliance's advertised library of "homosexual literature" were obscene, Goldberg found particularly odd Coleman's suggestion that the offer of "legal aid" gave the ad a "criminal taint." This implied a presumption on Coleman's part "of illegality whenever lawyers are involved—surely the level of respect for the profession has not reached this nadir," chided Goldberg. "The ad carried an informative statement with regard to a matter of social concern, and, as seen, its contents trigger none of the recognized exceptions to freedom of speech." The case had nothing to do with "unnatural intercourse," as implied by Coleman's opinion, and no "special reasons" presented themselves for suppressing this advertisement based on the Mississippi sodomy law.

Turning to the First Amendment problem, Goldberg characterized it as one of a "right of access" to a "public forum" created by the state. Despite the lack of direct editorial control by state officials, Goldberg concluded that the *Reflector* was a "state newspaper" for purposes of First Amendment analysis. He analogized to a "speakers corner" in a public park, where, he asserted, the government "could not constitutionally prohibit speeches dealing non-ob-

scenely with the topic of homosexuality." This was analogous to a newspaper "paid for and published by the state—call it the 'Open Forum'—in which all citizens are invited to express their views on any issue, subject only to reasonable space limitations and a small fee to help offset printing costs. Could the 'Open Forum' refuse to print a tendered statement on the ground that it expressed a political view contrary to that of the Governor, or on no stated ground at all," asked Goldberg. "Surely not. Conceivably, the state could place many non-content-oriented restrictions on the form of the messages, but the state could not refuse tendered statements otherwise similar in form to those regularly accepted solely because the proffered ads were disagreeable in content."

As to the *Reflector*'s status, "The absence of affirmative involvement by university officials in the decision to refuse the MGA ad should not end the state action inquiry," asserted Goldberg. The complaint alleged: "The *Reflector* is the official newspaper of MSU, a state supported and controlled institution of higher learning. The major portion of the *Reflector*'s financing comes from the Student Activity Fund which is collected by MSU and disbursed to the *Reflector*. The *Reflector* is printed on MSU facilities and it is an organ of MSU." Said Goldberg, "The *Reflector*'s funding is thus derived from what is in effect a tax charged by the state to the students." The "imprimatur of the state is clearly stamped on the paper." Even if his conclusions in this regard were questionable due to lack of full development of the facts because of Keady's insistence on ruling on stipulated facts rather than holding a trial, the Alliance was at least entitled to a remand for further development of the facts before a decision on state action was made.

Of course, finding that the editorial decision was a form of "state action" was not the end of the matter. There was, in Goldberg's view, a constitutionally protected right of editorial discretion. Several cases involving student newspapers had resulted in opinions holding that student editors normally have many of the same First Amendment rights as the editors of privately owned newspapers, for the simple reason that students did not give up their First Amendment rights at the school gate. While a school could engage in censorship of what appeared in a student publication where necessary to prevent disruption or damage to the educational program, normally student editors were to be accorded a wide range of discretion. He cited the Fifth Circuit's prior decision in *Bazaar v. Fortune*, a 1973 case upholding the right of student editors to include materials in a literary journal over the objections of administrators, while affording the administrators the right to insist on a notice disclaiming university approval for the editorial selection. He also noted the Fourth Circuit's decision in *Joyner v. Whiting* (1973), holding that the administration of a predominantly black state college had violated the rights of student editors by withdrawing financial support from the student newspaper after it published editorials supporting "black separatism." But, he noted, these decisions did not suggest that the *Reflector* be thought of as exactly like a privately owned newspaper because, as a state-funded medium of communication, he believed the *Reflector* was subject to the open forum doctrines he had previously described. While "a requirement of wide-open access to the pages of a student newspaper would sweep much too broadly," the right of access to a government-funded forum had to be accommodated. The way these competing interests should be reconciled, said Goldberg, was by recognizing a different degree of editorial discretion when it came to advertising and free notice columns as opposed to news stories and other purely editorial content.

Goldberg wrote that student editors should have "unfettered discretion over what might be termed the 'editorial product' of the newspaper," but when the state-funded paper provided space to "unedited advertisements or announcements from individuals outside the newspaper staff, access to such space must be made available to other similarly situated individuals on a nondiscriminatory basis." To Goldberg, accepting advertisements or notices from some political groups and not others on the basis of their content raised an equal protection issue within the context of the First Amendment issues in the case. Sharply restricting editorial discretion regarding advertisements overcame this difficulty. The editors would still be able to reject ads as unsuitable on bases not having to

do with their political content, such as problems of length or use of language that was not itself constitutionally protected. Indeed, said Goldberg, the paper might decide to limit advertising access to campus groups, or groups from the local community. But whatever non-content-based standards were adopted would have to be applied in a nondiscriminatory manner.

Goldberg concluded that this was "a most difficult area of conflicting first amendment interests," but that the majority had reached an erroneous result by failing to consider the difficult questions the case presented. The majority had merely concluded "no state action" based on a superficial analysis and ignored all the hard questions posed by a state-funded forum. Because of the difficulties, said Goldberg, he was suggesting his proposed rules with "extreme caution." He concluded: "The key to the reconciliation here is an emphasis in each situation on the powerful interests of speakers and listeners in free expression. In each context—officials attempting to censor students, and students attempting selectively to censor certain messages from the public on the basis of content—the court must balance the competing interests, but always with its thumb on the side of full and open discussion of public issues." Goldberg had, in fact, gone to the heart of the case hidden under the theoretical, doctrinal clash: it was really about the ability of a submerged minority to communicate its views to the public, and the core First Amendment value of "free expression" was not really advanced by a formulaic approach that cut off a government-funded forum for this group.

But Goldberg's view was a dissenting one, and the majority's opinion was denied rehearing by the circuit court and denied review by the U.S. Supreme Court on April 25, 1977.

A decade later, a smaller-scale version of the same controversy was played out at the University of Nebraska, when *The Daily Nebraskan*, a campus newspaper operated with university funding (and under the general policy supervision of a publications committee that included university faculty representatives), refused to accept "roommate" advertisements from two students, a man and a woman, who wanted to identify themselves in the advertisements as homosexuals. Once again, an entire legal controversy proceeded on two levels: at the public level, the publications committee and student editors insisted that their concern was with discrimination, and went so far as to adopt a policy of nondiscrimination by the newspaper on the basis of sexual orientation to reinforce their position that allowing advertisers to mention their sexual orientation would lead to discrimination because nongay readers would be deterred from responding to the advertisements. On a more realistic level, however, the issue was that lesbian and gay students seeking to associate with other lesbian and gay students as roommates were being denied the use of a state-funded forum for that purpose, and thus were being required to suppress their freedom of expression. The case for finding state action in *Sinn v. The Daily Nebraskan* (1987) was stronger than in the Mississippi Gay Alliance case, given the supervisory role of the publications committee, but the Eighth Circuit Court of Appeals, in a decision by Circuit Judge Frank J. Magill, found that this did not really matter. As long as the decision to refuse the ads was made by student editors, the action of the newspaper was not "fairly attributable" to the state, even though the trial judge had found that the paper was an "instrumentality of the state." This was because the university had taken great pains to insulate itself from direct participation in editorial decisions. By focusing entirely on the "state action" issue, the court of appeals avoided dealing with the difficult questions with which Judge Goldberg had dealt at such length in his dissent, and gave no notice whatever to the possible rights of freedom of expression and association that were being suppressed by the student editors in the case.

Press access questions are very difficult to reconcile because of the strong interests involved on all sides. Goldberg struggled to find a compromise that would promote maximum freedom of expression for members of the public and for student editors, and his efforts are there for those who seek to advance the struggle. Unfortunately, however, when courts are uncomfortable or embarrassed by the subject or the litigants before them, they indulge the seductive tendency to retreat to sterile formulas and to avoid harsh realities presented by oppressed minorities whose messages might prove controversial. Such seems to have been the case at MSU and the University of Nebraska.

Case References

Bazaar v. Fortune, 476 F.2d 570 (5th Cir. 1973), affirmedd as modified, 489 F.2d 225 (5th Cir.) (en banc), certiorari denied, 416 U.S. 995 (1974)

Columbia Broadcasting System v. Democratic National Committee, 412 U.S. 94 (1973)

Joyner v. Whiting, 477 F.2d 456 (4th Cir. 1973)

Miami Herald Publishing Co. v. Tornillo, 418 U.S. 241 (1974)

Sinn v. The Daily Nebraskan, 829 F.2d 662 (8th Cir. 1987), affirming 638 F. Supp. 143 (D. Neb. 1986)

State v. Mays, 329 So. 2d 65 (Miss.), certiorari denied, 429 U.S. 864 (1976)

104. PUBLIC SEXUALITY AND FITNESS TO TEACH

Board of Education of Long Beach Unified School District v. Jack M., 19 Cal. 3d 691, 139 Cal. Rptr. 700, 566 P.2d 602 (1977), vacating *Board of Education v. Millette*, 62 Cal. App. 3d 642, 133 Cal. Rptr. 275 (2d Dist. 1976).

Having determined in *Morrison v. State Board of Education* (1969) that a public school teacher could not be dismissed due to private, noncriminal homosexual conduct without a finding of unfitness to teach, the California Supreme Court was subsequently confronted with the more difficult issue of public sexual conduct. Jack Millette, a fifth grade teacher in the Long Beach schools, was arrested by an undercover vice officer in a public restroom on an accusation of public masturbation and solicitation. His school principal and the board of education sought his discharge. Did the accusation, if proved, constitute *per se* evidence of unfitness to teach elementary school?

Jack Millette had been a successful public schoolteacher without a blemish on his record for sixteen years when he encountered Vice Officer Wineinger on the afternoon of October 19, 1972, in a department store restroom. The officer was occupying the stall farthest from the door. According to the officer, Millette "entered the adjoining stall, bent down and looked up at the officer from under the partition separating the stalls. The officer dressed and, looking into [Millette]'s stall, observed [him] masturbating. [Millette] then beckoned to the officer, saying 'come here. You will like this.' The officer thereupon arrested [Millette] for lewd conduct in a public place." Millette later denied that he behaved as described by the officer, and the prosecuting authorities never pressed charges against him. However, worried about the impact of the arrest on his job, Millette called Joan White, his school principal, that same evening and told her about his arrest.

Under the California education laws in effect at that time, if a school board wanted to discharge a teacher on grounds of unfitness to teach and the teacher demanded a hearing, the board had to petition the superior court to hold a hearing. The legislature had amended the law to provide for administrative hearings within the state education department, but the new law would not go into effect until March 7, 1973. White decided to discharge Millette, who demanded a hearing. The day before the new law went into effect, the Long Beach Board of Education filed a petition in the Los Angeles County Superior Court, seeking a hearing to determine Millette's unfitness to teach. Cerritos, California, attorney John S. William represented Millette. Deputy County Counsels Louis V. Aguilar and Gregory Houle represented the school board. Superior Court Judge Vernon G. Foster presided at the hearing.

The school board presented Vice Officer Wineinger, who testified to his version of the events leading to Millette's arrest. Then the board called White, who admitted under questioning that she had no reason to believe that Millette could not perform his duties as a fifth grade teacher. She understood that he had been

under heavy stress at the time due to his mother's serious illness, but she felt that the conduct with which he was charged showed "unusual judgment and improper reaction to stress and pressure," rendering him unfit to continue teaching at her school. She also indicated, in response to questioning, that Millette's arrest and the reasons for it did not become known to students, parents, or school staff until the public hearing, and thus it was the school board, not Millette, that had made it a "public issue." The school board also called John A. Lepic, principal of the School for Adults Evening High School, as an expert on teacher credentials. Lepic testified that Millette's behavior rendered him unfit to teach because the notoriety stemming from the incident would hamper his relationship with students, parents, and school staff.

Millette testified that the allegations against him were untrue. He claimed that the vice officer had misunderstood his actions, which stemmed from a physical problem in urinating, and denied that he had been trying to solicit the officer. He also testified about the stress he had been under due to his mother's illness. Dr. Davis, a psychiatrist who specialized in diagnosing individuals charged with sexual offenses, also testified on Millette's behalf. After examining him, Davis had concluded that Millette was not a homosexual, and that the conduct on October 29, even if as described by the police officer, was a deviation from Millette's normal pattern of behavior that was unlikely to recur due to the trauma of the resulting employment problems and trial. To support his conclusions, Davis asserted that it would be highly unlikely for someone with "aggressive homosexual" tendencies to have not accrued a prior record of public sex offenses by Millette's age. Furthermore, such persons usually followed a similar pattern of behavior in their sexual exploits. If Millette were indeed somebody who regularly solicited sexual behavior from adults in public restrooms, that did not mean he was likely to solicit elementary school age children to commit sexual acts or to present any other threat to them.

The board presented its theory of the case. Seeking to distinguish the *Morrison* precedent, the board argued that it sought to dismiss

Millette not for homosexuality as such, but rather for poor judgment that made him a dubious role model, incapable of teaching moral conduct to his students. How could he teach respect for the law when he had flouted the law by engaging in public sexual conduct and solicitation, which were illegal? Even though he had not been prosecuted, the board argued, it was the fact of his behavior and what that said about his judgment that were relevant to his fitness to teach. Millette's counsel argued in response that the record gave no indication that what happened to Millette on October 29 was anything other than an isolated incident, unlikely to recur, and that the incident had not affected Millette's ability to teach and would not in the future.

Judge Foster believed Officer Wineinger's version of events and found as a matter of fact that Millette had behaved as charged. However, he also made the following findings of fact relevant to the issue of fitness to teach:

> Defendant's conduct did not come to the attention of the public, students, parents, fellow teachers, and other staff members other than to defendant's immediate superior to whom he reported the incident. Defendant's conduct was an isolated act precipitated by an unusual accumulation of pressure and stress. There is no danger that defendant will repeat the conduct. Defendant does not present a threat to students or fellow teachers. Defendant's conduct does not demonstrate an unfitness to teach.

On this basis, Foster denied the board's petition to uphold Millette's discharge and ordered him reinstated with full back pay and benefits.

The board appealed Foster's ruling to the Court of Appeal, Second District, which reversed in a 2–1 decision. Justice Edwin F. Beach's opinion of October 7, 1976, focused almost exclusively on Foster's finding that Millette had behaved as charged by Officer Wineinger. According to Beach, Foster's findings supported the conclusion that Millette had violated several provisions of the Penal Code, and that this by itself rendered him unfit *per se* to teach fifth grade students, regardless of any other extenuating circumstances or expert opinions. "It is immaterial that the defendant is or is not convicted of the criminal offense," said Beach. "It is the act, not the conviction thereof,

that formed the basis of his dismissal and evidences his unfitness." Accepting the school board's argument that Millette's public conduct was distinguishable from the private conduct involved in *Morrison*, and thus that the state supreme court's ruling was not dispositive of this case, Beach cited numerous subsequent decisions by the various California intermediate appellate courts upholding dismissals of teachers for a variety of public sexual acts.

Beach dismissed the significance of Foster's findings about whether the charged conduct was likely to recur and whether it presented any harm to students, asserting that they were not "true findings of fact" but rather "conclusions of law" which the appellate court was free to reject. He also asserted that the determination whether Millette presented a "threat" to students or to teachers was not a "requisite element" that the school board had to prove before it could dismiss him. Besides, asserted Beach, Foster's finding was "erroneous as a matter of law." It was enough for the board to show that Millette "committed an act that is regarded as immoral or unprofessional conduct or as conduct demonstrating evident unfitness to serve." The Education Code did not require, in so many words, that a "threat" be demonstrated. "The law implies a threat," insisted Beach. "The state, through its legislation, has mandated that where such outrageous criminal conduct as that presented here has taken place, the elementary school children need not hazard a risk of any kind whatever with the presence of such a person in the classroom." Indeed, under the prevailing law, had Millette been charged and convicted in a criminal proceeding for this conduct, he would have automatically lost his teaching license.

Beach expanded further on the nature of the threat that the law "implies":

> That threat lies in the fact that the children will not receive the full and effective teaching to which they are entitled. The teacher's ability to serve as an example is compromised. His ability to teach and demonstrate respect for the law and respect for the feelings of others has thus been reduced. This teacher has lost the self-respect and confidence with which he can fully and sincerely teach children obedience to reasonable rules and orders. The teaching of elementary school children is more than imparting of skills in the three 'R's.'

Because of the lack of judgment evidenced by Millette, Beach held that it was irrelevant that Foster found Millette was unlikely to repeat the conduct. Furthermore, said Beach, this case was entirely distinguishable from *Morrison* because the acts were public. Indeed, since *Morrison*, the legislature had decriminalized consensual homosexual acts between adults in private, but had retained criminal penalties for public sexual acts and solicitation, further distinguishing the facts of the two cases. As subsequent appellate rulings had shown, this distinction was crucial. "Masturbation is not illegal or abnormal," said Beach.

> That does not mean, however, that it must be condoned when done in a public place and coupled with public solicitation of homosexual conduct, any more than urinating or defecating in public would be condoned. Although we are not here concerned with whether and how the criminal law should deal with homosexuals, still we need not condone public solicitation of lewd homosexual acts by a teacher of fifth grade school children. . . . His act remains criminal by definition and entirely disgusting and abhorrent by any reasonable standard of decency. . . . We emphasize that in the case at bench the open masturbation by defendant and his solicitation of a total stranger to join defendant in homosexual conduct occurred in a place open to the public. It was not private conduct.

Consequently, Foster's opinion had to be reversed and judgment entered authorizing the board to dismiss Millette.

Beach's opinion drew an extended, impassioned dissenting opinion from Presiding Justice Lester W. Roth.

> The court's opinion selects from among the findings of fact "the finding" which describes the act upon which the Board predicated its charges of unfitness, declares that 'the finding' is *per se* a conclusive showing of unfitness, ignores the other findings of fact and the evidence upon which they are based, and concludes by substituting its findings and its judgment for that of the trier of fact.

Arguing that the appellate court had overstepped its role, Roth argued strongly that *Morrison* required the trier of fact to determine, as a matter of fact, the impact of the charged conduct on the school. *Morrison* required that a nexus be shown, not presumed, and that expert testimony, including that of psychiatric experts, be considered. Contrary to Beach, Roth asserted that these were all factual issues, as to which the trial judge's findings must be sustained if supported by evidence in the record. By treating as irrelevant Foster's findings on these issues, and giving no weight to the testimony of Dr. Davis, the appeals court had in effect substituted itself as a fact-finder and made highly personal judgments about Millette without ever having seen the man.

"We cannot operate with a blunt scalpel when we weigh the fitness of a person to continue to follow a profession he has been engaged in for 16 years," insisted Roth. "An appellate finding of '*per se*' unfitness, even if such were sanctioned by *Morrison*, which it is not, cuts a broad swath across the realities of this case." Not only had there been no criminal prosecution, in which Millette would have all the procedural protection incident to the state's burden of proof beyond reasonable doubt, but Judge Foster "*saw* and *heard* the witnesses (*and* applied *Morrison*) [and] came to a conclusion which differs from that of the appellate justices who have merely read the record." Roth appeared particularly incensed with the degree to which the private views of the majority justices had determined their approach to this case:

> One may well hold the private opinion, as the majority does, that respondent's acts show he lacks self-control, common sense and a regard for law and the feelings of others. Private opinions, however, cannot be substituted for principles established by the highest court of this state nor can private opinion, no matter from what exalted source, override medical testimony that respondent will not repeat this type of conduct. Yet the majority opines, in the teeth of the evidence and the trial court's finding, that respondent "lacks self-control." Appellate courts may be the repository of a great deal of wisdom but they have not as yet been certified to render *ex cathedra* psychiatric and medical opinions, especially about a person they have never seen.

Since Judge Foster had correctly applied the law "to a difficult case following the presentation of evidence," Roth would affirm the judgment, but he was the lonely dissenter, and the majority of the panel voted to deny a petition from Millette for rehearing. However, on

December 2, 1976, the state supreme court granted him a hearing, and ultimately (and unanimously) reversed, and reinstated Judge Foster's ruling in an *en banc* opinion by Justice Mathew Tobriner announced on July 21, 1977.

Tobriner adopted and embraced Roth's dissenting arguments at every turn. Most significantly, he indicated that the majority in the court of appeal had misconstrued the holding and significance of *Morrison*. The point of *Morrison*, said Tobriner, was not primarily that the teacher in that case had engaged in noncriminal homosexual conduct in the privacy of his home, but rather that his conduct had not been shown to destroy his ability to be an acceptable public schoolteacher. It was not enough that some might consider particular conduct "immoral" or "unprofessional." Although these were the words used in the Education Code, they were "so broad and vague that, standing alone, they could be constitutionally infirm." Hence, in *Morrison* the court had interpreted the Code to require a specific, factual finding of unfitness to teach before authorizing dismissal of a tenured public schoolteacher such as Millette.

> Observing that a statute can constitutionally bar a person from practicing a lawful profession only for reasons related to his fitness to practice that profession, we concluded in *Morrison* that the board cannot 'abstractly characterize the conduct in this case as "immoral," "unprofessional," or "involving moral turpitude" within the meaning of [the Education Code] . . . unless that conduct indicates that petitioner is unfit to teach.'

While it was true that the court had made reference to illegality of conduct as a factor to be considered, it was not the only factor. The trier of fact had to consider such factors as the likelihood the conduct would recur, whether it had become known to students and parents, and whether it would adversely affect the teacher's capabilities in the classroom, and make factual findings.

Reviewing the trial record in this case, Tobriner found that Judge Foster had made exactly the type of findings that were required by *Morrison* when he specifically found that the conduct was an isolated act unlikely to recur, that Millette did not present a threat to stu-

dents or to fellow teachers, and that his conduct did not demonstrate unfitness. Each of these findings was supported by evidence in the record, particularly the school principal's testimony that despite the conduct involved he was capable of performing his job duties, and Dr. Davis's testimony about the likelihood of recurrence. "[V]iewed in the light of defendant's proven 16–year record of competent teaching," this evidence fully supported Foster's final finding that Millette's conduct did not demonstrate unfitness to teach, and it was improper for the court of appeal to have substituted its own judgment on this matter.

In *Morrison*, the court had rejected the notion of *"per se"* unfitness based solely on the allegation of criminal acts. The legislature had subsequently gone even further, replacing the former statutes requiring automatic revocation of teaching licenses upon conviction of crimes with an administrative hearing process by which even those convicted of crimes had a right to attempt to show their continuing fitness to teach. Tobriner specifically rejected the board's argument that Millette's conduct rendered him unfit to teach his students respect for law, commenting in a footnote that "the teacher who committed an indiscretion, paid the penalty, and now seeks to discourage his students from committing similar acts may well be a more effective supporter of legal and moral standards than the one who has never been found to violate those standards."

Tobriner approvingly quoted from Roth's dissent: "It is inherently abhorrent to the American ethic of fair play to permit a state agency to dismiss a teacher by the use of the finding as if it had the effect of a final criminal judgment." Anybody charged with a crime in American society is entitled to the full panoply of due process attaching to criminal proceedings before suffering a penalty solely as a result of the charge. The legislature's subsequent action allowing convicted teachers an opportunity to prove their fitness at a hearing further supported this view. Since Judge Foster had properly considered all the evidence and made the kind of factual determinations mandated by the *Morrison* decision, the court of appeal's decision had to be vacated and Foster's decision affirmed.

The California Supreme Court's decision has proven highly influential in establishing the general proposition that government employees, even those charged with public sexual activity that might violate criminal statutes, should not be deemed unfit for continued public service. By holding that statutes authorizing dismissal for "immoral" or "unprofessional" conduct presented serious vagueness problems, and that only a demonstrated nexus between conduct and fitness would justify a discharge, the California courts took a major step toward protecting the public employment rights of sexual minorities. In so doing, they were in step with the federal system, in which the Civil Service Commission had issued a letter in 1973 establishing a similar approach for the federal civil service. Unfortunately, these principles, while established in law at the appellate level, are not always ideally protective, since they rely so heavily on fair-minded, unbiased judging at all stages of the administrative and judicial processes to be effective. As Justice Beach's opinion for the court of appeal majority showed, the "private opinions" of the judges may well influence their determination whether particular conduct has the required nexus with job fitness to justify discharge.

In this light, it is interesting to speculate whether Jack Millette would have won reinstatement had Dr. Davis concluded that he was a homosexual who was unlikely to engage in public solicitation in the future but who would most likely continue to engage in homosexual acts in private. Tobriner's opinion could support the conclusion that Millette should still be reinstated under such circumstances, but the outcome is not so certain, and it is clear from the other intermediate appellate decisions on which Beach relied that many California judges might find the required nexus based solely on the conclusion that the teacher in question was a noncelibate homosexual. Certainly, the cases from a variety of jurisdictions have shown intense judicial hostility to lesbian and gay public schoolteachers who do not take vows of chastity, or who find themselves caught up in the kinds of isolated incidents illustrated by this case. These cases raise larger issues about the degree to which a public employer, including a school board, has a legitimate interest in the off-duty conduct, both sexual and nonsexual, of its employees, and whether the profession of public schoolteacher does or should impose higher standards of conduct than are required in other areas of public employment.

Case References

Morrison v. State Board of Education, 1 Cal. 3d 214, 82 Cal. Rptr. 175, 461 P.2d 375 (1969), vacating 74 Cal. Rptr. 116 (App., 2d Dist. 1969), hearing granted, 3/12/69

105. A VIOLATION OF DUE PROCESS AGAINST A GAY TEACHER

Gaylord v. Tacoma School District No. 10, 88 Wash. 2d 286, 559 P.2d 1340 (en banc), certiorari denied, 434 U.S. 879 (1977). Prior decision: 85 Wash. 2d 348, 535 P.2d 804 (1975) (en banc).

James M. Gaylord, a public high school teacher in Tacoma, Washington, was removed from his job when the school administration learned that he was gay. Gaylord had never spoken a word about homosexuality to his students, colleagues, or bosses, and there was no indication that he had ever engaged in homosexual activity in a way that such conduct would come to public attention, until a chance occurrence brought his homosexuality to the attention of his school's assistant principal. Although the state of Washington had a sodomy law at the time of his discharge, by the time the state's supreme court upheld the discharge five years later, the state had repealed that law.

Gaylord was an honors graduate of the University of Washington, where he was elected to Phi Beta Kappa and received an award as the most outstanding student in his senior class. He began teaching in the Tacoma schools in 1960. During a sabbatical year, he earned a master's degree in library science from the University of Washington. All of his evaluations as a teacher were excellent, and he was apparently popular and respected by students and colleagues. But Gaylord had a secret: since his teen years, he had known that he was sexually oriented toward other men. Although he had sublimated this knowledge and not acted on it for many years, he was evidently affected by the new awakening consciousness among American homosexuals in the late 1960s and early 1970s. He joined the Dorian Society, a group of gays in Tacoma, and began to meet other people through the Society.

The Dorian Society published a newsletter that included "personals" advertisements. Gaylord responded to an advertisement and met Frank Rivers, with whom he began a relationship. Rivers, knowing that Gaylord was an intelligent, popular teacher at Wilson High School, mentioned to a casual acquaintance of his, a young man named Kim Balcolm who had recently graduated from Wilson High School and was confused about his own sexual identity, that Gaylord was somebody he could talk to about his problems. Gaylord met with young Balcolm and discussed the subject of homosexuality candidly with him. Balcolm prepared a written statement on October 24, 1972, about his conversation with Gaylord and took it to Wilson High School Assistant Principal Jack Beer. In the statement, Balcolm said he believed from Gaylord's comments that Gaylord was gay. Beer went to Gaylord's home that evening and confronted him with Balcolm's written statement. Gaylord was very open, stating that he had "come out of the closet" as a gay man, that it was irrelevant to his teaching, and that he hoped Beer would forget all about it.

Beer would not forget about it, however. He turned over Balcolm's written statement, together with his own report on his conversation with Gaylord, to the school's principal, Maynard Ponko, who brought the matter to the assistant superintendent of personnel. Soon the matter was before the board of directors of the school district, which sent Gaylord a letter dated November 21, 1972, stating that he was

being discharged: "The specific probable cause for your discharge is that you have admitted occupying a public status that is incompatible with the conduct required of teachers in this district. Specifically, that you have admitted being a publicly known homosexual."

Gaylord requested a hearing before the school board, which was held on December 19, 1972. At the hearing, Gaylord maintained that his homosexuality was not relevant to his teaching, that he had kept it private and confidential, and that his discharge was not justified. The board also heard testimony from officials of the high school and the district administration, who pointed to its Policy No. 4119, providing that "immorality" was one of the "justifiable causes for release or dismissal of school employees." After the hearing, the board adopted a written statement of its findings and conclusions.

The board found that Gaylord had admitted he was "a homosexual," that he had made this information known to Frank Rivers and ultimately to Kim Balcolm, "a student in the Tacoma School District No. 10," and thus that he had "made knowledge of his homosexuality public." Based on this, the board concluded "that being a publicly known homosexual is a [*sic*] moral conduct constituting just cause for dismissal as a teacher from Tacoma School District No. 10." In other words, clearly stated on the record, Gaylord was being discharged solely because he was a homosexual who had let three other men (Rivers, Balcolm, and Beer) know about his sexual orientation. There was no allegation that Gaylord had engaged in sexual activity with anybody or had done anything else to bring the fact of his sexual orientation to public attention.

Gaylord filed suit in the Pierce County Superior Court, seeking damages and reinstatement to his teaching position. He was represented by two women, identified in the published court opinions as Mrs. William R. Creech and Mrs. Christopher E. Young, of the Seattle firm of Peterson, Bracelin, Creech & Young. The school board was represented by Pierce County Prosecuting Attorney Don Herron and his deputy, Philip H. Brandt. Judge James V. Ramsdell held three days of hearings before arriving at his decision to uphold the discharge.

The hearings produced a wide range of evidence. Gaylord testified on his own behalf, and several teachers and students, and expert witnesses on the subject of homosexuality testified in support of his claims. The court also heard testimony from Beer, Ponko, and recently retired Tacoma School Assistant Superintendent of Personnel Trygve Blix. The flavor of the testimony comes through from extended quotes in the subsequent appellate decisions in the case.

The school district's argument was that Gaylord had to be dismissed because failure to do so would create disruption and unhappiness at the school, destroying the "optimum learning atmosphere of the classroom" which they were required to maintain by a Washington statute governing rules to be adopted by school boards. The district's testimony was intended to support its conclusions that retaining Gaylord as a "publicly known homosexual" would destroy such an atmosphere. Assistant Principal Beer testified, for example, that "homosexuality is out of place in a public school classroom."

I feel that a student from his initial years as a six-year-old until he graduates from a high school, at about 17 years, is going through his formative stages, and that a teacher, as well as a home or a church, but certainly a teacher is extremely instrumental in influencing a child in these developmental years. And I feel that consciously or unconsciously a teacher that is homosexual can do irrepairable [sic] damage in these formative years. . . . If a homosexual were on our faculty, a known homosexual on our faculty, No. 1, as an Assistant Principal I would have to defend his remaining there to other members of the staff. . . . It would be an extremely disruptive type of thing to have a homosexual serving as a staff member. . . . Well, I have already operated under the assumption that homosexuality is an abnormality and would be classified as immoral, and as such I don't believe that a homosexual meets the standards, the professional standards, the community standards, that we would expect of a classroom teacher.

The Wilson High School principal, Maynard Ponko, testified that had Gaylord not been promptly discharged, Ponko believed that

we would have had students come up and object . . . because they did not want to be put in his class. I had one, in particular, and he was rather violent about it. And I also feel a

responsibility to the whole community and our school and feel this is not the place for a homosexual, a known homosexual, to be working.

When asked what effect retaining Gaylord would have on the faculty, Ponko responded that "it would form isolations." When pressed what he meant by that, Ponko stated that "it had already started. Ridicule, disgust, contempt, for our housing the situation, and why don't we move faster? Doesn't the School Board have a right to move?"

The recently retired Blix testified that "fundamentally I don't think that homosexuality is a way of life that I can tolerate in my position."

I've worked with adolescents a long time and adolescents do admire adults, and adolescents also sometimes admire things that I don't think society accepts, as a whole. We have all seen a lot of that and I think that could be, if the word was out that there was a homosexual teaching, that youngsters even with those tendencies could well accept them and say, this person is a fine man, he's a homosexual, I can't see what's wrong with it . . . I think . . . that we've got to teach by examples as well as by discipline.

In other words, Gaylord had to be removed because he might serve as a positive role model for high school students who were concerned that they might be gay and would accept their sexual orientation as acceptable due to his example.

None of these three administrators was qualified as an expert witness in child psychology, moral philosophy, or any other learned profession relevant to allowing them to state as testimony such opinions going to the ultimate issue in the case. They were apparently considered "experts" on these issues by virtue of their qualifications as public school administrators and were free to spout their "feelings" and "beliefs" as if they were the conclusions of those who had formed such opinions through advance study and reflection.

But some actual "experts" were qualified, including University of Washington faculty in sociology and psychiatry and practicing professionals in the field. According to Judge Ramsdell's summary of the testimony, Drs. S. Harvard Kauffman and Jerman Rose, practicing child and adolescent psychiatrists, testified that "Gaylord's presence in the classroom did not pose any threat of harm to the personal or educational development of the students at Wilson High School, and that in their opinion James Gaylord would be able to function well as a teacher even if his students had knowledge of his homosexuality," even though some parents and students might object to his presence. "Both doctors also testified that homosexuality is acquired, not inherited, and that, while a student's sexual orientation was probably fixed by the time he got to high school, he still had a choice as to his behavior." Kauffman, the psychiatrist, spouted the "party line" of many (but by no means all or even most) American psychiatrists in the 1960s that "homosexuality is a deviation and disease and that if a homosexual wanted to change his behavior a psychiatrist would attempt to help him do so." (By the time Gaylord's case got to an appellate level, the American Psychiatric Association had completed its process of removing homosexuality from its official list of mental disorders, although it retained a category of mental disorders for those who were "disturbed" by their sexual orientation.)

Another expert witness, Dr. Stephen Sulzbacher, an educational psychologist from the University of Washington, also testified that Gaylord could continue to teach effectively, despite objections from some parents and students. Sulzbacher based his testimony on knowledge about homosexuals teaching in other school districts, although, when pressed, he admitted that none of them were "out of the closet" publicly. On cross-examination, he confirmed the speculation by the administrators that objecting parents could have a disruptive effect on the school program. When pushed on cross-examination, all the experts admitted that homosexuality was still a controversial subject, considered "immoral" by a majority of the public.

Gaylord's own testimony was quite poignant. He recounted how he had kept his homosexuality secret from his parents, colleagues, and students for more than twenty years as he struggled with his own identity, only venturing out of his closet discreetly in recent years by joining the Dorian Society and meeting people through its newsletter ads. He had no intention of making a public thing out of it, and it was the school district, not he, who had made it public by discharging him and dragging the whole matter before the school board. Gaylord ended his testimony on a note of frustration with the whole process:

> I quite frankly find it rather galling to have sat through the school board hearing and once again through this trial and hear administrators say that I'm a good teacher, I've been a very good teacher, and yet to be without a job, particularly when I see other people who still hold their jobs who haven't read a book or turned out a new lesson plan or come up with anything creative in years.

After the hearing, Ramsdell issued his findings of facts and conclusions of law, which significantly included that there was no allegation that Gaylord "has ever committed any overt acts of homosexuality. The sole basis for his discharge is James Gaylord's status as a homosexual." Ramsdell also found that Gaylord taught elective courses at Wilson High, so no objecting student would be required to take any of his courses. However, some administrators having testified that his continued employment would "impair the optimum learning atmosphere in a school district," the judge was obligated by statute to give their views extra weight. He based this conclusion on a Washington statute that required, with regard to rules to be promulgated by school administrators, that "the highest consideration is given to the judgment of qualified certificated educators regarding conditions necessary to maintain the optimum learning atmosphere." Even though homosexuality was not specifically stated as a basis for discharge for teachers in the statutes or in the published policy of the school board, Ramsdell found no due process violations in discharging him solely on that basis, for he found that there was a "rational nexus" between Gaylord's being "a publicly known homosexual" and preservation of an appropriate atmosphere for learning at Wilson High.

Dispensing with Gaylord's constitutional claims without substantive discussion or explanation, Ramsdell ruled that his suit must be dismissed. However, he stated some misgivings from the bench:

In the court's opinion under the evidence, and taking the evidence of the people who have to live with this, who seek under the statute to create the optimum learning atmosphere, the Court is going to rule for the Respondent [i.e., the school district]. I feel I have no choice. I can say this, that I expect and I hope that this matter is taken further and that we have a clarification under our own state law on this one question. I don't think it's open and shut, and I think this would be a good vehicle for having that question tested.

Gaylord appealed to the Washington Supreme Court, which heard the case *en banc* and issued a ruling reversing the trial court on May 15, 1975. The reversal was only a partial victory for Gaylord, however, for it was based not on the merits but rather on the court's view that Ramsdell had misconstrued the evidentiary burdens under Washington statutes governing the discharge of "certificated teachers" such as Gaylord.

The court found that Ramsdell had misconstrued the provisions about the weight to be given the views of school administrators. That provision, said Associate Justice Robert F. Utter, pertained only to the rules adopted to govern student behavior. Actually, the burden on the school district was to show by a preponderance of the evidence that Gaylord's continued employment would impair optimum teaching atmosphere, without giving any special weight to the school administrators over the other experts (who had unanimously testified that Gaylord's presence would not create such a problem). The case had to be remanded for a new factual determination applying the correct evidentiary burden. Three other members of the court specifically concurred with Utter.

Chief Justice Charles F. Stafford wrote an opinion "concurring specially," in which he agreed that the trial court had "misinterpreted" the relevant statutes. He indicated that the weight to be given evidence was within the trial judge's discretion and was not affected by the statute. Three other members of the court, two of whom had concurred with Utter's opinion, also concurred with Stafford.

Also concurring, at least in part, was a *pro tem* member of the court, Justice Ringold, who agreed that the trial court had improperly given extra weight to the administrators' testimony.

But he saw no need for a remand, because on the basis of Ramsdell's factual findings, he concluded that Gaylord could not be discharged. After reviewing Gaylord's biography and reproducing in full the written findings and conclusions of the school board and the findings of fact and conclusions of law of Judge Ramsdell (neither of which were otherwise published), Ringold asserted that there was no need to remand this case for further findings of fact because "there are no other relevant facts which can be found." In his view, the rather full trial record led inevitably to the conclusion that "the allegations of 'immorality' as sufficient cause for discharge were not maintained at the trial and are not seriously argued in this court." The record was clear that Gaylord was dismissed for his "status" as a homosexual, not for any behavior that could be characterized as "immoral." For Ringold, the case was open and shut: the statutory requirements for discharge had not been met because "the discharge was based upon a cause not specified in the letter of November 21, 1972 [from the school board to Gaylord] and defined by the stipulation of the parties as coming within Policy 4119 . . . (5) immorality." Ringold noted that the frequently quoted language from the statute, "optimum learning atmosphere," had been misappropriated for its application in this case, because it appeared in a section dealing with administrative promulgation of rules for student behavior, not with the basis for employee termination.

Harking back to a long line of Washington cases concerning grounds for teacher discharge, Ringold argued that the requisite of "sufficient cause" for discharge of a teacher under Washington cases had to be based on "conduct of the teacher which has adverse effects on the 'teacher's fitness to teach.'" The vaguely precatory language of the statute relied on by the court did not provide a definite enough standard to meet this fundamental due process requirement. "The desire to maintain the best learning atmosphere possible is not a sufficiently definite standard to deprive a teacher of his right to continue teaching," said Ringold. If such a standard were applied to this case, it would be "void for vagueness" in violation of the both the state and federal constitutional due process clauses. Nothing presented in the record would sustain any finding of "sufficient cause" to discharge Gaylord, so the case should be remanded, not for a new trial, but rather directing the trial judge to order Gaylord's reinstatement and determine the appropriate damages to be awarded him.

There was another opinion, by Justice Robert T. Hunter, whose conclusion was exactly the opposite of Ringold's. Quoting the testimony of the three school officials, Hunter found it quite clear that continued employment of Gaylord presented a danger that the school board should not be required to bear. He also felt that the majority of the court had adopted an interpretation of the statute that "disregards the entire purpose of the statute," because it was clear that teacher conduct as well as student conduct bore on the issue of "conditions necessary to maintain the optimum learning of the classroom." Since the principal, assistant principal, and former assistant superintendent of personnel were unanimous in concluding that "a teacher holding himself out as a homosexual would be damaging to the optimum learning atmosphere of the classroom," there was ample support in the record for the discharge. He felt that sending the case back to the trial court "can serve no useful purpose and will only cause undue delay in the final disposition of the case."

The case was returned to Judge Ramsdell, who determined that further factual hearing was unnecessary. He would evaluate the existing trial record and just not give any special weight to the administrators' opinions. Even so, he found the discharge to be justified. Despite the testimony by the defense experts, he found that Gaylord's continued employment would violate Policy No. 4119 on immorality. For one thing, although there was no evidence about Gaylord actually committing any sexual acts prohibited by Washington law, Ramsdell believed that an admission of homosexuality connoted illegal as well as immoral acts because "sexual gratification with a member of one's own sex is implicit in the term 'homosexual.'" The school board had a right to be concerned with the efficiency of accomplishing its educational mission, and Ramsdell concluded that once Gaylord's homosexuality became known, that efficiency would be impaired by the nega-

tive reactions of parents, students, and colleagues. If Gaylord was not discharged, the result would be "fear, confusion, suspicion, parental concern and pressure on the administration by students, parents, and other teachers." Ramsdell concluded that "appellant was properly discharged by respondent upon a charge of immorality upon his admission and disclosure that he was a homosexual," and again denied the relief requested.

Once again Gaylord appealed his case to the Supreme Court of Washington, which again considered the case *en banc*, having heard argument from Christopher E. Young on behalf of Gaylord and Prosecuting Attorney Don Herron, of Tacoma, for the school board. This time, the court voted overwhelmingly to affirm Ramsdell's opinion upholding the discharge. In an opinion by Justice Charles Horowitz issued on January 20, 1977, the court concluded that substantial evidence supported Ramsdell's finding that Gaylord was "guilty of immorality," and further that substantial evidence supported Ramsdell's conclusion that Gaylord's "fitness as a teacher was impaired to the injury of Wilson High School, justifying his discharge."

Horowitz first considered whether Gaylord was guilty of "immorality." He quoted a Washington statute to the effect that it was "the duty of all teachers to 'endeavor to impress on the minds of their pupils the principles of morality, truth, justice, temperance, humanity and patriotism.'" The laws governing certification of teachers required "a person of good moral character" to occupy such a position, and made "immorality" a ground for revoking a teacher's license. Other grounds included commission of "crimes against the laws of the state." However, said Horowitz, immorality could not constitutionally be the basis for a discharge without evidence of "actual or prospective adverse performance as a teacher." Because Washington statutes required that there be "sufficient cause" for the discharge of a certificated teacher, the cause "must adversely affect the teacher's performance before it can be invoked as a ground for discharge," as the court had held on the previous appeal of Gaylord's case.

Was homosexuality, without evidence of actual conduct, immoral within the meaning of the policy and statutes? After reviewing a range of dictionaries, encyclopedias, and medical works, Horowitz concluded that the sources generally agreed that a "homosexual" was "one whose sexual inclination is towards those of the individual's own sex rather than the opposite sex," but that a distinction had to be drawn between the "overt" and the "passive or latent" homosexual, the former being one who acted on his inclinations while the latter repressed them. In this case, Gaylord had admitted being a homosexual, and Ramsdell had found that "from appellant's own testimony it is unquestioned that homosexual acts were participated in by him, although there was no evidence of any overt act having been committed." Since Gaylord had testified that he had "been a homosexual for 20 years" and that in the two years prior to his discharge "he actively sought out the company of other male homosexuals and participated actively as a member of the Dorian Society (a society of homosexuals)," including responding to advertisements in its newsletter, it was appropriate to conclude that Gaylord was an overt homosexual (i.e., one who engaged in homosexual acts). Since Gaylord had made no attempt to prove that he was only a "passive or latent" homosexual, the court was justified in drawing this conclusion.

Since Horowitz had now established that Gaylord had engaged in homosexual activity, the question of immorality was easy to answer because "homosexuality is widely condemned as immoral and was so condemned as immoral during biblical times." Even the expert witnesses called on Gaylord's behalf had said that a majority of adults in this country "react negatively to homosexuality" and that "in our present culture and certainly, in the last few hundred years in Western Europe and in America this has been a frightening idea." That did not conclude the question for Horowitz, however:

> Volitional choice is an essential element of morality. One who has a disease, for example, cannot be held morally responsible for his condition. Homosexuality is not a disease, however. Gaylord's witness, a psychiatrist, testified on cross-examination that homosexuality except in a case of hormonal or congenital defect (not shown to be present here) is not inborn. Most homosexuals have a "psychological or acquired orientation." Only recently the Board of the American Psychiatric

Association has stated: "homosexuality . . . by itself does not necessarily constitute a psychiatric disorder." The Board explained that the new diagnostic category of Sexual Orientation Disturbance applies to: "individuals whose sexual interests are directed primarily towards people of the same sex and who are either disturbed by, in conflict with, or wish to change their sexual orientation. [This section] is distinguished from homosexuality, which by itself does not necessarily constitute a psychiatric disorder."

What did Horowitz conclude from this? That Gaylord chose to continue living as a homosexual rather than attempt to change. Having made such a "voluntary choice," he must be "held morally responsible" for it. In other words, any homosexual who decided not to attempt to change his sexual orientation was to be considered immoral because society considered homosexuality immoral. The repeal of Washington's sodomy statute made no difference to this determination, said Horowitz, because the statute was not relevant to deciding what was immoral, merely what was illegal. "Generally the fact that sodomy is not a crime no more relieves conduct of its immoral status than would consent to the crime of incest," Horowitz asserted.

Turning to the other question in the case, whether Gaylord's "immorality" had sufficiently impaired his performance as a teacher to constitute "sufficient cause" for discharge, Horowitz found that there was evidence in the record from which Ramsdell could properly draw that conclusion. First, Horowitz rejected Gaylord's argument that it was the school, not Gaylord, that was responsible for making his homosexuality public. "By seeking out homosexual company, he took the risk his homosexuality would be discovered," said Horowitz. Then, by actually speaking with "the boy" and subsequently confirming his homosexuality to Beer, Gaylord had voluntarily broken his previous secrecy. It was Gaylord, not the school, who made his homosexuality public.

Then Horowitz noted that one student had "expressly objected" to Gaylord teaching at the school, and that three fellow teachers had testified against his remaining on the faculty. The three administrators had also testified that his continuing presence on the faculty "would create problems." While there was conflicting testimony on this, "the court had the power to accept the testimony it did on which to base complained of findings." The testimony adverse to Gaylord was substantial enough, said Horowitz, to provide an adequate basis for Ramsdell's conclusions. Trying to soften the harshness of the decision, Horowitz asserted that the case had to be considered within the special context of the public school. Students might construe continued employment of Gaylord "as indicating adult approval of his homosexuality."

> It would be unreasonable to assume as a matter of law a teacher's ability to perform as a teacher required to teach principles of morality is not impaired and creates no danger of encouraging expression of approval and of imitation. Likewise to say that school directors must wait for prior specific overt expression of homosexual conduct before they act to prevent harm from one who chooses to remain "erotically attracted to a notable degree towards persons of his own sex and is psychologically, if not actually disposed to engage in sexual activity prompted by this attraction" is to ask the school directors to take an unacceptable risk in discharging their fiduciary responsibility of managing the affairs of the school district.

Maybe in other circumstances homosexuality would not be a disqualifying factor, but in the context of a public high school, said Horowitz, it significantly impaired the teacher's fitness, and was an adequate basis for discharge.

Horowitz's opinion drew strong dissents from two members of the court, Justices James M. Dolliver and Robert F. Utter, who had written the court's opinion on the first appeal. Dolliver's dissent was the more lengthy and developed. "For all the scholarly research done by the majority here," he said, "the most basic point has been missed; the respondent school board did not meet its burden of proof."

The error was in drawing an inference from status to conduct, said Dolliver. After quoting in full the Washington sodomy and lewdness statutes, the former of which had been repealed since Gaylord's discharge, Dolliver stated:

> There is not a shred of evidence in the record that Mr. Gaylord participated in any of the acts stated above. While we have held in the past that "sufficient cause" requires certain *conduct. . . .*, we are presented here with a

record showing no illegal or immoral conduct; we have only an admission of a homosexual status and Gaylord's testimony that he sought male companionship. . . . Undoubtedly there are individuals with a homosexual identity as there are individuals with a heterosexual identity, who are not sexually active. Mr. Gaylord, for all we know, may be one of these individuals. Certainly in this country we should be beyond drawing severe and far-reaching inferences from the admission of a status—a status which may be no more than a state of mind. Furthermore, there are homosexual activities involving a physical relationship which are not prohibited by statute.

Dolliver argued that the court had incorrectly placed on Gaylord the burden of proving that he had not engaged in any illegal or immoral conduct, when in fact the statute placed the burden on the school board of demonstrating the opposite. Given such a statutory burden of proof, it was incorrect to let the trial judge infer the commission of illegal or immoral acts. The supreme court should have required proof of conduct to justify dismissal, as it had in its past cases construing the "sufficient cause" requirement. "The only conceivable testimony on conduct was the comment of the student that Gaylord and another male were 'deeply involved' for about a month. This hardly qualifies as testimony either as to 'immorality,' sodomy or lewdness. Finding no conduct, I am unwilling to take the leap in logic accepted by the majority that admission of a status or identity implies the commission of certain illegal or immoral acts." Noting that the majority's approach to the proof issue was "novel," Dolliver exclaimed, "Presumably under this reasoning, an unmarried male who declares himself to be heterosexual will be held to have engaged in 'illegal or immoral acts.' The opportunities for industrious school districts seems unlimited."

While the majority had devoted great efforts to discussing "overt" as opposed to "latent" homosexuals, it had paid no attention to the absence of the term "homosexual" from the Revised Code of Washington. "There is no law in this state against being a homosexual," he asserted, and what was banned, prior to the July 1, 1976, repeal of the sodomy law, were "certain acts, none of which Mr. Gaylord was alleged to have committed and none of which can it be either assumed or inferred he committed simply because of his status as a homosexual."

An equally glaring error was upholding a discharge where the school district failed to establish that Gaylord's performance as a teacher was "impaired by his homosexuality." He had been teaching successfully for a dozen years, and was a homosexual the whole time. "In other words, homosexuality *per se* does not preclude competence," Dolliver asserted. Furthermore, Gaylord "carefully kept his private life quite separate from the school," where nobody knew about it until this matter arose. "Given the discretion with which Gaylord conducted his private life, it appears that public knowledge of Gaylord's homosexuality occurred, as the trial court found, at the time of his dismissal." As to the impact such public knowledge might have on the school, all the testimony was merely "speculation," which Dolliver found to be "an unacceptable method for justifying the dismissal of a teacher who has a flawless record of excellence in his classroom performance." What if parents or students objected to a teacher because he was black, a Roman Catholic, or a single heterosexual man? Any of these descriptive terms could be substituted for the word "homosexual" in Judge Ramsdell's finding on this point, which would bring the majority's errant approach "into sharp focus." The right to practice one's profession was "sufficiently precious" to surround it with "a panoply of legal protection," which was violated by the court's approach in this case.

Justice Utter's dissent, though shorter, was no less cutting. "At the conclusion of the only trial where testimony was taken," he commented, "the court found, 'There is no allegation or evidence that James Gaylord has ever committed any overt acts of homosexuality.'" Yet, after remand, on the basis of reviewing that trial record, Ramsdell found on the same issue, "It is unquestioned that homosexual acts were participated in by him, although there was no evidence of any overt acts having been committed." How could these opposite "findings" be based on the same trial record? "No one asked Gaylord whether he was involved in any overt act or acts," said Utter. Mere proof of "homosexuality" was "an insufficient basis for discharge of a teacher on the grounds of immo-

rality." Utter continued: "The burden of proof to establish something more was on the district, not Gaylord. The majority has concluded that Gaylord's admission of deep involvement with another male is sufficient to raise an inference of participation in immoral activity. His discharge should not be based upon this slimmest of inferences."

Despite these strong statements, however, Dolliver and Utter had been unable to convince their colleagues of the basic unfairness of the result. Gaylord petitioned the U.S. Supreme Court for review of the case, but on October 3, 1977, the Court declined to hear it, with only Justices William J. Brennan, Jr., and Thurgood Marshall publicly indicating that they would have granted review.

The Washington Supreme Court's second opinion in *Gaylord* shows basic ignorance about the nature of human sexuality. The court's attempt to deal with the concepts of homosexuality and immorality appears simplistic, for it rests on the premise that human beings have a "choice" as to any characteristic of their bodies or personalities that cannot be definitely labeled as being either "inborn" or the product of diseases. When the American Psychiatric Association's board voted that homosexuality *per se* was not a mental illness, it was not thereby also stating that it was merely a preference chosen by each individual that could be changed by psychiatric treatment. The question whether sexual orientation can be changed through therapy has been bitterly argued for decades, and most sex researchers have concluded that there is not good documentation that any person who was an exclusive homosexual had ever been "changed" to heterosexuality through therapy. Sexual orientation can be characterized as an aspect of human sexual response that some researchers believe may have biological and perhaps even genetic (the two are not necessarily the same) components, as well as environmental determinants. The testimony before Ramsdell from the "expert" psychiatrist who believed homosexuality was an "illness" was that it was "fixed" by adolescence. If so, how could a postadolescent, such as Gaylord, be considered to have a "choice" regarding his sexual orientation? His only choice was whether to act in accordance with it or to seek change. Horowitz branded as "immoral" the decision not to seek change, ignoring the significant body of knowledge accumulated by the late 1970s indicating that change was virtually impossible for the "exclusive homosexual."

Justice Horowitz ignored any distinction between sexual orientation and sexual conduct, conflating the two concepts under the broad label "homosexuality." Perhaps he could not be blamed for this, because the public is generally ignorant on the finer points of human sexuality as uncovered through the diligent but rarely well-understood efforts of sex researchers since the 1950s. Dictionaries and other sources he used (including the *New Catholic Encyclopedia*) to derive a definition of "homosexuality" were little help, since they also failed to make the distinction between same-sex orientation and

conduct. Even the dissenters, who might be expected to have taken on this issue more directly, aimed their fire solely at the evidentiary issue that no conduct had actually been proven. But what if it had been proven that Gaylord had engaged in sexual activity with another consenting male in the privacy of his home? How would they have decided the case then?

One must conclude that James Gaylord was the victim of an ignorant court, doing no more than one might expect in light of the broader societal ignorance it was reflecting. At the same time, however, one wonders how such a result could be obtained in a country whose Constitution proclaims that no person can be deprived of life, liberty, or property without due process of law.

106. IS HOMOSEXUALITY SPREAD LIKE "MEASLES"?

Gay Lib v. University of Missouri, 558 F.2d 848 (8th Cir. 1977), certiorari denied sub nom. *Ratchford v. Gay Lib*, 434 U.S. 1080 (1978). Decision below: 416 F. Supp. 1350 (W.D. Mo. 1976).

The only case in which members of the U.S. Supreme Court commented on whether a public university can deny official recognition to a gay student organization involved the University of Missouri at Columbia, where a formal denial of recognition to a student group called "Gay Lib" in 1973 led to federal litigation that fell one vote short of full plenary review by the Court. Dissenting from the denial of *certiorari*, then-Justice William H. Rehnquist, joined by Justice Harry A. Blackmun, suggested that the university's concern with the possible incitement of increased violations of Missouri's sodomy law might be analogized to a concern with keeping those infected with measles from congregating in order to avoid an epidemic. (Prior to modern innoculation campaigns, the highly infectious measles virus was greatly feared, leading to quarantines of infected schoolchildren.)

The controversy at the University of Missouri actually began in 1971, when a small group of self-identified gay students at the uni-

versity applied on February 25 to the Missouri Students Association to begin the process of seeking formal recognition. As required by university rules, they submitted a petition, a proposed constitution and bylaws, and a statement of purpose. The initial statement of purpose emphasized communication, specifying that the group sought to "provide a dialogue between the homosexual and heterosexual members of the university community," to "dispel the lack of information and develop an understanding of the homosexual at the University of Missouri." Of the other listed goals, which in some sense just paraphrased the first two, the only one that stood out as somewhat different was "to alleviate the unnecessary burden of shame felt by the local homosexual population." The student government was receptive to the application, approving it in committee and in full senate, and referring it on to the joint faculty and student Committee on Student Organizations, Government, and Activities.

Gay Lib's application languished for quite a while in this committee, mainly due to the opposition of several faculty members. While the petition was pending, Gay Lib, seeking to respond to some of the concerns that its statement of purpose was too general and contained inadequate assurances against disruption and other problems, drafted a new, much more detailed statement of purpose that was responsive to some of the objections faculty members had raised. This statement, submitted to the committee on November 22, 1971, once again emphasized the communicative and educative goals, this time explicitly talking about studying the Missouri sex crimes laws with a view toward their reform, promoting discussion about homosexuality in the university community (with an emphasis on the ability of gay students to learn from the dialogue with nongay faculty and students), providing information to those in the community who "really don't know what homosexuality or bisexual behavior is" in an attempt to reduce prejudice. Perhaps the key statement, whose substance was to become the center of the ensuing legal controversy, was: "Gay Lib does not seek to proselytize, convert, or recruit. On the other hand, people who have already established a pattern of homosexuality when they enter college must adjust to this fact." To this end, Gay Lib proposed to help those dealing with their own difficulties in sexual adjustment by providing a means for them to reach out and seek assistance. "While we do not pretend to have psychiatric expertise, we can reach people who do not trust normal channels for such help and enable them to contact professional help as required." Finally, "as an educational group, Gay Lib does not advocate any violation of state statutes. We serve as a forum for understanding and knowledge where this is now lacking."

This statement eventually swayed a majority of the committee, which voted on December 22 to recommend approval of Gay Lib as a recognized student organization. Five faculty members of the committee dissented, stating that their disapproval "is based upon the belief that recognition will damage the image of the University of Missouri-Columbia. Recognition gives tacit approval to all that Gay Liberation may stand for irrespective of whether the orga-nization is legal or illegal." Edwin Hutchins, then dean of student affairs, agreed with the faculty dissenters and vetoed the committee's recommendation on February 1, 1972, communicating his views in a lengthy letter to the chair of the committee that the federal district court quoted in full in its subsequent opinion in the case. The letter is a long, agonizing consideration of the difficulties felt by an administrator who does not want to take a public position but is required to rule on a controversial issue. It skirts around the edges of the topic, says nothing substantive, but concludes that the committee was rushed into making its recommendation without exploring all the ramifications of approval of the application. As long as there was a minority report from the committee expressing strong reservations, Hutchins was not going to stick his neck out and accept the recommendation. "This negative response to the committee recommendation should in no way be construed as an interpretation that we do not have an issue of importance presented to us," he wrote in the best, noncommittal bureaucratic prose, "that this is not an area of concern to our students or that such issues will not appear as agenda items in the future. But at this juncture I do not feel that the committee recommendation, lacking as it does the full support of the committee, is one timely for the University."

Rather than appeal this ruling immediately, the gay students went back to the student senate, which had supported their efforts, and sought to establish the Senate Committee on Sexual Freedom, which was approved with Lawrence Eggleston, one of the Gay Lib instigators, as its "chairone." The committee held weekly meetings, rather sparsely attended, to discuss sexual issues, and had guest speakers from the law enforcement community discuss the sodomy and solicitation laws of Missouri. The committee requested funding to subscribe to the national gay newspaper, *The Advocate*, which was approved by the senate but was vetoed by the administration. In December 1972, the new dean of student affairs, Edward Thelen, criticized the committee as a "subterfuge for accomplishing the recognition vetoed by Dean Hutchins," and instructed the director of student life to ignore their requests to schedule meeting rooms, pay out appropriated funds from student accounts, and the like. The chancellor of the university refused to overrule Thelen's directions, so Eggleston and his compatriots began, on January 22, 1973, the appeal process through the university's hierarchy on their original application for formal recognition as a student group. At the first step, Dean Thelen refused to reconsider Hutchins's veto. At the next step, Chancellor Schooling upheld Thelen's decision, stating that recognition "would not be in the best interests of the University." Gay Lib appealed to University President C. Brice Ratchford, who concluded that "the purposes [of Gay Lib] are not compatible with the overall educational mission of the University of Missouri and that recognition of an organization with those purposes would not be in the best interest of the University." Ratchford commented that the very name of the proposed organization implied activism rather than mere conversation. "They are in fact an attempt to actively promote the practices of homosexuality by claiming they are acceptable in our society," he proclaimed with alarm, and the bid for recognition was actually an attempt "to obtain the tacit approval of homosexuality" by the university. Since homosexuality "is generally treated in the State of Missouri as being a socially repugnant concept" as evidenced by the criminal laws of the state, denying recognition to Gay Lib would not infringe on any "rights or freedoms" that the students might claim, Ratchford asserted.

The final internal appeal was to the board of curators of the University of Missouri, which was simultaneously considering a similar appeal from the Kansas City campus of the university. Consolidating the two appeals, the board appointed a prominent Jefferson City attorney, Cullen Coil, to act as a hearing officer and to produce a report to the Board on how it should act. Coil held a hearing on August 13, 1973, at which students, administrators, and experts summoned by both sides produced extensive testimony contained in 290 pages of court reporters' transcript. Almost all the testimony related to one of three main issues, as later summarized by the federal district court: the procedural steps taken by Gay Lib to obtain recognition, "whether homosexuality is normal or ab-

normal," and "whether University recognition of a homosexual organization would produce increased violations of the Missouri Sodomy Law."

On the basis of the hearing, Coil produced a report with factual findings and his ultimate recommendation that the petition be denied. Coil concluded that formal recognition would

> give a formal status to and tend to reinforce the personal identities of the homosexual members . . . and will perpetuate and expand an abnormal way of life, unless contrary to their intention as stated in their written purposes, the homosexual members make a concerted effort to seek treatment, recognize homosexuality as abnormal and attempt to cease their homosexual practices.

Coil also argued that recognizing the group might tip "latent or potential" homosexuals among the student body in the direction of engaging in homosexual activity, and would tend to "expand homosexual behavior which will cause increased violations" of the Missouri sodomy law. He ridiculed the idea of homosexuals providing counseling to other homosexuals, which he characterized as "the sick and abnormal counselling others who are similarly ill and abnormal." University recognition would put an official seal of approval on the gay lifestyle, he asserted.

Coil's report convinced the board, which voted on November 16, 1973, to deny recognition to both campus groups. Concluding that the gay student organizations were premised on "homosexuality being normal behavior," contrary to the factual findings of Coil which the board was adopting, the board adopted verbatim Coil's final findings and recommendation, supplemented by its own reiteration that "homosexuality is an illness and should and can be treated as such."

The Gay Lib group's attorney, Lawrence P. Kaplan, of Clayton, Missouri, filed suit on behalf of the group and a handful of named members in the U.S. District Court for the Western District of Missouri. By agreement with the university's attorney, James S. Newberry, of Columbia, the 290-page transcript was submitted to District Judge Elmo B. Hunter, together with depositions taken from three witnesses who claimed expertise in the subject of homosexuality.

The main issue of the depositions, and the main concern of Judge Hunter, was whether formal recognition of Gay Lib would produce an increase in homosexual activity among students at the university. During the hearing before Coil, Dr. Harold Moser Voth, a faculty member of the Menninger School of Psychiatry, testified as an "expert" that "the forming of an organization would tend to reinforce the personal identity and behavior of the individual, bringing like people together; in the sense that it would reflect society's implicit, if not explicit condonement of this organization."

Yes, I think it would tend to further homosexual behavior. I think it would go on anyway, certainly, but giving it formal status I think would tend to perpetuate it or expand it. [Question: Are we talking about a near possibility or probability or what?] Well, it is an inference. I think when you institutionalize a cluster of behavior, you are giving it a thrust. You are bound to perpetuate it, as I see it. I can't imagine otherwise. [Question: But you would get activities which would be in breach of the sodomy laws of the State of Missouri?] Well, if they do those things, then they are going to be breaking the law.

One of the deponents was Dr. Charles Socarides, a New York psychiatrist whose views on homosexuality, formed through his experience with patients troubled by their homosexuality, were implicitly repudiated in 1973 by a vote of the membership of the American Psychiatric Association, but who was described by Judge Hunter in his 1976 opinion as "a highly qualified expert in the field" based on his textbook *The Overt Homosexual* and his professorship at Columbia University Medical School. Socarides was asked in his deposition whether formal recognition of Gay Lib would result in increased violations of the Missouri sodomy laws. His answer:

I believe that wherever you have a convocation of homosexuals, that you are going to have increased homosexual activities, which, of course, includes sodomy. It is one of the most prevalent forms of sexual expression in homosexuality. And I know that for a fact from hearing from my patients, who go to gatherings of homosexuals and where there is a great deal of cruising and a great deal of picking up of partners. So that any gathering would certainly promote such sexual contact.

Gay Lib had produced its own expert witness, Dr. Robert C. Kolodny, a medical doctor who was not a psychiatrist, who testified that in his opinion homosexuality was "a normal behavior." While he stated that he would not be "happy" if his child was homosexual, he believed that Gay Lib would neither increase homosexuality nor cause homosexual practices to proliferate on the campus. He said that he did not believe "that there would be any discernible effect upon the sexual behavior of the student population."

I make that statement for two reasons primarily. One is my clinical knowledge of human sexual behavior. The second is from actual knowledge of what, in fact, has occurred on several campuses where homosexual groups have been allowed to acquire office space, hold social functions, and sponsor university activities. In this situation, in the campuses that I am familiar with where data has been gathered, there has not been a change in the degree of homosexuality—I might alter that—there has not been a change in the percentage of students on that campus who are swinging toward homosexual behavior and leaving heterosexual behavior.

Judge Hunter spent considerable time pondering the hearing record and the depositions and finally decided to uphold the university's decision. His opinion of June 29, 1976, was largely devoted to procedural and jurisdictional matters. Gay Lib had asserted a wide variety of substantive federal and statutory claims, and named as defendants both the university and individual officials and board members. Hunter determined that the only claims over which he could assert jurisdiction were constitutional claims asserted against the president of the university and the board members as individuals acting in their official capacities. Thus, the case boiled down to whether the university's action violated the rights of Gay Lib and its named plaintiff members to freedom of association under the First Amendment or equal protection of the laws under the Fourteenth Amendment.

Turning to the merits of the First Amendment claim, Hunter recognized that there is a federal constitutional right to form associations to advocate changes in the laws and to promote common interests, and that this right had been extended to public university student groups by the U.S. Supreme Court in *Healy v. James*, a 1972 decision concerning a university's refusal to recognize the Students for a Democratic Society (SDS), a militant student antiwar protest group. But the right was not absolute, as the Court had commented in *Tinker v. Des Moines Independent Community School District* (1969), where it recognized "the need for affirming the comprehensive authority of the states and of school officials, consistent with fundamental constitutional safeguards, to prescribe and control conduct in the schools." It was clear, and Hunter easily found, that "nonrecognition prevented Gay Lib from being eligible to use University facilities for meetings and to receive support out of student activities money," the very findings that prompted the Supreme Court to find a burden on constitutional rights in *Healy*.

However, said Hunter, the Supreme Court in *Healy* had stated that a balance must be struck between the associational rights of the students and the interests of the university in pursuing its educational mission. "The burden is upon the University to justify its decision of rejection," said Hunter. "This burden is a 'heavy' one, because despite the University's legitimate interest in maintaining order and decorum on campus, a denial of recognition serves as a type of prior restraint of a First Amendment right." But Hunter declared that the heavy burden had been met, although he considered his determination "a close one," primarily by the expert testimony of Voth and Socarides, which he accepted as being "logical, convincing and persuasive on the critical issue of fact as to whether the recognition of Gay Lib by the University would likely result in the commission of felonious acts of sodomy proscribed by the Missouri Criminal Statute on the subject." He rejected Kolodny's testimony to the contrary on the basis of common sense: "It is well known that the sex drive is a basic drive of mankind and homosexuality according to Dr. Voth and Dr. Socarides can be expected to increase and to include sodomy 'whenever you have a convocation of homosexuals.'"

In *Healy*, the Supreme Court had made clear that the point at which a university could deny recognition to a student group was the point at which its activities crossed over into lawlessness. "The critical line heretofore drawn for determining the permissibility of regulation is the line between mere advocacy and advocacy 'directed to inciting or producing imminent lawless action and is likely to produce such action,'" said the *Healy* Court, quoting from a prior decision in *Brandenburg v. Ohio* (1969). While the university could not restrict Gay Lib's activities just because it found Gay Lib's views to be "abhorrent," "the First Amendment does not require that the University sanction and permit the free association of individuals as a student campus organization where, as the Court now finds from the evidence, that association is likely to incite, promote, and result in acts contrary to and in violation of the sodomy statute."

Turning to the equal protection claim, Hunter concluded that his findings on the likelihood of increased sodomy dictated the same result. Gay Lib was not like the other groups that had received official recognition, because the university had shown to Hunter's satisfaction that affording it formal recognition would lead to increased violations of Missouri law. This provided an adequate state interest under any standard of judicial review to justify treating Gay Lib differently.

Gay Lib filed an appeal to the U.S. Court of Appeals for the Eighth Circuit, where Kaplan and Newberry appeared to argue the case before a three-judge panel on February 17, 1977. The panel divided two to one in its June 8, 1977, decision, with a majority agreeing to overrule Hunter solely on First Amendment grounds, and an emphatic dissenter arguing that the majority had misconstrued its role in the litigation.

At the heart of Circuit Judge Donald P. Lay's opinion for the majority was his conclusion that, because Hunter had decided the case based on paper submission rather than on live testimony from the experts, the court of appeals could make factual findings on a *de novo* basis and relatively easily set aside Hunter's evaluation of the expert testimony.

Noting that both the First and Fourth Circuits had ruled since *Healy* that university recognition of gay student groups was required by the First Amendment, Lay was willing to give little weight to Hunter's decision. Hunter's reliance on the "expert testimony" of Voth and Socarides could be misplaced, since "as demonstrated by the substantial body of professional medical opinion conflicting with defendants' case, it must be acknowledged that there is no scientific certitude to the opinions offered." Furthermore, noted Lay, "recognition of Gay Lib is not determinative of whether its members will be allowed to meet or associate, but only of whether the group may use school facilities and become eligible for student activities funds." Kolodny had testified, based on experience at other campuses, that recognition of Gay Lib would not have "any discernible effect upon the sexual behavior of the student population." While the defendants claimed their experts were more worthy of belief than Kolodny, who was not a psychiatrist, Lay was unpersuaded. "We need not pause here since defendants' evidence turns solely on Dr. Voth's conclusory 'inference' and Dr. Socarides' 'belief,' for which no historical or empirical basis is disclosed."

Even if one were to accept Voth and Socarides at face value, however, "we find it insufficient to justify a governmental prior restraint on the right of a group of students to associate for the purposes avowed in their statement and revised statement of purposes." Without being able to quantify exactly how much proof the university might need of imminent danger to overcome the students' constitutional claims, Supreme Court precedents "make clear that the restriction of First Amendment rights in the present context may be justified only by a far greater showing of a likelihood of imminent lawless action than that presented here." Lay quoted Justice John Marshall Harlan's famous statement in *NAACP v. Alabama* (1958):

> It is beyond debate that freedom to engage in association for the advancement of beliefs and ideas is an inseparable aspect of the 'liberty' assured by the Due Process Clause of the Fourteenth Amendment, which embraces freedom of speech. . . . Of course, it is immaterial whether the beliefs sought to be advanced by association pertain to political, economic, religious or cultural matters, and state action which may have the effect of curtailing the freedom to associate is subject to the closest scrutiny.

Reviewing Gay Lib's statements of purpose, Lay found nothing to indicate that the group was bent on advocating or stimulating lawless activity. He found the purposes similar to those approved by the Fourth Circuit in *Gay Alliance of Students v. Matthews* (1976). "It is, at most, a 'pro-homosexual' organization, advocating a liberalization of legal restrictions against the practice of homosexuality and one seeking, by the educational and informational process, to generate understanding and acceptance of individuals whose sexual orientation is wholly or partly homosexual."

Said Lay, "It is difficult to singularly ascribe evil connotations to the group simply because they are homosexuals." This would blur the line between advocacy and conduct too much. "Finally, such an approach smacks of penalizing persons for their status rather than their conduct, which is constitutionally impermissible." While recognizing the need of university officials to carry out their educational mission, Lay saw no incompatibility between that and recognizing Gay Lib. "To invoke censorship in an academic environment is hardly the recognition of a healthy democratic society," he concluded. As a parting shot at the university, the majority also authorized an award of attorneys fees to Gay Lib for both the appeal and the original trials.

Circuit Judge William H. Webster, later to become director of the Federal Bureau of Investigation and the Central Intelligence Agency, concurred in this result, finding the university's evidence too "skimpy and speculative" to justify "prior restraint of First Amendment rights." He found no evidence that Gay Lib and its members "intend to violate any state law or regulation of the university or even that they will advocate such violations." It would be time enough for the university to act if violations occurred and came to its attention.

> I have no doubt that the ancient halls of higher learning at Columbia will survive even the most offensive verbal assaults upon traditional moral values; solutions to tough problems are not found in repression of ideas. I am equally certain that the university possesses the power and the right to deal with individuals and organizations, "recognized" or not, that violate either its lawful regulations or the laws of the state. There will be time for that if appellees'

dire predictions should somehow prove to be correct. The nature of our government demands that we abide that time.

The majority opinion drew outraged dissent from the third member of the panel, District Judge John K. Regan, who was sitting on the case by designation. He found a blatant violation of the rules governing appellate review, in that the panel was substituting its judgment on the credibility of the testimony for that of the district court. "The mere fact that the testimony was submitted to the district court in deposition and transcript form does not justify a completely *de novo* approach by this Court," he asserted. This was a case for the usual "clearly erroneous" rule, under which an appeals court respects the findings of a trial court so long as they are not clearly erroneous based on the record. Here, Regan found ample testimony in the record to support Hunter's conclusion that formal recognition of Gay Lib would lead to an increase in sodomy law violations on campus. Disapproval of Gay Lib was not based on "mere disagreement" with the group's "philosophy," as was the case in *Healy v. James*, but rather on a determination that the group's recognition would lead to "felonious" action under state law.

> Moreover, state university officials have a responsibility not only to taxpayers but to *all* students on campus, and that responsibility encompasses a right to protect latent or potential homosexuals from becoming overt homosexual students. In carrying out these responsibilities, they were aware that unlike recognition of political associations, whether of the right, center or left, an organization dedicated to the furtherance and advancement of homosexuality would, in any realistic sense, certainly so to impressionistic students, imply approval not only of the organization *per se* but of homosexuality and the normality of such conduct, and thus adversely affect potential homosexual students. In my opinion, the University was entitled to protect itself and the other students on campus, in this small way, against abnormality, illness and compulsive conduct of the kind here described in the evidence.

Encouraged by Regan's dissent, the university filed a petition for rehearing *en banc*. Sharply divided, the active judges of the circuit evenly split over the petition, denying it on

August 8, 1977, but three judges were moved to express public disagreement with the refusal to rehear the case. Chief Judge Floyd R. Gibson, joined by Judge J. Smith Henley, agreed with Regan that the panel majority had misapplied the rules on review of factual determinations, and took up Regan's concern for the "young, often impressionable" students who might be led into "probable illegal conduct on campus" as a result of formal recognition of Gay Lib. Circuit Judge Roy L. Stephenson also issued a brief statement, concurring with Gibson's substantive concerns, while agreeing with the panel majority that it was not necessarily bound by the district court's factual findings when they were based solely on evidence submitted by deposition or other documents.

The university filed a petition for *certiorari* with the U.S. Supreme Court, which fell one vote short. (The Court grants *certiorari* if four Justices agree that the case should be heard.) Announcing denial of the petition on February 21, 1978, the Court indicated that Chief Justice Warren E. Burger would have granted the petition and given plenary consideration to the case, and Justice William H. Rehnquist, joined by Justice Harry A. Blackmun, issued a dissenting opinion, arguing that the case presented a significant issue deserving Supreme Court review. While noting that the Court had discretion to decide which cases to take, Rehnquist felt the Court was shirking its duty here: "[The] existence of such discretion does not imply that it should be used as a sort of judicial storm cellar to which we may flee to escape from controversial or sensitive cases." What was the important issue to be decided? "Writ large, the issue posed in this case is the extent to which a self-governing democracy, having made certain acts criminal, may prevent or discourage individuals from engaging in speech or conduct which encourages others to violate those laws," said Rehnquist.

While the circuit panel's decision to review the factual determination of the district judge *de novo* itself presented sufficient grounds for Supreme Court review on that "procedural question," explained Rehnquist, the real issue "lurking behind" it "is one which surely goes to the heart of the inevitable clash between the authority of a State to prevent the subversion of the lawful rules of conduct which it has enacted pursuant to its police power and the right of individuals under the First and Fourteenth Amendments who disagree with various of those rules to urge that they be changed through democratic processes."

> The University in this case did not ban the discussion in the classroom, or out of it, of the wisdom of repealing sodomy statutes. The State did not proscribe membership in organizations devoted to advancing "gay liberation." The University merely refused to recognize an organization whose activities were found to be likely to incite a violation of a valid state criminal statute.

Reviewing Gay Lib's statement of purpose, Rehnquist found that it included purposes that the expert psychiatric witnesses had identified as having more effect than mere advocacy. In a university setting there were students who "are still coping with the sexual problems which accompany late adolescence and early adulthood." While Gay Lib was contending that the question presented was "little different from whether the university recognition of a college Democratic club in fairness also requires recognition of a college Republican club," to the university much more was at stake:

> From the point of view of the University, however, the question is more akin to whether those suffering from measles have a constitutional right, in violation of quarantine regulations, to associate together and with others who do not presently have measles, in order to urge repeal of a state law providing that measles sufferers be quarantined. The very act of assemblage under these circumstances undercuts a significant interest of the State which a plea for the repeal of the law would nowise do.

The even split among the judges of the Eighth Circuit on the petition for *en banc* rehearing indicated the sharpness and importance of the controversy, Rehnquist asserted, and the need for Supreme Court plenary review. Invoking Justice Oliver Wendell Holmes's famous "clear and present danger" test for government overriding First Amendment rights, Rehnquist asserted that this case was distinguishable from *Healy*. In that case, the Court was dealing with an appeal from a motion to dismiss, where there was no record evidence before the trial court about the potential for campus disruption by SDS. The Court held that such evidence would be required to sustain a refusal to recognize the group and remanded the case for a factual determination. In this case, however, there was record evidence by "experts" supporting the university's conclusion. "By denying certiorari," Rehnquist argued, "we must leave university officials in complete confusion as to how, if ever, they may meet the standard that we laid out in *Healy*."

Rehnquist was unable to move even one more of his colleagues to agree to review the case, however, for a petition for reconsideration of the denial of *certiorari* was denied by the Court on April 17, 1978.

The Supreme Court's decision left undisturbed the growing body of circuit authority finding that public university officials were required by the First Amendment to extend formal recognition to gay students groups, so long as the groups complied with appropriate university rules. As had the Fourth Circuit in *Matthews*, the Eighth Circuit concluded that a sodomy law was not a bar to such recognition; one could not presume solely on the basis of homosexual identity or status that an organization of gay students was Socarides's feared "convocation of homosexuals" leading inevitably to unlawful conduct. As cases arose in other circuits, *Gay Lib v. University of Missouri* was seen as a compelling precedent, discounting the significance of testimony by Socarides (then the favorite "expert" psychiatric witness of defendants in cases where homosexuality was at issue due to his known views on the subject and the prestige of his Columbia University associations) and recognizing the fundamental right of gay people, whether at the college level or elsewhere, to form associations to advance their interests.

Case References

Brandenburg v. Ohio, 395 U.S. 444 (1969)

Gay Alliance of Students v. Matthews, 544 F.2d 162 (4th Cir. 1976)

Healy v. James, 408 U.S. 169 (1972)

NAACP v. Alabama, 357 U.S. 449 (1958)

Tinker v. Des Moines Independent Community School District, 393 U.S. 503 (1969)

107. THE PROM DATE AND THE PRINCIPAL

Fricke v. Lynch, 491 F. Supp. 381 (D.R.I. 1980).

Richard Lynch had a problem. As principal of Cumberland High School in Rhode Island, he was seriously concerned about the health and safety of his students. There were problems with drinking and driving and occasional fights over girlfriends or at sports events. Keeping a school full of teenagers under control was not easy, but Lynch usually rose to the challenge. Now, however, he faced an unprecedented situation: the gay liberation movement had finally reached his school and was providing (or so he thought) another cause for concern about student health and safety.

The problem first reared its head in the spring of 1979, when Paul Guilbert, a junior, wanted to bring a boy to the junior prom as his date. Since tickets to the prom were sold only to couples, Paul had to identify his date when he purchased his ticket and was referred to Lynch for permission. Lynch turned down his request, feeling that adverse reaction by other students could disrupt the dance and lead to injury of Paul and his date. Paul's attempt to make a statement for gay rights did provoke a reaction, even though he was not allowed to attend the prom. Several students began to harass Paul, and Lynch had to escort him between classes to protect his safety. Only a handful of students actively supported Paul's request. One was Aaron Fricke, another junior and a friend of Paul.

In April 1980, the senior class of Cumberland High School met to plan its graduation activities, including the senior prom, which was to be held at the Pleasant Valley Country Club, in Sutton, Massachusetts. Aaron, who had decided that he was gay like his friend Paul, also decided that he wanted to bring a male date to the prom. Aaron approached Lynch for permission, which was promptly denied. Then, during spring break, Aaron contacted Paul (now living in New York) and asked him to be his date for the prom if he could get permission to attend. Paul agreed.

After the break, Aaron again pressed his case with Lynch. They discussed Aaron's deci-

sion that he was gay. Aaron insisted that he could not conscientiously date girls. After their meeting, Lynch personally delivered a letter to the Fricke home, with one copy for Aaron and one for Aaron's parents, in which he explained his reasons for denying Aaron's request:

1. The real and present threat of physical harm to you, your male escort and to others;

2. The adverse effect among your classmates, other students, the School and the Town of Cumberland, which is certain to follow approval of such a request for overt homosexual interaction (male or female) at a class function;

3. Since the dance is being held out of state and this is a function of the students of Cumberland High School, the School Department is powerless to insure protection in Sutton, Massachusetts. That protection would be required of property as well as persons and would expose all concerned to liability for harm which might occur;

4. It is long standing school policy that no unescorted student, male or female, is permitted to attend. To enforce this rule, a student must identify his or her escort before the committee will sell the ticket.

I suspect that other objections will be raised by your fellow students, the Cumberland School Department, Parents and other citizens, which will heighten the potential for harm.

Lynch concluded with an explanation of how Aaron could appeal the decision to the school district superintendent and the school board. Aaron received no satisfaction from the appeal process, and found two lawyers, John P. Ward, of Boston, and Lynette Labinger, of Providence, to file suit on his behalf in the U.S. District Court in Providence. They contended that Lynch's denial of permission had violated Aaron's constitutional rights under the First and Fourteenth amendments to freedom of speech and association and equal protection of the laws.

As soon as the lawsuit was filed, the media became interested. *The Boston Globe* provided coverage on May 20 and May 21, and *The New York Times* ran a story on May 21, giving Aaron's case national exposure as television and radio picked it up from *The Times*. Local newspapers in Rhode Island were full of the controversy, and some students at Cumberland High School began to react to Aaron's stand. One student was so outraged that he physically attacked Aaron in the school's parking lot, punching him in the face and requiring five stitches under Aaron's right eye. Lynch promptly suspended the assaulter and assigned Aaron a parking space closer to the school entrance. Lynch also resumed the escort service he had provided for Paul the year before, accompanying Aaron through the halls of the school between classes. The furor at the school quickly died down, and there were no further disruptive incidents.

Attorneys Labinger and Ward promptly moved for a preliminary injunction, requiring Lynch (sued in his official capacity as principal of Cumberland High School) to permit Aaron to bring Paul to the prom. The case was scheduled for hearing before U.S. District Judge Raymond Pettine, then a fourteen-year veteran of the federal bench and reputed to be one of the most liberal district court judges in the nation. V. James Santaniello of Providence represented Lynch in opposing the motion for injunctive relief.

At the hearing, Aaron testified about his reasons for wanting to take Paul to the prom. He explained that as a class member, he had a right to participate in the senior prom but that due to his sexual identity it would be dishonest to bring a girl as his date. He also contended that his attendance with Paul would make a statement for equal rights and human rights.

Lynch testified about the incidents that had occurred the year before after Paul requested permission to bring a male date to the junior prom, and about the assault on Aaron after he filed suit. Lynch contended it would be difficult to guarantee the safety of Aaron and Paul if they were allowed to attend the dance. He said that his disapproval had nothing to do with the sex of Aaron's proposed date, but everything to do with the possibility of disruption and physical harm. Lynch testified that he did not know whether adequate security could be provided and had not devised a security plan for the prom in case Aaron was allowed to attend. He emphasized that the location of the prom in Massachusetts was an additional complication. Under questioning, Lynch indicated that teachers and police officers were normally scheduled to be present at the prom to deal with any problems, and that in the past they had been able to control the situation.

Aaron's case presented difficult legal issues for Judge Pettine. There was the question whether the First Amendment had any relevance to the issue of attendance at a dance. This was complicated by Aaron's status as a minor student, since there were arguments that the full panoply of First Amendment rights might not extend into school activities and to students with regard to whom the school principal stands *in loco parentis*. Furthermore, the equal protection argument presented difficulties if it was conceptualized as sexual orientation discrimination, since no court had yet recognized homosexuality to be a suspect classification.

In tackling these issues, Judge Pettine decided to focus on the First Amendment freedom of speech claim, since that area of the law provided the clearest precedential guidance. He chose to rely on a 1974 decision, *Gay Students Organization v. Bonner*, in which the U.S. Court of Appeals for the First Circuit (which would hear any appeal from Judge Pettine's decision) ruled that First Amendment free speech rights were violated when the University of New Hampshire refused to allow the Gay Students Organization to hold dances and other social events on the campus. University officials argued that purely social events of the type they had forbidden did not involve traditional First Amendment rights of expression. The First Circuit disagreed, pointing out that discussion and exchange of ideas takes place at informal social events, and that the event itself contained a political message concerning the existence and aspirations of homosexuals to equal treatment in society.

Judge Pettine found this highly relevant to the issues before him. Aaron had testified that attending the dance with Paul would be a political statement, and his testimony on this point seemed to be sincere. Since Lynch's refusal of permission would be restricting Aaron's freedom of speech, the refusal would have to be tested against the standards the U.S. Supreme Court had established in *United States v. O'Brien* (1968) for evaluating restrictions imposed on fundamental rights guaranteed under the U.S. Constitution: Did the restriction further an important or substantial governmental interest which was unrelated to suppression of free expression, and was the incidental restriction on speech no greater than necessary to further that interest?

Judge Pettine found that Lynch, as principal of Cumberland High School, believed he was acting in Aaron's best interest because Lynch genuinely believed that allowing Aaron to attend with a male date would provoke disruption and violence. Lynch also sincerely believed that he would have trouble controlling the situation. The school clearly had an important interest in student safety and the authority to regulate student conduct to advance that interest. Furthermore, it appeared that Lynch was not forbidding Aaron from attending in order to suppress the content of Aaron's message, but rather out of a genuine concern for Aaron's safety. That left the hardest question: was it really necessary to forbid Aaron and Paul from attending to preserve order and avoid physical injury, or could a less restrictive alternative be found?

Acknowledging the sincerity of Lynch's beliefs as to the risks involved, Judge Pettine concluded that those risks were speculative and not a firm foundation for refusing permission. He pointed out that the brief flurry of problems accompanying Aaron's lawsuit had quickly died down, and that the school had always provided sufficient security in the past to ensure the safety of students attending the prom. Lynch had testified that he had not yet actually focused on the necessary arrangements for security. Pettine concluded that "additional school or law enforcement personnel could be used to 'shore up security' and would be effective." He also indicated that "a firm, clearly communicated attitude by the administration that any disturbance will not be tolerated" would also help to avoid disruption.

This was a standard First Amendment analysis of the issue, but Pettine also had to consider whether the context of the controversy might alter the usual analysis. During the Vietnam War era, federal courts had to deal with political activities by high school students opposed to the war, resulting in several impor-

tant decisions about the constitutional rights of high school students. Perhaps the best known and most influential decision was *Tinker v. Des Moines Independent Community School District*, a 1969 ruling by the U.S. Supreme Court which held that high school students do not "shed their constitutional rights at the schoolhouse gate." Justice Abe Fortas, writing for the Court, stated that when school officials wanted to justify prohibiting "a particular expression of opinion," they had to be able to show that their action "was caused by something more than a mere desire to avoid the discomfort and unpleasantness that always accompany an unpopular viewpoint." In particular, the school officials would have the burden of showing that there would be material and substantial interference with the normal operation of the school.

Applying the *Tinker* standard, Pettine concluded that whatever justification might be found for restrictions due to possible disruption at the school were very slight in the case of a prom to be held off the regular school campus. Although Aaron had been punched and slightly injured on the school grounds after filing his lawsuit, the subsequent escort measures taken on his behalf had been effective. The major disruptions necessary for a *Tinker* defense—cancellation of classes, serious injuries—had not occurred, and there was no indication that allowing Aaron to attend the dance with Paul would materially and substantially interfere with school discipline.

Going further, Pettine asserted that if protected expressive activity was likely to provoke a disruptive response, it was more consistent with U.S. political traditions to provide protection for the speaker than to forbid the speech. Although the case arose in a high school rather than in a political hall, Pettine concluded that "even a legitimate interest in school discipline does not outweigh a student's right to peacefully express his views in an appropriate time, place, and manner." Pettine rejected Lynch's argument that the senior prom was not such an appropriate time, place, and manner for making a symbolic statement in support of gay rights by bringing a same-sex date.

Since he found it possible to rule in Aaron's favor based on the First Amendment free speech claim, Pettine did not address the First Amendment right of association claim. He did, however, briefly indicate that he would also have ruled for Aaron on his equal protection claim. Although Aaron's attorneys had conceded that "homosexuals are not a suspect class sufficient to trigger a higher standard of scrutiny," Pettine indicated that because the "government classification impinges on a first amendment right" a higher level of scrutiny would be appropriate, leading to the same result he had reached under the more direct First Amendment speech analysis.

Pettine issued his decision on May 28, 1980, ruling that Aaron Fricke was entitled to attend the senior prom with his preferred date, Paul Guilbert. The decision was an important landmark in recognizing the rights of openly lesbian and gay high school students to participate as full and equal members of the school community. Aaron and Paul attended the prom without serious problems, and Aaron later wrote a book about his experiences as an openly gay high school senior.

There has been little subsequent litigation about the rights of lesbian and gay high school students, but it seems likely as the AIDS epidemic continues to spread that those rights will figure prominently in controversies over "safer sex" education in the public schools. In such controversies, some of the issues explored in this case will take on new significance. For now, the case is perhaps most important for illustrating the particular problems faced by adolescents coping with their newly discovered sexuality and the need to affirm their self-worth by achieving recognition and respect for their relationships. The intervention of a thoughtful federal district judge played an important role in calming the fears at Cumberland High School and making it possible for Aaron Fricke and Paul Guilbert to make an eloquent statement for human dignity.

Case References

Gay Students Organization of the University of New Hampshire v. Bonner, 509 F.2d 652 (1st Cir. 1974)

Tinker v. Des Moines Independent Community School District, 393 U.S. 503 (1969)

United States v. O'Brien, 391 U.S. 367, rehearing denied, 393 U.S. 900 (1968)

108. CAN EDUCATORS SPEAK ABOUT THEIR SEXUALITY?

Rowland v. Mad River Local School District, 730 F.2d 444 (6th Cir. 1984), certiorari denied, 470 U.S. 1009 (Brennan, J., dissenting), rehearing denied, 471 U.S. 1062 (1985).

Few decisions more graphically illustrate the second-class citizenship of sexual minorities than that of the U.S. Court of Appeals for the Sixth Circuit in *Rowland v. Mad River Local School District*. In that case, the court upheld the dismissal of a professional guidance counselor solely because she revealed to a handful of her colleagues that she was bisexual. The decision, which provoked outraged dissent by one member of the court and an extensive dissent from denial of review by U.S. Supreme Court Justice William J. Brennan, Jr., marks one of the low points in the history of the federal judiciary's treatment of the rights of sexual minorities.

Marjorie Rowland was hired to work as a vocational guidance counselor at Stebbins High

School, in Montgomery County, Ohio, beginning in August 1974. She was hired under a limited one-year contract, subject to renewal, without any promise of job tenure under Ohio public education laws. Her sexual orientation was at that time unknown to school officials. Shortly after she began working, Rowland came to school one morning in an exceptionally bright and cheerful mood. Responding to repeated questioning by her secretary, Elaine Monell, about the reason for her mood, Rowland finally responded that she was in love with a woman. Rowland told Monell that she was bisexual and asked her to keep that information confidential. Monell, apparently upset by this information, violated Rowland's confidence by telling Mr. DeNino, the school principal.

Shortly after this incident, Rowland also mentioned to Monell that two students she was counseling were bisexual. This apparently arose from an incident where Rowland was counseling a gay student in the presence of the student's mother, urging the student, who was concerned about her homosexual feelings, to come to terms with them. The mother became angry at Rowland, demanding to know why Rowland would give such advice, when homosexuality was "against the Bible." Rowland did not tell the mother that she was bisexual, but, concerned that the mother might make trouble for her with the school, Rowland went to the assistant principal, Mr. Goheen, and confided that she was "uneasy" about the incident because she feared that if the mother complained, Rowland's "job would be at stake." Goheen reassured her about this, but she remained concerned.

Finally, in December, Rowland had a meeting with the principal during which he encouraged her to resign. She refused, and, alarmed at this development, began to "come out" to other teachers, seeking to enlist their support. In a subsequent meeting involving DeNino, School Superintendent Hopper, attorneys for the school district, and Rowland, she again refused to resign. Hopper and DeNino decided to suspend Rowland with full pay for the remainder of her one-year contract. Rowland filed suit in the U.S. District Court for the Southern District of Ohio in Dayton, alleging that her suspension violated her rights to due process and attacking various Ohio statutes under which Hopper and DeNino purported to ground their decision. The district court issued a preliminary injunction against the suspension, and Rowland was reassigned to a non-student-contact position in curriculum development for career education for the balance of the school year.

In March 1975, the principal recommended to the school board that Rowland's contract not be renewed. The school board unanimously voted to accept this recommendation, without performing any independent investigation of the facts underlying the recommendation. (At the same meeting, the board voted not to renew several teacher contracts, all on the rec-

ommendation of district administrators.) Rowland filed a second lawsuit, contending that the refusal to renew her contract (in effect, a dismissal) violated her First and Fourteenth amendment rights under the U.S. Constitution.

At first, the district court dismissed all of Rowland's claims, finding that "sexual preference" was "not a constitutionally protected interest." Rowland appealed this determination to the Sixth Circuit, which reversed in an unpublished order noting that "none of the circumstances surrounding Ms. Rowland's contract had been developed" and concluding that "dismissal on the pleadings was improper." The case was remanded to the district court, where it was sent to trial by agreement of the parties before U.S. Magistrate Robert A. Steinberg. After the jury had heard all the evidence and attorneys for the parties had submitted proposed charges Magistrate Steinberg announced that he would not give the jury a general charge because to do so would require an extensive seminar in constitutional law. Instead, to simplify matters, Steinberg prepared a detailed set of "special verdict" questions to submit to the jury, calling only for factual conclusions, on which he could subsequently render judgment by applying to the facts his understanding of relevant constitutional principles.

The jury's findings in response to these questions constituted an apparently clear victory for Rowland. The jury found that her revelation of her bisexuality to Monell and school authorities and colleagues had not in any way interfered with the school's functioning or disrupted its operations, but that the decision to suspend Rowland was at least in part motivated by her statements about her bisexuality. While finding that the recommendation and decision to terminate her were not motivated by her having filed suit against her suspension, the jury did conclude that in their dealings with Rowland the school officials had treated her differently from "similarly situated" employees "because she was homosexual/bisexual." The jury also found, however, that at the time of her suspension Rowland's performance as a guidance counselor was not "satisfactory" because she had revealed to her secretary the sexual orientation of two students she was counseling "when it was not necessary to do so."

The jury found that the school officials had acted in good faith. After instructing the jury that a school official would be acting in good faith if he was sincere and believed he was doing the right thing based on an objective belief that his conduct was lawful, Magistrate Steinberg said: "During the 1974–75 school year, there was no clearly established constitutional right to be homosexual or bisexual, or to have as one's sexual orientation and preference homosexuality or bisexuality. The law was uncertain concerning whether or not statements regarding bisexuality made in a high school setting were constitutionally protected." This was a rather stark statement of the lack of judicial recognition for the right of homosexual or bisexual persons to exist. As such, it is not surprising that the jury could conclude that school officials, presumably advised by counsel, would have believed that what they were doing raised no constitutional issues.

The jury found that the school board's decision not to renew Rowland's contract was premised solely on the recommendation of District Superintendent Hopper. The jury specifically found that if Rowland "had not been bisexual and if she had not told Mrs. Monell, the secretary, of her sexual preference," she would not have been suspended or transferred, and that the board of education would not have failed to renew her contract "anyway for other reasons." This conclusion would seem at first contradictory to the jury's finding that Rowland's performance as a guidance counselor was unsatisfactory at the time of her suspension, but it might have reflected the jury's conclusion that the one incident on which it based that conclusion would not have been considered sufficient, by itself, to justify a discharge. The Sixth Circuit, however, was ultimately unwilling to give it such a logical reading.

Based on the special verdicts, Magistrate Steinberg concluded that the individual defendants, who had been found to have acted in "good faith," could not be held personally liable to Rowland. However, he concluded that they were acting in an official capacity, thus incurring liability on behalf of the school district. Based on the jury's specific findings, Steinberg ruled that the suspension and transfer had violated Rowland's rights "to equal pro-

tection of the law and free speech," and that the nonrenewal of her contract specifically violated her "right to free speech," since it was apparently premised on her statements about her sexual orientation. Steinberg then submitted the issue of damages to the jury, which awarded $13,500 for personal humiliation, mental anguish, and suffering caused by the suspension, no damages for the transfer, and damages of $26,947 for lost earnings caused by the nonrenewal of Rowland's contract. The jury specifically rejected the claim that Rowland was entitled to additional damages beyond lost pay for the nonrenewal, since it found that she had "suffered no loss of reputation or standing in the community and no personal humiliation, mental anguish or suffering as the result of the failure to renew her contract."

After the district court affirmed the magistrate's order, the school board appealed the case to the Sixth Circuit Court of Appeals, which heard argument on June 29, 1983. (Among other things, the case dramatically illustrates the time-consuming nature of federal litigation, since the appeal was argued almost eight years after Rowland's nonrenewal.) Michael J. Burdge, of Dayton, argued on behalf of the school board. Michael D. Simpson, an attorney from the National Education Association in Washington, argued on behalf of Rowland, whose counsel at trial and of record was Alexander M. Spater, of Columbus, Ohio. National Gay Rights Advocates, a California public interest law firm, filed an *amicus* brief in support of Rowland's trial victory. The divided Sixth Circuit panel issued its decision on March 22, 1984, reversing the trial verdict and dismissing the case over a strongly argued dissent by Circuit Judge George Clifton Edwards, Jr. Chief Judge Pierce Lively wrote the opinion for the court.

Lively noted that although Rowland did not have a tenured position, she could challenge her suspension, transfer, and nonrenewal if she could show that these actions by the school district had violated her constitutional rights. He asserted, however, that the jury's factual findings did not support a legal conclusion that any constitutional rights had been violated. Turning first to Rowland's First Amendment claims, Lively contended that the case was controlled by *Connick v. Myers*, a 1983 U.S. Supreme Court decision that had been issued after the district court entered its final order in Rowland's case. In *Connick*, the Supreme Court had cut back somewhat on the broad constitutional protection for public employee speech it had recognized in *Pickering v. Board of Education* (1968). *Pickering*, a case where a schoolteacher was discharged for taking a public position critical of the board of education, had been construed by some federal district courts to provide broad protection against discharge for public employees who took public positions in opposition to the views of their employers, so long as that speech did not disrupt the public workplace or undermine its mission. Magistrate Steinberg, in applying *Pickering*, had concluded that the jury's findings of nondisruption stemming from Rowland's comments to Monell, Goheen, DeNino, and some of her teaching colleagues compelled a conclusion that her speech was constitutionally protected. In *Connick*, however, the Court had appeared to cut back on the broad *Pickering* protection by specifying that to be protected, the disruptive or potentially disruptive speech had to be about a matter of public concern, rather than a purely personal concern of the employee. In that case, the Court upheld the discharge of a New Orleans assistant district attorney who had circulated a survey inside the local prosecutor's office among her fellow employees raising questions about working conditions in the office. The Court concluded that the survey pertained to the employee's personal gripes about working conditions, not about a matter of general public concern. The Court concluded that when such speech was the basis for a discharge, "absent the most unusual circumstances, a federal court is not the appropriate forum in which to review the wisdom of a personnel decision taken by a public agency allegedly in reaction to the employee's behavior." Indeed, at one point in the opinion, Justice Byron R. White had asserted that when the speech did not involve matters of public concern, it was "unnecessary" for the court "to scrutinize the reasons for [the] discharge."

Taking this as his cue, Lively asserted that Rowland's statements to Monell, Goheen, DeNino, and other faculty colleagues were purely personal in nature: "It is clear that she was speaking only in her personal interest. There was absolutely no evidence of any public concern in the community or at Stebbins High School with the issue of bisexuality among school personnel when she began speaking to others about her own sexual preference." Lively emphasized that Rowland had asked Monell and Goheen to keep her revelations confidential, which hardly suggested, in his view, an intent to participate in a dialogue on a matter of public interest. Furthermore, her statements to her colleagues were made to enlist them in support of her position in a personal dispute. Her "own treatment of the issue of her sexual preference indicates that she recognized that the matter was not one of public concern," asserted Lively. Consequently, there was no need under *Connick* for the court even to get into the reasons for her discharge, if motivated by this particular speech.

As to the equal protection claim, Lively found that there was no evidence in the record to support the jury's finding that Rowland had been treated differently from "similarly situated" colleagues. Indeed, the jury had itself been puzzled about this point, said Lively, having questioned the magistrate during its deliberations about what was meant by the phrase "similarly situated," since it had received no testimony about treatment of other employees with whom to compare Rowland, and the magistrate had commented, on the record, that "there really isn't any evidence in this case on any similarly situated employee anyway." Lively was also impressed by the jury's finding that Rowland's job performance was "unsatisfactory" at the time of her suspension. This clearly indicated to him that the school district had a substantial justification for its actions apart from Rowland's bisexuality or statements about it, satisfying the Supreme Court's test for "dual motive" cases set forth in *Mt. Healthy City School District v. Doyle* (1977). (In *Mt. Healthy*, the Court held that where a plaintiff shows that constitutionally protected activity was a motivating factor in a discharge, the defendant could still prevail by showing that a sufficient independent justification for the discharge existed.) Although the jury had found specifically that the school board would not have voted against renewing

Rowland's contract "anyway for other reasons" had the issue of her bisexuality not arisen, Lively asserted that this finding was not sufficient under *Mt. Healthy* to find a constitutional violation, because the question as posed to the jury did not incorporate reference to its finding about her "unsatisfactory" performance.

Lively also questioned Magistrate Steinberg's conclusion that the school district should be held liable for Hopper's decisions. While it was true that the Supreme Court had held in several cases that the government could be held responsible when its policymaking employees violated the constitutional rights of individuals while carrying out government policies, it was not clear in this case that Hopper had been carrying out any "policy" of the school district. "The district cannot be held liable for an action of an employee which was totally unrelated to any policy or custom of the public employer," said Lively. The board of education was not directly involved in the suspension and transfer decisions, which were made by Hopper, and merely acted on Hopper's recommendation in the nonrenewal decision. Lively concluded that the district should not be held liable on any of Rowland's claims.

Finally, Lively rejected Edwards's contention in dissent that the majority was ignoring the reality of the case or treating Rowland as a "sick" person. Said Lively,

> [H]er personal sexual orientation is not a matter of public concern, and we have decided the First Amendment issue on the basis of the latest Supreme Court treatment of legally similar claims. And, as we have pointed out, the plaintiff sought to prevail on her equal protection claim without any showing that heterosexual school employees in situations similar to hers have been, or would be, treated differently for making their personal sexual preferences the topic of comment and discussion in the high school community.

Insisting that the court had done no more than "the required analysis" of Rowland's claims, Lively held that the trial decision must be reversed and judgment entered for the school district.

Edwards insisted in dissent that the court's preoccupation with "legal analysis" had missed the point of the case: "This school teacher has been deprived of her job solely because she let it be known to some colleagues, and through them, to her administrative superiors that her sexual preference was for another woman." A jury in her community had found in her favor on a claim of constitutional rights violations and awarded her damages, and the magistrate and district court had entered judgment in her favor. "This record presents a clear cut issue as to whether a citizen's mere statement of a homosexual preference may be punished by job loss by the joint decision of a school superintendent, a public school principal and assistant principal, and the school board, as a matter of institutional policy," said Edwards.

> I find no language in the Constitution of the United States which excludes citizens who are bisexual or homosexual from its protection, and particularly of the protection of the first and fourteenth amendments thereto. The Constitution protects all citizens of the United States; no language therein excludes the homosexual minority. Like all citizens, homosexuals are protected in these great rights, certainly to the extent of being homosexual and stating their sexual preference in a factual manner where there is no invasion of any other person's rights.

Tackling the First Amendment claim, Edwards disagreed with the majority's application of *Connick v. Myers* to this case. Contrary to *Connick*, this case did not involve an employee's "behavior," said Edwards. There was no proof that Rowland did anything that led to her termination, apart from "being bisexual and expressing the fact." The jury had found that Rowland would not have been suspended or transferred if she had not been bisexual and expressed that fact to Elaine Monell, and that the school board's decision against renewing her contract would not have been taken "anyway for other reasons." Also, said Edwards, it was clear that the jury did not believe that Rowland's mentioning to Monell that two of the students were gay was a basis for her discharge. More to the point, however, was Edwards's disagreement with Lively's characterization of Rowland's speech. Edwards insisted that speech about sexual orientation is speech on a matter of public interest. "Long before her nonrenewal/discharge, plaintiff became a center of public controversy in the Mad River School community involving the same issue of homosexual rights which has swirled nation-wide for many years," insisted Edwards. "This record leaves no doubt but that her statements about her status resulted in 'public concern'—both pro and con."

> To summarize the first amendment aspects of this case, the speech may not have had its origin in an overt attempt to exercise freedom of speech. But speech it was. It revealed plaintiff's status as a homosexual in what at the outset she may have presumed to be a confidential relationship. When, however, that speech was spread to school authorities and the community, plaintiff's adherence to her right both to be what she was and to state the fact brought down on her head the wrath of some parents and termination of her job by the ruling authorities of her school. There is evidence in this record that organized parental pressures were involved in the ultimate nonrenewal/discharge. Clearly at the point of discharge, there was a controversy in process over an important public issue. While this incident did not generate national attention, in southern Ohio it was an important matter of public concern. It thus became a part of the nationwide debate on homosexuality and the rights or lack thereof of homosexuals—a debate of far greater significance than the majority opinion recognizes.

As to the equal protection issue, Edwards found that the majority had once again ignored the reality of the case. What if the case involved a guidance counselor who appeared white skinned but who revealed to a secretary that she had a black parent? "If community protests in this rural southwest Ohio county had convinced the principal and school board to nonrenew that teacher, would there be any doubt about whether or not this was 'policy' and a case for a federal constitutional remedy?" asked Edwards, who found "no logical equal protection distinction between these two minority discrimination situations, both of which evoke deeply felt prejudices and fears on the part of many people." Furthermore, Edwards found the invocation of *Mt. Healthy* in this case to be totally unjustified: "She was bisexual by preference. She said so. She was fired because she was a homosexual who revealed her sexual preference—and, as the jury found, for no other reason." This was not a "dual motive" case.

Edwards also found meritless the majority's contention that there was no evidence from which the jury could conclude that Rowland was treated "differently" from "similarly situated" colleagues. "The jury clearly did not believe that the above actions would have been taken against Rowland if she had not admitted a sexual preference which Superintendent Hopper, Principal DeNino and, ultimately, the School Board disapproved of," he said. This was adequate to support the finding of discrimination. He further disputed Lively's conclusion that the board could not be held liable in this case for the decisions of Hopper.

Finally, in a section of his dissent headed "The Reality of This Case," Edwards submitted:

> My colleague's opinion seems to me to treat this case, *sub silentio*, as if it involved only a single person and a sick one at that—in short, that plaintiff's admission of homosexual status was sufficient in itself to justify her termination. To the contrary, this record does not disclose that she is subject to mental illness; nor is she alone.

Edwards then cited and quoted from the memorandum issued by U.S. Surgeon General Julius Richmond in 1979, in which he instructed the Public Health Service to cease "diagnosing" homosexuality for purposes of excluding homosexuals from the United States under the Immigration and Nationality Act, on the ground that medical science no longer considered homosexuality a mental disorder, and from the Kinsey Report and subsequent scholarly works on the proportion of the population that is believed to be bisexual and homosexual. Edwards appended to his dissent the complete special verdict questions and answers from the jury trial.

The Sixth Circuit voted to deny Rowland's petition for rehearing or rehearing *en banc* on June 4, 1984. She filed a petition for *certiorari* with the U.S. Supreme Court, which was denied on February 25, 1985, with two justices, Brennan and Thurgood Marshall, dissenting. In an unusual step, Brennan issued an extended discussion of his reasons for dissenting, arguing that it was time for the Supreme Court to hear a gay equal protection case because of the importance of the issues presented. (The Court has repeatedly and consistently refused to take cases that would directly present the issue whether governmental discrimination against gay people violates the Equal Protection Clause.)

"This case starkly presents issues of individual constitutional rights that have, as the dissent below noted, 'swirled nationwide for many years,'" said Brennan. "The court below reversed [Rowland's trial victory] based on a crabbed reading of our precedents and unexplained disregard of the jury and judge's factual findings. Because they are so patently erroneous, these maneuvers suggest only a desire to evade the central question: may a State dismiss a public employee based on her bisexual status alone?"

Turning to the speech issue, Brennan argued that the Sixth Circuit had completely misapplied *Connick*, which dealt with circumstances where disruptive speech was the basis for a discharge. The court of appeals' application of *Connick* could be questioned on two grounds: first, Rowland's speech did touch on matters of public concern, and second, even if speech is private, it would be protected if it did not interfere with the public employer's operation. As to the first point, "I think it impossible not to note that a . . . public debate is currently ongoing regarding the rights of homosexuals. The fact of petitioner's bisexuality, once spoken, necessarily and ineluctably involved her in that debate. Speech that 'touches upon' this explosive issue is no less deserving of constitutional attention than speech relating to more widely condemned forms of discrimination." Furthermore, *Connick* did not suggest that an employee's "first statement" had to be part of a public debate initiated by somebody else in order for protection to attach to it; this would relegate public employees to the role of "second-class speakers" who could never initiate a policy debate. It was "the topic of the speech" that was the critical factor in determining whether it related to a matter of public concern, and "homosexuality" as a topic of speech certainly qualified.

Furthermore, Brennan argued that *Connick* had not really dealt with the issue of nondisruptive speech because the speech at issue in that case was disruptive to the working of the New Orleans District Attorney's Office. The whole point in these public employee speech cases was to "balance" the interests of the individual and the employer. The First Amendment does not protect only political speech; because of the need to balance rights in the public sector, however, the Court had decided to give greater protection to political speech in the balance. But where the speech involved did not in any way interfere with the public employer's functioning, as the jury found in this case, the balance weighed in favor of the employee. Unlike *Connick* or *Pickering*, this case "involves no critical statements, but rather an entirely harmless mention of a fact about petitioner that apparently triggered certain prejudices held by her supervisors." Thus, the case posed a question left open by *Connick* that deserved an answer from the Court on plenary consideration: whether nondisruptive speech of a personal nature by a public employee would be considered protected.

Turning to the equal protection issue, Brennan noted that the Court had held almost thirty years earlier in *Schware v. Board of Bar Examiners* (1957) that a "State cannot exclude a person from . . . any . . . occupation . . . for reasons that contravene the Due Process or Equal Protection Clause of the Fourteenth Amendment." The equal protection claim became particularly compelling when it involved a so-called suspect class or a fundamental right. "Under this rubric," asserted Brennan, "discrimination against homosexuals or bisexuals based solely on their sexual preference raises significant constitutional questions under both prongs of our settled equal protection analysis."

First, homosexuals constitute a significant and insular minority of this country's population. Because of the immediate and severe opprobrium often manifested against homosexuals once so identified publicly, members of this group are particularly powerless to pursue their rights openly in the political arena. Moreover, homosexuals have historically been the object of pernicious and sustained hostility, and it is fair to say that discrimination against homosexuals is "likely . . . to reflect deep-seated prejudice rather than . . . rationality." State action taken against members of such groups based simply on their status as members of the group traditionally has been subjected to strict, or at least heightened, scrutiny by this Court.

Brennan then noted that many federal and state courts had found sexual orientation discrimination in particular situations to violate fundamental rights, including rights of free speech and privacy. As Brennan had noted in an earlier dissent from a denial of *certiorari* in *Whisenhunt v. Spradlin* (1983), public employees were entitled to the same extent as other citizens to make "private choices involving family life and personal autonomy." This case now posed the question directly whether the public employer could take action against an employee solely because the employee revealed such an inherently private matter as her choice of sexual partner.

While conceding that "traditional equal protection principles" might not interfere with a public employer's actions taken because of employee conduct, "such approval would not answer the question, posed here, whether the mere nondisruptive *expression* of homosexual preference can pass muster even under a minimal rationality standard as the basis for discharge from public employment," insisted Brennan, who noted that the school board had introduced no evidence in support of its actions apart from Rowland's nondisruptive statements. In a footnote, Brennan asserted that Rowland's speech "is perhaps better evaluated as no more than a natural consequence of her sexual orientation, in the same way that co-workers generally know whom their fellow employees are dating or to whom they are married. Under this view, petitioner's First Amendment and equal protection claims may be seen to converge, because it is realistically impossible to separate her spoken statements from her status." Failure to acknowledge this convergence and insistence on treating the two claims as conceptually distinct had led the court of appeals to erroneous conclusions about the sufficiency of the evidence for the jury. Given the jury's findings on nondisruption and lack of other justifications for the nonrenewal, it was not necessary to find "suspect class" standing for homosexuals in order to rule in Rowland's favor, Brennan implied, stating, "I have serious doubt in light of that finding whether the result below can be upheld under any standard of equal protection review."

By reversing the jury's verdict, the Court of Appeals necessarily held that adverse state action taken against a public employee based solely on his or her expressed sexual preference is constitutional. Nothing in our precedents requires that result; indeed, we have never addressed the topic. Because petitioner's case raises serious and unsettled constitutional questions relating to this issue of national importance, an issue that cannot any longer be ignored, I respectfully dissent from the decision to deny this petition for a writ of certiorari.

Despite this impassioned dissent, joined by Justice Marshall, the Court voted again in April 1985 not to consider the case.

The decision in *Rowland* stands, as noted at the outset, as the low-water mark for gay rights in the federal courts. Even the Supreme Court's subsequent decision in *Bowers v. Hardwick* (1986), dismissive as it was of the fundamental interest in sexual expression as a part of human behavior, was not as demeaning to the humanity of sexual minorities as this *de facto* assertion that the state could discriminate against a person solely on the basis of his or her known sexual orientation, without any showing that the government's legitimate interests were compromised in any way by continuing to employ that individual. Debate has raged, and will continue to rage, on whether the military, with its "special needs," or agencies that perform national security functions, with their fears of vulnerability to subversion, are justified in rejecting gay people as employees. But this case was in an entirely different category, highlighting yet again the unspoken or unarticulated fears upon which the courts seem to act when they are confronted with an unashamed, openly gay person who wishes to pursue a vocation in public education. Such decisions stand as a sharp rebuke to the contention, asserted in dissent by Judge Edwards, that homosexuals have the same constitutional rights as other citizens, an argument frequently voiced by "principled" opponents of gay rights legislation who contend that no need has been shown for specific statutory protection against employment discrimination based on sexual orientation.

Case References

Bowers v. Hardwick, 478 U.S. 186 (1986)

Connick v. Myers, 461 U.S. 138 (1983)

Mt. Healthy City School District v. Doyle, 429 U.S. 274 (1977)

Pickering v. Board of Education, 391 U.S. 563 (1968)

Schware v. Board of Bar Examiners, 353 U.S. 232 (1957)

Whisenhunt v. Spradlin, 464 U.S. 965 (1983)

109. CAN PUBLIC SCHOOLTEACHERS ADVOCATE SODOMY LAW REFORM?

National Gay Task Force v. Board of Education of the City of Oklahoma City, 729 F.2d 1270 (10th Cir. 1984), affirmed without opinion by equally divided court, 470 U.S. 903 (1985).

In 1980, conservative California state legislator John Briggs collected enough voter signatures on petitions to introduce a ballot initiative calling for the discharge of any public school employee with student contact who had engaged in homosexual activity in public or engaged in gay rights advocacy or "promotion" in a manner that might come to the attention of students. A direct offspring of the "save our children" campaign mounted by popular singer Anita Bryant, in Dade County, Florida, in 1977, which resulted in the repeal of a county ordinance prohibiting sexual orientation discrimination, the Briggs Initiative spurred a statewide mobilization of gay rights and civil liberties groups and received national press attention. Presidential candidates Jimmy Carter and Ronald Reagan both went on record as opposing the initiative, as did most political leaders of both major parties in California, and it went down to defeat by a comfortable margin. But the initiative struck sparks with conservative Oklahoma state officials, who enacted their own version of Briggs's proposal in 1981 as an amendment to the state's laws governing the conduct and discipline of public school teachers, codified as 70 Oklahoma Statutes section 6–103.15.

Oklahoma has an archaic "crime against nature" law, 21 Oklahoma Statutes section 886, which provides, in classic style: "Every person who is guilty of the detestable and abominable crime against nature, committed with mankind or with a beast, is punishable by imprisonment in the penitentiary not exceeding ten (10) years." The Oklahoma Court of Criminal Appeals, the state's highest tribunal for criminal cases, had construed this in 1955 as proscribing "oral and anal copulation," regardless of the genders of the participants, in addition to bestiality. The Oklahoma legislators, in their 1981 enactment, provided for the discharge of any teacher, student teacher, or teacher's aide who engaged in "public homosexual activity or conduct" in a manner that rendered them "unfit" to hold their position. "Public homosexual activity" was defined as any violation of the sodomy law that was "committed with a person of the same sex" and was "indiscreet and not practiced in private." "Public homosexual conduct" was defined as "advocating, soliciting, imposing, encouraging or promoting public or private homosexual activity in a manner that creates a substantial risk that such conduct will come to the attention of school children or school employees." As to unfitness, the new law provided that the following factors "shall be considered" in deciding whether a person had been rendered unfit for public school employment as a teacher:

1. The likelihood that the activity or conduct may adversely affect students or school employees; 2. The proximity in time or place [of] the activity or conduct to the teacher's, student teacher's or teachers' aide's official duties; 3. Any extenuating or aggravating circumstances; and 4. Whether the conduct or activity is of a repeated or continuing nature which tends to encourage or dispose school children toward similar conduct or activity.

This law seemed, on its face, to authorize the discharge of any teacher who publicly advocated repeal or modification of the Oklahoma sodomy law to decriminalize consensual sodomy between adults in private. It might even be construed to authorize discharge of a teacher who spoke publicly in favor of banning discrimination or violence against gays, since such public statements might be seen as "encouraging" or "promoting" private homosexual activity. Teachers and civil liberties advocates in Oklahoma were determined to challenge the constitutionality of the law, but they could not find a teacher, student teacher, or teacher's aide willing to come forward as the plaintiff, since to do so could well subject them to discharge and significant harassment in this very conservative state. However, the National Gay Task Force, then under the leadership of Virginia Apuzzo, a lesbian former nun and New York political activist, stepped forward and offered to serve as an organizational plaintiff representing those of its members who were Oklahoma school teachers.

Suit was filed in the U.S. District Court for the Western District of Oklahoma against the Oklahoma City Board of Education and the state of Oklahoma by William B. Rogers, an American Civil Liberties Union cooperating attorney representing the National Gay Task Force, seeking an injunction against enforcement of the law. The complaint alleged that there were teachers employed by the board whose constitutional rights to privacy, equal protection, and due process were violated by the law, which was also claimed to violate the First Amendment free speech and establishment clauses. San Francisco attorneys Leonard Graff and Donald Knutson, of Gay Rights Advocates, Inc., joined Rogers in drafting a brief that argued that the "public homosexual activity" provisions violated constitutional privacy rights recognized by the federal district court in Texas in *Baker v. Wade* (1982) and the New York Court of Appeals in *People v. Onofre* (1980). Referring to the debates in the Oklahoma legislature and the historic derivation of Oklahoma's archaically worded sodomy law from English canon law, they argued that a primary motivation for the law's enactment was theological doctrine, and that it effectively "punished" political speech within the core of First Amendment protection. They also contended that the law in effect created a class of openly gay teachers and singled them out for irrational discrimination, noting that Oklahoma's sodomy law did not itself focus on homosexual activity as such and thus provided no public policy basis

for distinguishing homosexual teachers in this manner. Besides, they argued, the sodomy statute was facially vague, since the particular acts prohibited were not specified. The board of education retained Oklahoma City attorney Larry Lewis, who contended that the sodomy law was constitutional and that the discharge of teachers who engaged in public homosexual activity or conduct was fully within the police powers of the Oklahoma legislature to protect the morals and welfare of public school students. Lewis also contended that the statute could be construed to be consistent with U.S. Supreme Court decisions protecting the political speech rights of schoolteachers, since the "factors" for determining "unfitness" arguably required a determination that the teacher's activity had some negative effect on the school and its students before a teacher could be discharged.

Chief Judge Luther B. Eubanks agreed with Lewis and ruled, in an unpublished decision, that the statute was constitutional in all respects. Although he found that the "public homosexual conduct" provisions reached constitutionally protected speech, he held that it was possible to limit the statute by construction to teacher activities that caused a "material and substantial disruption" of the public school's activities. Noting that the U.S. Supreme Court had ruled in *Wainwright v. Stone* (1973) that archaic sodomy laws were saved from vagueness challenges if they had been construed by state courts to apply only to specifically described acts, and that the Oklahoma courts had done so in *Berryman v. State* (1955), Eubanks dismissed outright the vagueness challenge to the "public homosexual activity" portion of the law and noted that privacy concerns were not implicated by public homosexual activity.

The National Gay Task Force appealed this ruling to the U.S. Court of Appeals for the Tenth Circuit. By now, the case had attracted nationwide attention from the lesbian and gay community, and *amicus* briefs were filed by the Speech Communication Association, the Gay and Lesbian Rights Chapter of the American Civil Liberties Union of Southern California, and the Lambda Legal Defense and Education Fund. A divided panel of the Tenth Circuit issued its ruling on March 14, 1984, upholding the portions of the law dealing with "public homosexual activity," but striking down those dealing with "public homosexual conduct" as overbroad in violation of the First Amendment.

Writing for the majority of the panel, Circuit Judge James K. Logan disagreed with Eubanks that a "material and substantial disruption" test could be read into the statute and, consequently, ruled that it was "facially overbroad" because it clearly covered constitutionally protected speech.

Briefly dealing first with the "public homosexual activity" portion of the law, Logan noted, as had Eubanks, that so long as the law imposed penalties only for the commission of public sex acts, there was no violation of the constitutional privacy principles identified in *Baker v. Wade* and *Onofre*, which extended only to such activities between consenting adults in private. The vagueness contentions were properly rejected, said Logan, because "the Oklahoma cases construing the 'crime against nature' statute have clearly defined the acts that the statute proscribes," and there could be no equal protection argument here because "we cannot find that a classification based on the choice of sexual partners is suspect, especially since only four members of the Supreme Court have viewed gender as a suspect classification. . . . Surely a school may fire a teacher for engaging in an indiscreet public act of oral or anal intercourse." Logan dismissed the establishment of religion claim without discussion, merely citing the Supreme Court's decision in *Harris v. McCrae* (1980), which had rejected an establishment clause attack on an abortion law.

The "public homosexual conduct" provision, however, posed serious constitutional questions for Logan. Although the overbreadth doctrine had been described as "strong medicine" that should be used "sparingly and only as a last resort," this provision was capable of regulating "pure speech," which was the paradigm situation for applying overbreadth concerns to strike down a statute. The U.S. Supreme Court had held in *Brandenburg v. Ohio* (1969) that advocacy of illegal activity, such as sodomy in this case, would be constitutionally protected unless it was "directed to inciting or producing imminent lawless action and is likely to incite or produce such action." While a schoolteacher who went on television to urge people to commit sodomy might not be protected by the First Amendment, surely one who went on television or testified before a legislative committee advocating the repeal of the sodomy law would be protected, and both speeches would be covered by this statute. "The First Amendment does not permit someone to be punished for advocating illegal conduct at some indefinite future time," Logan asserted. "'Encouraging' and 'promoting,' like 'advocating,' do not necessarily imply incitement to imminent action," he contended. Indeed, he would even find protected a public statement that it was "psychologically damaging for people with homosexual desires to suppress those desires" in support of decriminalization. Since such statements were "aimed at legal and social change," they were at the core of First Amendment protection and would likely have a substantial deterrent effect on the free speech rights of those employed by the Oklahoma public schools.

Finding that the speech had constitutional protection in the first instance did not decide the case, however, for Eubanks had also found that protected speech was involved but upheld the law nonetheless by imposing a limiting construction on it. Logan concluded that there was no basis in the statute for a limiting construction, which would be required by the Supreme Court's cases on the First Amendment rights of students and teachers. Only protected speech that caused a "material or substantial interference or disruption in the normal activities of the school" could be singled out for adverse consequences, under the Court's rulings in *Pickering v. Board of Education* (1968) and *Tinker v. Des Moines Independent Community School District* (1969). The statute's "unfitness" provision, while appearing to try to circumscribe the discharge decision by tying the speech to adverse effects on the school, had not posed a stringent enough test. "An adverse effect on students or other employees is the only factor among those listed . . . that is even related to a material and substantial disruption," said Logan. "And although a material and substantial disruption is an adverse effect, many adverse effects are not material and substantial disruptions." The law did not limit its reach to statements made in the classroom, but broadly swept in all speech that might come to the attention of almost anyone who might object to a school official, and did not even require a finding of adverse effect, which was only one of several factors that might be the basis for an "unfitness" determination. Unless the law as drafted was "readily subject" to a narrowing construction, it could not be saved, and Logan did not see how a federal court could impose such a construction, given the sweep of the statutory language.

Finally, Logan concluded that the statute's distinction between "activity" and "conduct," through its definition section, made it possible to sever the provisions in such a way as to uphold the former and strike the latter as unconstitutional.

Circuit Judge James E. Barrett filed a heated dissenting opinion, arguing that the entire statute was constitutional. He revealed his emotional reaction to the case by repeated quotation of the "abominable and detestable" language from the Oklahoma sodomy law, and by apparently misreading the statutory prohibition struck down by the majority. Arguing that severing the statute made it "ineffective," Barrett contended that the Oklahoma legislature had a right to authorize the dismissal of any teacher who encouraged school children to engage in homosexual activities. "Oklahoma has clearly announced that the offense of sodomy is not to be countenanced within its borders," declared Barrett. "Federal courts should not function as superlegislatures in order to judge the wisdom or desirability of legislative policy determinations in areas that neither affect fundamental rights nor proceed along suspect lines."

Barrett argued that the statute could be given a limiting construction to avoid any overbreadth problems. "Sodomy is *malum in se,* i.e., immoral and corruptible in its nature without regard to the fact of its being noticed or punished by the law of the state," asserted Barrett, referring without citation to the fact that the old statute of Henry VIII had been absorbed into the English common law, resulting in treatment of sodomy as a common-law offense in some of the states prior to its statutory prohibition. "It is not *malum prohibitum,* i.e., wrong only because it is forbidden by law

and not involving moral turpitude. It is on this principle that I must part with the majority's holding that the 'public homosexual conduct' portion of the Oklahoma statute is overbroad." For Barrett, the statute was appropriately aimed at getting rid of schoolteachers who were "in truth *inciting* school children to participate in the abominable and detestable crime against nature," and there was "no need to demonstrate that such conduct would bring about a material or substantial interference or disruption in the normal activities of the school. A teacher advocating the practice of sodomy to school children is without First Amendment protection." Any overbreadth in the statute was overcome by the "important and substantial" governmental interest of preventing sodomy.

Barrett disputed the relevance of *Tinker v. Des Moines* as a precedent, noting that *Tinker* involved schoolchildren disciplined for protesting the Vietnam War. "Political expression and association is at the very heart of the First Amendment," he said, but "the advocacy of a practice as universally condemned as the crime of sodomy hardly qualifies as such." Barrett was apparently ignorant of the historical and anthropological studies showing that sodomy was not "universally condemned" and was, in fact, lawful in many countries and half the states of the United States. He found no need to show that such "advocacy" would materially disrupt a public school, regardless of where statements were made or how carefully worded to bear solely on legislative issues. He saw the majority's ruling as a "bow to permissiveness" and not supported by the Supreme Court precedents on which it relied, especially those that dealt with speech solely in the context of adults.

At first it appeared that Oklahoma officials would not appeal the ruling, but Dennis Arrow, a conservative lawyer, stepped forward to bring the case to the U.S. Supreme Court on behalf of the Oklahoma City school board through direct appeal, as provided in cases where a state statute had been invalidated by a lower federal court. The Court noted "probable jurisdiction" of the case on October 1, 1984, setting oral argument for January 1985. Virginia Apuzzo, of the National Gay Task Force, invited Harvard Law School Professor Laurence H. Tribe, one of the nation's most famous and successful Supreme Court litigators, to take on the case on a *pro bono* basis in the Supreme Court. Tribe, who had never previously argued a "gay rights" case, was assisted on the brief by Bill Rogers and Leonard Graff. Other *amicus* briefs urging affirmance of the Tenth Circuit's opinion were filed by the American Association for Personal Privacy, the American Association of University Professors (concerned with the impact a Supreme Court opinion could have on the free speech rights of public university teachers), the Center for Constitutional Rights, the National Education Association, and Lambda Legal Defense and Education Fund. In addition to these private-sector organizations, *amicus* support came from the state of New York, in a brief filed by Attorney General Robert Abrams and joined by California Attorney General John Van de Kamp.

This time, however, the defenders of the statute were not alone in advocating reversal to the Court. *Amicus* briefs came from the Concerned Women for America Education and Legal Defense Fund, the National School Boards Association (fearful of a Supreme Court decision further limiting the discretion of school boards in discharging teachers), the Washington Legal Foundation (a conservative think tank), and the state of Oklahoma.

Before the oral argument could be held, Justice Lewis F. Powell, Jr., required surgery and as a result announced that he would miss the January argument Term of the Court. The case was argued on January 14, 1985, to an eight-member bench, some of whose members expressed great hostility to Tribe and his arguments, unprecedented for him in his dealings with the Court. The eight members of the Court who participated in the argument were deadlocked, four to four, on whether to affirm or to reverse the lower court's ruling, so the case awaited Justice Powell's return to active duty. When he did return in March, the Court had to make practical decisions about which cases to settle by reargument and which cases to affirm without opinion by the equally divided Court, many of which had accumulated during Powell's absence. For reasons not explained by

the Court, it decided to let the Tenth Circuit's opinion stand without explanation. Presumably this meant that Powell was satisfied with the Tenth Circuit's disposition of the matter and felt that no purpose would be served in rehearing the case just so he could vote to uphold it directly, although this conclusion is merely speculative. (After all, several years after the *Bowers v. Hardwick* decision, Justice Powell commented that he had thought that a trivial case, perhaps indicating that he found gay rights issues of little constitutional moment.)

Although the Supreme Court did not produce an opinion in the Oklahoma case, its affirmance of the lower court opinion was the first substantive victory for the gay rights movement in the Supreme Court in almost a quarter century. Not since the Court struck down postal regulations that had been used to bar gay-oriented literature from the mails had it shown any approval of constitutional protection for gays. More importantly, the Court's decision took the wind out of the sails of the Briggs movement, since conservative legislators in some other states abandoned plans to introduce similar legislation. The Tenth Circuit's opinion, standing as the "law of the case," was a strong endorsement of First Amendment protection for gay rights advocacy. Nonetheless, Judge Barrett's dissenting opinion showed the depth of hostility against gays that persists in some quarters, even on the federal bench.

Case References

Baker v. Wade, 553 F. Supp. 1121 (N.D. Tex. 1982), appeal dismissed, 743 F.2d 236 (5th Cir. 1984), reversed en banc, 769 F.2d 289 (5th Cir. 1985), certiorari denied, 478 U.S. 1022 (1986)

Berryman v. State, 283 P.2d 558 (Okla. Crim. App.), appeal dismissed for want of a substantial federal question, 350 U.S. 878 (1955)

Bowers v. Hardwick, 478 U.S. 186 (1985)

Brandenburg v. Ohio, 395 U.S. 444 (1969)

Harris v. McCrae, 448 U.S. 297 (1980)

People v. Onofre, 51 N.Y.2d 476 (1980), certiorari denied, 451 U.S. 987 (1981)

Pickering v. Board of Education, 391 U.S. 563 (1968)

Tinker v. Des Moines Independent Community School District, 393 U.S. 503 (1969)

Wainwright v. Stone, 414 U.S. 21 (1973)

110. "INTOLERANCE DAY" AT MADISON HIGH

Solmitz v. Maine School Administrative District No. 59, 495 A.2d 812 (Me. 1985).

Societal prejudice against sexual minorities is widespread and expresses itself in many ways, including a general reluctance to hear the message of tolerance. Studies of the attitudes of young people reveal a horrifying hatred of those who are perceived as "different" in ways that challenge the self-image and self-esteem of the study subjects. In some cases, this hatred, grounded in ignorance and fear, actually explodes into violence, as it did in Bangor, Maine, when a group of three teenagers taunted and harassed a young gay man and assaulted him on a bridge, resulting in his drowning. The tragedy greatly alarmed the small, organized gay community in Maine, and stimulated others concerned about the mounting violence and intolerance to confront the issue head-on in the schools.

One such person was David O. Solmitz, a social studies teacher at Madison High School. Solmitz believed strongly in introducing reality into the classroom by inviting speakers from the outside world to talk about their lives and the problems they experienced. He contacted Dale McCormick, a prominent lesbian activist, and asked her to participate in devising a program through which the Madison High School students could confront various kinds of bigotry and work through their own anxieties and ignorance. The resulting program that Solmitz proposed to the school's principal, Anthony Krapf, was a "Tolerance Day" event that would include representative speakers from a wide range of groups that experienced prejudice in society, including lesbians and gay men (whom McCormick would represent). Tolerance Day, which Solmitz proposed to stage on Friday, January 25, 1985, would involve an assembly for the entire student body at which all the guest speakers would address the students, and then separate workshop sessions in classrooms devoted to particular groups, among which students could select.

Solmitz and Krapf met on January 14 to discuss the proposed program. Krapf instructed Solmitz that he should not invite a homosexual to speak at Tolerance Day. Solmitz expressed disagreement with this instruction, so the two men met the next day with the superintendent of schools in School Administrative District No. 59, Robert Woodbury, who echoed Krapf's view that inviting a homosexual to speak would cause too many problems. Solmitz was unwilling to take no for an answer, however, and continued discussions with Woodbury and Krapf. They reached a compromise agreement on January 18, under which the program would be modified so that the guest speakers would not address the assembly, but merely be introduced there, and students who did not want to hear any of the guest speakers could attend a study hall.

While discussing these plans with Krapf and Woodbury, Solmitz, who feared that his proposed program was falling apart, began consulting attorneys to consider legal action. Solmitz's lawyers contacted the superior court to schedule a hearing date in case it was necessary to seek injunctive relief in order to have Tolerance Day take place. This brought the matter to the attention of the local newspapers, which ran articles on Saturday morning, January 19. Over the weekend, school administrators and school board members received approximately fifty telephone calls and visits from people, all critical of allowing McCormick to appear at the school. Some callers said that picketing would occur, some parents said they would not allow their children to attend or that they would attend themselves to see what was going on, and a few calls warned of possible bomb threats and sabotage of the school's furnace (in the heart of the frigid Maine winter) if the program went on as scheduled.

The calls, visits, and threats prompted the school board to call an emergency session on Monday night, January 21. Superintendent Woodbury summarized the Tolerance Day proposal and ensuing discussions for the board, and reported on the threats of disruption he had received. The board members went into a closed session to discuss the matter. Upon resuming the meeting, they unanimously approved a resolution canceling the Tolerance Day program, specifically because of their concerns about "safety, order and security" at Madison High School. The next day, Solmitz, McCormick, and one of Solmitz's students who had been active in planning the program, Sonja Roach, filed suit against the school board, as well as Woodbury and Krapf and the individual board members in their official capacities, alleging a violation of constitutional rights. All three plaintiffs contended that their own First Amendment rights were violated, and McCormick additionally alleged that the board's order that she not speak at the school violated her right to equal protection of the laws.

The Kennebec County Superior Court justice (unnamed in the only published opinion in the case) held a hearing on motion for a temporary restraining order on January 23. Augusta attorneys Jim Mitchell and Jed Davis represented the plaintiffs, and Portland lawyers Merton Henry and Brian C. Shaw appeared for the school board and individual defendants. The next day, the judge announced that he would not order the school to go forward with the program on January 25, and set down the matter for a hearing on the merits on February 8. Several members of the school board testified about the reason for their vote to cancel, all unanimously asserting that they had no desire to censor the subjects to be discussed at Madison High School, but were all concerned about potential harm to students and disruption of the academic program if the Tolerance Day events were held as scheduled. The hearing continued on February 11, and the judge ruled on February 14, denying permanent injunctive relief and refusing to rule on the requests for attorney's fees made by both sides. Based on the hearing testimony, the judge found that "concerns about disruptions and the fact that such disruptions might make Tolerance Day a 'lost day educationally' . . . were the *decisive factors* in the decision to vote to cancel." Believing the denials by the board members and administrators, the judge found that no "desire to suppress ideas" was involved in the cancellation decision. Consequently, the judge held that the cancellation was not motivated by the content of the proposed program and did not raise First

Amendment concerns. The judge also ruled that McCormick had not experienced invidious discrimination; after all, the entire program was canceled and nobody was allowed to speak, so she had not been singled out for differential treatment.

Solmitz, Roach, and McCormick immmediately filed an appeal to the Maine Supreme Judicial Court, which scheduled arguments for April 29. The case had by now attracted national attention, for the spectacle of a proposed "Tolerance Day" being canceled due to intolerance by the local community was an irony deemed worthy of commentary by many in the national media. *Amicus* briefs were filed in support of the plaintiffs by the Center for Constitutional Rights and allied groups, Lambda Legal Defense and Education Fund, the Maine Teachers Association, and the Student Press Law Center. The defendants drew *amicus* support from the Christian Civil League of Maine and the Maine School Management Association. That *amicus* briefs were drafted and submitted from so many groups on such short notice speaks loudly of the passions immediately provoked by this dispute.

The court quickly reached a unanimous determination in the case, ruling on July 12, 1985, that the superior court had correctly refused to order the school board to allow the Tolerance Day program to be held, and further that neither party should be awarded attorney's fees. The opinion for the court by Chief Justice Vincent L. McKusick echoed the trial judge by finding that the evidence presented at the hearing supported a determination that the board was not engaging in unconstitutional censorship when it voted to cancel the program.

For McKusick, the case was really about the appropriate scope of authority of a school board to deal with its "broad power to manage the curriculum." McKusick derived much of his First Amendment analysis from the U.S. Supreme Court's opinions in *Tinker v. Des Moines Independent Community School District* (1969) and *Board of Education, Island Trees Union Free School District v. Pico* (1982). In these cases the Court had to confront claims involving the First Amendment rights of high school students to express political views through symbolic action or to receive information through the school's library collection, respectively. In both, the Court had held that school officials had broad management authority, but that students (and teachers) retained First Amendment rights, requiring a balance to be struck between the two in order to advance the public goal of providing an education program for the students. In both cases, the Court was concerned that school officials retain enough authority to be able to assure that the educational program went forward without disruption and the burden was squarely placed, as it must be in a First Amendment context, on the school board to show that disruption would result if First Amendment activities were not restricted. Furthermore, in *Pico* the Court held that decisons about the educational program and curriculum were primarily entrusted to professional educators and elected school board officials.

McKusick characterized this case as, at bottom, a curriculum dispute. Solmitz was proposing an "addition" to the curriculum at Madison High School, and school authorities had discretion to decide whether to accept his proposal.

> In the case at bar, plaintiffs could make no realistic claim that the Tolerance Day program was anything other than a proposed addition to the course of instruction at Madison High School. Even the compromise Tolerance Day program would have required all students to attend a morning assembly and would have displaced the school's regular classes for part of the day. We must address the arguments of the teacher Solmitz, the student Roach, and the speaker McCormick, in the context of the broad discretion granted school boards in discharging their responsibilities for the curriculum of public schools.

McKusick turned first to Solmitz, who claimed that the cancellation of his program amounted to violation of "academic freedom" under the First Amendment, a right recognized as a "special concern" by the U.S. Supreme Court in *Keyishian v. Board of Regents* (1967). McKusick denied that academic freedom was at stake in this case. "Solmitz, however, does not, nor could he, contend that the Board's veto infringed in any way upon his right to teach his assigned courses as he deemed appropriate, or to express himself freely on tolerance, prejudice against homosexuals, or any other subject."

McKusick asserted that no matter how broad a recognition courts gave to the academic freedom of individual teachers, that did not mean that a teacher could "insist upon a given curriculum for the whole school where he teaches," which Solmitz sought to do in his Tolerance Day program. Tolerance Day would be part of the "school-wide curriculum," and as to this no one teacher had a greater right than the school administration.

McKusick insisted, furthermore, that the board's reason for canceling the event, as found by the superior court, was not to stifle discussion, but rather to prevent disruption and possible injury to the students and damage to school property as a result of the threats received over the weekend of January 19 and 20. There was no reason to disturb those findings, said McKusick, because they were not clearly erroneous, given the testimony presented on the record to the trial judge, and appellate courts were not supposed to substitute their view of the evidence unless it provided no support for the trial judge's conclusions on issues of fact. Six of the nine board members had testified as to their reasons for canceling the event, and the parties had stipulated that the testimony of the three missing board members would have been to the same effect.

The plaintiffs had argued that this finding should not be the end of the inquiry, but rather the court should look to the motivations of the townspeople whose calls and threats had led to the cancellation. If the school board's vote was not motivated by a desire to stifle free speech, surely the stimulus for the vote was. "We decline to take the novel step of declaring that a permissible decision of elected officials is infected with the invidious motives of their constituents," said McKusick.

> Plaintiffs have cited no authority from this, or any other jurisdiction, to support their demand that we delve into the minds of citizens who lobbied their elected officials. Indeed, courts are generally hesitant to require even the decisionmakers themselves to explain in court testimony the motivation of their official actions. . . . It was entirely appropriate for the Superior Court to refuse to substitute the motives of the complaining citizens for those of the Board.

McKusick found that the board's cancellation vote was a "reasonable" response to the threat that the educational program of Madison High School would be "seriously disrupted" had the Tolerance Day program been held. In *Tinker*, the Supreme Court had made clear that free speech rights would have to give way if the board could credibly show that allowing the speech would result in serious disruption of the program. McKusick stated: "Surely then, in the present case the Board could permissibly veto a teacher's proposed addition to the curriculum that threatened to force the entire school to suffer 'a lost day educationally.'" McKusick noted that the board had imposed no discipline on Solmitz for his role in provoking the controversy and did not order him to refrain from discussing homosexuality or any other issue consistent with the school's curriculum in his history classes. He concluded that the board's action neither infringed on Solmitz's rights as a teacher nor impermissibly restricted "the free marketplace of ideas at Madison High School."

Turning to Roach's claims, the court conceded that as a student Roach had certain First Amendment rights as a potential listener and participant in the Tolerance Day exercise, but concluded that these rights were not violated by the cancellation of the program because the program was not canceled for the purpose of depriving her of those rights, but rather for "safety, order, and security reasons." In *Pico*, where the Supreme Court was concerned with the removal of controversial books from the school library collection by vote of the board, only a plurality of the Court had agreed to the proposition that the First Amendment rights of a student might place an affirmative obligation on school officials to present instruction on any particular topic or issue. Said McKusick, "*Pico* was limited to the removal of library books from the school, and even the plurality opinion recognized the broad power of school boards in controlling curriculum."

Finally, turning to McCormick, McKusick asserted that she "has no right to speak at Madison High School arising from the invitation she received from Solmitz, and she could demand successfully to address the student body only if the school had become a public forum." While several speakers were invited to talk to students at Madison High School each year, the court found that the school had not been transformed into the kind of "public forum" where any and every outside speaker had a right of access. McKusick drew support from the Supreme Court's decision in *Perry Education Association v. Perry Local Educators' Association* (1983), a dispute about access to teachers' school mailboxes by the teachers' union. The Supreme Court had there held that a public school was not considered a public forum; rather, it was public property dedicated to a particular use which government could preserve for that use. McKusick concluded that Madison High School was not even the sort of "limited public forum" as to which members of the public had at least some First Amendment rights of access to speak. The school had promulgated a policy statement indicating that "controversial questions shall have a legitimate place in the work of the public schools," but that "no individual or group may claim the right to present arguments directly to students." McKusick implicitly endorsed this policy statement as an accurate characterization of the constitutional principles at stake. Furthermore, as he had found in discussing the other plaintiffs, the board's veto of the event (and, by implication, McCormick's participation in it) was motivated not by hostility to her message but rather by concerns of security. Said McKusick, "[W]e are unable to hold that the Board acted to suppress a point of view to which its members were opposed. The Board cancelled the *entire* program in the face of threats of disruptive activity by some members of the community." Thus, the cancellation did not violate McCormick's free speech rights. Furthermore, McKusick agreed with the trial judge that there was no "invidious discrimination" against McCormick because she was a lesbian. All of the invited Tolerance Day speakers had been precluded from speaking at the school by the cancellation vote.

Turning finally to the legal fees question, McKusick noted that normally only the prevailing party had a right to assert a claim for such fees in civil rights litigation, and clearly the plaintiffs had not prevailed. However, the right of defendants to claim fees in such litigation did not automatically follow because the policy on awarding fees to defendants was based on concerns of preventing frivolous litigation, which this was not. "Plaintiff's arguments in this lawsuit were not wholly without merit," conceded McKusick, "and they litigated their case fully, in a manner that was helpful to the courts." Consequently, even though the school board and individual defendants had prevailed, they were not entitled to have their fees paid by the plaintiffs.

The Tolerance Day controversy at Madison High School had many ironic aspects, not least of them the name of the school, honoring the legislative parent of the Bill of Rights (including the First Amendment). Perhaps the very act of cancellation sent a stronger message than any Tolerance Day program could have done (i.e., that intolerance thrives on fear and ignorance, and that the intolerant are most resistant to hearing the truth about the objects of their fear). By approving the school board's actions, the Maine Supreme Judicial Court was enforc-

ing a "heckler's veto." Indeed, there was no evidence that the threats received by school board members was any more than that—threats that might be no more than a bluff. On the other hand, when the safety of schoolchildren and school staff was at stake, the school board could legitimately fear the consequences if it allowed the Tolerance Day program to occur and actual harm resulted. The case demonstrates the fragility of free speech rights, and the ability of a handful of prejudiced individuals to prevent the kind of civilizing discussion that might reduce the overall level of bigotry.

Case References

Board of Education, Island Trees Union Free School District No. 26 v. Pico, 457 U.S. 853 (1982)

Keyishian v. Board of Regents, 385 U.S. 589 (1967)

Perry Education Association v. Perry Local Educators' Association, 460 U.S. 37 (1983)

Tinker v. Des Moines Independent Community School District, 393 U.S. 503 (1969)

111. IS "RECOGNITION" A FORM OF "ENDORSEMENT"?

Gay Rights Coalition of Georgetown University Law Center v. Georgetown University, 536 A.2d 1 (D.C. App. 1987) (en banc), application for stay denied, 484 U.S. 999, 484 U.S. 1039 (1988), vacating 496 A.2d 567 (D.C. App. 1985).

By the mid-1980s, it was well established that public universities must, consistent with the First Amendment, extend official recognition to gay student organizations on their campuses on the same basis that recognition is extended to other student organizations. But what of private universities, and particularly those with religious origins or affiliations? Clearly, the First Amendment rights of lesbian and gay students could not be asserted against a nongovernmental actor, but demands for recognition might be premised on statutes or ordinances forbidding discrimination on the basis of sexual orientation, where those existed. In that case, however, what about First Amendment claims by the university to be free from government dictates regarding "political" positions, such as endorsement of lesbian and gay rights? And to

complicate things further, what about the claims of religiously affiliated or operated universities to be free of government dictation in matters of religious belief and practice? All of these questions came together in the attempts by lesbian and gay students at Georgetown University and its affiliated law school to achieve official recognition for their organizations beginning in 1979.

The District of Columbia Council adopted a comprehensive human rights ordinance which provided, *inter alia*, that educational institutions may not discriminate on the basis of sexual orientation. What the D.C. Code specifically prohibited was "for an educational institution . . . to deny, restrict, or to abridge or condition the use of, or access to, any of its facilities and services to any person otherwise qualified, wholly or partially, for a discriminatory reason, based upon the . . . sexual orientation . . . of any individual." In 1979, lesbian and gay students at Georgetown University, a 200-year-old institution founded by the Society of Jesus (Catholic Jesuits) and still operated under contract with that religious order as one of two pontifical universities in the United States, formed two organizations: Gay People of Georgetown University on the "main campus" and Gay Rights Coalition at the Georgetown University Law Center. Both groups applied to the respective student government organizations and received votes of approval for their formation and operation as student organizations. However, on their formal application for official university recognition, university administrators of their respective campuses denied the requests by both groups, and the president of the university, Reverend Timothy S. Healy, backed up his administrators.

Healy premised his denial on Roman Catholic doctrine concerning homosexuality, indicating that it would be inconsistent with such doctrine for the university to extend official recognition, which it considered a form of "endorsement," to gay rights groups. On the other hand, Healy indicated, the groups still had their student government endorsements, which entitled them to meet and hold events on campus, and the university would allow this status to continue. In terms of tangible benefits, the lack of official university endorsement meant that the gay student groups would not receive office space, telephone and mail services, and other amenities extended to officially recognized groups, and their lower priority for room reservations might at times cause some inconvenience when demand for meeting rooms was high.

The gay student groups renewed their demands for recognition in the fall term of 1979, but recognition was again denied. In the interim since their first applications in the spring term of 1979, the university had published a new set of guidelines on "recognition criteria." These guidelines refined the various forms of recognition available to student groups. The lowest level was "student body endorsement," based on a vote by the representative student government organization. The next level was "university recognition," which signified "endorsement of the various co-curricular activities undertaken by a specific club," and finally, there was "university funding," which involved actual appropriation of financial assistance to a particular club or organization. Both of the gay student organizations had student body endorsement, but were denied official recognition and funding from the university.

Obtaining the services of Leonard Graff and Ronald Bogard, gay attorneys active in Washington, the student groups filed suit against the university in the District of Columbia Superior Court, contending that denial of official recognition violated the Human Rights Act. Georgetown defended on two theories: first, that its denial of recognition did not violate the D.C. Code because it was based not on the sexual orientation of the members of the groups but rather on the "purposes and activities" of their organizations. Alternatively, Georgetown argued that even if it were found that it had discriminated on the basis of sexual orientation, such discrimination was privileged by the Free Exercise Clause of the First Amendment. The student groups argued that "recognition" and "endorsement" should not be equated, pointing to other officially "recognized" groups, such as Jewish and Moslem student organizations, which held and promoted views contrary to Catholic teaching.

The plaintiffs filed a motion for summary judgment, arguing there were no significant facts in dispute between the parties, which was heard by Superior Court Judge Leonard Braman. On March 9, 1981, Judge Braman issued an order, granting the motion in part, finding that Georgetown's actions had violated the D.C. Code. Braman concluded that, as a matter of law, refusing to grant university recognition to the student groups constituted discrimination on the basis of sexual orientation, and that Georgetown's claim that such recognition would actually constitute an endorsement which could not be compelled by the government was irrelevant to this aspect of the case. However, Braman concluded that there were factual disputes to be resolved before Georgetown's First Amendment defense could be properly evaluated, not least of which was the plaintiffs' argument that Georgetown, despite its religious foundation, had become a secular institution which could not raise a First Amendment defense in this instance.

The case was set for trial before Superior Court Judge Sylvia Bacon, who held seven days of hearings, consumed with testimony about Georgetown's alleged religious or nonreligious status, the Catholic Church's views on homosexuality, and the asserted impact or lack of impact on those views of requiring recognition of the student groups. Judge Bacon ultimately ruled, a year after the conclusion of the trial, that it would violate the First Amendment rights of Georgetown for the court to order official recognition of the student groups.

Bacon found that Georgetown was "a religiously affiliated educational institution which serves both sectarian and secular purposes" and that denial of official recognition had been premised on the "moral or normative teachings of the Roman Catholic Church," which had been established at trial through expert testimony and official Church documents. As later summarized by the court of appeals of the District,

> Under Catholic doctrine, sexual function has its true meaning and moral rectitude only in heterosexual marriage. Homosexual acts—as distinguished from a homosexual orientation—are morally wrong and must be viewed as "gravely evil and a disordered use of the sexual faculty." Persons of homosexual orientation have an obligation to "try as is reasonably possible to change if they find themselves in such orientation" and must in any event conform their conduct to the normative teachings on human sexuality. No believer affiliated with the Roman Catholic Church may condone, endorse, approve or be neutral about homosexual orientation, homosexual lifestyle or homosexual acts.

Finding that the major purpose of university recognition was "endorsement" of the activities of the recognized student club, Bacon found that the refusal to extend such endorsement was based on religious belief by a religious institution, and that forcing the university to extend recognition "would be inconsistent with Church normative teachings and with the basic obligation not to undermine the normative teachings of the Church." She also noted, however, that the university allowed clubs to form and operate on campus without official

endorsement, and that in the District of Columbia it was also possible for gay student organizations to find off-campus opportunities to meet and hold programs. Bacon concluded, as to questions of law raised by the case, that Georgetown's receipt of federal funds to advance its secular educational purposes did not defeat its claim to free exercise rights, which it was entitled to claim due to its church affiliation. Since ordering Georgetown to extend official recognition would require it to act in a manner "inconsistent with its duties as a Catholic institution," so ordering would place a burden on the free exercise of religion, and since there was no "national" policy requiring the state to prevent discrimination on the basis of sexual orientation, the Human Rights Act of the District did not present the kind of "compelling state interest" necessary to outweigh the burden on religious freedom. To Bacon, the city ordinance was little more than a "local enactment of well-motivated purpose but impermissible reach" in this case.

The student groups appealed Bacon's ruling to the District of Columbia Court of Appeals. That court, not to be confused with the U.S. Court of Appeals for the District of Columbia Circuit, is the highest appellate court for the District on matters of District law. A three-judge panel of the court heard oral argument on October 24, 1984, from Washington attorneys Richard Gross for the plaintiffs and Charles H. Wilson for the university. The city of Washington's government submitted a brief arguing for a reversal of Bacon's ruling.

In an opinion issued on July 30, 1985, the three-judge panel ruled by a 2–1 vote that the First Amendment did not exempt Georgetown from its legal requirement under the Human Rights Act to refrain from discriminating on the basis of sexual orientation, and reversed Bacon's decision. The opinion for the court by Judge John M. Ferren drew a strong dissenting opinion from Judge Julia Cooper Mack, who argued that "recognition," as understood to mean "endorsement," was not required as such by the terms of the Human Rights Act. Ferren rejected the argument that requiring the university to extend recognition to the student groups constituted an "endorsement," or indeed any form of coerced speech or belief, so that no First Amendment issue was presented in his view.

As was customary in the D.C. court of appeals, the opinion had been circulated to all the members of the court before being issued. A majority of the members decided that the case presented significant issues on which all members of the court should have an opportunity to rule. While allowing the panel's decision to be published, the court issued an order vacating the opinion and setting the case for reargument *en banc*, which was held on October 16, 1985. While the appeal before the three-judge panel had drawn some *amicus* interest, primarily from gay rights groups and the state of Wisconsin (which, being the only state with a gay rights law, had an interest in how the novel questions in this case would be resolved), the *en banc* reconsideration drew an enormous amount of *amicus* participation as a result of the provocative opinion issued by the panel. Nine *amicus* briefs were filed, taking a variety of views. Perhaps the most interesting *amicus* participation involved the American Civil Liberties Union (ACLU). The director of the ACLU's Washington, D.C., affiliate, who had been unable to persuade the local board of directors to side with the university, filed his own individual *amicus* brief on behalf of the university, arguing that First Amendment rights of freedom of speech were vitally implicated in an order that the university "endorse" a group having a particular political viewpoint. The ACLU's national office in New York filed an *amicus* brief on behalf of the student groups, arguing that recognition of the student groups did not significantly encroach on any free speech or free exercise rights the university might enjoy.

The sharply split court took more than two years to issue its decision, with seven opinions representing the views of the seven judges. A majority of the court concluded that the Human Rights Act did not require the university to extend official recognition to the gay student organizations, but a different majority concluded that the Act did require the University to accord the student groups various tangible benefits that would normally accompany recognition on the same basis that they were accorded to other student groups. The result was a sort of "*de facto*" recognition.

The holding of the case was in the opinion by Judge Julia Cooper Mack, who straddled the various factions. Chief Judge William C. Pryor wrote separately, concurring in the judgment. Judge Theodore R. Newman, Jr., also concurred, with an opinion more fully articulating the second part of the holding, which had the partial concurrence of Mack and Judges John M. Ferren and John A. Terry. Ferren and Terry had constituted the majority of the three-judge panel; they adhered to their view that the Act required recognition of the student groups and that such recognition would not violate the First Amendment rights of the university, so they wrote separate opinions as well, explaining their dissent from the first part of the court's holding. Finally, Judges James A. Belson and Frank Q. Nebeker wrote separate opinions, partially concurring in the first part of the court's holding but dissenting from the conclusion that the university must extend any tangible benefits to the gay student groups.

Mack began her opinion with a lengthy, detailed description of Georgetown University and the history of the lesbian and gay student groups' attempts to gain recognition, during the course of which she endorsed most of Judge Bacon's factual findings, including that Georgetown was a religious institution to the extent necessary to find that it could raise a free exercise claim under the First Amendment.

Proceeding to the question whether denial of official recognition to the student groups violated the Human Rights Act, Mack expanded on her dissenting opinion in the three-judge panel, in which she argued that the Act should not be construed to require the university to recognize any politically oriented student organization, since recognition involved a form of endorsement that the government could not compel of any private institution. Mack invoked the "deeply rooted" interpretive doctrine that when application of a statute in a particular way would raise serious constitutional issues, courts should try to find an interpretation that would make decision of the constitutional issue unnecessary. Mack found that this goal could be achieved by construing the Human Rights Act so it would not require anyone subject to the Act to endorse any particular point of view.

The plaintiffs had argued on appeal that Bacon erred in finding that university recognition constituted an endorsement. They based their argument on the wide array of student organizations that had received official recognition, many pursuing political or religious agendas that were assertedly at odds with Catholic doctrine. Among these were organizations of Jewish and Arab students, the Young Americans for Freedom, and the Democratic Socialist Organizing Committee. At trial, Reverend Healy had testified that it was not inconsistent with the Church's doctrinal teachings to extend official recognition to groups organized by students of other religious faiths:

> It is the understanding of the Roman Catholic Church that faiths other than the Roman Catholic Church are, to put it in the technical terms, carriers of grace and as such are good. The Roman Catholic Church would feel that they are incomplete, but in the context of a complex university, it is the clear and stated purpose of the Roman Catholic Church that those of other faiths receive the same pastoral and intellectual sustenance in their faith as far as it is possible for the University to grant it, given the multiplicity, as Catholic students receive from a Catholic university.

The student groups also pointed to the university's recognition of the Women's Rights Collective and the Women's Political Caucus, and argued that those groups had advanced or publicized positions involving birth control and abortion. Healy and other witnesses denied that the women's groups took official positions on these questions, and pointed out that in one instance where the collective had posted some notices from another organization about birth control and abortion, university officials had investigated and determined that these were "minor incidents" not sufficient to withdraw university recognition. Healy saw the gay groups in a different light, since the purposes set forth in their constitutions seemed to present direct contradictions to Catholic theology. Most particularly, Healy testified, there was objection to a statement in the main campus group's constitution about a commitment to "the development of responsible sexual ethics consonant with one's personal beliefs." It was clear from expert testimony that Catholic doctrine did not allow personal belief to play a role in sexual ethics,

which must be derived solely from Church teachings. Healy also testified that recognizing the group would leave the university open to "endorsing" a wide range of activities that might place it in conflict with Church teaching.

Given Georgetown's role as a "Catholic university," Healy asserted that the university had a special responsibility to refrain from lending its support or prestige to organizations that stood in direct contradiction to Church teachings. The university had presented theological expert testimony to the effect that homosexual activity was always morally objectionable. Healy asserted that it was not enough for the university to remain "neutral" on moral questions. It was impelled by its mission and religious affiliation to take a firm position in opposition to activities seen as sinful by the Church, including homosexuality.

Reviewing Bacon's factual findings under the clearly erroneous standard, Mack said the court could not find clearly erroneous Judge Bacon's conclusion that ordering University recognition of the gay student groups would constitute an endorsement of the type that would be contrary to Georgetown's religious status and mission. But, on the other hand, Mack felt that it was possible to separate conceptually the issues of endorsement and tangible benefits, which both attached to university recognition. She found this distinction "fundamental from both a statutory and constitutional perspective." Mack found that the endorsement was an "intangible," "symbolic" thing, separate and apart from such tangible things as access to university facilities and funding, which did not, in themselves, necessarily implicate an endorsement in her mind. Mack agreed with an argument made in the *amicus* brief from the Governor's Council on Lesbian and Gay Issues of the state of Wisconsin that tying the tangible and intangible benefits of recognition together was not necessary. "While the 'endorsement' and the tangible benefits may be one for Georgetown's administrative purposes, they are not so in the eyes of the Human Rights Act," she asserted, "nor are they so in the eyes of the First Amendment." The District of Columbia government argued in its brief that the "constitutionality of the statute cannot depend on the University's internal linkages." Mack agreed.

As applied to the endorsement part of the recognition package, Mack found that the Human Rights Act could not require endorsement for two reasons. First, the Act by its terms applied only to discriminatory denial of access to "facilities and services," which an endorsement was not. Said Mack, the Act was to "ensure equality of *treatment*, not equality of *attitudes*." There was nothing in the Act to suggest that it reached beyond treatment and sought to make "a discriminatory state of mind unlawful in itself. Still less does the statute reveal any desire to force a private actor to express an idea that is not truly held." Thus, Judge Braman's initial ruling conflicted with the "literal meaning" of the law. Second, it was the duty of the court to embrace a construction of the Act, if possible, that avoided the constitutional questions that would naturally arise if the Act were construed to require a private actor to endorse a particular idea or point of view, whether religious or political. Since a "literal" construction avoided this problem, it should be embraced by the court. Mack noted that the university's First Amendment claim need not even rest primarily on its religious status, since it could make the same sort of argument under the freedom of speech protection of the Amendment. After reciting a long history of Supreme Court cases striking down attempts by government to get private institutions, whether religious or secular, to lend their support to particular points of view, Mack noted that as recently as 1986 the Court had ruled in *Pacific Gas and Electric Co. v. Public Utilities Commission* that a state regulatory body could not compel a public utility to include in billing envelopes "the speech of a third party with whom the utility disagreed." Freedom of speech meant freedom from being compelled to assist the speech of one with whom the private actor disagreed. It would be different if the private actor was essentially providing a public forum, as was the case of a shopping center owner in *PruneYard Shopping Center v. Robins*, a 1980 case in which the Court held that a state requirement that the center owner allow distribution of pamphlets by a third party did not offend the First Amendment rights of the center's owner. Mack asserted that "Georgetown's scheme of 'University recognition' cannot be analogized to a public forum,

nor can its campus be equated with 'a business establishment that is open to the public to come and go as they please.'" It was a long way from a shopping center being required to let pamphleteers distribute pamphlets with which the owner disagreed to requiring a university to endorse through official recognition a student organization with whose views the university disagreed.

To illustrate her point, Mack posed a "world turned upside down" hypothetical case, in which a Gay University of America was petitioned for official recognition by a Roman Catholic Ethics Association formed by some of its students for the purpose of promoting the Catholic Church's views on homosexuality. Surely, she contended, the Gay University, founded on an attitude of support for "gay practices and the philosophies that support them," could not be compelled by the government to endorse the views of the Catholic Church by recognizing the student group. "Insincere statements of opinion are not what the Human Rights Act requires," she said. "On the other hand, the statute would require equal distribution of any attendant tangible benefits if [Gay University of America's] denial of these was based on the religion of [Roman Catholic Ethics Association] members. Georgetown's protection against compelled expression is no more and no less."

Turning from the issue of official recognition to tangible benefits, Mack held that the denial of the tangible benefits that went with recognition was a violation of the Human Rights Act. "Where, as here, those possessing characteristics identified by the legislature as irrelevant to individual merit are treated less favorably than others, the Human Rights Act imposes a burden upon the regulated actor to demonstrate that the irrelevant characteristic played no part in its decision," which Georgetown had failed to do. Mack found that the reasons given by the university for denying the benefits all conceptually related back to the issue of endorsement, which she had held could be separated out from the tangible benefits. In particular, Mack rejected the university's contention that its denial of recognitional benefits based on the purposes and activities of the student groups could stand as a nondiscriminatory decision. Clearly, the denial was based on or influenced by the sexual orientation of the students, and thus tainted under the Act, as shown by statements by university administrators in their communications with the student groups and in their testimony.

Mack noted with approval Judge Braman's reliance on a provision of the Human Rights Act that made clear that "disparate impact" theories could be used to find a violation of the Act. This meant that "despite the absence of any intention to discriminate, practices are unlawful if they bear disproportionately on a protected class and are not independently justified for some nondiscriminatory reason." Legislative history showed that the D.C. City Council had expressly desired to enact this theory, derived from the Supreme Court's 1971 decision in *Griggs v. Duke Power Co.*, as part of its Human Rights Act. Even if the university here had no direct intent to discriminate on the basis of sexual orientation, its denial of recognition certainly had that effect, in that gay students were denied certain benefits that were routinely extended to nongay students with regard to their student organization activities.

Having concluded that the university's denial of tangible benefits of recognition violated the Act, Mack turned to the question whether it would violate Georgetown's First Amendment rights to order it to extend those tangible benefits to the student groups. Here, the court was venturing into new territory, since neither Braman nor Bacon had conceptualized the case in this way. Bacon's holding that ordering recognition would impermissibly impair Georgetown's free exercise rights had depended on the endorsement aspects of recognition. Once the endorsement aspect was stripped away, the remaining question was whether requiring extension of tangible benefits would mark a similar impairment. Although the case had been litigated at trial on an "all-or-nothing" basis, Mack concluded that there was enough evidence in the record from which to conclude that requiring extension of tangible benefits would present some burden to the university's free exercise rights. Thus, the statutory remedy could be imposed only if the government had a compelling interest that could not be vindicated

other than by ordering extension of these benefits.

Mack contended that the D.C. city government had a compelling interest in eradicating sexual orientation discrimination, as shown by the legislative history and debate leading to enactment of the Act. Placing "sexual orientation" in the list of forbidden bases for discrimination, the council had implicitly stated that "all forms of discrimination based on anything other than individual merit are equally injurious, to the immediate victims and to society as a whole." Mack stated:

> The Council determined that a person's sexual orientation, like a person's race and sex, for example, tells nothing of value about his or her attitudes, characteristics, abilities or limitations. It is a false measure of individual worth, one unfair and oppressive to the person concerned, one harmful to others because discrimination inflicts a grave and recurring injury upon society as a whole. To put an end to this evil, the Council outlawed sexual orientation discrimination.

The council had first legislated on this matter as a regulation; then, after receiving home rule legislative authority from Congress in 1977, the council had reenacted the prohibition as a part of the D.C. Code, accompanied by a committee report indicating the council's intent that the Human Rights Act provisions be given "vigorous enforcement."

Of course, the question whether the interest was "compelling" could not rest solely on legislative pronouncements, said Mack. It was a question of law, as to which no appellate court had unequivocally pronounced itself.

> We approach that task, therefore, with more than a little trepidation. Our society is built upon a heterosexual model. We are met at the outset with centuries of attitudinal thinking, often colored by sincerely held religious beliefs, that has obscured scientific appraisal and stunted the growth of legal theories protecting homosexual persons from invidious discrimination. We know one basic fact—that homosexual and bisexual citizens have been part of society from time immemorial. These orientations, like that of heterosexuals, have cut across all diverse classifications—race, sex, national origin, and religion, to name but a few. After careful reflection, we cannot conclude that one's sexual orientation is a characteristic reflecting upon individual merit.

Mack then reviewed the evidence presented by sex researchers, beginning with the historic reports of Dr. Alfred Kinsey in the 1940s, documenting the widespread incidence of homosexual and bisexual orientation, and suggesting that homosexuality was as "deeply ingrained" as heterosexuality and largely impervious to change. She noted the rejection by professional associations of the contention that homosexuality was a "mental disorder," while noting that gay people could be subject to particular psychological stresses due to the discriminatory attitudes and actions of society. She also noted that homosexuals were as diverse a group as heterosexuals, so that knowing one's sexual orientation did not automatically reveal anything about "abilities or commitments in work, religion, politics, personal and social relationships, or social activities, except to the extent that in many areas the lives of gay people are frequently conditioned by the attitudes of others." In particular, she noted that homosexuals tended to be thought of stereotypically in relation to their sexuality, while their diversity and humanity were frequently ignored. "Despite its irrelevance to individual merit, a homosexual or bisexual orientation invites ongoing prejudice in all walks of life, ranging from employment to education, and for most of which there is currently no judicial remedy outside the District of Columbia or the State of Wisconsin," said Mack, citing instances of governmental and private-sector discrimination documented in a wide variety of studies and official documents. "Such discrimination has persisted throughout most of history," she commented, including, in its "most virulent form," the Nazi death camps of World War II.

While such a finding was not a prerequisite to finding a compelling state interest, she noted "that sexual orientation appears to possess most or all of the characteristics that have persuaded the Supreme Court to apply strict or heightened constitutional scrutiny to legislative classifications under the Equal Protection Clause." Among these characteristics were that sexual orientation seemed to be determined by causes beyond the control of the individual, and that gays were subjected to "unique disabilities on the basis of stereotyped characteristics not truly indicative of their abilities." Taken together with the long history of discrimination, this resulted in a group that was like the "discrete and insular minorities" specified in the famous footnote four of *United States v. Carolene Products Co.* (1938), who were traditionally neglected by the "political processes ordinarily to be relied upon to protect minorities." Said Mack:

> The compelling interests, therefore, that any state has in eradicating discrimination against the homosexually or bisexually oriented include the fostering of individual dignity, the creation of a climate and environment in which each individual can utilize his or her potential to contribute to and benefit from society, and equal protection of the life, liberty and property that the Founding Fathers guaranteed to us all. . . . We consider that the Council of the District of Columbia acted on the most pressing of needs when incorporating into the Human Rights Act its view that discrimination based on sexual orientation is a grave evil that damages society as well as its immediate victims. The eradication of sexual orientation discrimination is a compelling governmental interest.

Here, of course, one came to the matter of "balancing" a compelling governmental interest against a fundamental right guaranteed by the First Amendment, free exercise of religion. Mack had little difficulty striking a balance in favor of a remedy for the student groups because she found that "compelling equal access to the tangible benefits, without requiring the intangible 'endorsement' contained in 'University Recognition,' imposes a relatively slight burden on Georgetown's religious practice." The tangible benefits were relatively insignificant; Georgetown's main objections all along had been to the endorsement aspects of official recognition, which were removed from the case, said Mack, by the court's decision that the Act did not require official recognition. Mack found reinforcement for this view by the university's unprotesting extension of some tangible benefits to the gay student groups upon their approval by the student government. Finally, she found that requiring the extension of tangible benefits on an equal basis was the least restrictive means available to achieve the government's compelling interest. To order less, she said, "would be to defeat its compelling purpose."

Chief Judge Pryor wrote a brief separate opinion to emphasize his view that nothing in the court's ruling "requires the University, over its constitutional objections, to publicly associate itself or affirmatively support the goals or activities of the gay student organizations." For Pryor, this meant that Georgetown could refuse to allow the student groups to use the name of the university and could also deny any requests by the student groups for funding in support of their causes.

> Lastly, I would observe that our Human Rights Act is broad and comprehensive. It covers a wide range of possible discriminatory practices. Necessarily our decisions will reflect the nature of the asserted discrimination, the presence or absence of historic conditions which surround the question, legislative intent, and case precedent. For me, the decision in this instance reflects those considerations and does not, in any way, signal a weakening of the purposes the Act was intended to serve.

Pryor thus rebutted the views of the partial dissenters who would have compelled university recognition for the gay student groups.

Judge Newman's opinion endorsed Mack's conclusion that denial of tangible benefits to the student groups violated the Human Rights Act, but made some distinctions in reasoning and took a different tack on the free exercise claim. For example, Newman found much of Mack's discussion of the "compelling interest" issue superfluous. For him, it was enough that the District council decided to include sexual orientation in the Human Rights Act, a finding to which courts should defer in determining whether there was a compelling interest. As far as he was concerned, the legislative branch, not the judiciary, was better placed to determine in the first instance which interests of the government were compelling, and courts should defer to that determination to some extent. Deference was especially appropriate where, as here, it was clear from the legislative record that the council recognized the conflicting interests involved. "In enacting the Human Rights Act, the District of Columbia Council included a section that permits religious institutions to discriminate in favor of co-religionists when doing so is designed to further the institution's religious principles." This decision signified the council's recognition of the special claims of religion.

At the same time, however, in prohibiting discrimination on grounds other than religion or political affiliation, or in any circumstances other than those embraced by the terms of these exceptions, the Council made plain that no further exception should be tolerated. In taking this view, our legislature implicitly determined that the importance of outlawing discrimination on the basis of sexual orientation outweighs competing religious claims. This least restrictive means determination, along with the Council's assessment of the overall importance of the governmental interest, is entitled to at least a modicum of this court's deference.

Newman reviewed some of the cases in which the Supreme Court had to balance free exercise claims against state interests and noted that in most cases the Court would enforce the government policy if it actually served some significant public interest to do so. Cases in which government regulations were not enforced were frequently decided on the ground that the government regulation did not actually do much to advance a significant public interest, when weighed against the interest in protecting religious diversity. "While government cannot compel religious or other belief," said Newman, "it can require persons and institutions to comport their behavior to secular moral norms," of which nondiscrimination was one. "In a series of recent decisions, the Supreme Court has extinguished any doubt that the enforcement of antidiscrimination laws is a compelling governmental interest when poised against a First Amendment objection." In *Bob Jones University v. United States*, a 1983 case, the Court had upheld withdrawal of tax-exempt status from a private university that maintained racially discriminatory policies based on the religious beliefs of the university's founder. The Court found that the government's interest in combatting discrimination outweighed the First Amendment interest of the university. Finally, the Court had recognized that "the nature of the burden imposed on the religious objector" was also a relevant factor. "I do not understand Georgetown to argue that discrimination against any persons or groups is a tenet of its faith," said Newman. "Rather, it claims that providing the disputed facilities and services to the gay student organizations infringes that University's religious interest in embracing a particular doctrine of sexual ethics." Thus, what the court was ordering in this case would work only an "indirect infringement" of the university's religious interests, for, said Newman, enforcement of the Human Rights Act did not "signify endorsement by the government or by the covered entity of any particular doctrine of sexual ethics.... Rather, it simply recognizes as irrelevant a person's sexual orientation in the provision of facilities and services by an educational institution."

Finally, Newman disputed the assertion by dissenting Judge Belson that the Human Rights Act's provisions against racial discrimination were any more important or carried more compelling weight than the provisions on sexual orientation discrimination. While this might be a valid observation about *national* policy, that was not really relevant in determining the issue under local law. "Moreover," he said, "an interest need not be identical in weight to some other compelling interest in order to be compelling itself." And, responding to Judge Ferren's partial dissent, Newman indicated that it was not necessary in this case, as far as he was concerned, to decide whether the gay student groups had a right to use the university's name in their organizational titles, since that question was not directly presented to the court for decision.

Judge Ferren, writing for himself and Judge Terry, wanted to stay with his original opinion for the three-judge panel, holding that university recognition could be compelled without violating the First Amendment and that such was required by the Human Rights Act. Ferren believed that the constitutional issue was "the only issue in the case," since any unequal treatment on the basis of sexual orientation, including denial of recognition, violated the antidiscrimination command of the Human Rights Act. He saw no basis for separating out the issues of recognition and tangible benefits and holding that the Act applied only to the latter. And, as to the constitutional issue, he insisted that the government's compelling interest in prohibiting discrimination on the basis of sexual orientation was sufficient to overcome any First Amendment interest the university might have in refraining from impliedly "endorsing" the gay rights groups by extending

formal recognition to them. Ferren called "altogether gratuitous" Judge Belson's dissenting opinion on the issue of tangible benefits, since at oral argument counsel for Georgetown "expressly waived . . . any First Amendment objection to providing such benefits," calling them "relatively insignificant" in his brief.

Ferren's argument on the statutory construction issue was essentially that Mack and her concurrers on this point were creating a serious "equal protection" type of problem, by holding that groups of gay students could be treated differently from groups of nongay students by the university. The language of the Human Rights Act was broad enough, taken together with its express command for "broad" interpretation, to comprehend both aspects of the recognition controversy. In essence, Mack's opinion allowed the university to discriminate, argued Ferren, drawing an analogy from the Supreme Court's recent decision finding a "hostile environment" on the basis of sex to constitute a violation of the federal Civil Rights Act in *Meritor Savings Bank v. Vinson* (1986). "I find no difficulty concluding that withholding such a significant form of citizenship in a university community results in a demeaning, and thus conditional, access to facilities and services that violates the plain language of the statute," argued Ferren.

All the agonizing about separating out the "recognition" from the "benefits" was unnecessary, said Ferren, because the court was incorrect in concluding that extending recognition should be treated as a form of endorsement for the particular views that the gay student group might express on any particular issue. "Assuming that 'recognition' is a form of 'endorsement,' what exactly is it an endorsement *of*—a student group's values or, instead, merely a group's right to exist on campus and to advocate its values? The former is speech; the latter may not be," insisted Ferren. This issue was a question of fact, not law, as to which the court of appeals should make an independent determination, especially since it was not really addressed at the trial level. Ferren could agree that "regulations literally compelling someone to speak moral or ideological statements are directly and extremely intrusive upon the individual's freedom of belief and expression" such that "no countervailing state interest could render such compulsions constitutional." But that was not this case, Ferren argued. All the Human Rights Act required was that the university, having established a system of university recognition for student groups, administer the forum equally. There was no implication that the operator of the forum necessarily endorsed the views of any group that was entitled by principles of equality to have access. As such, Ferren rejected the relevance of most of the cases on which Mack relied to bolster her conclusion that the Act could not be construed to require recognition without raising a constitutional issue. Furthermore, Ferren found Mack's opinion lacking in any valid explanation why requiring the tangible benefits would not raise the same issues that requiring recognition would raise.

Next, Ferren took on Judge Belson, who argued in partial dissent that the university would have a right to take the actions it did if it was motivated "solely by a desire to suppress advocacy of homosexual conduct." Belson had argued that the Act forbade discrimination based on "preference or practice," not discrimination based on advocacy. Ferren rejected Belson's view that the factual findings below would not support a conclusion that the Act was violated, or that Georgetown's actions could be excused on the basis of its First Amendment right to prevent advocacy of dissident viewpoints on its private campus.

Coming to what he considered the "fundamental question" in the case, "whether plaintiffs' request for 'University recognition'—meaning full citizenship as student groups at Georgetown University—may be denied, even though in violation of the Human Rights Act, because of Georgetown's first amendment rights," Ferren reasserted his answer from the panel decision. He indicated that he saw no constitutional conflict because, "on this record, 'University recognition' or 'endorsement' of the plaintiff student groups does not mean, explicitly or implicitly, a statement of approval—or even of neutrality—toward homosexuality, gay rights, or related matters."

In context—and context is critically important—the Act only requires Georgetown not to discriminate against student groups

that wish to express their own views in what I believe we may call, without fear of contradiction, a typical private university marketplace of ideas, which inherently stands for freedom of expression. That marketplace is analogous, for constitutional purposes, to the shopping center in *PruneYard*. There, the Supreme Court held that the first amendment rights of the shopping center owner did not justify barring pamphleteers from exercising their own free speech rights in the common areas open to the public. A legal requirement that Georgetown make its university-wide forum available on a nondiscriminatory basis to all student citizens of the university does not, in my view, imply in any way that the university corporation/administration itself can be reasonably identified with the views of any particular student organization or that the university, as such, has a position—pro, con, or neutral—on any particular message a student group happens to spread. The Human Rights Act, therefore, does not require Georgetown to espouse any view or to intimate even a neutral opinion.

Furthermore, Georgetown was free to make any statement it liked disavowing any positions that might be taken by the gay student organizations, although it was not required to do so in order to overcome any implication that it endorsed the students' views, as opposed to their equal right to have and express views. Georgetown was, by its very nature, "a forum for its students, teachers, administrators and alumni." As such, it was "akin to a public forum in that a variety of constituent groups has automatic access, there is a tradition of wide open debate, and thus, given this very nature of a university, there is no implication" that the university endorses any one point of view expressed by a group of students.

Judge Belson's decision, in which Judge Nebeker joined, concurred with Mack's holding that the Human Rights Act did not require official recognition, but dissented from the holding on tangible benefits and free exercise rights. Belson found that Georgetown's free exercise and free speech rights were "paramount" in this situation, and that the university could not be compelled either to extend formal recognition or tangible benefits to the gay student groups.

As a preliminary matter, Belson contended that summary judgment had been improperly granted on the question whether the Human Rights Act was violated, since, in his view, there were pertinent factual disputes. "One central issue was whether the university withheld recognition because of the sexual orientation of the members of the groups, or instead because of the groups' advocacy of homosexual life-styles, conduct inconsistent with religious beliefs to which Georgetown adheres." Further hearing would be needed to make this factual finding, Belson insisted.

More important, however, was his disagreement with Mack's legal conclusion on the First Amendment issue. He accused her of "consistent short-weighting of Georgetown's first amendment rights in the constitutional balancing process." He agreed with Mack that the statute should be construed to avoid the constitutional issue if at all possible, but here he contended it might not even be necessary to get to that point, had a proper job been done in determining whether the statute was actually violated. The university insisted that the sexual orientation of the members of the student groups was not the motivation for its decision; if this were so, argued Belson, then there could be no violation of the Act. Belson found that the papers filed by the university in opposition to the motion for summary judgment on this issue clearly raised factual disputes as to motivation that would have to be resolved before it could properly be concluded that the Act had been violated. Indeed, for Judge Braman to have premised a finding of violation on the view that a university may not discriminate on the basis of the viewpoint taken by a student, as he may have done, would have independently raised constitutional issues not even examined in Judge Mack's opinion. "The Human Rights Act," said Belson, "by its plain language does not prohibit discrimination against persons or groups based upon their advocacy. Rather, it prohibits discrimination against persons based upon their 'sexual orientation' which, in the words of the statute, 'means male or female homosexuality, heterosexuality and bisexuality, by preference or practice.'" Thus, contended Belson, Judge Braman erred if he held for the plaintiffs on the theory that the Act was violated "by denying recognition because of the groups' advocacy of homosexual life-styles."

Belson asserted that the Act should be construed solely to be concerned with status-based discrimination. If the university denied recognition because the gay student organizations consisted primarily of gay students, that would violate the Act. If the denial was premised, as the university argued, on the advocacy activities of the groups, then the Act was not violated. A statutorily imposed requirement of "neutrality toward the promotion of an idea, viz., the morality of homosexual life-styles, would abridge first amendment rights," asserted Belson.

But even if Georgetown were found to have violated the Human Rights Act, Belson argued that it still had a valid First Amendment defense, based on freedom of speech. "Georgetown has a free speech defense based on its right not to endorse or subsidize the groups' promotion of ideas and activities with which it disagrees," asserted Belson. For Belson, even requiring extension of tangible benefits without recognition implicated this right. "Any such forced subsidization of these groups will abridge Georgetown's free speech and free exercise rights." The free speech defense did not depend on Georgetown's status as a Catholic institution, either, since any private citizen has a First Amendment right to freedom of speech as against government dictates.

Belson argued that the *PruneYard* precedent did not support the students' case here. In that case, a shopping center was merely required to allow access. It was not ordered to subsidize the pamphleteers in any direct way, whereas Georgetown would be providing a direct subsidy if ordered to provide the tangible benefits, no matter how trivial, embodied in the court's order. The issue was compounded precisely because Georgetown was a university, which might be expected to take positions on moral and ethical issues, unlike PruneYard, a shopping center. In addition, since Georgetown was a Catholic institution, its free exercise rights were also implicated. "It has long been part of this country's first amendment jurisprudence that an individual cannot be compelled to fund the dissemination of religious views of others," said Belson, citing James Madison and Thomas Jefferson for this principle. Indeed, given the fundamental nature of the rights at issue, Belson was ready to argue that there should not be any sort of "balancing" of rights in this type of case, although the Supreme Court's use of balancing tests in free exercise cases made it necessary to do so.

As to any balancing, Belson disputed the court's contention that prevention of sexual orientation discrimination was the same type of compelling interest that could be found in attempts to end racial discrimination. Whether under the Equal Protection Clause, where the U.S. Court of Appeals for the District of Columbia Circuit had recently held in *Padula v. Webster* (1987) that sexual orientation classifications were not entitled to heightened scrutiny, or in the lack of federal legislation barring sexual orientation discrimination, Belson saw no indication that American society considered eradicating sexual orientation discrimination to be a compelling interest of government. That the D.C. council decided to ban such discrimination, taken by itself, did not signify a compelling government interest, in Belson's view. While the court had to accord "substantial weight" to the council's determination, it was not dispositive. Furthermore, the tangible benefits at issue here were rather minor, and it was difficult to assert that the District had any "compelling interest" in, for example, making sure the gay students at Georgetown could use the university's internal mail services. This case did not involve the sort of significant deprivations— discrimination in housing or employment, for example—that were the prime motivators for passage of the Human Rights Act. Indeed, it appeared that Georgetown allowed the gay student groups to meet and function on campus "without hindrance, merely requiring that they do so without university subsidization or endorsement." Since Georgetown was asserting fundamental First Amendment claims in the balance, Belson did not find that the balance could plausibly be struck in favor of the students' claim.

Judge Terry, in addition to concurring with Ferren, wrote his own separate brief opinion, to reiterate his view that the court's opinion did not go "far enough," since he saw "no meaningful difference between the tangible and intangible benefits which these appellants are seeking from the university." He further could not agree that university recognition equated to endorsement, since the university had rec-

ognized such groups as the Jewish Students Association, without anyone believing that it was thereby endorsing Judaism. If the university feared misconstruction by others of its intentions, it could always issue a disclaimer.

Judge Nebeker concluded the blizzard of opinions with his own separate partial concurrence and dissent. "Today the court uses the state's power to force a religious body, contrary to its basic tenets, to provide services and facilities to those who advocate and proselytize abnormal and criminal sexual practices," he commented, citing the sodomy law provisions in the D.C. Code, which the U.S. Senate had maintained by voting to disapprove a repeal bill passed by the council. Nebeker agreed with Belson's analysis, but wrote separately to emphasize the criminal nature of homosexual activity in the District. If a balancing test was appropriate, said Nebeker, it was

> important to recognize that the homosexual orientation, as defined by one's sexual practice, at issue here has a stark inconsistency with established criminal law. The conduct inherent in homosexual 'life-style' is felonious. Accordingly, I find no factor favoring a state interest under the Act which can be balanced against Georgetown's rights. Indeed, there is every reason in law to hold absolute Georgetown's first amendment rights.

To "prove" his point, Nebeker attached to his opinion some flyers produced by the gay student group at George Washington University to promote social events, including a dance to benefit the gay student groups at Georgetown. These flyers, reproduced with the published report of the case, include cartoon depictions of naked figures in sexually charged poses. Attorney Bogard had objected strenuously when the attorneys for the university sought to introduce them at trial, pointing out that they were not produced by the Georgetown gay student groups, but Judge Bacon, trying the case without a jury, indicated she would take them anyway and give them the appropriate weight or lack of weight in her deliberations. Now Nebeker seized on them as evidence of the sort of use to which the Georgetown University name would be put if the student groups were allowed to operate on campus. "They are examples of propaganda used to announce dances and gatherings (one for the 'benefit for gay people of Georgetown University') in the Washington, D.C. area. They are also examples of the sort of promotion the court's holding would require a religiously-affiliated university to subsidize," Nebeker asserted. "One might ask whether by our holding a student group dedicated to heterosexual relations with girls under the age of sixteen would likewise derive 'sexual orientation' benefits under the Act in the face of first amendment assertions."

The university immediately sought a stay of the court's decision while it decided whether to appeal to the U.S. Supreme Court. Chief Justice William H. Rehnquist twice granted a brief stay while the members of the Court interrupted their Christmas holidays to confer. On January 11, 1988, the Court denied the university's request for a stay, with Justice Antonin Scalia not participating.

When the Court denied a renewed application for a stay on January 25, Georgetown capitulated and negotiated a settlement with the student groups rather than seek further review. Under the settlement, the groups would have to indicate on any publicity materials they distributed that any views they expressed should not be attributed to Georgetown University. Reactionary forces in Congress quickly responded, adding an amendment proposed by Senator William Armstrong to the District of Columbia's municipal appropriation, requiring the council to amend its Human Rights Act so as to exempt religious and religiously affiliated organizations from having to refrain from discrimination on the basis of sexual orientation, or face a cut-off of all federal funding to the District government.

The District council, claiming that the First Amendment rights of its members were violated by this enactment, refused to amend the law, and the council members filed suit to have the budget amendment declared unconstitutional, which it subsequently was by the federal district and appeals courts in *Clarke v. United States*. However, after the district court opinion was issued, Congress relied on its ultimate legislative authority over the District to amend the Human Rights Act directly to the same effect. The D.C. Circuit Court of Appeals subsequently vacated its decision in *Clarke* as moot,

over the protests of some dissenting judges who contended that this was the type of problem that was likely to recur.

By then, however, the gay student groups at Georgetown had been operating under this "*de facto*" recognition arrangement without incident for many years. Soon after the D.C. court of appeals decision, a group of gay students at neighboring Catholic University of America also petitioned for recognition, which was granted voluntarily by the university. Similar recognition was soon obtained by a gay student organization at Fordham University Law School, a Catholic institution in New York, where a municipal gay rights ordinance might have been construed to cover the situation, although it was not as broadly drafted as the D.C. Human Rights Act.

Ultimately, the reconciliation of conflicting rights provided by the D.C. court of appeals seemed to achieve a peaceful settlement of the underlying dispute, although it turned on such subtle distinctions of "tangible" and "intangible" benefits that it was difficult for anybody other than a lawyer to find convincing. There could be little doubt that many church leaders were unhappy with the result, as were many in the gay community who insisted, with Judge Ferren, that anything less than full recognition was a type of "second-class citizenship" that the Human Rights Act was intended to prohibit. In a society that highly values religious freedom, however, this compromise was about the best that the gay community could have expected under the circumstances from a judiciary that, by the late 1980s, was becoming much more conservative as a result of several years of appointments by the administration of President Ronald Reagan.

Case References

Bob Jones University v. United States, 461 U.S. 574 (1983)

Clarke v. United States, 705 F. Supp. 605 (D.D.C. 1988), affirmed, 886 F.2d 404 (D.C. Cir. 1989), vacated as moot and remanded, 915 F.2d 699 (D.C. Cir. 1990)

Griggs v. Duke Power Co., 401 U.S. 424 (1971)

Meritor Savings Bank v. Vinson, 477 U.S. 57 (1986)

Pacific Gas & Electric Co. v. Public Utilities Commission, 475 U.S. 1 (1986)

Padula v. Webster, 822 F.2d 97 (D.C. Cir. 1987)

PruneYard Shopping Center v. Robins, 447 U.S. 74 (1980)

United States v. Carolene Products Co., 304 U.S. 144 (1938)

112. GAY STUDENTS ENTITLED TO NONDISCRIMINATORY FUNDING

Gay and Lesbian Students Association v. Gohn, 850 F.2d 361 (8th Cir. 1988), reversing 656 F. Supp. 1045 (W.D. Ark. 1987).

During the first decade of gay liberation activity following the 1969 Stonewall Riots in New York, some of the most active battlefronts were the campuses of colleges and universities, where lesbian and gay students formed associations and sought the recognition and privileges routinely accorded to other student groups. While a series of lawsuits had firmly established by the end of the 1970s that state colleges and universities were required to recognize such groups under the First Amendment, the battle continued during the 1980s as groups attempted to organize at private colleges and universities and as previously recognized groups at state schools attempted to gain access to university funding to support their activities.

Student groups faced the most difficult battles in states that still retained criminal penalties for consensual sodomy, where student government leaders, school administrators, and state legislators who had a vote on university funding all argued that the state should have a right to refrain from providing assistance or support to people who, in their view, habitually engaged in criminal activity. These disputes came to a head at the University of Arkansas in Fayetteville, where the Gay and Lesbian Students Association (GLSA), accorded official recognition and access to university facilities in 1983, applied to the Associated Student Government for funds to support some of its educational programs.

The GLSA claimed that its purpose was to educate people about homosexuality and to provide a support group for homosexuals. Its activities included sponsoring workshops, films, and panel discussions on homosexuality, in the hope that such activities would lead to greater understanding and a decrease in discriminatory attitudes. Under the student government system at the university, there were two classifications of funds: "A" funds, which supported such ongoing activities as the student newspaper, and "B" funds, which were provided for particular one-time projects or events. Requests for such funds were submitted to the finance committee of the elected student senate, which would review the requests for compliance with funding rules. These rules included a requirement that the organization attempt to do some fundraising of its own before applying for funds and that the event be for a primarily educational rather than social purpose. The finance committee would then make a recommendation to the senate, which would vote on the funding. Senate denials of funds could be appealed to the vice-chancellor for student services.

Shortly after it was formally established, GLSA applied for funds in January 1983 to present two films and to hold a panel discussion. The finance committee recommended that GLSA receive $136 for these purposes, and the proposal went to the senate floor. There was a "heated" debate, during which one senator argued, "The key word is 'support.' . . . This is a group that supports gay and lesbian homosexuality. We cannot use state money to support a homosexual group. What if a group of students/arsonists wanted to start an arsonists club and start fires. Would you fund them? . . . It's the same thing as funding homosexuals." Another senator remarked, "Why is it that this group is being subjected to a review . . . when other groups on campus who request funding are not treated like this?" The funding proposal was defeated by a vote of 35 to 17. Vice Chancellor Lyle Gohn was present at the senate meeting and heard the debate, about which he later testified in a deposition.

The GLSA appealed the denial of its funding request to Gohn. Gohn denied the appeal, claiming he did not know the reason why the senate rejected the request, but "I would hope that you . . . would accept the decision of your fellow student senators." Successive appeals to the chancellor of the university and its vice president for academic affairs were also unsuccessful. Chancellor B. A. Nugent wrote GLSA that there was "no evidence that discrimination was present among those who voted against funding" and that "determining the motives or rationale of the individual student senators . . . has no relevancy." He also mentioned in his letter that some "B" funds were left over that year, but stated his belief that the senate's action was based on purely financial considerations. Responding to publicity about the funding denial and appeal at the university, Arkansas State Representative Travis Dowd introduced resolutions in the legislature urging the university to "refrain from assisting in any manner whatsoever the gay community on campus," and to "institute any and all lawful measures to stem the tide of homosexuality on the campuses of our colleges and universities." The resolutions were narrowly defeated in committee, but copies ended up in Gohn's correspondence file of his dealings with the GLSA.

GLSA applied for "B" funds again in 1984. This time, a sympathetic finance committee chair successfully employed the strategem of "packaging" GLSA's request with funding requests from several other student groups. Although several senators tried to separate GLSA's request during the floor debate in order to vote it down, they were unsuccessful. GLSA members present for the debate characterized it as "horrible," "emotional," and "vulgar," but GLSA received its $70 request for a program. The reaction to the funding decision was "swift and severe," according to the ultimate decision by the court of appeals. The senate passed a rule prohibiting funding of any group organized on the basis of "sexual preference," which the student government president vetoed, calling it "discriminatory." The brouhaha on campus led to a meeting between university officials and members of the legislature, at which the funding issue was discussed and concern was expressed about the adverse impact of publicity about support for gay groups on campus. When Chancellor Willard Gatewood attended a meeting in June 1985 to discuss a proposed human rights program at the university that would examine various types of prejudice, he objected to the inclusion of a segment on homophobia, stating the university would not

fund it and implicitly threatening to withdraw all university funding for the whole program if the segment on homosexuality was included.

GLSA applied for funds again in the fall of 1985 in support of a campus showing of the film *Before Stonewall* and two planned workshops on racism and homophobia. GLSA sought $295, but revised its request to $165 after a meeting with the finance committee, which endorsed the smaller request. Fearful about the upcoming senate debate, the chair of the finance committee sought advice from Vice Chancellor Gohn, who told her to handle it as best she could. Hoping to avoid jeopardizing funding for other groups in light of the charged political atmosphere, she presented GLSA's request individually rather than in a package as had been done in 1984. At the senate meeting, a GLSA member stood up to address the meeting and one senator called out a comment expressing surprise at how "normal" the speaker looked. There was a brief debate during which opponents argued that funding would be illegal due to the state's sodomy law or would violate their religious beliefs. The funding request was voted down, forty-three to twenty-one. The GLSA request was the only one endorsed by the finance committee that was voted down, and the decision left some student activity funds still unspent. The senate even approved appropriations for three groups that had not received finance committee endorsement.

GLSA appealed again to Gohn, who again denied the appeal. While acknowledging that GLSA had complied with all the rules and that some other groups had been funded without complying with all the rules, he argued that the senate's decision should be respected, and that he did not know why the request was voted down and thought the reasons would be irrelevant in any case. Gohn's decision was upheld on appeal to the chancellor and the president of the university, who stated that this was a matter within the jurisdiction of the vice chancellor. Having exhausted its internal appeal rights, GLSA filed a lawsuit against Gohn and the trustees of the university in the federal district court in Fayetteville, seeking a declaration by the court that the constitutional rights of GLSA and its members had been violated and ordering Gohn to overrule any future discriminatory funding denials by the senate. The substantive basis for the lawsuit was 42 U.S.C. section 1983, a provision that authorizes suits for violation of civil rights by the government. GLSA claimed that the actions of the senate and Gohn were "state action" as required by the statute, due to the university's funding by the state legislature.

The case was heard by Chief Judge H. Franklin Waters of the Western District of Arkansas. Attorneys Clayton Blackstock and Marcia Barnes, of the Little Rock firm of Mitchell and Roachell, represented GLSA as cooperating attorneys for the Arkansas chapter of the American Civil Liberties Union. The university's general counsel, Fred H. Harrison, headed a defense team of several attorneys from the university and the state Attorney General's Office. The parties having stipulated the facts relevant to their dispute, the university moved to dismiss the case, arguing that the controversy was moot because each annual funding cycle was a separate event and turnover in the composition of the senate from year to year meant that it was essentially a different body for the next funding cycle. The university also argued that the complaint failed to satisfy the "state action" requirements under section 1983 because the student senators were not state officials, and, in any event, that the university was not required by the U.S. Constitution to provide funding for any particular student activities.

In his March 23, 1987, opinion, Judge Waters rejected the university's procedural arguments. He found that the controversy was of a type that was "capable of repetition, yet evading review," relying on the U.S. Supreme Court's 1982 decision in *Murphy v. Hunt*. That is, because of the brevity of the academic year and the funding cycle, and the time-consuming nature of internal appeals, the same funding controversy could theoretically recur year after year and the GLSA would never have an available judicial forum to rule on its constitutional claims. The history of the past three years provided justification for concluding that it was reasonably likely that the problem would recur, despite the university's assertion that GLSA's lobbying efforts had resulted in the election of more senators favorable to its funding requests.

As to the state action requirement, Waters found that the student senate was "the creation of the state"; its constitution had been approved by the board of trustees, which was established by a state law granting authority to the trustees to govern the university. Furthermore, the offices and funding for the student government came from the state, "B" funds came out of the university's state appropriation, and the vice chancellor, an appointee of the trustees and thus a state official, had authority to review the funding denial. Waters concluded that this university was "fully public," and its actions (including actions of the senate upheld on review by administrators) "are fairly attributable to the state." He found support for this conclusion in several cases decided by other federal courts, focusing particularly on *Sellman v. Baruch College of the City University of New York*, a 1979 district court opinion that specifically held that action by the student government was "state action" for purposes of the statute.

On the substantive issues in the case, however, Waters decided to rule against GLSA. This result was surprising, given Waters's analysis of the legal issues. He found that the existing case law on gay and lesbian student groups at public universities created an unequivocal right to recognition, but that there was no substantive right to receive funding. "A finding that the right to funding is encompassed within or is an essential element of the right of association would appear to limit a university's determination of how to divide up available funds," he asserted. There were 200 registered student organizations at the university, and only $6,200 in "B" funds were available during the 1985–86 school year, so it was clear that some discretion had to be used to decide which groups would receive funding, since there was not enough for all groups. On the other hand, it was also clear that under the First Amendment, the exercise of that discretion could not be carried out in a way infringing protected constitutional rights. As the U.S. Supreme Court had stated in 1972 in *Perry v. Sindermann*:

> [The government] may not deny a benefit to a person on a basis that infringes his constitutionally protected interests—especially, his interest in freedom of speech. For if the government could deny a benefit to a person

because of his constitutionally protected speech or associations, his exercise of those freedoms would in effect be penalized and inhibited. This would allow the government to "produce a result which [it] could not command directly." [citation omitted]. Such interference with constitutional rights is impermissible.

GLSA argued that since in the past the senate had routinely funded any group that met the technical requirements for funding and was recommended by the finance committee, it had created a "public forum" for speech activities from which no group could be excluded on the basis of the content of its speech. GLSA charged that its requests had been denied precisely because of the content of the programs it would be presenting, violating First Amendment principles. Waters disagreed, relying primarily on the U.S. Supreme Court's decision in *Maher v. Roe*, a 1977 ruling holding that a state could adopt a regulation prohibiting use of state funds for abortion-related services. While the state could not directly prohibit speech on a particular topic, it could refrain from supporting that speech through funding of the speaker. "The student senate has discretion whether to accept the recommendations of the finance committee as to which groups should be funded," wrote Waters.

Funding is approved through a democratic process and the ultimate decision is based on the vote of the student senate. In such a process a certain amount of discretion and subjective consideration is essential. Undoubtedly, the denial of funding to any group will have an impact, but it will not prevent the organization from advocating its views. To date there has not developed any firm policy concerning the constitutional value in sexual preference nondiscrimination. The University did not infringe upon GLSA's right of free speech or right of free association, but merely refused to affirmatively aid these rights through funding.

Waters also denied GLSA's claim that the funding denials violated the Equal Protection Clause. For one thing, he held, the funding decision could not be challenged under the "strict scrutiny" standard, since "homosexuals have not been determined to be a suspect class." Without pronouncing further on the subject, Waters silently indicated he was not about to undertake such a determination. Alternatively, "strict scrutiny" might apply if a fundamental

right were at issue, but Waters had already determined in denying the First Amendment claim that there was no fundamental right to university funding for a student organization; such funding was discretionary. Having determined that GLSA's claim did not invoke "strict scrutiny" of the university's actions, Waters said that the issue was whether the university's grant of discretion to the senate to make decisions on funding of student activities was "rational." He concluded that it was. "There is no guarantee that a given group will be funded or, if funded, that they will receive the full amount of their request," he wrote after summarizing yet again the funding procedure. "The ultimate decision is in the hands of those elected by the general population of the University." Thus, again without expressly articulating his reason, Waters implicitly held that it was within the discretion of the senate to deny funding on any ground it collectively thought appropriate.

GLSA appealed to the U.S. Court of Appeals for the Eighth Circuit. At the request of GLSA and its attorneys, the director of the ACLU's Lesbian and Gay Rights Project, Nan Hunter of New York, argued their appeal on January 14, 1988. University General Counsel Harrison argued for the respondent. The university cross-appealed on the issue of state action and also raised the mootness issue at oral argument. The three-judge panel issued its decision on June 22, affirming Waters's procedural rulings but reversing on the merits. In an opinion by Circuit Judge Richard S. Arnold, the court ruled that GLSA's First Amendment rights had been violated by the denial of its funding requests.

Arnold wrote that Waters had correctly summarized the First Amendment law up to a point, but seemed to have missed the point that the record evidenced content-based discrimination by the student senators in voting against the funding requests, and political sensitivity by Gohn and other administrators to the concerns of particular legislators in refusing to overrule the senate. Waters erred, wrote Arnold, "in overemphasizing . . . that the GLSA has no right to funding." The cases on which Waters had relied all involved content-neutral government policies that might be argued to have had a discriminatory or exclusionary effect on particular individuals. But that was not the situation in this case.

> The University claims the denial of funding was for a number of valid reasons related to the educational merit and benefit to the community of the GLSA's planned activities. But these reasons were not mentioned in the course of the denial of funds. Indeed, there is evidence that many senators voted against funding for other reasons, such as their disagreement with the GLSA's beliefs. In response to this, the University argues that the motive of the Student Senate is irrelevant, and in any case cannot be determined, since each senator may have a different rationale. Every claim of viewpoint discrimination requires, by its very nature, that the purposes or motives of governmental officials be determined. When the body involved has many members, the question is harder to answer, but it still must be faced.

Arnold found that "the First Amendment violation is apparent" in this case. GLSA had met all criteria for funding but was denied, even though funds were available and other groups that had not met all criteria were funded. Furthermore, the one time the senate did vote to fund a GLSA event, it promptly passed a resolution barring GLSA from future funding. Some student senators freely stated their content-based reasons for voting against GLSA's request, and university administrators "were feeling pressure from state legislators not to fund GLSA or to allow in any way the dissemination of opinions tolerant towards homosexuals." Under the circumstances, it was apparent that the denial of funding to GLSA was based on the content of the views it espoused, and there was no compelling state interest to justify the senate's denial of these funds. While a senator had referred to the sodomy law, "the GLSA does not advocate sodomy, and, even if it did," insisted Arnold, "its speech about an illegal activity would still be protected by the First Amendment. People may extol the virtues of arson or even cannibalism. They simply may not commit the acts." While the university could ban conduct, it could not "discriminate against people because it dislikes their ideas, not even when the ideas include advocating that certain conduct now criminal be legalized."

Arnold concluded that a First Amendment violation had occurred in this case and that no useful purpose would be served by remanding the matter to Waters to make new factual findings, since the record was replete with the necessary evidence for the court of appeals to draw its own conclusions. "This record leaves no reasonable doubt that funds were denied because of disagreement with GLSA's speech. A finding the other way would be clearly erroneous," asserted Arnold. Thus, the remand to Waters was solely for the purpose of providing GLSA with "appropriate relief in accordance with this opinion." The university sought rehearing from the panel and *en banc* review from the circuit, but an order denying both requests was issued on August 18, 1988.

The Eighth Circuit's decision in *GLSA v. Gohn* marked a major step in the ongoing effort to enable sexual minorities to organize and present their messages at state-funded colleges and universities. Because of the nature of views about sexuality in American culture, the "coming out" process for young people can be rather protracted. At college age, many homosexual individuals have yet to discover and accept their sexuality, and the number of openly lesbian and gay students in a position to present a positive argument for acceptance and understanding is small. Recognition of their associations (which might have an active membership of at most a few dozen people on a campus with thousands of students) without any financial support would necessarily limit the message and make it difficult to reach many who need to hear it, whether they are themselves gay or nongay. The principle that such funding decisions must be made on a nondiscriminatory basis under the First Amendment can have a significant effect in amplifying the message and broadening the discussion of human sexuality at American institutions of higher education.

Case References

Maher v. Roe, 432 U.S. 464 (1977)

Murphy v. Hunt, 455 U.S. 478 (1982)

Perry v. Sindermann, 408 U.S. 593 (1972)

Sellman v. Baruch College of the City University of New York, 482 F. Supp. 475 (S.D.N.Y. 1979)

CHAPTER 8
IMMIGRATION AND NATURALIZATION

One of the by-products of the anti-Communist crusades of the late 1940s and early 1950s was the introduction in American immigration and naturalization law of provisions excluding homosexuals from immigrating to the United States or from becoming U.S. citizens. Reflecting the testimony of medical "experts" on homosexuality, the original language of exclusion concerned "sexual psychopaths" and limited citizenship to those of "good moral character." Subsequent litigation led the U.S. Supreme Court to announce that the exclusionary language was not unduly vague and clearly reflected the intent of Congress to exclude homosexuals. Just to be sure, Congress amended the law in the 1960s specifically to exclude those "afflicted" with "sexual deviation."

But by the 1970s the medical establishment's consensus that "non-standard" sexuality was inevitably a form of mental illness had fallen apart, as the National Institutes of Health issued a report by a committee chaired by Dr. Evelyn Hooker proclaiming that homosexuality did not necessarily indicate sexual psychopathology, and members of the American Psychiatric Association voted to support a decision by their executive board to delete "homosexuality" from the list of pathologies in the profession's standard diagnostic manual. Later in the 1970s, Surgeon General Julius Richmond declared that the Public Health Service (PHS) would no longer attempt to "diagnose" homosexuality in arriving immigrants, leaving the Immigration and Naturalization Service (INS) with a dilemma: the law required that the PHS examine incoming immigrants to determine whether they were excludable on medical grounds. If the PHS would no longer diagnose homosexuality, how could lesbian or gay male immigrants be excluded under the law? Furthermore, how could they be stigmatized as not being of "good moral character" and thus denied citizenship solely on the basis of their sexual orientation?

The INS decided to exclude any immigrants who were identified by themselves or those accompanying them (or as a result of property they were bringing in with them, such as homosexually oriented publications, buttons, or insignia or slogans on clothing) as homosexuals, without obtaining PHS diagnostic certification, and to oppose grants of citizenship to those who had managed to obtain entry prior to the PHS policy change by concealing their homosexuality. Lesbian and gay activist groups challenged these policies, claiming that the change in medical views on homosexuality meant that the statutory exclusions were no longer enforceable or operative. Circuit courts divided on the question but the U.S. Supreme Court refused to act, setting the stage for Congress to repeal the exclusionary provisions in 1990 as part of a general reform of the INA provisions concerning grounds for exclusion.

Thus, the exclusion of homosexual immigrants from entry or citizenship in the United States is now an issue solely of historical interest (unlike most of the other issues addressed in this book). Nonetheless, the handful of cases discussed in this chapter provide an interesting insight into the evolution of views about homosexuality over the course of the past fifty years, and, in *Adams v. Howerton*, illustrates a problem that continues after the removal of the homosexual exclusion—nonrecognition of lesbian and gay relationships under rules governing the admission of spouses and family members of United States citizens.

Immigration and Naturalization: Readings

Carro, J.L., "From Constitutional Psychopathic Inferiority to AIDS: What Is in the Future for Homosexual Aliens?" 7 *Yale Law & Policy Review* 201 (Fall-Winter 1989)

Green, R., "Give Me Your Tired, Your Poor, Your Huddled Masses (of Heterosexuals): An Analysis of American and Canadian Immigration Policy," 16 *Anglo-American Law Review* 139 (May-July 1987)

Loue, S., "Homosexuality and Immigration Law: A Reexamination," 18 *Journal of Psychiatry & Law* 109 (Summer 1990)

Lundy, S.E., "I Do But I Can't: Immigration Policy and Gay Domestic Relationships," 5 *Yale Law & Policy Review* 185 (Fall-Winter 1986)

Wheatley, M., "Lesbian and Gay Aliens Denied Naturalization," 8 *Loyola of Los Angeles International and Comparative Law Journal* 161 (Winter 1985)

113. GAY ALIENS AS EXCLUDABLE PSYCHOPATHS

Boutilier v. Immigration & Naturalization Service, 387 U.S. 118 (1967), affirming 363 F.2d 488 (2d Cir. 1966).

There have undoubtedly always been people in the United States who engaged in homosexual activity, but the way in which legislative functions were divided in the United States between the states and the federal government meant that issues surrounding homosexuality were primarily a matter of state concern during the 19th century. In the totally federal sphere of immigration, there was little direct legislation concerning the admission or exclusion of particular groups until late in the century, when Congress became concerned with Asian immigration. Early in the 20th century, a major overhaul of the immigration laws expanded the concept of the medical exclusion. Ironically, as medical science began to see "sexual deviation" as a matter of illness rather than criminality, the result was to channel a newly emerging congressional desire to exclude "sexual deviates" into the sphere of medical exclusion. The 1917 Immigration Act provided for the exclusion of "persons of constitutional psychopathic inferiority," which some took to include "sex perverts." If persons suspected of falling into such a category presented themselves for admission, they were to be referred to the Public Health Service (PHS) for examination, diagnosis, and certification of status. If an alien who had entered the country was later found to have been excludable at the time of entry, the government could petition for deportation.

After World War II, during the height of the anti-Communist hysteria of the McCarthy period, a concern with homosexuals in government as a source of subversion and undermining of public morality undoubtedly contributed to the desire to make the exclusion of homosexuals more explicit as part of a major revision in the immigration laws undertaken early in the 1950s. While considering bills leading to enactment of the 1952 Immigration and Naturalization Act, the Senate Judiciary Committee replaced the term "constitutional psychopathic inferiority" with the more compact and modern "persons afflicted with psychopathic personality," which the PHS had advised would be "sufficiently broad to provide for the exclusion of homosexuals and sex perverts." At the time, the weight of psychiatric opinion was that homosexuals, or at least the ones who were troubled or dysfunctional enough to end up in a psychiatrist's office, were suffering from a serious mental defect or disease.

The legislative history makes clear that congressional proponents of the legislation certainly intended to exclude homosexuals by including this language, but it was the source of some trouble to the lower federal courts, since the term "psychopathic personality" was not ideally clear and specific with regard to sexual conduct and orientation. The U.S. Court of Appeals for the Ninth Circuit, based in San Francisco, found the term so indefinite that in two cases it found deportation of the alien in question would offend the due process guarantees in the Fifth Amendment of the U.S. Constitution.

The constitutional rights of aliens have always been a matter of some dispute. Since the Constitution gives Congress plenary authority in the area of immigration policy, the Supreme Court has held that basic guarantees of due process and equal protection in the Fifth Amendment do not apply to issues of exclusion and admission. The Fourteenth Amendment's Equal Protection Clause, from which Fifth Amendment equal protection doctrine derives, is limited in its application to all persons born or naturalized in the United States. However, once an alien has achieved admission and resides in the United States, due process and equal protection guarantees become relevant in proceedings to deport. When the deportation is initiated for reasons that existed prior to admission, however, the constitutional principles become muddled and confused, as examination of the Supreme Court's most significant ruling with regard to homosexuals under the 1952 Act, *Boutilier v. Immigration & Naturalization Service*, makes clear.

Clive Michael Boutilier, a native of Canada, came to the United States with his family in 1955, when he was 21 years old. He had been sexually active as a teenager, having had occasional sexual contacts with both men and women since the age of 14. He continued to be sexually active in New York City, where he settled. He had one scrape with the law, being charged with unlawful anal and oral sex with a minor male in 1959, but the charge was reduced to simple assault and dismissed when the complaining party failed to appear in court. Boutilier shared an apartment with a male sex partner, and had been classified 4–F in the draft after a Selective Service psychiatric examination revealed his homosexuality.

In 1963, Boutilier filed a petition for naturalization as a U.S. citizen. The documents required him to list any legal problems while residing in the United States, and he truthfully listed the 1959 sex charges. This led the Immigration Service to ask for more detailed information about his sexual activities before and after entry in the United States, and he truthfully supplied the information in writing. Immigration officials sent Boutilier's documentation to the PHS, which reviewed the documents and issued a certificate stating that Boutilier "was afflicted with a class A condition, namely, psychopathic personality, sexual deviate, at the time of his admission to the United States for permanent residence on June 22nd, 1955." After receiving this certification, the government filed a petition to deport Boutilier.

A hearing was held on the deportation petition before a special inquiry officer of the Immigration Service. Boutilier declined the opportunity to submit to a personal examination by PHS doctors, but offered letters from two private psychiatrists describing his condition. Both psychiatrists concluded that Boutilier was not a "psychopathic personality" as that term was understood in the medical profession, although each psychiatrist described him as having some sort of mental problem.

These opinions were not considered dispositive on the issue of deportation for sev-eral reasons. First, they concerned Boutilier's condition in 1963 when his application for naturalization and the government's deportation proceeding were pending, but the relevant time for considering Boutilier's condition, by strict reading of the statute, was when he first applied for admission to the United States, since his deportation was sought not for conduct after entry but for excludability at the time of entry. Second, and more important given the due process issues in the case, the psychiatrists' reports placed labels on Boutilier's condition based on current medical opinion, but current medical opinion was of no concern to the special inquiry officer, who concluded that Congress had used "psychopathic personality" as a legal term of art rather than a medical formulation. The opinions of psychiatrists were deemed irrelevant, except to establish Boutilier's sexual orientation at the time of entry, since Congress had intended to exclude homosexuals by using the terminology suggested by the PHS at the time of enactment of the law.

The immigration officer, concluding that Boutilier had been a homosexual at the time of his entry, ruled that he should be deported. Boutilier's appeal to the Board of Immigration Appeals was unsuccessful, and he filed suit against the Immigration Service in the U.S. Court of Appeals for the Second Circuit, seeking to have the deportation order vacated. The court heard argument on June 2, 1966, and dismissed Boutilier's petition on July 8, 1966. Judge Irving Kaufman wrote an opinion for the court, essentially agreeing with the rulings of the special inquiry officer. Kaufman rejected a variety of new arguments raised by Boutilier's attorneys, Blanche and David Freedman, including that Boutilier could not be deported without a medical examination by the PHS. Kaufman noted that Boutilier's current medical status was not the issue, so such an examination would be irrelevant. Furthermore, Kaufman accepted the Immigration Service's contention, argued by Special Assistant U.S. Attorney Francis J. Lyons, that Congress had used the phrase "psychopathic personality" instead of "homosexual" or "sexual deviate" solely on the advice of PHS officials that this would be the appropriate medical nomenclature for describing homosexuality as a medical basis for exclusion. Whether all homosexuals necessarily had a psychopathic personality was irrelevant.

The court's ruling drew a spirited dissent from Circuit Judge Leonard P. Moore, who argued that Boutilier's deportation would violate due process of law. For one thing, Boutilier was labeled by the PHS as having had a psychopathic personality at the time of his entry to the United States solely on the basis of his own admissions of having previously engaged in some homosexual activity. According to Moore, the PHS followed a rote procedure of labeling all those who engaged in homosexual conduct as psychopathic, without regard to their actual physical or mental condition. As such, the PHS violated the fundamental due process precept that the government may not label persons in a way that affects their rights without a "careful case-by-case determination." He noted the great hardship "involved in uprooting an alien from a country once he has developed economic and social ties there and slackened or severed those which bound him to his country of origin." Boutilier's deportation would separate him from his parents and siblings now settled in the United States.

Judge Moore also disagreed with the conclusion that Congress intended the phrase "psychopathic personality" to apply automatically "to cover anyone who had ever had a homosexual experience." Since the Kinsey Report of 1948 estimated that "at least 37 percent" of the male population had at least one homosexual experience, that would presume that Congress considered more than a third of the male population of the United States afflicted with a psychopathic personality—an absurd result. Citing famous characters in world history who would be excludable under this standard, and noting that the list could be extended to include "more than a few members of legislative bodies," Moore argued that a more plausible interpretation would be that Congress intended to exclude "someone with a long-lasting and perhaps compulsive orientation towards homosexual or otherwise 'abnormal' behavior." Delving futher into the PHS report on which congressional committees had relied, Moore singled out such phrases as "developmental defects" and "pathological trends in personality structure," and commented that such language indicated

Congress intended the PHS to undertake "an inquiry in each case, to be performed by skilled psychiatrists," rather than a cursory adoption of the alien's own description of a few past homosexual experiences as conclusively justifying the "psychopathic" label.

Finally, noting the Ninth Circuit authorities, Judge Moore contended that the term "psychopathic personality" presented problems of vagueness. It was unlikely that an alien applying for admission to the United States would consider the term to apply to himself, even if he had engaged in discreet, private, and consensual homosexual activity in the past. Moore then revealed his own limited understanding of the nature of human sexuality (probably not unusual for those who took a "humane" stance toward homosexuals at the time) by contending that had Boutilier known that "sexual deviation" was unacceptable for U.S. entry, he could have obtained psychiatric assistance to modify his behavior. This was based on the letters from Boutilier's psychiatric consultants, who had written that his sexual orientation was still fluid and subject to change.

Boutilier appealed to the U.S. Supreme Court, which heard argument on March 14, 1967, and announced its opinion affirming the court of appeals on May 22, 1967, in an opinion by Justice Tom C. Clark. Blanch Freedman argued Boutilier's appeal. Nathan Lewin, of the Solicitor General's Office, argued for the government. The case attracted *amicus* briefs on Boutilier's behalf from the American Civil Liberties Union and the Homosexual Law Reform Society of America (a group that may have been formed primarily to file a brief in this case).

Justice Clark concluded for the Court that "[t]he legislative history of the Act indicates beyond a shadow of a doubt that the Congress intended the phrase 'psychopathic personality' to include homosexuals such as petitioner." Justice Clark focused particularly on the Senate Judiciary Report, which, after indicating that the phrase "psychopathic personality" had been adopted on recommendation of the PHS, concluded: "This change of nomenclature is not to be construed in any way as modifying the intent to exclude all aliens who are sexual deviates." Similar statements from House committee reports were also invoked. In the Court's view, Congress had merely used the phrase "psychopathic personality" as a code word to cover all homosexuals. Clark asserted that the "[g]overnment clearly established that petitioner was a homosexual at entry" (even though Boutilier's psychiatrists had asserted in their letters that his sexuality was actually fluid and not permanently established).

The Court also rejected Boutilier's arguments about the vagueness of the Act. Vagueness, according to Clark, was a doctrine used to criticize laws that did not give fair notice to persons that they should not engage in certain conduct. The doctrine was inapplicable here because Boutilier engaged in the conduct before ever becoming concerned with the statute as an applicant for entry to the United States. The regulation, in Clark's view, "imposes neither regulation of nor sanction for conduct. . . . Here, when petitioner first presented himself at our border for entrance, he was already afflicted with homosexuality. The pattern was cut, and under it he was inadmissible." Until one had entered the United States, one was not entitled to due process of law, since Congress had plenary authority to exclude aliens. Since Boutilier's postentry conduct was not the basis for his deportation, merely serving as confirmation that he was correctly labeled by the PHS as a homosexual based on his preentry conduct, due process considerations were irrelevant.

Justice William O. Douglas issued a lengthy dissenting opinion, joined by Justice Abe Fortas. Justice William J. Brennan, Jr., separately adopted Judge Moore's dissent from the court of appeals as his own.

Justice Douglas immediately went to the heart of the matter. The exclusion of homosexuals was essentially political rather than medical: "The term 'psychopathic personality' is a treacherous one like 'communist' or in an earlier day 'Bolshevik.' A label of this kind when freely used may mean only an unpopular person. It is much too vague by constitutional standards for the imposition of penalties or punishment." After reviewing various medical texts about "psychopathic personality" and "homosexuality," Douglas reproduced a lengthy excerpt from the 1948 Kinsey report arguing that

it was improper to label homosexuals as necessarily suffering from mental illness or defect.

Douglas then essentially adopted Judge Moore's argument that it would not be credible to attribute to Congress the desire to exclude anybody who had ever had a homosexual experience, "no matter how blameless his social conduct had been nor how creative his work nor how valuable his contribution to society." Returning to the inherent vagueness of the term "psychopathic personality" as it was defined in a variety of published sources, Douglas contrasted it with the term "moral turpitude," which been upheld by the Court against vagueness challenges as a basis for deportation. Douglas noted that the latter term had deep roots in legal history, unlike "psychopathic personality," which had been adopted in 1952 even though the PHS had itself admitted, as noted in a House Committee report, that the term is "vague and indefinite." Equating deportation to "banishment or exile," and calling it "practically" criminal, Douglas argued that a high standard of due process should be applied. A hearing should be afforded and the PHS required to determine in the individual case whether the alien was "afflicted with a psychopathic personality."

Noting that "at least half of the questioning of this petitioner related to his postentry conduct," Douglas scoffed at the Court's assertion that the deportation decision was based solely on his conduct prior to entry. Douglas then quoted the letters from Boutilier's psychiatrists, and argued that they did not support a finding that Boutilier was "afflicted" and that a rigid application of the label violated Congress's intention that a medical determination be made on each application. "We cruelly mutilate the Act when we hold otherwise," he concluded, "for we make the word of the bureaucrat supreme, when it was the expertise of the doctors and psychiatrists on which Congress wanted the administrative action to be dependent."

The *Boutilier* decision laid bare the schizophrenic nature of Congress's dealing with homosexuals. Homosexuals were singled out by Senator Joseph McCarthy and others as security risks and traitors, and it seems clear that Congress intended to exclude them as a group.

By grouping them with the other medical exclusions, however, Congress was saying in effect that the reason for exclusion was medical: that persons who were mentally flawed should not be admitted to the United States.

At the time Congress made that determination, the medical establishment, as reflected in the PHS report, believed that homosexuality was a form of mental illness or defect. Over the 1950s and 1960s, a variety of studies significantly undermined the medical consensus, and by the late 1960s there were insistent voices among mental health practitioners calling for a change in the profession's position on homosexuality. Although the leading medical professional organizations did not formally vote to change their positions until after the *Boutilier* decision, it was possible by 1967 for Boutilier's advocates and *amici* to assemble impressive support from medical authorities to the effect that the automatic labeling of all homosexuals as "psychopathic" was mistaken. To surmount this problem, the Court had to lay bare that Congress was not concerned with the facts about homosexuality as such; that antipathy toward homosexuals as a group rather than a more general concern for the mental health of the nation was the motivating factor for the exclusion, so

that the exclusion should continue consistent with the intent of Congress, even though the words used to describe the basis for the exclusion were no longer deemed valid by the very medical community that had supplied Congress with its pretextual rationale for exclusion.

Even as *Boutilier* was pending in the lower courts, Congress had reacted to claims that the exclusionary language was unduly vague by amending the law to add the term "sexual deviation," so that there would be no mistake about congressional intent to exclude homosexuals under the medical exclusion section of the law. However, because Congress did not move the exclusion out of the medical sections, there would be further difficulties for enforcement of the exclusion when the PHS, following the lead of medical professional associations, determined more than a decade later that it could not "diagnose" homosexuality as a medical condition and would henceforth refuse to "diagnose" aliens as homosexuals.

Case References

Fleuti v. Rosenberg, 302 F.2d 652 (9th Cir. 1962), remanded, 374 U.S. 449 (1963)

Lavoie v. United States Immigration & Naturalization Service, 360 F.2d 27 (9th Cir. 1966), reversed, 387 U.S. 572 (1967)

114. IS HOMOSEXUALITY A DISQUALIFICATION FOR CITIZENSHIP?

Nemetz v. Immigration & Naturalization Service, 647 F.2d 432 (4th Cir. 1981), reversing 485 F. Supp. 470 (E.D. Va. 1980).

Horst Nemetz, a native of Germany, came to the United States in 1967 as a permanent resident. He moved to Virginia and resided there with a male roommate, with whom he had a sexual relationship. In 1976, Nemetz petitioned the federal district court in Alexandria to become a naturalized U.S. citizen. Following normal procedures, the Immigration and Naturalization Service (INS) of the U.S. Justice Department called Nemetz for a hearing on his petition, during which it came out that Nemetz was gay. Nemetz was represented by his attorney, Richard Murray, of Washington, at this

interview, and Murray continually interposed objections to some of the questions, but the hearing record contained admissions by Nemetz to being homosexual, to living with his male sexual partner, and to engaging in sexual relations with him on a regular basis. Nemetz's partner was a consenting adult, and their sexual activities took place in private.

Based on this hearing record, the INS concluded that Nemetz lacked the requisite "good moral character" for naturalization, referring to the Virginia sodomy law whose constitutionality had recently been sustained by a federal court in *Doe v. Commonwealth's Attorney for City of Richmond* (1975). Consequently, the INS recommended to the federal district court in Alexandria that Nemetz's petition be denied. Senior District Judge Oren R. Lewis held a hearing on the petition on February 15, 1980. Nemetz was represented at the hearing by Carolyn S. Motes, of Fairfax, and Murray, and the government was represented by Robert N. Herman, an INS attorney. The parties agreed to introduce the transcript of Nemetz's INS hearing as the factual record for decision, and engaged in oral argument over whether the Virginia sodomy law could be the basis for determining good moral character when Nemetz had never been convicted of violating it and had kept his sexual activities private.

In an opinion issued on February 26, Judge Lewis concluded that Nemetz's petition must be denied. Asserting that Nemetz had the burden of proving good moral character, Lewis concluded that Nemetz's own admissions made that impossible in this case. Motes's argument that Nemetz's private sexual activities "fall far short of conduct of a sufficiently reprehensible nature as to render [Nemetz] a person of bad moral character for purposes of the naturalization laws" was "not in accord with Virginia law," said Lewis, noting that "sodomy, as defined by Virginia law, is a crime involving moral turpitude." Lewis said that the federal court decision upholding the Virginia sodomy law, since affirmed by the U.S. Supreme Court, had commented that sodomy "is likely to end in a contribution to moral delinquency." To this, Lewis added: "The Virginia sodomy statute was adopted by the legislature in an attempt to quell the rising tide of this type of moral decay." (It is hard to know how Lewis had reached such a conclusion, since sodomy was a common-law crime that was codified, in Virginia as elsewhere, very early in U.S. history.)

Nemetz appealed this ruling to the U.S. Court of Appeals for the Fourth Circuit, which heard oral argument from Murray and Justice Department Attorney Margaret J. Perry on December 5, 1980. The court of appeals unanimously reversed in an opinion by Circuit Judge Sam J. Ervin, III, issued on April 24, 1981. For Ervin, the case raised issues of federalism, equal-

ity, and national uniformity of immigration policy. Reviewing the immigration and naturalization law, Ervin noted that it required disqualification of anybody who had been convicted of a "crime involving moral turpitude" or who "admit[s] having committed such a crime [or] committing acts which constitute the essential elements of such a crime."

Ervin was bothered about equality issues. He noted, "At oral argument the Service conceded that heterosexuals, whether married or unmarried, would not be subjected to questions concerning their private consensual sexual activities. As most states that proscribe consensual sodomy (including Virginia) make no distinction between homosexual and heterosexual acts, there appears to be no basis in law for treating the two classes differently." More significantly, Ervin rejected the government's contention that the determination of good moral character should be made by reference to state law. Nemetz had argued that the U.S. Constitution specifies that there be a "uniform rule of naturalization" in article I, section 8, clause 4. Defining "moral turpitude" in terms of state law would not provide a uniform rule, since some states criminalized consensual sodomy while many did not.

Said Ervin, "We agree with Nemetz that whether a person is of good moral character for purposes of naturalization is a question of federal law," which required construction of a uniform national rule. "[R]eferences to laws which vary from state to state can only lead to differing and often inconsistent results." This very case showed how that could happen, since by then at least nine states had repealed their sodomy laws legislatively and sodomy laws had been declared unconstitutional by the courts of two others. Ervin stated:

> At oral argument it was conceded that if Nemetz lived in Illinois, the Service would be unable to oppose his petition on the ground of bad moral character. In any state in which sodomy is not a crime, Nemetz could have freely admitted to committing acts of sodomy without placing his petition in jeopardy. In other words, but for an "accident of geography," Nemetz perhaps would be a naturalized citizen today. Such a result hardly contributes to any principle of uniformity and is, in fact, incongruous with common sense.

The INS argued that Congress traditionally ceded to the states the authority to legislate on matters of morality, but Ervin did not accept this as a good argument for sacrificing uniformity. The issue of federal citizenship was solely a matter of federal concern, and the determination of good moral character must proceed by reference solely to federal law, insisted Ervin. While it was appropriate to look to state law for guidance with regard to most crimes, which were essentially similar from state to state, on an issue where the states took disparate approaches it was not appropriate. "While we can assume without harm to the outcome of this case that states have a legitimate interest in regulating private acts, the federal government has none for the purposes of the naturalization laws," asserted Ervin, citing as an example *Wadman v. INS*, a 1964 case in which the Ninth Circuit had given a narrow construction to the use of "adultery" as a basis for finding bad moral character in a naturalization proceeding. Even though the federal statute specifically mentioned "adultery" as a basis for finding bad moral character, the Ninth Circuit had ruled that this should not necessarily be taken to include all fornication involving a married person. Ervin concluded that the Ninth Circuit had "implicitly recognized that it is the public rather than private aspect of adultery that makes it an act of moral turpitude" within the meaning of the immigration law.

"A close reading of the Act, moreover, lends support to the view that Congress did not intend to bar a finding of good moral character merely because of an alien's private consensual sexual activities. Although Congress excluded a wide range of people from entry into the country, the section on "bad moral character" as a disqualification for citizenship was much narrower and contained only a few specific references. Sodomy was never specifically mentioned, in fact, even though the exclusion provisions mentioned those "afflicted with . . . sexual deviation." "Had Congress intended homosexual acts to evince bad moral character," concluded Ervin, "it could easily have incorporated [the reference to sexual deviation] into [the moral character section] by reference, as it did with regard to other excludable classes. Its failure to do so leads us to the conclusion that it did not intend purely private sexual activities to act as an absolute bar to a finding of good moral character."

Turning to Nemetz's own case, Ervin concluded that the petition for naturalization should be granted. His homosexual activity should not be relied on as evidence of bad moral character, since it had been "purely private, consensual and without harm to the public." Nemetz had been steadily employed, and affidavits from witnesses indicated he had been a "good businessman and friend."

The *Nemetz* decision was an important breakthrough under the immigration laws, but it did not end the INS's practice of attempting to bar gay aliens from being granted citizenship. Instead, the INS switched its tactics, arguing in later cases that since the law excluded homosexuals from entry into the United States, homosexual aliens were not legally present in the United States, and thus could be denied naturalization because the law required that an alien have been lawfully present for at least five years. The INS successfully maintained this position in litigation in the Fifth Circuit in 1983, where the court of appeals held in *In re Longstaff* that a gay man of English nationality who had resided in Texas for many years must be denied naturalization because he had failed, upon applying for his entry visa more than twenty years before, to indicate that he was "afflicted with psychopathic personality." The U.S. Supreme Court refused to review that decision. The judicial stalemate surrounding the antigay immigration and naturalization policies was not finally resolved until 1990, when Congress repealed the offensive provision as part of a general overhaul of the sections dealing with medical exclusions.

Case References

Doe v. Commonwealth's Attorney for City of Richmond, 403 F. Supp. 1199 (E.D. Va. 1975), summarily affirmed without opinion, 425 U.S. 901, rehearing denied, 425 U.S. 985 (1976)

Longstaff, In re, 538 F. Supp. 589 (N.D. Tex. 1982), affirmed, 716 F.2d 1439 (5th Cir. 1983), certiorari denied, 467 U.S. 1219 (1984)

Wadman v. INS, 329 F.2d 812 (9th Cir. 1964)

115. A GAY FAMILY BATTLES THE IMMIGRATION SERVICE

Adams v. Howerton, 673 F.2d 1036 (9th Cir.), certiorari denied, 458 U.S. 1111 (1982), affirming 486 F. Supp. 1119 (C.D. Cal. 1980). Subsequent decision on deportation: *Sullivan v. Immigration & Naturalization Service*, 772 F.2d 609 (9th Cir. 1985).

One area where the definition of family relationships takes on supreme importance is the interpretation of immigration and naturalization law. Under U.S. immigration law, strict quotas are established limiting the number of immigrants who may enter the country for purposes of permanent settlement, and preferences are given to particular occupations. However, these quotas and preferences do not apply if the immigrant is an "immediate relative" of a U.S. citizen. Under section 201(b) of the Immigration and Naturalization Act, immediate relatives are "the children, spouses and parents of a citizen of the United States." When they met and fell in love early in the 1970s, Australian citizen Anthony Corbett Sullivan and U.S. citizen Richard Frank Adams initiated a legal controversy over whether the law should recognize gay families in this context.

Sullivan was in the United States on a student visa when he met and fell in love with Adams. They began to live together in 1971. Sullivan's visa expired and he was able to secure a nonimmigrant visitor's visa in 1973, which allowed him to remain in the country until January 7, 1974. As the time drew near for his visa expiration, Sullivan went through a marriage ceremony with an American citizen named Mary Egleston, hoping to be allowed permanent status in the United States as a spouse of a U.S. citizen. Sullivan's petition for permanent status, initially granted, was later revoked by the Immigration and Naturalization Service when an investigation showed that the marriage was a sham for purposes of qualifying for permanent residence. The Immigration Service began deportation proceedings against Sullivan.

While the deportation was proceeding, Adams and Sullivan acted on reports that the city clerk in Boulder, Colorado, was willing to issue marriage licenses to gay couples. (The Colorado marriage law did not then specify that marriage was limited to opposite-sex couples.)

The two men obtained a license and had a wedding ceremony performed by a minister on April 21, 1975. Local press coverage led a member of the state legislature to request an opinion from the Colorado attorney general as to the validity of the marriage; the attorney general, in an informal opinion, asserted that Colorado law would not recognize a same-sex marriage as valid. However, no steps were taken by law enforcement authorities to void the marriage.

Meanwhile, four days after the marriage ceremony, Adams filed a petition with the Immigration Service to have his new spouse, Sullivan, classified as his "immediate relative." The Service denied the petition, and the denial was upheld by the Board of Immigration Appeals in an unpublished opinion based solely on the Board's view that Colorado law did not authorize same-sex marriages. Adams and Sullivan then filed suit in the U.S. District Court for the Central District of California, represented by attorney David M. Brown and the American Civil Liberties Union Foundation of California.

Adams and Sullivan argued that since the Immigration and Naturalization Act did not define "spouse," the court should look to the law of the jurisdiction in which they were married to determine whether they were spouses. Since the Colorado marriage law did not expressly require that marital partners be of opposite sex, the clerk had issued a license and a minister duly licensed to perform marriages had performed a ceremony, they claimed that their marriage under Colorado law should be binding on the Service. They also noted that there was no Colorado case law on point, and that the attorney general's letter to a state legislator was not a formal opinion of any legal effect. They also argued that if the Colorado marriage law did not allow for same-sex marriage, it was in violation of the federal constitutional requirement of equal protection of the laws.

Opposing the petition, Assistant U.S. Attorney Eva Halbreich argued that the Board had correctly concluded that the marriage was invalid under Colorado law and cited the growing body of law upholding the constitutional validity of limiting marriage to opposite-sex couples. She also argued that even if the marriage was valid in Colorado, that would not be binding on the Board, which was construing a federal statute.

Chief Judge Irving Hill of the district court issued his ruling orally from the bench on February 25, 1980. (An edited transcript of his opinion was later published in the *Federal Supplement* law reports.) Hill upheld the decision by the Board of Immigration Appeals.

Addressing first the question of whether the marriage was valid, Hill concluded that a determination whether Adams and Sullivan were spouses was a matter of federal law. Although the law of the jurisdiction where a marriage purportedly took place would be important in determining the validity of the marriage, "that is not an absolute and totally governing criterion." Noting that the Immigration Act itself specified some circumstances where marriages valid under state law would not be considered binding under immigration law, Hill concluded that ultimately the test was whether recognizing the marriage would create a result "which offends federal public policy."

Giving closer examination to the Colorado law on marriage, Hill found hints in the state law that the Colorado legislature expected marriages to be conducted between opposite-sex couples and noted that standard reference sources all defined marriage with relation to opposite-sex couples. Indeed, no court had ever held that a state was required to recognize a same-sex marriage.

But even if a gay marriage were recognized in Colorado, Hill held that it would not be recognized for purposes of the immigration law. In determining what policy Congress would intend on the subject, Hill argued that "one ought to explore the societal values which underlie the recognition of marriage and the reasons that it has been a preferred and protected legal institution." In Hill's view, those values had entirely to do with propagation of the species and had no reference to any other value.

Since a same-sex couple would be biologically incapable of generating offspring, there would be no basis for recognizing their marriage as a matter of federal policy.

Adams and Sullivan had argued alternatively that they be treated as "putative spouses." The doctrine of putative spouses had been adopted in some jurisdictions as a necessary legal fiction to deal with circumstances where important property or support issues were at stake and it was necessary to treat somebody as a spouse to avoid unconscionable results; normally, the doctrine was applied where parties believed themselves to be married but it was found that no marriage existed due to some technicality of the law. Hill found that the concept of putative spouse required a good-faith belief on the part of one claiming that status that they were actually married, and asserted that nobody in American society could believe in good faith that any court would recognize a same-sex marriage as valid.

As to the constitutional challenge mounted by Adams and Sullivan to the unavailability of marriage for same-sex couples, Hill relied on the refusal by the U.S. Supreme Court to review the Minnesota Supreme Court's 1971 decision in *Baker v. Nelson*, which had rejected a constitutional challenge on this question. The Supreme Court had dismissed the petition to review in that case as not presenting a substantial federal question. Hill reasoned that if no substantial federal question was presented, it was obvious that the policy did not violate the equal protection obligation.

Even if *Baker* were not controlling on the question, Hill said, he would have decided it the same way. Hill found that the state had a rational basis for restricting marriage to opposite-sex couples as a way of promoting the survival of the species, and rejected the argument that allowing nonprocreative opposite-sex couples to marry contradicted this goal:

> There is no real alternative to some overbreadth in achieving this goal. The state has chosen to allow legal marriage as between all couples of the opposite sex. The alternative would be to inquire of each couple, before issuing a marriage license, as to their plans for children and to give sterility tests to all applicants, refusing licenses to those found sterile or unwilling to raise a family. Such tests and inquiries would

themselves raise serious constitutional questions.

Hill concluded by recognizing that society's views were changing, and that it was possible that in the future states might recognize some sort of contractual familial structure for same-sex relations, but insisted that such structure would not be the same as marriage:

> [E]ven such a substantial change in the prevailing mores would not reach the point where such relationships would be characterized as "marriages." At most, they would become personal relationships having some, but not all, of the legal attributes of marriage. And even when and if that day arrives, two persons of the same sex, like those before the Court today, will not be thought of as being "spouses" to each other within the meaning of the immigration laws. For that result to obtain, an affirmative enactment of Congress will be required.

Adams and Sullivan appealed this decision to the U.S. Court of Appeals for the Ninth Circuit in San Francisco. A three-judge panel heard arguments on October 7, 1981, and issued its unanimous opinion affirming the district court on February 25, 1982.

Circuit Judge J. Clifford Wallace dealt only briefly with the issue of Colorado law in his opinion for the court. Wallace found that it was "not clear" whether Colorado "would recognize a homosexual marriage," but that it was unnecessary for the court to take a position on this question because the case could be disposed of entirely as a matter of interpretation of the federal law. The court believed that Congress had clearly not intended to let state law control the question whether somebody was a "spouse" of a U.S. citizen under immigration law. This was because the statute contained its own express limitations on "persons who may be deemed spouses" which would clearly exclude certain marriages that would be valid under state law, such as marriages in which the spouses did not intend to live together. Furthermore, where a word in common use is not specifically defined in a statute, the court will normally give it the meaning it carries in common use. Wallace found that in common use, "spouse" did not refer to the parties in a same-sex couple.

More significantly, Wallace found that the same 1965 Congress that adopted the provision governing "immediate relatives" and their immigration rights had also adopted language expressly excluding homosexuals from obtaining permanent immigration visas, consistent with the Immigration Service's position in the then pending *Boutilier* case. In determining congressional intent with regard to whether a same-sex marriage should be recognized under the immigration law, he said, "We think it unlikely that Congress intended to give homosexual spouses preferential admission treatment under section 201(b) of the Act when, in the very same amendments adding that section, it mandated their exclusion."

As to the argument that section 201(b) thus construed violated the equal protection obligations of the federal government under the Fifth Amendment's due process clause, Wallace referred to the well-established plenary power of Congress in the area of immigration policy mandating great deference by the courts. The Supreme Court had regularly upheld immigration rules that would be deemed unconstitutional if applied to U.S. citizens, and the courts had routinely rejected attempts to subject immigration regulations to the same searching due process or equal protection reviews that would apply in other areas of legal regulation.

Given this deferential standard, it was not difficult for Wallace to find that Congress had a rational basis for extending special admission preferences to the traditionally defined spouses of U.S. citizens as a way of manifesting its "concern for family integrity." No further explanation was deemed necessary to uphold the law.

Adams and Sullivan promptly petitioned the U.S. Supreme Court for review, but their petition was quickly denied without comment on June 28, 1982, and the Immigration Service activated its deportation proceedings against Sullivan. Sullivan requested a continuance of the proceedings while he applied to the Immigration Service for suspension of deportation on the ground that his deportation would cause extreme hardship to himself and Adams. Sullivan argued that they had been together for twelve years as a couple and that a forced breakup of their relationship would cause great personal anguish. He also argued that immigration by Adams to Australia was not a viable alternative because Australia was less tolerant than the United States toward homosexuals. His own family had cut off all relations with him over the issue of his sexual orientation, and the notoriety his case had already achieved in Australia would make it difficult for him to resume living there. Furthermore, after living for many years in the Los Angeles area he had become an active and respected member of the community.

The Board of Immigration Appeals rejected all these arguments. The Board took the position that any anguish Sullivan and Adams might suffer would be no greater than that suffered by other nonrelatives separated due to immigration law restrictions, and that problems he might encounter in Australia would be the same "experienced by most aliens who have spent time abroad." The Board discounted his community ties in Los Angeles, commenting that they had been formed during the course of the litigation when Sullivan's status in the United States was in doubt.

Sullivan appealed this decision to the Ninth Circuit, which heard argument December 5, 1984, and rendered a decision affirming the Board on September 30, 1985. Judge Anthony M. Kennedy (later appointed to the U.S. Supreme Court by President Ronald Reagan) wrote for the panel majority; Judge Harry Pregerson dissented.

Kennedy's decision for the court was a virtual rubber stamp of the Board of Immigration Appeals' decision. Holding that the standard of review was whether the Board had abused its discretion and had addressed the arguments raised by the petitioner, Kennedy concluded that each argument Sullivan made was individually dealt with in the Board's opinion. In a conclusory summation, Kennedy asserted that "deportation rarely occurs without personal distress and emotional hurt," but noted that the courts had in the past upheld deportation orders separating families and remanding immigrants to war-torn countries, so Sullivan's case did not appear to the court to be an abuse of discretion. Kennedy concluded that the Board "has discretion to construe extreme hardship narrowly."

Judge Pregerson disagreed, noting that although the Board had addressed all of Sullivan's claims, its decision was "arbitrary" because "important aspects of the individual claim are distorted or disregarded." The conclusory statements employed by the Board in dismissing Sullivan's petition failed to explain why his case should be dealt with in the same way as other cases. Pregerson criticized the Board for giving "no recognition to the strain Sullivan would experience if he were forced to separate from the person with whom he has lived and shared a close relationship for the past twelve years. This failure to recognize Sullivan's emotional hardship is particularly troublesome because he and Adams have lived together as a family."

Furthermore, the Board's response to Sullivan's arguments about the special difficulties he would encounter in Australia due to the notoriety of his case constituted "short shrift," according to Pregerson.

> Sullivan's readjustment to life in Australia would be quite *contrary* to that of "most aliens." As Sullivan points out, most deported aliens do not return to their native country as virtual outcasts from their friends and family. And, most deported aliens can return to their native lands with their closest companions. But Sullivan would be precluded from doing so because Adams allegedly would not be permitted to emigrate to Australia.

Thus, the Board had not given individual consideration to Sullivan's case, but had arbitrary dealt with him as fungible with all other aliens. Pregerson criticized the Board's discounting of Sullivan's community ties in the United States, noting that their foundation had been laid several years before the legal controversy began, and he also noted that there was precedent for considering hardship with regard to separation of relatives not specified in the "immediate relative" portion of the statute, such as siblings.

Finally, and most seriously, Pregerson contended that the statute required the Board to consider all the factors urged by Sullivan cumulatively. The Board's approach had been to take each individual factor and discount its significance, without considering the cumulative impact of all the factors in making an overall determination whether Sullivan's case presented extreme hardship. To Pregerson, failure to take a totality-of-the-circumstances approach constituted arbitrariness. Pregerson concluded that the case should be sent back to the Board with directions to give Sullivan appropriate individual consideration.

Although they had garnered a strong dissenting opinion, Adams and Sullivan decided not to carry their legal struggle further, having been advised that it was unlikely the Supreme Court would reverse the court of appeals. Instead, they took their case to the media, appearing on the *Phil Donahue* television program to publicize the injustice they charged was being done to them, and attempted to stave off the final deportation. On that program, Richard Adams announced that he would leave the United States if necessary to remain with Tony Sullivan.

The renewed publicity from the case had an impact in Australia, where government officials decided to create a new immigration regulation authorizing preferred status for "domestic partners" of Australian citizens. While this was being worked out, Adams and Sullivan traveled in Europe. They were finally issued one of the new visas and settled in Australia.

Adams and Sullivan's ten-year legal struggle to be able to live together permanently in the United States vividly illustrates the failure of American institutions to come to grips with the new lifestyles emerging from the sexual revolution of the 1970s. Mired in Victorian notions of "family" and ignoring the increasing number of couples—heterosexual and homosexual—who live together in long-term relationships

without marriage, Congress has made no adjustment in the basic immigration law requirements of family status. As international travel increases and international couples become more common, the failure to recognize alternative relationships is likely to create similar tragic stories in the future.

The case of *Adams v. Howerton* raises other interesting questions of international import. Is the U.S. position in this matter consistent with international treaties and accords governing free immigration across national borders? Will the European trend toward legal recognition of homosexual marriages initiated in Denmark in 1989 and Sweden in 1990 result in the formation of gay families that would be cognizable as such under U.S. immigration law, particularly after Congress repealed the express exclusion of homosexuals in 1990? Finally, would the recent trend of enactment of domestic partnership ordinances at the municipal level in the United States (which in some ways resemble the kinds of legal constructs described by Judge Hill) encourage the courts or Congress to embrace a broader concept of "family" for purposes of the immigration law? Only time will tell.

Case References

Baker v. Nelson, 291 Minn. 310, 191 N.W.2d 185 (1971), certiorari denied, 409 U.S. 810 (1972)

Boutilier v. Immigration & Naturalization Service, 387 U.S. 118 (1967), affirming 363 F.2d 488 (2d Cir. 1966)

116. PARSING THE IMMIGRATION LAW: WHEN IS A "PSYCHOPATH" NOT?

Lesbian/Gay Freedom Day Committee, Inc. v. U.S. Immigration & Naturalization Service, 541 F. Supp. 569 (N.D. Cal. 1982), affirmed in part, vacated in part, sub nom. *Hill v. U.S. Immigration & Naturalization Service,* 714 F.2d 1470 (9th Cir. 1983). *In re Longstaff,* 538 F. Supp. 589 (N.D. Tex. 1982), affirmed, 716 F.2d 1439 (5th Cir. 1983), certiorari denied, 467 U.S. 1219 (1984). Interim rulings: 631 F.2d 731 (5th Cir.), rehearing, 634 F.2d 629 (5th Cir. 1980).

Two cases decided by federal appeals courts within weeks of each other in 1983 showed how U.S. immigration and nationality laws dating from the early years of the century had failed to keep up with the developing knowledge of human sexuality. By perpetuating earlier beliefs about variant sexuality as a mental illness or defect, these laws were among the few federal statutes that on their face discriminated on the basis of sexual orientation. However, because they practiced their discrimination on nonresidents of the United States, they had proven virtually invulnerable to constitutional attack, since the U.S. Constitution gave Congress plenary authority to regulate this area of law and the Fifth Amendment's Due Process Clause had been construed by the U.S. Supreme Court as applying only to those resident in the United States. The appeals courts disagreed on how these laws should be interpreted in light of current circumstances, but the Supreme Court refused to involve itself in this disagreement, leaving the problem to linger until November 1990, when Congress finally amended the law to remove the exclusionary language.

Although the chain of events leading to the conflicting appellate rulings began first in Texas with the naturalization petition of Richard John Longstaff, it was the litigation arising in San Francisco that led to the first of these conflicting rulings. The California litigation arose from two separate complaints filed in the federal district court in San Francisco. In one, British gay journalist Carl Hill petitioned for a writ of *habeas corpus* after the Board of Immigration Appeals ruled in 1981 that he was excludable as a self-proclaimed homosexual. In the other, the Lesbian/Gay Freedom Day Committee, which organized San Francisco's annual gay pride celebration, sought a declaration that the Immigration and Naturalization Service's policy of excluding identified homosexuals from entering the country violated the First Amendment by interfering with the rights of San Franciscans participating in the celebration to associate with foreign gays who wanted to participate in these activities.

Both cases were deliberately set up as "test cases" to challenge a new policy that the Immigration and Naturalization Service (INS) had recently announced. Under immigration laws deriving from enactments as early as 1917, Congress had specified that "psychopathic" persons would be excluded from entry into the United States as visitors or as immigrants. At the time, the medical profession took the view that homosexuality was a symptom of a psychopathic personality, and this remained the predominant view of American psychiatry until the 1960s, when new studies began to question whether variant sexuality was by itself an indicator of mental illness. Enough doubts were created, in fact, that Congress revised the immigration law in 1965 to make absolutely clear that it sought to exclude homosexuals, regardless of the evolving views of the medical establishment, by adding the term "sexual deviation" to the list of excludable medical conditions contained in 8 U.S.C. section 1182(a)(4). It was clear that the basis for excluding homosexuals was as much political as medical. However, by adding sexual deviation in that subsection of the statute, Congress continued to apply the medical exclusion apparatus, under which applicants for visas who were believed by INS officers to be homosexuals would be referred to medical officers of the Public Health Service (PHS) for examination and certification of their status. Only upon such certification would a "homosexual alien" be considered excludable.

In 1973, the Board of Trustees of the American Psychiatric Association decided that the mounting evidence justified removing homosexuality from the list of mental disorders to be contained in the next edition of its comprehensive Diagnostic and Statistical Manual, the standard reference work on psychiatry. This decision was affirmed by a poll of its members completed the following year. The American Psychological Association, the American Public Health Association, the American Nurses Association, and the Council of Advanced Practitioners in Psychiatric and Mental Health Nursing of the American Nurses Association all subsequently endorsed this view. By the end of the 1970s, it had become clear that a strong majority of the mental health professions had rejected the old orthodoxy, and the requirement that a PHS psychiatrist "diagnose" a visa applicant as "suffering from psychopathic personality" or "sexual deviation" because the applicant was homosexual had become professionally untenable.

On August 2, 1979, Surgeon General Julius Richmond wrote a letter to the INS indicating that on the basis of the current position of the mental health professional associations, he was instructing PHS professionals to cease from "diagnosing" homosexuals as having one of the excludable conditions under the immigration law unless there was evidence other than their homosexuality to support such a determination.

His decision was based on two reasons: "current and generally accepted canons of medical practice" no longer considered homosexuality *per se* a mental disorder, and, as such, "the determination of homosexuality is not made through a medical diagnostic procedure." The INS applied to the attorney general for an opinion as to how it should proceed under the circumstances. On August 15, 1979, the Office of Legal Counsel of the Justice Department issued its opinion that the surgeon general had "discretion to promulgate policies regarding the description and diagnosis of disease," but that this discretion was bounded by the clear intent of Congress to exclude homosexuals regardless of current medical views. Consequently, the Justice Department advised the INS to adopt a uniform policy for investigating suspected homosexual visa applicants that did not rely on the PHS's cooperation.

On September 9, 1980, the INS adopted new guidelines, under which aliens arriving in the United States would no longer be asked whether they suffered from "psychopathic personality" or "sexual deviation," or any other direct questions about their sexual orientation, unless the alien or somebody traveling with him or her made an unsolicited statement that the alien was a homosexual. If such a statement was made, the alien would be examined further by an INS official and asked to sign a written declaration of homosexuality. The "confessed" homosexual would then be passed on to an immigration judge, who would be authorized to exclude the alien based on his or her admissions.

Carl Hill was determined to challenge these procedures, since it had been the position of gay rights groups that the surgeon general's position should put an end entirely to the exclusionary policy. Alerting gay rights organizations in San Francisco to his plans, Hill landed at San Francisco International Airport on November 5, 1980, with a valid visitor's visa, and made an unsolicited statement to the immigration inspector that he was gay. The inspector ordered Hill to appear on November 7 for a hearing before an immigration judge. Gay Rights Advocates, a San Francisco public interest law firm, represented Hill, with its founder, Donald Knutson, as lead counsel. The immigration judge held that Hill could not be excluded from the United States on the basis of his statements, because the statute required a medical certificate. The INS appealed this ruling to the Board of Immigration Appeals, which held that a medical certificate was not required to exclude a self-proclaimed homosexual because the burden of proving admissibility was on the alien, not the INS. Hill promptly petitioned the federal district court for a writ of *habeas corpus*, which Judge Robert P. Aguilar granted, finding that the medical certificate was a statutory prerequisite to exclusion for a medical reason. Judge Aguilar gave the INS thirty days to initiate new proceedings including the requisite medical examination. When the INS failed to initiate the new proceedings, Hill was admitted into the United States as a visitor.

Meanwhile, the Lesbian/Gay Freedom Day Committee had mounted its own challenge to the new INS policies, filing its complaint six days before the 1981 gay pride celebrations in San Francisco. The June 22 complaint filed by attorney Mary C. Dunlap alleged that the INS policy violated the rights of U.S. citizens under the First and Fifth amendments by depriving them of the freedom to associate and to discuss political issues with homosexual aliens on grounds violative of due process and equal protection. This case was also assigned to Judge Aguilar, who at first denied the accompanying motion for a temporary restraining order, but then, in light of the imminent gay pride celebration and the lack of any demonstrated harm to the United States of admitting gay aliens to participate in those proceedings, issued a preliminary injunction prohibiting the INS from barring entry to any alien solely on the grounds of homosexuality.

Aguilar consolidated the two cases for argument, at which Assistant U.S. Attorney Michael J. Tonsing represented the INS. Aguilar issued a lengthy opinion on June 17, 1982, less than a month before the next scheduled gay pride celebration in San Francisco. Aguilar found for the gay petitioners in both cases, ruling that the INS could not exclude homosexuals without the cooperation of the PHS. Basing his decision in Hill's case solely on statutory construction, Aguilar found determinative the placement of the exclusionary language in the medical category. "A reading of the applicable portions of the Immigration and Nationality Act, and corresponding legislative history, indicates the intent of Congress that homosexuality be a medical exclusion, and that therefore a medical certificate is required to exclude a homosexual from entry into the United States," said Aguilar. He carefully reviewed all the provisions of the Act relating to medical exclusions and found that while they did not expressly state that no alien could be excluded for a medical reason without a medical certificate, they added up to a statutory scheme having that result.

Aguilar's conclusion was based on his finding that Congress's decision to exclude homosexuals was "based upon the premise that homosexuality is a medical illness." This premise was itself based on a searching review of the legislative history, where reference to homosexuality as a medical condition was repeated many times. Since Congress had explicitly based the exclusion of homosexuals on a medical rationale, only the procedure for medical exclusions could be used. "The Act nowhere provides that an immigration officer may make the determination that an alien is afflicted with a medical condition that constitutes a medical exclusion to admission," asserted Aguilar. "Rather, exclusive authority over such medical determinations is placed in the Public Health Service officers (or designated civil surgeons)." To support this conclusion, Aguilar cited numerous decisions by the Board of Immigration Appeals as well as the federal courts in which the lack of a proper medical certificate had been found determinative in barring the INS from excluding or deporting a suspected homosexual alien.

Turning to the Lesbian/Gay Freedom Day Committee's case, Aguilar found that the Committee had a clear First Amendment claim. By the time of the argument of the case, the Committee had focused its theory solely on the First Amendment, and was no longer arguing based on the Fifth Amendment due process or equal protection claims. Aguilar found that the Committee's chances of success hinged entirely on the precedential scope of three U.S. Supreme Court rulings dealing with the immigration laws: *Boutilier v. INS* (1967), *Kleindienst v. Mandel* (1972), and *Fiallo v. Bell* (1977).

In *Boutilier*, the Supreme Court construed the predecessor to the current exclusionary statute. Presented with evidence that the medical profession no longer uniformly considered all homosexuals afflicted with "psychopathic personality," the only specified basis for exclusion under the pre-1965 law, the Court held that this was irrelevant to the determination of congressional intent because the legislative history showed that Congress had been advised by the PHS that it could achieve its goal of excluding homosexuals by using the term "psychopathic personality" in the statute without making explicit reference to homosexuals. Congress had not used the term in "the clinical sense," ruled the Court, but rather as a description encompassing homosexuals.

In *Kleindienst*, the Court considered what standard of review should be applied when it was charged that the INS had violated the Constitution in enforcing the immigration law. As in Lesbian/Gay Freedom Day Committee's case, *Kliendienst* involved an assertion that U.S. citizens had been deprived of their First Amendment rights when the INS refused to allow a visit to the United States by a foreign Marxist scholar, who had been invited to the country to lecture. The Court held that U.S. citizens do have a First Amendment right to hear foreign speakers, but that the decision whether to exclude such persons was vested in the discretion of the attorney general, who was authorized by statute to waive a particular exclusion. If the attorney general exercised his authority for "facially legitimate and bona fide" reasons, said the Court, further judicial review was not required. In *Fiallo*, the Court addressed the question, left open in *Kleindienst*, whether the same standard of review was to be applied when the constitutional challenge was to the statute itself, rather than merely to its administration. The Court determined that the same standard should be used. Thus, whether reviewing the statute itself or its administration by the INS and the Justice Department, a court must uphold the validity of the statute and its administration if there appeared a facially legitimate and *bona fide* reason for maintaining a particular exclusion.

656

In attacking the statute directly, the Committee argued that a facially legitimate and *bona fide* basis for continuing the exclusion of homosexuals under the terms "psychopathic personality" and "sexual deviation" no longer pertained because of the changing view of the mental health professions concerning the status of homosexuals. Since Congress had embodied this exclusion in the medical provision, it was clear that the basis for exclusion was a belief, however phrased, that homosexuality was a medical problem. The problem with this argument, of course, was that the Supreme Court had rejected it in *Boutilier* when it held that these terms were not used in their "clinical" meanings but rather as signifiers for homosexuality as such. But Aguilar did not feel that this ended the matter, arguing that where the medical profession "has not changed the medical illness label applied to a homosexual (the situation in *Boutilier*), but rather has determined that homosexuality is no longer a medical illness, mental disorder, or a sexual deviation at all," the logic of *Boutilier* no longer pertains. As Aguilar saw it, the controversy in *Boutilier*, which predated by almost a decade the action of mental health professional associations in proclaiming that homosexuality was not a mental illness, was not over whether homosexuality was a mental illness, but rather over whether it was properly described by the term "psychopathic personality." By construing that term to include "homosexuals," the Court was doing no more than clarifying the intent of Congress to exclude "homosexuals" due to their medical condition, whatever it was called. The Court was not, according to Aguilar, ruling on whether homosexuality was a medical condition.

Once homosexuality was no longer considered a medical illness or mental disorder, said Aguilar, "no medical grounds for the exclusion of a homosexual due solely to his or her homosexuality exists. . . . Congress could not have intended that an alien who has no medically recognized mental disorder or sexual deviation be excluded under section 1182(a)(4)," which dealt with medical exclusion grounds. Thus, Congress could no longer be held to have intended to exclude homosexuals, therefore Aguilar could grant the requested relief without having to reach the First Amendment issue,

since he had determined as a matter of statutory interpretation that homosexuals, as such, were no longer excluded by the statute.

Perhaps fearing to premise his holding solely on this highly formalistic reading of the statute, which overlooked the likely political basis for the homosexual exclusion, Aguilar proceeded to reach the merits of the First Amendment claim anyway and ruled that the INS's decision in light of the surgeon general's policy change to adopt its new policy was an act of discretion that could be reviewed based on the *Kliendienst* and *Fiallo* standards. Having already concluded that the medical premises underlying the 1952 and 1965 immigration laws no longer applied, it was easy for Aguilar to conclude that there remained no facially legitimate or *bona fide* reason to continue to maintain a medical exclusion of gays. Furthermore, he found that the government had made no showing of public interest in excluding gays sufficient to overcome the First Amendment detriments the plaintiffs would suffer were the policy to continue being enforced. In particular, Aguilar rejected the government's argument of an interest based on the remaining state sodomy laws in about half the states to be unavailing, since the immigration policy had nothing to do directly with sodomy. The INS made no attempt to exclude only those homosexuals who might commit sodomy in the United States, he said. "Rather, the policy excludes any person who is a homosexual, based merely on their 'status' as a homosexual, without reference to their proposed activities in the United States."

Aguilar attempted to bolster his decision further with a quote from Benjamin Cardozo's influential book, *The Nature of the Judicial Process* (1921), in which the then-chief judge of the New York Court of Appeals (and later Supreme Court Justice) stated:

> [W]hen a rule, after it has been duly tested by experience, has been found to be inconsistent with the sense of justice or with the social welfare, there should be less hesitation in frank avowal and full abandonment. . . . If judges have . . . misinterpreted the mores of their day, or if the mores of their day are no longer those of ours, they ought not to tie, in helpless submission, the hands of their successors.

The INS promptly appealed Aguilar's rulings to the U.S. Court of Appeals for the Ninth Circuit, which heard argument on April 12, 1983. James Hunolt, of Washington, represented the government. San Francisco attorneys Jeff T. Appleman and Mary C. Dunlap represented Hill and the Lesbian/Gay Freedom Day Committee on the appeal, with the assistance of Los Angeles attorney Laurence R. Sperber. The opinion by Circuit Judge Robert Boochever, issued September 7, 1983, agreed with Aguilar's interpretation of the Act and upheld his ruling with regard to Hill, but vacated the injunctive relief granted on behalf of the gay pride committee on the ground that it was unnecessary, since the INS would not be able to exclude gay visitors due to the *Hill* ruling.

The court reiterated Aguilar's conclusion that "it would . . . violate Congress' direction to allow INS officers who are not medically trained to determine psychopathic personality, sexual deviation, or mental defect by interrogation." Since the statute clearly set out a procedure involving PHS physicians in all cases where homosexuality was suspected, it was clear that Congress was concerned about leaving the diagnosis of such conditions to lay persons. These provisions meant that "immigration officers are not to perform physical and mental examinations by obtaining admissions; doctors are to perform the mental and physical examinations," said Boochever, who also placed particular weight on the string of Board of Immigration Appeals cases holding that medical certificates were necessary. The construction by an agency of its own enabling statute was due "great respect," he said, and "since the adoption of the 1952 Act and continuing consistently up until the INS' recent change of heart, it has required a medical examination and certificate for exclusion on medical grounds." Furthermore, as the Board of Immigration Appeals had itself stated in a 1967 case, "neither the special inquiry officer nor this Board has the expertise or the authority to make a determination on respondent's medical admissibility or inadmissibility." The INS did not consider itself "competent or authorized to make medical determinations." Since Congress had prescribed the medical examination procedure, it was not for the INS to

attempt by regulation or by "guidelines" to bypass that procedure. And, since that procedure was no longer available due to the policy change by the surgeon general, there was no need to enjoin the INS from barring gay visitors from the United States, since it had lost the mechanism for carrying out the ban.

As the *Hill* and *Committee* cases were working their way through the federal judicial system in San Francisco, the Fifth Circuit was nearing its decision in Richard John Longstaff's petition for naturalization. Longstaff, a British subject, had immigrated to the United States in 1965 at the age of 25. He was interviewed for his visa just weeks after Congress had amended the immigration law to add "sexual deviation" to the list of excludable medical conditions. In fact, the questionnaire Longstaff completed did not use that term. Rather, buried in a long list referring to a variety of conditions was the phrase "psychopathic personality." Longstaff, who was a healthy, sexually active gay man, saw nothing in any of the questions about homosexuality, and answered "No" to the question. He was admitted and lived first in Oklahoma and then in Dallas.

By the time he applied for naturalization as a U.S. citizen in 1975, Longstaff was the proprietor of two businesses in Dallas and Houston and a well-known and respected member of the Dallas gay community. The INS's investigation of his petition for naturalization turned up those facts, and led to further questioning about his sexual practices. After initially denying his homosexuality, Longstaff confirmed that he was gay and had been sexually active both before and after his admission to the United States. Concluding that since Longstaff knew he was gay at the time of entry, he had not been lawfully admitted to the United States and that his continued sex life was in violation of Texas sodomy laws, the INS moved the federal district court to deny Longstaff's application. Attorney Brian K. Bates represented Longstaff before the district court, and INS officer James A. Curry represented the government.

On March 9, 1979, District Judge Joe Ewing Estes denied Longstaff's petition for naturalization. Longstaff appealed to the Fifth Circuit, which at first affirmed the denial on the ground that Longstaff had failed to sustain his burden of proof of good moral character as required by the naturalization provisions. On rehearing, the court remanded the case to give Longstaff an opportunity to present more testimony on this issue. He was interviewed again by an INS examiner, who filed a recommendation with the court that the petition be denied on grounds of unlawful entry.

Longstaff returned to court with character witnesses who affirmed that he was an honest, productive citizen, but this cut little ice with District Judge Estes, who ruled again, on March 25, 1982, that Longstaff was not entitled to become a U.S. citizen. Longstaff had "not met his burden of proof that he has been lawfully admitted for permanent residence," concluded Estes, who found that Longstaff was excludable both as a homosexual and as somebody who had "committed sodomy in England before his entry." In addition to the homosexual exclusion, said Estes, Longstaff had to deal with the good moral character problem, since sodomy was a crime of "moral turpitude" that went to the issue of character. Estes reviewed several Texas cases holding that violations of the sodomy law, even though it had been reformed in recent years to be a misdemeanor statute rather than a felony statute, were crimes of moral turpitude. Finally, said Estes, Longstaff had exhibited a "lack of candor" by concealing his homosexuality when first questioned by the INS. For all these reasons, he was not entitled to become a U.S. citizen.

Longstaff appealed to the Fifth Circuit, which heard argument from attorney Bates and Justice Department attorney Margaret Perry. Leonard Graff, a San Francisco attorney, filed an *amicus* brief on Longstaff's behalf under the sponsorship of Gay Rights Advocates and the National Gay Task Force.

The Fifth Circuit panel produced a curious opinion by Circuit Judge Alvin B. Rubin on September 28, 1983. It upheld Estes's ruling solely on the basis that Longstaff had not lawfully been admitted to the United States, without reaching the issue of good moral character. Rubin's opinion was highly formalistic and seemed designed to highlight the shortcomings of the statute in light of intervening events, while at the same time applying it. For example, in summarizing the facts of the case, Rubin noted

Longstaff's negative answer in 1965 to the question whether he was "afflicted with psychopathic personality, epilepsy, mental defect, fits, fainting spells, convulsions or a nervous breakdown," and commented that "no evidence suggests that Longstaff knew or had reason to know that 'psychopathic personality' was a term of art that included homosexuals and consequently excluded them from admission to the United States." Indeed, noted Rubin, Longstaff "had reason to anticipate progressive social tolerance toward homosexuality" in light of the recent law reform efforts in England accompanying release of the Wolfenden Report, which recommended ending penalties for consensual sodomy.

Rubin noted that INS examiner Lee Reinfeld had concluded, after the Fifth Circuit's prior remand, that Longstaff had the requisite good moral character but recommended against naturalization based on the issue of unlawful entry. Rubin concluded, apparently reluctantly, that Reinfeld's recommendation was appropriate. Naturalization was a procedure that was available only to those who were lawfully present in the United States, said Rubin, and it would "distort" the meaning of the law to hold that Longstaff was lawfully present when he had incorrectly responded to the question concerning his status as a psychopathic personality. Even though he did not know what that meant, it was clear at the time that Congress intended it to exclude homosexuals, as the Supreme Court subsequently held in *Boutilier*. Since Congress had plenary power to decide whom to exclude and had decided to exclude homosexuals, it could not be said that Longstaff was lawfully present merely because of his incorrect response to the question.

Of course, Longstaff's attorneys had brought to the panel's attention Judge Aguilar's decision, which was affirmed by the Ninth Circuit shortly before the Fifth Circuit's opinion was released, and argued that since there had been no medical certification of homosexuality in Longstaff's case, his admission had been lawful. Rubin was not buying this argument, however. While agreeing that the statute made a medical certification "conclusive evidence of excludibility," said Rubin, "this does not necessarily mean, however, that the absence of certification is conclusive evidence of admissibility." The question was whether the alien applying for admission was a homosexual, and Longstaff was not denying that.

Rubin found that the Ninth Circuit's reasoning placed too much power in the hands of the surgeon general to stymie the will of Congress. While Congress intended to ensure that only competent medical evidence would be considered in immigration proceedings by requiring the participation of the PHS, "there is no reason why an informed applicant's admission that he falls within an excludable class is not competent evidence on which to base on exclusion decision," said Rubin, who characterized such a declaration as "primary" evidence. Furthermore, there was no bar under the statute to reconsidering the lawfulness of entry if new evidence came to light, as Rubin found to be illustrated in a variety of cases in which the INS sought to deport an alien when new information came to light that the alien had been excludable at the time of entry. Indeed, Rubin turned back on the Ninth Circuit the argument that an agency's interpretation of its own statute should be given great weight, noting that the new guidelines on dealing with homosexual applicants were just such an interpretation and thus presumptively valid.

While he found that the law did not provide for Longstaff's naturalization (and might require his deportation), Rubin clearly was not happy about this situation:

> Longstaff is thus barred from naturalization by his own truthful statements that he was excludable as a homosexual at the time of his entry, and, therefore, was not lawfully admitted for permanent residence. There is no evidence that, when he sought a visa eighteen years ago, he was asked any question that would indicate to him or to any other intelligent layman that his sexual preferences might affect the issuance of a visa, or that he knowingly gave a false answer to any question asked of him. In the eighteen years of his residence, he has led a constructive life. We are, however, bound to decide according to a law made in the exercise of a power that is plenary. If Congress' policy is misguided, Congress must revise that policy. If the result achieved by the policy is unfair to a deserving person who desires to become a citizen, the injustice must be corrected by lawmakers.

This ruling drew a spirited dissent from Circuit Judge Albert Tate, Jr., who was thoroughly convinced by the Ninth Circuit's opinion that Longstaff should be awarded citizenship. While conceding that Rubin's decision had "certainly reached a logical conclusion, based upon its intelligent analysis of applicable legislation and jurisprudential authority," Tate felt that the Ninth Circuit's opinion had clearly established that a homosexual was excludable based only on a medical certification. Since Longstaff had never been diagnosed as afflicted by a psychopathic personality or sexual deviation by a PHS physician, and the current controversy was based solely on his own admissions, he could not have been barred from entry and should be allowed to be naturalized, given all the circumstances. He agreed with the Ninth Circuit that Congress had intended that medical professionals, not "the non-medical judgment of bureaucratic agencies," make the decisions whether aliens had medical conditions justifying exclusion.

For Tate, the court's decision presented a serious injustice that transcended Longstaff's individual situation, although he noted that the decision made Longstaff "subject to deportation many, many years after his presumably lawful entry to the United States and his constructive life here." "Of far greater importance," said Tate, was the shadow now cast on the status of "all other persons against whom a governmental agency may assert as a reason for deportation—perhaps (as in the case of Longstaff) many years after presumably lawful entry into the United States—a newly discovered pre-admission 'medical' cause for exclusion from entry." This made the continued residence of such people "dependent on the uncertainties and indefiniteness of medical science," which Tate characterized as a "spectre" that might lead to "the possibility of abuse of bureaucratic deportation powers" justifying Congress's decision to require that medical professionals rather than bureaucrats make the key determination in these cases. Judge Tate's concern was borne out in Longstaff's case, since the INS instituted deportation proceedings that were terminated only when Longstaff sold his businesses and moved to the West Coast, where the Ninth Circuit's ruling held sway.

The circuit voted to deny rehearing *en banc*. Despite the split in circuit authority created by the decision, the U.S. Supreme Court announced on May 29, 1984, that it would not review the *Longstaff* case, with only Justice William J. Brennan publicly registering that he would have granted *certiorari*. Thus, an issue of crucial importance to the international lesbian and gay community was left in suspended animation, as efforts for a legislative solution sponsored by openly gay U.S. Representative Barney Frank went nowhere for many years (despite affirmative endorsement for a legislative end to the antigay exclusion from the Reagan Administration) and different rules pertained in different parts of the country. Attorneys advised gay aliens seeking admission to the United States to come through a West Coast port or to take pains that nothing they said, wore, or carried in their luggage might prompt an immigration officer to question their sexual orientation.

The problem intensified in 1990 when a great controversy sprang up surrounding immigration policy concerning those infected with HIV, a virus associated with acquired immune deficiency syndrome (AIDS), during an international AIDS medical conference held in San Francisco. The daily press contained stories that the Justice Department had demanded that the PHS provide extra officers to issue medical certificates of HIV status and homosexuality, and that the administration, prompted by conservative members of Congress, might try to enforce the antigay ban to keep international AIDS activists from attending the conference. Although the administration backed down and nobody was prevented from attending the conference, there was new impetus in Congress to do something about the issue. As part of a general immigration reform bill that came up in the final days of the congressional session that fall, section 1182(a)(1) was amended to exclude all mention of particular medical conditions as grounds for exclusion. In place of the prior language, Congress enacted a provision giving the secretary of Health and Human Services authority to issue regulations listing communicable diseases "of public health significance" that could be a basis for exclusion, and authorizing as well the exclusion of aliens determined "to have a physical or mental disorder and behavior associated with the disorder" that would pose a threat to the property, safety, or welfare of the alien or others. This "health-related grounds" exclusion also specifically barred drug abusers or addicts. Any reference to homosexuality or sexual deviation was omitted.

Due to the 1990 amendments, the *Hill* and *Longstaff* cases are now primarily of historical interest. They strikingly illustrate how attempts by Congress to hide prejudice under medical terminology backfired when medical science advanced to new levels of understanding, and how some federal judges were willing to strike through the pretense of "scientific" terminology to expose the underlying politics of the antigay exclusion. While no longer of any precedential significance, these cases are still worth studying for what they reveal about the nature of the legislative and judicial systems in their dealings with the issues posed by sexual variety in modern society.

Case References

Boutilier v. Immigration & Naturalization Service, 387 U.S. 118 (1967)

Fiallo v. Bell, 430 U.S. 787 (1977)

Kleindienst v. Mandel, 408 U.S. 753 (1972)

CHAPTER 9
ESTATES AND TRUSTS

The cases in this chapter might well have been included in Chapter 4 (The Family), since the particular problems faced by sexual minorities in the area of estates law derive from the failure of the law to recognize nontraditional families in this context. Lacking access to marriage, same-sex couples and transsexuals are unable to rely on many of the normal processes of the law in the disposition of their estates. The three cases discussed are among the few reported court decisions dealing with a problem that is quite widespread and manifests itself in two situations: contests over the validity of wills, and the distribution of assets when a lesbian or gay person dies intestate (i.e. without a will).

Before the modern gay liberation movement began to change attitudes about human sexuality, courts were willing to entertain the presumption that homosexuals were mentally ill, and thus that testamentary dispositions to their same-sex partners did not represent the disposition of one of sound mind, or alternatively reflected the "undue influence" the sinister partner exerted over the decedent. Perhaps the leading case to take this view is *In re Kaufmann's Will*, in which the New York Court of Appeals overturned the testamentary disposition of a wealthy gay man to his life partner when it was challenged by surviving legal relatives. More recently, suggestions that testamentary dispositions to homosexual lovers are automatically tainted have been dismissed by many courts with little or no comment or analysis, and there is virtually no appellate case law on the subject to discuss. These days, the question of capacity is raised instead (at least in the case of gay men) when a person dies from AIDS. Early in 1992, a surrogate court judge in New York County (New York) resolved a four-year court battle over the multimillion dollar estate of a gay man who had died from AIDS and who had left the bulk of his estate to create a foundation for AIDS medical research. His surviving relatives contended that his testamentary disposition was flawed by the ravages of his disease, but the surrogate ultimately ordered that the foundation be established.

At least one innovative lawyer has advanced the argument, unsuccessfully at the trial stage, that a surviving gay partner should be entitled to benefit from the "elective share" that New York law guarantees to a surviving spouse. And a Louisiana lawyer has unsuccessfully asserted the argument that a surviving gay partner is a "concubine," under a law that limits the percentage of an estate that a concubine can inherit from a person who also leaves surviving relatives. As family relationships continue to evolve in new ways reflecting the diversity of human sexuality and psychology, it is likely that the estates and trusts field will yield fertile ground for innovative legal thinking. The 1990s will probably see interesting cases in jurisdictions that pass domestic partnership laws extending recognition to nonmarital relationships, whose outcome is impossible to foretell.

Estates and Trusts: Readings

Anderson, L., "Property Rights of Same-Sex Couples: Toward a New Definition of Family," 26 *Journal of Family Law* 357 (Winter 1987)

Lovas, S., "When is a Family Not a Family? Inheritance and the Taxation of Inheritance Within the Non-Traditional Family," 24 *Idaho Law Review* 353 (Summer 1988)

Roberts, "Will Drafting and Property Ownership: Bearing in Mind Cohabitees and Lesbian and Gay Couples," 22 *Family Law* 77 (February 1992)

Sherman, J.G., "Undue Influence and the Homosexual Testator," 42 *University of Pittsburgh Law Review* 225 (Winter 1981)

117. UNDUE INFLUENCE AND THE HOMOSEXUAL TESTATOR

In re Kaufmann's Will (Weiss v. Kaufmann), 20 App. Div. 2d 464, 247 N.Y.S.2d 664 (1st Dept. 1964), affirmed per curiam memorandum, 15 N.Y.2d 825, 257 N.Y.S.2d 941 (1965). Prior decisions: 11 App. Div. 2d 759, 202 N.Y.S.2d 423 (1st Dept. 1960); 14 App. Div. 2d 411, 221 N.Y.S.2d 601 (1st Dept. 1961).

One way in which society has traditionally discriminated against sexual minorities is by refusing to honor their testamentary wishes. Challenges to wills in which bequests to surviving homosexual lovers were claimed by relatives to be the product of "undue influence" were common before the advent of the modern gay liberation movement. The epidemic of acquired immune deficiency syndrome (AIDS) among gay men during the 1980s, leading to the deaths of many in middle-age who left businesses, homes, and other assets to gay life partners, saw a new resurgence of such contests. Perhaps the most celebrated early case in which surviving relatives successfully challenged such a will was the litigation over probate of the last will and testament of Robert D. Kaufmann, a millionaire heir of the Kay Jewelry business. Kaufmann, who died in his sleep during a fire at his Key West vacation house on April 18, 1959, left virtually his entire estate to his apparent life partner, Walter A. Weiss.

It is difficult to reconstruct the facts of Kaufmann's life and his relationship with Weiss from the published opinions of the courts due to the great "delicacy" of language with which courts of the period prior to the advent of the modern gay rights movement spoke of gay relationships, especially where wealthy parties were concerned. But it seems likely from comments in the dissenting opinion by Justice G. Robert Witmer that Weiss and Kaufmann were gay life partners, and that many of the "facts" recited in the majority opinion were based on ignorance about the covert life styles of wealthy gay men. (Such ignorance would be quite understandable at the time, since sodomy was a serious felony in New York and gay men had every incentive to keep their lives as secret as possible.) Weiss and Kaufmann apparently first met in 1946 when both men were in their early to mid-thirties, Weiss a few years older than

Kaufmann. The circumstances of their meeting and becoming friendly are not revealed by the published opinions, but might have been the result of personal introductions, social gatherings, or "street cruising" or the like, for all one knows, since Kaufmann later commented in a letter that before meeting Weiss his sex life had been "spotty, furtive and destructive." After meeting Weiss, the wealthy young man, indifferent to business affairs (managed largely by his father and his older brother Joel, the business genius of the family), discovered a talent for painting. He nurtured the talent through professional instruction, eventually producing a body of art that achieved exhibition during the 1950s in numerous galleries and museums. Kaufmann was evidently invigorated by his developing relationship with Weiss, moving his home to New York City from Washington, purchasing a townhouse on East 74th Street in Manhattan, and developing a degree of independence from his family that was unprecedented for him. With Weiss's encouragement, Kaufmann entered psychotherapy and developed new confidence and self-esteem.

In 1948, Kaufmann and Weiss entered into a contractual arrangement making Weiss a salaried financial advisor to Kaufmann. Apparently, Weiss was not a particularly savvy financial advisor, since most of his recommendations led to losses rather than gains. But Kaufmann apparently placed full trust and confidence in Weiss, eventually opening bank accounts for which Weiss had signing authority, changing over his insurance policies to make Weiss a beneficiary, executing a medical power of attorney giving Weiss authority to make medical decisions if Kaufmann became incapable, and even directing that Weiss make and execute all funeral arrangements for him, if necessary. Weiss did not apparently bring any financial assets of his own to their relationship. He was a lawyer admitted to practice, but evidently was not engaged in an active practice of law. The two men took such steps as gay men could take to simulate a marital relationship through merging finances and living arrangements, but nowhere in any of the documents, drafted with the assistance of highly skilled and reputable legal specialists, was there any direct mention that the two men had a sexual relationship. After all, gay sex was a serious felony offense in New York (and every other state in the nation) at that time.

Prior to developing this close and loving relationship with Weiss, Kaufmann had executed a will leaving his estate to members of his family, variously distributed. By 1951, his relationship with Weiss had become so close that he made a new will, leaving a significant portion of his estate to Weiss. At the same time the will was executed on June 13, 1951, Kaufmann also wrote a letter in longhand to explain to his family his reasons for leaving such a major bequest to a nonrelative. After affirming that the will contained unusual provisions in that "a sizable portion" of the estate went to a man who was "not a member of my family," Kaufmann explained how he had met Weiss in 1946, at a time when his outlook on life was then "approaching a nadir," that he was then a "frustrated time-wasting little boy, . . . terribly unhappy, highly emotional and filled to the brim with a grandly variegated group of fears, guilt and assorted complexes." Kaufmann wrote that he fortunately met Weiss, who encouraged him to go into psychotherapy, where he found himself.

> Walter gave me the courage to start something which slowly but eventually permitted me to supply for myself everything my life had heretofore lacked: an outlet for my long-latent but strong creative ability in painting . . . a balanced, healthy sex life which before had been spotty, furtive and destructive; an ability to reorientate myself to actual life and to face it calmly and realistically. All of this adds up to Peace of Mind—and what a delight, what a relief after so many wasted, dark, groping, fumbling immature years to be reborn and become adult! I am eternally grateful to my dearest friend—best pal, Walter A. Weiss. What could be more wonderful than a fruitful, contented life and who more deserving of gratitude now, in the form of an inheritance,

> than the person who helped most in securing that life? I cannot believe my family could be anything else but glad and happy for my own comfortable self-determination and contentment and equally grateful to the friend who made it possible. Love to you all, Bob.

At the time of this will execution, the portion of Kaufmann's estate that Weiss would have inherited if Kaufmann then died was about half a million dollars. Weiss and Kaufmann grew ever closer through the 1950s, as Kaufmann retreated from his family, devoting himself extensively to painting and entertaining and traveling on a lavish scale. The two men traveled to Europe together, and Weiss managed all of Kaufmann's affairs, including screening his mail and calls, advising on all business decisions, and suggesting several times over the decade that Kaufmann continually revise his will to reflect new business developments and changes in family relationships. At Weiss's recommendation, Kaufmann had moved his legal business from the family's lawyers in Washington to prominent New York estates attorney Lloyd Garrison. Garrison and his partners prepared a series of wills for Kaufmann during the 1950s, each leaving more of Kaufmann's estate to Weiss than the previous one. The final will, signed in 1958, made Weiss virtually sole beneficiary and co-executor with Garrison. Kaufmann's 1951 letter, carefully preserved, accompanied each will.

Weiss's relationship with Kaufmann's family was not very good. Evidently, he got along quite poorly with Joel Kaufmann, who was the chief manager of the family's business affairs after the death of their father. Joel had two sons upon whom Robert evidently doted, and who were specifically remembered in his various wills. There is also evidence that Robert always retained a certain affection for his brother Joel, but that Walter was convinced that Joel's business decisions were not in Robert's (and Walter's) best interests. With Walter's prompting, Robert and Joel were on the opposite sides of several lawsuits and other business controversies during the 1950s, through which Robert eventually withdrew or liquidated all his interests in the various family businesses, so that by the end of the decade Joel had no control over any of Robert's assets, all of which were effectively controlled by Walter as Robert's financial manager and advisor.

In 1955, Robert began to suffer from pronounced insomnia, and could obtain restful sleep only by taking a variety of prescription drugs. This condition continued until his death, and may even explain his death, since he was sound asleep, drugged as usual, when the fire broke out in his Key West vacation home on April 18, 1959. Walter was in New York at the time, and the opinions contain no hint of any foul play in Robert's death.

After Robert died and Walter entered his will for probate, all hell broke loose in the Kaufmann family, since Joel apparently had not known about the series of wills. Robert's 1951 letter was produced and became the subject of much conjecture, providing the theory under which Joel and attorneys for Joel's children and Robert's invalid brother Aron eventually challenged the will: undue influence. They claimed that Walter, who was an attorney at law, was actually either in an attorney-client relationship with Robert, which would require him to prove affirmatively that he had not taken advantage of the relationship to have himself named chief beneficiary and executor, or that by virtue of the relationship that had grown over time, Walter had so overborne Robert's will that he had not freely left his estate to Walter.

Joel retained Milton Levy, a partner at Lord, Day and Lord to represent the family in its contest of the will. Weiss retained Milton Pollack, since Garrison and his firm would have to serve as witnesses. The case went through two jury trials in the surrogate's court in Manhattan, the first presided over by Surrogate Joseph A. Cox, the second by Surrogate S. Samuel DiFalco.

As the proponent of the will, Weiss was subjected to pretrial examination by Levy, attorney for the contestants. Pollack objected to attempts by Levy to question Weiss about the men's relationship dating back to the late 1940s, on the ground that the normal rule limited examinations regarding the relationship of a beneficiary to the testator to a period beginning three years prior to the death. Surrogate Cox issued an order limiting examination based on this rule, which was overturned on appeal by the appellate division in a unanimous *per curiam* decision of July 5, 1960. "Special circumstances are demonstrated in this case arising from the long continued personal relationship between the testator and the proponent, who is a stranger to the blood, to indicate that on the issues of testamentary capacity and undue influence affecting the execution of the will, an examination in full scope is warranted," said the appeals court. The three-year "rule" was made for the "average case," said the court, but this was not the "average case."

In both trials, Weiss decided not to testify. Both times, the jury accepted Levy's argument that undue influence was the only explanation for this bizarre will, under which the lonely, bachelor millionaire had left his fortune to the "mysterious" Walter Weiss, the evil genius who had taken over his mind and soul and twisted them against his loving family, but who had not testified at trial as to the reasons for such an unusual bequest.

On appeal from the first trial, the appellate division reversed on November 30, 1961, and directed a new trial on the issue of undue influence. According to the *per curiam* opinion of the appellate court, the surrogate had made errors "which were calculated to and which may have had a material influence upon the verdict of the jury." One was that the surrogate "received testimony as to family relationship, property and financial transactions and records and declarations of the testator, so remote in time as to have no bearing upon the issue of undue influence affecting the testamentary act." The court emphasized that much of the historical evidence that appeared to play such a large part in the case was not directly relevant to the issue whether Walter had asserted undue influence at the time the final will was executed. According to the court, the surrogate should have charged the jury, as Weiss's attorney requested, that "it must be shown that such coercion, duress or domination was exercised over the very testamentary act itself."

The court found that the surrogate had made "an improper reference and charge with respect to a relationship of attorney and client between the principal beneficiary Weiss and the decedent." According to the surrogate's charge, if the jury found that the bequest to

Weiss was a result of such a relationship between himself and Kaufmann, and that Weiss had any role in the preparation of the will, "then a duty of explanation is imposed upon Mr. Weiss to satisfy you that the propounded paper was the free, untrammeled and intelligent expression of the wishes and intentions of the testator. If such an explanation is called for by the proof and has not been given in the proof to satisfy you, you may find that undue influence has been established." The court held on appeal that there was no evidence in the record from which the jury could have concluded that Weiss and Kaufmann had an attorney and client relationship, thus this charge and the placement of a burden of proof on Weiss were improper. Weiss was not practicing as an attorney; Kaufmann had retained other lawyers to handle his legal work; these other lawyers drafted his will, so the burden of proof did not shift to Weiss. The contestants had the burden of showing undue influence. Indeed, in reviewing the record, a majority of the appellate panel (Justices Francis L. Valente, Harold A. Stevens, and Samuel W. Eager) felt that there was not sufficient evidence to justify submitting the question of undue influence to the jury.

A biting dissent by Justice James B. M. McNally, joined by Presiding Justice Benjamin A. Rabin, took issue with the ruling of the court. To McNally, there were too many unusual, unexplained facts in this case to support the majority's conclusions. "It was for the jury to say under all the facts and circumstances whether or not the acts of Weiss were artful and cunning contrivances which so overcame testator's independent volition as to induce him to do what he otherwise would not have done," insisted McNally. McNally quickly summarized the relationship of Weiss and Kaufmann over the past decade, emphasizing the escalating control Weiss had over Kaufmann's business and personal affairs, and asserted that it was "for the jury to say whether this relation and the activities of Weiss intruded directly upon the planning, preparation and execution of the instrument offered for probate." McNally insisted that the jury could have found that virtually every move Kaufmann made to increase Weiss's control and financial interests was taken at the prompting and instigation of Weiss, in-

dicating a degree of control that removed any free will of Kaufmann's in their relationship. Weiss did not testify at trial, although he had been deposed during pre-trial discovery. Much of the trial testimony consisted of attempts by attorney Levy to discredit Weiss's deposition testimony, which attempts McNally found very convincing. It was clear that Weiss, fearing a challenge to Kaufmann's will, had lied to Joel and others at various times. Given the time and place, it is not surprising that a gay man seeking to avoid public exposure of the nature of his illegal sexual activities and relationship would attempt in conversation with others to cover it up, but McNally seized on the various lies, emphasized them, and argued that the jury could properly have found them dispositive of many key points.

On the second trial before Surrogate DiFalco, Levy evidently changed strategy, seizing on the arguments in McNally's dissent. Since the attorney-client confidential relationship was apparently not available as a basis for challenging the will, Levy concentrated on piling up more and more evidence about how much Weiss had moved in and taken over total control of Kaufmann's life and affairs. The new jury was evidently convinced by all this, since it rendered the same verdict as the first jury: undue influence by Weiss made the will invalid.

On the subsequent appeal, unfortunately for Weiss, the appellate panel included the two prior dissenters, McNally and Rabin, but only one member of the prior majority, Stevens. The two other members of the panel, Presiding Justice Charles D. Breitel (later to become chief judge of the New York Court of Appeals) and Justice G. Robert Witmer were evenly divided on the case. The result was a 3–2 majority to sustain the challenge and disqualify the will, with McNally writing this time for a majority of the court and Witmer writing for himself and Stevens in dissent in the opinions issued on March 19, 1964.

McNally's opinion, which occupies twenty pages in the *New York Supplement*, rakes over every factual discrepancy between the documents and Weiss's version of events (based again on Weiss's original pretrial depositions, since he again refrained from testifying at trial) to argue that the jury had sufficient basis to discredit Weiss's account of things and to find undue influence. McNally suggested that letters and memoranda attributed to Kaufmann were actually the work of Weiss, either dictated to Kaufmann or to a secretary and typed for Kaufmann's signature. Indeed, it appeared that some business letters may even have been signed with Kaufmann's name by the secretary. McNally aimed special fire at the crucial letter of June 13, 1951, in which Kaufmann explained why he was making Weiss a major beneficiary. McNally suggested that Weiss had a hand in drafting this letter, and that it contained numerous factual discrepancies, including the date when Weiss and Kaufmann first met and the sequence of events leading from that meeting. McNally insisted on an interpretation of events that assumed Weiss and Kaufmann had not met until shortly before they concluded their business arrangement of 1948, whereas the letter indicated a 1946 meeting. If one accepted McNally's conclusion on this, much of the letter appears in error, since Kaufmann began art lessons and started asserting independence from his family prior to the 1948 agreement. Weiss's deposition, in which he may have lied about the true date of first meeting to avoid questions about the nature of his relationship with Kaufmann, came back to haunt him here, since there was no independent evidence in the record to support the 1946 date mentioned in the letter. "The 1951 letter is not based on reality," said McNally, who also noted that the letter suggested "that Weiss in some fashion was identified with Robert's sex life," but that Weiss's deposition "emphatically denied" sexual involvement with Robert. (What was Weiss to do? Gay sex was a serious felony in New York in 1959. Although it is possible that Weiss and Robert did not have a sexual relationship, it seems highly unlikely. Perhaps Weiss thought that by denying the sexual relationship, he could escape the imputation of undue influence.) According to McNally, "The emotional base reflected in the letter of June 13, 1951, is gratitude utterly unreal, highly exaggerated and pitched to a state of fervor and ecstasy." Similar discrepancies between deposition, testimony, and documents led McNally to find much of Weiss's story lacking in credibility.

Although he concluded that "Robert was endowed with a good mind, sensitivity, artistic ability and generous disposition," McNally asserted that the evidence would support the conclusion that Robert's total inexperience and disinterest in his financial affairs had led him virtually to turn over the management of his life to Weiss. "The arrangement was not one of master and servant or principal and agent," said McNally; "It was a confidential relationship more in the nature of teacher and pupil in the area of finance with specific application to the resources and assets of Robert." McNally claimed that the relationship had an "ominous inception," arguing that the 1948 agreement establishing Weiss as Kaufmann's "advisor" was very one-sided and had been prepared by Weiss, "a lawyer by training," and that Weiss's attitude as reflected in this agreement "did not auger [sic] well for the qualities of fairness and loyalty required on his part to achieve Robert's desire for the capacity to be independent in matters of business."

> Weiss and Robert lived together from 1949 to the date of Robert's death. The evidence enabled the jury to find that Robert became increasingly dependent on Weiss socially and businesswise. Moreover, it supports the view that this dependence was encouraged and that Weiss took affirmative steps to insulate Robert from his family and persons he sought to cultivate. Robert gave Weiss his unbounded confidence and trust. Weiss exploited Robert, induced him to transfer to him the stewardship formerly exercised by Joel, increased Robert's need for dependency, prevented and curtailed associations which threatened his absolute control of Robert and alienated him from his family.

This, in short, may well be an accurate picture of what would happen if two gay men fell in love, one wealthy and very controlled by his family, the other not wealthy but well educated and assertive. Indeed, this might well be an accurate picture of a situation where a will challenge would not easily be tolerated if one changed the sex of Robert to female and the sexual orientation of Robert and Walter to heterosexual. The lack of a legal vehicle for social recognition of a gay marriage at that time, when homosexuality was held in high disrepute and scorn and subject to criminal punishment in

New York, made a situation that might appear in some circles today to be entirely normal to appear at that time highly suspicious to a moralistic judge, who could not believe that a wealthy heir such as Robert Kaufmann would allow somebody like Walter Weiss to exert such influence unless his free will was entirely overborne. Concluded McNally, "The record becomes clear if it is viewed in the light of a skillfully executed plan by Weiss to gain the confidence of Robert, displace Joel as manager of his financial affairs, assume control of Robert's bank accounts, safe deposit box, household and property as if it were his." McNally found the June 13, 1951, letter to be part of Weiss's overall scheme, and seized on Weiss's later disavowal of earlier knowledge of this letter as prime evidence of his plot.

> The record enabled the jury to find that the instrument of June 19, 1958 [the final will] was the end result of an unnatural, insidious influence operating on a weak-willed, trusting, inexperienced Robert whose natural warm family attachment had been attenuated by false accusations against Joel, subtle flattery suggesting an independence he had not realized and which, in fact, Weiss had stultified, and planting in Robert's mind the conviction that Joel and other members of the family were resentful of and obstructing his drive for independence.

"Here, the circumstances spell out a confidential relationship between proponent and decedent which gave rise to an obligation on the part of the proponent-devisee to offer an explanation," said McNally. This time he commanded a majority for the point he had lost on the previous appeal, yet "[t]he issue of undue influence was submitted to the jury without the benefit to the contestants of any presumption," and the jury had found against Weiss. "The record overwhelmingly sustains the verdict on undue influence on the basis of the charge made."

Witmer's dissent, although also couched in the delicate language of the time and never once referring directly to homosexuality, condemns the majority for imposing its moral views in a situation where the only issue was the intent of Kaufmann, who was entitled to leave his estate to anybody he wished. "The case for the contestants is grounded completely upon cir-cumstantial evidence," he said, "and consists of evidence of a relationship between the testator and the proponent Weiss begun in the late 1940s and continuing until testator's death in April 1959. No specific act is relied upon as constituting the alleged undue influence inducing the propounded will; but the claim is that from about 1950 testator was under the complete domination of Weiss."

Witmer could not agree with this conclusion, noting several points in the detailed evidence of Kaufmann's conduct over the crucial decade when he had acted independently of Weiss, meeting with attorneys and business associates without Weiss's participation, and exhibiting all the competence necessary to make a valid will. While the evidence had been sufficient to lead two juries to find undue influence, Witmer questioned whether it was sufficient as a matter of New York law for such a finding. "It is elementary that the statutory right of a competent person to dispose of his property as he wishes may not be thwarted by disappointed relatives nor by jurors who think that the testator used bad judgment or was misled," insisted Witmer, quoting authority indicating that only where undue influence was the "necessary conclusion" to be drawn from the evidence would an otherwise validly executed will be set aside. "The verdict in this case rests upon surmise, suspicion, conjecture and moral indignation and resentment, not upon the legally required proof of undue influence; and it cannot stand," insisted Witmer.

> The record shows that the testator was intelligent and generally healthy. . . . True, the testator was not wholly like other people. He had little zest for business, which fact set him apart from his family. He had artistic ability, and particularly loved to paint. So did Weiss. They had common interests. Testator felt and said that he had uncommon ability as a painter and that some day he would be known for his artistic work. In this, he was not wholly wrong, for it appears that eighty museums have accepted his work for permanent display. The record is replete with evidence of the friendly relations, indeed love and affection, that existed between testator and Weiss for a decade. There is no substantial evidence that their relationship was not one of mutual esteem and self-respect.

While conceding that the evidence showed instances where Kaufmann had bowed to Weiss's judgment on financial matters, this was only to be expected when Weiss was retained and paid by Kaufmann as his financial advisor. Furthermore, Kaufmann had remembered his nephews in all his wills, including the final one, and had written out only a maiden aunt after having "spent considerable money refurbishing her apartment" for her. Indeed, as indication that Kaufmann was not totally under Weiss's thumb, just weeks before his death, when Weiss and Kaufmann were both in Key West, Weiss wanted to go up north and Kaufmann wanted to stay longer, so Weiss went back to New York and Kaufmann, lingering in Key West, died in the fire.

Witmer concluded that the June 13, 1951, letter, the genuineness of which he did not question, was the key to the relationship between the two men:

> This letter appears to lay bare the fact and prove the suspicion which members of testator's family had of the intimate relationship which existed between the two men. That and the falsehoods told by Weiss may have been among the reasons why Weiss failed to take the witness stand upon the trial. In our opinion, however, there was no legal compulsion upon Weiss to testify beyond the testimony which he gave on the examination before trial and which was read at length upon the trial of this case. The issue in this case is not what were the morals of these men, nor whether testator led a normal life, nor whether Weiss has been proved a liar. The issue is, does the propounded instrument represent the intrinsic wishes and will of the testator, or was it the product of the command of Weiss which the testator did not really want to follow, but was unable to resist?

Witmer asserted that "every act" of Kaufmann from the date of the disputed letter was "consistent with what he expressed in that letter" and that the argument that the letter was written at Weiss's inducement did not "ring true." Why would the letter refer, if obliquely, to a sexual relationship between the two men, a fact Weiss tried to keep secret, if Weiss was its true author? As to why Kaufmann would treat Weiss in his will as if Weiss was a spouse, Witmer found little mystery:

> As far as the motive is concerned the relationship may be likened to that of one who has a mistress. Morals aside, upon the facts of this case "proof of the circumstance that the will was an unnatural one is lacking." Of course, the court does not condone the relationship, but the moral law may not be substituted for the law of wills; and it should not be overlooked that difficult cases tend to make bad law. Undoubtedly the testator was influenced, but the evidence in this case is entirely consistent with the complete lack of undue influence. Yet, because of the suspicious circumstances involved, the majority of this Court as well as the Court below would deny him his legal right to dispose of his property as he has chosen to do.

As far as Witmer was concerned, there was no factual issue regarding undue influence for the jury to decide, and Pollack's motion for a directed verdict in favor of probate of the will should have been granted by the surrogate.

There being a dissent in the appellate division, Weiss appealed as of right to the court of appeals, which quickly disposed of the matter in a unanimous *per curiam* decision of February 11, 1965. Finding that the record "indicates that testator was pliable and easily taken advantage of, as proponent admitted, that there was a long and detailed history of dominance and subservience between them, that testator relied exclusively upon proponent's knowledge and judgment in the disposition of almost all of the material circumstances affecting the conduct of his life, and proponent is willed virtually the entire estate," the Court concluded that there was a factual issue of undue influence suitable for jury consideration, and affirmed the decision below with no further explanation.

This decision caused great concern to attorneys assisting gay people in planning for their estate dispositions. Although the judges in the appellate division majority waltzed around the issue and never came right out and said that it could be presumed in a homosexual relationship that the more "dominant" or "knowledgeable" member would have the burden of proof in refuting a claim of undue influence, that was the natural conclusion to be drawn from the dissent's criticism of how the majority handled the case. Furthermore, this decision was rendered at a time when the predominant view of homosexuality, both in the medical profession and in the courts, was that those of "deviant" sexual orientation suffered from mental illness, and thus their competency to deal with business affairs was subject to question. Justice Witmer alluded to this point when he asserted, at the end of his dissent, that the evidence that Kaufmann went through psychotherapy did not necessarily support any conclusion that he was incapable of exercising free will in the disposition of his estate.

The change of view by professional associations of psychiatrists and psychologists concerning the etiology and consequences of nonconventional sexual orientation may have contributed to the gradual change in judicial views on this issue. By the mid-1980s, it was

possible for a New York judge to say in a case concerning a challenge to the will of a decedent with AIDS that the homosexual relationship between the decedent and the beneficiary was not a basis for asserting a claim of undue influence. AIDS will contests were normally phrased as "competency" challenges, but lurking under the surface, especially when families did not discover their sons' homosexuality until after the AIDS diagnosis, was the subtle but persistent theme of "undue influence." Thus it may long be, when homosexual testators cut off or sharply curtail bequests to biological family members in preference to their gay life partners and friends.

118. ARE GAY DOMESTIC PARTNERS "CONCUBINES"?

In re Bacot, 502 So. 2d 1118 (La. App., 4th Cir.), certiorari denied, 503 So. 2d 466 (La. 1987).

The refusal of the law to authorize same-sex marriages has created significant ambiguity about the legal status (or lack of legal status) of same-sex couples who live together and conduct their lives as if they were legal spouses. While many of the complications will appear obvious to anyone who contemplates the matter, perhaps the least obvious complication arose in 1984 when the courts of Louisiana, applying statutes derived from the French Napoleonic Code, had to determine whether such same-sex couples occupied the legal status of "concubines" for purposes of the laws of succession.

The question arose when Samuel Wilds Bacot, Jr., who had lived for nine years as the domestic partner of Danny Washington, died after executing a one-sentence hand-written will (referred to in Louisiana as an "olographic testament") purporting to leave his entire estate to "Danny." The ensuing litigation between claimants to the estate spawned numerous disputes, but none so peculiar as the question whether statutory limitations on bequests to concubines would apply to Washington.

Bacot and Washington began to live together in a homosexual relationship in the mid-

1970s. They shared household chores and duties, maintained joint bank accounts, jointly entered into a signed rental agreement, and were reciprocal beneficiaries on each other's life insurance policies. Although they had occasional fights about Washington's alcoholism, those who knew them testified that they still cared for one another deeply and that Washington took care of Bacot during all his illnesses. Among those who testified to the nature of their relationship were their landlord, Bacot's cousin Mary Etta Jolly Fizer, and James Louis Anderson, a longtime friend of Bacot.

For some reason, however, Bacot decided to adopt one Elmo Orgeron, Jr., as his son, executor, and heir, executing adoption papers and a last will and testament to that effect on January 5, 1982. Although court papers do not reveal the reason for this action, perhaps it occurred during a falling out between Bacot and Washington over Washington's drinking. In any event, Washington remained the beneficiary of Bacot's life insurance policy.

In September 1984, Bacot entered Charity Hospital in New Orleans suffering acute chronic virulent type B herpes simplex. The disease affected Bacot's brain due to a buildup of toxic ammonia, producing sharp swings in his mental state and lucidity, according to his treating physician, Dr. Bonnie Boyd, who later testified that his mental state "waxed and waned." At 2 A.M. on October 4, Bacot rang for his nurse, quite agitated, demanding a pen and paper so he could make a will. Bacot feared that he might die before his last wishes could be carried out. Carolyn McLain, the supervising nurse, tried to dissuade Bacot, but he insisted on doing this right away. Finally, McLain gave him paper and a pen, and Bacot wrote: "I leave all to Danny." He signed the paper "Wilds Bacot," and scrawled a date that might either be 10/4/84 or 4/10/84. Both McLain and Mildred Dix, the licensed practical nurse who was attending Bacot, agreed that he was quite lucid through the whole incident, knew who he was and what he was doing, and seemed determined to accomplish the task. McLain took the paper, wrote Bacot's patient number on it, signed her own name and dated it, and placed it in his medical file. Shortly after this incident, Bacot slipped into a coma and eventually died on October 14.

Five days later, Orgeron presented the January 1982 will for probate at the Civil District Court of Orleans Parish. Then "Dannys" came out of the woodwork, claiming to be Bacot's heir under the "olographic testament" found in his medical records. In addition to Danny Washington, claims were filed by Danny Poirier and Danny Butler, each claiming they had engaged in sexual relationships with Bacot for some period and were intended as his sole heir. In addition, Bacot's cousins, H. William Jolly, III, Mary Etta Jolly Fizer, and Bob Conway Jolly, intervened in the proceeding, claiming that the January 1982 will was invalid and that they were entitled to inherit Bacot's estate under the laws of intestate succession. After striking a deal with Danny Washington under which they would get half the estate if he won, the Jolly cousins amended their original petition to allege instead that the olographic testament was valid and superseded the 1982 will.

The probate court found that the olographic testament was valid and met all statutory requirements under the Louisiana Code, thereby rejecting Orgeron's claim under the 1982 will. However, the court held that the case was controlled by article 1481 of the Civil Code, which limited the portion of an estate that a testator could leave to an "open concubine" to ten percent of the "movables" in the estate; real property could not be left to a concubine. The probate court found that Danny Washington was the only "Danny" with a valid claim under the olographic testament, but that he was the "open concubine" of Bacot. Since Washington could inherit only ten percent of Bacot's personal property, the court determined that the rest of the estate would pass by the laws of intestate succession to Bacot's "son," Orgeron, who had filed a copy of the 1982 adoption papers with the court.

The probate court's opinion caused consternation in the lesbian and gay community in Louisiana, since it cast into question the validity of wills made by lesbian and gay domestic partners leaving more than ten percent of their personal property to their partners. It also caused consternation for Washingon and the Jollys, since they considered Orgeron a usurper who had not been validly adopted. The other "Dannys" were also upset. (Either Bacot's estate must have been significant to have engendered such passions, or the contestants were all upset as a matter of principle. In any event, one wonders why he died at the Charity Hospital.) Everybody retained counsel and an appeal was taken by all parties to the Louisiana Court of Appeal for the Fourth Circuit. A unanimous panel of Judges James C. Gulotta, Philip C. Ciaccio, and Robert L. Lobrano issued an opinion by Judge Lobrano on January 14, 1987, after lengthy deliberation.

After disposing of the numerous procedural preliminaries, which included approving the probate court's findings that the olographic testament was a valid expression of Bacot's testamentary intent and that only Danny Washington could be the "Danny" referred to in the document, the court tackled the interesting and vital question whether Washington and Bacot were "open concubines" and concluded that they were not.

The court traced the history of the concubinage statute prior to 1808, when the Louisiana Territory's government was first enacting laws after President Thomas Jefferson had negotiated the purchase of the Louisiana Territory from Emperor Napoleon of France, who previously controlled the territory through the French conquest of Spain and the placement of Joseph Bonaparte on the Spanish throne. French law predating the Code Napoleon had placed limitations on bequests to concubines, based on the policy of reinforcing legal marriage and protecting the property rights of family members against unrecognized usurpers. "Concubinage was frowned upon as a means of avoiding the responsibilities of family associated with marriage," commented Lobrano, "especially the obligations associated with the birth of children." These considerations were carried over into the 1825 Louisiana Civil Code, which narrowed the prior prohibition, however, "by limiting a donation to only a percentage of the movables, and excepting those who later married." Lobrano found that the current article 1481 was "nearly identical" to the 1825 Code provision.

At all points in the historical record, which Judge Lobrano traced to biblical references and ancient Roman law, concubines had always been described as mixed-sex couples living together openly in an unmarried, spousal-type relationship. He noted that recent amendments to Louisiana Code provisions and all prior case law that had occasion to discuss the matter had either implicitly or expressly indicated that concubinage consisted of a man and woman living together without benefit of marriage. Indeed, the parties had to be "capable of contracting marriage" for the relationship to be considered concubinage, otherwise the policy justification of reinforcing marriage and discouraging people from seeking to evade the responsibilities of marriage would not be served by placing the testamentary limitation on the parties. "There is not now, nor has there ever been in our law a legal mechanism for recognizing marriage between persons of the same sex," said Lobrano. "Homosexuals living together, no matter what the duration, can never marry, and therefore such individuals can never be concubines to one another. A concubine is as essential to a state of concubinage as a ghost is to Hamlet. Thus, a man cannot live in open concubinage with another man."

Consequently, Washington was not limited by law to inheriting no more than ten percent of Bacot's personal property, and the probate court's judgment decreeing Danny Washington to be Bacot's concubine was reversed. The court ordered the case remanded for consistent proceedings in the probate court. Left open by the court of appeal's decision was the validity of Orgeron's adoption by Bacot. The probate court had ruled that, as Bacot's "son," Orgeron was entitled to take the balance of the estate through intestate succession. The Jollys objected that the validity of Orgeron's adoption (which was sought to be proved by uncertified documents) was not properly before the probate court, which was concerned only with the validity of the wills. The court of appeal agreed with the Jollys and vacated the probate court's decision, finding the adoption valid for reconsideration at such time as Orgeron might make a claim for possession of property against the estate.

Orgeron, apparently out in the cold, was not ready to give up, however, and filed a petition for *certiorari* in the Louisiana Supreme Court. The court denied the writ, two justices dissenting, on March 13, 1987.

While the *Bacot* decision has little precedential significance outside of Louisiana, the only state that derives its law from French sources, the case is interesting in illustrating the difficulties that arise from the continued failure to accord some legal status or recognition to sexual and emotional long-term relationships other than traditional "marriage." While the same-sex case appeared clear cut to the court of appeal, one wonders how it might have dealt with a case involving a man and a male-to-female postoperative transsexual. Such a couple might be denied a marriage license, even though the transsexual might be able to obtain a revised birth certificate indicating female sex. Would such a couple be considered living in concubinage for purposes of succession in Louisiana?

119. CAN GAYS CLAIM SPOUSAL SHARES FROM THEIR LOVERS' ESTATES?

Estate of Cooper, 149 Misc. 2d 282, 564 N.Y.S.2d 684 (Sur. Ct. Kings Co. 1990).

By the end of the 1980s, gay marriage and an alternative—domestic partnership—had become hot topics for debate within the lesbian and gay community and even in the mainstream press. During the March on Washington for Lesbian and Gay Rights held on Columbus Day weekend in 1987, hundreds of lesbian and gay couples participated in a mass mock wedding ceremony in front of the Internal Revenue Service building. The purpose of the ceremony was to protest the inability of gay people to marry their same-sex partners and share in the benefits marriage bestowed, not least of them the ability of spouses to inherit significant amounts of personal and real property without being taxed under the "spousal exclusion" of the Internal Revenue Code. The lack of a right to marry also caused problems under the estates laws of the states, which provide that when a person dies without a will, his or her property is to be distributed by statutory formula to spouses, offspring, and other family members, to the exclusion of those not deemed relatives by the law.

The AIDS epidemic that began in the late 1970s and accelerated in ferocity through the 1980s dramatically illustrated the problems that arose when same-sex couples were excluded from the operation of these estates laws. AIDS struck young and middle-aged men quickly, and many died without having had the opportunity to make a will. Many were the stories of gay men returning from the funerals of their lovers only to discover family members removing property from their apartments, contesting their continued ownership of cooperative or condominium apartments, and even attempting to claim a share of businesses jointly established and developed over the years. While AIDS produced many will contests, with claims of incapacity and undue influence echoing through judicial chambers, some of the saddest cases to contemplate were those where the deceased left no will, or had neglected to revise a will that predated his or her last serious relationship.

In one of the few reported decisions about an attempt by a gay litigant to escape some of the complications of his lover's early death from AIDS, a New York State surrogate court judge in Brooklyn faced a novel claim in 1990: that a surviving gay life partner should be allowed to claim an "elective share" against the estate of his partner, using a device under the New York Estate Powers and Trust Law that seeks to guarantee that surviving spouses cannot be completely disinherited.

Ernest Chin and William Thomas Cooper became lovers in 1984, and lived together in a spousal-type relationship until Cooper's death on February 19, 1988. Cooper had apparently made a will before becoming involved with Chin and had not revised it prior to his death; as a result, Chin faced dispossession from his home and economic loss. According to Chin, "the only reason Mr. Cooper and I were not legally married is because marriage license clerks in New York State will not issue licenses to persons of the same sex." Chin claimed that, except for the fact that he and Cooper were both men, their lives "were identical to that of husband and wife. We kept a common home; we shared expenses, our friends recognized us as spouses; we had a physical relationship." Under the circumstances, Chin claimed that he should be entitled to the rights of a "surviving spouse" under the law and that the failure to accord him such rights, due to New York's refusal to allow same-sex marriage, constituted a denial of equal protection of the laws.

After considering the arguments of attorneys Bradley B. Davis for Chin and Ethel Fitzgerald for the estate of Cooper, Judge Vincent Pizzuto issued a decision on December 19, 1990, dismissing Chin's claim against the estate. For Pizzuto, the dispositive question was whether New York's refusal to let same-sex couples marry violated their constitutional rights, and he could find no violation under either the due process or equal protection clauses. Pizzuto relied mainly on *Baker v. Nelson*

(1971), in which the Minnesota Supreme Court denied a marriage license to a same-sex couple, and on *Adams v. Howerton* (1982), in which the U.S. Court of Appeals for the Ninth Circuit held that a gay male couple that had obtained a marriage license and gone through a ceremony with a municipal clerk nonetheless was not entitled to the recognition accorded spouses under the federal Immigration and Naturalization Act. In both cases, the courts had taken the view that a marriage is, by definition, the legal union of a man and a woman, so by definition same-sex couples could not marry or qualify to be treated as spouses. "This court could find no authority in any jurisdiction of the United States, either authorizing marriages between people of the same sex, or elevating homosexual unions to the same level achieved by the marriage of two people of the opposite sex," said Pizzuto.

However, Pizzuto was confronted with the recent decision of the New York Court of Appeals in *Braschi v. Stahl Associates Co.* (1989), in which the highest court of New York had ruled that a gay male couple could be considered a family unit for purposes of New York rent control regulations that guaranteed the right of family members in residence to continue living in rent-controlled apartments after the death of the primary tenant. Remarking on "the reality of family life" in contemporary New York, the court of appeals stated that "in the context of eviction, a more realistic, and certainly equally valid, view of a family includes two adult lifetime partners whose relationship is long term and characterized by an emotional and financial commitment and interdependence. This view comports both with our society's traditional concept of 'family' and with the expectations of individuals who live in nuclear units." Thus, the court concluded that it was reasonable to bring a same-sex couple within the protections extended to family members under the rent regulations.

On the other hand, noted Pizzuto, in an earlier case, *People v. Allen* (1970), the court of appeals, in construing the jurisdiction of the family court, had adopted a much stricter, more legalistic definition of "family," commenting that the court's jurisdiction arose "in relationships only where there is legal interdependence, either through a solemnized marriage or a recognized marriage or a recognized common-law union." Although in *Allen* it was alleged that the nonmarital heterosexual couple were engaged in a long-term relationship, the court of appeals held this was not sufficient to bring their dispute under the family court's jurisdiction: "It matters not that, in reality, many such informal relationships exist in our State. Regardless of the frequency of its occurrence, such informal or illicit relationships remain unrecognized and should not be afforded the protective jurisdiction of the Family Court." Pizzuto suggested that *Allen*, as much as *Braschi*, represented a policy-driven decision responsive to the particular factual context. *Braschi* dealt with determining who was a family member, not who was a spouse, and *Allen* had rejected analogizing nonmarital partners to spouses for purposes of family court jurisdiction where the benefits to be gained were intended by the legislature to be conferred on lawful spouses. "There is a great distinction between being part of a family entitled to the protection of rent control laws because of public policy and legislative intent, and in being a surviving spouse of a decedent," Pizzuto asserted.

The Estates Powers and Trust Law of New York specifically defined a surviving spouse as being a husband or a wife of a decedent. (By contrast, the disputed regulation in *Braschi* had not contained a definition of "family members" who were to benefit from noneviction protection.) The purpose of the elective share statute was to protect a surviving spouse, defined as a husband or a wife, from being disinherited. "Mr. Chin would have this court hold that persons of the same sex who opt to live in a 'spousal relationship' should be given similar rights to those granted to a surviving spouse by the Legislature. To do so would be impermissible judicial legislating and contrary to the public policy expressed by our Legislature," concluded Pizzuto. He went on to find that the legislature's restriction of marriage to oppositesex couples "has a rational basis" and "does not offend the equal protection right of the Fourteenth Amendment or due process." Pizzuto grounded this conclusion in the state's "compelling interest in fostering the traditional institution of marriage (whether based on self-preservation, procreation, or in nurturing and keeping alive the concept of marriage and family as a basic fabric of our society), as old and as fundamental as our entire civilization, which institution is deeply rooted and long established in firm and rich societal values." Pizzuto gave no explanation as to how denying Ernest Chin an elective share in his deceased lover's estate would help to preserve traditional marriage.

The *Cooper* decision was representative of the continuing litigation over gay marriage that began to spring up in the early 1990s, as gay couples, who had abandoned attempting to sue for marriage licenses ever since the negative gay marriage decisions of the 1970s, decided to reassert their arguments in light of intervening developments in federal and state constitutional law and increased societal acceptance for gay people and their relationships. As of the end of 1991, none of the new round of gay marriage cases pending in courts in Hawaii, Illinois, and the District of Columbia had advanced to an appellate decision, but it seemed unlikely that any such litigation would ultimately be successful. On such a controversial issue, the courts were most likely to disclaim authority to engage in legislative revisionism (as did Pizzuto), leaving those dissatisfied with the marriage laws to pursue legislative reforms.

Meanwhile, gay political activists were increasingly successful in persuading city councilors and some private-sector employers that they should begin to recognize "domestic partnerships" as an alternative to gay marriage. As the 1990s began, it seemed likely that the stopgap of "domestic partnership," with its conferral of some benefits of marriage (normally not including spousal status for purposes of intestacy), would gain wider acceptance than actual marriage for same-sex couples. At the same time, lesbian and gay couples were bombarded with messages from the lesbian and gay media and the newly emerging professional associations of lesbian and gay lawyers to engage in creative "gay family planning," using interwoven legal documents such as wills, trusts, powers of attorney, and partnership agreements, hoping to simulate to the extent possible a desirable legal status for their relationships that would avoid the worst problems that arose due to their inability to marry.

Case References

Adams v. Howerton, 673 F.2d 1036 (9th Cir. 1982), affirming 486 F. Supp. 1119 (C.D. Cal. 1980), certiorari denied, 458 U.S. 1111 (1982)

Baker v. Nelson, 291 Minn. 310, 191 N.W.2d 185 (1971), appeal dismissed, 409 U.S. 810 (1972)

Braschi v. Stahl Associates Co., 74 N.Y.2d 201, 544 N.Y.S.2d 784, 543 N.E.2d 49 (1989)

People v. Allen, 27 N.Y.2d 108, 313 N.Y.S.2d 719, 261 N.E.2d 637 (1970)

TABLE OF CASES

INDEX